Introduction to Management Accounting

Prentice Hall Series in Accounting
Charles T. Horngren, Consulting Editor

Introduction to Management Accounting

Tenth Edition

Charles T. Horngren
Stanford University

Gary L. Sundem
University of Washington—Seattle

William O. Stratton
University of Southern Colorado

 Prentice-Hall International, Inc.

Executive Editor: P.J. Boardman
Marketing Manager: Debbie Emry
Production: Editorial Services of New England
Managing Editor: Katherine Evancie
Interior Designer: Jean Hammond
Cover Designer: Lorraine Castellano
Design Director: Patricia Wosczyk
Manufacturing Buyer: Paul Smolenski
Associate Editor: Diane deCastro
Editorial Assistant: Jane Avery
Production Coordinator: Renée Pelletier
Cover Art: Pete Saloutos/ The Stock Market

© 1996, 1993, 1990, 1987, 1984, 1981, 1978, 1974, 1970, 1965 by Prentice-Hall, Inc.
A Simon & Schuster Company
Upper Saddle River, NJ 07458

Printed in the United States of America

10 9 8 7 6 5 4 3 2 1

ISBN 0-13-213638-4

Prentice-Hall International (UK) Limited, *London*
Prentice-Hall of Australia Pty. Limited, *Sydney*
Prentice-Hall Canada Inc., *Toronto*
Prentice-Hall Hispanoamericana, S.A., *Mexico*
Prentice-Hall of India Private Limited, *New Delhi*
Prentice-Hall of Japan, Inc., *Tokyo*
Simon & Schuster Asia Pte. Ltd., *Singapore*
Editora Prentice-Hall do Brasil, Ltda., *Rio de Janeiro*
Prentice-Hall, Upper Saddle River, New Jersey

To Joan, Scott, Mary, Susie, Cathy,
Liz, Garth, Jens,
Norma, Gina, and Adam

■ **Charles T. Horngren** (center) is the Edmund W. Littlefield Professor of Accounting at Stanford University. A graduate of Marquette University, he received his MBA from Harvard and his Ph.D. from the University of Chicago. He is also the recipient of honorary doctorates from Marquette as well as De Paul University.

A Certified Public Accountant, Horngren has served on the Accounting Principles Board, the Financial Accounting Standards Board Advisory Council, the Council of the American Institute of Certified Public Accountants, and as a trustee of the Financial Accounting Foundation.

A member of the American Accounting Association, Horngren has been its President and its Director of Research. He received the Outstanding Accounting Educator Award in 1973. The California Certified Public Accountants Foundation gave Horngren its Faculty Excellence Award in 1975 and its Distinguished Professor Award in 1983. In 1985 the AICPA presented its first Outstanding Accounting Educator Award to Horngren. In 1990 he was elected to the Accounting Hall of Fame.

Professor Horngren is also a member of the National Association of Accountants. He was a member of the Board of Regents, Institute of Certified Management Accountants, which administers the CMA examinations.

Horngren is the co-author of four other books published by Prentice Hall: *Cost Accounting: A Managerial Emphasis, Eighth Edition*, 1994 (with George Foster and Srikant M. Datar); *Introduction to Financial Accounting, Sixth Edition*, 1996 (with Gary L. Sundem and John A. Elliott); *Accounting, Third Edition*, 1996 (with Walter T. Harrison, Jr.), and *Financial Accounting, Second Edition*, 1995 (also with Harrison). In addition he is the Consulting Editor for the Prentice Hall Series in Accounting.

■ **Gary L. Sundem** (left) is Professor of Accounting at the University of Washington, Seattle. He received his B.A. degree from Carleton College and his MBA and Ph.D. degrees from Stanford University.

Professor Sundem was the 1992–93 President of the American Accounting Association. He was Executive Director of the Accounting Education Change Commission, 1989–91, and served as Editor of *The Accounting Review*, 1982–86.

A member of the National Association of Accountants, Sundem is past president of the Seattle chapter. He has served on NAA's national Board of Directors, the Committee on Academic Relations, and the Research Committee.

Professor Sundem has numerous publications in accounting and finance journals including *Issues in Accounting Education*, *The Accounting Review*, *Journal of Accounting Research*, and *The Journal of Finance*. He received an award for the most notable contribution to accounting literature in 1978; he was selected Outstanding Accounting Educator by the Washington Society of CPAs in 1987. He has made more than 100 presentations at universities in the United States and abroad.

■ **William O. Stratton** (right) is Department Chairman and Associate Professor of Accounting at the University of Southern Colorado. He received B.S. degrees from Florida State University and Pennsylvania State University, his MBA from Boston University, and his Ph.D. from the Claremont Graduate School.

A Certified Management Accountant, Stratton has lectured extensively at management accounting conferences in North America and Europe. He has developed and delivered workshops on activity-based management to manufacturing and service organizations throughout the United States. In 1993, Professor Stratton was awarded the Boeing Competition prize for classroom innovation.

Stratton has numerous publications in accounting and international business journals including *Management Accounting*, *Decision Sciences*, *IIE Transactions*, and *Synergie*.

Brief Contents

Contents

Part Four  Product Costing

16   Overhead Application: Variable and Absorption Costing   600

Part Five ■ Basic Financial Accounting

17   Basic Accounting: Concepts, Techniques, and Conventions   638

18   Understanding Corporate Annual Reports: Basic Financial Statements   684

Preface

Introduction to Management Accounting is the second member of a matched pair of books that provides full coverage of the essentials of financial and managerial accounting. The first book is *Introduction to Financial Accounting*. In combination, the pair can be used throughout two semesters or three quarters of introductory accounting.

This book is an introduction to internal accounting—most often called management accounting. It deals with important topics that all students of management and business should study. The book is written primarily for students who have had one or two terms of basic accounting. It is also appropriate for continuing educational programs of varying lengths in which the students have had no formal training in accounting. The four financial accounting chapters (Chapters 17–20) make it especially appropriate for short courses introducing managers to accounting because both financial and management accounting can be presented from a user's perspective using one textbook.

The twin objectives in this revision are to recognize current trends in management accounting and to clearly present the basic concepts and techniques. Although basic concepts in management accounting have not changed dramatically, the application of those concepts has been significantly influenced by a changing world-wide competitive environment and significant changes in the cost accounting systems used by world-class companies. The focus of the text remains the understanding of costs and cost behavior and the use of cost information for planning and control decisions, but both terminology and applied settings have been revised to reflect the changes in the real world of management accounting.

This book attempts a balanced, flexible approach. For example, it deals as much with nonprofit, retail, wholesale, selling, and administrative situations as it does with manufacturing. The fundamental accounting concepts and techniques for planning and control are applicable to all types and functions of organizations, not just to manufacturing. This more general approach makes it easier for the student to relate the book's examples and problems to his or her particular interests. Moreover, many valuable concepts (for example, master budgets) are more easily grasped if they are not complicated by intricate manufacturing situations.

Stress is on planning and control, not on product costing for purposes of inventory valuation and income determination. Our approach, which excludes the troublesome but unimportant complications introduced by changes in inventory levels, simplifies the presentation of planning and control techniques in the classroom. Instead of the simultaneous discussion of costs for control and for product costing found in most texts, this text concentrates on planning and control without dwelling on details of product costing until Chapter 13. At that point, cost allocation, job costing, process costing, and the implications of overhead application for product costing may be considered in perspective and in relation to management policy decisions regarding the "best" inventory valuation method.

A chapter-by-chapter description of the noteworthy changes in this edition is given in the front section of the solutions manual. Significant aspects of the Tenth Edition include the following:

1. Coverage of modern trends in management accounting has been integrated into most of the chapters. Instead of presenting a traditional approach and then appending coverage of new topics, the current environment of management accounting is the setting for the basic description and explanations of concepts and techniques. See, for example, the introduction to current trends in Chapter 1, activity analysis in Chapter 3, activity-based costing in Chapters 4 and 13, nonfinancial measures of performance in Chapter 9, capital budgeting for investments in technology in Chapter 11, selection of cost drivers for overhead in Chapter 14, and coverage of backflush costing in Chapter 15.

2. Emphasis on understanding cost behavior is increased. Part One includes an entire chapter on cost behavior, Chapter 3. Cost behavior, including identifying an organization's activities and the cost drivers for those activities, is fundamental to understanding management accounting.

3. International examples have been expanded. Suppliers and customers, no matter what their size or country, are increasingly affected by dealings with and within other nations. Each chapter has at least one homework problem that has a setting outside the United States, and international dimensions of issues are introduced throughout the text.

4. Ethical issues are covered in Chapter 1 to emphasize their importance.

5. Cost allocation is covered in Chapter 13. Many of the details of cost allocation are driven by product costing considerations, so the chapter is included in Part Four, "Product Costing."

6. Chapter 15 minimizes coverage of the technical details of process costing. Notably, a long section on process costing in a subsequent department that appeared in previous editions has been replaced by a brief explanation of a transferred-in cost, the only new step students need to learn.

7. Chapter 17 in the Ninth Edition, "Quantitative Techniques Used in Management Accounting," has been deleted in this edition. Relevant quantitative materials have been integrated into other chapters.

8. The financial accounting chapters have been fully updated to reflect new pronouncements.

9. All chapters have undergone major revisions for clarity. Redundancies have been eliminated, topics have been reorganized, and illustrations have been expanded. Ease of reading has been a constant goal.

10. Learning objectives and accounting vocabulary definitions have been placed both at the beginning of each chapter and in chapter margins for emphasis.

11. Boxed examples, drawn from articles in the business press, have been updated and expanded.

Alternative Ways of Using This Book

In our opinion, the first nine chapters provide the foundation of the field of management accounting. These nine chapters may be amplified by assigning the subsequent chapters in the given order or by inserting them after the earlier chapters as desired. Such insertion may be achieved without disrupting the readers' flow of thought. The most obvious candidates for insertion are indicated below:

Chapters   1   2   3   4   5   6   7   8   9 → 10–20

	2			5		7		8
	↑			↑		↑		↑
	17			13		11		16
	18			14		12		
	19			15				
	20							

If some of the basics of financial accounting are to be included in a course in management accounting, any or all of the financial accounting chapters (17–20) may be undertaken anytime. (For example, to provide a change of pace, such chapters have even been used in the midst of a course.)

Instructors tend to disagree markedly about the sequence of topics in a course in management accounting. Criticisms of any sequence in a textbook are inevitable. Consequently, this book tries to provide a modular approach that permits hopping and skipping back and forth with minimal inconvenience. In a nutshell, our rationale is to provide a loosely constrained sequence to ease diverse approaches to teaching. Content is of primary importance; sequence is secondary.

Teaching is highly personal and is heavily influenced by the backgrounds and interests of assorted students in miscellaneous settings. To satisfy this audience, a book must be pliable, not a straitjacket.

As the authors, we prefer to assign the chapters in the sequence provided in the book. But we are not enslaved by the sequence. Through the years, we have assigned an assortment of sequences, depending on the readers' backgrounds.

Part One, "Focus on Decision Making," provides a bedrock introduction, so we assign all six chapters. Sometimes we assign Chapter 17 immediately after Chapter 1—particularly if the readers have little or no background in financial accounting. Moreover, if there is time in the course for students to become more familiar with product costing, we frequently assign Chapters 13 and 14 immediately after Chapter 4. Furthermore, there is much logical appeal to studying the chapters on capital budgeting (Chapters 11 and 12) immediately after the chapters on relevant costs (Chapters 5 and 6). However, tradition, plus the fact that capital budgeting is often amply covered in other courses, have prevented our placing such chapters there. In addition, the master budget is often covered in finance courses, so Chapter 7 is frequently skipped.

Part Two, "Accounting for Planning and Control," emphasizes the attention-directing functions of accounting. We often assign Chapter 16 immediately after Chapter 8 because it stresses the product-costing aspects of standard costs, whereas Chapter 8 focuses on the control aspects.

The coverage of product costing in Part Four has been revised to include many of the new developments in cost accounting. All of these topics are important; however, the decision to study them will depend on the teacher's preferences, the other courses in the curriculum, and the students' previous courses.

Part Five introduces, interprets, and appraises basic financial accounting. These chapters form a unified package that covers all elementary financial accounting in capsule form with heavy stress on interpretation and uses and, except in Chapter 17, with little attention given to the accumulation of the information. In our view, a major objective of basic financial accounting should be to equip the student with enough fundamental concepts and terminology so that he or she can reasonably comprehend any industrial corporate annual report.

Chapters 17–20 may be skipped entirely or may be used in a variety of ways:

1. In courses or executive programs where the students have no accounting background but where the main emphasis is on management rather than financial accounting
2. In courses where the chapters may be used as a quick review by students who have had some financial accounting previously
3. In courses where one or two of Chapters 17–20 may be chosen to remedy weaknesses or gaps in the background of the students

Chapters 17–20 need not be used in total, page by page, or topic by topic. Teachers are free to pick and choose those topics (particularly in Chapters 19 and 20) that seem most suitable for their students.

Some teachers may want to use these chapters to teach the fundamentals of financial accounting to students with no prior background in accounting. Classroom testing has shown that such teaching can be done successfully, provided that the homework material is chosen carefully.

The front of the solutions manual contains several alternate detailed assignment schedules and ample additional recommendations to teachers regarding how best to use this book.

Supplements for the Instructor

- Instructor's Manual—includes chapter learning objectives, chapter overviews, chapter outlines, quizzes, transparency masters for key exhibits in the text, selected readings, and video write-ups.
- Solutions Manual—provides solutions for all end-of-chapter assignment material. All solutions were prepared by the authors.
- Solutions Transparencies—provide solutions on acetates.
- Test Item File—consists of approximately 15 true/false questions, 50 multiple-choice questions, and 10 exercises per chapter. The appropriate learning objective and level of difficulty are indicated for each question.
- ABC News/Prentice Hall Video Library—offers high-quality feature and documentary-style videos with carefully researched selections from award-winning ABC news shows. The accompanying video guide provides a synopsis, learning objectives, and discussion questions for each video segment.
- PH custom test—DOS- and Windows-based computerized testing package in $3^1/_2$" format.
- PowerPoint Transparencies—this classroom presentation package on PowerPoint 3.0 can be used to present chapter material using colorful graphics, outlines of chapter material, and additional examples and explanations of difficult topics.

Supplements for the Student

- Study Guide—includes a detailed review of key ideas for each chapter plus practice test questions and problems along with the worked-out solutions.
- Spreadsheet Templates—provide pre-prepared templates for selected problems from the text in $3^1/_2$" format and can be used with both Lotus 1-2-3 and Excel.
- Like Magic: A Series of Computerized Cases for Managerial and Cost Accounting— a Lotus® 1-2-3® based computerized practice set for management or cost accounting. (A solutions manual is available for instructors.)

Acknowledgments

We have received ideas, assistance, miscellaneous critiques, and assorted assignment material in conversations and by mail from many students, professors, and business leaders. Each has our gratitude, but the list is too long to enumerate here.

Jim Smith and John Harris of The Marmon Group, Inc., provided the chapter heading photographs with captions for Chapters 1–4, 6–8, and 10–20. Laney Pomp of H.G. Engineering provided the Chapter 5 photogragh and caption. Kathy Jensen, Manager of Integrated Performance Systems at Health Systems International provided the caption for the Chapter 9 photograph by Judy Kruesch.

Joanne Cook and Donna Kilpatrick provided extensive assistance in the development and editing of exercises and problems. Barbara Pearson cheerfully and expertly typed the solutions manual.

The Chapter 4 illustration of activity-based costing is based (in part) on a case developed by Sapling Corporation. Derek Sandison of Sapling provided useful suggestions for this illustration.

The following professors supplied helpful comments and reviews of the previous edition or drafts of this edition: Donald Bedell; Mary Beth Caldwell, University of Arkansas, Fayetteville; William A. Chamberlin, Embry Riddle Aeronautical University; Randolph S. Coyner, Florida Atlantic University; David Croll; Dean Edmiston, Emporia State University; Dan Elnathan; Nabil Hassan, Wright State University; Michael Kinney; Anne Kotheimer; Wallace R. Leese, California State University, Chico; C. Angela Letourneau, Winthrop University; Rich Mayer; Gary L. Merz, Clarion University of Pennsylvania; Roland Minch; Greta Mortimer; Bruce R. Neumann, University of Colorado, Denver; Charles Pineno; Gary Rholl, Lane Community College; William G. Shenkir, University of Virginia; John Temmerman; and Joseph Weintrop.

Appreciation also goes to The Institute of Certified Management Accountants for their generous permission to use or adapt problems (designated as CMA) from their publications.

And, finally, our thanks to P.J. Boardman, Rich Wohl, Debbie Emry, Catharine Grimes, Diane deCastro, Jane Avery, Katherine Evancie, Paul Smolenski, Patricia Wosczyk, and Vincent Scelta at Prentice Hall.

Comments from readers are welcome.

Charles T. Horngren
Gary L. Sundem
William O. Stratton

1 Perspective: Scorekeeping, Attention Directing, and Problem Solving

The evolving role of cost accountants is evident at Rochester Instrument Systems Inc., a worldwide supplier of electronic instrumentation equipment. Among the company's products is a device to monitor nuclear power plant safety equipment. A cost accountant discusses reports with the supervisor of a work cell.
Courtesy Rochester Instrument Systems, Inc.

Learning Objectives

When you have finished studying this chapter, you should be able to

1 Describe the major users of accounting information.

2 Name the types of questions an accounting system helps to answer.

3 Distinguish service organizations from manufacturing organizations.

4 Explain the cost-benefit and behavioral issues involved in designing an accounting system.

5 Explain the role of budgets and performance reports in planning and control.

6 Discuss the effect of product life cycles on assessing product profitability.

7 Distinguish between line and staff roles in an organization.

8 Contrast functions of controllers and treasurers.

9 Identify current trends in management accounting.

10 Explain a management accountant's ethical responsibilities.

Accounting information can help managers in all types of organizations answer vital questions. Consider the following broad range of problems that demand solutions:

- Boeing engineers have prepared manufacturing specifications for a new airplane, the 7X7. There are three possible ways to organize the assembly of the plane. Which is the most cost-effective approach?
- A product manager at Kellogg's is designing a new marketing plan for Frosted Flakes. Market research predicts that distributing free samples in the mail will increase annual sales by 4%. How will the cost of the free samples (including the cost of distributing them) compare with the profits from the added sales?
- University National Bank offers free checking to customers who keep a minimum balance of $300 in their account. How much does it cost the bank to provide this free service?
- Kitsap County Special Olympics holds a series of athletic events for disabled youth. How much money must be raised in the group's annual fund drive to support its planned activities?

- Chez Bonaparte is a dinner-only restaurant located in a middle-class neighborhood. The proprietor is considering opening for lunch. To be competitive, the average lunch must be priced about $7, and about 40 patrons can be served. Can the restaurant produce a lunch that meets its quality standards at an average cost of less than $7?
- The Monroe County School District is negotiating with the teacher's union. Among the issues are teachers' salaries, class size, and number of extracurricular activities offered. The union and the district have each made several proposals. How much will each of the various proposals cost? If class size were to increase by one student per class, what would be the added cost, and would these costs differ for elementary, junior high, and high school levels?

In answering these and a wide variety of other questions, managers turn to accounting for information. In this chapter, we consider the purposes and roles of accounting and accountants in different types of organizations as well as some of the trends and challenges faced by accountants today.

■ PURPOSES OF ACCOUNTING

Ultimately, all accounting information is accumulated to help someone make decisions. That someone may be a company president, a production manager, a hospital or school administrator, a sales manager, a shareholder, a small-business owner, a politician—the list is almost infinite. Almost all managers in every organization are better equipped to perform their duties when they have a reasonable grasp of accounting data. For example, a knowledge of accounting is crucial for decisions by government agencies regarding research contracts, defense contracts, and loan guarantees. The U.S. government continually makes decisions about loan guarantees to tiny businesses (for instance, through the Small Business Administration) and large corporations (such as Chrysler) as well as to banks and savings and loan companies. In fact, a survey of managers ranked accounting as the most important business course for future managers.

Objective 1

Describe the major users of accounting information

Users of Accounting Information

In general, users of accounting information fall into three categories.

1. Internal managers who use the information for short-term planning and controlling routine operations.
2. Internal managers who use the information for making nonroutine decisions (e.g., investing in equipment, pricing products and services, choosing which products to emphasize or de-emphasize) and formulating overall policies and long-range plans.
3. External parties, such as investors and government authorities, who use the information for making decisions about the company.

Both internal parties (managers) and external parties share an interest in accounting information, but their uses differ. Therefore, the types of accounting information they demand may also differ. *Management accounting* refers to accounting information developed for managers within an organization. In other words, **management accounting** is the process of identifying, measuring, accumulating, analyzing, preparing, interpreting, and communicating information that helps managers fulfill organizational objectives. In contrast, **financial accounting** refers to accounting information developed for the use of

management accounting The process of identifying, measuring, accumulating, analyzing, preparing, interpreting, and communicating information that helps managers fulfill organizational objectives.

financial accounting The field of accounting that develops information for external decision makers such as stockholders, suppliers, banks, and government regulatory agencies.

external parties such as stockholders, suppliers, banks, and government regulatory agencies.[1] The major distinctions between management accounting and financial accounting are listed in Exhibit 1-1.

	Management Accounting	Financial Accounting
Primary users	Organization managers at various levels.	Outside parties such as investors and government agencies but also organization managers.
Freedom of choice	No constraints other than costs in relation to benefits of improved management decisions.	Constrained by generally accepted accounting principles (GAAP).
Behavioral implications	Concern about how measurements and reports will influence managers' daily behavior.	Concern about how to measure and communicate economic phenomena. Behavioral considerations are secondary, although executive compensation based on reported results may have behavioral impacts.
Time focus	Future orientation: formal use of budgets as well as historical records. Example:19X6 budget versus 19X6 actual performance.	Past orientation: historical evaluation. Example: 19X6 actual performance versus 19X5 actual performance
Time span	Flexible, varying from hourly to 10 to 15 years.	Less flexible; usually 1 year or 1 quarter.
Reports	Detailed reports: concern about details of parts of the entity, products, departments, territories, etc.	Summary reports: concern primarily with entity as a whole.
Delineation of activities	Field is less sharply defined. Heavier use of economics, decision sciences, and behavioral sciences.	Field is more sharply defined. Lighter use of related disciplines.

The Need for Accounting Systems

accounting system A formal mechanism for gathering, organizing, and communicating information about an organization's activities.

Despite these differences, most organizations prefer a general-purpose accounting system that can supply appropriate information to all three types of users. An **accounting system** is a formal mechanism for gathering, organizing, and communicating information about an organization's activities. A good accounting system helps an organization achieve its goals and objectives by helping to answer three types of questions.

---

[1] For a book-length presentation of the subject, see Charles T. Horngren, Gary L. Sundem, and John A. Elliott, *Introduction to Financial Accounting* (Englewood Cliffs, NJ: Prentice Hall, 1996), the companion to this textbook.

scorekeeping The accumulation and classification of data.

attention directing Reporting and interpreting information that helps managers to focus on operating problems, imperfections, inefficiencies, and opportunities.

problem solving Aspect of accounting that quantifies the likely results of possible courses of action and often recommends the best course of action to follow.

Objective 2

Name the types of questions an accounting system helps to answer

1. *Scorecard questions*: Am I doing well or poorly? **Scorekeeping** is the accumulation and classification of data. This aspect of accounting enables both internal and external parties to evaluate organizational performance. The collection, classification, and reporting of scorekeeping information is the task that dominates day-to-day accounting.

2. *Attention-directing questions*: Which problems should I look into? **Attention directing** means reporting and interpreting information that helps managers to focus on operating problems, imperfections, inefficiencies, and opportunities. This aspect of accounting helps managers to concentrate on important areas of operations promptly enough for effective action. Attention directing is commonly associated with current planning and control, and with the analysis and investigation of recurring *routine* internal accounting reports.

3. *Problem-solving questions*: Of the several ways of doing a job, which is the best? The **problem-solving** aspect of accounting quantifies the likely results of possible courses of action and often recommends the best course to follow. Problem solving is commonly associated with nonrecurring decisions, situations that require special accounting analyses or reports.

The scorecard and attention-directing uses of information are closely related. The same information may serve a scorecard function for a manager and an attention-directing function for the manager's superior. For example, many accounting systems provide performance reports in which actual results of decisions and activities are compared with previously determined plans. By pinpointing where actual results differ from plans, such performance reports can show managers how they are doing and show the managers' superiors where to take action. In addition, the actual results help answer scorecard questions of financial accounting, which is chiefly concerned with reporting the results of the organization's activities to external parties.

In contrast, problem-solving information may be used in long-range planning and in making special, nonrecurring decisions, such as whether to make or buy parts, replace equipment, or add or drop a product. These decisions often require expert advice from specialists such as industrial engineers, budgetary accountants, and statisticians.

Sometimes all three facets of accounting overlap, making it difficult to classify a particular accounting task as a scorekeeping, attention-directing, or problem-solving task. Nevertheless, attempts to make these distinctions provide insight into the objectives and tasks of both accountants and managers. Exhibit 1-2 summarizes the relationships among the types of accounting information and their uses. Remember, however, that accounting systems are worthwhile only if they lead to better decisions.

Internal Versus External Accounting Systems

generally accepted accounting principles (GAAP) Broad concepts or guidelines and detailed practices, including all conventions, rules, and procedures that together make up accepted accounting practice at a given time.

Using one accounting system for both financial and management purposes sometimes creates problems. External forces (for example, income tax authorities and regulatory bodies such as the U.S. Securities and Exchange Commission and the California Health Facility Commission) often limit management's choices of accounting methods for external reports. Many organizations develop systems primarily to satisfy legal requirements imposed by external parties. These systems often neglect the needs of internal users.

Consider the annual financial reports by public corporations. These reports must adhere to a set of standards known as **generally accepted accounting principles (GAAP)**. GAAP includes broad concepts or guidelines and detailed

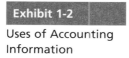

Exhibit 1-2

Uses of Accounting
Information

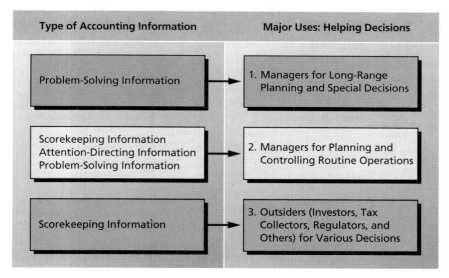

Type of Accounting Information	Major Uses: Helping Decisions
Problem-Solving Information	1. Managers for Long-Range Planning and Special Decisions
Scorekeeping Information Attention-Directing Information Problem-Solving Information	2. Managers for Planning and Controlling Routine Operations
Scorekeeping Information	3. Outsiders (Investors, Tax Collectors, Regulators, and Others) for Various Decisions

practices, including all conventions, rules, and procedures, that together make up accepted accounting practice at a given time. However, internal accounting reports need not be restricted by GAAP. For instance, GAAP requires that organizations account for their assets (economic resources) according to their historical cost. For its own management purpose, however, an organization can account for its economic resources on the basis of their *current values*, as measured by estimates of replacement costs. No outside agency can prohibit such accounting. Managers can create whatever kind of internal accounting system they want—-provided they are willing to pay the cost of developing and operating the system.

Of course, satisfying internal demands for information (as well as external demands) means that organizations may have to keep more than one set of records. At least in the United States, there is nothing immoral or unethical about having simultaneous sets of books—but they are expensive. Because external financial reports are required by authorities, many organizations do not choose to invest in a separate system for internal management purposes. Managers are forced to use information designed to meet external users' needs instead of information designed for their specific decisions.

Effects of Government Regulation

Even when management is willing to pay for a separate internal accounting system, that system may be affected by government regulation. The reason is that government agencies have legal power to order into evidence any internal document that they deem necessary.

Universities and defense contractors, for example, must allocate costs to government contracts in specified ways or risk government's refusal to pay. For example, in a widely publicized case in the early 1990s, Stanford University and several other prominent universities were denied reimbursement for certain costs that the government deemed inappropriate.

Foreign Corrupt Practices Act U.S. law forbidding bribery and other corrupt practices, and requiring that accounting records be maintained in reasonable detail and accuracy, and that an appropriate system of internal accounting controls be maintained.

management audit A review to determine whether the policies and procedures specified by top management have been implemented.

The **Foreign Corrupt Practices Act** is a U.S. law forbidding bribery and other corrupt practices. This law also requires that accounting records be maintained in reasonable detail and accuracy, and that an appropriate system of internal accounting controls be maintained. The title is misleading because the act's provisions apply to all publicly held companies, even if they conduct no business outside the United States.

The greatest impact of the act on accounting systems stems from the requirement that management must document the adequacy of internal accounting controls. As a result, many companies have greatly increased their internal auditing staffs and have elevated the status of such staffs. Often the internal audit staff reports directly to the president, sometimes even to the board of directors.

Internal auditors help review and evaluate systems to help minimize errors, fraud, and waste. More important, many internal auditing staffs have a primary responsibility for conducting management audits. A **management audit** is a review to determine whether the policies and procedures specified by top management have been implemented. Management audits are not confined to profit-seeking organizations. The General Accounting Office (GAO) of the U.S. government conducts these audits on a massive scale. Most states also have audit agencies that audit departments of the state government. Some also audit municipalities and other local government organizations.

The overall impact of government regulation is very controversial. Many managers insist that the extra costs of compliance far exceed any possible benefits. One benefit, however, is that operating managers, now more than ever, must become more intimately familiar with their accounting systems. The resulting changes in the systems sometimes provide stronger controls and more informative reports.

■ MANAGEMENT ACCOUNTING IN SERVICE AND NONPROFIT ORGANIZATIONS

The basic ideas of management accounting were developed in manufacturing organizations. These ideas, however, have evolved so that they are applicable to all types of organizations including service organizations. Service organizations, for our purposes, are all organizations other than manufacturers, wholesalers, and retailers. That is, they are organizations that do not make or sell tangible goods. Public accounting firms, law firms, management consultants, real estate firms, transportation companies, banks, insurance companies, and hotels are profit-seeking service organizations.

Almost all nonprofit organizations, such as hospitals, schools, libraries, museums, and government agencies, are also service organizations. Managers and accountants in nonprofit organizations have much in common with their counterparts in profit-seeking organizations. There is money to be raised and spent. There are budgets to be prepared and control systems to be designed and implemented. There is an obligation to use resources wisely. If used intelligently, accounting contributes to efficient operations and helps nonprofit organizations achieve their objectives.

The characteristics of both profit-seeking and nonprofit service organizations include the following:

1. *Labor is intensive*: The highest proportion of expenses in schools and law firms are wages, salaries, and payroll-related costs, not the costs relating to the use of machinery, equipment, and physical facilities.
2. *Output is usually difficult to define*: The output of a university might be defined as the number of degrees granted, but many critics would maintain that the real output is "what is contained in the students' brains." Therefore, measuring output is often considered impossible.
3. *Major inputs and outputs cannot be stored*: An empty airline seat cannot be saved for a later flight, and a hotel's available labor force and rooms are either used or unused as each day occurs.

In this book, references are made to service industry and nonprofit organization applications as the various management accounting techniques are discussed. A major generalization is worth mentioning at the outset. Simplicity is the watchword for installation of systems in service industries and nonprofit organizations. In fact, many professionals such as physicians, professors, or government officials resist even filling out a time card. In fact, simplicity is a fine watchword for the design of any accounting system. Complexity tends to generate costs of gathering and interpreting data that often exceed prospective benefits. Concern for simplicity is sometimes expressed as KISS (which means "keep it simple, stupid").

■ COST-BENEFIT AND BEHAVIORAL CONSIDERATIONS

In addition to simplicity, two major themes should guide the design of all accounting systems: (1) cost-benefit balances and (2) behavioral implications. Both will be described briefly now. Because of their importance, both will also be mentioned often in succeeding chapters.

cost-benefit balance
Weighing estimated costs against probable benefits, the primary consideration in choosing among accounting systems and methods.

The **cost-benefit balance**—weighing estimated costs against probable benefits—is the primary consideration in choosing among accounting systems and methods. The need to balance costs and benefits dominates management accounting and will dominate this book. Systems and methods are economic goods available at various costs. Which system does a manager want to buy? A simple file drawer for amassing receipts and canceled checks? An elaborate budgeting system based on computerized descriptive models of the organization and its subunits? Or something in between?

The answer depends on the buyer's perceptions of the expected benefits in relation to the costs. For example, a hospital administrator may contemplate the installation of a TECHNICON computerized system for controlling hospital operations. Users of such a system need only enter a piece of information once. The system automatically incorporates that datum into financial records, medical records, costs by departments, nurse staffing requirements, drug administration, billings for patients, revenue generated by physicians, and so forth. Such a system is highly efficient and is subject to few errors. The system costs $14 million, however. Thus the system is neither a "good buy" nor a "bad buy" in itself. Rather, it must meet the test of the economics of information—its value must exceed its cost.

The value of a loaf of bread may exceed a cost of 50¢ a loaf, but it may not exceed a cost of $5 per loaf. Similarly, a particular accounting system may be a wise investment if its cost is sufficiently small. Like a consumer who switches from bread to potatoes if the cost of bread is too high, managers seek other sources of information if accounting systems are too expensive. In many organizations it may be more economical to gather some kinds of data by one-shot special efforts than by a ponderous system that repetitively gathers rarely used data.

The need to balance costs and benefits appeals to both the hard-headed manager and the theoretician. Managers have been using the cost-benefit test for years, even though they may refer to it as "just being practical."

behavioral implications The accounting system's effect on the behavior (decisions) of managers.

In addition to the costs and benefits of an accounting system, the buyer of such a system should also consider **behavioral implications**, that is, the system's effect on the behavior (decisions) of managers. The system must provide accurate, timely budgets and performance reports in a form useful to managers. If managers do not use accounting reports, the reports create no benefits.

Management accounting reports affect employees' feelings and behavior. Consider a performance report that is used to evaluate the operations under the responsibility of a particular manager. If the report unfairly attributes excessive costs to the operation, the manager may lose confidence in the system and not let it influence future decisions. In contrast, a system that managers believe in and trust can be a major influence on their decisions and actions.

In a nutshell, management accounting can best be understood as a balance between costs and benefits coupled with an awareness of the importance of behavioral effects. Even more than financial accounting, management accounting spills over into related disciplines, such as economics, the decision sciences, and the behavioral sciences.

■ THE MANAGEMENT PROCESS AND ACCOUNTING

Regardless of the type of organization, managers benefit when accounting provides information that helps them plan and control the organization's operations.

The Nature of Planning and Controlling

decision making The purposeful choice from among a set of alternative courses of action designed to achieve some objective.

The management process is a series of activities in a cycle of planning and control. **Decision making**—the purposeful choice from among a set of alternative courses of action designed to achieve some objective—is the core of the management process. Decisions range from the routine (making daily production schedules) to the nonroutine (launching a new product line).

Decisions within an organization are often divided into two types: (1) planning decisions and (2) control decisions. In practice, planning and control are so intertwined that it seems artificial to separate them. In studying management, however, it is useful to concentrate on either the planning phase or the control phase to simplify the analysis.

Objective 5

Explain the role of budgets and performance reports in planning and control

The left side of Exhibit 1-3 demonstrates the planning and control cycle of current operations. Planning (the top box) refers to setting objectives and outlining how they will be attained. Thus planning provides the answers to two questions: What is desired? When and how is it to be accomplished? In contrast, controlling (the two boxes labeled "Action" and "Evaluation") refers to *implementing* plans and *using feedback* to attain objectives. Feedback is crucial to the cycle of planning and control. Planning determines action, action generates feedback, and feedback influences further planning. Timely, systematic reports provided by the internal accounting system are the chief source of useful feedback.

Management by Exception

budget A quantitative expression of a plan of action, and an aid to coordinating and implementing the plan.

The right side of Exhibit 1-3 shows that accounting formalizes *plans* by expressing them as budgets. A **budget** is a quantitative expression of a plan of action; it is also an aid to coordinating and implementing the plan. Budgets are the chief devices for compelling and disciplining management planning. Without budgets, planning may not get the front-and-center focus that it usually deserves.

Exhibit 1-3

Accounting Framework for Planning and Control

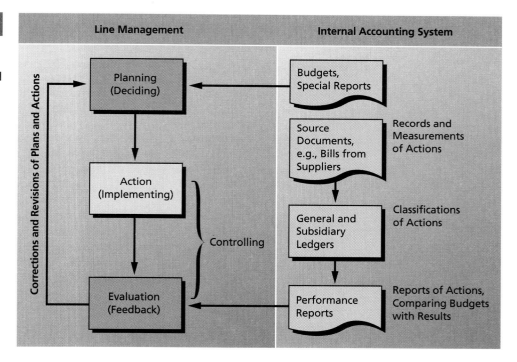

performance reports Feedback provided by comparing results with plans and by highlighting variances.

variances Deviations from plans.

management by exception Concentrating on areas that deviate from the plan and ignoring areas that are presumed to be running smoothly.

Accounting formalizes control as **performance reports** (the last box), which provide feedback by comparing results with plans and by highlighting **variances**, which are deviations from plans. The accounting system records, measures, and classifies actions in order to produce performance reports.

Exhibit 1-4 shows a simple performance report for a law firm. Performance reports are used to judge decisions and the productivity of organizational units and managers. By comparing actual results to budgets, performance reports motivate managers to achieve the budgeted objectives.

Performance reports spur investigation of exceptions—items for which actual amounts differ significantly from budgeted amounts. Operations are then brought into conformity with the plans, or the plans are revised. This is often called **management by exception**, which means concentrating on areas that deviate from the plan and ignoring areas that are presumed to be running smoothly. Thus the management-by-exception approach frees managers from needless concern with those phases of operations that are adhering to plans. However, well-conceived plans should incorporate enough discretion or flexibility so that the manager may feel free to pursue any unforeseen opportunities. In other words, control should not be a straightjacket. When unfolding events call for actions not specifically authorized in the plan, managers should be able to take these actions.

Exhibit 1-4

Performance Report

	Budgeted Amounts	Actual Amounts	Deviations or Variances	Explanation
Revenue from fees	XXX	XXX	XX	—
Various expenses	XXX	XXX	XX	—
Net income	XXX	XXX	XX	—

Illustration of Budgets and Performance Reports

Suppose the Casaverde Company manufactures electric fans. Consider the department that assembles the fans. Workers assemble the parts and install the motor largely by hand. They then inspect each fan before transferring it to the packaging and shipping department. The present sales forecast has led managers to plan a production schedule of 10,000 fans for the coming month. The assembly department budget in Exhibit 1-5 shows cost classifications.

Exhibit 1-5

Casaverde Company Assembly Department Budget for the Month Ended March 31, 19X1

Production activity	10,000 fans
Material (detailed by type: metal stampings, motors, etc.)	$ 68,000
Assembly labor (detailed by job classification, number of workers, etc.)	43,000
Other labor (managers, inspectors)	12,000
Utilities, maintenance, etc.	7,500
Supplies (small tools, lubricants, etc.)	2,500
Total	$133,000

The operating plan for the department, in the form of a department budget for the coming month, is prepared in conferences attended by the department manager, the manager's supervisor, and an accountant. They scrutinize each of the costs subject to the manager's control. They often use the average amount of the cost for the past few months as a guide, especially if past performance has been good. However, the budget is a *forecast* of costs for the projected level of production activity. Hence, conference members must predict each cost in light of trends, price changes, alterations in product mix and characteristics, production methods, and changes in the level of production activity from month to month. Only then can they formulate the budget that becomes the manager's target for the month.

As actual factory costs are incurred, Casaverde's accounting system collects them and classifies them by department. At the end of the month (or weekly, or even daily, for such key items as materials or assembly labor), the accounting department prepares an assembly department performance report. Exhibit 1-6 is a simplified report. In practice, this report may be very detailed and contain explanations of variances from the budget.

Department heads and their superiors use the performance report to help appraise how effectively and efficiently the department is operating. Their focus is on the variances—the deviations from the budget. Casaverde's assembly department performance report (Exhibit 1-6) shows that although the department produced 140 fewer fans than planned, material costs were $1,000 over budget, and assembly labor was $1,300 over budget. By investigating such variances managers may find better ways of doing things.

Exhibit 1-6		Budget	Actual	Variance
Casaverde Company Assembly Department Performance Report for the Month Ended March 31, 19X1	Production activity in units	10,000	9,860	140 U
	Material (detailed by type: metal stampings, motors, etc.)	$ 68,000	$ 69,000	$1,000 U
	Assembly labor (detailed by job classification, number of workers, etc.)	43,000	44,300	1,300 U
	Other labor (managers, inspectors)	12,000	11,200	800 F
	Utilities, maintenance, etc.	7,500	7,400	100 F
	Supplies (small tools, lubricants, etc.)	2,500	2,600	100 U
	Total	$133,000	$134,500	$1,500 U

U = Unfavorable; actual exceeds budget
F = Favorable; actual is less than budget

Notice that although budgets aid planning and performance reports aid control, it is not accountants but other managers and their subordinates who evaluate accounting reports and actually plan and control operations. Accounting *assists* the managerial planning and control function by providing prompt measurements of actions and by systematically pinpointing trouble spots.

■ PLANNING AND CONTROL FOR PRODUCT LIFE CYCLES

product life cycle
The various stages through which a product passes, from conception and development through introduction into the market through maturation and, finally, withdrawal from the market.

Many management decisions relate to a single good or service, or to a group of related products. To effectively plan for and control production of such goods or services, accountants and other managers must consider the product's life cycle. **Product life cycle** refers to the various stages through which a product passes, from conception and development through introduction into the market through maturation and, finally, withdrawal from the market. At each stage, managers face differing costs and potential returns. Exhibit 1-7 shows a typical product life cycle.

Exhibit 1-7	No Sales	Sales Growth	Stable Sales Level	Low Sales ⟶ No Sales
Typical Product Life Cycle	Product Development	Introduction to Market	Mature Market	Phase-out of Product

Product life cycles range from a few months (for fashion clothing or faddish toys) to many years (for automobiles or refrigerators). Some products, such as many computer software packages, have long development stages and relatively short market lives. Others, such as Boeing 727 airplanes, have market lives many times longer than their development stage.

In the planning process, managers must recognize revenues and costs over the entire life cycle—however long or short. Accounting needs to track actual costs and revenues throughout the life cycle, too. Periodic comparisons between *planned* costs and revenues and *actual* costs and revenues allow managers to assess the current profitability of a product, determine its current product life-cycle stage, and make any needed changes in strategy.

For example, suppose a pharmaceutical company is developing a new drug to reduce high blood pressure. The budget for the product should plan for costs without revenues in the product development stage. Most of the revenues come in the introduction and mature-market stages, and a pricing strategy should recognize the need for revenues to cover both development and phase-out costs as well as the direct costs of producing the drug. During phase-out, costs of producing the drug must be balanced with both the revenue generated and the need to keep the drug on the market for those who have come to rely on it.

Objective 6

Discuss the effect of product life cycles on assessing product profitability

■ ACCOUNTING'S POSITION IN THE ORGANIZATION

To assist other managers in the decision making vital to an organization's success, most companies (and many nonprofit organizations and government agencies) employ a variety of accounting personnel with various types of authority and responsibility.

Line and Staff Authority

line authority
Authority exerted downward over subordinates.

staff authority
Authority to advise but not command. It may be exerted downward, laterally, or upward.

controller (comptroller)
The top accounting officer of an organization. The term comptroller is used primarily in government organizations.

The organization chart in Exhibit 1-8 shows how a typical manufacturing company divides responsibilities. Notice the distinction between line and staff authority. **Line authority** is authority exerted downward over subordinates. **Staff authority** is authority to advise but not command. It may be exerted downward, laterally, or upward.

Most organizations specify certain activities as their basic mission. Most missions involve the production and sale of goods or services. All subunits of the organization that are directly responsible for conducting these basic activities are called line departments. The others are called staff departments because their principal task is to support or service the line departments. Thus staff activities are indirectly related to the basic activities of the organization. Exhibit 1-8 shows a series of factory-service departments that perform staff functions supporting the line functions carried on by the production departments.

The top accounting officer of an organization is often called the **controller** or, especially in a government organization, a **comptroller**. This executive, like virtually everyone in an accounting function, fills a staff role, whereas sales and production executives and their subordinates fill line roles. The accounting

Exhibit 1-8

Partial Organization Chart of a Manufacturing Company

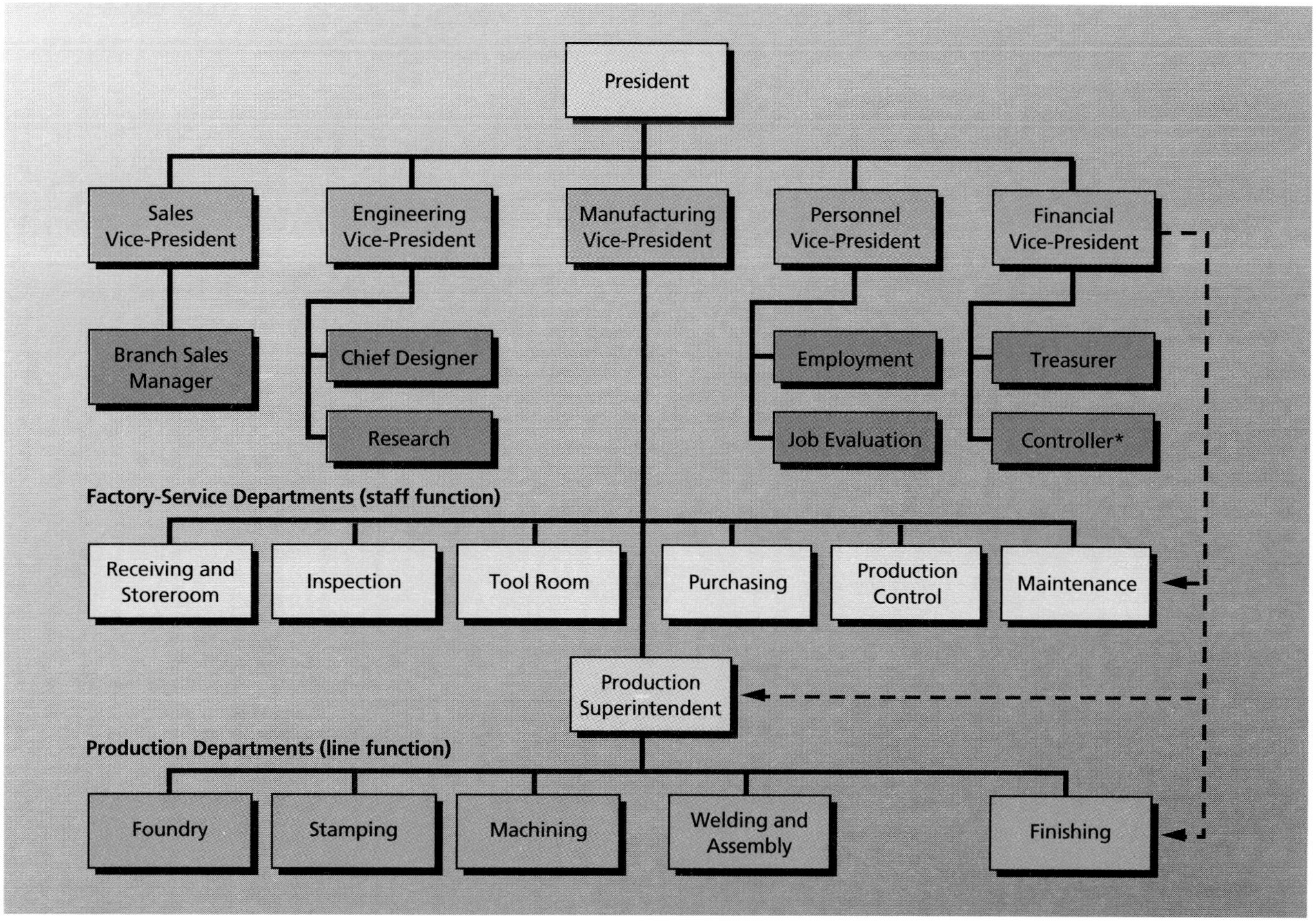

Factory-Service Departments (staff function)

Production Departments (line function)

For detailed organization of a controller's department, see Exhibit 1-9. Dashed line represents staff authority of the finance staff to advise those in manufacturing operations.

department does not exercise direct authority over line departments. Rather, the accounting department provides other managers with specialized service including advice and help in budgeting, analyzing variances, pricing, and making special decisions.

Objective 7

Distinguish between line and staff roles in an organization

Exhibit 1-9 shows how a controller's department may be organized. In particular, note the distinctions among the scorekeeping, attention-directing, and problem-solving roles of various personnel. Unless some internal accountants are given the last two roles as their primary responsibilities, the scorekeeping tasks tend to dominate and the system becomes less responsive to management's decision making.

Exhibit 1-9   Organization Chart of a Controller's Department

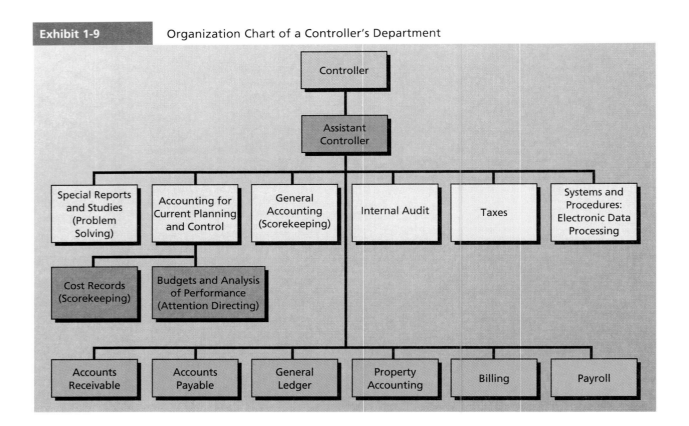

The Controller

The controller position varies in stature and duties from company to company. In some firms the controller is confined to compiling data, primarily for external reporting purposes. In others, such as General Electric, the controller is a key executive who aids managerial planning and control throughout the company's subdivisions. In most firms controllers have a status somewhere between these two extremes. For example, their opinions on the tax implications of certain management decisions may be carefully weighed, yet their opinions on other aspects of these decisions may not be sought.

Although controllers (or comptrollers) have a staff role, they are generally empowered by the firm's president to approve, install, and oversee the organization's accounting system to ensure uniform accounting and reporting methods. In theory, the controller proposes these systems and methods to the president, who approves and orders compliance with them on the part of line personnel (thus preserving the "staff" advisory role of accounting). In practice, however, controllers usually directly specify how production records should be kept or how time records should be completed. The controller holds delegated authority from top-line management over such matters.

In theory, then, controllers have no line authority except over the accounting department. Yet, by reporting and interpreting relevant data, controllers do exert a force or influence that leads management toward logical decisions that are consistent with the organization's objectives.

Distinctions Between Controller and Treasurer

Many people confuse the offices of controller and treasurer. The Financial Executives Institute, an association of corporate treasurers and controllers, distinguishes their functions as follows:

Objective 8

Contrast functions of controllers and treasurers

CONTROLLERSHIP	TREASURERSHIP
1. Planning for control	1. Provision of capital
2. Reporting and interpreting	2. Investor relations
3. Evaluating and consulting	3. Short-term financing
4. Tax administration	4. Banking and custody
5. Government reporting	5. Credits and collections
6. Protection of assets	6. Investments
7. Economic appraisal	7. Risk management (insurance)

Management accounting is the primary means of implementing the first three functions of controllership.

The treasurer is concerned mainly with the company's financial matters, the controller with operating matters. The exact division of accounting and financial duties varies from company to company. In a small organization, the same person might be both treasurer and controller.

The controller has been compared with a ship's navigator. The navigator uses specialized training to assist the captain. Without the navigator, the ship may founder on reefs or miss its destination entirely. The navigator guides and informs the captain as to how well the ship is being steered, but the captain exerts the right to command. This navigator role is especially evident in the first three functions listed for controllership.

■ CAREER OPPORTUNITIES IN MANAGEMENT ACCOUNTING

The many types and levels of accounting personnel found in the typical organization mean that there are broad opportunities awaiting those who master the accounting discipline.

Certified Management Accountant

Certified Public Accountant (CPA) In the United States, an accountant earns this designation by a combination of education, qualifying experience, and the passing of a two-day written national examination.

Certified Management Accountant (CMA) The management accountant's counterpart to the CPA.

Institute of Management Accountants (IMA) The largest U.S. professional organization of accountants whose major interest is management accounting.

When accounting is mentioned, most people think first of independent auditors who reassure the public about the reliability of the financial information supplied by company managers. These external auditors are called certified public accountants in the United States and chartered accountants in many other English-speaking nations. In the United States, an accountant earns the designation of **Certified Public Accountant (CPA)** by a combination of education, qualifying experience, and the passing of a two-day written national examination. The major U.S. professional association in the private sector that regulates the quality of outside auditors is the American Institute of Certified Public Accountants (AICPA).

In recent years, increased interest in and demand for management accounting has led to development of the **Certified Management Accountant (CMA)** designation, the internal accountant's counterpart to the CPA. The **Institute of Management Accountants (IMA)**, formerly called the National Association of Accountants, is the largest U.S. professional organization of accountants whose major interest is management accounting. The IMA oversees the CMA program, which has three main objectives:

1. To establish management accounting as a recognized profession by identifying the role of the management accountant and the underlying body of knowledge and by outlining a course of study by which such knowledge can be acquired
2. To foster higher educational standards in the field of management accounting
3. To establish an objective measure of an individual's knowledge and competence in the field of management accounting

The highlight of the CMA program is a two-day qualifying examination in four parts: (1) economics, finance, and management; (2) financial accounting and reporting; (3) management reporting, analysis, and behavioral issues; and (4) decision analysis and information systems.[2] The CMA designation is gaining increased stature in the management community as a credential parallel to the CPA.

Training for Top Management Positions

In addition to preparing you for a position in an accounting department, studying accounting—and working as a management accountant—can prepare you for the very highest levels of management. Accounting deals with all facets of an organization, no matter how complex, so it provides an excellent opportunity to gain broad knowledge. Accounting must embrace all management functions, including purchasing, manufacturing, wholesaling, retailing, and a variety of marketing and transportation activities. Senior accountants or controllers in a corporation are sometimes picked as production or marketing executives. Why? Because they may have impressed other executives as having acquired general management skills. A number of recent surveys have indicated that more chief executive officers began their careers in an

---

[2] Information can be obtained from the IMA, 10 Paragon Drive, Montvale, NJ 07645-1759.

accounting position than in any other area, including marketing, production, and engineering.

Former controllers have risen to the top of such mammoth companies as Pepsico and Pfizer. According to *Business Week*, controllers

> are now getting involved with the operating side of the company, where they give advice and influence production, marketing, and investment decisions as well as corporate planning. Moreover, many controllers who have not made it to the top have won ready access to top management. . . . Probably the main reason the controller is getting the ear of top management these days is that he or she is virtually the only person familiar with all the working parts of the company.

ADAPTATION TO CHANGE

The growing interest in management accounting also stems from its ability to help managers adapt to change. Indeed, the one constant in the world of business is change. Today's economic decisions differ from those of 10 years ago. As decisions change, demands for information change. *Accountants must adapt their systems to the changes in management practices and technology.* A system that produces valuable information in one setting may be valueless in another.

Accountants have not always been responsive to the need to change. A decade ago many managers complained about the irrelevance of accounting information. Why? Because their decision environment had changed but accounting systems had not. However, most progressive companies have now changed their accounting systems to recognize the realities of today's complex, technical, and global business environment. Instead of being irrelevant, accountants in such companies are adding more value than ever. For example, *Management Accounting* (September, 1994) reported on a Champion International Corporation paper mill that made major changes in its accounting system. By working with managers to produce the information considered relevant for their decisions, accountants became regarded as "business partners." Previously, managers had considered accountants to be a "financial police department." Instead of merely pointing out problems, the accountants became part of the solution.

Current Trends

Three major factors are causing changes in management accounting today:

1. Shift from a manufacturing-based to a service-based economy
2. Increased global competition
3. Advances in technology

Objective 9

Identify current trends in management accounting

Each of these factors will affect your study of management accounting.

The service sector now accounts for almost 80% of the employment in the United States. Service industries are becoming increasingly competitive, and their use of accounting information is growing. Basic accounting principles are applied to service organizations throughout this book.

Global competition has increased in recent years as many international barriers to trade, such as tariffs and duties, have been lowered. In addition, there has been a worldwide trend toward deregulation. The result has been a shift in the balance of economic power in the world. Nowhere has this been more evident than in the United States. To regain their competitive edge, many U.S. companies are redesigning their accounting systems to provide more accurate and timely information about the cost of activities, products, or services. To be competitive, managers must understand the effects of their decisions on costs, and accountants must help managers predict such effects.

By far the most dominant influence on management accounting over the past decade has been technological change. This change has affected both the production and the use of accounting information. The increasing capabilities and decreasing cost of computers, especially personal computers (PCs), has changed how accountants gather, store, manipulate, and report data. Most accounting systems, even small ones, are automated. In addition, computers enable managers to access data directly and to generate their own reports and analyses in many cases. By using spreadsheet software and graphics packages, managers can use accounting information directly in their decision process. Thus, all managers need a better understanding of accounting information now than they may have needed in the past. In addition, accountants need to create databases that can be readily understood by managers.

Technological change has also dramatically changed the manufacturing environment for many companies, causing changes in how accounting information is used. Manufacturing processes are increasingly automated. Automated manufacturing processes make extensive use of robots and other computer-controlled equipment and less use of human labor for direct production activities. Many early accounting systems were designed primarily to measure and report the cost of labor. Why? Because human labor was the largest cost in the production of many products and services. Clearly, such systems are not appropriate in automated environments. Accountants in such settings have had to change their systems to produce information for decisions about how to acquire and use materials and automated equipment efficiently.

Just-in-Time Philosophy and Computer-Integrated Manufacturing

just-in-time (JIT) philosophy A philosophy to eliminate waste by reducing the time products spend in the production process and eliminating the time products spend on activities that do not add value.

Accompanying technological change has been a change in management philosophy. The most important recent change leading to increased efficiency in American factories has been the adoption of a **just-in-time (JIT) philosophy**. The essence of the philosophy is to eliminate waste. Managers try to (1) reduce the time that products spend in the production process and (2) eliminate the time that products spend on activities that do not add value (such as inspection and waiting time).

Process time can be reduced by redesigning and simplifying the production process. Companies can use *computer-aided design (CAD)* to design products that can be manufactured efficiently. Even small changes in design often lead to large manufacturing cost savings. Companies can also use *computer-aided manufacturing (CAM)*, in which computers direct and control production equipment. CAM often leads to a smoother, more efficient flow of production with fewer delays.

computer-integrated manufacturing (CIM) systems Systems that use computer-aided design and computer-aided manufacturing, together with robots and computer-controlled machines.

Systems that use CAD and CAM together with robots and computer-controlled machines are called **computer-integrated manufacturing (CIM) systems**. Companies that install a full CIM system use very little labor. Robots and computer-controlled machines perform the routine jobs that were previously done by assembly-line workers. In addition, well-designed systems provide great flexibility because design changes require alterations only in computer programs, not retraining of an entire work force.

Time spent on activities that do not add value to the product can be eliminated or reduced by focusing on quality, improving plant layout, and cross-training workers. Achieving zero production defects ("doing it right the first time") reduces inspection time and eliminates rework time. One midwestern factory saved production time by redesigning its plant layout so that the distance products traveled from one operation to the next during production was reduced from 1,384 feet to 350 feet. Another company reduced setup time on a machine from 45 minutes to 1 minute by storing the required tools nearby and training the machine operator to do the setup. A British company reduced the time to manufacture a vacuum pump from 3 weeks to 6 minutes by switching from long assembly lines to manufacturing cells that accomplish the entire process in quick succession.

Originally, JIT referred only to an inventory system that minimized inventories by arranging for materials and subcomponents to arrive just as they were needed and for goods to be made just in time to be shipped to customers—no sooner and no later. But JIT has become the cornerstone of a broad management philosophy. It originated in Japanese companies such as Toyota and Kawasaki, and now has been adopted by many large U.S. companies including Hewlett-Packard and Xerox. Many small firms have also embraced JIT.

Implications for the Study of Management Accounting

As you read the remainder of this book, remember that accounting systems change as the world changes. The techniques presented in this book are being applied in real organizations today. Tomorrow may be different, however. *To adapt to changes, you must understand why the techniques are being used, not just how they are used. We urge you to resist the temptation simply to memorize rules and techniques.* Instead, develop your understanding of the underlying concepts and principles. These will continue to be useful in developing and understanding new techniques for changing environments.

■ IMPORTANCE OF ETHICAL CONDUCT

Although accounting systems may change, the need for accountants to adhere to high ethical standards of professional conduct has never been greater.

Standards of Ethical Conduct

Public opinion surveys consistently rank accountants high in terms of their professional ethics. CPAs and CMAs adhere to codes of conduct regarding competence, confidentiality, integrity, and objectivity. Exhibit 1-10 contains the

Standards of Ethical Conduct for Management Accountants
Codes of conduct developed by the Institute of Management Accountants, which include competence, confidentiality, integrity, and objectivity.

Standards of Ethical Conduct for Management Accountants developed by the IMA. Professional accounting organizations have procedures for reviewing alleged behavior not consistent with the standards.

Preparing objective, accurate external and internal financial reports is primarily the responsibility of line managers. However, management accountants are also responsible for the reports. Ensuring that accounting systems, procedures, and compilations are reliable and free of manipulation is ultimately the responsibility of every accountant.

Ethical Dilemmas

What makes an action by an accountant unethical? An unethical act is one that violates the ethical standards of the profession. The standards, however, leave much room for individual interpretation and judgment.

When one action is clearly unethical and another alternative is clearly ethical, managers and accountants should have no difficulty choosing between them. Unfortunately, most ethical dilemmas are not that clear-cut. The most difficult situations arise when there is strong pressure to take an action that is borderline or when two ethical standards conflict.

Suppose you are an accountant who has been asked to supply the company's banker with a profit forecast for the coming year. A badly needed bank loan rides on the prediction. The company president is absolutely convinced that profits will be at least $500,000. Anything less than that and the loan is not likely to be approved.

Your analysis shows that if the planned introduction of a new product goes extraordinarily well, profits will exceed $500,000. The most likely outcome, however, is for a modestly successful introduction and a $100,000 profit. If the product fails, the company stands to lose $600,000. Without the loan, the new product cannot be taken to the market, and there is no way the company can avoid a loss for the year. Bankruptcy is even a possibility.

What forecast would you make? There is no easy answer. A forecast of less than $500,000 seems to guarantee financial problems, perhaps even bankruptcy. Stockholders, management, employees, suppliers, and customers may all be hurt. But a forecast of $500,000 may not be fair and objective. The bank may be misled by it. Still, the president apparently thinks a $500,000 forecast is reasonable, and you know that there is some chance it will be achieved. Perhaps the potential benefit to the company of an overly optimistic forecast is greater than the possible cost to the bank.

There is no right answer to this dilemma. The important point is to recognize the ethical dimensions and weigh them when forming your judgment.

The tone set by top management can have a great influence on managers' ethics. Complete integrity and outspoken support for ethical standards by senior managers is the single greatest motivator of ethical behavior throughout an organization. In the final analysis, however, ethical standards are personal and depend on the values of the individual.

Exhibit 1-10

Standards of Ethical Conduct for Management Accountants

Objective 10

Explain a management accountant's ethical responsibilities

Management accountants have an obligation to the organizations they serve, their profession, the public, and themselves to maintain the highest standards of ethical conduct. In recognition of this obligation, the Institute of Management Accountants has adopted the following standards of ethical conduct for management accountants. Adherence to these standards is integral to achieving the objectives of management accounting. Management accountants shall not commit acts contrary to these standards nor shall they condone the commission of such acts by others within their organizations.

Competence

Management accountants have a responsibility to
- Maintain an appropriate level of professional competence by ongoing development of their knowledge and skills.
- Perform their professional duties in accordance with relevant laws, regulations, and technical standards.
- Prepare complete and clear reports and recommendations after appropriate analyses of relevant and reliable information.

Confidentiality

Management accountants have a responsibility to
- Refrain from disclosing confidential information acquired in the course of their work except when authorized, unless legally obligated to do so.
- Inform subordinates as appropriate regarding the confidentiality of information acquired in the course of their work and monitor their activities to assure the maintenance of that confidentiality.
- Refrain from using or appearing to use confidential information acquired in the course of their work for unethical or illegal advantage either personally or through third parties.

Integrity

Management accountants have a responsibility to
- Avoid actual or apparent conflicts of interest and advise all appropriate parties of any potential conflict.
- Refrain from engaging in any activity that would prejudice their ability to carry out their duties ethically.
- Refuse any gift, favor, or hospitality that would influence or would appear to influence their actions.
- Refrain from either actively or passively subverting the attainment of the organization's legitimate and ethical objectives.
- Recognize and communicate professional limitations or other constraints that would preclude responsible judgment or successful performance of an activity.
- Communicate unfavorable as well as favorable information and professional judgments or opinions.
- Refrain from engaging in or supporting any activity that would discredit the profession.

Objectivity

Management accountants have a responsibility to
- Communicate information fairly and objectively.
- Disclose fully all relevant information that could reasonably be expected to influence an intended user's understanding of the reports, comments, and recommendations presented.

Ethics at General Motors

The importance of ethics to management accountants was emphasized when *Management Accounting*, the journal of the Institute of Management Accountants, put out a special issue on ethics in June 1990. Two thrusts run through the articles in the issue: (1) business schools must make students aware of the ethical dimension of the decisions they will face in the business world, and (2) business firms must recognize that establishing standards of ethical conduct for their employees is important to financial success. As a follow-up, *Management Accounting* instituted a regular column on ethics. A recent column presented a case on the ethics of planned obsolescence of products. Many readers submitted solutions to the case, some of which were published in *Management Accounting*, showing that ethical dilemmas generate a great deal of interest.

Roger B. Smith, former Chairman and Chief Executive Officer of General Motors, stated that "ethical practice is, quite simply, good business." Since 1977 GM has had a policy on personal integrity. But GM recognizes that making ethical decisions is not always easy. Because the world is complex, there are often competing obligations to shareholders, customers, suppliers, fellow managers, society, and self and family. As Smith says, "It is easy to do what is right; it is hard to know what is right." A basic rule used by GM is that employees "should never do anything [they] would be ashamed to explain to [their] families or be afraid to see on the front page of the local newspaper."

General Motors is not alone in promoting ethical conduct. Over half of the large companies in the United States have a "Corporate Code of Conduct." These codes provide support to employees who feel pressured to make decisions they believe to be unethical. They also provide training in the types of behavior expected of employees. ■

Sources: From Roger B. Smith, "Ethics in Business: An Essential Element of Success," Management Accounting, *Special Issue on Ethics in Corporate America (June 1990), p. 50; Robert B. Sweeney and Howard L. Siers, "Ethics in America,"* Management Accounting, *Special Issue on Ethics in Corporate America (June 1990), pp. 34–40; and James A. Healy and Roy L. Nersesian, "The Case of Planned Obsolescence,"* Management Accounting *(February 1994), pp. 67–68.*

Highlights to Remember

Accounting information is useful to internal managers for making short-term planning and control decisions, for making nonroutine decisions, and for formulating overall policies and long-range plans. The accounting information answers scorekeeping, attention-directing, and problem-solving questions. Management accounting focuses on information for internal decision makers (managers), and financial accounting focuses on information for external parties.

Many management accounting techniques were developed in profit-seeking manufacturing companies because such companies often had a greater need for sophisticated accounting information. However, there is increasing application of management accounting in service and nonprofit organizations.

Management accounting systems exist for the benefit of managers. Systems should be judged by a cost-benefit criterion—the benefits of better decisions should exceed the cost of the system. The benefit of a system will be affected by behavioral factors—how the system affects managers and their decisions.

An essential tool for performance evaluation is a budget. A performance report compares actual results to the budget. To interpret accounting information about a particular product appropriately, it is often important to recognize the product's position in its product life cycle.

Accountants are staff employees who provide information and advice for line managers. The head of accounting is often called the controller. Unlike the treasurer, who is concerned primarily with financial matters, the controller measures and reports on operating performance.

The future worth of an accounting system will be affected by how easily and well the system can adapt to change. A changing business environment may require the accounting system to collect and report new data and discontinue reporting information that is no longer needed. Changes affecting accounting systems include growth in the service sector of the economy, increased global competition, and advances in technology. Information needs of organizations that adopt a just-in-time philosophy or use computer-aided design and manufacturing systems differ from those of more traditional firms.

Finally, both external and internal accountants are expected to adhere to standards of ethical conduct. Many ethical dilemmas, however, require value judgments, not the simple application of standards.

Summary Problems for Your Review

Try to solve these problems before examining the solutions that follow.

Problem One

The scorekeeping, attention-directing, and problem-solving duties of the accountant have been described in this chapter. The accountant's usefulness to management is said to be directly influenced by how good an attention director and problem solver he or she is.

Evaluate this contention by specifically relating the accountant's duties to the duties of operating management.

Solution to Problem One

Operating managers may have to be good scorekeepers, but their major duties are to concentrate on the day-to-day problems that most need attention, to make longer-range plans, and to arrive at special decisions. Accordingly, because managers are concerned mainly with attention directing and problem solving, they will obtain the most benefit from the alert internal accountant who is a useful attention director and problem solver.

Problem Two

Using the organization charts in this chapter (Exhibits 1-8 and 1-9), answer the following questions:

1. Which of the following have line authority over the machining manager: maintenance manager, manufacturing vice-president, production superintendent, purchasing agent, scorekeeper, personnel vice-president, president, chief budgetary accountant, chief internal auditor?

2. What is the general role of service departments in an organization? How are they distinguished from operating or production departments?

3. Does the controller have line or staff authority over the cost accountants? The accounts receivable clerks?

4. What is probably the *major duty* (scorekeeping, attention directing, or problem solving) of the following:

Payroll clerk	Cost analyst
Accounts receivable clerk	Head of internal auditing
Cost record clerk	Head of special reports and studies
Head of general accounting	Head of accounting for planning
Head of taxes	and control
Budgetary accountant	Controller

Solution to Problem Two

1. The only executives having line authority over the machining manager are the president, the manufacturing vice-president, and the production superintendent.

2. A typical company's major purpose is to produce and sell goods or services. Unless a department is directly concerned with producing or selling, it is called a service or staff department. Service departments exist only to help the production and sales departments with their major tasks: the efficient production and sale of goods or services.

3. The controller has line authority over all members of his or her own department, all those shown in the controller's organization chart (Exhibit 1-9, p. 16).

4. The major duty of the first five—through the head of taxes—is typically scorekeeping. Attention directing is probably the major duty of the next three. Problem solving is probably the primary duty of the head of special reports and studies. The head of accounting for planning and control and the controller should be concerned with all three duties: scorekeeping, attention directing, and problem solving. However, there is a perpetual danger that day-to-day pressures will emphasize scorekeeping. Therefore accountants and managers should constantly see that attention directing and problem solving are also stressed. Otherwise the major management benefits of an accounting system may be lost.

Problem Three

Yang Electronics Company (YEC) developed a high-speed, low-cost copying machine. It marketed the machine primarily for home use. However, as YEC customers learned how easy and inexpensive it was to make copies with the YEC machine, its use by small businesses grew. Sales soared as some businesses ordered large numbers of the copiers. However, the heavier use by these companies caused breakdowns in a certain component of the equipment. The copiers were warrantied for two years, regardless of the amount of usage. Consequently, YEC experienced high costs for replacing the damaged components.

As the quarterly meeting of the Board of Directors of YEC approached, Mark Chua, assistant controller, was asked to prepare a report on the situation. Unfortunately, it was hard to predict the exact effects. However, it seemed that many business customers were starting to switch to more expensive copiers sold by competitors. And it was clear that the increased maintenance costs would significantly affect YEC's profitability. Mark summarized the situation as best he could for the Board.

Alice Martinez, the controller of YEC, was concerned about the impact of the report on the Board. She does not disagree with the analysis, but thinks it makes management look bad and might even lead the Board to discontinue the product. She is convinced from conversations with the head of engineering that the copier can be slightly redesigned to meet the needs of higher-volume users, so discontinuing it may pass up a potentially profitable opportunity.

Martinez called Chua into her office and asked him to delete the part of his report dealing with the component failures. She said it was all right to mention this orally to the Board, noting that engineering is nearing a solution to the problem. However, Chua feels strongly that such a revision in his report would mislead the Board about a potentially significant negative impact on the company's earnings.

Required   Explain why Martinez's request to Chua is unethical. How should Chua resolve this situation?

Solution to Problem Three

According to the Standards of Ethical Conduct for Management Accountants in Exhibit 1-10, Martinez's request violates requirements for competence, integrity, and objectivity. It violates competence because she is asking Chua to prepare a report that is not complete and clear, one that omits potentially relevant information. Therefore, the Board will not have all the information it should to make a decision about the component failure problem.

The request violates the integrity requirement because the revised report may subvert the attainment of the organization's objectives in order to achieve Martinez's objectives. Management accountants are specifically responsible for communicating unfavorable as well as favorable information.

Finally, the revised report would not be objective. It would not disclose all relevant information that could be expected to influence the Board's understanding of operations and therefore their decisions.

Chua's responsibility is to discuss this issue with increasingly higher levels of authority within YEC. First, he should let Martinez know about his misgivings. Possibly the issue can be resolved by her withdrawing the request. If not, he should inform her that he intends to take up the matter with her superior and then continue up to higher levels of authority, even to the Board, if necessary, until the issue is resolved. So that Chua does not violate the standard of confidentiality, he should not discuss the matter with persons outside of YEC.

Accounting Vocabulary

Vocabulary is an essential and often troublesome phase of the learning process. A fuzzy understanding of terms hampers the learning of concepts and the ability to solve accounting problems.

Before proceeding to the assignment material or to the next chapter, be sure you understand the words or terms listed below. Their meaning is explained in the chapter and in the glossary at the end of this book.

Fundamental Assignment Material

The assignment material for each chapter is divided into two groups: *fundamental* and *additional*. The fundamental assignment material consists of two sets of parallel problems that convey the essential concepts and techniques of the chapter. The additional assignment material consists of questions, exercises, problems, and cases that cover the chapter in more detail.

1-A1   Scorekeeping, Attention Directing, and Problem Solving

For each of the activities listed below, identify the function that the accountant is performing—scorekeeping, attention directing, or problem solving. Also state whether the departments mentioned are production or service departments.

1. Analyzing, for a Ford production superintendent, the impact on costs of some new drill presses.
2. Preparing a scrap report for the finishing department of a Honda parts factory.
3. Preparing the budget for the maintenance department of St. Jude's Hospital.
4. Interpreting why a Springfield foundry did not adhere to its production schedule.
5. Explaining the stamping department's performance report.
6. Preparing a monthly statement of European sales for the Ford marketing vice-president.
7. Preparing, for the manager of production control of an Inland Steel plant, a cost comparison of two computerized manufacturing control systems.
8. Interpreting variances on the Yale University purchasing department's performance report.
9. Analyzing, for a Honda international manufacturing manager, the desirability of having some auto parts made in Korea.
10. Preparing a schedule of depreciation for forklift trucks in the receiving department of a General Electric factory in Scotland.

1-A2   Management by Exception

The Gamma-Omega fraternity held a homecoming party. The fraternity expected attendance of 80 persons and prepared the following budget:

Room rental	$ 150
Food	800
Entertainment	600
Decorations	220
Total	$1,770

After all bills for the party were paid, the total cost came to $1,948, or $178 over budget. Details are $150 for room rental; $1,008 for food; $600 for entertainment; and $190 for decorations. Ninety-five persons attended the party.

Required

1. Prepare a performance report for the party that shows how actual costs differed from the budget. That is, include in your report the budget amounts, actual amounts, and variances.
2. Suppose the fraternity uses a management-by-exception rule. Which costs deserve further examination? Why?

1-A3   Accounting's Position in the Organization: Line and Staff Functions

1. Of the following, who has line authority over a cost record clerk: budgetary accountant, head of accounting for current planning and control, head of general accounting,

controller, storekeeper, production superintendent, manufacturing vice-president, president, production control chief?

2. Of the following, who has line authority over an assembler: stamping manager, assembly manager, production superintendent, production control chief, storekeeper, manufacturing vice-president, engineering vice-president, president, controller, budgetary accountant, cost record clerk?

1-B1   Scorekeeping, Attention Directing, and Problem Solving

For each of the activities listed below identify the function the accountant is performing—scorekeeping, attention directing, or problem solving. Also state whether the departments for which the tasks are performed are production or service departments. If a department is neither of these, name the department and indicate whether it is staff or line.

1. Daily recording of material purchase vouchers.
2. Analyzing the costs of acquiring and using each of two alternate types of welding equipment.
3. Preparing a report of overtime labor costs by production departments.
4. Posting daily cash collections to customers' accounts.
5. Estimating the costs of moving corporate headquarters to another city.
6. Interpreting increases in nursing costs per patient-day in a hospital.
7. Analyzing deviations from the budget of the factory maintenance department.
8. Assisting in a study by the manufacturing vice-president to determine whether to buy certain parts needed in large quantities for manufacturing products or to acquire facilities for manufacturing these parts.
9. Allocating factory service department costs to production departments.
10. Recording overtime hours of the product finishing department.
11. Compiling data for a report showing the ratio of advertising expenses to sales for each branch store.
12. Investigating reasons for increased returns and allowances for drugs purchased by a hospital.
13. Preparing a schedule of fuel costs by months and government departments.
14. Estimating the operating costs and outputs that could be expected for each of two large metal-stamping machines offered for sale by different manufacturers. Only one of these machines is to be acquired by your company.
15. Computing and recording end-of-year adjustments for expired fire insurance on the factory warehouse for materials.

1-B2   Management by Exception

The Lummi Indian Tribe sells fireworks for the 4 weeks preceding July 4th. The tribe's stand at the corner of Highway 104 and Acorn Road was the largest, with budgeted sales for 19X5 of $70,000. Expected expenses were as follows:

Cost of fireworks	$30,000
Labor cost	15,000
Other costs	8,000
Total costs	$53,000

Actual sales were $69,860, almost equal to the budget. The tribe spent $34,000 for fireworks, $13,000 for labor, and $8,020 for other costs.

Required

1. Compute budgeted profit and actual profit.
2. Prepare a performance report to help identify those costs that were significantly different from the budget.

3. Suppose the tribe uses a management-by-exception rule. What costs deserve further explanation? Why?

1-B3   Accounting's Position in Organization: Controller and Treasurer
For each of the following activities, indicate whether it is most likely to be performed by the controller (C) or treasurer (T):

1. Prepare credit checks on customers.
2. Help managers prepare budgets.
3. Advise which alternative action is least costly.
4. Prepare divisional financial statements.
5. Arrange short-term financing.
6. Prepare tax returns.
7. Arrange insurance coverage.
8. Meet with financial analysts from Wall Street.

Additional Assignment Material

Questions

1-1. Why does an organization invest resources in an accounting system?

1-2. Distinguish among scorekeeping, attention directing, and problem solving.

1-3. "The emphases of financial accounting and management accounting differ." Explain.

1-4. "The field is less sharply defined. There is heavier use of economics, decision sciences, and behavioral sciences." Identify the branch of accounting described in the quotation.

1-5. "Additional government regulation assists the development of management accounting systems." Do you agree? Explain.

1-6. "The Foreign Corrupt Practices Act applies to bribes paid outside the United States." Do you agree? Explain.

1-7. Give three examples of service organizations. What distinguishes them from other types of organizations?

1-8. What two major considerations affect all accounting systems? Explain each.

1-9. "The accounting system is intertwined with operating management. Business operations would be a hopeless tangle without the paperwork that is so often regarded with disdain." Do you agree? Explain, giving examples.

1-10. Distinguish among a budget, a performance report, and a variance.

1-11. "Management by exception means abdicating management responsibility for planning and control." Do you agree? Explain.

1-12. "Good accounting provides automatic control of operations." Do you agree? Explain.

1-13. Why are accountants concerned about the product life cycle?

1-14. Distinguish between line and staff authority.

1-15. "The controller does control in a special sense." Explain.

1-16. "Planning is much more vital than control." Do you agree? Explain.

1-17. Describe the contents of the qualifying examination for becoming a CMA.

1-18. How are changes in technology affecting management accounting?

1-19. What is the essence of the JIT philosophy?

1-20. Standards of ethical conduct for management accountants have been divided into four major responsibilities. Describe each of the four in 20 words or less.

1-21. "Why are there ethical dilemmas? I thought accountants had standards that specified what is ethical behavior." Discuss.

Exercises

1-22   Management Accounting and Financial Accounting
Consider the following short descriptions. Indicate whether each description more closely relates to a major feature of financial accounting (use FA) or management accounting (use MA).

1. Behavioral impact is secondary
2. Is constrained by generally accepted accounting principles
3. Has a future orientation
4. Is characterized by detailed reports
5. Field is more sharply defined
6. Has less flexibility

1-23   Line Versus Staff

For each of the following, indicate whether the employee has line (L) or staff (S) responsibility:

1. Production superintendent
2. Cost accountant
3. Market research analyst
4. District sales manager
5. Head of the legal department
6. President

1-24   Organization Chart

Draw an organization chart for a single-factory company with the personnel listed below. Which represent factory-service departments? Production departments?

Personnel vice-president
Maintenance manager
Sales vice-president
Production control chief
Production planning chief
Assembly manager
Purchasing agent
Secretary and treasurer
President

Punch press manager
Vice-president and controller
Scorekeeper
Drill press manager
Production superintendent
Chairman of the board
Engineering vice-president
Manufacturing vice-president

1-25   Objectives of Management Accounting

The IMA is composed of about 70,000 members. The IMA "Objectives of Management Accounting" states: "The management accountant participates, as part of management, in assuring that the organization operates as a unified whole in its long-run, intermediate, and short-run best interests."

Required Based on your reading in this chapter, prepare a 100-word description of the principal ways that accountants participate in managing an entity.

Problems

1-26   Management and Financial Accounting

Jan Harai, an able mechanical engineer, was informed that she would be promoted to assistant factory manager. Jan was pleased but uncomfortable. In particular, she knew little about accounting. She had taken one course in "financial" accounting.

Jan planned to enroll in a management accounting course as soon as possible. Meanwhile she asked Harland Young, a cost accountant, to state three or four of the principal distinctions between financial and management accounting.

Prepare Harland's written response to Jan.

1-27   Use of Accounting Information in Hospitals

Most revenues of U.S. hospitals do not come directly from patients. Instead, revenues come through third parties such as insurance companies and government agencies. Until the 1980s, these payments generally reimbursed the hospital's costs of serving patients. Such payments, however, are now generally flat fees for specified services. For example, the hospital might receive $5,000 for an appendectomy or $25,000 for heart surgery—no more, no less.

Required   How might the method of payment change the demand for accounting information in hospitals? Relate your answer to the decisions of top management.

1-28   Costs and Benefits

Marks & Spencer, a huge retailer in the United Kingdom, was troubled by its paper bureaucracy. Looked at in isolation, each form seemed reasonable, but overall a researcher reported that there was substantial effort in each department to verify the information. Basically, the effort seemed out of proportion to any value received, and, eventually, many of the documents were simplified or eliminated.

Describe the rationale that should govern systems design.

1-29   Importance of Accounting

A news story reported:

> Rockwell's Anderson, a veteran of the company's automotive operations, recalls that when he sat in on meetings at Rockwell's North American Aircraft Operations 20 years ago, "there'd be 60 or 70 guys talking technical problems, with never a word on profits." Such inattention to financial management helped Rockwell lose the F-15 fighter to McDonnell Douglas, Pentagon sources say. Anderson brought in profit-oriented executives, and he has now transformed North American's staff meetings to the point that "you seldom hear talk of technical problems any more," he says. "It's all financial."

What is your reaction to Anderson's comments? Are his comments related to management accounting?

1-30   Changes in Accounting Systems

In the early 1990s, the Boeing Company undertook a large-scale study of its accounting system. The study led to several significant changes. None of these changes was required for reporting to external parties. Management thought, however, that the new system gave more accurate costs of the airplanes and other products produced.

Required

1. Boeing had been a very successful company using its old accounting system. What might have motivated it to change the system?
2. When Boeing changed its system, what criteria might its managers have used to decide whether to invest in the new system?
3. Is changing to a system that provides more accurate product costs always a good strategy? Why or why not?

1-31   Ethical Issues

Suppose you are controller of a medium-sized oil exploration company in west Texas. You adhere to the standards of ethical conduct for management accountants. How would those standards affect your behavior in each of the following situations?

1. Late one Friday afternoon you receive a geologist's report on a newly purchased property. It indicates a much higher probability of oil than had previously been expected. You are the only one to read the report that day. At a party on Saturday night, a friend asks about the prospects for the property.
2. An oil industry stock analyst invites you and your spouse to spend a week in Hawaii free of charge. All she wants in return is to be the first to know about any financial information your company is about to announce to the public.
3. It is time to make a forecast of the company's annual earnings. You know that some additional losses will be recognized before the final statements are prepared. The company's president has asked you to ignore these losses in making your prediction because a lower-than-expected earnings forecast could adversely affect the chances of obtaining a loan that is being negotiated and will be completed before actual earnings are announced.

4. You do not know whether a particular expense is deductible for income tax purposes. You are debating whether to research the tax laws or simply to assume that the item is deductible. After all, if you are not audited, no one will ever know the difference. If you *are* audited, you can plead ignorance of the law.

Cases

1-32 Line and Staff Authority (CMA adapted)

Electronic Equipment Leasing Company (EEL) leases office equipment to a variety of customers. The company's organization chart follows:

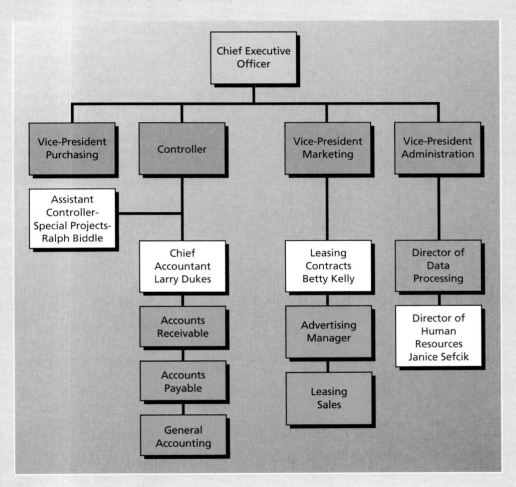

The four positions highlighted in the chart are described below:

- Ralph Biddle, Assistant Controller–Special Projects. Biddle works on projects assigned to him by the controller. The most recent project was to design a new accounts payable system.

- Betty Kelly, Leasing Contracts Manager. Kelly coordinates and implements leasing transactions. Her department handles all transactions after the sales department gets a signed contract. This includes requisitioning equipment from the purchasing department, maintaining appropriate insurance, delivering equipment, issuing billing statements, and seeking renewal of leases.

- Larry Dukes, Chief Accountant. Dukes supervises all the accounting functions. He produces reports for the four supervisors in the functional areas.
- Janice Sefcik, Director of Human Resources. Sefcik works with all departments of EEL in hiring of personnel. Her department advertises all positions and screens candidates, but the individual departments conduct interviews and make hiring decisions. Sefcik also coordinates employee evaluations and administers the company's salary schedule and fringe benefit program.

Required

1. Distinguish between line and staff positions in an organization and discuss why conflicts might arise between line and staff managers.
2. For each of the four managers described, identify whether their position is a line or staff position and explain why you classified it that way. Also, indicate any potential conflicts that might arise with other managers in the organization.

1-33   Ethics and Accounting Personnel

Mercury Shoe Company has an equal opportunity employment policy. This policy has the full support of the company's president, Beverly Watson, and is included in all advertisements for open positions.

Hiring in the accounting department is done by the controller, Dwight Laughton. The assistant controller, Jack Smith, also interviews candidates, but Laughton makes all decisions. In the last year, the department hired five new persons. There had been a total of 175 applications for the open positions. From this set, thirteen had been interviewed, including four minority candidates. The five hired included three sons of close friends of Laughton and no minorities. Smith had felt that at least two of the minority candidates were very well qualified and that the three sons of Laughton's friends were definitely not among the most qualified.

When Smith questioned Laughton concerning his reservations about the hiring practices, he was told that these decisions were Laughton's and not his, so he should not question them.

Required

1. Explain why Laughton's hiring practices were probably unethical.
2. What should Smith do about this situation?

1-34   Professional Ethics and Toxic Fluids

(CMA) Victoria Addison is the assistant director of financial reporting for Earth's Products Inc., a large processor of ores and minerals. The finance department is in the final stages of compiling the financial statements for the fiscal year ended April 30, 1993, and Addison is working late to complete the footnotes pertaining to long-term contracts. Addison has gathered several files that contain the information she needs to complete her work.

Among the contracts and other documents in the files, Addison has found a copy of a report from the Procurement Manager of Earth Products to the division manager of the company's coal cleaning plant regarding the procedures for disposing of plant wastes. Addison noticed some penciled calculations and notes on the bottom of the report. According to these notes, Earth Products has been using a nearby residential landfill to dump toxic coal-cleaning fluid wastes, and the dump site is nearing saturation making it necessary to locate a new disposal site for these toxic wastes. The calculations indicate that significant amounts of toxic cleaning fluids have been mixed with residential refuse over the past two years.

Determined to learn more about this situation, Addison kept the report. Uncertain how she should proceed, Addison began to ponder her options by outlining the following three alternative courses of action:

- Seek the advice of her boss, the director of financial reporting.
- Anonymously release the information to the local newspaper.
- Bring the information to the attention of an outside member of the board of directors with whom she was acquainted.

Required

1. Discuss why Victoria Addison has an ethical responsibility to take some action in the matter of Earth's Products Inc. and the dumping of toxic wastes.
2. For each of the three alternative courses of action that Victoria Addison has outlined, explain whether or not the action is appropriate.
3. Without prejudice to your answer in Requirement 2, assume that Victoria Addison sought the advice of her superior, the director of financial reporting, and discovered that the director was involved in the dumping of toxic wastes. Describe the steps that Victoria Addison should take in proceeding to resolve the conflict in this situation.

2

Introduction to Cost Behavior and Cost-Volume Relationships

Canadian-based Sterling Crane rents a wide assortment of hoisting equipment to the heavy construction industry. At this site in Alberta, a 550-ton crane is hoisting a 400-ton refinery vessel that is part of a natural gas production facility. Sterling Crane calculates the number of rental hours required to earn a target profit using cost-volume-profit analysis.
Courtesy Sterling Crane

Learning Objectives

When you have finished studying this chapter, you should be able to

1 Explain how cost drivers affect cost behavior.

2 Show how changes in cost-driver activity levels affect variable and fixed costs.

3 Calculate break-even sales volume in total dollars and total units.

4 Construct a cost-volume-profit graph.

5 Identify the limiting assumptions that underlie cost-volume-profit analysis.

6 Calculate sales volume in total dollars and total units to reach a target profit.

7 Distinguish between contribution margin and gross margin.

8 Explain the effects of sales mix on profits (Appendix 2A).

9 Compute cost-volume-profit relationships on an after-tax basis (Appendix 2B).

How do the costs and revenues of a hospital change as one more patient is admitted for a 4-day stay? How are the costs and revenues of an airline affected when one more passenger is boarded at the last moment, or when one more flight is added to the schedule? How should the budget request by the Arizona Department of Motor Vehicles be affected by the predicted increase in the state's population? These questions introduce one common question: What will happen to financial results if a specified level of activity or volume fluctuates? Answering this question is the first step in analyzing **cost behavior**—how the activities of an organization affect its costs. A knowledge of the patterns of cost behavior offers valuable insights in planning and controlling short- and long-run operations. While this lesson is emphasized throughout this book, in this introductory chapter, our goal is to provide perspective rather than to impart an intimate knowledge of the complexities of cost behavior.

cost behavior How the activities of an organization affect its costs.

■ COST DRIVERS

cost drivers
Activities that affect costs.

Activities that affect costs are often called **cost drivers**. An organization may have many cost drivers. Consider the costs of running a warehouse that receives and stores material and supplies. The costs of operating the warehouse may be driven by the total dollar value of items handled, the weight of the items handled, the number of different orders received, the number of different items handled, the number of different suppliers, the fragility of the items handled, and possibly several other cost drivers. A major task in specifying cost behavior is to identify the cost drivers—that is, to determine the activities that cause costs to be incurred.

To examine cost behavior without undue complexity, this chapter focuses on *volume-related cost drivers*. Later chapters will introduce cost drivers that are not related to volume. Volume-related cost drivers include the number of orders processed, the number of items billed in a billing department, the number of admissions to a theater, the number of pounds handled in a warehouse, the hours of labor worked in an assembly department, the number of rides in an amusement park, the seat-miles on an airline, and the dollar sales in a retail business. All of these cost drivers can serve either directly or indirectly as a measure of the volume of output of goods or services. Of course, when only one product is being produced, the units of production is the most obvious volume-related cost driver for production-related costs.

■ COMPARISON OF VARIABLE AND FIXED COSTS

A key to understanding cost behavior is distinguishing *variable costs* from *fixed costs*. Costs are classified as variable or fixed depending on how much they change as the level of a particular cost driver changes. A **variable cost** is a cost that changes in direct proportion to changes in the cost driver. In contrast, a **fixed cost** is not immediately affected by changes in the cost driver. Suppose units of production is the cost driver of interest. A 10% increase in the units of production would produce a 10% increase in variable costs. However, the fixed costs would remain unchanged.

variable cost A cost that changes in direct proportion to changes in the cost driver.
fixed cost A cost that is not immediately affected by changes in the cost driver.

Some examples may clarify the differences between fixed and variable costs. The costs of most merchandise, materials, parts, supplies, commissions, and many types of labor are generally variable with respect to most volume-related cost drivers. Real estate taxes, real estate insurance, many executive salaries, and space rentals tend to be fixed with respect to any volume-related cost driver.

Consider some variable costs. Suppose Watkins Products pays its door-to-door sales personnel a 40% straight commission on sales. The total cost of sales commissions to Watkins is 40% of sales dollars—a variable cost with respect to sales revenues. Or suppose Dan's Bait Shop buys bags of fish bait for $2 each. The total cost of fish bait is $2 times the number of bags purchased—a variable cost with respect to units (number of bags) purchased. Notice that variable costs are uniform *per unit*, but that the *total* fluctuates in direct proportion to the cost-driver activity. Exhibit 2-1 depicts these relationships between cost and cost-driver activity graphically.

Exhibit 2-1

Variable-Cost
Behavior

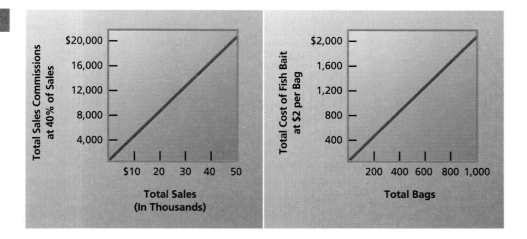

Now consider a fixed cost. Suppose Sony rents a factory to produce picture tubes for color television sets for $500,000 per year. The *total cost* of $500,000 is not affected by the number of picture tubes produced. The *unit cost* of rent applicable to each tube, however, does depend on the total number of tubes produced. If 100,000 tubes are produced, the unit cost will be $500,000 ÷ 100,000 = $5. If 50,000 tubes are produced, the unit cost will be $500,000 ÷ 50,000 = $10. Therefore, a fixed cost does not change *in total*, but it becomes progressively smaller on a *per-unit* basis as the volume increases.

Note carefully from these examples that the "variable" or "fixed" characteristic of a cost relates to its *total dollar amount* and not to its per-unit amount. The following table summarizes these relationships.

	If Cost-Driver Activity Level Increases (or Decreases):	
Type of Cost	Total Cost	Cost Per Unit*
Fixed costs	No change	Decrease (or increase)
Variable costs	Increase (or decrease)	No change

* Per unit of activity volume, for example, product units, passenger-miles, sales dollars.

When predicting costs, two rules of thumb are useful:

1. Think of fixed costs as a *total*. Total fixed costs remain unchanged regardless of changes in cost-driver activity.
2. Think of variable costs on a *per-unit* basis. The *per-unit* variable cost remains unchanged regardless of changes in cost-driver activity.

Relevant Range

Although we have just described fixed costs as unchanging regardless of cost-driver activity, this rule of thumb holds true only within reasonable limits. For example, rent costs will rise if increased production requires a larger or

relevant range The limit of cost-driver activity within which a specific relationship between costs and the cost driver is valid.

additional building—or if the landlord just decides to raise the rent. Conversely, rent costs may go down if decreased production causes the company to move to a smaller plant. The **relevant range** is the limit of cost-driver activity within which a specific relationship between costs and the cost driver is valid. In addition, remember that even within the relevant range, a fixed cost remains fixed only over a given period of time—usually the budget period. Fixed costs may change from budget year to budget year solely because of changes in insurance and property tax rates, executive salary levels, or rent levels. But these items are unlikely to change within a given year.

For example, suppose that a General Electric plant has a relevant range of between 40,000 and 85,000 cases of light bulbs per month and that total monthly fixed costs within the relevant range are $100,000. Within the relevant range, fixed costs will remain the same. If production falls below 40,000 cases, changes in personnel and salaries would slash fixed costs to $60,000. If operations rise above 85,000 cases, increases in personnel and salaries would boost fixed costs to $115,000.

These assumptions—a given period and a given activity range—are shown graphically at the top of Exhibit 2-2. It is highly unusual, however, for monthly operations to be outside the relevant range. Therefore, the three-level refinement at the top of Exhibit 2-2 is usually not graphed. Instead, a single horizontal line is typically extended through the plotted activity levels, as at the bottom of the exhibit. Often a dashed line is used outside the relevant range.

Exhibit 2-2

Fixed Costs and Relevant Range

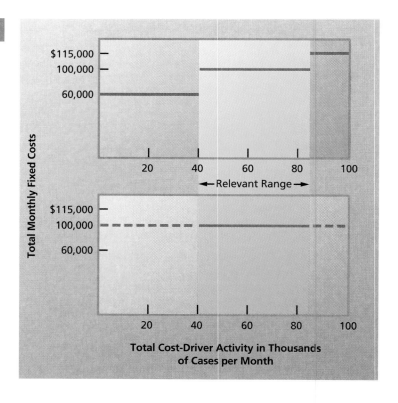

The basic idea of a relevant range also applies to variable costs. That is, outside a relevant range, some variable costs, such as fuel consumed, may behave differently per unit of cost-driver activity. For example, the efficiency of motors is affected if they are used too much or too little.

Differences in Classifying Costs

As you may suspect, it is often difficult to classify a cost as exactly variable or exactly fixed. Many complications arise including the possibility of costs behaving in some nonlinear way (not producing a straight line graph). For example, as tax preparers learn to process the new year's tax forms, their productivity rises. This means that total costs may actually behave as in Panel A that follows, not as in Panel B.

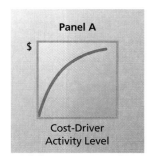

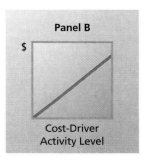

Moreover, costs may simultaneously be affected by more than one cost driver. For example, the costs of shipping labor may be affected by *both* the weight and the number of units handled. We shall investigate various facets of this problem in succeeding chapters; for now, we shall assume that any cost may be classified as either variable or fixed. We assume also that a given variable cost is associated with *only one* volume-related cost driver, and that relationship is *linear*.

Finally, in the real world, classifying costs as fixed or variable depends on the decision situation. More costs are fixed and fewer are variable when decisions involve very short time spans and very small changes in activity level. Suppose a United Airlines plane with several empty seats will depart from its gate in 2 minutes. A potential passenger is running down a corridor bearing a transferable ticket from a competing airline. Unless the airplane is held for an extra 30 seconds, the passenger will miss the departure and will not switch to United for the planned trip. What are the variable costs to United of delaying the departure and placing one more passenger in an otherwise empty seat? Variable costs (for example, one more meal) are negligible. Virtually all the costs in that decision situation are fixed. Now in contrast, suppose United's decision is whether to add another flight, acquire another gate, add another city to its routes, or acquire another airplane. Many more costs would be regarded as variable and fewer as fixed.

These examples underscore the importance of how the decision affects the analysis of cost behavior. Whether costs are really "fixed" depends heavily on the relevant range, the length of the planning period in question, and the specific decision situation.

■ COST-VOLUME-PROFIT ANALYSIS

Managers often classify costs as fixed or variable when making decisions that affect the volume of output. The managers want to know how such decisions will affect costs and revenues. They realize that many factors in addition to the volume of output will affect costs. Yet, a useful starting point in their decision process is to specify the relationship between the volume of output and costs and revenues.

cost-volume-profit (CVP) analysis The study of the effects of output volume on revenue (sales), expenses (costs), and net income (net profit).

The managers of profit-seeking organizations usually study the effects of output volume on revenue (sales), expenses (costs), and net income (net profit). This study is commonly called **cost-volume-profit (CVP) analysis**. The managers of nonprofit organizations also benefit from the study of CVP relationships. Why? No organization has unlimited resources, and knowledge of how costs fluctuate as volume changes helps managers to understand how to control costs. For example, administrators of nonprofit hospitals are constantly concerned about the behavior of costs as the volume of patients fluctuates.

To apply CVP analysis, managers usually resort to some simplifying assumptions. The major simplification is to classify costs as either variable or fixed with respect to a single measure of the volume of output activity. This chapter focuses on such a simplified relationship.

CVP Scenario

Amy Winston, the manager of food services for Middletown Community College, is trying to decide whether to rent a line of food vending machines. Although individual snack items have various acquisition costs and selling prices, Winston has decided that an average selling price of 50¢ per unit and an average acquisition cost of 40¢ per unit will suffice for purposes of this analysis. She predicts the following revenue and expense relationships.

	Per Unit	Percentage of Sales
Selling price	$ .50	100%
Variable cost of each item	.40	80
Selling price less variable cost	$ .10	20%
Monthly fixed expenses		
Rent	$1,000	
Wages for replenishing and servicing	4,500	
Other fixed expenses	500	
Total fixed expenses per month	$6,000	

We will next use these data to illustrate several applications of CVP analysis.

Break-Even Point—Contribution Margin and Equation Techniques

break-even point The level of sales at which revenue equals expenses and net income is zero.

The most basic CVP analysis computes the monthly break-even point in number of units and in dollar sales. The **break-even point** is the level of sales at which revenue equals expenses and net income is zero. The business press frequently refers to break-even points. For example, a news story on hotel occupancy rates in San Francisco in 1994 stated that "seventy percent [occupancy] is considered a break-even for hoteliers." Another news story stated that "the Big Three auto makers have slashed their sales break-even point in North America from 12.2 million cars and trucks to only 9.1 million this year." Finally, an article on Outboard Marine Corporation reported that, as a result of restructuring, the company's "break-even point will be $250 million lower than it was in 1993."

The study of cost-volume-profit relationships is often called *break-even analysis*. This term is misleading, because finding the break-even point is often just the first step in a planning decision. Managers usually concentrate on how the decision will affect sales, costs, and net income.

Break-Even in the Auto Industry

Increased world-wide competition in the automobile industry has made many companies acutely aware of their break-even points. In the early 1990s most auto companies were losing money. With dim prospects for large increases in volume of sales, profitability would result only if they could decrease their break-even points. That is exactly what most companies did.

Break-even points vary greatly for different auto companies. The larger companies have high fixed costs and therefore must achieve higher sales to break even. For example, Chrysler must sell 1.6 million vehicles to break even. The break-even volume is down from 1.9 million vehicles in the late 1980s, and it is well below the 2.3 million sold in 1993. Still, the reduction of 16% in the break-even point is less than that achieved by some competitors.

Saab, a Swedish company, has focused on bringing down the number of production hours per car. A reduction from 120 hours to 45 hours has decreased the break-even volume from 125,000 vehicles to 83,000. This is still above 1993 sales of 73,605 cars, but well below the 135,000 vehicles projected for the mid-1990s.

The assembly operations for Jaguar, located 100 miles north of London, have had a dual focus: quality and production time. Quality improvements were expected to increase sales, and this appears to be working. Warranty costs in the U.S. alone are down 60% and sales are up. Production improvements were intended to reduce the break-even volume. Since 1990, Jaguar has cut the time required to build a car by 54%. This has cut the break-even point from between 50,000 and 60,000 vehicles to 30,000 per year.

Another British company, Rolls-Royce, sells far fewer cars. In fact, sales dropped from 3,300 Rolls-Royces and Bentleys in 1990 to 1,360 in 1993.

At a break-even volume of about 2,600 cars, the company was profitable in 1990. However, the company faced serious difficulty as sales plunged to 1,480 in 1991 and further to 1,360 by 1993. Yet, by trimming its worldwide staff from 5,000 to 2,300 people, Rolls-Royce reduced its break-even volume to 1,300 cars by 1993, providing a small profit after two years of losses.

It is clear that break-even volumes differ greatly among automobile companies. Rolls-Royce can generate a profit at a sales level of 1,300 vehicles, but Saab, Jaguar, and Chrysler would go out of business at that volume. Similarly, Chrysler could not survive selling at volumes that are highly profitable to Saab and Jaguar. Each company must compute its own break-even volume based on its own fixed and variable costs. If a company's sales fall below its break-even point, it must either find a way to get more sales or it must restructure its production operations to reduce its break-even point. ■

Sources: From Paul A. Eisenstein, "Jaguar Ledgers to Feature Black, Not Red, Ink Next Year," The Washington Times, *September 16, 1994, p. D3; Mary Beth Vander Schaaf, "Saab Counts on V-6 to Boost 9000,"* Automotive News, *September 26, 1994, p.37; "GM's Saab Unit Climbs Back Into Black,"* Investor's Business Daily, *September 27, 1994, p. A4; James Bennet, "Chrysler Chief's World View: Place to Sell, Not Build, Cars,"* New York Times, *September 30, 1994, p. D1; Christopher Jensen, "Jaguar's Renaissance: Ford Helps Its British Acquisition Make Quality Job One,"* The Plain Dealer, *October 9, 1994, p. 1H; Dan Jedlicka, "Rebounding Rolls Needs a Partner,"* Chicago Sun-Times, *October 17, 1994, p.47.*

One direct use of the break-even point, however, is to assess possible risks. By comparing planned sales with the break-even point, managers can determine a **margin of safety**:

margin of safety
Equal to the planned unit sales less the break-even unit sales; it shows how far sales can fall below the planned level before losses occur.

margin of safety = planned unit sales – break-even unit sales

The margin of safety shows how far sales can fall below the planned level before losses occur.

We next explore two basic techniques for computing a break-even point: contribution margin and equation.

Contribution-Margin Technique

contribution margin (marginal income)
The sales price minus the variable cost per unit.

Consider the following commonsense arithmetic approach. Every unit sold generates a **contribution margin** or **marginal income,** which is the sales price minus the variable cost per unit. For the vending machine snack items, the contribution margin per unit is $.10:

Unit sales price	$.50
Unit variable cost	.40
Unit contribution margin to fixed costs and net income	$.10

Objective 3

Calculate break-even sales volume in total dollars and total units

When is the break-even point reached? When enough units have been sold to generate a *total* contribution margin (total number of units sold × contribution margin per unit) equal to the total fixed costs. Divide the $6,000 in fixed costs by the $.10 unit contribution margin. The number of units that must be sold to break even is $6,000 ÷ $.10 = 60,000 units. The sales revenue at the break-even point is 60,000 units × $.50 per unit, or $30,000.

Think about the contribution margin of the snack items. Each unit purchased and sold generates *extra* revenue of $.50 and *extra* cost of $.40. Fixed costs are unaffected. If zero units were sold, a loss equal to the fixed cost of $6,000 would be incurred. Each unit reduces the loss by $.10 until sales reach the break-even point of 60,000 units. After that point, each unit adds (or *contributes*) $.10 to profit.

The condensed income statement at the break-even point is

	Total	Per Unit	Percentage
Units	60,000		
Sales	$30,000	$.50	100%
Variable costs	24,000	.40	80
Contribution margin*	$ 6,000	$.10	20%
Fixed costs	6,000		
Net income	$ 0		

* Sales less variable costs.

Sometimes the unit price and unit variable costs are not known. This situation is common at companies that sell more than one product because no single price or variable cost applies to all products. For example, a grocery store sells hundreds of products at many different prices. A break-even point *in units* would not be meaningful. In such cases, you can use total sales and total variable costs to calculate variable costs as a *percentage of each sales dollar*.

Consider our vending machine example:

Sales price	100%
Variable expenses as a percentage of dollar sales	80
Contribution-margin percentage	20%

Therefore, 20% of each sales dollar is available for the recovery of fixed expenses and the making of net income: $6,000 ÷ .20 = $30,000 sales are needed to break even. The contribution-margin percentage is based on dollar sales and is often expressed as a ratio (.20 instead of 20%). Using the contribution-margin percentage, you can compute the break-even volume in dollar sales without determining the break-even point in units.

Equation Technique

The equation technique is the most general form of analysis, the one that may be adapted to any conceivable cost-volume-profit situation. You are familiar with a typical income statement. Any income statement can be expressed in equation form, or as a *mathematical model*, as follows:

$$\text{sales} - \text{variable expenses} - \text{fixed expenses} = \text{net income} \tag{1}$$

That is,

$$\left(\begin{array}{c}\text{unit} \\ \text{sales} \\ \text{price}\end{array} \times \begin{array}{c}\text{number} \\ \text{of} \\ \text{units}\end{array}\right) - \left(\begin{array}{c}\text{unit} \\ \text{variable} \\ \text{cost}\end{array} \times \begin{array}{c}\text{number} \\ \text{of} \\ \text{units}\end{array}\right) - \begin{array}{c}\text{fixed} \\ \text{expenses}\end{array} = \begin{array}{c}\text{net} \\ \text{income}\end{array}$$

At the break-even point net income is zero:

$$\text{sales} - \text{variable expenses} - \text{fixed expenses} = 0$$

Let N = number of units to be sold to break even. Then, for the vending machine example,

$$\$.50N - \$.40N - \$6,000 = 0$$
$$\$.10N = \$6,000$$
$$N = \$6,000 \div \$.10$$
$$N = 60,000 \text{ units}$$

Total sales in the equation is a price-times-quantity relationship, which was expressed in our example as $.50N. To find the *dollar* sales, multiply 60,000 *units* by $.50, which would yield the break-even dollar sales of $30,000.

You can also solve the equation for sales dollars without computing the unit break-even point by using the relationship of variable costs and profits as a *percentage* of sales:

$$\text{variable-cost ratio or percentage} = \frac{\text{variable cost per unit}}{\text{sales price per unit}}$$
$$= \frac{\$.40}{\$.50}$$
$$= .80 \text{ or } 80\%$$

Let S = sales in dollars needed to break even. Then

$$S - .80S - \$6,000 = 0$$
$$.20S = \$6,000$$
$$S = \$6,000 \div .20$$
$$S = \$30,000$$

Relationship Between the Two Techniques

You may have noticed that the contribution-margin technique is merely a shortcut version of the equation technique. Look at the last three lines in the two solutions given for equation 1. They read

Break-Even Volume	
Units	*Dollars*
$.10N = \$6,000$	$.20S = \$6,000$
$N = \dfrac{\$6,000}{\$.10}$	$S = \dfrac{\$6,000}{.20}$
$N = 60{,}000$ units	$S = \$30{,}000$

From these equations, we can derive the following general shortcut formulas:

$$\text{break-even volume in units} = \frac{\text{fixed expenses}}{\text{contribution margin per unit}} \qquad (2)$$

$$\text{break-even volume in dollars} = \frac{\text{fixed expenses}}{\text{contribution-margin ratio}} \qquad (3)$$

Which should you use, the equation or the contribution-margin technique? Use either. The choice is a matter of personal preference or convenience within a particular case.

Break-Even Point—Graphical Techniques

Exhibit 2-3 is a graph of the cost-volume-profit relationship in our vending machine example. Study the graph as you read the procedure for constructing it.

Objective 4

Construct a cost-volume-profit graph

1. Draw the axes. The horizontal axis is the sales volume, and the vertical axis is dollars of cost and revenue.
2. Plot sales volume. Select a convenient sales volume, say, 100,000 units, and plot point A for total sales dollars at that volume: 100,000 × $.50 = $50,000. Draw the revenue (i.e., sales) line from point A to the origin, point 0.
3. Plot fixed expenses. Draw the line showing the $6,000 fixed portion of expenses. It should be a horizontal line intersecting the vertical axis at $6,000, point B.
4. Plot variable expenses. Determine the variable portion of expenses at a convenient level of activity: 100,000 units × $.40 = $40,000. Add this to the fixed expenses: $40,000 + $6,000 = $46,000. Plot point C for 100,000 units and $46,000. Then draw a line between this point and point B. This is the total expenses line.
5. Locate the break-even point. The break-even point is where the total expenses line crosses the sales line, 60,000 units or $30,000, namely, where total sales revenues exactly equal total costs, point D.

Exhibit 2-3

Cost-Volume-Profit
Graph

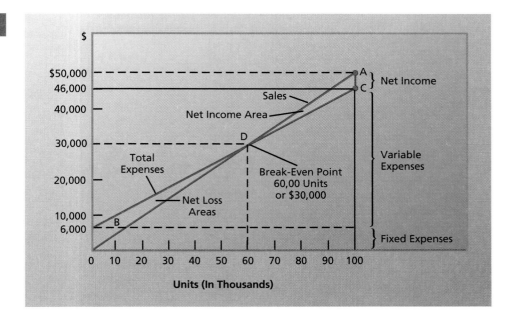

The break-even point is only one facet of this cost-volume-profit graph. More generally, the graph shows the profit or loss at *any* rate of activity. At any given volume, the vertical distance between the sales line and the total expenses line measures the net income or net loss.

Managers often use break-even graphs because they show potential profits over a wide range of volume more easily than numerical exhibits. Whether graphs or other types of exhibits are used depends largely on management's preference.

Objective 5

Identify the limiting assumptions that underlie cost-volume-profit analysis

Note that the concept of relevant range is applicable to the entire break-even graph. Almost all break-even graphs show revenue and cost lines extending back to the vertical axis as shown in Exhibit 2-4(A). This approach is misleading because the relationships depicted in such graphs are valid only within the relevant range that underlies the construction of the graph. Exhibit 2-4(B), a modification of the conventional break-even graph, partially demonstrates the multitude of assumptions that must be made in constructing the typical break-even graph. Some of these assumptions follow:

1. Expenses may be classified into variable and fixed categories. Total variable expenses vary directly with activity level. Total fixed expenses do not change with activity level.
2. The behavior of revenues and expenses is accurately portrayed and is linear over the relevant range. The principal differences between the accountant's break-even chart and the economist's are that (1) the accountant's sales line is drawn on the assumption that selling prices do not change with production or sales, and the economist assumes that reduced selling prices are normally associated with increased sales volume; and (2) the accountant usually assumes a constant variable expense per unit, and the economist assumes that variable expense per unit changes with production levels. Within the relevant range, the accountant's and the economist's sales and expense lines are usually close to one another, although the lines may diverge greatly outside the range.

3. Efficiency and productivity will be unchanged.

sales mix The relative proportions or combinations of quantities of products that constitute total sales.

4. Sales mix will be constant. The **sales mix** is the relative proportions or combinations of quantities of products that constitute total sales. (See Appendix 2A for more on sales mixes.)

5. The difference in inventory level at the beginning and at the end of a period is insignificant. (The impact of inventory changes on CVP analysis is discussed in Chapter 16.)

Exhibit 2-4

Conventional and Modified Break-Even Graphs

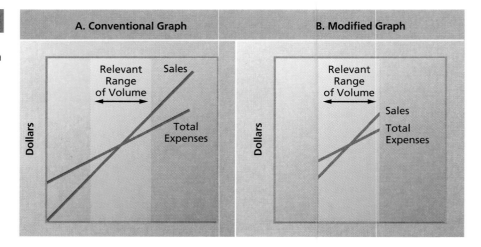

Changes in Fixed Expenses

Changes in fixed expenses cause changes in the break-even point. For example, if the $1,000 monthly rent of the vending machines were doubled, what would be the monthly break-even point in number of units and dollar sales?

The fixed expenses would increase from $6,000 to $7,000, so

$$\text{break-even volume in units} = \frac{\text{fixed expenses}}{\text{contribution margin per unit}} = \frac{\$7,000}{\$.10} = 70,000 \text{ units} \qquad (2)$$

$$\text{break-even volume in dollars} = \frac{\text{fixed expenses}}{\text{contribution-margin ratio}} = \frac{\$7,000}{.20} = \$35,000 \qquad (3)$$

Note that a one-sixth increase in fixed expenses altered the break-even point by one-sixth: from 60,000 to 70,000 units and from $30,000 to $35,000. This type of relationship always exists if everything else remains constant.

Companies frequently lower their break-even points by reducing their total fixed costs. For example, closing or selling factories decreases property taxes, insurance, depreciation, and managers' salaries.

Changes in Contribution Margin per Unit

Changes in variable costs also cause the break-even point to shift. Companies can reduce their break-even points by increasing their contribution margins per unit of product through either increases in sales prices or decreases in unit variable costs, or both.

For example, assume that the fixed rent is still $1,000. (1) If the owner is paid 1¢ rental per unit sold in addition to the fixed rent, find the monthly break-even point in number of units and in dollar sales. (2) If the selling price falls from 50¢ to 45¢ per unit, and the original variable expenses per unit are unchanged, find the monthly break-even point in number of units and in dollar sales.

Here's what happens to the break-even point:

1. The variable expenses would increase from 40¢ to 41¢, the unit contribution margin would decline from 10¢ to 9¢, and the contribution-margin ratio would become .18 ($.09 ÷ $.50).

   The original fixed expenses of $6,000 would be unaffected, but the denominators would change from those previously used. Thus,

$$\text{break-even point in units} \;=\; \frac{\$6,000}{\$.09} \;=\; 66,667 \text{ units} \tag{2}$$

$$\text{break-even point in dollars} \;=\; \frac{\$6,000}{.18} \;=\; \$33,333 \tag{3}$$

2. If the selling price fell from 50¢ to 45¢, and the original variable expenses were unchanged, the unit contribution would be reduced from 10¢ to 5¢ (i.e., 45¢ − 40¢), and the break-even point would soar to 120,000 units ($6,000 ÷ $.05). The break-even point in dollars would also change because the selling price and contribution-margin ratio change. The contribution-margin ratio would be .1111 ($.05 ÷ $.45). The break-even point, in dollars, would be $54,000 (120,000 units × $.45) or, using the formula:

$$\text{break-even point in dollars} \;=\; \frac{\$6,000}{.1111} \;=\; \$54,000 \tag{3}$$

Target Net Profit and an Incremental Approach

Managers can also use CVP analysis to determine the total sales, in units and dollars, needed to reach a target profit. For example, in our snack-vending example, suppose Winston considers $480 per month the minimum acceptable net income. How many units will have to be sold to justify the adoption of the vending machine plan? How does this figure "translate" into dollar sales?

Objective 6

Calculate sales volume in total dollars and total units to reach a target profit

The method for computing desired or target sales volume in units and the desired or target net income is the same as was used in our earlier break-even computations. Now the targets, however, are expressed in the equations:

$$\text{target sales} - \text{variable expenses} - \text{fixed expenses} = \text{target net income} \tag{4}$$

or

$$\text{target sales volume in units} = \frac{\text{fixed expenses} + \text{target net income}}{\text{contribution margin per unit}} \tag{5}$$

$$= \frac{\$6,000 + \$480}{\$.10} = 64,800 \text{ units}$$

incremental effect
The change in total results (such as revenue, expenses, or income) under a new condition in comparison with some given or known condition.

Another way of getting the same answer is to use your knowledge of the break-even point and adopt an incremental approach. The term **incremental** is widely used in accounting. It refers to the *change* in total results (such as revenue, expenses, or income) under a new condition in comparison with some given or known condition.

In this instance, the given condition is assumed to be the 60,000-unit break-even point. All expenses would be recovered at that volume. Therefore the *change* or *increment* in net income for every unit *beyond* 60,000 would be equal to the contribution margin of $.50 – $.40 = $.10. If $480 were the target net profit, $480 ÷ $.10 would show that the target volume must exceed the break-even volume by 4,800 units; it would therefore be 60,000 + 4,800 = 64,800 units.

To find the answer in terms of *dollar* sales, multiply 64,800 units by $.50 or use the formula:

$$\text{target sales volume in dollars} = \frac{\text{fixed expenses} + \text{target net income}}{\text{contribution-margin ratio}} \qquad (6)$$

$$= \frac{\$6,000 + \$480}{.20} = \$32,400$$

To solve directly for sales dollars with the alternative incremental approach, the break-even point, in dollar sales of $30,000, becomes the frame of reference. Every sales dollar beyond that point contributes $.20 to net profit. Divide $480 by .20. Dollar sales must exceed the break-even volume by $2,400 to produce a net profit of $480; thus the total dollar sales would be $30,000 + $2,400 = $32,400.

The following table summarizes these computations:

	Break-Even Point	Increment	New Condition
Volume in units	60,000	4,800	64,800
Sales	$30,000	$2,400	$32,400
Variable expenses	24,000	1,920	25,920
Contribution margin	$ 6,000	$ 480	$ 6,480
Fixed expenses	6,000	—	6,000
Net income	$ 0	$ 480	$ 480

Multiple Changes in Key Factors

In the real world, managers often must make decisions about the probable effects of multiple factor changes. For instance, suppose that after the vending machines have been in place a while, Winston is considering locking them from 6:00 P.M. to 6:00 A.M., which she estimates will save $820 in wages monthly. The cutback from 24-hour service would hurt volume substantially because many nighttime employees use the machines. Employees could find food elsewhere, however, so not too many complaints are expected.[1] Should the machines remain available 24 hours per day? Assume that monthly sales would decline by 10,000 units from current sales of (1) 62,000 units and (2) 90,000 units. Consider two approaches. One approach is to construct and solve equations for conditions that prevail under each alternative and select the volume level that yields the highest net income.

---

[1] The quality of overall working conditions might affect these decisions, even though such factors are difficult to quantify. In particular, if costs or profits do not differ much between alternatives, the nonquantifiable, subjective aspects may be the deciding factors.

Regardless of the current volume level, be it 62,000 or 90,000 units, if we accept the prediction that sales will decline by 10,000 units as accurate, the closing from 6:00 P.M. to 6:00 A.M. will decrease net income by $180.

	Decline from 62,000 to 52,000 Units		Decline from 90,000 to 80,000 Units	
Units	62,000	52,000	90,000	80,000
Sales	$31,000	$26,000	$45,000	$40,000
Variable expenses	24,800	20,800	36,000	32,000
Contribution margin	$ 6,200	$ 5,200	$ 9,000	$ 8,000
Fixed expenses	6,000	5,180	6,000	5,180
Net income	$ 200	$ 20	$ 3,000	$ 2,820
Change in net income	($180)		($180)	

A second approach—an incremental approach—is quicker and simpler. Simplicity is important to managers because it keeps the analysis from being cluttered by irrelevant and potentially confusing data.

What does the insightful manager see in this situation? First, whether 62,000 or 90,000 units are being sold is irrelevant to the decision at hand. The issue is the decline in volume, which would be 10,000 units in either case. The essence of this decision is whether the prospective savings in cost exceed the prospective loss in total contribution-margin dollars.

Lost total contribution margin, 10,000 units @ .10	$1,000
Savings in fixed expenses	$ 820
Prospective decline in net income	$ 180

Locking the vending machines from 6:00 P.M. to 6:00 A.M. would cause a $180 decrease in monthly net income. Whichever way you analyze it, locking the machines is not a sound financial decision.

CVP Analysis in the Computer Age

As we have seen, cost-volume-profit analysis is based on a mathematical model, the equation

$$\text{sales} - \text{variable expenses} - \text{fixed expenses} = \text{net income}$$

The CVP model is widely used as a *planning model*. Managers in a variety of organizations use a personal computer and a CVP modeling program to study combinations of changes in selling prices, unit variable costs, fixed costs, and desired profits. Many nonprofit organizations also use computerized CVP modeling. For example, some private universities have models that help measure how decisions such as raising tuition, adding programs, and closing dormitories during winter holidays will affect financial results. The computer quickly calculates the results of changes and can display them both numerically and graphically.

Exhibit 2-5 is a sample spreadsheet that shows what the sales level would have to be at three different fixed expense levels and three different variable expense levels to reach three different income levels. The computer calculates the 27 different sales levels rapidly and without error. Managers can insert any numbers they want for fixed expenses (column A), variable expense percentage (column B), target net income (row 3 of columns C, D, and E), or combinations thereof, and the computer will compute the required sales level.

Exhibit 2-5

Spreadsheet Analysis of CVP Relationships

	A	B	C	D	E
1			Sales Required to Earn		
2	Fixed	Variable	Annual Net Income of		
3	Expenses	Expense %	$2,000	$4,000	$6,000
4					
5	$4,000	0.40	$10,000*	$13,333	$16,667
6	$4,000	0.44	$10,714*	$14,286	$17,857
7	$4,000	0.48	$11,538*	$15,385	$19,231
8	$6,000	0.40	$13,333	$16,667	$20,000
9	$6,000	0.44	$14,286	$17,857	$21,429
10	$6,000	0.48	$15,385	$19,231	$23,077
11	$8,000	0.40	$16,667	$20,000	$23,333
12	$8,000	0.44	$17,857	$21,429	$25,000
13	$8,000	0.48	$19,231	$23,077	$26,923
15					
16	*(A5 + C3)/(1 − B5) = ($4,000 + $2,000)/(1 − $.40)				
17	(A6 + C3)/(1 − B6) = ($4,000 + $2,000)/(1 − $.44)				
18	(A7 + C3)/(1 − B7) = ($4,000 + $2,000)/(1 − $.48)				
19					

In addition to speed and convenience, computers allow a more sophisticated approach to CVP analysis than the one illustrated in this chapter. The assumptions listed on pages 47–48 are necessary to simplify the analysis enough for most managers to construct a CVP model by hand. Computer analysts, however, can construct a model that does not require all the simplifications. Computer models can include multiple cost drivers, nonlinear relationships between costs and cost drivers, varying sales mixes, and analyses that need not be restricted to a relevant range.

Use of computer models is a cost-benefit issue. Sometimes the costs of modeling are exceeded by the value of better decisions made using the models. However, the reliability of these models depends on the accuracy of their underlying assumptions about how revenues and costs will actually be affected. Moreover, in small organizations, simplified CVP models often are accurate enough that more sophisticated modeling is unwarranted.

■ ADDITIONAL USES OF COST-VOLUME ANALYSIS

Best Combination of Factors

The analysis of cost-volume-profit relationships is an important management responsibility. Managers usually try to obtain the most profitable combination of variable- and fixed-cost factors. For example, purchasing automated machinery may raise fixed costs but reduce labor cost per unit. Conversely, it may be wise to reduce fixed costs to obtain a more favorable combination. Thus, direct selling by a salaried sales force (a fixed cost) may be supplanted by the use of manufacturer's agents who are compensated via sales commissions (variable costs).

Generally, companies that spend heavily for advertising are willing to do so because they have high contribution-margin percentages (airlines, cigarette and cosmetic companies). Conversely, companies with low contribution-margin percentages usually spend less for advertising and promotion (manufacturers of industrial equipment). Obviously, two companies with the same unit sales volumes at the same unit prices could have different attitudes toward risking an advertising outlay. Assume the following:

	Perfume Company	Janitorial Service Company
Unit sales volume	100,000 bottles	100,000 square feet
Dollar sales at $20 per unit	$2,000,000	$2,000,000
Variable costs	200,000	1,700,000
Contribution margin	$1,800,000	$ 300,000
Contribution-margin percentage	90%	15%

Suppose each company wants to increase sales volume by 10%:

	Perfume Company	Janitorial Service Company
Increase in sales volume, 10,000 × $20	$200,000	$200,000
Increase in contribution margin, 90%, 15%	180,000	30,000

The perfume company would be inclined to increase advertising considerably to boost the contribution margin by $180,000. In contrast, the janitorial service company would be foolhardy to spend large amounts to increase the contribution margin by $30,000.

Note that when the contribution-margin percentage of sales is low, great increases in volume are necessary before significant increases in net profits can occur. As sales exceed the break-even point, a high contribution-margin percentage increases profits faster than does a small contribution-margin percentage.

Operating Leverage

operating leverage
A firm's ratio of fixed to variable costs.

In addition to weighing the varied effects of changes in fixed and variable costs, managers need to consider their firm's ratio of fixed to variable costs, called **operating leverage**. In highly leveraged companies—those with high fixed costs and low variable costs—small changes in sales volume result in large changes in net income. Companies with less leverage (that is, lower fixed costs and higher variable costs) are not affected as much by changes in sales volume.

Exhibit 2-6 shows cost behavior relationships at two firms, one highly leveraged and one with low leverage. The firm with higher leverage has fixed costs of

Lowering the Break-Even Point

One way that companies cope with hard economic times is to lower their break-even point. *Business Week* suggested that investors look for such firms "because efficiency gains at companies that have pared fixed costs as well as variable ones should be deep and lasting."

Why is lowering the break-even point important? Because a company that maintains its profitability in times of low sales is poised to take off when the economy improves. Baldwin, the piano maker, actually improved its profits in a time of decreasing sales by successfully cutting costs—especially fixed costs. If it maintains its new cost structure as sales

rebound, profits will soar. Lowering fixed costs is especially important because these costs will not necessarily increase as production increases to meet renewed demand for sales.

Chrysler is another example of a company that pared its fixed costs in the slow sales period in the early 1990s. According to *Business Week*, it became "close to being the low-cost producer among the Big Three . . . [and] will benefit most if an auto turnaround comes soon." ∎

Source: Adapted from "Lots of Companies Are Lean, But Which Are Mean?" Business Week, *February 3, 1992, p. 84.*

$14,000 and variable cost per unit of $.10. The firm with lower leverage has fixed costs of only $2,000 but variable costs of $.25 per unit. Expected sales at both companies are 80,000 units at $.30 per unit. At this sales level, both alternatives would have net incomes of $2,000. If sales fall short of 80,000 units, profits *drop* most sharply for the highly leveraged business. If sales exceed 80,000 units, however, profits *increase* most sharply for the highly leveraged concern.

The highly leveraged alternative is more risky. Why? Because it provides the highest possible net income and the highest possible losses. In other words, net income is highly variable, depending on the actual level of sales. The low-leverage alternative is less risky because variations in sales lead to only small variability in net income. At sales of 90,000 units, net income is $4,000 for the higher-leveraged firm but only $2,500 for the lower-leveraged firm. At sales of 70,000 units, however, the higher-leveraged firm has zero profits, compared to $1,500 for the lower-leveraged firm.

Contribution Margin and Gross Margin

variable-cost ratio (variable-cost percentage) All variable costs divided by sales.

gross margin (gross profit) The excess of sales over the total cost of goods sold.

cost of goods sold The cost of the merchandise that is acquired or manufactured and resold.

Contribution margin may be expressed as a *total* absolute amount, a *unit* absolute amount, a *ratio*, and a *percentage*. The **variable-cost ratio** or **variable-cost percentage** is defined as all variable costs divided by sales. Thus a contribution-margin ratio of 20% means that the variable-cost ratio is 80%.

Too often people confuse the terms *contribution margin* and *gross margin*. **Gross margin** (which is also called **gross profit**) is the excess of sales over the **cost of goods sold** (that is, the cost of the merchandise that is acquired or manufactured and then sold). It is a widely used concept, particularly in the retailing industry.

Compare the gross margin with the contribution margin:

gross margin = sales price − cost of goods sold
contribution margin = sales price − all variable expenses

Exhibit 2-6

High Versus Low
Leverage

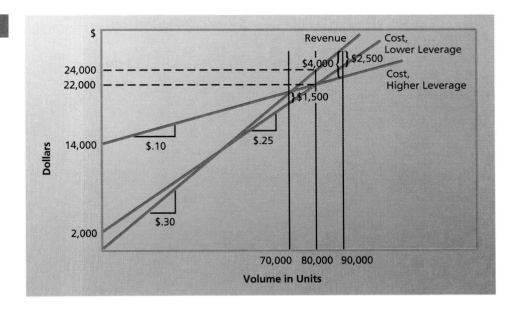

Objective 7

Distinguish between
contribution margin
and gross margin

The following comparisons from our vending machine illustration show the
similarities and differences between the contribution margin and the gross
margin in a retail store:

Sales	$.50
Variable costs: acquisition cost of unit sold	.40
Contribution margin and gross margin are equal	$.10

Thus the original data resulted in no difference between the measure of
contribution margin and gross margin. There *would* be a difference between
the two, however, if the firm had to pay additional rent of 1¢ per unit sold:

	Contribution Margin	Gross Margin
Sales	$.50	$.50
Acquisition cost of unit sold	$.40	.40
Variable rent	.01	
Total variable expense	.41	
Contribution margin	$.09	
Gross margin		$.10

As the preceding tabulation indicates, contribution margin and gross margin
are not the same concepts. Contribution margin focuses on sales in relation to
all variable costs, whereas gross margin focuses on sales in relation to cost of
goods sold. For example, consider MascoTech, a Detroit-based auto parts supplier. A newspaper article reported that MascoTech's "gross profit margin on
sales is about 21% today, but for each additional sales dollar the contribution
margin is more like 30%."

■ NONPROFIT APPLICATION

Consider how cost-volume-profit relationships apply to nonprofit organizations. Suppose a city has a $100,000 lump-sum budget appropriation for a government agency to conduct a counseling program for drug addicts. The variable costs for drug prescriptions are $400 per patient per year. Fixed costs are $60,000 in the relevant range of 50 to 150 patients. If all of the budget appropriation is spent, how many patients can be served in a year?

Let N be the number of patients.

revenue – variable expenses – fixed expenses = 0 if budget is completely spent
$100,000 lump sum – $400N – $60,000 = 0
$400N = $100,000 – $60,000
N = $40,000 ÷ 400
N = 100 patients

Suppose the total budget appropriation for the following year is cut by 10%. Fixed costs will be unaffected, but service will decline:

revenue – variable expenses – fixed expenses = 0
$90,000 – $400N – $60,000 = 0
$400N = $90,000 – $60,000
N = $30,000 ÷ $400
N = 75 patients

The reduction in service is more than the 10% reduction in the budget. Without restructuring operations, the service volume must be reduced 25% (from 100 to 75 patients) to stay within budget. Note that lump-sum revenue is a horizontal line on the graph:

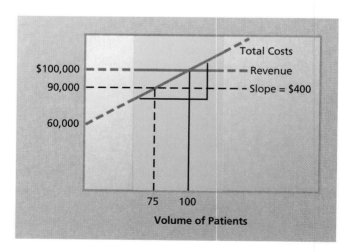

Highlights to Remember

Understanding cost behavior patterns and cost-volume-profit (CVP) relationships can help guide a manager's decisions. The first step in assessing cost behavior is to identify cost drivers. Variable costs and fixed costs have contrasting behavior patterns with respect to a particular cost driver—variable costs change in proportion to changes in the cost driver, whereas fixed costs are unaffected by cost-driver activity.

CVP analysis (sometimes called break-even analysis) can be approached graphically or with equations. Managers use CVP analysis to compute a break-even point, to compute a target net income, or to examine the effects on income of changes in factors such as fixed costs, variable costs, or volume. CVP analysis is used in nonprofit organizations as well as in profit-seeking companies.

Be sure to recognize the limitations of CVP analysis. Most important, it relies on the ability to separate costs into fixed and variable categories. Therefore, it is applicable only over a relevant range of activity. In addition, it assumes constant efficiency, sales mix, and inventory levels.

The contribution margin—the difference between sales price and variable costs—is an important concept. Do not confuse it with gross margin, the difference between sales price and cost of goods sold.

Summary Problem for Your Review

Problem

The budgeted income statement of Port Williams Gift Shop is summarized as follows:

Net revenue	$ 800,000
Less: expenses, including $400,000 of fixed expenses	880,000
Net loss	$ (80,000)

The manager believes that an increase of $200,000 on advertising outlays will increase sales substantially.

Required

1. At what sales volume will the store break even after spending $200,000 on advertising?
2. What sales volume will result in a net profit of $40,000?

Solution

1. Note that all data are expressed in dollars. No unit data are given. Most companies have many products, so the overall break-even analysis deals with dollar sales, not units. The variable expenses are $880,000 − $400,000, or $480,000. The variable-expense ratio is $480,000 ÷ $800,000, or .60. Therefore the contribution-margin ratio is .40. Let S = break-even sales in dollars. Then

$$S - \text{variable expenses} - \text{fixed expenses} = \text{net profit}$$
$$S - .60S - \left(\$400,000 + \$200,000\right) = 0$$
$$.40S = \$600,000$$
$$S = \frac{\$600,000}{.40} = \frac{\text{fixed expenses}}{\text{contribution-margin ratio}}$$
$$S = \$1,500,000$$

2.

$$\text{required sales} = \frac{\text{fixed expenses} + \text{target net profit}}{\text{contribution-margin ratio}}$$

$$\text{required sales} = \frac{\$600{,}000 + \$40{,}000}{.40} = \frac{\$640{,}000}{.40}$$

$$\text{required sales} = \$1{,}600{,}000$$

Alternatively, we can use an incremental approach and reason that all dollar sales beyond the $1.5 million break-even point will result in a 40% contribution to net profit. Divide $40,000 by .40. Sales must therefore be $100,000 beyond the $1.5 million break-even point to produce a net profit of $40,000.

Appendix 2A: Sales-Mix Analysis

Objective 8

Explain the effects of sales mix on profits

To emphasize fundamental ideas, the cost-volume-profit analysis in this chapter has focused on a single product. Nearly all companies, however, sell more than one product. *Sales mix* is defined as the relative proportions or combinations of quantities of products that comprise total sales. If the proportions of the mix change, the cost-volume-profit relationships also change.

Suppose Ramos Company has two products, wallets (W) and key cases (K). The income budget follows:

	Wallets (W)	Key Cases (K)	Total
Sales in units	300,000	75,000	375,000
Sales @ $8 and $5	$2,400,000	$375,000	$2,775,000
Variable expenses @ $7 and $3	2,100,000	225,000	2,325,000
Contribution margins @ $1 and $2	$ 300,000	$150,000	$ 450,000
Fixed expenses			180,000
Net income			$ 270,000

For simplicity, ignore income taxes. What would be the break-even point? The typical answer assumes a constant mix of 4 units of W for every unit of K. Therefore, let K = number of units of product K to break even, and 4K = number of units of product W to break even:

$$\text{sales} - \text{variable expenses} - \text{fixed expenses} = \text{zero net income}$$
$$\$8(4K) + \$5(K) - \$7(4K) - \$3(K) - \$180{,}000 = 0$$
$$\$32K + \$5K - \$28K - \$3K - \$180{,}000 = 0$$
$$\$6K = \$180{,}000$$
$$K = 30{,}000$$
$$4K = 120{,}000 = W$$

The break-even point is 30,000K + 120,000W = 150,000 units.

This is the only break-even point for a sales mix of four wallets for every key case. Clearly, however, there are other break-even points for other sales mixes. For instance, suppose only key cases were sold, fixed expenses being unchanged:

$$\text{break-even point} = \frac{\text{fixed expenses}}{\text{contribution margin per unit}}$$

$$= \frac{\$180,000}{\$2}$$

$$= 90,000 \text{ key cases}$$

If only wallets were sold:

$$\text{break-even point} = \frac{180,000}{\$1}$$

$$= 180,000 \text{ wallets}$$

Managers are not primarily interested in the break-even point for its own sake. Instead, they want to know how changes in a planned sales mix will affect net income. When the sales mix changes, the break-even point and the expected net income at various sales levels are altered. For example, suppose overall actual total sales were equal to the budget of 375,000 units. However, only 50,000 key cases were sold:

	Wallets (W)	Key Cases (K)	Total
Sales in units	325,000	50,000	375,000
Sales @ $8 and $5	$2,600,000	$250,000	$2,850,000
Variable expenses @ $7 and $3	2,275,000	150,000	2,425,000
Contribution margins @ $1 and $2	$ 325,000	$100,000	$ 425,000
Fixed expenses			180,000
Net income			$ 245,000

The change in sales mix has resulted in a $245,000 actual net income rather than the $270,000 budgeted net income, an unfavorable difference of $25,000. The budgeted and actual sales in number of units were identical, but the proportion of the product bearing the higher unit contribution margin declined.

Different advertising strategies may also affect the sales mix. Clearly, if a sales budget is not actually attained, the budgeted net income will be affected by the individual sales volume of each product. The fewer the units sold, the lower the profit, and vice versa. All other factors being equal, the higher the proportion of the more profitable products, the higher the profit. For example, Reynolds Industries sells highly profitable cigarettes (such as the Winston brand) and less profitable canned goods (such as the Del Monte brand). For any given level of total sales, the greater the proportion of the cigarettes, the greater the total profit.

Managers usually want to maximize the sales of all their products. Faced with limited resources and time, however, executives prefer to generate the most profitable sales mix achievable. For example, consider a recent annual report of Deere & Co., a manufacturer of farm equipment: "The increase in the ratio of cost of goods sold to net sales resulted from higher production costs [and] a less favorable mix of products sold."

Profitability of a given product helps guide executives who must decide to emphasize or de-emphasize particular products. For example, given limited production facilities or limited time of sales personnel, should we emphasize wallets or key cases? These decisions may be affected by other factors beyond the contribution margin per unit of product. Chapter 5 explores some of these factors including the importance of the amount of profit per *unit of time* rather than per *unit of product*.

Appendix 2B: Impact of Income Taxes

Objective 9

Compute cost-volume-profit relationships on an after-tax basis

Thus far we have (as so many people would like to) ignored income taxes. In most nations, however, private enterprises are subject to income taxes. Reconsider the vending machine example in the chapter. On page 49, as part of our CVP analysis, we discussed the sales necessary to achieve a target income before income taxes of $480. If an income tax were levied at 40%, the new result would be

Income before income tax	$480	100%
Income tax	192	40
Net income	$288	60%

Note that

$$\text{net income} = \text{income before income taxes} - .40 \text{ (income before income taxes)}$$
$$\text{net income} = .60 \text{ (income before income taxes)}$$
$$\text{income before income taxes} = \frac{\text{net income}}{.60}$$

or

$$\text{target income before income taxes} = \frac{\text{target after-tax net income}}{1 - \text{tax rate}}$$

$$\text{target income before income taxes} = \frac{\$288}{1 - .40} = \frac{\$288}{.60} = \$480$$

Suppose the target net income after taxes was $288. The only change in the general equation approach would be on the right-hand side of the following equation:

$$\text{target sales} - \text{variable expenses} - \text{fixed expenses} = \frac{\text{target after-tax net income}}{1 - \text{tax rate}}$$

Thus, letting N be the number of units to be sold at $.50 each with a variable cost of $.40 each and total fixed costs of $6,000,

$$\$.50N - \$.40N - \$6,000 = \frac{\$288}{1 - .4}$$
$$\$.10N = \$6,000 + \frac{\$288}{.6}$$
$$\$.06N = \$3,600 + \$288 = 3,888$$
$$N = \$3,888 \div \$.06 = 64,800 \text{ units}$$

Sales of 64,800 units produce an *after-tax* profit of $288 as shown here and a *before-tax* profit of $480 as shown in the chapter.

Suppose the target net income after taxes was $480. The volume needed would rise to 68,000 units, as follows:

$$\$.50N - \$.40N - \$6,000 = \frac{\$480}{1 - .4}$$

$$\$.10N = \$6,000 + \frac{\$480}{.6}$$

$$\$.06N = \$3,600 + \$480 = \$4,080$$

$$N = \$4,080 \div \$.06 = 68,000 \text{ units}$$

As a shortcut to computing the effects of volume on the change in after-tax income, use the formula

$$\begin{pmatrix} \text{change} \\ \text{in net} \\ \text{income} \end{pmatrix} = \begin{pmatrix} \text{change in volume} \\ \text{in units} \end{pmatrix} \times \begin{pmatrix} \text{contribution margin} \\ \text{per unit} \end{pmatrix} \times (1 - \text{tax rate})$$

In our example, suppose operations were at a level of 64,800 units and $288 after-tax net income. The manager is wondering how much after-tax net income would increase if sales become 68,000 units.

$$\text{change in net income} = (68,000 - 64,800) \times \$.10 \times (1 - .4)$$
$$= 3,200 \times \$.10 \times .60 = 3,200 \times \$.06$$
$$= \$192$$

In brief, each unit beyond the break-even point adds to after-tax net profit at the unit contribution margin multiplied by (1 – income tax rate).

Throughout our illustration, the break-even point itself does not change. Why? Because *there is no income tax at a level of zero profits.*

Accounting Vocabulary

break-even point, *p. 42*

contribution margin, *p. 44*

cost behavior, *p. 37*

cost drivers, *p. 38*

cost of goods sold, *p. 54*

cost-volume-profit (CVP) analysis, *p. 42*

fixed cost, *p. 38*

gross margin, *p. 54*

gross profit, *p. 54*

incremental effect, *p. 49*

marginal income, *p. 44*

margin of safety, *p. 44*

operating leverage, *p. 53*

relevant range, *p. 40*

sales mix, *p. 48*

variable cost, *p. 38*

variable-cost percentage, *p. 54*

variable-cost ratio, *p. 54*

Fundamental Assignment Material

2-A1   Cost-Volume-Profits and Vending Machines

Delgado Food Services Company operates and services snack vending machines located in restaurants, gas stations, factories, etc., in four Midwestern states. The machines are rented from the manufacturer. In addition, Delgado must rent the space occupied by its machines. The following expense and revenue relationships pertain to a contemplated expansion program of 20 machines.

Fixed monthly expenses follow:

Machine rental: 20 machines @ $21.75	$ 435
Space rental: 20 locations @ $14.40	288
Part-time wages to service the additional 20 machines	727
Other fixed costs	50
Total monthly fixed costs	$1,500

Other data follow:

	Per Unit	Per $100 of Sales
Selling price	$.50	100%
Cost of snack	.40	80
Contribution margin	$.10	20%

Required

These questions relate to the above data unless otherwise noted. **Consider each question independently.**

1. What is the monthly break-even point in number of units? In dollar sales?
2. If 18,000 units were sold, what would be the company's net income?
3. If the space rental cost were doubled, what would be the monthly break-even point in number of units? In dollar sales?
4. If, in addition to the fixed rent, Delgado Food Services Company paid the vending machine manufacturer 1¢ per unit sold, what would be the monthly break-even point in number of units? In dollar sales? Refer to the original data.
5. If, in addition to the fixed rent, Delgado paid the machine manufacturer 2¢ for each unit sold in excess of the break-even point, what would the new net income be if 18,000 units were sold? Refer to the original data.

2-A2   Exercises in Cost-Volume-Profit Relationships

The MacKenzie-Hawkins Transportation Company specializes in hauling heavy goods over long distances. The company's revenues and expenses depend on revenue miles, a measure that combines both weights and mileage. Summarized budget data for next year are based on predicted total revenue miles of 800,000.

	Per Revenue Mile
Average selling price (revenue)	$1.50
Average variable expenses	1.30
Fixed expenses, $110,000	

Required

1. Compute the budgeted net income. Ignore income taxes.
2. Management is trying to decide how various possible conditions or decisions might affect net income. Compute the new net income for each of the following changes. Consider each case independently.
   a. A 10% increase in revenue miles
   b. A 10% increase in sales price
   c. A 10% increase in variable expenses
   d. A 10% increase in fixed expenses
   e. An average decrease in selling price of 3¢ per mile and a 5% increase in revenue miles. Refer to the original data
   f. An average increase in selling price of 5% and a 10% decrease in revenue miles
   g. A 10% increase in fixed expenses in the form of more advertising and a 5% increase in revenue miles

2-B1   Basic CVP Exercises

Each problem is *unrelated* to the others.

1. Given: Selling price per unit, $20; total fixed expenses, $5,000; variable expenses per unit, $15. Find break-even sales in units.
2. Given: Sales, $40,000; variable expenses, $30,000; fixed expenses, $7,500; net income, $2,500. Find break-even sales.

3. Given: Selling price per unit, $30; total fixed expenses, $33,000; variable expenses per unit, $14. Find total sales in units to achieve a profit of $7,000, assuming no change in selling price.

4. Given: Sales, $50,000; variable expenses, $20,000; fixed expenses, $20,000; net income, $10,000. Assume no change in selling price; find net income if activity volume increases 10%.

5. Given: Selling price per unit, $40; total fixed expenses, $80,000; variable expenses per unit, $30. Assume that variable expenses are reduced by 20% per unit, and the total fixed expenses are increased by 10%. Find the sales in units to achieve a profit of $20,000, assuming no change in selling price.

2-B2   Basic CVP Analysis

Peter Landis opened his own small day care facility, Toys 'N Tots (TNT), just over 2 years ago. After a rocky start, TNT has been thriving. Peter is now preparing a budget for November 19X6.

Monthly fixed costs for TNT are

Rent	$ 800
Salaries	1,400
Other fixed costs	100
Total fixed costs	$2,300

The salary is for Lynn McGraw, the only employee, who works with Peter in caring for the children. Peter does not pay himself a salary, but he receives the excess of revenues over costs each month.

The cost driver for variable costs is "child-days." One child-day is one day in day care for one child, and the variable cost is $10 per child-day. The facility is open 6:00 A.M. to 6:00 P.M. weekdays (i.e., Monday through Friday), and there are 22 weekdays in November 19X6. An average day has 8 children attending TNT. State law prohibits TNT from having more than 14 children, a limit it has never reached. Peter charges $30 per day per child, regardless of how long the child is at TNT.

Required

1. Suppose attendance for November 19X6 is equal to the average, resulting in 22 × 8 = 176 child-days. What amount will Peter have left after paying all his expenses?
2. Suppose both costs and attendance are difficult to predict. Compute the amount Peter will have left after paying all his expenses for each of the following situations. Consider each case independently.
   a. Average attendance is 9 children per day instead of 8, generating 198 child-days.
   b. Variable costs increase to $11 per child-day.
   c. Rent is increased by $200 per month.
   d. Peter spends $300 on advertising (a fixed cost) in November, which increases average daily attendance to 9.5 children.
   e. Peter begins charging $33 per day on November 1, and average daily attendance slips to 7 children.

Additional Assignment Material

Questions

2-1. "Cost behavior is simply identification of cost drivers and their relationships to costs." Comment.

2-2. Give three examples of variable costs and of fixed costs.

2-3. "Fixed costs decline as volume increases." Do you agree? Explain.

2-4. "It is confusing to think of fixed costs on a per-unit basis." Do you agree? Why or why not?

2-5. "The relevant range pertains to fixed costs, not variable costs." Do you agree? Explain.

2-6. Identify two simplifying assumptions that underlie CVP analysis.

2-7. "Classification of costs into variable and fixed categories depends on the decision situation." Explain.

2-8. "Contribution margin is the excess of sales over fixed costs." Do you agree? Explain.

2-9. Why is "break-even analysis" a misnomer?

2-10. "Companies in the same industry generally have about the same break-even point." Do you agree? Explain.

2-11. Distinguish between the equation technique of CVP analysis and the unit contribution-margin technique.

2-12. Describe three ways of lowering a break-even point.

2-13. "Incremental analysis is quicker, but it has no other advantage over an analysis of all costs and revenues associated with each alternative." Do you agree? Why or why not?

2-14. Explain operating leverage and why a highly leveraged company is risky.

2-15. "CVP analysis is a common management use of personal computers." Do you agree? Explain.

2-16. "The contribution margin and gross margin are always equal." Do you agree? Explain.

2-17. "CVP relationships are unimportant in nonprofit organizations." Do you agree? Explain.

2-18. "Two products were sold. Total budgeted and actual total sales in number of units were identical to the units budgeted. Actual unit variable costs and sales prices were the same as budgeted. Actual contribution margin was lower than budgeted." What could be the reason for the lower contribution margin?

2-19. Present the CVP formula for computing the target income before income taxes.

2-20. Present the CVP formula for computing the effects of a change in volume on after-tax income.

Exercises

2-21 Nature of Variable and Fixed Costs

"As I understand it, costs such as the salary of the vice president of transportation operations are variable because the more traffic you handle, the less your unit cost. In contrast, costs such as fuel are fixed because each ton-mile should entail consumption of the same amount of fuel and hence bear the same unit cost." Do you agree? Explain.

2-22 Basic Review Exercises

Fill in the blanks for each of the following independent cases (ignore income taxes):

	Sales	Variable Expenses	Contribution Margin	Fixed Expenses	Net Income
1.	$900,000	$500,000	$ —	$350,000	$ —
2.	800,000	—	350,000	—	80,000
3.	—	600,000	340,000	250,000	—

2-23 Basic Review Exercises

Fill in the blanks for each of the following independent cases:

Case	(a) Selling Price per Unit	(b) Variable Cost per Unit	(c) Total Units Sold	(d) Total Contribution Margin	(e) Total Fixed Costs	(f) Net Income
1.	$25	$ —	120,000	$720,000	$640,000	$ —
2.	10	6	100,000	—	320,000	—
3.	20	15	—	100,000	—	15,000
4.	30	20	70,000	—	—	12,000
5.	—	9	80,000	160,000	110,000	—

2-24 Hospital Costs and Pricing

St. Vincent Hospital has overall variable costs of 30% of total revenue and fixed costs of $42 million per year.

Required

1. Compute the break-even point expressed in total revenue.
2. A patient-day is often used to measure the volume of a hospital. Suppose there are going to be 50,000 patient-days next year. Compute the average daily revenue per patient necessary to break even.

2-25 Motel Rentals

The Holiday Motel has annual fixed costs applicable to its rooms of $3.2 million for its 400-room motel, average daily room rents of $50, and average variable costs of $10 for each room rented. It operates 365 days per year.

Required

1. How much net income on rooms will be generated (1) if the motel is completely full throughout the entire year and (2) if the motel is half full?
2. Compute the break-even point in number of rooms rented. What percentage occupancy for the year is needed to break even?

2-26 Basic Relationships, Hotel

The Pippin Hotel in Chicago has 400 rooms, with a fixed cost of $350,000 per month during the busy season. Room rates average $62 per day with variable costs of $12 per rented room per day. Assume a 30-day month.

Required

1. How many rooms must be occupied per day to break even?
2. How many rooms must be occupied per month to make a profit of $100,000?
3. Assume that the Pippin Hotel has these average contribution margins per month from use of space in its hotel:

Leased shops in hotel	$60,000
Meals served, conventions	30,000
Dining room and coffee shop	30,000
Bar and cocktail lounge	20,000

Fixed costs for the total hotel are $350,000 per month. Variable costs are $12 per day per rented room. The hotel has 400 rooms and averages 80% occupancy per day. What average rate per day must the hotel charge to make a profit of $100,000 per month?

2-27 Sales-Mix Analysis

Study Appendix 2A. Tanaka Farms produces strawberries and raspberries. Annual fixed costs are $14,400. The cost driver for variable costs is pints of fruit produced. The variable cost is $.40 per pint of strawberries and $.60 per pint of raspberries. Strawberries sell for $.75 per pint, raspberries for $1.10 per pint. Two pints of strawberries are produced for every pint of raspberries.

Required

1. Compute the number of pints of strawberries and the number of pints of raspberries produced and sold at the break-even point.
2. Suppose only strawberries are produced and sold. Compute the break-even point in pints.
3. Suppose only raspberries are produced and sold. Compute the break-even point in pints.

2-28 Income Taxes

Review the illustration in Appendix 2B. Suppose the income tax rate were 20% instead of 40%. How many units would have to be sold to achieve a target net income of (1) $288 and (2) $480? Show your computations.

2-29 Income Taxes and Cost-Volume-Profit Analysis

Study Appendix 2B. Suppose Meola Security Company has a 20% income tax rate, a contribution-margin ratio of 30%, and fixed costs of $440,000. What sales volume is necessary to achieve an after-tax income of $80,000?

Problems

2-30 Fixed Costs and Relevant Range

Guiterro Systems Group (GSG) has a substantial year-to-year fluctuation in billings to clients. Top management has the following policy regarding the employment of key professional personnel:

If Gross Annual Billings Are	Number of Persons to be Employed	Key Professional Annual Salaries and Related Expenses
$2,000,000 or less	10	$1,000,000
$2,000,001–2,400,000	11	1,100,000
$2,400,001–2,800,000	12	1,200,000

Top management believes that a minimum of ten individuals should be retained for a year or more even if billings drop drastically below $2 million.

For the past five years, gross annual billings for GSG have fluctuated between $2,020,000 and $2,380,000. Expectations for next year are that gross billings will be between $2,100,000 and $2,300,000. What amounts should be budgeted for key professional personnel? Graph the relationships on an annual basis, using the two approaches illustrated in Exhibit 2-2. Indicate the relevant range on each graph. You need not use graph paper; simply approximate the graphical relationships.

2-31 Movie Manager

Julia Sanchez is the manager of Stanford's traditional Sunday Flicks. Each Sunday a film has two showings. The admission price is deliberately set at a very low $2. A maximum of 500 tickets is sold for each showing. The rental of the auditorium is $220 and labor is $290, including $60 for Sanchez. Sanchez must pay the film distributor a guarantee, ranging from $200 to $600 or 50% of gross admission receipts, whichever is higher.

Before and during the show, refreshments are sold; these sales average 12% of gross admission receipts and yield a contribution margin of 40%.

1. On June 3, Sanchez played *Forrest Gump*. The film grossed $1,500. The guarantee to the distributor was $500, or 50% of gross admission receipts, whichever is higher. What operating income was produced for the Students' Association, which sponsored the showings?

2. Recompute the results if the film grossed $900.

3. The "four-wall" concept is increasingly being adopted by movie producers. In this plan, the movie's producer pays a fixed rental to the theater owner for, say, a week's showing of a movie. As a theater owner, how would you evaluate a "four-wall" offer?

2-32 Promotion of Championship Fight

Newspaper accounts of a middle-weight boxing match stated that each fighter would receive a flat fee of $3 million in cash. The fight would be shown on closed-circuit television. The central promotor, Donald Prince, would collect 100% of the receipts and would return 30% to the individual local promoters. Prince expected to sell 1.1 million seats at a net average price of $13 each. Prince was also to receive $300,000 from Madison Square Garden (which had sold out its 19,500 seats, ranging from $150 for ringside down to $20, for a gross revenue of $1.25 million); Prince would not share the $300,000 with the local promoters.

Required

1. Donald Prince is trying to decide what amount to spend for advertising. What is the most Prince could spend and still break even on overall operations, assuming sales of 1.1 million tickets?
2. If Prince desired an operating income of $500,000, how many seats would have to be sold? Assume that the average price was $13 and the total fixed costs were $8 million.

2-33 Basic Relationships, Restaurant

(W. Crum, adapted.) Nicole Azarski owns and operates a restaurant. Her fixed costs are $10,500 per month. Luncheons and dinners are served. The average total bill (excluding tax and tip) is $9 per customer. Azarski's present variable costs average $4.80 per meal.

Required

1. How many meals must be served to attain a profit before taxes of $4,200 per month?
2. What is the break-even point in number of meals served per month?
3. Azarski's rent and other fixed costs rise to a total of $14,700 per month. Assume that variable costs also rise to $5.75 per meal. If Azarski increases her average price to $11, how many meals must she now serve to make $4,200 profit per month?
4. Azarski's accountant tells her she may lose 10% of her customers if she increases her prices. If this should happen, what would be Azarski's profit per month? Assume that the restaurant had been serving 3,500 customers per month.
5. To help offset the anticipated 10% loss of customers, Azarski hires a pianist to perform for 4 hours each night for $1,000 per month. Assume that this would increase the total monthly meals from 3,150 to 3,450. Would Azarski's total profit change? By how much?

2-34 Cost-Volume-Profit Analysis, Barbering

Michael's Hair Styling in Singapore has five barbers. (Michael is not one of them.) Each barber is paid $8.90 per hour and works a 40-hour week and a 50-week year. Rent and other fixed expenses are $1,750 per month. Assume that the only service performed is the giving of haircuts, the unit price of which is $11.

Required

1. Find the contribution margin per haircut. Assume that the barbers' compensation is a fixed cost.
2. Determine the annual break-even point, in number of haircuts.
3. What will be the operating income if 20,000 haircuts are sold?
4. Suppose Michael revises the compensation method. The barbers will receive $4 per hour plus $5 for each haircut. What is the new contribution margin per haircut? What is the annual break-even point (in number of haircuts)?
5. Ignore requirements 3 and 4 and assume that the barbers cease to be paid by the hour but receive $6 for each haircut. What is the new contribution margin per haircut? The annual break-even point (in number of haircuts)?
6. Refer to requirement 5. What would be the operating income if 20,000 haircuts are sold? Compare your answer with the answer in requirement 3.
7. Refer to requirement 5. If 20,000 haircuts are sold, at what rate of commission would Michael earn the same operating income as he earned in requirement 3?

2-35 CVP and Financial Statements

ConAgra, Inc., is an Omaha-based company that produces food products under brand names such as Healthy Choice, Armour, and Banquet. In 1994 the company's sales increased by 12% and its 1994 income statement showed the following (in millions):

Net Sales	$23,510
Costs of Goods Sold	20,450
Selling, Administrative, and General Expense	2,090
Interest Expense	250
Operating Income	$ 720

Suppose that the cost of goods sold is the only variable cost; selling, administrative, general, and interest expenses are fixed with respect to sales.

Required

Assume that ConAgra had another 12% increase in sales in 1995 and that there was no change in costs except for increases associated with the higher volume of sales. Compute the predicted 1995 operating profit for ConAgra and the percentage increase in operating profit. Explain why the percentage increase in profit differs from the percentage increase in sales.

2-36 Bingo and Leverage

A California law permits bingo games when offered by specified nonprofit institutions, including churches. Reverend Jill Bono, the pastor of a new parish in Marin County, is investigating the desirability of conducting weekly bingo nights. The parish has no hall, but a local hotel would be willing to commit its hall for a lump-sum rental of $600 per night. The rent would include cleaning, setting up and taking down the tables and chairs, and so on.

Required

1. Bingo cards would be provided by a local printer in return for free advertising thereon. Door prizes would be donated by local merchants. The services of clerks, callers, security force, and others would be donated by volunteers. Admission would be $3 per person, entitling the player to one card; extra cards would be $1.50 each. Reverend Bono also learns that many persons buy extra cards, so there would be an average of four cards played per person. What is the maximum in total cash prizes that the church may award and still break even if 200 persons attend each weekly session?

2. Suppose the total cash prizes are $900. What will be the church's operating income if 100 persons attend? If 200 persons attend? If 300 persons attend? Briefly explain the effects of the cost behavior on income.

3. After operating for 10 months, Reverend Bono is thinking of negotiating a different rental arrangement but keeping the prize money unchanged at $900. Suppose the rent is $200 weekly plus $2 per person. Compute the operating income for attendance of 100, 200, and 300 persons, respectively. Explain why the results differ from those in requirement 2.

2-37 Adding a Product

Andy's Ale House, a pub located near State University, serves as a gathering place for the university's more social scholars. Andy sells beer on draft and all brands of bottled beer at a contribution margin of 60¢ a beer.

Andy is considering also selling hamburgers during selected hours. His reasons are twofold. First, sandwiches would attract daytime customers. A hamburger and a beer are a quick lunch. Second, he has to meet competition from other local bars, some of which provide more extensive menus.

Andy analyzed the costs as follows:

	Per Month
Monthly fixed expenses	
Wages of part-time cook	$1,200
Other	360
Total	$1,560

	Per Hamburger
Variable expenses	
Rolls	$.12
Meat @ $2.80 per pound	
(7 hamburgers per pound)	.40
Other	.18
Total	$.70

Andy planned a selling price of $1.10 per hamburger to lure many customers.

For all questions, assume a 30-day month.

1. What are the monthly and daily break-even points, in number of hamburgers?
2. What are the monthly and daily break-even points, in dollar sales?
3. At the end of two months, Andy finds he has sold 3,600 hamburgers. What is the operating profit per month on hamburgers?
4. Andy thinks that at least 60 extra beers are sold per day because he has these hamburgers available. This means that 60 extra people come to the bar or that 60 buy an extra beer because they are attracted by the hamburgers. How does this affect Andy's monthly operating income?
5. Refer to requirement 3. How many extra beers would have to be sold per day so that the overall effects of the hamburger sales on monthly operating income would be zero?

2-38   Cost-Volume-Profit Relationships and a Dog Track

The Vegas Kennel Club is a dog-racing track. Its revenue is derived mainly from attendance and a fixed percentage of the parimutuel betting. Its expenses for a 90-day season are as follows:

Wages of cashiers and ticket takers	$150,000
Commissioner's salary	20,000
Maintenance (repairs, etc.)	20,000
Utilities	30,000
Other expenses (depreciation, insurance, advertising, etc.)	100,000
Purses: total prizes paid to winning racers	810,000

The track made a contract with AP Inc. to park the cars. AP charged the track $4.80 per car. A survey revealed that on the average three persons arrived in each car and that half the attendees arrived by private automobiles. The others arrived by taxi and public buses.

The track's sources of revenue are

Rights for concession and vending	$50,000
Admission charge (deliberately low)	$1 per person
Percentage of bets placed	10%

1. Assume that each person bets $25 a night.
   a. How many persons have to be admitted for the track to break even for the season?
   b. If the desired operating profit for the year is $270,000, how many people would have to attend?
2. If a policy of free admission brought a 20% increase in attendance, what would be the new level of operating profit? Assume that the previous level of attendance was 600,000 people.
3. If the purses were doubled in an attempt to attract better dogs and thus increase attendance, what would be the new break-even point? Refer to the original data and assume that each person bets $25 a night.

2-39   Traveling Expenses

An Huang is a traveling inspector for the State Auditor's Office. He uses his own car and the agency reimburses him at 23¢ per mile. An Huang claims he needs 27¢ per mile just to break even.

Shawn McHale, the district manager, looks into the matter and compiles the following information about Huang's expenses:

Oil change every 3,000 miles	$ 30
Maintenance (other than oil) every 6,000 miles	240
Yearly insurance	700
Auto cost $13,500 with an average cash trade-in value of $6,000; has a useful life of three years.	
Gasoline is approximately $1.70 per gallon and Huang averages 17 miles per gallon.	

When Huang is on the road, he averages 120 miles a day. McHale knows that Huang does not work Saturdays or Sundays, has 10 working days vacation and 6 holidays, and spends approximately 15 working days in the office.

Required

1. How many miles per year would Huang have to travel to break even at the current rate of reimbursement?
2. What would be an equitable mileage rate?

2-40 Government Organization

A social welfare agency has a government budget appropriation for 19X6 of $900,000. The agency's major mission is to help handicapped persons who are unable to hold jobs. On the average, the agency supplements each person's other income by $5,000 annually. The agency's fixed costs are $290,000. There are no other costs.

Required

1. How many handicapped persons are helped during 19X6?
2. For 19X7, the agency's budget appropriation has been reduced by 15%. If the agency continues the same level of monetary support per person, how many handicapped persons will be helped in 19X7? Compute the percentage decline in the number of persons helped.
3. Assume a budget reduction of 15%, as in requirement 2. The manager of the agency has discretion as to how much to supplement each handicapped person's income. She does not want to reduce the number of persons served. On the average, what is the amount of the supplement that can be given to each person? Compute the percentage decline in the annual supplement.

2-41 Analysis of Airline Results

Actual operating statistics for the three months ended June 30 in a Continental Airlines quarterly report follow:

	Current Year	Preceding Year
Revenue passengers carried	946,603	1,044,697
Revenue-passenger-miles (000s)[*]	549,179	577,071
Scheduled aircraft miles flown	9,472,766	8,595,308
Available seat-miles (000s)	971,028	839,720
Passenger load factor	56.6%	?
Yield per revenue-passenger-mile[†]	$?	$ .0884

[*] A revenue-passenger-mile is 1 passenger carried 1 mile. For example, 2 passengers carried 800 miles would be 1,600 revenue-passenger-miles.
[†] Total revenue divided by revenue-passenger-miles.

The president of Continental commented:

"In the second quarter, airline revenues were nearly $64 million, a 25.6% increase compared with the preceding year. Revenue-passenger-miles, however, declined 5%, primarily as a result of weakened economic conditions. Meanwhile, the yield per passenger-mile increased 32% as a result of several fare increases made to counter spiraling costs."

Required

1. **a.** Compute the total passenger revenue in the second quarter of the preceding year.
   b. Also compute the passenger load factor.
2. Compute the yield per revenue-passenger-mile in the current year.
3. Assume that variable costs during the current quarter were 5¢ per revenue-passenger-mile. Also assume that the yield per revenue-passenger-mile was unaffected by the increase in the load factor. Suppose the passenger load factor had increased from 56.6% to 57.6%; compute the increase in operating income that would have been attained.

2-42   Gross Margin and Contribution Margin

General Mills produces and sells food products such as cereals (Cheerios and Wheaties) and baking products (Gold Medal flour and Betty Crocker cake mixes). A condensed 1994 income statement follows (in millions):

Sales	$8,517
Costs of goods sold	4,458
Gross margin	4,059
Other operating expenses	3,306
Operating income	$ 753

Assume that $960 million of the cost of goods sold is a fixed cost representing depreciation and other production costs that do not change with the volume of production. In addition, $2,120 million of the other operating expenses is fixed.

Required

1. Compute the total contribution margin for 1994 and the contribution margin percentage. Explain why the contribution margin differs from the gross margin.
2. Suppose that sales for General Mills were predicted to increase by 10% in 1995 and that the cost behavior was expected to continue in 1995 as it did in 1994. Compute the predicted operating income for 1995. By what percentage did this predicted 1995 operating income exceed the 1994 operating income?
3. What assumptions were necessary to compute the predicted 1995 operating income in requirement 2?

2-43   Choosing Equipment for Different Volumes

(CMA, adapted.) Consolidated Cinema owns and operates a nationwide chain of movie theaters. The 500 properties in the Consolidated chain vary from low-volume, small-town, single-screen theaters to high-volume, big-city, multiscreen theaters.

The management is considering installing machines that will make popcorn on the premises. These machines would allow the theaters to sell popcorn that would be freshly popped daily rather than the prepopped corn that is currently purchased in large bags. This proposed feature would be properly advertised and is intended to increase patronage at the company's theaters.

The machines can be purchased in several different sizes. The annual rental costs and operating costs vary with the size of the machines. The machine capacities and costs are as follows:

	Popper Model		
	Economy	*Regular*	*Super*
Annual capacity	50,000 boxes	120,000 boxes	300,000 boxes
Costs			
Annual machine rental	$8,000	$11,200	$20,200
Popcorn cost per box	.13	.13	.13
Cost of each box	.08	.08	.08
Other variable costs per box	.22	.14	.05

Required

1. Calculate the volume level in boxes at which the Economy Popper and Regular Popper would earn the same operating profit (loss).
2. The management can estimate the number of boxes to be sold at each of its theaters. Present a decision rule that would enable Consolidated management to select the most profitable machine without having to make a separate cost calculation for each theater. That is, at what anticipated range of unit sales should the economy model be used? the regular model? the super model?
3. Could the management use the average number of boxes sold per seat for the entire chain and the capacity of each theater to develop this decision rule? Explain your answer.

2-44   Sales-Mix Analysis

Study Appendix 2A. The Pacific Catering Company specializes in preparing tasty main courses that are frozen and shipped to the finer restaurants in the Los Angeles area. When a diner orders the item, the restaurant heats and serves it. The budget data for 19X6 are

	Product	
	Chicken Cordon Bleu	*Veal Marsala*
Selling price to restaurants	$6	$8
Variable expenses	3	4
Contribution margin	$3	$4
Number of units	250,000	125,000

The items are prepared in the same kitchens, delivered in the same trucks, and so forth. Therefore, the fixed costs of $1,320,000 are unaffected by the specific products.

Required

1. Compute the planned net income for 19X6.
2. Compute the break-even point in units, assuming that the planned sales mix is maintained.
3. Compute the break-even point in units if only veal were sold and if only chicken were sold.
4. Suppose 99,000 units of veal and 297,000 units of chicken were sold. Compute the net income. Compute the new break-even point if these relationships persisted in 19X6. What is the major lesson of this problem?

2-45   Hospital Patient Mix

Study Appendix 2A. Hospitals measure their volume in terms of patient-days, which are defined as the number of patients multiplied by the number of days that the patients are hospitalized. Suppose a large hospital has fixed costs of $24 million per year and variable costs of $300 per patient-day. Daily revenues vary among classes of patients. For simplicity, assume that there are two classes: (1) self-pay patients (S) who pay an average of $500 per day and (2) non–self-pay patients (G) who are the responsibility of insurance companies and government agencies and who pay an average of $400 per day. Twenty percent of the patients are self-pay.

Required
1. Compute the break-even point in patient-days, assuming that the planned mix of patients is maintained.
2. Suppose that 200,000 patient-days were achieved but that 25% of the patient-days were self-pay (instead of 20%). Compute the net income. Compute the break-even point.

2-46   Income Taxes on Hotels
Study Appendix 2B. The State Street Hotel in downtown Chicago has annual fixed costs applicable to rooms of $10 million for its 600-room hotel, average daily room rates of $95, and average variable costs of $15 for each room rented. It operates 365 days per year. The hotel is subject to an income tax rate of 40%.

Required
1. How many rooms must the hotel rent to earn a net income after taxes of $1,200,000? Of $360,000?
2. Compute the break-even point in number of rooms rented. What percentage occupancy for the year is needed to break even?
3. Assume that the volume level of rooms sold is 150,000. The manager is wondering how much income could be generated by adding sales of 15,000 rooms. Compute the additional net income after taxes.

2-47   Tax Effects, Multiple Choice
(CMA.) Study Appendix 2B. DisKing Company is a wholesaler for video tapes. The projected after-tax net income for the current year is $120,000 based on a sales volume of 200,000 video tapes. DisKing has been selling the tapes at $16 each. The variable costs consist of the $10 unit purchase price and a handling cost of $2 per unit. DisKing's annual fixed costs are $600,000, and DisKing is subject to a 40% income tax rate.

Management is planning for the coming year when it expects that the unit purchase price will increase 30%.

1. DisKing Company's break-even point for the current year is (a) 150,000 units (b) 100,000 units (c) 50,000 units (d) 60,000 units (e) some amount other than those given.
2. An increase of 10% in projected unit sales volume for the current year would result in an increased after-tax income for the current year of (a) $80,000 (b) $32,000 (c) $12,000 (d) $48,000 (e) some amount other than those given.
3. The volume of sales in dollars that DisKing Company must achieve in the coming year to maintain the same after-tax net income as projected for the current year if unit selling price remains at $16 is (a) $12,800,000 (b) $14,400,000 (c) $11,520,000 (d) $32,000,000 (e) some amount other than those given.
4. To cover a 30% increase in the unit purchase price for the coming year and still maintain the current contribution-margin ratio, DisKing Company must establish a selling price per unit for the coming year of (a) $19.60 (b) $20.00 (c) $20.80 (d) $19.00 (e) some amount other than those given.

Cases

2-48   Hospital Costs
Metropolitan City Hospital is unionized. In 19X3 nurses received an average annual salary of $37,000. The hospital administrator is considering how the contract with nurses should be changed for 19X4. In turn, the charging of nursing costs to each department might also be changed.

Each department is accountable for its financial performance. Revenues and expenses are allocated to departments. Consider the expenses of the obstetrics department in 19X3:

Variable expenses (based on 19X3 patient-days) are

Meals	$ 310,000
Laundry	160,000
Laboratory	600,000
Pharmacy	400,000
Maintenance	50,000
Other	130,000
Total	$1,650,000

Fixed expenses (based on number of beds) are

Rent	$2,000,000
General administrative services	1,500,000
Janitorial	100,000
Maintenance	100,000
Other	200,000
Total	$3,900,000

Nurses are assigned to departments on the basis of annual patient-days as follows:

Volume Level in Patient-Days	Number of Nurses
10,000–12,500	30
12,500–16,000	35

Total patient-days are the number of patients multiplied by the number of days they are hospitalized. Each department is charged for the salaries of the nurses assigned to it.

During 19X3 the obstetrics department had a capacity of 60 beds, billed each patient an average of $500 per day, and had revenues of $7.5 million.

Required
1. Compute the 19X3 volume of activity in patient-days.
2. Compute the 19X3 patient-days that would have been necessary for the obstetrics department to recoup all fixed expenses except nursing expenses.
3. Compute the 19X3 patient-days that would have been necessary for the obstetrics department to break even including nurses' salaries as a fixed cost.
4. Suppose Obstetrics must pay $120 per patient-day for nursing services. This plan would replace the two-level fixed-cost system employed in 19X3. Compute what the break-even point in patient-days would have been in 19X3 under this plan.

2-49   CVP and Prediction of Income
According to an article in *Business Week* (July 25, 1994), T.J. Izzo had a great idea after a bad back almost forced him to give up golf. His problem was carrying a golf bag, not swinging a club. So he designed a harness-like golf bag strap that distributed the weight equally on both shoulders. In April 1992 he formed Izzo Systems Inc. In 1993 Izzo made operating income of $12,000 on revenue of $1 million from selling 75,000 straps. In 1994 Izzo expected to sell 92,000 straps for $1.7 million.

Required
1. Suppose that variable costs per strap are $10. Compute total fixed and total variable costs for 1993.

2. Suppose the cost behavior in 1994 was the same as in 1993. Estimate Izzo's operating income for 1994 (a) with sales at the predicted 92,000 straps, (b) with sales 10% above the predicted level, and (c) with sales 10% below the predicted level.

3. Explain why the predicted 1994 operating income was so much greater than the 1993 operating income.

2-50   CVP in a Modern Manufacturing Environment

A division of Hewlett-Packard Company changed its production operations from one where a large labor force assembled electronic components to an automated production facility dominated by computer-controlled robots. The change was necessary because of fierce competitive pressures. Improvements in quality, reliability, and flexibility of production schedules were necessary just to match the competition. As a result of the change, variable costs fell and fixed costs increased, as shown in the following assumed budgets:

	Old Production Operation	New Production Operation
Unit variable cost		
Material	$ .88	$ .88
Labor	1.22	.22
Total per unit	$2.10	$1.10
Monthly fixed costs		
Rent and depreciation	$450,000	$ 875,000
Supervisory labor	85,000	175,000
Other	50,000	90,000
Total per month	$585,000	$1,140,000

Expected volume is 600,000 units per month, with each unit selling for $3.10. Capacity is 800,000 units.

Required

1. Compute the budgeted profit at the expected volume of 600,000 units under both the old and the new production environments.
2. Compute the budgeted break-even point under both the old and the new production environments.
3. Discuss the effect on profits if volume falls to 500,000 units under both the old and the new production environments.
4. Discuss the effect on profits if volume increases to 700,000 units under both the old and the new production environments.
5. Comment on the riskiness of the new operation versus the old operation.

2-51   Multiproduct Break-Even in a Restaurant

Study Appendix 2A. An article in *Washington Business* included a 1990 income statement for La Brasserie, a French restaurant in Washington, D.C. A simplified version of the statement follows:

Revenues	$2,098,400
Cost of sales, all variable	1,246,500
Gross profit	851,900
Operating expenses	
Variable	222,380
Fixed	170,700
Administrative expenses, all fixed	451,500
Net income	$ 7,320

The average dinner tab at La Brasserie is $40, and the average lunch tab is $20. Assume that the variable cost of preparing and serving dinner is also twice that of a lunch. The restaurant serves twice as many lunches as dinners. Assume that the restaurant is open 305 days a year.

Required

1. Using the cost and revenue data for 1990, compute the daily break-even volume in lunches and dinners for La Brasserie. Compare this to the actual volume for 1990.
2. Suppose that an extra annual advertising expenditure of $12,000 would increase the average daily volume by three dinners and six lunches, and that there is plenty of capacity to accommodate the extra business. Prepare an analysis for the management of La Brasserie explaining whether this would be desirable.
3. La Brasserie uses only premium food, and the cost of food makes up 25% of the restaurant's total variable costs. Use of average rather than premium ingredients could cut the food cost by 20%. Assume that La Brasserie uses average-quality ingredients and does not change its prices. How much of a drop-off in volume could it endure and still maintain the same net income? What factors in addition to revenue and costs would influence the decision about the quality of food to use?

2-52 Effects of Changes in Costs, Including Tax Effects

(CMA.) Study Appendix 2B. Friendly Candy Company is a wholesale distributor of candy. The company services grocery, convenience, and drug stores in a large metropolitan area.

Small but steady growth in sales has been achieved by Friendly Candy Company over the past few years while candy prices have been increasing. The company is formulating its plans for the coming fiscal year. Presented below are the data used to project the current year's after-tax net income of $110,400.

Average selling price per box	$4.00
Average variable costs per box	
Cost of candy	$2.00
Selling expenses	.40
Total	$2.40
Annual fixed costs	
Selling	$160,000
Administrative	280,000
Total	$440,000
Expected annual sales volume (390,000 boxes)	$1,560,000
Tax rate	40%

Manufacturers of candy have announced that they will increase prices of their products an average of 15% in the coming year, owing to increases in raw material (sugar, cocoa, peanuts, etc.) and labor costs. Friendly Candy Company expects that all other costs will remain at the same rates or levels as in the current year.

1. What is Friendly Candy Company's break-even point in boxes of candy for the current year?
2. What selling price per box must Friendly Candy Company charge to cover the 15% increase in the cost of candy and still maintain the current contribution-margin ratio?
3. What volume of sales in dollars must the Friendly Candy Company achieve in the coming year to maintain the same net income after taxes as projected for the current year if the selling price of candy remains at $4 per box and the cost of candy increases 15%?
4. What strategies might Friendly Candy Company use to maintain the same net income after taxes as projected for the current year?

3 Variations of Cost Behavior

Understanding cost-behavior patterns is important for all organizations. Trans Union Corporation is a major supplier of personal credit information to mortgage and credit-card companies worldwide. As the volume of credit reports changes, the cost of data storage tape changes in direct proportion. Office space costs are fixed, and the costs of tape-driven units have step-cost behavior because they change in abrupt increments.
Courtesy Trans Union Corporation

Learning Objectives

When you have finished studying this chapter, you should be able to

1 Explain step- and mixed-cost behavior.

2 Explain management influences on cost behavior.

3 Measure cost functions and use them to predict costs.

4 Describe mathematical cost functions.

5 Describe the importance of activity analysis for measuring cost functions.

6 Use the account analysis, high-low, visual-fit, and least-squares regression methods for measuring cost functions.

Chapter 2 demonstrated the importance of understanding relationships between an organization's activities and its costs, revenues, and profits. This chapter focuses on **measurement of cost behavior,** which means under-standing and *quantifying* how activities of an organization affect levels of costs. Recall that the activities that affect costs are called *cost drivers*. Understanding relationships between costs and their cost drivers allows managers in all types of organizations—profit-seeking, nonprofit, and government—to

- Evaluate new manufacturing methods or service practices (Chapter 4)
- Make proper short-run marketing decisions (Chapter 5)
- Plan or budget the effects of future activities (Chapters 7 and 8)
- Design effective management control systems (Chapters 9 and 10)
- Make proper long-run decisions (Chapters 11 and 12)
- Design accurate and useful product costing systems (Chapters 13 to 16)
- Make short-run production decisions (Chapter 6)

measurement of cost behavior Under-standing and quantify-ing how activities of an organization affect levels of costs.

As you can see, understanding cost behavior is fundamental to management accounting. There are numerous real-world cases in which managers have made seriously wrong decisions to drop product lines, close manufacturing plants, or bid too high or too low on jobs because they had erroneous cost behavior information. This chapter, therefore, deserves careful study.

■ COST DRIVERS AND COST BEHAVIOR

linear-cost behavior
Activity that can be graphed with a straight line when a cost changes proportionately with changes in a cost driver.

Accountants and managers usually assume that cost behavior is *linear* over some *relevant range* of activities or change in cost drivers. **Linear-cost behavior** can be graphed with a straight line when a cost changes proportionately with changes in a single cost driver. Recall that the *relevant range* specifies the limits of cost driver activity within which a specific relationship between a cost and its cost driver will be valid. Managers usually define the relevant range based on their previous experience with different levels of activity and cost.

Many activities influence costs, but for some costs the *volume* of a product produced or service provided is the primary driver. These costs are easy to identify with, or trace to, products or services. Examples of volume-driven costs include the costs of printing labor, paper, ink, and binding to produce all the copies of this textbook. The number of copies printed obviously affects the total printing labor, paper, ink, and binding costs. Equally important, we could relatively easily *trace* the use of these resources to the copies of the text printed. Schedules, payroll records, and other documents show how much of each was used to produce the copies of this text.

Other costs are more affected by activities *not* directly related to volume and often have *multiple* cost drivers. Such costs are not easy to identify with or trace to outputs. Examples of costs that are difficult to trace include the wages and salaries of the editorial staff of the publisher of this textbook. These editorial personnel produce many different textbooks, and it would be very difficult to determine exactly what portion of their costs went into a specific book, such as *Introduction to Management Accounting*.

Understanding and measuring costs that are difficult to trace to outputs can be especially challenging. In practice, many organizations use a linear relationship with a single cost driver to describe each cost even though many have multiple causes. This approach is easier and less expensive than using nonlinear relationships or multiple cost drivers. *Careful use* of linear-cost behavior with a single cost driver often provides cost estimates that are accurate enough for most decisions. Linear-cost behavior with a single cost driver may seem at odds with reality and economic theory, but *the added benefit of understanding "true" cost behavior may be less than the cost of determining "true" cost behavior*.

For ease of communication and understanding, accountants usually describe cost behavior in visual or graphical terms. Exhibit 3-1 shows linear-cost behavior, the relevant range, and a cost driver. Note the similarity to the CVP charts of Chapter 2.

Exhibit 3-1

Linear-Cost Behavior

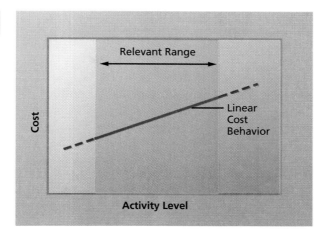

Types of Cost Behavior

Objective 1

Explain step- and mixed-cost behavior

Chapter 2 described two patterns of cost behavior: *variable* and *fixed* costs. Recall that a purely variable cost varies in proportion to its cost driver, while a purely fixed cost is not affected by cost-driver activity. In addition to these pure versions of cost, two additional types of costs combine characteristics of both fixed and variable cost behavior. These are *step* costs and *mixed* costs.

Step Costs

step costs Costs that change abruptly at intervals of activity because the resources and their costs come in indivisible chunks.

Step costs change abruptly at intervals of activity because the resources and their costs come in indivisible chunks. If the individual chunks of cost are relatively large and apply to a specific, broad range of activity, the cost is considered a fixed cost over that range of activity. An example is in panel (A) of Exhibit 3-2, which shows the cost of leasing oil and gas drilling equipment. When oil and gas exploration activity reaches a certain level in a given region, an entire additional rig must be leased. One level of oil and gas rig leasing, however, will support all volumes of exploration activity within a relevant range of drilling. Within each relevant range, this step cost behaves as a fixed cost. The total step cost at a level of activity is the amount of *fixed cost* appropriate for the range containing that activity level.

In contrast, accountants often describe step costs as variable when the individual chunks of costs are relatively small and apply to a narrow range of activity. Exhibit 3-2 (panel B) shows the wage cost of cashiers at a supermarket. Suppose one cashier can serve an average of twenty shoppers per hour and that within the relevant range of shopping activity, the number of shoppers can range from 40 per hour to 440 per hour. The corresponding number of cashiers would range between 2 and 22. Because the steps are relatively small, this step cost behaves much like a variable cost and could be used as such for planning with little loss of accuracy.

Exhibit 3-2

Step-Cost Behavior

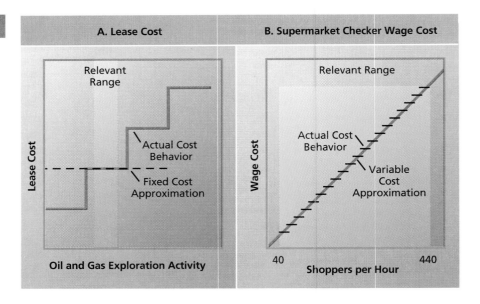

A. Lease Cost

Relevant Range

Actual Cost Behavior

Fixed Cost Approximation

Lease Cost

Oil and Gas Exploration Activity

B. Supermarket Checker Wage Cost

Relevant Range

Actual Cost Behavior

Variable Cost Approximation

Wage Cost

40   440

Shoppers per Hour

Mixed Costs

mixed costs Costs that contain elements of both fixed- and variable-cost behavior.

Mixed costs contain elements of both fixed- and variable-cost behavior. Like step costs, the fixed element is determined by the planned *range* of activity level. Unlike step costs, however, usually in a mixed cost there is only one relevant range of activity and one level of fixed cost. The variable-cost element of the mixed cost is a purely variable cost that varies proportionately with activity within the single relevant range. In a mixed cost the variable cost is incurred in addition to the fixed cost: the total mixed cost is the sum of the fixed cost plus the variable cost.

Many costs are mixed costs. For example, consider the monthly facilities maintenance department cost of the Parkview Medical Center, shown in Exhibit 3-3. Salaries of the maintenance personnel and costs of equipment are fixed at $10,000 per month. In addition, cleaning supplies and repair materials may vary at a rate of $5 per patient-day[1] delivered by the hospital.

An administrator at Parkview Medical Center could use knowledge of the facilities maintenance department cost behavior to:

1. *Plan costs*: Suppose the hospital expects to service 4,000 patient-days next month. The month's predicted facilities maintenance department costs are $10,000 fixed plus the variable cost of $20,000 (4,000 patient-days times $5 per patient-day), for a total of $30,000.

2. *Provide feedback to managers*: Suppose actual facilities maintenance costs were $34,000 in a month when 4,000 patient-days were serviced as planned. Managers would want to know why the hospital overspent by $4,000 ($34,000 less the planned $30,000) so that they could take corrective action.

---

[1] A patient-day is one patient spending 1 day in the hospital; one patient spending 5 days is 5 patient-days of service.

3. *Make decisions about the most efficient use of resources*: For example, managers might weigh the long-run tradeoffs of increased fixed costs of highly automated floor cleaning equipment against the variable costs of extra hours needed to clean floors manually.

Mixed-Cost Behavior

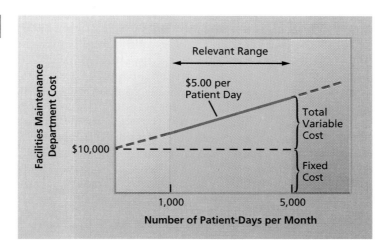

■ MANAGEMENT INFLUENCE ON COST BEHAVIOR

In addition to measuring and evaluating current cost behavior, management can influence cost behavior through decisions about such factors as *product* or *service attributes, capacity, technology,* and policies to create *incentives to control costs.*

Product and Service Decisions

Objective 2

Explain management influences on cost behavior

Perhaps the greatest influences on product and service costs are manager's choices of product mix, design, performance, quality, features, distribution, and so on. Each of these decisions contributes to the organization's performance and should be made in a cost/benefit framework. For example, Hertz, the car rental company, would add a feature to its services only if the cost of the feature (for example, free mileage) could be justified (more than recovered in profit from increased business).

Capacity Decisions

capacity costs The fixed costs of being able to achieve a desired level of production or to provide a desired level of service while maintaining product or service attributes, such as quality.

Strategic decisions about the scale and scope of an organization's activities generally result in fixed levels of *capacity costs.* **Capacity costs** are the fixed costs of being able to achieve a desired level of production or to provide a desired level of service while maintaining product or service attributes, such as quality. Companies in industries with long-term variations in demand must exercise caution when making capacity decisions. Fixed-capacity costs cannot be recovered when demand falls during an economic downturn. Consider the dilemma facing Ford. In the mid-1980s, Ford was operating at full capacity. To meet demand, workers were on overtime and Ford even contracted with Mazda to produce some of its Probe cars. Ford had to choose between building new plants and assembly lines or continuing to pay premiums for overtime and outside production. Building new plants would enable Ford to produce cars at less cost but the fixed-capacity costs would not be controllable. Overtime and outsourcing production to Mazda was expensive but Ford could control these variable costs much more easily during any business downturn. What did Ford do? According to executives at Ford, "We know in 1986 and 1987 we lost some sales. We could have probably had a higher market share. But we felt it was worth it to keep our costs under control. . . . Sooner or later there's going to be a downturn and we'll be running down days and short weeks even with the capacity we have." During the business downturn in the early 1990s, Ford was able to exercise more control over its costs. Again, in the mid-1990s, Ford faced the same strategic decision concerning scale and scope of operations.

Committed Fixed Costs

committed fixed costs Costs arising from the possession of facilities, equipment, and a basic organization: large, indivisible chunks of cost that the organization is obligated to incur or usually would not consider avoiding.

Short of drastically changing operations, every organization has some costs to which it is committed, perhaps for quite a few years. **Committed fixed costs** usually arise from the possession of facilities, equipment, and a basic organization. These are large, indivisible chunks of cost that the organization is obligated to incur or usually would not consider avoiding. Committed fixed costs include mortgage or lease payments, interest payments on long-term debt, property taxes, insurance, and salaries of key personnel. Only major changes in the philosophy, scale, or scope of operations could change these committed fixed costs in future periods. Recall the example of the facilities maintenance department for the Parkview Medical Center. The capacity of the facilities maintenance department was a management decision, and in this case the decision determined the magnitude of the equipment cost. Suppose Parkview Medical Center were to increase permanently its patient-days per month beyond the relevant range of 5,000 patient-days. Because more capacity would be needed, the committed equipment cost would rise to a new level per month.

Discretionary Fixed Costs

discretionary fixed costs Costs determined by management as part of the periodic planning process in order to meet the organization's goals.

Some costs are fixed at certain levels only because management decided that these levels of cost should be incurred to meet the organization's goals. These **discretionary fixed costs** have no obvious relationship to levels of output activity but are determined as part of the periodic planning process. Each planning period, management will determine how much to spend on discretionary items such as advertising and promotion costs, public relations, research and development costs, charitable donations, employee training programs, and purchased management consulting services.

Unlike committed fixed costs, managers can alter discretionary fixed costs easily—up or down—even within a budget period, if they decide that different levels of spending are desirable. Conceivably, managers could reduce such discretionary costs almost entirely for a given year in dire times, whereas they could not reduce committed costs. Discretionary fixed costs may be essential to the long-run achievement of the organization's goals, but managers can vary spending levels broadly in the short run.

Sometimes managers plan discretionary fixed costs, such as advertising or research and development, as a percentage of planned sales revenue. Of course, managers would not contract for advertising or conduct research and development only as current revenues are received. Rather, this planning is needed if the organization is to be able to pay for discretionary fixed costs.

Consider Marietta Corporation, which is experiencing financial difficulties. Sales for its major products are depressed, and Marietta's management is considering cutting back on costs *temporarily*. Marietta's management must determine which of the following fixed costs to reduce or eliminate and how much money each would save:

Fixed Costs	Planned Amounts
Advertising and promotion	$ 30,000
Depreciation	400,000
Employee training	100,000
Management salaries	800,000
Mortgage payment	250,000
Property taxes	600,000
Research and development	1,500,000
Total	$3,680,000

Should Marietta reduce or eliminate any of these fixed costs? The answer depends on Marietta's long-run outlook. Marietta could reduce costs but also greatly reduce its ability to compete in the future if it cuts carelessly. Rearranging these costs by categories of committed and discretionary costs yields the following analysis:

Fixed Costs	Planned Amounts
Committed	
Depreciation	$ 400,000
Mortgage payment	250,000
Property taxes	600,000
Total committed	$1,250,000
Discretionary (potential savings)	
Advertising and promotion	$ 30,000
Employee training	100,000
Management salaries	800,000
Research and development	1,500,000
Total discretionary	$2,430,000
Total committed and discretionary	$3,680,000

Eliminating all discretionary fixed costs would save Marietta $2,430,000 per year. As is clear from Chapter 2, reducing fixed costs lowers the break-even point or increases the profit at a given level of sales, which might benefit Marietta at this time. Marietta would be unwise to eliminate all of these costs arbitrarily. Nevertheless, distinguishing committed and discretionary fixed costs would be the company's first step to identifying where costs *could* be reduced.

Technology Decisions

One of the most critical decisions that managers make is the type of technology that the organization will use to produce its products or deliver its services. Choice of technology (for example, labor-intensive versus robotic manufacturing or traditional banking services versus automated tellers) positions the organization to meet its current goals and to respond to changes in the environment (for example, changes in customer needs or actions by competitors). Not surprisingly, technology may have a great impact on the costs of products and services.

Cost-Control Incentives

Finally, future costs may be affected by the *incentives* that management creates for employees to control costs. Managers use their knowledge of cost behavior to set cost expectations, and employees may receive compensation or other rewards that are tied to meeting these expectations. For example, the administrator of Parkview Medical Center may give the supervisor of the facilities maintenance department a favorable evaluation if the supervisor maintained quality of service *and* kept department costs below the expected amount for the level of patient-days serviced. This strong form of feedback could cause the supervisor to watch department costs carefully and to find ways to reduce costs without reducing quality of service.

■ MEASUREMENT OF COST BEHAVIOR

cost measurement
The first step in estimating or predicting costs as a function of appropriate cost drivers.

The decision making, planning, and control activities of management accounting require accurate and useful estimates of future fixed and variable costs. The first step in estimating or predicting costs is **cost measurement** or *measuring cost behavior* as a function of appropriate cost drivers. The second step is to use these cost measures to estimate future costs at expected, future levels of cost-driver activity.

Objective 3

Measure cost functions and use them to predict costs

It is usually easy to measure costs that are obviously linked with a volume-related cost driver. Why? Because you can trace such costs to particular cost drivers, and measurement simply requires a system for identifying the costs. For example, *systems* for controlling inventories measure the amount of materials issued for a particular product or service. Similarly, payroll systems that use labor records or time cards may detail the amount of time each worker spends on a particular product or service.

In contrast it is usually difficult to measure costs that have no obvious links to cost drivers, or those with multiple cost drivers. *Assumed* relationships between costs and cost drivers often are used because an observable link is not present.

cost function An algebraic equation used by managers to describe the relationship between a cost and its cost driver(s).

Cost Functions

To describe the relationship between a cost and its cost driver(s), managers often use an algebraic equation called a **cost function**. When there is only one cost driver, the cost function is similar to the algebraic CVP relationships discussed in Chapter 2. Consider the mixed cost graphed in Exhibit 3-3 on page 83, facilities maintenance department cost:

$$\begin{array}{l} \text{Total facilities maintenance} \\ \text{department costs} \end{array} = \begin{array}{l} \text{Total fixed} \\ \text{maintenance cost} \end{array} + \begin{array}{l} \text{Total variable} \\ \text{maintenance cost} \end{array}$$

$$= \begin{array}{l} \text{Fixed maintenance} \\ \text{per month} \end{array} + \left(\begin{array}{l} \text{Variable cost} \\ \text{per patient- day} \end{array} \times \begin{array}{l} \text{Number of} \\ \text{patient- days} \end{array} \right)$$

Let

Y = total facilities maintenance department cost
F = fixed maintenance cost
V = variable cost per patient-day
X = cost-driver activity in number of patient-days

Objective 4

Describe mathematical cost functions

We can rewrite the mixed-cost function as

$$Y = F + VX, \text{ or}$$
$$Y = \$10{,}000 + \$5.00X$$

This mixed-cost function has the familiar form of a straight line—it is called a *linear-cost function*. When graphing a cost function, F is the *intercept*, the point on the vertical axis where the cost function begins. In Exhibit 3-3 the intercept is the $10,000 fixed cost per month. V, the variable cost per unit of activity, is the *slope* of the cost function. In Exhibit 3-3 the cost function slopes upward at the rate of $5 for each additional patient-day.

Criteria for Choosing Functions

Two principles should be applied to obtain accurate and useful cost functions: plausibility and reliability.

1. The cost function must be plausible or believable. Personal observation of costs and activities, when it is possible, provides the best evidence of a plausible relationship between a cost and its driver. Some cost relationships, by nature, are not directly observable, so the cost analyst must be confident that the proposed relationship is sound. Many costs may move together with a number of cost drivers, but no cause-and-effect relationships may exist. A cause-and-effect relationship (that is, X causes Y) is desirable for cost functions to be accurate and useful.

2. In addition to being plausible, a cost function's estimates of costs at actual levels of activity must reliably conform with actually observed costs. Reliability can be assessed in terms of "goodness of fit"—how well the cost function explains past cost behavior. If the fit is good and conditions do not change, the cost function should be a reliable predictor of future costs.

Note especially that managers use these criteria *together* in choosing a cost function: each is a check on the other. Knowledge of operations and how costs are recorded is helpful in choosing a plausible and reliable cost function that links cause and effect. For example, maintenance is often performed when output is low, because that is when machines can be taken out of service. Lower output does not *cause* increased maintenance costs, however, nor does increased output cause *lower* maintenance costs. The timing of maintenance is somewhat discretionary. A more plausible explanation is that over a longer period increased output causes higher maintenance costs, but daily or weekly recording of maintenance costs may make it appear otherwise. Understanding the nature of maintenance costs should lead to a reliable, long-run cost function.

Choice of Cost Drivers: Activity Analysis

activity analysis
The process of indentifying appropriate cost drivers and their effects on the costs of making a product or providing a service.

cost prediction The application of cost measures to expected future activity levels to forecast future costs.

Incorrect assumptions about cost behavior may cause incorrect decisions. The remedy is a careful examination of cost behavior. To aid such an examination, managers apply **activity analysis**, which identifies appropriate cost drivers and their effects on the costs of making a product or providing a service. The final product or service may have a number of cost drivers because a number of separate activities may be involved. The greatest benefit of activity analysis is that it directs management accountants to the appropriate cost drivers for each cost.

Activity analysis is especially important for measuring and predicting costs for which cost drivers are not obvious. **Cost prediction** applies cost measures to expected future activity levels to forecast future costs. Earlier in this chapter we said that a cost is fixed or variable *with respect to a specific cost driver*. A cost that appears fixed in relation to one cost driver could in fact be variable in relation to another cost driver. For example, suppose the Jupiter automobile plant uses automated painting equipment. The cost of adjusting this equipment may be fixed with respect to the total *number* of automobiles produced; that is, there is no discernible cost relationship between these support costs and the number of automobiles produced. This same cost may vary dramatically, however, with the number of different *colors* and *types of finishes* of automobiles produced. Activity analysis examines various potential cost drivers for plausibility and reliability. As always, the expected benefits of improved decision making from using more accurate cost behavior should exceed the expected costs of the cost-driver search.

Identifying the appropriate cost drivers is the most critical aspect of any method for measuring cost behavior. For many years, most organizations used only one cost driver: the amount of labor used. In essence, they assumed that the only activity affecting costs was the use of labor. In the past decade, however, we have learned that previously "hidden" activities greatly influence cost behavior. Often, analysts in both manufacturing and service companies find that activities related to the complexity of performing tasks affect costs more directly than labor usage or other cost drivers that are related to the volume of output activity.

Consider Northwestern Computers, which makes two products for personal computers: a plug-in music board (Mozart-Plus) and a hard-disk drive (Powerdrive). When most of the work on Northwestern's products was done by hand, most costs, other than the cost of materials, were related to (driven by) labor cost. The use of computer-controlled assembly equipment, however, has increased the costs of support activities and has reduced labor cost. Labor cost is now only 5% of the total costs at Northwestern. Furthermore, activity analysis has shown that most of today's support costs are driven by the number of components added to products (a measure of product complexity), not by labor cost. Mozart-Plus has five component parts, and Powerdrive has nine.

On average, support costs were twice as much as labor costs. Suppose Northwestern wants to predict how much support cost is incurred in producing one Mozart-Plus and how much for one Powerdrive. Using the old cost driver, labor cost, the prediction of support costs would be

	Mozart-Plus	Powerdrive
Labor cost	$ 8.50	$130.00
Support cost:		
2 × Direct labor cost	$17.00	$260.00

Using the more appropriate cost driver, the *number of components added to products*, the predicted support costs are

	Mozart-Plus	Powerdrive
Support cost		
at $20 per component		
$20 × 5 components	$100.00	
$20 × 9 components		$180.00
Difference in predicted support cost	$ 83.00	$ 80.00
	higher	lower

By using an appropriate cost driver, Northwestern can predict its support costs much more accurately. Managers will make better decisions with this more accurate information. For example, prices charged for products can be more closely related to the costs of production.

Activity Analysis at Hughes Aircraft Company

The regulatory and competitive environment of Hughes Aircraft Company has changed dramatically over the past several years. Government agencies demand better cost estimates, and shrinking defense spending means more competition among government contractors. Hughes Aircraft found that its 50-year-old financial reporting system provided irrelevant and inaccurate measures of cost behavior for management decision making. These cost measures were based on labor usage, which is no longer a relevant cost driver at Hughes.

Managers at Hughes spent considerable time and money analyzing the firm's service and manufacturing activities to find more appropriate cost drivers than labor usage. Among other things, they found that human resource service costs are driven in part by the number of new hires and the number of training hours rather than total direct labor usage. In fact, very few of Hughes' major activities were found to be driven by labor usage.

Managers also had to convince Hughes' employees, managers, auditors, and customers (primarily the U.S. government) that the new activity analysis produces plausible and reliable cost estimates. Toward that end, Hughes conducted pilot studies at a few sites before moving to company-wide implementation of activity analysis for cost measurement. These pilot studies demonstrated that activity analysis greatly improved cost predictions and also streamlined the cost-impact studies required by government agencies. Both managers at Hughes and government auditors are convinced that the activity-based cost information will be more relevant and will result in more effective management of government contracts. ■

Source: Adapted from Jack Haedicke and David Feil, "Hughes Aircraft Sets the Standard for ABC," Management Accounting, *February 1991, pp. 29-33.*

■ METHODS OF MEASURING COST FUNCTIONS

Once managers for a firm have determined the most plausible drivers behind different costs, they can choose from a broad selection of methods of approximating cost functions, including (1) engineering analysis, (2) account analysis, (3) high-low analysis, (4) visual-fit analysis, (5) simple least-squares regression, and (6) multiple least-squares regression. These methods are not mutually exclusive; managers frequently use two or more together to avoid major errors in measuring cost behavior. Some organizations use each of these methods in succession over the years as the need for more accurate measures becomes evident and more hard evidence becomes available. The first two methods may rely only on logical analysis, whereas the last four involve analysis of past costs. In this section, we will discuss each of these methods, with the exception of multiple least-squares regression, which is a bit more complex and not often used in practice.

Engineering Analysis

engineering analysis
The systematic review of materials, supplies, labor, support services, and facilities needed for products and services; measuring cost behavior according to what costs should be, not by what costs have been.

The first method, **engineering analysis**, measures cost behavior according to what costs *should be*, not by what costs *have been*. It entails a systematic review of materials, supplies, labor, support services, and facilities needed for products and services. Analysts can even use engineering analysis successfully for new products and services, as long as the organization has had experience with similar costs. Why? Because measures can be based on information from personnel who are directly involved with the product or service. In addition to actual experience, analysts learn about new costs from experiments with prototypes, accounting and industrial engineering literature, the experience of competitors, and the advice of management consultants. From this information, cost analysts determine what future costs should be. If the cost analysts are experienced and understand the activities of the organization, then their engineering cost predictions may be quite reliable and useful for decision making. The disadvantages of engineering cost analysis are that the efforts are costly and often not timely.

Weyerhauser Company, producer of wood products, used engineering analysis to determine the cost drivers for its 14 corporate service departments. These cost drivers are used to measure the cost of corporate services used by three main business groups. For example, the drivers of accounts payable costs for each division are number of hours spent on each division, number of documents, and number of invoices. *This approach to measuring cost behavior also could be used by nearly any service organization.*

At Parkview Medical Center, introduced earlier, an assistant to the hospital administrator interviewed facilities maintenance personnel and observed their activities on several random days for a month. From these data, she confirmed that the most plausible cost driver for facilities maintenance cost is the number of patient-days. She also estimated from current department salaries and equipment charges that monthly fixed costs approximated $10,000 per month. From interviews and supplies usage during the month she observed, she estimated that variable costs are $5 per patient-day. She communicated this information to the hospital administrator but cautioned that her cost measures may be in error because

1. The month she observed may be abnormal.
2. The facilities maintenance personnel may have altered their normal work habits because she was observing them.
3. The facilities maintenance personnel may not have told the complete truth about their activities because of their concerns about the use of the information they revealed.

The assistant administrator observed that these problems are common to engineering approaches to cost measurement. She recommended analysis of more objective data to supplement her engineering analysis.

In the meantime, facilities maintenance cost in any month could be predicted by first forecasting that month's expected patient-days and then entering that figure into the following algebraic, mixed-cost function:

$$Y = \$10,000 \text{ per month} + (\$5 \times \text{patient-days})$$

For example, if the administrator expects 4,000 patient-days next month, she will predict facilities maintenance costs to be:

$$Y = \$10,000 + (\$5 \times 4,000 \text{ patient-days}) = \underline{\$30,000}$$

Account Analysis

account analysis
Selecting a volume-related cost driver and classifying each account as a variable cost or as a fixed cost.

In contrast to engineering analysis, users of *account analysis* look to the accounting system for information about cost behavior. The simplest method of **account analysis** selects a volume-related cost driver and classifies each account as a variable or fixed cost. The cost analyst then looks at each cost account balance and estimates either the variable cost per unit of cost-driver activity or the periodic fixed cost.

To illustrate this approach to account analysis, let's return to the facilities maintenance department at Parkview Medical Center and analyze costs for January 19X4. Recall that the most plausible driver for these costs is the number of patient-days serviced per month. The table below shows costs recorded in a month with 3,700 patient-days:

Monthly Cost	January 19X4 Amount
Supervisor's salary and benefits	$ 3,800
Hourly workers' wages and benefits	14,674
Equipment depreciation and rentals	5,873
Equipment repairs	5,604
Cleaning supplies	7,472
Total facilities maintenance cost	$37,423

Next, the analyst determines how much of each cost may be fixed and how much may be variable. Assume that the analyst has made the following judgments:

Monthly Cost	January 19X4 Amount	Fixed	Variable
Supervisor's salary and benefits	$ 3,800	$3,800	
Hourly workers' wages and benefits	14,674		$14,674
Equipment depreciation and rentals	5,873	5,873	
Equipment repairs	5,604		5,604
Cleaning supplies	7,472		7,472
Total	$37,423	$9,673	$27,750

Objective 6

Use the account analysis, high-low, visual-fit, and least-squares regression methods for measuring cost functions

Measuring total facilities maintenance cost behavior, then, requires only simple arithmetic. Add all the fixed costs to get the total fixed cost per month. Divide the total variable costs by the units of cost-driver activity to get the variable cost per unit of cost driver.

$$\text{Fixed cost per month} = \underline{\$9,673}$$
$$\text{Variable cost per patient-day} = \$27,750 \div 3,700 \text{ patient-days}$$
$$= \underline{\$7.50 \text{ per patient-day}}$$

The algebraic, mixed-cost function, measured by account analysis, is

$$Y = \$9,673 \text{ per month} + (\$7.50 \times \text{patient-days})$$

Account-analysis methods are less expensive to conduct than engineering analysis, but they require recording of relevant cost accounts and cost drivers. In addition, account analysis is subjective because the analyst decides whether each cost is variable or fixed based on judgment.

High-Low, Visual-Fit, and Least-Squares Methods

All three of these methods are more objective than the engineering analysis method because each is based on hard evidence as well as on judgment. They also can be more objective than account analysis because they use more than one period's cost and activity information. Because these methods require more past cost data, account analysis—and especially engineering analysis—probably will remain primary methods of measuring cost behavior, however. Products, services, technologies, and organizations are changing rapidly in response to increased global competition. *In some cases, by the time enough historical data are collected to support these analyses, the data are obsolete*—the organization has changed, the production process has changed, or the product has changed. The cost analyst must be careful that the historical data are from a past environment that still closely resembles the future environment for which costs are being predicted. Another concern is that historical data may hide past inefficiencies that could be reduced if they are identified.

Data for Illustration

In discussing the high-low, visual-fit, and least-squares regression methods, we will continue to use one consistent example: Parkview Medical Center's facilities maintenance department costs. The following table shows monthly data collected on facilities maintenance department costs and on the number of patient-days serviced over the past year:

Facilities
Maintenance
Department
Data, 19X4

Month	Facilities Maintenance Department Cost (Y)	Number of Patient-Days (X)
January	$37,000	3,700
February	23,000	1,600
March	37,000	4,100
April	47,000	4,900
May	33,000	3,300
June	39,000	4,400
July	32,000	3,500
August	33,000	4,000
September	17,000	1,200
October	18,000	1,300
November	22,000	1,800
December	20,000	1,600

high-low method
A simple method for measuring a linear cost function from past cost data, focusing on the highest-activity and lowest-activity points and fitting a line through these two points.

High-Low Method

When sufficient cost data are available, the cost analyst may use historical data to measure the cost function mathematically. A simple method to measure a linear-cost function from past cost data is the **high-low method** shown in Exhibit 3-4.

Exhibit 3-4

High-Low Method

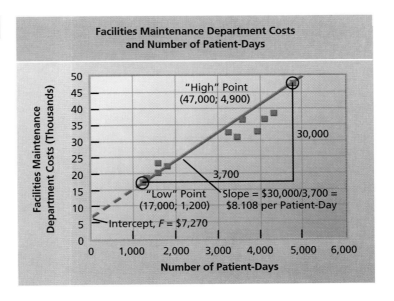

Facilities Maintenance Department Costs and Number of Patient-Days

The first step in analyzing historical data is to plot the data points on a graph. This visual display helps the analyst see whether there are obvious errors in the data. Even though many points are plotted, the focus of the high-low method is on the highest-activity and lowest-activity points. Normally, the next step is for the analyst to fit a line through these two points. If one of these points is an "outlier" that seems in error or nonrepresentative of normal operations, however, the analyst will use the next-highest or next-lowest activity point. For example, you should not use a point from a period with abnormally low activity caused by a labor strike or fire. Why? Because that point is not representative of a normal relationship between the cost and the cost driver.

After selecting the representative high and low points, the analyst can draw a line between them, extending the line to the vertical (*Y*) axis of the graph. Note that this extension in Exhibit 3-4 is a dashed line as a reminder that costs may not be linear outside the relevant range. Also, managers usually are concerned with how costs behave within the relevant range, not with how they behave either at zero activity or at impossibly high activity (given current capacity). Measurements of costs within the relevant range probably are not reliable measures or predictors of costs *outside* the relevant range.

The point at which the line intersects the *Y*-axis is the intercept, *F*, or estimate of fixed cost. The slope of the line measures the variable cost, *V*, per patient-day. The clearest way to measure the intercept and slope with the high-low method is to use algebra:

Month	Facilities Maintenance Department Cost (*Y*)	Number of Patient-Days (*X*)
High: April	$47,000	4,900
Low: September	17,000	1,200
Difference	$30,000	3,700

Variable cost per patient-day,

$$V = \frac{\text{change in costs}}{\text{change in activity}} = \frac{\$47,000 - \$17,000}{4,900 - 1,200 \text{ patient-days}}$$

$$V = \frac{\$30,000}{3,700} = \$8.1081 \text{ per patient-day}$$

Fixed cost per month, *F* = Total mixed cost less total variable cost

$$\text{at } X \text{ (high):} \quad F = \$47,000 - (\$8.1081 \times 4,900 \text{ patient-days})$$
$$= \$47,000 - \$39,730$$
$$= \$\ 7,270 \text{ per month}$$

$$\text{at } X \text{ (low):} \quad F = \$17,000 - (\$8.1081 \times 1,200 \text{ patient-days})$$
$$= \$17,000 - \$9,730$$
$$= \$\ 7,270 \text{ per month}$$

Therefore, the facilities maintenance department cost function, measured by the high-low method, is

$$Y = \$7,270 \text{ per month} + (\$8.1081 \times \text{patient-days})$$

The high-low method is easy to use and illustrates mathematically how a change in a cost driver can change total cost. The cost function that resulted in this case is *plausible*. Before the widespread availability of computers, managers often used the high-low method to measure a cost function quickly. Today, however, the high-low method is not used often in practice because of its unreliability and because it makes inefficient use of information, using only two periods' cost experience, regardless of how many relevant data points have been collected. Other methods that we now consider can use all the available data.

Visual-Fit Method

visual-fit method A method in which the cost analyst visually fits a straight line through a plot of all the available data, not just between the high point and the low point, making it more reliable than the high-low method.

Because it can use all the available data, the **visual-fit method** is more reliable than the high-low method. In the visual-fit method, the cost analyst visually fits a straight line through a plot of all the available data, not just between the high point and the low point. If the cost function for the data is linear, it is possible to visualize a straight line through the scattered points that comes reasonably close to most of them and thus captures the general tendency of the data. The analyst extends that line back until it intersects the vertical axis of the graph.

Exhibit 3-5 shows this method applied to the facilities maintenance department cost data for the past 12 months. By measuring where the line intersects the cost axis, the analyst can estimate the monthly fixed cost—in this case, about $10,000 per month. To find the variable cost per patient-day, select any activity level (say 1,000 patient-days) and find the total cost at that activity level ($17,000). Then divide the variable cost (which is total cost less fixed cost) by the units of activity.

Variable cost per patient-day = ($17,000 − $10,000) ÷ 1,000 patient-days
= $7 per patient-day

Exhibit 3-5	
Visual-Fit Method	

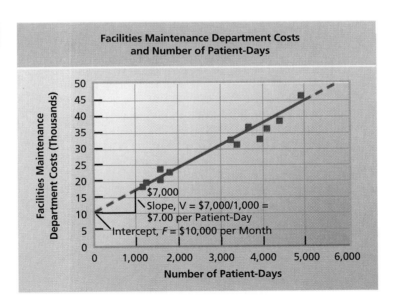

The linear-cost function measured by the visual fit method is:

Y = $10,000 per month + ($7 × patient-days)

Although the visual-fit method can use all the data, the placement of the line and the measurement of the fixed and variable costs are subjective. This subjectivity is the primary reason that the visual-fit method is now rarely used in practice, even though using computers to plot data and draw lines has made the method easier to implement. This method is a good introduction to what least-squares regression accomplishes with statistics.

Least-Squares Regression Method

least-squares regression (regression analysis) Measuring a cost function objectively by using statistics to fit a cost function to all the data.

Least-squares regression measures a cost function more objectively (with statistics rather than human eyesight) using the same data. Least-squares regression analysis (or simply, **regression analysis**) uses statistics to fit a cost function to all the data. Regression analysis that uses one cost driver to measure a cost function is called *simple regression*. The use of multiple cost drivers for a single cost is called *multiple regression*. Only a basic discussion of simple regression analysis is presented in this section of the chapter. Some statistical properties of regression and using computer regression software are discussed in Appendix 3.

Regression analysis usually measures cost behavior more reliably than other cost measurement methods. In addition, regression analysis yields important statistical information about the reliability of cost estimates, so analysts can assess confidence in the cost measures and select the best cost driver. One such measure of reliability, or goodness of fit, is the **coefficient of determination, R^2** (or R-squared), which measures how much of the fluctuation of a cost is explained by changes in the cost driver. Appendix 3 explains R^2 and discusses how to use it to select the best cost driver.

coefficient of determination (R^2) A measurement of how much of the fluctuation of a cost is explained by changes in the cost driver.

Exhibit 3-6 shows the linear, mixed-cost function for facilities maintenance costs as measured by simple regression analysis.

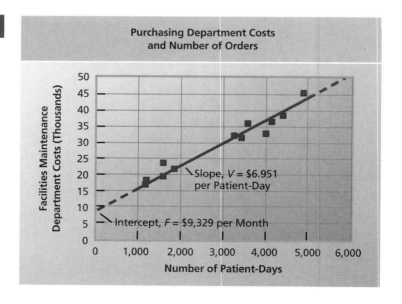

Exhibit 3-6

Least-Squares Regression Method

The fixed-cost measure is $9,329 per month. The variable-cost measure is $6.951 per patient-day. The linear-cost function is

Facilities maintenance department cost = $9,329 per month + $6.951 per patient-day

or

$$Y = \$9,329 + \$6.951 \times \text{patient-days}$$

Compare the cost measures produced by each of the five approaches:

Method	Fixed Cost per Month	Variable Cost per Patient-Day
Engineering analysis	$10,000	$5.000
Account analysis	9,673	7.500
High-low	7,270	8.108
Visual-fit	10,000	7.000
Regression	9,329	6.951

To see the differences in results between methods, we will use account-analysis and regression-analysis measures to predict total facilities maintenance department costs at 1,000 and 5,000 patient-days, the approximate limits of the relevant range:

	Account Analysis	Regression Analysis	Difference
1,000 patient-days:			
Fixed cost	$ 9,673	$ 9,329	$ 344
Variable costs			
$7.500 × 1,000	7,500		
$6.951 × 1,000		6,951	549
Predicted total cost	$17,173	$16,280	$ 893
5,000 patient-days:			
Fixed cost	$ 9,673	$ 9,329	$ 344
Variable costs			
$7.500 × 5,000	37,500		
$6.951 × 5,000		34,755	2,745
Predicted total cost	$47,173	$44,084	$3,089

At lower levels of patient-day activity both methods yield similar cost predictions. At higher levels of patient-day activity, however, the account-analysis cost function predicts much higher facilities maintenance department costs. The difference between the predicted total costs is due primarily to the higher variable cost per patient-day (approximately $0.55 more) measured by account analysis, which increases the difference in predicted total variable costs proportionately as the number of planned patient-days increases. Because of their grounding in statistical analysis, the regression-cost measures are probably more reliable than the others. Managers would have more confidence in cost predictions from the regression-cost function.

Measuring Cost Behavior at Hewlett-Packard

Consider how Hewlett-Packard (HP), the computer manufacturer, measured cost behavior as part of its company-wide implementation of activity-based costing. HP used detailed engineering analysis to revise its accounting system at many of its manufacturing sites. The old cost system at HP used labor cost as the cost driver for all nonmaterial costs, regardless of the actual cost drivers. On average, labor costs were only 2% of total costs, so it was unlikely that they were the major cause of most other costs. The result of using labor cost was significant cost distortion—products with higher labor costs were overcosted whereas products with lower labor costs were undercosted. Managers did not have confidence in the product cost predictions using this labor-based system.

Cost analysts spent several years talking with managers and engineers and carefully observing facilities maintenance, manufacturing support, and other activities to identify more appropriate cost drivers and their relationships to cost behavior.

At HP's Surface Mount Center at Boise, the ABC system has been fully operational since early in 1993. This facility manufactures about 50 different electronic circuit boards for internal customers within HP. The selection of cost drivers at the Center resulted from an "intense analysis of the production process

and cost behavior patterns by the accounting, production, and engineering staffs." This combination of account analysis and engineering analysis resulted in 10 different cost drivers.

One interesting aspect of the ABC system is the continuous involvement of managers and engineers in improving the system. "An almost daily dialogue goes on among production, engineering, and the accountants about how the ABC cost system could be improved to reflect product costs more accurately."

A series of simple linear regressions between overhead dollars and cost driver volumes was conducted to test the statistical validity of the cost drivers. For example, one of the regressions was "all automatic placement overhead costs" versus the cost-driver "number of automatic placements," which had a coefficient of determination (R^2) of 92%. Another regression measured the relationship between "material procurement overhead costs" and the cost-driver "number of distinct parts" and had an R^2 of 91%. The regression analyses tended to confirm that the cost drivers selected indeed were correlated with overhead costs. ■

Source: From Mike Merz and Arlene Hardy, "ABC Puts Accountants on Design Team at HP," Management Accounting, *September 1993, pp. 22–27.*

Highlights to Remember

Cost behavior refers to how costs change as levels of an organization's activities change. Costs can behave as fixed, variable, step, or mixed costs. Fixed costs may behave in a step manner and may be committed or discretionary. Committed fixed costs cannot be changed easily, but discretionary fixed costs may be changed at nearly any time as management sees fit. Management also may influence fixed- and variable-cost behavior by its choices of product or service attributes, capacity, technology, and incentives for cost control.

Cost measurement quantifies the behavior of costs into fixed and variable components. This behavior is measured with respect to appropriate cost drivers within the relevant range of cost-driver activity. Fixed costs usually are estimated per period. Variable costs are estimated per unit of cost driver. One of the most important aspects of cost measurement is activity analysis, or determination of the proper cost drivers and their effects on costs.

A cost function is the mathematical expression of cost behavior. The typical linear cost function is of the form:

$$Y = F + VX,$$

where

$$F = \text{fixed cost per time period}$$
$$V = \text{variable cost per unit of cost driver}$$
$$X = \text{the most plausible cost driver}$$

Three major approaches to measuring cost functions are engineering analysis, account analysis, and least-squares regression analysis methods. All these methods require expert judgment. Engineering analysis may be performed for new or revised processes, but account and regression analyses require historical cost data. All analyses may be combined. The most objective method usually is least-squares regression analysis, but this analysis requires considerable past data and statistical sophistication on the part of the analyst. The reliability of all methods may be improved if the analyst has relevant experience with similar costs and activities.

Summary Problems for Your Review

Problem One: Measurement of Cost Behavior

The Reetz Company has its own photocopying department. Reetz's photocopying costs include costs of copy machines, operators, paper, toner, utilities, and so on. We have the following cost and activity data:

Month	Total Photocopying Cost	Number of Copies
1	$25,000	320,000
2	29,000	390,000
3	24,000	300,000
4	23,000	310,000
5	28,000	400,000

Required

1. Use the high-low method to measure the cost behavior of the photocopy department in formula form.
2. What are the benefits and disadvantages of using the high-low method for measuring cost behavior?

Solution to Problem One

1. The lowest and highest activity levels are in months 3 (300,000 copies) and 5 (400,000 copies).

$$\text{Variable cost per copy} = \frac{\text{change in cost}}{\text{change in activity}} = \frac{\$28,000 - \$24,000}{400,000 - 300,000}$$

$$= \frac{\$4,000}{100,000} = \$0.04 \text{ per copy}$$

Fixed cost per month = total cost less variable cost
at 400,000 copies: $28,000 − ($0.04 × 400,000) = $12,000 per month
at 300,000 copies: $24,000 − ($0.04 × 300,000) = $12,000 per month

Therefore, the photocopy cost function is:

Y (total cost) = $12,000 per month + $0.04 × number of copies

2. The benefits of using the high-low method are:
- The method is easy to use.
- Not many data are needed.

The disadvantages of using the high-low method are:
- The choice of the high and low points is subjective.
- The method does not use all available data.
- The method may not be reliable.

Problem Two: Activity Analysis

The Reliable Insurance Company processes a variety of insurance claims for losses, accidents, thefts, and so on. Account analysis has estimated the variable cost of processing each claim at 0.5% (.005) of the dollar value of the claim. This estimate seemed reasonable because higher claims often involve more analysis before settlement. To control processing costs better, however, Reliable Insurance conducted an activity analysis of claims processing. The analysis suggested that more appropriate cost drivers and behavior for automobile accident claims are

    0.2% of Reliable Insurance policyholders' property claims
  + 0.6% of other parties' property claims
  + 0.8% of total personal injury claims

Data from two recent automobile accident claims follow:

	Automobile Claim No. 607788	Automobile Claim No. 607991
Policyholder claim	$ 4,500	$23,600
Other party claim	0	3,400
Personal injury claim	12,400	0
Total claim amount	$16,900	$27,000

Required

1. Estimate the cost of processing each claim using data from account analysis and then the activity analysis.
2. How would you recommend that Reliable Insurance estimate the cost of processing claims?

Solution to Problem Two

1.

	Automobile Claim No. 607788		Automobile Claim No. 607991	
	Claim Amount	Processing Cost	Claim Amount	Processing Cost
Using account analysis				
Total claim amount	$16,900		$27,000	
Estimated processing cost at 0.5%		$ 84.50		$135.00

continued

	Automobile Claim No. 607788		Automobile Claim No. 607991	
	Claim Amount	Processing Cost	Claim Amount	Processing Cost
Using activity analysis				
Policyholder claim	$ 4,500		$23,600	
Estimated processing cost at 0.2%		$ 9.00		$ 47.20
Other party claim	0		3,400	
Estimated processing cost at 0.6%		0		20.40
Personal injury claim	12,400		0	
Estimated processing cost at 0.8%		99.20		0
Total estimated processing cost		$108.20		$ 67.60

2. The activity analysis estimates of processing costs are considerably different from those using cost account analysis. If the activity analyses are reliable, then automobile claims that include personal injury losses are more costly to process than property damage claims. If these estimates are relatively inexpensive to keep current and to use, then it seems reasonable to adopt the activity analysis approach. Reliable Insurance will have more accurate cost estimates and will be better able to plan its claims processing activities. Reliable Insurance processes many different types of claims, however. Extending activity analysis to all types of claims would result in a complicated system for predicting costs—much more complex (and costly) than simply using the total dollar value of claims. Whether to adopt the activity approach overall depends on cost-benefit considerations that may be estimated by first adopting activity analysis for one type of claim and assessing the usefulness and cost of the more accurate information.

Appendix 3: Use and Interpretation of Least-Squares Regression

Regression analysis of historical cost data can be accomplished with no more than a simple calculator. It would be unusual, however, to find cost analysts doing regression analysis by hand—computers are much faster and less prone to error. Therefore, we focus on using a computer to perform regression analysis and on interpretation of the results.

This appendix should not be considered a substitute for a good statistics class. More properly, this appendix should be seen as a motivator for studying statistics so that analysts can provide and managers can interpret top-quality cost estimates.

Assume that there are two potential cost drivers for the costs of the facilities maintenance department in Parkview Medical Center: (1) number of patient-days and (2) total value of hospital room charges. Regression analysis helps to determine which activity is the better cost driver. Exhibit 3-7 shows the past 12 months' cost and cost-driver data for the facilities maintenance department.

Regression Analysis Procedures

Very good statistical software is available for both mainframes and personal computers (PCs). Most spreadsheet software available for PCs offers basic regression analysis in the "data" analysis or "tools" commands. We illustrate elements of these spreadsheet commands because many readers will be familiar with other aspects of spreadsheet software from work experience and from academic applications—*not* because spreadsheets are the best software to use for regression analysis. In general, sophisticated regression analysis, beyond what spreadsheets can offer, is easier with more specialized statistical software.

Exhibit 3-7				
Facilities Maintenance Department Data	**Month**	**Facilities Maintenance Cost (Y)**	**Number of Patient-Days (X₁)**	**Value of Room Charges (X₂)**
	January	$37,000	3,700	$2,983,000
	February	23,000	1,600	3,535,000
	March	37,000	4,100	3,766,000
	April	47,000	4,900	3,646,000
	May	33,000	3,300	3,767,000
	June	39,000	4,400	3,780,000
	July	32,000	3,500	3,823,000
	August	33,000	4,000	3,152,000
	September	17,000	1,200	2,625,000
	October	18,000	1,300	2,315,000
	November	22,000	1,800	2,347,000
	December	20,000	1,600	2,917,000

Entering Data

First create a spreadsheet with the historical cost data in rows and columns. Each row should be data from one period. Each column should be a cost category or a cost driver. For ease of analysis, all the potential cost drivers should be in adjacent columns. Each row and column should be complete (no missing data) and without errors.

Plotting Data

There are two main reasons why the first step in regression analysis should be to plot the cost against each of the potential cost drivers: (1) Plots may show obvious nonlinear trends in the data; if so, linear regression analysis may not be appropriate for the entire range of the data. (2) Plots help identify "outliers"—costs that are in error or are otherwise obviously inappropriate. There is little agreement about what to do with any outliers that are not the result of data-entry errors or nonrepresentative cost and activity levels (e.g., periods of labor strikes, natural catastrophes). After all, if the data are not in error and are representative, the process that is being studied generated them. Even so, some analysts might recommend removing outliers from the data set. Leaving these outliers in the data makes regression analysis statistically less appealing, because data far removed from the rest of the data set will not fit the line well. The most conservative action is to leave all data in the data set unless uncorrectable errors are detected or unless the data are known to be not representative of the process.

Plotting with spreadsheets uses "graph" commands on the columns of cost and cost-driver data. These graph commands typically offer many optional graph types (such as bar charts and pie charts), but the most useful plot for regression analysis usually is called the *XY* graph. This graph is the type shown earlier in this chapter—the *X*-axis is the cost driver, and the *Y*-axis is the cost. The *XY* graph should be displayed without lines drawn between the data points (called data symbols)—an optional command. (Consult your spreadsheet manual for details, because each spreadsheet program is different.)

Regression Output
The regression output is generated by commands that are unique to each software package but they identify the cost to be explained ("dependent variable") and the cost driver(s) ("independent variable[s]").

Producing regression output with spreadsheets is simple: Just select the "regression" command, specify (or "highlight") the *X*-dimension[s] (the cost driver[s]), and specify the *Y*-dimension or "series" (the cost). Next specify a blank area on the spreadsheet where the output will be displayed, and select "go." Below is a regression analysis of facilities maintenance department costs using one of the two possible cost drivers, number of patient-days, X_1. Note that this output can be modified somewhat by the analyst, and the values in the output can be used elsewhere in the spreadsheet.

Facilities Maintenance Department Cost
Explained by
Number of Patient-Days

Regression Output

Constant	$9,329
Standard error of *Y* estimate	$2,145.875
R^2	0.9546625
No. of observations	12
Degrees of freedom	10
X coefficient(s)	6.9506726
Standard error of coefficient(s)	0.478994

Interpretation of Regression Output
The fixed-cost measure is labeled "constant" or "intercept" and is $9,329 per month. The variable cost measure is labeled "*X* coefficient(s)" (or something similar in other spreadsheets) and is $6.9506726 per patient-day. The linear cost function (after rounding) is

$$Y = \$9{,}329 \text{ per month} + (\$6.951 \times \text{patient-days})$$

Typically, the computer output gives a number of statistical measures that indicate how well each cost driver explains the cost and how reliable the cost predictions are likely to be. A full explanation of the output is beyond the scope of this text. One of the most important statistics, the coefficient of determination or R^2, is very important to assessing the goodness of fit of the cost function to the actual cost data.

What the visual-fit method tried to do with eyesight, regression analysis has accomplished more reliably. In general, the better a cost driver is at explaining a cost, the closer the data points will lie to the line, and the higher will be the R^2, which varies between 0 and 1. An R^2 of 0 would mean that the cost driver does not explain the cost at all, whereas an R^2 of 1 would mean that the cost driver explains the cost perfectly. The R^2 of the relationship measured with number of patient-days as the cost driver is 0.955, which is quite high. This value indicates that number of patient-days explains facilities maintenance department cost extremely well and can be interpreted as meaning that number of patient-days explains 95.5% of the past fluctuation in facilities maintenance department cost.

In contrast, performing a regression analysis on the relationship between facilities maintenance department cost and value of hospital room charges produces the following results:

Facilities Maintenance Department Cost
Explained by
Value of Hospital Room Charges

Regression Output

Constant	– $8,627.01
Std error of *Y* estimate	$7,045.371
R^2	0.511284
No. of observations	12
Degrees of freedom	10
X coefficient(s)	0.011939
Standard error of coefficient(s)	0.003691

The R^2 value, 0.511, indicates that the cost function using value of hospital room charges does not fit facilities maintenance department cost as well as the cost function using number of patient-days.

To use the information generated by regression analysis fully, an analyst must understand the meaning of the statistics and must be able to determine whether the statistical assumptions of regression are satisfied by the cost data. Indeed one of the major reasons why cost analysts study statistics is to understand the assumptions of regression analysis better. With this understanding, analysts can provide their organizations with top-quality estimates of cost behavior.

Summary Problem for Your Review

Problem Three

Comtell, Inc., makes computer peripherals (disk drives, tape drives, and printers). Until recently, production scheduling and control (PSC) costs were predicted to vary in proportion to labor costs according to the following cost function:

PSC costs, $Y = 2 \times$ labor cost (or 200% of labor)

Because PSC costs have been growing at the same time that labor cost has been shrinking, Comtell is concerned that its cost estimates are neither plausible nor reliable. Comtell's controller has just completed activity analysis to determine the most appropriate drivers of PSC costs. She obtained two cost functions using different cost drivers:

$$Y = 2 \times \text{labor cost}$$
$$R^2 = 0.233$$

and

$$Y = \$10{,}000/\text{month} + (11 \times \text{number of components used})$$
$$R^2 = 0.782$$

Required

1. What would be good tests of which cost function better predicts PSC costs?
2. During a subsequent month, labor costs were $12,000 and 2,000 product components were used. Actual PSC costs were $31,460. Using each of the preceding cost functions, prepare reports that show predicted and actual PSC costs, and the difference or *variance* between the two.
3. What is the meaning and importance of each cost variance?

Solution to Problem Three

1. A statistical test of which function better explains past PSC costs compares the R^2 of each function. The second function, based on the number of components used, has a considerably higher R^2, so it better explains the past PSC costs. If the environment is essentially unchanged in the future, the second function probably will predict future PSC costs better than the first, too.

   A useful predictive test would be to compare the cost predictions of each cost function with actual costs for several months that were not used to measure the cost functions. The function that more closely predicted actual costs is probably the more *reliable* function.

2. Note that more actual cost data would be desirable for a better test, but the procedure would be the same.

   PSC cost predicted on a labor cost basis follows:

Predicted Cost	Actual Cost	Variance
2 x $12,000 = $24,000	$31,460	$7,460 underestimate

   PSC cost predicted on a component basis follows:

Predicted Cost	Actual Cost	Variance
$10,000 + ($11 x 2,000) = $32,000	$31,460	$540 overestimate

3. The cost function that relies on labor cost underestimated PSC cost by $7,460. The cost function that uses the number of components closely predicted actual PSC costs (off by $540). Planning and control decisions would have been based on more accurate information using this prediction than using the labor cost-based prediction. An issue is whether the benefits of collecting data on the number of components used exceed the added cost of so doing.

Accounting Vocabulary

account analysis, *p. 91*
activity analysis, *p. 88*
capacity costs, *p. 83*
coefficient of determination (R^2), *p. 96*
committed fixed costs, *p. 84*
cost function, *p. 86*

cost measurement, *p. 86*
cost prediction, *p. 88*
discretionary fixed costs, *p. 84*
engineering analysis, *p. 90*
high-low method, *p. 93*
least-squares regression, *p. 96*
linear-cost behavior, *p. 80*

measurement of cost behavior, *p. 79*
mixed cost, *p. 82*
regression analysis, *p. 96*
step costs, *p. 81*
visual-fit method, *p. 95*

Fundamental Assignment Material

3-A1   Types of Cost Behavior
Identify the following *planned costs* as (a) purely variable costs, (b) discretionary fixed costs, (c) committed fixed costs, (d) mixed costs, or (e) step costs. For purely variable costs and mixed costs, indicate the most likely cost driver.

1. Straight-line depreciation on desks in the office of a CPA.
2. Sales commissions based on revenue dollars. Payments to be made to advertising salespersons employed by radio station KVOD, Denver.
3. Jet fuel costs of American Airlines.
4. Total costs of renting trucks by the city of Anaheim. Charge is a lump sum of $300 per month plus $.20 per mile.
5. Total repairs and maintenance of a school building.
6. Advertising costs, a lump sum planned by ABC, Inc.
7. Rental payment by the Federal Bureau of Investigation on a five-year lease for office space in a private office building.
8. Advertising allowance granted to wholesalers by Pepsi Bottling on a per-case basis.
9. Compensation of lawyers employed internally by General Motors.
10. Crew supervisor in a Current, Inc., mail-order house. A new supervisor is added for every 12 workers employed.
11. Public relations employee compensation to be paid by Exxon Oil Company.

3-A2   Activity Analysis
Custom Signs makes customized wooden signs for businesses and residences. These signs are made of wood, which the owner glues and carves by hand or with power tools. After carving the signs, he paints them or applies a natural finish. He has a good sense of his labor and materials cost behavior, but he is concerned that he does not have good measures of other support costs. Currently, he predicts support costs to be 50% of the *cost of materials*. Close investigation of the business reveals that $30 times the *number of power tool operations* is a more plausible and reliable support cost relationship.

Consider estimated support costs of the following two signs that Custom Signs is making:

	SIGN ONE	SIGN TWO
Materials cost	$300	$150
Number of power tool operations	3	6
Support cost	?	?

Required

1. Prepare a report showing the support costs of both signs using each cost driver and showing the differences between the two.
2. What advice would you give Custom Signs about predicting support costs?

3-A3   Division of Mixed Costs into Variable and Fixed Components

Bonnie Martinez, the president of Martinez Mechanical, has asked for information about the cost behavior of manufacturing support costs. Specifically, she wants to know how much support cost is fixed and how much is variable. The following data are the only records available:

Month	Machine Hours	Support Costs
May	850	$ 9,000
June	1,400	13,000
July	1,000	7,900
August	1,250	11,000
September	1,750	13,500

Required

1. Find monthly fixed support cost and the variable support cost per machine hour by the high-low method.
2. Suppose a reliable least-squares regression analysis using additional data (within the relevant range) gave the following output:

Regression equation: $Y = \$1,500 + \$6.80X$

What recommendations would you give the president based on these analyses?

3-B1 Identifying Cost Behavior Patterns

At a seminar, a cost accountant spoke on identification of different kinds of cost behavior.

Josie Nightengale, a hospital administrator who heard the lecture, identified several hospital costs of concern to her. After her classification, Nightengale presented you with the following list of costs and asked you to (1) classify their behavior as one of the following: variable, step, mixed, discretionary fixed, committed fixed, and (2) to identify a likely cost driver for each variable or mixed cost.

1. Training costs of an administrative resident
2. Straight-line depreciation of operating room equipment
3. Costs of services of LMN Hospital Consulting
4. Nursing supervisors' salaries (a supervisor is needed for each 45 nursing personnel)
5. Operating costs of x-ray equipment ($95,000 a year plus $3 per film)
6. Blue Cross insurance for all full-time employees
7. Costs incurred by Dr. Brahn in cancer research
8. Repairs made on hospital furniture

3-B2 Activity Analysis

Midwest Circuits, a Kansas manufacturer of printed circuit boards, has always costed its circuits boards with a 100% "mark-up" over its material costs to cover its manufacturing support costs (which include labor). An activity analysis suggests that support costs are driven primarily by the number of manual operations performed on each board, estimated at $4 per manual operation. Compute the estimated support costs of two typical circuit boards below using the traditional mark-up and the activity analysis results:

	Card No. 2222	Card No. 5555
Material cost	$30.00	$55.00
Manual operations	15	6

Why are the cost estimates different?

3-B3 Division of Mixed Costs into Variable and Fixed Components

The president and the controller of Juan's Transformer Company (Mexico) have agreed that refinement of the company's cost measurements will aid planning and control decisions. They have asked you to measure the function for mixed-cost behavior of repairs and maintenance from the following sparse data. Currency is the Mexican peso ($).

Monthly Activity in Machine Hours	Monthly Repair and Maintenance Cost
8,000	$185,000,000
12,000	$255,000,000

Additional Assignment Material

Questions

3-1. What is a cost driver? Give three examples of costs and their possible cost drivers.

3-2. What is the "relevant range"? Why is it important?

3-3. Explain linear-cost behavior.

3-4. "Variable costs should fluctuate directly in proportion to sales." Do you agree? Explain.

3-5. Why are fixed costs also called capacity costs?

3-6. "Step costs can be fixed or variable depending on your perspective." Explain.

3-7. Explain how mixed costs are related to both fixed and variable costs.

3-8. What are the benefits of using "cost functions" to describe cost behavior?

3-9. How do management's product and service choices affect cost behavior?

3-10. How do committed fixed costs differ from discretionary fixed costs?

3-11. Why are committed fixed costs the most difficult to change of the fixed costs?

3-12. What are the primary determinants of the level of committed costs? Discretionary costs?

3-13. "Planning is far more important than day-to-day control of discretionary costs." Do you agree? Explain.

3-14. "Changing technology can make historically valid cost relationships misleading for planning and control." Explain.

3-15. Explain the use of incentives to control cost.

3-16. Describe the methods for measuring cost functions using past cost data.

3-17. Explain "plausibility" and "reliability" of cost functions. Which is preferred? Explain.

3-18. What is activity analysis?

3-19. What is engineering analysis? Account analysis?

3-20. How could account analysis be combined with engineering analysis?

3-21. Explain the strengths and weaknesses of the high-low and visual-fit methods.

3-22. Why is regression analysis usually preferred to the high-low method?

3-23. "You never know how good your fixed- and variable-cost measures are if you use account analysis or if you visually fit a line on a data plot. That's why I like least-squares regression analysis." Explain.

3-24. At a conference, a consultant stated, "Before you can control, you must measure." An executive complained, "Why bother to measure when work rules and guaranteed employment provisions in labor contracts prevent discharging workers, using part-time employees, and using overtime?" Evaluate these comments. Summarize your personal attitudes toward the usefulness of engineering analysis.

Exercises

3-25   Various Cost Behavior Patterns

In practice, there is often a tendency to simplify approximations of cost behavior patterns, even though the "true" underlying behavior is not simple. Choose from the accompanying graphs A through H the one that matches the numbered items. Indicate by letter which graph best fits each of the situations described. Next to each number-letter pair, identify a likely cost driver for that cost.

The vertical axes of the graphs represent total dollars of costs incurred, and the horizontal axes represent levels of cost driver activity *during a particular time period*. The graphs may be used more than once.

1. Availability of quantity discounts, where the cost per unit falls as each price break is reached

2. Price of an increasingly scarce raw material as the quantity used increases

3. Guaranteed annual wage plan, whereby workers get paid for 40 hours of work per week

even at zero or low levels of production that require working only a few hours weekly

4. Water bill, which entails a flat fee for the first 10,000 gallons used and then an increasing unit cost for every additional 10,000 gallons used

5. Cost of machining labor that tends to decrease as workers gain experience

6. Depreciation of office equipment

7. Cost of sheet steel for a manufacturer of farm implements

8. Salaries of supervisors, where one supervisor is added for every 12 phone solicitors

9. Natural gas bill consisting of a fixed component, plus a constant variable cost per thousand cubic feet after a specified number of cubic feet are used

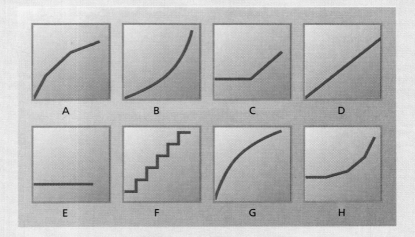

3-26 Predicting Costs

Given the following four cost behaviors and expected levels of cost-driver activity, predict total costs:

1. Fuel costs of driving vehicles, $.20 per mile, driven 20,000 miles per month

2. Equipment rental cost, $5,000 per piece of equipment per month for 7 pieces for three months

3. Ambulance and EMT personnel cost for a soccer tournament, $1,100 for each 250 tournament participants; the tournament is expecting 2,400 participants

4. Purchasing department cost, $7,500 per month plus $5 per material order processed at 4,000 orders in one month

3-27 Identifying Discretionary and Committed Fixed Costs

Identify and compute total discretionary fixed and total committed fixed costs from the following list prepared by the accounting supervisor for Nicholas, Inc.:

Advertising	$20,000
Depreciation	47,000
Company health insurance	15,000
Management salaries	85,000
Payment on long-term debt	50,000
Property tax	32,000
Grounds maintenance	9,000
Office remodeling	21,000
Research and development	36,000

3-28   Cost Effects of Technology

Bean Bauer, Inc., an outdoor sports retailer, is considering automating its order-taking process. The estimated costs of two alternative approaches are as follows:

	Alternative 1	Alternative 2
Annual fixed cost	$200,000	$400,000
Variable cost per order	$8	$4
Expected number of orders	80,000	80,000

At the expected level of orders, which automated approach has the lower cost? What is the indifference level of orders, or the "break-even" level of orders? What is the meaning of this level of orders?

3-29   Mixed Cost, Choosing Cost Drivers, High-Low and Visual-Fit Methods

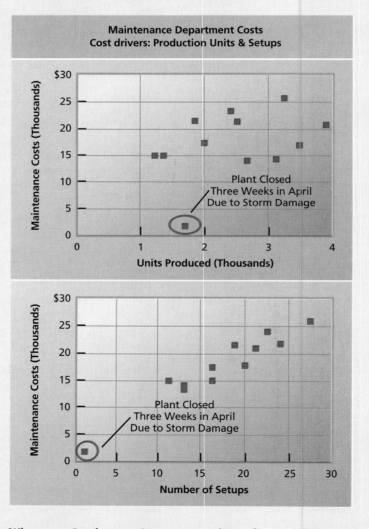

Wheatown Implement Company produces farm implements for various large vehicles used for farming. Wheatown is in the process of measuring its manufacturing costs and is particularly interested in the costs of the maintenance activity since maintenance is a significant mixed cost. Activity analysis indicates that maintenance activity consists primarily of maintenance labor setting up machines using certain supplies. A setup consists of preparing the necessary machines for a particular production run of a product. During setup, machines must still be running, which consumes energy. Thus the costs associated with maintenance include labor, supplies, and energy. Unfortunately, Wheatown's cost accounting system does not trace these costs to maintenance activity separately. Wheatown employs two full-time maintenance mechanics to perform maintenance. The annual salary of a maintenance mechanic is $25,000 and is considered a fixed cost. Two plausible cost drivers have been suggested: units produced and number of setups.

Data had been collected for the past 12 months and a plot made for the cost driver—units of production. The maintenance cost figures collected include estimates for labor, supplies, and energy. Toby Hatcher, controller at Wheatown, recently attended an activity-based costing seminar where she learned that some types of activities are performed each time a batch of goods is processed rather than each time a unit is produced. Based on this concept, she has gathered data on the number of setups performed over the past 12 months. The plots of monthly maintenance costs versus the two potential cost drivers are given at the beginning of this problem.

Required

1. Find monthly fixed maintenance cost and the variable maintenance cost per driver unit using the visual-fit method based on each potential cost driver. Explain how you treated the April data.
2. Find monthly fixed maintenance cost and the variable maintenance cost per driver unit using the high-low method based on each potential cost driver.
3. Which cost driver best meets the criteria for choosing cost functions? Explain.

3-30 Account Analysis

Indian Mascot Computers, Inc., is a company started by two university students to market and assemble IBM-clone computers to faculty and students. The company operates out of the garage of one of the student's homes. From the following costs of a recent month, compute the total cost function and total cost for the month.

- Telephone $ 60, fixed
- Utilities   260, 25% attributable to the garage, 75% to the house
- Advertising   75, fixed
- Insurance   80, fixed
- Materials   7,500, variable, for five computers
- Labor   1,700; $1,200 fixed plus $500 for hourly help for assembling five computers

3-31 Economic Plausibility of Regression Analysis Results

The head of the Industrial Plastics Manufacturing Department of the Charbon Co. was concerned about some cost behavior information given to him by the new assistant controller, who was hired because of his recent training in cost analysis. His first assignment was to apply regression analysis to various costs in the department. One of the results was presented as follows:

"A regression on monthly data was run to explain building maintenance cost as a function of direct labor hours as the cost driver. The results are

$$Y = \$7,542 - \$.54X$$

I suggest that we use the building as intensively as possible to keep the maintenance costs down."

The department head was puzzled. How could increased use cause decreased maintenance cost? Explain this counterintuitive result to the department head. What step(s) did the assistant controller probably omit in applying and interpreting the regression analysis?

Problems

3-32   Controlling Risk, Capacity Decisions, Technology Decisions

Consider the discussion of Ford Motor on page 84 of the text. Ford had been outsourcing production to Mazda and using overtime for as much as 20% of production—Ford's plants and assembly lines were running at 100% of capacity and demand was sufficient for an additional 20%. Ford had considered building new highly automated assembly lines and plants to earn more profits since overtime premiums and outsourcing were costly. However, the investment in high technology and capacity expansion was rejected.

Assume that all material and labor costs are variable with respect to the level of production and that all other costs are fixed. Consider one of Ford's plants that makes Probes. The cost to convert the plant to use fully automated assembly lines is $20 million. The resulting labor costs would be significantly reduced. The costs, in millions of dollars, of the build option and the outsource/overtime option are given in the table below.

Build Option			
Percent of capacity	60	100	120
Material costs	$18	$30	$36
Labor costs	6	10	12
Other costs	40	40	40
Total costs	$64	$80	$88

Outsource/Overtime Option			
Percent of capacity	60	100	120
Material costs	$18	$30	$36
Labor costs	18	30	44
Other costs	20	20	20
Total costs	$56	$80	$100

Required

1. Prepare a line graph showing total costs for the two options: (1) build new assembly lines, and (2) continue to use overtime and outsource production of Probes. Give an explanation of the cost behavior of the two options.
2. Which option enables Ford management to control risk better? Explain. Assess the cost-benefit trade-offs associated with each option.
3. A solid understanding of cost behavior is an important prerequisite to effective managerial control of costs. Suppose you are an executive at Ford and currently the production (and sales) level is approaching the 100% level of capacity and the economy is expected to remain strong for at least 1 year. While sales and profits are good now, you are aware of the cyclical nature of the automobile business. Would you recommend committing Ford to building automated assembly lines in order to service potential near-term increases in demand or would you recommend against building, looking to the likely future downturn in business? Discuss your reasoning.

3-33   Activity Analysis

Violet Blossom Technology develops and markets computer software for the agriculture industry. Because support costs comprise a large portion of the cost of software development, the director of cost operations of Violet Blossom, Ted Daleys, is especially concerned with understanding the effects of support cost behavior. Daleys has completed a preliminary activity analysis of one of Violet Blossom's primary software products: GroCare (software to manage fertilizer mixing). This product is a software "template" that is customized for specific customers, who are charged for the basic product plus customizing costs. The activity analysis is based on the number of customized lines of GroCare code. Currently, support cost estimates are based on a fixed rate of 50% of the basic cost. Data are shown for two recent customers:

	Customer	
	West Acres Plants	*Beautiful Blooms*
Basic cost of GroCare	$12,000	$12,000
Lines of customized code	525	180
Estimated cost per line of customized code	$23	$23

Required

1. Compute the support cost of customizing GroCare for each customer using each cost-estimating approach.
2. If the activity analysis is reliable, what are the pros and cons of adopting it for all of Violet Blossom's software products?

3-34 Government Service Cost Analysis

The Internal Revenue Service has an auditing system whereby an auditor scrutinizes income tax returns after they have been prescreened with the help of computer tests for normal ranges of deductions claimed by taxpayers. An expected cost of $7 per tax return has been used, based on measurement studies that allow 20 minutes per return. Each agent has a workweek of 5 days of 8 hours per day. Twenty auditors are employed at a salary of $840 each per week.

The audit supervisor has the following data regarding performance for the most recent 4-week period, when 8,000 returns were processed:

Actual Cost of Auditors	Expected Cost for Processing Returns	Difference or Variance
$67,200	?	?

Required

1. Compute the planned cost and the variance.
2. The supervisor believes that audit work should be conducted more productively and that superfluous personnel should be transferred to field audits. If the foregoing data are representative, how many auditors should be transferred?
3. List some possible reasons for the variance.
4. Describe some alternative cost drivers for processing income tax returns.

3-35 Separation of Drug Testing Laboratory Mixed Costs into Variable and Fixed Components

A staff meeting has been called at ProTest Laboratory, a drug-testing facility retained by several professional and college sport leagues and associations. The chief of testing, Dr. Steroid, has demanded an across-the-board increase in prices for a particular test because of the increased testing and precision that is now required.

The administrator of the laboratory has asked you to measure the mixed-cost behavior of this particular testing department and to prepare a short report she can present to Dr. Steroid. Consider the following limited data:

	Average Test Procedures per Month	Average Monthly Cost of Test Procedures
Monthly averages, 19X4	500	$ 60,000
Monthly averages, 19X5	600	70,000
Monthly averages, 19X6	700	147,000

3-36 University Cost Behavior

Waterloo Business College, a private institution, is preparing a planned income statement for the coming academic year ending August 31, 19X6. Tuition revenues for the past 2 years ending August 31 were 19X5: $600,000, and 19X4: $650,000. Total expenses for 19X5 were $610,000 and in 19X4 were $630,000. No tuition rate changes occurred in 19X4 or 19X5, nor are any expected to occur in 19X6. Tuition revenue is expected to be $620,000 for 19X6. What net income should be planned for 19X6, assuming that the implied cost behavior remains unchanged?

3-37 Interpretation of Regression Analysis
Study Appendix 3. Eleanor Bass Tent and Tarp (EBTT) Company has difficulty controlling its use of supplies. The company has traditionally regarded supplies as a purely variable cost. Nearly every time production was above average, however, EBTT spent less than predicted for supplies; when production was below average, EBTT spent more than predicted. This pattern suggested to Kerry Kane, the new controller, that part of the supplies cost was probably not related to production volume, or was fixed.

She decided to use regression analysis to explore this issue. After consulting with production personnel, she considered two cost drivers for supplies cost: (1) number of tents and tarps produced, and (2) square feet of material used. She obtained the following results based on monthly data:

	Cost Driver	
	Number of Tents and Tarps	*Square Feet of Material Used*
Constant	2,200	1,800
Variable coefficient	.033	.072
R^2	.220	.683

Required

1. Which is the preferred cost function? Explain.
2. What percentage of the fluctuation of supplies cost depends on square feet of materials? Do fluctuations in supplies cost depend on anything other than square feet of materials? What proportion of the fluctuations are not explained by square feet of materials?

3-38 Step Costs
Maverick County jail requires a staff of at least one guard for every four prisoners. The jail will hold 48 prisoners. Maverick County has a beach that attracts numerous tourists and transients in the spring and summer. However, the county is rather sedate in the fall and winter. The fall–winter population of the jail is generally between 12 and 16 prisoners. The numbers in the spring and summer can fluctuate from 12 to 48, depending on the weather, among other factors (including phases of the moon, according to some longtime residents).

Maverick County has four permanent guards hired on a year-round basis at an annual salary of $36,000 each. When additional guards are needed, they are hired on a weekly basis at a rate of $600 per week. (For simplicity, assume that each month has exactly 4 weeks).

Required

1. Prepare a graph with the weekly planned cost of jail guards on the vertical axis and the number of prisoners on the horizontal axis.
2. What would be the budgeted amount for jail guards for the month of January? Would this be a fixed or variable cost?
3. Suppose the jail population of each of the 4 weeks in July was 25, 38, 26, and 43, respectively. The actual amount paid for jail guards in July was $19,800. Prepare a report comparing the actual amount paid for jail guards with the amount that would be expected with efficient scheduling and hiring.

4. Suppose Maverick County treated jail-guard salaries for nonpermanent guards as a variable expense of $150 per week per prisoner. This variable cost was applied to the number of prisoners in excess of 16. Therefore, the weekly cost function was:

$$\text{Weekly jail-guard cost} = \$3{,}000 + \$150 \times (\text{total prisoners} - 16)$$

Explain how this cost function was determined.

5. Prepare a report similar to that in requirement 3 except that the cost function in requirement 4 should be used to calculate the expected amount of jail-guard salaries. Which report, this one or the one in requirement 3, is more accurate? Is accuracy the only concern?

3-39 Regression Analysis

Study Appendix 3. Noritake, Inc., a manufacturer of fine china and stoneware, is troubled by fluctuations in productivity and wants to compute how much manufacturing support costs are related to the various sizes of batches of output. The following data show the results of a random sample of 10 batches of one pattern of stoneware:

Sample	Batch Size, X	Support Costs, Y
1	15	$180
2	12	140
3	20	230
4	17	190
5	12	160
6	25	300
7	22	270
8	9	110
9	18	240
10	30	320

Required

1. Plot support costs, Y, versus batch size, X.
2. Using regression analysis, measure the cost function of support costs and batch size.
3. Predict the support costs for a batch size of 30.
4. Using the high-low method, repeat requirements 2 and 3. Should the manager use the high-low or regression method? Explain.

Cases

3-40 Government Health Cost Behavior

Dr. Sandy Turner, the chief administrator of a community mental health agency, is concerned about the dilemma of coping with reduced budgets next year and into the foreseeable future but increasing demand for services. In order to plan for reduced budgets, she first must identify where costs can be cut or reduced and still keep the agency functioning. Below are some data from the past year.

Program Area	Costs
Administration	
Salaries	
Administrator	$60,000
Assistant	30,000
Two secretaries	42,000

continued

Program Area	Costs
Supplies	35,000
Advertising and promotion	9,000
Professional meetings, dues, and literature	14,000
Purchased services	
Accounting and billing	15,000
Custodial and maintenance	13,000
Security	12,000
Consulting	10,000
Community mental health services	
Salaries (two social workers)	46,000
Transportation	10,000
Outpatient mental health treatment	
Salaries	
Psychiatrist	85,000
Two social workers	70,000

Required

1. Identify which costs you think are likely to be discretionary or committed costs.
2. One possibility is to eliminate all discretionary costs. How much would be saved? What do you think of this recommendation?
3. How would you advise Dr. Turner to prepare for reduced budgets?

3-41   Activity Analysis

The costs of the Information Systems (IS) department (and other service departments) of Northwest Wood Products have always been charged to the three business divisions (Forest Management, Lumber Products, and Paper Products) based on the *number of employees* in each division. This measure is easy to obtain and update, and until recently none of the divisions had complained about the charges. The Paper Products division has recently automated many of its operations and has reduced the number of its employees. At the same time, however, to monitor its new process, Paper Products has increased its requests for various reports provided by the IS department. The other divisions have begun to complain that they are being charged more than their fair share of IS department costs. Based on activity analysis of possible cost drivers, cost analysts have suggested using the number of reports prepared as a means of charging for IS costs and have gathered the following information:

	Forest Management	Lumber Products	Paper Products
19X3 Number of employees	762	457	502
19X3 Number of reports	410	445	377
19X3 IS Costs: $300,000			
19X4 Number of employees	751	413	131
19X4 Number of reports	412	432	712
19X4 IS Costs: $385,000			

Required

1. Discuss the *plausibility* and probable *reliability* of each of the cost drivers—number of employees or number of reports.
2. What are the 19X3 and 19X4 IS costs per unit of cost driver for each division using each cost driver? Do the Forest Management and Lumber Products divisions have

legitimate complaints? Explain.
3. What are the *incentives* that are implied by each cost driver?
4. Which cost driver should Northwest Wood Products use to charge its divisions for IS accounting services? For other services?

3-42   Choice of Cost Driver

Study Appendix 3. Rodney Ellis, the director of cost operations of Perpetual Storage Company, wishes to develop the most accurate cost function to explain and predict support costs in the company's printed circuit board assembly operation. Mr. Ellis is concerned that the cost function that he currently uses—based on direct labor costs—is not accurate enough for proper planning and control of support costs. Mr. Ellis directed one of his financial analysts to obtain a random sample of 25 weeks of support costs and three possible cost drivers in the circuit-board assembly department: direct labor hours, number of boards assembled, and average cycle time of boards assembled. (Average cycle time is the average time between start and certified completion—after quality testing—of boards assembled during a week.) Much of the effort in this assembly operation is devoted to testing for quality and reworking defective boards, all of which increase the average cycle time in any period. Therefore, Mr. Ellis believes that average cycle time will be the best support cost driver. Mr. Ellis wants his analyst to use regression analysis to demonstrate which cost driver best explains support costs.

Week	Circuit Board Assembly Support Costs Y	Direct Labor Hours X_1	Number of Boards Completed X_2	Average Cycle Time (Hours) X_3
1	$66,402	7,619	2,983	186.44
2	56,943	7,678	2,830	139.14
3	60,337	7,816	2,413	151.13
4	50,096	7,659	2,221	138.30
5	64,241	7,646	2,701	158.63
6	60,846	7,765	2,656	148.71
7	43,119	7,685	2,495	105.85
8	63,412	7,962	2,128	174.02
9	59,283	7,793	2,127	155.30
10	60,070	7,732	2,127	162.20
11	53,345	7,771	2,338	142.97
12	65,027	7,842	2,685	176.08
13	58,220	7,940	2,602	150.19
14	65,406	7,750	2,029	194.06
15	35,268	7,954	2,136	100.51
16	46,394	7,768	2,046	137.47
17	71,877	7,764	2,786	197.44
18	61,903	7,635	2,822	164.69
19	50,009	7,849	2,178	141.95
20	49,327	7,869	2,244	123.37
21	44,703	7,576	2,195	128.25
22	45,582	7,557	2,370	106.16
23	43,818	7,569	2,016	131.41
24	62,122	7,672	2,515	154.88
25	52,403	7,653	2,942	140.07

1. Plot support costs, Y, versus each of the possible cost drivers, X_1, X_2, and X_3.
2. Use regression analysis to measure cost functions using each of the cost drivers.
3. According to the criteria of plausibility and reliability, which is the best cost driver for support costs in the circuit board assembly department?
4. Interpret the economic meaning of the best cost function.

3-43   Use of Cost Functions for Pricing

Study Appendix 3. Read the previous problem. If you worked this problem, use your measured cost functions. If you did not work the previous problem, assume the following measured cost functions:

$$Y = \$9,000/\text{week} + (\$6 \times \text{direct labor hours}); R^2 = .10$$
$$Y = \$20,000/\text{week} + (\$14 \times \text{number of boards completed}); R^2 = .40$$
$$Y = \$5,000/\text{week} + (\$350 \times \text{average cycle time}); R^2 = .80$$

1. Which of the support cost functions would you expect to be the most reliable for explaining and predicting support costs? Why?
2. Perpetual Storage prices its products by adding a percentage mark-up to its product costs. Product costs include assembly labor, components, and support costs. Using each of the cost functions, compute the circuit board portion of the support cost of an order that used the following resources:
   a.   Effectively used the capacity of the assembly department for 3 weeks
   b.   Assembly labor hours: 20,000
   c.   Number of boards: 6,000
   d.   Average cycle time: 180 hours
3. Which cost would you recommend that Perpetual Storage use? Why?
4. Assume that the market for this product is extremely cost competitive. What do you think of Perpetual Storage's pricing method?

3-44   Identifying Relevant Data

SuperByte Company manufactures palm-sized, portable computers. Because these very small computers compete with larger portable computers that have more functions and flexibility, understanding and using cost behavior is very critical to SuperByte's profitability. SuperByte's controller, Kelly Hudson, has kept meticulous files on various cost categories and possible cost drivers for most of the important functions and activities of SuperByte. Because most of the manufacturing at SuperByte is automated, labor cost is relatively fixed. Other support costs comprise most of SuperByte's costs. Partial data that Hudson has collected over the past 25 weeks on one of these support costs, logistics operations (materials purchasing, receiving, warehousing, and shipping), follow:

Week	Logistics Costs Y	Number of Orders X
1	$23,907	1,357
2	18,265	1,077
3	24,208	1,383
4	23,578	1,486
5	22,211	1,292
6	22,862	1,425
7	23,303	1,306
8	24,507	1,373
9	17,878	1,031
10	18,306	1,020
11	20,807	1,097

continued

Week	Logistics Costs Y	Number of Orders X
12	19,707	1,069
13	23,020	1,444
14	20,407	733
15	20,370	413
16	20,678	633
17	21,145	711
18	20,775	228
19	20,532	488
20	20,659	655
21	20,430	722
22	20,713	373
23	20,256	391
24	21,196	734
25	20,406	256

Required

1. Plot logistics cost, Y, versus number of orders, X. What cost behavior is evident? What do you think happened in week 14?
2. What is your recommendation to Kelly Hudson regarding the relevance of the past 25 weeks of logistics cost and number of orders for measuring logistics cost behavior?
3. Hudson remarks that one of the improvements that SuperByte has made in the past several months was to negotiate just-in-time deliveries from its suppliers. This was made possible by substituting an automated ordering system for the previous manual (labor-intensive) system. Although fixed costs increased, the variable cost of placing an order was expected to drop greatly. Do the data support this expectation? Do you believe that the change to the automated ordering system was justified? Why or why not?

4

Introduction to Cost Management Systems

Marmon/Keystone Corporation is a leading distributor of steel and aluminum pipe and tubing. Tubing is used by companies such as Harley-Davidson for the frame of its motorcycles. Marmon/Keystone uses activity-based costing to accurately report the cost of selling and distributing its products. *Courtesy Marmon/Keystone Corporation*

Learning Objectives

When you have finished studying this chapter, you should be able to

1 Define the following terms and explain how they are related: cost, cost objective, cost accumulation, and cost allocation.

2 Distinguish between direct and indirect costs.

3 Define and identify examples of each of the three major categories of manufacturing costs.

4 Differentiate between product costs and period costs, identifying examples of each.

5 Explain how the financial statements of merchandisers and manufacturers differ because of the types of goods they sell.

6 Construct income statements of a manufacturing company in both the absorption and contribution formats.

7 Identify the steps involved in the design and implementation of an activity-based-costing system.

8 Calculate activity-based costs for cost objects.

9 Explain why activity-based-costing systems are being adopted by more and more organizations.

10 Explain how JIT systems can reduce non-value-added activities.

Managers rely on accountants to measure the cost of the goods and services the company produces. Consider the following commentaries on the modern role of management accountants:

> We (cost accountants) had to understand what the numbers mean, relate the numbers to business activity, and recommend alternative courses of action. Finally, we had to evaluate alternatives and make decisions to maximize business efficiency.
> —South Central Bell

> Because the ABC (Activity-Based Costing) system now mirrors the manufacturing process, the engineers and production staff believe the cost data produced by the accounting system. Engineering and production regularly ask accounting to help find the product design combination that will optimize costs. . . . The accountants now participate in product design decisions. They help engineering and production understand how costs behave. . . . The ABC system makes the professional lives of the accountants more rewarding. —Hewlett-Packard Company

cost accounting That part of the accounting system that measures costs for the purposes of management decision making and financial reporting.

As you can see, all kinds of organizations—manufacturing firms, service companies, and nonprofit organizations—need some form of **cost accounting**, that part of the accounting system that measures costs for the purposes of management decision making and financial reporting. Because it is the most general case, embracing production, marketing, and general administration functions, we will focus on cost accounting in a manufacturing setting. Remember, though, that you can apply this framework to any organization.

In this chapter we introduce the concepts of cost and management accounting appropriate to any manufacturing company. We also consider recent changes that have led to what is called the *new manufacturing environment*. Manufacturing companies are in the midst of great changes. The need to compete in global markets has changed the types of information useful to managers. At the same time technology has changed both the manufacturing processes and information-processing capabilities. Although the basic *concepts* of management accounting have not changed, their *application* is significantly different in many companies than it was a decade ago. Management accountants today must be able to develop systems to support globally oriented, technology-intensive companies, often called *world-class manufacturing companies*.

In addition, we discuss how cost accounting affects and is affected by financial reporting, and how the need to use costs for reported income statements and balance sheets influences the way cost accounting systems are structured. (A review of income statements and balance sheets is in Chapter 17.)

Objective 1

Define the following terms and explain how they are related: cost, cost objective, cost accumulation and cost allocation.

■ CLASSIFICATIONS OF COSTS

Costs may be classified in many ways—far too many to be covered in a single chapter. This chapter concentrates on the big picture of how manufacturing costs are accumulated and classified. Chapters 13 to 16 give details on how a variety of cost accounting systems measure the costs of products or services. Chapters 13 to 15 may be studied immediately after this chapter without losing continuity. Chapter 16 can be studied after Chapter 8.

Cost Accumulation and Cost Objectives

cost A sacrifice or giving up of resources for a particular purpose, frequently measured by the monetary units that must be paid for goods and services.

A **cost** may be defined as a sacrifice or giving up of resources for a particular purpose. Costs are frequently measured by the monetary units (for example, dollars or francs) that must be paid for goods and services. Costs are initially recorded in elementary form (for example, repairs or advertising). Then these costs are grouped in different ways to help managers make decisions, such as evaluating subordinates and subunits of the organization, expanding or deleting products or territories, and replacing equipment.

cost objective (cost object) Any activity or resource for which a separate measurement of costs is desired. Examples include departments, products, and territories.

To aid decisions, managers want to know the cost of something. This "something" is called a **cost objective** or **cost object**, defined as *any activity or resource for which a separate measurement of costs is desired*. Examples of cost

cost accumulation
Collecting costs by some natural classification such as materials or labor.

cost allocation Tracing and reassigning costs to one or more cost objectives such as departments, customers, or products.

objectives include departments, products, territories, miles driven, bricks laid, patients seen, tax bills sent, checks processed, student hours taught, and library books shelved.

The cost accounting system typically includes two processes:

1. **Cost accumulation:** Collecting costs by some "natural" classification such as materials or labor.
2. **Cost allocation:** Tracing and reassigning costs to one or more cost objectives such as departments, customers, or products.

Exhibit 4-1 illustrates these processes. First, the costs of all raw materials are *accumulated*. Then they are *allocated* to the departments that use them and further to the specific items made by these departments. The total raw materials cost of a particular product is the sum of the raw materials costs allocated to it in the various departments.

Exhibit 4-1

Cost Accumulation and Allocation

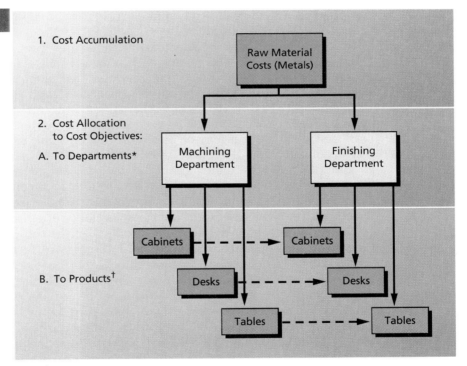

* Purpose: to evaluate performance of manufacturing departments.
† Purpose: to obtain costs of various products for valuing inventory, determining income, and judging product profitability.

To make intelligent decisions, managers want reliable measurements. An extremely large U.S. grocery chain, A&P, ran into profit difficulties. It began retrenching by closing many stores. Management's lack of adequate cost information about individual store operations made the closing program a hit-or-miss affair. A news story reported the following:

> Because of the absence of detailed profit-and-loss statements, and a cost-allocation system that did not reflect true costs, A&P's strategists could not be sure whether an individual store was really unprofitable. For example, distribution costs were shared equally among all the stores in a marketing area without regard to such factors as a store's distance from the warehouse. Says one close observer of the company: "When they wanted to close a store, they had to wing it. They could not make rational decisions, because they did not have a fact basis."

Direct and Indirect Costs

direct costs Costs that can be identified specifically and exclusively with a given cost objective in an economically feasible way.
indirect costs Costs that cannot be identified specifically and exclusively with a given cost objective in an economically feasible way.

A major feature of costs in both manufacturing and nonmanufacturing activities is whether the costs have a direct or an indirect relationship to a particular cost objective. **Direct costs** can be identified specifically and exclusively with a given cost objective in an economically feasible way. In contrast, **indirect costs** cannot be identified specifically and exclusively with a given cost objective in an economically feasible way.   *is cost effective*

Whenever it is "economically feasible," managers prefer to classify costs as direct rather than indirect. In this way, managers have greater confidence in the reported costs of products and services. "Economically feasible" means "cost effective," in the sense that managers do not want cost accounting to be too expensive in relation to expected benefits. For example, it may be economically feasible to trace the exact cost of steel and fabric (direct cost) to a specific lot of desk chairs, but it may be economically infeasible to trace the exact cost of rivets or thread (indirect costs) to the chairs.

Other factors also influence whether a cost is considered direct or indirect. The key is the particular cost objective. For example, consider a supervisor's salary in the maintenance department of a telephone company. If the cost objective is the department, the supervisor's salary is a direct cost. In contrast, if the cost objective is a service (the "product" of the company) such as a telephone call, the supervisor's salary is an indirect cost. In general, many more costs are direct when a department is the cost objective than when a service (a telephone call) or a physical product (a razor blade) is the cost objective.

Objective 2

Distinguish between direct and indirect costs

Frequently managers want to know both the costs of running departments and the costs of products, services, activities, or resources. Costs are inevitably allocated to more than one cost objective. Thus a particular cost may simultaneously be direct and indirect. As you have just seen, a supervisor's salary can be both direct (with respect to his or her department) and indirect (with respect to the department's individual products or services).

Categories of Manufacturing Costs

Any raw material, labor, or other input used by any organization could, in theory, be identified as a direct or indirect cost, depending on the cost objective. In manufacturing operations, which transform materials into other goods through the use of labor and factory facilities, products are frequently

Objective 3

Define and identify examples of each of the three major categories of manufacturing costs

direct-material costs
The acquisition costs of all materials that are physically identified as a part of the manufactured goods and that may be traced to the manufactured goods in an economically feasible way.

direct-labor costs The wages of all labor that can be traced specifically and exclusively to the manufactured goods in an economically feasible way.

factory-overhead costs (factory burden, manufacturing overhead) All costs other than direct material or direct labor that are associated with the manufacturing process.

the cost objective. As a result, manufacturing costs are most often divided into three major categories: (1) direct materials, (2) direct labor, and (3) factory overhead.

1. **Direct-material costs** include the acquisition costs of all materials that are physically identified as a part of the manufactured goods and that may be traced to the manufactured goods in an economically feasible way. Examples are iron castings, lumber, aluminum sheets, and subassemblies. Direct materials often do not include minor items such as tacks or glue because the costs of tracing these items are greater than the possible benefits of having more precise product costs. Such items are usually called *supplies* or *indirect materials*, which are classified as a part of the factory overhead described in this list.

2. **Direct-labor costs** include the wages of all labor that can be traced specifically and exclusively to the manufactured goods in an economically feasible way. Examples are the wages of machine operators and assemblers. Much labor, such as that of janitors, forklift truck operators, plant guards, and storeroom clerks, is considered to be *indirect labor* because it is impossible or economically infeasible to trace such activity to specific products. Such indirect labor is classified as a part of factory overhead. In highly automated factories, there may be no direct labor costs. Why? Because it may be economically infeasible to physically trace any labor cost directly to specific products.

3. **Factory-overhead costs** include all costs associated with the manufacturing process that are not classified as direct material or direct labor. Other terms used to describe this category are **factory burden** and **manufacturing overhead**. Examples are power, supplies, indirect labor, supervisory salaries, property taxes, rent, insurance, and depreciation.

In traditional accounting systems, all manufacturing overhead costs are considered to be indirect. However, computers have allowed modern systems to physically trace many overhead costs to products in an economically feasible manner. For example, meters wired to computers can monitor the electricity used to produce each product, and costs of setting up a batch production run can be traced to the items produced in the run. In general, the more overhead costs that can be traced directly to products, the more accurate the product cost.

Prime Costs, Conversion Costs, and Direct-Labor Costs

prime costs Direct labor costs plus direct materials costs.

conversion costs Direct labor costs plus factory overhead costs.

Exhibit 4-2 shows that direct labor is sometimes combined with one of the other types of manufacturing costs. The combined categories are **prime costs**—direct labor plus direct materials—or **conversion costs**—direct labor plus factory overhead.

The twofold categorization, direct materials and conversion costs, has replaced the threefold categorization, direct materials, direct labor, and factory overhead, in many modern, automated manufacturing companies. Why? Because direct labor in such a company is a small part of costs and not worth tracing directly to the products. In fact, some companies call their two categories direct materials and factory overhead, and simply include direct labor costs in the factory overhead category.

Exhibit 4-2

Relationships of
Key Categories of
Manufacturing Costs
for Product-Costing
Purposes

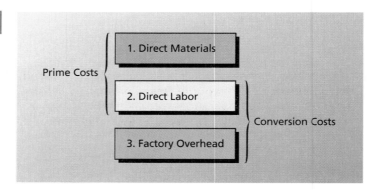

Why so many different systems? As mentioned earlier, accountants and managers weigh the costs and benefits of additional categories when they design their cost accounting systems. When the costs of any single category or item become relatively insignificant, separate tracking may no longer be desirable. For example, in highly automated factories direct labor is often less than 5% of total manufacturing costs. In such cases, it may make economic sense to combine direct-labor costs with one of the other major cost categories. Such is the case at several Hewlett-Packard plants, which collect direct labor as just another subpart of factory overhead.

To recap, the three major categories for manufacturing product costs are direct material, direct labor, and factory overhead. Some companies, however, have only two categories: direct materials and conversion costs. As information technology improves, some companies may have four or more. For instance, a company might have direct materials, direct labor, other direct costs (such as specifically metered power), and factory overhead.

In addition to direct-material, direct-labor, and factory-overhead costs, all manufacturing companies also incur selling and administrative costs. These costs are accumulated by departments such as advertising and sales departments. However, as you will see later in this chapter, most firm's *financial statements* do not allocate these costs to the physical units produced. In short, these costs do not become a part of the reported inventory cost of the manufactured products. To aid in decisions, however, managers often want to know the selling and administrative costs associated with each product. Therefore, *management reports* often include such costs as product costs.

■ COST ACCOUNTING FOR FINANCIAL REPORTING

Regardless of the type of cost accounting system used, the resulting costs are used in a company's financial statements. This section discusses how financial reporting requirements influence the design of cost accounting systems.

Costs are reported on both the income statement, as cost of goods sold, and the balance sheet, as inventory amounts. If you are not familiar with income statements and balance sheets, or with terms such as cost of goods sold and inventory costs, you will find an overview of them in Chapter 17.

Product Costs and Period Costs

product costs Costs identified with goods produced or purchased for resale.

period costs Costs that are deducted as expenses during the current period without going through an inventory stage.

When preparing both income statements and balance sheets, accountants frequently distinguish between *product costs* and *period costs*. **Product costs** are costs identified with goods produced or purchased for resale. Product costs are initially identified as part of the inventory on hand. These product costs (inventoriable costs) become expenses (in the form of *cost of goods sold*) only when the inventory is sold. In contrast, **period costs** are costs that are deducted as expenses during the current period without going through an inventory stage.

For example, look at the top half of Exhibit 4-3. A merchandising company (retailer or wholesaler) acquires goods for resale without changing their basic form. The only product cost is the purchase cost of the merchandise. Unsold goods are held as merchandise inventory cost and are shown as an asset on a balance sheet. As the goods are sold, their costs become expenses in the form of "cost of goods sold."

A merchandising company also has a variety of selling and administrative expenses. These costs are period costs because they are deducted from revenue as expenses without ever being regarded as a part of inventory.

Objective 4

Differentiate between product costs and period costs, identifying examples of each

The bottom half of Exhibit 4-3 illustrates product and period costs in a manufacturing firm. Note that direct materials are transformed into salable form with the help of direct labor and factory overhead. All these costs are product costs because they are allocated to inventory until the goods are sold. As in merchandising accounting, the selling and administrative expenses are not regarded as product costs but are treated as period costs.[1]

Be sure you are clear on the differences between merchandising accounting and manufacturing accounting for such costs as insurance, depreciation, and wages. In merchandising accounting, all such items are period costs (expenses of the current period). In manufacturing accounting, many of these items are related to production activities and thus, as factory overhead, are product costs (become expenses in the form of cost of goods sold as the inventory is sold).

In both merchandising and manufacturing accounting, selling and general administrative costs are period costs. Thus the inventory cost of a manufactured product *excludes* sales salaries, sales commissions, advertising, legal, public relations, and the president's salary. *Manufacturing overhead* is traditionally regarded as a part of finished-goods inventory cost, whereas *selling* expenses and *general administrative* expenses are not.

Objective 5

Explain how the financial statements of merchandisers and manufacturers differ because of the types of goods they sell

Balance Sheet Presentation

Examining both halves of Exhibit 4-3 together, you can see that the balance sheets of manufacturers and merchandisers differ with respect to inventories. The merchandiser's "inventory account" is supplanted in a manufacturing concern by three inventory classes that help managers trace all product costs through the production process to the time of sales.

---

[1] This distinction between product and period costs has a long tradition for both internal and external reporting. During the late 1980s new U.S. income tax requirements forced companies to treat many selling and administrative costs as product instead of period costs. These special requirements, however, are confined to reporting to income tax authorities only.

Exhibit 4-3   Relationships of Product Costs and Period Costs

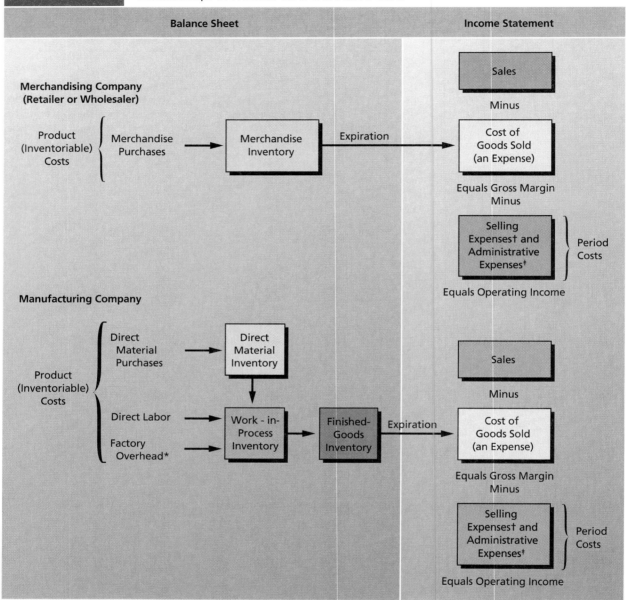

* Examples: indirect labor, factory supplies, insurance, and depreciation on plant.
† Examples: insurance on salespersons' cars, depreciation on salespersons' cars, salespersons' salaries.
‡ Examples: insurance on corporate headquarters building, depreciation on office equipment, clerical salaries.

Note particularly that when insurance and depreciation relate to the manufacturing function, they are inventoriable, but when they relate to selling and administration, they are not inventoriable.

These classes are:

- *Direct-materials inventory*: Materials on hand and awaiting use in the production process.
- *Work-in-process inventory*: Goods undergoing the production process but not yet fully completed. Costs include appropriate amounts of the three major manufacturing costs (direct material, direct labor, and factory overhead).
- *Finished-goods inventory*: Goods fully completed but not yet sold.

The only essential difference between the structure of the balance sheet of a manufacturer and that of a retailer or wholesaler would appear in their respective current asset sections:

Current Asset Sections of Balance Sheets

Manufacturer			Retailer or Wholesaler	
Cash		$ 4,000	Cash	$ 4,000
Receivables		25,000	Receivables	25,000
Finished goods	$32,000			
Work in process	22,000			
Direct material	23,000			
Total inventories		77,000	Merchandise inventories	77,000
Other current assets		1,000	Other current assets	1,000
Total current assets		$107,000	Total current assets	$107,000

Unit Costs for Product Costing

Reporting cost of goods sold or inventory values requires costs to be assigned to units of product. Assume the following:

Total cost of goods manufactured	$40,000,000
Total units manufactured	10,000,000
Unit cost of product for inventory purposes ($40,000,000 ÷ 10,000,000)	$ 4

If some of the 10 million units manufactured are still unsold at the end of the period, a part of the $40 million cost of goods manufactured will be "held back" as a cost of the ending inventory of finished goods (and shown as an asset on a balance sheet). The remainder becomes "cost of goods sold" for the current period and is shown as an expense on the income statement.

Costs and Income Statements

In income statements, the detailed reporting of selling and administrative expenses is typically the same for manufacturing and merchandising organizations, but the cost of goods sold is different:

Manufacturer	Retailer or Wholesaler
Manufacturing cost of goods produced and then sold, usually composed of the three major categories of cost: direct materials, direct labor, and factory overhead.	Merchandise cost of goods sold, usually composed of the purchase cost of items, including freight in, that are acquired and then resold.

Consider the additional details as they are presented in the model income statement of a manufacturing company in Exhibit 4-4. The $40 million cost of goods manufactured is subdivided into the major components of direct materials, direct labor, and factory overhead. In contrast, a wholesale or retail company would replace the entire "cost-of-goods-manufactured" section with a single line, "cost of goods purchased."

Exhibit 4-4				
Model Income Statement, Manufacturing Company	Sales (8,000,000 units @ $10)			$80,000,000
	Cost of goods manufactured and sold			
	Beginning finished-goods inventory		$ —0—	
	Cost of goods manufactured			
	Direct materials used	$20,000,000		
	Direct labor	12,000,000		
	Factory overhead	8,000,000	40,000,000	
	Cost of goods available for sale		$40,000,000	
	Ending finished-goods inventory, 2,000,000 units @ $4		8,000,000	
	Cost of goods sold (an expense)			32,000,000
	Gross margin or gross profit			$48,000,000
	Less: other expenses			
	Selling costs (an expense)		$30,000,000	
	General and administrative costs (an expense)		8,000,000	38,000,000
	Operating income*			$10,000,000

*Also net income in this example because other expenses such as interest and income taxes are ignored here for simplicity.

The terms "costs" and "expenses" are often used loosely by accountants and managers. "Expenses" denote all costs deducted from (matched against) revenue in a given period. On the other hand, "costs" is a much broader term and is used to describe both an asset (the cost of inventory) and an expense (the cost of goods sold). Thus manufacturing costs are funneled into an income statement as an expense (in the form of cost of goods sold) via the multistep inventory procedure shown earlier in Exhibit 4-3. In contrast, selling and general administrative costs are commonly deemed expenses immediately as they are incurred.

Transactions Affecting Inventories

The three manufacturing inventory accounts are affected by the following transactions:

- Direct Materials Inventory
    Increased by purchases of direct materials
    Decreased by use of direct materials
- Work-in-Process Inventory
    Increased by use of direct materials, direct labor, or factory overhead
    Decreased by transfer of completed goods to finished-goods inventory

- Finished-Goods Inventory
  Increased by transfers of completed goods from work-in-process inventory
  Decreased by the amount of cost of goods sold at time of sale

Direct labor and factory overhead are used at the same time they are acquired. Therefore, they are entered directly into work-in-process inventory and have no separate inventory account. In contrast, direct materials are often purchased in advance of their use and held in inventory for some time.

Exhibit 4-5

Inventory Transactions (in millions)

Transaction	Direct Materials Inventory	Work-in-Process Inventory	Finished-Goods Inventory
Beginning balance	$ 0	$ 0	$ 0
Purchase direct materials	+30	—	—
Use direct materials	–20	+20	—
Acquire and use direct labor	—	+12	—
Acquire and use factory overhead	—	+8	—
Complete production	—	–40	+40
Sell goods and record cost of goods sold	—	—	$–32
Ending balance	$ 10	$ 0	$ 8

Exhibit 4-5 traces the effects of each transaction. It uses the dollar amounts from Exhibit 4-4, with one exception. Purchases of direct materials totaled $30 million, with $20 million used in production (as shown in Exhibit 4-4) and $10 million left in inventory at the end of the period. As the bottom of Exhibit 4-5 indicates, the ending balance sheet amounts would be:

Direct-material inventory	$10,000,000
Work-in-process inventory	0
Finished-goods inventory	8,000,000
Total inventories	$18,000,000

■ COST BEHAVIOR AND INCOME STATEMENTS

In addition to differences between manufacturing and merchandising firms, manufacturers differ among themselves in accounting for costs on income statements, with some favoring an *absorption* approach and others using a *contribution* approach. To highlight the different effects of these approaches, we will assume that in 19X2 the Samson Company has direct-material costs of $7 million and direct-labor costs of $4 million. Assume also that the company incurred the factory overhead illustrated in Exhibit 4-6 and the selling and administrative expenses illustrated in Exhibit 4-7. Total sales were $20 million. Finally, assume that the units produced are equal to the units sold. That is, there is no change in inventory levels. (In this way, we avoid some complications that are unnecessary and unimportant at this stage.[2])

---

[2] These complexities are discussed in Chapters 15 and 16.

Exhibit 4-6

Samson Company
Schedules of Factory
Overhead (Product
Costs) for the Year
Ended December 31,
19X2 (thousands of
dollars)

Schedule 1: Variable Costs

Supplies (lubricants, expendable tools, coolants, sandpaper)	$ 150	
Material-handling labor (forklift operators)	700	
Repairs	100	
Power	50	$1,000

Schedule 2: Fixed Costs

Managers' salaries	$ 200	
Employee training	90	
Factory picnic and holiday party	10	
Supervisory salaries	700	
Depreciation, plant and equipment	1,800	
Property taxes	150	
Insurance	50	3,000
Total manufacturing overhead		$4,000

Exhibit 4-7

Samson Company
Schedules of Selling
and Administrative
Expenses (Period
Costs) for the Year
Ended December 31,
19X2 (thousands of
dollars)

Schedule 3: Selling Expenses

Variable		
Sales commissions	$ 700	
Shipping expenses for products sold	300	$1,000
Fixed		
Advertising	$ 700	
Sales salaries	1,000	
Other	300	2,000
Total selling expenses		$3,000

Schedule 4: Administrative Expenses

Variable		
Some clerical wages	$ 80	
Computer time rented	20	$ 100
Fixed		
Office salaries	$ 100	
Other salaries	200	
Depreciation on office facilities	100	
Public-accounting fees	40	
Legal fees	100	
Other	360	900
Total administrative expenses		$1,000

Objective 6

Construct income
statements of a
manufacturing
company in both
the absorption
and contribution
formats

Note that Exhibits 4-6 and 4-7 subdivide costs as variable or fixed. Many companies do not make such subdivisions in their income statements. Furthermore, when such subdivisions are made, sometimes arbitrary decisions are necessary as to whether a given cost is variable, fixed, or partially fixed (for example, repairs). Nevertheless, to aid decision making, many companies are attempting to report the extent to which their costs are approximately variable or fixed.

Absorption Approach

absorption approach
A costing approach that considers all factory overhead (both variable and fixed) to be product (inventoriable) costs that become an expense in the form of manufacturing cost of goods sold only as sales occur.

Exhibit 4-8 presents Samson's income statement using the **absorption approach** (*absorption costing*), the approach used by most companies. Firms that take this approach consider all factory overhead (both variable and fixed) to be product (inventoriable) costs that become an expense in the form of manufacturing cost of goods sold only as sales occur.

Note in Exhibit 4-8 that gross profit or gross margin is the difference between sales and the *manufacturing* cost of goods sold. Note too that the *primary classifications* of costs on the income statement are by three major management *functions*: manufacturing, selling, and administrative.

Exhibit 4-8			
Samson Company Absorption Income Statement for the Year Ended December 31, 19X2 (thousands of dollars)			

Sales			$20,000
Less: manufacturing costs of goods sold			
Direct material		$7,000	
Direct labor		4,000	
Factory overhead (Schedules 1 plus 2)*		4,000	15,000
Gross margin or gross profit			$ 5,000
Selling expenses (Schedule 3)		$3,000	
Administrative expenses (Schedule 4)		1,000	
Total selling and administrative expenses			4,000
Operating income			$ 1,000

* Note: Schedules 1 and 2 are in Exhibit 4-6. Schedules 3 and 4 are in Exhibit 4-7.

Contribution Approach

contribution approach A method of internal (management accounting) reporting that emphasizes the distinction between variable and fixed costs for the purpose of better decision making.

In contrast, Exhibit 4-9 presents Samson's income statement using the **contribution approach** (*variable costing* or *direct costing*). The contribution approach is not allowed for external financial reporting. However, many companies use this approach for internal (management accounting) purposes and an absorption format for external purposes, because they expect the benefits of making better decisions to exceed the extra costs of using different reporting systems simultaneously.

For decision purposes, the major difference between the contribution approach and the absorption approach is that the former emphasizes the distinction between variable and fixed costs. Its primary classifications of costs are by variable and fixed *cost behavior patterns*, not by *business functions*.

The contribution income statement provides a *contribution margin*, which is computed after deducting from revenue all variable costs including variable selling and administrative costs. This approach makes it easier to understand the impact of changes in sales demand on operating income. It also dovetails neatly with the CVP analysis illustrated in Chapter 2.

Exhibit 4-9

Samson Company
Contribution Income
Statement for
the Year Ended
December 31, 19X2
(thousands of
dollars)

Sales		$20,000
Less: variable expenses		
Direct material	$ 7,000	
Direct labor	4,000	
Variable indirect manufacturing costs (Schedule 1)*	1,000	
Total variable manufacturing cost of goods sold	$12,000	
Variable selling expenses (Schedule 3)	1,000	
Variable administrative expenses (Schedule 4)	100	
Total variable expenses		13,100
Contribution margin		$ 6,900
Less: fixed expenses		
Manufacturing (Schedule 2)	$ 3,000	
Selling (Schedule 3)	2,000	
Administrative (Schedule 4)	900	5,900
Operating income		$ 1,000

* Note: Schedules 1 and 2 are in Exhibit 4-6. Schedules 3 and 4 are in Exhibit 4-7.

The contribution approach stresses the lump-sum amount of fixed costs to be recouped before net income emerges. This highlighting of total fixed costs focuses management attention on fixed-cost behavior and control in making both short-run and long-run plans. Remember that advocates of the contribution approach do not maintain that fixed costs are unimportant or irrelevant. They do stress, however, that the distinctions between behaviors of variable and fixed costs are crucial for certain decisions.

The difference between the gross margin (from the absorption approach) and the contribution margin (from the contribution approach) is striking in manufacturing companies. Why? Because fixed manufacturing costs are regarded as a part of cost of goods sold, and these fixed costs reduce the gross margin accordingly. However, *fixed* manufacturing costs do not reduce the contribution margin, which is affected solely by revenues and *variable* costs.

The implications of the *absorption approach* and the *contribution approach* for decision making are discussed in the next chapter.

■ ACTIVITY-BASED ACCOUNTING, VALUE-ADDED COSTING, AND JUST-IN-TIME PRODUCTION

In the past decade, many companies in the United States, struggling to keep up with competitors from Japan, Germany, and other countries, adopted new management philosophies and developed new production technologies. In many cases, these changes prompted corresponding changes in accounting systems.

For example, Borg-Warner's Automotive Chain Systems Operation transformed its manufacturing operation to a just-in-time manufacturing system with work cells. This change in the way manufacturing was done made the traditional accounting system obsolete. A new cost accounting system coupled with the new production systems "improved the overall reporting, controls, and efficiency dramatically."[3]

[3] A. Phillips and Don Collins, "How Borg-Warner Made the Transition From Pile Accounting to JIT," *Management Accounting*, October 1990, pp. 32–35.

Contribution Approach and Activity-Based Costing

Since the 1950s a growing number of firms have used the contribution approach for internal income statements. However, with the emergence of activity-based costing (ABC) in the late 1980s, some ABC proponents suggested that absorption costing information from an ABC system was more appropriate than contribution-based information for decision making. Now in the 1990s, according to Robert Koehler, "the combination of activity-based costing . . . and the contribution-margin approach will give a true overview of the whole cost picture."

One company that has combined ABC with the contribution approach is the Elgin Sweeper Company, the leading manufacturer of motorized street sweepers in North America, with annual sales of $50 million. In the late 1980s Elgin set out to install a cost-management system so that the effects of management decisions on costs could be pinpointed. The first step was to perform a cost-behavior study to identify the costs of Elgin's various activities. The company compiled a list of cost drivers that included actual labor dollars, actual labor hours, units shipped, units produced, purchase orders, service parts sales dollars, service orders shipped, workdays, calendar days, completed engineering change notices, engineering hours worked, and many others. Then costs that varied with each cost driver were identified and measured.

After measuring cost behavior, product-line contribution statements were prepared. These were designed to help managers see the results of their resource-allocation decisions and to assess the outcomes of strategic decisions. Each statement had three sections for each product line: (1) contribution margin, (2) direct margin, and (3) pretax income.

To measure *contribution margin*, costs driven by volume-related cost drivers were deducted from revenues to show the effects of volume on profits. The *direct margin* included a deduction of costs directly related to the product line but not necessarily related to volume. This provided a measure of the economic results of the full product line. Finally, pretax income included a deduction of all remaining fixed costs.

Elgin is still in the process of improving its cost-management system. Refinements of its product line contribution statements are planned, as are increased involvement of production supervisors with the cost-driver concept and the elimination of non-value-added activity. Elgin expects the result of its cost-management system to be "people making intelligent, informed, and cost-effective decisions." ■

Source: Adapted from R. W. Koehler, "Triple-Threat Strategy," Management Accounting, October 1991, pp. 30–34; and J. Callan, W. Tredup, and R. Wissinger, "Elgin Sweeper Company's Journey Toward Cost Management," Management Accounting, July 1991, pp. 24–27.

Activity-Based Accounting

activity-based accounting (ABA) (activity-based costing [ABC]) A system that first accumulates overhead costs for each of the activities of an organization, and then assigns the costs of activities to the products, services, or other cost objects that caused that activity.

The primary focus of the changes in operations and accounting has been an increased attention to the cost of the *activities* undertaken to design, produce, sell, and deliver a company's products or services. **Activity-based accounting (ABA)** or **activity-based-costing (ABC)** systems first accumulate overhead costs for each of the *activities* of an organization, and then assign the costs of activities to the products, services, or other cost objects that caused that activity.

Consider the Salem manufacturing plant of a major appliance producer. Exhibit 4-10 contrasts the traditional costing system with an ABC system. In the traditional cost system, the portion of *total overhead* allocated to a product depends on the proportion of *total direct-labor-hours* consumed in making the product. In the ABC system, significant overhead activities (machining, assembly, quality inspection, etc.) and related resources are separately identified and traced to products using cost drivers—machine hours, number of parts, number of inspections, etc. In the ABC system, the amount of overhead costs allocated to a product depends on the proportion of total machine hours, total parts, total inspections, and so on, consumed in making the product. One large overhead cost pool has been broken into several pools, each associated with a key activity. We now consider a more in-depth illustration of the design of an ABC system.

| Exhibit 4-10 | Traditional and Activity-Based Cost Systems |

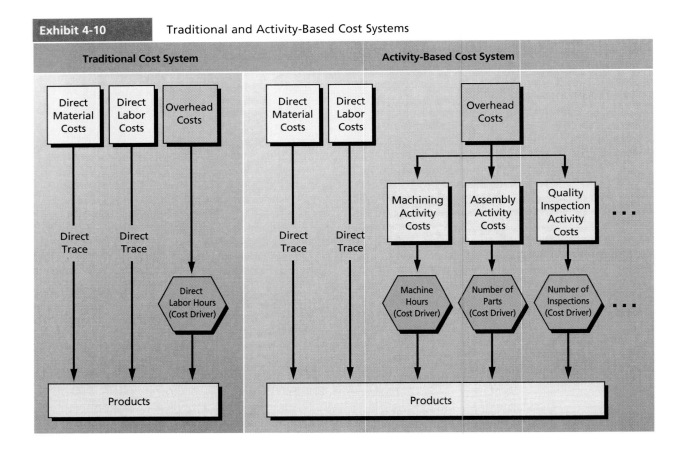

Illustration of Activity-Based Costing[4]

Consider the Billing Department at Portland Power Company (PPC), an electric utility. The Billing Department (BD) at PPC provides account inquiry and bill-printing services for two major classes of customers—residential and commercial. Currently, the BD services 120,000 residential and 20,000 commercial customer accounts.

Two factors are having a significant impact on PPC's profitability. First, deregulation of the power industry has led to increased competition and lower rates, so PPC must find ways of reducing its operating costs. Second, the demand for power in PPC's area will increase due to the addition of a large housing development and

[4]Much of the discussion in this section is based on an illustration used in "Implementing Activity-Based Costing—The Modeling Approach," a workshop sponsored by the Institute of Management Accountants and Sapling Corporation.

a shopping center. The marketing department estimates that residential demand will increase by almost 50% and commercial demand will increase by 10% during the next year. Since the BD is currently operating at full capacity, it needs to find ways to create capacity to service the expected increase in demand. A local service bureau has offered to take over the BD functions at an attractive lower cost (compared to the current cost). The service bureau's proposal is to provide all the functions of the BD at $3.50 per account regardless of the type of account.

Exhibit 4-11 depicts the residential and commercial customer classes (cost objects) and the resources used to support the BD. The costs associated with

| Exhibit 4-11 | Current (Traditional) Costing System: Portland Power Company—Billing Department |

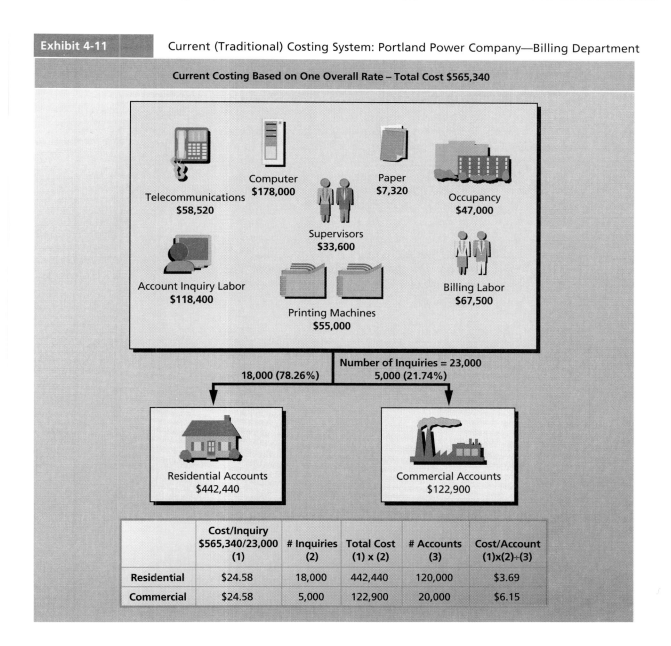

Current Costing Based on One Overall Rate – Total Cost $565,340

Telecommunications $58,520

Computer $178,000

Paper $7,320

Occupancy $47,000

Supervisors $33,600

Account Inquiry Labor $118,400

Billing Labor $67,500

Printing Machines $55,000

Number of Inquiries = 23,000
18,000 (78.26%)   5,000 (21.74%)

Residential Accounts $442,440

Commercial Accounts $122,900

	Cost/Inquiry $565,340/23,000 (1)	# Inquiries (2)	Total Cost (1) x (2)	# Accounts (3)	Cost/Account (1)x(2)÷(3)
Residential	$24.58	18,000	442,440	120,000	$3.69
Commercial	$24.58	5,000	122,900	20,000	$6.15

the BD are all indirect—they cannot be identified specifically and exclusively with either customer class in an economically feasible way. The BD used a traditional costing system that allocated all support costs based on the number of account inquiries of the two customer classes. Exhibit 4-11 shows that the cost of the resources used in the BD last month was $565,340. BD received 23,000 account inquiries during the month, so the cost per inquiry was $565,340 ÷ 23,000 = $24.58. There were 18,000 residential account inquiries, 78.26% of the total. Thus residential accounts were charged with 78.26% of the support costs while commercial accounts were charged with 21.74%. The resulting cost per account is $3.69 and $6.15 for residential and commercial accounts, respectively.

Management believed that the actual consumption of support resources was much greater than 22% for commercial accounts because of their complexity. For example, commercial accounts average 50 lines per bill compared with only 12 for residential accounts. Management was also concerned about activities such as correspondence (and supporting labor) resulting from customer inquiries because these activities are costly but do not add value to PPC's services from the customer's perspective. However, management wanted a more thorough understanding of key BD activities and their interrelationships before making important decisions that would impact PPC's profitability. The company decided to perform a study of the BD using activity-based costing. The following is a description of the study and its results.

The activity-based-costing study was performed by a team of managers from the BD and the chief financial officer from PPC. The team followed a four-step procedure to conduct the study.

Step 1: Determine cost objectives, key activities centers, resources, and related cost drivers. Management had set the objective for the study—determine the BD cost per account for each customer class. The team identified the following activities, and related cost drivers for the BD through interviews with appropriate personnel.

Objective 7

Identify the steps involved in the design and implementation of an activity-based-costing system

Activity Centers	Cost Drivers
Account billing	Number of lines
Bill verification	Number of accounts
Account inquiry	Number of labor hours
Correspondence	Number of letters

The four key BD activity centers are *account billing, bill verification, account inquiry, and correspondence*. The resources shown in Exhibit 4-11 support these major activity centers. Cost drivers were selected based on two criteria:

1. There had to be a reasonable cause-effect relationship between the driver unit and the consumption of resources and/or the occurrence of supporting activities.
2. Data on the cost-driver units had to be available.

Step 2: Develop a process-based map representing the flow of activities, resources, and their interrelationships. An important phase of any activity-based analysis is identifying the interrelationships between key activities and the resources consumed. This is typically done by interviewing key personnel. Once the linkages between activities and resources are identified, a process map is drawn that provides a visual representation of the operations of the BD.

Exhibit 4-12 is a process map that depicts the flow of activities and resources at the BD.[5] Note that there are no costs on Exhibit 4-12. The management team first

Exhibit 4-12 Process Map of Billing Department Activities

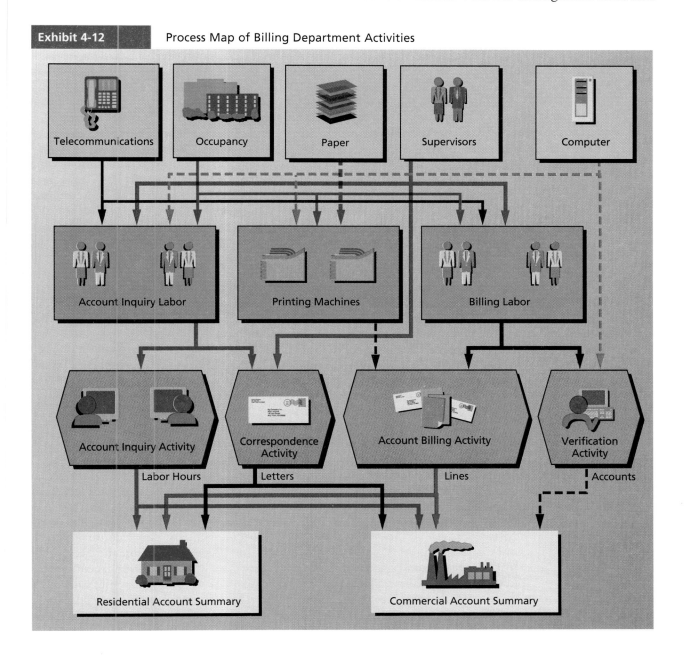

---

[5] This example illustrates the process-based modeling approach to activity-based costing. For a more detailed description of the process modeling approach see Raef A. Lawson, "Beyond ABC: Process-Based Costing," *Journal of Cost Management*, Vol. 8, No. 3 (Fall 1994), pp. 33–43. Also, for a discussion of how one major firm used process-based costing to implement ABC in its billing center, see T. Hobdy, J. Thomson, and P. Sharman, "Activity-Based Management at AT&T," *Management Accounting* (April 1994), pp. 35–39.

focused on understanding business processes. Costs were not considered until Step 3, after the key interrelationships of the business were understood.

Consider residential accounts. Three key activities support these accounts: account inquiry, correspondence, and account billing. Account inquiry activity consumes account inquiry labor time. Account inquiry laborers, in turn, use telecommunication and computer resources, occupy space, and are supervised. Correspondence is sometimes necessary as a result of inquiries. This activity requires account inquiry laborers who are supervised. The account billing activity is performed by billing laborers using printing machines The printing machines occupy space, and require paper and computer resources. Billing laborers also occupy space, use telecommunucations, and are supervised. The costs of each of the resources consumed were determined during Step 3—data collection.

Step 3: Collect relevant data concerning costs and the physical flow of the cost-driver units among resources and activities. Using the process map as a guide, BD accountants collected the required cost and operational data by further interviews with relevant personnel. Sources of data include the accounting records, special studies, and sometimes "best estimates of managers."

Exhibit 4-13 is a graphical representation of the data collected for the four activity centers identified in Step 1. For each activity center, data collected included traceable costs and the physical flow of cost-driver units. For example, Exhibit 4-13 shows traceable costs of $235,777 for the account billing activity. Traceable costs include the costs of the printing machines ($55,000 from Exhibit 4-11) plus portions of the costs of all other resources that support the billing activity (paper, occupancy, computer, and billing labor). Notice that the total traceable costs of $205,332 + $35,384 + $235,777 + $88,847 = $565,340 in Exhibit 4-13 equals the total indirect costs in Exhibit 4-11. Next, the physical flow of cost-driver units was determined for each activity or cost object. For each activity center, the traceable costs were divided by the sum of the physical flows to establish a cost per cost-driver unit.

Objective 8

Calculate activity-based costs for cost objects

Step 4: Calculate and interpret the new activity-based information. The activity-based cost per account for each customer class can be determined from the data in Step 3. Exhibit 4-14 shows the computations.

Examine the last two items in Exhibit 4-14. Notice that traditional costing overcosted the high-volume residential accounts and substantially undercosted the low-volume, complex commercial accounts. The cost per account for residential accounts using ABC is $2.28, which is $1.41 (or 38%) less than the $3.69 cost generated by the traditional costing system. The cost per account for commercial accounts is $14.57, which is $8.42 (or 137%) more than the $6.15 cost from the traditional cost system. Management's belief that traditional costing was undercosting commercial accounts was confirmed. PPC's management now has more accurate cost information for planning and decision-making purposes.

These results are common when companies perform activity-based-costing studies—high volume cost objects with simple processes are overcosted when only one volume-based cost driver is used. In the BD, this volume-based cost-driver was the number of inquiries. Which system makes more sense—the existing allocation system that "spreads" all support costs to customer classes based solely on the number of inquiries, or the activity-based-costing system that identifies key activities and assigns costs based on the consumption of units of cost drivers chosen for each

Exhibit 4-13   ABC System: Portland Power Company—Billing Department

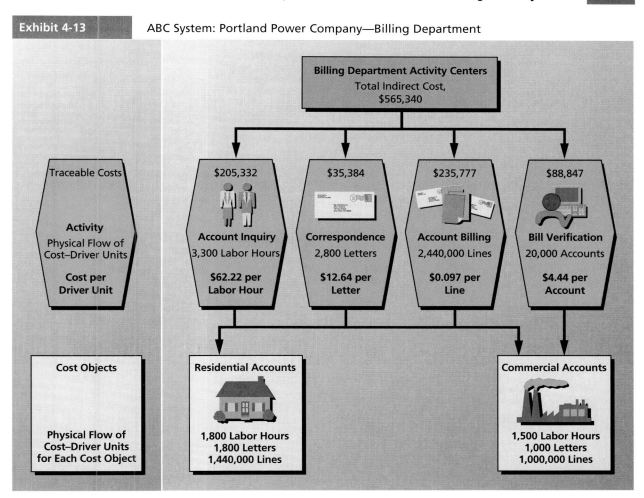

key activity? For PPC, the probable benefits of the new activity-based-costing system appear to outweigh the costs of implementing and maintaining the new cost system. However, the cost-benefit balance must be assessed on a case-by-case basis.

Summary of Activity-Based Costing

Activity-based accounting systems can turn many indirect manufacturing overhead costs into direct costs, costs identified specifically with given cost objectives. Appropriate selection of activities and cost drivers allows managers to trace many manufacturing overhead costs to cost objectives just as specifically as they have traced direct-material and direct-labor costs. Because activity-based accounting systems classify more costs as direct than do traditional systems, managers have greater confidence in the accuracy of the costs of products and services reported by activity-based systems.

Activity-based accounting systems are more complex and costly than traditional systems, so not all companies use them. But more and more organizations

Exhibit 4-14   Key Results of Activity-Based-Costing Study

Driver Costs

Activity/Resource (Driver Units)	Traceable Costs (From Exhibit 4-13) (1)	Total Physical Flow of Driver Units (From Exhibit 4-13) (2)	Cost per Driver Unit (1)÷(2)
Account inquiry (labor hours)	$205,332	3,300 Hours	$62.2218
Correspondence (letters)	35,384	2,800 Letters	12.6371
Account billing (lines)	235,777	2,440,000 Lines	0.09663
Bill verification (accounts)	88,847	20,000 Accounts	4.44235

Cost per Customer Class

		Residential		Commercial	
	Cost per Driver Unit	Physical Flow of Driver Units	Cost	Physical Flow of Driver Units	Cost
Account inquiry	$62.2218	1,800 Hrs.	$111,999	1,500 Hrs.	$ 93,333
Correspondence	$12.6371	1,800 Ltrs.	22,747	1,000 Ltrs.	12,637
Account billing	$0.09663	1,440,000 Lines	139,147	1,000,000 Lines	96,630
Bill verification	$4.44235	0	0	20,000 Accts.	88,847
Total cost			$273,893		$291,447
Number of accounts			120,000		20,000
Cost per account			$2.28		$14.57
Cost per account, traditional system from Exhibit 4-11			$3.69		$6.15

in both manufacturing and nonmanufacturing industries are adopting activity-based systems for a variety of reasons:

Objective 9

Explain why activity-based-costing systems are being adopted by more and more organizations

- Fierce competitive pressure has resulted in shrinking profit margins. Companies may know their overall margin, but they often do not believe in the accuracy of the margins for *individual* products or services. Some are winners and some are losers—but which ones? Accurate costs are essential for answering this question.

- Business complexity has increased, which results in greater diversity in the types of products and services as well as customer classes. Therefore, the consumption of a company's shared resources also varies substantially across products and customers.

- New production techniques have increased the proportion of indirect costs—that is, indirect costs are far more important in today's world-class manufacturing environment. In many industries direct labor is being replaced by automated equipment. Indirect costs are sometimes over 50 percent of total cost.

- The rapid pace of technological change has shortened product life cycles. Hence, companies do not have time to make price or cost adjustments once costing errors are discovered.

- The costs associated with bad decisions that result from inaccurate cost determinations are substantial (bids lost due to overcosted products, hidden losses from undercosted products, failure to detect activities that are not cost effective, etc.). Companies with accurate costs have a huge advantage over those with inaccurate costs.

- Computer technology has reduced the costs of developing and operating cost systems that track many activities.

Activity-Based Management

What's the next step beyond activity-based costing? Activity-based management. According to Peter Turney, one of the leaders in activity-based costing (ABC), ABC "can supply useful information, but what a company does with that information is what counts." In activity-based management, managers apply the information gathered using ABC to make better decisions.

In the broadest terms, activity-based management aims "to improve the value received by customers" and "to improve profits by providing this value," states Turney. How does activity-based management achieve these objectives?

Activity-based management focuses on managing activities—including identifying non-value-added activities that can be eliminated—and making sure that needed activities are carried out efficiently. Of course, each organization has its own set of activities. To improve operations, management must search out unnecessary or inefficient activities, determine the cost drivers for the activities, and change those cost drivers. For example, moving a partly finished product from the end of one production process to the start of another provides no value to the customer, but it is a necessary step. The distance between the processes drives this particular cost. By decreasing the distance, the cost can be reduced, if not eliminated.

Focusing on activities alerts managers to opportunities to save costs. Peter Turney cites Stockham Valve and Fittings, which used ABC to

- produce parts with the lowest cost process,

- design parts to minimize manufacturing costs,

- modify equipment to reduce costs,

- increase prices of products priced below ABC cost, and

- drop unprofitable products.

Using ABC information to improve operating decisions often justifies the added expense of an ABC system. ∎

Source: Adapted from Peter B. B. Turney, "Activity-Based Management," Management Accounting, *January 1992, pp. 20–25.*

---

cost-management system Identifies how management's decisions affect costs, by first measuring the resources used in performing the organization's activities and then assessing the effects on costs of changes in those activities.

value-added cost The necessary cost of an activity that cannot be eliminated without affecting a product's value to the customer.

non-value-added costs Costs that can be eliminated without affecting a product's value to the customer.

Cost-Management Systems and Value-Added Costing

To support managers' decisions better, accountants go beyond simply determining the cost of products and services. They develop cost-management systems. A **cost-management system** identifies how management's decisions affect costs. To do so, it first measures the resources used in performing the organization's activities and then assesses the effects on costs of changes in those activities. Cost management makes extensive use of *activity analysis*, which was introduced in Chapter 3, pages 88–89.

The cornerstone of cost management is distinguishing between value-added costs and non-value-added costs. A **value-added cost** is the cost of an activity that cannot be eliminated without affecting a product's value to the customer. Value-added costs are necessary (as long as the activity that drives such costs is performed efficiently). In contrast, companies try to minimize **non-value-added costs**, costs that *can* be eliminated without affecting a product's value to the customer. Activities such as handling and storing inventories, transporting partly finished products from one part of the plant to another, and changing the setup of production-line operations to produce a different model of the product are all non-value-adding activities that can be reduced, if not eliminated, by careful redesign of the plant layout and the production process. Often accounting is regarded as a non-value-adding activity. Although it cannot be eliminated, organizations should be sure that the benefits derived from accounting information exceed the costs.

Identifying Activities, Resources, and Cost Drivers

Arkansas Blue Cross Blue Shield (ABCBS) is the largest health insurer in the state of Arkansas with annual revenue of more than $450 million. Recently, ABCBS implemented activity-based management (ABM). ABM is using activity-based information in the decision-making process. The identification of key activities, resources, and cost drivers was one of the early steps performed.

- A pilot study was performed on one area of the firm—information management. The criteria for selection of a pilot area included significant costs, the possibility of improving the existing cost-allocation system, access to data, and a receptive staff.

- The cost objectives were defined—the internal customers of information management.

- Activities, resources, and cost drivers were identified based on meetings with managers. Examples of key activities are Production (job scheduling, production control), Electronic Media Claims Processing, Printing, and Mail Processing. Resources include Systems Programmers, Mail Labor, Print Labor, Tape Labor, Data Base Administrators, 3080 CPU, 3090 CPU, LSM (robotic cartridge system), DASD (hard disk storage), and Telecommunications. Cost drivers included CPU minutes, single-density volumes (DASD), number of tape/cartridge mounts (LSM), number of jobs, and number of CRTs (telecommunications).

- Once the key activities, resources, and drivers were identified, a process map of the operations

of the information management function was developed by the project team. This map reflected the flow of activities and resources in support of the cost centers. The map also identified the data that needed to be collected to complete the study. (Note that the process map is very similar to Exhibit 4-12 in appearance.)

- Once the ABC model was built and validated, the results were interpreted and recommendations for improvement were made.

As a result of the ABC study, the following actions were taken by management:

- A separate utility meter was placed on the computer room.

- CRT purchases are now charged directly to the user. Maintenance costs for CRTs are now assigned based on CRT count.

- Three new cost centers were created: EMC Systems, Change Control, and Production Control.

- CPU was upgraded.

ABCBS is now in the process of expanding the new ABM system corporate-wide to include purchasing, actuarial, advertising, and claims processing. The company is also using the new ABM system for activity-based budgeting. ■

Source: From "Implementing Activity-Based Costing— The Model Approach," Institute of Management Accountants and Sapling Corporation, Orlando, November 1994.

JIT Systems

just-in-time (JIT) production system
A system in which an organization purchases materials and parts and produces components just when they are needed in the production process, the goal being to have zero inventory, because holding inventory is a non-value-added activity.

Attempts to minimize non-value-added costs have led many organizations to adopt JIT systems (see Chapter 1, page 20) to eliminate waste and improve quality. In a **just-in-time (JIT) production system**, an organization purchases materials and parts and produces components *just* when they are needed in the production process. Goods are not produced until it is time for them to be shipped to a customer. The goal is to have zero inventory, because holding inventory is a non-value-added activity.

JIT companies are customer-oriented because customer orders drive the production process. An order triggers the immediate delivery of materials, followed by production and delivery of the goods. Instead of producing inventory and hoping an order will come, a JIT system produces products directly for received orders. Several factors are crucial to the success of JIT systems:

1. *Focus on quality*: JIT companies try to involve all employees in controlling quality. Although any system can seek quality improvements, JIT systems emphasize *total quality control (TQC)* and *continuous improvement in quality*. Having all employees striving for zero defects minimizes non-value-added activities such as inspection and rework for defective items.

production cycle time The time from initiating production to delivering the goods to the customer.

2. *Short* **production cycle times**, *the time from initiating production to delivering the goods to the customer*: Keeping production cycle times short allows timely response to customer orders and reduces the level of inventories. Many JIT companies have achieved remarkable reductions in production cycle times. For example, applying JIT methods in one AT&T division cut production cycle time by a factor of 12.

3. *Smooth flow of production*: Fluctuations in production rates inevitably lead to delays in delivery to customers and excess inventories. To achieve smooth production flow, JIT companies simplify the production process to reduce the possibilities of delay, develop close relationships with suppliers to assure timely delivery and high quality of purchased materials, and perform routine maintenance on equipment to prevent costly breakdowns.

Objective 10

Explain how JIT systems can reduce non-value-added activities

Many companies help achieve these objectives by improving the physical layout of their plants. In conventional manufacturing, similar machines (lathes, molding machines, drilling machines, etc.) are grouped together. Workers specialize in only one machine operation (operating either the molding or the drilling machine). There are at least two negative effects of such a layout. First, products must be moved from one area of the plant to another for required processing. This increases material handling costs and results in work-in-process inventories that can be substantial. These are non-value-added activities and costs. Second, the specialized labor resource is often idle—waiting for work-in-process. This wasted resource—labor time—is also non-value-added.

cellular manufacturing A production system in which machines are organized in cells according to the specific requirements of a product family.

In a JIT production system, machines are often organized in cells according to the specific requirements of a product family. This is called **cellular manufacturing**. Only the machines that are needed for the product family are in the cell, and these machines are located as close to each other as possible. Workers are trained to use all the cellular machines. Each cell (often shaped in the form of a "U") is a mini-factory or focused factory. Many problems associated with the conventional production layout are eliminated in cellular manufacturing. Work-in-process inventories are reduced or eliminated because there is no need for moving and storing inventory. Idle time is reduced or eliminated because workers are capable of moving from idle machine activity to needed activities. As a result, cycle times are reduced.

4. *Flexible production operations*: Two dimensions are important: facilities flexibility and employee flexibility. Facilities should be able to produce a variety of components and products to provide extra capacity when a particular product is in high demand and to avoid shut-down when a unique facility breaks down. Facilities should also require short setup times, the time it takes to switch from producing one product to another. Cross-training employees—training employees to do a variety of jobs—provides further flexibility. Multiskilled workers can fill in when a particular operation is overloaded and can reduce setup time. One company reported a reduction in setup time from 45 minutes to 1 minute by training production workers to perform the setup operations.

Accounting for a JIT system is often simpler than for other systems. Most cost accounting systems focus on determining product costs for inventory valuation. But JIT systems have minimal inventories, so there is less benefit from an elaborate inventory costing system. In true JIT systems, material, labor, and overhead costs can be charged directly to cost of goods sold because inventories are small enough to be ignored. All costs of production are assumed to apply to products that have already been sold. More details on accounting in JIT systems are found in Chapter 15.

Highlights To Remember

Many new terms were introduced in this chapter. Review those in bold print to make sure you know their exact meaning. Basic terms, such as cost, cost objective, cost accumulation, and cost allocation are especially important.

A major feature of costs for both manufacturing and nonmanufacturing organizations is whether the costs have a direct or an indirect relationship to cost objectives such as a department or product. Manufacturing costs (direct material, direct labor, and factory overhead) are traditionally regarded as product costs (inventoriable costs). In contrast, selling and administrative costs are period costs; hence they are typically deducted from revenue as expenses in the period incurred.

Financial statements for manufacturers differ from those of merchandisers. Costs such as utilities, wages, and depreciation, which are treated as period costs by a merchandising company, are product costs (part of factory overhead) for a manufacturing company if they are related to the manufacturing process. Balance sheets of manufacturers may include three inventory accounts: direct materials, work in process, and finished goods.

The contribution approach to preparing an income statement emphasizes the distinction between fixed and variable costs, and is a natural extension of the CVP analysis used in decisions. In contrast, the absorption approach emphasizes the distinction between manufacturing costs and selling and administrative costs.

Activity-based costing (ABC) and just-in-time (JIT) production systems are two approaches used by modern companies to improve their competitiveness. The focus of activity-based costing is on more accurate product or service costing. Management can then use ABC information to manage costs better. To manage costs, they try to eliminate non-value-added activities. The JIT approach focuses on improving operating efficiencies by reducing waste. JIT and ABC can be used separately or together—many modern companies use both.

Readers who now desire a more detailed treatment of product costing may jump to the study of Chapter 13 or 14 without losing continuity. In turn, Chapter 16 may be studied immediately after Chapter 8 if desired. Instructors differ regarding the appropriate sequence of chapters and topics.

Summary Problem for Your Review

Problem

1. Review the illustrations in Exhibits 4-6 through 4-9. Suppose that all variable costs fluctuate in direct proportion to units produced and sold, and that all fixed costs are unaffected over a wide range of production and sales. What would operating income have been if sales (at normal selling prices) had been $20.9 million instead of $20.0 million? Which statement, the absorption income statement or the contribution income statement, did you use as a framework for your answer? Why?

2. Suppose employee training (Exhibit 4-6) was regarded as a variable rather than a fixed cost at a rate of $90,000 ÷ 1,000,000 units, or $.09 per unit. How would your answer in part 1 change?

Solution

1. Operating income would increase from $1,000,000 to $1,310,500, computed as follows:

Increase in revenue	$ 900,000
Increase in total contribution margin:	
Contribution-margin ratio in contribution income statement (Exhibit 4-9) is $6,900,000 ÷ $20,000,000 = .345	
Ratio times revenue increase is .345 × $900,000	$ 310,500
Increase in fixed expenses	—0—
Operating income before increase	1,000,000
New operating income	$1,310,500

Computations are easily made by using data from the contribution income statement. In contrast, the traditional absorption costing income statement must be analyzed and divided into variable and fixed categories before the effect on operating income can be estimated.

2. The original contribution-margin ratio would be lower because the variable costs would be higher by $.09 per unit: ($6,900,000 – $90,000) ÷ $20,000,000 = .3405.

	Given Level	Higher Level	Difference
Revenue	$20,000,000	$20,900,000	$900,000
Variable expense ($13,100,000 + $90,000)	13,190,000	13,783,550	593,550
Contribution margin at .3405	$ 6,810,000	$ 7,116,450	$306,450
Fixed expenses ($5,900,000 – $90,000)	5,810,000	5,810,000	—
Operating income	$ 1,000,000	$ 1,306,450	$306,450

Appendix 4: More on Labor Costs

Classifications of Labor Costs

The terms used to classify labor costs are often confusing. Each organization seems to develop its own interpretation of various labor-cost classifications. We begin by considering some commonly encountered labor-cost terms:

- Direct labor (already defined)
- Factory overhead (examples of prominent labor components of these in ufacturing costs follow)
    - Indirect labor (wages)
        - Forklift truck operators (internal handling of materials)
        - Maintenance (to set up for production runs)

Janitors
Expediting (overseeing special orders, usually on a rush basis)
Plant guards
Rework labor (time spent by direct laborers redoing defective work)
Overtime premium paid to all factory workers
Idle time
Managers' salaries
Payroll fringe costs (for example, health care premiums, pension costs)

indirect labor All factory labor wages, other than those for direct labor and manager salaries.

All factory labor wages, other than those for direct labor and manager salaries, are usually classified as **indirect labor** costs, a major component of factory overhead. The term *indirect labor* is usually divided into many subsidiary classifications. The wages of forklift truck operators are generally not commingled with janitors' salaries, for example, although both are regarded as indirect labor.

Costs are classified in a detailed fashion primarily to associate a specific cost with its specific cost driver. Two classes of indirect labor deserve special mention: overtime premium and idle time.

overtime premium An indirect labor cost, consisting of wages paid to all factory workers in excess of their straight-time wage rates.

Overtime premium paid to all factory workers is usually considered a part of overhead. If a lathe operator earns $8 per hour for straight time and time and one-half for overtime, the premium is $4 per overtime hour. If the operator works 44 hours, including 4 overtime hours, in 1 week, the gross earnings are classified as follows:

Direct labor: 44 hours × $8	$352
Overtime premium (factory overhead): 4 hours × $4	16
Total earnings for 44 hours	$368

Why is overtime premium considered an indirect cost rather than direct? After all, it can usually be traced to specific batches of work. It is usually not considered a direct charge because the scheduling of production jobs is generally random. Suppose that at 8:00 A.M. you bring your automobile to a shop for repair. Through random scheduling, your auto is repaired between 5:00 and 6:00 P.M., when technicians receive overtime pay. Then, when you come to get your car, you learn that all the overtime premium had been added to your bill. You probably would not be overjoyed.

Thus, in most companies, the overtime premium is not allocated to any specific job. Instead, the overtime premium is considered to be attributable to the heavy overall volume of work, and its cost is thus regarded as part of the indirect manufacturing costs (factory overhead). The latter approach does not penalize a particular batch of work solely because it happened to be worked on during the overtime hours.

idle time An indirect labor cost consisting of wages paid for unproductive time caused by machine breakdowns, material shortages, and sloppy scheduling.

Another subsidiary classification of indirect-labor costs is **idle time**. This cost typically represents wages paid for unproductive time caused by machine breakdowns, material shortages, sloppy production scheduling, and the like. For example, if the same lathe operator's machine broke down for 3 hours during the week, the operator's earnings would be classified as follows:

Direct labor: 41 hours × $8	$328
Overtime premium (factory overhead): 4 hours × $4	16
Idle time (factory overhead): 3 hours × $8	24
Total earnings for 44 hours	$368

Manager salaries usually are not classified as a part of indirect labor. Instead, the compensation of supervisors, department heads, and all others who are regarded as part of manufacturing management are placed in a separate classification of factory overhead.

Payroll Fringe Costs

payroll fringe costs
Employer contributions to employee benefits such as social security, life insurance, health insurance, and pensions.

A type of labor cost that is growing in importance is **payroll fringe costs** such as employer contributions to employee benefits such as social security, life insurance, health insurance, and pensions. Most companies classify these as factory overhead. In some companies, however, fringe benefits related to direct labor are charged as an additional direct-labor cost. For instance, a direct laborer, such as a lathe operator or an auto mechanic, whose gross wages are computed on the basis of $10 an hour, may enjoy fringe benefits totaling $4 per hour. Most companies classify the $10 as direct-labor cost and the $4 as factory overhead. Other companies classify the entire $14 as direct-labor cost. The latter approach is conceptually preferable because these costs are a fundamental part of acquiring labor services.

Accountants and managers need to pinpoint exactly what direct labor includes and excludes. Such clarity may avoid disputes regarding cost reimbursement contracts, income tax payments, and labor union matters. For example, some countries offer substantial income tax savings to companies that locate factories there. To qualify, these companies' "direct labor" in that country must equal at least a specified percentage of the total manufacturing costs of their products. Disputes have arisen regarding how to calculate the direct-labor percentage for qualifying for such tax relief. Are payroll fringe benefits on direct labor an integral part of direct labor, or are they a part of factory overhead? Depending on how companies classify costs, you can readily see that the two identical firms may show different percentages of total manufacturing costs. Consider a company with $10,000 of payroll fringe costs:

Classification A			Classification B		
Direct materials	$ 80,000	40%	Direct materials	$ 80,000	40%
Direct labor	40,000	20	Direct labor	50,000	25
Factory overhead	80,000	40	Factory overhead	70,000	35
Total manufacturing costs	$200,000	100%	Total manufacturing costs	$200,000	100%

Classification A assumes that payroll fringe costs are part of factory overhead. In contrast, Classification B assumes that payroll fringe costs are part of direct labor.

Accounting Vocabulary

absorption approach, *p. 133*
activity-based accounting (ABA),
  p. 135
activity-based costing (ABC), *p. 135*
cellular manufacturing, *p. 145*
contribution approach, *p. 133*
conversion costs, *p. 125*
cost, *p. 122*
cost accounting, *p. 122*
cost accumulation, *p. 123*
cost allocation, *p. 123*

cost-management system, *p. 143*
cost object, *p. 122*
cost objective, *p. 122*
direct costs, *p. 124*
direct-labor costs, *p. 125*
direct-material costs, *p. 125*
factory burden, *p. 125*
factory-overhead costs, *p. 125*
idle time, *p. 148*
indirect costs, *p. 124*
indirect labor, *p. 148*

just-in-time (JIT) production
  system, *p. 144*
manufacturing overhead, *p. 125*
non-value-added costs, *p. 143*
overtime premium, *p. 148*
payroll fringe costs, *p. 149*
period costs, *p. 127*
prime costs, *p. 125*
product costs, *p. 127*
production cycle time, *p. 145*
value-added cost, *p. 143*

Fundamental Assignment Material

4-A1   Straightforward Income Statements

The Goldsmith Company had the following manufacturing data for the year 19X6 (in thousands of dollars):

Beginning and ending inventories	None
Direct material used	$425
Direct labor	350
Supplies	20
Utilities—variable portion	45
Utilities—fixed portion	15
Indirect labor—variable portion	100
Indirect labor—fixed portion	50
Depreciation	110
Property taxes	20
Supervisory salaries	50

Selling expenses were $325,000 (including $70,000 that were variable) and general administrative expenses were $148,000 (including $24,000 that were variable). Sales were $1.9 million.

Direct labor and supplies are regarded as variable costs.

Required

1. Prepare two income statements, one using the contribution approach and one using the absorption approach.

2. Suppose that all variable costs fluctuate directly in proportion to sales, and that fixed costs are unaffected over a very wide range of sales. What would operating income have been if sales had been $2.2 million instead of $1.9 million? Which income statement did you use to help obtain your answer? Why?

4-A2   Meaning of Technical Terms

Refer to the absorption income statement of your solution to the preceding problem. Give the amounts of the following: (1) prime cost, (2) conversion cost, (3) factory burden, (4) factory overhead, and (5) manufacturing overhead.

4-A3   Activity-Based Costing

Quality Machining Products (QMP) is an automotive component supplier. QMP has been approached by General Motors to consider expanding its production of part G108 to a total annual quantity of 2,000 units. This part is a low-volume, complex product with a high gross margin that is based on a proposed (quoted) unit sales price of $7.50. QMP uses a traditional costing system that allocates factory-overhead costs based on direct-labor costs. The rate currently used to allocate factory-overhead costs is 400% of direct-labor cost. This rate is based on the $3,300,000 annual factory overhead divided by $825,000 annual direct-labor cost. To produce 2,000 units of G108 requires $5,000 of direct materials and $1,000 of direct labor. The unit cost and gross margin percentage for Part G108 based on the traditional cost system are computed as follows:

	Total	Per Unit ($\div$2,000)
Direct material	$ 5,000	$2.50
Direct labor	1,000	.50
Factory overhead:		
[400% X direct labor]	4,000	2.00
Total cost	$10,000	$5.00
Sales price quoted		7.50
Gross margin		$2.50
Gross margin percentage		33.3%

The management of QMP decided to examine the effectiveness of their traditional costing system versus an activity-based-costing system. The following data have been collected by a team consisting of accounting and engineering analysts:

Activity Center	Traceable Factory Overhead Costs (Annual)
Quality	$ 800,000
Production scheduling	50,000
Setup	600,000
Shipping	300,000
Shipping administration	50,000
Production	1,500,000
Total factory overhead cost	$3,300,000

Activity Center: Cost Drivers	Annual Cost-Driver Quantity
Quality: number of pieces scrapped	10,000
Production scheduling and setup: number of setups	500
Shipping: number of containers shipped	60,000
Shipping administration: number of shipments	1,000
Production: number of machine hours	10,000

The accounting and engineering team has performed activity analysis and provides the following estimates for the total quantity of cost drivers to be used to produce 2,000 units of part G108:

Cost Driver	Cost-Driver Consumption
Pieces scrapped	120
Setups	4
Containers shipped	10
Shipments	5
Machine hours	15

Required

1. Prepare a schedule calculating the unit cost and gross margin of Part G108 using the activity-based-costing approach.
2. Based on the ABC results, which course of action would you recommend regarding the proposal by General Motors? List the benefits and costs associated with implementing an activity-based-costing system at QMP.

4-B1   Contribution and Absorption Income Statements

The following information is taken from the records of the Queensland Company for the year ending December 31, 19X5. There were no beginning or ending inventories.

Sales	$11,000,000	Long-term rent, factory	$ 110,000
Sales commissions	550,000	Factory superintendent's	
Advertising	225,000	salary	32,000
Shipping expenses	310,000	Supervisors' salaries	105,000
Administrative executive		Direct material used	4,100,000
salaries	100,000	Direct labor	2,200,000
Administrative clerical		Cutting bits used	60,000
salaries (variable)	450,000	Factory methods research	40,000
Fire insurance on		Abrasives for machining	100,000
factory equipment	2,000	Indirect labor	810,000
Property taxes on		Depreciation on	
factory equipment	10,000	equipment	300,000

Required

1. Prepare a contribution income statement and an absorption income statement. If you are in doubt about any cost behavior pattern, decide on the basis of whether the total cost in question will fluctuate substantially over a wide range of volume. Prepare a separate supporting schedule of indirect manufacturing costs subdivided between variable and fixed costs.
2. Suppose that all variable costs fluctuate directly in proportion to sales, and that fixed costs are unaffected over a wide range of sales. What would operating income have been if sales had been $12.5 million instead of $11 million? Which income statement did you use to help get your answer? Why?

4-B2   JIT and Non-Value-Added Activities

A motorcycle manufacturer was concerned with declining market share because of foreign competition. To become more efficient, the company was considering changing to a JIT production system. As a first step in analyzing the feasibility of the change, the company identified its major activities. Among the 120 activities were the following:

Materials receiving and inspection

Production scheduling

Production setup

Rear-wheel assembly

Movement of engine from fabrication to assembly building

Assembly of handlebars

Paint inspection

Reworking of defective brake assemblies

Installation of speedometer

Placement of completed motorcycle in finished goods storage

Required

1. From the preceding list of 10 activities, prepare two lists: one of value-added activities and one of non-value-added activities.
2. For each non-value-added activity, explain how a JIT production system might eliminate, or at least reduce, the cost of the activity.

4-B3   Activity-Based Costing

The cordless phone manufacturing division of a consumer electronics company uses activity-based accounting. For simplicity, assume that its accountants have identified only the following three activities and related cost drivers for manufacturing overhead:

Activity	Cost Driver
Materials handling	Direct materials cost
Engineering	Engineering change notices
Power	Kilowatt hours

Three types of cordless phones are produced: CL3, CL5, and CL9. Direct costs and cost-driver activity for each product for a recent month are as follows:

	CL3	CL5	CL9
Direct materials cost	$25,000	$50,000	$125,000
Direct labor cost	$4,000	$1,000	$3,000
Kilowatt hours	50,000	200,000	150,000
Engineering change notices	13	5	2

Manufacturing overhead for the month was:

Materials handling	$10,000
Engineering	30,000
Power	24,000
Total manufacturing overhead	$64,000

Required

1. Compute the manufacturing overhead allocated to each product with the activity-based accounting system.

2. Suppose all manufacturing overhead costs had been allocated to products in proportion to their direct-labor costs. Compute the manufacturing overhead allocated to each product.

3. In which product costs, those in requirement 1 or those in requirement 2, do you have the most confidence? Why?

Additional Assignment Material

Questions

4-1. Name four cost objectives or cost objects.

4-2. "Departments are not cost objects or objects of costing." Do you agree? Explain.

4-3. What is the major purpose of detailed cost-accounting systems?

4-4. "The same cost can be direct and indirect." Do you agree? Explain.

4-5. "Economic feasibility is an important guideline in designing cost-accounting systems." Do you agree? Explain.

4-6. How does the idea of economic feasibility relate to the distinction between direct and indirect costs?

4-7. "The typical accounting system does not allocate selling and administrative costs to units produced." Do you agree? Explain.

4-8. Distinguish between prime costs and conversion costs.

4-9. "For a furniture manufacturer, glue or tacks become an integral part of the finished product, so they would be direct material." Do you agree? Explain.

4-10. Many cost-accounting systems have a twofold instead of a threefold category of manufacturing costs. What are the items in the twofold category?

4-11. "Depreciation is an expense for financial statement purposes." Do you agree? Explain.

4-12. Distinguish between "costs" and "expenses."

4-13. "Unexpired costs are always inventory costs." Do you agree? Explain.

4-14. "Advertising is noninventoriable." Explain.

4-15. Why is there no direct-labor inventory account on a manufacturing company's balance sheet?

4-16. What is the advantage of the contribution approach as compared with the absorption approach?

4-17. Distinguish between manufacturing and merchandising companies.

4-18. "The primary classifications of costs are by variable- and fixed-cost behavior patterns, not by business functions." Name three commonly used terms that describe this type of income statement.

4-19. Name 4 steps in the design and implementation of an activity-based-costing system.

4-20. Refer to the Portland Power Company illustration on pages 136–142. Which BD resource costs depicted in Exhibit 4-11 would have variable cost behavior?

4-21. Why are more and more organizations adopting activity-based-costing systems?

4-22. Why do managers want to distinguish between value-added activities and non-value-added activities?

4-23. Name four factors crucial to the success of JIT production systems.

4-24. "ABC and JIT are alternative techniques for achieving competitiveness." Do you agree?

Exercises

4-25 Meaning of Technical Terms

Refer to Exhibit 4-4, page 130. Give the amounts of the following with respect to the cost of goods available for sale: (1) prime costs, (2) conversion costs, (3) factory burden, and (4) indirect manufacturing costs.

4-26 Presence of Ending Work in Process

Refer to Exhibits 4-4 and 4-5. Suppose manufacturing costs were the same, but there was an ending work-in-process inventory of $3 million. The cost of the completed goods would therefore be $37 million instead of $40 million. Suppose also that the cost of goods sold is unchanged.

Required
1. Recast the income statement of Exhibit 4-4, page 130.
2. What lines and ending balances would change in Exhibit 4-5 and by how much?

4-27   Relating Costs to Cost Objectives
A company uses an absorption cost system. Prepare headings for two columns: (1) assembly department and (2) products assembled. Fill in the two columns with a *D* for direct and an *I* for indirect for each of the costs below. For example, if a specific cost is direct to the department but indirect to the product, place a *D* in column 1 and an *I* in column 2. The costs are: materials used, supplies used, assembly labor, material-handling labor (transporting materials between and within departments), depreciation—building, assembly supervisor's salary, and the building and grounds supervisor's salary.

4-28   Classification of Manufacturing Costs
Classify each of the following as direct or indirect (*D* or *I*) with respect to product and as variable or fixed (*V* or *F*) with respect to whether the cost fluctuates in total as activity or volume changes over wide ranges of activity. You will have two answers, *D* or *I* and *V* or *F*, for each of the 10 items.

1. Food for a factory cafeteria
2. Workers' compensation insurance in a factory
3. Supervisor training program
4. Salary of a factory storeroom clerk
5. Paper towels for a factory washroom
6. Steel scrap for a blast furnace
7. Factory rent
8. Cutting bits in a machinery department
9. Cement for a roadbuilder
10. Abrasives (sandpaper, etc.)

4-29   Variable Costs and Fixed Costs; Manufacturing and Other Costs
For each of the numbered items, choose the appropriate classifications for a manufacturing company. If in doubt about whether the cost behavior is basically variable or fixed, decide on the basis of whether the total cost will fluctuate substantially over a wide range of volume. Most items have two answers among the following possibilities with respect to the cost of a particular job:

a. Selling cost
b. Manufacturing costs, direct
c. Manufacturing costs, indirect
d. General and administrative cost
e. Fixed cost
f. Variable cost
g. Other (specify)

Sample answers:

Direct material	e, f
President's salary	d, e
Bond interest expense	e, g (financial expense)

Items for your consideration:

1. Company picnic costs	11. Salespersons' commissions
2. Overtime premium, punch press	12. Salespersons' salaries
3. Idle time, assembly	13. Welding supplies
4. Freight out	14. Fire loss
5. Property taxes	15. Sandpaper
6. Paint for finished products	16. Supervisory salaries, production control
7. Heat and air conditioning, factory	
8. Material-handling labor, punch press	17. Supervisory salaries, assembly department
9. Straight-line depreciation, salespersons' automobiles storeroom	
10. Factory power for machines	18. Supervisory salaries, factory

4-30   Inventory Transactions

Review Exhibit 4-9, page 134. Assume that the Jenkins Company had no beginning inventories. The following transactions occurred in 19X6 (in thousands):

1.	Purchase of direct materials	$400
2.	Direct materials used	310
3.	Acquire direct labor	180
4.	Acquire factory overhead	210
5.	Complete all goods that were started	?
6.	Cost of goods sold (half of the goods completed were sold)	?

Required

Prepare an analysis similar to Exhibit 4-9. What are the ending balances of direct materials, work-in-process, and finished-goods inventories?

4-31   Inventory Transactions

Refer to the preceding problem. Suppose goods were still in process that cost $90,000. Half the goods completed were sold. What are the balances of all the accounts in the ending balance sheet?

4-32   Straightforward Absorption Statement

The Gomez Company had the following data (in thousands) for a given period:

Sales	$900
Direct materials	250
Direct labor	180
Indirect manufacturing costs	150
Selling and administrative expenses	170

Required

There were no beginning or ending inventories. Compute the (1) manufacturing cost of goods sold, (2) gross profit, (3) operating income, (4) prime cost, and (5) conversion cost.

4-33   Straightforward Contribution Income Statement

Yoko Ltd. had the following data (in millions of yen) for a given period:

Sales	¥750
Direct materials	280
Direct labor	150
Variable factory overhead	50
Variable selling and administrative expenses	90
Fixed factory overhead	100
Fixed selling and administrative expenses	50

Required There were no beginning or ending inventories. Compute the (1) variable manufacturing cost of goods sold, (2) contribution margin, and (3) operating income.

4-34 Straightforward Absorption and Contribution Statement
Martinez Company had the following data (in millions) for a recent period. Fill in the blanks. There were no beginning or ending inventories.

a.	Sales	$950
b.	Direct materials used	360
c.	Direct labor	200
	Factory overhead	
d.	Variable	110
e.	Fixed	50
f.	Variable manufacturing cost of goods sold	—
g.	Manufacturing cost of goods sold	—
	Selling and administrative expenses	
h.	Variable	100
i.	Fixed	50
j.	Gross profit	—
k.	Contribution margin	—
l.	Prime costs	—
m.	Conversion costs	—
n.	Operating income	—

4-35 Absorption Statement
Richard's Jewelry had the following data (in thousands) for a given period. Assume there are no inventories. Fill in the blanks.

Sales	$__
Direct materials	400
Direct labor	—
Factory overhead	—
Manufacturing cost of goods sold	800
Gross margin	130
Selling and administrative expenses	—
Operating income	40
Conversion cost	—
Prime cost	610

4-36 Contribution Income Statement

Nottingham Company had the following data (in thousands) for a given period. Assume there are no inventories.

Direct labor	$190
Direct materials	200
Variable factory overhead	140
Contribution margin	210
Fixed selling and administrative expenses	110
Operating income	20
Sales	980

Required

Compute the (1) variable manufacturing cost of goods sold, (2) variable selling and administrative expenses, and (3) fixed factory overhead.

4-37 Classifications of Direct Labor Cost

Study Appendix 4. A division of a machinery manufacturer has the following cost of goods manufactured:

Direct materials	$240,000	60%
Direct labor	60,000	15
Factory overhead	100,000	25
Cost of goods manufactured	$400,000	100%

The fringe benefits related to direct labor are 30% of the nominal direct-labor costs. They are currently included in factory overhead. If these benefits were regarded as part of direct labor rather than factory overhead, what percentage of cost of goods manufactured would direct labor represent?

4-38 Overtime Premium

Study Appendix 4. Downtown Auto has a service department. You have brought your car for repair at 8:00 A.M. When you come to get your car after 6:00 P.M., you notice that your bill contains a charge under "labor" for "overtime premium." When you inquire about the reason for the charge, you are told, "We worked on your car from 5:00 P.M. to 6:00 P.M. Our union contract calls for wages to be paid at time-and-a-half after 8 hours. Therefore our ordinary labor charge of $40 per hour was billed to you at $60."

Required

1. Should Downtown Auto allocate the overtime premium only to cars worked on during overtime hours? Explain.
2. Would your preceding answer differ if Downtown Auto arranged to service your car at 8:00 P.M. as a special convenience to you? Explain.

4-39 Value-Added Analysis in a Service Company

Refer to the Portland Power Company illustration and Exhibit 4-12 on page 139.
Some companies that perform value-added cost analysis subdivide non-value-added activities into two categories—essential and discretionary. An example of an essential but non-value-added activity is setting up the company's computer system for a billing run. An example of a discretionary non-value-added activity is monitoring telephone inquiries. Most non-value-added discretionary activities should be eliminated. Non-value-added essential activities are reduced through continuous improvement efforts. For each resource and activity listed below, indicate whether it is value-added (VA), non-value-added essential (NVA-E), or non-value-added discretionary (NVA-D). Also indicate

appropriate managerial actions to control costs for each type of resource and activity based on its classification.

Resource/Activity
Telecommunications
Paper
Computer
Supervisors
Account inquiry activity
Billing labor

4-40 Cost Allocation and Activity-Based Costing

Refer to the Portland Power Company illustration and Exhibit 4-14. The data used in the BD study are averages for each customer class. Based on the study results, the company conducted a thorough investigation of all commercial customers that received correspondence. On average, these accounts consumed 5 minutes of inquiry labor time and had 75 lines on the electric bill. What was the cost per account to service this customer class? (Assume only 1 letter per customer and that commercial accounts are verified only one time.)

Problems

4-41 Cost Accumulation and Allocation

Wang Manufacturing Company has two departments, machining and finishing. For a given period, the following costs were incurred by the company as a whole: direct material, $130,000; direct labor, $75,000; and manufacturing overhead, $80,000. The grand total costs were $285,000.

The machining department incurred 70% of the direct-material costs, but only 33⅓% of the direct-labor costs. As is commonplace, manufacturing overhead incurred by each department was allocated to products in proportion to the direct-labor costs of products within the departments.

Three products were produced.

Product	Direct Material	Direct Labor
X-1	40%	30%
Y-1	30%	30%
Z-1	30%	40%
Total for the machining department	100%	100%
X-1	33 ⅓ %	40%
Y-1	33 ⅓%	40%
Z-1	33 ⅓%	20%
Total added by finishing department	100%	100%

The manufacturing overhead incurred by the machining department and allocated to all products therein amounted to: machining, $38,000; finishing, $42,000.

Required

1. Compute the total costs incurred by the machining department and added by the finishing department.
2. Compute the total costs of each product that would be shown as finished-goods inventory if all the products were transferred to finished stock on completion. (There were no beginning inventories.)

4-42　Cost Allocation and Activity-Based Accounting

Quality Machining Products (QMP) is a discrete automotive component supplier. QMP has been approached by Chrysler with a proposal to significantly increase production of Part T151A to a total annual quantity of 100,000. Chrysler believes that by increasing the volume of production of Part T151A, QMP should realize the benefits of economies of scale and hence should accept a lower price than the current $6.00 per unit. Currently, QMP's gross margin on Part T151A is 3.3%, computed as follows:

	Total	Per Unit (÷100,000)
Direct materials	$150,000	$1.50
Direct labor	86,000	.86
Factory overhead (400% X direct labor)	344,000	3.44
Total cost	$580,000	$5.80
Sales price		6.00
Gross margin		$ .20
Gross margin percentage		3.3%

Part T151A seems to be a marginal profit product. If additional volume of production of Part T151A is to be added, QMP management believes that the sales price must be increased, not reduced as requested by Chrysler. The management of QMP sees this quoting situation as an excellent opportunity to examine the effectiveness of their traditional costing system versus an activity-based-costing system. Data have been collected by a team consisting of accounting and engineering analysts.

Activity Center: Cost Drivers	Annual Cost-Driver Quantity
Quality: number of pieces scrapped	10,000
Production scheduling and setup: number of setups	500
Shipping: number of containers shipped	60,000
Shipping administration: number of shipments	1,000
Production: number of machine hours	10,000

Activity Center	Traceable Factory Overhead Costs (Annual)
Quality	$ 800,000
Production scheduling	50,000
Setup	600,000
Shipping	300,000
Shipping administration	50,000
Production	1,500,000
Total costs	$3,300,000

The accounting and engineering team has provided the following cost-driver consumption estimates for the production of 100,000 units of Part T151A:

Cost Driver	Cost-Driver Consumption
Pieces scrapped	1,000
Setups	12
Containers shipped	500
Shipments	100
Machine hours	500

Required

1. Prepare a schedule calculating the unit cost and gross margin of Part T151A using the activity-based-costing approach.
2. Based on the ABC results, what course of action would you recommend regarding the proposal by Chrysler? List the benefits and costs associated with implementing an activity-based-costing system at QMP.

4-43 Financial Statements for Manufacturing and Merchandising Companies
Mountain Equipment Company (MEC) and Outdoor Supplies Inc. (OSI) both sell tents. MEC purchases its tents from a manufacturer for $100 each and sells them for $130. It purchased 10,000 tents in 19X6.

OSI produces its own tents. In 19X6 OSI produced 10,000 tents. Costs were as follows:

Direct materials purchased		$ 585,000
Direct materials used		570,000
Direct labor		300,000
Factory overhead		
Depreciation	$40,000	
Indirect labor	60,000	
Other	30,000	130,000
Total cost of production		$1,000,000

Assume that OSI had no beginning inventory of direct materials. There was no beginning inventory of finished tents, but ending inventory consisted of 1,000 finished tents. Ending work-in-process inventory was negligible.

Each company sold 9,000 tents for $1,170,000 in 19X6 and incurred the following selling and administrative costs:

Sales salaries and commissions	95,000
Depreciation on retail store	30,000
Advertising	25,000
Other	10,000
Total selling and administrative cost	$160,000

Required

1. Prepare the inventories section of the balance sheet for December 31, 19X6, for MEC.
2. Prepare the inventories section of the balance sheet for December 31, 19X6, for OSI.
3. Using Exhibit 4-4 on page 130 as a model, prepare an income statement for the year 19X6 for MEC.
4. Using Exhibit 4-4 on page 130 as a model, prepare an income statement for the year 19X6 for OSI.
5. Summarize the differences between the financial statements of MEC, a merchandiser, and OSI, a manufacturer.

4-44   Library Research in JIT or Activity-Based Accounting

Select an article from *Management Accounting* or *Journal of Cost Management* (available in most libraries) that describes a particular company's application of either (1) a JIT production system or (2) an activity-based accounting system. Prepare a summary of 300 words or less that includes the following:

Name of the company (if given)

Industry of the company

Description of the particular application

Assessment of the benefits the company received from the application

Any difficulties encountered in implementation

4-45   Review Of Chapters 2 to 4

The Dames Shoe Manufacturing Company provides you with the following miscellaneous data regarding operations in 19X5:

Gross profit	$ 30,000
Net loss	(10,000)
Sales	125,000
Direct material used	40,000
Direct labor	30,000
Fixed manufacturing overhead	15,000
Fixed selling and administrative expenses	15,000

There are no beginning or ending inventories.

Required   Compute the (1) variable selling and administrative expenses, (2) contribution margin in dollars, (3) variable manufacturing overhead, (4) break-even point in sales dollars, and (5) manufacturing cost of goods sold.

4-46   Review of Chapters 2 to 4

Sullivan Corporation provides you with the following miscellaneous data regarding operations for 19X6:

Break-even point (in sales dollars)	$125,000
Direct material used	40,000
Gross profit	25,000
Contribution margin	30,000
Direct labor	43,000
Sales	150,000
Variable manufacturing overhead	20,000

There are no beginning or ending inventories.

Required   Compute the (1) fixed manufacturing overhead, (2) variable selling and administrative expenses, and (3) fixed selling and administrative expenses.

4-47   Review of Chapters 2 to 4

(D. Kleespie.) U. Grant Company manufactured and sold 1,000 sabres during October. Selected data for this month follow:

Sales	$160,000
Direct materials used	42,000
Direct labor	38,000
Variable manufacturing overhead	22,000
Fixed manufacturing overhead	14,000
Variable selling and administrative expenses	?
Fixed selling and administrative expenses	?
Contribution margin	40,000
Operating income	19,000

There were no beginning or ending inventories.

Required

1. What were the variable selling and administrative expenses for October?
2. What were the fixed selling and administrative expenses for October?
3. What was the cost of goods sold under absorption costing during October?
4. Without prejudice to your earlier answers, assume that the fixed selling and administrative expenses for October amounted to $12,000.
   a. What was the break-even point in units for October?
   b. How many units must be sold to earn a target operating income of $14,000?
   c. What would the selling price per unit have to be if the company wanted to earn an operating income of $14,500 on the sale of 900 units?

4-48   Payroll Fringe Costs

Study Appendix 4. Direct labor is often accounted for at the gross wage rate, and the related "fringe costs," such as employer payroll taxes and employee contributions to health care plans, are accounted for as part of overhead. Suppose Amy O'Keefe, a direct laborer, works 40 hours during a particular week as an auditor for a public accounting firm. She receives $18 gross pay per hour plus related fringe costs of $10 per hour.

Required

1. What would be the weekly cost of O'Keefe's direct labor? Of related general overhead?
2. Suppose O'Keefe works 30 hours for Client A and 10 hours for Client B, and the firm allocates costs to each client. What would be the cost of O'Keefe's "direct labor" on the Client A job? The Client B job?
3. How would you allocate general overhead to the Client A job? The Client B job?
4. Suppose O'Keefe works a total of 50 hours (30 for Client A and 20 for Client B), 10 of which are paid on a time-and-one-half basis. What would be the cost of O'Keefe's "direct labor" on the Client A job? The Client B job? The addition to general overhead?

Cases

4-49   Identifying Activities, Resources, and Cost Drivers in Manufacturing

Extrusion Plastics is a multinational, diversified organization. One of its manufacturing divisions, Northeast Plastics Division, has become less profitable due to increased competition. The division produces three major lines of plastic products within its single plant. Product Line A is high-volume, simple pieces produced in large batches. Product Line B is medium-volume, more complex pieces. Product Line C is low-volume, small-order, highly complex pieces.

Currently, the division allocates indirect manufacturing costs based on direct labor. The V.P. Manufacturing is uncomfortable using the traditional cost figures. He thinks the company is under-pricing the more complex products. He decides to conduct an activity-based costing analysis of the business.

Interviews were conducted with the key managers in order to identify activities, resources, cost drivers, and their interrelationships.

Interviewee: Production Manager

Q1: What activities are carried out in your area?

A1: *All products are manufactured using three similar, complex, and expensive molding machines. Each molding machine can be used in the production of the three product lines. Each setup takes about the same time irrespective of the product.*

Q2: Who works in your area?

A2: *Last year, we employed thirty machine operators, two maintenance mechanics, and two supervisors.*

Q3: How are the operators used in the molding process?

A3: *It requires nine operators to support a machine during the actual production process.*

Q4: What do the maintenance mechanics do?

A4: *Their primary function is to perform machine setups. However, they were also required to provide machine maintenance during the molding process.*

Q5: Where do the supervisors spend their time?

A5: *They provide supervision for the machine operators and the maintenance mechanics. For the most part, the supervisors appear to spend the same amount of time with each of the employees that they supervise.*

Q6: What other resources are used to support manufacturing?

A6: *The molding machines use energy during the molding process and during the setups. We put meters on the molding machines to get a better understanding of their energy consumption. We discovered that for each hour that a machine ran, it used 6.3 kilo-watts of energy. The machines also require consumable shop supplies (e.g., lubricants, hoses, etc.). We have found a direct correlation between the amount of supplies used and the actual processing time.*

Q7: How is the building used, and what costs are associated with it?

A7: *We have a 100,000-square-foot building. The total rent and insurance costs for the year were $675,000. These costs are allocated to production, sales, and administration based on square footage.*

Required

1. Identify the activities, resources, and cost drivers for the division.
2. For each resource identified in requirement 1, indicate its cost behavior with respect to the activities it supports (assume a planning period of 1 month).

4-50   Analysis with Contribution Income Statement

The following data have been condensed from Chateau Corporation's report of 19X5 operations (in millions of French francs [FF]):

	Variable	Fixed	Total
Manufacturing cost of goods sold	FF420	FF200	FF620
Selling and administrative expenses	150	70	220
Sales			950

Required

1. Prepare the 19X5 income statement in contribution form, ignoring income taxes.
2. Chateau's operations have been fairly stable from year to year. In planning for the future, top management is considering several options for changing the annual pattern of operations. You are asked to perform an analysis of their estimated effects. Use your contribution income statement as a framework to compute the estimated

operating income (in millions) under each of the following separate and unrelated assumptions.

a. Assume that a 10% reduction in selling prices would cause a 40% increase in the physical volume of goods manufactured and sold.

b. Assume that an annual expenditure of FF30 million for a special sales promotion campaign would enable the company to increase its physical volume by 10% with no change in selling prices.

c. Assume that a basic redesign of manufacturing operations would increase annual fixed manufacturing costs by FF80 million and decrease variable manufacturing costs by 15% *per product unit*, but with no effect on physical volume or selling prices.

d. Assume that a basic redesign of selling and administrative operations would double the annual fixed expenses for selling and administration and increase the variable expenses for selling and administration by 25% *per product unit*, but would also increase physical volume by 20%. Selling prices would be increased by 5%.

e. Would you prefer to use the absorption form of income statement for the preceding analyses? Explain.

3. Discuss the desirability of alternatives *a* through *d* in requirement 2. If only one alternative could be selected, which would you choose? Explain.

5 Relevant Information and Decision Making: Marketing Decisions

HG Engineering, a Canadian-based company with operations in Canada and South America, provides engineering and project-management services to mining and mineral-processing companies. HG uses relevant cost analysis to price bids on projects such as this copper producing plant.
Courtesy HG Engineering

Learning Objectives

When you have finished studying this chapter, you should be able to

1 Discriminate between relevant and irrelevant information for making decisions.

2 Diagram the relationships among the main elements of the decision process.

3 Analyze data by the contribution approach to support a decision for accepting or rejecting a special sales order.

4 Explain the potential pitfalls of using a unit-cost approach for predicting the effect of a special order on operating income.

5 Analyze data by the relevant-information approach to support a decision for adding or deleting a product line.

6 Compute a measure of product profitability when production is constrained by a scarce resource.

7 Identify the role of costs in pricing decisions in perfect and imperfect markets.

8 Discuss the factors that influence pricing decisions in practice.

9 Compute a target sales price by various approaches and identify their advantages and disadvantages.

What price should a Safeway store charge for a pound of hamburger? What should Boeing charge for a 757 airplane? Should a clothing manufacturer accept a special order from Wal-Mart at a price lower than that generally charged? Should an appliance manufacturer add a new product, say an automatic bread maker, to its product line? Or should an existing product be dropped? Which product makes best use of a particular limited resource? All these questions relate to the marketing strategy of a firm, in which accounting information plays an important role.

At the start of this book, we emphasized that the purpose of management accounting is to provide information that enables managers to make sound decisions. In this chapter and the next we focus on identifying *relevant information* for particular management decisions,[1] with this chapter focusing primarily on marketing decisions. Although the word "relevant" has been much overworked in recent years, the ability to separate relevant from irrelevant information is often the difference between success and failure in modern business.

■ MEANING OF RELEVANCE: THE MAJOR CONCEPTUAL LESSON

What information is relevant depends on the decision being made. Decision making is essentially choosing among several courses of action. The available actions are determined by an often time-consuming formal or informal search and screening process, perhaps carried on by a company team that includes engineers, accountants, and operating executives. Accountants have an important role in the decision-making process, not as decision makers but as collectors and reporters of relevant information. (Although many managers want the accountant to recommend the proper decision, the final choice always rests with the operating executive.) The accountant's role in decision making is primarily that of a technical expert on financial analysis who helps managers focus on relevant data, information that will lead to the best decision.

Relevance Defined

In the final stages of the decision-making process, managers compare two or more alternative courses of action. The decision is based on the predicted difference in future performance under each alternative. The key question is: What difference will the choice make? **Relevant information** is the predicted future costs and revenues that will differ among the alternatives.

relevant information
The predicted future costs and revenues that will differ among alternative courses of action.

Note that relevant information is a prediction of the future, not a summary of the past. Historical (past) data have no *direct* bearing on a decision. Such data can have an *indirect* bearing on a decision because they may help in predicting the future. But past figures, in themselves, are irrelevant to the decision itself. Why? Because the decision cannot affect past data. Decisions affect the future. Nothing can alter what has already happened.

Of the expected future data, only those that will differ from alternative to alternative are relevant to the decision. Any item that will remain the same regardless of the alternative selected is irrelevant. For instance, if a department manager's salary will be the same regardless of the products stocked, the salary is irrelevant to the selection of products.

Accuracy and Relevance

In the best of all possible worlds, information used for decision making would be perfectly relevant *and* accurate. However, in reality, the cost of such information

---

[1] Throughout this and the next chapter, to concentrate on the fundamental ideas, we shall ignore the time value of money (discussed in Chapter 11) and income taxes (discussed in Chapter 12).

often exceeds its benefit. Accountants often trade off relevance versus accuracy. Of course, relevant information must be reasonably accurate but not precisely so.

Precise but irrelevant information is worthless for decision making. For example, a university president's salary may be $140,000 per year, to the penny, but may have no bearing on the question of whether to buy or rent data processing equipment. On the other hand, imprecise but relevant information can be useful. For example, sales predictions for a new product may be subject to great error, but they still are helpful to the decision of whether to manufacture the product.

The degree to which information is relevant or precise often depends on the degree to which it is *qualitative* or *quantitative*. Qualitative aspects are those for which measurement in dollars and cents is difficult and imprecise; quantitative aspects are those for which measurement is easy and precise. Accountants, statisticians, and mathematicians try to express as many decision factors as feasible in quantitative terms, because this approach reduces the number of qualitative factors to be judged. Just as we noted that relevance is more crucial than precision in decision making, so a qualitative aspect may easily carry more weight than a measurable (quantitative) financial impact in many decisions. For example, the opposition of a militant union to new labor-saving machinery may cause a manager to defer or even reject completely the contemplated installation even if it would save money. Alternatively, to avoid a long-run dependence on a particular supplier, a company may pass up the opportunity to purchase a component from the supplier at a price below the cost of producing it themselves.

On the other hand, managers sometimes introduce new technology (e.g., advanced computer systems or automated equipment) even though the expected quantitative results seem unattractive. Managers defend such decisions on the grounds that failure to keep abreast of new technology will surely bring unfavorable financial results sooner or later.

Examples of Relevance

The following examples will help you clarify the sharp distinctions needed to discriminate between relevant and irrelevant information.

Suppose you always buy gasoline from either of two nearby gasoline stations. Yesterday you noticed that one station was selling gasoline at $1.50 per gallon; the other, at $1.40. Your automobile needs gasoline, and in making your choice of stations, you *assume* that these prices have not changed. The relevant costs are $1.50 and $1.40, the expected future costs that will differ between the alternatives. You use your past experience (i.e., what you observed yesterday) for predicting today's price. Note that the relevant cost is not what you paid in the past, or what you observed yesterday, but what you *expect to pay* when you drive in to get gasoline. This cost meets our two criteria: (1) it is the expected future cost, and (2) it differs between the alternatives.

You may also plan to have your car lubricated. The recent price at each station was $12, and this is what you anticipate paying. This expected future cost is irrelevant because it will be the same under either alternative. It does not meet our second criterion.

On a business level, consider the following decision. A manufacturer is thinking of using aluminum instead of copper in a line of ashtrays. The cost of direct material will decrease from 30¢ to 20¢ per ashtray. The analysis in a nutshell is as follows:

	Aluminum	Copper	Difference
Direct material	$.20	$.30	$.10

The cost of copper used for this comparison probably came from historical cost records on the amount paid most recently for copper, but the *relevant* cost in the foregoing analysis is the expected future cost of copper compared with the expected future cost of aluminum.

The direct-labor cost will continue to be 70¢ per unit regardless of the material used. It is irrelevant because our second criterion—an element of difference between the alternatives—is not met.

	Aluminum	Copper	Difference
Direct material	$.20	$.30	$.10
Direct labor	.70	.70	—

Therefore we can safely exclude direct labor from the comparison of alternatives. There is no harm in including irrelevant items in a formal analysis, provided that they are included properly. However, confining the reports to the relevant items provides greater clarity and timesavings for busy managers.

Exhibit 5-1 provides a more elaborate view of this decision than is necessary for this simple decision, but it serves to show the appropriate framework for more complex decisions. Box 1(A) represents historical data from the accounting system. Box 1(B) represents other data, such as price indices or industry statistics, gathered from outside the accounting system. Regardless of their source, the data in step 1 help the formulation of *predictions* in step 2. (Remember that although historical data may act as a guide to predicting, they are irrelevant to the decision itself.)

In step 3 these predictions become inputs to the *decision model*. A **decision model** is defined as any method for making a choice. Such models often require elaborate quantitative procedures, such as a petroleum refinery's mathematical method for choosing what products to manufacture for any given day or week. A decision model, however, may also be simple. It may be confined to a single comparison of costs for choosing between two materials. In this instance our decision model is: Compare the predicted unit costs and select the alternative with the lesser cost.

We will be referring back to Exhibit 5-1 frequently because it displays the major conceptual lesson in this chapter. Above all, note the commonality of the relevant-information approach to the various special decisions explored in this and the next chapter. In all decisions managers should focus on predictions of future outcomes, not dwell on past outcomes. The major difficulty is predicting how revenues and costs will be affected under each alternative. No matter what the decision situation, the key question to ask is: What difference will it make?

Objective 2

Diagram the relationships among the main elements of the decision process

decision model
Any method for making a choice, sometimes requiring elaborate quantitative procedures.

Exhibit 5-1

Decision Process and
Role of Information

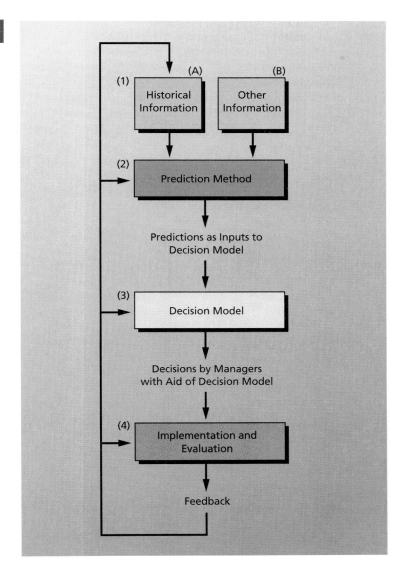

■ THE SPECIAL SALES ORDER

The first decision for which we examine relevant information is the special sales order.

Illustrative Example

Exhibit 5-2 illustrates the primary data from Exhibits 4-8 and 4-9, pages 133 and 134, two very important general exhibits. As you can see, the two income statements differ somewhat in format. The difference in format may be unimportant if the accompanying cost analysis leads to the same set of decisions. However, these two approaches sometimes lead to different *unit* costs that must be interpreted warily.

In our illustration, suppose 1 million units of product, such as some auto-mobile replacement part, were made and sold. Under the absorption-costing approach, the unit manufacturing cost of the product would be $15,000,000 ÷ 1,000,000, or $15 per unit. Suppose a mail-order house near year-end offered Samson $13 per unit for a 100,000-unit special order that (1) would not affect Samson's regular business in any way, (2) would not raise any antitrust issues concerning price discrimination, (3) would not affect total fixed costs, (4) would not require any additional variable selling and admin-istrative expenses, and (5) would use some otherwise idle manufacturing capacity. Should Samson accept the order? Perhaps the question should be stated more sharply: What is the difference in the short-run financial results between not accepting and accepting? As usual, the key question is: What difference will it make?

Exhibit 5-2

Absorption and
Contribution Forms
of the Income
Statement

Samson Company
Income Statement
for the Year Ended
December 31, 19X2
(thousands of
dollars)

Absorption Form		Contribution Form		
Sales	$20,000	Sales		$20,000
Less: manufacturing cost		Less: variable expenses		
of goods sold	15,000	Manufacturing	$12,000	
Gross margin or gross profit	$ 5,000	Selling and		
Less: selling and admin-		administrative	1,100	13,100
istrative expenses	4,000	Contribution margin		$ 6,900
Operating income	$ 1,000	Less: fixed expenses		
		Manufacturing	$ 3,000	
		Selling and		
		administrative	2,900	5,900
		Operating income		$ 1,000

Correct Analysis

The correct analysis employs the contribution approach and concentrates on the final *overall* results. As Exhibit 5-3 shows, only variable manufacturing costs are affected by the particular order, at a rate of $12 per unit. All other variable costs and all fixed costs are unaffected, so a manager may safely ignore them in making this special-order decision. Note how the contribution approach's dis-tinction between variable- and fixed-cost behavior patterns aids the necessary cost analysis. Total short-run income will increase by $100,000 if the order is accepted—despite the fact that the unit selling price of $13 is less than the absorption manufacturing cost of $15.

Exhibit 5-3 shows total fixed expenses in the first and last columns. There is no harm in including such irrelevant items in an analysis as long as they are included under every alternative at hand.

A fixed-cost element of an identical amount that is common among all alternatives is essentially irrelevant. Whether irrelevant items should be included in an analysis is a matter of taste, not a matter of right or wrong. However, if irrelevant items are included in an analysis, they should be inserted in a correct manner.

Exhibit 5-3

Comparative
Predicted Income
Statements,
Contribution
Approach

Samson Company
for Year Ended
December 31, 19X2

	Without Special Order, 1,000,000 Units	Effect of Special Order 100,000 Units		With Special Order, 1,100,000 Units
		Total	Per Unit	
Sales	$20,000,000	$1,300,000	$13	$21,300,000
Less: variable expenses				
Manufacturing	$12,000,000	$1,200,000	$12	$13,200,000
Selling and administrative	1,100,000	—	—	1,100,000
Total variable expenses	$13,100,000	$1,200,000	$12	$14,300,000
Contribution margin	$ 6,900,000	$ 100,000	$ 1	$ 7,000,000
Less: fixed expenses				
Manufacturing	$ 3,000,000	—	—	$ 3,000,000
Selling and administrative	2,900,000	—	—	2,900,000
Total fixed expenses	$ 5,900,000	—	—	$ 5,900,000
Operating income	$ 1,000,000	$ 100,000	$ 1	$ 1,100,000

Incorrect Analysis

Faulty cost analysis sometimes occurs because of misinterpreting unit fixed costs. For instance, managers might erroneously use the $15 absorption manufacturing cost per unit to make the following prediction for the year:

Objective 4

Explain the potential pitfalls of using a unit-cost approach for predicting the effect of a special order on operating income

Incorrect Analysis	Without Special Order 1,000,000 Units	Incorrect Effect of Special Order 100,000 Units	With Special Order 1,100,000 Units
Sales	$20,000,000	$1,300,000	$21,300,000
Less: manufacturing cost of goods sold @ $15	15,000,000	1,500,000	16,500,000
Gross margin	5,000,000	(200,000)	4,800,000
Selling and administrative expenses	4,000,000	—	4,000,000
Operating income	$ 1,000,000	$ (200,000)	$ 800,000

The incorrect prediction of a $1.5 million increase in costs results from multiplying 100,000 units by $15. Of course, the fallacy in this approach is that it treats a fixed cost (fixed manufacturing cost) as if it were variable. Avoid the assumption that unit costs may be used indiscriminately as a basis for predicting how total costs will behave. Unit costs are useful for predicting variable costs but often misleading when used to predict fixed costs.

Confusion of Variable and Fixed Costs

Consider the relationship between total fixed manufacturing costs and a fixed manufacturing cost per unit of product:

$$\text{fixed cost per unit of product} = \frac{\text{total fixed manufacturing costs}}{\text{some selected volume level used as the denominator}}$$

$$= \frac{\$3,000,000}{1,000,000 \text{ units}} = \$3 \text{ per unit}$$

As noted in Chapter 2, the typical cost accounting system serves two purposes simultaneously: *planning and control* and *product costing*. The total fixed cost for *budgetary planning and control purposes* can be graphed as a lump sum:

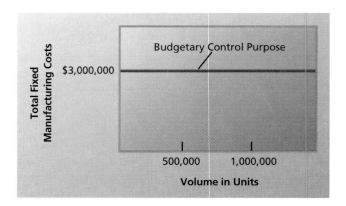

For *product-costing purposes*, however, the absorption-costing approach implies that these *fixed* costs have a *variable*-cost behavior pattern:

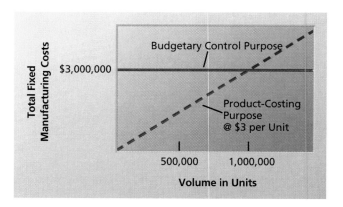

The addition of 100,000 units will not add any *total* fixed costs as long as total output is within the relevant range. The incorrect analysis, however, includes 100,000 × $3 = $300,000 of fixed cost in the predictions of increases in total costs.

In short, the increase in manufacturing costs should be computed by multiplying 1,000,000 units by $12, not by $15. The $15 includes a $3 component that will not affect the total manufacturing costs as volume changes.

Spreading Fixed Costs

As you have just seen, the distinction between unit cost and total cost can become particularly troublesome when analyzing fixed-cost behavior. Assume the same facts concerning the special order as before, except that the order was for 250,000 units at a selling price of $11.50. Then, to avoid the analytical pitfalls of unit-cost analysis, use the contribution approach and concentrate on *totals* instead of units (in thousands of dollars):

	Without Special Order	Effect of Special Order	With Special Order
	1,000,000 Units	*250,000 Units*	*1,250,000 Units*
Sales	20,000	2,875*	22,875
Variable manufacturing costs	12,000	3,000†	15,000
Other variable costs	1,100	—	1,100
Total variable costs	13,100	3,000	16,100
Contribution margin	6,900	(125)‡	6,775

*250,000 × $11.50 selling price of special order.
†250,000 × $12.00 variable manufacturing cost per unit of special order.
‡250,000 × $.50 negative contribution margin per unit of special order.

Short-run income will fall by $125,000 (that is, 250,000 units × $.50) if the special order is accepted. No matter how the fixed manufacturing costs are "unitized" and "spread" over the units produced, their total of $3 million will be *unchanged* by the special order (in thousands of dollars):

	Without Special Order	Effect of Special Order	With Special Order
	1,000,000 Units	*250,000 Units*	*1,250,000 Units*
Contribution margin (as above)	6,900	(125)	6,775
Total fixed costs			
At an average rate of $3.00*:			
1,000,000 × $3.00	3,000		
At an average rate of $2.40†:			
1,250,000 × $2.40		—	3,000
Contribution to other fixed			
costs and operating income	3,900	(125)	3,775

*$3,000,000 ÷ 1,000,000.
†$3,000,000 ÷ 1,250,000.

Notice that no matter how fixed costs are spread for *unit* product-costing purposes, *total* fixed costs are unchanged, even though fixed costs *per unit* fall from $3.00 to $2.40.

The lesson here is important. Do not be deceived. Follow what was called Robert McNamara's First Law of Analysis when he was U.S. Secretary of Defense: "Always start by looking at the grand total. Whatever problem you are studying, back off and look at it in the large." In this context, that law means, "Beware of unit costs. When in doubt, convert all unit costs into the total costs under each alternative to get the big picture." In particular, beware of unit costs when analyzing fixed costs. Think in terms of totals instead.

Multiple-Cost Drivers and Special Orders

To identify costs affected by a special order (or by other special decisions), more and more firms are going a step beyond simply identifying fixed and variable costs. As pointed out in Chapter 3, many different cost drivers may cause companies to incur costs. Businesses that have identified all their significant cost drivers can predict the effects of special orders more accurately.

Suppose Samson Company examined its $12 million of variable costs very closely and identified two significant cost drivers: $9 million that varies directly with *units produced* at a rate of $9 per unit and $3 million that varies with the *number of production setups*. Normally, for production of 1,000,000 units, Samson has 500 setups at a cost of $6,000 per setup, with an average of 2,000 units produced for each setup. Additional sales generally require a proportional increase in the number of setups.

Now suppose the special order is for 100,000 units that vary only slightly in production specifications. Instead of the normal 50 setups, Samson will need only 5 setups, and producing 100,000 units will take only $930,000 of additional variable cost:

Additional unit-based variable cost, 100,000 × $9	$900,000
Additional setup-based variable cost, 5 × $6,000	30,000
Total additional variable cost	$930,000

Instead of the original estimate of 100,000 × $12 = $1,200,000 additional variable cost, the special order will cost only $930,000, or $270,000 less than the original estimate. Therefore, the special order is $270,000 more profitable than predicted from the simple, unit-based assessment of variable cost.

A special order may also be more costly than predicted by a simple fixed- and variable-cost analysis. Suppose the 100,000-unit special order called for a variety of models and colors delivered at various times, so that 100 setups are required. The variable cost of the special order would be $1.5 million.

Additional unit-based variable cost, 100,000 × $9	$ 900,000
Additional setup-based variable cost, 100 × $6,000	600,000
Total additional variable cost	$1,500,000

Summary Problem for Your Review

Problem One

1. Return to the basic illustration in Exhibit 5-3, page 173. Suppose Samson Co. received a special order like that described in conjunction with Exhibit 5-3 that had the following terms: selling price would be $13.50 instead of $13.00, but a manufacturer's agent who had obtained the potential order would have to be paid a flat fee of $40,000 if the order were accepted. What would be the new special-order difference in operating income if the order were accepted?

2. Assume the original facts concerning the special order, except that the order was for 250,000 units at a selling price of $11.50. Some managers have been known to argue for acceptance of such an order as follows: "Of course, we will lose $.50 each on the variable manufacturing costs, but we will gain $.60 per unit by spreading our fixed manufacturing costs over 1.25 million units instead of 1 million units. Consequently, we should take the offer because it represents an advantage of $.10 per unit."

Old fixed manufacturing cost per unit, $3,000,000 ÷ 1,000,000	$3.00
New fixed manufacturing cost per unit, $3,000,000 ÷ 1,250,000	2.40
"Saving" in fixed manufacturing cost per unit	$ .60
Loss on variable manufacturing cost per unit, $11.50 − $12.00	.50
Net saving per unit in manufacturing cost	$ .10

Explain why this is faulty thinking.

Solution to Problem One

1. Focus on the *differences* in revenues and costs. In this problem, in addition to the difference in variable costs, there is a difference in fixed costs between the two alternatives.

Additional revenue, 100,000 units @ $13.50 per unit	$1,350,000
Less additional costs	
Variable costs, 100,000 units @ $12 per unit	1,200,000
Fixed costs, agent's fee	40,000
Increase in operating income from special order	$ 110,000

2. The faulty thinking comes from attributing a "savings" to the decrease in unit fixed costs. Regardless of how the fixed manufacturing costs are "unitized" or "spread" over the units produced, their *total* of $3 million will be *unchanged* by the special order. As the tabulation on page 175 indicates, short-run income will fall by 250,000 units × ($12.00 − $11.50) = $125,000 if the second special order is accepted.

■ DELETION OR ADDITION OF PRODUCTS OR DEPARTMENTS

The same principles of relevance applied to special orders apply—albeit in slightly different ways—to decisions about adding or deleting products or departments.

Avoidable and Unavoidable Costs

Consider a discount department store that has three major departments: groceries, general merchandise, and drugs. Management is considering dropping groceries, which have consistently shown a net loss. The following table reports the present annual net income (in thousands of dollars).

| | | | Departments | |
	Total	Groceries	General Merchandise	Drugs
Sales	$1,900	$1,000	$800	$100
Variable cost of goods sold and expenses*	1,420	800	560	60
Contribution margin	$ 480 (25%)	$ 200 (20%)	$240 (30%)	$ 40 (40%)
Fixed expenses (salaries, depreciation, insurance, property taxes, etc.):				
Avoidable	$ 265	$ 150	$100	$ 15
Unavoidable	180	60	100	20
Total fixed expenses	$ 445	$ 210	$200	$ 35
Operating income	$ 35	$ (10)	$ 40	$ 5

*Examples of variable expenses include paper bags and sales commissions.

avoidable costs
Costs that will not continue if an ongoing operation is changed or deleted.

unavoidable costs
Costs that continue even if an operation is halted.

common costs Those costs of facilities and services that are shared by users.

Notice that the fixed expenses are divided into two categories, *avoidable* and *unavoidable*. **Avoidable costs**—costs that will *not* continue if an ongoing operation is changed or deleted—are relevant. Avoidable costs include department salaries and other costs that could be eliminated by not operating the specific department. **Unavoidable costs**—costs that continue even if an operation is halted—are not relevant because they are not affected by a decision to delete the department. Unavoidable costs include many **common costs**, which are defined as those costs of facilities and services that are shared by users. Examples are store depreciation, heating, air conditioning, and general management expenses.[2]

Assume first that the only alternatives to be considered are dropping or continuing the grocery department, which shows a loss of $10,000. Assume further

[2] The concept of avoidable cost is used by government regulators as well as business executives. For example, Amtrak divides its costs into avoidable—costs that "would cease if the route were eliminated"—and fixed—costs that would "remain relatively constant if a single route were discontinued." The U.S. Interstate Commerce Commission then considers the avoidable costs when considering approval of a railroad's request to abandon a route. Similarly, the Canadian government looks at the avoidable cost when determining the amount of subsidy to give to the country's passenger-rail system. The Montreal *Gazette* reported that in 1993 revenues covered only 35% of the "$7 million in avoidable costs (costs that wouldn't exist if the train disappeared tomorrow—things like staff salaries, food, fuel, and upkeep of train stations)."

that the total assets invested would be unaffected by the decision. The vacated space would be idle, and the unavoidable costs would continue. Which alternative would you recommend? An analysis (in thousands of dollars) follows:

Income Statements	Store as a Whole		
	Total Before Change (a)	Effect of Dropping Groceries (b)	Total After Change (a) – (b)
Sales	$1,900	$1,000	$900
Variable expenses	1,420	800	620
Contribution margin	$ 480	$ 200	$280
Avoidable fixed expenses	265	150	115
Profit contribution to common space and other unavoidable costs	$ 215	$ 50	$165
Common space and other unavoidable costs	180	—	180
Operating income	$ 35	$ 50	$ (15)

The preceding analysis shows that matters would be worse, rather than better, if groceries were dropped and the vacated facilities left idle. In short, as the income statement shows, groceries bring in a contribution margin of $200,000, which is $50,000 more than the $150,000 fixed expenses that would be saved by closing the grocery department. The grocery department showed a loss in the first income statement because of the unavoidable fixed costs charged to it.

Assume now that the space made available by the dropping of groceries could be used to expand the general merchandise department. The space would be occupied by merchandise that would increase sales by $500,000, generate a 30% contribution-margin percentage, and have avoidable fixed costs of $70,000. The $80,000 increase in operating income of general merchandise more than offsets the $50,000 decline from eliminating groceries, providing an overall increase in operating income of $65,000 – $35,000 = $30,000.

(In thousands of dollars)	Effects of Changes			
	Total Before Change (a)	Drop Groceries (b)	Expand General Merchandise (c)	Total After Changes (a) – (b) + (c)
Sales	$1,900	$1,000	$500	$1,400
Variable expenses	1,420	800	350	970
Contribution margin	$ 480	$ 200	$150	$ 430
Avoidable fixed expenses	265	150	70	185
Contribution to common space and other unavoidable costs	$ 215	$ 50	$ 80	$ 245
Common space and other unavoidable costs*	180	—	—	180
Operating income	$ 35	$ 50	$ 80	$ 65

*Includes the $60,000 of former grocery fixed costs, which were allocations of unavoidable common costs that will continue regardless of how the space is occupied.

As the following summary analysis demonstrates, the objective is to obtain, from a given amount of space or capacity, the maximum contribution to the payment of those unavoidable costs that remain unaffected by the nature of the product sold (in thousands of dollars):

	Groceries	Profit Contribution of Given Space — Expansion of General Merchandise	Difference
Sales	$1,000	$500	$500 U
Variable expenses	800	350	450 F
Contribution margin	$ 200	$150	$ 50 U
Avoidable fixed expenses	150	70	80 F
Contribution to common space and other unavoidable costs	$ 50	$ 80	30 F

F = Favorable difference resulting from replacing groceries with general merchandise.
U = Unfavorable difference.

In this case, the general merchandise will not achieve the dollar sales volume that groceries will, but the higher contribution margin percentage and the lower wage costs (mostly because of the diminished need for stocking and checkout clerks) will bring more favorable net results.

This illustration contains another lesson. Avoid the idea that relevant-cost analysis merely says, "Consider all variable costs, and ignore all fixed costs." In this case, *some* fixed costs are relevant because they differ under each alternative.

■ OPTIMAL USE OF LIMITED RESOURCES

When a multiproduct plant is being operated at capacity, managers often must decide which orders to accept. The contribution approach also applies here, because the product to be emphasized or the order to be accepted is the one that makes the biggest *total* profit contribution per unit of the limiting factor. A **limiting factor** or **scarce resource** restricts or constrains the production or sale of a product or service. Limiting factors include labor-hours and machine-hours that limit production and hence sales in manufacturing firms, and square feet of floor space or cubic meters of display space that limit sales in department stores.

limiting factor (scarce resource)
The item that restricts or constrains the production or sale of a product or service.

The contribution approach must be used wisely, however. Managers sometimes mistakenly favor those products with the biggest contribution margin or gross margin per sales dollar, without regard to scarce resources.

Assume that a company has two products: a plain portable heater and a fancier heater with many special features. Unit data follow:

	Plain Heater	Fancy Heater
Selling price	$20	$30
Variable costs	16	21
Contribution margin	$ 4	$ 9
Contribution-margin ratio	20%	30%

Objective 6

Compute a measure of product profitability when production is constrained by a scarce resource

Which product is more profitable? On which should the firm spend its resources? The correct answer is: It depends. If sales are restricted by demand for only a limited *number* of heaters, fancy heaters are more profitable. Why? Because sale of a plain heater adds $4 to profit; sale of a fancy heater adds $9. If the limiting factor is *units* of sales, the more profitable product is the one with the higher contribution *per unit*.

Now suppose annual demand for heaters of both types is more than the company can produce in the next year. Productive capacity is the limiting factor. If 10,000 hours of capacity are available, and three plain heaters can be produced per hour in contrast to one fancy heater, the plain heater is more profitable. Why? Because it contributes more profit *per hour* of capacity:

	Plain Heater	Fancy Heater
1. Units per hour	3	1
2. Contribution margin per unit	$4	$9
Contribution margin per hour (1) × (2)	$12	$9
Total contribution for 10,000 hours	$120,000	$90,000

The criterion for maximizing profits when one factor limits sales is to obtain the greatest possible contribution to profit for each unit of the limiting or scarce factor. The product that is most profitable when one particular factor limits sales may be the least profitable if a different factor restricts sales.

When there are capacity limitations, the conventional contribution-margin or gross-margin-per-sales-dollar ratios provide an insufficient clue to profitability. Consider an example of two department stores. The conventional gross profit percentage (gross profit ÷ selling price) is an insufficient clue to profitability because profits also depend on the space occupied and the **inventory turnover** (number of times the average inventory is sold per year). Discount department stores such as Wal-Mart, Target, and K-Mart have succeeded while using lower markups than traditional department stores because they have been able to increase turnover and thus increase the contribution to profit per unit of space. Exhibit 5-4 illustrates the same product, taking up the same amount of space, in each of two stores. The contribution margins per unit and per sales dollar are less in the discount store, but faster turnover makes the same product a more profitable use of space in the discount store. In general, companies seek faster inventory turnover. A survey of retail shoe stores showed

inventory turnover The number of times the average inventory is sold per year.

that those with above-average financial performance had an inventory turnover of 2.6 compared to an industry average of 2.0.

Notice that throughout this discussion fixed costs have been correctly ignored. They are irrelevant unless their total is affected by the choices.

Exhibit 5-4

Effect of Turnover
on Profit

	Regular Department Store	Discount Department Store
Retail price	$4.00	$3.50
Cost of merchandise and other variable costs	3.00	3.00
Contribution to profit per unit	$1.00 (25%)	$ .50 (14%)
Units sold per year	10,000	22,000
Total contribution to profit, assuming the same space allotment in both stores	$10,000	$11,000

◾ ROLE OF COSTS IN PRICING DECISIONS

One of the major decisions managers face is pricing. Actually, pricing can take many forms. Among the many pricing decisions to be made are:

1. Setting the price of a new product
2. Setting the price of products sold under private labels
3. Responding to a new price of a competitor
4. Pricing bids in both sealed and open bidding situations

The pricing decision is extensively covered in the literature of economics and marketing. Our purpose here is not to provide a comprehensive review of that literature, but simply to highlight a few important points that help define the role of costs in pricing.

Economic Theory and Pricing

perfect competition
A market in which a firm can sell as much of a product as it can produce, all at a single market price.

Pricing decisions depend on the characteristics of the market a firm faces. In **perfect competition**, a firm can sell as much of a product as it can produce, all at a single market price. If it charges more, no customer will buy. If it charges less, it sacrifices profits. Therefore, every firm in such a market will charge the market price, and the only decision for managers is how much to produce.

marginal cost The additional cost resulting from producing and selling one additional unit.

Although costs do not directly influence prices in perfect competition, they affect the production decision. Consider the *marginal cost curve* in Exhibit 5-5. The **marginal cost** is the additional cost resulting from producing and selling one additional unit. The marginal cost often decreases as production increases up to a point because efficiencies are possible with larger production amounts. At some point, however, marginal costs begin to rise with increases in production because facilities begin to be overcrowded, resulting in inefficiencies.

marginal revenue
The additional revenue resulting from the sale of an additional unit.

Exhibit 5-5 also includes a *marginal revenue curve*. The **marginal revenue** is the additional revenue resulting from the sale of an additional unit. In perfect competition, the marginal revenue curve is a horizontal line equal to the price per unit at all volumes of sales.

As long as the marginal cost is less than the price, additional production and sales are profitable. When marginal cost exceeds price, however, the firm loses money on each additional unit. Therefore, the profit-maximizing volume is the quantity at which marginal cost equals price. In Exhibit 5-5, the firm should produce V_0 units. Producing fewer units passes up profitable opportunities; producing more units reduces profit because each additional unit costs more to produce than it generates in revenue.

Exhibit 5-5

Marginal Revenue and Cost in Perfect Competition

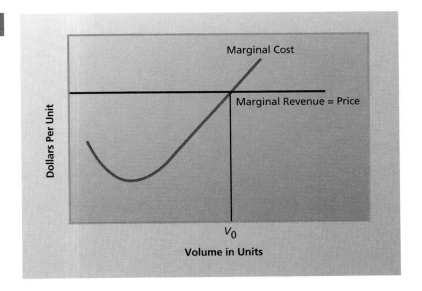

imperfect competition A market in which a firm's price will influence the quantity it sells.

In **imperfect competition**, a firm's price will influence the quantity it sells. At some point, price reductions are necessary to generate additional sales. Exhibit 5-6 contains a demand curve (also called the average revenue curve) for imperfect competition that shows the volume of sales at each possible price. To sell additional units, the price of *all units sold* must be reduced. Therefore, the marginal revenue curve, also shown in Exhibit 5-6, is below the demand curve. That is, the marginal revenue for selling one additional unit is less than the price at which it is sold because the price of all other units falls as well. For example, suppose 10 units can be sold for $50 per unit. The price must be dropped to $49 per unit to sell 11 units, to $48 to sell 12 units, and to $47 to sell 13 units. The fourth column of Exhibit 5-7 shows the marginal revenue for units 11 through 13. Notice that the marginal revenue decreases as volume increases.

price elasticity The effect of price changes on sales volumes.

To estimate marginal revenue, managers must predict the effect of price changes on sales volume, which is called **price elasticity**. If small price increases cause large volume declines, demand is highly *elastic*. If prices have little or no effect on volume, demand is highly *inelastic*.

Exhibit 5-6

Marginal Revenue
and Cost in
Imperfect
Competition

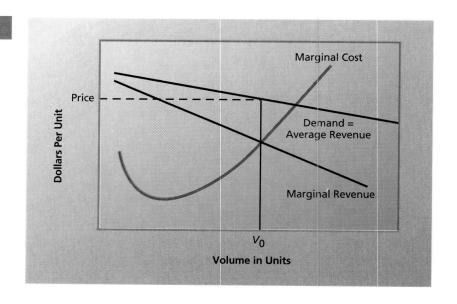

Exhibit 5-7 Profit Maximization in Imperfect Competition

Units Sold	Price per Unit	Total Revenue	Marginal Revenue	Marginal Cost	Profit from Production and Sale of Additional Unit
10	$50	10 × $50 = $500			
11	49	11 × 49 = 539	$539 − $500 = $39	$35	$39 − $35 = $4
12	48	12 × 48 = 576	576 − 539 = 37	36	37 − 36 = 1
13	47	13 × 47 = 611	611 − 576 = 35	37	35 − 37 = (2)

Objective 7

Identify the role
of costs in pricing
decisions in perfect
and imperfect
markets

Now suppose the marginal cost of the units is as shown in the fifth column of Exhibit 5-7. The optimal production and sales level would be 12 units. The last column illustrates that the 11th unit adds $4 to profit, the 12th adds $1, but production and sale of the 13th unit would *decrease* profit by $2. In general, firms should produce and sell units until the marginal revenue equals the marginal cost, represented by volume V_0 in Exhibit 5-6. The optimal price charged will be the amount that creates a demand for V_0 units.

Notice that in economic theory the *marginal cost* is relevant for pricing decisions. The accountant's approximation to marginal cost is *variable cost*. What is the major difference between the economist's marginal cost and the accountant's variable cost? Variable cost is assumed to be constant within a relevant range of volume, whereas marginal cost may change with each unit produced. Within large ranges of production volume, however, changes in marginal cost are often small. Therefore, using variable cost can be a reasonable approximation to marginal cost in many situations.

Maximization of Total Contribution

Managers seldom compute marginal revenue curves and marginal cost curves. Instead, they use estimates based on judgment to predict the effects of additional production and sales on profits. In addition, they examine selected volumes, not the whole range of possible volumes. Such simplifications are justified because the cost of a more sophisticated analysis would exceed the benefits.

Consider a division of General Electric (GE) that makes microwave ovens. Suppose market researchers estimate that 700,000 ovens can be sold if priced at $200 per unit, but 1,000,000 could be sold at $180. The variable cost of production is $130 per unit at production levels of both 700,000 and 1,000,000. Both volumes are also within the relevant range so that fixed costs are unaffected by the changes in volume. Which price should be charged?

The GE manager could compute the additional revenue and additional costs of the 300,000 additional units of sales at the $180 price:

Additional revenue: (1,000,000 × $180) – (700,000 × $200) =	$40,000,000
– Additional costs: 300,000 × $130	= 39,000,000
Additional profit:	$ 1,000,000

Alternatively, the manager could compare the total contribution for each alternative:

Contribution at $180: ($180 – $130) × 1,000,000 =	$50,000,000
Contribution at $200: ($200 – $130) × 700,000 =	49,000,000
Difference:	$ 1,000,000

Notice that comparing the total contributions is essentially the same as computing the additional revenues and costs. Further, both approaches correctly ignore fixed costs, which are unaffected by this pricing decision.

Objective 8

Discuss the factors that influence pricing decisions in practice

■ INFLUENCES ON PRICING IN PRACTICE

Several factors interact to shape the environment in which managers make pricing decisions. Legal requirements, competitors' actions, costs, and customer demands all influence pricing.

predatory pricing
Establishing prices so low that competitors are driven out of the market so that the predatory pricer then has no significant competition and can raise prices dramatically.

Legal Requirements

Pricing decisions must be made within constraints imposed by U.S. and international laws. In addition to prohibiting out-and-out collusion in setting prices, these laws generally prohibit prices that are *predatory* or *discriminatory*.

Predatory pricing is establishing prices so low that competitors are driven out of the market so that the predatory pricer then has no significant competition and can raise prices dramatically. For example, Wal-Mart has been accused of predatory pricing—selling at low cost to drive out local competitors.

U.S. courts have generally ruled that pricing is predatory only if companies set prices below average variable cost.

discriminatory pricing Charging different prices to different customers for the same product or service.

Discriminatory pricing is charging different prices to different customers for the same product or service. For example, a large group of neighborhood pharmacies sued several large drug companies, alleging that their practice of allowing discounts to mail-order drug companies, health maintenance organizations, and other managed-care entities constitutes discriminatory pricing. However, pricing is not discriminatory if it reflects a cost differential incurred in providing the good or service.

Businesses can defend themselves against charges of either predatory or discriminatory pricing by citing their costs as a basis for their prices. Therefore, a good understanding of the cost of a product or service, especially the activities that cause additional costs to be incurred, is useful in avoiding legal pitfalls. Our discussion here assumes that pricing practices do not violate legal constraints.

Competitors' Actions

Competitors usually react to the price changes of their rivals. Many companies will gather information regarding a rival's capacity, technology, and operating policies. In this way, managers make more informed predictions of competitors' reactions to a company's prices. The study of game theory, for which two economists won the 1994 Nobel Prize, focuses on predicting and reacting to competitors' actions.

Tinkering with prices is often most heavily affected by the price setter's expectations of competitors' reactions and of the overall effects on the total industry demand for the good or service in question. For example, an airline might cut prices even if it expects price cuts from its rivals, hoping that total customer demand for the tickets of all airlines will increase sufficiently to offset the reduction in the price per ticket.

Competition is becoming increasingly international. Overcapacity in some countries often causes aggressive pricing policies, particularly for a company's exported goods.

Costs

Costs influence the deliberate setting of prices in some industries, but not in others. Frequently, the market price is regarded as a given. Examples include the prices of metals and agricultural commodities. Consider gold. A mining company sells at the established market prices. Whether profits or losses are forthcoming depends on how well the company controls its costs and volume. Here cost data help managers decide on the level and mix of outputs.

The influence of costs on the setting of prices is often overstated. Nevertheless, many managers say that their prices are set by cost-plus pricing. For example, consider the construction and automobile industries. Their executives describe the procedure as computing an average unit cost and then adding a "reasonable" **markup** (i.e., the amount by which price exceeds cost) that will generate a target return on investment. The key, however, is the "plus" in cost plus. It is rarely an unalterable markup. Its magnitude depends on the behavior of competitors and customers.

markup The amount by which price exceeds cost.

Prices are most directly related to costs in industries where revenue is based on cost reimbursement. A prime example is defense contracting. Cost-reimbursement contracts generally specify how costs should be measured and what costs are allowable. For example, only coach-class (not first-class) fares are reimbursable for business air travel on government projects.

Ultimately, though, the market sets prices after all. Why? Because the price as set by a cost-plus formula is inevitably adjusted "in light of market conditions." The maximum price that may be charged is the one that does not drive the customer away. The minimum price might be considered to be zero (e.g., companies may give out free samples to gain entry into a market). A more practical guide is that, in the short run, the minimum price to be quoted, *subject to consideration of long-run effects*, should be equal to the costs that may be avoided by not landing the order—often all variable costs of producing, selling, and distributing the good or service. In the long run, the price must be high enough to cover all costs including fixed costs.

Customer Demands and Target Costing

More than ever before, managers are recognizing the needs of customers. Pricing is no exception. If customers believe a price is too high, they may turn to other sources for the product or service, substitute a different product, or decide to produce the item themselves.

Most companies have traditionally started with costs and added a markup to get prices. However, a growing number of companies are turning the equation around and developing costs based on prices. Companies that use **target costing** first determine the price at which they can sell a new product or service and then design a product or service that can be produced at a low enough cost to provide an adequate profit margin. Product designers thus become aware of the cost impacts of the design of both the product itself and the process used to produce it.

For example, market research may indicate that Toyota could sell 100,000 units of one model of a sports car annually at a list price of $35,000. The engineers who design the product might consider several different combinations of features bearing different costs. If the total product cost is sufficiently low, the product may be launched. Conversely, if the total product cost is too high, the product may be unjustified. Of course, the point here is that the customer helps determine the price. The product designers and the management accountants work together to see if a product can be developed at a target cost that will provide room for an attractive profit.

Target costing originated in Japan, but now it is used by many companies world-wide, including Chrysler, Mercedes-Benz, Procter & Gamble, and Caterpillar. Even some hospitals use target costing.

Whether a company sets prices based on costs or costs based on prices, it is inevitable that prices and costs interact. If the focus is on prices that are influenced primarily by market forces, managers must make sure that all costs can be covered in the long run. If prices are based on a markup of costs, managers must examine the actions of customers and competitors to ensure that products or services can be sold at the determined prices.

target costing A strategy in which companies first determine the price at which they can sell a new product or service and then design a product or service that can be produced at a low enough cost to provide an adequate profit margin.

Target Costing, ABC, and Service Companies

Many companies use target costing together with an activity-based-costing (ABC) system. Target costing requires a company to first determine what a customer will pay for a product and then work backwards to design the product and production process that will generate a desired level of profit. ABC provides data on the costs of the various activities needed to produce the product. Knowing the costs of activities allows product and production process designers to be able to predict the effects of their designs on the product's cost. Target costing essentially takes activity-based costs and uses them for strategic product decisions.

For example, Culp, Inc., a North Carolina textile manufacturer, uses target costing and ABC to elevate cost management into one of the most strategically imperative areas of the firm. Culp found that 80% of its product costs are predetermined at the design stage, but earlier cost control efforts had focused only on the other 20%. By shifting cost management efforts to the design stage and getting accurate costs of the various activities involved in production, cost management became an integral part of the strategic decisions of the firm.

Cost management at Culp evolved into a process of cutting costs when a product is being designed, not identifying costs that are out of line after the production is complete. A basic goal of target costing is to reduce costs before they occur. After all, once costs have been incurred they cannot be changed. Such a strategy is especially important if product life cycles are short—and, since most product life cycles are shrinking, use of target costing is expanding. Target costing focuses on reducing costs in the product design and development stages—when costs can really be affected. For example, Chrysler's design of the low-priced Neon was heavily influenced by the company's use of target costing, and Procter & Gamble's CEO credits target costing for helping eliminate costs that could lead products to be priced too high for the market.

Target costing has traditionally been applied in manufacturing companies. However, its use in service and nonprofit companies is growing. For example, a process nearly identical to target costing is being used in some hospitals. Development of treatment protocols, the preferred treatment steps for a patient with a particular diagnosis, is the "product design" phase for a hospital. Treatment protocols have short life cycles because of rapid advances in medical technology and knowledge. Therefore, with increased attention to cost containment in health care, it is important to consider the costs of the various activities in a treatment protocol at the time of designing the protocol.

Measuring the costs of a particular treatment protocol after it is in use was the best that could be done until recently, even in the most cost-conscious hospitals. But identifying cost overruns after the fact, although better than never measuring them, did not lead to good cost control. By using target costing techniques, that is, identifying the maximum amount that would be paid for a treatment, protocols can be designed to point out potential cost overruns before a treatment begins. This focuses cost containment on the patient level, where most decisions are made, not at the department level, where identifying the causes of cost overruns is more difficult. ■

Sources: J. Bohn, "Chrysler Cuts Costs by Nurturing Links with Suppliers," Automotive Age, *January 17, 1994, p.18; J. Brausch, "Target Costing for Profit Enhancement,"* Management Accounting, *November 1994, pp. 45–49; G. Hoffman, "Future Vision,"* Grocery Marketing, *March 1994, p. 6; D. Young, "Managing the Stages of Hospital Cost Accounting,"* Healthcare Financial Management, *April 1993, p. 58.*

Choice of Cost Words and Terms

full cost (fully allocated cost) The total of all manufacturing costs plus the total of all selling and administrative costs.

Earlier chapters have alerted you to the meanings of various accounting terms. Each organization has its own cost vocabulary, which often contains cost definitions that clash with their meanings in management accounting literature. In a specific situation, be sure to obtain the exact meaning of the terms used.

Exhibit 5-8 displays how the costs of products and services are usually described. Note particularly that **full cost** or **fully allocated cost** means the total of all manufacturing costs plus the total of all selling and administrative costs.

Exhibit 5-8		Cost per Unit of Product		
Variety of Cost Terms	Variable manufacturing cost	$12.00	$12.00	$12.00
	Variable selling and administrative cost	1.10		1.10
	Total variable cost	$13.10		
	Fixed manufacturing cost		3.00*	3.00
	Absorption cost		$15.00†	
	Fixed selling and administrative cost			2.90*
	Full cost (often called fully allocated cost)			$19.00

* Fixed manufacturing costs, $3,000,000 ÷ 1,000,000 = $3.00.
   Fixed selling and administrative costs, $2,900,000 ÷ 1,000,000 units = $2.90.

† This amount must be used by U.S. companies for inventory valuation in reports to shareholders.

Target Pricing

Cost plus is often the basis for target prices. The size of the "plus" depends on target (desired) operating incomes, which, in turn, frequently depend on the target return on investment for a division, a product line, or a product. Chapter 10 discusses return on investment. For simplicity here, we work with a target operating income.

Target prices can be based on a host of different markups based on a host of different definitions of cost. Thus, there are many ways to arrive at the *same target price*. They simply reflect different arrangements of the components of the same income statement.

Exhibit 5-9 displays the relationships of costs to target selling prices, assuming a target operating income of $1 million. The percentages there represent four popular markup formulas for pricing: (1) as a percentage of variable manufacturing costs, (2) as a percentage of total variable costs, (3) as a percentage of full costs, and (4) as a percentage of absorption costs.

Exhibit 5-9			Alternative Markup Percentages to Achieve Same Target Sales Prices
Relationships of Costs to Same Target Selling Prices	Target sales price	$20.00	
	Variable costs		
	(1) Manufacturing	$12.00*	($20.00 – $12.00) ÷ $12.00 = 66.67%
	Selling and administrative	1.10	
	(2) Unit variable costs	$13.10	($20.00 – $13.10) ÷ $13.10 = 52.67%
	Fixed costs		
	Manufacturing	$ 3.00*	
	Selling and administrative	2.90	
	Unit fixed costs	$ 5.90	
	(3) Full costs	$19.00	($20.00 – $19.00) ÷ $19.00 = 5.26%
	Target operating income	$ 1.00	

* (4) A frequently used formula is based on absorption costs:
[$20.00 – ($12.00 + $3.00)] ÷ $15.00 = 33.33%.

Of course, the percentages differ. For instance, the markup on variable manu-facturing costs is 66.67%, and on absorption costs it is 33.33%. Regardless of the formula used, the pricing decision maker will be led toward the *same* target price. For a volume of 1 million units, assume that the target selling price is $20 per unit. If the decision maker is unable to obtain such a price consistently, the company will not achieve its $1 million operating income objective.

■ ADVANTAGES OF VARIOUS APPROACHES TO PRICING DECISIONS

We have seen that prices can be based on various types of cost information, from variable costs to absorption costs to full costs. Each approach has advan-tages and disadvantages.

Contribution Approach Provides Detailed Information

Prices based on variable costs represent a contribution approach to pricing. When used intelligently, the contribution approach has some advantages over the absorption-costing and full-cost approaches, because the latter often fail to highlight different cost behavior patterns.

Obviously, the contribution approach offers more detailed information because it displays variable- and fixed-cost behavior patterns separately. Because the contribution approach is sensitive to cost-volume-profit relation-ships, it is a helpful basis for developing pricing formulas. Consequently, this approach makes it easier for managers to prepare price schedules at different volume levels.

The correct analysis in Exhibit 5-10 shows how changes in volume affect operating income. The contribution approach helps managers with pricing decisions because it readily displays the interrelationships among variable costs, fixed costs, and potential changes in selling prices.

Exhibit 5-10   Analyses of Effects of Changes in Volume on Operating Income

	Correct Analysis			Incorrect Analysis		
Volume in units	900,000	1,000,000	1,100,000	900,000	1,000,000	1,100,000
Sales @ $20.00	$18,000,000	$20,000,000	$22,000,000	$18,000,000	$20,000,000	$22,000,000
Total variable costs @ $13.10*	11,790,000	13,100,000	14,410,000			
Contribution margin	6,210,000	6,900,000	7,590,000			
Fixed costs†	5,900,000	5,900,000	5,900,000			
Full costs @ $19.00*				17,100,000	19,000,000	20,900,000
Operating income	$ 310,000	$ 1,000,000	$ 1,690,000	$ 900,000	$ 1,000,000	$ 1,100,000

* From Exhibit 5-8.

† Fixed manufacturing costs	$3,000,000
Fixed selling and administrative costs	2,900,000
Total fixed costs	$5,900,000

In contrast, target pricing with absorption costing or full costing presumes a given volume level. When volume changes, the unit cost used at the original planned volume may mislead managers. As our "incorrect analysis" on page 173 showed, managers sometimes erroneously assume that the change in total costs may be computed by multiplying any change in volume by the full unit cost.

The incorrect analysis in Exhibit 5-10 shows how managers may be misled if the $19 full cost per unit is used to predict effects of volume changes on operating income. Suppose a manager uses the $19 figure to predict an operating income of $900,000 if the company sells 900,000 instead of 1,000,000 units. If actual operating income is $310,000 instead, as the correct analysis predicts, that manager may be stunned—and possibly looking for a new job.

Other Advantages of Contribution Approach

Two other advantages of the contribution approach deserve mention. First, a normal or target-pricing formula can be developed as easily by the contribution approach as by absorption-costing or full-costing approaches, as Exhibit 5-9 showed.

Second, the contribution approach offers insight into the short-run versus long-run effects of cutting prices on special orders. For example, assume the same cost behavior patterns as at the Samson Co. (Exhibit 5-3, page 173). The 100,000-unit order added $100,000 to operating income at a selling price of $13, which was $7 below the target selling price of $20 and $2 below the absorption manufacturing cost of $15. Given all the stated assumptions, accepting the order appeared to be the better choice. No general answer can be given, but the relevant information was more easily generated by the contribution approach. Consider the contribution and absorption-costing approaches:

	Contribution Approach	Absorption- Costing Approach
Sales, 100,000 units @ $13	$1,300,000	$1,300,000
Variable manufacturing costs @ $12	1,200,000	
Absorption manufacturing costs @ $15		1,500,000
Apparent change in operating income	$ 100,000	($ 200,000)

Under the absorption approach, the decision maker has no direct knowledge of cost-volume-profit relationships. The decision maker must make the decision by hunch. On the surface, the offer is definitely unattractive because the price of $13 is $2 below absorption costs.

Under the contribution approach, the decision maker sees a short-run advantage of $100,000 from accepting the offer. Fixed costs will be unaffected by whatever decision is made and operating income will increase by $100,000. Still, there often are long-run effects to consider. Will acceptance of the offer undermine the long-run price structure? In other words, is the short-run advantage of $100,000 more than offset by highly probable long-run financial disadvantages? The decision maker may think so and may reject the offer. But—and this is important—by doing so the decision maker is, in effect, forgoing $100,000 now to protect certain long-run market advantages. Generally, the decision maker can assess problems of this sort by asking whether the probability of long-run benefits is worth an "investment" equal to the forgone contribution margin ($100,000 in this case). Under absorption approaches, the decision maker must ordinarily conduct a special study to find the immediate effects. Under the contribution approach, the manager has a system that will routinely and more surely provide such information.

Advantages of Absorption-Cost or Full-Cost Approaches

Our general theme of focusing on relevant information also extends into the area of pricing. To say that either a contribution approach or an absorption-cost approach or a full-cost approach provides the "best" guide to pricing decisions is a dangerous oversimplification of one of the most perplexing problems in business. Lack of understanding and judgment can lead to unprofitable pricing regardless of the kind of cost data available or cost accounting system used.

Frequently, managers do not employ a contribution approach because they fear that variable costs will be substituted indiscriminately for full costs and will therefore lead to suicidal price cutting. This problem should *not* arise if the data are used wisely. However, if top managers perceive a pronounced danger of underpricing when variable-cost data are revealed, they may justifiably prefer an absorption-costing approach or a full-cost approach for guiding pricing decisions.

Cost-plus pricing based on absorption costs or full costs entails circular reasoning. That is, price, which influences sales volume, is often based on an average absorption cost per unit, which in turn is partly determined by the underlying volume of sales.

Despite the criticism, absorption costs or full costs are far more widely used in practice than is the contribution approach. Why? In addition to the reasons already mentioned, the following have been offered:

1. In the long run, all costs must be recovered to stay in business. Sooner or later fixed costs do indeed fluctuate as volume changes. Therefore it is prudent to assume that all costs are variable (even if some are fixed in the short run).

2. Computing target prices based on cost plus may indicate what competitors might charge, especially if they have approximately the same level of efficiency as you and also aim at recovering all costs in the long run.

3. Absorption-cost or full-cost formula pricing meets the cost-benefit test. It is too expensive to conduct individual cost-volume tests for the many products (sometimes thousands) that a company offers.

4. There is much uncertainty about the shape of the demand curves and the correct price-output decisions. Absorption-cost or full-cost pricing copes with this uncertainty by not encouraging managers to take too much marginal business.

5. Absorption-cost or full-cost pricing tends to promote price stability. Managers prefer price stability because it eases their professional lives, primarily because planning is more dependable.

6. Absorption-cost pricing or full-cost pricing provides the most defensible basis for justifying prices to all interested parties including government antitrust investigators.

7. Absorption-cost or full-cost pricing provides convenient reference (target) points to simplify hundreds or thousands of pricing decisions.

No single method of pricing is always best. An interview study of executives reported use of *both* full-cost and variable-cost information in pricing decisions: "The full-vs.-variable-cost pricing controversy is not one of either black or white. The companies we studied used both approaches."[3]

The history of accounting reveals that most companies' systems have gathered costs via some form of full-manufacturing-cost system because this is what is required for financial reporting. In recent years, when systems are changed, variable costs and fixed costs are often identified. But managers have regarded this change as an addition to the existing full-manufacturing-cost system. That is, many managers insist on having information regarding both variable costs per unit and the allocated fixed costs per unit before setting selling prices. If the accounting system routinely gathers data regarding both variable and fixed costs, such data can readily be provided. However, most absorption-costing systems in practice do not organize their data collection so as to distinguish between variable and fixed costs. As a result, special studies or special guessing must be used to designate costs as variable or fixed.

Managers are especially reluctant to focus on variable costs and ignore allocated fixed costs when their performance evaluations, and possibly their bonuses, are based on income shown in published financial statements. Why? Because such statements are based on absorption costing and thus are affected by allocations of fixed costs.

Cost-Based Pricing for International Telephone Calls

Accounting has a direct effect on the revenue of many government contractors because prices are often simply costs plus a profit margin. Accounting costs also can directly affect the revenues of other companies, especially those subject to regulation.

An intriguing area of cost-based pricing is international telephone calls. When a customer in the United States calls someone (or receives a call from someone) in another country, the revenue from the call must be split between the telephone companies in the two countries. Under international agreements, revenues should be shared according to the costs of the two telephone companies, so that there is an equitable division of profits.

In the early 1990s the U.S. Federal Communications Commission (FCC) proposed changing the way revenues on international calls are shared among companies. Under current rules, U.S. firms pay foreign carriers about $.75 out of every dollar collected on overseas calls. The FCC suspected that payments above the foreign carriers' costs amounted to an overpayment of $1 billion a year. To ensure equitable revenues for U.S. telephone companies, the FCC wanted "to learn about the true costs, levels of profits, and how those costs and profits are shared among U.S. telephone companies and foreign telecommunications authorities."

At least two factors make the FCC's task difficult. First, it has no authority over foreign companies. Only U.S. companies must meet reporting requirements specified by the FCC. Second, accounting systems differ by country. For example, many South American countries explicitly adjust their accounting numbers for inflation, but U.S. companies do not. International cost comparisons will not be easy, but if cost-based pricing is to be used for international telephone calls, some method of comparison is necessary. This type of situation is leading many authorities to support more standardization of accounting measurement and reporting rules throughout the world. ∎

Source: Adapted from "Accounting Changes on International Calls Proposed by the FCC," The Wall Street Journal, July 13, 1990, p. A2.

---

[3] T. Bruegelmann, G. Haessly, C. Wolfangel, and M. Schiff, "How Variable Costing is Used in Pricing Decisions," *Management Accounting*, Vol. 65, no. 10, p. 65.

Formats for Pricing

Exhibit 5-9 showed how to compute alternative general markup percentages that would produce the same selling prices if used day after day. In practice, the format and arithmetic of quote sheets, job proposals, or similar records vary considerably.

Exhibit 5-11 is from an actual quote sheet used by the manager of a small job shop that bids on welding machinery orders in a highly competitive industry. The Exhibit 5-11 approach is a tool for informed pricing decisions. Notice that the *maximum* price is not a matter of cost at all; it is what you think you can obtain. The *minimum* price is the total variable cost.

Exhibit 5-11 Quote Sheet for Pricing		
Direct materials, at cost		$25,000
Direct labor and variable manufacturing overhead, 600 direct-labor-hours × $30		18,000
Sales commission (varies with job)		2,000
Total variable costs—minimum price*		45,000
Add fixed costs allocated to job, 600 direct-labor-hours × $20		12,000
Total costs		57,000
Add desired markup		30,000
Selling price—maximum price that you think you can obtain*		$87,000

* This sheet shows two prices, maximum and minimum. Any amount you can get above the minimum price is a contribution margin.

Of course, the manager will rarely bid the minimum price. To do so regularly would virtually ensure eventual bankruptcy. Still, the manager wants to know the effect of a job on the company's total variable costs. Occasionally, a bid near that minimum price may be justified because of idle capacity or the desire to establish a presence in new markets or with a new customer.

Note that Exhibit 5-11 classifies costs especially for the pricing task. Pricing decisions may be made by more than one person. The accountant's responsibility is to prepare an understandable format that involves a minimum of computations. Exhibit 5-11 combines direct labor and variable manufacturing overhead. All fixed costs, whether manufacturing, selling, or administrative, are lumped together and applied to the job using a single fixed-overhead rate per direct-labor-hour. Obviously, if more accuracy is desired, many more detailed cost items and overhead rates could be formulated. To obtain the desired accuracy, many companies are turning to activity-based costing, which was introduced in Chapter 4. For more details on how costs are applied to jobs in both manufacturing and service industries, see Chapter 14.

Some managers, particularly in construction and service industries such as auto repair, compile separate categories of costs of (1) direct materials, parts, and supplies and (2) direct labor. These managers then use different markup rates for each category. These rates are developed to provide revenue for both related overhead costs and operating profit. For example, an automobile repair shop might have the following format for each job:

	Billed to Customers
Auto parts ($200 cost plus 40% markup)	$280
Direct labor (Cost is $20 per hour. Bill at 300% to recover overhead and provide for operating profit. Billing rate is $20 × 300% = $60 per hour. Total billed for 10 hours is $60 × 10 = $600)	600
Total billed to customer	$880

Another example is an Italian printing company in Milan that wants to price its jobs so that each one generates a margin of 28% of revenues—14% to cover selling and administrative expenses and 14% for profit. To achieve this, the manager uses a pricing formula of 140% times predicted materials cost plus 25,000 Italian Lira (abbreviated Lit.) per hour of production time. The latter covers labor and overhead costs of Lit.18,000 per hour. For a product with Lit.400,000 of materials cost and 30 hours of production time, the price would be Lit.1,310,000:

	Cost	Price	Profit
Materials	Lit. 400,000	Lit. 560,000	Lit. 160,000
Labor and overhead	540,000	750,000	210,000
Total	Lit. 940,000	Lit. 1,310,000	Lit. 370,000

The profit of Lit.370,000 is approximately 40% of the cost of Lit.940,000 and 28% of the price of Lit.1,310,000.

Thus there are numerous ways to compute selling prices. However, some general words of caution are appropriate here. Managers are better able to understand their options and the effects of their decisions on profits if they know their costs. That is, it is more informative to pinpoint costs first, before adding markups, than to have a variety of markups already embedded in the "costs" used as guides for setting selling prices. For example, if materials cost $1,000, they should be shown on a price quotation guide at $1,000, not at, say, a marked-up $1,400 because that is what the seller hopes to get.

Highlights to Remember

The accountant's role in decision making is primarily that of a technical expert on financial analysis. The accountant's responsibility is to help the manager use relevant data as guidance for decisions. Accountants and managers must have a penetrating understanding of relevant information, especially costs.

To be relevant to a particular decision, a cost must meet two criteria: (1) it must be an expected *future* cost, and (2) it must have an element of *difference* among the alternatives. All *past* (*historical* or *sunk*) costs are in themselves irrelevant to any *decision* about the future, although they often provide the best available basis for the *prediction* of expected future data.

The combination of the relevant-costing and contribution approaches provides a commonality of approach, a fundamental framework, based on economic analysis, that applies to a vast range of problems. The following generalizations apply to a variety of decisions:

1. Whenever feasible, think in terms of total costs rather than unit costs. Too often, unit costs are regarded as an adequate basis for predicting changes in total costs. This assumption is satisfactory when analyzing variable costs but it is frequently misleading when analyzing fixed costs.

2. A common error is to regard all unit costs indiscriminately, as if all costs were variable costs. In the short run, changes in volume will affect *total* variable costs but not *total* fixed costs. The danger then is to predict total costs assuming that all unit costs are variable. The correct relationships are:

	Behavior as Volume Fluctuates	
	Variable Cost	*Fixed Cost*
Cost per unit	No change	Change
Total cost	Change	No change

Decisions to accept or reject a special sales order should focus on the *additional* revenues and *additional* costs of the order. Decisions on whether to delete a department or a product require analysis of the revenues forgone and the costs saved from the deletion. The key to obtaining the maximum profit from a given capacity is to obtain the greatest possible contribution to profit per unit of the limiting or scarce factor.

Pricing decisions are influenced by economics, the law, customers, competitors, and costs. Profit markups can be added to a variety of cost bases including variable manufacturing costs, all variable costs, absorption (full manufacturing) cost, or all costs. The contribution approach to pricing has the advantage of providing detailed information that is consistent with cost-volume-profit analysis.

Summary Problem for Your Review

Problem One appeared earlier in the chapter.

Problem Two

Custom Graphics is a Chicago printing company that bids on a wide variety of design and printing jobs. The owner of the company, Janet Solomon, prepares the bids for most jobs. Her cost budget for 19X6 is at the top of the next page.

Materials		$ 350,000
Labor		250,000
Overhead		
Variable	$300,000	
Fixed	150,000	450,000
Total production cost of jobs		1,050,000
Selling and administrative expenses		
Variable	$ 75,000	
Fixed	125,000	200,000
Total costs		$1,250,000

Solomon has a target profit of $250,000 for 19X6.

Required Compute the average target markup percentage for setting prices as a percentage of:

1. Prime costs (materials plus labor)
2. Variable production cost of jobs
3. Total production cost of jobs
4. All variable costs
5. All costs

Solution to Problem Two

The purpose of this problem is to emphasize that many different approaches to pricing might be used that, properly employed, would achieve the *same* target selling prices. To achieve $250,000 of profit, the desired revenue for 19X6 is $1,250,000 + $250,000 = $1,500,000. The target markup percentages are

1. Percent of prime cost = $\dfrac{(\$1,500,000 - \$600,000)}{(\$600,000)}$ = 150%

2. Percent of variable production cost of jobs = $\dfrac{(\$1,500,000 - \$900,000)}{(\$900,000)}$ = 66.7%

3. Percent of total production cost of jobs = $\dfrac{(\$1,500,000 - \$1,050,000)}{(\$1,050,000)}$ = 42.9%

4. Percent of all variable costs = $\dfrac{(\$1,500,000 - \$975,000)}{(\$975,000)}$ = 53.8%

5. Percent of all costs = $\dfrac{(\$1,500,000 - \$1,250,000)}{(\$1,250,000)}$ = 20%

Accounting Vocabulary

avoidable costs, *p. 178*
common costs, *p. 178*
decision model, *p. 170*
discriminatory pricing, *p. 186*
full cost, *p. 188*
fully allocated cost, *p. 188*
imperfect competition, *p. 183*

inventory turnover, *p. 181*
limiting factor, *p. 180*
marginal cost, *p. 182*
marginal revenue, *p. 183*
markup, *p. 186*
perfect competition, *p. 182*
predatory pricing, *p. 185*

price elasticity, *p. 183*
relevant information, *p. 168*
scarce resource, *p. 180*
target costing, *p. 187*
unavoidable costs, *p. 178*

Fundamental Assignment Material

5-A1   Special Order
Consider the following details of the income statement of the Moinpour Pen Company for the year ended December 31, 19X6:

Sales	$10,000,000
Less manufacturing cost of goods sold	6,000,000
Gross margin or gross profit	$ 4,000,000
Less selling and administrative expenses	3,300,000
Operating income	$ 700,000

Moinpour's fixed manufacturing costs were $2.4 million and its fixed selling and administrative costs were $2.5 million. Sales commissions of 3% of sales are included in selling and administrative expenses.

The company had sold 2 million pens. Near the end of the year, Pizza Hut Corporation offered to buy 150,000 pens on a special order. To fill the order, a special clip bearing the Pizza Hut emblem would have had to be made for each pen. Pizza Hut intended to use the pens in special promotions in an eastern city during early 19X7.

Even though Moinpour had some idle plant capacity, the president rejected the Pizza Hut offer of $660,000 for the 150,000 pens. He said:

> The Pizza Hut offer is too low. We'd avoid paying sales commissions, but we'd have to incur an extra cost of $.20 per clip for the emblem and its assembly with the pens. If Moinpour sells below its regular selling prices, it will begin a chain reaction of competitors' price cutting and of customers wanting special deals. I believe in pricing at no lower than 8% above our full costs of $9,300,000 ÷ 2,000,000 units = $4.65 per unit plus the extra $.20 per clip less the savings in commissions.

Required

1. Using the contribution approach, prepare an analysis similar to that in Exhibit 5-3, page 173. Use four columns: without the special order, the effect of the special order (total and per unit), and totals with the special order.
2. By what percentage would operating income increase or decrease if the order had been accepted? Do you agree with the president's decision? Why?

5-A2   Choice of Products
The Skill-Craft Company has two products: a plain electric mixer and a fancy electric mixer. The plain mixer sells for $64 and has a variable cost of $48. The fancy mixer sells for $100 and has a variable cost of $70.

Required

1. Compute contribution margins and contribution-margin ratios for plain and fancy mixers.
2. The demand is for more units than the company can produce. There are only 20,000 machine-hours of manufacturing capacity available. Two plain mixers can be produced in the same average time (1 hour) needed to produce one fancy mixer. Compute the total contribution margin for 20,000 hours for plain mixers only and for fancy mixers only.
3. Use two or three sentences to state the major lesson of this problem.

5-A3   Formulas for Pricing
Zeke Podolsky, a building contractor, constructs houses in tracts, often building as many as 20 homes simultaneously. Podolsky has budgeted costs for an expected number of houses in 19X7 as shown at the top of the next page.

Direct materials	$3,500,000
Direct labor	1,000,000
Job construction overhead	1,500,000
Cost of jobs	$6,000,000
Selling and administrative costs	1,500,000
Total costs	$7,500,000

The job construction overhead includes approximately $600,000 of fixed costs, such as the salaries of supervisors and depreciation on equipment. The selling and administrative costs include $300,000 of variable costs, such as sales commissions and bonuses that depend fundamentally on overall profitability.

Podolsky wants an operating income of $1.5 million for 19X7.

Required   Compute the average target markup percentage for setting prices as a percentage of

1. Prime costs (direct materials plus direct labor)
2. The full "cost of jobs"
3. The variable "cost of jobs"
4. The full "cost of jobs" plus selling and administrative costs
5. The variable "cost of jobs" plus variable selling and administrative costs

5-B1   Terminology and Straightforward Interpretations of Unit Costs
Following is the income statement of a manufacturer of blue jeans:

DANUBE COMPANY
Income Statement
for the Year Ended
December 31, 19X4

	Total	Per Unit
Sales	$40,000,000	$20.00
Less manufacturing cost of goods sold	24,000,000	12.00
Gross margin	$16,000,000	$ 8.00
Less selling and administrative expenses	15,000,000	7.50
Operating income	$ 1,000,000	$ .50

Danube had manufactured 2 million pairs of jeans, which had been sold to various clothing wholesalers and department stores. At the start of 19X5, the president, Rosemary Munoz, died from a stroke. Her son, Hector, became the new president. Hector had worked for 15 years in the marketing phases of the business. He knew very little about accounting and manufacturing, which were his mother's strengths. Hector has several questions for you including inquiries regarding the pricing of special orders.

Required

1. To prepare better answers, you decide to recast the income statement in contribution form. Variable manufacturing cost was $19 million. Variable selling and administrative expenses, which were mostly sales commissions, shipping expenses, and advertising allowances paid to customers based on units sold, were $9 million.
2. Hector asks, "I can't understand financial statements until I know the meaning of various terms. In scanning my mother's assorted notes, I found the following pertaining to both total and unit costs: *absorption cost, full manufacturing cost, variable cost, full cost, fully allocated cost, gross margin, contribution margin.* Using our data for 19X4, please give me a list of these costs, their total amounts, and their per-unit amounts."

3. "Near the end of 19X4 I brought in a special order from Sears for 100,000 jeans at $17 each. I said I'd accept a flat $20,000 sales commission instead of the usual 6% of selling price, but my mother refused the order. She usually upheld a relatively rigid pricing policy, saying that it was bad business to accept orders that did not at least generate full manufacturing cost plus 80% of full manufacturing cost.

"That policy bothered me. We had idle capacity. The way I figured, our manufacturing costs would go up by $100,000 \times \$12 = \$1,200,000$, but our selling and administrative expenses would go up by only $20,000. That would mean additional operating income of $100,000 \times (\$17 - \$12)$ minus $20,000, or $500,000 minus $20,000, or $480,000. That's too much money to give up just to maintain a general pricing policy. Was my analysis of the impact on operating income correct? If not, please show me the correct additional operating income."

4. After receiving the explanations offered in requirements 2 and 3, Hector said: "Forget that I had the Sears order. I had an even bigger order from J. C. Penney. It was for 500,000 units and would have filled the plant completely. I told my mother I'd settle for no commission. There would have been no selling and administrative costs whatsoever because J. C. Penney would pay for the shipping and would not get any advertising allowances.

"J. C. Penney offered $9.20 per unit. Our fixed manufacturing costs would have been spread over 2.5 million instead of 2 million units. Wouldn't it have been advantageous to accept the offer? Our old fixed manufacturing costs were $2.50 per unit. The added volume would reduce that cost more than our loss on our variable costs per unit.

"Am I correct? What would have been the impact on total operating income if we had accepted the order?"

5-B2   Unit Costs and Capacity
(CMA, adapted.) Moorhead Manufacturing Company produces two industrial solvents for which the following data have been tabulated. Fixed manufacturing cost is applied to products at a rate of $1.00 per machine-hour.

Per Unit	XY-7	BD-4
Selling price	$6.00	$4.00
Variable manufacturing costs	3.00	1.50
Fixed manufacturing cost	.80	.20
Variable selling cost	2.00	2.00

The sales manager has had a $160,000 increase in her budget allotment for advertising and wants to apply the money on the most profitable product. The solvents are not substitutes for one another in the eyes of the company's customers.

Required

1. How many machine-hours does it take to produce one XY-7? To produce one BD-4? (*Hint*: Focus on applied fixed manufacturing cost.)
2. Suppose Moorhead has only 100,000 machine-hours that can be made available to produce XY-7 and BD-4. If the potential increase in sales units for either product resulting from advertising is far in excess of these production capabilities, which product should be produced and advertised and what is the estimated increase in contribution margin earned?

5-B3   Dropping a Product Line
Hambley's Toy Store is on Regent Street in London. It has a magic department near the main door. Suppose that management is considering dropping the magic department, which has consistently shown an operating loss. The predicted income statements,

in thousands of pounds (£), follow (for ease of analysis, only three product lines are shown):

	Total	General Merchandise	Electronic Products	Magic Department
Sales	£6,000	£5,000	£400	£600
Variable expenses	4,090	3,500	200	390
Contribution margin	£1,910 (32%)	£1,500 (30%)	£200 (50%)	£210 (35%)
Fixed expenses (compensation, depreciation, property taxes, insurance, etc.)	1,110	750	50	310
Operating income	£ 800	£ 750	£150	£(100)

The £310,000 of magic department fixed expenses include the compensation of employees of £100,000. These employees will be released if the magic department is abandoned. All equipment is fully depreciated, so none of the £310,000 pertains to such items. Furthermore, disposal values of equipment will be exactly offset by the costs of removal and remodeling.

If the magic department is dropped, the manager will use the vacated space for either more general merchandise or more electronic products. The expansion of general merchandise would not entail hiring any additional salaried help, but more electronic products would require an additional person at an annual cost of £25,000. The manager thinks that sales of general merchandise would increase by £300,000; electronic products, by £200,000. The manager's modest predictions are partially based on the fact that she thinks the magic department has helped lure customers to the store and thus improved overall sales. If the magic department is closed, that lure would be gone.

Required   Should the magic department be closed? Explain, showing computations.

Additional Assignment Material

Questions

5-1 "The distinction between precision and relevance should be kept in mind." Explain.

5-2 Distinguish between the quantitative and qualitative aspects of decisions.

5-3 Describe the accountant's role in decision making.

5-4 "Any future cost is relevant." Do you agree? Explain.

5-5 Why are historical or past data irrelevant to special decisions?

5-6 Describe the role of past or historical costs in the decision process. That is, how do these costs relate to the prediction method and the decision model?

5-7 "There is a commonality of approach to various special decisions." Explain.

5-8 "No matter what the decision situation, the key question to ask is: What difference does it make?" Explain the nature of the difference.

5-9 "In relevant-cost analysis, beware of unit costs." Explain.

5-10 "Increasing sales will decrease fixed costs because it spreads them over more units." Do you agree? Explain.

5-11 "The key to decisions to delete a product or department is identifying avoidable costs." Do you agree? Explain.

5-12 "Avoidable costs are variable costs." Do you agree? Explain.

5-13 Give four examples of limiting or scarce factors.

5-14 Compare and contrast *marginal cost* and *variable cost*.

5-15 Describe four major factors that influence pricing decisions.

5-16 Why are customers one of the factors influencing price decisions?

5-17 "Basing pricing on only the variable costs of a job results in suicidal underpricing." Do you agree? Why?

5-18 Provide three examples of pricing decisions other than the special order.

5-19 List four popular markup formulas for pricing.

5-20 Describe two long-run effects that may lead to managers rejecting opportunities to cut prices and obtain increases in short-run profits.

5-21 Give two reasons why full costs are far more widely used than variable costs for guiding pricing.

5-22 Why do most executives use both full-cost and variable-cost information for pricing decisions?

5-23 "Target costing is the opposite of target pricing." Do you agree? Explain.

Exercises

5-24   Pinpointing of Relevant Costs

Today you are planning to see a motion picture and you can attend either of two theaters. You have only a small budget for entertainment, so prices are important. You have attended both theaters recently. One charged $6 for admission; the other charged $7. You habitually buy popcorn in the theater—each theater charges $2. The motion pictures now being shown are equally attractive to you, but you are virtually certain that you will never see the picture that you reject today.

Required

Identify the relevant costs. Explain your answer.

5-25   Information and Decisions

Suppose Radio Shack's historical costs for the manufacture of a calculator were as follows: direct materials, $4.60 per unit; direct labor, $3.00 per unit. Management is trying to decide whether to replace some materials with different materials. The replacement should cut material costs by 5% per unit. However, direct-labor time will increase by 5% per unit. Moreover, direct-labor rates will be affected by a recent 10% wage increase.

Prepare an exhibit like Exhibit 5-1 (p. 171), showing where and how the data about direct material and direct labor fit in the decision process.

5-26   Identification of Relevant Costs

Paul and Paula Petrocelli were trying to decide whether to go to the symphony or to the baseball game. They already have two nonrefundable tickets to "Pops Night at the Symphony" that cost $40 each. This is the only concert of the season they considered attending because it is the only one with the type of music they enjoy. The baseball game is the last one of the season, and it will decide the league championship. They can purchase tickets for $20 each.

The Petrocellis will drive 50 miles round trip to either event. Variable costs for operating their auto are $.14 per mile, and fixed costs average $.13 per mile for the 18,000 miles they drive annually. Parking at the symphony is free, but it costs $6 at the baseball game.

To attend either event, Paul and Paula will hire a baby-sitter at $4 per hour. They expect to be gone 5 hours to attend the baseball game but only 4 hours to attend the symphony.

Required

Compare the cost of attending the baseball game to the cost of attending the symphony. Focus on relevant costs. Compute the difference in cost, and indicate which alternative is more costly to the Petrocellis.

5-27   Straightforward Special-Order Decision

The Ventura Sport Shop makes game jerseys for athletic teams. The F. C. Strikers soccer club has offered to buy 100 jerseys for the teams in its league for $15 per jersey. The team price for such jerseys normally is $18, an 80% markup over Ventura's purchase price of $10 per jersey. Ventura adds a name and number to each jersey at a variable cost of $2 per jersey. The annual fixed cost of equipment used in the printing process is $6,000 and other fixed costs allocated to jerseys is $2,000. Ventura makes about 2,000 jerseys per year, making the fixed cost $4 per jersey. The equipment is used only for printing jerseys and stands idle 75% of the usable time.

The manager of Ventura Sport Shop turned down the offer, saying, "If we sell at $15 and our cost is $16, we lose money on each jersey we sell. We would like to help your league, but we can't afford to lose money on the sale."

Required

1. Compute the amount by which the operating income of Ventura Sport Shop would change if the F. C. Striker's offer were accepted.
2. Suppose you were the manager of Ventura Sport Shop. Would you accept the offer? In addition to considering the quantitative impact computed in requirement 1, list two qualitative considerations that would influence your decision—one qualitative factor supporting acceptance of the offer and one supporting rejection.

5-28 Unit Costs and Total Costs
You are a bank vice president who belongs to a downtown luncheon club. Annual dues are $120. You use the club solely for lunches, which cost $6 each. You have not used the club much in recent years and you are wondering whether to continue your membership.

Required

1. You are confronted with a variable-cost plus a fixed-cost behavior pattern. Plot each on a graph, where the vertical axis is total cost and the horizontal axis is annual volume in number of lunches. Also plot a third graph that combines the previous two graphs.
2. What is the cost per lunch if you pay for your own lunch once a year? Twelve times a year? Two hundred times a year?
3. Suppose the average price of lunches elsewhere is $10. (a) How many lunches must you have at the luncheon club so that the total costs of the lunches would be the same regardless of where you ate for that number of lunches? (b) Suppose you ate 250 lunches a year at the club. How much would you save in relation to the total costs of eating elsewhere?

5-29 Advertising Expenditures and Nonprofit Organizations

Many colleges and universities have been extensively advertising their services. For example, a university in Philadelphia used a biplane to pull a sign promoting its evening program, and one in Mississippi designed bumper stickers and slogans as well as innovative programs.

Suppose Central State University (CSU) charges a comprehensive annual fee of $14,000 for tuition, room, and board, and it has capacity for 2,500 students. Costs per student for the 19X1 academic year are:

	Variable	Fixed	Total
Educational programs	$4,000	$4,200	$ 8,200
Room	1,300	2,200	3,500
Board	2,600	600	3,200
	$7,900	$7,000*	$14,900

* Based on 2,000 to 2,500 students for the year.

The admissions department predicts enrollment of 2,000 students for 19X1. The assistant director of admissions has proposed a two-month advertising campaign, however, using radio and television advertisements together with an extensive direct mailing of brochures.

Required

1. Suppose the advertising campaign will cost $1.83 million. What is the minimum number of additional students the campaign must attract to make the campaign break even?
2. Suppose the admissions department predicts that the campaign will attract 350 additional students. What is the most CSU should pay for the campaign and still break even?

3. Suppose a three-month (instead of two-month) campaign will attract 450 instead of 350 additional students. What is the most CSU should pay for the one-month extension of the campaign and still break even?

5-30   Variety of Cost Terms

Consider the following data:

Variable selling and administrative costs per unit	$ 4.00
Total fixed selling and administrative costs	$2,900,000
Total fixed manufacturing costs	$3,000,000
Variable manufacturing costs per unit	$ 9.00
Units produced and sold	500,000

Required

1. Compute the following per unit of product: (a) total variable costs, (b) absorption cost, (c) full cost.
2. Give a synonym for *full cost*.

5-31   Profit per Unit of Space

1. Several successful chains of warehouse stores have merchandising policies that differ considerably from those of traditional department stores. Name some characteristics of these warehouse stores that have contributed to their success.
2. Food chains have typically regarded approximately 20% of selling price as an average target gross profit on canned goods and similar grocery items. What are the limitations of such an approach? Be specific.

5-32   A&P's Closing of Stores

A major U.S. grocery chain, A&P, recently ran into profit difficulties and closed many of its stores.

1. After the closures the company's labor costs as a percentage of sales increased in some markets, such as the Long Island and Pittsburgh divisions, even after allowing for normal increases in wage rates. How could this effect occur?
2. The company manufactured many of its own products in 46 company-operated plants. Twenty-one were bakeries. The others manufactured a variety of goods, from frozen potatoes to mouthwash. What impact would the store closings probably have on the manufacturing plants and on the total operating income?

5-33   Deletion of Product Line

Country Day School is a private elementary school. In addition to regular classes, after-school care is provided between 3:00 and 6:00 P.M. at $3 per child per hour. Financial results for the after-school care for a representative month are:

Revenue, 600 hours @ $3 per hour		$1,800
Less		
Teacher salaries	1,300	
Supplies	200	
Depreciation	325	
Sanitary engineering	25	
Other fixed costs	50	1,900
Operating income (loss)		$ (100)

The director of Country Day School is considering discontinuing the after-school care services because it is not fair to the other students to subsidize the after-school care program. He thinks that eliminating the program will free up $100 a month to be used in the regular classes.

Required

1. Compute the financial impact on Country Day School from discontinuing the after-school care program.
2. List three qualitative factors that would influence your decision.

5-34   Acceptance of Low Bid

The Hernandez Company, a maker of a variety of metal and plastic products, is in the midst of a business downturn and is saddled with many idle facilities. The National Hospital Supply Company has approached Hernandez to produce 300,000 nonslide serving trays. National will pay $1.20 each.

Hernandez predicts that its variable costs will be $1.30 each. Its fixed costs, which had been averaging $1 per unit on a variety of other products, will now be spread over twice as much volume, however. The president commented, "Sure we'll lose $.10 each on the variable costs, but we'll gain $.50 per unit by spreading our fixed costs. Therefore, we should take the offer, because it represents an advantage of $.40 per unit."

Required

Suppose the regular business had a current volume of 300,000 units, sales of $600,000, variable costs of $390,000, and fixed costs of $300,000. Do you agree with the president? Why?

5-35   Pricing by Auto Dealer

Many automobile dealers have an operating pattern similar to that of Ranch Motors, a dealer in Texas. Each month, Ranch initially aims at a unit volume quota that approximates a break-even point. Until the break-even point is reached, Ranch has a policy of relatively lofty pricing, whereby the "minimum deal" must contain a sufficiently high markup to ensure a contribution to profit of no less than $400. After the break-even point is attained, Ranch tends to quote lower prices for the remainder of the month.

Required

What is your opinion of this policy? As a prospective customer, how would you react to this policy?

5-36   Target Selling Prices

Consider the following data from Blackmar Company's budgeted income statement (in thousands of dollars):

Target sales	$60,000
Variable costs	
Manufacturing	30,000
Selling and administrative	6,000
Total variable costs	36,000
Fixed costs	
Manufacturing	8,000
Selling and administrative	6,000
Total fixed costs	14,000
Total of all costs	50,000
Operating income	$10,000

Required

Compute the following markup formulas that would be used for obtaining the same target sales as a percentage of (1) total variable costs, (2) full costs, (3) variable manufacturing costs, and (4) absorption costs.

5-37 Competitive Bids

Rimmer, Coles, and Diaz, a CPA firm, is preparing to bid for a consulting job. Although Alice Rimmer will use her judgment about the market in finalizing the bid, she has asked you to prepare a cost analysis to help in the bidding. You have estimated the costs for the consulting job to be:

Materials and supplies, at cost	$ 30,000
Hourly pay for consultants, 2,000 hours @ $35 per hour	70,000
Fringe benefits for consultants, 2,000 hours @ $12 per hour	24,000
Total variable costs	124,000
Fixed costs allocated to the job	
Based on labor, 2,000 hours @ $10 per hour	20,000
Based on materials and supplies, 80% of 30,000	24,000
Total cost	$168,000

Of the $44,000 allocated fixed costs, $35,000 will be incurred even if the job is not undertaken.

Alice normally bids jobs at the sum of (1) 150% of the estimated materials and supplies cost and (2) $80 per estimated labor-hour.

Required
1. Prepare a bid using the normal formula.
2. Prepare a minimum bid equal to the additional costs expected to be incurred to complete the job.
3. Prepare a bid that will cover full costs plus a markup for profit equal to 20% of full cost.

Problems

5-38 Pricing, Ethics, and the Law

Mega Pharmaceuticals, Inc., (MPI) produces both prescription and over-the-counter medications. In January MPI introduced a new prescription drug, Rythestan, to relieve the pain of arthritis. The company spent more than $50 million over the last five years developing the drug, and advertising alone during the first year of introduction will exceed $10 million. Production cost for a bottle of 100 tablets is approximately $12. Sales in the first three years are predicted to be 500,000, 750,000, and 1,000,000 bottles, respectively. To achieve these sales, MPI plans to distribute the medicine through three sources: directly from physicians, through hospital pharmacies, and through retail pharmacies. Initially, the bottles will be given free to physicians to give to patients, hospital pharmacies will pay $25 per bottle, and retail pharmacies will pay $40 per bottle. In the second and third year, the company plans to phase out the free distributions to physicians and move all other customers toward a $50 per bottle sales price.

Required
Comment on the pricing and promotion policies of MPI. Pay particular attention to the legal and ethical issues involved.

5-39 Pricing and Contribution Approach

The Concord Trucking Company has the following operating results to date for 19X3:

Operating revenues	$100,000,000
Operating costs	80,000,000
Operating income	$ 20,000,000

A large Boston manufacturer has inquired about whether Concord would be interested in trucking a large order of its parts to Atlanta. Steve Minkler, operations manager, investigated the situation and estimated that the "fully allocated" costs of servicing the order would be $40,000. Using his general pricing formula, he quoted a price of $50,000. The manufacturer replied: "We'll give you $37,000, take it or leave it. If you do not want our business, we'll truck it ourselves or go elsewhere."

A cost analyst had recently been conducting studies of how Concord's operating costs tended to behave. She found that $64 million of the $80 million could be characterized as variable costs. Minkler discussed the matter with her and decided that this order would probably generate cost behavior little different from Concord's general operations.

Required

1. Using a contribution format, prepare an analysis for Minkler.
2. Should Concord accept the order? Explain.

5-40   Cost Analysis and Pricing

The budget for the University Park Printing Company for 19X5 follows:

Sales		£1,100,000
Direct material	£280,000	
Direct labor	320,000	
Overhead	400,000	1,000,000
Net income		£ 100,000

The company typically uses a so-called cost-plus pricing system. Direct material and direct labor costs are computed, overhead is added at a rate of 125% of direct labor, and 10% of the total cost is added to obtain the selling price.

Carol Rosenthal, the sales manager, has placed a £22,000 bid on a particularly large order with a cost of £5,600 direct material and £6,400 direct labor. The customer informs her that she can have the business for £19,800, take it or leave it. If Rosenthal accepts the order, total sales for 19X5 will be £1,119,800.

Rosenthal refuses the order, saying: "I sell on a cost-plus basis. It is bad policy to accept orders at below cost. I would lose £200 on the job."

The company's annual fixed overhead is £160,000.

Required

1. What would net income have been with the order? Without the order? Show your computations.
2. Give a short description of a contribution approach to pricing that Rosenthal might follow. Include a stipulation of the pricing formula that Rosenthal should routinely use if she hopes to obtain a target net income of £100,000.

5-41   Pricing of Education

You are the director of continuing education programs for a well-known university. Courses for executives are especially popular, and you have developed an extensive menu of one-day and two-day courses that are presented in various locations throughout the nation. The performance of these courses for the current fiscal year, excluding the final course which is scheduled for the next Saturday, is:

Tuition revenue	$2,000,000
Costs of courses	800,000
Contribution margin	1,200,000
General administrative expenses	400,000
Operating income	$ 800,000

The costs of the courses include fees for instructors, rentals of classrooms, advertising, and any other items, such as travel, that can be easily and exclusively identified as being caused by a particular course.

The general administrative expenses include your salary, your secretary's compensation, and related expenses, such as a lump-sum payment to the university's central offices as a share of university overhead.

The enrollment for your final course of the year is 40 students, who have paid $200 each. Two days before the course is to begin, a city manager telephones your office. "Do you offer discounts to nonprofit institutions?" he asks. "If so, we'll send 10 managers. But our budget will not justify our spending more than $100 per person." The extra cost of including these ten managers would entail lunches at $20 each and course materials at $40 each.

Required

1. Prepare a tabulation of the performance for the full year including the final course. Assume that the costs of the final course for the 40 enrollees' instruction, travel, advertising, rental of hotel classroom, lunches, and course materials would be $4,600. Show a tabulation in four columns: before final course, final course with 40 registrants, effect of 10 more registrants, and grand totals.
2. What major considerations would probably influence the pricing policies for these courses? For setting regular university tuition in private universities?

5-42   Use of Passenger Jets
In 19X5 Continental Air Lines, Inc. filled about 50% of the available seats on its flights, a record about 15 percentage points below the national average.

Continental could have eliminated about 4% of its runs and raised its average load considerably. The improved load factor would have reduced profits, however. Give reasons for or against this elimination. What factors should influence an airline's scheduling policies?

When you answer this question, suppose that Continental had a basic package of 3,000 flights per month that had an average of 100 seats available per flight. Also suppose that 52% of the seats were filled at an average ticket price of $200 per flight. Variable costs are about 70% of revenue.

Continental also had a marginal package of 120 flights per month that had an average of 100 seats available per flight. Suppose that only 20% of the seats were filled at an average ticket price of $100 per flight. Variable costs are about 50% of this revenue. Prepare a tabulation of the basic package, marginal package, and total package, showing percentage of seats filled, revenue, variable expenses, and contribution margin.

5-43   Effects of Volume on Operating Income
The Brownell Division of Victoria Sports Company manufactures boomerangs, which are sold to wholesalers and retailers. The division manager has set a target of 250,000 boomerangs for next month's production and sales. The manager, however, has prepared an analysis of the effects on operating income of deviations from the target:

Volume in units	200,000	250,000	300,000
Sales @ $3.00	$600,000	$750,000	$900,000
Full costs @ $2.50	500,000	625,000	750,000
Operating income	$100,000	$125,000	$150,000

The costs have the following characteristics. Variable manufacturing costs are $1.00 per boomerang; variable selling costs are $.20 per boomerang. Fixed manufacturing costs per month are $275,000; fixed selling and administrative costs, $50,000.

Required

1. Prepare a correct analysis of the changes in volume on operating income. Prepare a tabulated set of income statements at levels of 200,000, 250,000, and 300,000 boomerangs. Also show percentages of operating income in relation to sales.
2. Compare your tabulation with the manager's tabulation. Why is the manager's tabulation incorrect?

5-44   Pricing of Special Order

The Drosselmeier Corporation makes Christmas Nutcrackers and has an annual plant capacity of 2,400 product units. Its predicted operations for the year are:

Production and sales of 2,000 units, total sales	$90,000
Manufacturing costs	
Fixed (total)	$30,000
Variable (per unit)	$13
Selling and administrative expenses	
Fixed (total)	$15,000
Variable (per unit)	$5

Required

Compute the following, ignoring income taxes:

1. If the company accepts a special order for 300 units at a selling price of $20 each, how would the *total* predicted net income for the year be affected, assuming no effect on regular sales at regular prices?
2. Without decreasing its total net income, what is the lowest *unit price* for which the Drosselmeier Corporation could sell an additional 100 units not subject to any variable selling and administrative expenses, assuming no effect on regular sales at regular prices?
3. List the numbers given in the problem that are irrelevant (not relevant) in solving requirement 2.
4. Compute the expected annual net income (with no special orders) if plant capacity can be doubled by adding additional facilities at a cost of $250,000. Assume that these facilities have an estimated life of 5 years with no residual scrap value, and that the current unit selling price can be maintained for all sales. Total sales are expected to equal the new plant capacity each year. No changes are expected in variable costs per unit or in total fixed costs except for depreciation.

5-45   Pricing and Confusing Variable and Fixed Costs

Goldwyn Electronics had a fixed factory overhead budget for 19X2 of $10 million. The company planned to make and sell 2 million units of the product, a communications device. All variable manufacturing costs per unit were $10. The budgeted income statement contained the following:

Sales	$40,000,000
Manufacturing cost of goods sold	30,000,000
Gross margin	10,000,000
Deduct selling and administrative expenses	4,000,000
Operating income	$ 6,000,000

For simplicity, assume that the actual variable costs per unit and the total fixed costs were exactly as budgeted.

1. Compute Goldwyn's budgeted fixed factory overhead per unit.
2. Near the end of 19X2 a large computer manufacturer offered to buy 100,000 units for $1.2 million on a one-time special order. The president of Goldwyn stated: "The offer is a bad deal. It's foolish to sell below full manufacturing costs per unit. I realize that this order will have only a modest effect on selling and administrative costs. They will increase by a $10,000 fee paid to our sales agent." Compute the effect on operating income if the offer is accepted.
3. What factors should the president of Goldwyn consider before finally deciding whether to accept the offer?
4. Suppose the original budget for fixed manufacturing costs was $10 million, but budgeted units of product were 1 million. How would your answers to requirements 1 and 2 change? Be specific.

5-46 Demand Analysis

(SMA, adapted.) Ross Manufacturing Limited produces and sells one product, a three-foot American flag. During 19X4 the company manufactured and sold 50,000 flags at $24 each. Existing production capacity is 60,000 flags per year.

In formulating the 19X5 budget, management is faced with a number of decisions concerning product pricing and output. The following information is available:

1. A market survey shows that the sales volume is largely dependent on the selling price. For each $1 drop in selling price, sales volume would increase by 10,000 flags.
2. The company's expected cost structure for 19X5 is as follows:
   a. Fixed cost (regardless of production or sales activities), $360,000
   b. Variable costs per flag (including production, selling, and administrative expenses), $15
3. To increase annual capacity from the present 60,000 to 90,000 flags, additional investment for plant, building, equipment, and the like, of $200,000 would be necessary. The estimated average life of the additional investment would be 10 years, so the fixed costs would increase by an average of $20,000 per year. (Expansion of less than 30,000 additional units of capacity would cost only slightly less than $200,000.)

Indicate, with reasons, what the level of production and the selling price should be for the coming year. Also indicate whether the company should approve the plant expansion. Show your calculations. Ignore income tax considerations and the time value of money.

5-47 Choice of Products

Florida Fashions sells both designer and moderately priced women's wear in Sarasota. Profits have been volatile. Top management is trying to decide which product line to drop. Accountants have reported the following relevant data:

	Per Item	
	Designer	Moderately Priced
Average selling price	$240	$140
Average variable expenses	120	75
Average contribution margin	$120	$ 65
Average contribution-margin percentage	50%	46%

The store has 8,000 square feet of floor space. If moderately priced goods are sold exclusively, 400 items can be displayed. If designer goods are sold exclusively, only 300 items can be displayed. Moreover, the rate of sale (turnover) of the designer items will be two-thirds the rate of moderately priced goods.

1. Prepare an analysis to show which product to drop.
2. What other considerations might affect your decision in requirement 1?

5-48   Analysis of Unit Costs

The Sunlight Company manufactures small appliances, such as electric can openers, toasters, food mixers, and irons. The peak season is at hand, and the president is trying to decide whether to produce more of the company's standard line of can openers or its premium line that includes a built-in knife sharpener, a better finish, and a higher-quality motor. The unit data follow:

	Product	
	Standard	*Premium*
Selling price	$26	$34
Direct material	$ 8	$12
Direct labor	2	1
Variable factory overhead	2	3
Fixed factory overhead	6	9
Total cost of goods sold	$18	$25
Gross profit per unit	$ 8	$ 9

The sales outlook is very encouraging. The plant could operate at full capacity by producing either product or both products. Both the standard and the premium products are processed through the same departments. Selling and administrative costs will not be affected by this decision, so they may be ignored.

Many of the parts are produced on automatic machinery. The factory overhead is allocated to products by developing separate rates per machine-hour for variable and fixed overhead. For example, the total fixed overhead is divided by the total machine-hours to get a rate per hour. Thus the amount of overhead allocated to products is dependent on the number of machine-hours allocated to the product. It takes one hour of machine time to produce one unit of the standard product.

Direct labor may not be proportionate with overhead because many workers operate two or more machines simultaneously.

Which product should be produced? If more than one should be produced, indicate the proportions of each. Show computations. Explain your answers briefly.

5-49   Use of Available Facilities

The Higashi Company manufactures electronic subcomponents that can be sold directly or can be processed further into "plug-in" assemblies for a variety of intricate electronic equipment. The entire output of subcomponents can be sold at a market price of $2 per unit. The plug-in assemblies have been generating a sales price of $5.50 for three years, but the price has recently fallen to $5.10 on assorted orders.

Nancy Ng, the vice-president of marketing, has analyzed the markets and the costs. She thinks that production of plug-in assemblies should be dropped whenever the price falls below $4.50 per unit. The total available capacity should currently be devoted to producing plug-in assemblies. She has cited the data at the top of the next page.

Direct-materials and direct-labor costs are variable. The total overhead is fixed; it is allocated to units produced by predicting the total overhead for the coming year and dividing this total by the total hours of capacity available.

The total hours of capacity available are 600,000. It takes 1 hour to make 60 subcomponents and 2 hours of additional processing and testing to make 60 plug-in assemblies.

	Sub-components
Selling price, after deducting relevant selling costs	$2.00
Direct materials	$ .90
Direct labor	.30
Manufacturing overhead	.60
Cost per unit	1.80
Operating profit	$ .20

	Plug-In Assemblies
Selling price, after deducting relevant selling costs	$5.10
Transferred-in variable cost for subcomponents	$1.20
Additional direct materials	1.45
Direct labor	.45
Manufacturing overhead	1.20*
Cost per unit	4.30
Operating profit	$ .80

* For additional processing to make and test plug-in assemblies.

Required

1. If the price of plug-in assemblies for the coming year is going to be $5.10, should sales of subcomponents be dropped and all facilities devoted to the production of plug-in assemblies? Show computations.
2. Prepare a report for the vice president of marketing to show the lowest possible price for plug-in assemblies that would be acceptable.
3. Suppose 40% of the manufacturing overhead is variable with respect to processing and testing time. Repeat requirements 1 and 2. Do your answers change? If so, how?

5-50   Target Costing

Knoxville Electrical, Inc., makes small electric motors for a variety of home appliances. Knoxville sells the motors to appliance makers, who assemble and sell the appliances to retail outlets. Although Knoxville makes dozens of different motors, it does not currently make one to be used in garage-door openers. The company's market research department has discovered a market for such a motor.

The market research department has indicated that a motor for garage-door openers would likely sell for $23. A similar motor currently being produced has the following manufacturing costs:

Direct materials	$12.00
Direct labor	5.00
Overhead	8.00
Total	$25.00

Knoxville desires a gross margin of 15% of the manufacturing cost.

Required

1. Suppose Knoxville used cost-plus pricing, setting the price 15% above the manufacturing cost. What price would be charged for the motor? Would you produce such a motor if you were a manager at Knoxville? Explain.

2. Suppose Knoxville uses target costing. What price would the company charge for a garage-door-opener motor? What is the highest acceptable manufacturing cost for which Knoxville would be willing to produce the motor?

3. As a user of target costing, what steps would Knoxville managers take to try to make production of this product feasible?

5-51   Review Of Chapters 2–5

The Disposable Camera division of Saari Optics Co. has the following cost behavior patterns:

Production range in units	0–5,000	5,001–10,000	10,001–15,000	15,001–20,000
Fixed costs	$15,000	$22,000	$25,000	$27,000

Maximum production capacity is 20,000 cameras per year. Variable costs per unit are $5 at all production levels.

Required   Each situation described below is to be considered independently.

1. Production and sales are expected to be 11,000 cameras for the year. The sales price is $7 per camera. How many additional cameras need to be sold, in an unrelated market, at $6 per camera to show a total overall net income of $900 for the year?

2. The company has orders for 23,000 cameras at $7. If it desired to make a minimum overall net income of $14,500 on these 23,000 cameras, what unit purchase price would it be willing to pay a subcontractor for 3,000 cameras? Assume that the subcontractor would act as Saari's agent, deliver the cameras to customers directly, and bear all related costs of manufacture, delivery, etc. The customers, however, would pay Saari directly as goods were delivered.

3. Production is currently expected to be 7,000 cameras for the year at a selling price of $7. By how much may advertising or special promotion costs be increased to bring production up to 14,500 cameras and still earn a total net income of 2% of dollar sales?

4. Net income is currently $12,500. Nonvariable costs are $25,000. Competitive pressures are mounting, however. A 5% decrease in price will not affect sales volume but will decrease net income by $4,750. What is the present volume, in units? What is the correct selling price? (Note: It is not $7.)

Cases

5-52   Use of Capacity

(CMA, adapted.) St. Tropez S. A. manufactures several different styles of jewelry cases in southern France. Management estimates that during the third quarter of 1996 the company will be operating at 80% of normal capacity. Because the company desires a higher utilization of plant capacity, it will consider a special order.

St. Tropez has received special-order inquiries from two companies. The first is from JCP, Inc., which would like to market a jewelry case similar to one of St. Tropez's cases. The JCP jewelry case would be marketed under JCP's own label. JCP, Inc., has offered St. Tropez FF57.5 per jewelry case for 20,000 cases to be shipped by October 1, 1996. The cost data for the St. Tropez jewelry case, which would be similar to the specifications of the JCP special order, are as follows:

Regular selling price per unit	FF90
Costs per unit:	
Raw materials	FF25
Direct labor .5 hr @ FF60	30
Overhead .25 machine-hr @ FF40	10
Total costs	FF65

According to the specifications provided by JCP, Inc., the special-order case requires less expensive raw materials, which will cost only FF22.5 per case. Management has estimated that the remaining costs, labor time, and machine time will be the same as those for the St. Tropez jewelry case.

The second special order was submitted by the Cannes Co. for 7,500 jewelry cases at FF75 per case. These cases would be marketed under the Cannes label and would have to be shipped by October 1, 1996. The Cannes jewelry case is different from any jewelry case in the St. Tropez line; its estimated per-unit costs are as follows:

Raw materials	FF32.5
Direct labor .5 hr @ FF60	30
Overhead .5 machine-hr @ FF40	20
Total costs	FF82.5

In addition, St. Tropez will incur FF15,000 in additional setup costs and will have to purchase a FF25,000 special device to manufacture these cases; this device will be discarded once the special order is completed.

The St. Tropez manufacturing capabilities are limited by the total machine-hours available. The plant capacity under normal operations is 90,000 machine-hours per year, or 7,500 machine-hours per month. The budgeted *fixed* overhead for 1996 amounts to FF2.16 million, or FF24 per hour. All manufacturing overhead costs are applied to production on the basis of machine-hours at FF40 per hour.

St. Tropez will have the entire third quarter to work on the special orders. Management does not expect any repeat sales to be generated from either special order. Company practice precludes St. Tropez from subcontracting any portion of an order when special orders are not expected to generate repeat sales.

Required   Should St. Tropez accept either special order? Justify your answer and show your calculations. (*Hint*: Distinguish between variable and fixed overhead.)

5-53   Review of Chapters 2–5

The Lopez Company is a processor of a Bacardi-mix concentrate. Sales are made principally to liquor distributors throughout the country.

The company's income statements for the past year and the coming year are being analyzed by top management and are shown at the top of the next page.

Required   Consider each requirement independently.

Unless otherwise stated, assume that all unit costs of inputs such as material and labor are unchanged. Also, assume that efficiency is unchanged—that is, the labor and quantity of material consumed per unit of output are unchanged. Unless otherwise stated, assume that there are no changes in fixed costs.

1. The president has just returned from a management conference at a local university, where he heard an accounting professor criticize conventional income statements. The professor had asserted that knowledge of cost behavior patterns was of key importance in determining managerial strategies. The president now feels that the income statement should be recast to harmonize with cost-volume-profit analysis— that is, the statement should have three major sections: sales, variable costs, and fixed costs. Using the 1995 data, prepare such a statement, showing the contribution margin as well as operating income.

2. Comment on the changes in each item in the 1996 income statement compared to the 1995 statement. What are the most likely causes for each increase? For example, have selling prices been changed for 1996? How do sales commissions fluctuate in relation to units sold or in relation to dollar sales?

LOPEZ COMPANY
Income Statements

	For the Year 1995 Just Ended		For the Year 1996 Tentative Budget	
Sales 1,500,000 units in 1995		$900,000		$1,000,000
Cost of goods sold				
Direct material	$450,000		$495,000	
Direct labor	90,000		99,000	
Factory overhead				
Variable	18,000		19,800	
Fixed	50,000	608,000	50,000	663,800
Gross margin		$292,000		$ 336,200
Selling expenses				
Variable				
Sales commissions (based on dollar sales)	$ 45,000		$ 50,000	
Shipping and other	90,000		99,000	
Fixed				
Salaries, advertising, etc.	110,000		138,000	
Administrative expenses				
Variable	12,000		13,200	
Fixed	40,000	297,000	40,000	340,200
Operating income		$ (5,000)		$ (4,000)

3. The president is unimpressed with the 1996 budget: "We need to take a fresh look in order to begin moving toward profitable operations. Let's tear up the 1996 budget, concentrate on 1995 results, and prepare a new comparative 1996 budget under each of the following assumptions:

   a. A 5% average price cut will increase unit sales by 20%.

   b. A 5% average price increase will decrease unit sales by 10%.

   c. A sales commission rate of 10% and a 3⅓% price increase will boost unit sales by 10%.

   Prepare the budgets for 1996, using a contribution-margin format and three columns. Assume that there are no changes in fixed costs.

4. The advertising manager maintains that the advertising budget should be increased by $125,000 and that prices should be increased by 10%. Resulting unit sales will soar by 25%. What would be the expected operating income under such circumstances?

5. A nearby distillery has offered to buy 300,000 units in 1996 if the unit price is low enough. The Lopez Company would not have to incur sales commissions or shipping costs on this special order, and regular business would be undisturbed. Assuming that 1996's regular operations will be exactly like 1995's, what unit price should be quoted in order for the Lopez Company to earn an operating income of $10,000 in 1996?

6. The company chemist wants to add a special ingredient, an exotic flavoring that will add $.02 per unit to the Bacardi-mix costs. He also wants to replace the ordinary grenadine now used, which costs $.03 per unit of mix, with a more exquisite type costing $.04 per unit. Assuming no other changes in cost behavior, how many units must be sold to earn an operating income of $10,000 in 1996?

6 Relevant Information and Decision Making: Production Decisions

Colson Caster Corporation in Arkansas produces virtually any size or style of caster, including the wheels used for office chairs, for hotel baggage carts, and for the massive equipment used to move portions of the space shuttle. Managers use relevant cost analysis to decide whether to buy the metal forks (seen here) overseas rather than making them in the U.S. *Courtesy Colson Caster Corporation*

Learning Objectives

When you have finished studying this chapter, you should be able to

1 Define opportunity cost and use it to analyze the income effects of a given alternative.

2 Analyze given data to support a decision to make or buy certain parts or products.

3 Use either a differential or an opportunity-cost analysis to determine whether a joint product should be processed beyond the split-off point.

4 Distinguish between relevant and irrelevant items for decisions concerning disposal of obsolete inventory.

5 Explain why book value is irrelevant for equipment replacement decisions.

6 Explain how unit costs can be misleading.

7 Identify the nature, causes, and remedies of a serious motivational problem that might block a desirable decision to dispose of old equipment and replace it with new equipment.

Should Chrysler make the tires it mounts on its cars, or should it buy them from suppliers? Should General Mills sell the flour it mills, or should it use the flour to make more breakfast cereal? Should American Airlines add routes to use idle airplanes, or should it sell the planes? Successful managers can discriminate between relevant and irrelevant information in making decisions such as these. In the preceding chapter we provided a framework for identifying relevant costs and applied the framework to various marketing decisions. In this chapter we extend the analysis by introducing the concepts of opportunity cost and differential costs and by examining some production decisions: make or buy, sell or process further, and replace or keep equipment.

   This chapter and the preceding one illustrate relevant costs for many types of decisions. Does this mean that each decision requires a different approach to identifying relevant costs? No. *The fundamental principle in all decision situations is that relevant costs are future costs that differ among alternatives*. The principle is simple, but its application is not always straightforward. Because it is so important to be able to apply this principle, we present multiple examples.

■ OPPORTUNITY, OUTLAY, AND DIFFERENTIAL COSTS

opportunity cost
The maximum available contribution to profit forgone (or passed up) by using limited resources for a particular purpose.
outlay cost A cost that requires a cash disbursement.

The concept of opportunity cost is often used by decision makers. An **opportunity cost** is the maximum available contribution to profit forgone (or passed up) by using limited resources for a particular purpose. This definition indicates that opportunity cost is not the usual outlay cost recorded in accounting. An **outlay cost**, which requires a cash disbursement sooner or later, is the typical cost recorded by accountants.

An example of an opportunity cost is the salary forgone by a person who quits a job to start a business. Consider Maria Morales, a certified public accountant employed by a large accounting firm at $60,000 per year. She is yearning to have her own independent practice.

Maria's alternatives may be framed in more than one way. A straightforward comparison follows:

Objective 1

Define opportunity cost and use it to analyze the income effects of a given alternative

| | Alternatives Under Consideration | | |
	Remain as Employee	Open an Independent Practice	Difference
Revenues	$60,000	$200,000	$140,000
Outlay costs (operating expenses)	—	120,000	120,000
Income effects per year	$60,000	$ 80,000	$ 20,000

The annual difference of $20,000 favors Maria's choosing independent practice.

This tabulation is sometimes called a *differential analysis*. The *differential revenue* is $140,000, the *differential cost* is $120,000, and the *differential income* is $20,000. Each amount is the difference between the corresponding items under each alternative being considered. **Differential cost** and **incremental cost** are widely used synonyms. They are defined as the difference in total cost between two alternatives. For instance, the differential costs or incremental costs of increasing production from 1,000 automobiles to 1,200 automobiles per week would be the additional costs of producing the additional 200 automobiles each week. In the reverse situation, the decline in costs caused by reducing production from 1,200 to 1,000 automobiles per week would often be called *differential* or *incremental savings*.

differential cost (incremental cost)
The difference in total cost between two alternatives.

Returning to Maria Morales, focus on the meaning of opportunity cost. What is the contribution to profit of the best of the rejected alternatives? Independent practice has an opportunity cost of $60,000, the forgone annual salary.

These same facts may also be presented as follows:

		Alternative Chosen: Independent Practice
Revenue		$200,000
Expenses		
Outlay costs (operating expenses)	$120,000	
Opportunity cost of employee salary	60,000	
Income effects per year		180,000
		$ 20,000

Ponder the two preceding tabulations. Each produces the correct key difference between alternatives, $20,000. The first tabulation does not mention opportunity cost because the economic impacts (in the form of revenues and outlay costs) are individually measured for each of the alternatives (two in this case). Neither alternative has been excluded from consideration. The second tabulation mentions opportunity cost because the $60,000 annual economic impact of the *best excluded* alternative is included as a cost of the chosen alternative. The failure to recognize opportunity cost in the second tabulation will misstate the difference between alternatives.

Suppose Morales prefers less risk and chooses to stay as an employee:

		Alternative Chosen: Remain as Employee
Revenue		$ 60,000
Expenses		
Outlay costs	$ 0	
Opportunity cost of independent practice	80,000	80,000
Decrease in income per year		$(20,000)

If the employee alternative is selected, the key difference in favor of independent practice is again $20,000. The opportunity cost is $80,000, the annual operating income forgone by rejecting the best excluded alternative. Morales is sacrificing $20,000 annually to avoid the risks of an independent practice. In sum, the opportunity cost is the contribution of the best alternative that is excluded from consideration.

The major message here is straightforward: Do not overlook opportunity costs. Consider a homeowner who has made the final payment on the mortgage. While celebrating, the owner says, "It's a wonderful feeling to know that future occupancy is free of any interest cost!" Many owners have similar thoughts. Why? Because no future outlay costs for interest are required. Nevertheless, there is an opportunity cost of continuing to live in the home. After all, an alternative would be to sell the home, place the proceeds in some other investment, and rent an apartment. The owner forgoes the interest in the other investment, so this forgone interest income becomes an opportunity cost of home ownership.

■ MAKE-OR-BUY DECISIONS

Companies often must decide whether to produce a product or service within the firm or purchase it from an outside supplier. They apply relevant cost analysis to a variety of such make-or-buy decisions, including:

- Boeing's decision whether to buy or make many of the tools used in assembling 747 airplanes.

- IBM's decision whether to develop its own operating system for a new computer or to buy it from a software vendor.
- A local school district's decision whether to use its own personnel or hire a consulting firm to design and implement a new computerized accounting system.

Make-or-Buy and Idle Facilities

Objective 2

Analyze given data to support a decision to make or buy certain parts or products

To focus on basic principles, we examine relatively straightforward make-or-buy decisions. Consider manufacturers who must often decide whether to make or buy a product. For example, should a firm manufacture its own parts and subassemblies or buy them from vendors? Sometimes qualitative factors dominate quantitative assessments of costs. Some manufacturers always make parts because they want to control quality, others because they possess special know-how, usually skilled labor or rare materials needed in production. Alternatively, some companies always purchase parts to protect mutually advantageous long-run relationships with their suppliers. These companies may deliberately buy from vendors even during slack times to avoid difficulties in obtaining needed parts during boom times, when there may well be shortages of materials and workers, but no shortage of sales orders.

What quantitative factors are relevant to the decision of whether to make or buy? The answer, again, depends on the situation. A key factor is whether there are idle facilities. Many companies make parts only when their facilities cannot be used to better advantage.

Assume that the following costs are reported:

General Electric
Company
Cost of Making
Part No. 900

	Total Cost for 20,000 Units	Cost per Unit
Direct material	$ 20,000	$ 1
Direct labor	80,000	4
Variable factory overhead	40,000	2
Fixed factory overhead	80,000	4
Total costs	$220,000	$11

Another manufacturer offers to sell General Electric (GE) the same part for $10. Should GE make or buy the part?

Although the $11 unit cost shown seemingly indicates that the company should buy, the answer is rarely so obvious. The essential question is the difference in expected future costs between the alternatives. If the $4 fixed overhead per unit consists of costs that will continue regardless of the decision, the entire $4 becomes irrelevant. Examples of such costs include depreciation, property taxes, insurance, and allocated executive salaries.

Again, are only the variable costs relevant? No. Perhaps $20,000 of the fixed costs will be eliminated if the parts are bought instead of made. For example, a supervisor with a $20,000 salary might be released. In other words, fixed costs that may be avoided in the future are relevant.

For the moment, suppose the capacity now used to make parts will become idle if the parts are purchased and the $20,000 supervisor's salary is the only fixed cost that would be eliminated. The relevant computations follow:

	Make		Buy	
	Total	*Per Unit*	*Total*	*Per Unit*
Purchase cost			$200,000	$10
Direct material	$ 20,000	$ 1		
Direct labor	80,000	4		
Variable factory overhead	40,000	2		
Fixed factory overhead that can be avoided by not making (supervisor's salary)	20,000*	1*		
Total relevant costs	$160,000	$ 8	$200,000	$10
Difference in favor of making	$ 40,000	$ 2		

* Note that unavoidable fixed costs of $80,000 – $20,000 = $60,000 are irrelevant. Thus the irrelevant costs per unit are $4 – $1 = $3.

The key to make-or-buy decisions is identifying the *additional costs* for making (or the *costs avoided* by buying) a part or subcomponent. Activity analysis, described in Chapter 3, helps identify these costs. Production of a product requires a set of activities. A company with accurate measurements of the costs of its various activities can better estimate the additional costs incurred to produce an item. GE's activities for production of part number 900 were measured by two cost drivers, units of production of $8 per unit and supervision at a $20,000 fixed cost. Sometimes identification and measurement of additional cost drivers, especially non-volume-related cost drivers, can improve the predictions of the additional cost to produce a part or subcomponent.

Essence of Make or Buy: Use of Facilities

The choice in our example is not only whether to make or buy; it is how best to use available facilities. Although the data indicate that making the part is the better choice, the figures are not conclusive—primarily because we have no idea of what can be done with the manufacturing facilities if the component is bought. Only if the released facilities will otherwise remain idle are the preceding figures valid.

Suppose the released facilities can be used advantageously in some other manufacturing activity (to produce a contribution to profits of, say, $55,000) or can be rented out (say, for $35,000). These alternatives merit consideration. The two courses of action now become four (figures are in thousands):

	Make	Buy and Leave Facilities Idle	Buy and Rent out Facilities	Buy and Use Facilities for Other Products
Rent revenue	$ —	$ —	$ 35	$ —
Contribution from other products	—	—	—	55
Obtaining of parts	(160)	(200)	(200)	(200)
Net relevant costs	$(160)	$(200)	$(165)	$(145)

The final column indicates that buying the parts and using the vacated facilities for the production of other products would yield the lowest net costs in this case.

In sum, the make-or-buy decision should focus on relevant costs in a particular decision situation. In all cases, companies should relate make-or-buy decisions to the long-run policies for the use of capacity:

> One company does subcontract work for *other* manufacturers during periods when sales of its own products do not fully use the plant, but such work could not be carried on regularly without expansion of its plant. The profit margin on subcontracts would not be large enough to cover the additional costs of operating an expanded plant, and hence work is accepted only when other business is lacking. The same company sometimes meets a period of high volume by *purchasing* parts or having them made by subcontractors. Although the cost of such parts is usually higher than the cost to make them in the company's own plant, the additional cost is less than it would be if they were made on equipment which could be used only part of the time.[1]

■ JOINT PRODUCT COSTS

Nature of Joint Products

joint products Two or more manufactured products that (1) have relatively significant sales values and (2) are not separately identifiable as individual products until their split-off point.

split-off point The juncture of manufacturing where the joint products become individually identifiable.

separable costs Any cost beyond the split-off point.

joint costs The costs of manufacturing joint products prior to the split-off point.

When two or more manufactured products (1) have relatively significant sales values and (2) are not separately identifiable as individual products until their split-off point, they are called **joint products**. The **split-off point** is that juncture of manufacturing where the joint products become individually identifiable. Any costs beyond that stage are called **separable costs** because they are not part of the joint process and can be exclusively identified with individual products. The costs of manufacturing joint products before the split-off point are called **joint costs**. Examples of joint products include chemicals, lumber, flour, and the products of petroleum refining and meat packing. A meat-packing company cannot kill a sirloin steak; it has to slaughter a steer, which supplies various cuts of dressed meat, hides, and trimmings.

---

[1] *The Analysis of Cost-Profit Relationships*, National Association of Accountants, Research Series No. 17, p. 552.

An Example of Make or Buy: Outsourcing

Make-or-buy decisions apply to services as well as to products. One type of make-or-buy decision faced by many companies in the early 1990s was whether to buy data processing and computer network services or to provide them internally. Many companies eliminated their internal departments and "outsourced" (or bought) data processing services and network services from companies such as Electronic Data Systems, a General Motors subsidiary.

One of the first major companies to outsource its data processing was Eastman Kodak. By hiring IBM and Digital Equipment, Kodak was able to eliminate 1,000 jobs and avoid huge capital investments. Another example is J. P. Morgan & Co., which hired BT North America to link 26 Morgan offices in 14 countries. The five-year, $20-million contract is expected to save Morgan $12.5 million. Other outsourcing agreements include Sprint running Unilever's network, MCI handling Sun Microsystem's Pacific Rim network, AT&T working on Chevron's network, and GE Information Services operating the Vatican's global data network. Some companies, such as Sun Microsystems, outsource everything except their core technologies. Sun focuses on hardware and software design and outsources nearly everything else. Its employees do not actually produce any of the products that bear the company's name.

The total value of outsourcing contracts in the United States was about $9 billion in 1995.

The driving forces behind most outsourcing decisions are access to technology and cost savings. As the complexity of data processing and especially networking has grown, companies have found it harder and harder to keep current with the technology.

Instead of investing huge sums in personnel and equipment and diverting attention from the value-added activities of their own businesses, many firms have found outsourcing attractive from a financial standpoint. The big stumbling block has been subjective factors, such as control. To make outsourcing attractive, the services must be reliable, be available when needed, and be flexible enough to adapt to changing conditions. Companies that have successful outsourcing arrangements have been careful to include the subjective factors in their decisions.

Outsourcing has become so profitable that 77% of the Fortune 500 companies outsource some aspect of their business support services. An association, the Outsourcing Institute, was formed to provide "objective, independent information on the strategic use of outside resources." The institute sponsored a 42-page special advertising section in *Fortune* magazine in 1994. ■

Sources: Adapted from "Telecommunications: More Firms 'Outsource' Data Networks," The Wall Street Journal, March 11, 1992, p. B1; R. Suh, "Guaranteeing that Outsourcing Serves Your Business Strategy," Information Strategy: The Executive's Journal, Spring 1992, pp. 39–42; R. Zahler, "Identifying the Key Issues for Assessing Outsourcing," Network World, March 30, 1992, pp. 21, 23; J. Radigan, "All Wired Up at Morgan," Bank Systems & Technology, March 1992, pp. 25, 27; R.E. Drtina, "The Outsourcing Decision," Management Accounting, March, 1994, pp. 56–62; and M.F. Corbett, "Outsourcing: Redefining the Corporation of the Future," Fortune, December 12, 1994, pp. 51–92.

To illustrate joint costs, suppose Dow Chemical Company produces two chemical products, X and Y, as a result of a particular joint process. The joint processing cost is $100,000. This includes raw material costs and the cost of processing to the point where X and Y go their separate ways. Both products are sold to the petroleum industry to be used as ingredients of gasoline. The relationships follow:

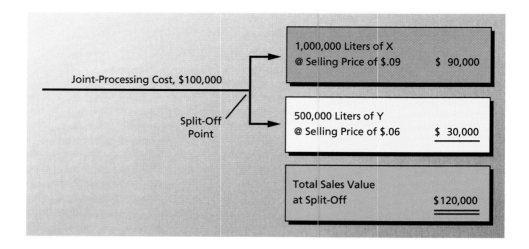

Sell or Process Further

Objective 3

Use either a differential or an opportunity-cost analysis to determine whether a joint product should be processed beyond the split-off point

Management frequently faces decisions of whether to sell joint products at split-off or to process some or all products further. Suppose the 500,000 liters of Y can be processed further and sold to the plastics industry as product YA, an ingredient for plastic sheeting. The additional processing cost would be $.08 per liter for manufacturing and distribution, a total of $40,000 for 500,000 liters. The net sales price of YA would be $.16 per liter, a total of $80,000.

Product X will be sold at the split-off point, but management is undecided about Product Y. Should Y be sold or should it be processed into YA? The joint costs must be incurred to reach the split-off point: They do not differ between alternatives and are completely irrelevant to the question of whether to sell or process further. The only approach that will yield valid results is to concentrate on the separable costs and revenue *beyond* split-off, as shown in Exhibit 6-1.

This analysis shows that it would be $10,000 more profitable to process Y beyond split-off than to sell Y at split-off. Briefly, it is profitable to extend processing or to incur additional distribution costs on a joint product *if* the additional revenue exceeds the additional expenses.

Exhibit 6-1

Illustration of Sell or Process Further

	Sell at Split-Off as Y	Process Further and Sell as YA	Difference
Revenues	$30,000	$80,000	$50,000
Separable costs beyond split-off @ $.08	—	40,000	40,000
Income effects	$30,000	$40,000	$10,000

Exhibit 6-2 illustrates another way to compare the alternatives of (1) selling Y at the split-off point and (2) processing Y beyond split-off. It includes the joint costs, which are the same for each alternative and therefore do not affect the difference.

Earlier discussions in this and the preceding chapter have emphasized the desirability of concentrating on totals and being wary of unit costs and allocations of fixed costs. Similarly, the allocation of joint product costs to units of product is fraught with analytical perils.

Exhibit 6-2

Sell or Process Further Analysis– Firm as Whole

	(1) Alternative One			(2) Alternative Two			(3) Differential Effects
	X	Y	Total	X	YA	Total	
Revenues	$90,000	$30,000	$120,000	$90,000	$ 80,000	$170,000	$50,000
Joint costs			$100,000			$100,000	—
Separable costs			—		40,000	40,000	40,000
Total costs			$100,000			$140,000	$ 40,000
Income effects			$ 20,000			$ 30,000	$ 10,000

The allocation of joint costs would not affect the decision, as Exhibit 6-2 demonstrates. The joint costs are not allocated in the exhibit, but no matter how they might be allocated, the total income effects would be unchanged. Additional coverage of joint costs and inventory valuation can be found in Chapter 13.

■ IRRELEVANCE OF PAST COSTS

The ability to recognize and thereby ignore irrelevant costs is sometimes just as important to decision makers as identifying relevant costs. How do we know that past costs, although sometimes predictors, are irrelevant in decision making? Consider such past costs as obsolete inventory and the book value of old equipment to see why they are irrelevant to decisions.

Obsolete Inventory

Objective 4

Distinguish between relevant and irrelevant items for decisions concerning disposal of obsolete inventory

Suppose General Dynamics has 100 obsolete aircraft parts in its inventory at a manufacturing cost of $100,000. General Dynamics can (1) remachine the parts for $30,000 and then sell them for $50,000 or (2) scrap them for $5,000. Which should it do?

This is an unfortunate situation, yet the $100,000 past cost is irrelevant to the decision to remachine or scrap. The only relevant factors are the expected future revenues and costs:

	Remachine	Scrap	Difference
Expected future revenue	$ 50,000	$ 5,000	$45,000
Expected future costs	30,000	—	30,000
Relevant excess of revenue over costs	$ 20,000	$ 5,000	$15,000
Accumulated historical inventory cost*	100,000	100,000	—
Net overall loss on project	$ (80,000)	$(95,000)	$15,000

* Irrelevant because it is unaffected by the decision.

We can completely ignore the $100,000 historical cost and still arrive at the $15,000 difference, the key figure in the analysis.

Book Value of Old Equipment

depreciation The periodic cost of equipment which is spread over (or charged to) the future periods in which the equipment is expected to be used.

book value (net book value) The original cost of equipment less accumulated depreciation, which is the summation of depreciation charged to past periods.

Like obsolete parts, the book value of equipment is not a relevant consideration in deciding whether to replace such equipment. When equipment is purchased, its cost is spread over (or charged to) the future periods in which the equipment is expected to be used. This periodic cost is called **depreciation**. The equipment's **book value** (or **net book value**) is the original cost less *accumulated depreciation*, which is the summation of depreciation charged to past periods. For example, suppose a $10,000 machine with a 10-year life has depreciation of $1,000 per year. At the end of 6 years, accumulated depreciation is 6 × $1,000 = $6,000, and the book value is $10,000 – $6,000 = $4,000.

Consider the following data for a decision whether to replace an old machine:

<table>
<tr><th></th><th>Old Machine</th><th>Replacement Machine</th></tr>
<tr><td>Original cost</td><td>$10,000</td><td>$8,000</td></tr>
<tr><td>Useful life in years</td><td>10</td><td>4</td></tr>
<tr><td>Current age in years</td><td>6</td><td>0</td></tr>
<tr><td>Useful life remaining in years</td><td>4</td><td>4</td></tr>
<tr><td>Accumulated depreciation</td><td>$ 6,000</td><td>0</td></tr>
<tr><td>Book value</td><td>$ 4,000</td><td>Not acquired yet</td></tr>
<tr><td>Disposal value (in cash) now</td><td>$ 2,500</td><td>Not acquired yet</td></tr>
<tr><td>Disposal value in 4 years</td><td>0</td><td>0</td></tr>
<tr><td>Annual cash operating costs (maintenance, power, repairs, coolants, etc.)</td><td>$ 5,000</td><td>$3,000</td></tr>
</table>

Objective 5

Explain why book value is irrelevant for equipment replacement decisions

We have been asked to prepare a comparative analysis of the two alternatives. Before proceeding, consider some important concepts. The most widely misunderstood facet of replacement decision making is the role of the book value of the old equipment in the decision. The book value, in this context, is sometimes called a **sunk cost**, which is really just another term for *historical* or *past cost*, a cost that has already been incurred and, therefore, is irrelevant to the decision-making process. At one time or another, we all try to soothe the wounded pride arising from having made a bad purchase decision by using an item instead of replacing it. It is a serious mistake to think, however, that a current or future action can influence the long-run impact of a past outlay. All past costs are down the drain. Nothing can change what has already happened.

sunk cost A cost that has already been incurred and, therefore, is irrelevant to the decision making process. Synonyms are *historical cost* and *past cost*.

The irrelevance of past costs for decisions does not mean that knowledge of past costs is useless. Often managers use past costs to help predict future costs. In addition, past costs affect future payments for income taxes (as explained in Chapter 12). However, the past cost *itself* is not relevant. The only relevant cost is the predicted future cost.

In deciding whether to replace or keep existing equipment, four commonly encountered items differ in relevance:[2]

- *Book value of old equipment*: Irrelevant, because it is a past (historical) cost. Therefore, depreciation on old equipment is irrelevant.
- *Disposal value of old equipment*: Relevant (ordinarily), because it is an expected future inflow that usually differs among alternatives.
- *Gain or loss on disposal*: This is the algebraic difference between book value and disposal value. It is therefore a meaningless combination of irrelevant and relevant items. The combination form, *loss* (or *gain*) *on disposal*, blurs the distinction between the irrelevant book value and the relevant disposal value. Consequently, it is best to think of each separately.
- *Cost of new equipment*: Relevant, because it is an expected future outflow that will differ among alternatives. Therefore depreciation on new equipment is relevant.

Exhibit 6-3 should clarify the foregoing assertions. It deserves close study. Book value of old equipment is irrelevant regardless of the decision-making technique used. The "difference" column in Exhibit 6-3 shows that the $4,000 book value of the *old* equipment is not an element of difference between alternatives. It should be completely ignored for decision-making purposes. The difference is merely one of timing. The amount written off is still $4,000, regardless of any available alternative. The $4,000 appears on the income statement either as a $4,000 deduction from the $2,500 cash proceeds received to obtain a $1,500 loss on disposal in the first year or as $1,000 of depreciation in each of 4 years. But how it appears is irrelevant to the replacement decision. In contrast, the $2,000 annual depreciation on the new equipment is relevant because the total $8,000 depreciation is a future cost that may be avoided by not replacing. The three relevant items, operating costs, disposal value, and acquisition cost give replacement a net advantage of $2,500.

Examination of Alternatives Over the Long Run

Exhibit 6-3 is the first example that looks beyond one year. Examining the alternatives over the entire lives ensures that peculiar nonrecurring items (such as loss on disposal) will not obstruct the long-run view vital to many managerial decisions.[3]

Exhibit 6-4 concentrates on relevant items only: the cash operating costs, the disposal value of the old equipment, and the depreciation on the new equipment. To demonstrate that the amount of the old equipment's book value will not affect the answer, suppose the book value of the old equipment is $500,000 rather than $4,000. Your final answer will not change. The cumulative advantage of replacement is still $2,500. (If you are in doubt, rework this example, using $500,000 as the book value.)

---

[2] For simplicity, we ignore income tax considerations and the effects of the interest value of money in this chapter. Book value is irrelevant even if income taxes are considered, however, because the relevant item is then the tax cash flow, not the book value. The book value is essential information for predicting the amount and timing of future tax cash flows, but, by itself, the book value is irrelevant. For elaboration, see Chapter 12.

[3] A more complete analysis that includes the timing of revenues and costs appears in Chapter 11.

Sunk Costs and Government Contracts

It is easy to agree that—in theory—sunk costs should be ignored when making decisions. But in practice sunk costs often influence important decisions, especially when a decision maker doesn't want to admit that a previous decision to invest funds was a bad decision.

Consider two examples from the *St. Louis Post Dispatch*: (1) Larry O. Welch, the air force chief of staff, was quoted as saying that "the B-2 already is into production; cancel it and the $17 billion front end investment is lost." (2) Les Aspin, chairman of the House Armed Services Committee, was quoted as stating that "with $17 billion already invested in it, the B-2 is too costly to cancel."

The $17 billion already invested in the B-2 is a sunk cost. It is "lost" regardless of whether production of the B-2 is canceled or not. And whether B-2 production is too costly to continue depends only on the future costs necessary to complete production compared to the value of the completed B-2s. The $17 billion was relevant when the original decision to begin development of the B-2 was made, but now that the money has been spent, it is no longer relevant. No decision can affect it.

Why would intelligent leaders consider the $17 billion relevant to the decision on continuing production of the B-2? Probably because it is difficult to admit that no benefit would be derived from the $17 billion investment. Those who favor canceling production of the B-2 would consider the outcome of the original investment decision to be unfavorable. With perfect hindsight, they believe the investment should not have been made. It is human nature to find unpleasant the task of admitting that $17 billion was wasted. Yet, it is more important to avoid throwing good money after bad—that is, if the value of the B-2 is not at least equal to the *future* investment in it, production should be terminated, regardless of the amount spent to date.

Ignoring sunk costs is not unique to the U.S. government. In reference to Russia's store of bomb-grade plutonium, the country's Minister of Atomic Energy stated, "We have spent too much money making this material to just mix it with radioactive wastes and bury it." Burying the plutonium may or may not be the best decision, but the amount already spent is not relevant to the decision. ■

Sources: J. Berg, J. Dickhaut, and C. Kanodia, "The Role of Private Information in the Sunk Cost Phenomenon," unpublished paper, November 12, 1991; M. Wald and M. Gordon, "Russia Treasures Plutonium, But U.S. Wants to Destroy It," New York Times, August 19, 1994, p. A1.

Exhibit 6-3

Cost Comparison—Replacement of Equipment Including Relevant and Irrelevant Items

	Four Years Together		
	Keep	*Replace*	*Difference*
Cash operating costs	$20,000	$12,000	$8,000
Old equipment (book value)			
Periodic write-off as depreciation	4,000	—	
or			—
Lump-sum write-off		4,000*	
Disposal value	—	–2,500*	2,500
New machine			
Acquisition			
Cost	—	8,000†	–8,000
Total costs	$24,000	$21,500	$2,500

The advantage of replacement is $2,500 for the four years together.

* In a formal income statement, these two items would be combined as "loss on disposal" of $4,000 − $2,500 = $1,500.

† In a formal income statement, written off as straight-line depreciation of $8,000 ÷ 4 = $2,000 for each of 4 years.

Exhibit 6-4

Cost Comparison—
Replacement of
Equipment, Relevant
Items Only

	Four Years Together		
	Keep	**Replace**	**Difference**
Cash operating costs	$20,000	$12,000	$8,000
Disposal value of old machine	—	–2,500	2,500
New machine, acquisition cost	—	8,000	–8,000
Total relevant costs	$20,000	$17,500	$2,500

■ IRRELEVANCE OF FUTURE COSTS THAT WILL NOT DIFFER

In addition to past costs, some *future* costs may be irrelevant because they will be the same under all feasible alternatives. These, too, may be safely ignored for a particular decision. The salaries of many members of top management are examples of expected future costs that will be unaffected by the decision at hand.

Other irrelevant future costs include fixed costs that will be unchanged by such considerations as whether machine X or machine Y is selected. However, it is not merely a case of saying that fixed costs are irrelevant and variable costs are relevant. Variable costs can be irrelevant, and fixed costs can be relevant. For instance, sales commissions might be paid on an order regardless of whether the order was filled from plant G or plant H. Variable costs are irrelevant whenever they do not differ among the alternatives at hand, and fixed costs are relevant whenever they differ under the alternatives at hand.

■ BEWARE OF UNIT COSTS

Objective 6

Explain how unit costs can be misleading

The pricing illustration in Chapter 5 showed that unit costs should be analyzed with care in decision making. There are two major ways to go wrong: (1) the inclusion of irrelevant costs, such as the $3 allocation of unavoidable fixed costs in the make-or-buy example (p. 221) that would result in a unit cost of $11 instead of the relevant unit cost of $8, and (2) comparisons of unit costs not computed on the same volume basis, as the following example demonstrates. Generally, be wary of unit fixed costs. Use total costs rather than unit costs. Then, if desired, the totals may be unitized. Machinery sales personnel, for example, often brag about the low unit costs of using the new machines. Sometimes they neglect to point out that the unit costs are based on outputs far in excess of the volume of activity of their prospective customer.

Assume that a new $100,000 machine with a five-year life can produce 100,000 units a year at a variable cost of $1 per unit, as opposed to a variable cost per unit of $1.50 with an old machine. A sales representative claims that the new machine will reduce cost by $.30 per unit. Is the new machine a worthwhile acquisition?

The new machine is attractive at first glance. If the customer's expected volume is 100,000 units, unit-cost comparisons are valid, provided that new depreciation is also considered. Assume that the disposal value of the old equipment is zero. Because depreciation is an allocation of *historical* cost, the depreciation on the old machine is irrelevant. In contrast, the depreciation on the new machine is relevant because the new machine entails a *future* cost that can be avoided by not acquiring it:

	Old Machine	New Machine
Units	100,000	100,000
Variable costs	$150,000	$100,000
Straight-line depreciation	—	20,000
Total relevant costs	$150,000	$120,000
Unit relevant costs	$ 1 .50	$ 1 .20

Apparently, the sales representative is correct. However, if the customer's expected volume is only 30,000 units per year, the unit costs change in favor of the old machine:

	Old Machine	New Machine
Units	30,000	30,000
Variable costs	$45,000	$30,000
Straight-line depreciation	—	20,000
Total relevant costs	$45,000	$50,000
Unit relevant costs	$ 1.50	$1.6667

CONFLICTS BETWEEN DECISION MAKING AND PERFORMANCE EVALUATION

Objective 7

Identify the nature, causes, and remedies of a serious motivational problem that might block a desirable decision to dispose of old equipment and replace it with new equipment

We have focused on using relevant information in decision making. To motivate people to make optimal decisions, methods of evaluating the performance of managers should be consistent with the decision analysis.

Consider the replacement decision shown in Exhibit 6-4, where replacing the machine had a $2,500 advantage over keeping it. To motivate managers to make the right choice, the method used to evaluate performance should be consistent with the decision model—that is, it should show better performance when managers replace the machine than when they keep it. Because performance is often measured by accounting income, consider the accounting income in the first year after replacement compared with that in years 2, 3, and 4.

	Year 1		Years 2, 3, and 4	
	Keep	*Replace*	*Keep*	*Replace*
Cash operating costs	$5,000	$3,000	$5,000	$3,000
Depreciation	1,000	2,000	1,000	2,000
Loss on disposal ($4,000 – $2,500)	—	$1,500	—	—
Total charges against revenue	$6,000	$6,500	$6,000	$5,000

If the machine is kept rather than replaced, first-year costs will be $6,500 – $6,000 = $500 lower, and first-year income will be $500 higher. Because managers naturally want to make decisions that maximize the measure of their performance, they may be inclined to keep the machine. This is an example of a conflict between the analysis for decision making and the method used to evaluate performance.

The conflict is especially severe if managers are transferred often from one position to another. Why? Because the $500 first-year advantage for keeping will be offset by a $1,000 annual advantage of replacing in years 2 to 4. (Note that the net difference of $2,500 in favor of replacement over the 4 years together is the same as in Exhibit 6-4.) A manager who moves to a new position after the first year, however, bears the entire loss on disposal without reaping the benefits of lower operating costs in years 2 to 4.

The decision to replace a machine earlier than planned also reveals that the original decision to purchase the machine may have been flawed. The old machine was bought 6 years ago for $10,000; its expected life was 10 years. However, if a better machine is now available, then the useful life of the old machine was really 6 years, not 10. This feedback on the actual life of the old machine has two possible effects, the first good and the second bad. First, managers might learn from the earlier mistake. If the useful life of the old machine was overestimated, how believable is the prediction that the new machine will have a 4-year life? Feedback can help avoid repeating past mistakes. Second, another mistake might be made to cover up the earlier one. A "loss on disposal" could alert superiors to the incorrect economic-life prediction used in the earlier decision. By avoiding replacement, the $4,000 remaining book value is spread over the future as "depreciation," a more appealing term than "loss on disposal." The superiors may never find out about the incorrect prediction of economic life. The accounting income approach to performance evaluation mixes the financial effects of various decisions, hiding both the earlier misestimation of useful life and the current failure to replace.

The conflict between decision making and performance evaluation is a widespread problem in practice. Unfortunately, there are no easy solutions. In theory, accountants could evaluate performance in a manner consistent with decision making. In our equipment example, this would mean predicting year-by-year income effects over the planning horizon for 4 years, noting that the first year would be poor, and evaluating actual performance against the predictions.

The trouble is that evaluating performance, decision by decision, is a costly procedure. Therefore aggregate measures are used. For example, an income statement shows the results of many decisions, not just the single decision of buying a machine. Consequently, in many cases like our equipment example, managers may be most heavily influenced by the first-year effects on the income statement. Thus managers refrain from taking the longer view that their superiors prefer.

Highlights to Remember

Chapters 5 and 6 have focused on identifying relevant information for a variety of decisions. Relevant costs are future costs that differ among alternatives. Past costs are not relevant, but they might help predict future costs.

Sometimes the notion of an opportunity cost is helpful in cost analysis. An opportunity cost is the maximum sacrifice in rejecting an alternative; it is the maximum earnings that might have been obtained if the productive good, service, or capacity had been applied to some alternative use. The opportunity-cost approach does not affect the important final differences between the courses of action, but the format of the analysis differs. This chapter also introduces differential costs or incremental costs, which are the differences in the total costs under each alternative.

Some generalizations about the decisions in this chapter follow:

* Make-or-buy decisions are, fundamentally, examples of obtaining the most profitable use of given facilities.
* Joint product costs are irrelevant in decisions about whether to sell at split-off or process further.
* The book value of old equipment is always irrelevant in replacement decisions. This cost is often called a sunk cost. Disposal value, however, is generally relevant.

Also, be aware that managers are often motivated to reject desirable economic decisions because of a conflict between the measures used in decision making and those used in performance evaluation.

Summary Problem for Your Review

Problem

Exhibit 6-5 contains data for the Block Company for the year just ended. The company makes industrial power drills. Exhibit 6-5 shows the costs of the plastic housing separately from the costs of the electrical and mechanical components.

Exhibit 6-5		A	B	A + B
Block Company Cost of Industrial Drills		Electrical and Mechanical Components*	Plastic Housing	Industrial Drills
	Sales: 100,000 units, @ $100			$10,000,000
	Variable costs			
	Direct material	$4,400,000	$ 500,000	$ 4,900,000
	Direct labor	400,000	300,000	700,000
	Variable factory overhead	100,000	200,000	300,000
	Other variable costs	100,000	—	100,000
	Sales commissions, @ 10% of sales	1,000,000	—	1,000,000
	Total variable costs	$6,000,000	$1,000,000	$ 7,000,000
	Contribution margin			$ 3,000,000
	Separable fixed costs	$1,900,000	$ 400,000	$ 2,300,000
	Common fixed costs	320,000	80,000	400,000
	Total fixed costs	$2,220,000	$ 480,000	$ 2,700,000
	Operating income			$ 300,000

* Not including the costs of plastic housing (column B).

1. During the year, a prospective customer in an unrelated market offered $82,000 for 1,000 drills. The latter would be in addition to the 100,000 units sold. The regular sales commission rate would have been paid. The president rejected the order because "it was below our costs of $97 per unit." What would operating income have been if the order had been accepted?
2. A supplier offered to manufacture the year's supply of 100,000 plastic housings for $13.50 each. What would be the effect on operating income if the Block Company purchased rather than made the housings? Assume that $350,000 of the separable fixed costs assigned to housings would have been avoided if the housings were purchased.
3. The company could have purchased the housings for $13.50 each and used the vacated space for the manufacture of a deluxe version of its drill. Assume that 20,000 deluxe units could have been made (and sold in addition to the 100,000 regular units) at a unit variable cost of $90, exclusive of housings and exclusive of the 10% sales commission. The 20,000 extra plastic housings could also be purchased for $13.50 each. The sales price would have been $130. All the fixed costs pertaining to the plastic housings would have continued, because these costs related primarily to the manufacturing facilities used. What would operating income have been if Block had bought the housings and made and sold the deluxe units?

Solution

1. The costs of filling the special order follow:

Direct material	$49,000
Direct labor	7,000
Variable factory overhead	3,000
Other variable costs	1,000
Sales commission @ 10% of $82,000	8,200
Total variable costs	$68,200
Selling price	82,000
Contribution margin	$13,800

Operating income would have been $300,000 + $13,800, or $313,800, if the order had been accepted. In a sense, the decision to reject the offer implies that the Block Company is willing to invest $13,800 in immediate gains forgone (an opportunity cost) in order to preserve the long-run selling-price structure.

2. Assuming that $350,000 of the fixed costs could have been avoided by not making the housings and that the other fixed costs would have been continued, the alternatives can be summarized as follows:

	Make	Buy
Purchase cost		$1,350,000
Variable costs	$1,000,000	
Avoidable fixed costs	350,000	
Total relevant costs	$1,350,000	$1,350,000

If the facilities used for plastic housings became idle, the Block Company would be indifferent as to whether to make or buy. Operating income would be unaffected.

3. The effect of purchasing the plastic housings and using the vacated facilities for the manufacture of a deluxe version of its drill is:

Sales would increase by 20,000 units, @ $130		$2,600,000
Variable costs exclusive of parts would increase by		
20,000 units, @ $90	$1,800,000	
Plus: sales commission, 10% of $2,600,000	260,000	2,060,000
Contribution margin on 20,000 units		$ 540,000
Housings: 120,000 rather than 100,000 would be needed		
Buy 120,000 @ $13.50	$1,620,000	
Make 100,000 @ $10 (only the variable costs are relevant)	1,000,000	
Excess cost of outside purchase		620,000
Fixed costs, unchanged		—
Disadvantage of making deluxe units		$ 80,000

Operating income would decline to $220,000 ($300,000 – $80,000). The deluxe units bring in a contribution margin of $540,000, but the additional costs of buying rather than making housings is $620,000, leading to a net disadvantage of $80,000.

Accounting Vocabulary

book value, *p. 226*
depreciation, *p. 226*
differential cost, *p. 218*
incremental cost, *p. 218*

joint costs, *p. 222*
joint products, *p. 222*
net book value, *p. 226*
opportunity cost, *p. 218*

outlay cost, *p. 218*
separable costs, *p. 222*
split-off point, *p. 222*
sunk cost, *p. 226*

Fundamental Assignment Material

6-A1   Replacing Old Equipment
Consider these data regarding Chippewa County's photocopying requirements:

	Old Equipment	Proposed Replacement Equipment
Useful life, in years	5	3
Current age, in years	2	0
Useful life remaining, in years	3	3
Original cost	$25,000	$15,000
Accumulated depreciation	10,000	0
Book value	15,000	Not acquired yet
Disposal value (in cash) now	3,000	Not acquired yet
Disposal value in 2 years	0	0
Annual cash operating costs for power, maintenance, toner, and supplies	14,000	7,500

The county administrator is trying to decide whether to replace the old equipment. Because of rapid changes in technology, she expects the replacement equipment to have only a three-year useful life. Ignore the effects of taxes.

Required

1. Tabulate a cost comparison that includes both relevant and irrelevant items for the next three years together. (*Hint*: See Exhibit 6-3, page 228.)
2. Tabulate a cost comparison of all relevant items for the next three years together. Which tabulation is clearer, this one or the one in requirement 1? (*Hint*: See Exhibit 6-4, page 229.)
3. Prepare a simple "shortcut" or direct analysis to support your choice of alternatives.

6-A2   Decision and Performance Models

Refer to the preceding problem.

1. Suppose the "decision model" favored by top management consisted of a comparison of a three-year accumulation of cash under each alternative. As the manager of office operations, which alternative would you choose? Why?
2. Suppose the "performance evaluation model" emphasized the minimization of overall costs of photocopying operations for the first year. Which alternative would you choose?

6-A3   Hospital Opportunity Cost

An administrator at University Hospital is considering how to use some space made available when the Family Medical Center moved to a new building. She has narrowed her choices as follows:

a. Use the space to expand laboratory testing. Expected future annual revenue would be $300,000; future costs, $270,000.
b. Use the space to expand the eye clinic. Expected future annual revenue would be $500,000; future costs, $480,000.
c. The gift shop is rented by an independent retailer who wants to expand into the vacated space. The retailer has offered a $9,000 yearly rental for the space. All operating expenses will be borne by the retailer.

The administrator's planning horizon is unsettled. However, she has decided that the yearly data given will suffice for guiding her decision.

Required

Tabulate the total relevant data regarding the decision alternatives. Omit the concept of opportunity cost in one tabulation, but use the concept in a second tabulation. As the administrator, which tabulation would you prefer to get if you could receive only one?

6-A4   Joint Products: Sell or Process Further

The Visqual Chemical Company produced three joint products at a joint cost of $105,000. These products were processed further and sold as follows:

Chemical Product	Sales	Additional Processing Costs
A	$260,000	$220,000
B	330,000	300,000
C	175,000	100,000

The company has had an opportunity to sell at split-off directly to other processors. If that alternative had been selected, sales would have been: A, $56,000; B, $28,000; and C, $54,000.

The company expects to operate at the same level of production and sales in the forthcoming year.

Required   Consider all the available information, and assume that all costs incurred after split-off are variable.

1. Could the company increase operating income by altering its processing decisions? If so, what would be the expected overall operating income?
2. Which products should be processed further and which should be sold at split-off?

6-B1   Role of Old Equipment Replacement

On January 2, 19X1, the K. Sung Company installed a brand-new $84,000 special molding machine for producing a new product. The product and the machine have an expected life of three years. The machine's expected disposal value at the end of 3 years is zero.

On January 3, 19X1, Jill Swain, a star salesperson for a machine tool manufacturer, tells Mr. Sung: "I wish I had known earlier of your purchase plans. I can supply you with a technically superior machine for $99,000. The machine you just purchased can be sold for $16,000. I guarantee that our machine will save $35,000 per year in cash operating costs, although it too will have no disposal value at the end of three years."

Sung examines some technical data. Although he has confidence in Swain's claims, Sung contends: "I'm locked in now. My alternatives are clear: (a) disposal will result in a loss, (b) keeping and using the 'old' equipment avoids such a loss. I have brains enough to avoid a loss when my other alternative is recognizing a loss. We've got to use that equipment until we get our money out of it."

The annual operating costs of the old machine are expected to be $60,000, exclusive of depreciation. Sales, all in cash, will be $850,000 per year. Other annual cash expenses will be $750,000 regardless of this decision. Assume that the equipment in question is the company's only fixed asset.

Required   Ignore income taxes and the time value of money.

1. Prepare statements of cash receipts and disbursements as they would appear in each of the next 3 years under both alternatives. What is the total cumulative increase or decrease in cash for the 3 years?
2. Prepare income statements as they would appear in each of the next 3 years under both alternatives. Assume straight-line depreciation. What is the cumulative increase or decrease in net income for the 3 years?
3. Assume that the cost of the "old" equipment was $1 million rather than $84,000. Would the net difference computed in requirements 1 and 2 change? Explain.
4. As Jill Swain, reply to Mr. Sung's contentions.
5. What are the irrelevant items in each of your presentations for requirements 1 and 2? Why are they irrelevant?

6-B2   Make or Buy

A Volkswagen executive in Germany is trying to decide whether the company should continue to manufacture an engine component or purchase it from Hanover Corporation for 50 deutsche marks (DM) each. Demand for the coming year is expected to be the same as for the current year, 200,000 units. Data for the current year follow:

Direct material	DM 5,000,000
Direct labor	2,000,000
Factory overhead, variable	1,000,000
Factory overhead, fixed	2,500,000
Total costs	DM10,500,000

If Volkswagen makes the components, the unit costs of direct material will increase 10%.

If Volkswagen buys the components, 40% of the fixed costs will be avoided. The other 60% will continue regardless of whether the components are manufactured or purchased. Assume that variable overhead varies with output volume.

Required

1. Tabulate a comparison of the make-or-buy alternatives. Show totals and amounts per unit. Compute the numerical difference between making and buying. Assume that the capacity now used to make the components will become idle if the components are purchased.
2. Assume also that the Volkswagen capacity in question can be rented to a local electronics firm for DM1,250,000 for the coming year. Tabulate a comparison of the net relevant costs of the three alternatives: make, buy and leave capacity idle, buy and rent. Which is the most favorable alternative? By how much in total?

6-B3 Sell or Process Further

ConAgra, Inc. produces meat products with brand names such as Swift, Armour, and Butterball. Suppose one of the company's plants processes beef cattle into various products. For simplicity, assume that there are only three products: steak, hamburger, and hides, and that the average steer costs $500. The three products emerge from a process that costs $100 per cow to run, and output from one steer can be sold for the following net amounts:

Steak (100 pounds)	$300
Hamburger (500 pounds)	500
Hides (120 pounds)	100
Total	$900

Assume that each of these three products can be sold immediately or processed further in another ConAgra plant. The steak can be the main course in frozen dinners sold under the Healthy Choice label. The vegetables and desserts in the 400 dinners produced from the 100 pounds of steak would cost $120, and production, sales, and other costs for the 400 meals would total $350. Each meal would be sold wholesale for $1.90.

The hamburger could be made into frozen Salisbury Steak patties sold under the Armour label. The only additional cost would be a $200 processing cost for the 500 pounds of hamburger. Frozen Salisbury Steaks sell wholesale for $1.50 per pound.

The hides can be sold before or after tanning. The cost of tanning one hide is $80, and a tanned hide can be sold for $175.

Required

1. Compute the total profit if all three products are sold at the split-off point.
2. Compute the total profit if all three products are processed further before being sold.
3. Which products should be sold at the split-off point? Which should be processed further?
4. Compute the total profit if your plan in requirement 3 is followed.

Additional Assignment Material

Questions

6-1. "Qualitative factors generally favor making over buying a component." Do you agree? Explain.

6-2. "Choices are often mislabeled as *make* or *buy*." Do you agree? Explain.

6-3. Distinguish between an opportunity cost and an outlay cost.

6-4. "I had a chance to rent my summer home for two weeks for $800. But I chose to have it idle. I didn't want strangers living in my summer house." What term in this chapter describes the $800? Why?

6-5. "Accountants do not ordinarily record opportunity costs in the formal accounting records." Why?

6-6. Distinguish between an incremental cost and a differential cost.

6-7. "Incremental cost is the addition to costs from the manufacture of one unit." Do you agree? Explain.

6-8. "The differential costs or incremental costs of increasing production from 1,000 automobiles to 1,200 automobiles per week would be the additional costs of producing the additional 200 automobiles." If production were reduced from 1,200 to 1,000 automobiles per week, what would the decline in costs be called?

6-9. "No technique used to assign the joint cost to individual products should be used for management decisions regarding whether a product should be sold at the split-off point or processed further." Do you agree? Explain.

6-10. "Past costs are indeed relevant in most instances because they provide the point of departure for the entire decision process." Do you agree? Why?

6-11. Which of the following items are relevant to replacement decisions? Explain.
 a. Book value of old equipment
 b. Disposal value of old equipment
 c. Cost of new equipment

6-12. Give an example of a situation in which the performance evaluation model is not consistent with the decision model.

6-13. "Evaluating performance, decision by decision, is costly. Aggregate measures, like the income statement, are frequently used." How might the wide use of income statements affect managers' decisions about buying equipment?

6-14. Explain the one-year-at-a-time approach for acquiring equipment in not-for-profit organizations.

6-15. "The financial consequences of Decision A regarding the acquisition of equipment should be separated from similar Decision B consequences made at a later date." Why?

6-16. "Some expected future costs may be irrelevant." Do you agree? Explain.

6-17. "Variable costs are irrelevant whenever they do not differ among the alternatives at hand." Do you agree? Explain.

6-18. There are two major reasons why unit costs should be analyzed with care in decision making. What are they?

6-19. "Machinery sales personnel sometimes erroneously brag about the low unit costs of using their machines." Identify one source of an error concerning the estimation of unit costs.

Exercises

6-20   Relevant Investment

Rhonda Timm had obtained a new truck with a list price, including options, of $16,000. The dealer had given her a "generous trade-in allowance" of $4,500 on her old truck that had a wholesale price of $3,000. Sales tax was $1,200.

The annual cash operating costs of the old truck were $4,200. The new truck was expected to reduce these costs by one-third.

Required   Compute the amount of the original investment in the new truck. Explain your reasoning.

6-21   Weak Division

Elgin Electronics Company paid $6 million in cash four years ago to acquire a company that manufactures magnetic tape drives. This company has been operated as a division of Elgin and has lost $500,000 each year since its acquisition.

The minimum desired return for this division is that, when a new product is fully developed, it should return a net profit of $500,000 per year for the foreseeable future.

Recently the IBM Corporation offered to purchase the division from Elgin for $4 million. The president of Elgin commented, "I've got an investment of $8 million to recoup ($6 million plus losses of $500,000 for each of four years). I have finally got this situation turned around, so I oppose selling the division now."

Prepare a response to the president's remarks. Indicate how to make this decision. Be as specific as possible.

6-22   Make Or Buy

Assume that a division of Sony makes an electronic component for its speakers. Its manufacturing process for the component is a highly automated part of a just-in-time production system. All labor is considered to be an overhead cost, and all overhead is regarded as fixed with respect to output volume. Production costs for 100,000 units of the component are as follows:

Direct materials		$300,000
Factory overhead		
Indirect labor	$80,000	
Supplies	30,000	
Allocated occupancy cost	40,000	150,000
Total cost		$450,000

A small, local company has offered to supply the components at a price of $3.45 each. If the division discontinued its production of the component, it would save two-thirds of the supplies cost and $30,000 of indirect labor cost. All other overhead costs would continue.

The division manager recently attended a seminar on cost behavior and learned about fixed and variable costs. He wants to continue to make the component because the variable cost of $3.00 is below the $3.45 bid.

Required

1. Compute the relevant cost of (a) making and (b) purchasing the component. Which alternative is less costly and by how much?
2. What qualitative factors might influence the decision about whether to make or buy the component?

6-23   Opportunity Costs

Esther Goldman is an attorney employed by a large law firm at $95,000 per year. She is considering whether to become a sole practitioner, which would probably generate annually $325,000 in operating revenues and $220,000 in operating expenses.

Required

1. Present two tabulations of the annual income effects of these alternatives. The second tabulation should include the opportunity cost of Goldman's compensation as an employee.
2. Suppose Goldman prefers less risk and chooses to stay as an employee. Show a tabulation of the income effects of rejecting the opportunity of independent practice.

6-24   Opportunity Cost of Home Ownership

Jerry Sikma has just made the final payment on his mortgage. He could continue to live in the home; cash expenses for repairs and maintenance (after any tax effects) would be $500 monthly. Alternatively, he could sell the home for $200,000 (net of any income taxes), invest the proceeds in 10% municipal tax-free bonds, and rent an apartment for $18,000 annually. The landlord would then pay for repairs and maintenance.

Required

Prepare two analyses of Sikma's alternatives, one showing no explicit opportunity cost and the second showing the explicit opportunity cost of the decision to hold the present home.

6-25   Opportunity Cost

Jennifer Foucade, M.D., is a psychiatrist who is in heavy demand. Even though she has raised her fees considerably during the past five years, Dr. Foucade still cannot accommodate all the patients who wish to see her.

Foucade has conducted 6 hours of appointments a day, 6 days a week, for 48 weeks a year. Her fee averages $150 per hour.

Her variable costs are negligible and may be ignored for decision purposes. Ignore income taxes.

Required

1. Foucade is weary of working a 6-day week. She is considering taking every other Saturday off. What would be her annual income (a) if she worked every Saturday and (b) if she worked every other Saturday?

2. What would be her opportunity cost for the year of not working every other Saturday?
3. Assume that Dr. Foucade has definitely decided to take every other Saturday off. She loves to repair her sports car by doing the work herself. If she works on her car during half a Saturday when she otherwise would not see patients, what is her opportunity cost?

6-26   Sell or Process Further

A Chevron petrochemical factory produces two products, L and M, as a result of a particular joint process. Both products are sold to manufacturers as ingredients for assorted chemical products.

Product L sells at split-off for $.25 per gallon; M, for $.30 per gallon. Data for April follow:

Joint processing cost	$1,500,000
Gallons produced and sold	
L	4,000,000
M	2,500,000

Suppose that in April the 2,500,000 gallons of M could have been processed further into Super M at an additional cost of $235,000. The Super M output could have been sold for $.38 per gallon. Product L would have been sold at split-off in any event.

Required   Should M have been processed further in April and sold as Super M? Show computations.

6-27   Joint Products, Multiple Choice

(CPA.) From a particular joint process, Watkins Company produces three products, X, Y, and Z. Each product may be sold at the point of split-off or processed further. Additional processing requires no special facilities, and production costs of further processing are entirely variable and traceable to the products involved. In 19X3 all three products were processed beyond split-off. Joint production costs for the year were $60,000. Sales values and costs needed to evaluate Watkins's 19X3 production policy follow:

Product	Units Produced	Net Realizable Values (Sales Values) at Split-Off	Additional Costs and Sales Values if Processed Further Sales Values	Additional Costs and Sales Values if Processed Further Added Costs
X	6,000	$25,000	$42,000	$9,000
Y	4,000	41,000	45,000	7,000
Z	2,000	24,000	32,000	8,000

Required   Answer the following multiple-choice questions

1. For units of Z, the unit production cost most relevant to a sell-or-process-further decision is (a) $5, (b) $12, (c) $4, (d) $9.
2. To maximize profits, Watkins should subject the following products to additional processing (a) X only, (b) X, Y, and Z, (c) Y and Z only, (d) Z only.

6-28 Obsolete Inventory

The local bookstore bought more Sierra Club calendars than it could sell. It was nearly June and 200 calendars remained in stock. The store paid $4.00 each for the calendars and normally sold them for $8.95. Since February, they had been on sale for $6.00, and 2 weeks ago the price was dropped to $5.00. Still, few calendars were being sold. The bookstore manager thought it was no longer worthwhile using shelf space for the calendars.

The proprietor of Mac's Collectibles offered to buy all 200 calendars for $300. He intended to store them a few years and then sell them as novelty items.

The bookstore manager was not sure she wanted to sell for $1.50 calendars that cost $4.00. The only alternative, however, was to scrap them because the publisher would not take them back.

Required

1. Compute the difference in profit between accepting the $300 offer and scrapping the calendars.
2. Describe how the $4.00 × 200 = $800 paid for the calendars affects your decision.

6-29 Replacement of Old Equipment

Three years ago the Broadway Dairy Queen bought a frozen yogurt machine for $8,000. A salesman has just suggested to the Broadway manager that she replace the machine with a new, $10,000 machine. The manager has gathered the following data:

	Old Machine	New Machine
Original cost	$8,000	$10,000
Useful life in years	8	5
Current age in years	3	0
Useful life remaining in years	5	5
Accumulated depreciation	$3,000	Not acquired yet
Book value	$5,000	Not acquired yet
Disposal value (in cash) now	$2,000	0
Disposal value in 5 years	0	0
Annual cash operating cost	$4,500	$2,500

Required

1. Compute the difference in total costs over the next 5 years under both alternatives, that is, keeping the original machine or replacing it with the new machine. Ignore taxes.
2. Suppose the Broadway manager replaces the original machine. Compute the "loss on disposal" of the original machine. How does this amount affect your computation in requirement 1? Explain.

Problems

6-30 Hotel Rooms and Opportunity Costs

The Sheraton Corporation operates many hotels throughout the world. Suppose one of its Los Angeles hotels is facing difficult times because of the opening of several new competing hotels.

To accommodate its flight personnel, United Airlines has offered Sheraton a contract for the coming year that provides a rate of $50 per night per room for a minimum of 50 rooms for 365 nights. This contract would assure Sheraton of selling 50 rooms of space nightly, even if some of the rooms are vacant on some nights.

The Sheraton manager has mixed feelings about the contract. On several peak nights during the year, the hotel could sell the same space for $100 per room.

Required

1. Suppose the contract is signed. What is the opportunity cost of the 50 rooms on October 20, the night of a big convention of retailers when every midtown hotel room is occupied? What is the opportunity cost on December 28, when only 10 of these rooms would be expected to be rented at an average rate of $80?

2. If the year-round rate per room averaged $90, what percentage of occupancy of the 50 rooms in question would have to be rented to make Sheraton indifferent about accepting the offer?

6-31   Extension of Preceding Problem

Assume the same facts as in the preceding problem. However, also assume that the variable costs per room per day are $10.

Required

1. Suppose the best estimate is a 53% general occupancy rate for the 50 rooms at an average $90 room rate for the next year. Should Sheraton accept the contract?

2. What percentage of occupancy of the 50 rooms in question would make Sheraton indifferent about accepting the offer?

6-32   Hotel Pricing and Discounts

(A. Wheelock.) A growing corporation in a large city has offered a 200-room Red Lion Motel a 1-year contract to rent 40 rooms at reduced rates of $48 per room instead of the regular rate of $83 per room. The corporation will sign the contract for 365-day occupancy because its visiting manufacturing and marketing personnel are virtually certain to use all the space each night.

Each room occupied has a variable cost of $8 per night (for cleaning, laundry, lost linens, and extra electricity).

The motel manager expects an 85% occupancy rate for the year, so she is reluctant to sign the contract. If the contract is signed, the occupancy rate on the remaining 160 rooms will be 95%.

Required

1. Compute the total contribution margin for the year with and without the contract.

2. Compute the lowest room rate that the motel should accept on the contract so that the total contribution margin would be the same with or without the contract.

6-33   Special Air Fares

The manager of operations of Qantas Airlines is trying to decide whether to adopt a new discount fare. Focus on one 134-seat 737 airplane now operating at a 56% load factor. That is, on the average the airplane has .56 × 134 = 75 passengers. The regular fares produce an average revenue of 12¢ per passenger mile.

Suppose an average 40% fare discount (which is subject to restrictions regarding time of departure and length of stay) will produce three new additional passengers. Also suppose that three of the previously committed passengers accept the restrictions and switch to the discount fare from the regular fare.

Required

1. Compute the total revenue per airplane mile with and without the discount fares.

2. Suppose the maximum allowed allocation to new discount fares is 50 seats. These will be filled. As before, some previously committed passengers will accept the restrictions and switch to the discount fare from the regular fare. How many will have to switch so that the total revenue per mile will be the same either with or without the discount plan?

6-34   Joint Costs and Incremental Analysis

(CMA.) LaFountaine de Paris, a high-fashion women's dress manufacturer, is planning to market a new cocktail dress for the coming season. LaFountaine de Paris supplies retailers in Europe and the United States.

Four yards of material are required to lay out the dress pattern. Some material remains after cutting, which can be sold as remnants. The leftover material could also be used to manufacture a matching cape and handbag. However, if the leftover material is to be used for the cape and handbag, more care will be required in the cutting, which will increase the cutting costs.

The company expects to sell 1,250 dresses if no matching cape or handbag is available. Market research reveals that dress sales will be 20% higher if a matching cape and handbag are available. The market research indicates that the cape and handbag will not be sold individually, but only as accessories with the dress. The various combinations of dresses, capes, and handbags that are expected to be sold by retailers are as follows:

	Percent of Total
Complete sets of dress, cape, and handbag	70%
Dress and cape	6%
Dress and handbag	15%
Dress only	9%
Total	100%

The material used in the dress costs FF62.5 a yard, or FF250 for each dress. The cost of cutting the dress if the cape and handbag are not manufactured is estimated at FF100 a dress, and the resulting remnants can be sold for FF25 for each dress cut out. If the cape and handbag are to be manufactured, the cutting costs will be increased by FF36 per dress. There will be no salable remnants if the capes and handbags are manufactured in the quantities estimated. The selling prices and the costs to complete the three items once they are cut are as follows:

	Selling Price per Unit	Unit Cost to Complete (Excludes Cost of Material and Cutting Operation)
Dress	FF1,000	FF400
Cape	140	100
Handbag	50	30

Required

1. Calculate the incremental profit or loss to LaFountaine de Paris from manufacturing the capes and handbags in conjunction with the dresses.
2. Identify any nonquantitative factors that could influence the company's management in its decision to manufacture the capes and handbags that match the dress.

6-35   Make or Buy

Dana Corporation manufactures automobile parts. It frequently subcontracts work to other manufacturers, depending on whether Dana's facilities are fully occupied. Dana is about to make some final decisions regarding the use of its manufacturing facilities for the coming year.

The following are the costs of making part KZ31, a key component of an emission control system:

	Total Cost for 60,000 Units	Cost per Unit
Direct material	$ 480,000	$ 8
Direct labor	360,000	6
Variable factory overhead	180,000	3
Fixed factory overhead	360,000	6
Total manufacturing costs	$1,380,000	$23

Another manufacturer has offered to sell the same part to Dana for $21 each. The fixed overhead consists of depreciation, property taxes, insurance, and supervisory salaries. All the fixed overhead would continue if Dana bought the component except that the cost of $120,000 pertaining to some supervisory and custodial personnel could be avoided.

Required

1. Assume that the capacity now used to make parts will become idle if the parts are purchased. Should the parts be made or bought? Show computations.
2. Assume that the capacity now used to make parts will either (a) be rented to a nearby manufacturer for $75,000 for the year or (b) be used to make oil filters that will yield a profit contribution of $240,000. Should part KZ31 be made or bought? Show computations.

6-36   New Machine

A new $250,000 machine is expected to have a five-year life and a terminal value of zero. It can produce 40,000 units a year at a variable cost of $4 per unit. The variable cost is $6 per unit with an old machine, which has a book value of $100,000. It is being depreciated on a straight-line basis at $20,000 per year. It too is expected to have a terminal value of zero. Its current disposal value is also zero because it is highly specialized equipment.

The salesman of the new machine prepared the following comparison:

	New Machine	Old Machine
Units	40,000	40,000
Variable costs	$160,000	$240,000
Straight-line depreciation	50,000	20,000
Total cost	$210,000	$260,000
Unit cost	$ 5.25	$ 6.50

He said, "The new machine is obviously a worthwhile acquisition. You will save $1.25 for every unit you produce."

Required

1. Do you agree with the salesman's analysis? If not, how would you change it? Be specific. Ignore taxes.
2. Prepare an analysis of total and unit costs if the annual volume is 20,000 units.
3. At what annual volume would both the old and new machines have the same total relevant costs?

6-37   Conceptual Approach

A large automobile-parts plant was constructed four years ago in an Ohio city served by two railroads. The PC Railroad purchased 40 specialized 60-foot freight cars as a direct result of the additional traffic generated by the new plant. The investment was based on an estimated useful life of 20 years.

Now the competing railroad has offered to service the plant with new 86-foot freight cars, which would enable more efficient shipping operations at the plant. The automobile company has threatened to switch carriers unless PC Railroad buys 10 new 86-foot freight cars.

The PC marketing management wants to buy the new cars, but PC operating management says, "The new investment is undesirable. It really consists of the new outlay plus the loss on the old freight cars. The old cars must be written down to a low salvage value if they cannot be used as originally intended."

Required   Evaluate the comments. What is the correct conceptual approach to the quantitative analysis in this decision?

6-38   Book Value of Old Equipment

Consider the following data:

	Old Equipment	Proposed New Equipment
Original cost	$24,000	$12,000
Useful life in years	8	3
Current age in years	5	0
Useful life remaining in years	3	3
Accumulated depreciation	$15,000	0
Book value	9,000	*
Disposal value (in cash) now	4,000	*
Annual cash operating costs (maintenance, power, repairs, lubricants, etc.)	$ 10,000	$ 6,000

* Not acquired yet.

Required

1. Prepare a cost comparison of all relevant items for the next three years together. Ignore taxes.
2. Prepare a cost comparison that includes both relevant and irrelevant items.
3. Prepare a comparative statement of the total charges against revenue for the first year. Would the manager be inclined to buy the new equipment? Explain.

6-39   Decision and Performance Models

Refer back to problem 6-B1.

1. Suppose the "decision model" favored by top management consisted of a comparison of a three-year accumulation of wealth under each alternative. Which alternative would you choose? Why? (Accumulation of wealth means cumulative increase in cash.)
2. Suppose the "performance evaluation model" emphasized the net income of a subunit (such as a division) each year rather than considering each project, one by one. Which alternative would you expect a manager to choose? Why?
3. Suppose the same quantitative data existed, but the "enterprise" was a city and the "machine" was a computer in the treasurer's department. Would your answers to the first two parts change? Why?

6-40   Relevant Costs

A cable television network is considering canceling the program "San Francisco Attorney" because it is watched by only 2.3% of the audience in its Monday evening time slot. It would be replaced by "Hawaiian Surfers," a new show being created from the same formula as the popular "Baywatch." Market research indicates that "Hawaiian Surfers" would be watched by 4% of the audience in the same time slot. For audiences between 1.5% and 5%, the network believes each 1% of audience in this time slot results in additional advertising revenue of $40,000 per week (including beneficial effects on other programs, both present and future). Replacement would come half-way through the 30-week season.

The network's accounting staff has prepared the following financial information to be used in making the decision:

- Developmental expenses for "San Francisco Attorney" were $600,000, and these are being amortized over the originally projected complete season (30 programs).

- Developmental expenses for "Hawaiian Surfers" were $900,000. If "Hawaiian Surfers" is shown for the second half of this season, the entire development cost must be amortized over those 15 programs. If it is not aired until next season, amortization will take place over 30 programs.

- The cost of a script for one program of "San Francisco Attorney" is $20,000 and for "Hawaiian Surfers" is $24,000. No contract for scripts for "Hawaiian Surfers" has yet been signed, but a contract for 20 programs of "San Francisco Attorney" was signed and the $400,000 was already paid.

- The star of "San Francisco Attorney" is under contract to the network for the entire season at $240,000. If "San Francisco Attorney" is canceled, the star will do one special in the spring; if "San Francisco Attorney" continues, he will not do the special. If the star does not do the special, another person (with completely equivalent audience appeal) will be hired for $40,000 to do the special.

- The star of "Hawaiian Surfers" has been hired for the next season for $180,000. If she does 15 shows this season, she will have to forego a part in a movie. Consequently, she must be paid $120,000 for 15 shows this season.

- Investment in the set for "San Francisco Attorney" was $100,000, which was immediately expensed. Additional expenses for the set average $10,000 per show. If "San Francisco Attorney" is canceled, the set can be sold for $20,000. Another alternative use of the set is for a TV movie the network is planning. Additional set expenses for the movie would be $50,000, but building a completely new set would cost $80,000.

- "Hawaiian Surfers" is filmed on location; thus, there is no investment required for a set. However, $20,000 per show is required to make the location suitable for filming.

- The production crew for "San Francisco Attorney" (including actors other than the star) receive $50,000 per show. Most of these people could be used profitably in other operations at the network. However, two actors must be fired if the show is canceled, and the actors' union requires severance pay of $4,000 each.

- There will be a large start-up cost of production for "Hawaiian Surfers" because it will be needed suddenly, six months ahead of schedule. This will amount to $150,000, only $60,000 of which would be necessary if it were not aired until next season. The production crew is very important for "Hawaiian Surfers," and they receive $80,000 per show.

- The network allocates corporate overhead to each show by a complex formula. Each program of "San Francisco Attorney" was allocated $20,000 of overhead; each program of "Hawaiian Surfers" will be allocated $30,000 of overhead. The only corporate overhead expense that would change if "Hawaiian Surfers" replaced "San Francisco Attorney" is the consultation time that corporate management spends with the production staff. This averages 10% of the total production crew expense.

- This decision is to be made by top management, who will invest about $20,000 of their time and effort in it. In addition, a consultant will be paid $4,000 to review the decision.

Required   Should the network cancel "San Francisco Attorney" and replace it with "Hawaiian Surfers" immediately? Explain. Be sure to describe the information that was relevant to this decision and compute the monetary advantage or disadvantage to switching from "San Francisco Attorney" to "Hawaiian Surfers."

6-41   Relevant Cost and Special Order

Estrada Company's *unit* costs of manufacturing and selling a given item at an activity level of 10,000 units per *month* are

Manufacturing costs	
Direct materials	$3.90
Direct labor	.60
Variable overhead	.80
Fixed overhead	.90
Selling expenses	
Variable	3.00
Fixed	1.10

Required Ignore income taxes in all requirements. These four parts have no connection with each other.

1. Compute the *annual* operating income at a selling price of $12 per unit.
2. Compute the expected *annual* operating income if the volume can be increased by 20% when the selling price is reduced to $11. Assume the implied cost behavior patterns are correct.
3. The company desires to seek an order for 5,000 units from a foreign customer. The variable selling expenses will be reduced by 40%, but the fixed costs for obtaining the order will be $6,000. Domestic sales will not be affected. Compute the minimum break-even price per unit to be considered.
4. The company has an inventory of 2,000 units of this item left over from last year's model. These must be sold through *regular channels* at reduced prices. The inventory will be valueless unless sold this way. What unit cost is relevant for establishing the minimum selling price of these 2,000 units?

6-42 Relevant-Cost Analysis

Following are the unit costs of making and selling a single product at a normal level of 5,000 units per month and a current unit selling price of $80:

Manufacturing costs	
Direct material	$25
Direct labor	12
Variable overhead	8
Fixed overhead (total for the year, $300,000)	5
Selling and administrative expenses	
Variable	15
Fixed (total for the year, $480,000)	8

Required Consider each requirement separately. Label all computations, and present your solutions in a form that will be comprehensible to the company president.

1. This product is usually sold at a rate of 60,000 units per year. It is predicted that a rise in price to $88 will decrease volume by 10%. How much may advertising be increased under this plan without having annual operating income fall below the current level?
2. The company has received a proposal from an outside supplier to make and ship this item directly to the company's customers as sales orders are forwarded. Variable selling and administrative costs would fall 40%. If the supplier's proposal is accepted, the company will use its own plant to produce a new product. The new

product would be sold through manufacturer's agents at a 10% commission based on a selling price of $20 each. The cost characteristics of this product, based on predicted yearly normal volume, are as follows:

	Per Unit
Direct material	$ 3
Direct labor	6
Variable overhead	4
Fixed overhead	3
Manufacturing costs	$16
Selling and administrative expenses	
Variable (commission)	10% of selling price
Fixed	$ 1

What is the maximum price per unit that the company can afford to pay to the supplier for subcontracting production of the entire old product? This is not easy. Assume the following:

- Total fixed factory overhead and total fixed selling expenses will not change if the new product line is added.
- The supplier's proposal will not be considered unless the present annual net income can be maintained.
- Selling price of the old product will remain unchanged.
- All $300,000 of fixed manufacturing overhead will be assigned to the new product.

6-43   Relevant Costs on Broadway

The *New York Times* reported that Neil Simon plans to open his latest play, *London Suite*, off Broadway. Why? For financial reasons. Producer Emanuel Azenberg predicted the following costs before the play even opens:

	On Broadway	Off Broadway
Sets, costumes, lights	$ 357,000	$ 87,000
Loading in (building set, etc.)	175,000	8,000
Rehearsal salaries	102,000	63,000
Director and designer fees	126,000	61,000
Advertising	300,000	121,000
Administration	235,000	100,000
Total	$1,295,000	$440,000

Broadway ticket prices average $55, and theaters can seat about 1,000 persons per show. Off-Broadway prices average only $40, and the theaters seat only 500. Normally plays run eight times a week, both on and off Broadway. Weekly operating expenses off Broadway average $82,000; they average an extra $124,000 on Broadway for a weekly total of $206,000.

Required   1. Suppose 400 persons attended each show, whether on or off Broadway. Compare the weekly financial results from a Broadway production to one produced off Broadway.

2. Suppose attendance averaged 75% of capacity, whether on or off Broadway. Compare the weekly financial results from a Broadway production to one produced off Broadway.

3. Compute the attendance per show required just to cover weekly expenses (a) on Broadway and (b) off Broadway.

4. Suppose average attendance on Broadway was 600 per show and off Broadway was 400. Compute the total net profit for a 26-week run (a) on Broadway and (b) off Broadway. Be sure to include the pre-opening costs.

5. Repeat requirement 4 for a 100-week run.

6. Using attendance figures from requirements 4 and 5, compute (a) the number of weeks a Broadway production must run before it breaks even, and (b) the number of weeks an off-Broadway production must run before it breaks even.

7. Using attendance figures from requirements 4 and 5, determine how long a play must run before the profit from a Broadway production exceeds that from an off-Broadway production.

8. If you were Neil Simon, would you prefer *London Suite* to play on Broadway or off Broadway? Explain.

Cases

6-44 Make or Buy

(CMA, adapted.) The Weisbrod Corporation, which produces and sells to wholesalers a highly successful line of summer lotions and insect repellents, has decided to diversify to stabilize sales throughout the year. The company is considering the production of winter lotions and creams to prevent dry and chapped skin.

After considerable research, a winter products line has been developed. Because of the conservative nature of the company management, however, Weisbrod's president has decided to introduce only one of the new products for this coming winter. If the product is a success, further expansion in future years will be initiated.

The product selected (called Chap-Off) is a lip balm that will be sold in a lipstick-type tube. The product will be sold to wholesalers in boxes of 24 tubes for $8 per box. Because of available capacity, no additional fixed charges will be incurred to produce the product. A $100,000 fixed charge will be absorbed by the product, however, to allocate a fair share of the company's present fixed costs to the new product.

Using the estimated sales and production of 100,000 boxes of Chap-Off as the expected volume, the accounting department has developed the following costs per box:

Direct labor	$3.50
Direct material	3.00
Total overhead	1.50
Total	$8.00

Weisbrod has approached a cosmetics manufacturer to discuss the possibility of purchasing the tubes for Chap-Off. The purchase price of the empty tubes from the cosmetics manufacturer would be $1.05 per 24 tubes. If the Weisbrod Corporation accepts the purchase proposal, it is predicted that direct-labor and variable-overhead costs would be reduced by 10% and direct-material costs would be reduced by 20%.

Required

1. Should the Weisbrod Corporation make or buy the tubes? Show calculations to support your answer.

2. What would be the maximum purchase price acceptable to the Weisbrod Corporation for the tubes? Support your answer with an appropriate explanation.

3. Instead of sales of 100,000 boxes, revised estimates show sales volume at 125,000 boxes. At this new volume, additional equipment, at an annual rental of $10,000, must be acquired to manufacture the tubes. This incremental cost would be the only additional fixed cost required even if sales increased to 300,000 boxes. (The 300,000 level is the goal for the third year of production.) Under these circumstances, should the Weisbrod Corporation make or buy the tubes? Show calculations to support your answer.

4. The company has the option of making and buying at the same time. What would be your answer to requirement 3 if this alternative were considered? Show calculations to support your answer.

5. What nonquantifiable factors should the Weisbrod Corporation consider in determining whether they should make or buy the lipstick-type tubes?

6-45   Make or Buy

The Rohr Company's old equipment for making subassemblies is worn out. The company is considering two courses of action: (a) completely replacing the old equipment with new equipment or (b) buying subassemblies from a reliable outside supplier, who has quoted a unit price of $1 on a seven-year contract for a minimum of 50,000 units per year.

Production was 60,000 units in each of the past two years. Future needs for the next seven years are not expected to fluctuate beyond 50,000 to 70,000 units per year. Cost records for the past two years reveal the following unit costs of manufacturing the subassembly:

Direct material	$ .30
Direct labor	.35
Variable overhead	.10
Fixed overhead (including $.10 depreciation and $.10 for direct departmental fixed overhead)	.25
	$1.00

The new equipment will cost $188,000 cash, will last seven years, and will have a disposal value of $20,000. The current disposal value of the old equipment is $10,000.

The sales representative for the new equipment has summarized her position as follows: The increase in machine speeds will reduce direct labor and variable overhead by 35 ¢ per unit. Consider last year's experience of one of your major competitors with identical equipment. They produced 100,000 units under operating conditions very comparable to yours and showed the following unit costs:

Direct material	$.30
Direct labor	.05
Variable overhead	.05
Fixed overhead, including depreciation of $.24	.40
	$.80

Required   For purposes of this case, assume that any idle facilities cannot be put to alternative use. Also assume that 5¢ of the old Rohr unit cost is allocated fixed overhead that will be unaffected by the decision.

1. The president asks you to compare the alternatives on a total-annual-cost basis and

on a per-unit basis for annual needs of 60,000 units. Which alternative seems more attractive?

2. Would your answer to requirement 1 change if the needs were 50,000 units? 70,000 units? At what volume level would Rohr be indifferent between making and buying subassemblies? Show your computations.

3. What factors, other than the preceding ones, should the accountant bring to the attention of management to assist them in making their decision? Include the considerations that might be applied to the outside supplier.

7

Master Budget: Overall Plan

Wells Lamont is one of the world's largest manufacturers and marketers of gloves for work and recreation. With operations in the U.S., China, Jamaica, and Mexico, well-developed sales forecasts are essential in maintaining sufficient stock and in managing plant and warehouse capacity.
Courtesy Wells Lamont

Learning Objectives

When you have finished studying this chapter, you should be able to

1 Distinguish between master budgets and long-range plans.

2 Distinguish between operating and financial budgets.

3 Identify a budget's major advantages to an organization.

4 Follow the principal steps in preparing a master budget.

5 Use sales and other cost drivers in preparing budgets.

6 Prepare the operating budget and the supporting schedules.

7 Prepare the financial budget.

8 Understand the difficulties of sales forecasting.

9 Anticipate problems of human behavior toward budgets.

10 Identify the uses of a financial planning model.

11 Use a spreadsheet to develop a budget (Appendix 7).

Planning is the key to good management. This is true for individuals, small family-owned companies, new high-technology companies, large corporations, government agencies, and nonprofit organizations. For example, most successful students who earn good grades, finance their education, and finish their degrees in a reasonable amount of time do so because they plan their time, their work, and their recreation. These students are *budgeting* their scarce resources to make the best use of their time, money, and energy. Likewise, owners of successful small companies who survive and grow even in difficult economic times carefully plan or budget their inventory purchases and their expansion of facilities so that they do not overextend themselves financially but are still able to meet customers' needs.

High-technology firms are often started by highly intelligent scientists and engineers who have valuable product ideas, but the high-technology firms that thrive are those whose managers also have superior planning and budgeting skills. Coordinating the use of scarce resources in a large, diverse corporation is an extremely complex and vital activity. Budgeting in these large corporations usually is ongoing throughout the year. Taxpayers demand that governments plan for the effective use of their hard-earned dollars, so government budgeting is especially important in difficult economic times, when tax dollars could otherwise have been spent for private purposes. Nonprofit organizations must develop more effective plans to achieve their objectives as they compete for scarce donations or grant monies. Not only are budgets critical to good planning in any endeavor, budgets are necessary for evaluation of performance. Keeping score is an American tradition, whether on the football field or in the boardroom. A *budget*—a formal, quantitative expression of plans (whether for an individual, business, or other organization)—provides a benchmark against which to measure actual performance.

As you will see in this chapter, a budget can be much more than a limit on expenditures. Although government agencies too often use a budget merely as a limit on their spending, businesses and other organizations generally use budgets to focus on operating or financial problems early, so that managers can take steps to avoid or remedy the problems. Thus a budget is a tool that helps managers both *plan* and *control* operations.

Surveys of company practices indicate the importance of budgeting. For example, in a recent survey of manufacturing companies, the top ranked technique for cost reduction and control was budgetary planning and control. Advocates of budgeting maintain that the process of budgeting *forces a manager to become a better administrator* and *puts planning in the forefront of the manager's mind*. Indeed, failure to draw up, monitor, and adjust budgets to changing conditions is one of the primary reasons behind the collapse of many businesses.

In this chapter we will look at the uses and benefits of budgets and consider the construction of the master budget.

■ BUDGETS: WHAT THEY ARE AND HOW THEY BENEFIT THE ORGANIZATION

Objective 1

Distinguish between master budgets and long-range plans

Another way to describe a budget is as a condensed business plan for the forthcoming year (or less). Few investors or bank loan officers today will provide funds for the would-be entrepreneur without a credible business plan. Similarly, within a firm, managers need budgets to guide them in allocating resources and maintaining control and to enable them to measure and reward progress.

Budgeting over Time

strategic plan A plan that sets the overall goals and objectives of the organization.

The planning horizon for budgeting may vary from one day to many years, depending on the organization's objectives and the uncertainties involved. The most forward-looking budget is the **strategic plan,** which sets the overall goals and objectives of the organization. (Note, though, that some business analysts do not call a strategic plan a budget because it covers no specific period and does not produce forecasted financial statements.)

long-range planning
Producing forecasted financial statements for five- or ten-year periods.

Long-range planning produces forecasted financial statements for 5- or 10-year periods. Decisions made during long-range planning include addition or deletion of product lines, design and location of new plants, acquisitions of buildings and equipment, and other long-term commitments. Long-range plans are coordinated with **capital budgets,** which detail the planned expenditures for facilities, equipment, new products, and other long-term investments. (Capital budgeting is the subject of Chapters 11 and 12.)

capital budget
A budget that details the planned expenditures for facilities, equipment, new products, and other long-term investments.

A master budget is essentially a more extensive analysis of the first year of the long-range plan. A *budget* is a formal, quantitative expression of management plans. A **master budget** summarizes the planned activities of all subunits of an organization—sales, production, distribution, and finance. The master budget quantifies targets for sales, cost-driver activity, purchases, production, net income, cash position, and any other objective that management specifies. *Thus, the master budget is a periodic business plan that includes a coordinated set of detailed operating schedules and financial statements.* It includes forecasts of sales, expenses, cash receipts and disbursements, and balance sheets. Master budgets are also called **pro forma statements**, another term for forecasted financial statements. Management might prepare monthly budgets for the year or perhaps monthly budgets for only the first quarter and quarterly budgets for the three remaining quarters. The master budget is the most detailed budget that is coordinated across the whole organization, but individual managers may also prepare daily or weekly *task-oriented* budgets to help them carry out their particular functions and meet operating and financial goals.

master budget (pro forma statement)
A budget that summarizes the planned activities of all subunits of an organization.

continuous budget (rolling budget)
A common form of master budget that adds a month in the future as the month just ended is dropped.

Continuous budgets or **rolling budgets** are a very common form of master budgets that add a month in the future as the month just ended is dropped. Continuous budgets compel mangers to think specifically about the forthcoming 12 months and thus maintain a stable planning horizon. As they add a new 12th month to a continuous budget, managers may update the other 11 months as well. Then they can compare actual monthly results with both the original plan and the most recently revised plan.

Components of Master Budget

The terms used to describe assorted budget schedules vary from organization to organization; however, most master budgets have common elements. The usual master budget for a nonmanufacturing company has the following components:

Objective 2

Distinguish between operating and financial budgets

A. Operating budget
   1. Sales budget (and other cost-driver budgets as necessary)
   2. Purchases budget
   3. Cost-of-goods-sold budget
   4. Operating expenses budget
   5. Budgeted income statement

B. Financial budget
   1. Capital budget
   2. Cash budget
   3. Budgeted balance sheet

Exhibit 7-1 presents a condensed diagram of the relationships among the various parts of a master budget for a nonmanufacturing company. In addition to these categories, manufacturing companies that maintain physical product inventories prepare ending inventory budgets and additional budgets for each type of resource activity (such as labor, materials, and factory overhead).

Exhibit 7-1

Preparation of
Master Budget for
Nonmanufacturing
Company

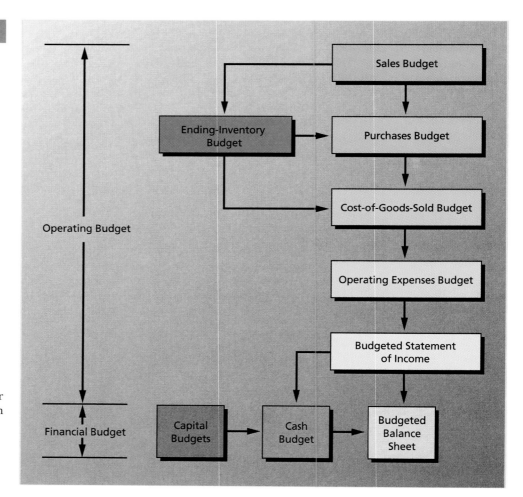

**operating budget
(profit plan)** A
major part of a master
budget that focuses on
the income statement
and its supporting
schedules.

financial budget
The part of a master
budget that focuses
on the effects that the
operating budget and
other plans (such as
capital budgets and
repayments of debt)
will have on cash.

The two major parts of a master budget are the operating budget and the financial budget. The **operating budget** focuses on the income statement and its supporting schedules. Though sometimes called the **profit plan**, an operating budget may show a budgeted *loss*, or even be used to budget expenses in an organization or agency with no sales revenues. In contrast, the **financial budget** focuses on the effects that the operating budget and other plans (such as capital budgets and repayments of debt) will have on cash.

In addition to the master budget, there are countless forms of special budgets and related reports. For example, a report might detail goals and objectives for improvements in quality or customer satisfaction during the budget period.

Advantages of Budgets

All managers do some kind of planning or budgeting. Sometimes plans and budgets are unwritten, especially in small organizations. This might work in a small organization, but as an organization grows, informal, seat-of-the-pants planning is not enough. A more formal budgetary system becomes more than an attractive alternative—it is a necessity.

Objective 3

Identify a budget's major advantages to an organization

Skeptical managers have claimed, "I face too many uncertainties and complications to make budgeting worthwhile for me." Be wary of such claims. Planning and budgeting are especially important in uncertain environments. A budget allows *systematic rather than chaotic reaction to change*. For example, the Natural Resources Group of W. R. Grace & Co. greatly reduced a planned expansion in reaction to a worldwide abundance of oil and gas. A top executive, quoted in the company's annual report, stated that "management used the business planning process to adjust to changes in operating conditions."

Three major benefits of budgeting are as follows:

1. Budgeting compels managers to think ahead by formalizing their responsibilities for planning.
2. Budgeting provides definite expectations that are the best framework for judging subsequent performance.
3. Budgeting aids managers in coordinating their efforts, so that the objectives of the organization as a whole match the objectives of its parts.

Let's look more closely at each of these benefits.

Formalization of Planning

Budgeting forces managers to think ahead—to anticipate and prepare for changing conditions. The budgeting process makes planning an *explicit* management responsibility. Too often, managers operate from day-to-day, extinguishing one business brush fire after another. They simply have "no time" for any tough-minded thinking beyond the next day's problems. Planning takes a back seat to or is actually obliterated by daily pressures.

The trouble with the day-to-day approach to managing an organization is that objectives are never crystallized. Managers react to current events rather than plan for the future. To prepare a budget, a manager should set goals and objectives, and establish policies to aid their achievement. The objectives are the destination points, and budgets are the road maps guiding us to those destinations. Without goals and objectives, company operations lack direction; problems are not foreseen; and results are difficult to interpret afterward.

Expectations: Framework for Judging Performance

Budgeted goals and performance are generally a better basis for judging actual results than is past performance. The news that a company had sales of $100 million this year, as compared with $80 million the previous year, may or may not indicate that the company has been effective and has met company objectives. Perhaps sales should have been $110 million this year. The major drawback of using historical results for judging current performance is that inefficiencies may be concealed in the past performance. Intervening changes in economic conditions, technology, maneuvers by competitors, personnel, and so forth also limit the usefulness of comparisons with the past.

Communication and Coordination

Another benefit of budgeting is that personnel are informed of what is expected of them. Nobody likes to drift along, not knowing what "the boss" expects or hopes to achieve. A good budget process communicates both from the top down and from the bottom up. Top management makes clear the goals and objectives of the organization in its budgetary directives to middle- and lower-level managers, and increasingly to all employees. Employees and lower-level managers then inform higher-level managers how they plan to achieve the goals and objectives.

Budgets also help managers coordinate objectives. For example, a budget forces purchasing personnel to integrate their plans with production requirements, while production managers use the sales budget and delivery schedule to help them anticipate and plan for the employees and physical facilities they will require. Similarly, financial officers use the sales budget, purchasing requirements, and so forth to anticipate the company's need for cash. Thus the budgetary process forces managers to visualize the relationship of their department's activities to other departments and to the company as a whole.

▦ ILLUSTRATION OF PREPARATION OF MASTER BUDGET

Now that you know what budgets are and why they are important, we can return to Exhibit 7-1 and trace the preparation of the master budget components. *Do not rush; follow each step carefully and completely.* Although the process may seem largely mechanical, remember that the master-budgeting process generates key decisions regarding pricing, product lines, capital expenditures, research and development, personnel assignments, and so forth. Therefore, the first draft of the budget leads to decisions that prompt subsequent drafts before a final budget is chosen. Because budget preparation is somewhat mechanical, many organizations use powerful spreadsheet or modeling software to prepare and modify budget drafts. Appendix 7 discusses using personal computer spreadsheets for budgeting. You may want to refer to Chapter 17, which describes basic knowledge of financial accounting processes, terms, and calculations we will use to prepare a master budget.

Description of Problem

To illustrate the budgeting process we will use as an example the Cooking Hut Company (CHC), a local retailer of a wide variety of kitchen and dining room items. The company rents a retail store in a midsized community near a large

Communication and Coordination with Budgeting in a High-Technology Company

Photon Technology International, Inc., manufactures electro-optical instruments used for medical research and diagnostic procedures. Its products are state-of-the-art, but until recently, Photon did not have a formal budgeting procedure and found itself on the verge of financial failure. Collection of sales from customers was slow, research and development outlays were high, and Photon was fast running out of cash.

Photon hired a professional financial manager who has instituted a budget process that links cash flow, intensive high-technology research and development, customer training and education, and on-site customizing of the products. Coordination of all of these factors is absolutely critical in this new, high-technology firm. This budget process develops three "what-if" scenarios: (1) a best-case budget where everything goes as hoped, (2) a worst-case budget that predicts just the opposite, and (3) a most-likely-case budget where each budget forecast (sales, sales collections, cost-driver activity, cost behavior, and so on) is examined and set at a realistic level. This budget process allows Photon to anticipate cash flow problems before they threaten the company's survival and to communicate critical resource needs within the company. Photon believes that implementing a formal budget process is a critical step in its transition from a start-up to a maturing company. ■

Source: Adapted from Charles L. Grant, "High-Tech Budgeting," Management Accounting, *May 1991, pp. 30–31.*

metropolitan area. CHC's management prepares a continuous budget to aid financial and operating decisions. For simplicity in this illustration, the planning horizon is only 4 months, April through July. In the past, sales have increased during this season. Collections lag behind sales, and cash is needed for purchases, wages, and other operating outlays. In the past, the company has met this cash squeeze with the help of short-term loans from a local bank and will continue to do so, repaying those loans as cash is available.

Exhibit 7-2 is the closing balance sheet for the fiscal year just ended. Sales in March were $40,000. Monthly sales are forecasted as follows:

April	$50,000
May	$80,000
June	$60,000
July	$50,000
August	$40,000

Management expects future sales collections to follow past experience: 60% of the sales should be in cash and 40% on credit. All credit accounts are collected in the month following the sales. The $16,000 of accounts receivable on March 31 represents credit sales made in March (40% of $40,000). Uncollectible accounts are negligible and are to be ignored. Also ignore all local, state, and federal taxes for this illustration.

Because deliveries from suppliers and customer demands are uncertain, at the end of each month, CHC wants to have on hand a basic inventory of items valued at $20,000 plus 80% of the expected cost of goods sold for the following month. The cost of merchandise sold averages 70% of sales. Therefore, the inventory on March 31 is $20,000 + .7(.8 × April sales of $50,000) = $20,000 + $28,000 = $48,000. The purchase terms available to CHC are net, 30 days. CHC pays for each month's purchases as follows: 50% during that month and 50% during the next month. Therefore, the accounts payable balance on March 31 is 50% of March's purchases, or $33,600 × .5 = $16,800.

Exhibit 7-2	**Assets**		
The Cooking Hut Company	Current assets		
Balance Sheet	Cash	$10,000	
March 31, 19X1	Accounts receivable, net (.4 × March sales of $40,000)	16,000	
	Merchandise inventory, $20,000 +.7 (.8 x April sales of $50,000)	48,000	
	Unexpired insurance	1,800	$ 75,800
	Plant assets		
	Equipment, fixtures, and other	$37,000	
	Accumulated depreciation	12,800	24,200
	Total assets		$100,000
	Liabilities and Owners' Equity		
	Current liabilities		
	Accounts payable (.5 × March purchases of $33,600)	$16,800	
	Accrued wages and commissions payable ($1,250 + $3,000)	4,250	$ 21,050
	Owners' equity		78,950
	Total liabilities and owners' equity		$100,000

CHC pays wages and commissions semimonthly, half a month after they are earned. They are divided into two portions: monthly fixed wages of $2,500 and commissions, equal to 15% of sales, which we will assume are uniform throughout each month. Therefore, the March 31 balance of accrued wages and commissions payable is (.5 × $2,500) + .5(.15 × $40,000) = $1,250 + $3,000 = $4,250. CHC will pay this $4,250 on April 15.

In addition to buying new fixtures for $3,000 cash in April, CHC's other monthly expenses are as follows:

Miscellaneous expenses	5% of sales, paid as incurred
Rent	$2,000, paid as incurred
Insurance	$200 expiration per month
Depreciation, including new fixtures	$500 per month

The company wants a minimum of $10,000 as a cash balance at the end of each month. To keep this simple, we will assume that CHC can borrow or repay loans in multiples of $1,000. Management plans to borrow no more cash than necessary and to repay as promptly as possible. Assume that borrowing occurs at the beginning and repayment at the end of the months in question. Interest is paid, under the terms of this credit arrangement, when the related loan is repaid. The interest rate is 18% per year.

Steps in Preparation of Master Budget

The principal steps in preparing the master budget are:

Objective 4

Follow the principal steps in preparing a master budget

Operating Budget

1. Using the data given, prepare the following detailed schedules for each of the months of the planning horizon:
    a. Sales budget
    b. Cash collections from customers
    c. Purchases budget
    d. Disbursements for purchases
    e. Operating expense budget
    f. Disbursements for operating expenses
2. Using these schedules, prepare a budgeted income statement for the 4 months ending July 31, 19X1 (Exhibit 7-3).

Financial Budget

3. Using the data given and the supporting schedules, prepare the following forecasted financial statements:
    a. Cash budget including details of borrowings, repayments, and interest for each month of the planning horizon (Exhibit 7-4)
    b. Budgeted balance sheet as of July 31, 19X1 (Exhibit 7-5)

You will need schedules 1a, 1c, and 1e to prepare the budgeted income statement (Exhibit 7-3), and schedules 1b, 1d, and 1f to prepare the cash budget (Exhibit 7-4).

Organizations with effective budget systems have specific guidelines for the steps and timing of budget preparation. Although the details differ, the guidelines invariably include the preceding steps. As we follow these steps to examine the schedules of this illustrative problem, ***be sure that you understand the source of each figure in each schedule and budget.*** The logic of this manual example is identical to the logic used to prepare computerized budgeting models and systems (see Appendix 7).

Step 1: Preparation of Operating Budget

You should now be ready to trace the budgeting process.

Step 1a: Sales Budget

Objective 5

Use sales and other cost drivers in preparing budgets

The sales budget (Schedule a in the table on page 262) is the starting point for budgeting because inventory levels, purchases, and operating expenses are geared to the rate of sales activities (and other cost drivers that are not present in this example). Accurate sales and cost-driver activity forecasting is essential to effective budgeting; sales forecasting is considered in a later section of this chapter. March sales are included in Schedule a because they affect cash collections in April. Trace the final column in Schedule a to the first row of Exhibit 7-3 on page 264. In nonprofit organizations, forecasts of revenue or some level of services are also the focal points for budgeting. Examples are patient revenues and government reimbursement expected by hospitals and donations expected by churches. If no revenues are generated, as in the case of municipal fire protection, a desired level of service is predetermined.

Step 1b: Cash Collections

It is easiest to prepare Schedule b, cash collections, at the same time as preparing the sales budget. Cash collections include the current month's cash sales plus the previous month's credit sales. We will use total collections in preparing the cash budget—see Exhibit 7-4 on page 266.

	March	April	May	June	July	April–July Total
Schedule a: Sales Budget						
Credit sales, 40%	$16,000	$20,000	$32,000	$24,000	$20,000	
Plus cash sales, 60%	24,000	30,000	48,000	36,000	30,000	
Total sales	$40,000	$50,000	$80,000	$60,000	$50,000	$240,000
Schedule b: Cash Collections						
Cash sales this month		$30,000	$48,000	$36,000	$30,000	
Plus 100% of last month's credit sales		16,000	20,000	32,000	24,000	
Total collections		$46,000	$68,000	$68,000	$54,000	

Step 1c: Purchases Budget

After sales are budgeted, prepare the purchases budget (Schedule c). The total merchandise needed will be the sum of the desired ending inventory plus the

	March	April	May	June	July	April–July Total
Schedule c: Purchases Budget						
Desired ending inventory	$48,000*	$64,800	$ 53,600	$48,000	$42,400	
Plus cost of goods sold†	28,000	35,000	56,000	42,000	35,000	$168,000
Total needed	$76,000	$99,800	$109,600	$90,000	$77,400	
Less beginning inventory	42,400‡	48,000	64,800	53,600	48,000	
Purchases	$33,600	$51,800	$ 44,800	$36,400	$29,400	
Schedule d: Disbursements for Purchases						
50% of last month's purchases		$16,800	$ 25,900	$22,400	$18,200	
Plus 50% of this month's purchases		25,900	22,400	18,200	14,700	
Disbursements for purchases		$42,700	$ 48,300	$40,600	$32,900	

* $20,000 + (.8 × April cost of goods sold) = $20,000 + .8($35,000) = $48,000.
† .7 × March sales of $40,000 = $28,000; .7 × April sales of $50,000 = $35,000, and so on.
‡ $20,000 + (.8 × March cost of goods sold of $28,000) = $20,000 + $22,400 = $42,400.

Objective 6

Prepare the operating budget and the supporting schedules

amount needed to fulfill budgeted sales demand. The total need will be partially met by the beginning inventory; the remainder must come from planned purchases. These purchases are computed as follows:

budgeted purchases = desired ending inventory + cost of goods sold – beginning inventory

Trace the total purchases figure in the final column of Schedule c to the second row of Exhibit 7-3.

Step 1d: Disbursements for Purchases

Schedule d, disbursements for purchases, is based on the purchases budget. Disbursements include 50% of the current month's purchases and 50% of the previous month's purchases. We will use total disbursements in preparing the cash budget, Exhibit 7-4, for the financial budget.

Step 1e: Operating Expense Budget

The budgeting of operating expenses depends on various factors. Month-to-month fluctuations in sales volume and other cost-driver activities directly influence many operating expenses. Examples of expenses driven by sales volume include sales commissions and many delivery expenses. Other expenses are not influenced by sales or other cost-driver activity (such as rent, insurance, depreciation, and salaries) within appropriate relevant ranges and are regarded as fixed. Trace the total operating expenses in the final column of Schedule e, which summarizes these expenses, to the budgeted income statement, Exhibit 7-3.

	March	April	May	June	July	April–July Total
Schedule e: Operating Expense Budget						
Wages (fixed)	$2,500	$ 2,500	$ 2,500	$ 2,500	$ 2,500	
Commissions (15% of current month's sales)	6,000	7,500	12,000	9,000	7,500	
Total wages and commissions	$8,500	$10,000	$14,500	$11,500	$10,000	$46,000
Miscellaneous expenses (5% of current sales)		2,500	4,000	3,000	2,500	12,000
Rent (fixed)		2,000	2,000	2,000	2,000	8,000
Insurance (fixed)		200	200	200	200	800
Depreciation (fixed)		500	500	500	500	2,000
Total operating expenses		$15,200	$21,200	$17,200	$15,200	$68,800

Step 1f: Operating Expense Disbursements

Disbursements for operating expenses are based on the operating expense budget. Disbursements include 50% of last month's and this month's wages and commissions, and miscellaneous and rent expenses. We will use the total of these disbursements in preparing the cash budget, Exhibit 7-4.

	March	April	May	June	July	April–July Total
Schedule f: Disbursements for Operating Expenses						
Wages and commission						
50% of last month's expenses		$ 4,250	$ 5,000	$ 7,250	$ 5,750	
50% of this month's expenses		5,000	7,250	5,750	5,000	
Total wages and commissions		$ 9,250	$12,250	$13,000	$10,750	
Miscellaneous expenses		2,500	4,000	3,000	2,500	
Rent		2,000	2,000	2,000	2,000	
Total disbursements		$13,750	$18,250	$18,000	$15,250	

Step 2: Preparation of Budgeted Income Statement

Steps 1a through 1f provide enough information to construct a budgeted income statement *from operations* (Exhibit 7-3). The income statement will be complete after addition of the interest expense, which is computed after the cash budget has been prepared. Budgeted income from operations is often a benchmark for judging management performance.

Exhibit 7-3				Data	Source of Data
The Cooking Hut Company Budgeted Income Statement for 4 Months Ending July 31, 19X1	Sales			$240,000	Schedule a
	Cost of goods sold			168,000	Schedule c
	Gross margin			$ 72,000	
	Operating expenses:				
	Wages and commissions		$46,000		Schedule e
	Rent		8,000		Schedule e
	Miscellaneous		12,000		Schedule e
	Insurance		800		Schedule e
	Depreciation		2,000	68,800	Schedule e
	Income from operations			$ 3,200	
	Interest expense			675	Exhibit 7-4
	Net income			$ 2,525	

Step 3: Preparation of Financial Budget

Objective 7

Prepare the financial budget

The second major part of the master budget is the financial budget, which consists of the capital budget, cash budget, and ending balance sheet. This chapter focuses on the cash budget and the ending balance sheet. Chapters 11 and 12 discuss the capital budget. In our illustration, the $3,000 purchase of new fixtures would be included in the capital budget.

Step 3a: Cash Budget

cash budget A statement of planned cash receipts and disbursements.

The **cash budget** is a statement of planned cash receipts and disbursements. The cash budget is heavily affected by the level of operations summarized in the budgeted income statement. The cash budget has the following major sections, where the letters *w, x, y,* and *z* refer to the lines in Exhibit 7-4 that summarize the effects of that section.

The *total cash available before financing* (*w*) equals the beginning cash balance plus cash receipts. Cash receipts depend on collections from customers' accounts receivable and cash sales and on other operating income sources. Trace total collections from Schedule b to Exhibit 7-4.

Cash disbursements (*x*) for

1. Purchases depend on the credit terms extended by suppliers and the bill-paying habits of the buyer (disbursements for merchandise from Schedule d should be traced to Exhibit 7-4).

2. Payroll depends on wage, salary, and commission terms and on payroll dates (wages and commissions from Schedule f should be traced to Exhibit 7-4).

3. Some costs and expenses depend on contractual terms for installment payments, mortgage payments, rents, leases, and miscellaneous items (miscellaneous and rent from Schedule f should be traced to Exhibit 7-4).

4. Other disbursements include outlays for fixed assets, long-term investments, dividends, and the like (the $3,000 expenditure for new fixtures).

Management determines the *minimum cash balance desired* (*y*) depending on the nature of the business and credit arrangements.

Financing requirements (*z*) depend on how the *total cash available, w* in Exhibit 7-4, compares with the *total cash needed*. Needs include the disbursements, *x*, plus the desired ending cash balance, *y*. If the total cash available is less than the cash needed, borrowing is necessary—Exhibit 7-4 shows that CHC will borrow $14,000 in April to cover the planned *deficiency*. If there is an *excess*, loans may be repaid—$1,000, $9,000, and $4,000 are repaid in May, June, and July, respectively. The pertinent outlays for interest expenses are usually contained in this section of the cash budget. Trace the calculated interest expense to Exhibit 7-3, which then will be complete.

The *ending cash balance* is $w - x + z$. Financing, *z*, has either a positive (borrowing) or a negative (repayment) effect on the cash balance. The illustrative cash budget shows the pattern of short-term, "self-liquidating" financing. Seasonal peaks often result in heavy drains on cash—for merchandise purchases and operating expenses—before the sales are made and cash is collected from customers. The resulting loan is "self-liquidating"—that is, the borrowed money is used to acquire merchandise for sale, and the proceeds from sales are used to repay the loan. This "working capital cycle" moves from cash to inventory to receivables and back to cash.

Cash budgets help management to avoid having unnecessary idle cash, on the one hand, and unnecessary cash deficiencies, on the other. A well-managed financing program keeps cash balances from becoming too large or too small.

Exhibit 7-4	The Cooking Hut Company Cash Budget for 4 Months Ending July 31, 19X1			
	April	**May**	**June**	**July**
Beginning cash balance	$ 10,000	$10,550	$10,970	$10,965
Cash receipts				
Collections from customers (Schedule b)	46,000	68,000	68,000	54,000
Total cash available, before financing $(w)^*$	$ 56,000	$78,550	$78,970	$64,965
Cash disbursements				
Merchandise (Schedule d)	42,700	48,300	40,600	32,900
Operating expenses (Schedule f)	13,750	18,250	18,000	15,250
Purchase of new fixtures (given)	3,000	—	—	—
Total disbursements (x)	$ 59,450	$66,550	$58,600	$48,150
Minimum cash balance desired (y)	10,000	10,000	10,000	10,000
Total cash needed	$ 69,450	$76,550	$68,600	$58,150
Excess (deficiency) of total cash available over total cash needed before financing $(w - x - y)$	$(13,450)	$ 2,000	$10,370	$ 6,815
Financing				
Borrowing (at beginning of month)	$14,000[†]			
Repayments (at end of month)	—	$ (1,000)	$ (9,000)	$ (4,000)
Interest (at 18% per year) [‡]	—	(30)	(405)	(240)
Total cash increase (decrease) from financing (z)	$ 14,000	$ (1,030)	$ (9,405)	$ (4,240)
Ending cash balance $(w - x + z)$	$ 10,550	$10,970	$10,965	$12,575

* Letters are keyed to the explanation in the text.
† Borrowing and repayment of principal are made in multiples of $1,000, at an interest rate of 18% per year.
‡ Interest computations: .18 × $1,000 × 3/12; .18 × $9,000 x 3/12; .18 × $4,000 × 5/12.

Step 3b: Budgeted Balance Sheet

The final step in preparing the master budget is to construct the budgeted balance sheet (Exhibit 7-5) that projects each balance sheet item in accordance with the business plan as expressed in the previous schedules. Specifically, the beginning balances at March 31 would be increased or decreased in light of the expected cash receipts and cash disbursements in Exhibit 7-4 and in light of the effects of noncash items appearing on the income statement in Exhibit 7-3. For example, unexpired insurance would decrease from its balance of $1,800 on March 31 to $1,000 on July 31, even though it is a noncash item.

When the complete master budget is formulated, management can consider all the major financial statements as a basis for changing the course of events. For example, the initial formulation may prompt management to try new sales strategies to generate more demand. Alternatively, management may explore the effects of various adjustments in the timing of receipts and disbursements. The large cash deficiency in April, for example, may lead to an emphasis on cash sales or an attempt to speed up collection of accounts receivable. In any event, the first draft of the master budget is rarely the final draft. As it is reworked, the budgeting process becomes an integral part of the management process itself—budgeting is planning and communicating.

Exhibit 7-5

The Cooking Hut
Company
Budgeted
Balance Sheet
July 31, 19X1

Assets		
Current assets		
Cash (Exhibit 7-4)	$12,575	
Accounts receivable, net (.4 × July sales of $50,000, Schedule a)	20,000	
Merchandise inventory (Schedule c)	42,400	
Unexpired insurance ($1,800 – $800)	1,000	$ 75,975
Plant assets		
Equipment, fixtures, and other ($37,000 + $3,000 fixtures)	$40,000	
Accumulated depreciation ($12,800 + $2,000 depreciation expense)	(14,800)	25,200
Total assets		$101,175

Liabilities and Owners' Equity		
Current liabilities		
Accounts payable (.5 × July purchases of $29,400, Schedule c)	$14,700	
Accrued wages and commissions payable (.5 × $10,000, Schedule e)	5,000	$ 19,700
Owners' equity ($78,950 + $2,525 net income)		81,475
Total liabilities and owners' equity		$101,175

Note: Beginning balances are used as a start for the computations of unexpired insurance, plant, and owners' equity.

The Budgeting Process at Daihatsu

Daihatsu Motor Company is a Japanese-based mini-car manufacturer owned in part by Toyota. Daihatsu ranks seventh of the nine Japanese automakers in terms of their domestic sales volume. The annual budgeting process (short-term profit-planning process) at Daihatsu is the first-year segment of the five-year long-range plan.

Each year departments prepare six plans that are combined to form an operating profit budget. A brief description of these six plans follows:

1. Production, Distribution, and Sales
2. Projected Parts and Materials Costs
3. Plant Rationalization (projected reductions in variable costs)
4. Personnel (direct labor and service department)
5. Facility Investment (capital budget)
6. Fixed Expense (design costs, maintenance costs, advertising, general and administrative costs)

The starting point for each plan is the actual cost performance of the previous year—*actual cost performance of the previous year is used as the standard for the coming year*. The six plans are combined as follows:

Sales forecast	Plan 1
Less expected variable costs (standards)	Plan 1
Contribution margin	
Less expected *changes* in variable costs	Plans 2 and 3
Adjusted contribution margin	
Less expected fixed costs	Plans 4, 5, and 6
Budgeted operating profit	

■

Source: From Y. Monden and J. Lee, "How a Japanese Auto Maker Reduces Costs," Management Accounting, August 1993, pp. 22–26.

■ CAUTION: DIFFICULTIES OF SALES FORECASTING

As you have seen in the foregoing illustration, the sales budget is the foundation of the entire master budget. The accuracy of estimated purchases budgets, production schedules, and costs depends on the detail and accuracy (in dollars, units, and mix) of the budgeted sales.

Sales forecasting is a key to preparing the sales budget, but a forecast and a budget are not necessarily identical. A **sales forecast** is a *prediction* of sales under a given set of conditions. A **sales budget** is the result of *decisions* to create the conditions that will generate a *desired* level of sales. For example, you may have forecasts of sales at various levels of advertising. The forecast for the one level you decide to implement becomes the budget.

Sales forecasts are usually prepared under the direction of the top sales executive. Important factors considered by sales forecasters include the following:

> **sales forecast** A prediction of sales under a given set of conditions.
>
> **sales budget** The result of decisions to create conditions that will generate a desired level of sales.

> **Objective 8**
>
> Understand the difficulties of sales forecasting

1. *Past patterns of sales:* Past experience combined with detailed past sales by product line, geographical region, and type of customer can help predict future sales.
2. *Estimates made by the sales force:* A company's sales force is often the best source of information about the desires and plans of customers.
3. *General economic conditions:* Predictions for many economic indicators, such as gross domestic product and industrial production indexes (local and foreign), are published regularly. Knowledge of how sales relate to these indicators can aid sales forecasting.
4. *Competitors' actions:* Sales depend on the strength and actions of competitors. To forecast sales, a company should consider the likely strategies and reactions of competitors, such as changes in their prices, product quality, or services.
5. *Changes in the firm's prices:* Sales can be increased by decreasing prices and vice versa. A company should consider the effects of price changes on customer demand (see Chapter 5).
6. *Changes in product mix:* Changing the mix of products often can affect not only sales levels but also overall contribution margin. Identifying the most profitable products and devising methods to increase their sales is a key part of successful management.
7. *Market research studies:* Some companies hire market experts to gather information about market conditions and customer preferences. Such information is useful to managers making sales forecasts and product mix decisions.
8. *Advertising and sales promotion plans:* Advertising and other promotional costs affect sales levels. A sales forecast should be based on anticipated effects of promotional activities.

Sales forecasting usually combines various techniques. In addition to the opinions of the sales staff, statistical analysis of correlations between sales and economic indicators (prepared by economists and members of the market research staff) provide valuable help. The opinions of line management also heavily influence the final sales forecasts. Ultimately, no matter how many technical experts are used in forecasting, the *sales budget* is the responsibility of line management.

Sales forecasting is still somewhat mystical, but its procedures are becoming more formalized and are being reviewed more seriously because of the intensity of global competitive pressures. Although this book does not include a detailed discussion of the preparation of the sales budget, the importance of an accurate sales forecast cannot be overstressed.

Governments and other nonprofit organizations also face a problem similar to sales forecasting. For example, the budget for city revenues may depend on a variety of factors, such as predicted property taxes, traffic fines, parking fees, license fees, and city income taxes. In turn, property taxes depend on the extent of new construction and, in most localities, general increases in real estate values. Thus, a municipal budget may require forecasting that is just as sophisticated as that required by a private firm.

▮ PROCESS OF MAKING A BUDGET WORK: ANTICIPATING HUMAN BEHAVIOR

Objective 9

Anticipate problems of human behavior toward budgets

No matter how accurate sales forecasts are, if budgets are to benefit an organization, they need the support of all the firm's employees. Lower-level workers and managers' attitudes toward budgets will be heavily influenced by the attitude of top management. Even with the support of top management, however, budgets—and the managers who implement them—can run into opposition.

Managers often compare actual results with budgets in evaluating subordinates. Few individuals are immediately ecstatic about techniques used to check their performance. Lower-level managers sometimes regard budgets as embodiments of restrictive, negative top-management attitudes. Accountants reinforce this view if they use a budget only to point out managers' failings. Such negative attitudes are even greater when the budget's primary purpose is to limit spending. For example, budgets are generally unpopular in government agencies where their only use is to request and authorize funding. To avoid negative attitudes toward budgets, accountants and top management must demonstrate how budgets can *help each manager and employee* achieve better results. Only then will the budgets become a positive aid in motivating employees at all levels to work toward goals, set objectives, measure results accurately, and direct attention to the areas that need investigation.

Another serious human relations problem, which may preclude some of these benefits of budgeting, can result if budgets stress one set of performance goals, but employees and managers are rewarded for performance on other dimensions. For example, a budget may concentrate on current costs of production, but managers and employees may be rewarded on quality of production and on timely delivery of products to customers. These dimensions of performance could be in direct conflict.

participative budgeting Budgets formulated with the active participation of all affected employees.

The overriding importance of the human aspects of budgeting cannot be overemphasized. Too often, top management and accountants are overly concerned with the mechanics of budgets, ignoring the fact that the effectiveness of any budgeting system depends directly on whether the affected managers and employees understand and accept the budget. Budgets formulated with the active participation of all affected employees are generally more effective than budgets imposed on subordinates. This involvement is usually called **participative budgeting**.

▮ FINANCIAL PLANNING MODELS

Properly constructed and implemented, the master budget is the best practical approximation to a formal *model* of the total organization: its objectives, inputs, constraints, and outputs. Managers try to predict how various decisions will affect the master budget. This is a step-by-step process whereby tentative plans are revised as managers exchange views on various aspects of expected activities.

financial planning models
Mathematical models of the master budget that can react to any set of assumptions about sales, costs, or product mix.

Objective 10

Identify the uses of a financial planning model

Today, most large companies have developed **financial planning models**, mathematical models of the master budget that can react to any set of assumptions about sales, costs, product mix, and so on. For instance, Dow Chemical's model uses 140 separate, constantly revised cost inputs that are based on several different cost drivers.

By mathematically describing the relationships among all the operating and financial activities and among the other major internal and external factors that can affect the results of management decisions, financial planning models allow managers to assess the predicted impacts of various alternatives before final decisions are selected. For example, a manager might want to predict the consequences of changing the mix of products offered for sale to emphasize several products with the highest prospects for growth. A financial planning model would provide operational and financial budgets well into the future under alternative assumptions about the product mix, sales levels, production constraints,

Activity-Based Budgeting

Financial planning models can use activity-based cost information for budgeting. This is a different view of costs. For example, a purchasing department's previous-year results might appear as follows, based on a traditional view of costs:

Purchasing Department	
Salaries	$200,000
Benefits	75,000
Supplies	30,000
Travel	10,000
Total	$315,000

If management wants to reduce costs by 10% overall ($31,500), purchasing may simply reduce each cost category by 10%. This method of cost reduction is sometimes referred to as "slash and burn." For example, at Borg-Warner Automotive, virtually all managers expressed dissatisfaction with the budgeting process. Each year managers made cost estimates as part of the annual budgeting procedure. But since these budgets "almost surely" would be returned as being too high, along with a directive to *cut costs by a prescribed percentage*, managers were motivated to "play games" by overestimating costs.

Using activity-based cost information, the purchasing department's budget would appear as follows:

Purchasing Department	
Activity	
Certify 10 new vendors	$ 65,450
Issue 450 purchase orders	184,640

continued

Purchasing Department	
Activity	
Issue 275 releases	64,910
	$315,000

Activity-based budgeting links financial data with the activity that consumed the related resource. Instead of the "slash and burn" method, the department now targets specific activities that can be reduced without impairing its overall effectiveness. For example, it may be possible to reduce the number of vendor certifications to five. Assuming that vendor certification costs are variable with respect to the number of vendors, this would reduce certification costs by $5 \times (\$65,450 \div 10)$ or $32,725, enabling the department to meet or exceed its budget target.

Many companies that implement activity-based costing primarily for product costing purposes realize many more benefits after implementation. For example, a snack-food processor used one financial planning model for activity-based product costing purposes but, after implementing the model, the company now uses it for budgeting, manpower projections, new pricing strategies, and product rationalization. ■

Sources: Adapted from "Implementing Activity-Based Costing: The Model Approach," Institute of Management Accounting and Sapling Corporation, *November 1994; G. Hanks, M. Fried, and J. Huber, "Shifting Gears at Borg-Warner Automotive,"* Management Accounting, *February 1994, pp. 25–29.*

quality levels, scheduling, and so on. Most important, managers can get answers to "what if" questions, such as "What if sales are 10% below forecasts? What if material prices increase 8% instead of 4% as expected? What if the new union contract grants a 6% raise in consideration for productivity improvements?" Building models that can help answer "what if" questions is the subject of Appendix 7.

Financial planning models have shortened managers' reaction times dramatically. A revised plan for a large company that took many accountants many days to prepare by hand can be prepared in minutes. Public Service Electric & Gas, a New Jersey utility, can run its total master budget several times a day, if necessary.

Warning: The use of spreadsheet software on personal computers has put financial planning models within reach of even the smallest organizations. The ready access to powerful modeling, however, does not guarantee plausible or reliable results. Financial planning models are only as good as the assumptions and the inputs used to build and manipulate them—what computer specialists call GIGO (garbage in, garbage out). Nearly every chief financial officer has a horror story to tell about following bad advice from a faulty financial planning model.

Highlights to Remember

A budget outlines an organization's objectives and possible steps for achieving them. The budgetary process compels managers to think and to prepare for changing conditions. Budgets are aids in planning, communicating, setting standards of performance, motivating personnel toward goals, measuring results, and directing attention to the areas that need investigation.

Master budgets typically cover relatively short periods—usually 1 month to 1 year. Long-range plans, however, may extend over a much longer time horizon, up to 10 years ahead. Because the future is uncertain, long-range plans focus on strategic considerations. The master budget is more detailed and offers specific guidance over the immediate budget period. Within the master budget are operating budgets, which detail resource requirements, and financial budgets, which are forecasted financial plans. The steps involved in preparing a master budget vary across organizations but follow the general outline given on page 261. Invariably, the first step is to forecast sales or service levels, which can be quite difficult. The next step should be to forecast cost-driver activity levels, given expected sales and service. From these forecasts and knowledge of cost behavior, collection patterns, and so on, the operating and financing budgets can be prepared.

One of the most crucial determinants of successful budgeting is how the organization includes and considers the people who are directly affected by the budget. Negative attitudes toward budgets usually prevent realization of many of the benefits of budgeting. Such attitudes are usually caused by managers who use budgets to force behavior or to punish substandard performance. Budgets generally are more useful when they are formulated with the willing participation of all affected parties.

Financial planning models are mathematical representations of the organization's master budget. Most large companies use financial planning models, and many small companies are beginning to use them. These models usually are prepared with computer spreadsheet software that allows powerful budget analysis and flexible planning (see Appendix 7).

Summary Problem for Your Review

Do not attempt to solve this problem until you understand the *step-by-step* illustration in this chapter.

Problem

The Country Store is a retail outlet for a variety of hardware and homewares. The owner of the Country Store is anxious to prepare a budget for the next quarter, which is typically quite busy. She is most concerned with her cash position because she expects that she will have to borrow to finance purchases in anticipation of sales. She has gathered all the data necessary to prepare a simplified budget. Exhibit 7-6 shows these data in tabular form. In addition, equipment will be purchased in April for $19,750 cash, and dividends of $4,000 will be paid in June. Review the structure of the example in the chapter and then prepare the Country Store's master budget for the months of April, May, and June. The solution follows after the budget data. Note that there are a few minor differences between this example and the one in the chapter. These are identified in Exhibit 7-6 and in the solution. The primary difference is in the payment of interest on borrowing. Borrowing occurs at the end of a month when cash is needed. Repayments (if appropriate) occur at the end of a month when cash is available. Interest also is paid in cash at the end of the month at an annual rate of 12% on the amount of note payable outstanding during that month.

Exhibit 7-6	The Country Store Budget Data Balance Sheet as of March 31, 19X4		
Assets		Budgeted Sales	
Cash	$ 9,000	March (actual)	$60,000
Accounts receivable	48,000	April	70,000
Inventory	12,600	May	85,000
Plant and equipment (net)	200,000	June	90,000
Total assets	$269,600	July	50,000
Liabilities and equities		Required minimum cash balance	$ 8,000
Interest payable	0	Sales mix, cash/credit:	
Note payable	0	Cash sales	20%
Accounts payable	18,300	Credit sales (collected the following	
Capital stock	180,000	month)	80%
Retained earnings	71,300	Gross profit rate	40%
Total liabilities and equities	$269,600	Loan interest rate (interest paid in cash	
Budgeted expenses (per month)		monthly)	12%
Wages and salaries	$ 7,500	Inventory paid for in:	
Freight out as a % of sales	6%	Month purchased	50%
Advertising	$ 6,000	Month after purchase	50%
Depreciation	$ 2,000		
Other expense as a % of sales	4%		
Minimum inventory policy as a % of next month's cost of goods sold	30%		

Solution

Schedule a: Sales budget

	April	May	June	Total
Credit sales, 80%	$56,000	$68,000	$72,000	$196,000
Cash sales, 20%	14,000	17,000	18,000	49,000
Total sales	$70,000	$85,000	$90,000	$245,000

Schedule b: Cash collections

	April	May	June	Total
Cash sales	$14,000	$17,000	$18,000	$ 49,000
Collections from prior month	48,000	56,000	68,000	172,000
Total collections	$62,000	$73,000	$86,000	$221,000

Schedule c: Purchases budget

	April	May	June	Total
Desired ending inventory	$15,300	$16,200	$ 9,000	$ 40,500
Plus cost of goods sold	42,000	51,000	54,000	147,000
Total needed	$57,300	$67,200	$63,000	$187,500
Less beginning inventory	12,600	15,300	16,200	44,100
Total purchases	$44,700	$51,900	$46,800	$143,400

Schedule d: Cash disbursements for purchases

	April	May	June	Total
For March*	$18,300			$ 18,300
For April	22,350	$22,350		44,700
For May		25,950	$25,950	51,900
For June			23,400	23,400
Total disbursements	$40,650	$48,300	$49,350	$138,300

* The amount payable from the previous month.

Schedules e and f: Operating expenses and disbursements for expenses (except interest)

	April	May	June	Total
Cash expenses				
Salaries & wages	$ 7,500	$ 7,500	$ 7,500	$22,500
Freight-out	4,200	5,100	5,400	14,700
Advertising	6,000	6,000	6,000	18,000
Other expenses	2,800	3,400	3,600	9,800
Total disbursements for expenses	$20,500	$22,000	$22,500	$65,000
Noncash expenses				
Depreciation	2,000	2,000	2,000	6,000
Total expenses	$22,500	$24,000	$24,500	$71,000

The Country Store
Cash Budget
April–June, 19X4

	April	May	June
Beginning cash balance	$ 9,000	$ 8,000	$ 8,000
Cash collections	62,000	73,000	86,000
Total cash available	71,000	81,000	94,000
Cash disbursements			
Inventory purchases	40,650	48,300	49,350
Operating expenses	20,500	22,000	22,500
Equipment purchases	19,750	0	0
Dividends	0	0	4,000
Interest*	0	179	154
Total disbursements	80,900	70,479	76,004
Minimum cash balance	8,000	8,000	8,000
Total cash needed	$ 88,900	$78,479	$84,004
Cash excess (deficit)	$(17,900)	$ 2,521	$ 9,996
Financing			
Borrowing†	17,900	0	0
Repayments	0	(2,521)	(9,996)
Total cash from financing	17,900	(2,521)	(9,996)
Ending cash balance	$ 8,000	$ 8,000	$ 8,000

* In this example interest is paid on the loan amounts outstanding during the month; May: $(0.12 \div 12) \times (\$17,900) = \$179$; June: $(0.12 \div 12) \times (\$17,900 - \$2,521) = \$154$.
† In this example, borrowings are at the end of the month in the amounts needed. Repayments also are made at the end of the month as excess cash permits.

The Country Store
Budgeted Income
Statement
April–June, 19X4

	April	May	June	April–June Total
Sales	$70,000	$85,000	$90,000	$245,000
Cost of goods sold	42,000	51,000	54,000	147,000
Gross margin	28,000	34,000	36,000	98,000
Operating expenses				
Salaries and wages	7,500	7,500	7,500	22,500
Freight-out	4,200	5,100	5,400	14,700
Advertising	6,000	6,000	6,000	18,000
Other	2,800	3,400	3,600	9,800
Interest*	–	179	154	333
Depreciation	2,000	2,000	2,000	6,000
Total expense	$22,500	$24,179	$24,654	$ 71,333
Net operating income	$ 5,500	$ 9,821	$11,346	$ 26,667

* Note that interest expense is the monthly interest rate times the borrowed amount held for the month: May $(0.12 \div 12) \times \$17,900 = \$179$; June: $(0.12 \div 12) \times \$15,379 = \$154$.

The Country Store
Budgeted Balance
Sheets as of the Ends
of April–June, 19X4

	April	May	June*
Assets			
Current assets			
Cash	$ 8,000	$ 8,000	$ 8,000
Accounts receivable	56,000	68,000	72,000
Inventory	15,300	16,200	9,000
Total current assets	79,300	92,200	89,000
Plant, less accumulated depreciation†	217,750	215,750	213,750
Total assets	$297,050	$307,950	$302,750
Liabilities and Equities			
Liabilities			
Accounts payable	$ 22,350	$ 25,950	$ 23,400
Notes payable	17,900	15,379	5,383
Total liabilities	40,250	41,329	28,783
Stockholders equity			
Capital stock	180,000	180,000	180,000
Retained earnings	76,800	86,621	93,967
Total equities	256,800	266,621	273,967
Total liabilities & equities	$297,050	$307,950	$302,750

* The June 30, 19X4 balance sheet is the ending balance sheet for the entire three-month period.
† $200,000 + $19,750 − $2,000 = $217,750.

Appendix 7: Use of Spreadsheets for Budgeting

Objective 11

Use a spreadsheet
to develop a budget

Spreadsheet software for personal computers is an extremely powerful and flexible tool for budgeting. An obvious advantage of the spreadsheet is that arithmetic errors are virtually nonexistent. The real value of spreadsheets, however, is that they can be used to make a mathematical model (a financial planning model) of the organization. This model can be used repeatedly at a very low cost and can be altered to reflect possible changes in expected sales, cost drivers, cost functions, and so on. The objective of this appendix is to illustrate *sensitivity analysis*, one aspect of the power and flexibility of spreadsheet software that has made this software an indispensable budgeting tool.

Recall the chapter's master budgeting example. Suppose CHC has prepared its master budget using spreadsheet software. To simplify making changes to the budget, the relevant forecasts and other budgeting details have been placed in Exhibit 7-7. Note that for simplification, only the data necessary for the purchases budget have been shown here; the full master budget would require a larger table with all the data given in the chapter. Each part of the table can be identified by its column and row intersection or "cell address." For example, the beginning inventory for the budget period can be located with the cell address "D4," which is shown as $48,000.

The Cooking Hut Company

Exhibit 7-7   Budget Data (Column and row labels are given by the spreadsheet)

	A	B	C	D	E	F	G
1	Budget data						
2	Sales forecasts		Other information				
3							
4	March (actual)	$40,000	Beginning inventory	$48,000			
5	April	50,000	Desired ending inventory: Base amount	$20,000			
6	May	80,000	Plus percent of next				
7	June	60,000	month's cost of				
8	July	50,000	goods sold	80%			
9	August	40,000	Cost of goods sold				
10			as percent of sales	70%			

By referencing the budget data's cell addresses, you can generate the purchases budget (Exhibit 7-8) within the same spreadsheet by entering *formulas* instead of numbers into the schedule. Consider Exhibit 7-8. Instead of typing $48,000 as April's beginning inventory in the purchases budget at cell D17, type a "formula" with the cell address for the beginning inventory from the preceding *table*, + D4 (the cell address preceded by a "+" sign—a spreadsheet rule to identify a formula; some spreadsheets use " = " to indicate a formula). Likewise, all the cells of the purchases budget will be composed of formulas containing cell addresses instead of numbers. The *total needed* in April (D16) is + D13 + D14, and *purchases* in April (D19) are budgeted to be + D16 – D17. The figures for May, June, and July are computed similarly within the respective columns. This approach gives the spreadsheet the most flexibility, because you could change any number in the budget data in Exhibit 7-7 (e.g., a sales forecast), and the software automatically recalculates the numbers in the entire purchases budget. Exhibit 7-8 shows the formulas used for the purchases budget. Exhibit 7-9 is the purchases budget displaying the numbers generated by the formulas in Exhibit 7-8.

Now, what if sales could be 10% higher than initially forecasted during April through August? What effect will this alternative forecast have on budgeted purchases? Even to revise this simple purchases budget would require a considerable number of manual recalculations. Merely changing the sales forecasts in spreadsheet Exhibit 7-7, however, results in a nearly instantaneous revision of the purchases budget. Exhibit 7-10 shows the alternative sales forecasts (in colored type) and other unchanged data along with the revised purchases budget. We could alter every piece of budget data in the table, and easily view or print out the effects on purchases. This sort of

sensitivity analysis
The systematic varying of budget data input to determine the effects of each change on the budget.

analysis, assessing the effects of varying one of the budget inputs, up or down, is called *sensitivity analysis*. **Sensitivity analysis** for budgeting is the systematic varying of budget data input to determine the effects of each change on the budget. This type of "what if" analysis is one of the most powerful uses of spreadsheets for financial planning models. Note, though, that it is not generally a good idea to vary more than one of the types of budget inputs at a time, unless they are obviously related, because doing so makes it difficult to isolate the effect of each change.

Exhibit 7-8   The Cooking Hut Company   Purchases Budget Formulas

	A	B	C	D	E	F	G
11	Schedule c						
12	Purchases budget			April	May	June	July
13	Desired ending inventory			+ D5 + D8 D10*B6	+ D5 + D8 D10*B7	+ D5 + D8 D10*B8	+ D5 + D8 D10*B9
14	Plus cost of goods sold			+ D10*B5	+ D10*B6	+ D10*B7	+ D10*B8
15							
16	Total needed			+ D13 + D14	+ E13 + E14	+ F13 + F14	+ G13 + G14
17	Less beginning inventory			+ D4	+ D13	+ E13	+ F13
18							
19	Purchases			+ D16 – D17	+ E16 – E17	+ F16 – F17	+ G16 – G17
20							

Exhibit 7-9   The Cooking Hut Company   Purchases Budget

	A	B	C	D	E	F	G
11	Schedule c						
12	Purchases budget			April	May	June	July
13	Desired ending inventory			$64,800	$ 53,600	$48,000	$42,400
14	Plus cost of goods sold			35,000	56,000	42,000	35,000
15							
16	Total needed			99,800	109,600	90,000	77,400
17	Less beginning inventory			48,000	64,800	53,600	48,000
18							
19	Purchases			$51,800	$ 44,800	$36,400	$29,400
20							

Exhibit 7-10   The Cooking Hut Company   Purchases Budget

	A	B	C	D	E	F	G
1	Budgeted data						
2	Sales forecasts		Other information				
3							
4	March (actual)	$40,000	Beginning inventory	$ 48,000			
5	April	55,000	Desired ending inventory: Base amount	$ 20,000			
6	May	88,000	Plus percent of next				
7	June	66,000	month's cost of				
8	July	55,000	goods sold	80%			
9	August	44,000	Cost of goods sold				
10			as percent of sales	70%			
11	Schedule c						
12	Purchases budget			April	May	June	July
13	Desired ending inventory			$ 69,280	$ 56,960	$50,800	$44,640
14	Plus cost of goods sold			38,500	61,600	46,200	38,500
15							
16	Total needed			107,780	118,560	97,000	83,140
17	Beginning inventory			48,000	69,280	56,960	50,800
18							
19	Purchases			59,780	49,280	$40,040	$32,340
20							

Every schedule, operating budget, and financial budget of the master budget can be prepared on the spreadsheet. Each schedule would be linked by the appropriate cell addresses just as the budget input data (Exhibit 7-7) are linked to the purchases budget (Exhibits 7-8 and 7-9). As in the purchases budget, ideally all cells in the master budget are formulas, not numbers. That way, every budget input can be the subject of sensitivity analysis, if desired, by simply changing the budget data in Exhibit 7-7.

Preparing the master budget on a spreadsheet is time-consuming—the first time. After that, the time savings and planning capabilities through sensitivity analysis are enormous compared with a manual approach. A problem can occur, however, if the master budget model is not well documented when a person other than the author attempts to modify the spreadsheet model. Any assumptions that are made should be described either within the spreadsheet or in a separate budget preparation document.

Accounting Vocabulary

Fundamental Assignment Material

Special note: Problems 7-A1 and 7-B1 provide single-problem reviews of most of the chapter topics. Those readers who prefer to concentrate on the fundamentals in smaller chunks should consider any of the other problems.

7-A1   Prepare Master Budget

A wholesaling subsidiary of Paul Lamb Industries has a strong belief in using highly decentralized management. You are the new manager of one of its small "Apex" stores (Store No. 82). You know much about how to buy, how to display, how to sell, and how to reduce shoplifting. You know little about accounting and finance, however.

Top management is convinced that training for higher management should include the active participation of store managers in the budgeting process. You have been asked to prepare a complete master budget for your store for June, July, and August. You are responsible for its actual full preparation. All accounting is done centrally, so you have no expert help on the premises. In addition, tomorrow the branch manager and the assistant controller will be here to examine your work; at that time they will assist you in formulating the final budget document. The idea is to have you prepare the budget a few times so that you gain more confidence about accounting matters. You want to make a favorable impression on your superiors, so you gather the following data as of May 31, 19X6:

		Recent and Projected Sales	
Cash	$ 29,000		
Inventory	420,000	April	$300,000
Accounts receivable	369,000	May	350,000
Net furniture and fixtures	168,000	June	700,000
Total assets	$986,000	July	400,000
Accounts payable	$475,000	August	400,000
Owners' equity	511,000	September	300,000
Total liabilities and owners' equities	$986,000		

Credit sales are 90% of total sales. Credit accounts are collected 80% in the month following the sale and 20% in the following month. Assume that bad debts are negligible and can be ignored. The accounts receivable on May 31 are the result of the credit sales for April and May: $(.20 \times .90 \times \$300,000 = \$54,000) + (1.00 \times .90 \times \$350,000 = \$315,000) = \$369,000$. The average gross profit on sales is 40%.

The policy is to acquire enough inventory each month to equal the following month's projected sales. All purchases are paid for in the month following purchase.

Salaries, wages, and commissions average 20% of sales; all other variable expenses are 4% of sales. Fixed expenses for rent, property taxes, and miscellaneous payroll and other items are $55,000 monthly. Assume that these variable and fixed expenses require cash disbursements each month. Depreciation is $2,500 monthly.

In June, $55,000 is going to be disbursed for fixtures acquired in May. The May 31 balance of accounts payable includes this amount.

Assume that a minimum cash balance of $25,000 is to be maintained. Also assume that all borrowings are effective at the beginning of the month and all repayments are made at the end of the month of repayment. Interest is paid only at the time of repaying principal. The interest rate is 12% per annum; round interest computations to the nearest ten dollars. All loans and repayments of principal must be made in multiples of a thousand dollars.

Required

1. Prepare a budgeted income statement for the coming quarter, a budgeted statement of monthly cash receipts and disbursements (for the next 3 months), and a budgeted balance sheet for August 30, 19X6. All operations are evaluated on a before-income-tax basis. Also, because income taxes are disbursed from corporate headquarters, they may be ignored here.
2. Explain why there is a need for a bank loan and what operating sources supply cash for repaying the bank loan.

7-B1   Prepare Master Budget

The Little Teddy Company wants a master budget for the next 3 months, beginning January 1, 19X7. It desires an ending minimum cash balance of $5,000 each month. Sales are forecasted at an average selling price of $4 per miniature teddy bear. In January, Little Teddy is beginning JIT deliveries from suppliers, which means that purchases equal expected sales. On January 1, purchases will cease until inventory reaches $6,000, after which time purchases will equal sales. Merchandise costs are $2 per bear. Purchases during any given month are paid in full during the following month. All sales are on credit, payable within 30 days, but experience has shown that 60% of current sales is collected in the current month, 30% in the next month, and 10% in the month thereafter. Bad debts are negligible.

Monthly operating expenses are as follows:

Wages and salaries	$15,000
Insurance expired	125
Depreciation	250
Miscellaneous	2,500
Rent	250/month + 10% of quarterly sales over $10,000

Cash dividends of $1,500 are to be paid quarterly, beginning January 15, and are declared on the 15th of the previous month. All operating expenses are paid as incurred, except insurance, depreciation, and rent. Rent of $250 is paid at the beginning of each month, and the additional 10% of sales is paid quarterly on the 10th of the month following the end of the quarter. The next settlement is due January 10.

The company plans to buy some new fixtures for $3,000 cash in March.

Money can be borrowed and repaid in multiples of $500 at an interest rate of 12% per annum. Management wants to minimize borrowing and repay rapidly. Interest is computed and paid when the principal is repaid. Assume that borrowing occurs at the beginning, and repayments at the end, of the months in question. Money is never borrowed at the beginning and repaid at the end of the *same* month. Compute interest to the nearest dollar.

Assets as of December 31, 19X6		Liabilities as of December 31, 19X6	
Cash	$ 5,000	Accounts payable	
Accounts receivable	12,500	(merchandise)	$35,550
Inventory*	39,050	Dividends payable	1,500
Unexpired insurance	1,500	Rent payable	7,800
Fixed assets, net	12,500		$44,850
	$70,550		

* November 30 inventory balance = $16,000

Recent and forecasted sales:

October	$38,000	December	$25,000	February	$75,000	April	$45,000
November	25,000	January	62,000	March	38,000		

Required

1. Prepare a master budget including a budgeted income statement, balance sheet, statement of cash receipts and disbursements, and supporting schedules for the months January through March 19X7.
2. Explain why there is a need for a bank loan and what operating sources provide the cash for the repayment of the bank loan.

Additional Assignment Material

Questions

7-1. Is budgeting used primarily for scorekeeping, attention directing, or problem solving?

7-2. "Budgets are okay in relatively certain environments. But everything changes so quickly in the electronics industry that budgeting is a waste of time." Comment on this statement.

7-3. What are the major benefits of budgeting?

7-4. Why is budgeted performance better than past performance as a basis for judging actual results?

7-5. What is the major technical difference between historical and budgeted financial statements?

7-6. "Budgets are primarily a tool used to limit expenditures." Do you agree? Explain.

7-7. How do strategic planning, long-range planning, and budgeting differ?

7-8. "Capital budgets are plans for managing long-term debt and common stock." Do you

agree? Explain.

7-9. "I oppose continuous budgets because they provide a moving target. Managers never know what to aim at." Discuss.

7-10. "Pro forma statements are those statements prepared in conjunction with continuous budgets." Do you agree? Explain.

7-11. Differentiate between an operating budget and a financial budget.

7-12. Why is the sales forecast the starting point for budgeting?

7-13. What is the principal objective of a cash budget?

7-14. Differentiate between a sales forecast and a sales budget.

7-15. What factors influence the sales forecast?

7-16. "Education and salesmanship are key features of budgeting." Explain.

7-17. What are financial planning models?

7-18. "Budgeting for a manufacturing firm is fundamentally different from budgeting for a retail firm." Do you agree? Explain.

7-19. "I cannot be bothered with setting up my monthly budget on a spreadsheet. It just takes too long to be worth the effort." Comment.

7-20. Explain the importance of understanding cost behavior to preparing the master budget.

7-21. Explain the relationship between the sales (or service) forecast and cost-driver activity.

Exercises

7-22 Multiple Choice

(CMA.) Answer the following selected multiple choice questions from the CMA examination.

1. The financial budget process includes
   a. the cash budget.
   b. the capital budget.
   c. the budgeted statement of cash flows.
   d. the budgeted balance sheet.
   e. all of the above.

2. The master budget process usually begins with the
   a. production budget.
   b. operating budget.
   c. financial budget.
   d. capital budget.
   e. sales budget.

3. The production budget process usually begins with the
   a. direct labor budget.
   b. direct materials budget.
   c. manufacturing overhead budget.
   d. sales budget.
   e. ending inventory budget.

4. A continuous (rolling) budget
   a. presents the plan for only one level of activity and does not adjust to changes in the level of activity.
   b. presents the plan for a range of activity so the plan can be adjusted for changes in activity.
   c. is a plan that is revised monthly or quarterly, dropping one period and adding another.
   d. is one of the budgets that is part of a long-range strategic plan, unchanged unless the strategy of the company changes.
   e. works best for a company that can reliably forecast its sales revenue and expenses.

5. Which one of the following management considerations is usually addressed first in strategic planning?
   a. Outsourcing
   b. Overall goals of the firm
   c. Organizational structure
   d. Recent annual budgets
   e. Being an industry leader

7-23   Multiple Choice

(CPA.) The James Co., a wholesaler, budgeted the following sales for the indicated months:

	June 19X6	July 19X6	August 19X6
Sales on account	$1,800,000	$1,920,000	$2,040,000
Cash sales	240,000	250,000	260,000
Total sales	$2,040,000	$2,170,000	$2,300,000

All merchandise is marked up to sell at its invoice cost plus 25%. Merchandise inventories at the beginning of each month are at 30% of that month's projected cost of goods sold.

Select the best answer for each of the following items:

1. The cost of goods sold for the month of June 19X6 is anticipated to be (a) $1,632,000, (b) $1,428,000, (c) $1,836,000, (d) $1,530,000, (e) none of these.

2. Merchandise purchases for July 19X6 are anticipated to be (a) $1,736,000, (b) $1,926,600, (c) $1,767,200, (d) $1,658,700, (e) none of these.

7-24   Purchases and Sales Budgets

(CMA, adapted.) The Pitts Pony Corporation is a retailer whose sales are all made on credit. Sales are billed twice monthly, on the 10th of the month for the last half of the prior month's sales and on the 20th of the month for the first half of the current month's sales. The terms of all sales are 2/10, net 30. Based on past experience, the collection experience of accounts receivable is as follows:

Within the discount period	80%
On the 30th day	18%
Uncollectible	2%

The sales value of shipments for May 19X5 and the forecast for the next 4 months are:

May (actual)	$700,000
June	800,000
July	900,000
August	900,000
September	600,000

Pitts Pony's average markup on its products is 20% of the sales price.

Pitts Pony purchases merchandise for resale to meet the current month's sales demand and to maintain a desired monthly ending inventory of 25% of the next month's sales. All purchases are on credit with terms of net 30. Pitts Pony pays for one-half of a month's purchases in the month of purchase and the other half in the month following the purchase.

All sales and purchases occur uniformly throughout the month.

Required   1. How much cash can Pitts Pony Corporation plan to collect from accounts receivable collections during July 19X5?

    a. $801,400   **d.** $794,000
    b. $842,600   **e.** None of these
    c. $815,000

2. How much can Pitts Pony plan to collect in September from sales made in August 19X5?

    a. $441,000   **d.** $337,000
    b. $400,400   **e.** None of these
    c. $433,800

3. The budgeted dollar value of Pitts Pony inventory on August 31, 19X5 will be

    a. $150,000   **d.** $120,000
    b. $130,000   **e.** None of these
    c. $180,000

4. How much merchandise should Pitts Pony plan to purchase during June 19X5?

    a. $650,000   **d.** $740,000
    b. $680,000   **e.** None of these
    c. $620,000

5. The amount Pitts Pony should budget in August 19X5 for the payment of merchandise is

    a. $720,000   **d.** $660,000
    b. $690,000   **e.** None of these
    c. $780,000

7-25   Sales Budget

Eckart's Runners, Inc., has the following data:

- Accounts receivable, May 31: (.3 × May sales of $500,000) = $150,000
- Monthly forecasted sales: June, $400,000; July, $440,000; August, $500,000; September, $530,000

    Sales consist of 70% cash and 30% credit. All credit accounts are collected in the month following the sales. Uncollectible accounts are negligible and may be ignored.

Required Prepare a sales budget schedule and a cash collections budget schedule for June, July, and August.

7-26   Sales Budget

Minoura Steel Company was preparing its sales budget for the first quarter of 19X6. Forecast sales are (in thousands of yen)

January	¥180,000
February	¥210,000
March	¥270,000

    Sales are 20% cash and 80% on credit. Fifty percent of the credit accounts are collected in the month of sale, 40% in the month following the sale, and 10% in the following month. No uncollectible accounts are anticipated. Accounts receivable at the beginning of 19X6 are ¥96 million (10% × November credit sales of ¥200 million and 50% of December credit sales of ¥152 million).

Required Prepare a schedule showing sales and cash collections for January, February, and March, 19X6.

7-27   Cash Collection Budget

Cassandra's Casters has found that cash collections from customers tend to occur in the following pattern:

Collected within cash discount period in month of sale	50%
Collected within cash discount period in first month after month of sale	10
Collected after cash discount period in first month after month of sale	25
Collected after cash discount period in second month after month of sale	12
Never collected	3
Total sales in any month (before cash discounts)	100%
Cash discount allowable as a percentage of invoice price	1%

Compute the total cash budgeted to be collected in March if sales are predicted as $300,000 for January, $400,000 for February, and $500,000 for March.

7-28   Purchase Budget

Arnold's Country Store plans inventory levels (at cost) at the end of each month as follows: May, $250,000; June, $220,000; July, $270,000; August, $230,000.

Sales are expected to be: June, $440,000; July, $350,000; August, $400,000. Cost of goods sold is 60% of sales.

Purchases in April were $250,000; in May, $180,000. A given month's purchases are paid as follows: 10% during that month; 80% the next month; and the final 10% the next month.

Required   Prepare budget schedules for June, July, and August for purchases and for disbursements for purchases.

7-29   Purchase Budget

The inventory of the Mega Ram Computer Company store was $200,000 on May 31. The manager was upset because the inventory was too high. She has adopted the following policies regarding merchandise purchases and inventory. At the end of any month, the inventory should be $15,000 plus 90% of the cost of goods to be sold during the following month. The cost of merchandise sold averages 60% of sales. Purchase terms are generally net, 30 days. A given month's purchases are paid as follows: 20% during that month and 80% during the following month.

Purchases in May had been $150,000. Sales are expected to be: June, $300,000; July, $280,000; August, $340,000; and September, $380,000.

Required   1. Compute the amount by which the inventory on May 31 exceeded the manager's policies.
2. Prepare budget schedules for June, July, and August for purchases and for disbursements for purchases.

Problems

7-30   Cash Budget

Consider the income statement at the top of the next page.

The cash balance, May 31, 19X6, is $12,000. Sales proceeds are collected as follows: 80% month of sale, 10% second month, 10% third month.

Accounts receivable are $40,000 on May 31, 19X6, consisting of $16,000 from April sales and $24,000 from May sales.

Accounts payable on May 31, 19X6, are $145,000. Johnson Company pays 25% of purchases during the month of purchase and the remainder during the following month. All operating expenses requiring cash are paid during the month of recognition. Insurance and property taxes are paid annually in December, however.

Johnson Company	Sales		$290
Budgeted Income	Inventory, May 31	$ 50	
Statement for the	Purchases	192	
Month Ended	Available for sale	242	
June 30, 19X6	Inventory, June 30	40	
(in thousands)	Cost of goods sold		202
	Gross margin		$ 88
	Operating expenses		
	Wages	$ 36	
	Utilities	3	
	Advertising	10	
	Depreciation	1	
	Office expenses	4	
	Insurance and property taxes	3	57
	Operating income		$ 31

Required   Prepare a cash budget for June. Confine your analysis to the given data. Ignore income taxes and other possible items that might affect cash.

7-31   Cash Budget

Karen Tucker is the manager of an extremely successful gift shop, Benefits Gifts, which is operated for the benefit of local charities. From the following data, she wants a cash budget showing expected cash receipts and disbursements for the month of April, and the cash balance expected as of April 30, 19X7:

- Bank note due April 10: $90,000 plus $4,500 interest
- Depreciation for April: $2,000
- Two-year insurance policy due April 14 for renewal: $1,500, to be paid in cash
- Planned cash balance, March 31, 19X7: $80,000
- Merchandise purchases for April: $500,000, 40% paid in month of purchase, 60% paid in next month
- Customer receivables as of March 31: $60,000 from February sales, $450,000 from March sales
- Payrolls due in April: $90,000
- Other expenses for April, payable in April: $45,000
- Accrued taxes for April, payable in June: $7,500
- Sales for April: $1,000,000, half collected in month of sale, 40% in next month, 10% in third month
- Accounts payable, March 31, 19X7: $450,000

Required   Prepare the cash budget.

7-32   Cash Budget

Prepare a statement of estimated cash receipts and disbursements for October 19X6 for the Penrose Apple Cider Company, which sells one product, raw, unprocessed apple cider, by the case. On October 1, 19X6, part of the trial balance showed:

Cash	$ 4,800	
Accounts receivable	15,600	
Allowance for bad debts		$1,900
Merchandise inventory	11,500	
Accounts payable, merchandise		7,200

The company's purchases are payable within 10 days. Assume that one-third of the purchases of any month are due and paid for in the following month.

The unit invoice cost of the merchandise purchased is $12. At the end of each month it is desired to have an inventory equal in units to 50% of the following month's sales in units.

Sales terms include a 1% discount if payment is made by the end of the calendar month. Past experience indicates that 60% of the billings will be collected during the month of the sale, 30% in the following calendar month, 6% in the next following calendar month. Four percent will be uncollectible. The company's fiscal year begins August 1.

Unit selling price	$ 20
August actual sales	12,000
September actual sales	36,000
October estimated sales	30,000
November estimated sales	22,000
Total sales expected in the fiscal year	$360,000

Exclusive of bad debts, total budgeted selling and general administrative expenses for the fiscal year are estimated at $54,300, of which $16,800 is fixed expense (inclusive of a $7,200 annual depreciation charge). These fixed expenses are incurred uniformly throughout the year. The balance of the selling and general administrative expenses varies with sales. Expenses are paid as incurred.

7-33 Spreadsheets and Sensitivity Analysis of Income Statement
Study Appendix 7. The Six-Star Store has the following budgeted sales, which are uniform throughout the month:

May	$450,000
June	375,000
July	330,000
August	420,000

Cost of goods sold averages 70% of sales and is purchased essentially as needed. Employees earn fixed salaries of $21,000 (total) monthly and commissions of 10% of the current month's sales, paid as earned. Other expenses are rent, $6,000, paid on the first of each month for that month's occupancy; miscellaneous expenses, 6% of sales, paid as incurred; insurance, $450 per month, from a 1-year policy that was paid for on January 2; and depreciation, $2,850 per month.

Required

1. Using spreadsheet software, prepare a table of budget data for the Six-Star Store.
2. Continue the spreadsheet in part 1 to prepare budget schedules for (a) disbursements for operating expenses and (b) operating income for June, July, and August.
3. Adjust the budget data appropriately for each of the following scenarios independently and recompute operating income using the spreadsheet:

a. A sales promotion that will cost $30,000 in May could increase sales in each of the following 3 months by 5%.
b. Eliminating the sales commissions and increasing employees' salaries to $52,500 per month could decrease sales thereafter by a net of 2%.

7-34   Spreadsheets and Sensitivity Analysis of Operating Expenses

Study Appendix 7. The Disk Drive Division (DDD) of Intelligent Storage, Inc., produces highest quality floppy- and hard-disk drives for personal computers. The disk drives are assembled from purchased components. The costs (value) added by DDD are indirect costs (which include assembly labor), packaging, and shipping. Cost behavior of DDD is as follows:

	Fixed	Variable
Purchased components		
Hard-disk drives		$100 per component
Floppy-disk drives		40 per component
Indirect costs	$40,000	16 per component
Packaging	8,000	4 per disk drive
Shipping	8,000	2 per disk drive

Both disk drives require five components. Therefore, the total cost of components for hard-disk drives is $500 and for floppy-disk drives is $200. DDD uses a 6-month continuous budget that is revised monthly. Sales forecasts for the next 8 months are as follows:

	Hard Disk Drives	Floppy Disk Drives
October	3,200 units	4,000 units
November	2,400	3,000
December	5,600	7,000
January	3,200	4,000
February	3,200	4,000
March	2,400	3,000
April	2,400	3,000
May	2,800	3,500

Required   Treat each event in succession.

1. Use spreadsheet software to prepare a table of budgeting information and an operating expense budget for the Disk Drive Division for October through March. Incorporate the expectation that sales of floppy-disk drives will be 125% of hard-disk drives. Prepare a spreadsheet that can be revised easily for succeeding months.
2. October's actual sales were 2,800 hard-disk drives and 3,600 floppy-disk drives. This outcome has caused DDD to revise its sales forecasts downward by 10%. Revise the operating expense budget for November through April.
3. At the end of November, DDD decides that the proportion of hard drives to floppy drives is changing. Sales of floppy-disk drives are expected to be 150% of hard-disk drive sales. Expected sales of hard-disk drives are unchanged from part 2. Revise the operating expense budget for December through May.

Cases

7-35   Cash Budgeting for Hospital

(CMA, adapted.) General Hospital provides a wide range of health services in its community. General's board of directors has authorized the following capital expenditures:

Interaortic balloon pump	$1,300,000
Computed tomographic scanner	850,000
X-ray equipment	750,000
Laboratory equipment	1,700,000
	$4,600,000

The expenditures are planned for October 1, 19X7, and the board wishes to know the amount of borrowing, if any, necessary on that date. Mark Spillman, hospital controller, has gathered the following information to be used in preparing an analysis of future cash flows.

1. Billings, made in the month of service, for the first 6 months of 19X7 are

Month	Actual Amount
January	$5,300,000
February	5,300,000
March	5,400,000
April	5,400,000
May	6,000,000
June	6,000,000

Ninety percent of General's billings are made to third parties such as Blue Cross, federal or state governments, and private insurance companies. The remaining 10% of the billings are made directly to patients. Historical patterns of billing collections are:

	Third-Party Billings	Direct Patient Billings
Month of service	20%	10%
Month following service	50	40
Second month following service	20	40
Uncollectible	10	10

Estimated billings for the last 6 months of 19X7 are listed next. The same billing and collection patterns that have been experienced during the first 6 months of 19X7 are expected to continue during the last 6 months of the year.

Month	Estimated Amount
July	$5,400,000
August	6,000,000
September	6,600,000
October	6,800,000
November	7,000,000
December	6,600,000

2. The purchases that have been made during the past 3 months and the planned purchases for the last 6 months of 19X7 are presented in the schedule on the next page:

Month	Amount
April	$1,300,000
May	1,450,000
June	1,450,000
July	1,500,000
August	1,800,000
September	2,200,000
October	2,350,000
November	2,700,000
December	2,100,000

All purchases are made on account, and accounts payable are remitted in the month following the purchase.

3. Salaries for each month during the remainder of 19X7 are expected to be $1,800,000 per month plus 20% of that month's billings. Salaries are paid in the month of service.
4. General's monthly depreciation charges are $150,000.
5. General incurs interest expenses of $180,000 per month and makes interest payments of $540,000 on the last day of each calendar quarter.
6. Endowment fund income is expected to continue to total $210,000 per month.
7. General has a cash balance of $350,000 on July 1, 19X7, and has a policy of maintaining a minimum end-of-month cash balance of 10% of the current month's purchases.
8. General Hospital employs a calendar-year reporting period.

Required

1. Prepare a schedule of budgeted cash receipts by month for the third quarter of 19X7.
2. Prepare a schedule of budgeted cash disbursements by month for the third quarter of 19X7.
3. Determine the amount of borrowing, if any, necessary on October 1, 19X7, to acquire the capital items totaling $4,600,000.

7-36   Comprehensive Budgeting for University
(CPA, adapted.) Suppose you are the controller of Southern State University. The university president, Robert James, is preparing for his annual fund-raising campaign for 19X8–X9. To set an appropriate target, he has asked you to prepare a budget for the academic year. You have collected the following data for the current year (19X7–X8):

1.	Undergraduate Division	Graduate Division
Average salary of faculty member	$45,000	$45,000
Average faculty teaching load in semester credit hours per year (eight undergraduate or six graduate courses)	24	18
Average number of students per class	30	20
Total enrollment (full-time and part-time students)	3,600	1,800
Average number of semester credit hours carried each year per student	25	20
Full-time load, semester hours per year	30	24

For 19X8–X9, all faculty and staff will receive a 6% salary increase. Undergraduate enrollment is expected to decline by 2%, but graduate enrollment is expected to increase by 5%.

2. The 19X7–X8 budget for operation and maintenance of facilities is $500,000, which includes $240,000 for salaries and wages. Experience so far this year indicates that the budget is accurate. Salaries and wages will increase by 6% and other operating costs will increase by $12,000 in 19X8–X9.

3. The 19X7–X8 and 19X8–X9 budgets for the remaining expenditures are:

	19X7–X8	19X8–X9
General administrative	$500,000	$525,000
Library		
Acquistions	150,000	155,000
Operations	190,000	200,000
Health services	48,000	50,000
Intramural athletics	56,000	60,000
Intercollegiate athletics	240,000	245,000
Insurance and retirement	520,000	560,000
Interest	75,000	75,000

4. Tuition is $70 per credit hour. In addition, the state legislature provides $780 per full-time-equivalent student. (A full-time equivalent is 30 undergraduate hours or 24 graduate hours.) Tuition scholarships are given to 30 *full-time* undergraduates and 50 *full-time* graduate students.

5. Revenues other than tuition and the legislative apportionment are:

	19X7–X8	19X8–X9
Endowment income	$200,000	$210,000
Net income from auxiliary services	325,000	335,000
Intercollegiate athletic receipts	290,000	300,000

6. The chemistry/physics classroom building needs remodeling during the 19X8–X9 period. Projected cost is $550,000.

Required

1. Prepare a schedule for 19X8–X9 that shows, by division, (a) expected enrollment, (b) total credit hours, (c) full-time-equivalent enrollment, and (d) number of faculty members needed. Assume that part-time faculty can be hired at one-half the salary per credit hour as full-time faculty.
2. Calculate the budget for faculty salaries for 19X8–X9 by division.
3. Calculate the budget for tuition revenue and legislative apportionment for 19X8–X9 by division.
4. Prepare a schedule for President James showing the amount that must be raised by the annual fund-raising campaign.

8 Flexible Budgets and Standards for Control

Getz Bros. & Co., Inc. markets many North American packaged foods and products to supermarkets in Asia and Central Europe for companies such as Tootsie Roll, Borden, and Treetop. Flexible budgeting enables Getz Bros. to adjust to changing market conditions. *Courtesy, Getz Bros. & Co., Inc.*

Learning Objectives

When you have finished studying this chapter, you should be able to

1 Distinguish between flexible budgets and master (static) budgets.

2 Use flexible-budget formulas to construct a flexible budget based on the volume of sales.

3 Use flexible-budget formulas to construct a flexible budget for an activity center.

4 Understand the performance evaluation relationship between master (static) budgets and flexible budgets.

5 Compute flexible-budget variances and sales-activity variances.

6 Distinguish between expectations, standard costs, and standard cost systems.

7 Compute and interpret price and usage variances for inputs based on cost-driver activity.

As we have seen in Chapter 7, formal budgeting procedures result in comprehensive operational and financial plans for future periods. These budgets guide managers and employees as they make their daily decisions and as they try to anticipate future problems and opportunities. As the budget period unfolds, it is only natural that employees and managers want to know, "How did we do?" Employees and their supervisors at the shop floor or at the customer service desk should know how they are doing in meeting their nonfinancial objectives (such as making on-time deliveries and resolving customer problems). Upper-level managers also want to know how the organization is meeting its financial objectives as spelled out in the master budget. Managers obtain feedback on how effectively economic conditions were forecast and how well plans were executed by comparing budgets to actual results. Knowing what went right and what went wrong should help managers plan and manage more effectively in future periods. The accounting system in most organizations is designed to record transactions continuously and report actual financial results at designated intervals. The way budgets and actual results are compared, however, determines the value of financial feedback.

This chapter introduces flexible budgets, which are budgets designed to direct management to areas of actual financial performance that deserve attention. (Managers can apply this same basic process to control of other important areas of performance such as quality or customer service.) After discussing flexible budgets and basic budget variances that are applicable to all organizations, we take a detailed look at variances for traditional manufacturing inputs such as material, labor, and overhead.

■ FLEXIBLE BUDGETS: BRIDGE BETWEEN STATIC BUDGETS AND ACTUAL RESULTS

Static Budgets

All the *master budgets* discussed in Chapter 7 are *static* or inflexible, because even though they may be easily revised, the budgets as accepted assume fixed levels of future activity. A master budget is prepared for only one level of activity (for example, one volume of sales activity). To illustrate, a typical master budget is a plan tailored to a single target sales level of, say, 9,000 units. The terms *static budget* and *master budget* are usually regarded as synonyms.

All *actual* results could be compared with the original plan, regardless of changes in ensuing conditions—even though, for example, sales volume turned out to be only 7,000 units instead of the originally planned 9,000 units. Suppose the Dominion Company, a one-department firm in Toronto, manufactures and sells a wheeled, collapsible suitcase carrier that is popular with airline flight crews. Manufacture of this suitcase carrier requires several manual and machine operations. The product has some variations, but may be viewed for our purposes essentially as a single product bearing one selling price.

The master (static) budget for June 19X4 included the condensed income statement shown in Exhibit 8-1, column 2. The actual results for June 19X4 are in column 1. Differences or variances between actual results and the master budget are in column 3. The master budget called for production and sales of 9,000 units, but only 7,000 units were actually produced and sold. There were no beginning or ending inventories, so the units made in June were sold in June.

The master budget was based on carefully forecasted sales and operations. The performance report in Exhibit 8-1 compares the actual results with the master budget. *Performance report* is a generic term that usually means a comparison of actual results with some budget. A helpful performance report will include *variances* that direct upper management's attention to significant deviations from expected results, allowing *management by exception* (see p. 11). Recall that a *variance* is a deviation of an actual amount from the expected or budgeted amount. Exhibit 8-1 shows variances of actual results from the master budget; these are called **master (static) budget variances**. Actual revenues that exceed expected revenues result in favorable revenue variances; when actual revenues are below expected revenues, variances are unfavorable. Similarly, actual expenses that exceed budgeted expenses result in **unfavorable expense variances**; actual expenses that are less than budgeted expenses, result in **favorable expense variances**. Each significant variance

master budget variance (static budget variance) The variance of actual results from the master budget.

unfavorable expense variance A variance that occurs when actual expenses are more than budgeted expenses.

favorable expense variance A variance that occurs when actual expenses are less than budgeted expenses.

should cause a manager to ask "Why?" By explaining why a variance occurs, managers are forced to recognize changes that have affected costs and that might affect future decisions.

	Actual (1)	Master Budget (2)	Master Budget Variances (3)
Units	7,000	9,000	2,000
Sales	$217,000	$279,000	$62,000 U
Variable expenses			
Variable manufacturing expenses	$151,270	$189,000	$37,730 F
Shipping expenses (selling)	5,000	5,400	400 F
Administrative expenses	2,000	1,800	200 U
Total variable expenses	$158,270	$196,200	$37,930 F
Contribution margin	$ 58,730	$ 82,800	$24,070 U
Fixed expenses			
Fixed manufacturing expenses	$ 37,300	$ 37,000	$ 300 U
Fixed selling and administrative expenses	33,000	33,000	—
Total fixed expenses	$ 70,300	$ 70,000	$ 300 U
Operating income (loss)	$ (11,570)	$ 12,800	$24,370 U

U = **Unfavorable expense variances** occur when actual expenses are more than budgeted expenses.
F = **Favorable expense variances** occur when actual expenses are less than budgeted expenses.

Suppose the president of Dominion Company asks you to explain *why* there was an operating loss of $11,570 when a profit of $12,800 was budgeted. Clearly, sales were below expectations, but the favorable variances for the variable costs are misleading. Considering the lower-than-projected level of sales activity, was cost control really satisfactory? The comparison of actual results with a master budget does not give much help in answering that question. Master budget variances are not very useful for management by exception.

Flexible Budgets

flexible budget (variable budget)
A budget that adjusts for changes in sales volume and other cost-driver activities.

In contrast to the performance report based only on comparing the master budget to actual results, a more helpful benchmark for analysis is the *flexible budget*. A **flexible budget** (sometimes called **variable budget**) is a budget that adjusts for changes in sales volume and other cost-driver activities. The flexible budget is identical to the master budget in format, but managers may prepare it for any level of activity. For performance evaluation, the flexible budget would be prepared at the actual levels of activity achieved. In contrast, the master budget is kept fixed or static to serve as the primary benchmark for evaluating performance. It shows revenues and costs at only the originally *planned* levels of activity.

Objective 1

Distinguish
between flexible
budgets and master
(static) budgets

To reiterate, flexible budgets have the following distinguishing features: (1) they may be prepared for a range of activity (as shown in Appendix 7, this is a natural use of financial planning software), and (2) they provide a dynamic basis for comparison with the actual results because they are automatically matched to changes in activities.

The flexible-budget approach says, "Give me any activity level you choose, and I'll provide a budget tailored to that particular level." Many companies routinely "flex" their budgets to help evaluate recent financial performance. For example, Procter & Gamble evaluates monthly financial performance of all its business units by comparing actual results to new, flexible budgets that are prepared for actual levels of activity.

Flexible-Budget Formulas

Objective 2

Use flexible-budget
formulas to construct a flexible
budget based on
volume of sales

The flexible budget is based on the same assumptions of revenue and cost behavior (within the relevant range) as the master budget. It is based on knowledge of cost behavior regarding appropriate cost drivers—*cost functions* or *flexible-budget formulas*. The cost functions that you used in Chapter 2 and estimated in Chapter 3 can be used as flexible-budget formulas. Recall that these cost functions had units of volume as the single cost driver. The flexible budget incorporates effects on each cost and revenue caused by changes in activity. Exhibits 8-2 and 8-3 show Dominion Company's simple flexible budget, which has a single cost driver, units of output. Dominion Company's cost functions or flexible budget formulas are believed to be valid within the relevant range of 7,000 to 9,000 units. Be sure that you understand that each column of Exhibit 8-2 (7,000, 8,000, and 9,000 units, respectively) is prepared using the same flexible-budget formulas—and any activity level within this range could be used, as shown in the graph in Exhibit 8-3. Note that fixed costs are expected to be constant across this range of activity.

Exhibit 8-2

Dominion Company
Flexible Budgets

		Flexible Budgets for Various Levels of Sales/Production Activity		
BUDGET FORMULA PER UNIT				
Units		7,000	8,000	9,000
Sales	$ 31.00	$217,000	$248,000	$279,000
Variable costs/expense				
Variable manufacturing costs	$ 21.00	$147,000	$168,000	$189,000
Shipping expenses (selling)	.60	4,200	4,800	5,400
Administrative	.20	1,400	1,600	1,800
Total variable costs/expenses	$ 21.80	$152,600	$174,400	$196,200
Contribution margin	$ 9.20	$ 64,400	$ 73,600	$ 82,800
BUDGET FORMULA PER MONTH				
Fixed costs				
Fixed manufacturing costs	$37,000	$ 37,000	$ 37,000	$ 37,000
Fixed selling and administrative costs	33,000	33,000	33,000	33,000
Total fixed costs	$70,000	$ 70,000	$ 70,000	$ 70,000
Operating income (loss)		$ (5,600)	$ 3,600	$ 12,800

Exhibit 8-3

Dominion Company
Graph of Flexible
Budget of Costs

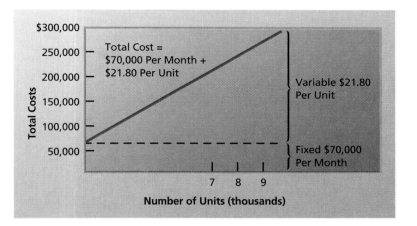

Objective 3

Use flexible-budget
formulas to
construct a flexible
budget for an
activity center

Activity-Based Flexible Budgets

As discussed in Chapters 3 and 4, more and more organizations are adopting activity-based-costing (ABC) systems that have multiple cost drivers. The focus of ABC systems is on activities as the primary cost objects. Managers identify activity centers and their associated cost drivers that are used to assign costs to final cost objects such as products or customer classes. Companies that use ABC systems develop a flexible budget for each activity center. Consider the Portland Power Company, an electric utility.[*] The Billing Department of the Portland Power Company has four activity centers: account inquiry, correspondence, account billing, and bill verification. The Billing Department would develop four flexible budgets, one for each activity center. The costs for each activity center would be analyzed to determine fixed and variable components.

We illustrate a flexible budget for the "account billing" activity center. The total costs of the account billing activity center is $235,777. Assume that cost behavior analysis indicates that fixed costs are $81,400. Thus, variable costs are $235,777 – $81,400 = $154,377. Activity analysis indicates that the cost driver for account billing activity is the number of lines printed, and the total lines printed is 2,440,000. Thus, the variable cost per line is $154,377 ÷ 2,440,000 = $0.063. The resulting cost function for the account billing activity center is [($0.063 × number of lines) plus $81,400]. The account billing activity center's cost function is believed to be valid within the relevant range of 2,000,000 to 3,000,000 lines.[†] A flexible budget for the account billing activity center is illustrated below. Similar flexible budgets would be developed for the other three activity centers. ∎

Flexible Budget—Account Billing Activity Center

Portland Power Company Billing Department Activity-Based Flexible Budget	Budget Formula	Cost Driver: Number of Lines		
		2,000,000	2,500,000	3,000,000
Variable Costs (Detailed)	$.063/line	$126,000	$157,500	$189,000
Fixed Costs (Detailed)	$81,400	81,400	81,400	81,400
Total Flexible Budget		$207,400	$238,900	$270,400

[*] This example is based on the Portland Power Company that was illustrated in Chapter 4 (pages 136–142) although it is not necessary to have covered Chapter 4 or the illustration to understand this example.

[†] This example ignores the interrelationships between activities in the Billing Department. For example, reduced demand by residential and/or commercial customers that cause the number of lines to decrease to 2,000,000 will cause other driver levels to change (number of inquiries, number of accounts, etc.). As these levels change, the proportions of fixed costs that are traced to the various activity centers will change. The variable cost per line will remain at $.063 but the fixed costs allocated to the billing activity center will change. Normally, the magnitude of the change in fixed cost is not significant so the budget formulas are still valid. The data for the Portland Power Company was entered in financial planning software that enables detailed tracing of costs, the resulting total flexible budget amounts varied by less than 2% from the amounts above.

Evaluation of Financial Performance Using Flexible Budgets

Objective 4

Understand the performance evaluation relationship between master (static) budgets and flexible budgets

Comparing the flexible budget to actual results accomplishes an important performance evaluation purpose. There are basically two reasons why actual results might not have conformed to the master budget. One is that sales and other cost-driver activities were not the same as originally forecasted. The second is that revenues or variable costs per unit of activity and fixed costs per period were not as expected. Though these reasons may not be completely independent (for example, higher sales prices may have caused lower sales levels), it is useful to separate these effects because different people may be responsible for them and because different management actions may be indicated. The intent of using the flexible budget for performance evaluation is to isolate unexpected effects on actual results that can be corrected if adverse or enhanced if beneficial. Because the flexible budget is prepared at the actual levels of activity (in our example, sales volume), any variances between the flexible budget and actual results cannot be due to activity levels (again, assuming cost and revenue functions are valid). These *variances between the flexible budget and actual results* are called **flexible-budget variances** and must be due to *departures of actual costs or revenues from flexible-budget formula amounts*—because of pricing or cost control. In contrast, any differences or *variances between the master budget and the flexible budget are due to activity levels*, not cost control. These latter differences between the master budget amounts and the amounts in the flexible budget are called **activity-level variances**.

flexible-budget variances The variances between the flexible budget and the actual results.

activity-level variances The differences between the master budget amounts and the amounts in the flexible budget.

Consider Exhibit 8-4. The flexible budget (column 3) taken from Exhibit 8-2 (and simplified) provides an explanatory bridge between the master budget (column 5) and the actual results (column 1). The variances for operating income are summarized at the bottom of Exhibit 8-4. Note that the sum of the activity-level variances (here sales-activity variances because sales is the only activity used as a cost driver) and the flexible-budget variances equals the total of the master budget variances. The difference between actual results and the original master budget has two components: the sales-activity variances and the flexible-budget variances.

■ ISOLATION OF BUDGET VARIANCES AND THEIR CAUSES

effectiveness The degree to which a goal, objective, or target is met.

efficiency The degree to which inputs are used in relation to a given level of outputs.

Managers use comparisons between actual results, master budgets, and flexible budgets to evaluate organizational performance. When evaluating performance, it is useful to distinguish between **effectiveness**—the degree to which a goal, objective, or target is met—and **efficiency**—the degree to which inputs are used in relation to a given level of outputs.

Performance may be effective, efficient, both, or neither. For example, Dominion Company set a master budget objective of manufacturing and selling 9,000 units. Only 7,000 units were actually made and sold, however. Performance, as measured by sales-activity variances, was ineffective because the sales objective was not met.

Was Dominion's performance efficient? Managers judge the degree of efficiency by comparing actual outputs achieved (7,000 units) with actual inputs (such as the costs of direct materials and direct labor). *The less input used to produce a given output, the more efficient the operation.* As indicated by the flexible-budget variances, Dominion was inefficient in its use of a number of inputs. Later in this chapter we consider in detail direct material, direct labor, and variable overhead flexible-budget variances.

| Exhibit 8-4 | | Dominion Company   Summary of Performance for the Month Ended June 30, 19X4 | | | | |

	Actual Results at Actual Activity Level* (1)	Flexible-Budget Variances[†] (2) = (1) – (3)	Flexible-Budget for Actual Sales Activity[‡] (3)	Sales-Activity Variances (4) = (3) – (5)	Master Budget (5)
Units	7,000	—	7,000	2,000 U	9,000
Sales	$217,000	—	$217,000	$62,000 U	$ 279,000
Variable costs	158,270	5,670 U	152,600	43,600 F	196,200
Contribution margin	$ 58,730	$5,670 U	$ 64,400	$18,400 U	$ 82,800
Fixed costs	70,300	300 U	70,000	—	70,000
Operating income	$ (11,570)	$5,970 U	$ (5,600)	$18,400 U	$ 12,800

Total flexible-budget variances, $5,970 U

Total sales-activity variances, $18,400 U

Total master budget variances, $24,370 U

U = Unfavorable. F = Favorable.
* Figures are from Exhibit 8-1.
† Figures are shown in more detail in Exhibit 8-5.
‡ Figures are from the 7,000-unit column in Exhibit 8-2.

Flexible-Budget Variances

Flexible budget variances measure the efficiency of operations at the actual level of activity. The first three columns of Exhibit 8-4 compare the actual results with the flexible-budget amounts. The flexible-budget variances are the differences between columns 1 and 3, which total $5,970 unfavorable because:

total flexible-budget variance = total actual results – total flexible budget, planned results
$$= (- \$11,570) - (- \$5,600)$$
$$= \$ - 5,970, \text{ or } \$5,970 \text{ unfavorable}[1]$$

The total flexible-budget variance arises from sales prices received and the variable and fixed costs incurred. Dominion Company had no difference between actual sales price and the flexible-budgeted sales price, so the focus is on the differences between actual costs and flexible-budgeted costs at the actual 7,000-unit level of activity. Without the flexible budget in column 3, we cannot separate the effects of differences in cost behavior from the effects of changes in sales activity. The flexible-budget variances indicate whether operations were efficient or not, and may form the basis for periodic performance evaluation. Operations managers are in the best position to explain flexible-budget variances.

Companies that use variances primarily to fix blame, however, often find that managers resort to cheating and subversion to beat the system. Managers

[1] What if the total flexible budget results were positive—say, $4,000? The total flexible-budget variance would be (– $11,570) – ($4,000) = $ – 15,570, or $15,570 unfavorable.

of operations usually have more information about those operations than higher-level managers. If that information is used against them, lower-level managers can be expected to withhold or misstate valuable information for their own self-protection. For example, one manufacturing firm actually *reduced* the next period's departmental budget by the amount of the department's unfavorable variances in the current period. If a division had a $50,000 expense budget and experienced a $2,000 unfavorable variance, the following period's budget would be set at $48,000. This system led managers to cheat and to falsify reports to avoid unfavorable variances. We can criticize departmental managers' ethics, but the system was as much at fault as the managers.

Exhibit 8-5 gives an expanded, line-by-line computation of variances for all master budget items at Dominion. Note how most of the costs that had seemingly favorable variances when a master budget was used as a basis for comparison have, in reality, unfavorable variances. Do not conclude automatically that favorable flexible-budget variances are good and unfavorable flexible-budget variances are bad. Instead, *interpret all variances as signals that actual operations have not occurred exactly as anticipated* when the flexible-budget formulas were

Exhibit 8-5				Dominion Company Cost-Control Performance Report for the Month Ended June 30, 19X4
	Actual Costs Incurred	**Flexible Budget***	**Flexible Budget Variances†**	**Explanation**
Units	7,000	7,000	—	
Variable costs				
Direct material	$ 69,920	$ 70,000	$ 80 F	Lower prices but higher usage
Direct labor	61,500	56,000	5,500 U	Higher wage rates and higher usage
Indirect labor	9,100	11,900	2,800 F	Decreased setup time
Idle time	3,550	2,800	750 U	Excessive machine breakdowns
Cleanup time	2,500	2,100	400 U	Cleanup of spilled solvent
Supplies	4,700	4,200	500 U	Higher prices and higher usage
Variable manufacturing costs	$151,270	$147,000	$4,270 U	
Shipping	5,000	4,200	800 U	Use of air freight to meet delivery
Administration	2,000	1,400	600 U	Excessive copying and long distance calls
Total variable costs	$158,270	$152,600	$5,670 U	
Fixed costs				
Factory supervision	$ 14,700	$ 14,400	$ 300 U	Salary increase
Factory rent	5,000	5,000	—	
Equipment depreciation	15,000	15,000	—	
Other fixed factory costs	2,600	2,600	—	
Fixed manufacturing costs	$ 37,300	$ 37,000	$ 300 U	
Fixed selling and administrative costs	33,000	33,000	—	
Total fixed costs	$ 70,300	$ 70,000	$ 300 U	
Total variable and fixed costs	$228,570	$222,600	$5,970 U	

* From 7,000-unit column of Exhibit 8-2.
† This is a line-by-line breakout of the variances in column 2 of Exhibit 8-4.

set. Any cost that differs significantly from the flexible budget deserves an explanation. The last column of Exhibit 8-5 gives possible explanations for Dominion Company's variances.

Sales-Activity Variances

sales-activity variances Variances that measure how effective managers have been in meeting the planned sales objective, calculated as actual unit sales less master budget unit sales times the budgeted unit contribution margin.

Sales-activity variances measure how effective managers have been in meeting the planned sales objective. In Dominion Company, sales activity fell 2,000 units short of the planned level. The final three columns of Exhibit 8-4 clearly show how the sales-activity variances (totaling $18,400 U) are unaffected by any changes in unit prices or variable costs. Why? Because the same budgeted unit prices and variable costs are used in constructing both the flexible and master budgets. Therefore, all unit prices and variable costs are held constant in columns 3 through 5.

The total of the sales-activity variances informs the manager that falling short of the sales target by 2,000 units caused operating income to be $18,400 lower than initially budgeted (a $5,600 loss instead of a $12,800 profit). In summary, the shortfall of sales by 2,000 units caused Dominion Company to incur a total sales activity variance of 2,000 units at a contribution margin of $9.20 per unit (from the first column of Exhibit 8-2, page 296).

$$\begin{matrix} \text{total sales-activity} \\ \text{variance} \end{matrix} \quad \left(\begin{matrix} \text{actual sales units } - \\ \text{master budget sales units} \end{matrix} \right) \times \left(\begin{matrix} \text{budgeted contribution} \\ \text{margin per unit} \end{matrix} \right)$$
$$= (9,000 - 7,000) \times \$9.20$$
$$= \$18,400 \text{ Unfavorable}$$

Who has responsibility for the sales-activity variance? Marketing managers usually have the primary responsibility for reaching the sales level specified in the static budget. Of course variations in sales may be attributable to many factors.[2] Nevertheless, marketing managers are typically in the best position to explain why sales activities attained differed from plans.

Expectations, Standard Costs, and Standard Cost Systems

expected cost The cost most likely to be attained.

standard cost A carefully determined cost per unit that should be attained.

standard cost systems Accounting systems that value products according to standard costs only.

Expectations or *standard costs* are the building blocks of a planning and control system. An **expected cost** is the cost that is most likely to be attained. A **standard cost** is a carefully developed cost per unit that *should be* attained. It is often synonymous with the expected cost, but some companies intentionally set standards above or below expected costs to create desired incentives. Do not confuse having expectations or standards with having a *standard cost system*. **Standard cost systems** value products according to standard costs only.[3] These inventory valuation systems simplify financial reporting, but in most companies they are expensive to install and to maintain. Therefore, standard

---

[2] For example, sales-activity variances can be subdivided into sales quantity, sales mix, market size, and market share variances. This more advanced treatment of sales activity variances is covered in Charles T. Horngren, George Foster, and Srikant M. Datar, *Cost Accounting: A Managerial Emphasis* (Englewood Cliffs, NJ: Prentice Hall, 1994), pp. 758–763. These sales activity variances might result from changes in the product, changes in customer demand, effective advertising, and so on.

[3] Details of standard cost systems for financial reporting are covered in Charles T. Horngren, George Foster, and Srikant M. Datar, *Cost Accounting: A Managerial Emphasis* (Upper Saddle River, NJ: Prentice Hall, 1994), Chapters 7 and 8, pp. 225–296.

Caterpillar Tracks Multiple Cost Systems Through Master Budget

Caterpillar, Inc., the world-wide manufacturer of heavy construction equipment, found that its standard cost system, while efficient for financial reporting, was too cumbersome to support its many decision-making needs. For example, a product designer, who recognizes that most of a product's costs are determined at the design stage, could not determine what expected costs of alternative designs would be for a new product. Current or expected costs would be more useful for decision making, but Caterpillar determined that developing a standard cost system that reflected current or expected costs would be infeasible. Caterpillar decided instead to use three cost systems, linked through the master budget, to meet all its accounting and decision-making needs.

Caterpillar retained the standard cost system for financial reporting, but developed two additional cost systems. To support planning and decision making, Caterpillar has a separate product costing system based on activity-based costing (discussed in

Chapters 3 and 4). This system is kept current to reflect changes in activities and cost drivers. Caterpillar also developed an operational control system for evaluating performance. This system compares actual performance to budgets and targets, computing new flexible budgets for changes in product mix, quantities, and other operations.

The new cost systems provide immediate cost feedback to product development, component design, sourcing decisions, quality and cost improvements, investment analysis, pricing, competitive cost analyses, and manufacturing design and process improvements. As a result, cost estimates are more reliable, and the time to make critical decisions has been shortened considerably—both critical components of effective decision making in a competitive environment. ■

Source: Adapted from Lou F. Jones, "Product Costing at Caterpillar," Management Accounting, *February 1991, pp. 34–42.*

Objective 6

Distinguish between expectations, standard costs, and standard cost systems

costs may not be revised often enough to be useful for management decision making regarding specific products or services. (Ideally, only one cost system should be necessary in any organization, but in practice many organizations have developed multiple cost systems.) The expected costs used in flexible budgets also may be called standards because they are benchmarks or objectives to be attained. The fact that they are called standards does not imply that the organization also must have a *standard cost system* for inventory valuation or that it must use the standard cost system for planning and control.

Current Attainability: Most Widely Used Standard

What standard of expected performance should be used in flexible budgets? Should it be so strict that it is rarely, if ever, attained? Should it be attainable 50% of the time? 90%? 20%? Individuals who have worked a lifetime setting and evaluating standards for performance disagree, so there are no universal answers to this question.

perfection standards (ideal standards)
Expressions of the most efficient performance possible under the best conceivable conditions, using existing specifications and equipment.

Perfection standards (also called **ideal standards**) are expressions of the most efficient performance possible under the best conceivable conditions, using existing specifications and equipment. No provision is made for waste, spoilage, machine breakdowns, and the like. Those who favor using perfection standards maintain that the resulting unfavorable variances will constantly remind personnel of the continuous need for improvement in all phases of operations. Though concern for continuous improvement is widespread, these standards are not widely used because they have an adverse effect on employee motivation. Employees tend to ignore unreasonable goals, especially if they would not share the gains from meeting imposed perfection standards.

Organizations that apply the JIT philosophy (discussed in Chapter 4) attempt to achieve continuous improvement from "the bottom up," not by prescribing what should be achieved via perfection standards.

currently attainable standards Levels of performance that can be achieved by realistic levels of effort.

Currently attainable standards are levels of performance that can be achieved by realistic levels of effort. Allowances are made for normal defectives, spoilage, waste, and nonproductive time. There are at least two popular interpretations of the meaning of currently attainable standards. The first interpretation has standards set just tightly enough that employees regard their attainment as highly probable if normal effort and diligence are exercised. That is, variances should be random and negligible. Hence, the standards are predictions of what will indeed occur, anticipating some inefficiencies. Managers accept the standards as being reasonable goals. The major reasons for "reasonable" standards, then, are:

1. The resulting standards serve multiple purposes. For example, the same cost can be used for financial budgeting, inventory valuation, and budgeting departmental performance. In contrast, perfection standards cannot be used for inventory valuation or financial budgeting, because the costs are known to be inaccurate.

2. Reasonable standards have a desirable motivational impact on employees, especially when combined with incentives for continuous improvement. The standard represents reasonable future performance, not fanciful goals. Therefore, unfavorable variances direct attention to performance that is not meeting reasonable expectations.

A second interpretation of currently attainable standards is that standards are set tightly. That is, employees regard their fulfillment as possible, though unlikely. Standards can be achieved only by very efficient operations. Variances tend to be unfavorable; nevertheless, employees accept the standards as being tough but not unreasonable goals. Is it possible to achieve continuous improvement using currently attainable standards? Yes, but expectations must reflect improved productivity and must be tied to incentive systems that reward continuous improvement.

Trade-offs Among Variances

Because the operations of organizations are linked, the level of performance in one area of operations will affect performance in other areas. Nearly any combination of effects is possible: Improvements in one area could lead to improvements in others and vice versa. Likewise, substandard performance in one area may be balanced by superior performance in others. For example, a service organization may generate favorable labor variances by hiring less-skilled customer representatives, but this favorable variance may lead to unfavorable customer satisfaction and future unfavorable sales-activity variances. In another situation, a manufacturer may experience unfavorable materials variances by purchasing higher-quality materials at a higher than planned price, but this variance may be more than offset by the favorable variances caused by lower inventory handling costs (e.g., inspections) and higher-quality products (such as favorable scrap and rework variances).

Because of the many interdependencies among activities, an "unfavorable" or "favorable" label should not lead the manager to jump to conclusions. By themselves, such labels merely raise questions and provide clues to the causes of performance. *They are attention directors, not problem solvers.* Furthermore, the cause of variances might be faulty expectations rather than the execution of plans by managers. One of the first questions a manager should consider when explaining a large variance is whether expectations were valid.

When to Investigate Variances

When should variances be investigated? Frequently the answer is based on subjective judgments, hunches, guesses, and rules of thumb that have proved to be useful. The most troublesome aspect of using the feedback from flexible budgeting is deciding when a variance is large enough to warrant management's attention. The master and flexible budgets imply that the standard cost is the only permissible outcome. Practically speaking, the accountant (and everybody else) realizes that the standard is one of the many possible acceptable cost outcomes. Consequently, the accountant expects variances to fluctuate randomly within some normal limits. Of course, an activity that allows wildly fluctuating variances as "normal" may be a poorly designed activity. A random variance from a well-designed activity, by definition, is not caused by controllable actions and calls for no corrective action. In short, a random variance is attributable to chance rather than to management's implementation of plans. Consequently, the more a variance randomly fluctuates, the larger the variance required to make investigation worthwhile. There are two questions: First, what is a large versus a small variance? Second, is a large variance random or controllable? Usually, the second question is answered only after an investigation, so answering the first question is critical.

Managers recognize that, even if everything operates as planned, variances are unlikely to be exactly zero. They predict a range of "normal" variances; this range may be based on economic criteria (i.e., how big a variance must be before investigation could be worth the effort) or on statistical criteria. For some critical items, any deviation may prompt a follow-up. For most items, a minimum dollar or percentage deviation from budget may be necessary before investigations are expected to be worthwhile. For example, a 4% variance in a $1 million material cost may deserve more attention than a 20% variance in a $10,000 repair cost. Because knowing exactly when to investigate is difficult, many organizations have developed such rules of thumb as, "Investigate all variances exceeding $5,000 or 25% of expected cost, whichever is lower."

Comparisons with Prior Period's Results

Some organizations compare the most recent budget period's actual results with last year's results for the same period rather than use flexible budget benchmarks. For example, an organization might compare June 19X4's actual results to June 19X3's actual results. In general these comparisons are not as useful for evaluating performance of an organization as comparisons of actual outcomes with planned results for the same period. Why? Because many changes probably have occurred in the environment and in the organization that make a comparison across years invalid. Very few organizations and environments are so stable that the only difference between now and a year ago is merely the passage of time. Even comparisons with last month's actual results may not be as useful as comparisons with flexible budgets. Comparisons over time may be useful for analyzing *trends* in such key variables as sales volume, market share, and product mix, but they do not help answer questions such as "Why did we have a loss of $11,570 in June, when we expected a profit of $12,800?"

Summary Problem for Your Review

Problem One

Refer to the data contained in Exhibits 8-1 and 8-2. Suppose actual production and sales were 8,500 units instead of 7,000 units; actual variable costs were $188,800; and actual fixed costs were $71,200. The selling price remained at $31 per unit.

Required

1. Compute the master budget variance. What does this tell you about the efficiency of operations? The effectiveness of operations?
2. Compute the sales-activity variance. Is the performance of the marketing function the sole explanation for this variance? Why?
3. Using a flexible budget at the actual activity level, compute the budgeted contribution margin, budgeted operating income, and flexible-budget variance. What do you learn from this variance?

Solution to Problem One

1.
$$\text{actual operating income} = (8{,}500 \times \$31) - \$188{,}800 - \$71{,}200 = \$3{,}500$$
$$\text{master budget operating income} = \$12{,}800 \text{ (from Exhibit 8-1)}$$
$$\text{master budget variance} = \$12{,}800 - \$3{,}500 = \$9{,}300 \text{ U}$$

Three factors affect the master budget variance: sales activity, efficiency, and price changes. There is no way to tell from the master budget variance alone how much of the $9,300 U was caused by any of these factors alone.

2. sales-activity variance = budgeted unit contribution margin × difference between the master budget unit sales and the actual unit sales
= $9.20 per unit CM × (9,000 − 8,500)
= $4,600 U

This variance is labeled as a sales-activity variance because it quantifies the impact on operating income of the deviation from an original sales target while holding price and efficiency factors constant. This is a measure of the effectiveness of the operations— Dominion was ineffective in meeting its sales objective. Of course, the failure to reach target sales may be traceable to several causes beyond the control of marketing personnel including material shortages, factory breakdowns, and so on.

3. The budget formulas in Exhibit 8-2 are the basis for the following answers:

flexible-budget contribution margin = $9.20 × 8,500 = $78,200
flexible-budget operating income = $78,200 − $70,000 fixed costs = $8,200
actual operating income = $3,500 (from requirement 1)
flexible-budget variance = $8,200 − $3,500 = $4,700 U

The flexible-budget variance shows that the company spent $4,700 more to produce and sell the 8,500 units than it should have if operations had been efficient and unit costs had not changed. Note that this variance plus the $4,600 U sales-activity variance total to the $9,300 U master budget variance.

Objective 7

Compute and interpret price and usage variances for inputs based on cost-driver activity

◼ FLEXIBLE-BUDGET VARIANCES IN DETAIL

The rest of this chapter probes the analysis of variances in detail. The emphasis is on subdividing labor, material, and overhead cost variances into usage and price or spending components. Note that in companies where direct-labor costs are small in relation to total costs (that is, in highly automated companies) direct-labor costs may be treated as an overhead-cost item, so separate labor standards, budgets, or variances need not be analyzed.

Variances from Material and Labor Standards

Consider Dominion Company's $10 standard cost of direct materials and $8 standard cost of direct labor. These standards per unit are derived from two components: a standard quantity of an input and a standard price for the input.

	Standards		
	Standard Inputs Expected per Unit of Output	*Standard Price Expected per Unit of Input*	*Standard Cost Expected per Unit of Output*
Direct material	5 pounds	$ 2	$10
Direct labor	½ hour	16	8

Once standards are set and actual results are observed, we can measure variances from the flexible budget. To show how the analysis of variances can be pursued more fully, we will reconsider Dominion's direct-material and direct-labor costs, as shown in Exhibit 8-5, and assume that the following actually occurred for the production of 7,000 units of output:

- *Direct material:* 36,800 pounds of material were purchased and *used* at an actual unit *price* of $1.90 for a total actual cost of $69,920.
- *Direct labor:* 3,750 hours of labor were *used* at an actual hourly *price* (rate) of $16.40, for a total cost of $61,500.

Note that the flexible-budget variances for direct labor and direct material can be attributed to (1) using more or less of the resource than planned and (2) spending more or less for the resource than planned at the actual level of output achieved. These additional data enable us to subdivide the flexible-budget variances (column 3) from Exhibit 8-5 into the separate *usage* and *price* components, which are shown below in columns 4 and 5.

	(1) Actual Costs	(2) Flexible- Budget	(3) Flexible- Budget Variance	(4) Price Variance*	(5) Usage Variance*
Direct material	$69,920	$70,000	$ 80 F	$3,680 F	$3,600 U
Direct labor	61,500	56,000	5,500 U	1,500 U	4,000 U

* Computations to be explained shortly.

The flexible-budget totals for direct materials and direct labor are the amounts that would have been spent with expected efficiency. They are often labeled total *standard costs allowed*, computed as follows:

$$\begin{matrix} \text{flexible} \\ \text{budget or} \\ \text{total standard} \\ \text{cost allowed} \end{matrix} = \begin{matrix} \text{units of good} \\ \text{output} \\ \text{achieved} \end{matrix} \times \begin{matrix} \text{input allowed} \\ \text{per unit of} \\ \text{output} \end{matrix} \times \begin{matrix} \text{standard unit} \\ \text{price of input} \end{matrix}$$

$$\begin{matrix} \text{standard direct-materials} \\ \text{cost allowed} \end{matrix} = 7{,}000 \text{ units} \times 5 \text{ pounds} \times \$2.00 \text{ per pound} = \$70{,}000$$

$$\begin{matrix} \text{standard direct-labor cost} \\ \text{allowed} \end{matrix} = 7{,}000 \text{ units} \times \tfrac{1}{2} \text{ hour} \times \$16.00 \text{ per hour} = \$56{,}000$$

Before reading on, note particularly that the flexible-budget amounts (i.e., the standard costs allowed) are tied to an initial question: What was the output achieved? Always ask yourself: What was the good output? Then proceed with your computations of the total standard cost allowed for the good output achieved.

Price and Usage Variances

As noted earlier, we computed the flexible-budget amounts using the flexible-budget formulas, or currently attainable standards. Flexible-budget variances measure the relative efficiency of achieving the actual output. Price and usage variances subdivide each flexible-budget variance into the following:

price variance The difference between actual input prices and expected input prices multiplied by the actual quantity of inputs used.

usage variance (quantity variance, efficiency variance) The difference between the quantity of inputs actually used and the quantity of inputs that should have been used to achieve the actual quantity of output multiplied by the expected price of the input.

1. **Price variance**—difference between actual input prices and standard input prices multiplied by the actual quantity of inputs used.
2. **Usage variance**—difference between the quantity of inputs actually used and the quantity of inputs that should have been used to achieve the actual quantity of output multiplied by the expected price of the input (also called a **quantity variance** or **efficiency variance**).

When feasible, you should separate the variances that are subject to a manager's direct influence from those that are not. This aids scorekeeping, attention directing, and problem solving. The usual approach is to separate price factors from usage factors. Price factors are less subject to immediate control than are usage factors, principally because of external forces, such as general economic conditions, that can influence prices. Even when price factors are regarded as being outside management control, isolating them helps to focus on the efficient usage of inputs. For example, the commodity prices of wheat, oats, corn, and rice are outside the control of General Mills. By separating price variances from usage variances, the breakfast cereal maker can focus on whether grain was used efficiently.

Price and usage variances are helpful because they provide feedback to those responsible for inputs. These variances should not be the only information used for decision making, control, or evaluation, however. Exclusive focus on material price variances by purchasing agents or buyers, for example, can work against an organization's JIT and total quality management goals. A buyer may be motivated to earn favorable material price variances by buying in large quantities and by buying low-quality material. The result could then be excessive inventory-handling and opportunity costs and increased manufacturing defects owing to faulty material. Similarly, exclusive focus on labor price and usage variances could motivate supervisors to use lower-skilled workers or to rush workers through critical tasks, both of which could impair quality of products and services.

Price and Usage Variance Computations

We now consider the detailed calculation of price and usage variances. The objective of these variance calculations is to hold either price or usage constant so that the effect of the other can be isolated. When calculating the price variance, you hold use of inputs constant at the actual level of usage. When calculating the usage variance, you hold price constant at the standard price. For Dominion Company the price variances are:

Direct-material price variance = (actual price − standard price) × actual quantity
= ($1.90 − $2.00) per pound × 36,800 pounds
= $3,680 favorable

Direct-labor price variance = (actual price − standard price) × actual quantity
= ($16.40 − $16.00) per hour × 3,750 hours
= $1,500 unfavorable

The usage variances are:

Direct-material usage variance = (actual quantity used − standard quantity allowed)
× standard price
= [36,800 − (7,000 × 5)] pounds × $2.00 per pound
= (36,800 − 35,000) × $2
= $3,600 unfavorable

Direct-labor usage variance = (actual quantity used − standard quantity allowed)
× standard price
= [3,750 − (7,000 × ½)] hours × $16 per hour
= (3,750 − 3,500) × $16
= $4,000 unfavorable

To determine whether a variance is favorable or unfavorable, use logic rather than memorizing a formula. A price variance is favorable if the actual price is less than the standard. A usage variance is favorable if the actual quantity used is less than the standard quantity allowed. The opposite relationships imply unfavorable variances.

Note that the sum of the direct-labor price and usage variances equals the direct labor flexible-budget variance. Furthermore, the sum of the direct-material price and usage variances equals the total direct-material flexible-budget variance.

Direct-materials flexible-budget variance = $80 favorable = $3,680 favorable + $3,600 unfavorable

Direct-labor flexible-budget variance = $5,500 unfavorable = $1,500 unfavorable + $4,000 unfavorable

Variances themselves do not show why the budgeted operating income was not achieved. They raise questions, provide clues, and direct attention, however. For instance, one possible explanation for this set of variances is that a manager might have made a trade-off—the manager might have purchased at a favorable price some materials that were substandard quality, saving $3,680 (the materials price variance). Excessive waste might have nearly offset this savings, as indicated by the $3,600 unfavorable material usage variance and net flexible-budget variance of $80 favorable. The material waste also might have caused at least part of the excess use of direct labor. Suppose more than $80 of the $4,000 unfavorable direct-labor usage variance was caused by reworking units with defective materials.

Then the manager's trade-off was not successful. The cost inefficiencies caused by using substandard materials exceeded the savings from the favorable price.

Exhibit 8-6 shows the price and usage variance computations for labor graphically. The standard cost (or flexible budget) is the standard quantity multiplied by the standard price—the square shaded light blue. The price variance is the difference between the unit prices, actual and standard, multiplied by actual quantity used—the rectangle shaded dark blue. The usage variance is the standard price multiplied by the difference between the actual quantity used and the standard quantity allowed for the good output achieved—the area of the shaded rectangle on the lower right. (Note that for clarity the graph portrays only unfavorable variances.)

Exhibit 8-6

Graphical Representation of Price and Usage Variances for Labor

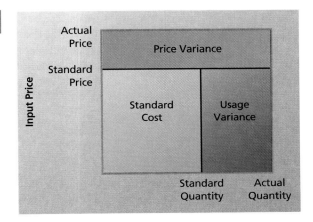

Effects of Inventories

Analysis of Dominion Company was simplified because (1) there were no finished goods inventories—any units produced were sold in the same period—and (2) there was no direct-material inventory—the materials were purchased and used in the same period.

What if production does not equal sales? The sales-activity variance then is the difference between the static budget and the flexible budget for the number of units *sold*. In contrast, the flexible-budget cost variances compare actual costs with flexible-budgeted costs for the number of units *produced*.

Generally managers want quick feedback and want variances to be identified as early as is practical. In the case of direct materials, that time is when the materials are purchased rather than when they are used, which may be much later. Therefore, the material price variance is usually based on the quantity purchased, measured at the time of purchase. The material usage variance remains based on the quantity used. Suppose Dominion Company purchased 40,000 pounds of material (rather than the 36,800 pounds used) at $1.90 per pound. The material price variance would be (actual price – standard price) × material *purchased* = ($1.90 – $2.00) per pound × 40,000 pounds = $4,000 favorable. The material usage variance would remain at $3,600 unfavorable because it is based on the material *used*.

■ OVERHEAD VARIANCES

Direct-material and direct-labor variances are often subdivided into price and usage components. In contrast, many organizations believe that it is not worth-while to monitor individual overhead items to the same extent. Therefore, over-head variances often are not subdivided beyond the flexible-budget variances—the complexity of the analysis may not be worth the effort.

But in some cases, it may be worthwhile to subdivide the flexible-budget overhead variances, especially those for variable overhead. Part of the variable-overhead flexible-budget variance is related to control of the cost driver and part to the control of overhead spending itself. When actual cost-driver activity differs from the standard amount allowed for the actual output achieved, a **variable-overhead efficiency variance** will occur. Suppose that Dominion Company's cost of supplies, a variable-overhead cost, is driven by direct-labor hours. A vari-able-overhead cost rate of $.60 per unit at Dominion would be equivalent to $1.20 per direct-labor hour (because ½ hour is allowed per unit of output). Of the $500 unfavorable variance, $300 unfavorable is due to using 3,750 direct-labor hours rather than the 3,500 allowed by the flexible budget, as calculated below:

variable-overhead efficiency variance When actual cost-driver activity differs from the standard amount allowed for the actual output achieved.

$$\begin{array}{l} \text{Variable - overhead} \\ \text{efficiency variance} \\ \text{for supplies} \end{array} = \left(\begin{array}{cc} \text{actual direct} & \text{standard direct labor} \\ \text{labor hours} & - \quad \text{hours allowed} \end{array} \right) \times \begin{array}{c} \text{standard} \\ \text{variable - overhead} \\ \text{rate per hour} \end{array}$$

$$= \left(\begin{array}{cc} 3,750 \text{ actual} & 3,500 \text{ standard} \\ \text{hours} & - \quad \text{hours allowed} \end{array} \right) \times \$1.20 \text{ per hour}$$

$$= \$300 \text{ unfavorable}$$

This $300 excess usage of supplies is attributable to inefficient use of cost-driver activity, direct-labor hours. Whenever actual cost-driver activity exceeds that allowed for the actual output achieved, overhead efficiency variances will be unfavorable and vice versa. In essence this efficiency variance tells manage-ment the cost of *not* controlling the use of cost-driver activity. The remainder of the flexible-budget variance measures control of overhead spending itself, given actual cost-driver activity.

$$\begin{array}{l} \text{variable - overhead spending} \\ \text{variance for supplies} \end{array} = \begin{array}{c} \text{actual variable} \\ \text{overhead} \end{array} - \left(\begin{array}{cc} \text{expected variable} & \text{actual direct} \\ \text{overhead rate} & \times \quad \text{labor hours used} \end{array} \right)$$

$$= \$4,700 - (\$1.20 \times 3,750 \text{ hours})$$

$$\text{rs} = \$4,700 - \$4,500$$

$$= \$200 \text{ unfavorable}$$

variable-overhead spending variance The difference between the actual variable overhead and the amount of variable overhead budgeted for the actual level of cost-driver activity.

That is, the **variable-overhead spending variance** is the difference between the actual variable overhead and the amount of variable overhead budgeted for the actual level of cost-driver activity.

Like other variances, the overhead variances by themselves cannot identify causes for results that differ from the static and flexible budgets. The only way for management to discover why overhead performance did not agree with the budget is to investigate possible causes. The distinction between spending and usage variances provides a springboard for more investigation, however.

■ GENERAL APPROACH

Exhibit 8-7 presents the analysis of direct material and direct labor in a format that deserves close study. The general approach is at the top of the exhibit; the specific applications then follow. Even though the exhibit may seem unnecessarily complex at first, its repeated use will solidify your understanding of variance analysis. Of course, the other flexible-budget variances in Exhibit 8-5 could be further analyzed in the same manner in which direct labor and direct material are analyzed in Exhibit 8-7. Such a detailed investigation depends on the manager's perception of whether the extra benefits will exceed the extra costs of the analysis.

Column A of Exhibit 8-7 contains the actual costs incurred for the inputs during the budget period being evaluated. Column B is the flexible-budgeted costs for the inputs *given the actual inputs used*, using expected prices but actual usage. Column C is the flexible budget amount using both expected prices and expected usage for the outputs actually achieved. (This is the flexible budget amount from Exhibit 8-5 for 7,000 units.) Column B is inserted between A and C by using *expected* prices and *actual* usage. The difference between columns A and B is attributed to changing prices because usage is held constant between A and B at actual levels. The difference between columns B and C is attributed to changing usage because price is held constant between B and C at expected levels.

Exhibit 8-7

General Approach to Analysis of Direct-Labor and Direct-Material Variances

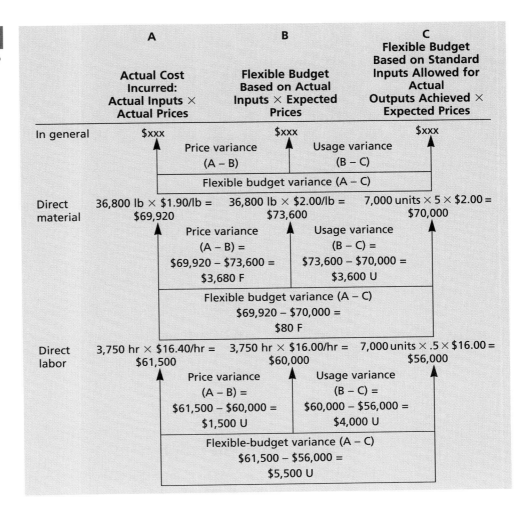

Actual output achieved in Column C is measured in units of product. However, most organizations manufacture a variety of products. When the variety of units are added together, the sum is frequently a nonsensical number (such as apples and oranges). Therefore, all units of output are often expressed in terms of the standard inputs allowed for their production, such as pounds of fruit. Labor hours may also become the common denominator for measuring total output volume. Thus production, instead of being expressed as 12,000 chairs and 3,000 sofas, could be expressed as 20,000 standard hours allowed (or more accurately as *standard hours of input allowed for outputs achieved*). Remember that *standard hours allowed* is a measure of actual *output* achieved. A key idea illustrated in Exhibit 8-7 is the versatility of the flexible budget. A flexible budget is geared to activity volume, and Exhibit 8-7 shows that activity volume can be measured in terms of either *actual inputs used* (columns A and B) or *standard inputs allowed* for *actual outputs achieved* (column C).

Exhibit 8-8 summarizes the general approach to overhead variances. The flexible-budget variances for fixed-overhead items are not subdivided here. Fixed-overhead flexible-budget variances are discussed in more detail in Chapter 16. Note that the sales activity variance for fixed overhead is zero, because as long as activities remain within relevant ranges, the fixed-overhead budget is the same at both planned and actual levels of activity.

Exhibit 8-8

General Approach to Analysis of Overhead Variances

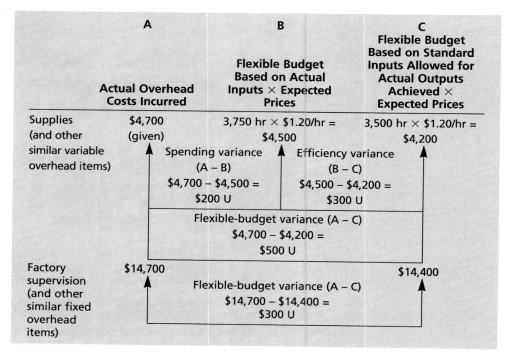

Highlights to Remember

Flexible budgets are geared to changing levels of activity rather than to the single, static level of the master budget. Flexible budgets may be tailored to particular levels of sales or cost-driver activity—before or after the fact. They tell how much revenue and cost to expect for any level of activity.

Cost functions, or flexible-budget formulas, reflect fixed- and variable-cost behavior and allow managers to compute budgets for any desired output or cost-driver activity level. The flexible budget amounts are computed by multiplying the variable cost per unit of activity times the level of activity expected for the actual outputs achieved.

The evaluation of performance is aided by feedback that compares actual results with budgeted expectations. The flexible-budget approach helps managers explain why the master budget was not achieved. Master budget variances are divided into (sales) activity and flexible-budget variances. Activity variances reflect the organization's effectiveness in meeting financial plans. Flexible-budget variances reflect the organization's efficiency at actual levels of activity.

Expectations form the basis for budgeting and performance evaluation. Expectations may be formalized as standard costs and may be incorporated into standard cost systems, but only expectations (which may be called standards) are required for master and flexible budgets. The most commonly used standards are considered to be attainable with reasonable effort.

Flexible-budget variances for variable inputs can be further broken down into price (or spending) and usage (or efficiency) variances. Price variances reflect the effects of changing input prices, holding usage of inputs constant at actual use. Usage variances reflect the effects of different levels of input usage, holding prices constant at expected prices.

Summary Problem for Your Review

Problem One appeared earlier in this chapter.

Problem Two

The following questions are based on the data contained in the Dominion Company illustration used in this chapter, on page 306.

- Direct materials: standard, 5 pounds per unit @ $2 per pound
- Direct labor: standard, 1/2 hour @ $16 per hour

Suppose the following were the actual results for production of 8,500 units:

1. Direct material: 46,000 pounds purchased and used at an actual unit price of $1.85 per pound, for an actual total cost of $85,100
2. Direct labor: 4,125 hours of labor used at an actual hourly rate of $16.80, for a total actual cost of $69,300

Required

1. Compute the flexible-budget variance and the price and usage variances for direct labor and direct material.
2. Suppose the company is organized so that the purchasing manager bears the primary responsibility for purchasing materials, and the production manager is responsible for the use of materials. Assume the same facts as in requirement 1 except that the purchasing manager bought 60,000 pounds of material. This means that there is an ending inventory of 14,000 pounds of material. Recompute the materials variances.

Solution to Problem Two

1. The variances are:

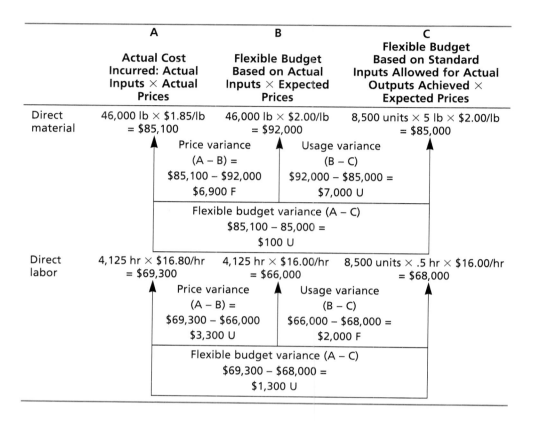

	A **Actual Cost Incurred: Actual Inputs × Actual Prices**	B **Flexible Budget Based on Actual Inputs × Expected Prices**	C **Flexible Budget Based on Standard Inputs Allowed for Actual Outputs Achieved × Expected Prices**
Direct material	46,000 lb × $1.85/lb = $85,100	46,000 lb × $2.00/lb = $92,000	8,500 units × 5 lb × $2.00/lb = $85,000

Price variance
(A – B) =
$85,100 – $92,000
$6,900 F

Usage variance
(B – C)
$92,000 – $85,000 =
$7,000 U

Flexible budget variance (A – C)
$85,100 – 85,000 =
$100 U

Direct labor	4,125 hr × $16.80/hr = $69,300	4,125 hr × $16.00/hr = $66,000	8,500 units × .5 hr × $16.00/hr = $68,000

Price variance
(A – B) =
$69,300 – $66,000
$3,300 U

Usage variance
(B – C)
$66,000 – $68,000 =
$2,000 F

Flexible budget variance (A – C)
$69,300 – $68,000 =
$1,300 U

2. Price variances are isolated at the most logical control point—time of purchase rather than time of use. In turn, the operating departments that later use the materials are generally charged at some predetermined budget, expected or standard price rather than at actual prices. This represents a slight modification of the approach in requirement 1 as shown at the top of the next page.

Note that this favorable price variance on balance may not be a good outcome—Dominion Company may not desire the extra inventory in excess of its immediate needs, and the favorable price variance may reflect that quality of the material is lower than planned. Note also that the usage variance is the same in requirements 1 and 2. Typically, the price and usage variances for materials now would be reported separately and not added together because they are based on different measures of volume. The price variance is based on inputs *purchased*, but the usage variance is based on inputs *used*.

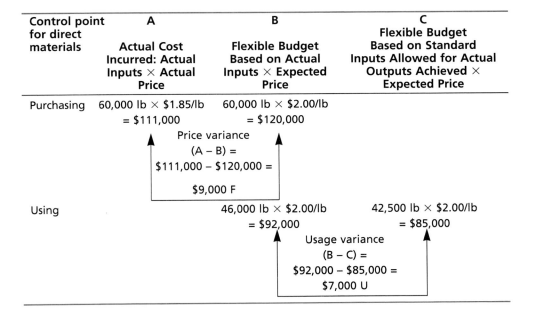

Control point for direct materials	A Actual Cost Incurred: Actual Inputs × Actual Price	B Flexible Budget Based on Actual Inputs × Expected Price	C Flexible Budget Based on Standard Inputs Allowed for Actual Outputs Achieved × Expected Price
Purchasing	60,000 lb × $1.85/lb = $111,000	60,000 lb × $2.00/lb = $120,000	
		Price variance (A − B) = $111,000 − $120,000 = $9,000 F	
Using		46,000 lb × $2.00/lb = $92,000	42,500 lb × $2.00/lb = $85,000
			Usage variance (B − C) = $92,000 − $85,000 = $7,000 U

Accounting Vocabulary

activity-level variance, *p. 298*
currently attainable standards, *p. 303*
effectiveness, *p. 298*
efficiency, *p. 298*
efficiency variance, *p. 307*
expected cost, *p. 301*
favorable expense variances, *p. 294*
flexible budget, *p. 295*
flexible-budget variances, *p. 298*

ideal standards, *p. 302*
master (static)-budget variances, *p. 294*
perfection standard, *p. 302*
price variance, *p. 307*
quantity variance, *p. 307*
sales-activity variance, *p. 301*
standard cost, *p. 301*
standard cost system, *p. 301*
static budget variance, *p. 294*

unfavorable expense variances, *p. 294*
usage variance, *p. 307*
variable budget, *p. 295*
variable-overhead spending variance, *p. 310*
variable-overhead efficiency variance, *p. 310*

Fundamental Assignment Material

8-A1   Flexible and Static Budgets

RDC Transportation Company's manager has had trouble interpreting operating performance for several years. The company has used a budget based on detailed expectations for the forthcoming quarter. For example, the condensed performance report for a recent quarter is shown at the top of the next page.

Although the manager was upset about not obtaining enough revenue, she was happy that her cost performance was favorable; otherwise her net operating income would be even worse.

The president was totally unhappy and remarked: "I can see some merit in comparing actual performance with budgeted performance because we can see whether actual revenue coincided with our best guess for budget purposes. But I can't see how this performance report helps me evaluate cost control performance."

	Budget	Actual	Variance
Net revenue	$8,000,000	$7,600,000	$400,000 U
Fuel	$ 160,000	$ 157,000	$ 3,000 F
Repairs and maintenance	80,000	78,000	2,000 F
Supplies and miscellaneous	800,000	788,000	12,000 F
Variable payroll	5,360,000	5,200,000	160,000 F
Total variable costs*	$6,400,000	$6,223,000	$177,000 F
Supervision	$ 160,000	$ 160,000	—
Rent	160,000	160,000	—
Depreciation	480,000	480,000	—
Other fixed costs	160,000	160,000	—
Total fixed costs	$ 960,000	$ 960,000	—
Total costs charged against revenue	$7,360,000	$7,183,000	$177,000 F
Operating income	$ 640,000	$ 417,000	$223,000 U

U = Unfavorable. F = Favorable.

* For purposes of this analysis, assume that all these costs are totally variable with respect to sales revenue. In practice, many are mixed and have to be subdivided into variable and fixed components before a meaningful analysis can be made. Also assume that the prices and mix of services sold remain unchanged.

Required

1. Prepare a columnar flexible budget for RDC at revenue levels of $7,000,000, $8,000,000 and $9,000,000. Use the format of the last three columns of Exhibit 8-2, page 296. Assume that the prices and mix of products sold are equal to the budgeted prices and mix.
2. Express the flexible budget for costs in formula form.
3. Prepare a condensed table showing the static (master) budget variance, the sales activity variance, and the flexible-budget variance. Use the format of Exhibit 8-4, page 299.

8A-2   Direct-Material and Direct-Labor Variances

The Handy Dandy Company manufactures metal giftware that is hand-shaped and hand-finished. The following standards were developed for a line of vases:

	Standard Inputs Expected for Each Unit of Output Achieved	Standard Price per Unit of Input
Direct materials	10 pounds	$ 6 per pound
Direct labor	5 hours	$25 per hour

During April, 550 vases were scheduled for production. However, only 525 were actually produced.

Direct materials purchased and used amounted to 5,500 pounds at a unit price of $5.25 per pound. Direct labor was actually paid $26.00 per hour, and 2,850 hours were used.

Required

1. Compute the standard cost per vase for direct materials and direct labor.
2. Compute the price variances and usage variances for direct materials and direct labor.
3. Based on these sketchy data, what clues for investigation are provided by the variances?

8-A3   Activity Level Variances

DataTech Company provides information systems services to local businesses. The costs of these services are driven by customer demand. One important cost is the cost of systems consultants who design data collecting, encoding, and reporting systems to fit customers' special needs. An overall cost driver is believed to be the number of these requests made to the systems consulting department. The expected variable cost of handling a request for June 19X7 was $60, and the number of requests expected was 75. Monthly fixed costs for the department (salaries, equipment depreciation, space costs) were budgeted at $7,000.

The actual number of requests serviced by systems consulting in June 19X7 was 90, and the total costs incurred by the department was $12,300. Of that amount, $7,800 was for fixed costs.

Required | Compute the master (static) budget variances and the flexible-budget variances for the systems consulting department for June 19X7.

8-B1   Summary Performance Reports

Consider the following data for Monarch Escrow Company:

1. Master budget data: sales, 2,500 clients at $35 each; variable costs, $25 per client; fixed costs, $15,000.
2. Actual results at actual prices: sales, 3,000 clients at $36 per client; variable costs, $80,000; fixed costs, $15,750.

Required | 1. Prepare a summary performance report similar to Exhibit 8-4, page 299.
2. Fill in the blanks:

Master budget operating income	$—
Variances	
Sales-activity variances	$ —
Flexible-budget variances	— —
Actual operating income	$—

8-B2   Material and Labor Variances

Consider the following data:

	Direct Material	Direct Labor
Actual price per unit of input (lb and hr)	$18	$12
Standard price per unit of input	$14	$13
Standard inputs allowed per unit of output	5	2
Actual units of input	56,000	30,000
Actual units of output (product)	14,400	14,400

Required | 1. Compute the price, usage, and flexible-budget variances for direct material and direct labor. Use U or F to indicate whether the variances are unfavorable or favorable.
2. Prepare a plausible explanation for the performance.

8-B3   Variable-Overhead Variances

You have been asked to prepare an analysis of the overhead costs in the billing department of a hospital. As an initial step, you prepare a summary of some events that bear on overhead for the most recent period. The variable-overhead flexible-budget variance was $5,000 unfavorable. The standard variable-overhead price per billing was $.06. Ten bills per hour is regarded as standard productivity per clerk. The total overhead incurred was $202,200, of which $134,500 was fixed. There were no variances for fixed overhead. The variable-overhead spending variance was $2,500 favorable.

Required

Find the following:
1. Variable-overhead efficiency variance
2. Actual hours of input
3. Standard hours allowed for output achieved

Additional Assignment Material

Questions

8-1. "The flex in the flexible budget relates solely to variable costs." Do you agree? Explain.

8-2. "We want a flexible budget because costs are difficult to predict. We need the flexibility to change budgeted costs as input prices change." Does a flexible budget serve this purpose? Explain.

8-3. "Effectiveness and efficiency go hand in hand. You can't have one without the other." Do you agree? Explain.

8-4. Differentiate between a master-budget variance and a flexible-budget variance.

8-5. Why do some companies classify direct-labor costs as part of factory overhead?

8-6. Differentiate between perfection standards and currently attainable standards.

8-7. What are two possible interpretations of "currently attainable standards"?

8-8. Why should a budgeted cost not be merely an extension of past experience?

8-9. "Price variances should be computed even if prices are regarded as being outside of company control." Do you agree? Explain.

8-10. Are direct-material price variances generally recognized when the materials are purchased or when they are used? Why?

8-11. Explain the role of understanding cost behavior and cost-driver activities for flexible budgeting.

8-12. Why do the techniques for controlling overhead differ from those for controlling direct materials?

8-13. How does the variable-overhead spending variance differ from the direct-labor price variance?

8-14. "Failure to meet price standards is the responsibility of the purchasing officer." Do you agree? Explain.

8-15. "A standard is one point in a band or range of acceptable outcomes." Evaluate this statement.

8-16. "A good control system places the blame for every unfavorable variance on someone in the organization. Without affixing blame, no one will take responsibility for cost control." Do you agree? Explain.

8-17. What are the key questions in the analysis and follow-up of variances?

8-18. What are some common causes of usage variances?

8-19. When should managers investigate variances?

Exercises

8-20 Flexible Budget

Elvira Company made 200,000 fountain pens in a given year. Its total manufacturing costs of $240,000 included $70,000 of fixed costs. Assume that no price changes will occur in the following year and that no changes in production methods are applicable. Compute the budgeted cost for producing 250,000 units in the following year.

8-21 Basic Flexible Budget

The superintendent of police of the city of Wichita is attempting to predict the costs of operating a fleet of police cars. Among the items of concern are fuel, $.18 per mile, and depreciation, $6,000 per car per year.

Required

The manager is preparing a flexible budget for the coming year. Prepare the flexible-budget amounts for fuel and depreciation for each car at a level of 40,000, 50,000, and 60,000 miles.

8-22   Flexible Budget

Consider the following data for the Boulder Delivery Service for a given month:

	Budget Formula per Unit	Various Levels of Output		
Units	—	6,000	7,000	8,000
Sales	$20	$?	$?	$?
Variable costs				
Direct material	?	48,000	?	?
Fuel	2	?	?	?
Fixed costs				
Depreciation		?	15,000	?
Salaries		?	?	55,000

Required   Fill in the unknowns.

8-23   Basic Flexible Budget

The budgeted prices for materials and direct labor per unit of finished product are $12 and $5, respectively. The production manager is delighted about the following data:

	Static (Master) Budget	Actual Costs	Variance
Direct materials	$96,000	$88,000	$8,000 F
Direct labor	40,000	37,600	2,400 F

Required   Is the manager's happiness justified? Prepare a report that might provide a more detailed explanation of why the static (master) budget was not achieved. Good output was 6,800 units.

8-24   Material and Labor Variances

Consider the following data:

	Direct Material	Direct Labor
Costs incurred: actual inputs × actual prices incurred	$150,000	$105,000
Actual inputs × expected prices	165,000	97,500
Standard inputs allowed for actual outputs achieved × expected prices	172,500	91,500

Required   Compute the price, usage, and flexible-budget variances for direct material and direct labor. Use U or F to indicate whether the variances are unfavorable or favorable.

8-25   Usage Variances

Assume that 9,000 plastic mannikins were produced. Suppose the standard direct-material allowance is two pounds per unit, at a cost per pound of $3. Actually, 20,000 pounds of materials (input) were used to produce the 9,000 units (output).

Similarly, assume that it is supposed to take 5 direct-labor hours to produce one unit, and that the standard hourly labor cost is $3. But 46,500 hours (input) were used to produce the 9,000 units in this Hong Kong factory.

Required   Compute the usage variances for direct material and direct labor.

8-26   Direct-Material Variances

The Morton Company uses a special fabric in the production of jackets. During August Morton purchased 10,000 square yards of the fabric @ $6.90 per yard and used 8,000 square yards in the production of 3,800 jackets. The standard allows 2 yards @ $7.10 per yard for each jacket.

Required   Calculate the material price variance and the material usage variance.

8-27   Labor Variances

The city of Austin has a sign shop where street signs of all kinds are manufactured and repaired. The manager of the shop uses standards to judge performance. Because a clerk mistakenly discarded some labor records, however, the manager has only partial data for October. She knows that the total direct-labor variance was $1,680 favorable, and that the standard labor price was $14 per hour. Moreover, a recent pay raise produced an unfavorable labor price variance for October of $1,120. The actual hours of input were 1,750.

Required   1. Find the actual labor price per hour.
2. Determine the standard hours allowed for the output achieved.

8-28   Activity-Level Variances

Materials support costs for the Martin Heavy Equipment Manufacturing Company depend on the weight of material (plate steel, castings, etc.) moved. For the current budget period and based on scheduled production, Martin expected to move 750,000 pounds of material at a cost of $.25 per pound. Several orders were canceled by customers, and Martin moved only 650,000 pounds of material. Total materials support costs for the period were $175,000.

Required   Compare actual support costs to the master-budget support costs by computing master budget, activity-level, and flexible-budget variances for materials support costs.

8-29   Multiple Choice
(CPA, adapted.)

1. Information on Barton Company's direct-labor costs is as follows:

Standard direct-labor rate	$ 12.50
Actual direct-labor rate	$ 11.25
Standard direct-labor-hours	12,000
Direct-labor usage variance—unfavorable	$14,500

What were the actual hours worked, rounded to the nearest hour? (a) 14,622, (b) 13,289, (c) 13,160, (d) 15,460.

2. Information on Kim Soon Company's direct-material costs is as follows:

Standard unit price	$ 4.50
Actual quantity purchased	1,800
Standard quantity allowed for actual production	1,650
Materials purchase price variance—favorable	$ 288

What was the actual purchase price per unit, rounded to the nearest penny? (a) $4.06, (b) $4.34, (c) $4.18, (d) $4.66.

Problems

8-30 National Park Service

The National Park Service prepared the following budget for one of its national parks for 19X8:

Revenue from fees	$6,000,000
Variable costs (miscellaneous)	600,000
Contribution margin	$5,400,000
Fixed costs (miscellaneous)	5,400,000
Operating income	$ 0

The fees were based on an average of 60,000 vehicle-admission days (vehicles multiplied by number of days in parks) per week for the 20-week season, multiplied by average entry and other fees of $6 per vehicle-admission day.

The season was booming for the first 4 weeks. There were major forest fires during the fifth week, however. A large percentage of the park was scarred by the fires. As a result, the number of visitors to the park dropped sharply during the remainder of the season.

Total revenue fell $1 million short of the original budget. Variable costs fell as expected, and fixed costs were unaffected except for hiring extra firefighters at a cost of $360,000.

Required

Prepare a columnar summary of performance, showing the original (static) budget, sales-activity variances, flexible budget, flexible-budget variances, and actual results.

8-31 Similarity of Direct-Labor and Variable-Overhead Variances

The V.X. Yee Company has had great difficulty controlling costs in Singapore during the past 3 years. Last month a standard cost and flexible-budget system was installed. A condensation of results for a department follows:

	Expected Cost per Standard Direct-Labor-Hour	Flexible-Budget Variance
Lubricants	$ .60	$ 300 F
Other supplies	.30	225 U
Rework	.60	450 U
Other indirect labor	1.50	450 U
Total variable overhead	$3.00	$ 825 U

F = Favorable. U = Unfavorable.

The department had initially planned to manufacture 9,000 audio speaker assemblies in 6,000 standard direct-labor-hours allowed. Material shortages and a heat wave resulted in the production of 8,100 units in 5,700 actual direct-labor-hours, however. The standard wage rate is $5.25 per hour, which was $.30 higher than the actual average hourly rate.

Required

1. Prepare a detailed performance report with two major sections: direct labor and variable overhead.
2. Prepare a summary analysis of price and usage variances for direct labor and spending and efficiency variances for variable overhead.

3. Explain the similarities and differences between the direct-labor and variable-overhead variances. What are some of the likely causes of the overhead variances?

8-32 Activity-Based Flexible Budget

This problem is based on the Chapter 4 discussion of activity-based costing on pages 136–142 and the Portland Power Company illustration. However, all the information needed is given here in the problem. Cost behavior analysis for the four activity centers in the Billing Department of Portland Power Company is given below.

Activity Center	Traceable Costs		Cost-Driver Activity
	Variable	Fixed	
Account inquiry	$ 79,910	$155,270	3,300 labor hours
Correspondence	$ 9,800	$ 25,584	2,800 letters
Account billing	$154,377	$ 81,400	2,440,000 lines
Bill verification	$ 10,797	$ 78,050	20,000 accounts

The Billing Department constructs a flexible budget for each activity center based on the following ranges of cost-driver activity:

Activity Center	Cost Driver	Relevant Range	
Account inquiry	Labor hours	3,000	5,000
Correspondence	Letters	2,500	3,500
Account billing	Lines	2,000,000	3,000,000
Bill verification	Accounts	15,000	25,000

Required

1. Develop flexible-budget formulas for each of the four activity centers.
2. Compute the budgeted total cost in each activity center for each of these levels of cost driver activity: (a) the smallest activity in the relevant range, (b) the midpoint of the relevant range, and (c) the highest activity in the relevant range.
3. Determine the total cost function for the Billing Department.
4. The following table gives the actual results for the Billing Department. Prepare a cost-control performance report comparing the flexible budget to actual results for each activity center. Compute flexible budget variances.

Activity Center	Cost-Driver Level (Actual)	Actual Cost
Account Inquiry	4,400 labor hours	$229,890
Correspondence	3,250 letters	$ 38,020
Account Billing	2,900,000 lines	$285,000
Bill Verification	22,500 accounts	$105,320

8-33 Variance Analysis

The Stanko Company uses standard costs and a flexible budget to control its manufacture of fine chocolates. The purchasing agent is responsible for material price variances, and the production manager is responsible for all other variances. Operating data for the past week are summarized as follows:

1. Finished units produced: 4,000 cases of chocolates.
2. Direct material: Purchases, 6,400 pounds @ 15 Swiss francs (SF) per pound; standard price is 16 SF per pound. Used, 4,300 pounds. Standard allowed per case produced, 1 pound.
3. Direct labor: Actual costs, 6,400 hours @ 30.5 SF, or 195,200 SF. Standard allowed per good case produced, 1½ hours. Standard price per direct-labor-hour, 30 SF.
4. Variable manufacturing overhead: Actual costs, 70,400 SF. Budget formula is 10 SF per standard direct-labor-hour.

Required

1. a. Material purchase-price variance
   b. Material usage variance
   c. Direct-labor price variance
   d. Direct-labor usage variance
   e. Variable manufacturing-overhead spending variance
   f. Variable manufacturing-overhead efficiency variance

(*Hint*: For format, see the solution to the second Summary Problem for Your Review, pages 314–15.)

2. a. What is the budget allowance for direct labor?
   b. Would it be any different if production were 5,000 cases?

8-34 Summary Explanation
Consider the following data. Except for physical units, all quantities are in dollars:

	Actual Results at Actual Prices	Flexible-Budget Variances	Flexible Budget	Sales-Activity Variances	Static (Master) Budget
Physical units	80,000	—	?	?	72,000
Sales	?	6,400 F	?	?	720,000
Variable costs	496,000	?	480,000	?	?
Contribution margin	?	?	?	?	?
Fixed costs	?	8,000 U	?	?	192,000
Operating income	?	?	?	?	?

Required

1. Fill in the unknowns.
2. Give a brief summary explanation of why the original target operating income was not attained.

8-35 Explanation of Variance in Income
The T & J Income Tax Service processes income tax returns that result in standard contribution margins averaging 70% of dollar sales and average selling prices of $50 per return. Average productivity is four returns per hour. Some preparers work for sales commissions and others for an hourly rate. The master budget for 19X6 had predicted processing 800,000 returns, but only 700,000 returns were processed.

Fixed costs of rent, supervision, advertising, and other items were budgeted at $21.5 million, but the budget was exceeded by $800,000 because of extra advertising in an attempt to boost revenue.

There were no variances from the average selling prices, but the actual commissions paid to preparers and the actual productivity per hour resulted in flexible-budget variances (i.e., total price and efficiency variances) for variable costs of $900,000 unfavorable.

The president was unhappy because the budgeted operating income of $6.5 million was not achieved. He said, "Sure, we had unfavorable variable-cost variances, but our operating income was down far more than that. Please explain why."

Required Explain why the budgeted operating income was not attained. Use a presentation similar to Exhibit 8-4, page 299. Enough data have been given to permit you to construct the complete exhibit by filling in the known items and then computing the unknown. Complete your explanation by summarizing what happened, using no more than three sentences.

8-36 Summary of Airline Performance
Consider the performance (in thousands of dollars) of Economy Airlines for a given year in the following table.

	Actual Results at Actual Prices	Master Budget	Variance
Revenue	$?	$300,000	$?
Variable expenses	200,000	195,000*	5,000U
Contribution margin	?	105,000	?
Fixed expenses	77,000	75,000	2,000U
Operating income	$?	30,000	$?

* Includes jet fuel of $90,000.

The master budget had been based on a budget of $.20 per revenue passenger mile. A revenue passenger mile is one paying passenger flown one mile. An average airfare decrease of 8% had helped generate an increase in passenger miles flown that was 10% in excess of the static budget for the year.

The price per gallon of jet fuel rose above the price used to formulate the static budget. The average jet fuel price increase for the year was 12%.

Required 1. As an explanation for the president, prepare a summary performance report that is similar to Exhibit 8-4, page 299.
2. Assume that jet fuel costs are purely variable and the use of fuel was at the same level of efficiency as predicted in the static budget. What portion of the flexible-budget variance for variable expenses is attributable to jet fuel expenses? Explain.

8-37 Flexible and Static Budgets
Beta Alpha Psi, the accounting fraternity, recently held a dinner dance. The original (static) budget and actual results were as follows:

	Budget	Actual	Variance
Attendees	75	90	
Revenue	$2,625	$3,255	$630 F
Chicken dinners @ $17.60	1,320	1,668	348U
Beverages, $6 per person	450	466	16U
Club rental, $75 plus 8% tax	81	81	0
Music, 3 hours @ $250 per hour	750	875	125U
Profit	$ 24	$ 165	$141 F

Required   **1.** Subdivide each variance into a sales activity variance portion and a flexible-budget variance portion. Use the format of Exhibit 8-4, page 299.
2. Provide possible explanations for the variances.

8-38   University Flexible Budgeting

(CMA, adapted.) The University of Coyne offers an extensive continuing education program in many cities throughout the state. For the convenience of its faculty and administrative staff and also to save costs, the university operates a motor pool. The motor pool operated with 25 vehicles until February of this year, when an additional automobile was acquired. The motor pool furnishes gasoline, oil, and other supplies for the cars and hires one mechanic who does routine maintenance and minor repairs. Major repairs are done at a nearby commercial garage. A supervisor manages the operations.

Each year the supervisor prepares an operating budget, informing university management of the funds needed to operate the pool. Depreciation on the automobiles is recorded in the budget in order to determine the cost per mile.

The schedule below presents the annual budget approved by the university. The actual costs for March are compared with one-twelfth of the annual budget.

University
Motor Pool
Budget Report for
March 19X6

	Annual Budget	One-Month Budget	March Actual	Over (Under)
Gasoline	$ 49,500	$ 4,125	$ 6,400	$2,275
Oil, minor repairs, parts, and supplies	9,000	750	800	50
Outside repairs	3,600	300	60	(240)
Insurance	7,500	625	650	25
Salaries and benefits	33,600	2,800	2,800	—
Depreciation	33,000	2,750	2,860	110
	$136,200	$11,350	$13,570	$2,220
Total miles	900,000	75,000	84,000	
Cost per mile	$ .1513	$ .1513	$ .1615	
Number of automobiles	25	25	26	

The annual budget was constructed based on the following assumptions:

1. 25 automobiles in the pool
2. 36,000 miles per year per automobile
3. 20 miles per gallon per automobile
4. $1.10 per gallon of gas
5. $.01 per mile for oil, minor repairs, parts, and supplies
6. $144 per automobile in outside repairs

The supervisor is unhappy with the monthly report comparing budget and actual costs for March; he claims it presents his performance unfairly. His previous employer used flexible budgeting to compare actual costs with budgeted amounts.

Required   **1.** Employing flexible-budgeting techniques, prepare a report that shows budgeted amounts, actual costs, and monthly variation for March.
2. Explain briefly the basis of your budget figure for outside repairs.

8-39   Straightforward Variance Analysis

Soft Rock Inc. uses a standard cost system. The month's data regarding its iron castings follow:

- Material purchased and used, 3,400 pounds
- Direct-labor costs incurred, 5,500 hours, $20,900
- Variable-overhead costs incurred, $4,750
- Finished units produced, 1,000
- Actual material cost, $.90 per pound
- Variable overhead rate, $.80 per hour
- Standard direct-labor cost, $4 per hour
- Standard material cost, $1 per pound
- Standard pounds of material in a finished unit, 3
- Standard direct-labor hours per finished unit, 5

Required   Prepare schedules of all variances, using the format of Exhibit 8-7, p. 311.

8-40   Standard Material Allowances

(CMA.) Branson Company is a chemical manufacturer that supplies industrial users. The company plans to introduce a new chemical solution and needs to develop a standard product cost for this new solution.

The new chemical solution is made by combining a chemical compound (nyclyn) and a solution (salex), boiling the mixture, adding a second compound (protet), and bottling the resulting solution in 20-liter containers. The initial mix, which is 20 liters in volume, consists of 24 kilograms of nyclyn and 19.2 liters of salex. A 20% reduction in volume occurs during the boiling process. The solution is then cooled slightly before 10 kilograms of protet are added; the addition of protet does not affect the total liquid volume.

The purchase prices of the raw materials used in the manufacture of this new chemical solution are as follows:

Nyclyn	$1.50 per kilogram
Salex	2.10 per liter
Protet	2.80 per kilogram

Required   Determine the standard quantity for each of the raw materials needed to produce 20 liters of Branson Company's new chemical solution and the standard materials cost of 20 liters of the new product.

8-41   Role of Defective Units and Nonproductive Time in Setting Standards

Yong Chee owns and operates Westward Machining, a subcontractor to several aerospace industry contractors. When Mr. Chee wins a bid to produce a piece of equipment, he sets standard costs for the production of the item. Actual manufacturing costs are compared with the standards to judge the efficiency of production.

In April 19X6 Westward won a bid to produce 15,000 units of a shielded component used in a navigation device. Specifications for the components were very tight, and Mr. Chee expected that 20% of the components would fail his final inspection, even if every care was exercised in production. There was no way to identify defective items before production was complete. Therefore 18,750 units had to be produced to get 15,000 good components. Standards were set to include an allowance for the expected number of defective items.

Each final component contained 2.7 pounds of direct materials, and normal scrap from production was expected to average .5 pounds per unit. The direct material was expected to cost $12.25 per pound plus $.75 per pound for shipping and handling.

Machining of the components required close attention by skilled machinists. Each component required 4 hours of machining time. The machinists were paid $22 per hour and worked 40-hour weeks. Of the 40 hours, an average of 32 hours was spent directly on production. The other 8 hours consisted of time for breaks and waiting time when machines were broken down or there was no work to be done. Nevertheless, all payments to machinists were considered direct labor, whether or not they were for time spent directly on production. In addition to the basic wage rate, Westward paid fringe benefits averaging $5 per hour and payroll taxes of 10% of the basic wages.

Required   Determine the standard cost of direct materials and direct labor for each good unit of output.

8-42   Automation and Direct Labor as Overhead

The Durango Company has a highly automated manufacturing process for producing a variety of airplane parts. Through the use of computer-aided manufacturing and robotics, the company has reduced its labor costs to only 5% of total manufacturing costs. Consequently, labor is not accounted for as a separate item but is considered part of overhead.

The static budget for producing 750 units of part Z624 in March 19X8 is:

Direct materials	$18,000*
Overhead	
Supplies	1,875
Power	1,310
Rent and other building services	2,815
Factory labor	1,500
Depreciation	4,500
Total manufacturing costs	$30,000

* 3 pounds per unit x $8 per pound x 750 units

Supplies and power are considered to be variable overhead. The other overhead items are fixed costs.

Actual costs in March 19X8 for producing 900 units of Z624 were:

Direct materials	$21,645*
Overhead	
Supplies	2,100
Power	1,612
Rent and other building services	2,775
Factory labor	1,650
Depreciation	4,500
Total manufacturing costs	$34,282

* 2,775 pounds purchased and used @ $7.80 per pound

Required

1. Compute (a) the direct-materials price and usage variances and (b) the flexible-budget variance for each overhead item.
2. Comment on the way Durango Company accounts for and controls factory labor.

8-43   Review of Major Points in Chapter

The following questions are based on the Dominion Company data contained in the illustration used in the chapter, p. 295 and 306.

1. Suppose actual production and sales were 8,000 units instead of 7,000 units. (a) Compute the sales-activity variance. Is the performance of the marketing function the sole explanation for this variance? Why? (b) Using a flexible budget, compute the budgeted contribution margin, the budgeted operating income, budgeted direct material, and budgeted direct labor.

2. Suppose the following were the actual results for the production of 8,000 units:

   Direct material: 42,000 pounds were used at an actual unit price of $1.80, for a total actual cost of $75,600.

   Direct labor: 4,125 hours were used at an actual hourly rate of $16.40, for a total actual cost of $67,650.

   Compute the flexible-budget variance and the price and usage variances for direct materials and direct labor. Present your answers in the form shown in Exhibit 8-7, p. 311.

3. Suppose the company is organized so that the purchasing manager bears the primary responsibility for the acquisition prices of materials, and the production manager bears the primary responsibility for usage but not responsibility for unit prices. Assume the same facts as in requirement 2 except that the purchasing manager acquired 60,000 pounds of materials. This means that there is an ending inventory of 18,000 pounds. Would your variance analysis of materials in requirement 2 change? Why? Show computations.

8-44   Hospital Costs and Explanation of Variances

The emergency room at Doctor's Hospital uses a flexible budget based on patients seen as a measure of activity. An adequate staff of attending and on-call physicians must be maintained at all times, so physician scheduling is unaffected by patient activity. Nurse scheduling varies as volume changes, however. A standard of .5 nurse-hours per patient visit was set. Average hourly pay for nurses is $14, ranging from $8 to $17 per hour. All materials are considered to be supplies, a part of overhead; there are no direct materials. A statistical study showed that the cost of supplies and other variable overhead is more closely associated with nurse-hours than with patient visits. The standard for supplies and other variable overhead is $10 per nursing hour.

The head physician of the emergency room unit, Sandy Cox, is responsible for control of costs. During December the emergency room unit treated 4,000 patients. The budget and actual costs were as follows:

	Budget	Actual	Variance
Patient visits	3,800	4,000	200
Nursing hours	1,900	2,070	170
Nursing cost	$ 26,600	$ 31,000	$4,400
Supplies and other variable overhead	19,000	20,320	1,320
Fixed costs	92,600	92,600	0
Total cost	$138,200	$144,920	$6,720

Required

1. Calculate price and usage variances for nursing costs.
2. Calculate spending and efficiency variances for supplies and other variable overhead.
3. Dr. Cox has been asked to explain the variances to the chief of staff. Provide possible explanations.

8-45   Review Problem on Standards and Flexible Budgets; Answers Are Provided
The Cowboy Leather Company makes a variety of leather goods. It uses standard costs and a flexible budget to aid planning and control. Budgeted variable overhead at a 45,000-direct-labor-hour level is $27,000.

During April the company had an unfavorable variable-overhead efficiency variance of $1,150. Material purchases were $241,900. Actual direct-labor costs incurred were $140,700. The direct-labor usage variance was $5,100 unfavorable. The actual average wage rate was $.20 lower than the average standard wage rate.

The company uses a variable-overhead rate of 20% of standard direct-labor *cost* for flexible-budgeting purposes. Actual variable overhead for the month was $30,750.

Required Compute the following amounts; then use *U* or *F* to indicate whether requested variances are unfavorable or favorable.
1. Standard direct-labor cost per hour
2. Actual direct-labor hours worked
3. Total direct-labor price variance
4. Total flexible budget for direct-labor costs
5. Total direct-labor variance
6. Variable-overhead spending variance in total

Answers to Problem 8-45.

1. $3. The variable-overhead rate is $.60, obtained by dividing $27,000 by 45,000 hours. Therefore the direct-labor rate must be $.60 ÷ .20 = $3.
2. 50,250 hours. Actual costs, $140,700 ÷ ($3 – $.20) = 50,250 hours.
3. $10,050 F. 50,250 actual hours × $.20 = $10,050.
4. $145,650. Usage variance was $5,100 U. Therefore, excess hours must have been $5,100 ÷ $3 = 1,700. Consequently, standard hours allowed must be 50,250 – 1,700 = 48,550. Flexible budget = 48,550 × $3 = $145,650.
5. $4,950 F. $145,650 – $140,700 = $4,950 F; or $10,050 F – $5,100 U = $4,950 F.
6. $470 U. Flexible budget = 48,550 × $.60 = $29,130. Total variance = $30,750 – $29,130 = $1,620 U. Price variance = $1,620 – $1,150. Efficiency variance = $470 U.

Case

8-46   Activity-Based Costing and Flexible Budgeting
The new printing department provides printing services to the other departments of Shark Advertising, Inc. Before the establishment of the in-house printing department, other departments contracted with external printers for their printing work. The Shark printing policy is that using departments are charged for the variable printing costs on the basis of number of pages printed. Fixed costs are recovered in pricing of external jobs.

The first year's budget for the printing department was based on the department's expected total costs divided by the planned number of pages to be printed.

The projected annual number of pages to be printed was 420,000, and total variable costs were budgeted to be $420,000. Most government accounts and all internal jobs were expected to use only single color printing. Variable costs were estimated based on the average variable cost of composing and printing a four-color page that is one-fourth graphics and three-fourths text. The amount of graphics also affects prepress or layout work. The expected annual costs for each division were as follows:

Department	Planned Pages Printed	Variable Cost per Page	Budgeted Charges
Government accounts	90,000	$1	$ 90,000
Commercial accounts	300,000	1	300,000
Central administration	30,000	1	30,000
Total	420,000		$420,000

After the first month of using the internal printing department, the printing department announced that its variable cost estimate of $1 per page was too low. The first month's actual costs were $48,000 to print 40,000 pages.

Government accounts	9,000 pages
Commercial accounts	27,500
Central administration	3,500

Three reasons were cited for higher than expected costs: All departments were using more printing services than planned, and government and internal jobs were using more four-color printing and more graphics than expected. The printing department also argued that additional four-color printing equipment would have to be purchased if demand for four-color printing continued to grow.

1. Compare the printing department actual results, static budget, and flexible budget for the month just completed.

2. Discuss possible reasons why the printing department static budget was inaccurate.

3. An activity-based costing (ABC) study completed by a consultant indicated that printing costs are driven by number of pages (@ $.30 per page), number of colors (@ $.25 per color per page), and hours of prepress (layout) work ($40 per hour).

   a. Discuss the likely effects of using the ABC results for budgeting and control of printing department use.

   b. Discuss the assumptions regarding cost behavior implied in the ABC study results.

   c. Central administration accounts during the first month (3,500 pages) used four colors per page, and required 6 hours of prepress work. Compare the cost of central administration accounts under the old and the proposed ABC system.

9 Management Control Systems and Responsibility Accounting

QualMed Plans for Health uses a powerful management information system and video teleconferencing network to improve company performance by assuring the highest quality health care and controling costs. *Courtesy QualMed*

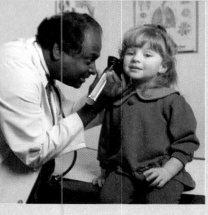

Learning Objectives

When you have finished studying this chapter, you should be able to

1 Describe the relationship of management control systems to organizational goals and subgoals.

2 Explain how the concept of responsibility accounting defines an organizational subunit as a cost center, a profit center, or an investment center.

3 Explain the importance of evaluating performance and how it impacts motivation, goal congruence, and employee effort.

4 Compare financial and nonfinancial performance, how they are interdependent, and why planning and control systems should consider both.

5 Prepare segment income statements for evaluating profit and investment centers using the contribution margin and controllable-cost concepts.

6 Measure performance against quality, cycle time, and productivity objectives.

7 Describe the difficulties of management control in service and nonprofit organizations.

8 Explain how management control systems must evolve with changing times.

The previous chapters have presented many important tools of management accounting. Tools such as activity-based costing, relevant costing, budgeting, and variance analysis are each useful by themselves. They are most useful, however, when they are parts of an integrated *system*—an orderly, logical plan to coordinate and evaluate all the activities of the organization, from the long-range planning of the chief executive officer, to the individual responses to customer or client inquiries, to the maintenance of physical assets. Managers of most organizations today, for example, realize that long-run success depends on focusing on cost, quality, and service—three components of the competitive edge. This chapter considers how management accounting tools combined into a management control system focus resources and talents of the individuals in an organization on such goals as cost, quality, and service. As you will see, no single system is inherently superior to another. The "best" system is the one that consistently leads to decisions that meet the organization's goals and objectives.

This chapter builds on previous ones to present how the individual tools of management accounting are blended systematically to help achieve organizational goals. The chapter discusses a rough sequence of steps to follow to design a successful management control *system*:

- Specify organizational goals, subgoals, and objectives.
- Identify responsibility centers.
- Develop measures of performance for motivation and goal congruence.
- Measure and report financial performance.
- Measure and report nonfinancial performance.

The chapter also discusses management control in service, government, and nonprofit organizations.

■ MANAGEMENT CONTROL SYSTEMS AND ORGANIZATIONAL GOALS

management control system A logical integration of management accounting tools to gather and report data and to evaluate performance.

The foundation of control is the planning process. The outcome of planning, whether it be a mission statement, long-range objectives, or operating budgets, provides the basis for control. A **management control system** is a logical integration of management accounting tools to gather and report data and to evaluate performance. A well-designed management control system aids and coordinates the process of making decisions and motivates individuals throughout the organization to act in concert. A management control system coordinates forecasting sales and cost-driver activity levels, budgeting, measuring and evaluating performance, and motivating employees. Indeed, explicit coordination of individuals' activities, actions, and choices is the hallmark of the management control system.

Information to support the management control system often comes primarily from the organization's financial accounting system. Yet, too often, financial accounting systems focus on technical details of data processing or external financial reporting, or emphasize compliance with legal requirements or detection of fraud, but give little consideration to employee motivation, performance evaluation, or management decision making. For example, most financial accounting systems do not distinguish between fixed- and variable-cost behavior and are not concerned with using appropriate cost drivers, both of which may be critical for management decision making. Thus, some organizations maintain multiple accounting systems—one for financial reporting and one to support management control. Whether it is part of one large system or a separate system, however, the *management control system* should be designed to improve decision making within an organization. The management control system is distinguished from a financial accounting system by its focus on organizational goals and objectives, internal management decision making, and motivation and evaluation of performance consistent with the organization's goals.

Objective 1

Describe the relationship of management control systems to organizational goals and subgoals

Organizational Goals

The first step in designing a management control system is to specify the organization's goals. Every organization exists because some individuals, acting alone or collectively, seek to achieve some *purpose* over the long run. These individuals are called stakeholders. In open organizations, stakeholders include a variety of groups—shareholders, employees, customers, suppliers, and community organizations. All of these groups have interests in the organization's activities, and each provides input to the planning process. The goals of the organization should reflect the interests of these groups. For example, UNICEF's long-run purpose and goal is to improve the condition of children throughout the world, especially in developing and underdeveloped countries. For another example, the long-run goal of profit-seeking firms (such as IBM) in a market economy is to generate competitive levels of profit. Organizations' goals vary across individuals, ownership, cultures, political systems, and time, to mention just a few factors.

Organizational Subgoals and Objectives

Broad goals, such as achieving competitive profits, usually are too vague to provide guidance for individuals who manage and work in the organizations. Consequently, the top managers of most successful organizations (those that meet their overriding goal) specify *subgoals* and *objectives*, and develop means of motivating and evaluating performance in achieving them *as a means of achieving the organization's overall goal.*

An organization's *subgoals* are usually called other names, such as *critical success factors, key variables, critical variables,* or *key result areas*. Top management judges these subgoals to be more specific than the dominant, overall goal, such as long-run, competitive profitability. Surveys indicate that many executives believe that to be successful in the 1990s, businesses need to focus on the following five critical success factors:

1. Customer responsiveness
2. Profitability
3. Quality
4. Innovation
5. Flexibility

Although subgoals give members of an organization more focus than an overall goal, they still do not give lower-level managers and employees the direction they need to guide their daily actions. Objectives—*specific tangible achievements* that can be observed on a short-term basis—provide this direction. For example, consider AMP Incorporated (1994 annual sales of over $4 billion and over 30,000 employees), producer of electronic connection devices and related tools and machines. To achieve its subgoal of "industry leadership in quality, delivery, service, and innovation," AMP launched a broad system (its "Plan for Excellence") for continuous improvement in the areas of quality, delivery, and service. This program counts on employee-generated, "bottom-up" improvements in such specific *objectives* as scrap rates, response times, and on-time deliveries. Progress is monitored and compared with the performance of companies noted for their "world-class" success in those areas. By meeting such objectives as on-time delivery, AMP Incorporated expects to attain industry leadership in customer deliveries and service, and, in turn, its overriding goal of competitive profitability.

Balance of Goals, Subgoals, and Objectives

While working toward subgoals and objectives is critical in any organization, be aware of their *short-run* nature. Overemphasis on any single subgoal or objective can easily create a focus on the short run, to the detriment of the long-run organizational goals. For example, some critics insist that many U.S. companies overstress short-run profits in contrast to successful Japanese and European companies. Although not all U.S. firms are short-run oriented, examples of a short-run focus abound. According to a former chief executive of ITT: "Every CEO says he plans for the long term. But every CEO lies. He's always temporizing with quarterly earnings. If he doesn't hack it quarter to quarter, he doesn't survive." In one study, the average holding period of stock of U.S. companies went from 7 years to less than 2 years during 1960–1990. Thus, key stakeholders have a short-run focus that often is reflected in management's actions.

Pressure for short-term profits can come from inside and outside a business. CEOs worry about how stock analysts will respond if profits drop even briefly. They and other top managers feel the pull of compensation plans that are based on short-term profit measures. Lower-level managers feel pressure to demonstrate that they deserve promotion, so they too have incentives to work for short-term profits that may not be beneficial in the long run. We may deplore these decisions, but our criticism should be aimed at the objectives and the management control systems as much as at the individuals involved. The objectives and systems were misspecified—they emphasized short-run performance at the expense of long-run performance. Design of a management control system that emphasizes short-run objectives that are congruent with long-run goals is both a challenging and vital task.

To encourage a longer-term view, for example, many companies are changing the way they pay bonuses. In 1992 AT&T changed from paying bonuses in cash or stock to paying them in AT&T stock *options* that require increases in stock prices before they can be exercised (a stock option is the right to purchase a share of a firm at a stated price) to shift the strategic orientation of AT&T's senior management to a more long-term view. Many companies also have instituted Employee Stock Ownership Plans (ESOPs) in part to promote a long-run focus for all employees.

Balancing the various subgoals and objectives is a critical part of management control. Sometimes the management control system ignores key success factors or inadvertantly emphasizes the wrong factors. Managers often face trade-off decisions. For example, a manager can increase market share, at least in the short run, by cutting prices, but this may also mean cutting profits. Making wise trade-offs or finding other, innovative solutions to the trade-offs often makes the difference between success and failure of managers and the organizations they oversee.

■ DESIGNING MANAGEMENT CONTROL SYSTEMS

To create a management control system that meets the organization's needs, designers need to recognize existing constraints, identify responsibility centers, weigh costs and benefits, provide motivations to achieve goal congruence and managerial effort, and install internal controls.

Process of Working Within Constraints

Every management control system needs to fit the organization's goals. In addition, a management control system must fit into the organization's structure. Some firms are organized primarily by *functions* such as manufacturing, sales, and service. Others are organized by *divisions* that bear profit responsibility along product or geographical lines. Still others may be organized by some hybrid arrangement, as in the case of Barleycorn, Inc., a retail grocery company with the basic organizational structure shown in Exhibit 9-1.

Exhibit 9-1

Organization Chart of Barleycorn, Inc.

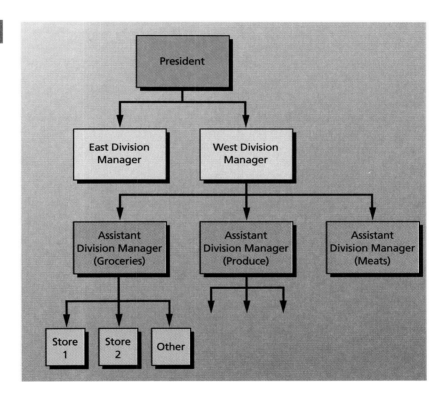

Most of the time, changes in control systems are piecemeal improvements rather than complete replacements. Occasionally, however, the management control system designer is able to persuade top management to change the organization structure before redesigning the system. Large companies may use an autonomous division to experiment with changes in organization structure and management control systems before implementing wholesale changes throughout the organization. For example, Champion International Corporation's mill in Hamilton, Ohio, which produces products for the premium paper market, changed its organizational structure when it implemented flexible manufacturing and just-in-time production. Newly adopted goals such as reduced cycle time and first-pass yield (the percentage of product flowing directly without rework to its intended destination) resulted in new demands on the accounting function. Accountants now include nonfinancial performance measures along with financial results and work with production management as "business partners."

Identification of Responsibility Centers

responsibility center
A set of activities assigned to a manager, a group of managers, or other employees.

In addition to organizational structures, designers of management control systems must consider the desired *responsibility centers* in an organization. A **responsibility center** is defined as a set of activities assigned to a manager, a group of managers, or other employees. A set of machines and machining tasks, for example, may be a responsibility center for a production supervisor; the full production department may be a responsibility center for the department head; and the entire organization may be a responsibility center for the president. In some organizations, management responsibility is shared by groups of employees to create wide "ownership" of management decisions, allow creative decision making, and prevent one person's concern (or lack of concern) for risks of failure to dominate decisions.

responsibility accounting
Identifying what parts of the organization have primary responsibility for each objective, developing measures of achievement of objectives, and creating reports of these measures by organization subunit or responsibility center.

cost center A responsibility center for which costs are accumulated.

An effective management control system gives each lower-level manager responsibility for a group of activities and objectives and then reports on (1) the results of the activities, (2) the manager's influence on those results, and (3) effects of uncontrollable events. Such a system has innate appeal for most top managers because it helps them delegate decision making and frees them to plan and control. Lower-level managers appreciate the autonomy of decision making they inherit. Thus system designers apply **responsibility accounting** to identify what parts of the organization have primary responsibility for each objective, develop measures of achievement of objectives, and create reports of these measures by organization subunit or responsibility center. Responsibility centers usually have multiple objectives (e.g., cost and quality) that the management control system monitors. Responsibility centers usually are classified according to their *financial* responsibility as cost centers, profit centers, or investment centers.

Cost, Profit, and Investment Centers

Objective 2

Explain how the concept of responsibility accounting defines an organizational subunit as a cost center, a profit center, or an investment center

profit centers A responsibility center for controlling revenues as well as costs (or expenses)—that is, profitability.

A **cost center** is a responsibility center for which costs are accumulated. Its financial responsibilities are to control and report costs only. An entire department may be considered a single cost center, or a department may contain several cost centers. For example, although an assembly department may be supervised by one manager, it may contain several assembly lines and regard each assembly line as a separate cost center. Likewise, within each line, separate machines or test equipment may be regarded as separate cost centers. The determination of the number of cost centers depends on cost-benefit considerations—do the benefits of smaller cost centers (for planning, control, and evaluation) exceed the higher costs of reporting?

Unlike cost centers, **profit centers** have responsibility for controlling revenues as well as costs (or expenses)—that is, profitability. Despite the name, a profit center can exist in nonprofit organizations (though it might not be referred to as such) when a responsibility center receives revenues for its services. For example, the Western Area Power Authority (WAPA) is charged with recovering its costs of operations through sales of power to electric utilities in the western United States. WAPA essentially is a profit center with the objective of breaking even. All profit center managers are responsible for both revenues and costs, but they may not be expected to maximize profits.

An **investment center** goes a step further. Its success is measured not only by its income but also by relating that income to its invested capital, as in a ratio of income to the value of the capital employed. In practice, the term investment center is not widely used. Instead, the term profit center is used indiscriminately to describe centers that are always assigned responsibility for revenues and expenses, but may or may not be assigned responsibility for the capital investment.

investment center A responsibility center whose success is measured not only by its income but also by relating that income to its invested capital, as in a ratio of income to the value of the capital employed.

Weighing of Costs and Benefits

The designer of the management control system must also weigh the costs and benefits of various alternatives, given the circumstances of the specific organization. No system is perfect, but one system may be better than another if it can improve operating decisions at a reasonable cost.

Both benefits and costs of management control systems are often difficult to measure, and both may become apparent only after experimentation or use. For example, the director of accounting policy of Citicorp has stated that, after several years of experience with a very detailed management control system, the system has proved to be too costly to administer relative to the perceived benefits. Accordingly, Citicorp planned to return to a simpler, less costly—though less precise—management control system.

Motivation of Employees to Achieve Goal Congruence and Exert Managerial Effort

goal congruence A condition where employees, working in their own personal interests, make decisions that help meet the overall goals of the organization.

managerial effort Exertion toward a goal or objective including all conscious actions (such as supervising, planning, and thinking) that result in more efficiency and effectiveness.

To achieve maximum benefits at minimum cost, a management control system must foster *goal congruence* and *managerial effort*. **Goal congruence** exists when individuals and groups aim at the same organizational goals. Goal congruence is achieved when employees, working in their own perceived best interests, make decisions that help meet the overall goals of the organization. **Managerial effort** is defined as exertion toward a goal or objective. Effort here means not merely working faster but also working *better*. Effort includes all conscious actions (such as supervising, planning, and thinking) that result in more efficiency and effectiveness. Effort is a matter of degree—it is optimized when individuals and groups *strive* for their objectives.

Goal congruence can exist with little accompanying effort, and vice versa, but *incentives* are necessary for both to be achieved. The challenge of management control system design is to specify objectives and rewards that induce (or at least do not discourage) employee decisions that would achieve organizational goals. For example, an organization may specify one of its subgoals to be continuous improvement in employee efficiency and effectiveness. Employees, however, might perceive that continuous improvements will result in tighter standards, faster pace of work, and loss of jobs. Even though they may agree with management that continuous improvements are competitively necessary, they should not be expected to exert effort for continuous improvements unless incentives are in place to make this effort in their own best interests. You may

Objective 3

Explain the importance of evaluating performance and how it impacts motivation, goal congruence, and employee effort be pleasantly surprised that some individuals will act selflessly, but management control systems should be designed to take advantage of more typical human behavior. Be aware that self-interest may be perceived differently in different cultures.

As another example, students may enroll in a college course because their goal is to learn about management accounting. The faculty and the students share the same goal, but goal congruence is not enough. Faculty also introduce incentives in the form of a grading system to spur student effort. Grading is a form of *performance evaluation*, as is use of management control reports for raises, promotions, and other forms of rewards in other settings. Performance evaluation is a widely used means of improving congruence and effort because most individuals tend to perform better when they receive feedback that is tied to their own self-interest. Thus Allen-Bradley Co., Corning, and other manufacturers who set quality improvements as critical subgoals put quality objectives into the bonus plans of top managers. Corning has quality incentives for factory workers as well.

To achieve goal congruence and managerial effort, designers of management control systems focus on *motivating* employees. **Motivation** has been defined as a drive toward some selected goal that creates effort and action toward that goal. Yet employees differ widely in their motivations. The system designer's task is more complex, ill structured, and more affected by human behavior than many people believe at first. The system designer must align individuals' self-interest with the goals of the organization. Thus the designer must focus on the different motivational impact—how each system will cause people to respond—of one management control system versus another.

To see how failure to anticipate motivational impact can cause problems, consider that some years ago in Russia, managers of the Moscow Cable Company decided to reduce copper wastage and actually slashed it by 60% that year. As a result they had only $40,000 worth of scrap instead of the $100,000 originally budgeted. Top management in the central government then fined the plant $45,000 for not meeting its scrap budget. What do you think this did to the cable company managers' motivation to control waste?

Responsibility accounting, budgets, variances, and the entire inventory of management control tools should constructively influence behavior. They may, however, be misused as negative weapons to punish, place blame, or find fault. Viewed positively, they assist employees to improve decisions. Used negatively, they pose a threat to employees, who will resist and undermine the use of such techniques.

motivation The drive for some selected goal that creates effort and action toward that goal.

Design of Internal Controls

One of the few external constraints on management control systems in the United States was imposed by the Foreign Corrupt Practices Act, passed in 1977. Despite its title, it requires *all* publicly owned U.S. companies to maintain accurate and detailed accounting records and a documented system of *internal control*. Both managers and accountants are responsible for developing, maintaining, and evaluating internal control systems. An **internal control system** consists of methods and procedures to:

internal control system Methods and procedures to prevent errors and irregularities, detect errors and irregularities, and promote operating efficiency.

1. Prevent errors and irregularities by a system of authorization for transactions, accurate recording of transactions, and safeguarding of assets

2. Detect errors and irregularities by reconciling accounting records with independently kept records and physical counts and reviewing accounts for possible reductions of values

3. Promote operating efficiency by examining policies and procedures for possible improvements

A management control system encompasses *administrative controls* (such as budgets for planning, controlling, and evaluating operations) and *accounting controls* (such as the common internal control procedure of separating the duties of the person who counts cash from the duties of the person who has access to the accounts receivable records). This text concentrates on the administrative control aspects of the management control system.

Occasional breakdowns in systems, controls, and communication at the top of an organization may not be completely preventable because of human errors. John Teets, chairman, president, and chief executive officer of Dial Corp. (consumer products, services, and passenger buses), recalled in *Institutional Investor* (July 1991) that one such breakdown occurred because an engineering manager in charge of redesigning a bus for a large customer let the redesign proceed far beyond the original scope of the contract. The manager thought the customer and his top management would interpret his checking with his managers to be a sign of weakness. The redesign changes would cost Dial upward of $25 million and resulted in legal actions, strained customer relations, and, likely, difficulties for the engineering manager involved.

Development of Measures of Performance

Objective 4

Compare financial and nonfinancial performance, how they are interdependent, and why planning and control systems should consider both

Because most responsibility centers have multiple objectives, only some of these objectives are expressed in financial terms, such as operations budgets, profit targets, or required return on investment, depending on the financial classification of the center. Other objectives, which are to be achieved concurrently, are nonfinancial in nature. The well-designed management control system functions alike for both financial and nonfinancial objectives to develop and report measures of performance. Good performance measures will:

1. Relate to the goals of the organization
2. Balance long-term and short-term concerns
3. Reflect the management of key activities
4. Be affected by actions of employees
5. Be readily understood by employees
6. Be used in evaluating and rewarding employees
7. Be reasonably objective and easily measured
8. Be used consistently and regularly

Both financial and nonfinancial performance measures are important. Sometimes accountants and managers focus too much on financial measures such as profit or cost variances because they are readily available from the accounting system. Managers, however, can improve operational control by also considering nonfinancial measures of performance. Such measures may be more timely and more closely affected by employees at lower levels of the organization, where the product is made or the service is rendered.

Nonfinancial measures are often easier to quantify and understand. Hence, employees can be easily motivated toward achieving performance goals. For example, AT&T Universal Card Services, which was awarded the prestigious Baldridge National Quality Award (presented by the U.S. Department of Commerce), uses 18 performance measures for its customer inquiries process. These measures include average speed of answer, abandon rate, and application processing time (3 days compared to the industry average of 34 days).

Often the effects of poor nonfinancial performance (quality, productivity, and customer satisfaction) do not show up in the financial measures until considerable ground has been lost. As a result, many companies now stress management of the *activities* that drive revenues and costs rather than waiting to explain the revenues or costs themselves after the activities have occurred. Superior financial performance usually follows from superior nonfinancial performance.

In the rest of this chapter, we consider both financial and nonfinancial measures of performance used in many management control systems.

■ CONTROLLABILITY AND MEASUREMENT OF FINANCIAL PERFORMANCE

Management control systems often distinguish between controllable and uncontrollable events and between controllable and uncontrollable costs. Usually, responsibility center managers are in the best position to explain their center's results even if the managers had little influence over them. For example, an importer of grapes from Chile to the United States suffered a sudden loss of sales several years ago after a few of the grapes were found to contain poisonous cyanide. The tampering was beyond the importer's control, so the importer's management control system compared actual profits to flexible-budgeted profits (see Chapter 8), given that actual sales were unusually depressed. This separated effects of activity volume—sales levels—from effects of efficiency, and reported the importer's profitability *given* the uncontrollable drop in sales.

uncontrollable cost
Any cost that cannot be affected by the management of a responsibility center within a given time span.

An **uncontrollable cost** is any cost that cannot be affected by the management of a responsibility center within a given time span. For example, a mail-order supervisor may be responsible only for costs of labor, shipping costs, ordering errors and adjustments, and customer satisfaction. The supervisor would not be responsible for costs of the supporting information system because the supervisor cannot control that cost.

controllable cost
Any cost that is influenced by a manager's decisions and actions.

Controllable costs should include all costs that are *influenced* by a manager's decision and actions. For example, the costs of the mail-order information system, though uncontrollable by the mail-order supervisor, are controllable by the manager in charge of information systems.

In a sense, the term "controllable" is a misnomer because no cost is completely under the control of a manager. The term is widely used, however, to refer to any cost that is affected by a manager's decisions, even if not totally "controlled." Thus the cost of operating the mail-order information system may be affected by equipment or software failures that are not completely—but are partially—under the control of the manager of information systems, who would be held responsible for all of the costs of the information system, even the costs of downtime.

The distinction between controllable and uncontrollable costs serves an information purpose. Costs that are completely uncontrollable tell nothing about a manager's decisions and actions because, by definition, nothing the manager does will affect the costs. Such costs should be ignored in evaluating the responsibility center manager's performance. In contrast, reporting controllable costs provides evidence about a manager's performance.

Because responsibility for costs may be widespread, systems designers must depend on understanding cost behavior to help identify controllable costs. This understanding is increasingly gained through activity-based costing (see Chapters 3 and 4). Both Procter & Gamble and Upjohn, Inc., for example, are experimenting with activity-based costing systems in some divisions. Procter & Gamble credits its experimental activity-based management control system for identifying controllable costs in one of its detergent divisions, which led to major strategic changes.

Contribution Margin

Many organizations combine the contribution approach to measuring income with responsibility accounting—that is, they report by cost behavior as well as by degrees of controllability.

Objective 5

Prepare segment income statements for evaluating profit and investment centers using the contribution-margin and controllable-cost concepts

Exhibit 9-2 on page 344 displays the contribution approach to measuring the financial performance of the various organizational units of Barleycorn, Inc., which we encountered earlier in Exhibit 9-1. Study this exhibit carefully. It provides perspective on how a management control system can be designed to stress cost behavior, controllability, manager performance, and responsibility center performance simultaneously.

Line a in Exhibit 9-2 shows the contribution margin (see Chapter 2), sales revenues less all variable expenses. The contribution margin is especially helpful for predicting the impact on income of short-run changes in activity volume. Managers may quickly calculate any expected changes in income by multiplying increases in dollar sales by the contribution margin ratio. The contribution margin ratio for meats in the West Division is $180 ÷ $900 =.20. Thus a $1,000 increase in sales of meats in the West Division should produce a $200 increase in income (.20 × $1,000 = $200) if there are no changes in selling prices, operating expenses, or mix of sales between stores 1 and 2.

Contribution Controllable by Segment Managers

segments
Responsibility centers for which a separate measure of revenues and costs is obtained.

Lines b and c in Exhibit 9-2 separate the contribution that is controllable by segment managers (b) and the overall segment contribution (c). Responsibility also defines *segments*. **Segments** are responsibility centers for which a separate measure of revenues and costs is obtained. Designers of management control systems distinguish between the *segment* as an economic investment and the *manager* as a professional decision maker. For instance, an extended period of drought coupled with an aging population may adversely affect the desirability of continued economic investment in a ski resort, but the resort manager may be doing an excellent job under the circumstances.

Exhibit 9-2

Barleycorn, Inc.   Contribution Approach: Model Income Statement, by Segments* (Thousands of Dollars)

	Company as a Whole	Company Breakdown into Two Divisions		Breakdown of West Division Only				Breakdown of West Division, Meats Only		
		East Division	West Division	Not Allocated†	Groceries	Produce	Meats	Not Allocated†	Store 1	Store 2
Net sales	$4,000	$1,500	$2,500	—	$1,300	$300	$900	—	$600	$300
Variable costs										
Cost of merchandise sold	$3,000	$1,100	$1,900	—	$1,000	$230	$670	—	$450	$220
Variable operating expenses‡	260	100	160	—	100	10	50	—	35	15
Total variable costs	$3,260	$1,200	$2,060	—	$1,100	$240	$720	—	$485	$235
(a) Contribution margin	$ 740	$ 300	$ 440	—	$ 200	$ 60	$180	—	$115	$ 65
Less: fixed costs controllable by segment managers§	260	100	160	$ 20	40	10	90	$ 30	35	25
(b) Contribution controllable by segment managers	$ 480	$ 200	$ 280	$ (20)	$ 160	$ 50	$ 90	$ (30)	$ 80	$ 40
Less: fixed costs controllable by others‖	200	90	110	20	40	10	40	10	22	8
(c) Contribution by segments	$ 280	$ 110	$ 170	$ (40)	$ 120	$ 40	$ 50	$ (40)	$ 58	$ 32
Less: unallocated costs‖	100									
(d) Income before income taxes	$ 180									

*Three different types of segments are illustrated here: divisions, product lines, and stores. As you read across, note that the focus becomes narrower; from East and West divisions to West Division only, to meats in West Division only.

†Only those costs clearly identifiable to a product line should be allocated.

‡Principally wages and payroll-related costs.

§Examples are certain advertising, sales promotion, salespersons' salaries, management consulting, training and supervision costs.

‖Examples are depreciation, property taxes, insurance, and perhaps the segment manager's salary.

‖These costs are not clearly or practically allocable to any segment except by some highly questionable allocation base.

The manager of store 1 may have influence over some local advertising but not other advertising, some fixed salaries but not other salaries, and so forth. Moreover, the meat manager at both the division and store levels may have zero influence over store depreciation or the president's salary. Therefore, Exhibit 9-2 separates costs by controllability. Managers on all levels are asked to explain the total segment contribution but are held responsible only for the controllable contribution.

Note that fixed costs controllable by the segment managers are deducted from the contribution margin to obtain the *contribution* controllable by segment managers. These controllable costs are usually discretionary fixed costs such as local advertising and some salaries, but not the manager's own salary. Other, noncontrollable, fixed costs (shown between lines a and b) are not allocated in the breakdown because they are not considered controllable this far down in the organization. That is, of the $160,000 fixed cost that is controllable by the manager of the West Division, $140,000 is also controllable by subordinates (grocery, produce, and meat managers), but $20,000 is not. The latter is controllable by the West Division manager but not by lower managers. Similarly, the $30,000 in that same line are costs that are attributable to the meat department of the West Division but not to individual stores.

In many organizations, managers have latitude to trade off some variable costs for fixed costs. To save variable material and labor costs, managers might make heavier outlays for automation, quality management and employee training programs, and so on. Moreover, decisions on advertising, research, and sales promotion have effects on sales activity and hence on contribution margins. The controllable contribution includes these expenses and attempts to capture the results of these trade-offs.

The distinctions in Exhibit 9-2 among which items belong in what cost classification are inevitably not clear-cut. For example, determining controllability is always a problem when service department costs are allocated to other departments. Should the store manager bear a part of the division headquarters costs? If so, how much and on what basis? How much, if any, store depreciation or lease rentals should be deducted in computing the controllable contribution? There are no easy answers to these questions. Each organization picks ways that benefit it most with the lowest relative cost (unlike the situation in external financial accounting systems, which must follow strict regulations).

Contribution by Segments

The *contribution by segments*, line c in Exhibit 9-2, is an attempt to approximate the financial performance of the *segment*, as distinguished from the financial performance of its *manager*, which is measured in line b. The "fixed costs controllable by others" typically include committed costs (such as depreciation and property taxes) and discretionary costs (such as the segment manager's salary). These costs are attributable to the segment but primarily are controllable only at higher levels of management.

Unallocated Costs

Exhibit 9-2 shows "unallocated costs" immediately before line d. They might include central corporate costs such as the costs of top management and some corporate-level services (e.g., legal and taxation). When a persuasive cause and effect or activity-based justification for allocating such costs cannot be found, many organizations favor not allocating them to segments.

The contribution approach highlights the relative objectivity of various means of measuring financial performance. The contribution margin itself tends to be the most objective. As you read downward in the report, the allocations become more subjective, and the resulting measures of contributions or income become more subject to dispute. Though such disputes may be unproductive uses of management time, the allocations do direct managers' attention to the costs of the entire organization and lead to organizational cost control.

■ NONFINANCIAL MEASURES OF PERFORMANCE

Objective 6

Measure performance against quality, cycle time, and productivity objectives

For many years organizations have monitored their nonfinancial performance. Sales organizations have followed up on customers to ensure their satisfaction. Manufacturers have tracked manufacturing defects and product performance. Government health organizations have kept meticulous statistics on disease incidence and reduction, which indicate the effectiveness of disease control efforts such as education, sanitation, and innoculation. In recent years, most organizations have developed a new awareness of the importance of controlling such nonfinancial performance as quality, cycle time, and productivity.

quality control The effort to ensure that products and services perform to customer requirements.

Quality control is the effort to ensure that products and services perform to customer requirements. Organizations around the globe have adopted formal quality management programs. It has also become apparent that improvements in quality (from inception of the product to delivery and after-sales service) lead to reduced cycle time and increased productivity.

Because these factors are closely related, it is not coincidental that all types of organizations are concerned about quality, cycle time, and productivity. They are key subgoals that lead to long-term profitability for privately owned companies and are increasingly important in nonprofit and government organizations, where tighter appropriations and increasing demands for services are facts of life.

Control of Quality

In essence, customers or clients define quality by comparing their needs to the attributes of the product or service. For example, buyers judge the quality of an automobile based on reliability, performance, styling, safety, and image relative to their needs, budget, and the alternatives. Defining quality in terms of customer requirements is only half the battle. There remains the problem of reaching and maintaining the desired level of quality. There are many approaches to controlling quality. The traditional approach in the United States was to inspect products after they were completed, and reject or rework those that failed the inspections. Because testing is expensive, often only a sample of products were inspected. The process was judged to be in control as long as the number of defective products did not exceed an *acceptable quality level*. This meant that some defective products could still make their way to customers.

Implementing Quality Programs at Grand Rapids Spring & Wire

Grand Rapids Spring & Wire Products, Inc. (GRSW), manufactures a variety of products for the automotive, appliance, furniture, and electronic industries. GRSW products include compression, extension, and torsion springs; stampings from progressive dies and four-slide stampings; roll forming; wire and grommet molding; and various assembly processes. In the mid-1980s, GRSW began an aggressive quality program designed to create a *quality culture*. Various quality theories were carefully studied by management and employees.

GRSW restructured its organization into mini-companies—cross functional, self-directed units that would enhance continuous improvement. The four mini-companies are Small Metal Stamping, Four-Slide Stamping, Spring Torsion, and Secondary. Each mini-company was assigned support personnel including accounting, engineering, and quality experts. This new organization has created a much flatter organizational structure and has improved communications. Each mini-company develops its own mission statement and plans. For example, the mission of the Secondary mini-company is:

> Boosting our attendance and participation while maintaining/increasing quality and delivery levels will lead to the continous improvement of quality (Q), cost (C), delivery (D), safety (S), morale (M), and ultimate customer satisfaction.

Performance indicators have been developed to measure quality, cost, delivery, safety, and morale. Examples of performance indicators include:

Mission Component	Performance Indicator	Goal
Quality	Defective parts per million	< 200
	Returns and allowances	< .5%
	Customer concerns	< 3 per month
Cost	Sales: sales/payroll	Increase
	Finished goods inventory as % of sales	< 15%
Delivery	Percent on time	> 97%
Safety	Reported accidents	0
	Outside medical aid required	0
Morale	Tardy, leave early, absences	< 12 per month
	Implemented suggestions	> 11 per month

Any time a process fails to achieve a performance goal, a team is formed to define and solve the problem. Each week employees meet with the support people to review progress on each mission component (QCDSM). Twice a year the company holds a stakeholders' meeting for all employees to review how the mini-company is progressing toward its mission and goals. ■

Source: From H. Roehm, D. Klein, and J. Castellano, "Blending Quality Theories for Continuous Improvement," Management Accounting, February 1995, pp. 26–32.

cost of quality report
A report that displays the financial impact of quality.

In recent years, however, U.S. companies, confronted with the success of Japanese products, have learned that this is a very costly way to control quality. All the resources consumed to make a defective product and to detect it are wasted, or considerable rework may be necessary to correct the defects. In addition, it is very costly to repair products in use by a customer or to win back a dissatisfied customer. IBM's Chief Executive Officer John Akers was quoted in the *Wall Street Journal* as saying, "I am sick and tired of visiting plants to hear nothing but great things about quality and cycle time—and then to visit customers who tell me of problems."[1] The high costs of achieving quality by "inspecting it in" are evident in a **cost of quality report**, which displays the financial impact of quality. The quality cost report shown in Exhibit 9-3 measures four categories of quality costs:

---

[1] Quoted in Graham Sharman, "When Quality Control Gets in the Way of Quality," *Wall Street Journal*, February 24, 1992, p. A14.

1. Prevention—costs incurred to prevent the production of defective products or delivery of substandard services including engineering analyses to improve product design for better manufacturing, improvements in production processes, increased quality of material inputs, and programs to train personnel

2. Appraisal—costs incurred to identify defective products or services including inspection and testing

3. Internal failure—costs of defective components and final products or services that are scrapped or reworked; also costs of delays caused by defective products or services

4. External failure—costs caused by delivery of defective products or services to customers, such as field repairs, returns, and warranty expenses

Poor Quality Nearly Short-Circuits Electronics Company

Penril DataComm, a Maryland designer and maker of data communications equipment, was on the brink of financial disaster resulting from the cost of poor quality. Penril was performing 100% inspection in many of its manufacturing processes and reworking or scrapping one-third of everything it produced. Penril turned its financial fortunes around based on a total quality effort. The results of a customized quality program included:

1. 1,266% increase in profits per employee
2. 95% increase in revenues
3. 81% decrease in defects per unit
4. 83% decrease in out-of-box failures (failures during the first three months in the field)
5. 73% decrease in first-year warranty service repairs
6. reduced response time to customer's orders from 10 weeks to 3 days

Penril's new mission is "to build an environment where internal and external customer expectations are met in every transaction." Penril supports this mission by following six principles:

1. Quality is the number-one priority. This requires a shift from short-term to long-term thinking. Resources are allocated for quality efforts, and quality teams are rewarded for improvements.

2. Customer focus. Customers and suppliers serve on concurrent engineering teams to "build the voice of the customer into all aspects of the business."

3. Emphasize prevention and continuous improvement. "Inspection only maintains the status quo."

Total quality means reforming designs, modifying policies and procedures, and training people in correct practices.

4. Management using data. Statistical analysis is used for control of processes.

5. Total employee involvement. According to Penril, the most important measure in the race for quality leadership is the rate of improvement, and this rate is maximized by involving everyone on a team. The team concept at Penril unleashes employee energy that improves morale, communication, respect, and trust. Training includes job skills, total quality management concepts, statistics, statistical process control, problem-solving skills, presentation skills, and communication skills.

6. Cross-functional management. Processes cross departments so each cross-functional team includes members from all areas involved in the process. Communication is enhanced by frequent meetings and newsletters. Employees present quality reports that document improvement efforts.

Perhaps the best measure of the success of Penril's new quality focus is in customer reaction—the number of original equipment manufacturers (OEMs) has doubled in the three years since the program began. "We know of no greater testimony to a company's quality than to have another company ask it to design a product for them, build it for them, and put the customer's name on it." ■

Source: From "Poor Quality Nearly Short Circuits Electronics Company," in Chet Marchwinski ed., Productivity, February 1993, pp. 1–3.

Exhibit 9-3   Eastside Manufacturing Company   Quality Cost Report* (Thousands of Dollars)

Month			Quality Cost Area	Year to Date		
Actual	Plan	Variance		Actual	Plan	Variance
			1. Prevention Cost			
3	2	1	A. Quality—administration	5	4	1
16	18	(2)	B. Quality—engineering	37	38	(1)
7	6	1	C. Quality—planning by others	14	12	2
5	7	(2)	D. Supplier assurance	13	14	(1)
31	33	(2)	Total prevention cost	69	68	1
5.5%	6.1%		% of Total quality cost	6.2%	6.3%	
			2. Appraisal cost			
31	26	5	A. Inspection	55	52	3
12	14	(2)	B. Test	24	28	(4)
7	6	1	C. Insp. & test of purchased mat.	15	12	3
11	11	0	D. Product quality audits	23	22	1
3	2	1	E. Maint. of insp. & test equip.	4	4	0
2	2	0	F. Mat. consumed in insp. & test	5	4	1
66	61	5	Total appraisal cost	126	122	4
11.8%	11.3%		% of Total quality cost	11.4%	11.3%	
			3. Internal failure cost			
144	140	4	A. Scrap & rework—manuf.	295	280	15
55	53	2	B. Scrap & rework—engineering	103	106	(3)
28	30	(2)	C. Scrap & rework—supplier	55	60	(5)
21	22	(1)	D. Failure investigation	44	44	0
248	245	3	Total internal failure cost	497	490	7
44.3%	45.4%		% of Total quality cost	44.9%	45.3%	
345	339	6	Total internal quality cost(1 + 2 + 3)	692	680	12
61.6%	62.8%		% of Total quality cost	62.6%	62.8%	
			4. External failure quality cost			
75	66	9	A. Warranty exp.—manuf.	141	132	9
41	40	1	B. Warranty exp.—engineering	84	80	4
35	35	0	C. Warranty exp.—sales	69	70	(1)
46	40	6	D. Field warranty cost	83	80	3
18	20	(2)	E. Failure investigation	37	40	(3)
215	201	14	Total external failure cost	414	402	12
38.4%	37.2%		% of Total quality cost	37.4%	37.2%	
560	540	20	Total quality cost	1,106	1,082	24
9,872	9,800		Total product cost	20,170	19,600	
5.7%	5.5%		%Tot. qual. cost to tot. prod. cost	5.5%	5.5%	

* Adapted from Allen H. Seed III, *Adapting Management Accounting Practice to an Advanced Manufacturing Environment* (National Association of Accountants, 1988). Table 5–2, p. 76.

This report shows that most of the costs incurred by Eastside Manufacturing Company are due to internal or external failures. These costs almost certainly are understated, however. Poor quality can result in large opportunity costs because of internal delays and lost sales. For example, quality problems in American-built automobiles in the 1970s and 1980s probably caused forgone sales that were significantly more costly than the tangible costs measured in any quality cost report.

In recent years, more and more U.S. companies have been rethinking this approach to quality control. Instead, they have adopted an approach first espoused by an American, W. Edwards Deming, and embraced by Japanese companies decades ago: *total quality management* (TQM). Following the old adage, "an ounce of prevention is worth a pound of cure," it focuses on *prevention* of defects and on customer satisfaction. The TQM approach is based on the assumption that the cost of quality is minimized when a firm achieves high quality levels. **Total quality management** is the application of quality principles to *all* of the organization's endeavors to satisfy customers. The U.S. Department of Commerce presents the Baldridge Award to companies that excel in quality, based on their customer-oriented quality achievements. TQM has significant implications for organization goals, structure, and management control systems. A complete discussion of TQM is beyond the scope of this text, but it includes delegating responsibility for many management functions to employees. For TQM to work, though, employees must be very well trained in the process, the product or service, and the use of quality-control information.

To implement TQM, employees are trained to prepare, interpret, and act on *quality-control charts*, such as that shown in Exhibit 9-4. The **quality-control chart** is a statistical plot of measures of various product dimensions or attributes. This plot helps detect process deviations before the process generates defects. These plots also identify excessive variation in product dimensions or attributes that should be addressed by process or design engineers. The chart in Exhibit 9-4 shows that the Eastside Manufacturing Company generally is not meeting its defects objective of .5% defects (which is a relatively high defect rate). Corrective action is indicated.

total quality management (TQM) The application of quality principles to all of the organization's endeavors to satisfy customers.

quality-control chart The statistical plot of measures of various product dimensions or attributes.

Exhibit 9-4

Eastside Manufacturing Company Quality Control Chart

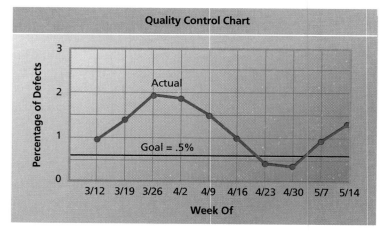

cycle time The time taken to complete a product or service, or any of the components of a product or service.

Control of Cycle Time

One key to improving quality is to reduce *cycle time*. **Cycle time**, or throughput time, is the time taken to complete a product or service, or any of the components of a product or service. It is a summary measure of manufacturing or service

Measuring the Cost of Quality

In a survey, controllers of companies with quality programs were asked if the cost of quality was being calculated. The answer: 51% said yes, 21% said no, and 31% said no but felt that it should be calculated. The same survey indicated that the cost of quality was between 11 and 30% of *revenue* for about one out of every three companies. Why don't more companies measure the cost of their quality programs? The reason often given is that it is very difficult to measure the various costs of quality. Companies often hesitate to invest in equipment that promotes quality for the same reason: it is difficult to measure the benefits and costs of quality. Accountants are beginning to create systems that effectively measure quality costs. We consider two illustrations.

The Quality Cost Report

The monthly quality cost report (QCR) at Gilroy foods consists of the four categories described in Exhibit 9-3 and contains about 40 items. Gilroy's QCR has two parts—a narrative and data. The narrative part is considered as important as the data. A monthly topic discusses ideas for quality improvement, areas needing attention, and explanations of prior events. Examples include onion and garlic slicing thickness, utilizing packaging drums more efficiently, and worker safety. Total employee involvement is facilitated through the monthly meetings when the narrative topics are dicussed.

Gilroy's quality target is set at 4% of sales. When this target is achieved, a new target will be established. The ultimate goal is to eliminate all quality costs since they are considered non-value-added.

Measuring the Cost of Investment in Quality Equipment

Often, companies do not invest in equipment that promotes quality because it is difficult to quantify all the benefits and costs of using such equipment. One company has developed a software program that enables a better measurement of these benefits and costs. Perceptron, Inc., based in Farmington Hills, Michigan, produces industrial measurement systems such as laser-based, optical, noncontact systems for automotive, appliance, aerospace, and furniture companies. These systems are used to measure product assembly accuracy. Assembly-line technicians can use the data provided by Perceptron's equipment to take preventive action to correct problems immediately, virtually eliminating the need for highly paid quality control inspectors.

Perceptron developed a computer software program that helps plant personnel to identify and quantify the hidden benefits and costs of acquiring and using quality equipment. Some of the major benefits and costs of the investment in in-line measurement systems and associated preventive activities are

QUANTIFIABLE BENEFITS	COSTS
quicker response to variation problems leading to reduced average cost of manufacturing process problems	acquisition cost of equipment including transportation and installation
reduced production costs of scrap and repair from early detection of defects	training
reduced work-in-process and parts inventories reduce the carrying costs of inventory and the costs of obsolescence because of engineering changes	initial programming labor
higher uptime and throughput from more stable processes reduces the costs of overtime and outsourcing	maintenance
reduced downstream production and warranty costs	measurement labor
higher quality of supplier parts due to early in-process detection of defects ■	process inspection

Sources: From "Cost Management-Quality Link," Cost Management Update, *September 1992, p. 1; Stephen L. Brinkman and Mark A. Appelbaum, "The Quality Cost Report: It's Alive and Well at Gilroy Foods,"* Management Accounting, *September 1994, pp. 61–65; Alahassane Diallon Zafar, U. Khan, and Curtis F. Vail, "Measuring the Cost of Investment in Quality Equipment,"* Managment Accounting, *August 1994, pp. 32–35.*

Time for a Change at Coleman

Coleman Co.—the Wichita, Kansas, maker of camping and recreational products—was rapidly losing market share to competitors such as Rubbermaid and Igloo. New management traced the root of the problem to excess cycle time. There were too many non-value-added steps in every process of the company, from product development to manufacturing to sales and service. Working to reduce cycle time by cutting out these steps also exposed quality problems and faulty incentives for workers. Any changes in processes and products required as many as 16 levels of approval. As a result, employees were reluctant to initiate changes because they were unlikely to be approved. Under the old piece-rate system, workers were even paid for defective parts. The quality problems were hidden by long cycle times, which resulted in extensive rework, and by large inventories, which resulted in large numbers of defective parts to be replaced. Coleman aggressively eliminated non-value-added process steps, revised processes and the workers' incentive systems, and introduced just-in-time methods. Now—several years later—cycle times have dropped dramatically, inventories are much lower, and profits are up markedly, as are cash flows. In addition, the value of the company has increased significantly. The company credits all of these improvements to controlling cycle time. ∎

Source: Adapted from Brian Dumaine, "Earning More by Moving Faster," Fortune, *October 7, 1991, pp. 89–94.*

efficiency and effectiveness, and an important cost driver. The longer a product or service is in process, the more costs are consumed. Low cycle time means quick completion of a product or service (without defects). Lowering cycle time requires smooth-running processes and high quality, and also creates increased flexibility and quicker reactions to customer needs. As cycle time is decreased, quality problems become apparent throughout the process and must be solved if quality is to be improved. Decreasing cycle time also results in bringing products or services more quickly to customers, a product or service characteristic customers value.

Firms measure cycle time for the important stages of a process and for the process as a whole. An effective means of measuring cycle time is to use *barcoding*, where a barcode (similar to symbols on most grocery products) is attached to each component or product, and read at the end of each stage of completion. Cycle time is measured for each stage as the time between readings of barcodes. Barcoding also permits effective tracking of materials and products for inventories, scheduling, and delivery.

Exhibit 9-5 shows a sample cycle-time report. (Cycle time can also be displayed on a control chart.) This report shows that Eastside Manufacturing Company is meeting its cycle-time objectives at two of its five production process stages. This report is similar to the flexible budget reports of Chapter 8. Explanations of the variances indicate that poor quality materials and poor design led to extensive rework and retesting.

Exhibit 9-5

Eastside
Manufacturing
Company
Cycle Time Report
for the Second Week
of May, 19X3

Process Stage	Actual Cycle Time*	Standard Cycle Time	Variance	Explanation
Materials processing	2.1	2.5	0.4 F	
Circuit board assembly	44.7	28.8	15.9 U	Poor quality materials caused rework
Power unit assembly	59.6	36.2	23.4 U	Engineering change required rebuilding all power units
Product assembly	14.6	14.7	0.1 F	
Functional and environmental test	53.3	32.0	21.3 U	Software failure in test procedures required retesting

F = Favorable.
U = Unfavorable.
* Average time per stage over the week.

Control of Productivity

More than half the companies in the United States manage productivity as part of the effort to improve their competitiveness. In concept, defining productivity is simple. **Productivity** is a measure of outputs divided by inputs. The fewer inputs needed to produce a given output, the more productive the organization. This simple definition, however, raises difficult measurement questions. How should outputs and inputs be measured? Specific management control problems usually determine the most appropriate measures of inputs and outputs. Labor-intensive (especially service) organizations are concerned with increasing the productivity of labor, so labor-based measures are appropriate. Highly automated companies are concerned with machine use and productivity of capital investments, so capacity-based measures, such as the percentage of time machines are available, may be most important to them. Manufacturing companies in general are concerned with the efficient use of materials, and so for them measures of material *yield* (a ratio of material outputs over material inputs) may be useful indicators of productivity. In all cases of productivity ratios, a measure of the resource that management wishes to control is in the denominator (the input) and some measure of the objective of using the resource is in the numerator (the output).

Exhibit 9-6 shows 12 possible productivity measures. As you can see, they vary widely according to the type of resource with which management is concerned.

productivity A measure of outputs divided by inputs.

Exhibit 9-6

Measures of
Productivity

Resource	Possible Outputs (Numerator)		Possible Inputs (Denominator)
Labor	Standard direct labor hours allowed for good output	÷	Actual direct labor hours used
	Sales revenue	÷	Number of employees
	Sales revenue	÷	Direct labor cost
	Bank deposit/loan activity (by a bank)	÷	Number of employees
	Service calls	÷	Number of employees
	Customer orders	÷	Number of employees
Materials	Weight of output	÷	Weight of input
	Number of good units	÷	Total number of units
Equipment, capital, physical capacity	Time (e.g., hours) used	÷	Time available for use
	Time available for use	÷	Time (e.g., 24 hours per day)
	Expected machine hours for good output	÷	Actual machine hours
	Sales revenue	÷	Direct labor cost

Choice of Productivity Measures

Which productivity measures should a company choose to manage? The choice depends on the behaviors desired. Managers generally concentrate on achieving the performance levels desired by their superiors. Thus, if top management evaluates subordinates' performance based on direct-labor productivity, lower-level managers will focus on improving that specific measure.

The challenge in choosing productivity measures is that a manager may be able to improve a single measure but hurt performance elsewhere in the organization. For example, long production runs may improve machine productivity but result in excessive inventories. Alternatively, improved labor productivity in the short run may be accompanied by a high rate of product defects.

Use of a single measure of productivity is unlikely to result in overall improvements in performance. As before, choice of management controls requires balancing trade-offs that employees can be expected to make to improve their performance evaluations. Many organizations focus management control on more fundamental activities, such as control of quality and service, and use productivity measures to monitor the actual benefits of improvements in these activities.

Caveat

Be careful with comparing productivity measures over time. Changes in the process or in the rate of inflation can prove misleading. For example, consider labor productivity at Ameritech Corporation (the Midwest U.S. telecommunications company). One measure of productivity tracked by Ameritech is *sales revenue per employee.*

	1990	1985	Percent Change
Total revenue (millions)	$4,788.8	$4,364.7	9.7%
Employees	75,780	74,883	1.2%
Revenue per employee (unadjusted for inflation)	$ 63,193	$ 58,287	8.4%

By this measure, Ameritech appears to have achieved an 8.4% increase in the productivity of labor. Total revenue has not been adjusted for the effects of inflation, however. Because of inflation, each 1985 dollar was equivalent to 1.207 1990 dollars. Therefore, Ameritech's 1985 sales revenue, expressed in 1990 dollars (to be equivalent with 1990 sales revenue) is $4,364.7 × 1.207 = $5,268.19. The adjusted 1985 sales revenue per employee is as follows:

	1990	1985 (Adjusted)	Percent Change
Total revenue ($millions)	$4,788.8	$5,268.2	− 9.1%
Employees	75,780	74,883	+ 1.2%
Revenue per employee (adjusted for inflation)	$ 63,193	$70,352	− 10.2%

Adjusting for the effects of inflation reveals that Ameritech's labor productivity has dropped dramatically rather than improved. This is a signal to management that corrective action should be taken to reverse this slide—such as raising prices or reducing the number of employees. This slide in productivity in the United States may explain why Ameritech purchased an *unregulated* New Zealand telephone company, where prices and lines of business may be managed more freely and where there is greater potential for higher productivity (i.e., increases in the numerator, revenue).

The Balanced Scorecard

balanced scorecard
A performance measurement system that strikes a balance between financial and operating measures, links performance to rewards, and gives explicit recognition to the diversity of stakeholder interests.

A world-class company today requires a state-of-the-art performance measurement system that monitors the vital signs (critical success factors) of the company. One newly evolving approach to the design of a performance measurement system is the balanced scorecard. A **balanced scorecard** is a performance measurement system that strikes a balance between financial and operating measures, links performance to rewards, and gives explicit recognition to the diversity of stakeholder interests. Companies such as Champion International (see p. 337) and Apple Computer use the balanced scorecard to focus management's attention on items subject to action on a month-by-month and day-by-day basis. One key advantage of this approach is that line managers can understand the numbers presented due to the use of nonfinancial measures.

■ MANAGEMENT CONTROL SYSTEMS IN SERVICE, GOVERNMENT, AND NONPROFIT ORGANIZATIONS

Most service, government, and nonprofit organizations have more difficulty implementing management control systems than do manufacturing firms. The main problem is that the outputs of service and nonprofit organizations are more difficult to measure than the cars or computers that are produced by manufacturers. As a result, it may be more difficult to know whether the service provided is, for example, of top quality until (long) after the service has already been delivered.

Objective 7

Describe the difficulties of management control in service and nonprofit organizations

The key to successful management control in any organization is proper training and motivation of employees to achieve goal congruence and effort, followed by consistent monitoring of objectives set in accordance with critical subgoals, but it is even more important in service-oriented organizations. For example, MBNA America, a large issuer of bank credit cards, identifies customer retention as its primary subgoal. MBNA trains its customer representatives carefully, each day measures and reports performance on 14 objectives consistent with customer retention (such as answering every call by the second ring, keeping the computer up 100% of the time, processing credit-line requests within 1 hour), and rewards every employee based on those 14 objectives. Employees have earned bonuses as high as 20% of their annual salaries by meeting those objectives.

Nonprofit and government organizations have additional problems designing and implementing an objective that is analogous to the financial "bottom line" that so often serves as a powerful incentive in private industry. Furthermore, many people seek positions in nonprofit organizations primarily for other than monetary rewards. For example, volunteers in the Peace Corps receive very little pay but derive much satisfaction from helping to improve conditions in underdeveloped countries. Thus monetary incentives are generally less effective in nonprofit organizations. Control systems in nonprofit organizations probably will never be as highly developed as in profit-seeking firms because:

1. Organizational goals and objectives are less clear. Moreover, they are often multiple, requiring difficult trade-offs.

2. Professionals (for example, teachers, attorneys, physicians, scientists, economists) tend to dominate nonprofit organizations. Because of their perceived professional status, they have been less receptive to the installation or improvement of formal control systems.

3. Measurements are more difficult because
    a. There is no profit measure.
    b. There are heavy amounts of discretionary fixed costs, which makes the relationships of inputs to outputs difficult to specify and measure.

4. There is less competitive pressure from other organizations or "owners" to improve management control systems. As a result, for example, many cities in the United States are "privatizing" some essential services such as sanitation by contracting with private firms.

5. The role of budgeting is often more a matter of playing bargaining games with sources of funding to get the largest possible authorization than it is rigorous planning.

6. Motivations and incentives of individuals may differ from those in for-profit organizations.

■ FUTURE OF MANAGEMENT CONTROL SYSTEMS

As organizations mature and as environments change, managers cope with their responsibilities by expanding and refining their management control tools. The management control techniques that were quite satisfactory 10 or 20 years ago may not be adequate for many organizations today. One often hears accounting systems criticized for being especially slow to adapt to organizational change.

Objective 8

Explain how management control systems must evolve with changing times

A changing environment often means that organizations must set different subgoals or critical success factors. Different subgoals create different objectives to be used as targets and create different benchmarks for evaluating performance. Obviously, the management control system must evolve, too, or the organization may not manage its resources effectively or efficiently. Thus the management control tools presented in this text may not be adequate even a short time from now.

Does this mean that the time spent studying this material has been wasted? No. Certain management control principles that will always be important and that can guide the redesign of systems to meet new management needs follow:

1. Always expect that individuals will be pulled in the direction of their own self-interest. You may be pleasantly surprised that some individuals will act selflessly, but management control systems should be designed to take advantage of more typical human behavior. Be aware that self-interest may be perceived differently in different cultures.

2. Design incentives so that individuals who pursue their own self-interest are also achieving the organization's objectives. If there are multiple objectives (as is usually the case), then multiple incentives are appropriate. Do not underestimate the difficulty of balancing these incentives—some experimentation may be necessary to achieve multiple objectives.

3. Evaluate actual performance based on expected or planned performance, revised, if possible, for actual output achieved. The concept of flexible budgeting can be applied to most subgoals and objectives, both financial and nonfinancial.

4. Consider nonfinancial performance to be just as important as financial performance. In the short run, a manager may be able to generate good financial performance while neglecting nonfinancial performance, but it is not likely over a longer haul.

value chain The sequence of functions that adds value to the company's products or services.

5. Array performance measures across the entire value chain of the company. The **value chain** is the sequence of functions that adds value to the company's products or services. These functions include research and development, product process design, production, marketing, distribution, and customer service. This ensures that all activities that are critical to the long-run success of the company are integrated into the management control system.

6. Periodically review the success of the management control system. Are objectives being met? Does meeting the objectives mean that subgoals and goals are being met, too? Do individuals have, understand, and use the management control information effectively?

7. Learn from the management control successes (and failures) of competitors around the world. Despite cultural differences, human behavior is remarkably similar. Successful applications of new technology and management controls may be observed in the performance of others.

Highlights to Remember

The starting point for designing and evaluating a management control system is the identification of organizational goals, subgoals, and objectives as specified by top management. Systems are typically designed within the constraints of a given set of goals and a given organizational structure.

The evolutionary design of management control systems depends on criteria of cost benefit, goal congruence, and employee effort. The design should be the one that is expected to produce the best decisions at a reasonable cost.

The way performance is measured and evaluated affects individuals' behavior. Measuring performance in areas such as quality and productivity causes employees to direct attention to those areas. The more rewards are tied to performance measures, the more incentive there is to improve the measures.

Measures of performance must be carefully thought out for their behavioral effects. Improving the measures should improve organizational performance toward achieving its goals. Poorly designed or balanced measures may actually work against the organization's goals.

Responsibility accounting assigns particular revenue or cost objectives to the management of the subunit that has the greatest influence over them. Responsibility accounting classifies organizational subunits as cost, profit, or investment centers according to their financial responsibilities. The contribution approach to measuring income aids performance evaluation by separating a segment's costs into those controllable by the segment management and those beyond management's control.

Nonfinancial performance is as important as financial performance. In fact, nonfinancial performance usually leads to financial performance in time. Many companies focus on short-term nonfinancial performance measures, knowing that financial results will follow.

Management control in service, government, and nonprofit organizations is difficult because of a number of factors, chief of which is a relative lack of clearly observable outcomes. Systems designers in these organizations must contend with particularly difficult trade-offs among objectives.

Management control systems must evolve with changing economic and organizational conditions if the systems are to continue to assist managers in their decision making, controlling, and evaluation tasks.

Summary Problem for Your Review

Problem

The Book & Game Company has two bookstores: Auntie's and Merlin's. Each store has a manager who has a great deal of decision authority over the individual stores. Advertising, market research, acquisition of books, legal services, and other staff functions, however, are handled by a central office. The Book & Game Company's current accounting system allocates all costs to the stores. Results for 19X6 were

Item	Total Company	Auntie's	Merlin's
Sales revenue	$700,000	$350,000	$350,000
Cost of merchandise sold	450,000	225,000	225,000
Gross margin	250,000	125,000	125,000
Operating expenses			
Salaries and wages	63,000	30,000	33,000
Supplies	45,000	22,500	22,500
Rent and utilities	60,000	40,000	20,000
Depreciation	15,000	7,000	8,000
Allocated staff costs	60,000	30,000	30,000
Total operating expenses	243,000	129,500	113,500
Operating income (loss)	$ 7,000	$ (4,500)	$ 11,500

Each bookstore manager makes decisions that affect salaries and wages, supplies, and depreciation. In contrast, rent and utilities are beyond the managers' control because the managers did not choose the location or the size of the store.

Supplies are variable costs. Variable salaries and wages are equal to 8% of the cost of merchandise sold; the remainder of salaries and wages is a fixed cost. Rent, utilities, and depreciation also are fixed costs. Allocated staff costs are unaffected by any events at the bookstores, but they are allocated as a proportion of sales revenue.

1. Using the contribution approach, prepare a performance report that distinguishes the performance of each bookstore from that of the bookstore manager.
2. Evaluate the financial performance of each bookstore.
3. Evaluate the financial performance of each manager.

Solution

1.

Item	Total Company	Auntie's	Merlin's
Sales revenue	$700,000	$350,000	$350,000
Variable costs			
Cost of merchandise sold	450,000	225,000	225,000
Salaries and wages	36,000	18,000	18,000
Supplies	45,000	22,500	22,500
Total variable costs	531,000	265,500	265,500
Contribution margin by bookstore	169,000	84,500	84,500
Less: fixed costs controllable by bookstore managers			
Salaries and wages	27,000	12,000	15,000
Depreciation	15,000	7,000	8,000
Total controllable fixed costs	42,000	19,000	23,000
Contribution controllable by managers	127,000	65,500	61,500
Less: fixed costs controllable by others			
Rent and utilities	60,000	40,000	20,000
Contribution by bookstore	67,000	$ 25,500	$ 41,500
Unallocated costs	60,000		
Operating income	$ 7,000		

2. The financial performances of the bookstores (i.e., segments of the company) are best evaluated by the line "contribution by bookstores." Merlin's has a substantially higher contribution, despite equal levels of sales revenues in the two stores. The major reason for this advantage is the lower rent and utilities paid by Merlin's.

3. The financial performance by managers is best judged by the line "contribution controllable by managers." By this measure, the performance of Auntie's manager is better than that of Merlin's. The contribution margin is the same for each store, but Merlin's manager paid $4,000 more in controllable fixed costs than did Auntie's manager. Of course, this decision could be beneficial in the long run. What is missing from each of these segment reports is the year's master budget and a flexible budget, which would be the best benchmark for evaluating both bookstore and bookstore manager.

Accounting Vocabulary

balanced scorecard, *p. 355*	investment center, *p. 339*	quality-control chart, *p. 350*
controllable cost, *p. 342*	management control system, *p. 334*	responsibility accounting, *p. 338*
cost center, *p. 338*	managerial effort, *p. 339*	responsibility center, *p. 338*
cost of quality report, *p. 347*	motivation, *p. 340*	segments, *p. 343*
cycle time, *p. 350*	productivity, *p. 353*	total quality management, *p. 350*
goal congruence, *p. 339*	profit center, *p. 338*	uncontrollable cost, *p. 342*
internal control system, *p. 340*	quality control, *p. 346*	value chain, *p. 357*

Fundamental Assignment Material

9-A1   Responsibility of Purchasing Agent

Acme Electronics Company, a privately held enterprise, has a subcontract from a large aerospace company on the West Coast. Although Acme was a low bidder, the aerospace company was reluctant to award the business to Acme, a newcomer to this kind of activity. Consequently, Acme assured the aerospace company of its financial strength by submitting its audited financial statements. Moreover, Acme agreed to a penalty clause of $2,000 per day to be paid by Acme for each day of late delivery for whatever cause.

Jean Lou, the Acme purchasing agent, is responsible for acquiring materials and parts in time to meet production schedules. She placed an order with an Acme supplier for a critical manufactured component. The supplier, who had a reliable record for meeting schedules, gave Lou an acceptable delivery date. Lou checked up several times and was assured that the component would arrive at Acme on schedule.

On the date specified by the supplier for shipment to Acme, Lou was informed that the component had been damaged during final inspection. It was delivered 10 days late. Lou had allowed 4 extra days for possible delays, but Acme was 6 days late in delivering to the aerospace company and so had to pay a penalty of $12,000.

Required   What department should bear the penalty? Why?

9-A2   Contribution Approach to Responsibility Accounting

George McBee owns a small chain of specialty toy stores in Denver and Kansas City. The company's organization chart follows:

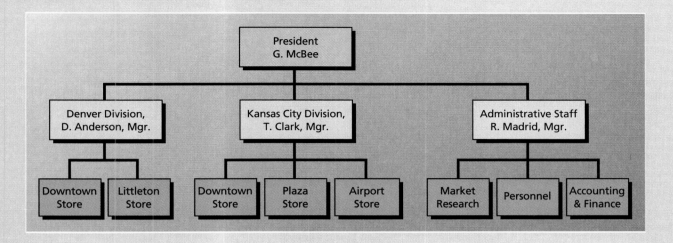

Financial results for 19X7 were

Sales revenue	$8,000,000
Cost of merchandise sold	5,000,000
Gross margin	3,000,000
Operating expenses	2,200,000
Income before income taxes	$ 800,000

The following data about 19X7 operations were also available:

1. All five stores used the same pricing formula; therefore all had the same gross margin percentage.
2. Sales were largest in the two Downtown stores, with 30% of the total sales volume in each. The Plaza and Airport stores each provided 15% of total sales volume, and the Littleton store provided 10%.
3. Variable operating costs at the stores were 10% of revenue for the Downtown stores. The other stores had lower variable and higher fixed costs. Their variable operating costs were only 5% of sales revenue.
4. The fixed costs over which the store managers had control were $125,000 in each of the Downtown stores, $160,000 at Plaza and Airport, and $80,000 at Littleton.
5. The remaining $910,000 of operating costs consisted of
   a. $180,000 controllable by the Kansas City division manager, but not by individual stores
   b. $130,000 controllable by the Denver division manager, but not by individual stores
   c. $600,000 controllable by the administrative staff
6. Of the $600,000 spent by the administrative staff, $350,000 directly supported the Kansas City division, with 20% for the Downtown store, 30% for each of the Plaza and Airport stores, and 20% for Kansas City operations in general. Another $150,000 supported the Denver division, 50% for the Downtown store, 25% for the Littleton store, and 25% supporting Denver operations in general. The other $100,000 was for general corporate expenses.

Required   Prepare an income statement by segments using the contribution approach to responsibility accounting. Use the format of Exhibit 9-2, page 344. Column headings should be

Company as a Whole	Breakdown into Two Divisions		Breakdown of Denver Division			Breakdown of Kansas City Division			
	Denver	Kansas City	Not allocated	Downtown	Littleton	Not allocated	Downtown	Plaza	Airport

9-A3   Comparison of Productivity

World Comm and Intertel are communications companies. Comparative data for 1989 and 1995 are

		World Comm	Intertel
Sales revenue	1989	$5,824,000,000	$7,658,000,000
	1995	$6,764,000,000	$9,667,000,000
Number of employees	1989	56,600	75,900
	1995	54,800	76,200

Assume that each 1989 dollar is equivalent to 1.2 1995 dollars, owing to inflation.

Required   1. Compute 1989 and 1995 productivity measures in terms of revenues per employee for World Comm and Intertel.
2. Compare the change in productivity between 1989 and 1995 for World Comm with that for Intertel.

9-B1   Responsibility Accounting

(CMA, adapted.) The Filler Company operates a standard cost system, calculates standard cost variances for each department, and reports them to department managers. Managers are supposed to use the information to improve their operations. Superiors use the same information to evaluate managers' performance.

Sharon Keller was recently appointed manager of the assembly department of the company. She has complained that the system as designed is disadvantageous to her department. Included among the variances charged to the departments is one for rejected units. The inspection occurs at the end of the assembly department. The inspectors attempt to identify the cause of the rejection so that the department where the error occurred can be charged with it. Not all errors can easily be identified with a department, however. The nonidentified units are totaled and apportioned to the departments according to the number of identified errors. The variance for rejected units in each department is a combination of the errors caused by the department plus a portion of the unidentified causes of rejects.

Required   1. Is Keller's complaint valid? Explain the reason(s) for your answer.
2. What would you recommend that the company do to solve its problem with Keller and her complaint?

9-B2   Divisional Contribution, Performance, and Segment Margins

The president of the Northwest Railroad wants to obtain an overview of his operations, particularly with respect to comparing freight and passenger business. He has heard about "contribution" approaches to cost allocations that emphasize cost behavior

patterns and *contribution margins, contributions controllable by segment managers,* and *contributions by segments.* Pertinent data for the year ended December 31, 19X6, follow.

Total revenue was $80 million, of which $72 million was freight traffic and $8 million was passenger traffic. Fifty percent of the latter was generated by Division 1; 40% by Division 2; and 10% by Division 3.

Total variable costs were $45 million, of which $36 million was freight traffic. Of the $9 million allocable to passenger traffic, $3.3, $2.8, and $2.9 million could be allocated to Divisions 1, 2, and 3, respectively.

Total separable discretionary fixed costs were $8 million, of which $7.6 million applied to freight traffic. Of the remainder, $80,000 could not be allocated to specific divisions, although it was clearly traceable to passenger traffic in general. Divisions 1, 2, and 3 should be allocated $240,000, $60,000, and $20,000, respectively.

Total separable committed costs, which were not regarded as being controllable by segment managers, were $25 million, of which 90% was allocable to freight traffic. Of the 10% traceable to passenger traffic, Divisions 1, 2, and 3 should be allocated $1.5 million, $350,000, and $150,000, respectively; the balance was unallocable to a specific division.

The common fixed costs not clearly allocable to any part of the company amounted to $800,000.

Required

1. The president asks you to prepare statements, dividing the data for the company as a whole between the freight and passenger traffic and then subdividing the passenger traffic into three divisions.
2. Some competing railroads actively promote a series of one-day sightseeing tours on summer weekends. Most often, these tours are timed so that the cars with the tourists are hitched on with regularly scheduled passenger trains. What costs are relevant for making decisions to run such tours? Other railroads, facing the same general cost picture, refuse to conduct such sightseeing tours. Why?
3. For purposes of this analysis, even though the numbers may be unrealistic, suppose that Division 2's figures represented a specific run for a train instead of a division. Suppose further that the railroad has petitioned government authorities for permission to drop Division 2. What would be the effect on overall company net income for 19X7, assuming that the figures are accurate and that 19X7 operations are in all other respects a duplication of 19X6 operations?

Exhibit 9-7

Green River
Quality Cost Report
(thousands of dollars)

Quality Cost Area	19X4 Cost	19X6 Cost
1. Prevention cost	45	107
% of Total quality cost	3.3%	12.4%
2. Appraisal cost	124	132
% of Total quality cost	9.1%	15.2%
3. Internal failure cost	503	368
% of Total quality cost	36.9%	42.5%
Total internal quality cost (1 + 2 + 3)	672	607
% of Total quality cost	49.3%	70.1%
4. External failure cost	691	259
% of Total quality cost	50.7%	29.9%
Total quality cost	1,363	866
Total product cost	22,168	23,462

9-B3 Quality Cost Report

The manufacturing division of Green River, Inc., makes a variety of home furnishings. In 19X4 the company installed a system to report on quality costs. At the end of 19X6, Amy Green, the division general manager, wanted an assessment of whether quality costs in 19X6 differed from those in 19X4. Each month the actual costs had been compared with the plan, but at this time Green wanted to see only total annual numbers for 19X6 compared with 19X4. The production supervisor prepared the report shown in Exhibit 9-7 on page 363.

Required

1. For each of the four quality cost areas, explain what types of costs are included and how those costs have changed between 19X4 and 19X6.
2. Assess overall quality performance in 19X6 compared with 19X4. What do you suppose has caused the changes observed in quality costs?

Additional Assignment Material

Questions

9-1. What are stakeholder groups? Which stakeholder groups are most important? Why?

9-2. "There are corporate objectives other than profit." Name three.

9-3. Give three examples of how managers may improve short-run performance to the detriment of long-run results.

9-4. "Performance evaluation seeks to achieve *goal congruence* and *managerial effort*." Describe what is meant by this statement.

9-5. "Control systems in nonprofit organizations will never be as highly developed as in profit-seeking organizations." Do you agree? Explain.

9-6. "We evaluate the performance of managers using accounting reports based on whatever rules are required for financial reporting." Is this a desirable policy? Explain.

9-7. The head of the public library in a major city said, "Budgeting is a necessary evil for us. We would rather spend the time providing help to library users, but we have to prepare a budget to get city funding." Discuss this statement.

9-8. "Variable costs are controllable and fixed costs are uncontrollable." Do you agree? Explain.

9-9. "Managers of profit centers should be held responsible for the center's entire profit. They are responsible for profit even if they cannot control all factors affecting it." Discuss.

9-10. Name two major factors that influence controllability.

9-11. What is the most controversial aspect of the contribution approach to responsibility accounting?

9-12. Give four examples of segments.

9-13. "Always try to distinguish between the performance of a segment and its manager." Why?

9-14. "The contribution margin is the best measure of short-run performance." Do you agree? Explain.

9-15. What is the most important criterion in judging the effectiveness of a measure of performance?

9-16. What does the Foreign Corrupt Practices Act have to do with accounting?

9-17. Identify the three goals of an internal control system.

9-18. What are four nonfinancial measures of performance that managers find useful?

9-19. There are four categories of cost in the quality cost report; explain them.

9-20. Why are companies increasing their quality control emphasis on the prevention of defects?

9-21. Discuss how quality, cycle time, and productivity are related.

9-22. "Nonfinancial measures of performance can be controlled just like financial measures." Do you agree? Explain.

9-23. Identify three measures of labor productivity, one using all physical measures, one using all financial measures, and one that mixes physical and financial measures.

9-24. Discuss the difficulties of comparing productivity measures over time.

Exercises

9-25 Management Control Systems and Innovation

The president of a fast-growing high-technology firm remarked, "Developing budgets and comparing performance with the budgets may be fine for some firms. But we want to encourage innovations and entrepreneurship. Budgets go with bureaucracy, not innovation." Do you agree? How can a management control system encourage innovation and entrepreneurship?

9-26   Municipal Responsibility Accounting

In 1975 New York City barely avoided bankruptcy. By the late 1980s it had one of the most sophisticated budgeting and reporting systems of any municipality, and its budgetary problems had nearly disappeared. The Integrated Financial Management System (IFMS), "clearly identifies managers in line agencies, and correlates allocations and expenditures with organizational structure... In addition, managers have more time to take corrective measures when variances between budgeted and actual expenditures start to develop." (*FE—The Magazine for Financial Executives*, vol. 1, no. 8, p. 26.)

Discuss how a responsibility accounting system such as IFMS can help manage a municipality such as New York City.

9-27   Responsibility for Stable Employment Policy

The Sargent Metal Fabricating Company has been manufacturing machine tools for a number of years and has had an industrywide reputation for doing high-quality work. The company has been faced with irregularity of output over the years. It has been company policy to lay off welders as soon as there was insufficient work to keep them busy and to rehire them when demand warranted. The company, however, now has poor labor relations and finds it very difficult to hire good welders because of its layoff policy. Consequently, the quality of the work has been declining steadily.

The plant manager has proposed that the welders, who earn $18 per hour, be retained during slow periods to do menial plant maintenance work that is normally performed by workers earning $14 per hour in the plant maintenance department.

You, as controller, must decide the most appropriate accounting procedure to handle the wages of the welders doing plant maintenance work. What department(s) should be charged with this work, and at what rate? Discuss the implications of your plan.

9-28   Salesclerk's Compensation Plan

You are manager of a discount software store in Tokyo. Sales are subject to month-to-month variations, depending on the individual salesclerk's efforts. A new salary-plus-bonus plan has been in effect for four months, and you are reviewing a sales performance report. The plan provides for a base salary of ¥45,000 per month, a ¥68,000 bonus each month if the monthly sales quota is met, and an additional commission of 5% of all sales over the monthly quota. The quota is set approximately 3% above the previous month's sales to motivate clerks toward increasing sales (in thousands):

		Salesclerk A	Salesclerk B	Salesclerk C
January	Quota	¥4,500	¥1,500	¥7,500
	Actual	1,500	1,500	9,000
February	Quota	¥1,545	¥1,545	¥9,270
	Actual	3,000	1,545	3,000
March	Quota	¥3,090	¥1,590	¥3,090
	Actual	5,250	750	9,000
April	Quota	¥5,400	¥ 775	¥9,270
	Actual	1,500	780	4,050

Required

1. Compute the compensation for each salesclerk for each month.
2. Evaluate the compensation plan. Be specific. What changes would you recommend?

9-29   Internal Control

The Fortune Company keeps careful control over its inventory. An important factor in its internal control is *separation of duties*. The purchasing personnel are not authorized to sign for the receipt of physical inventories, and those in charge of inventory records do not perform the regular count of the physical inventory.

Required   Briefly describe an irregularity that would probably be discovered or prevented by each of the two separations of duties described.

9-30   Performance Evaluation

Matthew Kennedy is a stock brokerage firm that evaluates its employees on sales activity generated. Recently the firm also began evaluating its stockbrokers on the number of new accounts generated.

Required   Discuss how these two performance measures are consistent and how they may conflict. Do you believe that these measures are appropriate for the long-term goal of profitability?

9-31   Quality Theories Compared

Sketch the two graphs as they appear below. Compare the total quality management approach by Deming to the traditional theory of quality. Complete the graphs by identifying which graph represents the total quality management approach versus the traditional theory. Which theory do you believe represents the current realities of today's global competitive environment?

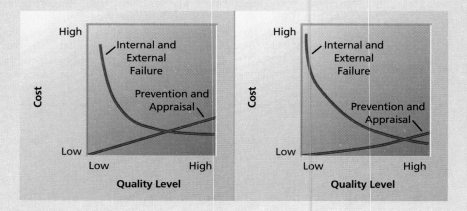

9-32   Cycle-Time Reporting

MainFrame Computers monitors its cycle time closely to prevent schedule delays and excessive costs. The standard cycle time for the manufacture of printed circuit boards for one of its computers is 25.5 hours. Consider the following cycle time data from the past 6 weeks of circuit board production:

Week	Units Completed	Total Cycle Time
1	564	14,108 hours
2	544	14,592
3	553	15,152
4	571	16,598
5	547	17,104
6	552	16,673

Required   Analyze circuit board cycle time performance in light of the 25.5-hour objective.

Problems

9-33 Multiple Goals and Profitability

The following multiple goals were identified by the General Electric company:

Profitability	Employee attitudes
Market position	Public responsibility
Productivity	Balance between short-range and
Product leadership	long-range goals
Personnel development	

General Electric is a huge, highly decentralized corporation. It had approximately 170 responsibility centers called "departments," but that is a deceiving term. In most other companies, these departments would be called divisions. For example, some GE departments have sales of over $500 million.

Each department manager's performance is evaluated annually in relation to the specified multiple goals. A special measurements group was set up to devise ways of quantifying accomplishments in each of the areas. In this way, the evaluation of performance would become more objective as the various measures were developed and improved.

Required

1. How would you measure performance in each of these areas? Be specific.
2. Can the other goals be encompassed as ingredients of a formal measure of profitability? In other words, can profitability per se be defined to include the other goals?

9-34 Responsibility Accounting, Profit Centers, and Contribution Approach

Consider the following data for the year's operations of an automobile dealer:

General dealership overhead	$ 120,000
Advertising of vehicles	120,000
Sales commissions, vehicles	48,000
Sales salaries, vehicles	60,000
Sales of vehicles	2,400,000
Sales of parts and service	600,000
Cost of vehicle sales	1,920,000
Parts and service materials	180,000
Parts and service labor	240,000
Parts and service overhead	60,000

The president of the dealership has long regarded the markup on material and labor for the parts and service activity as the amount that is supposed to cover all parts and service overhead plus all general overhead of the dealership. In other words, the parts and service department is viewed as a cost-recovery operation, and the sales of vehicles as the income-producing activity.

Required

1. Prepare a departmentalized operating statement that harmonizes with the views of the president.
2. Prepare an alternative operating statement that would reflect a different view of the dealership operations. Assume that $12,000 and $60,000 of the $120,000 general overhead can be allocated with confidence to the parts and service department and to sales of vehicles, respectively. The remaining $48,000 cannot be allocated except in some highly arbitrary manner.
3. Comment on the relative merits of requirements 1 and 2.

9-35 Incentives in Former Soviet Union

Before the country's breakup, officials in what had been the Soviet Union had been rewarding managers for exceeding a five-year-plan target for production quantities. A problem arose, however, because managers naturally tended to predict low volumes so that the targets would be set low. This hindered planning; good information about production possibilities was lacking.

The Soviets then devised a new performance evaluation measure. Suppose F is the forecast of production, A is actual production, and X, Y, and Z are positive constants set by top officials, with $X, Y, Z > 0$. The following performance measure was designed to motivate both high production and accurate forecasts.

$$\text{performance} = \begin{cases} (Y \times F) + [X \times (A - F)] & \text{if } F \le A \\ (Y \times F) - [Z \times (F - A)] & \text{if } F > A \end{cases}$$

Consider the Moscow Automotive Factory. During 1994 the factory manager, Nicolai Konstantin, had to predict the number of automobiles that could be produced during the next year. He was confident that at least 700,000 autos could be produced in 1995, and most likely they could produce 800,000 autos. With good luck, they might even produce 900,000. Government officials told him that the new performance evaluation measure would be used, and that $X = .50$, $Y = .80$, and $Z = 1.00$ for 1995 and 1996.

Required

1. Suppose Konstantin predicted production of 800,000 autos and 800,000 were produced. Calculate the performance measure.
2. Suppose again that 800,000 autos were produced. Calculate the performance measure if Konstantin had been conservative and predicted only 700,000 autos. Also calculate the performance measure if he had predicted 900,000 autos.
3. Now suppose it is November 1995 and it is clear that the 800,000 target cannot be achieved. Does the performance measure motivate continued efforts to increase production? Suppose it is clear that the 800,000 target will be met easily. Will the system motivate continued effort to increase production?

9-36   Productivity
NorthernComm, a telephone communications company, purchased the controlling interest in Telecom Corporation in an eastern European country. A key productivity measure monitored by NorthernComm is the number of customer telephone lines per employee. Consider the following data:

	19X6 without Telecom	19X6 with Telecom	19X5
Customer lines	15,054,000	19,994,000	14,615,000
Employees	74,520	114,590	72,350
Lines per employee	202	174	202

Required

1. What are NorthernComm's 19X5 productivity and its 19X6 productivity without Telecom?
2. What are NorthernComm's 19X6 productivity with Telecom and Telecom's 19X6 productivity?
3. What difficulties do you foresee if NorthernComm brings Telecom's productivity in line?

9-37   Productivity Measurement
Grace Laundry had the following results in 19X4 and 19X7:

	19X4	19X7
Pounds of laundry processed	1,360,000 pounds	1,525,000 pounds
Sales revenue	$720,000	$1,394,000

continued

	19X4	19X7
Direct-labor-hours worked	45,100 hours	46,650 hours
Direct-labor cost	$316,000	$498,000

Grace used the same facilities in 19X7 as in 19X4. During the past 3 years, however, the company put more effort into training its employees. The manager of Grace was curious about whether the training had increased labor productivity.

Required

1. Compute a measure of labor productivity for 19X7 based entirely on physical measures. Do the same for 19X4. That is, from the data given, choose measures of physical output and physical input, and use them to compare the physical productivity of labor in 19X7 with that in 19X4.

2. Compute a measure of labor productivity for 19X7 based entirely on financial measures. Do the same for 19X4. That is, from the data given, choose measures of financial output and financial input, and use them to compare the financial productivity of labor in 19X7 with that in 19X4.

3. Suppose the following productivity measure were used:

$$\text{productivity} = \frac{\text{sales revenue}}{\text{direct-labor-hours worked}}$$

Because of inflation each 19X4 dollar is equivalent to 1.4 19X7 dollars. Compute appropriate productivity numbers for comparing 19X7 productivity with 19X4 productivity.

Cases

9-38   Trade-Offs among Objectives

Datanet Company performs routine and custom information systems services for many other companies in a large midwestern metropolitan area. Datanet has built a reputation for high-quality customer service and job security for its employees. Quality service and customer satisfaction have been Datanet's primary subgoals—retaining a skilled and motivated work force has been an important factor in achieving those goals. In the past, temporary downturns in business did not mean layoffs of employees, though some employees were required to perform other than their usual tasks. In anticipation of growth in business, Datanet leased new equipment that, beginning in August, added $10,000 per month in operating costs. Three months ago, however, a new competitor began offering the same services to Datanet customers at prices averaging 20% lower than Datanet. Roger Jones, the company founder and president, believes that a significant price reduction is necessary to maintain the company's market share and avoid financial ruin, but he is puzzled about how to achieve it without compromising quality, service, and the goodwill of his work force.

Datanet has a productivity objective of 20 accounts per employee. Jones does not think that he can increase this productivity and still maintain both quality and flexibility to customer needs. Datanet also monitors average cost per account and the number of customer satisfaction adjustments (resolutions of complaints). The average billing markup rate is 25%. Consider the following data from the past 6 months:

	June	July	August	September	October	November
Number of accounts	797	803	869	784	723	680
Number of employees	40	41	44	43	43	41
Average cost per account	$153	$153	$158	$173	$187	$191
Average salary per employee	$3,000	$3,000	$3,000	$3,000	$3,000	$3,000

Required   **1.** Discuss the trade-offs facing Roger Jones.
       2. Can you suggest solutions to his trade-off dilemma?

9-39   Review of Chapters 1–9

As you are about to depart on a business trip, your accountant hands you the following information about your Thailand division:

1. The master budget for the fiscal year just ended on October 31, 19X6:

Sales	$850,000
Manufacturing cost of goods sold	670,000
Manufacturing margin	$180,000
Selling and administrative expenses	120,000
Operating income	$ 60,000

2. The budgeted sales and production mix:

Product A	50,000 units
Product B	70,000 units

3. The standard variable manufacturing cost per unit:

Product A		
Direct material	10 pieces @ $0.25	$2.50
Direct labor	1 hour @ $3.00	3.00
Variable overhead	1 hour @ $2.00	2.00
		$7.50

Product B		
Direct material	5 pounds @ $0.10	$0.50
Direct labor	.3 hours @ $2.50	0.75
Variable overhead	.3 hours @ $2.50	0.75
		$2.00

4. All budgeted selling and administrative expenses are common, fixed expenses; 60% are discretionary expenses.

5. The actual income statement for the fiscal year ended October 31, 19X6:

Sales	$850,000
Manufacturing cost of goods sold	685,200
Manufacturing margin	$164,800
Selling and administrative expenses	116,000
Operating income	$ 48,800

6. The actual sales and production mix:

Product A	53,000 units
Product B	64,000 units

7. The budgeted and actual sales prices

Product A	$10
Product B	5

8. The schedule of the actual *variable* manufacturing cost of goods sold by product (actual quantities in parentheses):

Product A:	Material	$134,500 (538,000 pieces)
	Labor	156,350 (53,000 hours)
	Overhead	108,650 (53,000 hours)
Product B:	Material	38,400 (320,000 pounds)
	Labor	50,000 (20,000 hours)
	Overhead	50,000 (20,000 hours)
		$537,900

9. Products A and B are manufactured in separate facilities. Of the *budgeted* fixed manufacturing cost, $130,000 is separable as follows: $45,000 to product A and $85,000 to product B. Ten percent of these separate costs are discretionary. All other budgeted fixed manufacturing expenses, separable and common, are committed.

The purpose of your business trip is a board of directors meeting. During the meeting it is quite likely that some of the information from your accountant will be discussed. In anticipation you set out to prepare answers to possible questions. (There are no beginning or ending inventories.)

Required

1. Determine the firm's *budgeted* break-even point in dollars, overall contribution-margin ratio, and contribution margins per unit by product.
2. Considering products A and B as *segments* of the firm, find the *budgeted* "contribution by segments" for each.
3. It is decided to allocate the *budgeted* selling and administrative expenses to the segments (in requirement 2) as follows: committed costs on the basis of budgeted unit sales mix and discretionary costs on the basis of actual unit sales mix. What are the final expense allocations? Briefly appraise the allocation method.
4. How would you respond to a proposal to base commissions to salespersons on the sales (revenue) value of orders received? Assume all salespersons have the opportunity to sell both products.
5. Determine the firm's *actual* "contribution margin" and "contribution controllable by segment managers" for the fiscal year ended October 31, 19X6. Assume *no* variances in committed fixed costs.
6. Determine the "sales-activity variance" for each product for the fiscal year ended October 31, 19X6.
7. Determine and identify all variances in *variable* manufacturing costs by product for the fiscal year ended October 31, 19X6.

10 Management Control in Decentralized Organizations

Three divisions of LA Darling Company located in Missouri and Arkansas supply the metal racks, wooden cases, and metal shelves for this computer software retailer. LA Darling's division managers use negotiated transfer prices when supplying parts to other divisions.
Courtesy LA Darling Company

Learning Objectives

When you have finished studying this chapter, you should be able to

1   Define decentralization and identify its expected benefits and costs.

2   Distinguish between profit centers and decentralization.

3   Define transfer prices and identify their purpose.

4   Identify the relative advantages and disadvantages of basing transfer prices on total costs, variable costs, and market prices.

5   Identify the factors affecting multinational transfer prices.

6   Explain how the linking of rewards to responsibility center results affects incentives and risk.

7   Compute ROI and residual income and contrast them as criteria for judging the performance of organization segments.

8   Identify the advantages/disadvantages of using various bases for measuring the invested capital used by organization segments.

As organizations grow and undertake more diverse and complex activities, many elect to delegate decision-making authority to managers throughout the organization. This delegation of the freedom to make decisions is called **decentralization**. The lower in the organization that this freedom exists, the greater the decentralization. Decentralization is a matter of degree along a continuum:

decentralization The delegation of freedom to make decisions. The lower in the organization that this freedom exists, the greater the decentralization.

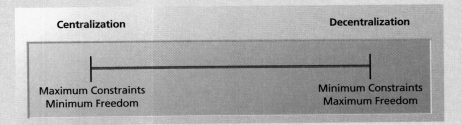

This chapter focuses on the role of management control systems in decentralized organizations. After providing an overview of decentralization, the chapter addresses the special problems created when one segment of an organization charges another for providing goods or services. Then it discusses how performance measures can be used to motivate managers. Finally, measures used to assess the profitability of decentralized units are introduced and compared.

Objective 1

Define decentralization and identify its expected benefits and costs

373

Decentralization was a popular response to the declining economy and increasing global competition in the mid-1990s. IBM is a typical example. A reorganization that began in 1988 and was expanded in late 1991 was the most drastic decentralization in IBM's history. The goal was to break IBM into numerous business units that act as if they were independent of one another. Similarly, General Electric has 13 "strategic business units" that act independently. Internationally, Siemens, which is Germany's counterpart to General Electric, has separate units, each with its own chief executive officer and board of directors.

Increasing sophistication of telecommunications—especially electronic mail and facsimile machines—aids decentralization. Geographical separation no longer must mean lack of access to information. Both sales and production units are being relocated far from headquarters without top management losing knowledge of what is happening in the units.

■ CENTRALIZATION VERSUS DECENTRALIZATION

At any time, some firms will see advantages in decentralization and some in centralization. Consider the international airline industry in the mid-1990s. Most airlines, such as South China Airlines, Iberia Airlines, and Air France, were decentralizing. In contrast, at the same time, Sabena, Belgium's state-owned airline, was reorganizing to *reverse* its trend toward decentralization. In the insurance industry, Aetna was decentralizing at the same time Equitable was centralizing. Even the United States Army, a very centralized organization, has started some decentralization in recent years.

Costs and Benefits

There are many benefits of at least some decentralization for most organizations. First, lower-level managers have the best information concerning local conditions and therefore may be able to make better decisions than their superiors. Second, managers acquire decision-making ability and other management skills that help them move upward in the organization, assuring continuity of leadership. In addition, managers enjoy higher status from being independent and thus are better motivated.

Of course, decentralization is not without costs. Managers may make decisions that are not in the organization's best interests, either because they act to improve their own segment's performance at the expense of the organization or because they are not aware of relevant facts from other segments. Managers in decentralized organizations also tend to duplicate services that might be less expensive if centralized (e.g., accounting, advertising, and personnel). Furthermore, under decentralization, costs of accumulating and processing information frequently rise because responsibility accounting reports are needed for top management to learn about and evaluate decentralized units and their managers. Finally, managers in decentralized units may waste time dickering with other units about goods or services one unit provides to the other.

Decentralization is more popular in profit-seeking organizations (where outputs and inputs can be measured) than in nonprofit organizations.

Decentralization in the 1990s

Many companies moved to decentralize their operations in one way or another during the 1990s, among them PepsiCo, DuPont, and Procter & Gamble. But the two companies that stood out in their efforts to decentralize were IBM and Johnson & Johnson. The two companies approached decentralization from very different perspectives.

Johnson & Johnson (1994 sales of $15.7 billion and net income of over $2 billion), maker of Tylenol, Band Aids, Johnson's Baby Powder, Ortho birth control pills, and many other products, has a long history of decentralization, beginning in the 1930s. Its 166 separately chartered companies are empowered to act independently. Although ultimately accountable to executives at J & J headquarters in New Brunswick, New Jersey, some segment presidents see their bosses as few as four times a year. An article in *Business Week* called J & J "a model of how to make decentralization work." CEO Ralph Larson says that decentralization "provides a sense of ownership and responsibility for a business that you simply cannot get any other way." Larson sees his role as providing direction but giving managers creative freedom.

J & J spent the early 1990s fine-tuning its decentralized system to erase costly mistakes that could have been avoided with more guidance from top management. Also, J & J had incurred high overhead costs as independent units duplicated many functions. Larson introduced methods of coordinating the independent units while still preserving the basics of decentralization. Although perhaps toning down the degree of decentralization, Larson vows that J & J

"will never give up the principle of decentralization, which is to give our operating executives ownership of a business. They are ultimately responsible."

IBM, in contrast, entered the 1990s a highly centralized firm. Its growth, though, had stalled, and it lost more than $15 billion during 1991–1993. Chairman John Akers instituted a vast reorganization that grants managers great autonomy but also puts pressure on them to perform. The plan is to make IBM a set of "wholly owned but more or less autonomous marketing, service, product development, and manufacturing companies." Segment managers will have far more decision-making freedom, but they will also have to show results on the bottom line.

IBM's new structure includes 13 distinct businesses, nine in manufacturing and development and four in marketing and services. Each of the 13 managers will be measured against targets in seven areas: revenue growth, profit, return on assets, cash flow, customer satisfaction, quality, and employee morale. Heavy incentives are tied to making performance targets. IBM hopes the reorganization will unleash the energy and creativity that were part of IBM's past but have been lacking in recent years. IBM earned a profit in 1994 that may indicate its efforts are paying off. ■

Source: Adapted from "A Big Company That Works," Business Week, *May 4, 1992, pp. 124–130, and D. Kirkpatrick, "Breaking Up IBM," Fortune, July 27, 1992, pp. 44–58.*

Managers can be given freedom when their results are measurable so that they can be held accountable for them. Poor decisions in a profit-seeking firm become apparent from the inadequate profit generated. Most nonprofit organizations lack such a reliable performance indicator, so granting managerial freedom is more risky.

Middle Ground

Philosophies of decentralization differ considerably. Cost-benefit considerations usually require that some management decisions be highly decentralized and others centralized. To illustrate, much of the controller's problem-solving and attention-directing functions may be decentralized and handled at lower levels, whereas income tax planning and mass scorekeeping such as payroll may be highly centralized.

Decentralization is most successful when an organization's segments are relatively independent of one another—that is, the decisions of a manager in one segment will not affect the fortunes of another segment. If segments do much internal buying or selling, much buying from the same outside suppliers, or much selling to the same outside markets, they are candidates for heavier centralization.

In Chapter 9 we stressed that cost-benefit tests, goal congruence, and managerial effort must all be considered when designing a control system. If management has decided in favor of heavy decentralization, **segment autonomy,** the delegation of decision-making power to managers of segments of an organization, is also crucial. For decentralization to work, however, this autonomy must be real, not just lip service. In most circumstances top managers must be willing to abide by decisions made by segment managers.

segment autonomy
The delegation of decision-making power to managers of segments of an organization.

Profit Centers and Decentralization

Do not confuse *profit centers* (accountability for revenue and expenses) with *decentralization* (freedom to make decisions). They are entirely separate concepts, although profit centers clearly are accounting devices that can aid decentralization. One can exist without the other. Some profit center managers possess vast freedom to make decisions concerning labor contracts, supplier choices, equipment purchases, personnel decisions, and so on. In contrast, other profit center managers may need top-management approval for almost all the decisions just mentioned. Indeed, cost centers may be more heavily decentralized than profit centers if cost center managers have more freedom to make decisions.

The literature contains many criticisms of profit centers on the grounds that managers are given profit responsibility without commensurate authority. Therefore, the criticism continues, the profit center is "artificial" because the manager is not free to make a sufficient number of the decisions that affect profit.

Such criticisms confuse profit centers and decentralization. The fundamental question in deciding between using a cost center or a profit center for a given segment is not whether heavy decentralization exists. Instead, the fundamental question is: Will a profit center better solve the problems of goal congruence and management effort than a cost center? In other words, do I predict that a profit center will induce the managers to make a better collective set of decisions from the viewpoint of the organization as a whole?

All control systems are imperfect. Judgments about their merits should concentrate on which alternative system will bring more of the actions top management seeks. For example, a plant may seem to be a "natural" cost center because the plant manager has no influence over decisions concerning the marketing of its products. Still, some companies evaluate a plant manager by the plant's profitability. Why? Because this broader evaluation base will affect the plant manager's behavior. Instead of being concerned solely with running an efficient cost center, the plant manager now "naturally" considers quality control more carefully and reacts to customers' special requests more sympathetically. A profit center may thus obtain the desired plant-manager behavior that a cost center cannot. In designing accounting control systems then, top managers must consider the system's impact on behavior desired by the organization.

■ TRANSFER PRICING

Very few problems arise in decentralized organizations when all the segments are independent of one another. Segment managers can then focus only on their own segments without hurting the organization as a whole. In contrast, when segments interact greatly, there is an increased possibility that what is best for one segment hurts another segment badly enough to have a negative effect on the entire organization. Such a situation may occur when one segment provides products or services to another segment and charges that segment a *transfer price*. **Transfer prices** are the amounts charged by one segment of an organization for a product or service that it supplies to another segment of the same organization. Most often, the term is associated with materials, parts, or finished goods. The transfer price is revenue to the segment producing the product or service, and it is a cost to the acquiring segment.

transfer price The amount charged by one segment of an organization for a product or service that it supplies to another segment of the same organization.

Purposes of Transfer Pricing

Why do transfer-pricing systems exist? The principal reason is to communicate data that will lead to goal-congruent decisions. For example, transfer prices should guide managers to make the best possible decisions regarding whether to buy or sell products and services inside or outside the total organization. Another important reason is to evaluate segment performance and thus motivate both the selling manager and the buying manager toward goal-congruent decisions. Finally, companies that are multinational in scope use transfer pricing to minimize their worldwide taxes, duties, and tariffs. These are easy aims to describe, but they are difficult aims to achieve.

Organizations solve their problems by using cost-based prices for some transfers, market-based prices for other transfers, and negotiated prices for others. Therefore, do not expect to obtain a single, universally applicable answer in the area of transfer pricing. It is a subject of continuous concern to top management. Whenever there is a lull in a conversation with a manager, try asking, "Do you have any transfer-pricing problems?" The response is usually, "Let me tell you about the peculiar transfer-pricing difficulties in my organization." A manager in a large wood products firm called transfer pricing his firm's most troublesome management control issue.

Transfers at Cost

Approximately half of the major companies in the world transfer items at cost. However, there are many possible definitions of cost. Some companies use only variable cost, others use full cost, and still others use full cost plus a profit markup. Some use standard costs and some use actual costs.

When the transfer price is some version of cost, transfer pricing is nearly identical to cost allocation (see Chapters 4 and 13). Costs are accumulated in one segment and then assigned to (or transferred to) another segment. Details of this process are covered in Chapter 13, but two important points deserve mention here.

First, transferring or allocating costs can disguise a cost's behavior pattern. Consider a computer manufacturer, such as Apple, that makes keyboards in one division and transfers them to another division for assembly into personal computers. The manager of the Keyboard Division may have good knowledge of the cost drivers affecting the costs of keyboards. But if a single transfer price per unit is charged when transferring the keyboards to the Assembly Division, the only cost driver affecting the cost to the Assembly Division is "units of keyboards." Cost drivers other than units produced are ignored, and distinctions between fixed and variable costs are blurred. The Assembly Division manager sees the entire cost of keyboards as a variable cost, regardless of what the true cost behavior is.

Other problems arise if *actual* cost is used as a transfer price. Because actual cost cannot be known in advance, the buying segment lacks a reliable basis for planning. More important, because inefficiencies are merely passed along to the buying division, the supplying division lacks incentive to control its costs. Thus, using budgeted or standard costs instead of actual costs is recommended for both cost allocation and transfer pricing.

Market-Based Transfer Prices

If there is a competitive market for the product or service being transferred internally, using the market price as a transfer price will generally lead to the desired goal congruence and managerial effort. The market price may come from published price lists for similar products or services, or it may be the price charged by the producing division to its external customers. If the latter, the internal transfer price may be the external market price less the selling and delivery expenses that are not incurred on internal business. The major drawback to market-based prices is that market prices are not always available for items transferred internally.

Consider a major outdoor equipment manufacturer that makes clothing and gear for all kinds of outdoor activities. One division of the company makes fabrics that are used in many final products as well as being sold directly to external customers, and another division makes tents. A particular tent requires 5 square yards of a special waterproof fabric. Should the Tent Division obtain the fabric from the Fabric Division of the company or purchase it from an external supplier?

Suppose the market price of the fabric is $10 per square yard, or $50 per tent, and assume for the moment that the Fabric Division can sell its entire production to external customers without incurring any marketing or shipping costs. The Tent Division manager will refuse to pay a transfer price greater than $50 for the fabric for each tent. Why? Because if the transfer price is greater than $50, she will purchase the fabric from the external supplier in order to maximize her division's profit.

Furthermore, the manager of the Fabric Division will not sell five square yards of fabric for less than $50. Why? Because he can sell it on the market for $50, so any lower price will reduce his division's profit. The only transfer price that allows both managers to maximize their division's profit is $50, the market price. If the managers had autonomy to make decisions, one of them would decline the internal production of fabric at any transfer price other than $50.

Now suppose the Fabric Division incurs a $1 per square yard marketing and shipping cost that can be avoided by transferring the fabric to the Tent Division instead of marketing it to outside customers. Most companies would then use a transfer price of $9 per square yard, or $45 per tent, often called a "market-price-minus" transfer price. The Fabric Division would get the same net amount from the transfer ($45 with no marketing or shipping costs) as from an external sale ($50 less $5 marketing and shipping costs), whereas the Tent Division saves $5 per tent. Thus the organization overall benefits.

<table>
<tr><td>Exhibit 10-1</td><td colspan="3">Sell Fabric Outside</td><td colspan="4">Use Fabric to Make Tent</td></tr>
<tr><td>Data for Analysis of
Transfer Prices</td><td>Market price per yard
of fabric to outsiders</td><td>$10</td><td></td><td>Sales price of
finished tent</td><td></td><td></td><td>$100</td></tr>
<tr><td></td><td>Variable costs per yard
of fabric</td><td>8</td><td></td><td>Variable costs</td><td></td><td></td><td></td></tr>
<tr><td></td><td>Contribution margin
per yard</td><td>$ 2</td><td></td><td>Fabric Division
(5 yds @ $8)
Tent Division</td><td></td><td>$40</td><td></td></tr>
<tr><td></td><td>Total contribution for
50,000 yards</td><td>$100,000</td><td></td><td>Processing
Selling</td><td>$41
12</td><td>
53</td><td>
93</td></tr>
<tr><td></td><td></td><td></td><td></td><td>Contribution
margin</td><td></td><td></td><td>$ 7</td></tr>
<tr><td></td><td></td><td></td><td></td><td>Total contribution
for 10,000 tents</td><td></td><td></td><td>$70,000</td></tr>
</table>

Variable-Cost Pricing

Market prices have innate appeal in a profit-center context, but they are not cure-all answers to transfer-pricing problems. Sometimes market prices do not exist, are inapplicable, or are impossible to determine. For example, no intermediate markets may exist for specialized parts, or markets may be too thin or scattered to permit the determination of a credible price. In these instances, versions of "cost-plus-a-profit" are often used in an attempt to provide a fair or equitable substitute for regular market prices.

To illustrate, consider again the outdoor equipment manufacturer. Exhibit 10-1 shows its selling prices and variable costs per unit. In this example the Fabric Division's variable costs of $8 per yard are the only costs affected by producing the additional fabric for transfer to the Tent Division. On receiving 5 yards of fabric, the Tent Division spends an additional $53 to process and sell each tent. Whether the fabric should be manufactured and transferred to the Tent Division depends on the existence of idle capacity in the Fabric Division (insufficient demand from outside customers).

As Exhibit 10-1 shows, if there were no *idle capacity* in the Fabric Division, the optimum action for the company as a whole would be for the Fabric Division to sell outside at $50, because the Tent Division would incur $53 of additional variable costs but add only $50 of additional revenue ($100 − $50). Using market price would provide the correct motivation for such a decision because, if the fabric were transferred, the Tent Division's cost would be $50 + $53 or $103, which would be $3 higher than its prospective revenue of $100 per unit. So the Tent Division would choose not to buy from the Fabric Division at the $50 market price. Of course, the Tent Division also would not buy from outside suppliers at a price of $50. If fabric is not available at less than $50 per tent, this particular tent will not be produced.

What if the Fabric Division has idle capacity sufficient to meet all the Tent Division's requirements? The optimum action would be to produce the fabric and transfer it to the Tent Division. Idle capacity implies that the Fabric Division could not sell the fabric to external customers and therefore would have zero contribution. If there were no production and transfer, the Tent Division and the company as a whole would forgo a total contribution of $70,000. In this situation, variable cost would be the better basis for transfer pricing and would lead to the optimum decision for the firm as a whole. To be more precise, the transfer price would be all additional costs that will be incurred by the production of the fabric to be transferred. For example, if a lump-sum setup cost is required to produce the 50,000 square yards of fabric required, the setup cost should be added to the variable cost in calculating the appropriate transfer price. (In the example there is no such cost.)

Negotiated Transfer Prices

Companies heavily committed to segment autonomy often allow managers to negotiate transfer prices. The managers may consider both costs and market prices in their negotiations, but no policy requires them to do so. Supporters of negotiated transfer prices maintain that the managers involved have the best knowledge of what the company will gain or lose by producing and transferring the product or service, so open negotiation allows the managers to make optimal decisions. Critics focus on the time and effort spent negotiating, an activity that adds nothing directly to the profits of the company.

Dysfunctional Behavior

dysfunctional behavior Any action taken in conflict with organizational goals.

Virtually any type of transfer pricing policy can lead to **dysfunctional behavior**—actions taken in conflict with organizational goals. Gulf Oil provides a clear example. Segments tried to make their results look good at each other's expense. One widespread result: inflated transfer payments among the Gulf segments as each one vied to boost its own bottom line. A top manager, quoted in *Business Week*, commented, "Gulf doesn't ring the cash register until we've made an outside sale."

What prompts such behavior? Reconsider the situation depicted in Exhibit 10-1. Suppose the Fabric Division *has idle capacity*. As we saw earlier, when there is idle capacity, the optimal transfer price is the variable cost of $40 (i.e., $8 per yard). As long as the fabric is worth at least $40 to the Tent Division, the company as a whole is better off with the transfer. Nevertheless, in a decentralized company the Fabric Division manager, working in the division's best interests, may argue that the transfer price should be based on the market price instead of variable cost. If the division is a profit center, the objective is to obtain as high a price as possible because such a price maximizes the contribution to the division's profit. (This strategy assumes that the number of units transferred will be unaffected by the transfer price—an assumption that is often shaky.)

If the company uses a market-based transfer-pricing policy when the Fabric Division has idle capacity, dysfunctional behavior can occur. At a $50 transfer price, the Tent Division manager will not purchase the fabric and make the tent. Why? Because at a transfer price of $50 and with additional processing costs of $53, the division's cost of $103 will exceed the tent's $100 selling price. Because the true *additional* cost of the fabric to the company is $40, the company forgoes a contribution of $100 − ($40 + $53) = $7 per tent.

Now suppose the Fabric Division has *no idle capacity*. A variable-cost transfer-pricing policy can lead to dysfunctional decisions. The Tent Division manager might argue for a variable-cost-based transfer price. After all, the lowest possible transfer price will maximize the Tent Division's profit. But such a policy will not motivate the Fabric Division to produce fabric for the Tent Division. As long as output can be sold on the outside market for any price above the variable cost, the Fabric Division will use its capacity to produce for the market, regardless of how valuable the fabric might be to the Tent Division.

How are such dilemmas resolved? One possibility is for top management to impose a "fair" transfer price and insist that a transfer be made. But managers in a decentralized company often regard such orders as undermining their autonomy.

Alternatively, managers might be given the freedom to negotiate transfer prices on their own. The Tent Division manager might look at the selling price of the tent, $100, less the additional cost the division incurs in making it, $53, and decide to purchase fabric at any transfer price less than $100 − $53 = $47. The Tent Division will add to its profit by making the tent if the transfer price is below $47.

Similarly, the Fabric Division manager will look at what it costs to produce and transfer the fabric. If there is idle capacity, any transfer price above $40 will increase the Fabric Division's profit. However, if there is no idle capacity, so that transferring a unit causes the division to give up an external sale at $50, the minimum transfer price acceptable to the Fabric Division is $50.

Negotiation will result in a transfer if the maximum transfer price the Tent Division is willing to pay is greater than the minimum transfer price the Fabric Division is willing to accept. When the Fabric Division has idle capacity, a transfer at a price between $40 and $47 will occur. The exact transfer price may depend on the negotiating ability of the two division managers. However, if the Fabric Division has no idle capacity, a transfer will not occur. Therefore, the manager's decisions are congruent with the company's best interests.

Use of Incentives

What should top management of a decentralized organization do if it sees segment managers making dysfunctional decisions? As usual, the answer is, "It depends." Top management can step in and force transfers, but doing so undermines segment managers' autonomy and the overall notion of decentralization. Frequent intervention results in recentralization. Indeed, if more centralization is desired, the organization could be redesigned by combining segments.

Top managers who wish to encourage decentralization will often make sure that both producing and purchasing division managers understand all the facts and then allow the managers to negotiate a transfer price. Even when top managers suspect that a dysfunctional decision might be made, they may swallow hard and accept the segment manager's judgment as a cost of decentralization. (Of course, repeated dysfunctional decision making may be a reason to change the organizational design or to change managers.)

Well-trained and informed segment managers who understand opportunity costs and fixed and variable costs will often make better decisions than will top managers. The producing division manager knows best the various uses of its capacity, and the purchasing division manager knows best what profit can be made on the items to be transferred. In addition, negotiation allows segments to respond flexibly to changing market conditions when setting transfer prices. One transfer price may be appropriate in a time of idle capacity, and another when demand increases and operations approach full capacity.

To increase segment managers' willingness to accommodate one another's needs and benefit the organization as a whole, top managers rely on both formal and informal communications. They may informally ask segment managers to be "good company citizens" and to sacrifice results for the good of the organization. They may also formalize this communication by basing performance evaluation and rewards on companywide as well as segment results. In the case of our outdoor equipment maker, the contribution to the company as a whole, $70,000 in the idle capacity case, could be split between the Fabric and Tent Divisions, perhaps equally, perhaps in proportion to the variable costs of each, or perhaps via negotiation.

The Need for Many Transfer Prices

As you can see, there is seldom a single transfer price that will ensure the desired decisions. The "correct" transfer price depends on the economic and legal circumstances and the decision at hand. Organizations may have to make trade-offs between pricing for congruence and pricing to spur managerial effort. Furthermore, the optimal price for either may differ from that employed for tax reporting or for other external needs.

Income taxes, property taxes, and tariffs often influence the setting of transfer prices so that the firm as a whole will benefit, even though the performance of a segment may suffer. For example, to maximize tax deductions for percentage depletion allowances, which are based on revenue, a petroleum company may want to transfer crude oil to other segments at as high a price as legally possible.

Transfer pricing is also influenced in some situations by state fair-trade laws and national antitrust acts. Because of the differences in national tax structures around the world or because of the differences in the incomes of various divisions and subsidiaries, the firm may wish to shift profits and "dump" goods, if legally possible. These considerations further illustrate the limits of decentralization where heavy interdependencies exist and explain why the same company may use different transfer prices for different purposes.

Multinational Transfer Pricing

Objective 5

Identify the factors affecting multinational transfer prices

Transfer-pricing policies of domestic companies focus on goal congruence and motivation. In multinational companies, other factors may dominate. For example, multinational companies use transfer prices to minimize worldwide income taxes, import duties, and tariffs.

Suppose a division in a high-income-tax-rate country produces a subcomponent for another division in a low-income-tax-rate country. By setting a low transfer price, most of the profit from the production can be recognized in the low-income-tax-rate country, thereby minimizing taxes. Likewise, items produced by divisions in a low-income-tax-rate country and transferred to a division in a high-income-tax-rate country should have a high transfer price to minimize taxes.

Sometimes income tax effects are offset by import duties. Usually import duties are based on the price paid for an item, whether bought from an outside company or transferred from another division. Therefore low transfer prices generally lead to low import duties.

Of course, tax authorities recognize the incentive to set transfer prices to minimize taxes and import duties. Therefore most countries have restrictions on allowable transfer prices. U.S. multinationals must follow an Internal Revenue Code rule specifying that transfers be priced at "arm's-length" market values, or at the values that would be used if the divisions were independent companies. Even with this rule, companies have some latitude in deciding an appropriate "arm's-length" price.

Consider an item produced by Division A in a country with a 25% income tax rate and transferred to Division B in a country with a 50% income tax rate. In addition, an import duty equal to 20% of the price of the item is assessed. Suppose the full unit cost of the item is $100, and the variable cost is $60. If tax authorities allow either variable- or full-cost transfer prices, which should be chosen? By transferring at $100 rather than $60, the company gains $2 per unit:

Effect of Transferring at $100 Instead of at $60	
Income of A is $40 higher; therefore A pays 25% × $40 more income taxes	$(10)
Income of B is $40 lower; therefore B pays 50% × $40 less income taxes	20
Import duty is paid by B on an additional $100 – $60 = $40; therefore B pays 20% × $40 more duty	(8)
Net savings from transferring at $100 instead of $60	$ 2

Companies may also use transfer prices to avoid financial restrictions imposed by some governments. For example, a country might restrict the amount of dividends paid to foreign owners. It may be easier for a company to get cash from a foreign division as payment for items transferred than as cash dividends.

In summary, transfer pricing is more complex in a multinational company than in a domestic company. Multinational companies have more objectives to be achieved through transfer-pricing policies, and some of the objectives often conflict with one another.

■ PERFORMANCE MEASURES AND MANAGEMENT CONTROL

Transfer pricing affects segment profit, thereby affecting the performance measures of profit centers. This section looks more generally at how performance measures affect managers' incentives.

Motivation, Performance, and Rewards

Exhibit 10-2 shows the criteria and choices faced by top management when designing a management control system. Using the criterion of cost-benefit and

incentives Those formal and informal performance-based rewards that enhance managerial effort toward organizational goals.

the motivational criteria of congruence and effort, top management chooses responsibility centers (e.g., cost center versus profit center), performance measures, and rewards. The term *incentives* was used on page 381. As used in this context, **incentives** are defined as those informal and formal performance-based rewards that enhance managerial effort toward organizational goals. For example, how the $70,000 contribution in Exhibit 10-1 is split between the Fabric and Tent Divisions affects the measures of their performance. In turn, the performance measures may affect the managers' rewards.

Exhibit 10-2

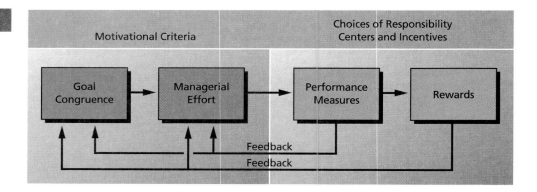

Objective 6

Explain how the linking of rewards to responsibility center results affects incentives and risk

Numerous performance measurement choices have been described in this book. Examples include whether to use tight or loose standards, whether to measure divisional performance by contribution margins or operating incomes, and whether to use both financial and nonfinancial measures of performance.

Research about rewards has generated a basic principle that is simple and important: Managers tend to focus their efforts in areas where performance is measured and where their performance affects rewards. Research also shows that the more objective the measures of performance, the more likely the manager will provide effort. Thus accounting measures, which provide relatively objective evaluations of performance, are important. Moreover, if individuals believe that there is no connection between their behavior and their measure of performance, they will not see how to alter their performance to affect their rewards.

The choice of rewards clearly belongs with an overall system of management control. Rewards may be both monetary and nonmonetary. Examples include pay raises, bonuses, promotion, praise, self-satisfaction, elaborate offices, and private dining rooms. However, the design of a reward system is mainly the concern of top managers, who frequently get advice from many sources besides accountants.

Agency Theory, Performance, Rewards, and Risk

Linking rewards to performance is desirable. But often a manager's performance cannot be measured directly. For example, responsibility center results may be measured easily, but a manager's effect on those results (i.e., managerial performance) may not. Ideally, rewards should be based on managerial performance, but in practice the rewards usually depend on the financial results in the manager's responsibility center. Managerial performance and responsibility center results are certainly related, but factors beyond a manager's control also affect results. The greater the influence of noncontrollable factors on responsibility center results, the more problems there are in using the results to represent a manager's performance.

agency theory A theory used to describe the formal choices of performance measures and rewards.

Economists describe the formal choices of performance measures and rewards as **agency theory**. For top management to hire a manager, both need to agree to an employment contract that includes specification of a performance measure and how it will affect rewards.[1] For example, a manager might receive a bonus of 15% of her salary if her responsibility center achieves its budgeted profit. According to agency theory, employment contracts will trade off three factors:

1. *Incentive*: The more a manager's reward depends on a performance measure, the more incentive the manager has to take actions that maximize that measure. Top management should define the performance measure to promote *goal congruence* and base enough reward on it to achieve *managerial effort*.

2. *Risk*: The greater the influence of uncontrollable factors on a manager's reward, the more risk the manager bears. People generally avoid risk, so managers must be paid more if they are expected to bear more risk. Creating incentive by linking rewards to responsibility center results, which is generally desirable, has the undesirable side effect of imposing risk on managers.

3. *Cost of measuring performance*: The incentive versus risk trade-off is not necessary if a manager's performance is perfectly measured. Why? Because then a manager could be paid a fixed amount if he or she performs as expected, and nothing if not. Whether to perform or not is completely controllable by the manager, and observation of the level of performance is all that is necessary to determine the compensation earned. But directly measuring a manager's performance is usually expensive and sometimes infeasible. Responsibility center results are more readily available. The cost-benefit criterion usually indicates that perfect measurement of a manager's performance is not worth its cost.

Consider a concert manager hired by a group of investors to promote and administer an outdoor rock performance. If the investors cannot directly measure the manager's effort and judgment, they would probably pay a bonus that depended on the economic success of the concert. The bonus would motivate the manager to put his effort toward generating a profit. On the other hand, it creates risk. Factors such as bad weather also could affect the concert's economic success. The manager might do an outstanding job and still not receive a bonus. Suppose the investors offer a contract with part guaranteed pay and part bonus. A larger bonus portion compared with the guaranteed portion creates more incentive, but it also means a larger expected total payment to compensate the manager for the added risk.

Summary Problem for Your Review

Problem One

Examine Exhibit 10-1, page 379. In addition to the data there, suppose the Fabric Division has annual fixed manufacturing costs of $800,000 and expected annual

---

[1] Often performance measures and rewards are implicit. For example, promotion is a reward, but usually the requirements for promotion are not explicit.

production of 500,000 square yards. The "fully allocated cost" per square yard was computed as follows:

Variable costs per square yard	$8.00
Fixed costs, $800,000 ÷ 500,000 square yards	1.60
Fully allocated cost per square yard	$9.60

Therefore the "fully allocated cost" of the 5 square yards required for one tent is 5 × $9.60 = $48.

Required Assume that the Fabric Division has idle capacity. The Tent Division is considering whether to buy enough fabric for 10,000 tents. Each tent will be sold for $100. The additional costs shown in Exhibit 10-1 for the Tent Division would prevail. If transfers were based on fully allocated cost, would the Tent Division manager buy? Explain. Would the company as a whole benefit if the Tent Division manager decided to buy? Explain.

Solution to Problem One

The Tent Division manager would not buy. The resulting transfer price of $48 would make the acquisition of the fabric unattractive to the Tent Division:

Tent Division			
Sales price of final product			$100
Deduct costs			
Transfer price paid to the Fabric Division (fully allocated cost)		$48	
Additional costs (from Exhibit 10-1)			
Processing	$41		
Selling	12	53	
Total costs to the Tent Division			101
Contribution to profit of the Tent Division			$ −1
Contribution to company as a whole (from Exhibit 10-1)			$ 7

As Exhibit 10-1 shows, the company as a whole would benefit by $70,000 (10,000 tents × $7) if the fabric were transferred.

The major lesson here is that, when idle capacity exists in the supplier division, transfer prices based on fully allocated costs may induce the wrong decisions. Working in her own best interests, the Tent Division manager has no incentive to buy from the Fabric Division.

■ MEASURES OF PROFITABILITY

A favorite objective of top management is to maximize profitability. Segment managers are often evaluated based on their segment's profitability. The trouble is that profitability does not mean the same thing to all people. Is it net income? Income before taxes? Net income percentage based on revenue? Is it an absolute amount? A percentage? In this section we consider the strengths and weaknesses of several commonly used measures.

Return on Investment

Too often, managers stress net income or income percentages without tying the measure into the investment associated with generating the income. To say that project A has an income of $200,000 and project B has an income of $150,000 is an insufficient statement about profitability. A better test of profitability is the rate of **return on investment (ROI),** which is income (or profit) divided by the investment required to obtain that income or profit. Given the same risks, for any given amount of resources required, the investor wants the maximum income. If project A requires an investment of $500,000 and project B requires only $250,000, all other things being equal, where would you put your money?

return on investment (ROI) A measure of income or profit divided by the investment required to obtain that income or profit.

$$ROI = \frac{income}{investment}$$

$$ROI \text{ project } A = \frac{\$200,000}{\$500,000} = 40\%$$

$$ROI \text{ project } B = \frac{\$150,000}{\$250,000} = 60\%$$

Objective 7

Compute ROI and residual income and contrast them as criteria for judging the performance of organization segments

ROI is a useful common denominator. It can be compared with rates inside and outside the organization, and with opportunities in other projects and industries. It is affected by two major ingredients:

$$\frac{\text{rate of return on}}{\text{invested capital}} = \frac{income}{\text{invested capital}}$$

$$= \frac{income}{revenue} \times \frac{revenue}{\text{invested capital}}$$

$$= \text{income percentage of revenue} \times \text{capital turnover}$$

The terms of this equation are deliberately vague at this point because various versions of income, revenue, and invested capital are possible. As you can see, the rate of return is the result of combining two items, **income percentage of revenue** (also called **return on sales**)—income divided by revenue—and **capital turnover**—revenue divided by invested capital. An improvement in either without changing the other will improve the rate of return on invested capital.

income percentage of revenue (return on sales) Income divided by revenue.
capital turnover Revenue divided by invested capital.

Consider an example of these relationships:

	Rate of Return on Invested Capital (%)	=	$\dfrac{\text{Income}}{\text{Revenue}}$	×	$\dfrac{\text{Revenue}}{\text{Invested Capital}}$
Present outlook	20	=	$\dfrac{16}{100}$	×	$\dfrac{100}{80}$
Alternatives					
1. Increase income percentage by reducing expenses	25	=	$\dfrac{20}{100}$	×	$\dfrac{100}{80}$
2. Increase turnover by decreasing investment in inventories	25	=	$\dfrac{16}{100}$	×	$\dfrac{100}{64}$

Alternative 1 is a popular way to improve performance. Alert managers try to decrease expenses without reducing sales or to boost sales without increasing related expenses. Alternative 2 is less obvious, but it may be a quicker way to improve performance. Increasing the turnover of invested capital means generating higher revenue for each dollar invested in such assets as cash, receivables, inventories, or equipment. There is an optimal level of investment in these assets. Having too much is wasteful, but having too little may hurt credit standing and the ability to compete for sales. Increasing turnover is one of the advantages of implementing the JIT philosophy (see Chapters 1 and 4). Many companies implementing JIT purchasing and production systems have realized dramatic improvements in their ROI.

Residual Income

residual income Net income less "imputed" interest.

cost of capital What a firm must pay to acquire more capital, whether or not it actually has to acquire more capital to take on a project.

Most managers agree that measuring return in relation to investment provides the ultimate test of profitability. ROI is one such comparison. However, some companies favor emphasizing an *absolute amount* of income rather than a percentage rate of return. They use **residual income**, defined as net income less "imputed" interest. "Imputed" interest refers to the **cost of capital**, what the firm must pay to acquire more capital—whether or not it actually has to acquire more capital to take on this project. For example, suppose a division's net income was $900,000, the average invested capital in the division for the year was $10 million, and the corporate headquarters assessed an imputed interest charge of 8%:

Divisional net income after taxes	$900,000
Minus imputed interest on average invested capital (.08 × $10,000,000)	800,000
Equals residual income	$100,000

Note that the cost of capital is the minimum acceptable rate of return for investments in a project or division. Modern finance theory and practice have shown that the cost of capital depends on the risk of the investment. If divisions have different levels of risk, they should have different imputed interest rates.

ROI or Residual Income?

Why do some companies prefer residual income to ROI? The ROI approach shows:

Divisional net income after taxes	$ 900,000
Average invested capital	$10,000,000
Return on investment	9%

Under ROI, the basic message is: Go forth and maximize your rate of return, a percentage. Thus, if performance is measured by ROI, managers of divisions currently earning 20% may be reluctant to invest in projects at 15% because doing so would reduce their average ROI.

However, from the viewpoint of the company as a whole, top management may want this division manager to accept projects that earn 15%. Why? Suppose the company's cost of capital is 8%. Investing in projects earning 15%

will increase the company's profitability. When performance is measured by residual income, managers tend to invest in any project earning more than the imputed interest rate and thus raise the firm's profits. That is, the residual income approach fosters goal congruence and managerial effort. Its basic message is: Go forth and maximize residual income, an absolute amount.

General Electric (GE) was one of the first companies to adopt a residual income approach. Consider two divisions of GE as an example. Division A has net income of $200,000; Division B has $50,000. Both have average invested capital of $1 million. Suppose a project is proposed that can be undertaken by either A or B. The project will earn 15% annually on a $500,000 investment, or $75,000 a year. The cost of capital for the project is 8%. ROI and residual income with and without the project are as follows:

| | Without Project | | With Project | |
	Division A	Division B	Division A	Division B
Net income	$ 200,000	$ 50,000	$ 275,000	$ 125,000
Invested capital	$1,000,000	$1,000,000	$1,500,000	$1,500,000
ROI (net income ÷ invested capital)	20%	5%	18.3%	8.3%
Capital charge (8% × invested capital)	$ 80,000	$ 80,000	$ 120,000	$ 120,000
Residual income (net income − capital charge)	$ 120,000	$(− 30,000)	$ 155,000	$ 5,000

Suppose you are the manager of Division A. If your evaluation is based on ROI, would you invest in the project? No. It would decrease your ROI from 20% to 18.3%. But suppose you are in Division B. Would you invest? Yes, because ROI increases from 5% to 8.3%. In general, in companies using ROI the least-profitable divisions have more incentive to invest in new projects than do the most profitable divisions.

Now suppose you are evaluated using residual income. The project would be equally attractive to either division. Residual income increases by $35,000 for each division, $155,000 − $120,000 for A and $5,000 − (− $30,000) for B. Both divisions have the same incentive to invest in the project, and the incentive depends on the profitability of the project compared with the cost of the capital used by the project.

In general, use of residual income will promote goal congruence and lead to better decisions than using ROI. Still, most companies use ROI. Why? Probably because it is easier for managers to understand, and it facilitates comparison across divisions. Furthermore, combining ROI with appropriate growth and profit targets can minimize its dysfunctional motivations.

Objective 8

Identify the advantages/disadvantages of using various bases for measuring the invested capital used by organization segments

■ A CLOSER LOOK AT INVESTED CAPITAL

To apply either ROI or residual income, both income and invested capital must be measured. However, there are many different interpretations of these concepts. To understand what ROI or residual income figures really mean, you must first determine how invested capital and income are being defined and measured. We discussed various definitions of income in Chapter 9, pages 343–346, so we will not repeat them here. We will, however, explore various definitions of invested capital.

Definition of Invested Capital

Consider the following balance sheet classifications:

Current assets	$ 400,000	Current liabilities	$ 200,000
Property, plant, and equipment	800,000	Long-term liabilities	400,000
Construction in progress	100,000	Stockholders' equity	700,000
Total assets	$1,300,000	Total liab. and stk. eq.	$1,300,000

Possible definitions of invested capital and their values on the preceding balance sheet include

1. *Total assets*: All assets are included, $1,300,000.
2. *Total assets employed*: All assets except agreed-on exclusions of vacant land or construction in progress, $1,300,000 – $100,000 = $1,200,000.
3. *Total assets less current liabilities*: All assets except that portion supplied by short-term creditors, $1,300,000 – $200,000 = $1,100,000. This is sometimes expressed as *long-term invested capital*; note that it can also be computed by adding the long-term liabilities and the stockholders' equity, $400,000 + $700,000 = $1,100,000.
4. *Stockholders' equity*: Focuses on the investment of the owners of the business, $700,000.

(All the preceding should be computed as averages for the period under review. These averages may be based on simply the beginning and ending balances or on more complicated averages that weigh changes in investments through the months.)

For measuring the performance of division managers, any of the three asset bases is recommended rather than stockholders' equity. If the division manager's mission is to put *all* assets to their best use without regard to their financing, then base 1 is best. If top management directs the manager to carry extra assets that are not currently productive, then base 2 is best. If the manager has direct control over obtaining short-term credit and bank loans, then base 3 is best. A key behavioral factor in choosing an investment base is that *managers will focus attention on reducing those assets and increasing those liabilities that are included in the base*. In practice, most companies using ROI or residual income include all assets in invested capital, and about half deduct some portion of current liabilities.

A few companies allocate long-term debt to their divisions and thus have an approximation of the stockholders' equity in each division. However, this practice has doubtful merit. Division managers typically have little responsibility for the long-term *financial* management of their divisions, as distinguished from *operating* management. The investment bases of division managers from two companies could differ radically if one company has heavy long-term debt and the other is debt-free.

Allocation to Divisions

Just as cost allocations affect income, so asset allocations affect the invested capital of particular divisions. The aim is to allocate this capital in a manner that will be goal congruent, will spur managerial effort, and will recognize segment autonomy insofar as possible. (As long as the managers feel that they are being treated uniformly, though, they tend to be more tolerant of the imperfections of the allocation.)

A frequent criterion for asset allocation is avoidability. That is, the amount allocable to any given segment for the purpose of evaluating the division's performance is the amount that the corporation as a whole could avoid by not having that segment. Commonly used bases for allocation, when assets are not directly identifiable with a specific division, include:

Asset Class	Possible Allocation Base
Corporate cash	Budgeted cash needs
Receivables	Sales weighted by payment terms
Inventories	Budgeted sales or usage
Plant and equipment	Usage of services in terms of long-run forecasts of demand or area occupied

The allocation base should be the activity that *caused* the asset to be acquired. When the allocation of an asset would indeed be arbitrary (i.e., no causal activity can be identified), many managers think that it is better not to allocate.

Should cash be included in a division's investment if the cash balances are strictly controlled by corporate headquarters? Arguments can be made for both sides, but the manager is usually regarded as being responsible for the volume of business generated by the division. In turn, this volume is likely to have a direct effect on the overall cash needs of the corporation.

A popular allocation base for cash is sales dollars. However, the allocation of cash on the basis of sales dollars seldom gets at the economic rationale of cash holdings. As Chapter 7 explains, cash needs are influenced by a host of factors including payment terms of customers and creditors.

Central control of cash is usually undertaken to reduce the holdings from what would be used if each division had a separate account. Fluctuations in cash needs of each division offset one another somewhat. For example, Division A might have a cash deficiency of $1 million in February, but Division B might have an offsetting cash excess of $1 million. Taken together for the year, Divisions A, B, C, D, and E might require a combined investment in cash of, say, $16 million if all were independent entities, but only $8 million if cash were controlled centrally. Hence, if Division C would ordinarily require a $4 million investment in cash as a separate entity, it would be allocated an investment of only $2 million as a segment of a company in which cash was controlled centrally.

Valuation of Assets

Whatever assets are included in a division's invested capital must be measured in some way. Should the assets contained in the investment base be valued at *gross book value* (original cost) or *net book value* (original cost less accumulated depreciation)? Should values be based on historical cost or some version of current value? Practice is overwhelmingly in favor of using net book value based on historical cost. Very few firms use replacement cost or any other type of current value. Historical cost has been widely criticized for many years as providing a faulty basis for decision making and performance evaluation. As Chapters 5 and 6 point out, historical costs per se are irrelevant for making economic decisions. Despite these criticisms, managers have been slow to depart from historical cost.

Why is historical cost so widely used? Some critics would say that sheer ignorance is the explanation. But a more persuasive answer comes from cost-benefit analysis. Accounting systems are costly. Historical records must be kept for many legal purposes, so they are already in place. No additional money must be spent to evaluate performance based on historical costs. Furthermore, many top managers believe that such a system provides the desired goal congruence and managerial effort and that a more sophisticated system will not radically improve collective operating decisions. Some believe, in fact, that using current values would cause confusion unless huge sums were spent educating personnel.

Historical costs may even improve some decisions because they are more objective than current costs. Moreover, managers can better predict the historical-cost effects of their decisions, so their decisions may be more influenced by the control system. Furthermore, the uncertainty involved with current-cost measures may impose undesirable risks on the managers. In short, the historical-cost system may be superior for the *routine* evaluation of performance. In nonroutine instances, such as replacing equipment or deleting a product line, managers should conduct special studies to gather any current valuations that seem relevant.

Finally, although historical-cost systems are common, most well-managed organizations do not use historical-cost systems alone. The alternatives available to managers are not

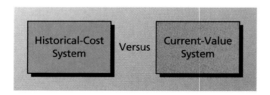

More accurately stated, the alternatives are

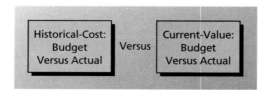

A budget system, whether based on historical cost or current value, causes managers to worry about inflation. Most managers seem to prefer to concentrate on improving their existing historical-cost budget system.

In sum, our cost-benefit approach provides no universal answers with respect to such controversial issues as historical values versus current values or return on investment versus residual income. Instead, using a cost-benefit test, each organization must judge for itself whether an alternative control system or accounting technique will improve collective decision making. The latter is the primary criterion.

Too often, the literature engages in pro-and-con discussions about which alternative is more nearly perfect or truer than another in some logical sense. The cost-benefit approach is not concerned with "truth" or "perfection" by itself. Instead it asks: Do you think your perceived "truer" or "more logical" system is worth its added cost? Or will our existing imperfect system provide about the same set of decisions if it is skillfully administered?

Plant and Equipment: Gross or Net?

net book value The original cost of an asset less any accumulated depreciation.

gross book value The original cost of an asset before deducting accumulated depreciation.

In valuing assets, it is important to distinguish between net and gross book values. **Net book value** (often called simply *book value*) is the original cost of an asset less any accumulated depreciation. **Gross book value** is the original cost of an asset before deducting accumulated depreciation. Most companies use net book value in calculating their investment base. However, according to a recent survey, a significant minority uses gross book value. The proponents of gross book value maintain that it facilitates comparisons between years, and between plants or divisions.

Consider an example of a $600,000 piece of equipment with a three-year life and no residual value.

Year	Operating Income Before Depreciation	Depreciation	Operating Income	Average Investment			
				Net Book Value*	Rate of Return	Gross Book Value	Rate of Return
1	$260,000	$200,000	$60,000	$500,000	12%	$600,000	10%
2	260,000	200,000	60,000	300,000	20	600,000	10
3	260,000	200,000	60,000	100,000	60	600,000	10

*($600,000 + $400,000) ÷ 2; ($400,000 + $200,000) ÷ 2; etc.

The rate of return on net book value goes up as the equipment ages. It could increase even if operating income gradually declined through the years. In contrast, the rate of return on gross book value is unchanged if operating income does not change. The rate would decrease if operating income gradually declined through the years.

Advocates of using net book value maintain that:

1. It is less confusing because it is consistent with the assets shown on the conventional balance sheet and with the net income computations.

2. The major criticism of net book value is not peculiar to its use for ROI purposes. It is really a criticism of using historical cost as a basis for evaluation.

The effect on motivation should be considered when choosing between net and gross book value. Managers evaluated using gross book value will tend to replace assets sooner than those in firms using net book value. Consider a

4-year-old machine with an original cost of $1,000 and net book value of $200. It can be replaced by a new machine that also costs $1,000. The choice of net or gross book value does not affect net income. However, the investment base increases from $200 to $1,000 in a net-book-value firm, but it remains at $1,000 in a gross-book-value firm. To maximize ROI or residual income, managers want a low-investment base. Managers in firms using net book value will tend to keep old assets with their low book value. Those in firms using gross book value will have less incentive to keep old assets. Therefore, to motivate managers to use state-of-the-art production technology, gross book value is preferred. Net asset value promotes a more conservative approach to asset replacement.

■ KEYS TO SUCCESSFUL MANAGEMENT CONTROL SYSTEMS

Successful management control systems have several key factors in addition to appropriate measures of profitability. We next explore some of these factors.

Focus on Controllability

As Chapter 9 explained (see Exhibit 9-2, p. 344), a distinction should be made between the performance of the division manager and the performance of the division as an investment by the corporation. Managers should be evaluated on the basis of their controllable performance (in many cases some controllable contribution in relation to controllable investment). However, decisions such as increasing or decreasing investment in a division are based on the economic viability of the *division*, not the performance of its *managers*.

This distinction helps to clarify some vexing difficulties. For example, top management may want to use an investment base to gauge the economic performance of a retail store, but the *manager* may best be judged by focusing on income and forgetting about any investment allocations. If investment is assigned to the manager, the aim should be to assign only that investment the manager can control. Controllability depends on what *decisions* managers can make regarding the size of the investment base. In a highly decentralized company, for instance, managers can influence the size of these assets and can exercise judgment regarding the appropriate amount of short-term credit and perhaps some long-term credit.

Management by Objectives

management by objectives (MBO)
The joint formulation by a manager and his or her superior of a set of goals and plans for achieving the goals for a forthcoming period.

Management by objectives (MBO) describes the joint formulation by a manager and his or her superior of a set of goals and plans for achieving the goals for a forthcoming period. For our purposes here, the terms *goals* and *objectives* are synonyms. The plans often take the form of a responsibility accounting budget (together with supplementary goals such as levels of management training and safety that may not be incorporated into the accounting budget). The manager's performance is then evaluated in relation to these agreed-on budgeted objectives.

Regardless of whether it is so labeled, a management-by-objectives approach lessens the complaints about lack of controllability because of its stress on *budgeted results*. That is, a budget is negotiated between a particular manager and his or her superior for a *particular* period and a *particular* set of expected outside and inside influences. In this way, a manager may more readily accept an assignment to a less successful segment. This is preferable to a system that emphasizes absolute profitability for its own sake. Unless focus is placed on currently attainable results, able managers will be reluctant to accept responsibility for segments that are in economic trouble.

Thus, skillful budgeting and intelligent performance evaluation will go a long way toward overcoming the common lament: "I'm being held responsible for items beyond my control."

Tailoring Budgets for Managers

Many of the troublesome motivational effects of performance evaluation systems can be minimized by the astute use of budgets. The desirability of tailoring a budget to particular managers cannot be overemphasized. For example, either an ROI or a residual income system can promote goal congruence and managerial effort if top management gets everybody to focus on what is currently attainable in the forthcoming budget period. Typically, divisional managers do not have complete freedom to make major investment decisions without checking with senior management.

Alternatives of Timing

Accounting textbooks, including this one, do not discuss at length the problem of timing. However, timing is an important factor to consider when a management control system is designed. For instance, the costs of gathering and processing information and the need for frequent feedback for controlling current operations may lead to using historical-cost measures rather than replacement costs. The need for replacement costs, realizable values, and economic values tends to be less frequent, so the systems are not designed to provide such information routinely. The essence of the matter is that management seems unwilling to pay for more elegant information because its extra costs exceed its prospective benefits.

Another aspect of timing underscores why management accounting systems are seldom static. A system that works well in 1993 may not suffice in 1998. Top management's desires and the attitudes of various managers may change. For example, top management may not allocate the costs of the internal auditing department in 1993 to encourage all managers to use auditing services. In 1998 top management may begin allocating auditing services to discourage use.

Highlights to Remember

As organizations grow, decentralization of some management functions becomes desirable. Decentralization immediately raises problems of obtaining decisions that are coordinated with the objectives of the organization as a whole. Ideally, planning and control systems should provide information that (1) aims managers toward decisions that are goal congruent, (2) provides feedback (evaluation of performance) that improves managerial effort, and (3) preserves segment autonomy. Note that the common thread of these problems is motivation.

Profit centers are usually associated with heavily decentralized organizations, whereas cost centers are usually associated with heavily centralized organizations. However, profit centers and decentralization are separate ideas; one can exist without the other.

Transfer-pricing systems are often used as a means of communicating information among segments and of measuring their performance. Problems of transfer pricing and cost allocations are similar. Proper choices vary from situation to situation. Multinational companies use transfer prices to minimize worldwide income taxes and import duties in addition to achieving goal congruence and motivation. Transfer prices can be based on costs or on market prices, or set by negotiation. If the item can be sold to external customers, a transfer price based on market price is usually preferable.

Choices of performance measures (such as return on investment and residual income) and rewards (such as bonuses and increases in salaries) can heavily affect goal congruence and managerial effort. To affect managerial behavior, strong links must exist between effort, performance, and rewards.

ROI and residual income are measures of investment center performance. Theorists tend to prefer residual income. Why? Because it focuses on an absolute amount of income after paying for the capital used. In practice, ROI is more popular. Why? Probably because it is easier to understand and, though imperfect, leads to reasonably good motivations.

Both ROI and residual income require measures of income and invested capital. The way these items are measured can greatly affect managers' incentives.

Summary Problem for Your Review

Problem One appeared earlier in the chapter.

Problem Two

A division has assets of $200,000 and operating income of $60,000.

1. What is the division's ROI?
2. If interest is imputed at 14%, what is the residual income?
3. What effects on management behavior can be expected if ROI is used to gauge performance?
4. What effects on management behavior can be expected if residual income is used to gauge performance?

Solution to Problem Two

1. ROI = $60,000 ÷ $200,000 = 30%.
2. Residential Income = $60,000 − .14($200,000) = $60,000 − $28,000 = $32,000.

3. If ROI is used, the manager is prone to reject projects that do not earn an ROI of at least 30%. From the viewpoint of the organization as a whole, this may be undesirable because its best investment opportunities may lie in that division and have a rate of, say, 22%. If a division is enjoying a high ROI, it is less likely to expand if it is judged via ROI than if it is judged via residual income.

4. If residual income is used, the manager is inclined to accept all projects whose expected rate of return exceeds the minimum desired rate. The manager's division is more likely to expand because his or her goal is to maximize a dollar amount rather than a rate.

Accounting Vocabulary

agency theory, *p. 385*
capital turnover, *p. 387*
cost of capital, *p. 388*
decentralization, *p. 373*
dysfunctional behavior, *p. 380*
gross book value, *p. 393*

incentives, *p. 384*
income percentage of revenue,
  p. 387
management by objectives (MBO),
  p. 394
net book value, *p. 393*

residual income, *p. 388*
return on investment (ROI),
  p. 387
return on sales, *p. 387*
segment autonomy, *p. 376*
transfer price, *p. 377*

Fundamental Assignment Material

10-A1   Rate of Return and Transfer Pricing

Consider the following data regarding budgeted operations of the Atlanta Division of Machine Products Inc.:

Average available assets	
Receivables	$150,000
Inventories	300,000
Plant and equipment, net	450,000
Total	$900,000
Fixed overhead	$300,000
Variable costs	$1 per unit
Desired rate of return on average available assets	25%
Expected volume	150,000 units

Required

1. a. What average unit sales price is needed to obtain the desired rate of return on average available assets?
   b. What would be the expected asset turnover?
   c. What would be the operating income percentage on dollar sales?
2. a. If the selling price is as computed above, what rate of return will be earned on available assets if sales volume is 180,000 units?
   b. If sales volume is 120,000 units?
3. Assume that 45,000 units are to be sold to another division of the same company and that only 105,000 units can be sold to outside customers. The other division manager has balked at a tentative selling price of $4. She has offered $2.25, claiming that she can manufacture the units herself for that price. The manager of the selling division has examined his own data. He had decided that he could eliminate

$60,000 of inventories, $90,000 of plant and equipment, and $22,500 of fixed over-head if he did *not* sell to the other division and sold only 105,000 units to outside customers. Should he sell for $2.25? Show computations to support your answer.

10-A2   Transfer-Pricing Dispute

A transportation equipment manufacturer, Mason Corporation, is heavily decentralized. Each division head has full authority on all decisions regarding sales to internal or exter-nal customers. The Pacific Division has always acquired a certain equipment component from the Southern Division. However, when informed that the Southern Division was increasing its unit price to $330, the Pacific Division's management decided to purchase the component from outside suppliers at a price of $300.

The Southern Division had recently acquired some specialized equipment that was used primarily to make this component. The manager cited the resulting high deprecia-tion charges as the justification for the price boost. He asked the president of the com-pany to instruct the Pacific Division to buy from Southern at the $330 price. He supplied the following data to back his request:

Pacific's annual purchases of component	2,000 units
Southern's variable costs per unit	$285
Southern's fixed costs per unit	$ 30

Required

1. Suppose there are no alternative uses of the Southern facilities. Will the company as a whole benefit if Pacific buys from the outside suppliers for $300 per unit? Show computations to support your answer.
2. Suppose internal facilities of Southern would not otherwise be idle. The equipment and other facilities would be assigned to other production operations that would otherwise require an additional annual outlay of $40,500. Should Pacific purchase from outsiders at $300 per unit?
3. Suppose that there are no alternative uses for Southern's internal facilities and that the selling price of outsiders drops by $30. Should Pacific purchase from outsiders?
4. As the president, how would you respond to the request of the manager of Southern? Would your response differ, depending on the specific situations described in requirements 1 through 3 above? Why?

10-A3   Transfer Pricing

Refer to Problem 10-A2, requirement 1 only. Suppose the Southern Division could mod-ify the component at an additional variable cost of $12 per unit and sell the 2,000 units to other customers for $330. Then would the entire company benefit if Pacific purchased the 2,000 components from outsiders at $300 per unit?

10-A4   Simple ROI and Residual Income Calculations

Consider the following data:

	Division		
	A	B	C
Invested capital	$1,000,000	$ 600,000	$ 800,000
Revenue	3,600,000	1,800,000	8,000,000
Income	180,000	126,000	80,000

Required

1. For each division, compute the income percentage of revenue, the capital turnover, and the rate of return on invested capital.

2. Which division is the best performer? Explain.
3. Suppose each division is assessed an imputed interest rate of 10% on invested capital. Compute the residual income for each division. Which division is the best performer based on residual income? Explain.

10-B1   Transfer Pricing

Burger-Rama Enterprises runs a chain of drive-in hamburger stands on Cape Cod during the ten-week summer season. Managers of all stands are told to act as if they owned the stand and are judged on their profit performance. Burger-Rama Enterprises has rented an ice-cream machine for the summer to supply its stands with ice cream. Rent for the machine is $1,800. Burger-Rama is not allowed to sell ice cream to other dealers because it cannot obtain a dairy license. The manager of the ice-cream machine charges the stands $4 per gallon. Operating figures for the machine for the summer are as follows:

Sales to the stands (8,000 gallons at $4)		$32,000
Variable costs, @ $2.10 per gallon	$16,800	
Fixed costs		
Rental of machine	1,800	
Other fixed costs	5,000	23,600
Operating margin		$ 8,400

The manager of the Cape Drive-In, one of the Burger-Rama drive-ins, is seeking permission to sign a contract to buy ice cream from an outside supplier at $3.30 a gallon. The Cape Drive-In uses 1,500 gallons of ice cream during the summer. Jane Garton, controller of Burger-Rama, refers this request to you. You determine that the other fixed costs of operating the machine will decrease by $480 if the Cape Drive-In purchases from an outside supplier. Garton wants an analysis of the request in terms of overall company objectives and an explanation of your conclusion. What is the appropriate transfer price?

10-B2   Rate of Return and Transfer Pricing

The Tokyo division of Toy King manufactures units of the game "Go" and sells them in the Japanese market for ¥6,000 each. The following data are from the Tokyo Division's 19X6 budget:

Variable cost	¥3,800 per unit
Fixed overhead	¥6,080,000
Total assets	¥12,500,000

Toy King has instructed the Tokyo Division to budget a rate of return on total assets (before taxes) of 20%.

Required

1. Suppose the Tokyo Division expects to sell 3,400 units of the game during 19X6:
   a.   What rate of return will be earned on total assets?
   b.   What would be the expected capital turnover?
   c.   What would be the operating income percentage of sales?
2. The Tokyo Division is considering adjustments in the budget to reach the desired 20% rate of return on total assets:
   a.   How many units must be sold to obtain the desired return if no other part of the budget is changed?
   b.   Suppose sales cannot be increased beyond 3,400 units. How much must total assets be reduced to obtain the desired return? Assume that for every ¥1,000 decrease in total assets, fixed costs decrease by ¥100.

3. Assume that only 2,400 units can be sold in the Japanese market. However, another 1,400 units can be sold to the American Marketing Division of Toy King. The Tokyo manager has offered to sell the 1,400 units for ¥5,500 each. The American Marketing Division manager has countered with an offer to pay ¥5,000 per unit, claiming that she can subcontract production to an American producer at a cost equivalent to ¥5,000. The Tokyo manager knows that if his production falls to 2,400 units he could eliminate some assets, reducing total assets to ¥10 million and annual fixed overhead to ¥4.9 million. Should the Tokyo manager sell for ¥5,000 per unit? Support your answer with the relevant computations. Ignore the effects of income taxes and import duties.

10-B3   ROI or Residual Income

T. A. Lincoln Co. is a large integrated conglomerate with shipping, metals, and mining operations throughout the world. The general manager of the Heavy Metals Division has been directed to submit a proposed capital budget for 19X7 for inclusion in the companywide budget.

The division manager has for consideration the following projects, all of which require an outlay of capital. All projects have equal risk.

Project	Investment Required	Return
1	$4,800,000	$1,200,000
2	1,900,000	627,000
3	1,400,000	182,000
4	950,000	152,000
5	650,000	130,000
6	300,000	90,000

The division manager must decide which of the projects to take. The company has a cost of capital of 15%. An amount of $12 million is available to the division for investment purposes.

Required

1. What will be the total investment, total return, return on capital invested, and residual income of the rational division manager if:
   a. The company has a rule that all projects promising at least 20% or more should be taken
   b. The division manager is evaluated on his ability to maximize his return on capital invested (assume that this is a new division with no invested capital)
   c. The division manager is expected to maximize residual income as computed by using the 15% cost of capital
2. Which of the three approaches will induce the most effective investment policy for the company as a whole? Explain.

Additional Assignment Material

Questions

10-1. "Decentralization has benefits and costs." Name three of each.

10-2. "The essence of decentralization is the use of profit centers." Do you agree? Explain.

10-3. Why is decentralization more popular in profit-seeking organizations than in nonprofit organizations?

10-4. What kinds of organizations find decentralization to be preferable to centralization?

10-5. Why are transfer-pricing systems needed?

10-6. Why are cost-based transfer prices in common use?

10-7. How does the presence or absence of idle capacity affect the optimal transfer-pricing policy?

10-8. "We use variable-cost transfer prices to ensure that no dysfunctional decisions are made." Discuss.

10-9. Why does top management sometimes accept division managers' judgments, even if the division manager appears to be wrong?

10-10. According to agency theory, employment contracts trade off three factors. Name the three.

10-11. Discuss two factors that affect multinational transfer prices but have little effect on purely domestic transfers.

10-12. Why are interest expense and income taxes ordinarily excluded in computing incomes that are related to asset bases?

10-13. What is the major benefit of the ROI technique for measuring performance?

10-14. "Both ROI and residual income use profit and invested capital to measure performance. Therefore it really doesn't matter which we use." Do you agree? Explain.

10-15. "We budget different rates of return for different divisions in the short run. But in the long run our desired rate of return for all divisions is the same." Do you agree with this policy? Why?

10-16. Division A's ROI is 20%, and B's is 10%. Each manager is paid a bonus based on his or her division's ROI. Discuss whether each division manager would accept or reject a proposed project with a rate of return of 15%. Would either of them make a different decision if managers were evaluated using residual income with an imputed interest rate of 11%? Explain.

10-17. Give four possible definitions of invested capital that can be used in measuring ROI or residual income.

10-18. "Managers who use a historical-cost accounting system look backward at what something cost yesterday, instead of forward to what it will cost tomorrow." Do you agree? Why?

10-19. Ross Company uses net book value as a measure of invested capital when computing ROI. A division manager has suggested that the company change to using gross book value instead. What difference in motivation of division managers might result from such a change? Do you suppose most of the assets in the division of the manager proposing the change are relatively new or old? Why?

10-20. Describe MBO.

Exercises

10-21   Multiple Choice (CMA)

1. The imputed interest rate used in the residual income approach to performance evaluation can **best** be described as the
   a. average lending rate for the year being evaluated.
   b. weighted average cost of capital for the company.
   c. target average return on investment set by the company's management.
   d. average return on investment for the company over the last several years.
   e. marginal after-tax cost of capital on new equity capital.

2. Decentralized firms can delegate authority and yet retain control and monitor managers' performance by structuring the organization into responsibility centers. Which one of the following organizational segments is most like an independent business?
   a. Revenue center
   b. Profit center
   c. Cost center
   d. Investment center
   e. Activity center

3. One approach to measuring divisional performance is return on investment. One way of expressing return on investment is expressed as operating income
   a. divided by the current year's capital expenditures plus cost of capital.

   b. minus imputed interest charged for invested capital.

   c. divided by fixed assets.

   d. divided by current assets.

   e. divided by total assets.

4. An appropriate transfer price between two divisions of the Cook Company can be determined from the following data.

Fabricating Division	
Market price of subassembly	$50
Variable cost of subassembly	$20
Excess capacity (in units)	1,000
Assembly Division	
Number of units needed	900

   What is the natural bargaining range for the two divisions?

   a. Between $20 and $50

   b. Between $50 and $70

   c. Any amount less than $50

   d. $50 is the only acceptable price

   e. $20 is the only acceptable price

10-22   Variable Cost as a Transfer Price

A three-ring binder's variable cost is $5 and its market value is $6.25 at a transfer point from the Printing Division to the Binding Division. The Binding Division's variable cost of processing the notebook further is $2.80, and the selling price of the final notebook is $8.50.

Required

1. Prepare a tabulation of the contribution margin per unit for the Binding Division's performance and overall performance under the two alternatives of (a) processing further and (b) selling to outsiders at the transfer point.

2. As Binding Division manager, which alternative would you choose? Explain.

10-23   Maximum and Minimum Transfer Price

Benson Company makes bicycles. Components are made in various divisions and transferred to the Omaha Division for assembly into final products. The Omaha Division can also buy components from external suppliers. The wheels are made in the Lincoln Division, which also sells wheels to external customers. All divisions are profit centers, and managers are free to negotiate transfer prices. Prices and costs for the Lincoln and Omaha divisions are:

Lincoln Division	
Sales price to external customers	$12
Internal transfer price	?
Costs	
Variable costs per wheel	$8
Total fixed costs	$320,000
Budgeted production	64,000 wheels*

* Includes production for transfer to Omaha.

Omaha Division

Sales price to external customers	$160
Costs	
Wheels, per bicycle	?
Other components, per bicycle	$80
Other variable costs, per bicycle	$40
Total fixed costs	$640,000
Budgeted production	16,000 bicycles

Fixed costs in both divisions will be unaffected by the transfer of wheels from Lincoln to Omaha.

Required

1. Compute the maximum transfer price per wheel the Omaha Division would be willing to pay to buy wheels from the Lincoln Division.
2. Compute the minimum transfer price per wheel at which the Lincoln Division would be willing to produce and sell wheels to the Omaha Division. Assume that Lincoln has excess capacity.

10-24   Simple ROI Calculations

You are given the following data:

Sales	$130,000,000
Invested capital	$ 50,000,000
Return on investment	12%

Required

1. Turnover of capital
2. Net income
3. Net income as a percentage of sales

10-25   Simple ROI Calculations

Fill in the blanks:

	Division		
	A	B	C
Income percentage of revenue	7%	3%	%
Capital turnover	4	___	4
Rate of return on invested capital	%	24%	20%

10-26   Simple ROI and Residual Income Calculations

Consider the following data:

	Division		
	X	Y	Z
Invested capital	$2,000,000	$ _____	$1,250,000
Income	$ _____	$ 182,000	$ 150,000
Revenue	$4,000,000	$3,640,000	$ _____
Income percentage of revenue	2.5%	%	%
Capital turnover	___	___	3
Rate of return on invested capital	%	14%	%

Required

1. Prepare a similar tabular presentation, filling in all blanks.
2. Which division is the best performer? Explain.
3. Suppose each division is assessed an imputed interest rate of 12% on invested capital. Compute the residual income for each division.

10-27 Comparison of Asset and Equity Bases

Alamo Footwear has assets of $2 million and a long-term, 10% debt of $800,000. Shirley Shoes has assets of $2 million and no long-term debt. The annual operating income (before interest) of both companies is $500,000.

Required

1. Compute the rate of return on
   a. Assets available
   b. Stockholders' equity
2. Evaluate the relative merits of each base for appraising operating management.

10-28 Finding Unknowns

Consider the following data:

	Division		
	J	K	L
Income	$140,000	$	$
Revenue	$	$	$
Invested capital	$	$3,000,000	$16,000,000
Income percentage of revenue	7%	4%	%
Capital turnover	4		3
Rate of return on invested capital	%	20%	15%
Imputed interest rate on invested capital	20%	12%	%
Residual income	$	$	$ 480,000

Required

1. Prepare a similar tabular presentation, filling in all blanks.
2. Which division is the best performer? Explain.

Problems

10-29 Profit Centers and Transfer Pricing in an Automobile Dealership

A large automobile dealership is installing a responsibility accounting system and three profit centers: parts and service, new vehicles, and used vehicles. The three department managers have been told to run their shops as if they were in business for themselves. However, there are interdepartmental dealings. For example:

a. The parts and service department prepares new cars for final delivery and repairs used cars prior to resale.

b. The used-car department's major source of inventory has been cars traded in as partial payment for new cars.

The owner of the dealership has asked you to draft a company policy statement on transfer pricing, together with specific rules to be applied to the examples cited. He has told you that clarity is of paramount importance because your statement will be relied on for settling transfer-pricing disputes.

10-30 Role of Economic Value and Replacement Value

(This problem requires understanding of the concept of present values. See Appendix B, pp. 807–814.) "To me, economic value is the only justifiable basis for measuring plant assets for purposes of evaluating performance. By economic value, I mean the present value of expected future services. Still, we do not even do this on acquisition of new assets—that is, we may compute a positive net present value, using discounted cash flow; but we record the asset at no more than its cost. In this way, the excess present value is not shown in the initial balance sheet. Moreover, the use of replacement costs in subsequent years is also unlikely to result in showing economic values. The replacement cost will probably be less than the economic value at any given instant of an asset's life.

"Market values are totally unappealing to me because they represent a second-best alternative value—that is, they ordinarily represent the maximum amount obtainable from an alternative that has been rejected. Obviously, if the market value exceeds the economic value of the assets in use, they should be sold. However, in most instances, the opposite is true; market values of individual assets are far below their economic value in use.

"The obtaining and recording of total present values of individual assets based on discounted-cash-flow techniques is an infeasible alternative. I, therefore, conclude that replacement cost (less accumulated depreciation) of similar assets producing similar services is the best practical approximation of the economic value of the assets in use. Of course, it is more appropriate for the evaluation of the division's performance than the division manager's performance."

Required
Critically evaluate these comments. Please do not wander; concentrate on the issues described by the quotation.

10-31 Transfer Pricing

The Ripley Pump Division of Dependable Motors Company produces water pumps for automobiles. It has been the sole supplier of pumps to the Automotive Division and charges $30 per unit, the current market price for very large wholesale lots. The pump division also sells to outside retail outlets, at $38 per unit. Normally, outside sales amount to 25% of a total sales volume of 1 million pumps per year. Typical combined annual data for the division follows:

Sales	$32,000,000
Variable costs, @ $24 per pump	$24,000,000
Fixed costs	3,000,000
Total costs	$27,000,000
Gross margin	$ 5,000,000

The Farmington Pump Company, an entirely separate entity, has offered the Automotive Division comparable pumps at a firm price of $28 per unit. The Ripley Pump Division claims that it cannot possibly match this price because it could not earn any margin at $28.

Required
1. Assume that you are the manager of the Automotive Division. Comment on the Ripley Pump Division's claim. Assume that normal outside volume cannot be increased.
2. The Ripley Pump Division feels that it can increase outside sales by 750,000 pumps per year by increasing fixed costs by $2 million and variable costs by $3 per unit while reducing the selling price to $36. Assume that maximum capacity is 1 million pumps per year. Should the division reject intracompany business and concentrate on outside sales?

10-32 Transfer-Pricing Concession
(CMA, adapted.) The Tucson Division of Allenham Corporation, operating at capacity, has been asked by the Santa Fe Division of Allenham to supply it with electrical fitting no. LX29. Tucson sells this part to its regular customers for $10.00 each. Santa Fe, which is operating at 50% capacity, is willing to pay $6.90 each for the fitting. Santa Fe

---

will put the fitting into a brake unit that it is manufacturing on essentially a cost-plus basis for a commercial airplane manufacturer.

Tucson has a variable cost of producing fitting no. LX29 of $6.00. The cost of the brake unit as being built by Santa Fe is as follows:

Purchased parts—outside vendors	$28.10
Tucson fitting no. LX29	6.90
Other variable costs	17.50
Fixed overhead and administration	10.00
	$62.50

Santa Fe believes the price concession is necessary to get the job.

The company uses return on investment and dollar profits in the measurement of division and division-manager performance.

Required

1. Consider that you are the division controller of Tucson. Would you recommend that Tucson supply fitting no. LX29 to Santa Fe? Why or why not? (Ignore any income tax issues.)
2. Would it be to the short-run economic advantage of the Allenham Corporation for the Tucson Division to supply the Santa Fe Division with fitting no. LX29 at $6.90 each? (Ignore any income tax issues.) Explain your answer.
3. Discuss the organizational and manager-behavior difficulties, if any, inherent in this situation. As the Allenham controller, what would you advise the Allenham Corporation president to do in this situation?

10-33   Transfer Prices and Idle Capacity

The Furniture Division of Washington Woodcraft purchases lumber, which it uses to fabricate tables, chairs, and other wood furniture. Most of the lumber is purchased from Southshore Mill, also a division of Washington Woodcraft. Both the Furniture Division and Southshore Mill are profit centers.

The Furniture Division proposes to produce a new Danish-designed chair that will sell for $92. The manager is exploring the possibility of purchasing the required lumber from Southshore Mill. Production of 800 chairs is planned, using capacity in the Furniture Division that is currently idle.

The Furniture Division can purchase the lumber from an outside supplier for $72. Washington Woodcraft has a policy that internal transfers are priced at *fully allocated cost*.

Assume the following costs for the production of one chair and the lumber required for the chair:

Southshore Mill		Furniture Division		
Variable cost	$48	Variable costs		
Allocated fixed cost	22	Lumber from Southshore Mill		$70
Fully allocated cost	$70	Furniture Division variable costs		
		Manufacturing	$19	
		Selling	6	25
		Total cost		$95

Required

1. Assume that the Southshore Mill has idle capacity and therefore would incur no additional fixed costs to produce the required lumber. Would the furniture division manager buy the lumber for the chair from the Southshore Mill, given the existing

transfer-pricing policy? Why or why not? Would the company as a whole benefit if the manager decides to buy from the Southshore Mill? Explain.

2. Assume that there is no idle capacity at the Southshore Mill and the lumber required for one chair can be sold to outside customers for $72. Would the company as a whole benefit if the manager decides to buy? Explain.

10-34   Transfer-Pricing Principles

A consulting firm, TAC, is decentralized with twenty-five offices around the country. The headquarters is based in Orange County, California. Another operating division is located in Los Angeles, 50 miles away. A subsidiary printing operation, Kwik Print, is located in the headquarters building. Top management has indicated the desirability of the Los Angeles office's using Kwik Print for printing reports. All charges are eventually billed to the client, but TAC was concerned about keeping such charges competitive.

Kwik Print charges Los Angeles the following:

Photographing page for offset printing (a setup cost)	$.25
Printing cost per page	.013

At this rate, Kwik Print sales have a 60% contribution margin to fixed overhead.

Outside bids for 100 copies of a 120-page report needed immediately have been:

Print 4U	$192.00
Jiffy Press	168.25
Kustom Print	174.00

These three printers are located within a 5-mile radius of TAC Los Angeles and can have the reports ready in 2 days. A messenger would have to be sent to drop off the original and pick up the copies. The messenger usually goes to headquarters, but in the past, special trips have been required to deliver the original or pick up the copies. It takes 3 to 4 days to get the copies from Kwik Print (because of the extra scheduling difficulties in delivery and pickup).

Quality control of Kwik Print is poor. Reports received in the past have had wrinkled pages and have occasionally been miscollated or had pages deleted. (In one circumstance an intracompany memorandum indicating TAC's economic straits was inserted in a report. Fortunately, the Los Angeles office detected the error before the report was distributed to the clients.) The degree of quality control in the three outside prints shops is unknown.

(Although the differences in costs may seem immaterial in this case, regard the numbers as significant for purposes of focusing on the key issues.)

Required

1. If you were the decision maker at TAC Los Angeles, to which print shop would you give the business? Is this an optimal economic decision from the entire corporation's viewpoint?

2. What would be the ideal transfer price in this case, if based only on economic considerations?

3. Time is an important factor in maintaining the goodwill of the client. There is potential return business from this client. Given this perspective, what might be the optimal decision for the company?

4. Comment on the wisdom of top management in indicating that Kwik Print should be used.

10-35 Multinational Transfer Prices

Malone's Medical Instruments, Inc., produces a variety of medical products at its plant in Seattle, Washington. The company has sales divisions worldwide. One of these sales divisions is located in Oslo, Norway. Assume that the U.S. income tax rate is 34%, the Norwegian rate is 60%, and a 15% import duty is imposed on medical supplies brought into Norway.

One product produced in Seattle and shipped to Norway is a heart monitor. The variable cost of production is $300 per unit, and the fully allocated cost is $550 per unit.

Required

1. Suppose the Norwegian and U.S. governments allow either the variable or fully allocated cost to be used as a transfer price. Which should Medical Instruments, Inc., choose to minimize the total of income taxes and import duties? Compute the amount the company saves if it uses your suggested transfer price instead of the alternative.
2. Suppose the Norwegian parliament passed a law decreasing the income tax rate to 50% and increasing the duty on heart monitors to 20%. Repeat requirement 1, using these new facts.

10-36 Agency Theory

The Lambo Company plans to hire a manager for its division in Kenya. Lambo's president and vice-president of personnel are trying to decide on an appropriate incentive employment contract. The manager will operate far from the London corporate headquarters, so evaluation by personal observation will be limited. The president insists that a large incentive to produce profits is necessary; he favors a salary of £12,000 and a bonus of 10% of the profits above £120,000. If operations proceed as expected, profits will be £480,000, and the manager will receive £48,000. But both profits and compensation might be more or less than planned.

The vice-president of personnel responds that £48,000 is more than most of Lambo's division managers make. She is sure that a competent manager can be hired for a guaranteed salary of £36,000. "Why pay £48,000 when we can probably hire the same person for £36,000?" she argued.

Required

1. What factors would affect Lambo's choice of employment contract? Include a discussion of the pros and cons of each proposed contract.
2. Why is the expected compensation more with the bonus plan than with the straight salary?

10-37 Margins and Turnover

Return on investment is often expressed as the product of two components—capital turnover and return on sales. You are considering investing in one of three companies, all in the same industry, and are given the following information:

	Company		
	X	Y	Z
Sales	$6,000,000	$ 2,500,000	$37,500,000
Income	900,000	375,000	375,000
Capital	3,000,000	12,500,000	12,500,000

Required

1. Why would you desire the breakdown of return on investment into return on sales and turnover on capital?
2. Compute the return on sales, turnover on capital, and return on investment for the three companies, and comment on the relative performance of the companies as thoroughly as the data permit.

10-38   ROI by Business Segment

Weston Services Inc. does business in three different business segments: (1) Entertainment, (2) Publishing/Information, and (3) Consumer/Commercial Finance. Results for a recent year were (in millions):

	Revenues	Operating Income	Total Assets
Entertainment	$1,272.2	$223.0	$1,120.1
Publishing/Information	705.5	121.4	1,308.7
Consumer/Commercial Finance	1,235.0	244.6	924.4

Required

1. Compute the following for each business segment:
   a.   Income percentage of revenue
   b.   Capital turnover
   c.   ROI
2. Comment on the differences in return on investment among the business segments. Include reasons for the differences.

10-39   Evaluation of Divisional Performance

As the chief executive officer of Polanski Company, you examined the following measures of the performance of three divisions (in thousands of dollars):

Division	Net Assets Based on		Operating Income Based on*	
	Historical Cost	Replacement Cost	Historical Cost	Replacement Cost
Marine Products	$15,000	$15,000	$2,700	$2,700
Sporting Goods	45,000	54,000	6,750	6,150
Outdoor Equipment	30,000	48,000	4,800	3,900

* The differences in operating income between historical and replacement cost are attributable to the differences in depreciation expenses.

Required

1. Calculate for each division the rate of return on net assets and the residual income based on historical cost and on replacement cost. For purposes of calculating residual income, use 10% as the minimum desired rate of return.
2. Rank the performance of each division under each of the four different measures computed in requirement 1.
3. What do these measures indicate about the performance of the divisions? Of the division managers? Which measure do you prefer? Why?

10-40   Use of Gross or Net Book Value of Fixed Assets

Assume that a particular plant acquires $800,000 of fixed assets with a useful life of 4 years and no residual value. Straight-line depreciation will be used. The plant manager is judged on income in relation to these fixed assets. Annual net income, after deducting depreciation, is $80,000.

Assume that sales, and all expenses except depreciation, are on a cash basis. Dividends equal net income. Thus, cash in the amount of the depreciation charge will accumulate each year. The plant manager's performance is judged in relation to fixed assets because all current assets, including cash, are considered under central-company control. Assume (unrealistically) that any cash accumulated remains idle. Ignore taxes.

1. Prepare a comparative tabulation of the plant's rate of return and the company's overall rate of return based on
   a. Gross (i.e., original cost) assets.
   b. Net book value of assets.
2. Evaluate the relative merits of gross assets and net book value of assets as investment bases.

10-41 Review of Major Points in Chapter

(D. Kleespie.) The Antonio Company uses the decentralized form of organizational structure and considers each of its divisions as an investment center. Division L is currently selling 15,000 air filters annually, although it has sufficient productive capacity to produce 21,000 units per year. Variable manufacturing costs amount to $18 per unit, while the total fixed costs amount to $90,000. These 15,000 air filters are sold to outside customers at $38 per unit.

Division M, also a part of the Antonio Company, has indicated that it would like to buy 1,500 air filters from Division L, but at a price of $37 per unit. This is the price Division M is currently paying an outside supplier.

Required

1. Compute the effect on the operating income of the company as a whole if Division M purchases the 1,500 air filters from Division L.
2. What is the minimum price that Division L should be willing to accept for these 1,500 air filters?
3. What is the maximum price that Division M should be willing to pay for these 1,500 air filters?
4. Suppose instead that Division L is currently producing and selling 21,000 air filters annually to outside customers. What is the effect on the overall Antonio Company operating income if Division L is required by top management to sell 1,500 air filters to Division M at (a) $18 per unit and (b) $37 per unit?
5. For this question only, assume that Division L is currently earning an annual operating income of $36,000, and the division's average invested capital is $300,000. The division manager has an opportunity to invest in a proposal that will require an additional investment of $20,000 and will increase annual operating income by $2,200. (a) Should the division manager accept this proposal if the Antonio Company uses ROI in evaluating the performance of its divisional managers? (b) If the company uses residual income? (Assume an "imputed interest" charge of 9%.)

Cases

10-42 Management by Objectives

(CMA.) Tom Clay is the chief executive officer of Mayberry Company. Clay has a financial management background and is known throughout the organization as a "no-nonsense" executive. When Clay became chief executive officer, he emphasized cost reduction and savings and introduced a comprehensive cost control and budget system. The company goals and budget plans were established by Clay and given to his subordinates for implementation. Some of the company's key executives were dismissed or demoted for failing to meet projected budget plans. Under the leadership of Tom Clay, Mayberry has once again become financially stable and profitable after several years of poor performance.

Recently Clay has become concerned with the human side of the organization and has become interested in the management technique referred to as "management by objectives" (MBO). If there are enough positive benefits of MBO, he plans to implement the system throughout the company. However, he realizes that he does not fully understand MBO because he does not understand how it differs from the current system of establishing firm objectives and budget plans.

Required

1. Briefly explain what MBO entails and identify its advantages and disadvantages.
2. Does the management style of Tom Clay incorporate the human value premises and goals of MBO? Explain your answer.

10-43   Profit Centers and Central Services

EZtronics, manufacturer of small appliances, has an Engineering Consulting Department (ECD). The department's major task has been to help the production departments improve their operating methods and processes.

For several years the consulting services have been charged to the production departments based on a signed agreement between the managers involved. The agreement specifies the scope of the project, the predicted savings, and the number of consulting hours required. The charge to the production departments is based on the costs to the Engineering Department of the services rendered. For example, senior engineer hours cost more per hour than junior engineer hours. An overhead cost is included. The agreement is really a "fixed-price" contract. That is, the production manager knows the total cost of the project in advance. A recent survey revealed that production managers have a high level of confidence in the engineers.

The ECD department manager oversees the work of about 40 engineers and 10 technicians. She reports to the engineering manager, who reports to the vice-president of manufacturing. The ECD manager has the freedom to increase or decrease the number of engineers under her supervision. The ECD manager's performance evaluation is based on many factors including the annual incremental savings to the company in excess of the costs of operating the ECD department.

The production departments are profit centers. Their goods are transferred to subsequent departments, such as a sales department or sales division, at prices that approximate market prices for similar products.

Top management is seriously considering a "no-charge" plan. That is, engineering services would be rendered to the production departments at absolutely no cost. Proponents of the new plan maintain that it would motivate the production managers to take better advantage of engineering talent. In all other respects, the new system would be unchanged from the present system.

Required

1. Compare the present and proposed plans. What are their strong and weak points? In particular, will the ECD manager tend to hire the "optimal" amount of engineering talent?
2. Which plan do you favor? Why?

11

Capital Budgeting: An Introduction

The Hyatt Corporation owns and operates luxury hotels around the world. Managers evaluate proposed major capital expenditures in a new hotel property using discounted-cash-flow models such as net present value. *Courtesy Hyatt Corporation*

Learning Objectives

When you have finished studying this chapter, you should be able to

1 Compute a project's net present value (NPV).

2 Compute a project's internal rate of return (IRR).

3 Identify the assumptions of the two discounted-cash-flow (DCF) models.

4 Apply the decision rules for the DCF models.

5 Use sensitivity analysis in evaluating projects.

6 Use both the total project and differential approaches to determine the NPV difference between two projects.

7 Identify relevant cash flows for DCF analyses.

8 Use the payback model and the accounting rate-of-return model and compare them with the DCF models.

9 Identify the methods for reconciling the conflict between using a DCF model for making a decision and using accounting income for evaluating the related performance.

Managers often must make important strategic decisions. For example:

- Should Roosevelt High School purchase new laboratory equipment?
- Should partners of Stone, Goldberg, and Gomez (a law firm) buy personal computers for the staff?
- Should Boeing begin production of a proposed new airplane?
- Should Kellogg's introduce a new breakfast cereal?

Such decisions, which have significant financial effects beyond the current year, are called **capital-budgeting decisions**. Capital-budgeting decisions are faced by managers in all types of organizations including religious, medical, and government enterprises.

Capital budgeting has three phases: (1) identifying potential investments, (2) selecting the investments to undertake (including the gathering of data to aid the decision), and (3) follow-up monitoring, or "postaudit," of investments. Accountants usually are not involved in the first phase, but they play important roles in phases 2 and 3.

capital-budgeting decisions Decisions that have significant financial effects beyond the current year.

413

Managers use many different capital-budgeting models in *selecting* investments. Each model summarizes facts and forecasts about an investment in a way that provides information for a decision maker. Accountants contribute to this choice process in their problem-solving role. In this chapter we compare the uses and limitations of various capital-budgeting models, with particular attention to relevant-cost analysis. Accountants' scorekeeping is important to the *postaudit* of investments, discussed later in the chapter.

■ FOCUS ON PROGRAMS OR PROJECTS

In planning and controlling operations, managers typically focus on reports covering a particular time period. For example, the chief administrator of a university will be concerned with all activities for a given academic year. But the administrator will also be concerned with individual *programs* or *projects* that have a longer-range focus. Examples are new programs in educational administration or health care education, joint law-management programs, new athletic facilities, new trucks, or new parking lots. In fact, many organizations may be perceived as a collection of individual investment projects.

This chapter concentrates on the planning and controlling of those programs or projects that affect more than one year's financial results. Such decisions require investments of resources that are often called *capital outlays*. Hence the term *capital budgeting* has arisen to describe the long-term planning for making and financing such outlays.

All capital outlays involve risk. The organization must commit funds to the project or program but cannot be sure what—if any—returns this investment will yield later. Many factors affecting future returns are unknowable, but well-managed organizations try to gather and quantify as many knowable or predictable factors as possible before making a decision. Capital-budgeting models facilitate this process.

Most large organizations use more than one capital-budgeting model. Why? Because each model summarizes information in a different way and reveals various useful perspectives on investments. There are three general types of capital-budgeting models: discounted-cash-flow models, payback models, and rate-of-return models. We look at each of these model types in turn in this chapter.

discounted-cash-flow (DCF) models A type of capital-budgeting model that focuses on cash inflows and outflows and explicitly and systematically incorporates the time value of money.

■ DISCOUNTED-CASH-FLOW MODELS

Discounted-cash-flow (DCF) models focus on a project's cash inflows and outflows and explictly and systematically incorporate the time value of money. They are based on the old adage that a bird in the hand is worth two in the bush—that a dollar in the hand today is worth more than a dollar to be received (or spent) 5 years from today. This adage applies because the use of money has a cost (interest), just as the use of a building or an automobile may have a cost (rent). DCF models, conceptually the most attractive models, are used by more than 85% of the large industrial firms in the United States and are the best measures of the financial effects of an investment.

Major Aspects of DCF

DCF models focus on expected *cash* inflows and outflows rather than on *net income*. It is important to recognize that injecting net income into discounted-cash-flow analysis is incorrect. Analysis of periodic *cash flows* is critical to DCF analysis.

There are two main variations of DCF: (1) net present value (NPV) and (2) internal rate of return (IRR). Both variations are based on the theory of compound interest. A brief summary of the tables and formulas used is included in Appendix B at the end of this book. ***Before reading on, examine Appendix B, pages 807–814, and be sure you understand the concept of compound interest and how to use Table 1 (p. 813) and Table 2 (p. 814).*** The mechanics of compound interest may appear formidable to those readers who are encountering them for the first time. However, a little practice with the interest tables should easily clarify the mechanical aspect.

Example

Throughout the rest of this section, we use the following example to illustrate the major concepts: A buildings and grounds manager at the University of Minnesota is contemplating the purchase of some lawn maintenance equipment that is expected to increase efficiency and produce cash-operating savings of $2,000 per year. The useful life of the equipment is 4 years, after which it will have a net disposal value of zero. The equipment will cost $6,075 now, and the minimum desired rate of return is 10% per year.

Net Present Value (NPV)

net-present-value (NPV) method A discounted-cash-flow approach to capital budgeting that discounts all expected future cash flows to the present using a minimum desired rate of return.

required rate of return (hurdle rate, discount rate) The minimum desired rate of return, based on the firm's cost of capital.

The **net-present-value (NPV) method** is a DCF approach to capital budgeting that discounts all expected future cash flows to the present using a minimum desired rate of return. To apply the NPV method to a proposed investment project, a manager first determines some minimum desired rate of return. The rate depends on the risk of a proposed project—the higher the risk, the higher the minimum desired rate of return. The minimum rate is based on the *cost of capital*—what the firm pays to acquire more capital—and it is also called the **required rate of return, hurdle rate,** or **discount rate**. Managers then determine the present values of all expected cash flows from the project, using this minimum desired rate. If the sum of the present values of the cash flows is positive, the project is desirable. If the sum is negative, it is undesirable. Why? A positive NPV means that accepting the project will increase the value of the firm because the present value of the project's cash inflows exceeds the present value of its cash outflows. (If by some chance, the NPV is exactly zero, a decision maker would be indifferent between accepting and rejecting the project.) When choosing among several investments, the one with the greatest net present value is the most desirable.

Applying the NPV method

The NPV method is applied in the following three steps, which are shown in Exhibit 11-1:

1. *Prepare a diagram of relevant expected cash inflows and outflows:* The right-hand side of Exhibit 11-1 shows how these cash flows are sketched. Outflows are in parentheses. Be sure to include the outflow at time zero, the date of acquisition. Although a sketch is not essential, it clarifies thought.

2. *Find the present value of each expected cash inflow or outflow:* Examine Table 1 in Appendix B on page 813. Find the present value (PV) factor from the correct row and column of the table. Multiply each expected cash inflow or outflow by the appropriate present value factor. For example, the $2,000 cash savings that will occur 2 years hence is worth $2,000 × .8264 = $1,653 today.

3. *Sum the individual present values:* The sum is the project's NPV. Accept a project whose NPV is positive, and reject a project whose NPV is negative.

Exhibit 11-1 shows a positive net present value of $265, so the investment is desirable. The value today (i.e., at time zero) of the four $2,000 cash inflows is $6,340. The manager pays only $6,075 to obtain these cash inflows. Thus a favorable difference can be achieved at time zero: $6,340 − $6,075 = $265.

Choice of the Correct Table

Exhibit 11-1 also shows another way to calculate the NPV, shown here as approach 2. The basic steps are the same as for approach 1. The only difference is that approach 2 uses Table 2 in Appendix B (see page 814) instead of Table 1. Table 2 is an annuity table that provides a shortcut to reduce hand calculations. It gives discount factors for computing the present value of a *series of equal* cash flows at equal intervals. Because the four cash flows in our example are all equal, you can use Table 2 to make one present-value computation instead of four individual computations. Table 2 is merely a summation of the pertinent present-value factors of Table 1. Therefore the annuity factor for 4 years at 10% is:

$$.9091 + .8264 + .7513 + .6830 = 3.1698$$

In this example, Table 2 accomplishes in one computation what Table 1 accomplishes in four multiplications and one summation.[1]

Beware of using the wrong table. Table 1 should be used for discounting individual amounts, Table 2 for a *series* of equal amounts. Of course, Table 1 is the fundamental table. If shortcuts are not desired, Table 1 can be used for all present-value calculations.

The use of Tables 1 and 2 can be avoided entirely by those with a present value function on their hand-held calculator or those who use the present value function on a spreadsheet program on their personal computer. However, we encourage you to use the tables when learning the NPV method. Using the tables leads to an understanding of the process that does not come if calculators or computers are used exclusively. Once you are comfortable with the method, you can take advantage of the speed and convenience of calculators and computers.

---

[1] Rounding error causes a .0001 difference between the Table 2 factor and the summation of Table 1 factors.

Exhibit 11-1 Net-Present-Value Technique

Original investment, $6,075. Useful life, 4 years. Annual cash inflow from operations, $2,000. Minimum desired rate of return, 10%. Cash outflows are in parentheses; cash inflows are not. Total present values are rounded to the nearest dollar.

	Present Value of $1, Discounted at 10%	Total Present Value	Sketch of Cash Flows at End of Year				
			0	1	2	3	4

Approach 1: Discounting Each Year's Cash Inflow Separately*

Cash flows							
Annual savings	.9091	$1,818	←	$2,000			
	.8264	1,653	←		$2,000		
	.7513	1,503	←			$2,000	
	.6830	1,366	←				$2,000
Present value of future inflows		$6,340					
Initial outlay	1.0000	(6,075)	$(6,075)				
Net present value		$ 265					

Approach 2: Using Annuity Table†

Annual savings	3.1699	$6,340	←	$2,000	$2,000	$2,000	$2,000
Initial outlay	1.0000	(6,075)	$(6,075)				
Net present value		$ 265					

* Present values from Table 1, Appendix B, page 813.
† Present values of annuity from Table 2, Appendix B, page 814. (Incidentally, calculators or computers may give slightly different answers than tables because of rounding differences.)

Effect of Minimum Rate

The minimum desired rate of return can have a large effect on NPVs. The higher the minimum desired rate of return, the lower the present value of each future cash inflow and thus the lower the NPV of the project. At a rate of 16%, the NPV of the project in Exhibit 11-1 would be – $479 (i.e., $2,000 × 2.7982 = $5,596, which is $479 less than the required investment of $6,075), instead of the +$265 computed with a 10% rate. (Present-value factor 2.7982 is taken from Table 2 in Appendix B on page 814.) When the desired rate of return is 16% rather than 10%, the project is undesirable at a price of $6,075.

Internal Rate of Return (IRR)

internal rate of return (IRR) The discount rate that makes the net present value of the project equal to zero.

Another way to decide whether to make a capital outlay is to calculate a project's **internal rate of return (IRR)**, the discount rate that makes the NPV of the project equal to zero, as Exhibit 11-2 shows. Expressed another way, the IRR is the discount rate that makes the present value of a project's expected cash inflows equal to the present value of the expected cash outflows, including the investment in the project.

Objective 2

Compute a project's internal rate of return (IRR)

Applying the IRR Method

The following three steps in calculating IRR are shown in Exhibit 11-2.

1. *Prepare a diagram of the expected cash inflows and outflows*: Follow this step exactly as you did in calculating the NPV (see Exhibit 11-1).

2. *Find an interest rate that equates the present value of the cash inflows to the present value of the cash outflows*: In other words, find an interest rate that produces an NPV of zero. Approach 1 uses Table 1 in Appendix B and can be used with any set of cash flows. However, if one outflow is followed by a series of equal inflows, you can use approach 2 and the following equation:

$$\text{initial investment} = \text{annual cash inflow} \times \text{annuity PV factor (F)}$$
$$\$6{,}075 = \$2{,}000 \times F$$
$$F = \frac{\$6{,}075}{\$2{,}000} = 3.0375$$

   In Table 2 of Appendix B (see p. 814), scan the row that represents the relevant life of the project, row 4 in our example. Select the column with an entry closest to the annuity PV factor that was calculated. The factor closest to 3.0375 is 3.0373 in the 12% column. Because these factors are extremely close, the IRR is almost exactly 12%. Approach 2, like approach 1, shows that an interest rate of 12% indeed produces an NPV of zero.

3. *Compare the IRR with the minimum desired rate of return*: If the IRR is greater than the minimum desired rate, the project should be accepted. Otherwise it should be rejected.

Interpolation and Trial and Error

Not all IRR calculations work out this neatly. Suppose the expected cash inflow in step 1 were $1,800 instead of $2,000. The equation in step 2 would produce

$$\$6{,}075 = \$1{,}800 \times F$$
$$F = \frac{\$6{,}075}{\$1{,}800} = 3.3750$$

Exhibit 11-2   Two Proofs of Internal Rate of Return

Original investment, $6,075. Useful life, 4 years. Annual cash inflow from operations, $2,000. Internal rate of return (selected by trial-and-error methods), 12%. Total present values are rounded to the nearest dollar.

	Present Value of $1, Discounted at 12%	Total Present Value			Sketch of Cash Flows at End of Year			
				0	1	2	3	4

Approach 1: Discounting Each Year's Cash Inflow Separately*

Cash flows			
Annual savings	.8929	$1,786	←------------- $2,000
	.7972	1,594	←------------------------ $2,000
	.7118	1,424	←------------------------------------- $2,000
	.6355	1,271	←-- $2,000
		$6,075	
Present value of future inflows		$6,075	
Initial outlay	1.0000	(6,075)	$(6,075)
Net present value (the zero difference proves that the rate of return is 12%)		$ 0	

Approach 2: Using Annuity Table†

Annual savings	3.0373	$6,075	←------------- $2,000 $2,000 $2,000 $2,000
Initial outlay	1.0000	(6,075)	$(6,075)
Net present value		$ 0	

* Present values from Table 1, Appendix B, page 813.
† Present values of annuity from Table 2, Appendix B, page 814.

419

On the period 4 line of Table 2, the column closest to 3.3750 is 7%, which may be close enough for most purposes. To obtain a more accurate rate, you must interpolate. The factor 3.3750 is between the 7% factor (3.3872) and the 8% factor (3.3121):

	Present-Value Factors	
7%	3.3872	3.3872
Approximate rate		3.3750
8%	3.3121	
Difference	.0751	.0122

Thus,

$$\text{approximate rate} = 7\% + \left(\frac{.0122}{.0751} \times 1\% \right) = 7.16\%$$

These hand computations become even more complex when the cash inflows and outflows are not uniform. Then trial-and-error methods are needed. See Appendix 11, page 438, for examples. Of course, in practice, managers today use computer programs and spreadsheets to greatly simplify trial-and-error procedures.

Meaning of Internal Rate of Return

Exhibit 11-2 shows that the present value of four annual cash inflows of $2,000 each is $6,075, assuming a rate of return of 12%. That is, 12% is the rate that equates the amount invested ($6,075) with the present value of the cash inflows ($2,000 per year for 4 years). Exhibit 11-3 shows that, if money were obtained at an effective interest rate of 12%, the cash inflow produced by the project would exactly repay the principal plus the interest over the 4 years. If money is available at less than 12%, the organization will have cash left over after repaying the principal and interest.

Exhibit 11-3 also highlights how the IRR is computed on the basis of the investment tied up in the project from period to period instead of solely on the initial investment. The internal rate is 12% of the capital invested during each year. The $2,000 inflow is composed of two parts, as analyzed in columns 3 and 4. Consider year 1. Column 3 shows the interest on the $6,075 invested capital as .12 × $6,075 = $729. Column 4 shows that the amount of investment recovered at the end of the year is $2,000 – $729 = $1,271. By the end of year 4, the series of four cash inflows exactly recovers the initial investment plus annual interest at a rate of 12% on the as yet unrecovered capital.

Exhibit 11-3 can be interpreted from either the borrower's or the lender's vantage point. Suppose the university borrowed $6,075 from a bank at an interest rate of 12% per annum, invested in the project, and repaid the loan with the $2,000 saved each year. Each $2,000 payment would represent interest of 12% plus a reduction of the loan balance. At a rate of 12%, the borrower would end up with an accumulated wealth of zero. Obviously, if the borrower could borrow at 12%, and the project could generate cash at more than the 12% rate (i.e., in excess of $2,000 annually), the borrower would be able to keep some cash—and the internal rate of return, *by definition*, would exceed 12%. Again the internal rate of return is the discount rate that would provide a net present value of zero (no more, no less).

Exhibit 11-3

Rationale Underlying Internal-Rate-of-Return Model (Same data as in Exhibit 11-2)

Original investment, $6,075. Useful life, 4 years. Annual cash savings from operations, $2,000. Internal rate of return, 12%. Amounts are rounded to the nearest dollar.

Year	(1) Unrecovered Investment at Beginning of Year	(2) Annual Cash Savings	(3) Interest at 12% per Year (1) × 12%	(4) Amount of Investment Recovered at End of Year (2) – (3)	(5) Unrecovered Investment at End of Year (1) – (4)
1	$6,075	$2,000	$729	$1,271	$4,804
2	4,804	2,000	576	1,424	3,380
3	3,380	2,000	406	1,594	1,786
4	1,786	2,000	214	1,786	0

Assumptions: Unrecovered investment at beginning of each year earns interest for whole year. Annual cash inflows are received at the end of each year. For simplicity in the use of tables, all operating cash inflows are assumed to occur at the end of the years in question. This is unrealistic because such cash flows ordinarily occur uniformly throughout the given year, rather than in lump sums at the end of the year. Compound interest tables especially tailored for these more stringent conditions are available, but we shall not consider them here.

Assumptions of DCF Models

Objective 3

Identify the assumptions of the two discounted-cash-flow (DCF) models

Although both DCF models are good, neither is perfect. Two major assumptions underlie DCF models. First, we assume a world of certainty. That is, we act as if the predicted cash inflows and outflows are certain to occur at the times specified. Second, we assume perfect capital markets. That is, if we have extra cash at any time, we can borrow or lend money at the same interest rate. This rate is our minimum desired rate of return for the NPV model and the internal rate of return for the IRR model. If these assumptions are met, no model could possibly be better than a DCF model.

Unfortunately, our world has neither certainty nor perfect capital markets. Nevertheless, the DCF models are usually preferred to other models. The assumptions of most other models are even less realistic. The DCF models are not perfect, but they generally meet our cost-benefit criterion. The payoff from better decisions is greater than the cost of applying one of the DCF models. More sophisticated models often do not improve decisions enough to be worth their cost.

■ USE OF DCF MODELS

In using DCF models of both types, managers must keep in mind the limitations of these models. Using such models is also complicated by the difficulties of determining a desired rate of return.

Choice of the Minimum Desired Rate

There are two key aspects of capital budgeting: investment decisions and financing decisions. *Investment decisions* focus on whether to acquire an asset, a project, a company, a product line, and so on. *Financing decisions* focus on whether to raise the required funds via some form of debt or equity or both.

Property Valuation and DCF

The use of discounted-cash-flow (DCF) analysis began to be widely applied in industrial firms in the 1950s. By the 1970s a majority of large companies used DCF. In the 1980s, real estate appraisers began using DCF to estimate the value of commercial properties. By the mid 1990s, lenders of all types (including appraisers, banks, insurance companies, pension funds, etc.) routinely used DCF to value properties for purposes such as determining offering prices for properties for sale, establishing limits on loans for which property was used as collateral, and for estimating market prices for portfolios that include real estate.

In addition to using DCF to value specific properties, most corporations acquiring another firm use DCF to establish an appropriate bid price. E.L. Morris, president of Fortune Finance Inc., a St. Louis investment banking firm, indicates that buyers find DCF "indisputably superior" to less sophisticated valuation methods.

For example, consider TeleWest, a British cable television company. Before being listed on both U.S. and U.K. stock markets in 1995, TeleWest used discounted cash flow to estimate its market value. The securities house of Kleinwort Benson computed net present values of £1.379 billion using a 17% rate and £1.667 billion using a rate of 15%. Kleinwort Benson also estimated the net present value of a single cable subscriber. Using a rate of 16%, each cable subscriber is worth £876. Using this figure, investors could use their own estimates of population, cable penetration rates, and churn rates (rates at which current subscribers cancel their subscriptions) to predict TeleWest's market value.

Despite its widespread use, not everyone is convinced that DCF is superior to other valuation methods. A recent controversy in Britain was prompted by the failure of the Queens Moat chain of hotels. Two different appraisers came up with estimates of the value of the chain's assets that diverged by more than £1 billion. The British Association of Hotel Accountants supported a valuation based on DCF, while the Royal Institute of Chartered Surveyors (RICS) backed a method based on applying a multiple to the company's accounting earnings. RICS believes an earnings-based valuation is more objective because it is based on "achieved" profits, not simply on cash flow estimates. Supporters of DCF would argue that estimates based on "best predictions" of cash flow are more accurate than those based on current earnings. After all, earnings are based on costs such as depreciation that may have little relation to the current values of the assets being used. ∎

Sources: Adapted from R. J. Okaneski, "Present Values: A Useful Underwriting Tool?," Appraisal Journal, October 1994, p. 609; "TeleWest Is Good Four-Way Bet, Says Kleinwort Benson," New Media Markets, October 27, 1994; S. London, "Facts and Forecasts: The Paucity of Credible Market Analysis," Financial Times, September 23, 1994, p. 12.

This textbook concentrates on the investment decision. Finance textbooks provide ample discussions of financing decisions.

Depending on a project's risk (i.e., the probability that the expected cash inflows will not be achieved) and what alternative investments are available, investors usually have some notion of a minimum rate of return that would make various projects desirable investments. The problem of choosing this required rate of return is complex and is really more a problem of finance than of accounting. In general, the higher the risk, the higher the required rate of return. In this book we assume that the minimum acceptable rate of return is given to the accountant by management. It represents the rate that can be earned by the best alternative investments of similar risk.

Note too that the minimum desired rate is not affected by whether the *specific project* is financed by all debt, all ownership capital, or some of each. Thus the cost of capital is not "interest expense" on borrowed money as the accountant ordinarily conceives it. For example, a mortgage-free home still has a cost of capital—the maximum amount that could be earned with the proceeds if the home were sold.

Depreciation and DCF

Accounting students are sometimes mystified by the apparent exclusion of depreciation from DCF computations. A common homework error is to deduct depreciation from cash inflows. This is a misunderstanding of one of the basic ideas involved in the concept of the discounting. Because the DCF approach is fundamentally based on inflows and outflows of *cash* and not on the accounting concepts of revenues and expenses, no adjustments should be made to the cash flows for depreciation expense (which is not a cash flow).[2] In the DCF approach, the entire cost of an asset is typically a *lump-sum* outflow of cash at time zero. Therefore it is wrong to also deduct depreciation from operating-cash inflows. To deduct periodic depreciation would be a double-counting of a cost that has already been considered as a lump-sum outflow.

Use of DCF Models by Nonprofit Organizations

Religious, educational, health care, government, and other nonprofit organizations face a variety of capital-budgeting decisions. Examples include investments in buildings, equipment, national defense systems, and research programs. Thus, even when no revenue is involved, organizations try to choose projects with the least cost for any given set of objectives.

The unsettled question of the appropriate discount rate plagues all types of organizations, profit-seeking and nonprofit. One point is certain: As all cash-strapped organizations soon discover, capital is not cost-free. A discussion of the appropriate required rate of return is beyond the scope of this book. Often departments of the federal government use 10%. It represents a crude approximation of the opportunity cost to the economy of having investments made by public agencies instead of by private organizations.

Progress in management practices and in the use of sophisticated techniques has generally tended to be faster in profit-seeking organizations. Although DCF is used by many federal departments, it is less frequently used at state and local levels of government. Thus, in general, managers have more opportunities in nonprofit than in profit-seeking organizations to contribute to improved decision making by introducing newer management decision models such as DCF.[3]

Review of Decision Rules

Objective 4

Apply the decision rules for the DCF models

Before proceeding, take time to review the basic ideas of discounted cash flow. The decision maker in our example cannot readily compare an immediate outflow of $6,075 with a series of future inflows of $2,000 each because the

---

[2] Throughout this and the next chapter, our examples often assume that cash inflows are equivalent to revenues and that cash outflows are equivalent to expenses (except for depreciation). Of course, if the revenues and expenses are accounted for on the accrual basis of accounting, there will be leads and lags of cash inflows and cash outflows that a precise DCF model must recognize. For example, a $10,000 sale on credit may be recorded as revenue in one period, but the related cash inflow would not be recognized in a DCF model until collected, which may be in a second period. Such refinements are not made in this chapter.

[3] An extensive study by the General Accounting Office cited the U.S. Postal Service as being the best of the federal agencies regarding capital budgeting. The Postal Service uses discounted cash flow, sensitivity analysis, and postaudits.

outflows and inflows do not occur simultaneously. The NPV model expresses all amounts in equivalent terms; that is, in today's monetary units (e.g., dollars, francs, marks, yen) at time zero. An interest rate measures the cost of using money. At a rate of 12%, the comparison would be:

Outflow in today's dollars	$(6,075)
Inflow equivalent in today's dollars @ 12%	6,075
Net present value	$ 0

Therefore, at a required rate of return of 12%, the decision maker is indifferent between having $6,075 now or having a stream of four annual inflows of $2,000 each. If the interest rate were 16%, the decision maker would find the project unattractive because the net present value would be negative:

Outflow	$(6,075)
Inflow equivalent in today's dollars @ 16% = $2,000 × 2.7982 (from Table 2) =	5,596
Net present value	$ (479)

At 10%, the NPV is positive, and the project is desirable:

Outflow	$(6,075)
Inflow equivalent in today's dollars @ 10% = $2,000 × 3.1699 from Table 2 =	6,340
Net present value	$ 265

We can summarize the decision rules offered by these two models as follows:

Net-Present-Value (NPV) Model	Internal Rate-of-Return (IRR) Model
1. Calculate the NPV, using the minimum desired rate of return as the discount rate.	1. Compute the IRR by trial and error (e.g., by using present-value tables).
2. If the NPV is positive, accept the project; if negative, reject the project.	2. If this rate exceeds the minimum desired rate of return, accept the project; if not, reject the project.

A report in *Business Week* provided an example of using an NPV model:

> Like many of the amounts being paid in big acquisitions of the last year, the $350 million that Eaton Corp. will have paid this January to acquire Cutler-Hammer, Inc., appears to be a stiff price. . . . Eaton is justifying the price in large part by using an old but increasingly popular financial tool: discounted-cash-flow analysis (DCF). To set the price, Eaton projected the future cash flows it expects from Cutler over the next 5 to 10 years and then discounted them, using a rate that reflects the risks involved in the investment and the time value of the money used. Eaton figures that, based on DCF, Cutler will return at least 12% on its $350 million outlay.

■ SENSITIVITY ANALYSIS AND ASSESSMENT OF RISK IN DCF MODELS

Capital investments entail risk. Why? Because the actual cash inflows may differ from what was expected or predicted. When considering a capital-budgeting project, a manager should first determine the riskiness of the investment. Then the inputs to the capital-budgeting model should be adjusted to reflect the risk.

There are three common ways to recognize risk. They can be used singly or in combination:

1. Increase the minimum desired rate of return for riskier projects.
2. Reduce individual expected cash inflows or increase expected cash outflows by an amount that depends on their riskiness.
3. Reduce the expected life of riskier projects.

In the examples in this book we assume that an appropriate risk adjustment is included in the minimum desired rate of return.

One method that helps identify the riskiness of a project is to compare the results of different capital-budgeting models. For example, a manager can compare the NPV and IRR results with those of simpler measures such as the payback period and accounting rate of return (discussed later in this chapter).

Another approach is the use of sensitivity analysis, which shows the financial consequences that would occur if actual cash inflows and outflows differed from those expected. It can be usefully applied whenever a decision requires predictions. It answers such "what-if" questions as: What will happen to my NPV or IRR if my predictions of useful life or cash flows are inaccurate? Spreadsheet software is ideally suited for this type of analysis.

There are two major types of sensitivity analysis: (1) comparing the optimistic, pessimistic, and most likely predictions and (2) determining the amount of deviation from expected values before a decision is changed. These analyses produce results such as the following:

Objective 5

Use sensitivity analysis in evaluating projects

1. Suppose the forecasts of annual cash inflows in Exhibit 11-1 could range from a low of $1,700 to a high of $2,300. The pessimistic, most likely, and optimistic NPV predictions are

   Pessimistic: ($1,700 × 3.1699) − $6,075 = $5,389 − $6,075 = −$686
   Most likely: ($2,000 × 3.1699) − $6,075 = $6,340 − $6,075 = $265
   Optimistic: ($2,300 × 3.1699) − $6,075 = $7,291 − $6,075 = $1,216

   Although the expected NPV is $265, the actual NPV might turn out to be as low as −$686 or, as high as $1,216.

2. A manager would reject a project if its expected NPV were negative. How far below $2,000 must the annual cash inflow drop before the NPV becomes negative? The cash inflow at the point where NPV = 0 is the "break-even" cash flow:

   NPV = 0
   (3.1699 × cash flow) − $6,075 = 0
   cash flow = $6,075 ÷ 3.1699
   = $1,916

   If the annual cash inflow is less than $1,916, the project should be rejected. Therefore annual cash inflows can drop only $2,000 − $1,916 = $84, or 4%, before the manager would change the decision. Thus managers must decide whether a given margin of error is acceptable or whether undertaking a project represents too great a risk.

Sensitivity analysis can also be performed on predictions of the useful life of capital equipment. Suppose 3 years is a pessimistic prediction, and 5 years is optimistic. Using present-value factors from the third, fourth, and fifth rows of the 10% column of Table 2 in Appendix B (see page 814), the NPVs are as follows:

$$\text{Pessimistic: } (2.4869 \times \$2{,}000) - \$6{,}075 = -\$1{,}101$$
$$\text{Most likely: } (3.1699 \times \$2{,}000) - \$6{,}075 = \$265$$
$$\text{Optimistic: } (3.7908 \times \$2{,}000) - \$6{,}075 = \$1{,}507$$

If the useful life is even 1 year less than predicted, the investment will be undesirable.

Sensitivity analysis provides an immediate financial measure of the consequences of possible errors in forecasting. Why is this useful? It helps to identify decisions that may be readily affected by prediction errors. After managers identify such decisions, they can gather additional information to help them better predict cash flows or useful life before making their decisions.

■ THE NPV COMPARISON OF TWO PROJECTS

Seldom are managers asked to perform analyses on a single option. More often, managers want to compare several alternatives.

Total Project Versus Differential Approach

total project approach An approach that compares two or more alternatives by computing the total impact on cash flows for each alternative and then converting these total cash flows to their present values.

differential approach An approach that compares two alternatives by computing the differences in cash flows between alternatives and then converting these differences in cash flows to their present values.

Two common methods for comparing alternatives are (1) the *total project approach* and (2) the *differential approach*.

The **total project approach** compares two or more alternatives by computing the total impact on cash flows for each alternative and then converting these total cash flows to their present values. It is the most popular approach and can be used for any number of alternatives. The alternative with the largest NPV of total cash flows is preferred.

The **differential approach** compares two alternatives by computing the *differences* in cash flows between alternatives and then converting these differences in cash flows to their present values. Its use is restricted to cases in which only two alternatives are being examined. (There are always at least two alternatives. One is the status quo—that is, doing nothing.)

To compare these approaches, suppose a company owns a packaging machine that it purchased 3 years ago for $56,000. The machine has a remaining useful life of 5 years but will require a major overhaul at the end of 2 more years at a cost of $10,000. Its disposal value now is $20,000. In 5 years its disposal value is expected to be $8,000, assuming that the $10,000 major overhaul will be done on schedule. The cash-operating costs of this machine are expected to be $40,000 annually. A sales representative has offered a substitute machine for $51,000, or for $31,000 plus the old machine. The new machine will reduce annual cash-operating costs by $10,000, will not require any overhauls, will have a useful life of 5 years, and will have a disposal value of $3,000.

Objective 6

Use both the total project and differential approaches to determine the NPV difference between two projects

If the minimum desired rate of return is 14%, what should the company do to minimize long run costs? (Try to solve this problem yourself before examining the solution that follows.)

A difficult part of long-range decision making is the structuring of the data. We want to see the effects of each alternative on future cash inflows and outflows. To apply either the total project or the differential approach, the first step is to arrange the relevant cash flows by project. Exhibit 11-4 shows how the cash flows for each alternative are sketched. The next step depends on the approach used:

Total Project Approach: Determine the net present value of the cash flows for each individual project. Choose the project with the largest positive present value (i.e., largest benefit) or smallest negative present value (i.e., smallest cost).

Differential Approach: Compute the differential cash flows; that is, subtract the cash flows for project B from the cash flows from project A for each year. Calculate the present value of the differential cash flows. If this present value is positive, choose project A; if it is negative, choose project B.

Exhibit 11-4 illustrates both the total project approach and the differential approach. Which approach you use when there are only two alternatives is a matter of preference. (The total project approach is necessary when analyzing three or more alternatives simultaneously.) However, to develop confidence in this area, you should work with both at the start. One approach can serve as proof of the accuracy of the other. In this example, the $8,429 net difference in favor of replacement is the result under either approach.

Analysis of Typical Items Under DCF

Objective 7

Identify relevant cash flows for DCF analyses

When you array the relevant cash flows, be sure to consider four types of inflows and outflows: (1) initial cash inflows and outflows at time zero, (2) investments in receivables and inventories, (3) future disposal values, and (4) operating cash flows.

Initial cash inflows and outflows at time zero. These cash flows include both outflows for the purchases and installation of equipment and other items required by the new project, and either inflows or outflows from disposal of any items that are replaced. In Exhibit 11-4 the $20,000 received from selling the old machine was offset against the $51,000 purchase price of the new machine, resulting in a net cash outflow of $31,000. If the old machine could not be sold, any cost incurred to dismantle and discard it would have been *added* to the purchase price of the new machine.

Investments in receivables and inventories. Investments in receivables, inventories, and intangible assets are basically no different from investments in plant and equipment. In the DCF model, the initial outlays are entered in the sketch of cash flows at time zero. At the end of the useful life of the project, the original outlays for machines may not be recouped at all or may be partially recouped in the amount of the salvage values. In contrast, the entire original investments in receivables and inventories are usually recouped when the project ends. Therefore all initial investments are typically regarded as outflows at time zero, and their terminal disposal values, if any, are regarded as inflows at the end of the project's useful life.

Exhibit 11-4 Total Project Versus Differential Approach to Net Present Value

	Present Value Discount Factor, at 14%	Total Present Value	Sketch of After-Tax Cash Flows at End of Year					
			0	1	2	3	4	5
I. Total Project Approach								
A. Replace								
Recurring cash operating costs, using an annuity table*	3.4331	$(102,993)		($30,000)	($30,000)	($30,000)	($30,000)	($30,000)
Disposal value, end of year 5	.5194	1,558						$3,000
Initial required investment	1.0000	(31,000)	($31,000)					
Present value of net cash outflows		$(132,435)						
B. Keep								
Recurring cash operating costs, using an annuity table*	3.4331	$(137,324)		($40,000)	($40,000)	($40,000)	($40,000)	($40,000)
Overhaul, end of year 2	.7695	(7,695)			($10,000)			
Disposal value, end of year 5	.5194	4,155						$8,000
Present value of net cash outflows		$(140,864)						
Difference in favor of replacement		$ 8,429						
II. Differential Approach								
A–B. Analysis Confined to Differences								
Recurring cash operating savings, using an annuity table*	3.4331	$ 34,331		$10,000	$10,000	$10,000	$10,000	$10,000
Overhaul avoided, end of year 2	.7695	7,695			$10,000			
Difference in disposal values, end of year 5	.5194	(2,597)						$(5,000)
Incremental initial investment	1.0000	(31,000)	($31,000)					
Net present value of replacement		$ 8,429						

* Table 2, page 814.

The example in Exhibit 11-4 required no additional investment in inventory or receivables. However, the expansion of a retail store, for example, entails an additional investment in a building and fixtures *plus* inventories. Such investments would be shown in the format of Exhibit 11-4 as follows:

	Sketch of Cash Flows				
End of year	0	1	2 . . . 19	20
Investment in building and fixtures	(10)				1
Investment in working capital (inventories)	(6)				6

As the sketch shows, the residual value of the building and fixtures might be small. However, the entire investment in inventories would ordinarily be recouped when the venture is terminated.

The difference between the initial outlay for working capital (mostly receivables and inventories) and the present value of its recovery is the present value of the cost of using working capital in the project. Working capital is constantly revolving in a cycle from cash to inventories to receivables and back to cash throughout the life of the project. But to be sustained, the project requires that money be tied up in the cycle until the project ends.

Future disposal values. The disposal value at the date of termination of a project is an increase in the cash inflow in the year of disposal. Errors in forecasting terminal disposal values are usually not crucial because the present value is usually small.

Operating cash flows. The major purpose of most investments is to affect revenues or costs (or both). The cash inflows and outflows associated with most of these effects may be difficult to measure, and three points deserve special mention.

First, in relevant-cost analysis, the only pertinent overhead costs are those that will differ among alternatives. Fixed overhead under the available alternatives needs careful study. In practice, this is an extremely difficult phase of cost analysis, because it is difficult to relate the individual costs to any single project.

Second, depreciation and book values should be ignored. The cost of assets is recognized by the initial outlay, not by depreciation as computed under accrual accounting.

Third, a reduction in a cash outflow is treated the same as a cash inflow. Both signify increases in value.

Cash Flows for Investments in Technology

Many capital-budgeting decisions compare a possible investment with a continuation of the status quo. One such decision is investment in a highly automated production system to replace a traditional system. Suppose a manufacturing company is considering investment in a computer integrated manufacturing (CIM) system. One of the most difficult parts of the decision is predicting relevant cash flows. It is easy to overlook some benefits of such a system and thereby underestimate its desirability.

Cash flows predicted for the CIM system should be compared with those *predicted for continuation of the present system into the future.* The latter are not necessarily the cash flows currently being experienced. Why? Because the competitive environment is changing. If others invest in CIM systems, failure to invest may cause a decline in market share and therefore lower revenues. Competitors may use their CIM systems to increase quality, change product designs more readily, and be more responsive to customer demands. Instead of predicting a future similar to the present situation, the future without a CIM might be a continual decline in revenues and a noncompetitive cost structure.

A CIM system can also lead to unanticipated cost savings. Certainly some savings, such as lower inventory levels, reduced machine downtime, and shorter cycle times, can be predicted and the savings quantified. However, others, such as flexibility to change product mix easily, ability to implement design changes quickly and cheaply, and general reduction of non-value-added activities, may be difficult to predict and especially difficult to measure.

There are two ways to deal with difficult-to-predict revenue and cost effects. First, they can be quantified as best as possible and included in an NPV analysis. Second, they can be recognized subjectively. For example, investment in a CIM may have a *negative* NPV of $500,000 without considering subjective effects. A manager must then decide whether the potential losses in contribution margin from a decline in competitiveness—plus possible nonquantified cost savings—exceed $500,000. If so, the CIM is a desirable investment, despite its negative NPV.

Complications

The foregoing material has been an *introduction* to the area of capital budgeting. In practice, a variety of factors complicate the analysis, including

1. *Income taxes*: Comparison between alternatives is best made after considering tax effects, because the tax impact may alter the picture. (The effects of income taxes are considered in Chapter 12.)

2. *Inflation*: Predictions of cash flows and discount rates should be based on consistent inflation assumptions. (This concept is explained in more detail in Chapter 12.)

3. *Mutually exclusive projects*: When the projects are mutually exclusive, so that the acceptance of one automatically entails the rejection of the other (e.g., buying Toyota or Ford trucks), the project that has the largest net present value should be undertaken.

4. *Unequal lives*: If alternative projects have unequal lives, comparisons may be made over the useful life of either the longer-lived project or the shorter-lived one. For our purposes, we will use the life of the longer-lived project. To provide comparability, we assume reinvestment in the shorter-lived project at the end of its life and give it credit for any residual value at the time the longer-lived project ends. The important consideration is what would be done in the time interval between the termination dates of the shorter- and longer-lived projects.

■ OTHER MODELS FOR ANALYZING LONG-RANGE DECISIONS

Although the use of DCF models for business decisions has increased steadily over the past four decades, simpler models are also used. Often managers use them in *addition* to DCF analyses.

These models, which we are about to explain, are conceptually inferior to DCF approaches. Then why do we bother studying them? First, because the simpler models might provide some useful information to supplement the DCF analysis. Second, because changes in business practice occur slowly. Many businesses still use the simpler models. Finally, because when simpler models are in use, they should be used properly, even if better models are available.

Of course, as always, the accountant and manager face a cost-and-value-of-information decision when they choose a decision model. Reluctance to use DCF models may be justified if the more familiar payback model or other simple models lead to the same investment decisions.

One existing technique may be called the emergency-persuasion method. No formal planning is used. Fixed assets are operated until they crumble, product lines are carried until they are obliterated by competition, and requests by managers for authorization of capital outlays are judged on the basis of their ability to convince top management that the investment is necessary. These approaches to capital budgeting are examples of the unscientific management that often leads to bankruptcy.

In contrast, both the payback and the accounting rate-of-return models, although flawed, are attempts to approach capital budgeting systematically.

Payback Model

payback time (payback period)
The measure of the time it will take to recoup, in the form of cash inflows from operations, the initial dollars of outlay.

Payback time or **payback period** is the measure of the time it will take to recoup, in the form of cash inflows from operations, the initial dollars of outlay. Assume that $12,000 is spent for a machine with an estimated useful life of 8 years. Annual savings of $4,000 in cash outflows are expected from operations. Depreciation is ignored. The payback period is 3 years, calculated as follows:

$$\text{payback time} = \frac{\text{initial incremental amount invested}}{\text{equal annual incremental cash}}$$
$$\text{inflow from operations}$$

Objective 8

Use the payback model and the accounting rate-of-return model and compare them with the DCF models

$$P = \frac{I}{O} = \frac{\$12,000}{\$4,000} = 3 \text{ years}$$

The payback model merely measures how quickly investment dollars may be recouped—it does not measure profitability. This is its major weakness. A project with a shorter payback time is not necessarily preferable to one with a longer payback time. On the other hand, the payback model can provide a rough estimate of riskiness, especially in decisions involving areas of rapid technological change.

Assume that an alternative to the $12,000 machine is a $10,000 machine whose operation will also result in a reduction of $4,000 annually in cash outflow. Then the payback periods are:

$$P_1 = \frac{\$12,000}{\$4,000} = 3.0 \text{ years}$$
$$P_2 = \frac{\$10,000}{\$4,000} = 2.5 \text{ years}$$

The $10,000 machine has a shorter payback time, and therefore it may appear more desirable. However, one fact about the $10,000 machine has been purposely withheld. What if its useful life is only 2.5 years? Ignoring the impact of compound interest for the moment, the $10,000 machine results in zero benefit, whereas the $12,000 machine (useful life 8 years) generates cash inflows for 5 years beyond its payback period.

The main objective in investing is profit, not the recapturing of the initial outlay. If a company wants to recover its outlay fast, it need not spend in the first place. Then no waiting time is necessary, because the payback time is zero. When a wealthy investor was assured by the promoter of a risky oil venture that he would have his money back within 2 years, the investor replied, "I already have my money."

The formula for payback time on page 431 can be used with assurance only when there are equal annual cash inflows from operations. When annual cash inflows are not equal, the payback computation must take a cumulative form—that is, each year's net cash flows are accumulated until the initial investment is recouped.

Assume a cash flow pattern as follows:

End of Year	0	1	2	3
Investment	($31,000)			
Cash inflows		$10,000	$20,000	$10,000

The calculation of the payback period is:

Year	Initial Investment	Net Cash Inflows Each Year	Net Cash Inflows Accumulated
0	$31,000	—	—
1	—	$10,000	$10,000
2	—	20,000	30,000
2.1	—	1,000	31,000

In this case, the payback time is slightly beyond the second year. Interpolation within the third year reveals that the final $1,000 needed to recoup the investment would be forthcoming in 2.1 years:

$$2 \text{ years } + \left(\frac{\$1,000}{\$10,000} \times 1 \text{ year} \right) = 2.1 \text{ years}$$

Accounting Rate-of-Return Model

Another non-DCF capital-budgeting model is the **accounting rate-of-return (ARR) model:**

accounting rate-of-return (ARR) model
A non-DCF capital-budgeting model expressed as the increase in expected average annual operating income divided by the initial increase in required investment.

$$\text{accounting rate-of-return} = \frac{\text{increase in expected average annual operating income}}{\text{initial increase in required investment}}$$

$$\text{ARR} = \frac{O - D}{I}$$

where ARR is the average annual accounting rate of return on initial additional investment, O is the average annual incremental cash inflow from operations, D is the incremental average annual depreciation, and I is the initial incremental amount invested. The accounting rate-of-return model is also known as the *accrual accounting rate-of-return model* (a more accurate description), the *unadjusted rate-of-return model*, and the *book-value model*. Its computations dovetail most closely with conventional accounting models of calculating income and required investment, and they show the effect of an investment on an organization's financial statements.

Assume the same facts as in Exhibit 11-1: Investment is $6,075, useful life is 4 years, estimated disposal value is zero, and expected annual cash inflow from operations is $2,000. Annual depreciation would be $6,075 ÷ 4 = $1,518.75, rounded to $1,519. Substitute these values in the accounting rate-of-return equation:

$$ARR = \frac{\$2,000 - \$1,519}{\$6,075} = 7.9\%$$

Some companies use the "average" investment (often assumed for equipment as being the average book value over the useful life) instead of original investment in the denominator. Therefore, the denominator becomes $6,075 ÷ 2 = $3,037.5, and the rate doubles:[4]

$$ARR = \frac{\$2,000 - \$1,519}{\$3,037.50} = 15.8\%$$

With the original investment in the denominator, the ARR is usually less than the IRR. When the "average" investment is used, the ARR generally exceeds the IRR.

Defects of Accounting Rate-of-Return Model

The accounting rate-of-return model is based on the familiar financial statements prepared under accrual accounting. Unlike the payback model, the accounting model at least has profitability as an objective. Nevertheless, it has a major drawback. The accounting model ignores the time value of money. Expected future dollars are erroneously regarded as equal to present dollars. The DCF model explicitly allows for the force of interest and the timing of cash flows. In contrast, the accounting model is based on *annual averages*.

The accounting model uses concepts of investment and income that were originally designed for the quite different purpose of accounting for periodic income and financial position. The resulting *accounting* rate of return may differ greatly from the project's *internal* rate of return.

To illustrate, consider a petroleum company with three potential projects to choose from: an expansion of an existing gasoline station, an investment in an oil well, and the purchase of a new gasoline station. To simplify the calculations, assume a 3-year life for each project. Exhibit 11-5 summarizes the comparisons. The projects differ only in the timing of the cash inflows. Note that the accounting rate of return indicates that all three projects are equally desirable. In contrast, the *internal* rate of return properly discriminates in favor of earlier cash inflows.

---

[4] The measure of the investment recovered in the preceding example is $1,519 per year, the amount of the annual depreciation. Consequently, the average investment committed to the project would decline at a rate of $1,519 per year from $6,075 to zero; hence the average investment would be the beginning balance plus the ending balance ($6,075+0) divided by 2, or $3,037.50. Note that when the ending balance is not zero, the average investment will *not* be half the initial investment.

	Expansion of Existing Gasoline Station	Investment in an Oil Well	Purchase of New Gasoline Station
Initial investment	$ 90,000	$ 90,000	$ 90,000
Cash inflows from operations			
Year 1	$ 40,000	$ 80,000	$ 20,000
Year 2	40,000	30,000	40,000
Year 3	40,000	10,000	60,000
Totals	$120,000	$120,000	$120,000
Average annual cash inflow	$ 40,000	$ 40,000	$ 40,000
Less: average annual depreciation ($90,000 ÷ 3)	30,000	30,000	30,000
Increase in average annual net income	$ 10,000	$ 10,000	$ 10,000
Accounting rate of return on initial investment	11.1%	11.1%	11.1%
Internal rate of return, using discounted-cash-flow techniques	16.0%*	23.3%*	13.4%*

* Computed by trial-and-error approaches using Tables 1 and 2, pages 813 and 814. See Appendix 11, page 438, for a detailed explanation.

■ PERFORMANCE EVALUATION

Potential Conflict

Many managers are reluctant to accept DCF models as the best way to make capital-budgeting decisions. Their reluctance stems from the wide usage of accounting income for evaluating performance. That is, managers become frustrated if they are instructed to use a DCF model for making decisions that are evaluated later by a non-DCF model, such as the typical accounting rate-of-return model, which is based on accounting income instead of cash flows.

To illustrate, consider the potential conflict that might arise in the example of Exhibit 11-1. Recall that the internal rate of return was 12%, based on an outlay of $6,075 that would generate cash savings of $2,000 for each of 4 years and no terminal disposal value. Using accounting income computed with straight-line depreciation, the evaluation of performance for years one through four would be:

	Year 1	Year 2	Year 3	Year 4
Cash-operating savings	$2,000	$2,000	$2,000	$2,000
Straight-line depreciation, $6,075 ÷ 4	1,519	1,519	1,519	1,519*
Effect on operating income	481	481	481	481
Book value at beginning of year	6,075	4,556	3,037	1,518
Accounting rate of return	7.9%	10.6%	15.8%	31.7%

* Total depreciation of 4 × $1,519 = $6,076 differs from $6,075 because of rounding error.

Many managers would be reluctant to replace equipment, despite the internal rate of 12%, if their performance were evaluated by accounting income. They might be especially reluctant if they are likely to be transferred to new positions every year or two. Why? This accrual accounting system understates the return in early years, and a manager might not be around to reap the benefits of the later overstatement of returns.

As Chapter 6 indicated, managerial reluctance to replace is reinforced if a heavy book loss on old equipment would appear in year 1's income statement (see page 230)—even though such a loss would be irrelevant in a properly constructed decision model. Thus performance evaluation based on typical accounting measures can cause the rejection of major, long-term projects such as investments in technologically advanced production systems. This pattern may help explain why many U.S. firms seem to be excessively short-term oriented.

Reconciliation of Conflict

How can the foregoing conflict be reconciled? Many organizations use the typical accounting model both for making capital-budgeting decisions *and* for evaluating performance and do not use DCF models at all. Yet, as we noted earlier, DCF models remain the best tool for capital-budgeting decisions, so this is not often a good solution.

Another obvious solution would be to use DCF for both capital-budgeting decisions and performance evaluation. A recent survey showed that most large companies (approximately 76%) conduct a follow-up evaluation of at least some capital-budgeting decisions, often called a **postaudit**. The purposes of postaudits include

postaudit A follow-up evaluation of capital-budgeting decisions.

1. Seeing that investment expenditures are proceeding on time and within budget
2. Comparing actual cash flows with those originally predicted, in order to motivate careful and honest predictions
3. Providing information for improving future predictions of cash flows
4. Evaluating the continuation of the project

Objective 9

Identify the methods for reconciling the conflict between using a DCF model for making a decision and using accounting income for evaluating the related performance

By focusing the postaudit on actual versus predicted *cash flows*, the evaluation is consistent with the decision process.

However, postauditing of all capital-budgeting decisions is costly. Most accounting systems are designed to evaluate operating performances of products, departments, divisions, territories, and so on, *year by year*. In contrast, capital-budgeting decisions frequently deal with individual *projects*, not the collection of projects that are usually being managed simultaneously by divisional or department managers. Therefore, usually only selected capital-budgeting decisions are audited.

The conflicts between the longstanding, pervasive accrual accounting model and various formal decision models represent one of the most serious unsolved problems in the design of management control systems. Top management cannot expect goal congruence if it favors the use of one type of model for decisions and the use of another type for performance evaluation.

Postaudits: Are They Worth Their Cost?

Most companies perform some kind of postaudit of capital investments. But the extent and methods of postaudits vary greatly.

A study published in *Management Accounting* gave the results of a survey of 690 large firms. Most companies agreed on the importance of postaudits and their objectives. One company's response was typical: Postaudits help evaluate "(1) the financial and nonfinancial impact of the project on the company, whether positive or negative; (2) how the actual results of the project compare to data and assumptions included in the program request; and (3) future actions that are necessary or expected regarding the project." Postaudits also provide information for future capital-budgeting decisions and give managers an incentive to be accurate when preparing data to support capital budgeting requests.

Despite agreement on the value and objectives of postaudits, practices differ. For example, most companies postaudit only selected projects—the larger and more strategically important the project, the more likely it is to be postaudited. Frequency of postaudits also varies. Some companies postaudit a project only once, others for a finite period of time, such as two years, and still others at regular intervals ranging from once a year to once every three years. Frequency often depends on the importance of the project.

Postaudits do not always solve the conflict between decision making and performance evaluation. Of the firms that use DCF for decision making, only 76% use a comparison of actual to predicted cash flows in their postaudits. The other 24% use data such as the payback period or accounting rate of return in their postaudits.

Why do postaudit practices vary? Most often cost/benefit considerations are the major influence. Postaudits are expensive, and only those methods that are worth their cost are employed. As data-processing costs have come down during the last decade, more and more companies are expanding their postaudit activities. ■

Sources: Adapted from L. A. Gordon and M. D. Myers, "Postauditing Projects," Management Accounting, *January 1991, pp. 39-42; B. J. Pierce and J. J. Tsay, "A Study of the Post-Completion Audit Practices of Large American Corporations: Experience from 1978 and 1988,"* Journal of Management Accounting Research, *Fall 1992, pp. 131–155.*

Highlights to Remember

Capital budgeting is long-term planning for proposed capital outlays and their financing. Because the DCF model explicitly and automatically weighs the time value of money, it is the best method to use for long-range decisions. The overriding goal is maximum long-run net cash inflows.

The DCF model has two variations: IRR and NPV. Both models consider the timing of cash flows and are thus superior to other models. Common errors in DCF analysis include deducting depreciation from operating cash inflows, using the wrong present-value table, ignoring disposal values on old equipment or future disposal values on new equipment, and incorrectly analyzing investments in working capital (e.g., inventories).

Risk is present in almost all capital investments. Sensitivity analysis helps to assess the riskiness of a project.

The payback model is a popular approach to capital-spending decisions. It is simple and easily understood, but it neglects profitability.

The accounting rate-of-return model is also widely used in capital budgeting, although it is conceptually inferior to DCF models. It fails to recognize explicitly the time value of money. Instead, the accounting model depends on averaging techniques that may yield inaccurate answers, particularly when cash flows are not uniform through the life of a project.

Performance evaluation using accounting income can conflict with the DCF analyses used for decisions. Frequently, the optimal decisions under discounted cash flow will not produce good accounting income in the early years. For example, heavy depreciation charges and the expensing rather than capitalizing of initial development costs will hurt reported income for the first year. Postaudits help to limit the effect of this conflict.

Summary Problem for Your Review

Problem

Review the problem and solution shown in Exhibit 11-4, page 428. Conduct a sensitivity analysis as indicated below. Consider each requirement as independent of other requirements.

1. Compute the NPV if the minimum desired rate of return were 20%.
2. Compute the NPV if predicted cash-operating costs were $35,000 instead of $30,000, using the 14% discount rate.
3. By how much may the cash operating savings fall short of the $30,000 predicted before reaching the point of indifference, the point where the NPV of the project is zero, using the original discount rate of 14%?

Solution

1. Either the total project approach or the differential approach could be used. The differential approach would show:

	Total Present Value
Recurring cash operating savings, using an annuity table (Table 2, p. 814): 2.9906 × $10,000 =	$29,906
Overhaul avoided: .6944 × $10,000 =	6,944
Difference in disposal values: .4019 × $5,000 =	(2,010)
Incremental initial investment	(31,000)
NPV of replacement	$ 3,840

2. NPV value in Exhibit 11-4 .... $ 8,429

   Present value of additional $5,000 annual operating costs 3.4331 × $5,000 .... (17,166)

   New NPV .... $ (8,737)

3. Let X = annual cash operating savings and find the value of X such that NPV = 0. Then

$$0 = 3.4331(X) + \$7{,}695 - \$2{,}597 - \$31{,}000$$
$$3.4331X = \$25{,}902$$
$$X = \$ 7{,}545$$

(Note that the $7,695, $2,597, and $31,000 are at the bottom of Exhibit 11-4.)

If the annual savings fall from $10,000 to $7,545, a decrease of $2,455 or almost 25%, the point of indifference will be reached.

An alternative way to obtain the same answer would be to divide the NPV of $8,429 (see bottom of Exhibit 11-4) by 3.4331, obtaining $2,455, the amount of the annual difference in savings that will eliminate the $8,429 of NPV.

Appendix 11: Calculations of Internal Rates of Return

This appendix shows how to compute internal rates of return. It uses data from Exhibit 11-5, p. 433.

Expansion of Existing Gasoline Station

The IRR formula (see page 418) can be used in evaluating the expansion of the existing gas station:

$90,000 = present value of annuity of $40,000 at X percent for 3 years, or what factor F in the table of the present values of an annuity will satisfy the following equation

$90,000 = $40,000 × F

F = $90,000 ÷ $40,000 = 2.2500

Now, on the year 3 line of Table 2 in Appendix B (see page 814), find the column that is closest to 2.2500. You will find that 2.2500 is extremely close to a rate of return of 16%—so close that interpolation between 14% and 16% is unnecessary. Therefore the internal rate of return is approximately 16%.

Investment in an Oil Well

Trial-and-error methods must be used to calculate the rate of return that will equate the future cash flows with the $90,000 initial investment for the investment in an oil well. Why? Because cash inflows vary from year to year. As a start, note that the 16% rate was applicable to a uniform annual cash inflow. But now use Table 1 in Appendix B (see p. 813) and try a higher rate, 22%, because you know that the cash inflows are coming in more quickly than under the uniform inflow:

		Trial at 22%		Trial at 24%	
Year	Cash Inflows	Present-Value Factor	Total Present Value	Present-Value Factor	Total Present Value
1	$80,000	.8197	$65,576	.8065	$64,520
2	30,000	.6719	20,157	.6504	19,512
3	10,000	.5507	5,507	.5245	5,245
			$91,240		$89,277

Because $91,240 is greater than $90,000, the true rate must be greater than 22%. Try 24%. Now $89,277 is less than $90,000 so the true rate lies somewhere between 22% and 24%. It can be approximated by interpolation:

Interpolation	Total Present Values	
at 22%	$91,240	$91,240
at True rate		90,000
at 24%	89,277	
Difference	$ 1,963	$ 1,240

$$\text{approximate rate} = 22\% + \left(\frac{1,240}{1,963} \times 2\%\right)$$
$$= 22\% + 1.3\% = 23.3\%$$

Purchase of a New Gasoline Station

In contrast to the oil-well project, a new gasoline station will have slowly increasing cash inflows. Thus the trial rate should be *lower* than the 16% rate applicable to the expansion project. Let us try 12%:

Year	Cash Inflows	Trial at 12%		Trial at 14%	
		Present-Value Factor	Total Present Value	Present-Value Factor	Total Present Value
1	$20,000	.8929	$17,858	.8772	$17,544
2	40,000	.7972	31,888	.7695	30,780
3	60,000	.7118	42,708	.6750	40,500
			$92,454		$88,824

Because $92,454 is greater than $90,000, try 14%. Then interpolate a rate between 12% and 14%:

Interpolation	Total Present Values	
at 12%	$92,454	$92,454
at True rate		$90,000
at 14%	88,824	
Difference	$ 3,630	$ 2,454

$$\text{approximate rate} = 12\% + \left(\frac{2,454}{3,630} \times 2\%\right)$$
$$= 12\% + 1.4\% = 13.4\%$$

Accounting Vocabulary

accounting rate-of-return (ARR) model, *p. 432*
capital-budgeting decisions, *p. 413*
differential approach, *p. 426*
discount rate, *p. 415*
discounted-cash-flow (DCF)

models, *p. 414*
hurdle rate, *p. 415*
internal rate of return (IRR), *p. 418*
net-present-value (NPV) method, *p. 415*

payback period, *p. 431*
payback time, *p. 431*
postaudit, *p. 435*
required rate of return, *p. 415*
total project approach, *p. 426*

Fundamental Assignment Material

11-A1   Exercises in Compound Interest: Answers Supplied

Use the appropriate interest table from Appendix B (see pp. 813 or 814) to complete the following exercises:

The answers appear at the end of the assignment material for this chapter, p. 454.

1. It is your 60th birthday. You plan to work 5 more years before retiring. Then you want to take $10,000 for a round-the-world tour. What lump sum do you have to invest now to accumulate the $10,000? Assume that your minimum desired rate of return is

    a.   4%, compounded annually

    b.   10%, compounded annually

    c.   20%, compounded annually

2. You want to spend $2,000 on a vacation at the end of each of the next 5 years. What lump sum do you have to invest now to take the five vacations? Assume that your minimum desired rate of return is

    a.   4%, compounded annually

    b.   10%, compounded annually

    c.   20%, compounded annually

3. At age 60, you find that your employer is moving to another location. You receive termination pay of $50,000. You have some savings and wonder whether to retire now.

    a.   If you invest the $50,000 now at 4%, compounded annually, how much money can you withdraw from your account each year so that at the end of 5 years there will be a zero balance?

    b.   If you invest it at 10%?

4. Two NBA basketball players, Johnson and Jackson, signed 5-year, $30 million contracts. At 16%, compounded annually, which of the following contracts is more desirable in terms of present values? Show computations to support your answer.

	Annual Cash Inflows (000)	
Year	*Johnson*	*Jackson*
1	$10,000	$ 2,000
2	8,000	4,000
3	6,000	6,000
4	4,000	8,000
5	2,000	10,000
	$30,000	$30,000

11-A2   Comparison of Capital-Budgeting Techniques

St. Luke's Hospital is considering the purchase of a new exercise machine at a cost of $20,000. It should save $4,000 in cash operating costs per year. Its estimated useful life is 8 years, and it will have zero disposal value.

Required

1. What is the payback time?

2. Compute the net present value if the minimum rate of return desired is 10%. Should the company buy? Why?

3. Compute the internal rate of return.
4. Using the accounting rate-of-return model, compute the rate of return on the initial investment.

11-A3   Sensitivity Analysis

Hewitt Dental Group is considering the replacement of an old billing system with new software that should save $5,000 per year in net cash operating costs. The old system has zero disposal value, but it could be used for the next 12 years. The estimated useful life of the new software is 12 years and it will cost $25,000.

Required

1. What is the payback period?
2. Compute the internal rate of return.
3. Management is unsure about the useful life. What would be the internal rate of return if the useful life were (a) 6 years instead of 12 or (b) 20 years instead of 12?
4. Suppose the life will be 12 years, but the savings will be $3,000 per year instead of $5,000. What would be the internal rate of return?
5. Suppose the annual savings will be $4,000 for 8 years. What would be the internal rate of return?

11-B1   Exercises in Compound Interest

Use the appropriate table to compute the following:

1. You have always dreamed of taking an African safari. What lump sum do you have to invest today to have the $12,000 needed for the safari in 3 years? Assume that you can invest the money at
   a.   5%, compounded annually
   b.   10%, compounded annually
   c.   16%, compounded annually

2. You are considering partial retirement. To do so you need to use part of your savings to supplement your income for the next 5 years. Suppose you need an extra $15,000 per year. What lump sum do you have to invest now to supplement your income for 5 years? Assume that your minimum desired rate of return is
   a.   5%, compounded annually
   b.   10%, compounded annually
   c.   16%, compounded annually

3. You just won a lump sum of $400,000 in a local lottery. You have decided to invest the winnings and withdraw an equal amount each year for 10 years. How much can you withdraw each year and have a zero balance left at the end of 10 years if you invest at
   a.   6%, compounded annually
   b.   12%, compounded annually

4. A professional athlete is offered the choice of two 4-year salary contracts, contract A for $1.4 million and contract B for $1.3 million:

	Contract A	Contract B
End of year 1	$ 200,000	$ 450,000
End of year 2	300,000	350,000
End of year 3	400,000	300,000
End of year 4	500,000	200,000
Total	$1,400,000	$1,300,000

Which contract has the higher present value at 14% compounded annually? Show computations to support your answer.

11-B2 NPV, IRR, ARR, and Payback

Sally's Subs is considering a proposal to invest in a speaker system that would allow its employees to service drive-through customers. The cost of the system (including installation of special windows and driveway modifications) is $60,000. Sally Holding, manager of Sally's Subs, expects the drive-through operations to increase annual sales by $50,000, with a 40% contribution margin ratio. Assume that the system has an economic life of 6 years, at which time it will have no disposal value. The required rate of return is 14%.

Required

1. Compute the payback period. Is this a good measure of profitability?
2. Compute the NPV. Should Holding accept the proposal? Why or why not?
3. Compute the IRR. How should the IRR be used to decide whether to accept or reject the proposal?
4. Using the accounting rate of return model, compute the rate of return on the initial investment.

11-B3 NPV and Sensitivity Analysis

Kittitas County Jail currently has its laundry done by a local cleaners at an annual cost of $36,000. It is considering a purchase of washers, dryers, and presses at a total installed cost of $50,000 so that inmates can do the laundry. The county expects savings of $15,000 per year, and the machines are expected to last 5 years. The desired rate of return is 10%.

Required

Answer each part separately.

1. Compute the NPV of the investment in laundry facilities.
2. **a.** Suppose the machines last only 4 years. Compute the NPV.
   b. Suppose the machines last 7 years. Compute the NPV.
3. **a.** Suppose the annual savings are only $12,000. Compute the NPV.
   b. Suppose the annual savings are $18,000. Compute the NPV.
4. **a.** Compute the most optimistic estimate of NPV, combining the best outcomes in requirements 2 and 3.
   b. Compute the most pessimistic estimate of NPV, combining the worst outcomes in requirements 2 and 3.
5. Accept the expected life estimate of 5 years. What is the minimum annual savings that would justify the investment in the laundry facilities?

Additional Assignment Material

Questions

11-1. Capital budgeting has three phases: (1) identification of potential investments, (2) selection of investments, and (3) postaudit of investments. What is the accountant's role in each phase?

11-2. Why is discounted cash flow a superior method for capital budgeting?

11-3. Distinguish between simple interest and compound interest.

11-4. Can NPV ever be negative? Why?

11-5. Distinguish among the models DCF, NPV, and IRR.

11-6. "The higher the minimum desired rate of return, the higher the price that a company will be willing to pay for cost-saving equipment." Do you agree? Explain.

11-7. "The DCF model assumes certainty and perfect capital markets. Thus it is impractical to use it in most real-world situations." Do you agree? Explain.

11-8. "Double-counting of costs occurs if depreciation is separately considered in DCF analysis." Do you agree? Explain.

11-9. "Nonprofit organizations do not use DCF because their cost of capital is zero." Do you agree? Explain.

11-10. "We can't use sensitivity analysis because our

cash-flow predictions are too inaccurate." Comment.

11-11. Name three common ways to recognize risk in capital budgeting.

11-12. Why should the differential approach to alternatives always lead to the same decision as the total project approach?

11-13. "The higher the interest rate, the less I worry about errors in predicting terminal values." Do you agree? Explain.

11-14. "The NPV model should not be used for investment decisions about advanced technology such as computer-integrated manufacturing systems." Do you agree? Explain.

11-15. "DCF approaches will not work if the competing projects have unequal lives." Do you agree? Explain.

11-16. "It is important that a firm use one and only one capital-budgeting model. Using multiple models may cause confusion." Do you agree? Explain.

11-17. "If DCF approaches are superior to the payback and the accounting rate-of-return methods, why should we bother to learn the others? All it does is confuse things." Answer this contention.

11-18. What is the basic flaw in the payback model?

11-19. Compare the accounting rate-of-return approach and the DCF approach with reference to the time value of money.

11-20. Explain how a conflict can arise between capital-budgeting decision models and performance evaluation methods.

Exercises

11-21 Exercise in Compound Interest

Rhonda Reynolds wishes to purchase a $230,000 house. She has accumulated a $30,000 down-payment, but she wishes to borrow $200,000 on a 30-year mortgage. For simplicity, assume annual mortgage payments at the end of each year and no loan fees.

Required

1. What are Reynolds's annual payments if her interest rate is (a) 8%, (b) 10%, and (c) 12%, compounded annually?
2. Repeat requirement 1 for a 15-year mortgage.
3. Suppose Reynolds had to choose between a 30-year and a 15-year mortgage, either one at a 10% interest rate. Compute the total payments and total interest paid on (a) a 30-year mortgage and (b) a 15-year mortgage.

11-22 Exercise in Compound Interest

Suppose General Electric (GE) wishes to borrow money from the Prudential Insurance Company. They agree on an annual rate of 12%.

Required

1. Suppose GE agrees to repay $500 million at the end of 5 years. How much will Prudential lend GE?
2. Suppose GE agrees to repay a total of $500 million at a rate of $100 million at the end of each of the next 5 years. How much will Prudential lend GE?

11-23 Exercise in Compound Interest

1. First National Bank offers depositors a lump-sum payment of $30,000 six years hence. If you desire an interest rate of 8% compounded annually, how much would you be willing to deposit now? At an interest rate of 16%?

2. Repeat requirement 1, but assume that the interest rates are compounded semi-annually.

11-24 Exercise in Compound Interest

A building contractor has asked you for a loan. You are pondering various proposals for repayment:

1. Lump sum of $600,000 four years hence. How much will you lend if your desired rate of return is (a) 10%, compounded annually, and (b) 20%, compounded annually?

2. Repeat requirement 1, but assume that the interest rates are compounded semi-annually.

3. Suppose the loan is to be paid in full by equal payments of $150,000 at the end of each of the next 4 years. How much will you lend if your desired rate of return is (a) 10%, compounded annually, and (b) 20%, compounded annually?

11-25   Basic Relationships in Interest Tables

1. Suppose you borrow $80,000 now at 16% interest, compounded annually. The borrowed amount plus interest will be repaid in a lump sum at the end of 8 years. How much must be repaid? Use Table 1 (p. 813) and the basic equation PV = future amount × conversion factor.

2. Assume the same facts as previously except that the loan will be repaid in equal installments at the end of each of 8 years. How much must be repaid each year? Use Table 2 (p. 814) and the basic equation: PV = future annual amounts × conversion factor.

11-26   Deferred Annuity Exercise

It is your 20th birthday. On your 25th birthday, and on three successive birthdays thereafter, you intend to spend exactly $1,000 for a birthday celebration. What lump sum do you have to invest now to have the four celebrations? Assume that the money will earn interest, compounded annually, of 12%.

11-27   Present Value and Sports Salaries

Because of a salary cap, National Basketball Association teams are not allowed to exceed a certain annual limit in total player salaries. Suppose the Chicago Bulls had scheduled salaries exactly equal to their cap of $12 million for 19X4. Michael Pippin, a star player, was scheduled to receive $3 million in 19X4. To free up money to pay a prize rookie, Pippin agreed to defer $1 million of his salary for 2 years, by which time the salary cap will have been increased. His contract called for salary payments of $3 million in 19X4, $3.5 million in 19X5, and $4 million in 19X6. Now he will receive $2 million in 19X4, still $3.5 million in 19X5, and $5 million in 19X6. For simplicity, assume that all salaries are paid on July 1 of the year they are scheduled. Pippin's minimum desired rate of return is 12%.

Required   Did the deferral of salary cost Pippin anything? If so, how much? Compute the present value of the sacrifice on July 1, 19X4. Explain.

11-28   IRR

Fill in the blanks:

	Number Of Years		
	10	*20*	*30*
Amount of annual cash inflow*	$ 5,000	$ ____	$10,000
Required initial investment	$19,615	$22,000	$ ____
IRR	____ %	16%	20%

* To be received at the end of each year.

11-29   Internal Rate and NPV

Fill in the blanks:

	Number of Years		
	8	*18*	*28*
Amount of annual cash inflow*	$10,000	$ ____	$ 7,000
Required initial investment	$ ____	$80,000	$29,099
IRR	18%	16%	____ %
Minimum desired rate of return	14%	____ %	26%
NPV	$ ____	($13,835)	$ ____

* To be received at the end of each year.

11-30   Illustration of Trial-and-Error Method of Computing Rate of Return
Study Exhibit 11-2, page 419. Suppose the annual cash inflow will be $2,500 rather than $2,000.

Required   What is the internal rate of return?

11-31   New Equipment
The Office Equipment Company has offered to sell some new packaging equipment to the Diaz Company. The list price is $42,000, but Office Equipment has agreed to accept some old equipment in trade. A trade-in allowance of $9,000 was agreed on. The old equipment was carried at a book value of $7,700 and could be sold outright for $6,000 cash. Cash-operating savings are expected to be $5,000 annually for the next 12 years. The minimum desired rate of return is 12%. The old equipment has a remaining useful life of 12 years. Both the old and the new equipment will have zero disposal values 12 years from now.

Required   Should Diaz buy the new equipment? Show your computations, using the NPV method. Ignore income taxes.

11-32   Present Values of Cash Inflows
Orlando Novelty Company has just been established. Operating plans indicate the following expected cash flows:

	Outflows	Inflows
Initial investment now	$210,000	$ —
End of year: 1	150,000	200,000
2	200,000	250,000
3	250,000	300,000
4	300,000	400,000
5	350,000	450,000

Required   1. Compute the NPV for all of these cash flows. This should be a single amount. Use a discount rate of 14%.
2. Is the IRR more than 14% or less than 14%? Explain.

11-33   Capital Budgeting with Uneven Cash Flows
MIT's Engineering School is considering the purchase of a special-purpose machine for $60,000. It is expected to have a useful life of 3 years with no terminal salvage value. The university's controller estimates the following savings in cash operating costs:

Year	Amount
1	$28,000
2	26,000
3	24,000

Required   Compute:
1. Payback period
2. Net present value if the required rate of return is 12%
3. IRR
4. Accounting rate of return (a) on the initial investment and (b) on the "average" investment

Problems

11-34   Rationale of NPV Model

Evergreen Outdoor School (EOS) has a chance to invest $10,000 in a project that is certain to pay $4,500 at the end of each of the next three years. The minimum desired rate of return is 10%.

Required

1. What is the project's net present value?
2. Show that EOS would be equally as well off undertaking the project or having its present value in cash. Do this by calculating the cash available at the end of 3 years if (a) $10,000 is borrowed at 10%, with interest paid at the end of each year, and the investment is made, or (b) cash equal to the project's NPV is invested at 10% compounded annually for 3 years. Use the following formats. Year 1 for the first alternative is completed for you.

	Alternative (a)—Invest in Project				
	(1)	(2)	(3)	(4)	(5)
			(1) + (2)		(3) – (4)
	Loan				Loan
	Balance at	Interest	Accumulated	Cash for	Balance
	Beginning	at 10%	Amount at	Repayment	at End
Year	of Year	Per Year	End of Year	of Loan	of Year
1	$10,000	$1,000	$11,000	$4,500	$6,500
2					
3					

	Alternative (b)—Keep Cash		
	(1)	(2)	(3)
	Investment		(1) + (2)
	Balance	Interest	Accumulated
	at Beginning	at 10%	Amount at
Year	of Year	Per Year	End of Year
1			
2			
3			

11-35   Replacement of Equipment

Refer to Problem 6-B1, page 236. Assume that the new equipment will cost $99,000 in cash and that the old machine cost $84,000 and can be sold now for $16,000 cash.

Required

1. Compute the net present value of the replacement alternative, assuming that the minimum desired rate of return is 10%.
2. What will be the IRR?
3. How long is the payback period on the incremental investment?

11-36   Investment in Solar Water Heater

A brochure entitled "A Guide to Buying a Solar Water Heater" contained an example showing how a homeowner could save $14 more than the cost of a solar water heater over 7 years. The total purchase price of the water heater, after all tax effects, was $1,575. Savings of $168 were predicted for the 1st year. The amount saved increased by 10% each year because the cost of heating water was expected to increase at a 10% annual rate. Therefore the 7-year savings were $168 + $185 + $203 + $223 + $245 + $269 + $296 = $1,589. (Note that $185 = 1.1 × $168, $203 = 1.1 × $185, etc.) Assume that the cost of capital for investing in a solar water heater is 8%.

Required

1. Do you agree that a homeowner could save a net amount of $14 during the 7 years by purchasing a solar water heater? Explain.
2. Assume that a homeowner bought a solar water heater for a net outlay of $1,575 and received the savings promised in the brochure. What was the net present value of the purchase of the heater at the time it was acquired? Assume that all savings occur at the end of the year.

11-37   Replacement of Office Equipment

New York University is considering replacing some Xerox copiers with faster copiers purchased from Kodak. The administration is very concerned about the rising costs of operations during the last decade.

To convert to Kodak, two operators would have to be retrained. Required training and remodeling would cost $5,000.

NYU's three Xerox machines were purchased for $10,000 each, 5 years ago. Their expected life was 10 years. Their resale value now is $2,000 each and will be zero in 5 more years. The total cost of the new Kodak equipment will be $49,000; it will have zero disposal value in 5 years.

The three Xerox operators are paid $8 an hour each. They usually work a 40-hour week. Machine breakdowns occur monthly on each machine, resulting in repair costs of $50 per month and overtime of 4 hours, at time-and-one-half, per machine per month, to complete the normal monthly workload. Toner, supplies, and so on, cost $100 a month for each Xerox copier.

The Kodak system will require only two regular operators, on a regular work week of 40 hours each, to do the same work. Rates are $10 an hour, and no overtime is expected. Toner, supplies, and so on, will cost a total of $3,300 annually. Maintenance and repairs are fully serviced by Kodak for $1,050 annually. (Assume a 52-week year.)

Required

1. Using DCF techniques, compute the present value of all relevant cash flows, under both alternatives, for the 5-year period discounted at 12%.
2. Should NYU keep the Xerox copiers or replace them if the decision is based solely on the given data?
3. What other considerations might affect the decision?

11-38   Replacement Decision for Railway Equipment

The Wabash Railroad is considering replacement of a Kalamazoo Power Jack Tamper, used for maintenance of track, with a new automatic raising device that can be attached to a production tamper.

The present power jack tamper cost $18,000 five years ago and had an estimated life of 12 years. A year from now the machine will require a major overhaul estimated to cost $5,000. It can be disposed of now via an outright cash sale for $3,500. There will be no value at the end of another 7 years.

The automatic raising attachment has a delivered selling price of $72,000 and an estimated life of 12 years. Because of anticipated future developments in combined maintenance machines, it is felt that the machine would be disposed of at the end of the seventh year to take advantage of newly developed machines. Estimated sales value at the end of 7 years is $5,000.

Tests have shown that the automatic raising machine will produce a more uniform surface on the track than the power jack tamper now in use. The new equipment will eliminate one laborer whose annual compensation, including fringe benefits, is $30,000.

Track maintenance work is seasonal, and the equipment normally works from May 1 to October 31 each year. Machine operators and laborers are transferred to other work after October 31, at the same rate of pay.

The salesman claims that the annual normal maintenance of the new machine will run about $1,000 per year. Because the automatic raising machine is more complicated than the manually operated machine, it will probably require a thorough overhaul at the end of the fourth year at an estimated cost of $7,000.

Records show the annual normal maintenance of the Kalamazoo machine to be $1,200. Fuel consumption of the two machines is equal.

Required   Should the Wabash keep or replace the Kalamazoo Power Jack Tamper? A 10% rate of return is desired. Compute present values. Ignore income taxes.

11-39   Discounted Cash Flow, Uneven Revenue Stream, Relevant Costs

Gloria Driver, the owner of a nine-hole golf course on the outskirts of a large city, is considering a proposal that the course be illuminated and operated at night. Ms. Driver purchased the course early last year for $80,000. Her receipts from operations during the 28-week season were $25,000. Total disbursements for the year, for all purposes, were $16,500.

The required investment in lighting this course is estimated at $19,000. The system will require 150 lamps of 1,000 watts each. Electricity costs $.032 per kilowatt-hour. The expected average hours of operation per night is five. Because of occasional bad weather and the probable curtailment of night operation at the beginning and end of the season, it is estimated that there will be only 130 nights of operation per year. Labor for keeping the course open at night will cost $15 per night. Lamp renewals are estimated at $300 per year; other maintenance and repairs, per year, will amount to 4% of the initial cost of the lighting system. Property taxes on this equipment will be about 2% of its initial cost. It is estimated that the average revenue, per night of operation, will be $90 for the first 2 years.

Considering the probability of competition from the illumination of other golf courses, Ms. Driver decides that she will not make the investment unless she can make at least 10% per annum on her investment. Because of anticipated competition, revenue is expected to drop to $60 per night for years 3 through 5. It is estimated that the lighting equipment will have a salvage value of $7,000 at the end of the 5-year period.

Required   Using DCF techniques, determine whether Ms. Driver should install the lighting system.

11-40   Minimization of Transportation Costs

The Luxor Company produces industrial and residential lighting fixtures at its manufacturing facility located in Los Angeles. Shipment of company products to an eastern warehouse is presently handled by common carriers at a rate of $.25 per pound of fixtures. The warehouse is located in Cleveland, 2,500 miles from Los Angeles.

Joanne Harris, the treasurer of Luxor, is presently considering whether to purchase a truck for transporting products to the eastern warehouse. The following data on the truck are available:

Purchase price	$40,000
Useful life	5 years
Salvage value after 5 years	0
Capacity of truck	10,000 lb
Cash costs of operating truck	$.90 per mile

Harris feels that an investment in this truck is particularly attractive because of her successful negotiation with Retro, Inc., to back-haul Retro's products from Cleveland to Los Angeles on every return trip from the warehouse. Retro has agreed to pay Luxor $2,400 per load of Retro's products hauled from Cleveland to Los Angeles up to and including 100 loads per year.

Luxor's marketing manager has estimated that 500,000 pounds of fixtures will have to be shipped to the eastern warehouse each year for the next 5 years. The truck will be fully loaded on each round trip.

Ignore income taxes.

1. Assume that Luxor requires a minimum rate of return of 20%. Should the truck be purchased? Show computations to support your answer.
2. What is the minimum number of trips that must be guaranteed by Retro, Inc., to make the deal acceptable to Luxor, based on the foregoing numbers alone?
3. What qualitative factors might influence your decision? Be specific.

11-41 Investment in Machine and Working Capital

The Akahita Company has an old machine with a net disposal value of $15,000 now and $4,000 five years from now. A new Speedo machine is offered for $62,000 cash or $47,000 with a trade-in. The new machine will result in an annual operating cash outflow of $40,000 as compared with the old machine's annual outflow of $50,000. The disposal value of the new machine 5 years hence will be $4,000.

Because the new machine will produce output more rapidly, the average investment in inventories by using the new machine will be $160,000 instead of $200,000.

The minimum desired rate of return is 20%. The company uses DCF techniques to guide these decisions.

Should the Speedo machine be acquired? Show your calculations. Company procedures require the computing of the present value of each alternative. The most desirable alternative is the one with the least cost. Assume that the PV of $1 at 20% for 5 years is $.40; the present value of an annuity of $1 at 20% for 5 years is $3.

11-42 Comparison of Investment Models

Dominique's Frozen Food Company makes frozen dinners and sells them to retail outlets near London. Dominique has just inherited £10,000 and has decided to invest it in the business. She is trying to decide between:

Alternative 1: Buy a £10,000 contract, payable immediately, from a local reputable sales promotion agency. The agency would provide various advertising services, as specified in the contract, over the next 10 years. Dominique is convinced that the sales promotion would increase net cash inflow from operations, through increased volume, by £2,000 per year for the first 5 years, and by £1,000 per year thereafter. There would be no effect after the 10 years had elapsed.

Alternative 2: Buy new mixing and packaging equipment, at a cost of £10,000, which would reduce operating cash outflows by £1,500 per year for the next 10 years. The equipment would have zero salvage value at the end of the 10 years.

Ignore any tax effect.

1. Compute the accounting rate of return on initial investment for both alternatives.
2. Compute the internal rate of return by the DCF model for both alternatives.
3. Are the internal rates of return different? Explain.

11-43 Make or Buy, Discounted Cash Flow, and Accounting Rate of Return

Refer to case 6-45, requirement 1, page 250.

1. Using an NPV analysis, which alternative is more attractive? Assume that the minimum rate of return desired is 8%.
2. Using the accounting rate-of-return method, what is the rate of return on the initial investment in the new machine?

11-44 Fixed and Current Assets; Evaluation of Performance

Metro Medical Center has been under pressure to keep costs down. Indeed, the hospital administrator has been managing various revenue-producing centers to maximize contributions to the recovery of the operating costs of the medical center as a whole. The administrator has been considering whether to buy a special-purpose X-ray machine for $187,000. Its unique characteristics would generate additional cash operating income of $50,000 per year for the medical center as a whole.

The machine is expected to have a useful life of 6 years and a terminal salvage value of $22,000.

The machine is delicate. It requires a constant inventory of various supplies and spare parts. When these items can no longer be used, they are instantly replaced, so an investment of $15,000 must be maintained at all times. However, this investment is fully recoverable at the end of the useful life of the machine.

Required

1. Compute NPV if the required rate of return is 14%.
2. Compute the internal rate of return (to the nearest whole percentage).
3. Compute the accounting rate of return on (a) the initial investment and (b) the "average" investment.
4. Why might the administrator be reluctant to base her decision on the DCF model?

11-45   Capital Budgeting, Sensitivity Analysis, and Ethics

James LaGrande had recently been appointed Controller of the Breakfast Cereals Division of a major food company. The Division Manager, Renee Osterland, was known as a hard-driving, intelligent, noncompromising manager. She had been very successful, and was rumored to be on the fast-track to corporate top management, maybe even in line for the company presidency. One of Jim's first assignments was to prepare the financial analysis for a new cold cereal, Krispie Krinkles. This product was especially important to Ms. Osterland because she was convinced that it would be a success and thereby a springboard for her ascent to top management.

Mr. LaGrande discussed the product with the food lab that had designed it, with the market research department that had tested it, and with the finance people who would have to fund its introduction. After putting together all the information, he developed the following optimistic and pessimistic sales projections:

	Optimistic	Pessimistic
Year 1	$ 1,600,000	$ 800,000
Year 2	3,600,000	1,200,000
Year 3	5,000,000	1,000,000
Year 4	8,000,000	800,000
Year 5	10,000,000	400,000

The optimistic predictions assume a successful introduction of a popular product. The pessimistic predictions assume that the product is introduced but does not gain wide acceptance and is terminated after 5 years. LaGrande thinks the most likely results are half-way between the optimistic and pessimistic predictions.

LaGrande learned from finance that this type of product introduction requires a predicted rate of return of 16% before top management will authorize funds for its introduction. He also determined that the contribution margin should be about 50% on the product, but could be as low as 42% or as high as 58%. Initial investment would include $3 million for production facilities, $2.5 million for advertising and other product introduction expenses, and $500,000 for working capital (inventory, etc.). The production facilities would have a value of $800,000 after 5 years.

Based on his preliminary analysis, LaGrande recommended to Osterland that the product not be launched. Osterland was not pleased with the recommendation. She claimed that LaGrande was much too pessimistic and asked him to redo his numbers so that she could justify the product to top management.

LaGrande carried out further analysis, but his predictions came out no differently. In fact, he became even more convinced that his projections were accurate. Yet, he was certain that if he returned to Osterland with numbers that did not support introduction of the product, he would incur her wrath. And, in fact, she could be right—that is, there is so much uncertainty in the forecasts that he could easily come up with believable numbers that would support going forward with the product. He would not believe them, but he thinks he could convince top management that they are accurate.

Required

1. Prepare the capital budgeting analysis that LaGrande used for his first meeting with Osterland.
2. How might LaGrande change his numbers to make the project acceptable?
3. What would you do if you were in LaGrande's position?

11-46   Replacement Decision

Amtrak, a passenger train company subsidized by the U.S. government, has included a dining car on the passenger train it operates from Buffalo to Albany, New York. Yearly operations of the dining car have shown a consistent loss, which is expected to persist, as follows:

Revenue (in cash)		$200,000
Expenses for food, supplies, etc. (in cash)	$100,000	
Salaries	110,000	210,000
Net loss (ignore depreciation on the dining car itself)		$ 10,000

The Auto-vend Company has offered to sell automatic vending machines to Amtrak for $22,000, less a $3,000 trade-in allowance on old equipment (which is carried at $3,000 book value, and which can be sold outright for $3,000 cash) now used in the dining car operation. The useful life of the vending equipment is estimated at 10 years, with zero scrap value. Experience elsewhere has led executives to predict that the equipment will serve 50% more food than the dining car, but prices will be 50% less, so the new revenue will probably be $150,000. The variety and mix of food sold are expected to be the same as for the dining car. A catering company will completely service and supply food and beverages for the machines, paying 10% of revenue to the Amtrak company and bearing all costs of food, repairs, etc. All dining car employees will be discharged immediately. Their termination pay will total $28,000. However, an attendant who has some general knowledge of vending machines will be needed for one shift per day. The annual cost to Amtrak for the attendant will be $13,000.

For political and other reasons, the railroad will definitely not abandon its food service. The old equipment will have zero scrap value at the end of 10 years.

Required

Using the preceding data, compute the following. Label computations. Ignore income taxes.

1. Use the NPV method to analyze the incremental investment. Assume that Congress has specified that a minimum desired rate of return of 10% be used for these types of investments. For this problem, assume that the PV of $1 at 10% to be received at the end of ten years is $.400 and that the PV of an annuity of $1 at 10% for 10 years is $6.000.
2. What would be the minimum amount of annual *revenue* that Amtrak would have to receive from the catering company to justify making the investment? Show computations.

Cases

11-47   Investment in CAD/CAM

The Romanov Manufacturing Company is considering the installation of a computer-aided design/computer-aided manufacturing (CAD/CAM) system. The current proposal calls for implementation of only the CAD portion of the system. Juanita Sanchez, the manager in charge of production design and planning, has estimated that the CAD portion of CAD/CAM could do the work of five designers, who are each paid $52,000 per year (52 weeks × 40 hours × $25/hour).

The CAD/CAM system can be purchased for $320,000. (The CAD portion cannot be purchased separately.) The annual out-of-pocket costs of running the CAD portion of the system are $180,000. The system is expected to be used for 8 years. Romanov's minimum desired rate of return is 12%.

Required

1. Compute the NPV and IRR of the investment in the CAD/CAM system. Should the system be purchased? Explain.
2. Suppose Sanchez was not certain about her predictions of savings and economic life. Possibly only four designers will be replaced, but if everything works out well, as many as six might be replaced. If better systems become available, the CAD/CAM system might be used only 5 years, but it might last as long as 10 years. Prepare pessimistic, most likely, and optimistic predictions of NPV. Would this analysis make you more confident or less confident in your decision in requirement 1? Explain.
3. What subjective factors might influence your decision?

11-48   Cafeteria Facilities

The cafeteria in Haakon Towers, an office building in downtown Oslo, is open 250 days a year. It offers typical cafeteria-line service. At the noon meal (open to the public), serving-line facilities can accommodate 200 people per hour for the 2-hour serving period. The average customer has a 30-minute lunch period. Serving facilities are unable to handle the overflow of noon customers with the result that, daily, 20 dissatisfied customers who do not wish to stand in line choose to eat elsewhere. Projected over a year, this results in a considerable loss to the cafeteria.

To tap this excess demand, the cafeteria is considering two alternatives: (1) installing two vending machines, at a cost of NK 25,000 apiece (NK means Norwegian kroner), or (2) completely revamping present serving-line facilities with new equipment, at a cost of NK 150,000. The vending machines and serving-line equipment have a useful life of 10 years and will be depreciated on a straight-line basis. The minimum desired rate of return for the cafeteria is 10%. The average sale is NK 15, with a contribution margin of 30%. This will remain the same if new serving-line facilities are installed.

Data for alternative 1, vending machines, are as follows:

- Service cost per year is NK 2,000; salvage value of each machine at the end of 10 years is NK 5,000.
- Contribution margin is 20%. It is estimated that 60% of the dissatisfied customers will use the vending machines and spend an average of NK 15. The estimated salvage value of the present equipment will net NK 20,000 at the end of the 10-year period.

Data for alternative 2, new serving-line facilities, are as follows:

- Yearly salary for an extra part-time cashier is NK 8,000; salvage value today of old equipment is NK 50,000; salvage value of new equipment, at the end of 10 years, is NK 50,000; cost of dismantling old equipment is NK 5,000. It is estimated that all the previously dissatisfied customers will use the new facilities.

All other costs are the same under both alternatives and need not be considered.

Required   Using the NPV model, which is the better alternative?

11-49   Investment in Technology

Indiana Auto Parts Company is considering installation of a computer-integrated manufacturing (CIM) system as part of its implementation of a JIT philosophy. Jacob Goldworthy, company president, is convinced that the new system is necessary, but he needs the numbers to convince the Board of Directors. This is a major move for the company, and approval at board level is required.

Jennifer Goldworthy, Jacob's daughter, has been assigned the task of justifying the investment. She is a business school graduate and understands the use of NPV for capital budgeting decisions. To identify relevant costs she developed the following information.

Indiana Auto Parts Company produces a variety of small automobile components and sells them to auto manufacturers. It has a 40% market share, with the following condensed results expected for 19X0:

Sales		$12,000,000
Cost of goods sold		
Variable	$4,000,000	
Fixed	4,300,000	8,300,000
Selling and administrative expenses		
Variable	$2,000,000	
Fixed	400,000	2,400,000
Operating income		$ 1,300,000

Installation of the CIM system will cost $6 million, and the system is expected to have a useful life of 6 years with no salvage value. In 19X1, the training costs for personnel will exceed any cost savings by $400,000. In years 19X2 through 19X6, variable cost of goods sold will decrease by 40%, an annual savings of $1.6 million. There will be no savings in fixed cost of goods sold—in fact, it will increase by the amount of the straight-line depreciation on the new system. Selling and administrative expenses will not be affected. The required rate of return is 12%. Assume that all cash flows occur at the end of the year, except the initial investment, which occurs at the beginning of 19X1.

Required

1. Suppose that Jennifer Goldworthy assumes that production and sales would continue for the next 10 years as they were in 19X0 in the absence of investment in the CIM. Compute the NPV of investing in the CIM.
2. Now suppose Jennifer predicts that it will be difficult to compete if the CIM is not installed. In fact, she has undertaken market research that estimates a drop in market share of 3 percentage points a year starting in 19X1 in the absence of investment in the CIM (i.e., market share will be 37% in 19X1, 34% in 19X2, 31% in 19X3, etc.). Her study also showed that the total market sales level will stay the same, and market prices are not expected to change. Compute the NPV of investing in the CIM.
3. Prepare an explanation from Jennifer Goldworthy to the Board of Directors of Indiana Auto Parts Company explaining why the analysis in requirement 2 is appropriate and why analyses such as that in requirement 1 cause companies to underinvest in high-technology projects. Include an explanation of qualitative factors that are not included in the NPV calculation.

11-50   Investment in Quality

The Woolongong Manufacturing Company produces a single model of a CD player that is sold to Australian manufacturers of sound systems. Each CD player is sold for $210, resulting in a contribution margin of $70 before considering any costs of inspection, correction of product defects, or refunds to customers.

In 19X0 top management at Woolongong is contemplating a change in its quality control system. Currently, $40,000 is spent annually on quality control inspections. Woolongong produces and ships 50,000 CD players a year. In producing those CD players, an average of 2,000 defective units are produced. Of these, 1,500 are identified by the inspection process, and an average of $85 is spent on each to correct the defects. The other 500 players are shipped to customers. When a customer discovers a defective CD player, Woolongong refunds the $210 purchase price.

As more and more customers change to JIT inventory systems and automated production processes, the receipt of defective goods poses greater and greater problems for them. Sometimes a defective CD player causes them to delay their whole production line while the CD player is being replaced. Companies competing with Woolongong recognize this situation, and most have already begun extensive quality control programs. If Woolongong does not improve quality, sales volume is expected to fall by 5,000 CD players a year, beginning in 19X1:

	Predicted Sales Volume in Units Without Quality Control Program	Predicted Sales Volume in Units With Quality Control Program
19X1	50,000	50,000
19X2	45,000	50,000
19X3	40,000	50,000
19X4	35,000	50,000

The proposed quality control program has two elements. First, Woolongong would spend $900,000 immediately to train workers to recognize and correct defects at the time they occur. This is expected to cut the number of defective CD players produced from 2,000 to 500 without incurring additional manufacturing costs. Second, an earlier inspection point would replace the current inspection. This would require purchase of an x-ray machine at a cost of $200,000 plus additional annual operating costs of $50,000 more than the current inspection costs. Early detection of defects would reduce the average amount spent to correct defects from $85 to $50, and only 50 defective CD players would be shipped to customers. To compete, Woolongong would refund one-and-one-half times the purchase price ($315) for defective CD players delivered to customers.

Top management at Woolongong has decided that a 4-year planning period is sufficient for analyzing this decision. The minimum required rate of return is 20%. For simplicity, assume that under the current quality control system, if the volume of production decreases, the number of defective CD players produced remains at 2,000. Also assume that all annual cash flows occur at the end of the relevant year.

Required Should Woolongong Manufacturing Company undertake the new quality control program? Explain, using the NPV model.

Solutions to Exercises in Compound Interest, Problem 11-A1

The general approach to these exercises centers on one fundamental question: Which of the two basic tables am I dealing with? No calculations should be made until after this question is answered with assurance. If you made any errors, it is possible that you used the wrong table.

1. From Table 1, page 813:
   a. $8,219
   b. $6,209
   c. $4,019

The $10,000 is an *amount of future worth*. You want the present value of that amount:

$$PV = \frac{\$10,000}{(1 + i)^n}$$

The conversion factor, $1/(1 + i)^n$, is on line 5 of Table 1. Substituting:

$$PV = \$10,000(.8219) = \$8,219$$
$$PV = \$10,000(.6209) = \$6,209$$
$$PV = \$10,000(.4019) = \$4,019$$

Note that the higher the interest rate, the lower the present value.

2. From Table 2, page 814:
   a. $8,903.60
   b. $7,581.60
   c. $5,981.20

The $2,000 withdrawal is a uniform annual amount, an annuity. You need to find the present value of an annuity for five years:

$$PV_A = \text{annual withdrawal} \times F, \text{ where F is the conversion factor.}$$

Substituting:

$$PV_A = \$2,000(4.4518) = \$8,903.60$$
$$PV_A = \$2,000(3.7908) = \$7,581.60$$
$$PV_A = \$2,000(2.9906) = \$5,981.20$$

3. From Table 2:
   a. $11,231.41
   b. $13,189.83

You have $50,000, the present value of your contemplated annuity. You must find the annuity that will just exhaust the invested principal in 5 years:

$$PV_A = \text{annual withdrawal} \times F$$
$$\$50,000 = \text{annual withdrawal} \times 4.4518$$
$$\text{annual withdrawal} = \$50,000 \div 4.4518$$
$$= \$11,231.41$$

$$\$50,000 = \text{annual withdrawal} \times 3.7908$$
$$\text{annual withdrawal} = \$50,000 \div 3.7908$$
$$= \$13,189.83$$

4. Amounts are in thousands. From Table 1: Johnson's contract is preferable; its present value exceeds that of Jackson's contract by $21,572 – $17,720 = $3,852. Note that the nearer dollars are more valuable than the distant dollars.

Year	Present Value @ 16% from Table 1	Present Value of Johnson's Contract	Present Value of Jackson's Contract
1	.8621	$ 8,621	$ 1,724
2	.7432	5,946	2,973
3	.6407	3,844	3,844
4	.5523	2,209	4,418
5	.4761	952	4,761
		$21,572	$17,720

12 Capital Budgeting: Taxes and Inflation

Union Tank Car Company, with Procor Limited, is the largest lessor and manufacturer of railway cars in North America. These cars are purchased or leased to move chemicals, petroleum, and food products. Customers evaluate the capital investment by considering cash flows and related tax effects. *Courtesy Union Tank Car Company*

Learning Objectives

When you have finished studying this chapter, you should be able to

1 Analyze a typical income statement to determine the net after-tax cash inflow from operations.

2 Compute the after-tax net present values of projects using straight-line depreciation.

3 Use double-declining-balance to determine the present value of tax savings from depreciation.

4 Explain the after-tax effect on cash of disposing of assets.

5 Demonstrate how depreciation affects capital-budgeting decisions.

6 Compute the impact of inflation on a capital-budgeting project.

Capital budgeting, as we learned in Chapter 11, requires making decisions that will have significant financial impacts beyond the current year. This chapter examines how two major factors, taxes and inflation, affect capital budgeting decisions.

Nearly all economic decisions affect taxes. Companies certainly recognize this truth as they write large tax checks to the government. Annual tax bills for some major U.S. corporations exceed $1 billion. To avoid paying more taxes than are required, companies need to consider the tax effects when making capital-budgeting decisions. This chapter introduces tax considerations. However, the tax law is exceedingly complex, so qualified counsel should be sought when the slightest doubt exists.

Inflation is nearly as pervasive as taxes. **Inflation** is the decline in the general purchasing power of the monetary unit. For example, a dollar today will buy only half as much as it did in the late 1970s. Although inflation in the U.S. is well below the double-digit level of a decade or so ago, it still persists. Even a 5% annual rate results in a rise of more than 60% in average prices over 10 years. In countries such as Brazil and Argentina, triple-digit annual inflation rates (i.e., average prices more than doubling each year) are commonplace. Therefore, inflation can greatly influence the cash flow predictions used in capital-budgeting decisions.

inflation The decline in the general purchasing power of the monetary unit.

■ INCOME TAXES AND CAPITAL BUDGETING

Income taxes are cash disbursements. Income taxes can influence the *amount* and the *timing* of cash flows. Their basic role in capital budgeting is no different from that of any other cash disbursement. However, taxes tend to narrow the cash differences between projects. Cash savings in operations will cause an increase in taxable income and thus a partially offsetting increase in tax outlays. For example, a 40% income tax rate would reduce the net attractiveness of $1 million in cash operating savings to $600,000, because $400,000 of the $1 million would be paid in taxes.

The U.S. federal government and most states raise money through corporate income taxes. State income tax rates differ considerably from state to state. Therefore, overall corporate income tax rates can vary widely.

marginal income tax rate The tax rate paid on additional amounts of pretax income.

U.S. federal income tax rates also depend on the amount of pretax income. Larger income is taxed at higher rates. (See page 475 of Appendix 12A for specific details about the current tax rates.) In capital budgeting, the relevant rate is the **marginal income tax rate,** that is, the tax rate paid on additional amounts of pretax income. Suppose corporations pay income taxes of 15% on the first $50,000 of pretax income and 30% on pretax income over $50,000. What is the *marginal income tax rate* of a company with $75,000 of pretax income? It is 30%, because 30% of any *additional* income will be paid in taxes. In contrast, the company's *average income tax rate* is only 20% (i.e., 15% $\times$ $50,000 + 30% $\times$ $25,000 = $15,000 of taxes on $75,000 of pretax income). When we assess tax effects of capital-budgeting decisions, we will always use the *marginal* tax rate because that is the rate applied to the additional cash flows generated by a proposed project.

Effects of Depreciation Deductions

Organizations that pay income taxes generally keep two sets of books—one for reporting to the public and one for reporting to the tax authorities. In the United States this practice is not illegal or immoral—in fact, it is necessary. Tax reporting must follow detailed rules designed to achieve certain social goals. These rules do not lead to financial statements that best measure an organization's financial results and position, so it is more informative to financial statement users if a separate set of rules is used for financial reporting. In this chapter we are concerned with measuring cash payments for taxes. Therefore we focus on the *tax reporting* rules, not those for public financial reporting.

Objective 1

Analyze a typical income statement to determine the net after-tax cash inflow from operations

One item that often differs between tax reporting and public reporting is depreciation. Recall that depreciation spreads the cost of an asset over its useful life. Income tax laws and regulations have increasingly permitted the cost to be spread over *depreciable lives* that are shorter than the assets' useful lives. In addition, for tax purposes, *accelerated depreciation* is often allowed, which charges a larger proportion of an asset's cost to the earlier years and less to later years. In contrast, an asset's depreciation for public reporting purposes is usually the same each year, called straight-line depreciation. For example, a $10,000 asset depreciated over a 5-year useful life would result in straight-line depreciation of $10,000 $\div$ 5 = $2,000 each year and accelerated depreciation of more than $2,000 per year in the early years and less than $2,000 in the later years.

Exhibit 12-1 shows the interrelationship of income before taxes, income taxes, and depreciation for Martin's Printing. Please examine this key exhibit carefully before reading on. Assume that the company has a single fixed asset, a printing press, which was purchased for $125,000 cash. The number of years over which an asset is depreciated for tax purposes is called the **recovery period**. The press has a 5-year recovery period for tax purposes. It is used to produce annual sales revenue of $130,000 and expenses (excluding depreciation) of $70,000. The purchase cost of the press is tax deductible in the form of yearly depreciation. Depreciation deductions (and similar deductions that are non-cash expenses when deducted) have been called **tax shields** because they protect that amount of income from taxation. However, all allowable expenses, both cash and noncash items, could be called tax shields because they reduce taxable income and thereby reduce income taxes.

Depreciating a fixed asset such as the press creates future tax deductions. In this case, these deductions will total $125,000. The present value of this deduction depends directly on its specific yearly effects on future income tax payments. Therefore the present value is influenced by the recovery period, the depreciation method selected, the tax rates, and the discount rate.

Exhibit 12-2 shows two methods for analyzing the data for capital budgeting, assuming straight-line depreciation. Both lead to the same final answer, a net present value of $40,821 for the investment in this asset. The choice of analytical method is a matter of personal preference. However, we will use method 2 in this chapter because it highlights the impact of the alternative depreciation methods on present values.

recovery period
The number of years over which an asset is depreciated for tax purposes.

tax shields
Depreciation deductions and similar deductions that protect that amount of income from taxation. All allowable expenses, both cash and non-cash items, could be called tax shields because they reduce income and thereby reduce income taxes.

Exhibit 12-1

Martin's Printing Basic Analysis of Income Statement, Income Taxes, and Cash Flows

Objective 2

Compute the after-tax net present values of projects using straight-line depreciation

Traditional Annual Income Statement		
(S) Sales		$130,000
(E) Less: Expenses, excluding depreciation		$ 70,000
(D) Depreciation (straight-line)		25,000
Total expenses		$ 95,000
Income before taxes		$ 35,000
(T) Income taxes @ 40%		14,000
(I) Net income		$ 21,000

Total after-tax effect on cash is
either S − E − T = $130,000 − $70,000 − $14,000 = $46,000
or I + D = $21,000 + $25,000 = $46,000

Analysis of the Same Facts for Capital Budgeting		
Cash effects of operations:		
(S–E) Cash inflow from operations: $130,000 − $70,000		$ 60,000
Income tax outflow @ 40%		24,000
After-tax inflow from operations (excluding depreciation)		$ 36,000
Cash effects of depreciation:		
(D) Straight-line depreciation: $125,000 ÷ 5 = $25,000		
Income tax savings @ 40%		10,000
Total after-tax effect on cash		$ 46,000

The $125,000 investment really buys two streams of cash: (1) net inflows from operations plus (2) savings of income tax outflows (which have the same effect in capital budgeting as additions to cash inflows) because the depreciation is deductible in computing taxable income. The choice of depreciation method will not affect the cash inflows from operations. But different depreciation methods will affect the cash outflows for income taxes. That is, a straight-line method will produce one present value of tax savings, and an accelerated method will produce a different present value. It is easier to pinpoint such differences by using method 2.

Tax Deductions, Cash Effects, and Timing

Before proceeding, review the basic relationships just portrayed:

Line	(A) Items Used in Computing Taxable Income	(B) Current Pretax Cash Effect	(C) Effect on Income Tax Cash Outflows at 40%	(B)–(C) Net After-Tax Cash Effect
1. Sales	$130,000	$130,000	$52,000	$78,000
2. Expenses, excluding depreciation	70,000	70,000	28,000	42,000
3. Cash effect of operations	$ 60,000	$ 60,000	$24,000	$36,000
4. Depreciation	25,000	0	(10,000)	10,000
5. Net cash effects		$ 60,000	$14,000	$46,000
6. Income before income taxes	$ 35,000			
7. Income taxes	14,000			
8. Net income	$ 21,000			

This tabulation highlights why the net cash effects of operations (the items on lines 1 to 3) are computed by multiplying the pretax amounts by 1 – the tax rate, or 1 – .40 = .60. The total effect is the cash flow itself less the tax effect. Each additional $1 of sales also adds $.40 of taxes, leaving a net cash inflow of $.60. Therefore, the after-tax cash inflow from sales is $130,000 × .6 = $78,000. Each additional $1 of cash expense reduces taxes by $.40, leaving a net cash outflow of $.60. Thus the after-tax effect of the $70,000 of *cash* expenses (line 2) is a cash outflow of $70,000 × .60 = $42,000. The net effect is a cash inflow of $78,000 – $42,000 = $36,000, or $60,000 × .6 = $36,000.

In contrast, the after-tax effects of the *noncash* expenses (depreciation on line 4) are computed by multiplying the tax deduction of $25,000 by the tax rate itself, or $25,000 × .40 = $10,000. Note that this is a cash *inflow* because it is a decrease in the tax payment. The total cash effect of a noncash expense is *only* the tax-savings effect.

Throughout the illustrations in this chapter, we assume that all income tax flows occur simultaneously with the related pretax cash flows. For example, we assume that both the net $60,000 pretax cash inflow and the related $24,000 tax payment occurred in year 1 and that no part of the tax payment was delayed until year 2.

Exhibit 12-2 Impact of Income Taxes on Capital-Budgeting Analysis

Assume: original cost of equipment, $125,000; 5-year life; zero terminal disposal value; pretax annual cash inflow from operations, $60,000; income tax rate, 40%; required after-tax rate of return, 12%. All items are in dollars except discount factors. The after-tax cash flows are from Exhibit 12-1.

	12% Discount Factor, from Appropriate Tables	Total Present Value at 12%	Sketch of After-Tax Cash Flows at End of Year					
			0	1	2	3	4	5
Method 1 (Discount the total annual effects together)								
Total after-tax effect on cash (see Exhibit 12-1)	3.6048	$ 165,821		←———46,000	46,000	46,000	46,000	46,000
Investment	1.0000	(125,000)	(125,000)					
Net present value of the investment		$ 40,821						
Method 2 (Discount two annual effects separately)								
Cash effects of operations, excluding depreciation	3.6048	$ 129,773		←———36,000	36,000	36,000	36,000	36,000
Cash effects of straight-line depreciation: savings of income taxes	3.6048	36,048		←———10,000	10,000	10,000	10,000	10,000
Total after-tax effect on cash		165,821						
Investment	1.0000	(125,000)	(125,000)					
Net present value of the investment		$ 40,821						

461

This assumption of no lags in income tax effects is also largely in accordance with the facts in the real world. Why? Because both individual and corporate taxpayers generally "pay-as-you-go." That is, estimated tax payments are made in installments at least quarterly, not in one lump sum in the subsequent year.

Another assumption throughout this chapter is that the companies in question are profitable. That is, the companies will have enough taxable income from all sources to use all income tax benefits in the situations described.

Accelerated Depreciation

accelerated depreciation Any pattern of depreciation that writes off depreciable assets more quickly than does ordinary straight-line depreciation.

Governments have frequently enacted income tax laws that permit accelerated depreciation instead of straight-line depreciation. **Accelerated depreciation** is any pattern of depreciation that writes off depreciable assets more quickly than does ordinary straight-line depreciation. These laws are aimed at encouraging investments in long-lived assets.

An extreme example clearly demonstrates why accelerated depreciation is attractive to investors. Reconsider the facts in Exhibit 12-2. Suppose, as is the case in some countries, that the entire initial investment can be written off immediately for income tax reporting. Using method 2 we see that net present value will rise from $40,821 to 54,773:

| | Present Values | |
	As in Exhibit 12-2	Complete Write-Off Immediately
Cash effects of operations	$ 129,773	$ 129,773
Cash effects of depreciation	36,048	50,000*
Total after-tax effect on cash	165,821	179,773
Investment	(125,000)	(125,000)
Net present value	$ 40,821	$ 54,773

* Assumes that the tax effect occurs simultaneously with the investment at time zero: $125,000 × .40 = $50,000.

In summary, the earlier you can take the depreciation, the greater the *present value* of the income tax savings. The *total* tax savings will be the same regardless of the depreciation method. In the example, the tax savings from the depreciation deduction is either .40 × $125,000 = $50,000 immediately or .40 × $25,000 = $10,000 per year for 5 years, a total of $50,000. However, the time value of money makes the immediate savings worth more than future savings. The mottoes in income tax planning are: "When there is a legal choice, take the *deduction sooner* rather than later," and "Recognize *taxable income later* rather than sooner."

Managers have an obligation to stockholders to minimize and delay taxes to the extent permitted by law. This is called tax avoidance. Astute tax planning can have large financial payoffs. In contrast, tax evasion, which is *illegally* reducing taxes by recording fictitious deductions or failing to recognize income, is not to be condoned.

Double-Declining-Balance Depreciation

A popular accelerated depreciation schedule uses the *double-declining-balance* (DDB) method. This method is the basis for most depreciation or cost recovery schedules in U.S. tax law. See Appendix 12A for details.

The DDB method divides 100% by the number of years over which an asset is to be depreciated, then doubles the resulting rate. For example, the DDB rate for 5-year assets is (100% ÷ 5) × 2 = 40%. This percentage is applied to the *undepreciated amount* each year to compute the annual depreciation. A 5-year DDB schedule has depreciation of 40% × 100% = 40% of the original investment in the first year, 40% × (100% – 40%) = 24% of the original investment in the second, 40% × (100% – 40% – 24%) = 14.4% of the original investment in the third, and so on.

A DDB schedule includes a switch to straight-line depreciation for the remaining undepreciated amount at the time when straight-line depreciation over the remaining recovery period provides more depreciation for the next year than would continuation of DDB. For a 5-year asset the switch comes in the fourth year, as the following DDB schedule for a $1,000 asset shows:

Year	Beginning Undepreciated Amount (1)	DDB Rate (2)	Depreciation (3) = (1) × (2)	Ending Undepreciated Amount (4) = (1) – (3)	Depreciation as a Percentage of Initial Investment (5) = (3) ÷ $1,000
1	$1,000	.40	$400	$600	40.0%
2	600	.40	240	360	24.0%
3	360	.40	144	216	14.4%
4	216	*	108	108	10.8%
5	108	*	108	0	10.8%

* Switch to straight line with 2 years remaining. Depreciation for years 4 and 5 is $216 ÷ 2 = $108. Continuation of DDB would have provided fourth-year depreciation of .40 × $216 = $86.40, which is less than the $108 straight-line amount.

Objective 3
Use double-declining-balance to determine the present value of tax savings from depreciation

Exhibit 12-3 presents DDB depreciation schedules for recovery periods of 3 through 10 years. DDB depreciation can be applied to the example in Exhibit 12-2 as follows:

Year	Tax Rate (1)	PV Factor @ 12% (2)	Depreciation (3)	Present Value of Tax Savings (1) × (2) × (3)
1	.40	.8929	$125,000 × .400 = $50,000	$17,858
2	.40	.7972	125,000 × .240 = 30,000	9,566
3	.40	.7118	125,000 × .144 = 18,000	5,125
4	.40	.6355	125,000 × .108 = 13,500	3,432
5	.40	.5674	125,000 × .108 = 13,500	3,064
				$39,045

How much was gained by using DDB instead of straight-line depreciation? The $39,045 present value of tax savings is $2,997 higher with DDB than the $36,048 achieved with straight-line depreciation (see Exhibit 12-2 Method 2, on p. 461).

Present Value of DDB Depreciation

In capital-budgeting decisions managers often want to know the present value of the tax savings from depreciation tax shields. Exhibit 12-9 in Appendix 12B (page 476) provides present values for $1 to be depreciated over double-declining-balance schedules for 3-, 5-, 7-, and 10-year recovery periods. You can find the present value of tax savings in three steps:

1. Find the factor from Exhibit 12-9 for the appropriate recovery period and required rate of return.
2. Multiply the factor by the tax rate to find the tax savings per dollar of investment.
3. Multiply the result by the amount of the investment to find the total tax savings.

For example, consider our investment of $125,000 in equipment with a 5-year DDB depreciation schedule. A 12% after-tax required rate of return and a 40% tax rate produce a tax savings with a present value of .7809 × .40 × $125,000 = $39,045.

Exhibit 12-3	Selected Double-Declining-Balance Depreciation Schedules

Recovery Period

Depreciation in Year	3 Years	4 Years	5 Years	6 Years	7 Years	8 Years	9 Years	10 Years
1	66.7%	50.0%	40.0%	33.3%	28.6%	25.0%	22.2%	20.0%
2	22.2%	25.0%	24.0%	22.2%	20.4%	18.8%	17.3%	16.0%
3	11.1%	12.5%	14.4%	14.8%	14.6%	14.1%	13.4%	12.8%
4		12.5%	10.8%	9.9%	10.4%	10.5%	10.5%	10.2%
5			10.8%	9.9%	8.7%	7.9%	8.1%	8.2%
6				9.9%	8.7%	7.9%	7.1%	6.6%
7					8.6%*	7.9%	7.1%	6.6%
8						7.9%	7.1%	6.6%
9							7.2%*	6.5%*
10								6.5%*

* Rounded to make the total 100%.

Objective 4	### Gains or Losses on Disposal

Explain the after-tax effect on cash of disposing of assets

The disposal of equipment for cash can also affect income taxes. Suppose the press purchased for $125,000 is sold. Consider three different assumptions about cash proceeds and when the sale occurs. For simplicity, straight-line depreciation is assumed:

	Press Sold at End of Year		
	5	3	3
(a) Cash proceeds of sale	$10,000	$70,000	$ 20,000
Book value: zero and [$125,000 − 3 ($25,000)]	0	50,000	50,000
Gain (loss)	$10,000	$20,000	$(30,000)
Effect on income taxes at 40%:			
(b) Tax saving, an inflow effect: .40 × loss			$ 12,000
(c) Tax paid, an outflow: .40 × gain	$ (4,000)	$ (8,000)	
Net cash inflow from sale:			
(a) plus (b)			$ 32,000
(a) minus (c)	$ 6,000	$62,000	

Ponder these calculations. Note especially the third column, which shows that the total cash inflow effect of a disposal at a loss is the cash proceeds *plus* the income tax savings ($20,000 + $12,000 = $32,000).

The often-heard expression "What the heck, it's deductible" sometimes warps perspective. Even though losses bring income tax savings and gains bring additional income taxes, gains are still more desirable than losses. In the foregoing tabulation, the $30,000 loss in the last column produces income tax savings of $12,000.[1] Each $1,000 of additional proceeds would reduce the tax savings by $400, but it would still result in $600 more cash. Suppose proceeds equal to book value ($50,000) were received. The total cash inflow would be $50,000 instead of $32,000; no tax effect would occur.

Income Tax Complications

It may come as a shock, but in the foregoing illustrations we deliberately avoided many possible income tax complications. Income taxes are affected by many intricacies including progressive tax rates, loss carrybacks and carryforwards, state income taxes, short- and long-term gains, distinctions between capital assets and other assets, offsets of losses against related gains, exchanges of property of like kind, exempt income, and so forth.[2]

Now keep in mind that miscellaneous changes in the tax law occur each year. An example is the *investment tax credit*, which provided lump-sum tax reductions to companies making qualified investments. The credit was equal to a specified percentage of the investment. It was first available in the United States in 1962, and since then it has been suspended and reinstated, and the allowable percentage has been changed several times. Most recently it was again suspended. Always check the current tax law before calculating the tax consequences of a decision.

---

[1] In this case, the old equipment was sold outright. Where there is a trade-in of old equipment for new equipment of like kind, special income tax rules result in the gain or loss being added to, or deducted from, the capitalized value of the new equipment. The gain or loss is not recognized in the year of disposal; instead, it is spread over the life of the new asset as an adjustment of the new depreciation charges.

[2] For book-length coverage of these and other complications, see *Federal Tax Course* (Upper Saddle River, NJ: Prentice Hall), published annually.

Summary Problem for Your Review

Problem One

Consider the investment opportunity presented in Exhibit 12-2, page 461: original cost of equipment, $125,000; 5-year economic life; zero terminal salvage value; pretax annual cash inflow from operations, $60,000; income tax rate, 40%; required after-tax rate of return, 12%. Assume that the equipment is depreciated on a 5-year DDB schedule for tax purposes. The net present value (NPV) is:

	Present Values (PV)
Cash effects of operations,* $60,000 × (1 − .40) × 3.6048	$129,773
Cash effects of depreciation on income tax savings using DDB $125,000 × .40 × .7809†	39,045
Total after-tax effect on cash	$168,818
Investment	125,000
Net present value	$ 43,818

* See Exhibit 12-2, page 461, for details.
† Factor .7809 is from Exhibit 12-9, page 476.

Required   Consider each requirement independently.

1. Suppose the equipment was expected to be sold for $20,000 cash immediately after the end of year 5. Compute the net present value of the investment.
2. Ignore the assumption in requirement 1. Return to the original data. Suppose the economic life of the equipment was 8 years rather than 5 years. However, DDB depreciation over 5 years is still allowed for tax purposes. Compute the net present value of the investment.

Solution to Problem One

1. Net present value as given $43,818
   Cash proceeds of sale .... $ 20,000
   Book value 0
   Gain .... $ 20,000
   Income taxes at 40% 8,000
      Total after-tax effect on cash .... $ 12,000
   PV of $12,000 to be received in
      5 years at 12%, $12,000 ×.5674 6,809
   NPV of investment $50,627

2. Net present value as given $43,818
   Add the present value of $36,000 per year for 8 years
      Discount factor of 4.9676 × $36,000 = ... $178,834
      Deduct the present value of $36,000 per year for 5 years ... 129,773
   Increase in present value 49,061
   Net present value $92,879

The investment would be very attractive. Note especially that the depreciation period for tax purposes and the economic useful life of the asset need not be equal. The tax law specifies lives (or recovery periods) for various types of depreciable assets. The tax life is unaffected by the economic useful lives of the assets. Thus a longer useful life for an asset increases operating cash flows without decreasing the present value of the tax savings.

CONFUSION ABOUT DEPRECIATION

Objective 5

Demonstrate how depreciation affects capital-budgeting decisions

The meanings of *depreciation* and *book value* are widely misunderstood. Pause and consider their role in decisions. Suppose a bank is considering the replacement of some old copying equipment with a book value of $30,000, an expected terminal disposal value of zero, a current disposal value of $12,000, and a remaining useful life of three years. For simplicity, assume that the bank will take straight-line depreciation of $10,000 yearly. The tax rate is 40%.

These data should be examined in perspective, as Exhibit 12-4 indicates. In particular, note that the inputs to the decision model are the predicted income tax effects on cash. Book values and depreciation may be necessary for making *predictions*. By themselves, however, they are not inputs to DCF decision models.

The following points summarize the role of depreciation regarding the replacement of equipment:

Exhibit 12-4

Perspective on Book Value and Depreciation

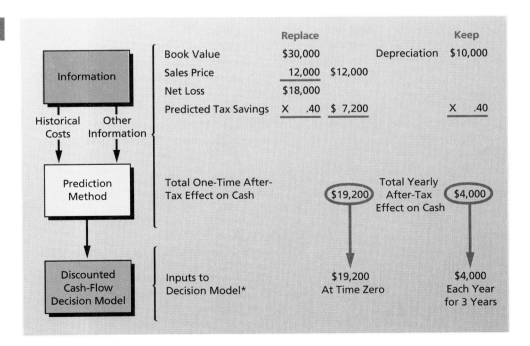

* There can, of course, be other related inputs to this decision model, for example, future annual cash flows from operations.

1. *Initial investment.* As Chapter 6 explained (p. 216), the amount paid for (and hence depreciation on) old equipment is irrelevant except for its effect on tax cash flows. In contrast, the amount paid for new equipment is relevant because it is an expected future cost that will not be incurred if replacement is rejected.

2. *Do not double-count.* The investment in equipment is a one-time outlay at time zero, so it should not be double-counted as an outlay in the form of depreciation. Depreciation by itself is irrelevant; it is not a cash outlay. However, depreciation must be considered when *predicting income tax cash outflows.*

3. *Relation to income tax cash flows.* Relevant quantities are expected future data that will differ among alternatives. Thus book values and past depreciation are irrelevant in all capital-budgeting decision models. The relevant item is the *income tax cash effect,* not the book value or the depreciation. Using the approach in Exhibit 12-4, the book value and depreciation are essential data for the *prediction method,* but the expected future income tax cash disbursements are the relevant data for the DCF decision model.

▓ CAPITAL BUDGETING AND INFLATION

In addition to taxes, capital-budgeting decision makers should consider the effects of inflation on their cash flow predictions. If significant inflation is expected over the life of a project, it should be specifically and consistently analyzed in a capital-budgeting model. Indeed, even a relatively small inflation rate, say, 3%, can have sizable cumulative effects over many years.

Watch for Consistency

nominal rate Quoted market interest rate that includes an inflation element.

The key to appropriate consideration of inflation in capital budgeting is *consistent* treatment of the minimum desired rate of return and the predicted cash inflows and outflows. Such consistency can be achieved by including an element for inflation in *both* the minimum desired rate of return and in the cash-flow predictions.

Many firms base their minimum desired rate of return on market interest rates, also called **nominal rates**, that include an inflation element. For example, consider three possible components of a 15% nominal rate:

(a) Risk-free element—the "pure" rate of interest that is paid on long-term federal bonds	6%
(b) Business-risk element—the "risk" premium that is demanded for taking larger risks	5
(a) + (b) Often called the "real rate"	11%
(c) Inflation element—the premium demanded because of expected deterioration of the general purchasing power of the monetary unit	4
(a) + (b) + (c) Often called the "nominal rate"	15%

Four percentage points out of the 15% return compensate an investor for receiving future payments in inflated dollars, that is, in dollars with less purchasing power than those invested. Therefore, basing the minimum desired rate of return on quoted market rates automatically includes an inflation element in the rate. *Companies that base their minimum desired rate of return on market rates should also adjust their cash-flow predictions for anticipated inflation.* For example, suppose 1,000 units of a product are expected to be sold in each of the next 2 years. Assume this year's price is $50, and inflation causes next year's price to be $52.50. This year's predicted cash inflow is 1,000 × $50 = $50,000 and next year's *inflation adjusted* cash inflow is 1,000 × $52.50 = $52,500. Inflation-adjusted cash flows are the inflows and outflows expected after adjusting prices to reflect anticipated inflation.

Consider another illustration: purchase cost of equipment, $200,000; useful life, 5 years; zero terminal salvage value; pretax operating cash savings per year, $83,333 (in 19X0 dollars); income tax rate, 40%. For simplicity, we assume ordinary straight-line depreciation of $200,000 ÷ 5 = $40,000 per year. The after-tax minimum desired rate, based on quoted market rates, is 25%. It includes an inflation factor of 10%.

Exhibit 12-5 displays correct and incorrect ways to analyze the effects of inflation. The key words are *internal consistency*. The correct analysis (1) uses a minimum desired rate that includes an element attributable to inflation and (2) explicitly adjusts the predicted operating cash flows for the effects of inflation. Note that the correct analysis favors the purchase of the equipment, but the incorrect analysis does not.

The incorrect analysis in Exhibit 12-5 is inherently inconsistent. The predicted cash inflows *exclude* adjustments for inflation. Instead, they are stated in 19X0 dollars. However, the discount rate *includes* an element attributable to inflation. Such an analytical flaw may induce an unwise refusal to purchase.[3]

---

[3] Another correct analysis of inflation uses "real" monetary units (real dollars) exclusively. To be internally consistent, the DCF model would use an inflation-free required rate of return and inflation-free operating cash flows. Using the numbers in Exhibit 12-5, the 25% minimum desired rate would be lowered to exclude the 10% expected inflation rate, the $50,000 operating cash savings in 19X0 dollars would be used in 19X1, 19X2, 19X3, 19X4, and 19X5, and the tax savings from depreciation would be reduced to 19X0 dollars. Properly used, this type of analysis would lead to the same net present value as the analysis used in Exhibit 12-5. In this case, the inflation-free minimum desired rate, also called a *real* rate, would be calculated as follows: (1 + nominal rate) ÷ (1 + inflation rate) = (1 + inflation-free rate), or 1.25 ÷ 1.10 = 1.13636. The inflation-free rate is 1.13636 − 1 = 13.636%. The net present value can be calculated as follows:

(1) After-Tax Savings in 19X0 Dollars	(2) Depreciation Tax Savings in 19X0 Dollars*	(3) Total Cash Savings (1) + (2)	(4) PV Factor at 13.636%†	(5) Present Value (3) × (4)
$50,000	$14,545	$64,545	.8800	$ 56,800
50,000	13,223	63,223	.7744	48,960
50,000	12,021	62,021	.6815	42,267
50,000	10,928	60,928	.5997	36,539
50,000	9,935	59,935	.5277	31,628
			Total present value =	$216,194

* $16,000 ÷ 1.10; $16,000 ÷ 1.10²; etc.

† 1 ÷ 1.13636; 1 ÷ 1.13636²; 1 ÷ 1.13636³; etc.

This analysis yields a net present value of $216,194 − $200,000 = $16,194, the same as in Exhibit 12-5 (except for a $2 rounding error).

Exhibit 12-5   Inflation and Capital Budgeting

Description	At 25%		Sketch of Relevant Cash Flows (in Dollars)					
	PV Factor	Present Value	0	1	2	3	4	5
End of year								
Correct Analysis (Be sure the discount rate includes an element attributable to inflation and adjust the predicted cash flows for inflationary effects.)								
Cash operating inflows:								
Pretax inflow in 19X0 dollars								
Income tax effect at 40%								
After-tax effect on cash				$55,000*	$60,500	$66,550	$73,205	$80,526
	.8000	$ 44,000						
	.6400	38,720						
	.5120	34,074						
	.4096	29,985						
	.3277	26,388						
Subtotal		$ 173,167						
Annual depreciation $200,000 ÷ 5 = $40,000								
Cash effect of depreciation								
Savings in income taxes @ 40% = $40,000 × .40 = $16,000	2.6893	43,029		$16,000†	$16,000	$16,000	$16,000	$16,000
Investment in equipment	1.0000	(200,000)	(200,000)					
Net present value		$ 16,196						
Incorrect Analysis (A common error is to include an inflation element in the discount rate as above, but *not* adjust the predicted cash inflows.)								
Cash operating inflows after taxes	2.6893	$134,465		$ 50,000	$50,000	$50,000	$50,000	$50,000
Tax effect of depreciation	2.6893	43,029		16,000	16,000	16,000	16,000	16,000
Investment in equipment	1.0000	(200,000)	($200,000)					
Net present value		$ (22,506)						

$83,333
33,333
$50,000

* Each year is adjusted for anticipated inflation: $50,000 × 1.10, $50,000 × 1.10^2, $50,000 × 1.10^3, and so on.
† The annual savings in income taxes from depreciation will be unaffected by inflation. Why? Because the income tax deduction must be based on original cost of the asset in 19X0 dollars.

Role of Depreciation

The correct analysis in Exhibit 12-5 shows that the tax effects of depreciation are *not* adjusted for inflation. Why? Because U.S. income tax laws permit a depreciation deduction based on the 19X0 dollars invested, nothing more.

Critics of income tax laws emphasize that capital investment is discouraged by not allowing the adjusting of depreciation deductions for inflationary effects. For instance, the net present value in Exhibit 12-5 would be larger if depreciation were not confined to the $40,000 amount per year. The latter generates a $16,000 saving in 19X1 dollars, then $16,000 in 19X2 dollars, and so forth. Defenders of existing U.S. tax laws assert that capital investment is encouraged in many other ways. The most prominent example is provision for accelerated depreciation over lives that are much shorter than the economic lives of the assets.

Improvement of Predictions with Feedback

The ability to forecast and cope with changing prices is a valuable management skill, especially when inflation is significant. Auditing and feedback should help evaluate management's predictive skills.

The adjustment of the operating cash flows in Exhibit 12-5 uses a *general-price-level* rate of 10%. However, where feasible managers should use *specific* rates or tailor-made predictions for price changes in materials, labor, and other items. These predictions may have different percentage changes from year to year.

Highlights to Remember

Income taxes can have a significant effect on the desirability of an investment. An outlay for a depreciable asset results in two streams of cash: (1) inflows from operations plus (2) savings in income tax outflows that may be analyzed as additions to cash inflows. The after-tax impact of operating cash inflows is obtained by multiplying the inflows by 1 minus the tax rate. In contrast, the impact of depreciation on cash flows is obtained by multiplying the depreciation by the tax rate itself.

Accelerated depreciation and short recovery periods increase net present values of depreciation tax shields. They have been heavily used by the U.S. government to encourage investments. When income tax rates and required rates of return are high, the attractiveness of immediate deductions heightens. Generally, depreciation deductions should be taken as early as legally possible. Managers have an obligation to minimize and delay income tax payments to the extent allowed by law. This is called tax avoidance. Tax evasion, the use of illegal means, is not to be condoned.

Taxes are also affected by the disposal of assets. Gains on disposal require additional tax payments, whereas losses create a tax shield.

The correct analysis in capital budgeting provides an internally consistent analysis of inflationary aspects. For example, the required rate of return should include an element attributable to anticipated inflation, and predicted operating cash flows should be adjusted for the effects of anticipated inflation.

Summary Problems for Your Review

Problem One appeared earlier in this chapter.

Problem Two

Examine the correct analysis in Exhibit 12-5, page 470. Suppose the cash operating inflows persisted for an extra year. Compute the present value of the inflow for the sixth year. Ignore depreciation.

Solution to Problem Two

The cash operating inflow would be $50,000 × 1.10⁶, or $80,526 × 1.10, or $88,579. Its present value would be $88,579 × .2621, the factor from Table 1 of Appendix B (period 6 row, 25% column), or $23,217.

Problem Three

Examine the DDB depreciation schedule on page 463. Assume an anticipated inflation rate of 12%. How would you change the present values of depreciation to accommodate the inflation rate?

Solution to Problem Three

The computations on page 463 would not be changed. The tax effects of depreciation are unaffected by inflation. U.S. income tax laws permit a deduction based on the original dollars invested, nothing more.

Appendix 12A: Modified Accelerated Cost Recovery System (MACRS)

Under U.S. income tax laws, most assets purchased since 1987 are depreciated using the Modified Accelerated Cost Recovery System (MACRS). Under MACRS, each asset is placed in one of the eight classes shown in Exhibit 12-6.

Exhibit 12-6

Examples of Assets in Modified Accelerated Cost Recovery System (MACRS) Classes

3-year	Special tools for several specific industries; tractor units for over-the-road.
5-year	Automobiles; trucks; research equipment; computers; machinery and equipment in selected industries.
7-year	Office furniture; railroad tracks; machinery and equipment in a majority of industries.
10-year	Water transportation equipment; machinery and equipment in selected industries.
15-year	Most land improvements; machinery and equipment in selected industries.
20-year	Farm buildings; electricity generation and distribution equipment.
27.5-year	Residential rental property.
31.5-year	Nonresidential real property.

MACRS Schedules

half-year convention
A requirement of the modified accelerated cost recovery system that treats all assets as if they were placed in service at the midpoint of the tax year.

MACRS depreciation schedules for 3-, 5-, 7-, and 10-year assets are based on the double-declining-balance (DDB) method described in the body of the chapter.[4] However, MACRS requires application of the **half-year convention**, which treats all assets as if they had been placed in service at the midpoint of the tax year. One-half year of depreciation is taken for tax purposes in the year an asset is acquired, regardless of whether it is purchased in January, July, or December. The DDB rate is then applied to the remaining undepreciated amount each year, until a switch to straight line is advantageous. The tax depreciation schedule for a 5-year asset is shown in Part A of Exhibit 12-7. Note that a half-year's depreciation is carried over to the sixth year. Schedules for 3-, 5-, 7-, and 10-year assets are shown in Exhibit 12-8.

To compute the tax depreciation that applies to each year of an asset's life, you must recognize that each year of an asset's life does not match perfectly with a tax year. For example, suppose a 5-year asset is purchased on July 1, 19X0. The first year of the asset's life overlaps two tax years, 19X0 and 19X1, as shown below:

1/1/X0	1/1/X1	1/1/X2	1/1/X3	1/1/X4	1/1/X5	1/1/X6
	Tax Year 1	Tax Year 2	Tax Year 3	Tax Year 4	Tax Year 5	Tax Year 6
		Asset Year 1	Asset Year 2	Asset Year 3	Asset Year 4	Asset Year 5
7/1/X0	7/1/X1	7/1/X2	7/1/X3	7/1/X4	7/1/X5	
Purchase Asset					Dispose of Asset	

Part B of Exhibit 12-7 shows how to use the 5-year MACRS schedule to determine the tax depreciation for each of the 5 years of the asset's life.

Example

Suppose a manufacturing company purchased a $125,000 machine on July 1, 19X0, and expected it to provide pretax cash inflows from operations of $60,000 annually for 10 years. Despite the 10-year *useful* life of the machine, it qualifies as a 5-year property for MACRS purposes. The tax rate is 40%, and the required after-tax rate of return is 12%.

The annual after-tax cash inflows from operations, excluding the tax effects of depreciation, are $60,000 × .60 = $36,000. Their present value is 5.6502 × $36,000 = $203,407. (The 5.6502 factor comes from the 12% column and 10-year row, Table 2 in Appendix B, p. 814.)

The present value of the tax savings from depreciation depends on the method of depreciation and the recovery period used. The tax savings can be computed independently of the cash effects of operations.

Suppose for a moment that the company used straight-line depreciation over the useful life of 10 years to compute tax depreciation. Annual tax savings would be ($125,000 ÷ 10) ×.40 = $5,000. Using the 12% column and 10-year row of Table 2 in Appendix B (p. 814), we find the present value of the tax savings to be 5.6502 × $5,000 = $28,251.

---

[4] MACRS schedules for 15- and 20-year assets are based on the 150 percent declining-balance method, and schedules for 27.5- and 31.5-year assets are based on straight-line depreciation. Details about these schedules are beyond the scope of this text.

But suppose the company's management, following the motto "Take the deduction sooner rather than later," decides to depreciate the machine over 5 years (as allowed by MACRS), rather than 10 years. If the company would continue to use straight-line depreciation, the annual tax savings would be ($125,000 ÷ 5) ×.40 = $10,000. The present value is 3.6048 × $10,000 = $36,048. The company would gain $36,048 – $28,251 = $7,797 in present value by taking the same total $125,000 depreciation over 5 rather than 10 years, using the straight-line method.

Exhibit 12-7				Five-Year MACRS Schedule for $10,000 Asset Purchased at Midpoint of Tax Year			
Part A: Computation of Depreciation on Tax Statements				**Part B: Computation of Depreciation for Each Year of an Asset's Life**			
Tax Year	*DDB Rate*	*Undepreciated Amount*	*Depreciation*	*Asset Year**	*Depreciation Amount*		*Depreciation Rate*
1	.40 ÷ 2 =.20†	$10,000	$2,000				
				1	2,000 + [(½) × 3,200] = $3,600		36.00%
2	.40	8,000	3,200				
				2	[(½) × 3,200] + [(½) × 1,920] = 2,560		25.60%
3	.40	4,800	1,920				
				3	[(½) × 1,920] + [(½) × 1,152] = 1,536		15.36%
4	.40	2,880	1,152				
				4	[(½) × 1,152] + [(½) × 1,152] = 1,152		11.52%
5	‡	1,728	1,152				
				5	[(½) × 1,152] + 576 = 1,152		11.52%
6	‡	576	576				

* Assumes the asset is acquired at the midpoint of the year. Therefore the first tax year plus half of the second tax year comprise the first year of the asset's life, and so on.
† Half-year convention applied.
‡ Switch to straight-line with 1½ years remaining. Fifth-year depreciation is (⅔) × $1,728 = $1,152; sixth-year depreciation is (⅓) × $1,728 = $576.

Finally, suppose management also realizes that accelerated depreciation is better than straight line for tax purposes. Therefore they decide to use the MACRS tax depreciation rates shown in the last column of Part B of Exhibit 12-7:

Asset Year	Tax Rate (1)	PV Factor @ 12% (2)	Depreciation (3)	Present Value of Tax Savings (4) = (1) × (2) × (3)
1	.40	.8929	$125,000 × .3600 = $45,000	$16,072
2	.40	.7972	125,000 × .2560 = 32,000	10,204
3	.40	.7118	125,000 × .1536 = 19,200	5,467
4	.40	.6355	125,000 × .1152 = 14,400	3,660
5	.40	.5674	125,000 × .1152 = 14,400	3,268
Total present value of tax savings				$38,671

Accelerated depreciation adds $38,671 – $36,048 = $2,623 to the present value of the tax savings. By using the MACRS 5-year recovery period instead of 10 years and accelerated (DDB) depreciation rather than straight line, the company gained $7,797 + $2,623 = $10,420 in present value. That is, the present value of the MACRS tax savings (which uses DDB depreciation over 5 years) exceeds the present value of the tax savings from straight-line depreciation for 10 years by $38,671 − $28,251 = $10,420.

Income Tax Rates

The U.S. federal government and most states levy corporate income taxes. The current federal tax rate on ordinary corporate taxable income below $50,000 is 15%. Rates then increase until companies with taxable income over $335,000 pay between 34% and 38% on additional income. These rates are sometimes subject to additional surcharges that may vary from year to year. Congress also makes frequent changes in the rates. Therefore, it is important to consult the most current schedules when analyzing tax effects.

State income tax rates vary considerably. Consequently, different companies may have widely different total income tax rates, depending on the states in which they operate as well as their overall level of taxable income.

Exhibit 12-8

Selected MACRS Depreciation Schedules

Tax Year	3-Year Property	5-Year Property	7-Year Property	10-Year Property
1	33.33%	20.00%	14.29%	10.00%
2	44.45	32.00	24.49	18.00
3	14.81	19.20	17.49	14.40
4	7.41	11.52	12.49	11.52
5		11.52	8.93	9.22
6		5.76	8.92	7.37
7			8.93	6.55
8			4.46	6.55
9				6.56
10				6.55
11				3.28

Appendix 12B: Present Value of Double-Declining-Balance Depreciation

Investment in a depreciable asset results in a tax savings because each dollar of depreciation is deductible in computing income taxes. Most investments are depreciated by accelerated methods for tax purposes. Exhibit 12-9 provides the present value of double-declining-balance depreciation on a $1.00 investment over 3-, 5-, 7-, and 10-year recovery periods for several different interest rates. For instance, for a 5-year asset and a 10% desired rate of return, the present value is (assuming depreciation is at the end of each year[5]) as follows:

---

[5] The year refers to a year of the asset's life. This may not correspond to a calendar (or tax) year. See Exhibit 12-7 on page 474.

Year	(1) Depreciation	(2) PV Factor @ 10%	(1) × (2) Present Value of Depreciation
1	$0.40	0.9091	$0.3636
2	0.24	0.8264	0.1983
3	0.144	0.7513	0.1082
4	0.108	0.6830	0.0738
5	0.108	0.6209	0.0671

Total depreciation $1.000
Present value of $1 of depreciation, shown in Exhibit 12-9 $0.8110

Exhibit 12-9

Present Value of $1 of Double-Declining-Balance Depreciation

Discount Rate	3-Year	5-Year	7-Year	10-Year
3%	.9584	.9355	.9138	.8827
4%	.9453	.9156	.8879	.8487
5%	.9325	.8965	.8633	.8170
6%	.9200	.8781	.8399	.7872
7%	.9079	.8604	.8175	.7593
8%	.8960	.8433	.7963	.7331
9%	.8845	.8269	.7760	.7085
10%	.8732	.8110	.7566	.6853
12%	.8515	.7809	.7203	.6429
14%	.8308	.7528	.6872	.6050
15%	.8208	.7394	.6716	.5876
16%	.8111	.7265	.6567	.5711
18%	.7922	.7019	.6286	.5406
20%	.7742	.6788	.6027	.5130
22%	.7570	.6571	.5788	.4879
24%	.7405	.6367	.5566	.4651
25%	.7325	.6270	.5461	.4545
26%	.7247	.6175	.5359	.4443
28%	.7095	.5993	.5167	.4252
30%	.6950	.5821	.4987	.4077
40%	.6301	.5088	.4245	.3378

To find the present value of the *tax savings* from $1.00 of investment, multiply the present value of $1 of depreciation (from Exhibit 12-9) by the income tax rate. If the tax rate is 40%, the present value of the tax savings for the example is 0.40 × $0.8110 = $0.3244, or 32.44% of the acquisition cost of the asset.

Accounting Vocabulary

accelerated depreciation, *p. 462*

half-year convention, *p. 473*

inflation, *p. 457*

marginal income tax rate, *p. 458*

nominal rate, *p. 468*

recovery period, *p. 459*

tax shields, *p. 459*

Fundamental Assignment Material

Special note: Throughout this assignment material, *unless directed otherwise*, assume that (1) all income tax cash flows occur simultaneously with the pretax cash flows, and (2) the companies in question will have enough taxable income from other sources to use all income tax benefits from the situations described.

12-A1   Straight-Line Depreciation and Present Values
A manager of Lotus is contemplating acquiring 60 computers used for designing software. The computers will cost $300,000 cash and will have zero terminal salvage value. The recovery period and useful life are both 3 years. Annual pretax cash savings from operations will be $150,000. The income tax rate is 40%, and the required after-tax rate of return is 16%.

Required

1. Compute the net present value, assuming straight-line depreciation of $100,000 yearly for tax purposes. Should Lotus acquire the computers? Explain.
2. Suppose the computers will be fully depreciated at the end of year 3 but can be sold for $40,000 cash. Compute the net present value. Should Lotus acquire the computers? Explain.
3. Ignore requirement 2. Suppose the required after-tax rate of return is 12% instead of 16%. Should the computers be acquired? Show computations.

12-A2   DDB and Present Values
The president of Southern States Power Company is considering whether to buy some equipment for its White River plant. The equipment will cost $1.5 million cash and will have a 10-year useful life and zero terminal salvage value. Annual pretax cash savings from operations will be $360,000. The income tax rate is 40%, and the required after-tax rate of return is 16%.

Required

1. Compute the net present value, using a 7-year recovery period and DDB depreciation for tax purposes. Should the equipment be acquired?
2. Suppose the economic life of the equipment is 15 years, which means that there will be $360,000 additional annual cash savings from operations in years 11 to 15. Assume that a 7-year recovery period is used. Should the equipment be acquired? Show computations.

12-A3   Gains or Losses on Disposal
An asset with a book value of $50,000 was sold for cash on January 1, 19X6.

Required

Assume two selling prices: $65,000 and $30,000. For each selling price, prepare a tabulation of the gain or loss, the effect on income taxes, and the total after-tax effect on cash. The applicable income tax rate is 40%.

12-A4   Inflation and Capital Budgeting
The head of the corporate strategy division of a major consulting firm has proposed investing $300,000 in personal computers for the staff. The useful life and recovery period for the computers are both 5 years. DDB depreciation is used. There is no terminal salvage value. Labor savings of $125,000 per year (in year-zero dollars) are expected from the purchase. The income tax rate is 45%, the after-tax required rate of return is 20%, which includes a 4% element attributable to inflation.

Required

1. Compute the net present value of the computers. Use the nominal required rate of return and adjust the cash flows for inflation. (For example, year 1 cash flow = 1.04 × year 0 cash flow.)
2. Compute the net present value of the computers using the nominal required rate of return without adjusting the cash flows for inflation.
3. Compare your answers in requirements 1 and 2. Which is correct? Would using the incorrect analysis generally lead to overinvestment or underinvestment? Explain.

12-B1   Straight-Line Depreciation and Present Values
The president of a company specializing in the production of peripheral equipment for

personal computers is considering the purchase of some equipment used for research and development. The cost is $400,000, the recovery period is 5 years, and there is no terminal disposal value. Annual pretax cash inflows from operations would increase by $140,000, the income tax rate is 40%, and the required after-tax rate of return is 14%.

Required

1. Compute the net present value, assuming straight-line depreciation of $80,000 yearly for tax purposes. Should the equipment be acquired?
2. Suppose the asset will be fully depreciated at the end of year 5 but is sold for $20,000 cash. Should the equipment be acquired? Show computations.
3. Ignore requirement 2. Suppose the required after-tax rate of return is 10% instead of 14%. Should the equipment be acquired? Show computations.

12-B2   DDB and Present Values

The general manager of a cruise ship company has a chance to purchase a new navigation device for all its vessels at a total cost of $250,000. The recovery period is 5 years. Additional annual pretax cash inflow from operations is $84,000, the economic life of the equipment is 5 years, there is no salvage value, the income tax rate is 35%, and the after-tax required rate of return is 16%.

Required

1. Compute the net present value, assuming double-declining-balance depreciation for tax purposes. Should the equipment be acquired?
2. Suppose the economic life of the equipment is 6 years, which means that there will be an $84,000 cash inflow from operations in the sixth year. The recovery period is still 5 years. Should the equipment be acquired? Show computations.

12-B3   Income Taxes and Disposal of Assets

Assume that income tax rates are 30%.

1. The book value of an old machine is $20,000. It is to be sold for $8,000 cash. What is the effect of this decision on cash flows, after taxes?
2. The book value of an old machine is $20,000. It is to be sold for $30,000 cash. What is the effect on cash flows, after taxes, of this decision?

12-B4   Sensitivity of Capital Budgeting to Inflation

G. Esteban, the president of a Mexican trucking company, is considering whether to invest 405,000 pesos in new semiautomatic loading equipment that will last 5 years, have zero scrap value, and generate cash operating savings in labor usage of 160,000 pesos annually, using 19X4 prices and wage rates. It is December 31, 19X4.

The minimum desired rate of return is 18% per year after taxes.

Required

1. Compute the net present value of the project. Use 160,000 pesos as the savings for each of the 5 years. Assume a 40% tax rate and, for simplicity, assume ordinary straight-line depreciation of 405,000 pesos ÷ 5 = 81,000 pesos annually for tax purposes.
2. Esteban is wondering if the model in requirement 1 provides a correct analysis of the effects of inflation. She maintains that the 18% rate embodies an element attributable to anticipated inflation. For purposes of this analysis, she assumes that the existing rate of inflation, 10% annually, will persist over the next 5 years. Repeat requirement 1, adjusting the cash operating savings upward by using the 10% inflation rate.
3. Which analysis, the one in requirement 1 or 2, is correct? Why?

Additional Assignment Material

Questions

12-1. Distinguish between average and marginal tax rates.

12-2. "Congress should pass a law forbidding corporations to keep two sets of books." Do you agree? Explain.

12-3. Tax laws generally provide two types of acceleration of depreciation. Identify them.

12-4. "An investment in equipment really buys two streams of cash." Do you agree? Explain.

12-5. Why should tax deductions be taken sooner rather than later?

12-6. What are the major influences on the present value of a tax deduction?

12-7. "If income tax rates do not change through the years, my total tax payments will be the same under every depreciation method. Therefore I really do not care what depreciation schedule is permitted." Do you agree? Explain.

12-8. Distinguish between tax avoidance and tax evasion.

12-9. "Tax planning is unimportant because the total income tax bill will be the same in the long run, regardless of short-run maneuvering." Do you agree? Explain.

12-10. Explain why accelerated depreciation methods are superior to straight-line methods for income tax purposes.

12-11. How much depreciation is taken in the first year if a $10,000 asset is depreciated on a double-declining-balance schedule with a 4-year recovery period? How much in the second year?

12-12. "Immediate disposal of equipment, rather than its continued use, results in a full tax deduction of the undepreciated cost now—rather than having such a deduction spread over future years in the form of annual depreciation." Do you agree? Explain, using the $30,000 book value of old equipment in Exhibit 12-4, page 467, as a basis for your discussion.

12-13. "When there are income taxes, depreciation is a cash outlay." Do you agree? Explain.

12-14. What are the three components of market (nominal) interest rates?

12-15. Describe how internal consistency is achieved when considering inflation in a capital-budgeting model.

12-16. "Capital investments are always more profitable in inflationary times because the cash inflows from operations generally increase with inflation." Comment on this statement.

12-17. Explain how U.S. tax laws fail to adjust for inflation.

12-18. "The MACRS half-year convention causes assets to be depreciated beyond the lives specified in the MACRS recovery schedules." Do you agree? Explain.

12-19. Give the MACRS class for each of the following assets: automobiles, office furniture, farm buildings, and residential rental property.

Exercises

12-20 Role of Depreciation in Decision Models

A student of management accounting complained, "I'm confused about how depreciation relates to decisions. For example, Chapter 6 says that depreciation on old equipment is irrelevant, but depreciation on new equipment is relevant. Chapter 11 said that depreciation was irrelevant in discounted-cash-flow models, but Chapter 12 shows the relevance of depreciation."

Required Prepare a careful explanation that will eliminate the student's confusion.

12-21 Depreciation, Income Taxes, Cash Flows

Fill in the unknowns (in thousands of dollars):

(S)	Sales	520
(E)	Expenses excluding depreciation	350
(D)	Depreciation	100
	Total expenses	450
	Income before income taxes	?
(T)	Income taxes at 40%	?
(I)	Net income	?
	Cash effects of operations	
	Cash inflow from operations	?
	Income tax outflow at 40%	?
	After-tax inflow from operations	?
	Effect of depreciation	
	Depreciation, $100	
	Income tax savings	?
	Total after-tax effect on cash	?

12-22   Depreciation, Income Taxes, Cash Flows

Fill in the unknowns (in thousands of dollars):

(S) Sales	?
(E) Expenses excluding depreciation	?
(D) Depreciation	300
Total expenses	1,350
Income before income taxes	?
(T) Income taxes at 40%	?
(I) Net income	480
Cash effects of operations	
Cash inflow from operations	?
Income tax outflow at 40%	?
After-tax inflow from operations	?
Effect of depreciation	
Depreciation, $200	
Income tax savings	?
Total after-tax effect on cash	?

12-23   After-Tax Effect on Cash

The 19X6 income statement of Central Satellite TV Company included the following:

Sales	$1,200,000
Less: Expenses, excluding depreciation	$ 600,000
Depreciation	300,000
Total expenses	$ 900,000
Income before taxes	$ 300,000
Income taxes (35%)	105,000
Net income	$ 195,000

Required   Compute the total after-tax effect on cash. Use the format of the second part of Exhibit 12-1, page 459, "Analysis of the Same Facts for Capital Budgeting."

12-24   DDB Depreciation

Airborne Express provides overnight delivery of packages throughout the world. Consider a light-duty van acquired for $30,000. Using DDB and a 4-year recovery period, compute the depreciation schedule for tax purposes.

12-25   Computing a DDB Depreciation Schedule

Compute the amount of DDB depreciation each year for a $10,000 asset with an 8-year recovery period. Use the following format:

Year	Beginning Undepreciated Amount	DDB Rate	Depreciation	Ending Undepreciated Amount
1	$10,000	?	?	?
.	.	.	.	.
.	.	.	.	.
8	?	?	?	$0

12-26   MACRS Recovery Periods

Study Appendix 12A. Consider the following business assets: (a) a heavy-duty truck, (b) a personal computer, (c) a commercial building, (d) filing cabinets for an office, (e) an electron microscope used in industrial research, and (f) a residential apartment complex. What is the recovery period for each of these assets under the prescribed MACRS method?

12-27   MACRS Depreciation

Study Appendix 12A. In 1996 Eagleclaw Shoe Company acquired the following assets and immediately placed them into service:

1. Special tools (a 3-year–MACRS asset) that cost $40,000 on February 1.
2. A desk-top computer that cost $8,000 on December 15.
3. Special calibration equipment that was used in research and development and cost $5,000 on July 7.
4. A set of file cabinets that cost $3,000, purchased on March 1.

Required   Compute the depreciation for tax purposes, under the prescribed MACRS method, in 1996 and 1997.

12-28   Half-Year Convention

Study Appendix 12A. Suppose a $10,000 asset has a recovery period of 4 years. Compute a DDB depreciation schedule that includes application of the half-year convention. Also include a switch to straight-line depreciation at the appropriate point.

12-29   Present Value of DDB Depreciation

Study Appendix 12B. Compute the present value of the tax savings for each of the following five assets:

	Asset Cost	Recovery Period	Discount Rate	Tax Rate
(a)	$160,000	3-year	12%	30%
(b)	$560,000	5-year	10%	40%
(c)	$ 55,000	7-year	16%	50%
(d)	$910,000	10-year	8%	35%
(e)	$430,000	10-year	15%	25%

Problems

12-30   Effect of Recovery Period

Southwestern Bank is considering the purchase of some equipment for $900,000. The chief financial officer is not sure whether the tax authorities will allow a 5-year or a 3-year recovery period. She wants to know how much difference the classification makes. DDB depreciation is used for tax purposes. The tax rate is 35%, and the required after-tax rate of return is 12%.

Required
1. Compute the present value of the tax savings if the recovery period is (a) 5 years and (b) 3 years.
2. Which classification has the higher present value? By how much?

12-31   Straight-Line Depreciation, DDB Depreciation, and Immediate Write-Off

Mr. Tamura bought a new $30,000 freezer for his grocery store. The freezer has a 6-year recovery period, Mr. Tamura's minimum desired rate of return is 12%, and his tax rate is 40%.

Required
1. Suppose Mr. Tamura uses straight-line depreciation for tax purposes. Compute the present value of the tax savings from depreciation.
2. Suppose Mr. Tamura uses DDB depreciation for tax purposes. Compute the present value of the tax savings from depreciation.

3. Suppose Mr. Tamura was allowed to immediately deduct the entire cost of the freezer for tax purposes. Compute the present value of the tax savings from depreciation.
4. Which of the three methods of deducting the cost of the freezer would Mr. Tamura prefer if all three were allowable for tax purposes? Why?

12-32   Income Taxes and Incremental Costs

Yvette Thirdgill has a small sewing and tailoring shop in the basement of her home. She uses the single telephone line into the home for both business and personal calls. She estimates that 50% of the telephone use is for business. Until 1989 she allocated the basic cost of the telephone line, $20 per month, between business and personal use and charged $10 per month for telephone services on her business income statement submitted to the tax authorities.

Beginning in 1989, the Internal Revenue Service (IRS) ruled that no portion of the first telephone line into a residence is allowed as a business expense for tax purposes. However, if a second line is installed and used strictly for business purposes, its total cost is allowed as an expense. The telephone company charges $20 per month for a second line.

Thirdgill's marginal income tax rate is 40%.

Required

1. Under the old tax law (in effect before 1989), how much extra per month (after tax effects) would Thirdgill have paid for a second telephone line?
2. Under the new tax law (in effect beginning in 1989), how much extra per month (after tax effects) would Thirdgill pay for a second telephone line?
3. How might the new tax law affect the demand for second telephone lines?

12-33   Tax Incentives for Capital Investment

Galaden Vineyards is a successful small winery in California's Sonoma Valley. The owner, Gino Colucchio, is considering an additional line of business: selling wind-generated electricity to the local utility. California law requires power utilities to purchase windmill electricity. Gino could put windmills on his land without disturbing the grape crop. A windmill generates 200,000 kilowatt-hours annually, and the utility would pay $.07 per kilowatt-hour. There are essentially no operating costs.

At the time Gino considered purchasing his first windmill, the cost was $100,000 per windmill. Initially he was discouraged and almost abandoned the idea. But then he learned about three government tax credit programs that applied to investments in windmills. Each credit reduced tax payments in the year of the investment. First, a general investment tax credit of 8% could be taken. That is, Galaden's federal income taxes could be immediately reduced by 8% of the cost of the windmill. In addition, windmills qualified for a "business energy credit" of 15%, reducing federal income taxes by another 15% of the cost. Finally, windmills qualified for half of California's 25% solar investment tax credit. This reduced Galaden's California state income tax by 12.5% of the windmill's cost. Despite the tax credits, the full cost can be depreciated.

Assume that windmills are allowed a 5-year recovery period, although the economic life is 20 years. Galaden's required rate of return is 14% after taxes, and the combined federal and state income tax rate is 45%. Assume for simplicity that straight-line depreciation is used for tax purposes.

Required

1. Would Gino purchase a windmill without the tax credits? Calculate the net present value.
2. Would Gino purchase a windmill with the tax credits? Calculate net present value.
3. What is the most that Gino would pay for a windmill, provided the tax credits are available?
4. Evaluate the effect of tax credits on stimulating investment.

12-34   Present Value of After-Tax Cash Flows

Kobe Chemicals Company, located in Kobe, Japan, is planning to buy new equipment to expand their production of a popular solvent. Estimated data are (monetary amounts are in thousands of Japanese yen):

Cash cost of new equipment now	¥400,000
Estimated life in years	10
Terminal salvage value	¥ 50,000
Incremental revenues per year	¥320,000
Incremental expenses per year other than depreciation	¥165,000

Assume a 60% flat rate for income taxes. All revenues and expenses other than depreciation will be received or paid in cash. Use a 14% discount rate. Assume that ordinary straight-line depreciation based on a 10-year recovery period is used for tax purposes. Also assume that the terminal salvage value will affect the depreciation per year.

Required   Compute:
1. Depreciation expenses per year
2. Anticipated net income per year
3. Annual net cash flow
4. Payback period
5. Accounting rate of return on initial investment
6. Net present value

12-35   DDB and Replacement of Equipment
Refer to problem 6-B1, page 236. Assume that income tax rates are 60%. The minimum desired rate of return, after taxes, is 6%. Using the net-present-value technique, show whether the proposed equipment should be purchased. Present your solution on both a total project approach and a differential approach. For illustrative purposes, assume that the old equipment would have been depreciated on a straight-line basis and the proposed equipment on a DDB basis. Assume it has a 3-year recovery period.

12-36   DDB, Residual Value
The Maddux Company estimates that it can save $10,000 per year in annual operating cash costs for the next five years if it buys a special-purpose machine at a cost of $33,000. Residual value is expected to be $3,000, although no residual value is being provided for in using DDB depreciation (5-year recovery period) for tax purposes. The equipment will be sold at the beginning of the sixth year; for purposes of this analysis assume that the proceeds are received at the end of the fifth year. The minimum desired rate of return, after taxes, is 12%. Assume the income tax rate is 45%.

Required
1. Using the net-present-value model, show whether the investment is desirable.
2. Suppose the equipment will produce savings for seven years instead of five. Residual value is expected to be zero at the end of the seventh year. Using the net-present-value model, show whether the investment is desirable.

12-37   Purchase of Equipment
The Sea Pines Clinic, a for-profit medical facility, is planning to spend $45,000 for modernized x-ray equipment. It will replace equipment that has zero book value and no salvage value, although the old equipment would last another 7 years.

The new equipment will save $13,500 in cash operating costs for each of the next 7 years, at which time it will be sold for $4,000. A major overhaul costing $5,000 will occur at the end of the fourth year; the old equipment would require no such overhaul. The entire cost of the overhaul is deductible for tax purposes in the fourth year. The equipment has a 5-year recovery period. DDB depreciation is used for tax purposes.

The minimum desired rate of return after taxes is 12%. The applicable income tax rate is 40%.

Required   Compute the after-tax net present value. Is the new equipment a desirable investment?

12-38   Minimization of Transportation Costs
The Luxor Company produces industrial and residential lighting fixtures at its manufacturing facility in Los Angeles. Shipment of company products to an eastern warehouse is

presently handled by common carriers at a rate of 25¢ per pound of fixtures (expressed in year-zero dollars). The warehouse is located in Cleveland, 2,500 miles from Los Angeles.

Joanne Harris, the treasurer of Luxor, is presently considering whether to purchase a truck for transporting products to the eastern warehouse. The following data on the truck are available:

Purchase price	$35,000
Useful life	5 years
Terminal residual value	0
Capacity of truck	10,000 lb
Cash costs of operating truck (expressed in year-1 dollars)	$.90 per mile

Harris feels that an investment in this truck is particularly attractive because of her successful negotiation with Retro, Inc., to back-haul Retro's products from Cleveland to Los Angeles on every return trip from the warehouse. Retro has agreed to pay Luxor $2,400 per load of Retro's products hauled from Cleveland to Los Angeles for as many loads as Luxor can accommodate, up to and including 100 loads per year over the next 5 years.

Luxor's marketing manager has estimated that 500,000 pounds of fixtures will have to be shipped to the eastern warehouse each year for the next 5 years. The truck will be fully loaded on each round trip.

Make the following assumptions:

   a. Luxor requires a minimum 20% after-tax rate of return, which includes a 10% element attributable to inflation.

   b. A 40% tax rate.

   c. DDB depreciation based on 5-year cost recovery period.

   d. An inflation rate of 10%.

Required
   1. Should the truck be purchased? Show computations to support your answer.
   2. What qualitative factors might influence your decision? Be specific.

12-39   Inflation and Nonprofit Institution
The city of Bremerton is considering the purchase of a photocopying machine for $7,200 on December 31, 19X4. The machine will have a useful life of 5 years and no residual value. The cash operating savings are expected to be $2,000 annually, measured in 19X4 dollars.

The minimum desired rate is 14%, which includes an element attributable to anticipated inflation of 6%. (Remember that the city pays no income taxes.)

Required
Use the 14% minimum desired rate for requirements 1 and 2:
   1. Compute the net present value of the project without adjusting the cash operating savings for inflation.
   2. Repeat requirement 1, adjusting the cash operating savings upward in accordance with the 6% inflation rate.
   3. Compare your results in requirements 1 and 2. What generalization seems applicable about the analysis of inflation in capital budgeting?

12-40   Tax Law, Inflation, and PV of Depreciation Tax Shield
Study Appendix 12A. Congress often considers proposed changes to the U.S. tax laws. A recent GOP proposal included a recognition of inflation in the tax depreciation schedule. The proposed schedule would replace the MACRS schedule shown in Exhibit 12-8, p. 475. The amount of depreciation allowed each year would be based on an inflation-adjusted cost of the asset, not the original historical cost. For example, assuming a 3% inflation rate, a 7-year asset was proposed to have the following depreciation schedule:

Year 1	10.7%	Year 5	15.8%
Year 2	20.4%	Year 6	16.9%
Year 3	17.1%	Year 7	18.0%
Year 4	14.8%	Year 8	9.6%

The total depreciation under this schedule is 123.3%.

Required

1. Suppose on January 2, 19X0, Langsten Company was considering the purchase of a $100,000 machine and anticipated a 3% annual inflation rate for the 7-year life of the asset. Using either MACRS or the proposed schedule, depreciation would be spread over 8 years. Compute the present value of the depreciation tax shield at the time of investment using (a) MACRS and (b) the proposed schedule. Use a required rate of return of 12%.

2. Does the proposed schedule provide more incentives for making investment than does the MACRS schedule? Explain.

3. Repeat requirement 1 using a 20% required rate of return. Explain the effect of the required rate of return on the desirability of changing to the proposed schedule.

12-41   MACRS and Low-Income Housing

Study Appendix 12A. Hector Ramirez is a real estate developer who specializes in residential apartments. A complex of 20 run-down apartments has recently come on the market for $155,000. Ramirez predicts that after remodeling, the 12 one-bedroom units will rent for $190 per month and the 8 two-bedroom apartments for $220. He budgets 15% of the rental fees for repairs and maintenance. The apartments should last for 30 years if the remodeling is done well. Remodeling costs are $6,000 per apartment. Both purchase price and remodeling costs qualify as 27.5-year MACRS property.

Assume that the MACRS schedule assigns an equal amount of depreciation to each of the first 27 years and one-half year to the 28th year. The present value at 10% of $1 of cost recovery spread over the 28 years in this way is $.3372.

Ramirez does not believe he will keep the apartment complex for its entire 30-year life. Most likely he will sell it just after the end of the tenth year. His predicted sales price is $450,000.

Ramirez's after-tax required rate of return is 10%, and his tax rate is 38%.

Required

Should Ramirez buy the apartment complex? What is the after-tax net present value? Ignore the investment tax credit and other tax complications such as capital gains.

Case

12-42   Make or Buy and Replacement of Equipment

Study Appendix 12A. Toyland Company was one of the original producers of "transformers." An especially complex part of 'Sect-a-con needs special tools that are not useful for other products. These tools were purchased on July 1, 19X3, for $200,000.

It is now July 1, 19X7. The manager of the Transformer Division, Ramona Ruiz, is contemplating three alternatives. First, she could continue to produce 'Sect-a-con using the current tools; they will last another 5 years, at which time they would have zero terminal value. Second, she could sell the tools for $30,000 and purchase the parts from an outside supplier for $1.10 each. Third, she could replace the tools with new, more efficient tools costing $180,000.

Ruiz expects to produce 80,000 units of 'Sect-a-con each of the next 5 years. Manufacturing costs for the part have been as follows, and no change in costs is expected:

Direct material	$ .38
Direct labor	.37
Variable overhead	.17
Fixed overhead*	.45
Total unit cost	$1.37

* Depreciation accounts for two-thirds of the fixed overhead. The balance is for other fixed overhead costs of the factory that require cash outlays, 60% of which would be saved if production of the parts were eliminated.

The outside supplier offered the $1.10 price as a once-only offer. It is unlikely such a low price would be available later. Toyland would also have to guarantee to purchase at least 70,000 parts for each of the next 5 years.

The new tools that are available would last for 5 years with a disposal value of $40,000 at the end of 5 years. Both the old and new tools are 5-year MACRS property, and both use the current MACRS schedules. Straight-line depreciation is used for book purposes and MACRS for tax purposes. The sales representative selling the new tools stated, "The new tools will allow direct labor and variable overhead to be reduced by $.21 per unit." Ruiz thinks this estimate is accurate. However, she also knows that a higher quality of materials would be necessary with the new tools. She predicts the following costs with the new tools:

Direct material	$ .40
Direct labor	.25
Variable overhead	.08
Fixed overhead	.60*
Total unit cost	$1.33

* The increase in fixed overhead is caused by depreciation on the new tools.

The company has a 40% marginal tax rate and requires a 12% after-tax rate of return.

Required

1. Calculate the net present value of each of the three alternatives. Recognize the tax implications. Which alternative should Ruiz select?
2. What are some factors besides the net present value that should influence Ruiz's selection?

13 Cost Allocation and Activity-Based Costing

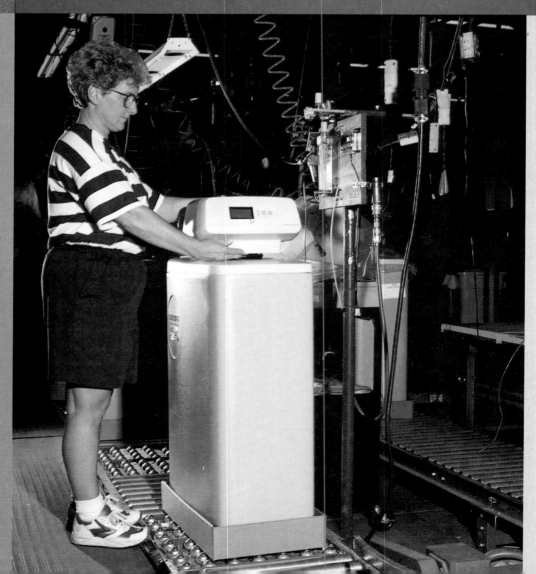

EcoWater Systems, Inc., is the world's largest manufacturer of residential water treatment and purification systems. The company has introduced activity-based costing to more accurately assign overhead to its products and customer types.
Courtesy EcoWater Systems, Inc.

Learning Objectives

When you have finished studying this chapter, you should be able to

1 Recognize the major purposes for allocating costs.

2 Explain the relationship between activities, resources, costs, and cost drivers.

3 Use recommended guidelines to allocate the variable and fixed costs of service departments to other organizational units.

4 Identify methods for allocating the central costs of an organization.

5 Use the direct and step-down methods to allocate service department costs to user departments.

6 Describe the general approach to allocating costs to products or services.

7 Use activity-based costing to allocate costs to products or services.

8 Use the physical-units and relative-sales-value methods to allocate joint costs to products.

A university's computer is used for teaching and for government-funded research. How much of its cost should be assigned to the research projects? A city creates a special police unit to investigate a series of related assaults. What is the total cost of the effort? A company uses a machine to make two different product lines. How much of the cost of the machine belongs to each product line? These are all problems of cost allocation, the subject of this chapter. University presidents, city managers, corporate executives, and many others face problems of cost allocation.

This is the first of three chapters on **cost accounting systems**—the techniques used to determine the cost of a product, service, or other cost objective. A cost accounting system collects and classifies costs and assigns them to cost objects. The goal of a cost accounting system is to measure the cost of designing, developing, producing (or purchasing), selling, distributing, and servicing particular products or services. Cost allocation is at the heart of most cost accounting systems.

The first part of this chapter describes general approaches to cost allocation. Although we present some factors to consider in selecting cost allocation methods, there are no easy answers. Recent attempts to improve cost allocation methods have focused on activity-based costing, the subject of the last part of the chapter.

cost accounting systems The techniques used to determine the cost of a product, service, or other cost objective by collecting and classifying costs and assigning them to cost objects.

■ COST ALLOCATION IN GENERAL

As Chapter 4 pointed out, cost allocation is fundamentally a problem of linking some cost or group of costs with one or more *cost objectives*, such as products, departments, customer classes, activities, and divisions. Ideally, cost allocation should assign each cost to the cost objective that *caused* it.

The linking of costs with cost objectives is accomplished by selecting cost drivers, activities that cause costs (see Chapter 2). When used for allocating costs, a cost driver is often called a **cost-allocation base**. Major costs such as newsprint for a newspaper and direct professional labor for a law firm may be allocated to departments, jobs, and projects on an item-by-item basis, using obvious cost drivers such as tons of newsprint consumed or direct-labor-hours used. Other costs, taken one at a time, are not important enough to justify being allocated individually. These costs are *pooled* and then allocated together. A **cost pool** is a group of individual costs that is allocated to *cost objectives* using a single cost driver. For example, building rent, utilities cost, and janitorial services may be in the same cost pool because all are allocated on the basis of square footage of space occupied. Or a university could pool all the operating costs of its registrar's office and allocate them to its colleges on the basis of the number of students in each college. In summary, all costs in a given cost pool should be caused by the same factor. That factor is the cost driver.

Many different terms are used to describe cost allocation in practice. You may encounter terms such as *allocate, attribute, reallocate, trace, assign, distribute, redistribute, load, burden, apportion,* and *reapportion* being used interchangeably to describe the allocation of costs to cost objectives. The terms *apply* or *absorb* tend to have the narrower meaning of costs allocated to products rather than to departments or divisions.

cost-allocation base A cost driver when it is used for allocating costs.

cost pool A group of individual costs that is allocated to cost objectives using a single cost driver.

Four Purposes of Allocation

What logic should be used for allocating costs? This question bothers many internal users and suppliers of services in all organizations. The answer depends on the principal purpose(s) of the cost allocation.

Costs are allocated for four major purposes.

Objective 1

Recognize the major purposes for allocating costs

1. *To predict the economic effects of planning and control decisions*: Managers within an organizational unit should be aware of all the consequences of their decisions, even consequences outside of their unit. Examples are the addition of a new course in a university that causes additional work in the registrar's office, the addition of a new flight or an additional passenger on an airline that requires reservation and booking services, and the addition of a new specialty in a medical clinic that produces more work for the medical records department.

2. *To obtain desired motivation*: Cost allocations are sometimes made to influence management behavior and thus promote goal congruence and managerial effort. Consequently, in some organizations there is no cost allocation for legal or internal auditing services or internal management consulting services because top management wants to encourage their use. In other organizations there is a cost allocation for such items to spur managers to make sure the benefits of the specified services exceed the costs.

3. *To compute income and asset valuations*: Costs are allocated to products and projects to measure inventory costs and cost of goods sold. These allocations frequently

serve financial accounting purposes. However, the resulting costs also are often used by managers in planning and performance evaluation.

4. *To justify costs or obtain reimbursement*: Sometimes prices are based directly on costs. For example, government contracts often specify a price that includes reimbursement for costs plus some profit margin. In these instances, cost allocations become substitutes for the usual working of the marketplace in setting prices.

The first two purposes specify planning and control uses for allocation. Purposes 3 and 4 show how cost allocations may differ for inventory costing (and cost of goods sold) and for setting prices. Moreover, different allocations of costs to products may be made for the various purposes. Thus full costs may guide pricing decisions (purpose 1), manufacturing costs may be proper for asset valuations (purpose 3), and some "in-between" cost may be negotiated for a government contract (purpose 4).

Ideally, all four purposes would be served simultaneously by a single cost allocation. But thousands of managers and accountants will testify that for most costs this ideal is rarely achieved. Instead, cost allocations are often a major source of discontent and confusion to the affected parties. Allocating fixed costs usually causes the greatest problems. When all four purposes cannot be attained simultaneously, the manager and the accountant should start attacking a cost-allocation problem by trying to identify which of the purposes should dominate in the particular situation at hand.

Often inventory-costing purposes dominate by default because they are externally imposed. When allocated costs are used in decision making and performance evaluation, managers should consider adjusting the allocations used to satisfy inventory-costing purposes. Often the added benefit of using separate allocations for planning and control and inventory-costing purposes is much greater than the added cost.

Three Types of Allocations

As Exhibit 13-1 shows, there are three basic types of cost allocations.

1. *Allocation of costs to the appropriate organizational unit*: Direct costs are physically traced to the unit, but costs used jointly by more than one unit are allocated based on cost-driver activity in the unit. Examples are allocating rent to departments based on floor space occupied, allocating depreciation on jointly used machinery based on machine-hours, and allocating general administrative expense based on total direct cost.

2. *Reallocation of costs from one organizational unit to another*: When one unit provides products or services to another, the costs are transferred along with the products or services. Some units, called **service departments**, exist only to support other departments, and their costs are totally reallocated. Examples include personnel departments, laundry departments in hospitals, and legal departments in industrial firms.

3. *Allocation of costs of a particular organizational unit or activity to products or services*: The pediatrics department of a medical clinic allocates its costs to patient visits, the assembly department of a manufacturing firm to units assembled, and the tax department of a CPA firm to clients served. The costs allocated to products or services include those allocated to the organizational unit in allocation types 1 and 2.

The major focus of this chapter is on type 2, the reallocation of costs from one

service departments
Units that exist only to support other departments.

organizational unit to another. However, all three types of allocations are fundamentally similar. Let us look first at how service department costs are allocated to production departments.

Exhibit 13-1

Three Types of Cost Allocations

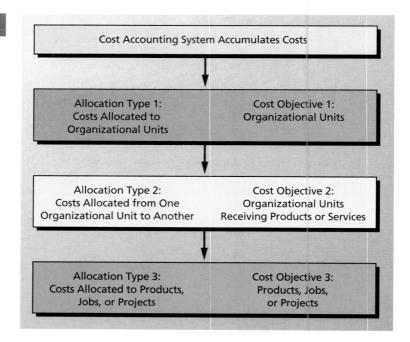

ALLOCATION OF SERVICE DEPARTMENT COSTS

Ideally, costs are allocated to organizational units because some activity in the unit caused the cost to be incurred. Therefore a cost allocation system should focus on the causes of costs—the cost drivers.

General Guidelines

Objective 2

Explain the relationship between activities, resources, costs, and cost drivers

What causes costs? Organizations incur costs to produce goods and services and to provide the support services required for that production. Essentially, costs are *caused* by the very same activities that are usually chosen as cost objectives. Examples are products produced, patients seen, orders processed, and legal consultations. The ultimate *effects* of these activities are various costs. It is important to understand how cost behavior relates to activities and the consumption of resources. To perform activities, resources are required. These resources have costs. Some costs vary in direct proportion to the consumption of resources. Examples are energy and supplies. Other costs do not vary (in the short run) with resource use. Examples are depreciation, supervisory salaries, and occupancy (rent, insurance). So we say that activities consume resources and the costs of these resources follow various behavioral patterns. When the manager and accountant search for cost drivers, they should focus on the relationship between activities and the consumption of resources. It is important to understand that cost drivers relate activities to the consumption of resources. Therefore the manager and the accountant should search for some cost driver that establishes a convincing relationship between the cause (activities being performed) and the effect (consumption of resources and related costs) and that permits *reliable predictions* of how costs will be affected by decisions regarding the activities.

To illustrate this important principle, we will consider allocation of service department costs. The preferred guidelines for allocating service department costs are as follows:

1. *Evaluate performance using budgets* for each service (staff) department, just as for each production or operating (line) department. The performance of a service department is evaluated by comparing actual costs with a budget, independent of how the costs are later allocated. From the budget, variable-cost pools and fixed-cost pools can be identified for use in allocation.

2. *Allocate variable- and fixed-cost pools separately* (sometimes called the dual method of allocation). Note that one service department (such as a computer department) can contain multiple cost pools if more than one cost driver causes the department's costs. At a minimum, there should be a variable-cost pool and a fixed-cost pool.

3. *Establish part or all of the details regarding cost allocation in advance* of rendering the service rather than after the fact. This approach establishes the "rules of the game" so that all departments can plan appropriately.

Objective 3

Use recommended guidelines to allocate the variable and fixed costs of service departments to other organizational units

Consider a simplified example of a computer department of a university that serves two major users, the School of Business and the School of Engineering. The computer mainframe was acquired on a 5-year lease that is not cancelable unless prohibitive cost penalties are paid.

How should the costs of the computer department (salaries, depreciation, energy, materials, etc.) be allocated to the user departments? Suppose there are two major purposes for the allocation: (1) predicting economic effects of the use of the computer, and (2) motivating departments and individuals to use its capabilities more fully.

To apply the first of the preceding guidelines, we need to analyze the costs of the computer department in detail. The primary activity performed is computer processing. Resources consumed include processing time, operator time, consulting time, energy, materials, and building space. Suppose cost behavior analysis has been performed and the budget formula for the forthcoming year is $100,000 monthly fixed cost plus $200 variable cost per hour of computer time used. Applying both guidelines 2 and 3 is the topic of the next two sections.

Variable-Cost Pool

The cost driver for the variable-cost pool is *hours of computer time used*. Therefore, variable costs should be allocated as follows:

budgeted unit rate × actual hours of computer time used

The cause-and-effect relationship is clear: The heavier the usage, the higher the total costs. In this example, the rate used would be the budgeted rate of $200 per hour.

The use of *budgeted* cost rates rather than *actual* cost rates for allocating variable costs of service departments protects the using departments from intervening price fluctuations and also often protects them from inefficiencies in the service departments. When an organization allocates *actual* total service department cost, it holds user department managers responsible for costs beyond their control and provides less incentive for service departments to be efficient. Both effects are undesirable.

Consider the allocation of *variable* costs to a department that uses 600 hours of computer time. Suppose inefficiencies in the computer department caused the variable costs to be $140,000 instead of the 600 hours × $200, or $120,000 budgeted. A good cost-allocation scheme would allocate only the $120,000 to the consuming departments and would let the $20,000 remain as an unallocated unfavorable budget variance of the computer department. This scheme holds computer department managers responsible for the $20,000 variance and reduces the resentment of user managers. User department managers sometimes complain more vigorously about uncertainty over allocations and the poor management of a service department than about the choice of a cost driver (such as direct-labor dollars or number of employees). Such complaints are less likely if the service department managers have budget responsibility and the user departments are protected from short-run price fluctuations and inefficiencies.

Most consumers prefer to know the total price in advance. They become nervous when an automobile mechanic or contractor undertakes a job without specifying prices. As a minimum, they like to know the hourly rates that they must bear. Therefore predetermined unit prices (at least) should be used. When feasible, predetermined total prices should be used for various kinds of work based on budgets and standards.

To illustrate, consider an automobile repair and maintenance department for a state government. Agencies who use the department's service should receive firm prices for various services. Imagine the feelings of an agency head who had an agency automobile repaired and was told, "Normally your repair would have taken 5 hours. However, we had a new employee work on it, and the job took him 10 hours. Therefore, we must charge you for 10 hours of labor time."

Fixed-Cost Pool

The cost driver for the fixed-cost pool is the amount of capacity required when the computer facilities were acquired. Therefore, fixed costs should be allocated as follows:

budgeted percent of capacity available for use × total budgeted fixed costs

Consider again our example of the university computer department. Suppose the deans had originally predicted the long-run average monthly usage by Business at 210 hours, and by Engineering at 490 hours, a total of 700 hours. The fixed-cost pool would be allocated as follows:

	Business	Engineering
Fixed costs per month		
210/700, or 30% of $100,000	$30,000	
490/700, or 70% of $100,000		$70,000

This predetermined lump-sum approach is based on the long-run capacity *available* to the user, regardless of actual usage from month to month. The reasoning is that the level of fixed costs is affected by *long-range* planning regarding the overall level of service and the *relative expected* usage, not by *short-run* fluctuations in service levels and *relative actual* usage.

A major strength of using capacity *available* rather than capacity *used* when allocating *budgeted* fixed costs is that short-run allocations to user departments are not affected by the *actual* usage of *other* user departments. Such a budgeted lump-sum approach is more likely to have the desired motivational effects with respect to the ordering of services in both the short run and the long run.

In practice, fixed-cost pools often are inappropriately allocated on the basis of capacity used, not capacity available. Suppose the computer department allocated the total actual costs after the fact. At the end of the month, total *actual* costs would be allocated in proportion to the *actual* hours used by the consuming departments. Compare the costs borne by the two schools when Business uses 200 hours and Engineering 400 hours:

Total costs incurred, $100,000 + 600($200) = $220,000	
Business: 200/600 × $220,000 =	$ 73,333
Engineering: 400/600 × $220,000 =	146,667
Total cost allocated	$220,000

What happens if Business uses only 100 hours during the following month, and Engineering still uses 400 hours?

Total costs incurred, $100,000 + 500($200) = $200,000	
Business: 100/500 × $200,000 =	$ 40,000
Engineering: 400/500 × $200,000 =	160,000
Total cost allocated	$200,000

Engineering has done nothing differently, but it must bear higher costs of $13,333, an increase of 9%. Its short-run costs depend on what other consumers have used, not solely on its own actions. This phenomenon is caused by a faulty allocation method for the *fixed* portion of total costs, a method whereby the allocations are highly sensitive to fluctuations in the actual volumes used by the various consuming departments. This weakness is avoided by using a predetermined lump-sum allocation of fixed costs, based on budgeted usage.

Consider another example, the automobile repair shop example introduced on page 494. You would not be happy if you came to get your car and were told, "Our daily fixed overhead is $1,000. Yours was the only car in our shop today, so we are charging you the full $1,000. If we had processed 100 cars today, your charge would have been only $10."

Troubles with Using Lump Sums

Using lump-sum allocations can cause problems, however. If fixed costs are allocated on the basis of long-range plans, there is a natural tendency on the part of consumers to underestimate their planned usage and thus obtain a smaller fraction of the cost allocation. Top management can counteract these tendencies by monitoring predictions and by following up and using feedback to keep future predictions more honest.

In some organizations there are even definite rewards in the form of salary increases for managers who make accurate predictions. Moreover, some cost-allocation methods provide for penalties for underpredictions. For example, suppose a manager predicts usage of 210 hours and then demands 300 hours. The manager either doesn't get the hours or pays a dear price for every hour beyond 210 in such systems.

Allocation of Central Costs

The seeming need to allocate central costs is a manifestation of a widespread, deep-seated belief that all costs must somehow be fully allocated to the revenue-producing (operating) parts of the organization. Such allocations are neither necessary from an accounting viewpoint nor useful as management information. However, most managers accept them as a fact of a manager's life—as long as all managers seem to be treated alike and thus "fairly."

Objective 4

Identify methods for allocating the central costs of an organization

Whenever possible, the preferred cost driver for central services is usage, either actual or estimated. But the costs of such services as public relations, top corporate management overhead, a real estate department, and a corporate-planning department are the least likely to be allocated on the basis of usage. Data processing, advertising, and operations research are the most likely to choose usage as a cost driver.

Companies that allocate central costs by usage tend to generate less resentment. Consider the experience of J. C. Penney Co. as reported in *Business Week*:

> The controller's office wanted subsidiaries such as Thrift Drug Co. and the insurance operations to base their share of corporate personnel, legal, and auditing costs on their revenues. The subsidiaries contended that they maintained their own personnel and legal departments, and should be assessed far less. . . . The subcommittee addressed the issue by asking the corporate departments to approximate the time and costs involved in servicing the subsidiaries. The final allocation plan, based on these studies, cost the divisions less than they were initially assessed but more than they had wanted to pay. Nonetheless, the plan was implemented easily.

Usage is not always an economically viable way to allocate central costs, however. Also, many central costs, such as the president's salary and related expenses, public relations, legal services, income tax planning, company-wide advertising, and basic research, are difficult to allocate on the basis of cause and effect. As a result, some companies use cost drivers such as the revenue of each division, the cost of goods sold by each division, the total assets of each division, or the total costs of each division (before allocation of the central costs) to allocate central costs.

The use of the foregoing cost drivers might provide a *rough* indication of cause-and-effect relationship. Basically, however, they represent an "ability to bear" philosophy of cost allocation. For example, the costs of company-wide advertising, such as the goodwill sponsorship of a program on a noncommercial television station, might be allocated to all products and divisions on the basis of the dollar sales in each. But such costs precede sales. They are discretionary costs as determined by management policies, not by sales results. Although 60 percent of the companies in a large survey treat sales revenue as a cost driver for cost allocation purposes, it is seldom truly a cost driver in the sense of being an activity that *causes* the costs.

Use of Budgeted Sales for Allocation

If the costs of central services are to be allocated based on sales even though the costs do not vary in proportion to sales, the use of *budgeted* sales is preferable to the use of *actual* sales. At least this method means that the short-run costs of a given consuming department will not be affected by the fortunes of other consuming departments.

For example, suppose $100 of fixed central advertising costs were allocated on the basis of potential sales in two territories:

	Territories		Total	Percent
	A	B		
Budgeted sales	$500	$500	$1,000	100
Central advertising allocated	$ 50	$ 50	$ 100	10

Consider the possible differences in allocations when actual sales become known:

	Territories	
	A	B
Actual sales	$300	$600
Central advertising		
1. Allocated on basis of budgeted sales	$ 50	$ 50
or		
2. Allocated on basis of actual sales	$ 33	$ 67

Compare allocation 1 with 2. Allocation 1 is preferable. It indicates a low ratio of sales to advertising in territory A. It directs attention where it is deserved. In contrast, allocation 2 soaks territory B with more advertising cost because of the *achieved* results and relieves territory A despite its lower success. This is another example of the analytical confusion that can arise when cost allocations to one consuming department depend on the activity of other consuming departments.

Reciprocal Services

Service departments often support other service departments in addition to producing departments. Consider a manufacturing company with two producing departments, molding and finishing, and two service departments, facilities management (rent, heat, light, janitorial services, etc.) and personnel. All costs in a given service department are assumed to be caused by, and therefore vary in proportion to, a single cost driver. The company has decided that the best cost driver for facilities management costs is square footage occupied and the best cost driver for personnel is the number of employees. Exhibit 13-2 shows the direct costs, square footage occupied, and number of employees for each department. Note that facilities management provides services for the personnel department in addition to providing services for the producing departments, and that personnel aids employees in facilities management as well as those in production departments.

Exhibit 13-2

Cost Drivers

	Service Departments		Production Departments	
	Facilities Management	*Personnel*	*Molding*	*Finishing*
Direct department costs	$126,000	$24,000	$100,000	$160,000
Square feet	3,000	9,000	15,000	3,000
Number of employees	20	30	80	320
Direct-labor hours			2,100	10,000
Machine-hours			30,000	5,400

Objective 5

Use the direct and step-down methods to allocate service department costs to user departments

There are two popular methods for allocating service department costs in such cases: the direct method and the step-down method.

Direct Method

direct method A method for allocating service department costs that ignores other service departments when any given service department's costs are allocated to the revenue-producing (operating) departments.

As its name implies, the **direct method** ignores other service departments when any given service department's costs are allocated to the revenue-producing (operating) departments. In other words, the fact that facilities management provides services for personnel is ignored, as is the support that personnel provides to facilities management. Facilities management costs are allocated based on the relative square footage occupied *by the production departments only*:

- Total square footage in production departments: 15,000 + 3,000 = 18,000
- Facilities management cost allocated to molding = (15,000 ÷ 18,000) × $126,000 = $105,000
- Facilities management cost allocated to finishing = (3,000 ÷ 18,000) × $126,000 = $21,000

step-down method A method for allocating service department costs that recognizes that some service departments support the activities in other service departments as well as those in production departments.

Likewise, personnel department costs are allocated *only to the production departments* on the basis of the relative number of employees in the production departments:

- Total employees in production departments = 80 + 320 = 400
- Personnel costs allocated to molding = (80 ÷ 400) × $24,000 = $4,800
- Personnel costs allocated to finishing = (320 ÷ 400) × $24,000 = $19,200

Step-down Method

The **step-down method** recognizes that some service departments support the activities in other service departments as well as those in production departments.

A sequence of allocations is chosen, usually by starting with the service department that renders the greatest service (as measured by costs) to the greatest number of other service departments. The last service department in the sequence is the one that renders the least service to the least number of other service departments. Once a department's costs are allocated to other departments, no subsequent service department costs are allocated back to it.

In our example, facilities management costs are allocated first. Why? Because facilities management renders more support to personnel than personnel provides for facilities management.[1] Examine Exhibit 13-3. After facilities management costs are allocated, no costs are allocated back to facilities management, even though personnel does provide some services for facilities management. The personnel costs to be allocated to the production departments include the amount allocated to personnel from facilities management ($42,000) in addition to the direct personnel department costs of $24,000.

Examine the last column of Exhibit 13-3. Before allocation, the four departments incurred costs of $410,000. In step 1, $126,000 was deducted from facilities management and added to the other three departments. There was no net effect on the total cost. In step 2, $66,000 was deducted from personnel and added to the remaining two departments. Again, total cost was unaffected. After allocation, all $410,000 remains, but it is all in molding and finishing. None was left in facilities management or personnel.

Exhibit 13-3		Step-Down Allocation			
	Facilities Management	**Personnel**	**Molding**	**Finishing**	**Total**
Direct department costs before allocation	$ 126,000	$ 24,000	$100,000	$160,000	$410,000
Step 1 Facilities management	$(126,000)	(9 ÷ 27) × $126,000 = $ 42,000	(15 ÷ 27) × $126,000 = $ 70,000	(3 ÷ 27) × $126,000 = $ 14,000	0
Step 2 Personnel		$(66,000)	(80 ÷ 400) × $66,000 = $ 13,200	(320 ÷ 400) × $66,000 = $ 52,800	0
Total cost after allocation	$ 0	$ 0	$ 183,200	$ 226,800	$ 410,000

Compare the costs of the production departments under direct and step-down methods, as shown in Exhibit 13-4. Note that the method of allocation can greatly affect the costs. Molding appears to be a much more expensive

[1] How should we determine which of the two service departments provides more service to the other? One way is to carry out step one of the step-down method with facilities management allocated first, and then repeat if assuming personnel is allocated first. With facilities management allocated first, $42,000 is allocated to personnel, as shown in Exhibit 13-3. If personnel had been allocated first, (20 ÷ 420) × $24,000 = $1,143 would have been allocated to facilities management. Because $1,143 is smaller than $42,000, facilities management is allocated first.

operation to a manager using the direct method than to one using the step-down method. Conversely, finishing seems more expensive to a manager using the step-down method.

Exhibit 13-4

Direct Versus Step-Down Method

	Molding		Finishing	
	Direct*	Step-down**	Direct*	Step-down**
Direct department costs	$100,000	$100,000	$160,000	$160,000
Allocated from facilities management	105,000	70,000	21,000	14,000
Allocated from personnel	4,800	13,200	19,200	52,800
Total costs	$209,800	$183,200	$200,200	$226,800

*From page 498.
**From Exhibit 13-3.

Which method is better? Generally, the step-down method.[2] Why? Because it recognizes the effects of the most significant support provided by service departments to other service departments. In our example, the direct method ignores the following possible cause-effect link: If the cost of facilities management is caused by the space used, then the space used by personnel causes $42,000 of facilities management cost. If the space used in personnel is caused by the number of production department employees supported, then the number of production department employees, not the square footage, causes $42,000 of the facilities management cost. The producing department with the most employees, not the one with the most square footage, should bear this cost.

The greatest virtue of the direct method is its simplicity. If the two methods do not produce significantly different results, many companies elect the direct method because it is easier for managers to understand.

Costs Not Related to Cost Drivers

Our example illustrating direct and step-down allocation methods assumed that a single cost driver caused all costs in a given service department. For example, we assumed that square footage occupied caused all facilities management costs. Additional square footage would result in additional facilities management cost. But what if some of the costs in facilities management are independent of square footage?

Three alternative methods of allocation should be considered:

1. Identify additional cost drivers. Divide facilities management costs into two or more different cost pools and use a different cost driver to allocate the costs in each pool.
2. Divide facilities management costs into two cost pools, one with costs that vary in proportion to the square footage (variable costs) and one with costs not affected by square footage (fixed costs). Allocate the former using the direct or step-down method, but do not allocate the latter. Costs not allocated are period costs for the organization but are not regarded as a cost of a particular production department.

---

[2] The most defensible theoretical accuracy is generated by the reciprocal cost method, which is rarely used in practice because it is more difficult to understand. Simultaneous equations and linear algebra are used to solve for the impact of mutually interacting services.

3. Allocate all costs by the direct or step-down method using square footage as the cost driver. This alternative implicitly assumes that, in the long run, square footage causes all facilities management costs—even if a short-term causal relationship is not easily identifiable. In other words, using more square footage may not cause an immediate increase in all facilities management costs, but eventually such costs will creep up in proportion to increases in square footage.

Suppose that most costs in a service department are caused by a single cost driver. Then alternatives 2 and 3 have much appeal. Only a small portion of costs would be unallocated (in alternative 2) or arbitrarily allocated (in alternative 3). But if large amounts of cost are not related to the single cost driver, alternative 1 should be seriously considered.

■ ALLOCATION OF COSTS TO OUTPUTS

cost application
The allocation of total departmental costs to the revenue-producing products or services.

Up to this point, we have concentrated on cost allocation to divisions, departments, and similar segments of an entity. Cost allocation is almost always carried one step further—to the outputs of these departments, however defined. Examples are *products*, such as automobiles, furniture, and newspapers, and *services*, such as banking, health care, and education. Sometimes the allocation of total departmental costs to the revenue-producing products or services is called **cost application** or *cost attribution*.

Costs are allocated to products for inventory valuation purposes and for decision purposes such as pricing, adding products, and promoting products. Cost allocation is also performed for cost-reimbursement purposes. As noted earlier, many defense contractors are reimbursed for the "costs" of producing products for the government.

General Approach

The general approach to allocating costs to final products or services is the following:

Objective 6

Describe the general approach to allocating costs to products or services

1. Allocate production-related costs to the operating (line), or production or revenue-producing departments. This includes allocating service department costs to the production departments following the guidelines listed on page 493. The production departments then contain all the costs: their direct department costs and the service department costs.

2. Select one or more cost drivers in each production department. Historically most companies have used only one cost driver per department. Recently a large number of companies have started using multiple cost pools and multiple cost drivers within a department. For example, a portion of the departmental costs may be allocated on the basis of direct-labor hours, another portion on the basis of machine-hours, and the remainder on the basis of number of machine setups.

3. Allocate (apply) the total costs accumulated in step 1 to products or services that are the outputs of the operating departments using the cost drivers specified in step 2. If only one cost driver is used, two cost pools should be maintained, one for variable costs and one for fixed costs. Variable costs should be allocated on the basis of actual cost-driver activity. Fixed costs should either remain unallocated or be allocated on the basis of budgeted cost-driver activity.

Consider our manufacturing example, and assume that the step-down method was used to allocate service department costs. Exhibit 13-3 showed total costs of $183,200 accumulated in molding and $226,800 in finishing. Note that all $410,000 total manufacturing costs reside in the production departments. To allocate these costs to the products produced, cost drivers must be selected for each department. We will use a single cost driver for each department and assume that all costs are caused by that cost driver. Suppose machine-hours is the best measure of what causes costs in the molding department, and direct-labor hours drive costs in finishing. Exhibit 13-2 showed 30,000 total machine-hours used in molding and 10,000 direct-labor hours in finishing. Therefore costs are allocated to products as follows:

Molding: $183,200 ÷ 30,000 machine-hours = $6.11 per machine-hour
Finishing: $226,800 ÷ 10,000 direct-labor hours = $22.68 per direct-labor hour

A product that takes 4 machine-hours in molding and 2 direct-labor hours in finishing would have a cost of

$$(4 \times \$6.11) + (2 \times \$22.68) = \$24.44 + \$45.36 = \$69.80$$

ACTIVITY-BASED COSTING (ABC)

In the past, most departments used direct-labor hours as the only cost driver for applying costs to products. But the use of direct-labor hours is not a very good measure of the cause of costs in modern, highly automated departments. Labor-related costs in an automated system may be only 5% to 10% of the total manufacturing costs and often are not related to the causes of most manufacturing overhead costs. Therefore many companies are implementing *activity-based costing* to develop measures that better reflect the consumption of resources and related costs in their environment.

Principles of Activity-Based Costing

Many managers in modern manufacturing firms and automated service companies believe it is inappropriate to allocate all costs based on measures of volume. Using direct-labor hours or cost—or even machine-hours—as the only cost driver seldom meets the cause-effect criterion desired in cost allocation. If many costs are caused by non-volume-based cost drivers, activity-based costing (ABC) should be considered. Recall from Chapter 4 that activity-based costing is a system that first accumulates the costs of each activity of an organization and then applies the costs of activities to the products, services, or other cost objects using appropriate cost drivers.

The goal of activity-based costing is to trace costs to products or services instead of arbitrarily allocating them. Direct materials and direct labor are directly traced to products because there is a physical measure of their consumption by a particular product. In activity-based costing, by using appropriate cost drivers, many manufacturing overhead costs can be accurately traced to products or services. For example, in traditional systems, engineering design costs are often part of an overhead cost pool that is allocated based on direct-labor hours. In many activity-based costing systems, such costs are assigned to products in proportion to the engineering design services received by the products.

To apply activity-based costing, an organization must first engage in *activity analysis* (see Chapter 3). Managers identify the major activities undertaken by each department as well as the resources consumed and select a cost driver for each activity. The cost driver should be a quantifiable measure of what causes resources to be used. In essence, the costs of the resources used to support a particular activity become a cost pool, and the cost driver is used to allocate the costs to products or services.

Most cost drivers are measures of the number of transactions involved in a particular activity. Therefore, activity-based costing is also called **transaction-based costing**. Examples of transactions that serve as cost drivers are production orders, material requisitions, machine setups, product inspections, material shipments received, and orders shipped. Low-volume products usually cause more transactions per unit of output than do high-volume products. Highly complex manufacturing processes have more transactions than do simple processes. If resources are used as a result of the number of transactions, allocations based totally on volume will assign too much cost to high-volume, low-complexity products and vice versa.

In activity-based costing systems, costs are not classified as either direct or indirect. They can fall at any point on a spectrum between a direct physical tracing and arbitrary allocation. Sophisticated and costly systems identify many activities, resources, and cost drivers so that most costs can be physically traced to products or services. Because of cost-benefit considerations, other activity-based costing systems have fewer activities, resources, and cost drivers. Such systems physically trace more costs to products than do traditional systems, but many costs continue to be allocated based on cost drivers that are only partly related to the consumption of resources.

Why are activity-based costing systems becoming popular? For two main reasons.[3] First, the profitability of products and customers is more accurately measured by an activity-based costing system. As global competition increases, product mix, pricing, and other decisions require better product cost information.

In addition, many managers have discovered that control of costs is best accomplished by focusing directly on efficient use of activities, not by focusing on products. For example, savings might be possible in the material-handling activity. This opportunity is seen most readily from activity-based costs, and incentives for improvement are more effective if the costs of the activity are being specifically measured and reported. Identifying cost drivers also reveals the possible cost reductions from limiting the number of transactions. For instance, if some costs are driven by the number of components in a final product, costs can be reduced by designing products with fewer components.

Notice that the main advantages of an activity-based costing system come from its use for planning and control.

Illustration of Activity-Based Costing

Chapter 4 introduced a four-step procedure for the design and implementation of activity-based-costing systems. We consider this same four-step procedure for the Molding Department of a manufacturing company that produces plastic parts using injection molding machines. The molding process produces three

transaction-based costing Activity-based costing.

---

[3] See Chapter 4, page 142, for a more detailed list of reasons why more and more organizations are adopting activity-based costing systems.

product lines with diverse demands on various activities and resources. Product line A consists of simple products that are produced in high volume (tape holders). Line B products are of medium volume and complexity (flashlight casings). Product line C consists of complex products that are produced in small lots (small camera casings). The former costing system allocated factory overhead costs based on the amount of direct-labor hours used to produce each product. The rate used to allocate factory overhead was $27 per direct-labor hour. This rate was calculated by dividing the total expected factory overhead ($1,080,000) by the total expected direct-labor hours (40,000). Product line C was allocated $6 \div 40 = 15\%$ of total overhead resource costs since 6,000 of the 40,000 total direct-labor hours were required to produce 150,000 units of C. The use of this volume-based driver to allocate factory overhead (indirect) cost resulted in the unit cost for the three product lines shown in Exhibit 13-5.

Exhibit 13-5		Product Line A	Product Line B	Product Line C
Product Cost Based on Former Costing System	Direct material	$1,050,000	$ 575,000	$240,000
	Direct labor (operators)	344,000	303,000	123,000
	Factory overhead @ $27 per DLH			
	Product line A (18,000 DLH)	486,000		
	Product line B (16,000 DLH)		432,000	
	Product line C (6,000 DLH)			162,000
	Total cost	$1,880,000	$1,310,000	$525,000
	Units produced	1,000,000	500,000	150,000
	Unit cost	$ 1.88	$ 2.62	$ 3.50

Management changed to activity-based costing in this manufacturing department. Product line C is typical of complex products that require relatively more indirect resources from setup and machining activity. Management believed that the former costing system may have undercosted such products. A study was performed to determine the activity-based costs for the three product lines.

Step 1: Determine the cost objective, key activity centers, resources, and related cost drivers. The costing objective is to determine the costs of product lines A, B, and C. Direct material and direct labor (machine operators) are traced directly to each product. The remaining overhead resources are listed in Exhibit 13-6 together with the two activity centers and chosen cost drivers.

Step 2: Develop a process-based map representing the flow of activities, resources, and their interrelationships. Based on interviews with key personnel, the interrelationships between activities and resources were determined. Exhibit 13-7 depicts the flow of activities and resources. Note that the cost behavior for each resource is also shown. Understanding the cost behavior of resources is vital during the planning process. For example, if the volume of product line A is expected to increase (within the relevant range of activity), machine-hours and the number of setups would increase. However, the only costs that would be expected to increase are direct materials, supplies, and energy since they are variable-cost resources (*VR*). Since the remaining resources are fixed-cost resources (*FR*), their costs would not increase in response to increased setups or machine hours.

	Activity Center	Cost Driver	Resources Consumed
Exhibit 13-6	Setup	Number of setups	Maintenance mechanic time
Activity Centers, Cost Drivers, and Resources Molding Department			Supervisor time
			Energy (machines had to remain on during setup activity)
			Occupancy space
			Molding machine time
	Molding process	Machine hours	Supplies
			Energy
			Supervisor time
			Molding machine time
			Occupancy space
			Maintenance mechanic time

Exhibit 13-7

Process-Based Map of the Molding Department Operations

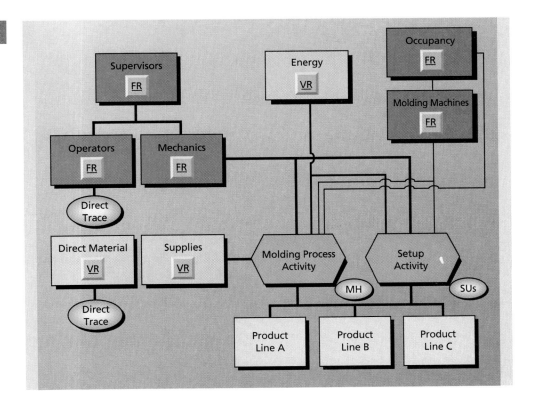

Step 3: Collect relevant data concerning costs and the physical flow of cost-driver units among resources and activities. Using the process map as a guide, accountants collected the required cost and operational data by further interviews with relevant personnel.

Exhibit 13-8 is a graphical representation and summary of the data collected for the two activity centers identified in Step 1. For each activity center, data collected included traceable overhead costs and the physical flow of cost-driver units.

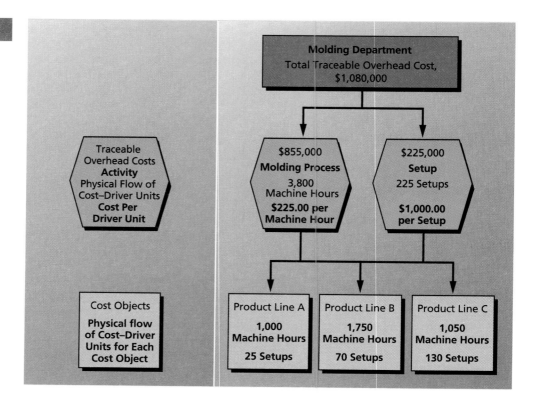

Step 4: Calculate and interpret the new activity-based information. Exhibit 13-9 shows the computations to determine the cost per unit for each product line. The results of the study confirmed management's belief—product line C was being under-costed by ($4.86 − $3.50) ÷ $3.50, or 39%. Exhibit 13-10 compares the allocation of factory overhead using the former costing system with the activity-based-costing system. Product line A's allocation of overhead decreased from 45% to 23.1% while product line C's allocation increased from 15% to 33.9%. Notice that the use of just two additional cost drivers (machine-hours and setups) can make a significant difference in product costing. Many companies use more than 20 different cost drivers to improve the accuracy of their costing system, but the costs associated with using many activity centers can be high. The benefit-cost criteria must be applied in each case.

Effect of Activity-Based Costing

Many companies have adopted activity-based costing in recent years. For example, consider Schrader Bellows, which increased the number of cost drivers used to allocate costs to products. Several of the new cost drivers are essentially measures of the number of transactions rather than measures of volume. The

Exhibit 13-9   Key Results of Activity-Based-Costing Study

Activity/Resource (Driver Units)	Traceable Costs (1)	Total Physical Flow of Driver Units (2)	Cost per Driver Unit (1)÷(2)
Setup [number of setups]	$225,000	225 Setups	$1,000
Molding process [machine-hours]	$855,000	3,800 Machine Hours	$ 225

		Product Line A		Product Line B		Product Line C	
	Cost per Driver Unit	Physical Flow of Driver Units	Cost	Physical Flow of Driver Units	Cost	Physical Flow of Driver Units	Cost
Direct material			$1,050,000		$ 575,000		$240,000
Direct labor			344,000		303,000		123,000
Setup costs	$1,000	25	25,000	70	70,000	130	130,000
Molding process	$ 225	1,000	225,000	1,750	393,750	1,050	236,250
Total			$1,644,000		$1,341,750		$729,250
Units produced			1,000,000		500,000		150,000
Cost per unit			$ 1.64		$ 2.68		$ 4.86

Exhibit 13-10

Comparison of Costing Systems

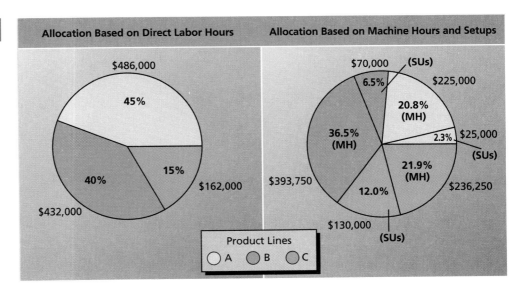

Allocation Based on Direct Labor Hours

$486,000 45%
15% $162,000
40% $432,000

Allocation Based on Machine Hours and Setups

$70,000 (SUs)
6.5% $225,000
20.8% (MH)
36.5% (MH) 2.3% $25,000 (SUs)
21.9% (MH) $236,250
$393,750 12.0%
$130,000 (SUs)

Product Lines
○ A ○ B ○ C

cost driver having the largest effects on unit costs is *number of machine setups*. The resulting changes in unit costs for the company's seven products were dramatic, as shown in Exhibit 13-11. Except for product 7, the products with low volume and a high number of setups per unit had large increases in unit costs. The products with high volume and fewer setups per unit had decreases in unit costs. Although product 7 had low volume, its unit cost dropped because it was assembled from components used in large volumes in other products. The unit cost of the components decreased because of their high volume and relatively few setups.

Activity-Based Costing at Hewlett-Packard

The Roseville Network Division (RND) of Hewlett-Packard was one of the first groups to use activity-based costing. The producer of computer-networking devices referred to its system as "cost-driver accounting." Because RND's products were increasing in number and decreasing in length of product life, the design of new products and their production processes was especially important to the division's success. But the old accounting system did not produce information helpful in comparing the production costs of different designs.

RND's new system focused on the costs of each production process—essentially, the different activities of the division. The system evolved from one with only two cost drivers—direct-labor hours and number of insertions—to one with the following nine cost drivers:

1. Number of axial insertions

2. Number of radial insertions

3. Number of DIP insertions

4. Number of manual insertions

5. Number of test hours

6. Number of solder joints

7. Number of boards

8. Number of parts

9. Number of slots

The increase in the number of cost drivers came about as accountants and managers developed a better understanding of the economics of the design and production process. By knowing the costs of the various activities, product designers could develop designs that would minimize costs for a given level of functionality and reliability.

Recognizing the average product life cycle of 24 months, RND built its cost system around its strategy to keep product lines as up-to-date as possible. RND also recognized a trade-off between accuracy and complexity. The initial two-cost-driver system was simple, but not accurate enough. But with the current nine cost drivers, concern grows that adding more cost drivers may make the system too complex—that is, make its costs greater than its benefits.

Engineering managers at RND were pleased with the activity-based-costing system. It greatly influenced the design of new products. For example, once it became clear that manual insertion was three times as expensive as automatic insertion, designs could be modified to include more automatic insertions. The system clearly had the desired effect of influencing the behavior of product designers. ■

Source: Adapted from R. Cooper and P. B. B. Turney, "Internally Forced Activity-Based Cost Systems," in R. S. Kaplan, ed., Measures for Manufacturing Excellence. *Boston, MA: Harvard Business School Press, 1990.*

Exhibit 13-11			Unit Cost		
	Product	**Sales Volume**	*Old System*	*Activity-based System*	**Percent Change**
Schrader Bellows* Costs Before and After Activity-Based Costing System	1	43,562 units	$ 7.85	$ 7.17	(8.7)
	2	500	8.74	15.45	76.8
	3	53	12.15	82.49	578.9
	4	2,079	13.63	24.51	79.8
	5	5,670	12.40	19.99	61.2
	6	11,169	8.04	7.96	(1.0)
	7	423	8.47	6.93	(18.2)

* This example is from "How Cost Accounting Systematically Distorts Product Costs" by R. Cooper and R. Kaplan, in *Accounting and Management: Field Study Perspectives* by W. Bruns, Jr., and R. Kaplan (Boston, MA: Harvard Business School Press, 1987), pp. 204–28.

■ ALLOCATION OF JOINT COSTS AND BY-PRODUCT COSTS

Joint costs and by-product costs create especially difficult cost-allocation problems. By definition, such costs relate to more than one product and cannot be separately identified with an individual product.

Joint Costs

So far we have assumed that cost drivers could be identified with an individual product. For example, if costs are being allocated to products or services on the basis of machine-hours, we have assumed that each machine-hour is used on a single final product or service. However, sometimes inputs are added to the production process before individual products are separately identifiable (i.e., before the *split-off point*). Recall from Chapter 6, page 222, that such costs are called *joint costs*. Joint costs include all inputs of material, labor, and overhead costs that are incurred before the split-off point.

Suppose a department has more than one product and some costs are joint costs. How should such joint costs be allocated to the products? As noted in Chapter 6, allocation of joint costs should not affect decisions about the individual products. Nevertheless, joint product costs are routinely allocated to products for purposes of *inventory valuation* and *income determination*.

Consider the example of joint product costs that we used in Chapter 6. A department in Dow Chemical Company produces two chemicals, X and Y. The joint cost is $100,000, and production is 1,000,000 liters of X and 500,000 liters of Y. X can be sold for $.09 per liter and Y for $.06 per liter. Ordinarily, some part of the $100,000 joint cost will be allocated to the inventory of X and the rest to the inventory of Y. Such allocations are useful for inventory purposes only. As explained in Chapter 6, joint cost allocations should be ignored for decisions such as selling a joint product or processing it further.

Two conventional ways of allocating joint costs to products are widely used: *physical units* and *relative sales values*. If physical units were used, the joint costs would be allocated as follows:

	Liters	Weighting	Allocation of Joint Costs	Sales Value at Split-Off
X	1,000,000	10/15 × $100,000	$ 66,667	$ 90,000
Y	500,000	5/15 × $100,000	33,333	30,000
	1,500,000		$100,000	$120,000

This approach shows that the $33,333 joint cost of producing Y exceeds its $30,000 sales value at split-off, seemingly indicating that Y should not be produced. However, such an allocation is not helpful in making production decisions. Neither of the two products could be produced separately.

A decision to produce Y must be a decision to produce X *and* Y. Because total revenue of $120,000 exceeds the total joint cost of $100,000, both will be produced. The allocation was not useful for this decision.

The physical-units method requires a common physical unit for measuring the output of each product. For example, board feet is a common unit for a variety of products in the lumber industry. However, sometimes such a common denominator is lacking. Consider the production of meat and hides from butchering a steer. You might use pounds as a common denominator, but pounds is not a good measure of the output of hides. As an alternative, many companies use the *relative-sales-value method* for allocating joint costs. The following allocation results from applying the relative-sales-value method to the Dow Chemical department:

	Relative Sales Value at Split-Off	Weighting	Allocation of Joint Costs
X	$ 90,000	90/120 × $100,000	$ 75,000
Y	30,000	30/120 × $100,000	25,000
	$120,000		$100,000

The weighting is based on the sales values of the individual products. Because the sales value of X at split-off is $90,000 and total sales value at split-off is $120,000, X is allocated 90/120 of the joint cost.

Now each product would be assigned a joint cost portion that is less than its sales value at split-off. Note how the allocation of a cost to a particular product such as Y depends not only on the sales value of Y but also on the sales value of X. For example, suppose you were the product manager for Y. You planned to sell your 500,000 liters for $30,000, achieving a profit of $30,000 − $25,000 = $5,000. Everything went as expected except that the price of X fell to $.07 per liter for revenue of $70,000 rather than $90,000. Instead of 30/120 of the joint cost, Y received 30/100 × $100,000 = $30,000 and had a profit of $0. Despite the fact that Y operations were exactly as planned, the cost-allocation method caused the profit on Y to be $5,000 below plan.

The relative-sales-value method can also be used when one or more of the joint products cannot be sold at the split-off point. To apply the method, we approximate the sales value at split-off as follows:

$$\text{Sales value at split-off} = \text{Final sales value} - \text{Separable costs}$$

For example, suppose the 500,000 liters of Y requires $20,000 of processing beyond the split-off point, after which it can be sold for $.10 per liter. The sales value at split-off would be ($.10 × 500,000) − $20,000 = $50,000 − $20,000 = $30,000.

By-Product Costs

by-product A product that, like a joint product, is not individually identifiable until manufacturing reaches a split-off point, but has relatively insignificant total sales value.

By-products are similar to joint products. A **by-product** is a product that, like a joint product, is not individually identifiable until manufacturing reaches a split-off point. By-products differ from joint products because they have relatively insignificant total sales values in comparison with the other products emerging at split-off. In contrast, joint products have relatively significant total sales values at split-off in comparison with the other jointly produced items. Examples of by-products are glycerine from soap making and mill ends of cloth and carpets.

If an item is accounted for as a by-product, only separable costs are allocated to it. All joint costs are allocated to the main products. Any revenues from by-products, less their separable costs, are deducted from the cost of the main products.

Consider a lumber company that sells sawdust generated in the production of lumber to companies making particle board. Suppose the company regards the sawdust as a by-product. In 19X6 sales of sawdust totaled $30,000, and the cost of loading and shipping the sawdust (that is, costs incurred beyond the split-off point) was $20,000. The inventory cost of the sawdust would consist of only the $20,000 separable cost. None of the joint cost of producing lumber and sawdust would be allocated to the sawdust. The difference between the revenue and separable cost, $30,000 – $20,000 = $10,000, would be deducted from the cost of the lumber produced.

Highlights to Remember

Costs are allocated for four major purposes: (1) prediction of economic effects of decisions, (2) motivation, (3) income and asset measurement, and (4) pricing.

Costs to be allocated are assigned to cost pools, preferably keeping variable costs and fixed costs in separate pools. Fixed costs of service departments should be allocated by using predetermined monthly lump sums for providing a basic capacity to serve. Variable costs should be allocated by using a predetermined standard unit rate for the services actually used. Often it is best to allocate only those central costs of an organization for which measures of usage by departments are available. Service department costs can be allocated using either the direct method or the step-down method.

Activity-based costing is growing in popularity. It first assigns costs to the activities of an organization. Then costs are allocated to products or services based on cost drivers that measure the causes of the costs of a particular activity.

Joint costs are often allocated to products for inventory valuation and income determination using the physical-units or relative-sales-value method. However, such allocations should not affect decisions.

Summary Problem for Your Review

Problem

Nonmanufacturing organizations often find it useful to allocate costs to final products or services. Consider a hospital. The output of a hospital is not as easy to define as the output of a factory. Assume the following measures of output in three revenue-producing departments:

Department	Measures of Output*
Radiology	X-ray films processed
Laboratory	Tests administered
Daily Patient Services†	Patient-days of care (i.e., the number of patients multiplied by the number of days of each patient's stay)

* These become the "product" cost objectives, the various revenue-producing activities of a hospital.
† There would be many of these departments, such as obstetrics, pediatrics, and orthopedics. Moreover, there may be both inpatient and outpatient care.

Budgeted output for 19X7 is 60,000 x-ray films processed in Radiology, 50,000 tests administered in the Laboratory, and 30,000 patient-days in Daily Patient Services.

In addition to the revenue-producing departments, the hospital has three service departments: Administrative and Fiscal Services, Plant Operations and Maintenance, and Laundry. (Of course, real hospitals have more than three revenue-producing departments and more than three service departments. This problem is simplified to keep the data manageable.)

The hospital has decided that the cost driver for Administrative and Fiscal Services costs is the direct department costs of the other departments. The cost driver for Plant Operations and Maintenance is square feet occupied, and for Laundry is pounds of laundry. The pertinent budget data for 19X7 are:

	Direct Department Costs	Square Feet Occupied	Pounds of Laundry
Administrative and Fiscal Services	$1,000,000	1,000	—
Plant Operations and Maintenance	800,000	2,000	—
Laundry	200,000	5,000	—
Radiology	1,000,000	12,000	80,000
Laboratory	400,000	3,000	20,000
Daily Patient Services	1,600,000	80,000	300,000
Total	$5,000,000	103,000	400,000

Required

1. Allocate service department costs using the direct method.
2. Allocate service department costs using the step-down method. Allocate Administrative and Fiscal Services first, Plant Operations and Maintenance second, and Laundry third.
3. Compute the cost per unit of output in each of the revenue-producing departments using (a) the costs determined using the direct method for allocating service department costs (requirement 1) and (b) the costs determined using the step-down method for allocating service department costs (requirement 2).

Solution

1. The solutions to all three requirements are shown in Exhibit 13-12. The direct method is presented first. Note that no service department costs are allocated to another service department. Therefore allocations are based on the relative amounts of the cost driver in the revenue-producing department only. For example, in allocating Plant Operations and Maintenance, square footage occupied by the service departments is ignored. The cost driver is the 95,000 square feet occupied by the revenue-producing departments.

Exhibit 13-12   Allocation of Service Department Costs: Two Methods

	Administrative and Fiscal Services	Plant Operations and Maintenance	Laundry	Radiology	Laboratory	Daily Patient Services
Accumulated Base	*Accumulated Costs*	*Sq. Footage*	*Pounds*			
1. Direct Method						
Direct departmental costs before allocation	$1,000,000	$ 800,000	$ 200,000	$1,000,000	$400,000	$1,600,000
Administrative and Fiscal Services	(1,000,000)	—	—	333,333*	133,333	533,334
Plant Operations and Maintenance		(800,000)	—	101,053†	25,263	673,684
Laundry			(200,000)	40,000‡	10,000	150,000
Total costs after allocation				$1,474,386	$568,596	$2,957,018
Product output in films, tests, and patient-days, respectively				60,000	50,000	30,000
3a. Cost per unit of output				$24.573	$11.372	$98.567
2. Step-down Method						
Direct departmental costs before allocation	$1,000,000	$ 800,000	$ 200,000	$1,000,000	$400,000	$1,600,000
Administrative and Fiscal Services	(1,000,000)	200,000§	50,000	250,000	100,000	400,000
Plant Operations and Maintenance		(1,000,000)	50,000¶	120,000	30,000	800,000
Laundry			(300,000)	60,000#	15,000	225,000
Total costs after allocation				$1,430,000	$545,000	$3,025,000
Product output in films, tests, and patient-days, respectively				60,000	50,000	30,000
3b. Cost per unit of output				$23.833	$10.900	$100.833

* $1,000,000 ÷ ($1,000,000 + $400,000 + $1,600,000) = 33⅓%; 33⅓% × $1,000,000 = $333,333; etc.

† $800,000 ÷ (12,000 + 3,000 + 80,000) = $8.4210526; $8.4210526 × 12,000 sq. ft. = $101,053; etc.

‡ $200,000 ÷ (80,000 + 20,000 + 300,000) = $.50; $.50 × 80,000 = $40,000; etc.

§ $1,000,000 ÷ ($800,000 + $200,000 + $1,000,000 + $400,000 + $1,600,000) = 25%; 25% × $800,000 = $200,000; etc.

¶ $1,000,000 ÷ (5,000 + 12,000 + 3,000 + 80,000) = $10.00; $10.00 × 5,000 sq. ft. = $50,000; etc.

$300,000 ÷ (80,000 + 20,000 + 300,000) = $.75; $.75 × 80,000 = $60,000; etc.

513

Note that the total cost of the revenue-producing departments after allocation, $1,474,386 + $568,596 + $2,957,018 = $5,000,000, is equal to the total of the direct department costs in all six departments before allocation.

2. The step-down method is shown in the lower half of Exhibit 13-12. The costs of Administrative and Fiscal Services are allocated to all five other departments. Because a department's own costs are not allocated to itself, the cost driver consists of the $4,000,000 direct department costs in the five departments excluding Administrative and Fiscal Services.

Plant Operations and Maintenance is allocated second on the basis of square feet occupied. No cost will be allocated to itself or back to Administrative and Fiscal Services. Therefore the square footage used for allocation is the 100,000 square feet occupied by the other four departments.

Laundry is allocated third. No cost would be allocated back to the first two departments, even if they had used laundry services.

As in the direct method, note that the total costs of the revenue-producing departments after allocation, $1,430,000 + $545,000 + $3,025,000 = $5,000,000, equals the total of the direct department costs before allocation.

3. The solutions are labeled 3a and 3b in Exhibit 13-12. Compare the unit costs derived from the direct method with those of the step-down method. In many instances, the final product costs may not differ enough to warrant investing in a cost-allocation method that is any fancier than the direct method. But sometimes even small differences may be significant to a government agency or anybody paying for a large volume of services based on costs. For example, in Exhibit 13-12 the "cost" of an "average" laboratory test is either $11.37 or $10.90. This may be significant for the fiscal committee of the hospital's board of trustees, who must decide on hospital prices. Thus cost allocation often is a technique that helps answer the vital question, "Who should pay for what, and how much?"

Accounting Vocabulary

by-product, *p. 510*
cost accounting systems, *p. 489*
cost-allocation base, *p. 490*

cost application, *p. 501*
cost pool, *p. 490*
direct method, *p.498*

service departments, *p. 491*
step-down method, *p. 498*
transaction-based costing, *p. 503*

Fundamental Assignment Material

13-A1   Allocation of Central Costs

The Central Railroad allocates all central corporate overhead costs to its divisions. Some costs, such as specified internal auditing and legal costs, are identified on the basis of time spent. However, other costs are harder to allocate, so the revenue achieved by each division is used as an allocation base. Examples of such costs were executive salaries, travel, secretarial, utilities, rent, depreciation, donations, corporate planning, and general marketing costs.

Allocations on the basis of revenue for 19X5 were (in millions):

Division	Revenue	Allocated Costs
Northern	$120	$ 6
Mesa	240	12
Plains	240	12
Total	$600	$30

In 19X6, Northern's revenue remained unchanged. However, Plains' revenue soared to $280 million because of unusually bountiful crops. The latter are troublesome to forecast because unpredictable weather has a pronounced influence on volume. Mesa had expected a sharp rise in revenue, but severe competitive conditions resulted in a decline to $200 million. The total cost allocated on the basis of revenue was again $30 million, despite rises in other costs. The president was pleased that central costs did not rise for the year.

Required

1. Compute the allocations of costs to each division for 19X6.
2. How would each division manager probably feel about the cost allocation in 19X6 as compared with 19X5? What are the weaknesses of using revenue as a basis for cost allocation?
3. Suppose the budgeted revenues for 19X6 were $120, $240, and $280, respectively, and the budgeted revenues were used as a cost driver for allocation. Compute the allocations of costs to each division for 19X6. Do you prefer this method to the one used in requirement 1? Why?
4. Many accountants and managers oppose allocating any central costs. Why?

13-A2 Direct and Step-Down Methods of Allocation

Pinney Tool and Die has three service departments:

	Budgeted Department Costs
Cafeteria, revenue of $100,000 less expenses of 250,000	$ 150,000
Engineering	2,500,000
General factory administration	950,000

Cost drivers are budgeted as follows:

Production Departments	Employees	Engineering Hours Worked for Production Departments	Total Labor Hours
Machining	100	50,000	250,000
Assembly	450	20,000	600,000
Finishing and painting	50	10,000	100,000

Required

1. All service department costs are allocated directly to the production departments without allocation to other service departments. Show how much of the budgeted costs of each service department are allocated to each production department. To plan your work, examine requirement 2 before undertaking this question.
2. The company has decided to use the step-down method of cost allocation. General factory administration would be allocated first, then cafeteria, then engineering. Cafeteria employees worked 30,000 labor hours per year. There were 50 engineering employees with 100,000 total labor hours. Recompute the results in requirement 1, using the step-down method. Show your computations. Compare the results in requirements 1 and 2. Which method of allocation do you favor? Why?

13-A3   Activity-Based Costing

Chen Company makes printed circuit boards in a suburb of Tokyo. The production process is automated with computer-controlled robotic machines assembling each circuit board from a supply of parts. Chen has identified four activities:

Activity	Cost Driver	Rate
Materials handling	Cost of direct materials	5% of materials cost
Assembly	Number of parts used	¥50 per part
Soldering	Number of circuit boards	¥1,500 per board
Quality assurance	Minutes of testing	¥350 per minute

Chen makes three types of circuit boards, models A, B, and C. Requirements for production of each circuit board are:

	Model A	Model B	Model C
Direct materials cost	¥4,000	¥6,000	¥8,000
Number of parts used	60	40	20
Minutes of testing	5	3	2

Required

1. Compute the cost of production of 100 of the three types of circuit boards and the cost per circuit board for each type.
2. Suppose the design of model A could be simplified so that it required only 30 parts (instead of 60) and took only 3 minutes of testing time (instead of 5). Compute the cost of 100 model A circuit boards and the cost per circuit board.

13-A4   Joint Products

Benjamin Metals, Inc., buys raw ore on the open market and processes it into two final products, A and B. The ore costs $12 per pound, and the process separating it into A and B has a cost of $4 per pound. During 19X6 Benjamin plans to produce 200,000 pounds of A and 600,000 pounds of B from 800,000 pounds of ore. A sells for $30 a pound and B for $15 a pound. The company allocated joint costs to the individual products for inventory valuation purposes.

Required

1. Allocate all the joint costs to A and B using the physical-units method.
2. Allocate all the joint costs to A and B using the relative-sales-value method.
3. Suppose B *cannot be sold* in the form in which it emerges from the joint process. Instead, it must be processed further at a fixed cost of $300,000 plus a variable cost of $1 per pound. Then it can be sold for $21.50 a pound. Allocate all the joint costs to A and B using the relative-sales-value method.

13-B1   Allocation of Computer Costs

Review the section "Allocation of Service Department Costs," pages 492–501, especially the example of the use of the computer by the university. Recall that the budget formula was $100,000 fixed cost monthly plus $200 per hour of computer time used. Based on long-run predicted usage, the fixed costs were allocated on a lump-sum basis, 30% to Business and 70% to Engineering.

Required

1. Show the total allocation if Business used 210 hours and Engineering used 390 hours in a given month. Assume that the actual costs coincided exactly with the budgeted amount for total usage of 700 hours.
2. Assume the same facts as in requirement 1 except that the fixed costs were allocated on the basis of actual hours of usage. Show the total allocation of costs to each school. As the dean of Business, would you prefer this method or the method in requirement 1? Explain.

13-B2   Allocation of Service Department Costs

Chief Cleaning, Inc. provides cleaning services for a variety of clients. The company has two producing divisions, Residential and Commercial, and two service departments, Personnel and Administrative. The company has decided to allocate all service department costs to the producing departments—Personnel on the basis of number of employees, and Administrative on the basis of direct department costs. The budget for 19X6 shows:

	Personnel	Administrative	Residential	Commercial
Direct department costs	$70,000	$90,000	$240,000	$400,000
Number of employees	6	10	24	36
Direct-labor hours			30,000	45,000
Square feet cleaned			4,500,000	9,970,000

Required

1. Allocate service department costs using the direct method.
2. Allocate service department costs using the step-down method. The Personnel Department costs should be allocated first.
3. Suppose the company prices by the hour in the Residential Department and by the square foot cleaned in Commercial. Using the results of the step-down allocations in requirement 2:
   a. Compute the cost of providing one direct-labor hour of service in the Residential Department.
   b. Compute the cost of cleaning one square foot of space in the Commercial Department.

13-B3   Activity-Based Costing

The Cunningham Novelty company makes a variety of souvenirs for visitors to New Zealand. The Beebee Division manufactures stuffed kiwi birds using a highly automated operation. A recently installed activity-based-costing system has four activity centers.

Activity Center	Cost Driver	Cost per Driver Unit
Materials receiving and handling	Kilograms of materials	$1.20 per kg
Production setup	Number of setups	$50 per setup
Cutting, sewing, and assembly	Number of units	$.40 per unit
Packing and shipping	Number of orders	$10 per order

Two products are called "standard kiwi" and "giant kiwi." They require .20 and .40 kg of materials, respectively, at a materials cost of $1.30 for standard kiwis and $2.20 for giant kiwis. One computer-controlled assembly line makes all products. When a production run of a different product is started, a setup procedure is required to reprogram the computers and make other changes in the process. Normally, 500 standard kiwis are produced per setup, but only 200 giant kiwis. Products are packed and shipped separately, so a request from a customer for, say, three different products is considered three different orders.

Ausiland Waterfront Market just placed an order for 100 standard kiwis and 50 giant kiwis.

Required

1. Compute the cost of the products shipped to Ausiland Waterfront Market.
2. Suppose the products made for Ausiland Waterfront Market required "AWM" to be printed on each kiwi. Because of the automated process, printing the initials takes no extra time or materials, but it requires a special production setup for each product. Compute the cost of the products shipped to the Ausiland Waterfront Market.
3. Explain how the activity-based-costing system helps Cunningham Novelty to

measure costs of individual products or orders better than a traditional system that allocates all non-materials costs based on direct labor.

13-B4   Joint Products

Manhattan Milling buys oats at $.50 per pound and produces MM Oat Flour, MM Oat Flakes, and MM Oat Bran. The process of separating the oats into oat flour and oat bran costs $.30 per pound. The oat flour can be sold for $1.50 per pound, the oat bran for $2.00 per pound. Each pound of oats has .2 pounds of oat bran and .8 pounds of oat flour. A pound of oat flour can be made into oat flakes for a fixed cost of $240,000 plus a variable cost of $.50 per pound. Manhattan Milling plans to process 1 million pounds of oats in 19X6, at a purchase price of $500,000.

Required

1. Allocate all the joint costs to oat flour and oat bran using the physical-units method.
2. Allocate all the joint costs to oat flour and oat bran using the relative-sales-value method.
3. Suppose there were no market for oat flour. Instead, it must be made into oat flakes to be sold. Oat flakes sell for $2.80 per pound. Allocate the joint cost to oat bran and oat flakes using the relative-sales-value method.

Additional Assignment Material

Questions

13-1. "A cost pool is a group of costs that is physically traced to the appropriate cost objective." Do you agree? Explain.

13-2. Give five terms that are sometimes used as substitutes for the term *allocate*.

13-3. What are the four purposes of cost allocation?

13-4. What are the three types of allocations?

13-5. Give three guides for the allocation of service department costs.

13-6. "Allocation is based on cause-effect." Explain.

13-7. Why should budgeted cost rates, rather than actual cost rates, be used for allocating the variable costs of service departments?

13-8. Why do many companies allocate fixed costs separately from variable costs?

13-9. "We used a lump-sum allocation method for fixed costs a few years ago, but we gave it up because managers always predicted usage below what they actually used." Is this a common problem? How might it be prevented?

13-10. "A commonly misused basis for allocation is dollar sales." Explain.

13-11. How should national advertising costs be allocated to territories?

13-12. Briefly describe the two popular methods for allocating service department costs.

13-13. "The step-down method allocates more costs to the producing departments than does the direct method." Do you agree? Explain.

13-14. How does the term *cost application* differ from *cost allocation*?

13-15. Many companies that previously applied costs to final products based on direct-labor hours have changed to another cost driver, such as machine hours. Why?

13-16. Why is activity-based costing also called transaction-based costing?

13-17. "Activity-based costing is useful for product costing, but not for planning and control." Do you agree? Explain.

13-18. Give five examples of transactions that can be used as cost drivers for transaction-based allocations.

13-19. Chapter 6 explained that joint costs should not be allocated to individual products for decision purposes. For what purposes are such costs allocated to products?

13-20. Briefly explain each of the two conventional ways of allocating joint costs of products.

13-21. What are by-products and how do we account for them?

Exercises

13-22   Fixed- and Variable-Cost Pools

The city of Cedarwood signed a lease for a photocopy machine at $2,000 per month and $.02 per copy. Operating costs for toner, paper, operator salary, and so on are all variable at $.03 per copy. Departments had projected a need for 50,000 copies a month. The Public Works Department predicted its usage at 18,000 copies a month. It made 21,000 copies in August.

Required

1. Suppose one predetermined rate per copy was used to allocate all photocopy costs. What rate would be used and how much cost would be allocated to the Public Works Department in August?
2. Suppose fixed- and variable-cost pools were allocated separately. Specify how each pool should be allocated. Compute the cost allocated to the Public Works Department in August.
3. Which method, the one in requirement 1 or the one in requirement 2, do you prefer? Explain.

13-23 Sales-Based Allocations

Pioneer Markets has three grocery stores in the metropolitan Topeka area. Central costs are allocated using sales as the cost driver. Following are budgeted and actual sales during November:

	Sunnyville	Wedgewood	Capitol
Budgeted sales	$600,000	$1,000,000	$400,000
Actual sales	600,000	700,000	500,000

Central costs of $180,000 are to be allocated in November.

Required

1. Compute the central costs allocated to each store with *budgeted* sales as the cost driver.
2. Compute the central costs allocated to each store with *actual* sales as the cost driver.
3. What advantages are there to using *budgeted* rather than *actual* sales for allocating the central costs?

13-24 Joint Costs

Robinson Company's production process for its two solvents can be diagrammed as follows:

The cost of the joint input, including processing costs before the split-off point, is $200,000. Solvent A can be sold at split-off for $10 per gallon and solvent B for $30 per gallon.

Required

1. Allocate the $200,000 joint cost to solvents A and B by the physical-units method.
2. Allocate the $200,000 joint cost to solvents A and B by the relative-sales-value method.

13-25 By-Product Costing

The Jones Press Company buys apples from local orchards and presses them to produce apple juice. The pulp that remains after pressing is sold to farmers as livestock food. This livestock food is accounted for as a by-product.

During the 19X5 fiscal year, the company paid $800,000 to purchase 8 million pounds of apples. After processing, 1 million pounds of pulp remained. Jones spent $30,000 to package and ship the pulp, which was sold for $50,000.

Required

1. How much of the joint cost of the apples is allocated to the pulp?

2. Compute the total inventory cost (and therefore the cost of goods sold) for the pulp.
3. Assume that $130,000 was spent to press the apples and $150,000 was spent to filter, pasteurize, and pack the apple juice. Compute the total inventory cost of the apple juice produced.

Problems

13-26   Hospital Allocation Base

Jade Soon, the administrator of Saint Jude Hospital, has become interested in obtaining more accurate cost allocations on the basis of cause and effect. The $150,000 of laundry costs had been allocated on the basis of 600,000 pounds processed for all departments, or $.25 per pound.

Soon is concerned that government health care officials will require weighted statistics to be used for cost allocation. She asks you, "Please develop a revised base for allocating laundry costs. It should be better than our present base, but not be overly complex either."

You study the situation and find that the laundry processes a large volume of uniforms for student nurses and physicians and for dietary, housekeeping, and other personnel. In particular, the coats or jackets worn by personnel in the radiology department take unusual handwork.

A special study of laundry for radiology revealed that 7,500 of the 15,000 pounds were jackets and coats that were five times as expensive to process as regular laundry items. Several reasons explained the difference, but it was principally because of handwork involved.

Assume that no special requirements were needed in departments other than radiology. Revise the cost-allocation base and compute the new cost-allocation rate. Compute the total cost charged to radiology using pounds and using the new base.

13-27   Cost of Passenger Traffic

Northern Pacific Railroad (NP) has a commuter operation that services passengers along a route between San Jose and San Francisco. Problems of cost allocation were highlighted in a news story about NP's application to the Public Utilities Commission (PUC) for a rate increase. The PUC staff claimed that the "avoidable annual cost" of running the operation was $700,000, in contrast to NP officials' claim of a loss of $9 million. PUC's estimate was based on what NP would be able to save if it shut down the commuter operation.

The NP loss estimate was based on a "full-allocation-of-costs" method, which allocates a share of common maintenance and overhead costs to the passenger service.

If the PUC accepted its own estimate, a 25% fare increase would have been justified, whereas NP sought a 96% fare increase.

The PUC stressed that commuter costs represent less than 1% of the system-wide costs of NP and that 57% of the commuter costs are derived from some type of allocation method—sharing the costs of other operations.

NP's representative stated that "avoidable cost" is not an appropriate way to allocate costs for calculating rates. He said that "it is not fair to include just so-called above-the-rail costs" because there are other real costs associated with commuter service. Examples are maintaining smoother connections and making more frequent track inspections.

Required
1. As public utilities commissioner, what approach toward cost allocation would you favor for making decisions regarding fares? Explain.
2. How would fluctuations in freight traffic affect commuter costs under the NP method?

13-28   Allocation of Automobile Costs

The motor pool of a major city provides automobiles for the use of various city departments. Currently, the motor pool has 50 autos. A recent study showed that it costs $2,400 of annual fixed cost per automobile plus $.10 per mile variable cost to own, operate, and maintain autos such as those provided by the motor pool.

Each month, the costs of the motor pool are allocated to the user departments on the basis of miles driven. On average, each auto is driven 24,000 miles annually, although wide month-to-month variations occur. In April 19X6, the 50 autos were driven a total of 50,000 miles. The motor pool's total costs for April were $19,000.

The chief planner for the city always seemed concerned about her auto costs. She was especially upset in April when she was charged $5,700 for the 15,000 miles driven in the department's five autos. This is the normal monthly mileage in the department. Her memo to the head of the motor pool stated, "I can certainly get autos at less than the $.38 per mile you charged in April." The response was, "I am under instructions to allocate the motor pool costs to the user departments. Your department was responsible for 30% of the April usage (15,000 miles ÷ 50,000 miles), so I allocated 30% of the motor pool's April costs to you (.30 × $19,000). That just seems fair."

Required

1. Calculate the city's average annual cost per mile for owning, maintaining, and operating an auto.
2. Explain why the allocated cost in April ($.38 per mile) exceeds the average in requirement 1.
3. Describe any undesirable behavioral effects of the cost-allocation method used.
4. How would you improve the cost-allocation method?

13-29   Allocation of Costs

The Vigil Transportation Company has one service department and two regional operating departments. The budgeted cost behavior pattern of the service department is $750,000 monthly in fixed costs plus $.75 per 1,000 ton-miles operated in the North and South regions. (Ton-miles are the number of tons carried times the number of miles traveled.) The actual monthly costs of the service department are allocated using ton-miles operated as the cost driver.

Required

1. Vigil processed 500 million ton-miles of traffic in April, half in each operating region. The actual costs of the service department were exactly equal to those predicted by the budget for 500 million ton-miles. Compute the costs that would be allocated to each operating region on an actual ton-miles basis.
2. Suppose the North region was plagued by strikes, so that the freight handled was much lower than originally anticipated. North moved only 150 million ton-miles of traffic. The South region handled 250 million ton-miles. The actual costs were exactly as budgeted for this lower level of activity. Compute the costs that would be allocated to North and South on an actual ton-miles basis. Note that the total costs will be lower.
3. Refer to the facts in requirement 1. Various inefficiencies caused the service department to incur total costs of $1,250,000. Compute the costs to be allocated to North and South. Are the allocations justified? If not, what improvement do you suggest?
4. Refer to the facts in requirement 2. Assume that assorted investment outlays for equipment and space in the service department were made to provide a basic maximum capacity to serve the North region at a level of 360 million ton-miles and the South region at a level of 240 million ton-miles. Suppose fixed costs are allocated on the basis of this capacity to serve. Variable costs are allocated by using a predetermined standard rate per 1,000 ton-miles. Compute the costs to be allocated to each department. What are the advantages of this method over other methods?

13-30   Hospital Equipment

Many states have a hospital commission that must approve the acquisition of specified medical equipment before the hospitals in the state can qualify for cost-based reimbursement related to that equipment. That is, hospitals cannot bill government agencies for the use of the equipment unless the commission originally authorized the acquisition.

Two hospitals in one such state proposed the acquisition and sharing of some expensive x-ray equipment to be used for unusual cases. The depreciation and related fixed costs of operating the equipment were predicted at $15,000 per month. The variable costs were predicted at $30 per patient procedure.

The commission asked each hospital to predict its usage of the equipment over its expected useful life of 5 years. Premier Hospital predicted an average usage of 75 x-rays per month; St. Mary's Hospital of 50 x-rays. The commission regarded this information as critical to the size and degree of sophistication that would be justified. That is, if the number of x-rays exceeded a certain quantity per month, a different configuration of space, equipment, and personnel would be required that would mean higher fixed costs per month.

Required

1. Suppose fixed costs are allocated on the basis of the hospitals' predicted average use per month. Variable costs are allocated on the basis of $30 per x-ray, the budgeted variable-cost rate for the current fiscal year. In October, Premier Hospital had 50 x-rays and St. Mary's Hospital had 50 x-rays. Compute the total costs allocated to Premier Hospital and to St. Mary's Hospital.

2. Suppose the manager of the equipment had various operating inefficiencies so that the total October costs were $19,500. Would you change your answers in requirement 1? Why?

3. A traditional method of cost allocation does not use the method in requirement 1. Instead, an allocation rate depends on the actual costs and actual volume encountered. The actual costs are totaled for the month and divided by the actual number of x-rays during the month. Suppose the actual costs agreed exactly with the budget for a total of 100 actual x-rays. Compute the total costs allocated to Premier Hospital and to St. Mary's Hospital. Compare the results with those in requirement 1. What is the major weakness in this traditional method? What are some of its possible behavioral effects?

4. Describe any undesirable behavioral effects of the method described in requirement 1. How would you counteract any tendencies toward deliberate false predictions of long-run usage?

13-31   Direct Method for Service Department Allocation

Sanders Instruments Company has two producing departments, Mechanical Instruments and Electronic Instruments. In addition, there are two service departments, Building Services and Materials Receiving and Handling. The company purchases a variety of component parts from which the departments assemble instruments for sale in domestic and international markets.

The Electronic Instruments division is highly automated. The manufacturing costs depend primarily on the number of subcomponents in each instrument. In contrast, the Mechanical Instruments division relies primarily on a large labor force to hand-assemble instruments. Its costs depend on direct-labor hours.

The costs of Building Services depend primarily on the square footage occupied. The costs of Materials Receiving and Handling depend primarily on the total number of components handled.

Instruments M1 and M2 are produced in the Mechanical Instruments department, and E1 and E2 are produced in the Electronic Instruments department. Data about these products follow:

	Direct-Material Cost	Number of Components	Direct-Labor Hours
M1	$74	25	4.0
M2	86	21	8.0
E1	63	10	1.5
E2	91	15	1.0

Budget figures for 19X5 include:

	Building Services	Materials Receiving and Handling	Mechanical Instruments	Electronic Instruments
Direct department costs (excluding direct materials cost)	$180,000	$120,000	$680,000	$548,000
Square footage occupied		5,000	50,000	25,000
Number of final instruments produced			8,000	10,000
Average number of components per instrument			10	16
Direct-labor hours			30,000	8,000

Required

1. Allocate the costs of the service departments using the direct method.
2. Using the results of requirement 1, compute the cost per direct-labor hour in the Mechanical Instruments Department and the cost per component in the Electronic Instruments Department.
3. Using the results of requirement 2, compute the cost per unit of product for instruments M1, M2, E1, and E2.

13-32   Step-Down Method for Service Department Allocation
Refer to the data in Problem 13-31.

Required

1. Allocate the costs of the service departments using the step-down method.
2. Using the results of requirement 1, compute the cost per direct-labor hour in the Mechanical Instruments Department and the cost per component in the Electronic Instruments Department.
3. Using the results of requirement 2, compute the cost per unit of product for instruments M1, M2, E1, and E2.

13-33   Direct and Step-Down Methods of Allocation

The Maton Company has prepared departmental overhead budgets for normal activity levels before reapportionments, as follows:

Building and grounds	$ 20,000
Personnel	1,200
General factory administration*	28,020
Cafeteria operating loss	1,430
Storeroom	2,750
Machining	35,100
Assembly	56,500
	$145,000

* To be reapportioned before cafeteria.

Management has decided that the most sensible product costs are achieved by using departmental overhead rates. These rates are developed after appropriate service department costs are allocated to production departments.

Cost drivers for allocation are to be selected from the following data:

Department	Direct-Labor Hours	Number of Employees	Square Feet of Floor Space Occupied	Total Labor Hours	Number of Requisitions
Building and grounds	—	—	—	—	—
Personnel*	—	—	2,000	—	—
General factory administration	—	35	7,000	—	—
Cafeteria operating loss	—	10	4,000	1,000	—
Storeroom	—	5	7,000	1,000	—
Machining	5,000	50	30,000	8,000	3,000
Assembly	15,000	100	50,000	17,000	1,500
	20,000	200	100,000	27,000	4,500

* Basis used is number of employees.

Required

1. Allocate service department costs by the step-down method. Develop overhead rates per direct-labor hour for machining and assembly.
2. Same as in requirement 1, using the direct method.
3. What would be the plantwide factory-overhead application rate, assuming that direct-labor hours are used as a cost driver?
4. Using the following information about two jobs, prepare three different total overhead costs for each job, using rates developed in requirements 1, 2, and 3.

	Direct-Labor Hours	
	Machining	*Assembly*
Job K10	19	2
Job K12	3	18

13-34 Joint Costs and Decisions

A petrochemical company has a batch process whereby 1,000 gallons of a raw material are transformed into 100 pounds of Z-1 and 400 pounds of Z-2. Although the joint costs of their production are $1,000, both products are worthless at their split-off point. Additional separable costs of $350 are necessary to give Z-1 a sales value of $900 as product A. Similarly, additional separable costs of $200 are necessary to give Z-2 a sales value of $900 as product B.

Required

You are in charge of the batch process and the marketing of both products. (Show your computations for each answer.)

1. **a.** Assuming that you believe in assigning joint costs on a physical basis, allocate the total profit of $250 per batch to products A and B.
   b. Would you stop processing one of the products? Why?
2. **a.** Assuming that you believe in assigning joint costs on a net-realizable-value (relative-sales-value) basis, allocate the total operating profit of $250 per batch to products A and B. If there is no market for Z-1 and Z-2 at their split-off point, a net realizable value is usually imputed by taking the ultimate sales values at the point of sale and working backward to obtain approximated "synthetic" relative sales values at the split-off point. These synthetic values are then used as weights for allocating the joint costs to the products.
   b. You have internal product-profitability reports in which joint costs are assigned on a net-realizable-value basis. Your chief engineer says that, after seeing these

reports, he has developed a method of obtaining more of product B and correspondingly less of product A from each batch, without changing the per-pound cost factors. Would you approve this new method? Why? What would the overall operating profit be if 50 pounds more of B were produced and 50 pounds less of A?

Cases

13-35 Allocation, Department Rates, and Direct-Labor Hours Versus Machine-Hours

The Tolbert Manufacturing Company has two producing departments, machining and assembly. Mr. Tolbert recently automated the machining department. The installation of a CAM system, together with robotic workstations, drastically reduced the amount of direct labor required. Meanwhile the assembly department remained labor-intensive.

The company had always used one firmwide rate based on direct-labor hours as the cost driver for applying all costs (except direct materials) to the final products. Mr. Tolbert was considering two alternatives: (1) continue using direct-labor hours as the only cost driver, but use different rates in machining and assembly, and (2) using machine-hours as the cost driver in the machining department while continuing with direct-labor hours in assembly.

Budgeted data for 19X6 are:

	Machining	Assembly	Total
Total cost (except direct materials), after allocating service department costs	$525,000	$420,000	$945,000
Machine-hours	105,000	*	105,000
Direct-labor hours	15,000	30,000	45,000

* Not applicable.

1. Suppose Tolbert continued to use one firmwide rate based on direct-labor hours to apply all manufacturing costs (except direct materials) to the final products. Compute the cost-application rate that would be used.
2. Suppose Tolbert continued to use direct-labor hours as the only cost driver but used different rates in machining and assembly:
   a. Compute the cost-application rate for machining.
   b. Compute the cost-application rate for assembly.
3. Suppose Tolbert changed the cost accounting system to use machine-hours as the cost driver in machining and direct-labor hours in assembly:
   a. Compute the cost-application rate for machining.
   b. Compute the cost-application rate for assembly.
4. Three products use the following machine-hours and direct-labor hours:

	Machine-Hours in Machining	Direct-Labor Hours in Machining	Direct-Labor Hours in Assembly
Product A	10.0	1.0	14.0
Product B	17.0	1.5	3.0
Product C	14.0	1.3	8.0

   a. Compute the manufacturing cost of each product (excluding direct materials) using one firm-wide rate based on direct-labor hours.
   b. Compute the manufacturing cost of each product (excluding direct materials) using direct-labor hours as the cost driver, but with different cost-application rates in machining and assembly.

c. Compute the manufacturing cost of each product (excluding direct materials) using a cost-application rate based on direct-labor hours in assembly and machine-hours in machining.

d. Compare and explain the results in requirements 4a, 4b, and 4c.

13-36 Multiple Allocation Bases

The Cozzetta Electronics Company produces three types of circuit boards; call them L, M, and N. The cost accounting system used by Cozzetta until 1994 applied all costs except direct materials to the products using direct-labor hours as the only cost driver. In 1994 the company undertook a cost study. The study determined that there were six main factors causing costs to be incurred. A new system was designed with a separate cost pool for each of the six factors. The factors and the costs associated with each are as follows:

1. Direct-labor hours—direct-labor cost and related fringe benefits and payroll taxes
2. Machine-hours—depreciation and repairs and maintenance costs
3. Pounds of materials—materials receiving, handling, and storage costs
4. Number of production setups—labor used to change machinery and computer configurations for a new production batch
5. Number of production orders—costs of production scheduling and order processing
6. Number of orders shipped—all packaging and shipping expenses

The company is now preparing a budget for 1996. The budget includes the following predictions:

	Board L	Board M	Board N
Units to be produced	10,000	800	5,000
Direct-material cost	£66/unit	£88/unit	£45/unit
Direct-labor hours	4/unit	18/unit	9/unit
Machine-hours	7/unit	15/unit	7/unit
Pounds of materials	3/unit	4/unit	2/unit
Number of production setups	100	50	50
Number of production orders	300	200	70
Number of orders shipped	1,000	800	2,000

The total budgeted cost for 1996 is £3,712,250, of which £955,400 was direct-materials cost, and the amount in each of the six cost pools defined above is:

Cost Pool*	Cost
1	£1,391,600
2	936,000
3	129,600
4	160,000
5	25,650
6	114,000
Total	£2,756,850

* Identified by the cost driver used.

Required

1. Prepare a budget that shows the total budgeted cost and the unit cost for each circuit board. Use the new system with six cost pools (plus a separate direct application of direct-materials cost).

2. Compute the budgeted total and unit costs of each circuit board if the old direct-labor-hour-based system had been used.
3. How would you judge whether the new system is better than the old one?

13-37 Case of Allocation of Data Processing Costs

(CMA, adapted.) The International Underwriters Insurance Co. (IUI) established a Systems Department two years ago to implement and operate its own data processing systems. IUI believed that its own system would be more cost-effective than the service bureau it had been using.

IUI's three departments—Claims, Records, and Finance—have different requirements with respect to hardware and other capacity-related resources and operating resources. The system was designed to recognize these differing needs. In addition, the system was designed to meet IUI's long-term capacity needs. The excess capacity designed into the system would be sold to outside users until needed by IUI. The estimated resource requirements used to design and implement the system are shown in the following schedule:

	Hardware and Other Capacity-Related Resources	Operating Resources
Records	25%	60%
Claims	50	15
Finance	20	20
Expansion (outside use)	5	5
Total	100%	100%

IUI currently sells the equivalent of its expansion capacity to a few outside clients.

At the time the system became operational, management decided to redistribute total expenses of the Systems Department to the user departments based on actual computer time used. The actual costs for the first quarter of the current fiscal year were distributed to the user departments as follows:

Department	Percentage Utilization	Amount
Records	60%	$330,000
Claims	15	82,500
Finance	20	110,000
Outside	5	27,500
Total	100%	$550,000

The three user departments have complained about the cost distribution method since the Systems Department was established. The Records Department's monthly costs have been as much as three times the costs experienced with the service bureau. The Finance Department is concerned about the costs distributed to the outside user category because these allocated costs form the basis for the fees billed to the outside clients.

Jerry Owens, IUI's controller, decided to review the cost-allocation method. The additional information he gathered for his review is reported in Tables 1 to 3.

Table 1		Annual Budget		First Quarter			
				Budget		Actual	
Systems Department Costs and Activity Levels		Hours	Dollars	Hours	Dollars	Hours	Dollars
Hardware and other capacity-related costs		—	$ 600,000	—	$150,000	—	$155,000
Software development		18,750	562,500	4,725	141,750	4,250	130,000
Operations							
Computer related		3,750	750,000	945	189,000	920	187,000
Input/output related		30,000	300,000	7,560	75,600	7,900	78,000
			$2,212,500		$556,350		$550,000

Table 2	Hardware and Other Capacity Needs	Software Development		Operations			
				Computer		Input/Output	
Historical Usage		Range	Average	Range	Average	Range	Average
Records	25%	0-30%	15%	55-65%	60%	10-30%	15%
Claims	50	15-60	40	10-25	15	60-80	75
Finance	20	25-75	40	10-25	20	3-10	5
Outside	5	0-25	5	3-8	5	3-10	5
	100%		100%		100%		100%

Table 3	Software Development	Operations	
		Computer Related	Input/Output
Usage of Systems Department's Services First Quarter (in hours)			
Records	450	540	1,540
Claims	1,800	194	5,540
Finance	1,600	126	410
Outside	400	60	410
Total	4,250	920	7,900

Owens has concluded that the method of cost allocation should be changed. He believes that the hardware and capacity-related costs should be allocated to the user departments in proportion to the planned long-term needs. Any difference between actual and budgeted hardware costs would not be allocated to the departments but remain with the Systems Department.

The costs for software development and operations would be charged to the user departments based on actual hours used. A predetermined hourly rate based on the annual budget data would be used. The hourly rates that would be used for the current fiscal year are as follows:

Function	Hourly Rate
Software development	$ 30
Operations	
Computer related	200
Input/output related	10

Owens plans to use first-quarter activity and cost data to illustrate his recommendations. The recommendations will be presented to the Systems Department and the user departments for their comments and reactions. He then expects to present his recommendations to management for approval.

Required

1. Calculate the amount of data processing costs that would be included in the Claims Department's first-quarter *budget* according to the method Jerry Owens has recommended.
2. Prepare a schedule to show how the actual first-quarter costs of the Systems Department would be charged to the users if Owens' recommended method were adopted.
3. Explain whether Owens' recommended system for charging costs to the user departments will:
   a. Improve cost control in the Systems Department
   b. Improve planning and cost control in the user departments

14

Job-Costing Systems, Overhead Application, Service Industries

Jamesway Incubator Company Ltd., based in Canada, is a leading international manufacturer of custom-made poultry incubator systems and controls. Jamesway uses job costing because of differences in customers' power requirements and differences in environmental and operating conditions. *Courtesy of Jamesway Incubator Company, Ltd.*

Learning Objectives

When you have finished studying this chapter, you should be able to

1 Distinguish between job-order costing and process costing.

2 Prepare summary journal entries for the typical transactions of a job-costing system.

3 Compute budgeted factory-overhead rates and factory overhead applied to production.

4 Use appropriate cost drivers for overhead application.

5 Identify the meaning and purpose of normalized overhead rates.

6 Demonstrate the two major methods for disposing of underapplied and overapplied overhead at year-end.

7 Show how job costing is used in service organizations.

Accountants compute product costs for both decision-making and financial-reporting purposes. They supply product costs to managers for evaluating pricing policy and product lines. For example, Chrysler managers need to know the cost of each kind of auto being produced to set prices, to determine marketing and production strategies for various models, and to evaluate production operations. At the same time, product costs appear as cost of goods sold in income statements and as finished-goods inventory values in balance sheets. Although it would be possible to have two product-costing systems, one for management decision making and one for financial reporting, seldom do the benefits of using two systems exceed the costs. Therefore, both decision-making and financial-reporting needs influence the design of product-costing systems.

In this chapter, we focus on one type of product-costing system, the job-order-costing system, looking at the elements of such systems and how they track the flow of costs. This system, designed primarily for external reporting, focuses on costs involved in the *production* of goods and services. Selling, administrative, distribution, and other nonmanufacturing costs are period costs, not product costs, and they are expensed immediately and excluded from the costs of *product* for inventory valuation and other external reporting purposes. Because this chapter draws heavily on terminology and concepts explained in Chapters 4 and 13, you might want to review those chapters before reading this one.

DISTINCTION BETWEEN JOB COSTING AND PROCESS COSTING

Objective 1

Distinguish between job-order costing and process costing

Recall that a *cost objective* (see Chapter 4) is any activity or resource for which a separate measurement of costs is desired. Cost accounting systems have a twofold purpose fulfilled by their day-to-day operations: (1) to allocate costs to departments for planning and control, hereafter for brevity's sake often called *control*, and (2) to allocate costs to units of product for *product costing*.

Two extremes of product costing are *job-order costing* and *process costing*. **Job-order costing** (or simply **job costing**) allocates costs to products that are readily identified by individual units or batches, each of which requires varying degrees of attention and skill. Industries that commonly use job-order methods include construction, printing, aircraft, furniture, special-purpose machinery, and any manufacture of tailor-made or unique goods.

job-order costing (job costing) The method of allocating costs to products that are readily identified by individual units or batches, each of which requires varying degrees of attention and skill.

Process costing averages costs over large numbers of nearly identical products. It is most often found in such industries as chemicals, oil, textiles, plastics, paints, flour, canneries, rubber, lumber, food processing, glass, mining, cement, and meat packing. These industries involve mass production of like units, which usually pass in continuous fashion through a series of uniform production steps called *operations* or *processes*.

process costing The method of allocating costs to products by averaging costs over large numbers of nearly identical products.

The distinction between the job-cost and the process-cost methods centers largely on how product costing is accomplished. Job costing applies costs to specific jobs, which may consist of either a single physical unit (such as a custom sofa) or a few like units (such as a dozen tables) in a distinct batch or job lot. In contrast, process costing deals with great masses of like units and broad averages of unit costs.

The most important point is that product costing is an *averaging* process. The unit cost used for inventory purposes is the result of taking some accumulated cost that has been allocated to production departments and dividing it by some measure of production. The basic distinction between job-order costing and process costing is the breadth of the denominator: In job-order costing, the denominator is small (e.g., one painting, 100 advertising circulars, or one special packaging machine); however, in process costing, the denominator is large (e.g., thousands of pounds, gallons, or board feet).

Job costing and process costing are extremes along a continuum of potential costing systems. Each company designs its own accounting system to fit its underlying production activities. Many companies use *hybrid* costing systems, which are blends of ideas from both job costing and process costing. Chapter 15 describes process costing.

ILLUSTRATION OF JOB-ORDER COSTING

Job costing is best learned by example. But first we examine the basic records used in a job-cost system.

job-cost record (job-cost sheet, job order) A document that shows all costs for a particular product, service, or batch of products.

Basic Records

The centerpiece of a job-costing system is the **job-cost record** (also called a **job-cost sheet** or **job order**), shown in Exhibit 14-1. All costs for a particular product, service, or batch of products are recorded on the job-cost record. A file of job-cost records for partially completed jobs provides supporting details for the Work-in-Process Inventory account, often simply called Work in Process (WIP). A file of completed job-cost records comprises the Finished-Goods Inventory account.

As Exhibit 14-1 shows, the job-cost record summarizes information contained on source documents such as *materials requisitions* and *labor time tickets*. **Materials requisitions** are records of materials issued to particular jobs. **Labor time tickets** (or **time cards**) record the time a particular direct laborer spends on each job.

Today job-cost records and source documents are likely to be computer files, not paper records. In fact, with on-line data entry, barcoding, and optical scanning, much of the information needed for such records enters the computer without ever being written on paper. Nevertheless, whether records are on paper or on computer files, the accounting system must collect and maintain the same basic information.

As each job begins, a job-cost record is prepared. As units are worked on, entries are made on the job-cost record. Three classes of costs are applied to the units as they pass through the departments: material requisitions are the source of direct-material costs, time tickets provide direct-labor costs, and budgeted overhead rates are used to apply factory overhead to products. (The computation of these budgeted rates will be described later in this chapter.)

materials requisitions Records of materials issued to particular jobs.

labor time tickets (time cards) The record of the time a particular direct laborer spends on each job.

Implementing Activity-Based Costing in a Job-Order and Process-Manufacturing Environment: Tredegar Molded Products

Tredegar Molded Products Company, a subsidiary of Tredegar Industries, Inc., is a diversified custom injection molder of plastics and metal products. Tredegar has six injection molding plants and one tooling facility and uses both job and process production and cost accounting systems. Examples of products manufactured are:

Job Order Production	Process Production
Steel molds	Deodorant canisters
Medical devices	Lip balm
	Closures (various sizes)
	Plugs and fitments

Recently, Tredegar began implementing activity-based costing (ABC) at three of its plants. The business issues leading to the implementation of ABC included the need for

- More accurate product costing
- Better understanding of key business processes
- Better utilization of resources

Specific applications of the new ABC information include:

- Activity-based budgeting
- Support for process improvement
- New product pricing
- Capital spending justification

Future uses of ABC at Tredegar include:

- Make or buy decisions
- Pricing of existing products ∎

Source: From Janet B. Wynn, "Beyond the Pilot at Tredegar," NetProphet User Conference, September 1994, Sapling Corporation, Toronto.

Exhibit 14-1

Completed Job-Cost
Record and Sample
Source Documents

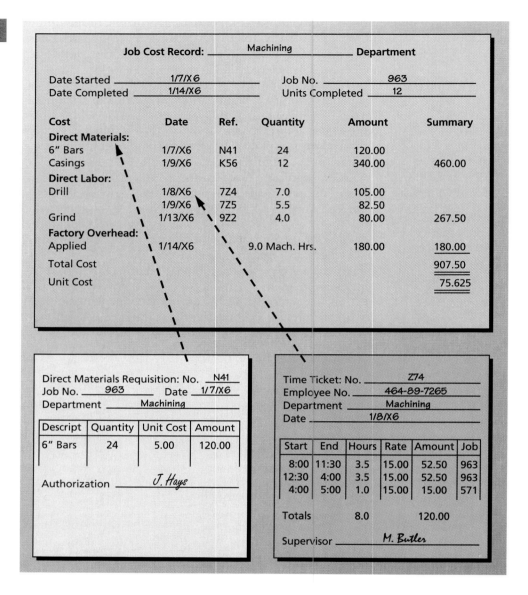

Data for Illustration

To illustrate the functioning of a job-order costing system, we will use the basic records and journal entries of the Enriquez Electronics Company. On December 31, 19X5, the firm had the following inventories:

Direct materials (12 types)	$110,000
Work in process	—
Finished goods (unsold units from two jobs)	12,000

The following is a summary of pertinent transactions for the year 19X6:

	Machining	Assembly	Total
1. Direct materials purchased on account	—	—	$1,900,000
2. Direct materials requisitioned for manufacturing	$1,000,000	$890,000	1,890,000
3. Direct-labor costs incurred	200,000	190,000	390,000
4a. Factory overhead *incurred*	290,000	102,000	392,000
4b. Factory overhead *applied*	280,000	95,000	375,000
5. Cost of goods completed and transferred to finished-goods inventory	—	—	2,500,000
6a. Sales on account	—	—	4,000,000
6b. Cost of goods sold	—	—	2,480,000

We explain the nature of *factory overhead applied* later in this chapter. First, however, we need to consider the accounting for these transactions.

Exhibit 14-2 is an overview of the general flow of costs through the Enriquez Electronics Company's job-order-costing system.[1] The exhibit summarizes the effects of transactions on the key manufacturing accounts in the firm's books. As you proceed through the detailed explanation of transactions, keep checking each explanation against the overview in Exhibit 14-2.

Objective 2

Prepare summary journal entries for the typical transactions of a job-costing system

Explanation of Transactions

The following transaction-by-transaction summary analysis will explain how product costing is achieved. Entries are usually made as transactions occur. However, to obtain a sweeping overview, our illustration uses a summary for the entire year 19X6. Further, explanations for the journal entries are omitted.

---

[1] Exhibit 14-2 and the following explanation of transactions assume knowledge of basic accounting procedures. These can be reviewed in Chapter 17, especially Appendix 17B. We will use the *T-account format* for a company's accounts. Entries on the left of the "T" are debits and those on the right are credits. Asset T-accounts, such as the inventory accounts, show increases on the left (debit) side and decreases on the right (credit) side of the "T":

Inventory	
Beginning Balance	Decreases
Increases	
Ending Balance	

Transactions affecting the accounts are recorded as *journal entries*. Debit (left side) entries are shown flush with the left margin, and credit (right side) entries are indented, and often an explanation is included. For example, a $10,000 transfer from Direct Materials Inventory to WIP Inventory would be shown as follows:

WIP Inventory	10,000	
Direct Materials Inventory		10,000
To increase WIP Inventory and decrease Direct Materials Inventory by $10,000.		

Exhibit 14-2   Job-Order Costing, General Flow of Costs (Thousands)

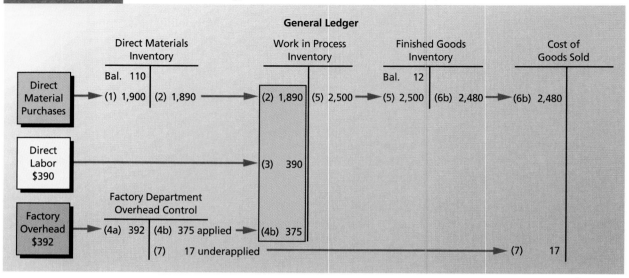

1. **Transaction:** Direct materials purchased, $1,900,000.
   Analysis: The asset Direct-Materials Inventory is increased. The liability Accounts Payable is increased.
   Journal Entry: Direct-Materials Inventory   1,900,000
                          Accounts Payable   1,900,000

2. **Transaction:** Direct materials requisitioned, $1,890,000.
   Analysis: The asset Work in Process (WIP) Inventory is increased. The asset Direct-Materials Inventory is decreased.
   Journal Entry: WIP Inventory   1,890,000
                          Direct-Materials Inventory   1,890,000

3. **Transaction:** Direct-labor cost incurred, $390,000.
   Analysis: The asset WIP Inventory is increased. The liability Accrued Payroll is increased.
   Journal Entry: WIP Inventory   390,000
                          Accrued Payroll   390,000

4a. **Transaction:** Factory overhead incurred, $392,000.
   Analysis: These actual costs are first charged to departmental overhead accounts, which may be regarded as assets until their amounts are later "cleared" or transferred to other accounts. Each department has detailed overhead accounts such as indirect labor, utilities, repairs, depreciation, insurance, and property taxes. These details support a summary Factory Department Overhead Control account. The managers are responsible for regulating these costs, item by item. As these costs are charged to the departments, the other accounts affected will be assorted assets and liabilities. Examples include cash, accounts payable, accrued payables, and accumulated depreciation.
   Journal Entry: Factory Department Overhead Control . .   392,000
                          Cash, Accounts Payable, and various
                          other balance sheet accounts . . .   392,000

4b. **Transaction:** Factory overhead applied, $95,000 + $280,000 = $375,000.
   Analysis: The asset WIP Inventory is increased. The asset Factory Department Overhead Control is decreased. (A fuller explanation occurs later in this chapter.)
   Journal Entry: WIP Inventory   375,000
   Factory Department Overhead Control   375,000

5. **Transaction:** Cost of goods completed, $2,500,000.
   Analysis: The asset Finished Goods Inventory is increased. The asset WIP Inventory is decreased.
   Journal Entry: Finished Goods Inventory   2,500,000
   WIP Inventory   2,500,000

6a. **Transaction:** Sales on account, $4,000,000.
   Analysis: The asset Accounts Receivable is increased. The revenue account Sales is increased.
   Journal Entry: Accounts Receivable   4,000,000
   Sales   4,000,000

6b. **Transaction:** Cost of goods sold, $2,480,000.
   Analysis: The expense Cost of Goods Sold is increased. The asset Finished Goods Inventory is decreased.
   Journal Entry: Cost of Goods Sold   2,480,000
   Finished Goods Inventory   2,480,000

Summary of Transactions

Exhibit 14-2 summarizes the Enriquez transactions for the year, focusing on the inventory accounts. WIP Inventory receives central attention. The costs of direct material used, direct labor, and factory overhead applied to product are brought into WIP. In turn, the costs of completed goods are transferred from WIP to Finished Goods. As goods are sold, their costs become expense in the form of Cost of Goods Sold. The year-end accounting for the $17,000 of under-applied overhead is explained later.

■ ACCOUNTING FOR FACTORY OVERHEAD

In the Enriquez Company example, factory overhead of $375,000 was applied to the WIP account. This section describes how to determine the amount of applied factory overhead.

Cost Application or Absorption

Recall that cost allocation refers to identifying or tracing accumulated costs to departments and products, and cost application (cost absorption) refers to allocation to products, as distinguished from allocation to departments.

   Few companies wait until the actual factory overhead is finally known before computing the costs of products. Instead, they compute a budgeted (pre-determined) overhead rate at the beginning of a fiscal year and use it to apply overhead costs as products are manufactured. Most managers want a close approximation of the costs of various products continuously, not just at the end of a year. Managers desire those costs for various ongoing uses including choosing which products to emphasize or de-emphasize, pricing products, producing interim financial statements, and managing inventories.

Budgeted Overhead Application Rates

The following steps summarize how to account for factory overhead:

1. Select one or more cost drivers to serve as a base for applying overhead costs. Examples include direct-labor hours, direct-labor costs, machine-hours, and production setups. The cost driver should be an activity that is the common denominator for systematically relating a cost or a group of costs, such as machinery cost, set-up costs, or energy cost, with products. The cost driver(s) should be the best available measure of the cause-and-effect relationships between overhead costs and production volume.

2. Prepare a factory-overhead budget for the planning period, ordinarily a year. The two key items are (1) budgeted overhead and (2) budgeted volume of the cost driver. There will be a set of budgeted overhead costs and an associated budgeted cost-driver level for each component of total overhead. In businesses with simple production systems there may be just one set.

3. Compute the **budgeted factory-overhead rate(s)** by dividing the budgeted total overhead by the budgeted cost driver activity.

4. Obtain actual cost-driver data (such as machine-hours) as the year unfolds.

5. Apply the budgeted overhead to the jobs by multiplying the budgeted rate(s) times the actual cost-driver data.

6. At the end of the year, account for any differences between the amount of overhead actually incurred and overhead applied to products.

budgeted factory-overhead rate The budgeted total overhead divided by the budgeted cost driver activity.

■ ILLUSTRATION OF OVERHEAD APPLICATION

To understand how to apply factory overhead to jobs, consider the Enriquez illustration again.

The following manufacturing-overhead budget has been prepared for the coming year, 19X7:

	Machining	Assembly
Indirect labor	$ 75,600	$ 36,800
Supplies	8,400	2,400
Utilities	20,000	7,000
Repairs	10,000	3,000
Factory rent	10,000	6,800
Supervision	42,600	35,400
Depreciation on equipment	104,000	9,400
Insurance, property taxes, etc.	7,200	2,400
	$277,800	$103,200

Objective 3

Compute budgeted factory-overhead rates and factory overhead applied to production

As products are worked on, Enriquez applies the factory overhead to the jobs. A budgeted overhead rate is used, computed as follows:

$$\text{budgeted overhead application rate} = \frac{\text{total budgeted factory overhead}}{\text{total budgeted amount of cost driver}}$$
$$\text{(such as direct-labor costs or machine-hours)}$$

Simplifying Product Costing at Harley-Davidson

When Harley-Davidson, the motorcycle manufacturer, adopted a just-in-time (JIT) philosophy in the early 1980s, it quickly discovered that its accounting system needed revision. The main focus of the accounting system was direct labor, which not only made up a part of product cost itself, but also functioned as an all-purpose base for allocating overhead. However, by the mid-1980s, direct labor was only 10% of total product cost. It certainly did not generate a majority of overhead costs. As Harley-Davidson's production process had changed, the accounting system had remained static.

The first point that became apparent with the JIT system was that detailed information on direct-labor costs was not useful to managers. It was costly to have each direct laborer record the time spent on each product or part and then enter the information from these time cards into the accounting system. For example, if each of 500 direct laborers works on 20 products per day, the system must record 10,000 entries per day, which is 200,000 entries per month. The time spent by direct laborers to record the time, by clerks to enter the data into the system, and by the accountants to check the data's accuracy is enormous—and all to produce product cost information that was used for financial reporting but was useless to managers.

The JIT system forced manufacturing managers to focus on satisfying customers and minimizing non-value-added activities. Gradually, accountants began to focus on the same objectives. Accounting's customers were the managers who used the accounting information, and effort put into activities that did not help managers was deemed counterproductive. Therefore, eliminating the costly, time-consuming recording of detailed labor costs became a priority. Direct labor was eliminated as a direct cost, and consequently it could not be used for overhead allocation. After considering process hours, flow-through time, material value, and individual cost per unit as possible cost drivers for allocating overhead, the company selected process hours. Direct labor and overhead were combined to form *conversion costs*, which were applied to products on the basis of total process hours. This did not result in costs significantly different than the old system, but the new system was much simpler and less costly. Only direct material was traced directly to the product. Conversion costs were applied at completion of production based on a simple measure of process time.

Accounting systems should generate benefits greater than their costs. More sophisticated systems are not necessarily better systems. Harley-Davidson's main objective in changing its accounting system was simplification—eliminating unnecessary tasks and streamlining others. These changes resulted in a revitalized accounting system. ∎

Source: Adapted from W. T. Turk, "Management Accounting Revitalized: The Harley-Davidson Experience," in B. J. Brinker, ed., Emerging Practices in Cost Management, *Warren, Gorham & Lamont, Boston, 1990, pp. 155–66.*

Suppose machine-hours are chosen as the only cost driver in the Machining Department, and direct-labor cost is chosen in the Assembly Department. The overhead rates are as follows:

	Year 19X7	
	Machining	*Assembly*
Budgeted manufacturing overhead	$277,800	$103,200
Budgeted machine-hours	69,450	
Budgeted direct-labor cost		$206,400
Budgeted overhead rate, per machine-hour: $277,800 ÷ 69,450 =	$4	
Budgeted overhead rate, per direct-labor dollar: $103,200 ÷ $206,400 =		50%

Note that the overhead rates are budgeted; they are estimates. These rates are then used to apply overhead based on *actual* events. That is, the total overhead applied in our illustration is the result of multiplying *actual* machine-hours or labor cost by the *budgeted* overhead rates:

Machining: actual machine-hours of 70,000 × $4 = $280,000
Assembly: actual direct-labor cost of $190,000 × .50 = 95,000
Total factory overhead applied $375,000

The summary journal entry for the application (entry 4b) is:

4b. WIP Inventory 375,000
      Factory Department Overhead Control 375,000

Choice of Cost Drivers

Objective 4

Use appropriate cost drivers for overhead application

Factory overhead is a conglomeration of manufacturing costs that, unlike direct material or direct labor, cannot conveniently be applied on an individual job basis. But such overhead is an integral part of a product's total cost. Therefore it is applied indirectly, using as a base a cost driver that is common to all jobs worked on and is the best available index of the product's relative use of, or benefits from, the overhead items. In other words, there should be a strong cause-and-effect relationship between the factory overhead cost incurred (the effect) and the cost driver chosen for its application.

As we have noted several times in this text, no one cost driver is right for all situations. The goal is to find the driver that best links cause and effect. In the Enriquez Machining Department, two or more machines can often be operated simultaneously by a single direct laborer. Use of machines causes most overhead cost in the Machining Department, for example, depreciation and repairs. Therefore machine-hours is the cost driver and the appropriate base for applying overhead costs. Thus Enriquez must keep track of the machine-hours used for each job, creating an added data collection cost. That is, both direct-labor costs and machine-hours must be accumulated for each job.

In contrast, direct labor is a principal cost driver in the Enriquez Assembly Department. It is an accurate reflection of the relative attention and effort devoted to various jobs. The workers are paid equal hourly rates. Therefore all that is needed is to apply the 50% overhead rate to the cost of direct labor already entered on the job-cost records. No separate job records have to be kept of the labor-hours. If the hourly labor rates differ greatly for individuals performing identical tasks, the hours of labor, rather than the dollars spent for labor, might be used as a base. Otherwise a $9-per-hour worker would cause more overhead applied than an $8-per-hour worker, even though the same time would probably be taken and the same facilities used by each employee for the same work.

Sometimes direct-labor cost is the best overhead cost driver even if wage rates vary within a department. For example, higher-skilled labor may use more costly equipment and have more indirect labor support. Moreover, many factory-overhead costs include costly labor fringe benefits such as pensions and payroll taxes. The latter are often more closely driven by direct-labor cost than by direct-labor hours.

If a department identifies more than one cost driver for overhead costs, these costs ideally should be put into as many cost pools as there are cost drivers. In practice, such a system is too costly for many organizations. Instead, these organizations select a few cost drivers (often only one) to serve as a basis for allocating overhead costs. The 80–20 rule can be used in these situations. In many cases, 80% of total overhead cost can be accounted for with just a few drivers (20% of all the drivers identified). For example, a company may identify 10 separate overhead pools with 10 different drivers. Often, approximately 80% of the total cost can be applied with only 2 drivers.

The selected cost drivers should be the ones that cause most of the overhead costs. For example, suppose machine-hours cause 70% of the overhead costs in a particular department, number of component parts cause 20%, and five assorted cost drivers cause the other 10%. Instead of using seven cost pools allocated on the basis of the seven cost drivers, most managers would use one cost driver, machine-hours, to allocate all overhead costs. Others would assign all cost to two cost pools, one allocated on the basis of machine-hours and one on the basis of number of component parts.

No matter which cost drivers are chosen, the overhead rates are applied day after day throughout the year to cost the various jobs worked on by each department. All overhead is applied to all jobs worked on during the year on the appropriate basis of machine-hours or direct-labor costs of each job. Suppose management predictions coincide exactly with actual amounts (an extremely unlikely situation). Then the total overhead applied to the year's jobs via these budgeted rates would be equal to the total overhead costs actually incurred.

■ PROBLEMS OF OVERHEAD APPLICATION

Normalized Overhead Rates

Objective 5

Identify the meaning and purpose of normalized overhead rates

Basically, our illustration has demonstrated the *normal costing* approach. Why the term "normal"? Because an annual average overhead rate is used consistently throughout the year for product costing, *without altering it from day to day and from month to month.* The resultant "normal" product costs include an average or normalized chunk of overhead.

As actual overhead costs are incurred by departments from month to month, they are charged to the departments. On a weekly or monthly basis, these actual costs are then compared with budgeted costs to obtain budget variances for performance evaluation. This *control* process is distinct from the *product-costing* process of applying overhead to specific jobs.

During the year and at year-end, the actual overhead amount incurred will rarely equal the amount applied. This variance between incurred and applied cost can be analyzed. The most common—and important—contributor to these variances is operating at a different level of volume than the level used as a denominator in calculating the budgeted overhead rate (e.g., using 100,000 budgeted direct-labor-hours as the denominator and then actually working only 80,000 hours). Other frequent contributory causes include: poor forecasting, inefficient use of overhead items, price changes in individual overhead items, erratic behavior of individual overhead items (e.g., repairs made only during slack time), and calendar variations (e.g., 20 workdays in one month, 22 in the next).

All these peculiarities of overhead are mingled in an *annual* overhead pool. Thus an annual rate is budgeted and used regardless of the month-to-month peculiarities of specific overhead costs. Such an approach is more defensible than, say, applying the actual overhead for *each month*. Why? Because a *normal* product cost is more useful for decisions, and more representative for inventory-costing purposes, than an "actual" product cost that is distorted by month-to-month fluctuations in production volume and by the erratic behavior of many overhead costs. For example, the employees of a gypsum plant using an "actual" product cost system had the privilege of buying company-made items "at cost." Employees joked about the benefits of buying "at cost" during high-volume months, when unit costs were lower because volume was higher:

	Actual Overhead			Direct-Labor Hours	Actual Overhead Application Rate* per Direct-Labor Hour
	Variable	*Fixed*	*Total*		
Peak-volume month	$60,000	$40,000	$100,000	100,000	$1.00
Low-volume month	30,000	40,000	70,000	50,000	1.40

* Divide total overhead by direct-labor hours. Note that the presence of fixed overhead causes the fluctuation in unit costs from $1.00 to $1.40. The variable component is $.60 an hour in both months, but the fixed component is $.40 in the peak-volume month ($40,000 ÷ 100,000) and $.80 in the low-volume month ($40,000 ÷ 50,000).

Disposition of Underapplied or Overapplied Overhead

Our Enriquez illustration contained the following data:

Transaction	
4a. Factory overhead incurred	$392,000
4b. Factory overhead applied	375,000
Underapplied factory overhead	$ 17,000

Total costs of $392,000 must eventually be charged to expense in some way. The $375,000 will become part of the Cost of Goods Sold expense when the products to which it is applied are sold. The remaining $17,000 must also become expense by some method.

When budgeted rates are used, the difference between incurred and applied overhead is typically allowed to accumulate during the year. When the amount applied to product *exceeds* the amount incurred by the departments, the difference is called **overapplied overhead.** When the amount applied is *less than* incurred, the difference is called **underapplied overhead.** At year-end, the difference ($17,000 underapplied in our illustration) is disposed of either through a *write-off* or through *proration*.

overapplied overhead The excess of overhead applied to products over actual overhead incurred.

underapplied overhead The excess of actual overhead over the overhead applied to products.

Immediate Write-Off

This is the most widely used approach. The $17,000 is regarded as a reduction in current income by adding the underapplied overhead to the cost of goods sold. The same logic is followed for overapplied overhead except that the result would be a decrease in cost of goods sold.

The theory underlying the direct write-off is that most of the goods worked on have been sold, and a more elaborate method of disposition is not worth the extra trouble. Another justification is that the extra overhead costs represented by underapplied overhead do not qualify as part of ending inventory costs because they do not represent assets. They should be written off because they largely represent inefficiency or the underutilization of available facilities in the current period.

The immediate write-off eliminates the $17,000 difference with a simple journal entry, labeled as transaction 7 in Exhibit 14-2.

7. Cost of Goods Sold (or a separate		
charge against revenue)	17,000	
Factory Department Overhead Control		17,000
To close ending underapplied overhead directly to Cost of Goods Sold.		

Objective 6

Demonstrate the two major methods for disposing of underapplied and overapplied overhead at year-end

prorate To assign underapplied overhead or overapplied overhead in proportion to the sizes of the ending account balances.

Proration Among Inventories

This method *prorates* underapplied overhead among three accounts. Theoretically, if the objective is to obtain as accurate a cost allocation as possible, all the overhead costs of the individual jobs worked on should be recomputed, using the actual, rather than the budgeted, rates. This approach is rarely feasible, so a practical attack is to prorate on the basis of the ending balances in each of three accounts (WIP, $155,000; Finished Goods, $32,000; and Cost of Goods Sold, $2,480,000). To **prorate** underapplied overhead means to assign it in proportion to the sizes of the ending account balances.

	(1)	(2)	(3)
	Unadjusted Balance, End of 19X2*	Proration of Underapplied Overhead	Adjusted Balance, End of 19X2
WIP	$ 155,000	155/2,667 × 17,000 = $ 988	$ 155,988
Finished Goods	32,000	32/2,667 × 17,000 = 204	32,204
Cost of Goods Sold	2,480,000	2,480/2,667 × 17,000 = 15,808	2,495,808
	$2,667,000	$17,000	$2,684,000

* See pages 536–37 for details.

The journal entry for the proration follows:

WIP	988	
Finished Goods	204	
Cost of Goods Sold	15,808	
Factory Department Overhead Control		17,000
To prorate ending underapplied overhead among three accounts.		

The amounts prorated to inventories here are not significant. In actual practice, prorating is done only when inventory valuations would be materially affected. Exhibit 14-3 provides a schematic comparison of the two major methods of disposing of underapplied (or overapplied) factory overhead.

The Use of Variable and Fixed Application Rates

As we have seen, overhead application is the most troublesome aspect of product costing. The presence of fixed costs is a major reason for the costing difficulties. Most companies have made no distinction between variable- and fixed-cost behavior in the design of their accounting systems. For instance, the Machining Department at Enriquez Electronics Company developed the following rate:

$$\text{budgeted overhead application rate} = \frac{\text{budgeted total overhead}}{\text{budgeted machine-hours}}$$

$$= \frac{\$277,800}{69,450} = \$4 \text{ per machine-hour}$$

Some companies distinguish between variable overhead and fixed overhead for product costing as well as for control purposes. If the Machining Department had made this distinction, then rent, supervision, depreciation, and insurance would have been considered the fixed portion of the total manufacturing overhead, and two rates would have been developed:

$$\text{budgeted variable-overhead application rate} = \frac{\text{budgeted total variable overhead}}{\text{budgeted machine-hours}}$$

$$= \frac{\$114,000}{69,450}$$

$$= \$1.64 \text{ per machine-hour}$$

$$\text{budgeted fixed-overhead application rate} = \frac{\text{budgeted total fixed overhead}}{\text{budgeted machine-hours}}$$

$$= \frac{\$163,800}{69,450}$$

$$= \$2.36 \text{ per machine-hour}$$

Exhibit 14-3   Year-end Disposition of Underapplied Factory Overhead (COGS = Cost of Goods Sold)

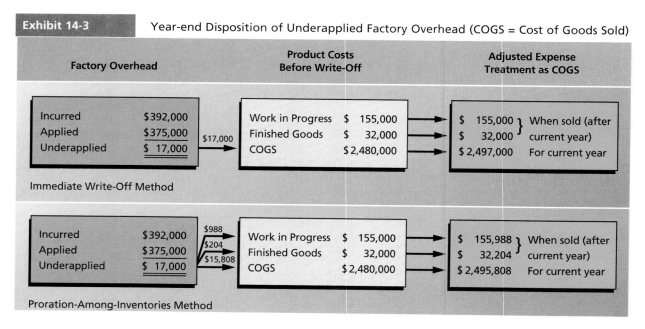

Such rates can be used for product costing. Distinctions between variable- and fixed-overhead incurrence can also be made for control purposes.

Actual Costing Versus Normal Costing

normal costing system The cost system in which overhead is applied on an average or normalized basis, in order to get representative or normal inventory valuations.

The overall system we have just described is sometimes called an *actual costing system* because every effort is made to trace the *actual* costs, as incurred, to the physical units benefited. However, it is only partly an actual system because overhead, by definition, cannot be traced to physical products. Instead, overhead is applied on an average or normalized basis to get representative or normal inventory valuations. Hence we shall label the system a **normal costing system.** The cost of the manufactured product is composed of *actual* direct material, *actual* direct labor, and *normal* applied overhead.

The two job-order costing approaches may be compared as follows:

	Actual Costing	Normal Costing
Direct materials	Actual	Actual
Direct labor	Actual	Actual
Manufacturing overhead	Actual	Budgeted rates*

* Actual inputs (such as direct-labor hours or direct-labor costs) multiplied by budgeted overhead rates (computed by dividing total budgeted manufacturing overhead by a budgeted cost driver such as direct-labor hours).

In a true actual costing system, overhead would not be applied as jobs were worked on, but only after all overhead costs for the year were known. Then, using an "actual" average rate(s) instead of a budgeted rate(s), costs would be applied to all jobs that had been worked on throughout the year. All costs incurred would be exactly offset by costs applied to the WIP Inventory. However, increased accuracy would be obtained at the serious sacrifice of timeliness in using costs for measuring operating efficiency, determining selling prices, and producing interim financial statements.

Normal costing has replaced actual costing in many organizations precisely because the latter approach fails to provide costs of products as they are worked on during the year. It is possible to use a normal costing system plus year-end adjustments to produce final results that closely approximate the results under actual costing. To do so in our illustration, the underapplied overhead is prorated among WIP, Finished Goods, and Cost of Goods Sold, as shown in Exhibit 14-3.

■ PRODUCT COSTING IN SERVICE AND NONPROFIT ORGANIZATIONS

This chapter has concentrated on how to apply costs to manufactured products. However, the job-costing approach is used in nonmanufacturing situations too. For example, universities have research "projects," airlines have repair and overhaul "jobs," and public accountants have audit "engagements." In such situations, the focus shifts from the costs of products to the costs of services.

In nonprofit organizations the "product" is usually not called a "job order." Instead, it may be called a program or a class of service. A "program" is an identifiable group of activities that frequently produces outputs in the form of services rather than goods. Examples include a safety program, an education program, and a family counseling program. Costs or revenues may be traced to individual hospital patients, individual social welfare cases, and individual university research projects. However, departments often work simultaneously on many programs, so the "job-order" costing challenge is to "apply" the various department costs to the various programs. Only then can managers make wiser decisions regarding the allocation of limited resources among competing programs.

In service industries—such as repairing, consulting, legal, and accounting services—each customer order is a different job with a special account or order number. Sometimes only costs are traced directly to the job, sometimes only revenue is traced, and sometimes both. For example, automobile repair shops typically have a repair order for each car worked on, with space for allocating materials and labor costs. Customers are permitted to see only a copy showing the retail prices of the materials, parts, and labor billed to their orders. If the repair manager wants cost data, a system may be designed so that the "actual" parts and labor costs of each order are traced to a duplicate copy of the repair order. That is why you often see auto mechanics "punching in" and "punching out" their starting and stopping times on "time tickets" as each new order is worked on.

Budgets and Control of Engagements

In many service organizations and some manufacturing operations, job orders are used not only for product costing, but also for planning and control purposes. For example, a public accounting firm might have a condensed budget for 19X1 as follows:

Revenue	$10,000,000	100%
Direct labor (for professional hours charged to engagements)	2,500,000	25%
Contribution to overhead and operating income	$ 7,500,000	75%
Overhead (all other costs)	6,500,000	65%
Operating income	$ 1,000,000	10%

In this illustration:

$$\text{budgeted overhead rate} = \frac{\text{budgeted overhead}}{\text{budgeted direct labor}}$$

$$= \frac{\$6,500,000}{\$2,500,000} = 260\%$$

As each engagement is budgeted, the partner in charge of the audit predicts the expected number of necessary direct-professional hours. Direct-professional hours are those worked by partners, managers, and subordinate auditors to complete the engagement. The budgeted direct-labor cost is the pertinent hourly labor costs multiplied by the budgeted hours. Partners' time is charged to the engagement at much higher rates than subordinates' time.

How is overhead applied? Accounting firms usually use either direct-labor cost or direct-labor hours as the cost driver for overhead application. In our example, the firm uses direct-labor cost. Such a practice implies that partners require proportionately more overhead support for each of their hours charged.

The budgeted total cost of an engagement is the direct-labor cost plus applied overhead (260% of direct-labor cost in this illustration) plus any other direct costs.

The engagement partner uses a budget for a specific audit that includes detailed scope and steps. For instance, the budget for auditing cash or receivables would specify the exact work to be done, the number of hours, and the necessary hours of partner time, manager time, and subordinate time. The partner monitors progress by comparing the hours logged to date with the original budget and with the estimated hours remaining on the engagement. Obviously, if a fixed audit fee has been quoted, the profitability of an engagement depends on whether the audit can be accomplished within the budgeted time limits.

Accuracy of Costs of Engagements

Suppose the accounting firm has costs on an auditing engagement as follows:

Direct-professional labor	$ 50,000
Applied overhead, 260% of $50,000	130,000
Total costs excluding travel costs	$180,000
Travel costs	14,000
Total costs of engagement	$194,000

Two direct costs, professional labor and travel costs, are traced to the jobs. But only direct-professional labor is a cost driver for overhead. (Note that costs reimbursed by the client—such as travel costs—do not add to overhead costs and should not be subject to any markups in the setting of fees.)

Managers of service firms, such as auditing and consulting firms, frequently use either the budgeted or "actual" costs of engagements as guides to pricing and to allocating effort among particular services or customers. Hence the accuracy of costs of various engagements may affect decisions.

Activity-Based Costing: Shifting Overhead to Direct Costs

Our accounting firm example described a widely used, relatively simple job-costing system. Only two direct-cost items (direct-professional labor and travel costs) are used, and only a single overhead application rate is used.

In recent years, to obtain more accurate costs, many professional service firms have refined their data processing systems and adopted activity-based costing. Computers help accumulate information that is far more detailed than was feasible a few years ago. As noted in earlier chapters, firms that use activity-based costing generally shift costs from being classified as overhead to being classified as direct costs. Using our previously assumed numbers for direct labor ($50,000) and travel ($14,000), we recast the costs of our audit engagement as follows:

Direct-professional labor	$ 50,000
Direct-support labor, such as secretarial costs	10,000
Fringe benefits for all direct labor*	24,000
Telephone calls	1,000
Photocopying	2,000
Computer time	7,000
Total direct costs	94,000
Applied overhead†	103,400
Total costs excluding travel costs	197,400
Travel costs	14,000
Total costs of engagement	$211,400

* 40% assumed rate multiplied by ($50,000 + $10,000) = $24,000.
† 110% assumed rate multiplied by total direct costs of $94,000 = $103,400.

Costs such as direct-support labor, telephone calls, photocopying, computer time, and travel costs are applied by directly measuring their usage on each engagement. The remaining costs to be allocated are assigned to cost pools based on their cause. The cost driver for fringe benefits is labor cost, and the cost driver for other overhead is total direct costs.

The more detailed approach of activity-based costing will nearly always produce total costs that differ from the total costs in the general approach shown earlier: $211,400 compared with $194,000. Of course, any positive or negative difference is attributable to having more types of costs traced directly to the engagement. For instance, secretarial time is directly tracked in the second but not the first example. Moreover, the fringe benefits are separately tracked. Some firms include such fringe benefits as an integral part of their direct-labor costs. Therefore, if fringe benefits are 40% of an auditor's hourly compensation of $25, some firms cost their labor at $25 plus 40% of $25, or $25 + $10 = $35. Other firms do as implied in the tabulation, compiling direct-professional labor at the $25 rate and separately compiling the related fringe benefits at the 40% rate.

Effects of Classifications on Overhead Rates

The activity-based-costing approach also has a lower overhead application rate, assumed at 110% of total direct costs instead of the 260% of direct labor used in the first example, for two reasons. First, there are fewer overhead costs because more costs are traced directly. Second, the application base is broader including all direct costs rather than only direct labor.

Even with activity-based costing, some firms may prefer to continue to apply their overhead based on direct-labor costs rather than total direct costs. Why? Because the partners believe that overhead is dominantly affected by the amount of direct-labor costs rather than other direct costs such as telephone calls. But at least the activity-based-costing firm has made an explicit decision that direct-labor costs are the best cost driver.

Whether the overhead cost driver should be total direct costs, direct-professional labor costs or hours, or some other cost driver is a knotty problem for many firms including most professional service firms. Ideally, activity analysis should uncover the principal cost drivers, and they should all be used for overhead application. In practice, only one or two cost drivers are usually used.

Multiple Overhead Rates

A growing minority of service and manufacturing organizations use more than one overhead rate to apply costs to engagements or jobs. For example, a professional services firm might apply some overhead on the basis of direct professional labor and other overhead on the basis of computer time. The latter cost driver is becoming more widely used as expensive computers assume a more prominent role in rendering service to clients or customers.

As might be expected, the activity-based-costing approach results in different total costs. Depending on how prices are set, these costs may lead to a different total revenue for the engagement. The activity-based-costing approach demonstrates a trend in both service and manufacturing industries. That is, as data processing becomes less expensive, more costs than just direct materials and direct labor will be classified as direct costs when feasible. Moreover, more than one cost driver will be used for overhead application. In these ways, there will be more accurate tracking of costs to specific jobs or engagements. Then managers will have improved information to guide their decisions.

Highlights to Remember

Accounting systems are designed to help satisfy control and product-costing purposes simultaneously. Costs are initially charged to departments; then they are applied to products to get inventory costs for balance sheets and income statements, to guide pricing, and to evaluate product performance.

Product costing is an averaging process. Process costing deals with broad averages and great masses of like units. Job costing deals with narrow averages and a unique unit or a small batch of like units. The job-cost sheet summarizes the costs of a particular job and holds the underlying detail for the WIP Inventory account.

Indirect manufacturing costs (factory overhead) are often applied to products using budgeted overhead rates. The rates are computed by dividing total budgeted overhead by a measure of cost-driver activity such as expected labor-hours or machine-hours. These rates are usually annual averages. The resulting product costs are normal costs, consisting of actual direct material plus actual direct labor plus applied overhead using budgeted rates. When actual overhead differs from applied overhead, overapplied or underapplied overhead arises, which is either written off at the end of the year or prorated to the inventory accounts.

The job-costing approach is used in nonmanufacturing as well as in manufacturing. Examples include costs of services such as auto repair, consulting, and auditing. For example, the job order is a key device for planning and controlling an audit engagement by a public accounting firm.

Exhibit 14-4	Relation of Costs to Financial Statements

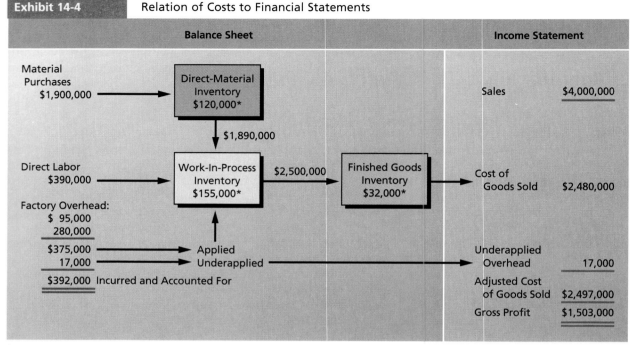

*Ending Balance

Summary Problem for Your Review

Problem

Review the Enriquez illustration, especially Exhibits 14-2 and 14-3, pages 536 and 544. Prepare an income statement for 19X6 through the gross profit line. Use the immediate write-off method for overapplied or underapplied overhead.

Solution

Exhibit 14-4 recapitulates the final impact of the Enriquez illustration on the financial statements. Note how the immediate write-off means that the $17,000 is added to the cost of goods sold. As you study Exhibit 14-4, trace the three major elements of cost (direct material, direct labor, and factory overhead) through the accounts.

Accounting Vocabulary

budgeted factory-overhead rate, p. 538
job costing, p. 532
job-cost record, p. 532
job-cost sheet, p. 532

job order, p. 532
job-order costing, p. 532
labor time tickets, p. 533
materials requisitions, p. 533
normal costing system, p. 545

overapplied overhead, p. 542
process costing, p. 532
prorate, p. 543
time cards, p. 533
underapplied overhead, p. 542

Fundamental Assignment Material

14-A1 Basic Journal Entries

The following data (in thousands) summarize the factory operations of the Lewis Manufacturing Co. for the year 19X5, its first year in business:

a.	Direct materials purchased for cash	$360
b.	Direct materials issued and used	330
c.	Labor used directly on production	125
d1.	Indirect labor	80
d2.	Depreciation of plant and equipment	55
d3.	Miscellaneous factory overhead (ordinarily would be detailed)	40
e.	Overhead applied: 180% of direct labor	?
f.	Cost of production completed	625
g.	Cost of goods sold	400

Required

1. Prepare summary journal entries. Omit explanations. For purposes of this problem, combine the items in *d* as "overhead incurred."
2. Show the T-accounts for all inventories, Cost of Goods Sold, and Factory Department Overhead Control. Compute the ending balances of the inventories. Do not adjust for underapplied or overapplied factory overhead.

14-A2 Accounting for Overhead, Budgeted Rates

McFarland Aeronautics Co. uses a budgeted overhead rate in applying overhead to individual job orders on a *machine-hour* basis for Department A and on a *direct-labor-hour* basis for Department B. At the beginning of 19X6, the company's management made the following budget predictions:

	Department A	Department B
Direct-labor cost	$1,500,000	$1,200,000
Factory overhead	$1,820,000	$1,000,000
Direct-labor hours	90,000	125,000
Machine-hours	350,000	20,000

Cost records of recent months show the following accumulations for Job Order No. 455:

	Department A	Department B
Material placed in production	$12,000	$32,000
Direct-labor cost	$10,800	$10,000
Direct-labor hours	900	1,250
Machine-hours	3,500	150

Required

1. What is the budgeted overhead *rate* that should be applied in Department A? In Department B?
2. What is the *total overhead* cost of Job Order No. 455?
3. If Job Order No. 455 consists of 120 units of product, what is the *unit cost* of this job?
4. At the *end* of 19X6, actual results for the year's operations were as follows:

	Department A	Department B
Actual overhead costs incurred	$1,300,000	$1,200,000
Actual direct-labor hours	80,000	120,000
Actual machine-hours	300,000	25,000

Find the underapplied or overapplied overhead for each department and for the factory as a whole.

14-A3 Disposition of Overhead

Shoreline Marine Manufacturing applies factory overhead using machine-hours and number of component parts as cost drivers. In 19X5, actual factory overhead incurred was $134,000 and applied factory overhead was $126,000. Before disposition of underapplied or overapplied factory overhead, the cost of goods sold was $525,000, gross profit was $60,000, and ending inventories were:

Direct materials	$ 25,000
WIP	75,000
Finished goods	150,000
Total inventories	$250,000

Required

1. Was factory overhead overapplied or underapplied? By how much?
2. Assume that Shoreline writes off overapplied or underapplied factory overhead as an adjustment to cost of goods sold. Prepare the journal entry, and compute adjusted gross profit.
3. Assume that Shoreline prorates overapplied or underapplied factory overhead based on end-of-the-year unadjusted balances. Prepare the journal entry, and compute adjusted gross profit.
4. Assume that actual factory overhead was $124,000 instead of $134,000, and that Shoreline writes off overapplied or underapplied factory overhead as an adjustment to cost of goods sold. Prepare the journal entry, and compute adjusted gross profit.

14-B1 Basic Journal Entries

Consider the following data for a London printing company (in thousands):

Inventories, December 31, 19X4	
Direct materials	£ 18
Work in process	25
Finished goods	100

Summarized transactions for 19X5:

a.	Purchases of direct materials	£109
b.	Direct materials used	95
c.	Direct labor	105
d.	Factory overhead incurred	90
e.	Factory overhead applied, 80% of direct labor	?
f.	Cost of goods completed and transferred to finished goods	280
g.	Cost of goods sold	350
h.	Sales on account	600

1. Prepare summary journal entries for 19X5 transactions. Omit explanations.
2. Show the T-accounts for all inventories, Cost of Goods Sold, and Factory Department Overhead Control. Compute the ending balances of the inventories. Do not adjust for underapplied or overapplied factory overhead.

14-B2 Disposition of Overhead

Baker Mfg. Co. had overapplied overhead of $50 in 19X6. Before adjusting for overapplied or underapplied overhead, the ending inventories for Direct Materials, WIP, and Finished Goods were $75, $100, and $150, respectively. Unadjusted cost of goods sold was $250.

1. Assume that the $50 was written off solely as an adjustment to cost of goods sold. Prepare the journal entry.
2. Management has decided to prorate the $50 to the appropriate accounts (using the unadjusted ending balances) instead of writing it off solely as an adjustment of cost of goods sold. Prepare the journal entry. Would gross profit be higher or lower than in requirement 1? By how much?

14-B3 Application of Overhead Using Budgeted Rates

The Mesa Clinic computes a cost of treating each patient. It allocates costs to departments and then applies departmental overhead costs to individual patients using a different budgeted overhead rate in each department. Consider the following predicted 19X7 data for two of Mesa's departments:

	Pharmacy	Medical Records
Department overhead cost	$180,000	$300,000
Number of prescriptions filled	90,000	
Number of patient visits		60,000

The cost driver for overhead in Pharmacy is *number of prescriptions filled*; in Medical Records it is *number of patient visits*.

In June 19X7, Luke Ashton paid two visits to the clinic and had four prescriptions filled at the pharmacy.

1. Compute departmental overhead rates for the two departments.
2. Compute the overhead costs applied to the patient Luke Ashton in June 19X7.
3. At the end of 19X7 actual overhead costs were:

Pharmacy	$175,000
Medical records	$325,000

The pharmacy filled 85,000 prescriptions, and the clinic had 63,000 patient visits during 19X7. Compute the overapplied or underapplied overhead in each department.

Additional Assignment Material

Questions

14-1. "There are different product costs for different purposes." Name at least two purposes.

14-2. Distinguish between job costing and process costing.

14-3. "The basic distinction between job-order costing and process costing is the breadth of the denominator." Explain.

14-4. How does hybrid costing relate to job costing and process costing?

14-5. Describe the subsidiary ledger for work in process in a job-cost system.

14-6. "The general ledger entries are only a small part of the accountant's daily work." Explain.

14-7. "Cost application or absorption is terminology related to the product-costing purpose." Explain.

14-8. "Job costs are accumulated for purposes of inventory valuation and income determination." State two other purposes.

14-9. Give four examples of cost drivers.

14-10. "Each department must choose one cost driver to be used for cost application." Do you agree? Explain.

14-11. "There should be a strong relationship between the factory overhead incurred and the cost driver chosen for its application." Why?

14-12. "Sometimes direct-labor cost is the best cost driver for overhead allocation even if wage rates vary within a department." Do you agree? Explain.

14-13. What are some reasons for differences between the amounts of *incurred* and *applied* overhead?

14-14. "Under actual overhead application, unit costs soar as volume increases and vice versa." Do you agree? Explain.

14-15. "Overhead application is overhead allocation." Do you agree? Explain.

14-16. Define *normal costing*.

14-17. What is the best theoretical method of allocating underapplied or overapplied overhead, assuming that the objective is to obtain as accurate a cost application as possible?

14-18. State three examples of service industries that use the job-costing approach.

14-19. "Service firms trace only direct-labor costs to jobs. All other costs are applied as a percentage of direct-labor cost." Do you agree? Explain.

14-20. "As data processing becomes more economical, more costs than just direct material and direct labor will be classified as direct costs wherever feasible." Give three examples of such costs.

Exercises

14-21 Direct Materials
For each of the following independent cases, fill in the blanks (in millions of dollars):

	1	2	3	4
Direct-materials inventory, Dec. 31, 19X5	8	8	5	–
Purchased	5	9	–	8
Used	7	–	7	3
Direct-materials inventory, Dec. 31, 19X6	–	6	9	7

14-22 Direct Materials
Genesis Athletic Shoes had an ending inventory of direct materials of $8 million. During the year the company had acquired $15 million of additional direct materials and had used $12 million. Compute the beginning inventory.

14-23 Use of WIP Inventory Account
September production resulted in the following activity in a key account of Colebury Casting Company (in thousands):

WIP Inventory	
September 1 balance	12
Direct material used	50
Direct labor charged to jobs	25
Factory overhead applied to jobs	55

Job Orders 13N and 37Q, with total costs of $70,000 and $54,000, respectively, were completed in September.

Required
1. Journalize the completed production for September.
2. Compute the balance in WIP Inventory, September 30, after recording the completed production.
3. Journalize the credit sale of Job 13N for $98,000.

14-24 Job-Cost Record

Yale University uses job-cost records for various research projects. A major reason for such records is to justify requests for reimbursement of costs on projects sponsored by the federal government.

Consider the following summarized data regarding Project No. 76 conducted by some physicists:

- Jan. 5   Direct materials, various metals, $825
- Jan. 7   Direct materials, various chemicals, $780
- Jan. 5–12   Direct labor, research associates, 120 hours
- Jan. 7–12   Direct labor, research assistants, 180 hours

Research associates receive $32 per hour; assistants, $19. The overhead rate is 80% of direct-labor cost.

Required
Sketch a job-cost record. Post all the data to the project-cost record. Compute the total cost of the project through January 12.

14-25 Analysis of Job-Cost Data

Job-cost records for Naomi's Remodeling, Inc., contained the following data:

Job No.	Dates			Total Cost of Job at May 31
	Started	*Finished*	*Sold*	
1	April 19	May 14	May 15	$2,800
2	April 26	May 22	May 25	8,800
3	May 2	June 6	June 8	7,200
4	May 9	May 29	June 5	8,100
5	May 14	June 14	June 16	3,900

Compute Naomi's (1) WIP Inventory at May 31, (2) Finished-Goods Inventory at May 31, and (3) Cost of Goods Sold for May.

14-26 Analysis of Job-Cost Data

The Cortez Construction Company constructs houses on speculation. That is, the houses are begun before any buyer is known. Even if the buyer agrees to purchase a house under construction, no sales are recorded until the house is completed and accepted for delivery. The job-cost records contained the following (in thousands):

	Dates			Total Cost of Job at Sept. 30	Total Construction Cost Added in Oct.
Job No.	*Started*	*Finished*	*Sold*		
43	4/26	9/7	9/8	$180	
51	5/17	9/14	9/17	170	
52	5/20	9/30	10/4	150	
53	5/28	10/14	10/18	200	$50
61	6/3	10/20	11/24	115	20
62	6/9	10/21	10/27	175	25
71	7/7	11/6	11/22	118	36
81	8/7	11/24	12/24	106	52

Required

1. Compute Cortez's cost of (a) construction-in-process inventory at September 30 and October 31, (b) finished-houses inventory at September 30 and October 31, and (c) cost of houses sold for September and October.
2. Prepare summary journal entries for the transfer of completed houses from construction in process to finished houses for September and October.
3. Record the cash sale and cost of house sold of Job 53 for $350,000.

14-27 Discovery of Unknowns
Kleen Plastics has the following balances on December 31, 19X5. All amounts are in millions:

Factory overhead applied	$200
Cost of goods sold	500
Factory overhead incurred	210
Direct-materials inventory	40
Finished-goods inventory	160
WIP inventory	110

The cost of goods completed was $420. The cost of direct materials requisitioned for production during 19X5 was $200. The cost of direct materials purchased was $225. Factory overhead was applied to production at a rate of 160% of direct-labor cost.

Required   Compute the beginning inventory balances of direct materials, WIP, and finished goods. Make these computations before considering any possible adjustments for overapplied or underapplied overhead.

14-28 Discovery of Unknowns
The Chickadee Manufacturing Company has the following balances (in millions) as of December 31, 19X6:

WIP inventory	$ 14
Finished-goods inventory	175
Direct-materials inventory	65
Factory overhead incurred	180
Factory overhead applied at 150% of direct-labor cost	150
Cost of goods sold	350

The cost of direct materials purchased during 19X6 was $275. The cost of direct materials requisitioned for production during 19X6 was $235. The cost of goods completed was $493, all in millions.

Required   Before considering any year-end adjustments for overapplied or underapplied overhead, compute the beginning inventory balances of direct materials, WIP, and finished goods.

14-29 Journal Entries for Overhead
Consider the following summarized data regarding 19X6:

	Budget	Actual
Indirect labor	$ 310,000	$ 325,000
Supplies	35,000	30,000
Repairs	80,000	75,000
Utilities	110,000	103,000
Factory rent	125,000	125,000
Supervision	60,000	70,000
Depreciation, equipment	220,000	220,000
Insurance, property taxes, etc.	40,000	42,000
a. Total factory overhead	$ 980,000	$ 990,000
b. Direct materials used	$1,650,000	$1,570,000
c. Direct labor	$1,225,000	$1,200,000

Required   Omit explanations for journal entries.
1. Prepare a summary journal entry for the actual overhead incurred for 19X6.
2. Prepare summary journal entries for direct materials used and direct labor.
3. Factory overhead was applied by using a budgeted rate based on budgeted direct-labor costs. Compute the rate. Prepare a summary journal entry for the application of overhead to products.
4. Post the journal entries to the T-accounts for WIP and Factory Department Overhead Control.
5. Suppose overapplied or underapplied factory overhead is written off as an adjustment to cost of goods sold. Prepare the journal entry. Post the overhead to the overhead T-account.

14-30 Relationships Among Overhead Items
Fill in the unknowns:

	Case A	Case B	Case C
Budgeted factory overhead	$3,600,000	?	$1,500,000
Budgeted cost drivers			
Direct-labor cost	$2,000,000		
Direct-labor hours		450,000	
Machine-hours			250,000
Overhead application rate	?	$5	?

14-31 Relationship Among Overhead Items

Fill in the unknowns:

	Case 1	Case 2
a. Budgeted factory overhead	$600,000	$420,000
b. Cost driver, budgeted direct-labor cost	400,000	?
c. Budgeted factory-overhead rate	?	120%
d. Direct-labor cost incurred	570,000	?
e. Factory overhead incurred	830,000	425,000
f. Factory overhead applied	?	?
g. Underapplied (overapplied) factory overhead	?	35,000

14-32 Underapplied and Overapplied Overhead

Starr Welding Company applies factory overhead at a rate of $8.50 per direct-labor hour. Selected data for 19X6 operations are (in thousands):

	Case 1	Case 2
Direct-labor hours	30	36
Direct-labor cost	$220	$245
Indirect-labor cost	32	40
Sales commissions	20	15
Depreciation, manufacturing equipment	22	32
Direct-material cost	230	250
Factory fuel costs	35	47
Depreciation, finished-goods warehouse	5	17
Cost of goods sold	420	510
All other factory costs	138	204

Required

Compute for both cases:
1. Factory overhead applied.
2. Total factory overhead incurred.
3. Amount of underapplied or overapplied factory overhead.

14-33 Disposition of Overhead

Assume the following at the end of 19X4 (in thousands):

Cost of goods sold	$250
Direct-materials inventory	80
WIP	100
Finished goods	150
Factory department overhead control (credit balance)	50

Required

1. Assume that the underapplied or overapplied overhead is regarded as an adjustment to cost of goods sold. Prepare the journal entry.

2. Assume that the underapplied or overapplied overhead is prorated among the appropriate accounts in proportion to their ending unadjusted balances. Show computations and prepare the journal entry.
3. Which adjustment, the one in requirement 1 or 2, would result in the higher gross profit? Explain, indicating the amount of the difference.

14-34 Disposition of Overhead
A French manufacturer uses a job-order system. At the end of 19X6 the following balances existed (in millions of French francs):

Cost of goods sold	FF150
Finished goods	120
WIP	30
Factory overhead (actual)	70
Factory overhead (applied)	50

1. Prepare journal entries for two different ways to dispose of the underapplied overhead.
2. Gross profit, before considering the effects in requirement 1, was FF50 million. What is the adjusted gross profit under the two methods demonstrated?

14-35 Disposition of Year-End Underapplied Overhead
Gloria Cosmetics uses a normal cost system and has the following balances at the end of its first year's operations:

WIP inventory	$200,000
Finished-goods inventory	200,000
Cost of goods sold	400,000
Actual factory overhead	409,000
Factory overhead applied	453,000

Required Prepare journal entries for two different ways to dispose of the year-end overhead balances. By how much would gross profit differ?

Problems

14-36 Relationships of Manufacturing Costs
(CMA adapted.) Selected data concerning the past fiscal year's operations of the Wallis Manufacturing Company are (in thousands):

	Inventories	
	Beginning	Ending
Raw materials	$ 70	$ 90
WIP	75	35
Finished goods	100	120
Other data		
Raw materials used		$ 468
Total manufacturing costs charged to production during the year (includes raw materials, direct labor, and factory overhead applied at a rate of 80% of direct-labor cost)		864
Cost of goods available for sale		1,026
Selling and general expenses		50

Required

Select the best answer for each of the following items:
1. The cost of raw materials purchased during the year amounted to
   - **a.** $430
   - **b.** $458
   - **c.** $488
   - **d.** $468
   - **e.** None of these
2. Direct-labor costs charged to production during the year amounted to
   - **a.** $162
   - **b.** $230
   - **c.** $396
   - **d.** $220
   - **e.** None of these
3. The cost of goods manufactured during the year was
   - **a.** $926
   - **b.** $914
   - **c.** $951
   - **d.** $906
   - **e.** None of these
4. The cost of goods sold during the year was
   - **a.** $991
   - **b.** $926
   - **c.** $906
   - **d.** $914
   - **e.** None of these

14-37 Relationship of Subsidiary and General Ledgers, Journal Entries

The following summarized data are available on three job-cost records of Weeks Company, a manufacturer of packaging equipment:

	412		413		414
	September	*October*	*September*	*October*	*October*
Direct materials	$8,000	$2,500	$12,000	—	$13,000
Direct labor	4,000	1,500	5,000	2,500	2,000
Factory overhead applied	8,000	?	10,000	?	?

The company's fiscal year ends on October 31. Factory overhead is applied as a percentage of direct-labor costs. The balances in selected accounts on September 30 were: direct-materials inventory, $19,000; and finished-goods inventory, $18,000.

Job 412 was completed during October and transferred to finished goods. Job 413 was still in process at the end of October, as was Job 414, which had begun on October 24. These were the only jobs worked on during September and October.

Job 412 was sold along with other finished goods by October 30. The total cost of goods sold during October was $32,000. The balance in Cost of Goods Sold on September 30 was $450,000.

Required

1. Prepare a schedule showing the balance of the WIP Inventory, September 30. This schedule should show the total costs of each job record. Taken together, the job-cost records are the subsidiary ledger supporting the general ledger balance of work in process.
2. What is the overhead application rate?
3. Prepare summary general journal entries for all costs added to WIP during October. Also prepare entries for all costs transferred from WIP to Finished Goods and from Finished Goods to Cost of Goods Sold. Post to the appropriate T-accounts.
4. Prepare a schedule showing the balance of the WIP Inventory, October 31.

14-38 Straightforward Job Costing

The Scott Custom Furniture Company has two departments. Data for 19X8 include the following:

Inventories, January 1, 19X8:

Direct materials (30 types)	$75,000
WIP (in assembly)	50,000
Finished goods	40,000

Manufacturing overhead budget for 19X8:

	Machining	Assembly
Indirect labor	$220,000	$ 410,000
Supplies	45,000	40,000
Utilities	95,000	75,000
Repairs	140,000	110,000
Supervision	105,000	215,000
Factory rent	75,000	75,000
Depreciation on equipment	160,000	105,000
Insurance, property taxes, etc.	60,000	70,000
	$900,000	$1,100,000

Budgeted machine-hours were 90,000; budgeted direct-labor cost in Assembly was $2,200,000. Manufacturing overhead was applied using budgeted rates on the basis of machine-hours in Machining and on the basis of direct-labor cost in Assembly.

Following is a summary of actual events for the year:

	Machining	Assembly	Total
a. Direct materials purchased			$ 1,900,000
b. Direct materials requisitioned	$1,100,000	750,000	1,850,000
c. Direct-labor costs incurred	900,000	2,800,000	3,700,000
d1. Factory overhead incurred	1,100,000	1,100,000	2,200,000
d2. Factory overhead applied	900,000	?	?
e. Cost of goods completed	—	—	7,820,000
f1. Sales	—	—	13,000,000
f2. Cost of goods sold	—	—	7,800,000

The ending work in process (all in Assembly) was $80,000.

Required

1. Compute the budgeted overhead rates.
2. Compute the amount of the machine-hours actually worked.
3. Compute the amount of factory overhead applied in the Assembly Department.
4. Prepare general journal entries for transactions *a* through *f*. Work solely with the total amounts, not the details for Machining and Assembly. Explanations are not required. Show data in thousands of dollars. Present T-accounts, including ending inventory balances, for direct materials, WIP, and finished goods.
5. Prepare a partial income statement similar to the one illustrated in Exhibit 14-4, page 550. Overapplied or underapplied overhead is written off as an adjustment of current cost of goods sold.

14-39 Nonprofit Job Costing

Job-order costing is usually identified with manufacturing companies. However, service industries and nonprofit organizations also use the method. Suppose a social service agency has a cost accounting system that tracks cost by department (for example, family counseling, general welfare, and foster children) and by case. In this way, Heather Long, the manager of the agency, is better able to determine how its limited resources (mostly professional social workers) should be allocated. Furthermore, the manager's interactions with superiors and various politicians are more fruitful when she can cite the costs of various types of cases.

The condensed line-item budget for the general welfare department of the agency for 19X7 showed:

Professional salaries		
Level 12	5 @ $35,000 = $175,000	
Level 10	21 @ $26,000 = 546,000	
Level 8	34 @ $18,000 = 612,000	$1,333,000
Other costs		479,880
Total costs		$1,812,880

For costing various cases, the manager favored using a single overhead application rate based on the ratio of total overhead to direct labor. The latter was defined as those professional salaries assigned to specific cases.

The professional workers filled out a weekly "case time" report, which approximated the hours spent for each case.

The instructions on the report were: "Indicate how much time (in hours) you spent on each case. Unassigned time should be listed separately." About 20% of available time was unassigned to specific cases. It was used for professional development (for example, continuing education programs). "Unassigned time" became a part of "overhead," as distinguished from the direct labor.

Required

1. Compute the "overhead rate" as a percentage of direct labor (that is, the assignable professional salaries).
2. Suppose that last week a welfare case, Client No. 537, required two hours of Level 12 time, four hours of Level 10 time, and nine hours of level 8 time. How much job cost should be allocated to Client No. 537 for the week? Assume that all professional employees work a 1,800-hour year.

14-40 Job Costing in a Consulting Firm

Link Engineering Consultants is a firm of professional civil engineers. It mostly does surveying jobs for the heavy construction industry throughout New England. The firm obtains its jobs by giving fixed-price quotations, so profitability depends on the ability to predict the time required for the various subtasks on the job. (This situation is similar to that in the auditing profession, where times are budgeted for such audit steps as reconciling cash and confirming accounts receivable.)

A client may be served by various professional staff, who hold positions in the hierarchy from partners to managers to senior engineers to assistants. In addition, there are secretaries and other employees.

Link Engineering has the following budget for 19X6:

Compensation of professional staff	$3,600,000
Other costs	1,300,000
Total budgeted costs	$4,900,000

Each professional staff member must submit a weekly time report, which is used for charging hours to a client job-order record. The time report has seven columns, one for each day of the week. Its rows are as follows:

- Chargeable hours
    Client 156
    Client 183
    Etc.
- Nonchargeable hours
    Attending seminar on new equipment
    Unassigned time
    Etc.

In turn, these time reports are used for charging hours and costs to the client job-order records. The managing partner regards these job records as absolutely essential for measuring the profitability of various jobs and for providing an "experience base for improving predictions on future jobs."

Required

1. This firm applies overhead to jobs at a budgeted percentage of the professional compensation charged directly to the job ("direct labor"). For all categories of professional personnel, chargeable hours average 85% of available hours. Nonchargeable hours are regarded as additional overhead. What is the overhead rate as a percentage of "direct labor," the chargeable professional compensation cost?
2. A senior engineer works 48 weeks per year, 40 hours per week. His compensation is $60,000. He has worked on two jobs during the past week, devoting 10 hours to Job 156 and 30 hours to Job 183. How much cost should be charged to Job 156 because of his work there?

14-41 Choice of Cost Drivers in Accounting Firm

Nicole Cookie, the managing partner of N&T Cookie Accounting, is considering the desirability of tracing more costs to jobs than just direct labor. In this way, the firm will be able to justify billings to clients.

Last year's costs were:

Direct-professional labor	$ 5,000,000
Overhead	10,000,000
Total costs	$15,000,000

The following costs were included in overhead:

Computer time	$ 950,000
Secretarial cost	900,000
Photocopying	350,000
Fringe benefits to direct labor	1,000,000
Phone call time with clients (estimated but not tabulated)	800,000
Total	$4,000,000

The firm's data processing techniques now make it feasible to document and trace these costs to individual jobs.

As an experiment, in December Nicole Cookie arranged to trace these costs to six audit engagements. Two job records showed the following:

	Engagement	
	Zeandale Milling	*Kaw Valley Bank*
Direct-professional labor	$15,000	$15,000
Fringe benefits to direct labor	3,000	3,000
Phone call time with clients	1,500	500
Computer time	3,000	700
Secretarial costs	2,000	1,500
Photocopying	500	300
Total direct costs	$25,000	$21,000

Required

1. Compute the overhead application rate based on last year's costs.
2. Suppose last year's costs were reclassified so that $4 million would be regarded as direct costs instead of overhead. Compute the overhead application rate as a percentage of direct labor and as a percentage of total direct costs.
3. Using the three rates computed in requirements 1 and 2, compute the total costs of engagements for Zeandale Milling and Kaw Valley Bank.
4. Suppose that client billing was based on a 30% markup of total job costs. Compute the billings that would be forthcoming in requirement 3.
5. Which method of job costing and overhead application do you favor? Explain.

14-42 Reconstruction of Transactions
(This problem is more challenging than the others in this chapter.)
   You are asked to bring the following incomplete accounts of a printing plant acquired in a merger up to date through January 31, 19X6. Also consider the data that appear after the T-accounts.

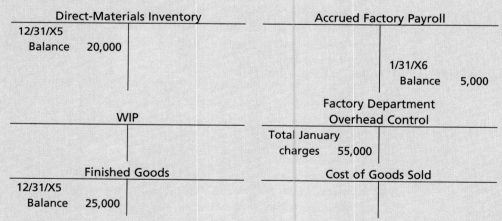

Additional information:

1. The overhead is applied using a budgeted rate that is set every December by forecasting the following year's overhead and relating it to forecasted direct-labor costs. The budget for 19X6 called for $640,000 of direct labor and $800,000 of factory overhead.
2. The only job unfinished on January 31, 19X6, was No. 419, on which total labor charges were $3,000 (200 direct-labor-hours), and total direct-material charges were $21,000.
3. Total materials placed into production during January totaled $140,000.

4. Cost of goods completed during January was $260,000.

5. January 31 balances of direct materials totaled $25,000.

6. Finished-goods inventory as of January 31 was $35,000.

7. All factory workers earn the same rate of pay. Direct-labor hours for January totaled 3,000. Indirect labor and supervision totaled $12,000.

8. The gross factory payroll paid on January paydays totaled $55,000. Ignore withholdings.

9. All "actual" factory overhead incurred during January has already been posted.

Required

a. Direct materials purchased during January

b. Cost of goods sold during January

c. Direct-labor costs incurred during January

d. Overhead applied during January

e. Balance, Accrued Factory Payroll, December 31, 19X5

f. Balance, WIP, December 31, 19X5

g. Balance, WIP, January 31, 19X6

h. Overapplied or underapplied overhead for January

Cases

14-43 Overhead Accounting for Control and for Product Costing

The games department of a major toy manufacturer has an overhead rate of $5 per direct-labor hour, based on expected variable overhead of $150,000 per year, expected fixed overhead of $350,000 per year, and expected direct-labor hours of 100,000 per year.

Data for the year's operations follow:

	Direct-Labor Hours Used	Overhead Costs Incurred*
First six months	55,000	$262,000
Last six months	41,000	236,500

* Fixed costs incurred were exactly equal to budgeted amounts throughout the year.

Required

1. What is the underapplied or overapplied overhead for each six-month period? Label your answer as underapplied or overapplied.

2. Explain *briefly* (not more than 50 words for each part) the probable causes for the underapplied or overapplied overhead. Focus on variable and fixed costs separately. Give the exact figures attributable to the causes you cite.

14-44 Multiple Overhead Rates and Activity-Based Costing

A division of Hewlett-Packard assembles and tests printed circuit (PC) boards. The division has many different products. Some are high volume; others are low volume. For years, manufacturing overhead was applied to products using a single overhead rate based on direct-labor dollars. However, direct labor has shrunk to 6% of total manufacturing costs.

Managers decided to refine the division's product-costing system. Abolishing the direct-labor category, they included all manufacturing labor as a part of factory overhead. They also identified several activities and the appropriate cost driver for each. The cost driver for the first activity, the start station, was the number of raw PC boards. The application rate was computed as follows:

$$\text{application rate for start station activity} = \frac{\text{budgeted total factory overhead at the activity}}{\text{budgeted raw PC boards for the year}}$$

$$= \frac{\$150,000}{125,000} = \$1.20$$

Each time a raw PC board passes through the start station activity, $1.20 is added to the cost of a product. The product cost is the sum of costs directly traced to the product plus the indirect costs (factory overhead) accumulated at each of the manufacturing activities undergone.

Using assumed numbers, consider the following data regarding PC Board 74:

Direct materials	$70.00
Factory overhead applied	?
Total manufacturing product cost	?

The activities involved and the related cost drivers chosen were:

Activity	Cost Driver	Factory-Overhead Costs Applied for Each Activity
1. Start station	No. of raw PC boards	1 × $ 1.20 = $1.20
2. Axial insertion	No. of axial insertions	42 × .07 = ?
3. Dip insertion	No. of dip insertions	? × .20 = 5.60
4. Manual insertion	No. of manual insertions	15 × ? = 6.00
5. Wave solder	No. of boards soldered	1 × 3.20 = 3.20
6. Backload	No. of backload insertions	8 × .60 = 4.80
7. Test	Standard time board is in test activity	.15 × 80.00 = ?
8. Defect analysis	Standard time for defect analysis and repair	.05 × ? = 4.50
Total		$?

Required

1. Fill in the blanks.
2. How is direct labor identified with products under this product-costing system?
3. Why would managers favor this multiple-overhead rate, activity-based costing system instead of the older system?

14-45 One or Two Cost Drivers
The Zoe Tool Co. in Geneva, Switzerland, has the following 19X7 budget for its two departments in Swiss francs (SF):

	Machining	Finishing	Total
Direct labor	SF 300,000	SF 800,000	SF 1,100,000
Factory overhead	SF 960,000	SF 800,000	SF 1,760,000
Machine-hours	60,000	20,000	80,000

In the past, the company has used a single plantwide overhead application rate based on direct-labor cost. However, as its product line has expanded and as competition has intensified, Mr. Zoe, the company president, has questioned the accuracy of the profits or losses shown on various products.

Zoe makes custom tools on special orders from customers. To be competitive and still make a reasonable profit, it is essential that the firm measure the cost of each customer order. Mr. Zoe has focused on overhead allocation as a potential problem. He knows that changes in costs are more heavily affected by machine-hours in the machining department and by direct-labor costs in the finishing department. As company controller, you have gathered the following data regarding two typical customer orders:

	Order Number	
	100361	*100362*
Machining		
Direct materials	SF 4,000	SF 4,000
Direct labor	SF 3,000	SF 1,500
Machine-hours	1,200	100
Finishing		
Direct labor	SF 1,500	SF 3,000
Machine-hours	120	120

Required

1. Compute six factory overhead application rates, three based on direct-labor cost and three based on machine-hours for machining, finishing, and for the plant as a whole.
2. Use the application rates to compute the total costs of orders 100361 and 100362 as follows: (a) plantwide rate based on direct-labor cost and (b) machining based on machine-hours and finishing based on direct-labor cost.
3. Evaluate your answers in requirement 2. Which set of job costs do you prefer? Why?

15

Process-Costing Systems

Eagle-Gypsum Products mines gypsum rock in the Colorado rockies and manufactures gypsum wallboard for commercial and residential construction. With backflush costing, costs are applied to wallboard only after production is complete.
Courtesy Eagle-Gypsum Products

Learning Objectives

When you have finished studying this chapter, you should be able to

1 Explain the basic ideas underlying process costing and how they differ from job costing.

2 Compute output in terms of equivalent units.

3 Compute costs and prepare journal entries for the principal transactions in a process-costing system.

4 Demonstrate how the presence of beginning inventories affects the computations of unit costs under the weighted-average method.

5 Demonstrate how the presence of beginning inventories affects the computation of unit costs under the first-in, first-out method.

6 Use backflush costing with a JIT production system.

7 Describe operation costing (Appendix 15).

Cost accounting systems fulfill two major purposes: (1) They allocate costs to departments for *planning and control*, and (2) they apply costs to units of product for *product costing*. Most of this book focuses on planning and control. This chapter, however, concentrates on a basic type of product costing called process costing and includes discussion of an adaptation of process costing called *backflush costing*. Appendix 15 describes hybrid-costing systems by illustrating operation costing.

The first part of the chapter (pages 569–576) presents the basic ideas of process costing. This coverage is sufficient for someone who wants just a general understanding of such systems. The second part introduces the complications arising from consideration of beginning inventories, which is important in applying process costing. The last part discusses backflush costing, a simplified version of process costing used by many companies that have adopted a JIT inventory system.

■ INTRODUCTION TO PROCESS COSTING

As noted in Chapter 14, all product costing uses averaging to determine costs per unit of production. The average unit cost may be relatively narrow, as in the production of a particular printing order in job-order costing. In contrast, the average may be broad, as in the production of beverages in process costing. *Process-costing systems* apply costs to like products that are usually mass produced in continuous fashion through a series of production *processes*. These processes are often organized as separate departments, although a single department sometimes contains more than one process.

Process Costing Compared with Job Costing

Job costing and process costing are used for different types of products. Firms in industries such as printing, construction, and furniture manufacturing, in which each unit or batch (job) of product is unique and easily identifiable, use job-order costing. Process costing is used when there is mass production through a sequence of several processes, such as mixing and cooking. Examples include chemicals, flour, glass, and toothpaste.

Exhibit 15-1

Comparison of Job-Order and Process Costing

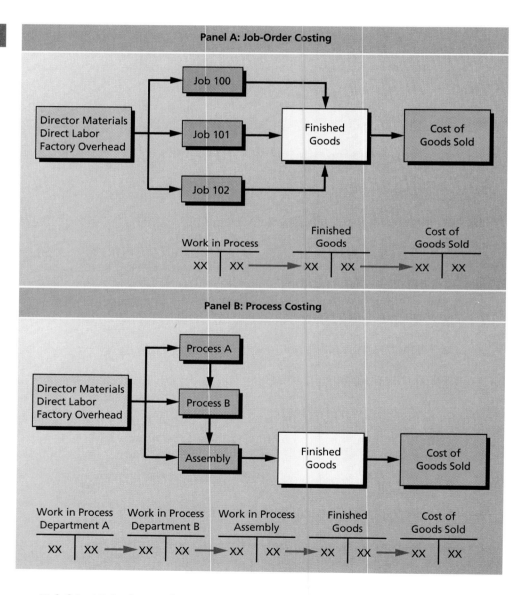

Exhibit 15-1 shows the major differences between job-order costing and process costing. Process costing requires several work-in-process accounts, one for each process or department. As goods move from process to process, their costs are transferred accordingly.

Process manufacturing systems vary in design. The design shown in panel B of Exhibit 15-1 is *sequential*—units pass from process A to process B. Many other designs are found in practice—each tailored to meet specific product requirements. For example, processes can be operated in *parallel* until final assembly. In this case process A and process B might simultaneously each produce a subcomponent of the final product. Whatever the specific layout, the basic principles of process costing are the same.

The process-costing approach does not distinguish among individual units of product. Instead, accumulated costs for a period are divided by quantities produced during that period to get broad, average unit costs. Process costing is applied to nonmanufacturing activities as well as manufacturing activities. Examples include dividing the costs of giving state automobile driver's license tests by the number of tests given and dividing the cost of a post office sorting department by the number of items sorted.

Process-costing systems are usually simpler and less expensive than job-order costing. Individual jobs do not exist. There are no job-cost records. The unit cost for inventory purposes is calculated by accumulating the costs of each processing department and dividing the total cost by an appropriate measure of output.

To get a rough feel for process costing, consider Magenta Midget Frozen Vegetables. It quick-cooks tiny carrots, beans, and so on before freezing them. As shown below, the costs of cooked vegetables (in millions of dollars) are transferred from the Cooking Department to the Freezing Department:

Work in Process—Cooking			Work in Process—Freezing	
Direct materials 14	Transfer cost of goods completed to next		Cost transferred in from	Transfer cost of goods completed to finished
Direct labor 4			cooking 24	goods 25
Factory overhead 8	department 24		Additional	
26			costs 3	
			27	
Ending inventory 2			Ending inventory 2	

The amount of cost to be transferred is determined by dividing the accumulated costs in the Cooking Department by the pounds of vegetables processed. The resulting cost per pound is then multiplied by the pounds of vegetables physically transferred to the Freezing Department.

The journal entries are similar to those for the job-order-costing system. That is, direct materials, direct labor, and factory overhead are accounted for as before. However, now there is more than a single work-in-process account for all units being manufactured. There is one work-in-process account for each processing department, Work in Process—Cooking and Work in Process—Freezing, in our example. The foregoing data would be recorded as follows:

1. Work in Process—Cooking 14
      Direct-materials inventory 14
    To record direct materials used

2.	Work in Process—Cooking	4	
	Accrued payroll		4
	To record direct labor		
3.	Work in Process—Cooking	8	
	Factory overhead		8
	To record factory overhead applied to product		
4.	Work in Process—Freezing	24	
	Work in Process—Cooking		24
	To transfer goods from the cooking process		
5.	Work in Process—Freezing	3	
	Accrued payroll		1
	Factory overhead		2
	To record direct labor and factory overhead applied to product		
6.	Finished goods	25	
	Work in Process—Freezing		25
	To transfer goods from the freezing process		

The central product-costing problem is how each department should compute the cost of goods transferred out and the cost of goods remaining in the department. If an identical amount of work was done on each unit transferred and on each unit in ending inventory, the solution is easy. Total costs are simply divided by total units. However, if the units in the inventory are each partially completed, the product-costing system must distinguish between the fully completed units transferred out and the partially completed units not yet transferred.

■ APPLICATION OF PROCESS COSTING

Consider another illustration. Suppose Oakville Wooden Toys, Inc., buys wood as a direct material for its Forming Department. The department processes only one type of toy, marionettes. The marionettes are transferred to the Finishing Department, where hand shaping, strings, paint, and clothing are added.

The Forming Department manufactured 25,000 identical units during April, and its costs that month were:

Direct materials		$ 70,000
Conversion costs		
Direct labor	$10,625	
Factory overhead	31,875	42,500
Costs to account for		$112,500

The unit cost of goods completed would simply be $112,500 ÷ 25,000 = $4.50. An itemization would show:

Direct materials, $70,000 ÷ 25,000	$2.80
Conversion costs, $42,500 ÷ 25,000	1.70
Unit cost of a whole completed marionette	$4.50

But what if not all 25,000 marionettes were completed during April? For example, assume that 5,000 were still in process at the end of April—only 20,000 were started and fully completed. All direct materials had been placed in process, but on average only 25% of the conversion costs had been applied to the 5,000 marionettes that remain in process. How should the Forming Department calculate the cost of goods transferred and the cost of goods remaining in the ending work-in-process inventory? The answer lies in the following five key steps:

- **Step 1:** Summarize the flow of physical units.
- **Step 2:** Calculate output in terms of equivalent units.
- **Step 3:** Summarize the total costs to account for, which are the costs applied to work in process.
- **Step 4:** Calculate unit costs.
- **Step 5:** Apply costs to units completed and to units in the ending work in process.

Physical Units and Equivalent Units (Steps 1 and 2)

Step 1, as the first column in Exhibit 15-2 shows, tracks the physical units of production. How should the output for April be measured? Not as 25,000 units. Instead, the output was 20,000 fully completed units and 5,000 partially completed units. A partially completed unit is not a perfect substitute for a fully completed unit. Accordingly, output is usually stated in *equivalent units*, not physical units.

equivalent units The number of completed units that could have been produced from the inputs applied.

Equivalent units are the number of completed units that could have been produced from the inputs applied. For example, four units each one-half completed represent two equivalent units. If each had been one-fourth completed, they would have represented one equivalent unit.

In our example, as step 2 in Exhibit 15-2 shows, the output would be measured as 25,000 equivalent units of direct-materials cost but only 21,250 equivalent units of *conversion costs*. Conversion costs include all manufacturing costs other than direct materials. Direct labor is usually not a major part of total costs, so it is combined with factory-overhead costs (such as the costs of energy, repairs, and material handling) as a major classification called conversion costs. Why only 21,250 equivalent units of conversion costs but 25,000 of direct-materials cost? Because direct materials had been added to all 25,000 units. In contrast, the conversion costs applied to the 5,000 partially completed units would have been sufficient to complete 1,250 units in addition to the 20,000 units that were actually completed.

Objective 2

Compute output in terms of equivalent units.

Computation of equivalent units requires estimates of degrees of completion for inventories in process. The accuracy of these estimates depends on the care and skill of the estimator and the nature of the process. Estimating the degree of completion is usually easier for materials than for conversion costs. The conversion sequence usually consists of a number of standard operations or a standard number of hours, days, weeks, or months for mixing, heating, cooling, aging, curing, and so forth. Thus the degree of completion for conversion costs depends on what proportion of the total effort needed to complete one unit or one batch has been devoted to units still in process. In industries where no exact estimate is possible, or, as in textiles, where vast quantities in process prohibit costly physical estimates, all work in process in every department is assumed to be one-third or one-half or two-thirds complete. In other cases, continuous processing entails little change of work-in-process levels from month to month. Consequently, in such cases, work in process is safely ignored, and monthly production costs are assigned solely to goods completed.

Exhibit 15-2

Forming Department Output in Equivalent Units for the Month Ended April 30, 19X1

Flow of Production	(Step 1) Physical Units	(Step 2) Equivalent Units	
		Direct Materials	Conversion Costs
Started and completed	20,000	20,000	20,000
Work in process, ending inventory	5,000	5,000	1,250*
Units accounted for	25,000		
Work done to date		25,000	21,250*

* 5,000 physical units × .25 degree of completion of conversion costs.

Measures in equivalent units are not confined to manufacturing situations. Such measures are a popular way of expressing workloads in terms of a common denominator. For example, radiology departments measure their output in terms of weighted units. Various x-ray procedures are ranked in terms of the time, supplies, and related costs devoted to each. A simple chest x-ray may receive a weight of one. But a skull x-ray may receive a weight of three because it uses three times the resources (e.g., technicians' time) as a procedure with a weight of one. Another example is the expression by universities of students enrolled in terms of full-time enrollment equivalents.

■ CALCULATION OF PRODUCT COSTS (STEPS 3 TO 5)

Objective 3

Compute costs and prepare journal entries for the principal transactions in a process-costing system

Exhibit 15-3 is a production-cost report. It shows steps 3 to 5 of process costing. Step 3 summarizes the total costs to account for (i.e., the total costs in, or debits to, Work in Process—Forming). Step 4 obtains unit costs by dividing total costs by the appropriate measures of equivalent units. The unit cost of a completed unit—material cost plus conversion costs—is $2.80 + $2.00 = $4.80.[1] Step 5 then uses these unit costs to apply costs to products.

Concentrate in Exhibit 15-3 on how the costs are applied to obtain an ending work in process of $16,500. The 5,000 physical units are fully completed in terms of direct materials. Therefore the direct materials applied to work in process are 5,000 equivalent units times $2.80, or $14,000. In contrast, the 5,000 physical units are 25% completed in terms of conversion costs. Therefore, the

---

[1] Why is the unit cost $4.80 instead of the $4.50 calculated earlier in this chapter (p. 572)? Because the $42,500 conversion cost is spread over 21,250 units instead of 25,000 units.

conversion costs applied to work in process are 1,250 equivalent units (25% of 5,000 physical units) times $2.00, or $2,500.

Exhibit 15-3

Forming Department Production Cost Report Month Ended April 30, 19X1

		Total Costs	Details Direct Materials	Details Conversion Costs
(Step 3)	Costs to account for	$112,500	$70,000	$42,500
(Step 4)	Divide by equivalent units		÷25,000	÷ 21,250
	Unit costs	$ 4.80	$ 2.80	$ 2.00
(Step 5)	Application of costs			
	To units completed and transferred to the Finishing Department, 20,000 units @$4.80	$ 96,000		
	To units not completed and still in process, April 30, 5,000 units			
	Direct materials	$ 14,000	5,000 ($2.80)	
	Conversion costs	2,500		1,250 ($2.00)
	Work in process, April 30	$ 16,500		
	Total costs accounted for	$112,500		

Journal entries for the data in our illustration would appear as:

1. Work in Process   70,000
      Direct-materials inventory   70,000
   Materials added to production in April

2. Work in Process—Forming   10,625
      Accrued payroll   10,625
   Direct labor in April

3. Work in Process—Forming   31,875
      Factory overhead   31,875
   Factory overhead applied in April

4. Work in Process—Finishing   96,000
      Work in Process—Forming   96,000
   Cost of goods completed and transferred in April from Forming to Assembly

The $112,500 added to the Work in Process—Forming account less the $96,000 transferred out leaves an ending balance of $16,500:

Work in Process—Forming			
1. Direct materials	$ 70,000	4. Transferred out	
2. Direct labor	10,625	to finishing	$96,000
3. Factory overhead	31,875		
Costs to account for	112,500		
Bal. April 30	16,500		

Summary Problem for Your Review

Problem One

Taylor Plastics makes a variety of plastic products. Its Extruding Department had the
following output and costs:

Units
  Started and completed: 30,000 units
  Started and still in process: 10,000 units; 100% completed for direct materials,
    but 60% completed for conversion costs
Costs applied
  Total: $81,600; direct materials, $60,000; conversion, $21,600

Compute the cost of work completed and the cost of the ending inventory of work in
process.

Solution to Problem One

		(Step 2) Equivalent Units	
Flow of Production	**(Step 1) Physical Units**	*Direct Materials*	*Conversion*
Started and completed	30,000	30,000	30,000
Ending work in process	10,000	10,000*	6,000*
Units accounted for	40,000		
Work done to date		40,000	36,000

* 10,000 x 100% = 10,000; 10,000 x 60% = 6,000.

				Details	
		Total Costs	*Direct Materials*	*Conversion Costs*
(Step 3)	Costs to account for	$81,600	$60,000	$21,600
(Step 4)	Divide by equivalent units		÷40,000	÷36,000
	Unit costs	$ 2.10*	$ 1.50	$ .60
(Step 5)	Application of costs			
	To units completed and transferred, 30,000 units @$2.10	$63,000		
	To ending work in process, 10,000 units			
	Direct materials	$15,000	10,000 ($1.50)	
	Conversion costs	3,600		6,000 ($.60)
	Work in process, ending inventory	$18,600		
	Total costs accounted for	$81,600		

* Unit cost ($2.10) = direct materials costs ($1.50) + conversion costs ($.60).

■ EFFECTS OF BEGINNING INVENTORIES

When beginning inventories are present, product costing becomes more complicated. Suppose Oakville Wooden Toys had 3,000 marionettes in work in process in its Forming Department on March 31. All direct materials had been placed in process, but on the average only 40% of the conversion costs had been applied to the 3,000 units. Because 25,000 units were worked on during April (20,000 units completed plus 5,000 still in process at the end of the month) and because there were 3,000 units in beginning inventory, 22,000 units must have been started in production during April.

The accompanying table presents the data we use in our illustrations:

Units		
Work in process, March 31: 3,000 units; 100% completed for materials, but only 40% completed for conversion costs		
Units started in April: 22,000		
Units completed in April: 20,000		
Work in process, April 30: 5,000 units; 100% completed for materials, but only 25% completed for conversion costs		
Costs		
Work in process, March 31		
Direct materials	$7,320	
Conversion costs	2,119	$ 9,439
Direct materials added during April		70,180
Conversion costs added during April		
($10,625 + $31,881)		42,506
Total costs to account for		$122,125

Note that the $122,125 total costs to account for include the $9,439 of beginning inventory in addition to the $112,686 added during April.

In this section, we discuss common inventory methods: the weighted-average method and the first-in, first-out method. The five-step approach is recommended for both methods.

■ WEIGHTED-AVERAGE METHOD

weighted-average (WA) process-costing method A process-costing method that adds the cost of (1) all work done in the current period to (2) the work done in the preceding period on the current period's beginning inventory of work in process and divides the total by the equivalent units of work done to date.

The **weighted-average (WA) process-costing method** adds the cost of (1) all work done in the current period to (2) the work done in the preceding period on the current period's beginning inventory of work in process. This total is divided by the equivalent units of work done to date, whether that work was done in the current period or previously.

Why is the term *weighted-average* used to describe this method? Primarily because the unit costs used for applying costs to products are affected by the *total cost incurred to date*, regardless of whether those costs were incurred during or before the current period.

Exhibit 15-4 shows the first two steps in this method, computation of physical units and equivalent units. Note that this illustration differs from the previous illustration in only one major respect, the presence of beginning work in process.

The computation of equivalent units ignores whether all 25,000 units to account for came from beginning work in process, or all were started in April,

Objective 4

Demonstrate how the presence of beginning inventories affects the computations of unit costs under the weighted-average method

or some combination thereof. Thus both Exhibits 15-2 and 15-4 show the total work done to date, 25,000 equivalent units of direct materials and 21,250 units of conversion costs. The equivalent units for work done to date, which is the divisor for unit costs, is unaffected by whether all work was done in April or some before April on the March 31 inventory of work in process.

Exhibit 15-5 presents a production-cost report. Its pattern is similar to that in Exhibit 15-3. That is, the report summarizes steps 3 to 5 regarding computations of product costs. The unit costs in Exhibit 15-5 are higher than those in Exhibit 15-3. Why? Because the equivalent units are the same, but the total costs include the costs incurred before April on the units in beginning inventory as well as those costs added during April.

Exhibit 15-4

Forming Department Output in Equivalent Units
Month Ended April 30, 19X1 (Weighted-Average Method)

		(Step 2) Equivalent Units	
Flow of Production	**(Step 1) Physical Units**	*Direct Materials*	*Conversion Costs*
Work in process, March 31	3,000 (40%)*		
Started in April	22,000		
To account for	25,000		
Completed and transferred out		20,000	20,000
during current period	20,000		
Work in process, April 30	5,000 (25%)*	5,000	1,250†
Units accounted for	25,000		
Work done to date		25,000	21,250

* Degrees of completion for conversion costs at the dates of inventories.
† .25 × 5,000 = 1,250.

To recap what has happened so far in this chapter:

1. In the first simple example, we assumed no beginning or ending inventories of work in process. Thus, when the $112,500 of costs incurred during April were applied to the 25,000 units worked on and fully completed during April, the unit cost (p. 572) was $2.80 + $1.70 = $4.50.

2. However, in the next example, we assumed that some of the units were not fully completed by the end of the month. This reduced the equivalent units and thus increased the unit cost (Exhibit 15-3, p. 575) to $2.80 + $2.00 = $4.80.

3. Then, in this latest example, we assumed that some of the units had also been worked on before April. The costs of that work are carried in work-in-process inventory, March 31. The addition of these costs (with no change in the equivalent units) increased the unit cost of work completed in April to $3.10 + $2.10 = $5.20.

first-in, first-out (FIFO) process-costing method
A process-costing method that sharply distinguishes the current work done from the previous work done on the beginning inventory of work in process.

■ FIRST-IN, FIRST-OUT METHOD

The **first-in, first-out (FIFO) process-costing method** sharply distinguishes the current work done from the previous work done on the beginning inventory of work in process. The calculation of equivalent units is confined to the work done in the current period (April in this illustration).

Exhibit 15-6 presents steps 1 and 2. The easiest way to compute equivalent units under the FIFO method is, first, compute the work done to date. Exhibit 15-6 shows these computations, which are exactly the same as in Exhibit 15-4. Second, deduct the work done *before* the current period. The remainder is the work done *during* the current period, which is the key to computing the unit costs by the FIFO method.

			Totals	Direct Materials	Conversion Costs
				Details	
(Step 3)	Work in process, March 31		$ 9,439	$ 7,320	$ 2,119
	Costs added currently		112,686	70,180	42,506
	Total costs to account for		$122,125	$77,500	$44,625
(Step 4)	Divisor, equivalent units for work done to date*			25,000	21,250
	Unit costs (weighted averages)		$ 5.20	$ 3.10	$ 2.10
(Step 5)	Application of costs				
	Completed and transferred, 20,000 units ($5.20)		$104,000		
	Work in process, April 30, 5,000 units				
	Direct materials		$ 15,500	5,000 ($3.10)	
	Conversion costs		2,625		1,250* ($2.10)
	Total work in process		$ 18,125		
	Total costs accounted for		$122,125		

Exhibit 15-5

Forming Department Production-Cost Report for the Month Ended April 30, 19X1 (Weighted-Average Method)

* Equivalent units of work done. For more details, see Exhibit 15-4.

Exhibit 15-6

Forming Department Output in Equivalent Units for the Month Ended April 30, 19X1 (FIFO Method)

Same as Exhibit 15-4

Flow of Production	(Step 1) Physical Units	(Step 2) Equivalent Units	
		Direct Materials	Conversion Costs
Work in process, March 31	3,000 (40%)*		
Started in April	22,000		
To account for	25,000		
Completed and transferred out	20,000	20,000	20,000
Work in process, April 30	5,000 (25%)*	5,000	1,250†
Units accounted for	25,000		
Work done to date		25,000	21,250
Less: equivalent units of work from previous periods included in beginning inventory		3,000‡	1,200§
Work done in current period only		22,000	20,050

* Degrees of completion for conversion costs at the dates of inventories.
† 5,000 × .25 = 1,250 equivalent units.
‡ 3,000 × 1.00 = 3,000 equivalent units.
§ 3,000 × .40 = 1,200 equivalent units.

Objective 5

Demonstrate how the presence of beginning inventories affects the computation of unit costs under the first-in, first-out method

FIFO is really a small step in the direction of job-order costing. Why? Because FIFO recognizes a distinct batch of production each period, whereas the weighted-average method does not. The divisor equivalent units for computing a unit cost are the equivalent units of only *current* work done.

Exhibit 15-7 is the production-cost report. It presents steps 3 to 5. The $9,439 beginning inventory balance is kept separate from current costs. The calculations of equivalent unit costs are confined to costs added in April only.

The bottom half of Exhibit 15-7 shows two ways to compute the costs of goods completed and transferred out. The first and faster way is to compute the $18,600 ending work in process and then deduct it from the $122,125 total costs to account for, obtaining $103,525. As a check on accuracy, it is advisable to use a second way: compute the cost of goods transferred in the detailed manner displayed in the footnote in Exhibit 15-7.

Exhibit 15-7

Forming Department Production-Cost Report for the Month Ended April 30, 19X1 (FIFO Method)

		Totals	**Details**	
			Direct Materials	***Conversion Costs***
(Step 3)	Work in process, March 31	$ 9,439	(work done before April)	
	Costs added currently	112,686	$70,180	$42,506
	Total costs to account for	$122,125		
(Step 4)	Divisor, equivalent units of work done in April only		22,000*	20,050*
	Unit costs (for FIFO basis)	$ 5.31	$ 3.19	$ 2.12
(Step 5)	Application of costs			
	Work in process, April 30			
	Direct materials	$ 15,950	5,000 ($3.19)	
	Conversion costs	2,650		1,250* ($2.12)
	Total work in process (5,000 units)	18,600		
	Completed and transferred out (20,000 units), $122,125 − $18,600	103,525†		
	Total costs accounted for	$122,125		

* Equivalent units of work done. See Exhibit 15-6 for more details.

† Check: Work in process, March 31 .... $ 9,439
    Additional costs to complete, conversion costs of 60% of
       3,000 × $2.12 = ... 3,816
    Started and completed, 22,000 − 5,000 = 17,000;
       17,000 × $5.31 = ... 90,270
    Total cost transferred $103,525
    Unit cost transferred, $103,525 ÷ 20,000 = $5.17625

Differences Between FIFO and Weighted-Average Methods

The key difference between the FIFO and weighted-average computations is equivalent units:

- FIFO—Equivalent units are the work done in the current period only.
- Weighted-average—Equivalent units are the work done to date including the earlier work done on the current period's beginning inventory of work in process.

These differences in equivalent units lead to differences in unit costs. Accordingly, there are differences in costs applied to goods completed and still in process. In our example, the FIFO method results in a larger work-in-process inventory on April 30 and a smaller April cost of goods transferred out:

	Weighted Average*	FIFO†
Cost of goods transferred out	$104,000	$103,525
Ending work in process	18,125	18,600
Total costs accounted for	$122,125	$122,125

* From Exhibit 15-5, page 579.
† From Exhibit 15-7, page 580.

Differences in unit costs between FIFO and weighted-average methods are ordinarily insignificant because (1) changes in material prices, labor wage rates, and other manufacturing costs from month to month tend to be small, and (2) changes in the volume of production and inventory levels also tend to be small.

The FIFO method involves more detailed computations than the weighted-average method. That is why FIFO is almost never used in practice in process costing *for product-costing purposes*. However, the FIFO *equivalent units* for current work done are essential *for planning and control purposes*. Why? Because they isolate the output for one particular period. Consider our example. The FIFO computations of equivalent units help managers to measure the efficiency of April's performance independently from March's performance. Thus budgets or standards for each month's departmental costs can be compared against actual results in light of the actual work done during any given month.

Transferred-in Costs

transferred-in costs
In process costing, costs incurred in a previous department for items that have been received by a subsequent department.

Many companies that use process costing have sequential production processes. For example, Oakville Wooden Toys transfers the items completed in its Forming Department to the Finishing Department. The Finishing Department would call the costs of the items it receives **transferred-in costs**—costs incurred in a previous department for items that have been received by a subsequent department. They are similar to but not identical to additional direct-material costs. Because transferred-in costs are a combination of all types of costs (direct-material and conversion costs) incurred in previous departments, they should not be called a direct-material cost in a subsequent department.

We account for transferred-in costs just as we account for direct materials, with one exception: Transferred-in costs are kept separate from the direct materials added in the department. Therefore, reports such as Exhibits 15-5 and 15-7 will include three columns of costs instead of two: transferred-in costs, direct-material costs, and conversion costs. The total unit cost will be the sum of all three types of unit costs.

Summary Problem for Your Review

Problem One appeared earlier in this chapter.

Problem Two

Consider the Cooking Department of Middleton Foods, a British food-processing company. Compute the cost of work completed and the cost of the ending inventory of work in process, using both the (1) weighted-average (WA) method and (2) FIFO method.

Units		
Beginning work in process: 5,000 units; 100% completed for materials, 40% completed for conversion costs		
Started during month: 28,000 units		
Completed during month: 31,000 units		
Ending work in process: 2,000 units; 100% completed for materials, 50% for conversion costs		
Costs		
Beginning work in process		
Direct materials	£8,060	
Conversion costs	1,300	£ 9,360
Direct materials added in current month		41,440
Conversion costs added in current month		14,700
Total costs to account for		£65,500

Solution to Problem Two

	(Step 1)	(Step 2) Equivalent Units	
Flow of Production	**Physical Units**	*Material*	*Conversion Cost*
Completed and transferred out	31,000	31,000	31,000
Ending work in process	2,000	2,000 *	1,000 *
1. Equivalent units, WA	33,000	33,000	32,000
Less: beginning work in process	5,000	5,000 †	2,000 †
2. Equivalent units, FIFO	28,000	28,000	30,000

* 2,000 × 100% = 2,000; 2,000 × 50% = 1,000.
† 5,000 × 100% = 5,000; 5,000 × 40% = 2,000.

Note especially that the work done to date is the basis for computing the equivalent units under the weighted-average method. In contrast, the basis for computing the equivalent units under the FIFO method is the work done in the current period only.

1.

Weighted-Average Method	Total Cost	Direct Materials	Conversion Costs
Beginning work in process	£ 9,360	£ 8,060	£ 1,300
Costs added currently	56,140	41,440	14,700
Total costs to account for	£65,500	£49,500	£16,000
Equivalent units, weighted-average		÷33,000	÷32,000
Unit costs, weighted-average	£ 2.00	£ 1.50	£ 0.50
Transferred out, 31,000 × £2.00	£62,000		
Ending work in process			
Direct materials	£ 3,000	(£ 1.50) 2,000	
Conversion cost	500		1,000 (£.50)
Total work in process	£ 3,500		
Total costs accounted for	£65,500		

2.

FIFO Method	Total Cost	Direct Materials	Conversion Costs
Beginning work in process	£ 9,360	(work done before month)	
Costs added currently	56,140	£41,440	£14,700
Total costs to account for	£65,500		
Equivalent units, FIFO		÷28,000	÷30,000
Unit costs, FIFO	£ 1.97	£ 1.48	£ 0.49
Ending work in process			
Direct materials	£ 2,960	2,000 (£1.48)	
Conversion cost	490		1,000 (£.49)
Total work in process	£ 3,450		
Transferred out, £65,500 − £3,450	£62,050*		
Total costs accounted for	£65,500		

* Check:

Beginning work in process	£ 9,360
Costs to complete, 60% × 5,000 × £.49	1,470
Started and completed, (31,000 − 5,000) (£1.48 + £.49)	51,220
Total cost transferred	£62,050

Unit cost transferred, £62,050 ÷ 31,000 = £2.00161

■ PROCESS COSTING IN A JIT SYSTEM: BACKFLUSH COSTING

Tracking costs through various stages of inventory—raw materials, work-in-process, and finished goods inventories—makes accounting systems complex. If there were no inventories, all costs would be charged directly to cost of goods sold, and accounting systems would be much simpler. Organizations using JIT

backflush costing
An accounting system that applies costs to products only when the production is complete.

production systems usually have very small inventories, and they may not want to bear the expense of a system that traces costs through all the inventory accounts. Such firms can use **backflush costing,** an accounting system that applies costs to products only when the production is complete.

Principles of Backflush Costing

Backflush costing has only two categories of costs: materials and conversion costs. Its unique feature is an absence of a work-in-process account. Actual material costs are entered into a *materials inventory* account, and actual labor and overhead costs are entered into a *conversion costs* account. Costs are transferred from these two temporary accounts directly into finished-goods inventories. Some backflush systems even eliminate the finished-goods inventory accounts and transfer costs directly to cost of goods sold, especially if goods are not kept in inventory but are shipped immediately on completion. Backflush systems rely on the assumption that completion of production follows so soon after the application of conversion activities that balances in the conversion costs accounts always should remain near zero. Costs are transferred out almost immediately after being initially recorded.

Example of Backflush Costing

Speaker Technology Inc. (STI) produces speakers for automobile stereo systems. STI recently introduced a JIT production system and backflush costing. Consider the July production for speaker model AX27. The standard material cost per unit of AX27 is $14, and the standard unit conversion cost is $21. During July, STI purchased materials for $5,600, incurred conversion costs of $8,400, which included all labor costs and manufacturing overhead, and completed and sold 400 units of AX27.

Backflush costing is accomplished in three steps:

1. Record actual materials and conversion costs. For simplicity, we assume for now that actual materials and conversion costs were identical to the standard costs. As materials are purchased, backflush systems add their cost to the materials inventory account:

Materials inventory	5,600	
Accounts payable (or cash)		5,600
To record material purchases		

Similarly, as direct labor and manufacturing overhead costs are incurred, they are added to the conversion-costs account:

Conversion costs	8,400	
Accrued wages and other accounts		8,400
To record conversion costs incurred		

2. Apply costs to completed units. When production is complete, costs from materials inventory and conversion-costs accounts are transferred directly to finished goods based on the number of units completed and a *standard cost* of each unit:

Finished goods inventory (400 × $35)	14,000	
Materials inventory		5,600
Conversion costs		8,400
To record costs of completed production		

Because of short production cycle times, there is little lag between additions to the conversion-costs account and transfers to finished goods. The conversion-costs account, therefore, remains near zero.

3. Record cost of goods sold during the period. The standard cost of the items sold is transferred from finished goods inventory to cost of goods sold:

Cost of goods sold	14,000	
Finished goods inventory		14,000
To record cost of 400 units sold @$35 per unit		

Suppose completed units are delivered immediately to customers, so that finished goods inventories are negligible. Steps 2 and 3 can then be combined and the finished goods inventory account eliminated:

Cost of goods sold	14,000	
Material inventory		5,600
Conversion costs		8,400

What if actual costs added to the conversion-costs account do not equal the standard amounts that are transferred to finished-goods inventory? Variances are treated like overapplied or underapplied overhead. Backflush systems assume that conversion-costs account balances should be approximately zero at all times. Any remaining balance in the account at the end of an accounting period is charged to cost of goods sold. Suppose actual conversion costs for July had been $8,600 and the amount transferred to finished goods (i.e., applied to the product) was $8,400. The $200 balance in the conversion-costs account at the end of the month would be written off to cost of goods sold:

Cost of goods sold	200	
Conversion costs		200
To recognize underapplied conversion costs		

Highlights to Remember

Process costing is used for inventory costing when there is continuous mass production of like units. The key concept in process costing is that of equivalent units, the number of fully completed units that could have been produced from the inputs applied. The concept of equivalent units is widely applied in both manufacturing and nonmanufacturing settings. For example, universities use the concept to measure full-time equivalent enrollment.

Five basic steps may be used to solve process-cost problems:

1. Summarize the flow of physical units.
2. Calculate output in terms of equivalent units.
3. Summarize the total costs to account for.
4. Calculate unit costs.
5. Apply costs to units completed and to units in the ending work in process.

Process costing is complicated by the presence of beginning inventories. Two methods can be used when these complications are present: the *weighted-average* and *first-in, first-out* methods. The FIFO method focuses on the work done only in the current period, whereas the weighted-average method focuses on the work done in previous periods on the current period's beginning inventory in addition to work done in the current period.

Many companies with JIT production systems use backflush costing. Such systems have no work-in-process inventory account and apply costs to products only after the production process is complete.

Summary Problem for Your Review

Problems One and Two appeared earlier in the chapter.

Problem Three

The most extreme (and simplest) version of backflush costing makes product costing entries at only one point. Suppose Speaker Technology Inc. (STI) had no materials inventory account (in addition to no work-in-process inventory account). Materials are not "purchased" until they are needed for production. Therefore, STI enters both material and conversion costs directly into its finished goods inventory account.

Required   Prepare journal entries (without explanations) and T-accounts for July's production of 400 units. As given earlier, materials purchases totaled $5,600, and conversion costs were $8,400. Why might a company use this extreme type of backflush costing?

Solution to Problem Three

In one step, material and conversion costs are applied to finished goods inventories:

Finished goods inventories	14,000	
Accounts payable		5,600
Wages payable and other accounts		8,400

Finished Goods Inventories		Accounts Payable, Wages Payable, and Other Accounts	
Materials	5,600		5,600
Conversion costs	8,400		8,400

This example of backflush costing illustrates a system that is simple and inexpensive. It provides reasonably accurate product costs if (1) materials inventories are low (most likely because of JIT delivery schedules), and (2) production cycle times are short, so that at any time only inconsequential amounts of material costs or conversion costs have been incurred for products that are not yet complete.

hybrid-costing system An accounting system that is a blend of ideas from both job costing and process costing.

operation costing A hybrid-costing system often used in the batch or group manufacturing of goods that have some common characteristics plus some individual characteristics.

Appendix 15: Hybrid Systems—Operation Costing

Job costing and process costing are extremes along a continuum of potential costing systems. Each company designs its own accounting system to fit its underlying production activities. Many companies use **hybrid-costing systems,** which are blends of ideas from both job costing and process costing. This appendix discusses one of many possible hybrid-costing systems, *operation costing.*

Nature of Operation Costing

Operation costing is a hybrid-costing system often used in the batch or group manufacturing of goods that have some common characteristics plus some individual characteristics. Examples of such goods include personal computers, clothing, and semiconductors. Such products are specifically identified by work orders. The goods are often variations of a single design but require a varying sequence of standardized operations. For instance, suits of clothes may differ, requiring various materials and hand operations. Similarly, a textile manufacturer may apply special chemical treatments (such as waterproofing) to some fabrics but not to others.

Operation costing may entail mass production, but there is sufficient product variety to have products scheduled in different batches or groups, each requiring a particular sequence of operations.

An *operation* is a standardized method or technique that is repetitively performed, regardless of the distinguishing features of the finished product. Examples include cutting, planing, sanding, painting, and chemical treating. Products proceed through the various operations in groups as specified by work orders or production orders. These work orders list the necessary direct materials and the step-by-step operations required to make the finished product.

Suppose a clothing manufacturer produces two lines of blazers. The wool blazers use better materials and undergo more operations than the polyester blazers, as follows:

	Wool Blazers	Polyester Blazers
Direct materials	Wool	Polyester
	Satin lining	Rayon lining
	Bone buttons	Plastic buttons
Operations	1. Cutting cloth	1. Cutting cloth
	2. Checking edges	—
	3. Sewing body	3. Sewing body
	4. Checking seams	—
	5. —	5. Sewing collars and lapels by machine
	6. Sewing collars and lapels by hand	—

The costs of the blazers are compiled by work order. As in job costing, the direct materials—different for each work order—are specifically identified with the appropriate order. Conversion costs—direct labor plus factory overhead—are initially compiled for each operation. A cost driver, such as the number of units processed or minutes or seconds used, is identified for each operation, and a conversion cost per unit of cost driver activity is computed. Then conversion costs are applied to products in a manner similar to the application of factory overhead in a job-cost system.

Example of Operation-Costing Entries

Suppose our manufacturer has two work orders, one for 100 wool blazers and the other for 200 polyester blazers, as follows:

Objective 7

Describe operation costing

	Wool Blazers	Polyester Blazers
Number of blazers	100	200
Direct materials	$2,500	$3,100
Conversion costs		
1. Cutting cloth	600	1,200
2. Checking edges	300	—
3. Sewing body	500	1,000
4. Checking seams	600	—
5. Sewing collars and lapels by machine	—	800
6. Sewing collars and lapels by hand	700	—
Total manufacturing costs	$5,200	$6,100

Direct labor and factory overhead vanish as separate classifications in an operation-costing system. The sum of these costs is most frequently called conversion cost. The conversion cost is applied to products based on the company's budgeted rate for performing each operation. For example, suppose the conversion costs of operation 1, cutting cloth, are driven by machine hours and are budgeted for the year as follows:

$$\text{budgeted rate for applying conversion costs for cutting cloth to product} = \frac{\text{budgeted conversion cost for cutting cloth for the year (direct labor, power, repairs, supplies, other factory overhead of this operation)}}{\text{budgeted machine-hours for the year for cutting cloth}}$$

$$\text{rate per machine-hours} = \frac{\$150,000 + \$450,000}{20,000 \text{ hours}} = \$30 \text{ per machine-hour}$$

As goods are manufactured, conversion costs are applied to the work orders by multiplying the $30 hourly rate times the number of machine-hours used for cutting cloth.

If 20 machine-hours are needed to cut the cloth for the 100 wool blazers, then the conversion cost involved is $600 (20 hours × $30 per hour). For the 200 polyester blazers, the conversion cost for cutting cloth is twice as much, $1,200 (40 hours × $30), because each blazer takes the same cutting time, and there are twice as many polyester blazers.

Summary journal entries for applying costs to the polyester blazers follow. (Entries for the wool blazers would be similar.)

The journal entry for the requisition of direct materials for the 200 polyester blazers is:

Work-in-process inventory (polyester blazers)	3,100	
Direct-materials inventory		3,100

Direct labor and factory overhead are subparts of a conversion-costs account in an operation-costing system. Suppose actual conversion costs of $3,150 were entered into the conversion-costs account:

Conversion costs	3,150	
Accrued payroll, accumulated depreciation,		
accounts payable, etc.		3,150

The application of conversion costs to products in operation costing is similar to the application of factory overhead in job-ordering costing. A *budgeted* rate per unit of cost-driver activity is used. To apply conversion costs to the 200 polyester blazers, the following summary entry is made for operations 1, 3, and 5 (cutting cloth, sewing body, and sewing collars and lapels by machine):

Work-in-process inventory (polyester blazers)	3,000	
Conversion costs, cutting cloth		1,200
Conversion costs, sewing body		1,000
Conversion costs, sewing collars and lapels by machine		800

After posting, work-in-process inventory has the following debit balance:

Work-in-Process Inventory (polyester blazers)		
Direct materials	$3,100	
Conversion costs applied	3,000	
Balance	$6,100	

As the blazers are completed, their cost is transferred to finished-goods inventory in the usual manner.

Any overapplication or underapplication of conversion costs is disposed of at the end of the year in the same manner as overapplied or underapplied overhead in a job-order costing system. In this case, conversion costs have been debited for actual cost of $3,150 and credited for costs applied of $3,000. The debit balance of $150 indicates that conversion costs are underapplied.

Accounting Vocabulary

backflush costing, *p. 584*
equivalent units, *p. 573*
first-in, first-out, (FIFO) process-costing method, *p. 578*

hybrid-costing system, *p. 586*
operation costing, *p. 586*
transferred-in costs, *p. 581*

weighted-average (WA) process-costing method, *p. 577*

Fundamental Assignment Material

15-A1 Basic Process Costing

Rockmania, Inc., produces portable compact disk (CD) players in large quantities. For simplicity, assume that the company has two departments, assembly and testing. The manufacturing costs in the Assembly Department during February were:

Direct materials added		$ 60,800
Conversion costs		
Direct labor	$50,000	
Factory overhead	40,000	90,000
Assembly costs to account for		$150,800

There was no beginning inventory of work in process. Suppose work on 19,000 CD players was begun in the assembly department during February, but only 17,000 CD players were fully completed. All the parts had been made or placed in process, but only half the labor had been completed for each of the CD players still in process.

Required
1. Compute the equivalent units and unit costs for February.
2. Compute the costs of units completed and transferred to the Testing Department. Also compute the cost of the ending work in process. (For journal entries, see Problem 15-21.)

15-A2   Weighted-Average Process-Costing Method

The Lucero Company manufactures electric drills. Material is introduced at the beginning of the process in the Assembly Department. Conversion costs are applied uniformly throughout the process. As the process is completed, goods are immediately transferred to the Finishing Department.

Data for the Assembly Department for the month of July 19X5 follow:

Work in process, June 30: $175,500 (consisting of $138,000 materials and $37,500 conversion costs); 100% completed for direct materials, but only 25% completed for conversion costs	10,000 units
Units started during July	80,000 units
Units completed during July	70,000 units
Work in process, July 31: 100% completed for direct materials, but only 50% completed for conversion costs	20,000 units
Direct materials added during July	$852,000
Conversion costs added during July	$634,500

Required
1. Compute the total cost of goods transferred out of the Assembly Department during July.
2. Compute the total costs of the ending work in process. Prepare a production-cost report or a similar orderly tabulation of your work. Assume weighted-average product costing. (For the FIFO method and journal entries, see Problems 15-31 and 15-37.)

15-A3   Backflush Costing

Thermo Controls, Inc., makes electronic thermostats for homes and offices. The Westplains Division makes one product, Autotherm, which has a standard cost of $37, consisting of $22 of materials and $15 of conversion costs. In January, actual purchases of materials totaled $45,000, labor payroll costs were $11,000, and manufacturing overhead was $19,000. Completed output was 2,000 units.

The Westplains Division uses a backflush-costing system that records costs in materials inventory and conversion costs accounts and applies costs to products at the time production is completed. There were no finished goods inventories on January 1 and 20 units on January 31.

Required
1. Prepare journal entries (without explanations) to record January's costs for the Westplains Division. Include the purchase of materials, incurrence of labor and manufacturing overhead costs, application of product costs, and recognition of cost of goods sold.
2. Suppose January's actual manufacturing overhead costs had been $22,000 instead of $19,000. Prepare the journal entry to recognize underapplied conversion costs at the end of January.

15-B1   Basic Process Costing

McClure Company produces digital watches in large quantities. The manufacturing costs of the Assembly Department were:

Direct materials added		$1,620,000
Conversion costs		
Direct labor	$415,000	
Factory overhead	260,000	675,000
Assembly costs to account for		$2,295,000

For simplicity, assume that this is a two-department company, assembly and finishing. There was no beginning work in process.

Suppose 900,000 units were begun in the Assembly Department. There were 600,000 units completed and transferred to the Finishing Department. The 300,000 units in ending work in process were fully completed regarding direct materials but half-completed regarding conversion costs.

Required
1. Compute the equivalent units and unit costs in the Assembly Department.
2. Compute the costs of units completed and transferred to the Finishing Department. Also compute the cost of the ending work in process in the Assembly Department.

15-B2 Weighted-Average Process-Costing Method

The Rainbow Paint Co. uses a process-cost system. Materials are added at the beginning of a particular process, and conversion costs are incurred uniformly. Work in process at the beginning is assumed 40% complete; at the end, 20%. One gallon of material makes 1 gallon of product. Data follow:

Beginning inventory	550 gal
Direct materials added	7,150 gal
Ending inventory	400 gal
Conversion costs incurred	$35,724
Cost of direct materials added	$65,340
Conversion costs, beginning inventory	$ 1,914
Cost of direct materials, beginning inventory	$ 3,190

Required
Use the weighted-average method. Prepare a schedule of output in equivalent units and a schedule of application of costs to products. Show the cost of goods completed and cost of ending work in process. (For journal entries see Problem 15-30. For the FIFO method see Problem 15-36.)

15-B3 Backflush Costing

ACME Auto Parts recently installed a backflush-costing system in its Audio Components Department. One cost center in the department makes 4-inch speakers with a standard cost as follows:

Materials	$ 9.80
Conversion costs	4.20
Total	$14.00

Speakers are scheduled for production only after orders are received, and products are shipped to customers immediately on completion. Therefore, no finished goods inventories are kept, and product costs are applied directly to cost of goods sold.

In October, 1,500 speakers were produced and shipped to customers. Materials were purchased at a cost of $15,500, and actual conversion costs (labor plus manufacturing overhead) of $6,300 were recorded.

Required

1. Prepare journal entries to record October's costs for the production of 4-inch speakers.
2. Suppose October's actual conversion costs had been $6,000 instead of $6,300. Prepare a journal entry to recognize overapplied conversion costs.

Additional Assignment Material

Questions

15-1. Give three examples of industries where process-costing systems are probably used.

15-2. Give three examples of nonprofit organizations where process-costing systems are probably used.

15-3. Give three examples of equivalent units in various organizations.

15-4. Under what conditions can significant amounts of work in process be safely ignored in process costing?

15-5. What is the central product-costing problem in process costing?

15-6. "There are five key steps in process-cost accounting." What are they?

15-7. "Equivalent units are the work done to date." What method of process costing is being described?

15-8. Identify the major distinction between the first two and the final three steps of the five major steps in accounting for process costs.

15-9. Present an equation that describes the physical flow in process costing.

15-10. Why is "work done in the current period only" a key measurement of equivalent units?

15-11. "The beginning inventory is regarded as if it were a batch of goods separate and distinct from the goods started *and* completed by a process during the current period." What method of process costing is being described?

15-12. "Ordinarily, the differences in unit costs under FIFO and weighted-average methods are insignificant." Do you agree? Explain.

15-13. "The total conversion costs are divided by the equivalent units for the work done to date." Does this quotation describe the weighted-average method or does it describe FIFO?

15-14. "Backflush-costing systems work only for companies using a JIT production system." Do you agree? Explain.

15-15. Explain what happens in a backflush-costing system when the amount of actual conversion cost in a period exceeds the amount applied to the products completed that period.

15-16. Give three examples of industries that probably use operation costing.

15-17. "In operation costing, average conversion costs are applied to products in a manner similar to the application of factory overhead in a job-cost system." Do you agree? Explain.

15-18. Prepare journal entries reflecting the application of conversion costs of $90,000 to work in process.

Exercises

15-19   Basic Process Costing

A department of Mayberry Textiles produces cotton fabric. All direct materials are introduced at the start of the process. Conversion costs are incurred uniformly throughout the process.

In May there was no beginning inventory. Units started, completed, and transferred: 650,000. Units in process, May 31: 220,000. Each unit in ending work in process was 60% converted. Costs incurred during May: direct materials, $3,654,000; conversion costs, $860,200.

Required

1. Compute the total work done in equivalent units and the unit cost for May.
2. Compute the cost of units completed and transferred. Also compute the cost of units in ending work in process.

15-20   Uneven Flow

One department of Wamego Technology Company manufactures basic hand-held calculators. Various materials are added at various stages of the process. The outer front shell and the carrying case, which represent 10% of the total material cost, are added at the final step of the assembly process. All other materials are considered to be "in process" by the time the calculator reaches a 50% stage of completion.

Seventy-four thousand calculators were started in production during 19X2. At year-end, 6,000 calculators were in various stages of completion, but all of them were beyond the 50% stage and on the average they were regarded as being 70% completed.

The following costs were incurred during the year: direct materials, $205,520; conversion costs, $397,100.

Required

1. Prepare a schedule of physical units and equivalent units.
2. Tabulate the unit costs, cost of goods completed, and cost of ending work in process.

15-21 Journal Entries

Refer to the data in Problem 15-A1. Prepare summary journal entries for the use of direct materials, direct labor, and factory overhead applied. Also prepare a journal entry for the transfer of goods completed and transferred. Show the postings to the Work-in-Process account.

15-22 Journal Entries

Refer to the data in Problem 15-B1. Prepare summary journal entries for the use of direct materials, direct labor, and factory overhead applied. Also prepare a journal entry for the transfer of goods completed and transferred. Show the posting to the Work-in-Process—Assembly Department account.

15-23 Physical Units

Fill in the unknowns in physical units:

	Case	
Flow of Production	A	B
Work in process, beginning inventory	1,500	4,000
Started	6,000	?
Completed and transferred	?	8,000
Work in process, ending inventory	2,000	3,000

15-24 Flow of Production, FIFO

Fill in the unknowns in physical or equivalent units:

		Equivalent Units	
Flow of Production	Physical Units	Direct Materials	Conversion Costs
Beginning work in process	1,000 (50%)*		
Started	?		
To account for	36,000		
Completed and transferred out	33,000	33,000	33,000
Ending work in process	? (30%)*	?	?
Units accounted for	?		
Work done to date		?	?
Equivalent units in beginning inventory		?	?
Work done in current period only		?	?

* Degree of completion of conversion costs at dates of inventory. Assume that all materials are added at the beginning of the process.

15-25   Multiple Choice

The Preparation Department of Blackburn, Inc., had the following flow of latex paint production (in gallons) for the month of April:

Units completed	
From work in process on April 1	5,000
From April production	25,000
	30,000

Direct materials are added at the beginning of the process. Units of work in process at April 30 were 10,000. The work in process at April 1 was 30% complete as to conversion costs, and the work in process at April 30 was 50% complete as to conversion costs. What are the equivalent units of production for the month of April using the FIFO method? Choose one of the following combinations:

	Direct Materials	Conversion Costs
a.	40,000	40,000
b.	35,000	33,500
c.	35,000	35,000
d.	40,000	35,000

15-26   Equivalent Units, FIFO

Fill in the unknowns:

		(Step 2) Equivalent Units	
Flow of Production in Units	**(Step 1) Physical Units**	**Direct Materials**	**Conversion Costs**
Work in process, beginning inventory	30,000*		
Started	45,000		
To account for	75,000		
Completed and transferred out	?	?	?
Work in process, ending inventory	2,000†	?	?
Units accounted for	75,000		
Work done to date		?	?
Less: Equivalent units of work from previous periods included in beginning inventory		?	?
Work done in current period only (FIFO method)		?	?

* Degree of completion: direct materials, 80%; conversion costs, 40%.
† Degree of completion: direct materials, 40%; conversion costs, 10%.

15-27   Compute Equivalent Units

Consider the following data for February:

	Physical Units
Started in February	80,000
Completed in February	90,000
Ending inventory, work in process	10,000
Beginning inventory, work in process	20,000

The beginning inventory was 80% complete regarding direct materials and 40% complete regarding conversion costs. The ending inventory was 20% complete regarding direct materials and 10% complete regarding conversion costs.

Required Prepare a schedule of equivalent units for the work done to date and the work done during February only.

15-28 FIFO and Unit Direct-Material Costs
The Lindberg Company uses the FIFO process-cost method. Consider the following for July:

- Beginning inventory, 15,000 units, 70% completed regarding direct materials, which cost $89,250
- Units completed, 80,000
- Cost of materials placed in process during July, $580,000
- Ending inventory, 5,000 units, 60% completed regarding materials

Required Compute the direct-material cost per equivalent unit for the work done in July only.

15-29 FIFO Method, Conversion Cost
Given the following information, compute the unit conversion cost for the month of June for the Abraham Company, using the FIFO process-cost method. Show details of your calculation.

- Units completed, 45,000
- Conversion cost in beginning inventory, $30,000
- Beginning inventory, 10,000 units with 75% of conversion cost
- Ending inventory, 15,000 units with 30% of conversion cost
- Conversion costs put into production in June, $180,600

15-30 Journal Entries
Refer to the data in Problem 15-B2. Prepare summary journal entries for the use of direct materials and conversion costs. Also prepare a journal entry for the transfer of goods completed, assuming that the goods are transferred to another department.

15-31 Journal Entries
Refer to the data in Problem 15-A2. Prepare summary journal entries for the use of direct materials and conversion costs. Also prepare a journal entry for the transfer of the goods completed and transferred from the Assembly Department to the Finishing Department.

Problems

15-32 Process and Activity-Based Costing
Consider the potato chip production process at a company such as Frito-Lay. Frito-Lay uses a continuous flow technology that is suited for high volumes of product. At the Plano, Texas, facility, between 6 and 7 thousand pounds of potato chips are produced each hour. The plant operates 24 hours a day. It takes 30 minutes to completely produce a bag of potato chips from the raw potato to the packed end-product.

Required 1. What product and process characteristics of potato chips dictate the cost accounting system used? Describe the costing system best suited to Frito-Lay.

2. What product and process characteristics dictate the use of an activity-based-costing system? What implications does this have for Frito-Lay?
3. When beginning inventories are present, product costing becomes more complicated. Estimate the relative magnitude of beginning inventories at Frito-Lay compared to total production. What implication does this have for the costing system?

15-33   Nonprofit Process Costing

The IRS must process millions of income tax returns yearly. When the taxpayer sends in a return, documents such as withholding statements and checks are matched against the data submitted. Then various other inspections of the data are conducted. Of course, some returns are more complicated than others, so the expected time allowed to process a return is geared to an "average" return.

Some work-measurement experts have been closely monitoring the processing at a particular branch. They are seeking ways to improve productivity.

Suppose 3 million returns were received on April 15. On April 22, the work-measurement teams discovered that all supplies (punched cards, inspection check-sheets, and so on) had been affixed to the returns, but 40% of the returns still had to undergo a final inspection. The other returns were fully completed.

Required

1. Suppose the final inspection represents 20% of the overall processing time in this process. Compute the total work done in terms of equivalent units.
2. The materials and supplies consumed were $600,000. For these calculations, materials and supplies are regarded just like direct materials. The conversion costs were $4,830,000. Compute the unit costs of materials and supplies and of conversion.
3. Compute the cost of the tax returns not yet completely processed.

15-34 Two Materials

The following data pertain to the Mixing Department at Foster Chemicals for April:

Units	
Work in process, March 31	0
Units started	60,000
Completed and transferred to finishing department	40,000
Costs	
Materials	
Plastic compound	$300,000
Softening compound	$ 80,000
Conversion costs	$192,000

The plastic compound is introduced at the start of the process, while the softening compound is added when the product reaches an 80% stage of completion. Conversion costs are incurred uniformly throughout the process.

The ending work in process is 40% completed for conversion costs. None of the units in process reached the 80% stage of completion.

Required

1. Compute the equivalent units and unit costs for April.
2. Compute the total cost of units completed and transferred to finished goods. Also compute the cost of the ending work in process.

15-35   Materials and Cartons

A Manchester, England, company manufactures and sells small portable tape recorders. Business is booming. Various materials are added at various stages in the assembly department. Costs are accounted for on a process-cost basis. The end of the process involves conducting a final inspection and adding a cardboard carton.

The final inspection requires 5% of the total processing time. All materials besides the carton are added by the time the recorders reach an 80% stage of completion of conversion.

There were no beginning inventories. One hundred fifty thousand recorders were started in production during 19X6. At the end of the year, which was not a busy time, 5,000 recorders were in various stages of completion. All the ending units in work in process were at the 95% stage. They awaited final inspection and being placed in cartons.

Total direct materials consumed in production, except for cartons, cost £2,250,000. Cartons used cost £319,000. Total conversion costs were £1,198,000.

Required

1. Present a schedule of physical units, equivalent units, and unit costs of direct materials, cartons, and conversion costs.
2. Present a summary of the cost of goods completed and the cost of ending work in process.

15-36 FIFO Computations
Refer to Problem 15-B2. Using FIFO, answer the same questions.

15-37 FIFO Methods
Refer to Problem 15-A2. Using FIFO costing, answer the same questions.

15-38 Backflush Costing
Everest Controls manufactures a variety of meters and other measuring instruments. One product is an altimeter used by hikers and mountain climbers. Everest adopted a JIT philosophy with an automated, computer-controlled, robotic production system. Production is scheduled after an order is received, materials and parts arrive just as they are needed, the production cycle time for altimeters is less than 1 day, and completed units are packaged and shipped as part of the production cycle.

Everest's backflush costing system has only three accounts related to production of altimeters: materials and parts inventory, conversion costs, and finished goods inventory. At the beginning of April (as at the beginning of every month) each of the three accounts had a balance of zero. Following are the April transactions related to the production of altimeters:

Materials and parts purchased	$287,000
Conversion costs incurred	$ 92,000
Altimeters produced	11,500 units

The budgeted (or standard) cost for one altimeter is $24 for materials and parts and $8 for conversion costs.

Required

1. Prepare summary journal entries for the production of altimeters in April.
2. Compute the cost of goods sold for April. Explain any assumptions you make.
3. Suppose the actual conversion costs incurred during April were $95,000 instead of $92,000, and all other facts were as given. Prepare the additional journal entry that would be required at the end of April. Explain why the entry was necessary.

15-39 Basic Operation Costing
Study Appendix 15. Hudson Co. manufactures a variety of wooden chairs. The company's manufacturing operations and costs applied to products for April were:

	Cutting	Assembly	Finishing
Direct labor	$ 60,000	$30,000	$ 90,000
Factory overhead	115,500	37,500	141,000

Three styles of chairs were produced in April. The quantities and direct material cost were:

Style	Quantity	Direct Materials
Standard	6,000	$108,000
Deluxe	4,500	171,000
Unfinished	3,000	63,000

Each unit, regardless of style, required the same cutting and assembly operations. The unfinished chairs, as the name implies, had no finishing operations whatsoever. Standard and deluxe styles required the same finishing operations.

Required

1. Tabulate the total conversion costs of each operation, the total units produced, and the conversion cost per unit.
2. Tabulate the total costs, the units produced, and the cost per unit.

15-40   Operation Costing with Ending Work in Process

Study Appendix 15. Squire Co. uses three operations in sequence to make video cameras. Using the information on the next page, complete the following:

Required

1. Operation 2 was highly automated. Product costs depended on a budgeted application rate for conversion costs based on machine-hours. The budgeted costs for 19X5 were $120,000 direct labor and $480,000 factory overhead. Budgeted machine-hours were 20,000. Each camera required 6 minutes of time in operation 2. Compute the costs of processing 1,000 cameras in operation 2.
2. Compute the total manufacturing costs of 1,000 cameras and the cost per standard-quality camera and better-quality camera.
3. Suppose that at the end of the year 500 standard-quality cameras were in process through operation 1 only and 600 better-quality cameras were in process through operation 2 only. Compute the cost of the ending work-in-process inventory. Assume that no direct materials are applied in operation 2, but that $10,000 of the $100,000 direct-material cost of the better-quality cameras are applied to each 1,000 cameras processed in operation 3.

	Production Orders	
	For 1,000 Standard-Quality Cameras	For 1,000 Better-Quality Cameras
Direct materials (actual costs applied)	$57,000	$100,000
Conversion costs (predetermined costs applied on the basis of machine-hours used)		
Operation 1	25,000	25,000
Operation 2	?	?
Operation 3	—	15,000
Total manufacturing costs applied	$?	$?

16 Overhead Application: Variable and Absorption Costing

Cerro Wire & Cable Co., Inc., makes wire used in residential, commercial, and industrial buildings as well as COAX cable used for televisions and VCRs. At Cerro Wire, absorption costs and related variances from under or over absorption are of limited use in controlling costs. Variable costing focuses managers' attention on costs they can control.
Courtesy Cerro Wire & Cable Co., Inc

Learning Objectives

When you have finished studying this chapter, you should be able to

1   Identify the basic feature that distinguishes the variable-costing approach from the absorption-costing approach.

2   Construct an income statement using the variable-costing approach.

3   Construct an income statement using the absorption-costing approach.

4   Identify the nature of the production-volume variance, compute it, and state how it should appear in the income statement.

5   Identify the differences among the three alternative cost bases of an absorption-costing system: actual, normal, and standard.

6   Explain why a company might prefer to use a variable-costing approach.

7   Identify the two methods for disposing of the standard cost variances at the end of a year and give the rationale for each.

8   Analyze and compare all the major variances in a standard absorption-costing system (Appendix 16).

The evaluation of managers is often based at least partly on the income of the organizational segment they manage. Therefore, managers strive to make their performance look good by making decisions that increase income. But how should we measure income? Accountants make many judgments when measuring income, and one of the most important is choosing the appropriate method for calculating product costs. Some managers think product costing is a subject of interest only to accountants. However, when they realize that product costs affect their evaluations, they quickly begin to pay attention to the determination of product costs. Only by knowing what influences product costs will they be able to predict how their decisions will affect income and hence their evaluations.

In the preceding three chapters, we concentrated on how an accounting system accumulates costs by departments or activities and *applies* costs to the products or services that are produced by those departments. This chapter focuses on two major variations of product costing: variable costing and absorption costing. Note that although we use a standard product-costing system here for illustrative purposes, these variations can be used in non-standard product-costing systems too.

VARIABLE VERSUS ABSORPTION COSTING

Accounting for Fixed Manufacturing Overhead

Objective 1

Identify the basic feature that distinguishes the variable-costing approach from the absorption-costing approach

Two major methods of product costing are compared in this chapter: *variable costing* (the contribution approach) and *absorption costing* (the functional, full-costing, or traditional approach). These methods differ in only one conceptual respect: Fixed manufacturing overhead is excluded from the cost of products under variable costing but is included in the cost of products under absorption costing. In other words, *variable costing* signifies that fixed factory overhead is not inventoried. In contrast, *absorption costing* indicates that inventory values include fixed factory overhead.

As Exhibit 16-1 shows, a variable-costing system regards fixed manufacturing overhead (fixed factory overhead) as an expired cost to be immediately charged against sales—not as an unexpired cost to be held back as inventory and charged against sales later as a part of cost of goods sold.

Exhibit 16-1

Comparison of Flow of Costs

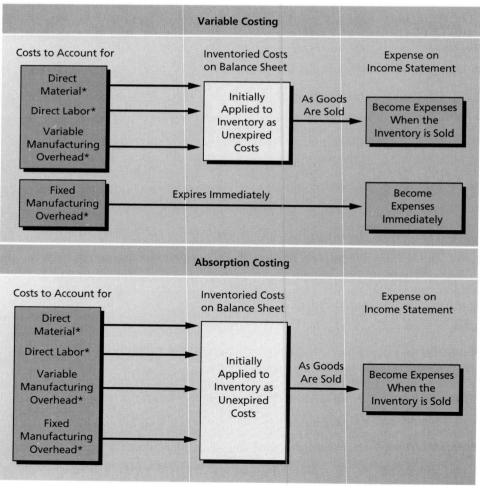

* As goods are manufactured, the costs are "applied" to inventory usually via the use of unit costs.

Variable costing is commonly called *direct costing*. However, this is a misnomer because the inventorying of costs is not confined to only "direct" materials and labor; it also includes an "indirect" cost–the *variable* manufacturing overhead. Such terminological confusion is unfortunate but apparently unavoidable in a field such as management accounting, where new analytical ideas or approaches arise in isolated fashion. Newly coined terms, which may not be accurately descriptive, often become embedded too deeply to be supplanted later.

Take a moment to reflect on Exhibit 16-1. Note that the only difference between variable and absorption costing is the accounting for fixed manufacturing overhead.

Absorption costing is more widely used than variable costing. However, the growing use of the contribution approach in performance measurement and cost analysis has led to increasing use of variable costing for internal-reporting purposes. Over half the major firms in the United States use variable costing for some internal reporting, and nearly a quarter use it as the primary internal format. For example, the Muncie, Indiana, plant of Borg-Warner Automotive Diversified Transmission Products Corporation recently changed its product-line performance reporting from an absorption-costing approach to variable costing. Why? Because variable costing "links manufacturing performance more closely with financial reporting by removing the impact of changing inventory levels from financial results." In contrast, neither the public accounting profession nor the U.S. IRS approves of variable costing for external-reporting or tax purposes. Therefore all U.S. firms use absorption costing for their reports to shareholders and tax authorities.

Until the last decade or two, use of variable costing for internal reporting was expensive. It requires information to be processed two ways, one for external reporting and one for internal reporting. The increasing use and decreasing cost of computers has reduced the added cost of a variable-costing system. Most managers no longer face the question of whether to invest in a separate variable-costing *system*. Rather, they simply choose a variable-costing or absorption-costing *format* for reports. Many well-designed accounting systems used today can produce either format.

Facts for Illustration

To make these ideas more concrete, consider the following example. In 19X6 and 19X7, the Greenberg Company had the following standard costs for production of its single product:

Basic Production
Data at Standard
Cost

Direct material	$1.30
Direct labor	1.50
Variable manufacturing overhead	.20
Standard variable costs per unit	$3.00

Fixed manufacturing overhead (fixed factory overhead) is budgeted at $150,000. Expected (or budgeted) production in each year is 150,000 units, and the sales price is $5 per unit. For simplicity, we will assume that the single cost driver for the $.20 per unit variable-manufacturing overhead is units produced.[1] Also we will assume that both budgeted and actual selling and administrative expenses are $65,000 yearly fixed cost plus sales commissions at 5% of dollar sales. Actual product quantities are:

	19X6	19X7
In units		
Opening inventory	—	30,000
Production	170,000	140,000
Sales	140,000	160,000
Ending inventory	30,000	10,000

There are no variances from the standard variable manufacturing costs, and fixed manufacturing overhead incurred is exactly $150,000 per year.

Based on this information, we can

1. Prepare income statements for 19X6 and 19X7 under variable costing.
2. Prepare income statements for 19X6 and 19X7 under absorption costing.
3. Show a reconciliation of the difference in operating income for 19X6, 19X7, and the two years as a whole.

Variable-Costing Method

We begin by preparing income statements under variable costing. The variable-costing statement shown in Exhibit 16-2 has a familiar contribution-approach format, the same format introduced in Chapter 4. The only new characteristic of Exhibit 16-2 is the presence of a detailed calculation of cost of goods sold, which is affected by changes in the beginning and ending inventories. (In contrast, the income statements in Chapters 4 through 9 assumed that there were no changes in the beginning and ending inventories.)

The costs of the product are accounted for by applying all *variable* manufacturing costs to the goods produced at a rate of $3 per unit; thus inventories are valued at standard variable costs. In contrast, fixed manufacturing costs are not applied to any products but are regarded as expenses in the period they are incurred.

Before reading on, be sure to trace the facts from the illustrative problem to the presentation in Exhibit 16-2, step by step. Note that both variable cost of goods sold and variable selling and administrative expense are deducted in computing the contribution margin. However, variable selling and administrative expense is not inventoriable. It is affected only by the level of sales, not by changes in inventory.

Absorption-Costing Method

Exhibit 16-3 shows the standard absorption-costing framework. As you can see, it differs from the variable-costing format in three ways.

---

[1] Increasingly, companies are using activity analysis to identify relevant cost drivers for manufacturing overhead. The use of cost drivers other than units of production does not affect the basic principles illustrated in the examples that follow.

Exhibit 16-2

Greenberg Company
Comparative Income
Statements Using
Variable Costing
(thousands of dollars)
Years 19X6 and 19X7
(data are in text)

		19X6		19X7	
Sales, 140,000 and 160,000 units, respectively (1)		$700		$800	
Variable expenses					
Variable manufacturing cost of goods sold					
Opening inventory, at standard variable costs of $3	$ —		$ 90		
Add: variable cost of goods manufactured at standard, 170,000 and 140,000 units, respectively	510		420		
Available for sale, 170,000 units in each year	$510		$510		
Deduct: ending inventory, at standard variable cost of $3	90*		30†		
Variable manufacturing cost of goods sold	$420		$480		
Variable selling expenses, at 5% of dollar sales	35		40		
Total variable expenses (2)		455		520	
Contribution margin (3) = (1) − (2)		$245		$280	
Fixed expenses					
Fixed factory overhead	$150		$150		
Fixed selling and administrative expenses	65		65		
Total fixed expenses (4)		215		215	
Operating income, variable costing (3) − (4)		$ 30		$ 65	

* 30,000 units x $3 = $90,000.
† 10,000 units x $3 = $30,000.

fixed-overhead rate
The amount of fixed manufacturing overhead applied to each unit of production. It is determined by dividing the budgeted fixed overhead by the expected volume of production for the budget period.

production-volume variance A variance that appears whenever actual production deviates from the expected volume of production used in computing the fixed overhead rate. It is calculated as (actual volume − expected volume) × fixed-overhead rate.

First, the unit product cost used for computing cost of goods sold is $4, not $3. Why? Because fixed manufacturing overhead of $1 is added to the $3 variable manufacturing cost. The $1 of fixed manufacturing overhead applied to each unit is the **fixed-overhead rate.** It is determined by dividing the budgeted fixed overhead by the expected cost-driver activity, in this case volume of production, for the budget period:

$$\text{fixed-overhead rate} = \frac{\text{budgeted fixed manufacturing overhead}}{\text{expected volume of production}} = \frac{\$150,000}{150,000 \text{ units}} = \$1$$

Second, fixed factory overhead does not appear as a separate line in an absorption-costing income statement. Instead, the fixed factory overhead is included in two places: as part of the cost of goods sold and as a *production-volume variance.*[2] A **production-volume variance** (which is explained further in the next section of this chapter) appears whenever actual production deviates from the expected volume of production used in computing the fixed overhead rate:

production-volume variance = (actual volume − expected volume) × fixed-overhead rate

Finally, the format for an absorption-costing income statement separates costs into the major categories of *manufacturing* and *nonmanufacturing*. In

---

[2] In general, this will be a *cost-driver activity variance*. In our example, production volume is the only cost driver, so it can be called a *production-volume variance*.

Objective 3

Construct
an income state-
ment using the
absorption-costing
approach

contrast, a variable-costing income statement separates costs into the major categories of *fixed* and *variable*. In an absorption-costing statement, revenue less *manufacturing* cost (both fixed and variable) is *gross profit* or *gross margin*. In a variable-costing statement, revenue less all *variable* costs (both manufacturing and nonmanufacturing) is the *contribution margin*. This difference is illustrated by a condensed comparison of 19X7 income statements (in thousands of dollars):

Variable Costing at Northern Telcom

Northern Telcom, the $7 billion Canadian designer and manufacturer of telecommunications equipment, gradually came to understand that its standard absorption costing income statement did not provide the information that managers needed. The company also realized that the problem was one of format more than of substance. The information needed for a more meaningful income statement was in the accounting system, but the traditional reported income statement did not present the information in the most useful way. Therefore, Northern Telcom's accountants adopted a "direct costing" approach to the income statement.

Statutory and regulatory reporting requirements did not allow Northern Telcom to completely abandon absorption costing. The company's solution left the top line—revenue—and the bottom line—earnings before tax—unchanged. But everything in between was reported differently, in the following format:

Revenue
   Product cost
Product margin
   Manufacturing/operational costs
   Inventory provisions
   New product introduction
   Selling and marketing
Direct Margin
   Administrative cost
   Other operating (income) expense
Operating profit
   Corporate assessments
   Other non-operating (income) expense
Earnings before balance sheet adjustments
   Balance sheet adjustment
Earnings before tax

This format represents an extreme application of variable costing. Only direct-material costs are considered product costs. All other costs, including direct labor and variable overhead, are period costs that are charged to expense when incurred, not added to inventory. For example, direct labor is part of manufacturing costs. The amount charged in any period is the amount actually incurred that period, regardless of whether the labor is related to goods sold or those still in inventory. Four measures of "profit" are used by managers: product margin (to measure the value added), direct margin (to measure results of product production and sales), operating profit (to measure total results of operations), and earnings before balance sheet adjustments (to measure effect of companywide profits).

The main difference between the old absorption costing system and the new system is that the new system expenses *all* costs except material costs, while the old system capitalized a portion of them. Reconciling the two systems was an accounting problem, unrelated to operating the business. Therefore, a final line was added to the income statement to provide a reconciliation—balance sheet adjustment. This represents the difference between the absorption and "direct" costing statements, as needed for statutory and regulatory reporting, but it can be ignored by managers.

Northern Telcom's efforts illustrate two important points. First, it is possible to adapt accounting methods to meet the specific needs of managers. Second, companies often do not have to choose between absorption and variable costing—either format can be produced by the same basic accounting system. ■

Source: From P. Sharman, "Time to Re-examine the P&L," CMA Magazine, September 1991, pp. 22–25.

Exhibit 16-3		19X6		19X7
Greenberg Company Comparative Income Statements Using Absorption Costing (thousands of dollars) Years 19X6 and 19X7 (data are in text)	Sales		700		800
	Cost of goods sold				
	Opening inventory, at standard absorption cost of $4*	—		120	
	Cost of goods manufactured at standard of $4	680		560	
	Available for sale	680		680	
	Deduct: ending inventory at standard absorption cost of $4	120		40	
	Cost of goods sold, at standard		560		640
	Gross profit at standard		140		160
	Production-volume variance†		20 F		10 U
	Gross margin or gross profit, at "actual"		160		150
	Selling and administrative expenses		100		105
	Operating income		60		45

```
* Variable cost                          $3
    Fixed cost ($150,000 ÷ 150,000)       1
    Standard absorption cost             $4
† Computation of production-volume variance based on expected volume of production of
   150,000 units:
            19X1              $20,000 F    (170,000 – 150,000) × $1
            19X2               10,000 U    (140,000 – 150,000) × $1
            Two years together $10,000 F   (310,000 – 300,000) × $1
 U = Unfavorable. F = Favorable.
```

Variable Costing		Absorption Costing	
Revenue	800	Revenue	800
All variable costs	520	All manufacturing costs*	650
Contribution margin	280	Gross margin	150
All fixed costs	215	All nonmanufacturing costs	105
Operating income	65	Operating income	45

* Standard absorption cost of goods sold plus production-volume variance.

Despite the importance of such differences in most industries, more and more firms are not concerned with the choice between variable and absorption costing. Why? Because they have implemented just-in-time (JIT) production methods (see Chapter 4) and sharply reduced inventory levels. There is no difference between variable-costing and absorption-costing income if the inventory level does not change, and companies with little inventory generally experience only insignificant *changes* in inventory.

■ FIXED OVERHEAD AND ABSORPTION COSTS OF PRODUCT

All three differences between variable- and absorption-costing formats arise solely because direct-costing treats fixed manufacturing overhead differently from absorption costing. In this and subsequent sections, we explore how to account for factory overhead in an absorption-costing system.

Variable and Fixed Unit Costs

Continuing our example of the Greenberg Company, we begin by comparing (1) the manufacturing overhead costs in the flexible budget used for departmental budgeting and control purposes with (2) the manufacturing overhead costs applied to products under an absorption-costing system. To stress the basic assumptions behind absorption costing, we will also split manufacturing overhead into variable and fixed components. (Most real absorption-costing systems do not make such a split.)

Consider the following graphs of *variable-overhead costs*:

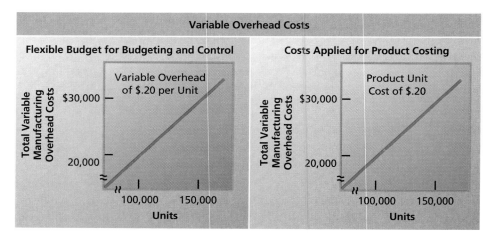

Note that the two graphs are identical. The expected variable-overhead costs from the flexible budget are the same as the variable-overhead costs applied to the products. Both *budgeted* and *applied* variable overhead are $.20 per unit. Each time 1,000 additional units are produced, we expect to incur an additional $200 of variable overhead, and $200 of variable-overhead cost is added to the inventory account for the items. The variable costs used for budgeting and control are the same as those used for product costing.

In contrast, the graph for *applied fixed-overhead costs* differs from that for the flexible budget:

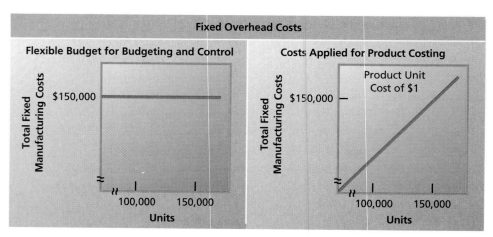

Note: These graphs are not to the same scale as the preceding graphs.

The flexible budget for fixed overhead is a lump-sum budgeted amount of $150,000. It is unaffected by volume. In contrast, the applied fixed cost depends on actual volume:

$$\text{fixed cost applied} = \text{actual volume} \times \text{fixed-overhead rate}$$
$$= \text{units produced} \times \$1$$

Suppose actual volume equals the expected volume of 150,000 units. Applied fixed overhead would be 150,000 units × $1 per unit = $150,000, the same as the flexible-budget amount. However, whenever actual volume differs from expected volume, the costs used for budgeting and control differ from those used for product costing. For budgeting and control purposes, managers use the actual cost behavior pattern for fixed costs. In contrast, as the graphs indicate, the absorption product-costing approach treats these fixed costs as though they had a variable-cost behavior pattern. The difference between applied and budgeted fixed overhead is the production-volume variance.

Nature of Production-Volume Variance

Objective 4

Identify the nature of the production-volume variance, compute it, and state how it should appear in the income statement

The *production-volume variance* can be calculated as follows:

$$\text{production-volume variance} = \text{applied fixed overhead} - \text{budgeted fixed overhead}$$
$$= (\text{actual volume} \times \text{fixed-overhead rate})$$
$$- (\text{expected volume} \times \text{fixed-overhead rate})$$

or

$$\text{production-volume variance} = (\text{actual volume} - \text{expected volume})$$
$$\times \text{fixed overhead rate}$$

volume variance A common name for production-volume variance.

In practice, the production-volume variance is usually called simply the **volume variance.** We use the term *production-volume variance* because it is a more precise description of the fundamental nature of the variance.

A production-volume variance arises when the actual production volume achieved does not coincide with the expected volume of production used as a denominator for computing the fixed-overhead rate for product-costing purposes:

1. When expected production volume and actual production volume are identical, there is no production-volume variance.
2. When actual volume is less than expected volume, the production-volume variance is unfavorable because usage of facilities is less than expected and fixed overhead is underapplied. It is measured in Exhibit 16-3 for 19X7 as follows:

$$(\text{expected volume} - \text{actual volume})$$
$$\times \text{budgeted fixed-overhead rate} = \text{production-volume variance}$$
$$(150,000 \text{ hours} - 140,000 \text{ hours}) \times \$1 = \$10,000 \text{ U}$$

or

$$\text{budget minus applied} = \text{production-volume variance}$$
$$\$150,000 - \$140,000 = \$10,000 \text{ U}$$

The $10,000 unfavorable production-volume variance increases the manufacturing costs shown on the income statement. Why? Recall that $150,000 of fixed manufacturing cost was incurred, but only $140,000 was applied to inventory. Therefore only $140,000 will be charged as expense when the inventory is sold. But all

$150,000 must be charged sometime, so the extra $10,000 is an added expense in the current income statement.

3. When actual volume exceeds expected volume, as was the case in 19X6, the production-volume variance is favorable because use of facilities is better than expected, and fixed overhead is overapplied:

production-volume variance = (150,000 units – 170,000 units) × $1 = $20,000 F

In this case, $170,000 will be charged through inventory. Because costs of only $150,000 are incurred, future expenses will be overstated by $20,000. Therefore current period expenses are reduced by the $20,000 favorable variance.

The production-volume variance is the conventional measure of the cost of departing from the level of activity originally used to set the fixed-overhead rate.[3] Most companies consider production-volume variances to be beyond immediate control, although sometimes a manager responsible for volume has to do some explaining or investigating. Sometimes failure to reach the expected volume is caused by idleness because of disappointing total sales, poor production scheduling, unusual machine breakdowns, shortages of skilled workers, strikes, storms, and the like.

There is no production-volume variance for variable overhead. The concept of production-volume variance arises for fixed overhead because of the conflict between accounting for control (by flexible budgets) and accounting for product costing (by application rates). Note again that the fixed-overhead budget serves the control purpose, whereas the development of a product-costing rate results in the treatment of fixed overhead as if it were a variable cost.

Above all, remember that fixed costs are simply not divisible as variable costs are. Rather, they come in big chunks and are related to the provision of big chunks of production or sales capability, not to the production or sale of a single unit of product.

Selection of Expected Activity Level for Computing the Fixed-Overhead Rate

The fixed-overhead rate in an absorption-costing framework depends on the expected activity level chosen as the denominator in the computation; the higher the level of activity, the lower the rate.

The selection of an appropriate activity level for the denominator is a matter of judgment. Management usually wants to apply a single representative standard fixed cost for a unit of product to apply over a period of at least 1 year, despite month-to-month changes in activity level. Therefore the predicted total fixed cost and the expected activity level used in calculating the fixed-overhead rate should cover at least a 1-year period. Most managers favor using the budgeted annual activity level as the expected activity level in the denominator. Others favor using some longer-run (3- to 5-year) approximation of "normal" activity. Still others favor using maximum or full capacity (often called **practical capacity**).

Although fixed-overhead rates are often important for product costing and long-run pricing, such rates have limited significance for control purposes. At

practical capacity
Maximum or full capacity.

---

[3] Do not confuse the production-volume variance described here with the sales-volume variance described in Chapter 8. Despite similar nomenclature, they are completely different concepts.

the lower levels of supervision, almost no fixed costs are under direct control. Even at higher levels of supervision, many fixed costs are uncontrollable in the short run within wide ranges of anticipated activity.

Actual, Normal, and Standard Costing

Overhead variances are not restricted to standard-costing systems. Many companies apply *actual* direct materials and actual direct-labor costs to products or services but use *standards* for applying overhead. Such a procedure is called **normal costing.** The following chart compares normal costing with two other basic ways for applying costs by the absorption-costing method:

normal costing A cost system that applies actual direct materials and actual direct-labor costs to products or services but uses standards for applying overhead.

	Actual Costing	Normal Costing	Standard Costing
Direct materials	Actual costs	Actual	Budgeted prices or
Direct labor	Actual	Actual	rates × standard inputs
Variable factory overhead	Actual	Budgeted	allowed
Fixed factory overhead		rates × actual inputs	for actual output achieved

Objective 5

Identify the differences among the three alternative cost bases of an absorption-costing system: actual, normal, and standard

Dropping fixed factory overhead from this chart produces a comparison of the same three basic ways of applying costs by the variable-costing method.

Both normal absorption costing and standard absorption costing generate production-volume variances. In addition, normal and standard-costing systems produce all other overhead variances under both variable and absorption formats.

Reconciliation of Variable Costing and Absorption Costing

Exhibit 16-4 reconciles the operating incomes shown in Exhibits 16-2 and 16-3. The difference in those two earlier exhibits is quickly explained by multiplying the fixed-overhead product-costing rate by the *change* in the total units in the beginning and ending inventories. Consider 19X7: The change in inventory was 20,000 units, so the difference in net income would be 20,000 units × $1.00 = $20,000.

The difference in income also equals the difference in the total amount of fixed manufacturing overhead charged as expense during a given year. (See Exhibits 16-5 and 16-6.) The $150,000 fixed manufacturing overhead incurred in 19X7 is automatically the amount recognized as an expense on a variable-costing income statement.

Under absorption costing, fixed manufacturing overhead appears in two places: cost of goods sold and production-volume variance. Note that $30,000 of these fixed costs were incurred before 19X7 and held over in the beginning inventory. During 19X7, $140,000 of fixed manufacturing overhead was added to inventory, and $10,000 was still lodged in the ending inventory of 19X7. Thus the fixed manufacturing overhead included in cost of goods sold for 19X7 was $30,000 + $140,000 − $10,000 = $160,000. In addition, the production-volume variance is $10,000, unfavorable. The total fixed manufacturing overhead charged as 19X7 expenses under absorption costing is $170,000, or $20,000 more than the $150,000 charged under variable costing. Therefore, 19X7 variable-costing income is higher by $20,000.

Remember that it is the relationship between sales and production that determines the difference between variable-costing and absorption-costing income. Whenever sales exceed production, that is, when inventory decreases, variable-costing income is greater than absorption-costing income.

Exhibit 16-4 Reconciliation of Operating Income Under Variable Costing and Absorption Costing		**19X6**	**19X7**	**Together**
	Operating income under			
	Absorption costing (see Exhibit 16-3, p. 607)	$60,000	$ 45,000	$105,000
	Variable costing (see Exhibit 16-2, p. 605)	30,000	65,000	95,000
	Difference to be explained	$30,000	$–20,000	$ 10,000
	The difference can be reconciled by multiplying the fixed-overhead rate by the *change* in the total inventory units			
	Fixed-overhead rate	$1	$1	$1
	Change in inventory units			
	Opening inventory	—	30,000	—
	Ending inventory	30,000	10,000	10,000
	Change	30,000	–20,000	10,000
	Difference in operating income explained	$30,000	$–20,000	$ 10,000

Why Use Variable Costing?

Why do many companies use variable costing for internal statements? One reason is that absorption-costing income is affected by production volume while direct-costing income is not. Consider the 19X7 absorption-costing statement in Exhibit 16-3, page 607, which shows operating income of $45,000. Suppose a manager decides to produce 10,000 additional units in December 19X7 even though they will remain unsold. Will this affect operating income? First, note that the gross profit will not change. Why? Because it is based on sales, not production. However, the production-volume variance will change:

$$\text{If production} = 140,000 \text{ units}$$
$$\text{Production-volume variance} = (150,000 - 140,000) \times \$1 = \$10,000 \text{ U}$$
$$\text{If production} = 150,000 \text{ units}$$
$$\text{Production-volume variance} = (150,000 - 150,000) \times \$1 = 0$$

Because there is no production-volume variance when 150,000 units are produced, the new operating income equals gross profit less selling and administrative expenses, $160,000 − $105,000 = $55,000. Therefore increasing *production* by 10,000 units without any increase in *sales* increases absorption-costing operating income by $10,000, from $45,000 to $55,000.

How will such an increase in production affect the variable-costing statement in Exhibit 16-2, page 605? Nothing will change. Production does not affect operating income under direct costing.

Suppose the evaluation of a manager's performance is heavily based on operating income. If the company uses the absorption-costing approach, a manager might be tempted to produce unneeded units just to increase reported operating income. No such temptation exists with variable costing.

| Exhibit 16-5 | Flow of Fixed Manufacturing Overhead Costs during 19X7 (Format Derived from Exhibit 16-1, page 602) |

Fixed Manufacturing Overhead Incurred   **Inventoried Costs on Balance Sheet**   **Expense on Income Statement**

Variable Costing

$150,000 → None → $150,000

Absorption Costing

Fixed Overhead Costs in Beginning Inventory, $30,000

$150,000 → $140,000 → Costs Added to Product, $140,000 → Cost of Goods Sold, $30,000 + $140,000 − $10,000 = $160,000

Fixed Overhead Costs in Ending Inventory, $10,000

Total Fixed Manufacturing Overhead Charged as Expense, $160,000 + $10,000 = $170,000

Unfavorable Production-Volume Variance, $10,000

$10,000 →

Companies also choose variable or absorption costing based on which system they believe gives a better signal about performance. A sales-oriented company may prefer variable costing because its income is affected primarily by the level of sales. In contrast, a production-oriented company, for example a company that can easily sell all the units it produces, might prefer absorption costing. Why? Because additional production increases the operating income with absorption costing but not with variable costing.

Exhibit 16-6		Inventory		Expense
Tracing Fixed Manufacturing Costs during 19X7 (data are from exhibits 16-2 and 16-3)	***Variable Costing***			
	No fixed overhead carried over from 19X6			
	Fixed overhead actually incurred in 19X7	$150,000		$150,000
	Absorption Costing		*Units*	*Dollars*
	Fixed overhead in beginning inventory	$ 30,000	30,000	$ 30,000
	Fixed overhead incurred in 19X7	150,000		
	To account for	$180,000		
	Applied to product, 140,000 @ $1		140,000	140,000
	Available for sale		170,000	$170,000
	Contained in standard cost of goods sold	$160,000	160,000	160,000 → $160,000
	In ending inventory	10,000	10,000	$ 10,000
	Not applied, so becomes unfavorable production-volume variance	10,000		10,000
	Fixed factory overhead charged against 19X7 operations			$170,000
	Accounted for, as above	$180,000		
	Difference in operating income occurs because $170,000 expires rather than $150,000			$ 20,000

■ EFFECT OF OTHER VARIANCES

So far, our example has deliberately ignored the possibility of any variance except the production-volume variance, which appears only on an absorption-costing statement. All other variances appear on both variable- and absorption-costing income statements. In this section we will consider other variances that were explained in Chapter 8.

Flexible-Budget Variances

Returning again to the Greenberg Company, we will assume some additional facts for 19X7 (the second of the 2 years covered by our example):

Flexible-budget variances	
Direct material	None
Direct labor	$34,000 U
Variable factory overhead	$ 3,000 U
Fixed factory overhead	$ 7,000 U
Supporting data (used to compute the above variances as shown in Appendix 16):	
Standard direct-labor-hours allowed for 140,000 units of output produced	35,000
Standard direct-labor rate per hour	$6.00
Actual direct-labor-hours of inputs	40,000
Actual direct-labor rate per hour	$6.10
Variable manufacturing overhead actually incurred	$31,000
Fixed manufacturing overhead actually incurred	$157,000

As Chapter 8 explains, flexible-budget variances may arise for both variable overhead and fixed overhead. Consider the following:

	Actual Amounts	Flexible-Budget Amounts @ 140,000 Units	Flexible-Budget Variances
Variable factory overhead	$ 31,000	$ 28,000	$3,000 U
Fixed factory overhead	157,000	150,000	7,000 U

Exhibit 16-7 shows the relationship between the fixed-overhead flexible-budget variance and the production-volume variance. The difference between the actual fixed overhead and that applied to products is the under-applied (or overapplied) overhead. Because the actual fixed overhead of $157,000 exceeds the $140,000 applied, fixed overhead is *underapplied* by $17,000, which means that the variance is *unfavorable*. The $17,000 under-applied fixed overhead has two components: (1) a production-volume variance of $10,000 U and (2) a fixed-overhead flexible-budget variance (also called the *fixed-overhead spending variance* or simply the *fixed-overhead budget variance*) of $7,000 U.

All variances other than the production-volume variance are essentially flexible-budget variances. They measure components of the differences between actual amounts and the flexible-budget amounts for the output achieved. Flexible budgets are primarily designed to assist planning and control rather than product costing. The production-volume variance is not a flexible-budget variance. It is designed to aid product costing.

Exhibit 16-8 contains the income statement under absorption costing that incorporates these new facts. These new variances hurt income by $44,000 because, like the production-volume variance, they are all unfavorable variances that are charged against income in 19X7. When cost variances are favorable, they increase operating income.

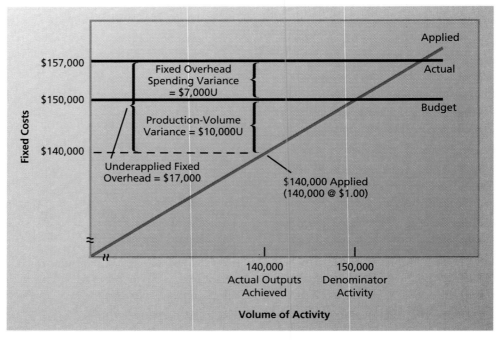

Disposition of Standard-Cost Variances

Advocates of standard costing contend that variances are generally subject to current control, especially when the standards are viewed as being currently attainable. Therefore variances are not inventoriable and should be considered as adjustments to the income of the period instead of being added to inventories. In this way, inventory valuations will be more representative of desirable and attainable costs.

	(in thousands)	
Sales, 160,000 at $5		$800
Opening inventory at standard, 30,000 at $4	$120	
Cost of goods manufactured at standard, 140,000 at $4	560	
Available for sale, 170,000 at $4	$680	
Deduct ending inventory at standard, 10,000 at $4	40	
Cost of goods sold at standard, 160,000 at $4		640
Gross profit at standard		$160
Flexible-budget variances, both unfavorable		
Variable manufacturing costs ($34,000 + $3,000)	$ 37	
Fixed factory overhead	7	
Production-volume variance (arises only because of fixed overhead), unfavorable	10	
Total variances		54
Gross profit at "actual"		$106
Selling and administrative expenses		105
Operating income		$ 1

prorating the variance Assigning the variances to the inventories and cost of goods sold related to the production during the period the variances arose.

The countervailing view favors assigning the variances to the inventories and cost of goods sold related to the production during the period the variances arose. This is often called **prorating the variances.** Prorating makes inventory valuations more representative of the *"actual"* costs incurred to obtain the products. In practice, unless variances and inventory levels are significant, the variances are usually not prorated.

Therefore, in practice, all cost variances are typically regarded as adjustments to current income. Where variances appear on the income statement is generally unimportant. Exhibit 16-8 shows variances as a component of gross profit at "actual." But the variances could appear instead as a completely separate section elsewhere in the income statement. Such placement would help to distinguish between product costing (i.e., the cost of goods sold, at standard) and loss recognition (unfavorable variances are "lost" or "expired" costs because they represent waste and inefficiency thereby not qualifying as inventoriable costs; i.e., waste is not an asset). The *placement* of the variance does not affect operating income.

Highlights to Remember

Cost accounting systems are usually designed to satisfy *control* and *product-costing* purposes simultaneously. Many varieties of product costing are in use. For years, manufacturing companies have regularly used absorption costing, which includes fixed factory overhead as a part of the cost of the product based on some predetermined application rate (variances are not inventoried). In contrast, variable costing charges fixed factory overhead to the period immediately—that is, fixed overhead is altogether excluded from inventories. Absorption costing continues to be much more widely used than variable costing, although the growing use of the contribution approach in performance measurement has led to increasing use of variable costing for internal purposes.

The production-volume variance is linked with absorption costing, not variable costing. It arises from the conflict between the control-budget purpose and the product-costing purpose of cost accounting. The production-volume variance is measured by the predetermined fixed overhead rate multiplied by the difference between expected production volume and actual production volume.

Actual-costing systems apply actual costs for direct materials, direct labor, and manufacturing overhead to the products produced. Normal-costing systems apply actual product costs for direct material and direct labor and budgeted product costs for manufacturing overhead. Standard-cost systems apply budgeted product costs for direct materials, direct labor, and manufacturing overhead.

No variances are charged to income in actual costing, only overhead variances are charged in normal costing, and direct material, direct labor, and overhead variances are charged in standard costing. If standards are currently attainable, the variances are generally not inventoried. Instead, they are directly charged or credited to current operations. The other alternative, proration of variances, splits variances between inventories and cost of goods sold. Proration is a close approximation to an actual-cost system.

Exhibit 16-9 summarizes the effects that variable costing and absorption costing have on income.

Exhibit 16-9	Comparative Income Effects			
	Variable Costing	**Absorption Costing**	**Comments**	
1. Fixed factory overhead inventoried?	No	Yes	Basic theoretical question of when a cost should become an expense.	
2. Production-volume variance?	No	Yes	Choice of expected volume of production affects measurement of operating income under absorption costing.	
3. Treatment of other variances?	Same	Same	Underscores the fact that the basic difference is the accounting for fixed factory overhead, not the accounting for variable factory overhead.	
4. Classifications between variable and fixed costs are routinely made?	Yes	No	However, absorption cost can be modified to obtain subclassifications of variable and fixed costs, if desired.	
5. Usual effects of changes in inventory levels on operating income			Differences are attributable to timing of the transformation of fixed factory overhead into expense.	
Production = sales	Equal	Equal		
Production > sales	Lower*	Higher†		
Production < sales	Higher	Lower		
6. Cost-volume-profit relationships	Tied to sales	Tied to production *and* sales	Management control benefit: Effects of changes in volume on operating income are easier to understand under variable costing.	

* That is, lower than absorption costing.
† That is, higher than variable costing.

Summary Problem for Your Review

Problem

1. Reconsider Exhibits 16-2 and 16-3, pages 605 and 607. Suppose production in 19X7 was 145,000 units instead of 140,000 units, but sales were 160,000 units. Assume that the net variances for all variable manufacturing costs were $37,000, unfavorable. Regard these variances as adjustments to the standard cost of goods sold. Also assume that actual fixed costs were $157,000. Prepare income statements for 19X7 under variable costing and under absorption costing.

2. Explain why operating income was different under variable costing from what it was under absorption costing. Show your calculations.

3. Without regard to requirement 1, would variable costing or absorption costing give a manager more leeway in influencing short-run operating income through production-scheduling decisions? Why?

Solution

1. See Exhibits 16-10 and 16-11. Note that the ending inventory will be 15,000 units instead of 10,000 units.

Exhibit 16-10				
Greenberg Company Income Statement (variable costing) Year 19X7 (thousands of dollars)	Sales			$800
	Opening inventory, at variable standard cost of $3	$ 90		
	Add: variable cost of goods manufactured	435		
	Available for sale	$525		
	Deduct: ending inventory, at variable standard cost of $3	45		
	Variable cost of goods sold, at standard		$480	
	Net flexible-budget variances for all variable costs, unfavorable		37	
	Variable cost of goods sold, at actual		$517	
	Variable selling expenses, at 5% of dollar sales		40	
	Total variable costs charged against sales			557
	Contribution margin			$243
	Fixed factory overhead		$157*	
	Fixed selling and administrative expenses		65	
	Total fixed expenses			222
	Operating income			$ 21†

* This could be shown in two lines, $150,000 budget plus $7,000 variance.
† The difference between this and the $65,000 operating income in Exhibit 16-2 occurs because of the $37,000 unfavorable variable-cost variances and the $7,000 unfavorable fixed-cost flexible-budget variance.

2. Decline in inventory levels is 30,000 – 15,000, or 15,000 units. The fixed-overhead rate per unit in absorption costing is $1. Therefore $15,000 more fixed overhead was charged against operations under absorption costing than under variable costing. The variable-costing statement shows fixed factory overhead of $157,000, whereas the absorption-costing statement includes fixed factory overhead in three places: $160,000 in cost of goods sold, $7,000 U in fixed factory overhead flexible-budget variance, and $5,000 U as a production-volume variance, for a total of $172,000. Generally, when inventories decline, absorption costing will show less income than will variable costing; when inventories rise, absorption costing will show more income than variable costing.

3. Some version of absorption costing will give a manager more leeway in influencing operating income via production scheduling. Operating income will fluctuate in harmony with changes in net sales under variable costing, but it is influenced by both production and sales under absorption costing. For example, compare the variable costing in Exhibits 16-2 and 16-10. As the second note to Exhibit 16-10 indicates, the operating income may be affected by assorted variances (but not the production-volume variance) under variable costing, but production scheduling per se will have no effect on operating income. On the other hand, compare the operating income of Exhibits 16-8 and 16-11.

As the third note to Exhibit 16-11 explains, production scheduling as well as sales influence operating income. Production was 145,000 rather than 140,000 units. So $5,000 of fixed overhead became a part of ending inventory (an asset) instead of part of the production-volume variance (an expense)—that is, the production-volume variance is $5,000 lower and the ending inventory contains $5,000 more fixed overhead in Exhibit 16-11 than in Exhibit 16-8. The manager adds $1 to 19X7 operating income with each unit of production under absorption costing, even if the unit is not sold.

Exhibit 16-11

**Greenberg Company
Income Statement
(absorption costing)
Year 19X7 (thou-
sands of dollars)**

Sales		$800
Opening inventory, at standard cost of $4	$120	
Cost of goods manufactured, at standard	580	
Available for sale	$700	
Deduct: ending inventory, at standard	60	
Cost of goods sold, at standard	$640	
Net flexible-budget variances for all variable manufacturing costs, unfavorable	$37	
Fixed factory overhead flexible-budget variance, unfavorable	7	
Production-volume variance, unfavorable	5*	
Total variances	49	
Cost of goods sold, at actual		689†
Gross profit, at "actual"		$111
Selling and administrative expenses		
Variable	40	
Fixed	65	105
Operating income		$ 6‡

* Production-volume variance is $1 x (150,000 expected volume – 145,000 actual production).
† This format differs slightly from Exhibit 16-8, page 616. The difference is deliberate; it illustrates that the formats of income statements are not rigid.
‡ Compare this result with the $1,000 operating income in Exhibit 16-8. The *only* difference is
traceable to the *production* of 145,000 units instead of 140,000 units, resulting in an unfavorable production-volume variance of $5,000 instead of $10,000.

Appendix 16: Comparisons of Production-Volume Variance with Other Variances

Objective 8

Analyze and com-
pare all the major
variances in a stand-
ard absorption-
costing system

The only new variance introduced in this chapter is the production-volume
variance, which arises because fixed-overhead accounting must serve two masters: the *control-budget* purpose and the *product-costing* purpose. Let us examine this variance in perspective by using the approach originally demonstrated
in Exhibit 8-8, page 311. The results of the approach appear in Exhibit 16-12,
which deserves your careful study, particularly the two footnotes. Please ponder the exhibit before reading on.

Exhibit 16-13 graphically compares the variable- and fixed-overhead costs
analyzed in Exhibit 16-12. Note how the control-budget line and the product-
costing line (the applied line) are superimposed in the graph for variable overhead but differ in the graph for fixed overhead.

Underapplied or overapplied overhead is always the difference between the
actual overhead incurred and the overhead applied. An analysis may then
be made:

$$\text{underapplied overhead} = \left(\begin{array}{c}\text{flexible-budget}\\\text{variance}\end{array}\right) + \left(\begin{array}{c}\text{production-volume}\\\text{variance}\end{array}\right)$$

$$\text{for variable overhead} = \$3,000 + 0 = \$3,000$$
$$\text{for fixed overhead} = \$7,000 + \$10,000 = \$17,000$$

Exhibit 16-12

Analysis of Variances (Data Are from Text for 19X7)

Inputs	(A) Costs Incurred: Actual Inputs × Actual Price	(B) Flexible Budget Based on Actual Inputs × Expected Prices	(C) Flexible Budget Based on Standard Inputs Allowed for Actual Outputs Achieved × Expected Prices	(D) Product Costing: Applied to Product
Direct labor	40,000 × $6.10 = $244,000	40,000 × $6 = $240,000	(35,000 × $6) or (140,000 × $1.50) = $210,000*	(35,000 × $6) or (140,000 × $1.50) = $210,000*
		40,000 × ($6.10 − 6) = price variance, $4,000 U	5,000 × $6 = usage variance, $30,000 U	Never a variance
		Flexible-budget variance, $34,000 U		Never a variance
Variable factory overhead	(given) $31,000	40,000 × $.80 = $32,000	(35,000 × $.80 or 140,000 × $.20) = $28,000*	$28,000*
		Spending variance, $1,000 F	5,000 × $.80 = efficiency variance, $4,000 U	Never a variance
		Flexible-budget variance, $3,000 U		Never a variance
		Underapplied overhead, $3,000 U		
Fixed factory overhead	$157,000	Lump sum $150,000	Lump sum $150,000†	140,000 × $1.00 = $140,000
		Spending variance, $7,000 U	Never a variance	Production-volume variance, $10,000 U
		Flexible-budget variance, $7,000 U		Production-volume variance, $10,000 U
		Underapplied overhead, $17,000 U		

U = Unfavorable. F = Favorable.

* Note especially that the flexible budget for variable costs rises and falls in direct proportion to production. Note also that the control-budget purpose and the product-costing purpose harmonize completely; the total costs in the flexible budget will always agree with the standard variable costs applied to the product because they are based on standard costs per unit multiplied by units produced.

† In contrast with variable costs, the flexible-budget total for fixed costs will always be the same regardless of the units produced. However, the control-budget purpose and the product-costing purpose conflict; whenever actual production differs from expected production, the standard costs applied to the product will differ from the flexible budget. This difference is the production-volume variance. In this case, the production-volume variance may be computed by multiplying the $1 rate times the difference between the 150,000 expected volume and the 140,000 units of output achieved.

| Exhibit 16-13 | Comparison of Control and Product-Costing Purposes, Variable Overhead and Fixed Overhead (not to scale) |

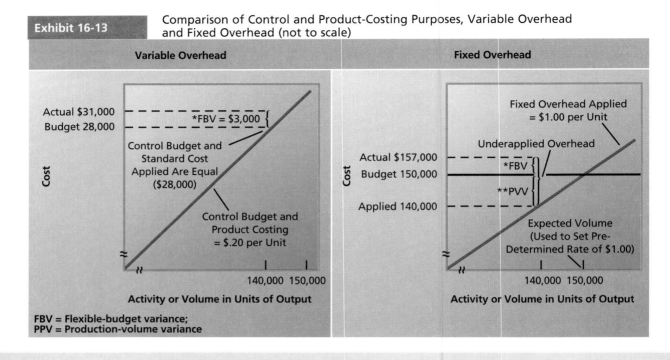

FBV = Flexible-budget variance;
PPV = Production-volume variance

Accounting Vocabulary

fixed-overhead rate, *p. 605*
normal costing, *p. 611*

practical capacity, *p. 610*
production-volume variance, *p. 605*

prorating the variance, *p. 617*
volume variance, *p. 609*

Fundamental Assignment Material

16-A1   Comparison of Variable Costing and Absorption Costing
From the following information pertaining to a year's operation, answer the questions below:

Units produced	3,000
Units sold	2,400
Direct labor	$4,500
Direct material used	3,000
Selling and administrative expenses (all fixed)	900
Fixed manufacturing overhead	2,000
Variable manufacturing overhead	2,500
All beginning inventories	0
Gross margin (gross profit)	2,400
Direct-materials inventory, end	400
Work-in-process inventory, end	0

Required

1. What is the ending finished-goods inventory cost under absorption costing?
2. What is the ending finished-goods inventory cost under variable-costing?
3. Would operating income be higher or lower under variable costing? By how much? Why? (Answer: $400 lower, but explain why.)

16-A2   Comparison of Absorption and Variable Costing

Examine the Stewart Company's simplified income statement based on variable costing. Assume that the budgeted volume for absorption costing in 19X5 and 19X6 was 1,400 units and that total fixed costs were identical in 19X5 and 19X6. There is no beginning or ending work in process.

Income Statement Year Ended December 31, 19X6			
Sales, 1,280 units @ $12			$15,360
Deduct variable costs			
Beginning inventory, 110 units @ $7		$ 770	
Variable manufacturing cost of goods manufactured, 1,200 units @ $7		8,400	
Variable manufacturing cost of goods available for sale		$9,170	
Ending inventory, 30 units @ $7		210	
Variable manufacturing cost of goods sold		$8,960	
Variable selling and administrative expenses		600	
Total variable costs			9,560
Contribution margin			$ 5,800
Deduct fixed costs			
Fixed factory overhead at budget		$2,800	
Fixed selling and administrative expenses		350	
Total fixed costs			3,150
Operating income			$ 2,650

Required

1. Prepare an income statement based on absorption costing. Assume that actual fixed costs were equal to budgeted fixed costs.
2. Explain the difference in operating income between absorption costing and variable costing. Be specific.

16-B1   Comparison of Variable Costing and Absorption Costing

From the following information pertaining to a year's operations, answer the questions below:

Units sold	1,200
Units produced	1,500
Direct labor	$4,200
Direct material used	3,500
Fixed manufacturing overhead	1,800
Variable manufacturing overhead	300
Selling and administrative expenses (all fixed)	700
Beginning inventories	0
Contribution margin	5,800
Direct-material inventory, end	800
There are no work-in-process inventories.	

Required

1. What is the ending finished-goods inventory cost under absorption costing?
2. What is the ending finished-goods inventory cost under variable-costing?

16-B2   Extension of Chapter Illustration

Reconsider Exhibits 16-2 and 16-3, pages 605 and 607. Suppose that in 19X7 production was 155,000 units instead of 140,000 units, and sales were 150,000 units. Also assume that the net variances for all variable manufacturing costs were $24,000, unfavorable. Also assume that actual fixed manufacturing costs were $156,000.

Required

1. Prepare income statements for 19X7 under variable costing and under absorption costing. Use a format similar to Exhibits 16-10 and 16-11, pages 619-620.
2. Explain why operating income was different under variable costing and absorption costing. Show your calculations.

Additional Assignment Material

Questions

16-1. "With variable costing only direct material and direct labor are inventoried". Do you agree? Why?

16-2. Why is direct costing a misnomer when referring to variable costing?

16-3. "Absorption costing regards more categories of costs as product costs." Explain. Be specific.

16-4. "An increasing number of companies are using variable costing in their corporate annual reports." Do you agree? Explain.

16-5. Why is variable costing used only for internal reporting and not for external financial reporting or tax purposes?

16-6. Why is it artificial to unitize fixed costs?

16-7. How is fixed overhead applied to products?

16-8. "Variable costing is consistent with cost-volume-profit analysis." Explain.

16-9. "In a standard absorption-costing system, the amount of fixed manufacturing overhead applied to the products rarely equals the budgeted fixed manufacturing overhead." Do you agree? Explain.

16-10. "The dollar amount of the production-volume variance depends on what expected volume of production was chosen to determine the fixed-overhead rate." Explain.

16-11. Why is there no production-volume variance for direct labor?

16-12. "An unfavorable production-volume variance means that fixed manufacturing costs have not been well controlled." Do you agree? Explain.

16-13. "The fixed cost per unit is directly affected by the expected volume selected as the denominator." Do you agree? Explain.

16-14. Why do advocates of currently attainable standard costs as a method for product costing claim that it is conceptually superior to actual costing?

16-15. "Production-volume variances arise with normal-absorption and standard-absorption costing, but not with actual costing." Explain.

16-16. "Absorption-costing income exceeds variable-costing income when the number of units sold exceeds the number of units produced." Do you agree? Explain.

16-17. Suppose a manager is paid a bonus only if standard absorption-costing operating income exceeds the budget. If operating income through November is slightly below budget, what might the manager do in December to increase his or her chance of getting the bonus?

16-18. Why are companies with small levels of inventory generally unconcerned with the choice of variable or absorption costing?

16-19. The IRS requires proration of any significant variances for tax reporting. Why do you suppose the IRS requires proration?

Exercises

16-20   Simple Comparison of Variable and Absorption Costing

Reeves Company began business on January 1, 19X4, with assets of $150,000 cash and equities of $150,000 capital stock. In 19X4 it manufactured some inventory at a cost of $60,000, including $12,000 for factory rent and other fixed factory overhead. In 19X5 it manufactured nothing and sold half of its inventory for $42,000 cash. In 19X6 it manufactured nothing and sold the remaining half for another $42,000 cash. It had no fixed expenses in 19X5 or 19X6.

There are no other transactions of any kind. Ignore income taxes.

Required   Prepare an ending balance sheet plus an income statement for 19X4, 19X5, and 19X6 under (1) absorption costing and (2) variable costing (direct costing).

16-21   Comparisons over Four Years

The Arnold Corporation began business on January 1, 19X3, to produce and sell a single product. Reported operating income figures under both absorption and variable (direct) costing for the first four years of operation are:

Year	Variable Costing	Absorption Costing
19X3	$70,000	$50,000
19X4	70,000	60,000
19X5	50,000	50,000
19X6	30,000	60,000

Standard production costs per unit, sales prices, application (absorption) rates, and expected volume levels were the same in each year. There were no underapplied or overapplied overhead costs, and no variances in any year. All nonmanufacturing expenses were fixed, and there were no nonmanufacturing cost variances in any year.

Required
1. In what year(s) did "units produced" equal "units sold"?
2. In what year(s) did "units produced" exceed "units sold"?
3. What is the dollar amount of the December 31, 19X6 finished-goods inventory? (Give absorption-costing value.)
4. What is the difference between "units produced" and "units sold" in 19X6, if you know that the absorption-costing fixed-manufacturing-overhead application rate is $3 per unit? (Give answer in units.)

16-22   Variable and Absorption Costing

Gillum Company data for 19X7 follow:

Sales: 12,000 units at $16 each	
Actual production	15,000 units
Expected volume of production	18,000 units
Manufacturing costs incurred	
Variable	$105,000
Fixed	63,000
Nonmanufacturing costs incurred	
Variable	$24,000
Fixed	18,000

Required
1. Determine operating income for 19X7, assuming the firm uses the variable-costing approach to product costing. (Do not prepare a statement.)
2. Assume that there is *no* January 1, 19X7 inventory; *no* variances are allocated to inventory; and the firm uses a "full absorption" approach to product costing. Compute (a) the cost assigned to December 31, 19X7, inventory; and (b) operating income for the year ended December 31, 19X7. (Do not prepare a statement.)

16-23   Computation of Production-Volume Variance

Wong Company budgeted its 19X6 variable overhead at ¥12,200,000 and its fixed overhead at ¥25,620,000. Expected 19X6 volume was 6,100 units. Actual costs for production of 5,900 units during 19X6 were:

Variable overhead	¥14,160,000
Fixed overhead	25,620,000
Total overhead	¥39,780,000

Required   Compute the production-volume variance. Be sure to label it favorable or unfavorable.

16-24   Reconciliation of Variable-Costing and Absorption-Costing Operating Income

Allie Associates produced 12,000 cameras during 19X5, although expected production was only 10,500 cameras. The company's fixed-overhead rate is $6 per camera. Absorption-costing operating income for the year is $18,000, based on sales of 11,000 units.

Required

1. Compute:
   a. Budgeted fixed overhead
   b. Production-volume variance
   c. Variable-costing operating income
2. Reconcile absorption-costing operating income and variable-costing operating income. Include the amount of the difference between the two and an explanation for the difference.

16-25   Overhead Variances

Study Appendix 16. Consider the following data for the Valenzuela Company:

	Factory Overhead	
	Fixed	*Variable*
Actual incurred	$14,000	$13,200
Budget for standard hours allowed for output achieved	12,500	11,000
Applied	11,600	11,000
Budget for actual hours of input	12,500	11,400

From the above information fill in the blanks below:

The flexible-budget variance is $_____	Fixed $_____
	Variable $_____
The production-volume variance is $_____	Fixed $_____
	Variable $_____
The spending variance is $_____	Fixed $_____
	Variable $_____
The efficiency variance is $_____	Fixed $_____
	Variable $_____

Mark your variances *F* for favorable and *U* for unfavorable.

16-26   Variances

Study Appendix 16. Consider the following data regarding factory overhead:

	Variable	Fixed
Budget for actual hours of input	$45,000	$70,000
Applied	41,000	64,800
Budget for standard hours allowed for actual output achieved	?	?
Actual incurred	48,000	68,500

Required Using the above data, fill in the following blanks with the variance amounts. Use *F* for favorable or *U* for unfavorable for each variance.

	Total Overhead	Variable	Fixed
1. Spending variance			
2. Efficiency variance			
3. Production-volume variance			
4. Flexible-budget variance			
5. Underapplied overhead			

Problems

16-27 Comparison of Variable Costing and Absorption Costing

Simple numbers are used in this problem to highlight the concepts covered in the chapter.

Assume that the Beretta Company produces one product—a bath mat—that sells for $10. Beretta uses a standard cost system. Total standard variable costs of production are $4 per mat, fixed manufacturing costs are $1,500 per year, and selling and administrative expenses are $300 per year, all fixed. Expected production volume is 500 mats per year.

Required 1. For each of the following nine combinations of actual sales and production (in *units*) for 19X7 prepare condensed income statements under variable costing and under absorption costing.

	(1)	(2)	(3)	(4)	(5)	(6)	(7)	(8)	(9)
Sales units	300	400	500	400	500	600	500	600	700
Production units	400	400	400	500	500	500	600	600	600

Use the following formats:

Variable Costing		Absorption Costing	
Revenue	$ aa	Revenue	$ aa
Cost of goods sold	(bb)	Cost of goods sold	(uu)
Contribution margin	$ cc	Gross profit at standard	$ vv
Fixed manufacturing costs	(dd)	Favorable (unfavorable) production-volume variance	ww
Fixed selling and administrative expenses	(ee)	Gross profit at "actual"	$ xx
		Selling and administrative expenses	(yy)
Operating income	$ ff	Operating income	$ zz

2. a. In which of the nine combinations is variable-costing income greater than absorption-costing income? In which is it lower? The same?

    b. In which of the nine combinations is the production-volume variance unfavorable? Favorable?

    c. How much profit is added by selling one more unit under variable costing? Under absorption costing?

    d. How much profit is added by producing one more unit under variable costing? Under absorption costing?

    e. Suppose sales, rather than production, is the critical factor in determining the success of Beretta Company. Which format, variable costing or absorption costing, provides the better measure of performance?

16-28   All-Fixed Costs

(Suggested by Raymond P. Marple.) The Raymond Company has built a massive water-desalting factory next to an ocean. The factory is completely automated. It has its own source of power, light, heat, and so on. The salt water costs nothing. All producing and other operating costs are fixed; they do not vary with output because the volume is governed by adjusting a few dials on a control panel. The employees have flat annual salaries.

    The desalted water is not sold to household consumers. It has a special taste that appeals to local breweries, distilleries, and soft-drink manufacturers. The price, $.25 per gallon, is expected to remain unchanged for quite some time.

    The following are data regarding the first two years of operations:

	In Gallons		Costs (All Fixed)	
	Sales	Production	Manufacturing	Other
19X5	3,000,000	6,000,000	$600,000	$200,000
19X6	3,000,000	0	600,000	200,000

Orders can be processed in four hours, so management decided, in early 19X6, to gear production strictly to sales.

Required
1. Prepare three-column income statements for 19X5, for 19X6, and for the 2 years together using (a) variable costing and (b) absorption costing.
2. What is the break-even point under (a) variable costing and (b) absorption costing?
3. What inventory costs would be carried on the balance sheets on December 31, 19X5 and 19X6, under each method?
4. Comment on your answers in requirements 1 and 2. Which costing method appears more useful?

16-29   Semifixed Costs

The Carley Company differs from the Raymond Company (described in Problem 16-28) in only one respect: It has both variable and fixed manufacturing costs. Its variable costs are $.07 per gallon, and its fixed *manufacturing* costs are $325,000 per year.

Required
1. Using the same data as in the preceding problem, except for the change in production-cost behavior, prepare three-column income statements for 19X5, for 19X6, and for the two years together using (a) variable costing and (b) absorption costing.
2. What inventory costs would be carried on the balance sheets on December 31, 19X5 and 19X6, under each method?

16-30   Absorption and Variable Costing

The Mueller Company had the following actual data for 19X6 and 19X7:

	19X6	19X7
Units of finished goods		
Opening inventory	—	2,000
Production	15,000	13,000
Sales	13,000	14,000
Ending inventory	2,000	1,000

The basic production data at standard unit costs for the 2 years were:

Direct materials	$22
Direct labor	18
Variable factory overhead	4
Standard variable costs per unit	$44

Fixed factory overhead was budgeted at $98,000 per year. The expected volume of production was 14,000 units, so the fixed overhead rate was $98,000 ÷ 14,000 = $7 per unit.

Budgeted sales price was $74 per unit. Selling and administrative expenses were budgeted at variable, $8 *per unit sold*, and fixed, $75,000 per month.

Assume that there were absolutely no variances from any standard variable costs or budgeted selling prices or budgeted fixed costs in 19X6.

There were no beginning or ending inventories of work in process.

Required
1. For 19X6, prepare income statements based on standard variable (direct) costing and standard absorption costing. (The next problem deals with 19X7.)
2. Explain why operating income differs between variable costing and absorption costing. Be specific.

16-31 Absorption and Variable Costing

Assume the same facts as in the preceding problem. In addition, consider the following actual data for 19X7:

Direct materials	$ 285,000
Direct labor	174,200
Variable factory overhead	36,000
Fixed factory overhead	95,000
Selling and administrative costs	
Variable	118,400
Fixed	75,000
Sales	1,054,000

Required
1. For 19X7, prepare income statements based on standard variable (direct) costing and standard absorption costing.
2. Explain why operating income differs between variable costing and absorption costing. Be specific.

16-32 Fundamentals of Overhead Variances

The Wilson Company is installing an absorption standard-cost system and a flexible-overhead budget. Standard costs have recently been developed for its only product and are as follows:

Direct material, 3 pounds @ $18	$54
Direct labor, 2 hours @ $14	28
Variable overhead, 2 hours @ $5	10
Fixed overhead	?
Standard cost per unit of finished product	$?

Expected production activity is expressed as 7,500 standard direct-labor-hours per month. Fixed overhead is expected to be $45,000 per month. The predetermined fixed-overhead rate for product costing is not changed from month to month.

Required

1. Calculate the proper fixed-overhead rate per standard direct-labor-hour and per unit.
2. Graph the following for activity from zero to 10,000 hours:
   a. Budgeted variable overhead
   b. Variable overhead applied to product
3. Graph the following for activity from zero to 10,000 hours:
   a. Budgeted fixed overhead
   b. Fixed overhead applied to product
4. Assume that 6,000 standard direct-labor-hours are allowed for the output achieved during a given month. Actual variable overhead of $30,600 was incurred; actual fixed overhead amounted to $47,000. Calculate the
   a. Fixed-overhead flexible-budget variance
   b. Fixed-overhead production-volume variance
   c. Variable-overhead flexible-budget variance
5. Assume that 7,800 standard direct-labor-hours are allowed for the output achieved during a given month. Actual overhead incurred amounted to $84,700, $47,200 of which was fixed. Calculate the
   a. Fixed-overhead flexible-budget variance
   b. Fixed-overhead production-volume variance
   c. Variable-overhead flexible-budget variance

16-33   Fixed Overhead and Practical Capacity

The expected activity of the paper-making plant of Bradford Paper Company was 45,000 machine-hours per month. Practical capacity was 60,000 machine-hours per month. The standard machine-hours allowed for the actual output achieved in January were 54,000. The budgeted fixed-factory-overhead items were:

Depreciation, equipment	$360,000
Depreciation, factory building	64,000
Supervision	47,000
Indirect labor	214,000
Insurance	18,000
Property taxes	17,000
Total	$720,000

Because of unanticipated scheduling difficulties and the need for more indirect labor, the actual fixed factory overhead was $747,000.

Required

1. Using practical capacity as the base for applying fixed factory overhead, prepare a summary analysis of fixed-overhead variances for January.

2. Using expected activity as the base for applying fixed factory overhead, prepare a summary analysis of fixed-overhead variances for January.
3. Explain why some of your variances in requirements 1 and 2 are the same and why some differ.

16-34 Selection of Expected Volume

Lilla Collins is a consultant to Portland Company. She is helping to install a standard cost system for 19X4. For product-costing purposes, the system must apply fixed factory costs to products manufactured. She has decided that the fixed-overhead rate should be based on machine hours, but she is uncertain about the appropriate volume to use in the denominator. Portland has grown rapidly; it has added production capacity approximately every 4 years. The last addition was completed in early 19X4, and the total capacity is now 2,800,000 machine-hours per year. Collins predicts the following operating levels (in machine hours) through 19X8:

Year	Capacity Used
19X4	2,250,000 hours
19X5	2,500,000 hours
19X6	2,700,000 hours
19X7	2,800,000 hours
19X8	3,000,000 hours

The current plan is to add another 500,000 machine hours of capacity in early 19X8. Collins has identified three alternatives for the allocation base:

1. Predicted volume for the year in question
2. Average volume over the 4 years of the current production setup
3. Practical (or full) capacity

Required

1. Suppose annual fixed factory overhead is expected to be $36,400,000 through 19X7. For simplicity, assume no inflation. Calculate the fixed-overhead rates (to the nearest cent) for 19X5, 19X6, and 19X7 using each of the three alternative allocation bases.
2. Provide a brief description of the effect of using each method of computing the allocation base.
3. Which method do you prefer? Why?

16-35 Extension of Appendix 16 Illustration

Study the format of the analysis of variances in Exhibit 16-12, page 621. Suppose production is 156,000 units. Also assume:

Standard direct-labor-hours allowed per unit produced	.25
Standard direct-labor-rate per hour	$6.00
Actual direct-labor-hours of input	42,000
Actual direct-labor-rate per hour	$6.15
Variable manufacturing overhead actually incurred	$35,000
Fixed manufacturing overhead actually incurred	$155,000

Other data are as shown in Exhibit 16-12.

Required Prepare an analysis of variances similar to that shown in Exhibit 16-12.

16-36   Analysis of Operating Results

(CMA, adapted.) Lance Company, a wholly owned subsidiary of Curtis, Inc., produces and sells three main product lines. The company employs a standard cost accounting system for record-keeping purposes.

At the beginning of 19X6, the president of Lance Company presented the budget to the parent company and accepted a commitment to contribute $16,400 to Curtis's consolidated profit in 19X6. The president has been confident that the year's profit would exceed the budget target, since the monthly sales reports that he has been receiving have shown that sales for the year will exceed budget by 10%. The president is both disturbed and confused when the controller presents an adjusted forecast as of November 30, 19X6, indicating that profit will be 11% under budget:

Lance Company
Forecasts of
Operating Results

	Forecasts as of	
	1/1/X6	*11/30/X6*
Sales	$156,000	$171,600
Cost of sales at standard	108,000*	118,800
Gross margin at standard	$ 48,000	$ 52,800
Over- (under-) absorbed fixed manufacturing overhead	0	(5,480)
Actual gross margin	$ 48,000	$ 47,320
Selling expenses	$ 11,200	$ 12,320
Administrative expenses	20,400	20,400
Total operating expenses	$ 31,600	$ 32,720
Earnings before tax	$ 16,400	$ 14,600

* Includes fixed manufacturing overhead of $18,000.

There have been no sales price changes or product-mix shifts since the 1/1/X6 forecast. The only cost variance on the income statement is the underabsorbed manufacturing overhead. This arose because the company produced only 16,000 standard machine-hours (budgeted machine-hours were 20,000) during 19X6 as a result of a shortage of raw materials while its principal supplier was closed by a strike. Fortunately, Lance's finished-goods inventory was large enough to fill all sales orders received.

Required

1. Analyze and explain why the profit has declined despite increased sales and good control over costs. Show computations.
2. What plan, if any, could Lance Company adopt during December to improve its reported profit at year-end? Explain your answer.
3. Illustrate and explain how Lance Company could adopt an alternative internal cost-reporting procedure that would avoid the confusing effect of the present procedure. Show the revised forecasts under your alternative.
4. Would the alternative procedure described in requirement 3 be acceptable to Curtis, Inc., for financial-reporting purposes? Explain.

16-37   Standard Absorption and Standard Variable Costing

Kasselman Company has the following results for a certain year. All variances are written off as additions to (or deductions from) the standard cost of goods sold. Find the unknowns, designated by letters.

Sales: 150,000 units, @ $22	$3,300,000
Net variance for standard variable manufacturing costs	$ 33,000, unfavorable
Variable standard cost of goods manufactured	$ 11 per unit
Variable selling and administrative expenses	$ 3 per unit
Fixed selling and administrative expenses	$ 650,000
Fixed manufacturing overhead	$ 165,000
Maximum capacity per year	190,000 units
Expected production volume for year	150,000 units
Beginning inventory of finished goods	15,000 units
Ending inventory of finished goods	10,000 units
Beginning inventory: variable-costing basis	a
Contribution margin	b
Operating income: variable-costing basis	c
Beginning inventory: absorption-costing basis	d
Gross margin	e
Operating income: absorption-costing basis	f

16-38 Disposition of Variances

In January 19X5 A. Lincoln Playtime, Inc., started a division for making "acrobots." Management hoped that these toys would be the new fad of 19X5. During 19X5 it produced 100,000 acrobots. Financial results were as follows:

- Sales: 75,000 units @ $25
- Direct labor at standard: 100,000 × $8 = $800,000
- Direct-labor variances: $34,000 U
- Direct material at standard: 100,000 × $5 = $500,000
- Direct-material variances: $9,500 U
- Overhead incurred at standard: 100,000 × $4 = $400,000
- Overhead variances: $3,500 F

A. Lincoln Playtime uses an absorption costing system and allows divisions to choose one of two methods of accounting for variances:

1. Direct charge to income.
2. Proration to the production of the period. Method 2 requires variances to be spread equally over the units produced during the period.

Required

1. Calculate the division's operating income (a) using method 1 and (b) using method 2. Assume no selling and administrative expenses.
2. Calculate ending inventory value (a) using method 1 and (b) using method 2. Note that there was no beginning inventory.
3. What is the major argument in support of each method?

16-39 Comparison of Performance of Two Plants

On your first day as assistant to the president of Harold Systems, Inc., your in-box contains the following memo:

To: Assistant to the President

From: The President

Subject: Beatles Watch Situation

This note is to bring you up to date on one of our acquisition problem areas. Market research detected the current nostalgia wave almost a year ago and concluded that HSI should acquire a position in this market. Research data showed that Beatles Watches could become profitable ($5 contribution margin on a $12 sales price) at a volume of 40,000 units per plant if they became popular. Consequently, we acquired closed-down facilities on each coast, staffed them, and asked them to keep us posted on operations.

Friday I got preliminary information from accounting that is unclear. I want you to find out why their costs of goods sold are far apart and how we should have them report in the future to avoid confusion. This is particularly important in the Beatles case, as market projections look bad and we may have to close one plant. I guess we'll close the West Coast plant unless you can show otherwise.

Preliminary
Accounting Report

	East	West
Sales	$480,000	$480,000
Cost of goods sold	280,000	450,000
Gross margin	$200,000	$ 30,000
Administration costs (fixed)	30,000	30,000
Net income	$170,000	$ 0
Production	80,000 units	40,000 units
Variances (included in cost of goods sold)	$170,000, F	$85,000, U

U = Unfavorable. F = Favorable.

Required   Reconstruct the given income statements in as much detail as possible. Then explain in detail why the income statements differ, and clarify this situation confronting the president. Assume that there are no price, efficiency, or spending variances.

16-40   Straightforward Problem on Standard Cost System
Study Appendix 16. The Bontale Company uses flexible budgets and a standard cost system.

- Direct-labor costs incurred, 12,000 hours, $138,000
- Variable-overhead costs incurred, $30,000
- Fixed-overhead flexible-budget variance, $1,600 favorable
- Finished units produced, 1,800
- Fixed-overhead costs incurred, $38,000
- Variable overhead applied at $2.75 per hour
- Standard direct-labor cost, $13 per hour
- Denominator production per month, 2,000 units
- Standard direct-labor hours per finished unit, 6

Required   Prepare an analysis of all variances (similar to Exhibit 16-12, p. 621).

16-41   Straightforward Problem on Standard Cost System
Study Appendix 16. The Brownstone Company uses a standard cost system. The month's data regarding its single product follow:

- Fixed-overhead costs incurred, $6,400
- Variable overhead applied at $1.10 per hour
- Standard direct-labor cost, $4.40 per hour

- Denominator production per month, 2,200 units
- Standard direct-labor hours per finished unit, 5
- Direct-labor costs incurred, 10,000 hours, $42,500
- Variable-overhead costs incurred, $10,500
- Fixed-overhead budget variance, $200, favorable
- Finished units produced, 1,800

Required Prepare an analysis of all variances (similar to Exhibit 16-12, p. 621).

Cases

16-42 Absorption Costing and Incentive to Produce

Allan McDonald is manager of the Pacific Division of Zenna, Inc. His division makes a single product that is sold to industrial customers. Demand is seasonal but is readily predictable. The division's budget for 19X5 called for production and sales of 120,000 units, with production of 10,000 units each month and sales varying between 8,000 and 13,000 units a month. The division's budget for 19X5 had operating income of $780,000:

Sales (120,000 x $50)	$6,000,000
Cost of goods sold (120,000 x $40)	4,800,000
Gross margin	$1,200,000
Selling and administrative expenses (all fixed)	420,000
Operating income	$ 780,000

By the end of November, sales had lagged projections, with only 105,000 units sold. Sales of 9,000 units were originally budgeted and are still expected in December. Production had remained stable at 10,000 units per month, and the cost of production had been exactly as budgeted:

Direct materials, 110,000 x $9	$ 990,000
Direct labor, 110,000 x $10	1,100,000
Variable overhead, 110,000 x $8	880,000
Fixed overhead	1,430,000
Total production cost	$4,400,000

The division's operating income for the first eleven months of 19X5 was:

Sales (105,000 x $50)	$5,250,000
Cost of goods sold (105,000 x $40)	4,200,000
Gross margin	$1,050,000
Selling and administrative expenses (all fixed)	385,000
Operating income	$ 665,000

McDonald receives an annual bonus only if his division's operating income exceeds the budget. He sees no way to increase sales beyond 9,000 units in December.

Required 1. From the budgeted and actual income statements shown, determine whether Zenna used direct or absorption costing.

2. Suppose Zenna uses a standard absorption-costing system. (a) Compute the 19X5 operating income if 10,000 units are produced and 9,000 units are sold in December. (b) How could McDonald achieve his budgeted operating income for 19X5?

3. Suppose Zenna uses a standard variable-costing system. (a) Compute the 19X5 operating income if 10,000 units are produced and 9,000 units are sold in December. (b) How could McDonald achieve his budgeted operating income for 19X5?

4. Which system motivates McDonald to make the decision that is in the best interests of Zenna? Explain.

16-43   Inventory Measures, Production Scheduling, and Evaluating Divisional Performance

The Paul Company stresses competition between the heads of its various divisions, and it rewards stellar performance with year-end bonuses that vary between 5% and 10% of division net operating income (before considering the bonus or income taxes). The divisional managers have great discretion in setting production schedules.

The Normandy Division produces and sells a product for which there is a long-standing demand but which can have marked seasonal and year-to-year fluctuations. On November 30, 19X6, Byron LeDoux, the Normandy Division manager, is preparing a production schedule for December. The following data are available for January 1 through November 30 (FF means French franc):

Beginning inventory, January 1, in units	10,000
Sales price, per unit	FF400
Total fixed costs incurred for manufacturing	FF9,350,000
Total fixed costs: other (not inventoriable)	FF9,350,000
Total variable costs for manufacturing	FF18,150,000
Total other variable costs (fluctuate with units sold)	FF4,000,000
Units produced	110,000
Units sold	100,000
Variances	None

Production in October and November was 10,000 units each month. Practical capacity is 12,000 units per month. Maximum available storage space for inventory is 25,000 units. The sales outlook for December through February is 6,000 units monthly. To retain a core of key employees, monthly production cannot be scheduled at less than 4,000 units without special permission from the president. Inventory is never to be less than 10,000 units.

The denominator used for applying fixed factory overhead is regarded as 120,000 units annually. The company uses a standard absorption-costing system. All variances are disposed of at year-end as an adjustment to standard cost of goods sold.

Required

1. Given the restrictions as stated, and assuming that the manager wants to maximize the company's net income for 19X6:
   a. How many units should be scheduled for production in December?
   b. What net operating income will be reported in 19X6 as a whole, assuming that the implied cost behavior patterns will continue in December as they did throughout the year to date? Show your computations.
   c. If December production is scheduled at 4,000 units, what would reported net income be?

2. Assume that standard variable costing is used rather than standard absorption costing:
   a. What would net income for 19X6 be, assuming that the December production schedule is the one in requirement 1, part a?

b. Assuming that December production was 4,000 units?

c. Reconcile the net incomes in this requirement with those in requirement 1.

3. From the viewpoint of the long-run interests of the company as a whole, what production schedule should the division manager set? Explain fully. Include in your explanation a comparison of the motivating influence of absorption and variable costing in this situation.

4. Assume standard absorption costing. The manager wants to maximize his after-income-tax performance over the long run. Given the data at the beginning of the problem, assume that income tax rates will be halved in 19X7. Assume also that year-end write-offs of variances are acceptable for income tax purposes. How many units should be scheduled for production in December? Why?

16-44   Performance Evaluation

Imperial Mills is a small flour company in the Midwest. Lloyd Vineland became president in 19X4. He is concerned with the ability of his production manager to control costs. To aid his evaluation, Vineland set up a standard cost system.

Standard costs were based on 19X4 costs in several categories. Each 19X4 cost was divided by 1,520,000 cwt, the volume of 19X4 production, to determine a standard for 19X5 (cwt means hundredweight, or 100 pounds):

	19X4 Cost (thousands)	19X5 Standard (per hundredweight)
Direct materials	$1,824	$1.20
Direct labor	836	.55
Variable overhead	1,596	1.05
Fixed overhead	2,432	1.60
Total	$6,688	$4.40

At the end of 19X5, Vineland compared actual results with the standards he established. Production was 1,360,000 cwt, and variances were as follows:

	Actual	Standard	Variance
Direct materials	$1,791	$1,632	$159 U
Direct labor	735	748	13 F
Variable overhead	1,423	1,428	5 F
Fixed overhead	2,418	2,176	242 U
Total	$6,367	$5,984	$383 U

Vineland was not surprised by the unfavorable variance in direct materials. After all, wheat prices in 19X5 averaged 10% above those in 19X4. But he was disturbed by the lack of control of fixed overhead. He called in the production manager and demanded an explanation.

Required

1. Prepare an explanation for the large unfavorable fixed-overhead variance.
2. Discuss the appropriateness of using one year's costs as the next year's standards.

17 Basic Accounting: Concepts, Techniques, and Conventions

The basic concepts of assets, liabilities, revenue, and expense apply to all organizations, whether they be profit-seeking or nonprofit. The University of Southern Colorado has an income statement although it is called the statement of revenues and expenditures. *Courtesy University of Southern Colorado*

Learning Objectives

When you have finished studying this chapter, you should be able to

1   Identify the meanings and interrelationships of the principal elements of financial statements.

2   Analyze typical business transactions using the balance sheet equation.

3   Distinguish between the accrual basis of accounting and the cash basis of accounting.

4   Relate the measurement of expenses to the expiration of assets.

5   Select relevant items from a set of data and assemble them into a balance sheet, an income statement, and a statement of retained income.

6   Explain the nature of dividends and retained income.

7   Distinguish between the reporting of corporate owners' equity and the reporting of owners' equity for partnerships and sole proprietorships.

8   Identify how the measurement conventions of recognition, matching, cost recovery, and stable monetary unit affect financial reporting.

Accounting is often called the language of business. It has a special vocabulary aimed at conveying the financial story of organizations. To understand corporate annual reports, you must learn at least the fundamentals of the language. This chapter introduces the basic words and ideas used by accountants and other managers when discussing financial matters.[1] It also introduces financial statements—what they say and, equally important, what they do not say.

You will explore the essence of profit-making activities and how accountants portray them. The more technical processes (e.g., ledger accounts) and language (e.g., debit and credit) are left for the chapter appendices. As we examine what accountants do, we introduce the relevant concepts and conventions. Although our focus will be on profit-seeking organizations, the main ideas also apply to nonprofit organizations.

---

[1] The aim of this section of the book (Chapters 17-20) is to provide an overview of *financial accounting*. Thus readers of the companion volume, *Introduction to Financial Accounting*, will find that these chapters provide a review rather than new material. For expanded coverage, see *Introduction to Financial Accounting* Charles T. Horngren, Gary L. Sundem, and John A. Elliott, (Prentice Hall, 1996).

■ THE NEED FOR ACCOUNTING

Most people think of accountants as scorekeepers who determine whether a business is making money (and how much, if any). In fact, all kinds of organizations (sometimes called *entities*)—government agencies, nonprofit organizations, and others—rely on accounting to gauge their progress.

Managers, investors, and other interest groups usually want the answers to two important questions about an organization: How well did the organization perform for a given period? Where does the organization stand at a given point? Accountants answer these questions with two major financial statements: an *income statement* and a *balance sheet*. To obtain these statements, accountants continually record the history of an organization. Through the financial accounting process, the accountant accumulates, analyzes, quantifies, classifies, summarizes, and reports events and their effects on the organization.

transaction Any event that affects the financial position of an organization and requires recording.

The accounting process focuses on transactions. A **transaction** is any event that affects the financial position of an organization and requires recording. Through the years, many concepts, conventions, and rules have been developed regarding what events are to be recorded as *accounting transactions* and how their financial impact is measured. These concepts will be introduced gradually over the remaining chapters.

■ FINANCIAL STATEMENTS

Objective 1

Identify the meanings and interrelationships of the principal elements of financial statements

Financial statements are summarized reports of accounting transactions. They can apply to any point in time and to any span of time.

An efficient way to learn about accounting is to study a specific illustration. Suppose King Hardware Company began business as a corporation on March 1. An opening *balance sheet* follows:

King Hardware Company Balance Sheet (Statement of Financial Position) As of March 1, 19X1

Assets		Equities	
Cash	$100,000	Paid-in capital	$100,000

balance sheet (statement of financial position, statement of financial condition) A snapshot of financial status at an instant of time.

assets Economic resources that are expected to benefit future activities.

equities The claims against, or interests in, an organization's assets.

The **balance sheet** (more accurately called **statement of financial position** or **statement of financial condition**) is a snapshot of financial status at an instant of time. It has two counterbalancing sections—assets and equities. **Assets** are economic resources that are expected to benefit future activities. **Equities** are the claims against, or interests in, the assets.

The accountant conceives of the balance sheet as an equation:

$$\text{assets} = \text{equities}$$

The equities side of this fundamental equation is often divided as follows:

$$\text{assets} = \text{liabilities} + \text{owners' equity}$$

Liabilities are the entity's economic obligations to nonowners. **Owners' equity** is the excess of the assets over the liabilities. For a **corporation**—a business organized as a separate legal entity and owned by its stockholders—the owners'

liabilities The entity's economic obligations to nonowners.

owners' equity The excess of the assets over the liabilities.

corporation A business organized as a separate legal entity and owned by its stockholders.

stockholders' equity The excess of assets over liabilities of a corporation.

paid-in capital The ownership claim against, or interest in, the total assets arising from any paid-in investment.

retained income (retained earnings) The ownership claim arising as a result of profitable operations.

accounts payable Amounts owed on open accounts whereby the buyer pays cash some time after the date of sale.

accounts receivable Amounts owed to a company by customers who buy on open account.

Analyze typical business transactions using the balance sheet equation

equity is called **stockholders' equity.** In turn, the stockholders' equity is composed of the ownership claim against, or interest in, the total assets arising from any paid-in investment (**paid-in capital**), plus the ownership claim arising as a result of profitable operations (**retained income** or **retained earnings**):

$$\text{assets} = \text{liabilities} + \text{stockholders' equity}$$
$$= \text{liabilities} + (\text{paid-in capital} + \text{retained earnings})$$

Consider a summary of King Hardware's *transactions* in March:

1. Initial investment by owners, $100,000 cash.
2. Acquisition of inventory for $75,000 cash.
3. Acquisition of inventory for $35,000 on open account. A purchase (or a sale) on open account is an agreement whereby the buyer pays cash some time after the date of sale, often in 30 days. Amounts owed on open accounts are usually called **accounts payable,** liabilities of the purchasing entity.
4. Merchandise carried in inventory at a cost of $100,000 was sold on open account for $120,000. These open customer accounts are called **accounts receivable,** assets of the selling entity.
5. Cash collections of accounts receivable, $30,000.
6. Cash payments of accounts payable, $10,000.
7. On March 1, $3,000 cash was disbursed for store rent for March, April, and May. Rent is $1,000 per month, payable quarterly in advance, beginning March 1.

Note that these are indeed *summarized* transactions. For example, all the sales did not occur at once, nor did all purchases of inventory, collections from customers, or disbursements to suppliers. Many repetitive transactions occur in practice, and specialized data collection techniques are used to measure their effects on the organization.

The foregoing transactions can be analyzed using the balance sheet equation, as shown in Exhibit 17-1.

Transaction 1, the initial investment by owners, increases assets and increases equities. That is, cash increases and so does paid-in capital—the claim arising from the owners' total initial investment in the corporation.

Transactions 2 and 3, the purchases of inventory, are steps toward the ultimate goal—the earning of a profit. But stockholders' equity is unaffected. That is, no profit is recorded until a sale is made.

Transaction 4 is the sale of $100,000 of inventory for $120,000. Two things happened simultaneously: a new asset, Accounts Receivable, is acquired (4a) in exchange for the giving up of Inventory (4b), and Stockholders' Equity is increased by the amount of the asset received ($120,000) and decreased by the amount of the asset given up ($100,000). The increase in Stockholders' Equity is called *revenue* or *sales*, and the decrease is an *expense* called *cost of goods sold*. Revenues and expenses will be discussed on page 644.

Transaction 5, cash collection of accounts receivable, is an example of an event that has no impact on stockholders' equity. Collections are merely the transformation of one asset (Accounts Receivable) into another (Cash).

Transaction 6, cash payment of accounts payable, also does not affect stockholders' equity—it affects assets and liabilities only. In general, collections from customers and payments to suppliers have no direct impact on stockholders' equity, unless part of the payment represents *interest expense*.

Transaction 7, the cash disbursement for rent, is made to acquire the right to use store facilities for the next 3 months. On March 1, the $3,000 measured the future benefit from these services, so the asset *Prepaid Rent* was created (7a). Prepaid rent is an asset even though you cannot see or touch it as you can such assets as cash or inventory. Assets also include legal rights to future services such as the use of facilities.

Transaction 7b recognizes that one-third of the rental services has expired during March, so the asset is reduced and stockholders' equity is also reduced by $1,000 as rent expense for March. This recognition of rent *expense* means that $1,000 of the asset Prepaid Rent has been "used up" (or has flowed out of the entity) in the conduct of operations during March.

For simplicity, we have assumed no expenses other than *cost of goods sold* and *rent*. Based on this information, King's accountant can prepare at least two financial statements—the balance sheet and the income statement—as follows:

King Hardware Co.
Income Statement
for the Month Ended
March 31, 19X1

Sales (revenue)		$120,000
Expenses		
Cost of goods sold	$100,000	
Rent	1,000	
Total expenses		101,000
Net income		$ 19,000

King Hardware Co.
Balance Sheet as of March 31, 19X1

Assets		Liabilities and Stockholders' Equity		
Cash	$ 42,000	Liabilities: accounts payable		$ 25,000
Accounts receivable	90,000	Stockholders' equity		
Inventory	10,000	Paid-in capital	$100,000	
Prepaid rent	2,000	Retained income	19,000	119,000
Total	$144,000	Total		$144,000

Relationship of Balance Sheet and Income Statement

income statement
A statement that measures the performance of an organization by matching its accomplishments (revenue from customers, which is usually called sales) and its efforts (cost of goods sold and other expenses).

The **income statement** measures the performance of an organization by matching its accomplishments (revenue from customers, which is usually called *sales*[2]) and its efforts (*cost of goods sold* and other expenses). The balance sheet shows the organization's financial position at an instant of time, but the income statement measures performance for a span of time, whether it be a month, a quarter, or longer. Thus, the income statement is the major link between balance sheets:

[2] Income statements for British companies use "turnover" instead of "sales." Other countries' financial statements use the same basic approach as U.S. statements, but terminology and specific measurement rules may differ.

Exhibit 17-1   King Hardware Co.   Analysis of Transactions (in Dollars) for March 19X1

	Assets				=	Liabilities +	Stockholders' Equity	
	Cash +	Accounts Receivable +	Inventory +	Prepaid Rent	=	Accounts Payable	Paid-in Capital +	Retained Income
Transactions								
1. Initial investment	+100,000				=		+100,000	
2. Acquire inventory for cash	− 75,000		+ 75,000		=			
3. Acquire inventory for credit			+ 35,000		=	+35,000		
4a. Sales on credit		+120,000			=			+120,000 (revenue)
4b. Cost of inventory sold			−100,000		=			−100,000 (expense)
5. Collect from customers	+ 30,000	− 30,000			=			
6. Pay accounts of suppliers	− 10,000				=	−10,000		
7a. Pay rent in advance	− 3,000			+3,000	=			
7b. Recognize expiration of rental services				−1,000	=			− 1,000 (expense)
Balance, 3/31X1	+ 42,000	+ 90,000	+ 10,000	+2,000	=	+25,000	+100,000	+ 19,000
	144,000						144,000	

643

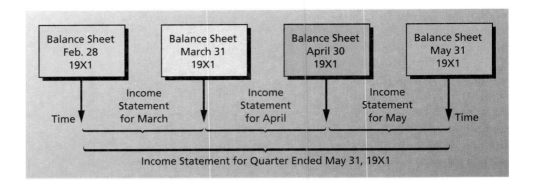

Examine the changes in retained income in Exhibit 17-1. The accountant records *revenue* and *expense* to indicate increases (revenues) and decreases (expenses) in the owners' claims. At the end of a given period, these items are summarized in the form of an income statement. The heading of a balance sheet indicates a *single date*. The heading of an income statement indicates a specific *period*. A balance sheet is a destination; an income statement is a journey.

account Each item in a financial statement.

Each item in a financial statement is frequently called an **account**. In the preceding example, the outflows of assets are represented by decreases in the inventory and prepaid rent accounts and corresponding decreases in stockholders' equity in the form of cost of goods sold and rent expense. Expense accounts are basically negative elements of stockholders' equity. Similarly, the sales (revenue) account is a positive element of stockholders' equity.

Revenues and Expenses

Return to Exhibit 17-1, and review transaction 4. Notice that this transaction has two phases, a revenue phase (4a) and an expense phase (4b) (dollar signs omitted):

Description of Transactions		Assets	=	Equities	
Balances after transaction 3 in Exhibit 17-1			135,000* =		135,000*
4a. Sales on account (inflow)	Accounts receivable	+120,000	=	Stockholders' equity	+120,000
4b. Cost of inventory sold (outflow)	Inventory	−100,000	=	Stockholders' equity	−100,000
Balances, after transaction 4		155,000	=		155,000

* Cash of $100,000 − $75,000	=	$ 25,000	Accounts payable	$ 35,000	
Inventory of $75,000 + $35,000	=	110,000	Paid-in capital	100,000	
		$135,000		$135,000	

revenue A gross increase in assets from delivering goods or services.

Transaction 4a illustrates the recognition of revenue. **Revenues** generally arise from gross increases in assets from delivering goods or services. To be recognized (i.e., formally recorded in the accounting records as revenue during the current period), revenue must ordinarily meet two tests. First, revenues must be *earned*. That is, the goods must be delivered or services must be fully rendered to customers. Second, revenues must be *realized*. That is, an exchange of resources evidenced by a market transaction must occur (e.g., the buyer pays or promises to pay cash and the seller delivers merchandise). If cash is not received directly, the collectibility of the asset (e.g., an account receivable) must be reasonably assured.

expenses Gross decreases in assets from delivering goods or services.

profits (earnings, income) The excess of revenues over expenses.

Transaction 4b illustrates the incurrence of an expense. **Expenses** generally arise from gross decreases in assets from delivering goods or services.

Transactions 4a and 4b also illustrate the fundamental meaning of **profits** or **earnings** or **income,** which is the excess of revenues over expenses.

As the Retained Income column in Exhibit 17-1 shows, increases in revenues also increase stockholders' equity. In contrast, increases in expenses decrease stockholders' equity.

Transactions 2 and 3 were purchases of merchandise inventory. They were steps toward the ultimate goal—the earning of a profit. But by themselves purchases earn no profit; remember that stockholders' equity was unaffected by the inventory acquisitions in transactions 2 and 3. That is, no profit is recognized until a sale is actually made to customers.

Transaction 4 is the $120,000 sale on open account of inventory that had cost $100,000. Two things happen simultaneously: a $120,000 inflow of assets in the form of accounts receivable (4a) in exchange for a $100,000 outflow of assets in the form of inventory (4b). Liabilities are completely unaffected, so owners' equity increases by $120,000 – $100,000, or $20,000.

Users of financial statements desire an answer to the question: How well did the organization perform for a given period? The income statement helps answer this question. King Hardware Co. has a positive change in stockholders' equity attributable solely to operations. This change is measured by the revenue and expenses that constitute income for the specific period.

For an example of a real company, consider Childrobics, Inc., the company that owns and operates "Play Centers" for children and families in the New York City metropolitan area. The company was incorporated in 1993, and at the end of its first year (on February 28, 1994) it reported:

Revenues	$250,393
Expenses	247,877
Net income	$ 2,516

The company paid no dividends, so its retained earnings increased from $0 to $2,516 during the year.

The Analytical Power of the Balance Sheet Equation

The balance sheet equation can highlight the link between the income statement and balance sheet. Indeed, the entire accounting system is based on the simple balance sheet equation:

$$\text{assets (A)} = \text{liabilities (L)} + \text{stockholders' equity (SE)} \qquad (1)$$

SE equals the original ownership claim plus the increase in ownership claim because of profitable operations. That is, SE equals the claim arising from paid-in capital plus the claim arising from retained income. Therefore:

$$A = L + \text{paid-in capital} + \text{retained income} \qquad (2)$$

Then, because retained income equals revenue minus expenses (see Exhibit 17-1):

$$A = L + \text{paid-in capital} + \text{revenue} - \text{expenses} \qquad (3)$$

Revenue and *expense accounts* are nothing more than subdivisions of stockholders' equity—temporary stockholders' equity accounts. Their purpose is to summarize the volume of sales and the various expenses, so that management is kept informed of the reasons for the continual increases and decreases in stockholders' equity in the course of ordinary operations. In this way, managers can make comparisons, set standards or goals, and exercise better control.

Notice in Exhibit 17-1 that, for each transaction, the equation is *always* kept in balance. If the items affected are confined to one side of the equation, you will find the total amount added equal to the total amount subtracted on that side. If the items affected are on both sides, then equal amounts are simultaneously added or subtracted on each side.

The striking feature of the balance sheet equation is its universal applicability. No transaction has ever been conceived, no matter how simple or complex, that cannot be analyzed via the equation. The top technical partners in the world's largest professional accounting firms, when confronted with the most intricate transactions of multinational companies, will inevitably discuss and think about their analyses in terms of the balance sheet equation. They focus on its major components: assets, liabilities, and owners' equity (including the explanations of changes in owners' equity that most often take the form of revenues and expenses in an income statement).

accrual basis A process of accounting that recognizes the impact of transactions on the financial statements in the time periods when revenues and expenses occur instead of when cash is received or disbursed.

ACCRUAL BASIS AND CASH BASIS

Measurements of income and financial position are anchored to the accrual basis of accounting, as distinguished from the cash basis. The **accrual basis** recognizes the impact of transactions on the financial statements in the periods when revenues and expenses occur instead of when cash is received or disbursed. That is, revenue is recorded as it is earned, and expenses are recorded as they are incurred—not necessarily when cash changes hands.

Transaction 4a in Exhibit 17-1, page 000, shows an example of the accrual basis. Revenue is recognized when sales are made on credit, not when cash is received. Similarly, transactions 4b and 7b (for cost of goods sold and rent) show that expenses are recorded as efforts are expended or services are used to obtain the revenue (regardless of when cash is disbursed). Therefore income is often affected by measurements of noncash resources and obligations. The accrual basis is the principal conceptual framework for relating accomplishments (revenues) with efforts (expenses).

More than 95% of all business is conducted on a credit basis; cash receipts and disbursements are not the critical transactions as far as the recognition of revenue and expense is concerned. Thus the accrual basis evolved in response to a desire for a more complete, and therefore more accurate, report of the financial impact of various events.

If the **cash basis** of accounting were used instead of the accrual basis, revenue and expense recognition would occur when cash is received and disbursed. In March, King Hardware would show $30,000 of revenue, the amount

Objective 3

Distinguish between the accrual basis of accounting and the cash basis of accounting

cash basis A process of accounting where revenue and expense recognition would occur when cash is received and disbursed.

of cash collected from customers. Similarly, cost of goods sold would be the $10,000 cash payment for the purchase of inventory, and rent expense would be $3,000 (the cash disbursed for rent) rather than the $1,000 rent applicable to March. A cash measurement of net income or net loss is obviously ridiculous in this case, and it could mislead those unacquainted with the fundamentals of accounting.

Ponder the rent example. Under the cash basis, March must bear expenses for the entire quarter's rent of $3,000 merely because cash outflows occurred then. In contrast, the accrual basis measures performance more sharply by allocating the rental expenses to the operations of each of the 3 months that benefited from the use of the facilities. In this way, the economic performance of each month will be comparable. Most accountants maintain that it is nonsense to say that March's rent expense was $3,000 and April's and May's was zero.

The major deficiency of the cash basis of accounting is that it is incomplete. It fails to match efforts and accomplishments (expenses and revenues) in a manner that properly measures economic performance and financial position. Moreover, it omits key assets (such as accounts receivable and prepaid rent) and key liabilities (such as accounts payable) from balance sheets.

Nonprofit Organizations

The examples in this chapter are focused on profit-seeking organizations, but balance sheets and income statements are also used by nonprofit organizations. For example, hospitals and universities have income statements, although they are called *statements of revenue and expense*. The "bottom line" is frequently called "excess of revenue over expense" rather than "net income."

The basic concepts of assets, liabilities, revenues, and expenses are applicable to all organizations, whether they be utilities, symphony orchestras, private, public, American, Asian, and so forth. However, some nonprofit organizations have been slow to adopt several ideas that are widespread in progressive companies. For example, many government organizations still use the cash basis of accounting. The lack of accrual-based financial statements has hampered the evaluation of the performance of such organizations.

■ ADJUSTMENTS TO THE ACCOUNTS

adjustments
Recording of implicit transactions, in contrast to the explicit transactions that trigger nearly all day-to-day routine entries.

source documents
Explicit evidence of any transactions that occur in the entity's operation, for example, sales slips and purchase invoices.

To measure income under the accrual basis, accountants use adjustments at the end of each reporting period. **Adjustments** record *implicit transactions*, in contrast to the *explicit transactions* that trigger nearly all day-to-day routine entries.

Earlier we defined a *transaction* as any economic event that should be recorded by the accountant. Note that this definition is not confined to market transactions, which are actual exchanges of goods and services between the entity and another party. For instance, the losses of assets from fire or theft are also transactions even though no market exchange occurs.

To illustrate, entries for explicit transactions such as credit sales, credit purchases, cash received on account, and cash disbursed on account are, supported by explicit evidence, is usually in the form of **source documents** (e.g., sales slips, purchase invoices, employee time records). On the other hand, adjustments for implicit transactions, such as unpaid wages, prepaid rent, interest owed, and the like, are prepared from special schedules or memorandums that recognize events (such as the passage of time) that are temporarily ignored in day-to-day recording procedures. Adjustments refine the accountant's accuracy and provide a more complete and significant measure of efforts, accomplishments, and financial position. Hence, they are an essential part of accrual accounting. They are generally made when the financial statements are about to be prepared.

The principal adjustments may be classified into four types:

1. Expiration of Unexpired Costs
2. Recognition (Earning) of Unearned Revenues
3. Accrual of Unrecorded Expenses
4. Accrual of Unrecorded Revenues

ADJUSTMENT TYPE I: EXPIRATION OF UNEXPIRED COSTS

Objective 4

Relate the measurement of expenses to the expiration of assets

Assets frequently expire because of the passage of time. This first type of adjustment was illustrated in Exhibit 17-1 by the recognition of rent expense in transaction 7b.

Assets may be viewed as bundles of economic services awaiting future use or expiration. It is helpful to think of assets, other than cash and receivables, as prepaid or stored costs that are carried forward to future periods rather than immediately charged against revenue:

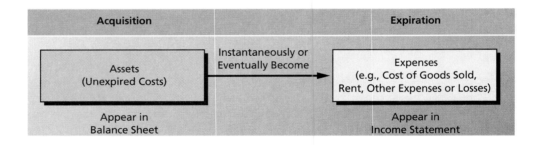

unexpired cost Any asset that ordinarily becomes an expense in future periods, for example, inventory and prepaid rent.

Expenses are used-up assets. An **unexpired cost** is any asset that ordinarily becomes an expense in future periods. Examples in our King Hardware Co. illustration are inventory and prepaid rent. Other examples are equipment and various prepaid expenses such as prepaid insurance and prepaid property taxes. When costs expire, accountants often say they are *written off* to expenses.

The analysis of the inventory and rent transactions in Exhibit 17-1 maintains this distinction of acquisition and expiration. The unexpired costs of inventory and prepaid rent are assets until they are used up and become expenses.

Timing of Asset Expiration

Sometimes services are acquired and used almost instantaneously. Examples are advertising services, interest services (the cost of money, which is a service), miscellaneous supplies, and sales salaries and commissions. Conceptually, these costs should, at least momentarily, be viewed as assets on acquisition before being written off as expenses. For example, suppose there was an eighth transaction in Exhibit 17-1, whereby newspaper advertising was acquired for $1,000 cash. To abide by the acquisition-expiration sequence, the transaction might be analyzed in two phases:

	Assets			= Liabilities +	Stockholders' Equity	
	Cash +	Other Assets +	Unexpired Advertising =		Paid-in Capital +	Retained Income
Transaction						
8a. Acquire advertising services	−1,000		+1,000 =			
8b. Use advertising services			−1,000 =			−1,000 (expense)

However, services are often acquired and used up so quickly that accountants do not bother recording an asset such as Unexpired Advertising or Prepaid Rent for them. Instead, they take a shortcut:

| Transaction | Cash + | Other Assets = | Liabilities + | Paid-in Capital + | Retained Income |
| 8 (a) and (b) together | −1,000 | | = | | −1,000 (expense) |

Making the entry in two steps instead of one may seem cumbersome, and it is—from a practical bookkeeping viewpoint. But our purpose is not to teach you to be efficient bookkeepers. We want you to develop an orderly way of thinking about what the manager does. The manager acquires goods and services, not expenses per se. These goods and services become expenses as they are used in obtaining revenue.

When does an asset expire and become an expense? Sometimes this question is not easily answered. For example, some accountants believe that research and development costs should be accounted for as assets (listed on balance sheets as "Deferred Research and Development Costs") and written off (charged as an expense) in some systematic manner over a period of years. But the regulators of financial accounting in the United States have ruled that such costs have vague future benefits that are difficult to measure reliably. Thus research costs must be written off as expenses immediately. In cases like this, research costs are not found in balance sheets. This is not always the case, however. Outside the United States, many countries, such as Japan and France, allow research and development to be recorded as an asset.

Depreciation

To keep the expense-adjustment illustration simple, until now we have deliberately ignored the accounting for long-lived assets such as equipment. Suppose King Hardware Co. had acquired some store equipment for $14,000 on March 1.

residual value
The predicted sales value of a long-lived asset at the end of its useful life.

Equipment is really a bundle of future services that will have a limited useful life. Accountants usually (1) predict the length of the useful life, (2) predict the ultimate **residual value** (the predicted sales value of a long-lived asset at the end of its useful life), and (3) allocate the *cost* of the equipment to the years of its useful life in some systematic way. This process is called the recording of depreciation expense; it applies to physical assets such as buildings, equipment, furniture, and fixtures owned by the entity. (Land is not subject to depreciation.)

The most popular depreciation method for financial reporting is the *straight-line method*, which depreciates an asset by the same amount each year. Suppose the predicted life of the equipment is 10 years, and the estimated residual value is $2,000:

$$\text{straight-line depreciation} = \frac{\text{original cost} - \text{estimated residual value}}{\text{years of useful life}}$$

$$= \frac{\$14,000 - \$2,000}{10}$$

$$= \$1,200 \text{ per year, or } \$100 \text{ per month}$$

We discuss depreciation in more detail in subsequent chapters. But the essence of the general concept of expense should be clear by now. The purchases and uses of goods and services (e.g., inventories, rent, equipment) ordinarily consist of two basic steps: (1) the *acquisition* of the *assets* (transactions 2, 3, and 7a) and (2) the *expiration* of the assets as *expenses* (transactions 4b and 7b). When these assets expire, the total assets and owners' equity are decreased.

Summary Problem for Your Review

This is an unusually long chapter, so pause. If you have never studied accounting before, or if you studied it long ago, do not proceed until you have solved the following problem. There are no shortcuts. Pushing a pencil is an absolute necessity for becoming comfortable with accounting concepts. The cost-benefit test will easily be met; the value of your gain in knowledge will exceed your investment of time. Another suggestion is to do the work on your own. In particular, do not ask for help from any professional accountants if they introduce any new terms beyond those already covered.

Problem One

The King Hardware Co. transactions for March were analyzed in Exhibit 17–1, page 643. The balance sheet showed the following balances as of March 31, 19X1:

	Assets	Equities
Cash	$ 42,000	
Accounts receivable	90,000	
Inventory	10,000	
Prepaid rent	2,000	
Accounts payable		$ 25,000
Paid-in capital		100,000
Retained income		19,000
	$144,000	$144,000

The following is a summary of the transactions that occurred during the next month, April:

1. Cash collections of accounts receivable, $88,000.
2. Cash payments of accounts payable, $24,000.
3. Acquisitions of inventory on open account, $80,000.
4. Merchandise carried in inventory at a cost of $70,000 was sold on open account for $85,000.
5. Adjustment for recognition of rent expense for April.
6. Some customers paid $3,000 in advance for merchandise that they ordered but did not expect in inventory until mid-May. (What asset must rise? Does this transaction increase liabilities or stockholders' equity?)
7. Total wages of $6,000 (which were ignored for simplicity in March) were paid on four Fridays in April. These payments for employee services were recognized by increasing Wages Expense and decreasing Cash.
8. Wages of $600 were incurred near the end of April, but the employees had not been paid as of April 30. Accordingly, the accountant increased Wages Expense and increased a liability, Accrued Wages Payable.
9. Cash dividends declared by the board of directors and disbursed to stockholders on April 29 equaled $18,000. (What account besides Cash is affected?) As will be explained on page 657, Cash and Retained Income are each decreased by $18,000.

Required

1. Using the *accrual basis* of accounting, prepare an analysis of transactions, employing the equation approach demonstrated in Exhibit 17-1. Be sure to leave plenty of columns for new accounts.
2. Prepare a balance sheet as of April 30, 19X1, and an income statement for the month of April.
3. Prepare a new report, the Statement of Retained Income, which should show the beginning balance in the Retained Income account, followed by a description of any major changes, and end with the balance as of April 30, 19X1.

Note: Entries 6 through 9 and the statement of retained income have not been explained. However, as a learning step, try to respond to the requirements here anyway. Explanations follow almost immediately.

Solution to Problem One

Objective 5

Select relevant items from a set of data and assemble them into a balance sheet, an income statement, and a statement of retained income

Part 1. ANALYSIS OF TRANSACTIONS. The answer is in Exhibit 17-2. The first five transactions are straightforward extensions or repetitions of the March transactions, but the rest of the transactions are new. They are discussed in the sections that follow the solution to the second part of this problem.

Parts 2 and 3. PREPARATION OF FINANCIAL STATEMENTS. See Exhibits 17-3, 17-4, and 17-5. The first two of these exhibits show financial statements already described in this chapter: the balance sheet and the income statement. Exhibit 17-5 presents a new statement, the *statement of retained income*, which is merely a formal presentation of the changes in retained income during the reporting period. It starts with the beginning balance, adds net income for the period in question, and deducts cash dividends to arrive at the ending balance. Frequently, this statement is tacked on to the bottom of an income statement. If so, the result is a *combined* statement of income and statement of retained income.

Exhibit 17-2 King Hardware Co. Analysis of Transactions (in Dollars) for April 19X1

Equities

Transaction	Assets					Liabilities				Stockholders' Equity	
	Cash +	Accounts Receivable +	Inventory +	Prepaid Rent	=	Accounts Payable +	Accrued Wages Payable +	Unearned Sales Revenue* +		Paid-in Capital +	Retained Income
Bal. 3/31/X1	+42,000	+90,000	+10,000	+2,000	=	+25,000				+100,000	+19,000
1.	+88,000	–88,000			=						
2.	–24,000				=	–24,000					
3.			+80,000		=	+80,000					
4a.		+85,000			=						+85,000 (revenue)
4b.			–70,000		=						–70,000 (expense)
5.				–1,000	=						– 1,000 (expense)
6.	+ 3,000				=			+3,000*			
7.	– 6,000				=						– 6,000 (expense)
8.					=		+600				– 600 (expense)
9.	–18,000				=						–18,000 (dividend)
4/30/X1	+85,000	+87,000	+20,000	+1,000	=	+81,000	+600	+3,000		+100,000	+ 8,400
		193,000			=			193,000			

* Some accountants would call this account "Customer Deposits," "Advances from Customers," "Deferred Sales Revenue," or "Unrealized Sales Revenue."

■ ADJUSTMENT TYPE II: RECOGNITION (EARNING) OF UNEARNED REVENUES

unearned revenue (deferred revenue) Collections from customers received and recorded before they are earned.

Transaction 6 in Exhibit 17-2 is $3,000 collected in advance from customers for merchandise they ordered. This transaction is an example of **unearned revenue,** sometimes called **deferred revenue.** It is a liability because the retailer is obligated to deliver the goods ordered or to refund the money if the goods are not delivered. Some companies call this account *advances from customers* or *customer deposits,* but it is an unearned revenue account no matter what its label. That is, it is revenue collected in advance that has not yet been earned. Advance collections of rent and magazine subscriptions are other examples.

Exhibit 17-3

King Hardware Company Balance Sheet as of April 30, 19X1

Assets		Liabilities and Stockholders' Equity		
Cash	$ 85,000	Liabilities		
Accounts receivable	87,000	Accounts payable	$ 81,000	
Inventory	20,000	Accrued wages payable	600	
Prepaid rent	1,000	Unearned sales revenue	3,000	$ 84,600
		Stockholders' equity		
		Paid-in capital	$100,000	
		Retained income	8,400	108,400
Total assets	$193,000	Total equities		$193,000

Exhibit 17-4

King Hardware Company Income Statement (Multiple-Step)* for the Month Ended April 30, 19X1

Sales		$85,000
Cost of goods sold		70,000
Gross profit		$15,000
Operating expenses		
Rent	$1,000	
Wages	6,600	7,600
Net income		$ 7,400

* A *"single-step" statement* would not draw the gross profit figure but would merely list all the expenses—including cost of goods sold—and deduct the total from sales. *Gross profit* is defined as the excess of sales over the cost of the inventory that was sold. It is sometimes called *gross margin.*

Exhibit 17-5

King Hardware Company Statement of Retained Income for the Month Ended April 30, 19X1

Retained income, March 31, 19X1	$19,000
Net income for April	7,400
Total	$26,400
Dividends	18,000
Retained income, April 30, 19X1	$ 8,400

Sometimes it is easier to see how accountants analyze transactions by visualizing the financial positions of both parties to a contract. For instance, consider the rent transaction of March 1. Compare the financial impact on King Hardware Co. with the impact on the landlord who received the rental payment:

	Owner of Property (Landlord, Lessor)				King Hardware Co. (Tenant, Lessee)			
	A	=	L	+	SE	A	= L +	SE
			Unearned Rent Revenue		*Rent Revenue*		*Prepaid Rent*	*Rent Expense*
	Cash					*Cash*		
(a) Explicit transaction (advance payment of three months' rent)	+3,000	=	+3,000			−3,000	+3,000 =	
(b) March adjustment (for one month's rent)		=	−1,000		+1,000		−1,000 =	−1,000
(c) April adjustment (for one month's rent)		=	−1,000		+1,000		−1,000 =	−1,000
(d) May adjustment (for one month's rent)		=	−1,000		+1,000		−1,000 =	−1,000

You are already familiar with the King Hardware analysis. The $1,000 monthly entries for King Hardware are examples of the first type of adjustments, the expiration of unexpired costs.

Now study the transactions from the viewpoint of the owner of the rental property. The first transaction recognizes *unearned revenue*, which is a *liability* because the lessor is obligated to deliver the rental services (or to refund the money if the services are not delivered).

As you can see from the preceding table, adjustments for the expiration of unexpired costs (Type I) and for the realization of unearned revenues (Type II) are really mirror images of each other. If one party to a contract has a prepaid expense, the other has unearned revenue. A similar analysis could be conducted for, say, a 3-year fire insurance policy or a 3-year magazine subscription. The buyer recognizes a prepaid expense (asset) and uses adjustments to spread the initial cost to expense over the life of the services. In turn, the seller, such as a magazine publisher, must initially recognize its liability, unearned subscription revenue. The *unearned* revenue is then systematically recognized as *earned* revenue as magazines are delivered throughout the life of the subscription.

You have now seen how two types of adjustments might occur: (1) expiration of unexpired costs and (2) recognition (earning) of unearned revenues. Next we consider the third type of adjustment: accrual of unrecorded expenses, as illustrated by wages.

accrue To accumulate a receivable or payable during a given period even though no explicit transaction occurs.

■ ADJUSTMENT TYPE III: ACCRUAL OF UNRECORDED EXPENSES

Accrue means to accumulate a receivable or payable during a given period even though no explicit transaction occurs. Examples of accruals are the wages of employees for partial payroll periods and the interest on borrowed money before the interest payment date. The receivables or payables grow as the clock ticks or as some services are continuously acquired and used, so they are said to accrue (accumulate).

Computerized accounting systems can make weekly, daily, or even "real-time" recordings in the accounts for many accruals. However, such frequent entries are often costly and unnecessary. Usually, adjustments are made to bring each expense (and corresponding liability) account up to date just before the formal financial statements are prepared.

Accounting for Payment of Wages

Consider wages. Most companies pay their employees at predetermined times. Here is a sample calendar for April:

	April					
S	M	T	W	T	F	S
	1	2	3	4	5	6
7	8	9	10	11	12	13
14	15	16	17	18	19	20
21	22	23	24	25	26	27
28	29	30				

Suppose King Hardware Co. pays its employees each Friday for services rendered during that week. For example, wages paid on April 26 would be compensation for the week ended April 26. The cumulative total wages paid on the Fridays during April were $6,000. Although day-to-day and week-to-week procedures may differ from entity to entity, a popular way to account for wages expense is the shortcut procedure described earlier for goods and services that are routinely consumed in the period of their purchase:

	Assets (A) = Liabilities (L) + Stockholders' Equity (SE)		
	Cash		*Wages Expense*
7. Routine entry for explicit transactions	−6,000	=	−6,000

Accounting for Accrual of Wages

King Hardware Co.'s wages are $300 per day. In addition to the $6,000 already paid, King Hardware owes $600 for employee services rendered during the last 2 days of April. The employees will not be paid for these services until the next regular weekly payday, May 3, so an accrual is necessary. No matter how simple or complex a set of accounting procedures may be in a particular entity, periodic adjustments ensure that the financial statements adhere to accrual accounting. The tabulation that follows repeats entry 7 for convenience and then adds entry 8:

	A	=	L	+	SE
			Accrued Wages Payable		*Wages Expense*
	Cash				
7. Routine entry for explicit transactions	–6,000	=			–6,000
8. Adjustment for implicit transaction, the accrual of unrecorded wages		=	+600		– 600
Total effects	–6,000	=	+600		–6,600

Conceptually, entries 7 and 8 could each be subdivided into the asset acquisition-asset expiration sequence, but this two-step sequence is not generally used in practice for such expenses that represent the immediate consumption of services.

Accrued expenses arise when payment *follows* the rendering of services; prepaid expenses arise when payment *precedes* the services. Other examples of accrued expenses include sales commissions, property taxes, income taxes, and interest on borrowed money. Interest is rent paid for the use of money, just as rent is paid for the use of buildings or automobiles. The interest accumulates (accrues) as time unfolds, regardless of when the actual cash for interest is paid.

■ ADJUSTMENT TYPE IV: ACCRUAL OF UNRECORDED REVENUES

The final type of adjustment, the realization of revenues that have been earned but not yet recorded as such in the accounts, is not illustrated in the "Summary Problem for Your Review." It is the mirror image of the accrual of unrecorded expenses. Suppose Security State Bank lends cash to King Hardware Co. on a 3-month promissory note for $50,000 with interest at 1% per month payable at maturity. The following tabulation shows the mirror-image effect of the adjustment for interest at the end of the first month (.01 × $50,000 = $500):

Security State Bank (Lender)						King Hardware Co. (Borrower)					
A	=	L	+	SE		A	=	L	+	SE	
Accrued Interest Receivable				*Interest Revenue*				*Accrued Interest Payable*		*Interest Expense*	
+500	=			+500			=	+500		–500	

To recapitulate, Exhibit 17-6 summarizes the four major types of adjustments needed to implement the accrual basis of accounting.

Exhibit 17-6	Four Major Types of Accounting Adjustments Before Preparation of Financial Statements

	Expense	Revenue
Payment Precedes Recognition of Expense or Revenue	I Expiration of unexpired costs. *Illustration:* The write-off of prepaid rent as rent expense (Exhibit 17-2, p. 652, entry 5)	II Recognition (earning) of unearned revenues. *Illustration:* The mirror image of Type I, whereby the landlord recognizes rent revenue and decreases unearned rent revenue (rent collected in advance)
Recognition of Expense or Revenue Precedes Payment	III Accrual of unrecorded expenses. *Illustration:* Wage expense for wages earned by employees but not yet paid (Exhibit 17-2, entry 8)	IV Accrual of unrecorded revenues. *Illustration:* Interest revenue earned but not yet collected by a financial institution

■ DIVIDENDS AND RETAINED INCOME

Exhibit 17-2 shows how revenues increase and expenses decrease the retained income portion of stockholders' equity. Transaction 9 shows another type of transaction that affects retained income—payment of dividends.

Dividends Are Not Expenses

dividends Distributions of assets to stockholders that reduce retained income.

Objective 6

Explain the nature of dividends and retained income

Dividends are distributions of assets to stockholders that reduce retained income. (Cash dividends are distributions of *cash* rather than some other asset.) Dividends are not expenses like rent and wages. They should not be deducted from revenues because dividends are not directly related to the generation of sales or the conduct of operations.

The ability to pay dividends is fundamentally caused by profitable operations. Retained income increases as profits accumulate and decreases as dividends occur.

The entire right-hand side of the balance sheet equation can be thought of as claims against the total assets. The liabilities are the claims of creditors. The stockholders' equity represents the claims of owners arising out of their initial investment (paid-in capital) and subsequent profitable operations (retained income). As a company grows, the retained income account can soar enormously if dividends are not paid. Retained income is frequently the largest stockholders' equity account. For example, H.J. Heinz, the food products company, had retained income of $3,633 million in 1994 compared to paid-in capital of only $242 million.

Retained Income Is Not Cash

Although retained income is a result of profitable operations, it is not a pot of cash awaiting distribution to stockholders. Consider the following illustration:

Step 1. Assume an opening balance sheet of:

Cash	$100	Paid-in capital	$100

Step 2. Purchase inventory for $50 cash. The balance sheet now reads:

Cash	$50	Paid-in capital	$100
Inventory	50		
	$100		

Steps 1 and 2 demonstrate a fundamental point. Ownership equity (paid-in capital, here) is an undivided claim against the total assets (in the aggregate). For example, half the shareholders do not have a specific claim on cash, and the other half do not have a specific claim on inventory. Instead, all the shareholders have an undivided claim against (or, if you prefer, an undivided interest in) all the assets.

Step 3. Now sell the inventory for $80, which produces a retained income of $80 – $50 = $30:

Cash	$130	Paid-in capital	$100
		Retained income	30
		Total equities	$130

At this stage, the retained income might be related to a $30 increase in cash. But the $30 in retained income connotes only a *general* claim against *total* assets. This may be clarified by the transaction that follows.

Step 4. Purchase equipment and inventory, in the amounts of $70 and $50, respectively. Now cash is $130 – $70 – $50 = $10:

Cash	$ 10	Paid-in capital	$100
Inventory	50	Retained income	30
Equipment	70		
Total assets	$130	Total equities	$130

To what assets is the $30 in retained income related? Is it linked to Cash, to Inventory, or to Equipment? The answer is all three. This example helps to explain the nature of the Retained Income account. It is a claim, not a pot of gold. You cannot buy a loaf of bread with retained income.

Retained income is increased by profitable operations, but the cash inflow from sales is an increment in assets (see step 3). When the cash inflow takes place, management will use the cash, most often to buy more inventory or equipment (step 4). Retained income (and also paid-in capital) is a general claim against, or undivided interest in, total assets, not a specific claim against cash or against any other particular asset. Do not confuse the assets themselves with the claims against the assets.

Nature of Dividends

As stated earlier, dividends are distributions of assets that reduce ownership claims. The cash assets that are disbursed typically arose from profitable operations. Thus dividends or withdrawals are often spoken of as "distributions of profits" or "distributions of retained income." Dividends are often erroneously described as being "paid *out* of retained income." In reality, cash dividends are distributions of assets that liquidate a portion of the ownership claim. The distribution is made possible by profitable operations.

The amount of cash dividends declared by the board of directors of a company depends on many factors, the least important of which is usually the balance in retained income. Although profitable operations are generally essential, dividend policy is also influenced by the company's cash position and future needs for cash to pay debts or to purchase additional assets. It is also influenced by whether the company is committed to a stable dividend policy or to a policy that normally ties dividends to fluctuations in net income. Under a stable policy, dividends may be paid consistently even if a company encounters a few years of little or no net income.

■ SOLE PROPRIETORSHIPS AND PARTNERSHIPS

sole proprietorship
A business entity with a single owner.

partnership An organization that joins two or more individuals together as co-owners.

This chapter has focused on the accounting for a corporation, King Hardware Co. However, the basic accounting concepts that underlie the owners' equity are unchanged regardless of whether ownership takes the form of a corporation, a **sole proprietorship**—a business entity with a single owner, or a **partnership**—an organization that joins two or more individuals together as co-owners. However, in proprietorships and partnerships, distinctions between paid-in capital (i.e., the investments by owners) and retained income are rarely made. Compare the possibilities for King Hardware Co. as of April 30:

Objective 7

Distinguish between the reporting of corporate owners' equity and the reporting of owners' equity for partnerships and sole proprietorships

Owners' Equity for a Corporation		
Stockholders' equity		
Capital stock (paid-in capital)	$100,000	
Retained income	8,400	
Total stockholders' equity		$108,400

Owner's Equity for a Sole Proprietorship	
Alice Walsh, capital	$108,400

Owners' Equity for a Partnership	
Susan Zingler, capital	$ 54,200
John Martin, capital	54,200
Total partners' equity	$108,400

In contrast to corporations, sole proprietorships and partnerships are not legally required to account separately for paid-in capital (i.e., proceeds from issuances of capital stock) and for retained income. Instead, they typically accumulate a single amount for each owner's original investments, subsequent investments, share of net income, and withdrawals. In the case of a sole proprietorship, then, the owner's equity will consist of a lone capital account.

net worth A synonym for owner's equity.

Note that, although owners' equity is sometimes called **net worth,** owners' equity is not a measure of the "current value" of the business to an outside buyer. The selling price of a business depends on future profit projections that may have little relationship to the existing assets or equities of the entity as measured by its accounting records.

■ GENERALLY ACCEPTED ACCOUNTING PRINCIPLES

Accounting is more an art than a science. It is based on a set of principles on which there is general agreement, not on rules that can be "proved."

Auditor's Independent Opinion

The financial statements of publicly held corporations and many other corporations are subject to an *independent audit* that forms the basis for a professional accounting firm's opinion, typically including the following key phrasing:

> In our opinion, such financial statements present fairly, in all material respects, the financial position of Microsoft Corporation and subsidiaries as of June 30, 1993 and 1994, and the results of their operations and their cash flows for each of the 3 years in the period ended June 30, 1994, in conformity with generally accepted accounting principles.

audit An examination or in-depth inspection that is made in accordance with generally accepted auditing standards. It culminates with the accountant's testimony that management's financial statements are in conformity with generally accepted accounting principles.

An accounting firm must conduct an audit before it can render the foregoing opinion. An **audit** is an "examination" or in-depth inspection that is made in accordance with generally accepted auditing standards, which have been developed primarily by the American Institute of Certified Public Accountants (AICPA), the leading organization of auditors. An audit includes tests of the accounting records, internal control systems, and other procedures as deemed necessary. After auditing a company, an accountant issues an *independent opinion*—the accountant's testimony that *management's* financial statements are in conformity with generally accepted accounting principles.

The auditor's opinion usually appears at the end of annual reports prepared for the stockholders and other external users. Investors often mistakenly rely on the opinion as an infallible guarantee of financial truth. Somehow accounting is thought to be an exact science, perhaps because of the aura of precision that financial statements possess. But, as noted earlier, accounting is more art than science. The financial reports may appear accurate because of their neatly integrated numbers, but they are the result of a complex measurement process that rests on a huge bundle of assumptions and conventions.

The conventions, rules, and procedures that together make up accepted accounting practice at any given time are called generally accepted accounting principles (GAAP). Accounting principles become "generally accepted" by agreement. Such agreement is not influenced solely by formal logical analysis. Experience, custom, usage, and practical necessity contribute to the set of principles. Accordingly, it might be better to call them *conventions*, because principles suggest that they are the product of airtight logic.

FASB and SEC

Financial Accounting Standards Board (FASB) The primary regulatory body over accounting principles and practices. Consisting of seven full-time members, it is an independent creation of the private sector.

Securities and Exchange Commission (SEC) By federal law, the agency with the ultimate responsibility for specifying the generally accepted accounting principles for U.S. companies whose stock is held by the general investing public.

American GAAP is largely the work of the **Financial Accounting Standards Board (FASB)**. The FASB, consisting of seven full-time members, is an independent creation of the private sector. It is financially supported by various companies and professional accounting associations.

By federal law, the **Securities and Exchange Commission (SEC),** a government agency, has the ultimate responsibility for specifying GAAP for U.S. companies whose stock is held by the general investing public. However, the SEC has informally delegated much rule-making power to the FASB. This public-sector–private-sector relationship may be sketched as follows:

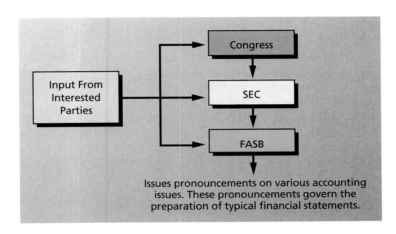

The FASB issues pronouncements on various accounting issues. These pronouncements govern the preparation of typical financial statements.

Consider this three-tiered structure. Note that Congress can overrule both the SEC and FASB, and the SEC can overrule the FASB. Such undermining of the FASB occurs rarely, but pressure is exerted on all three tiers by corporations and other interested parties if they think an impending pronouncement is "wrong." Hence the setting of accounting principles is a complex process involving heavy interactions among the affected parties: public regulators (Congress and SEC), private regulators (FASB), companies, the public accounting profession, representatives of investors, and other interested groups.

■ THREE MEASUREMENT CONVENTIONS

Three broad measurement or valuation conventions (principles) underlie accrual accounting: *recognition* (when to record revenue), *matching* and *cost recovery* (when to record expense), and the *stable monetary unit* (what unit of measure to use).

Recognition

The first broad measurement or valuation convention, *recognition*, was discussed earlier in this chapter in the section "Revenues and Expenses." In general, revenue is recognized when the goods or services in question are delivered to customers.

Matching and Cost Recovery

matching The relating of accomplishments or revenues (as measured by the selling prices of goods and services delivered) and efforts or expenses (as measured by the cost of goods and services used) to a particular period for which a measurement of income is desired.

cost recovery A concept in which assets such as inventories, prepayments, and equipment are carried forward as assets because their costs are expected to be recovered in the form of cash inflows (or reduced cash outflows) in future periods.

You may often encounter a favorite buzzword in accounting: **matching**. Matching is the relating of accomplishments or revenues (as measured by the selling prices of goods and services delivered) and efforts or expenses (as measured by the cost of goods and services used) to a *particular period* for which a measurement of income is desired. In short, matching is a short description of the accrual basis for measuring income.

Accountants apply matching as follows:

1. Identify the revenue recognized during the period.
2. Link the expenses to the recognized revenue directly (e.g., sales commissions or costs of inventories sold to customers) or indirectly (e.g., wages of janitors and supplies used). The latter expenses are costs of operations during a specific time period that have no measurable benefit for a *future* period.

The heart of recognizing expense is the **cost recovery** concept. That is, assets such as inventories, prepayments, and equipment are carried forward as assets because their costs are expected to be recovered in the form of cash inflows (or reduced cash outflows) in future periods. At the end of each period, the accountant (especially the outside auditor at the end of each year) carefully examines the evidence to be assured that these assets—these unexpired costs—should not be written off as an expense of the current period. For instance, in our chapter example, prepaid rent of $2,000 was carried forward as an asset as of March 31 because the accountant is virtually certain that it represents a future benefit. Why? Because without the prepayment, cash outflows of $2,000 would have to be made for April and May. So the presence of the prepayment is a benefit in the sense that future cash outflows will be reduced by $2,000. Furthermore, future revenue (sales) will be high enough to ensure the recovery of the $2,000.

Stable Monetary Unit

The monetary unit (e.g., the dollar) is the principal means for measuring assets and equities. It is the common denominator for quantifying the effects of a wide variety of transactions. While companies in the United States, Canada, Australia, and New Zealand use the dollar as the mometary unit, in other countries they use the franc, pound, mark, yen, or some other monetary unit.

Such measurement assumes that the monetary unit—the dollar, for example—is an unchanging yardstick. Yet we all know that a 1997 dollar does not have the same purchasing power as a 1987 or 1977 dollar. Therefore users of accounting statements that include dollars from different years must recognize the limitations of the basic measurement unit.

Accountants have been extensively criticized for not making explicit and formal adjustments to remedy the defects of their measuring unit. In the face of this, some accountants maintain that price-level adjustments would lessen objectivity and would add to the general confusion. They claim that the price-level problem has been exaggerated, and that the adjustments would not significantly affect the vast bulk of corporate statements because most accounts are in current or nearly current dollars.

On the other hand, inflation has been steady and its effects are sometimes surprisingly pervasive. Several countries, including Brazil and Argentina, routinely adjust their accounting numbers for the effects of inflation. The most troublesome aspect, however, is how to interpret the results after they are measured. Investors and managers in the United States are accustomed to the conventional statements. The intelligent interpretation of statements adjusted for changes in the price level will require extensive changes in the habits of users.

The body of generally accepted accounting principles contains more than the measurement conventions just discussed. Other major concepts include going concern, objectivity, materiality, and cost benefit. These are discussed in Appendix 17A.

Summary Problem for Your Review

Problem One appeared earlier in this chapter.

Problem Two

The following interpretations and remarks are sometimes encountered regarding financial statements. Do you agree or disagree? Explain fully.

1. "If I purchase 100 shares of the outstanding common stock of General Motors Corporation (or King Hardware Co.), I invest my money directly in that corporation. General Motors must record that transaction."
2. "Sales show the cash coming in from customers and the various expenses show the cash going out for goods and services. The difference is net income."
3. Consider the following recent accounts of Walgreens, the largest U.S. drugstore chain:

Paid-in capital	$ 76,919,000
Retained earnings	1,496,721,000
Total stockholders' equity	$1,573,640,000

A shareholder commented, "Why can't that big drugstore pay higher wages and dividends too? It can use its hundreds of millions of dollars of retained earnings to do so."
4. "The total Walgreens stockholders' equity measures the amount that the shareholders would get today if the corporation were liquidated."

Solution to Problem Two

1. Money is invested directly in a corporation only upon original issuance of the stock by the corporation. For example, 100,000 shares of stock may be issued at $80 per share, bringing in $8 million to the corporation. This is a transaction between the corporation and the stockholders. It affects the corporate financial position:

Cash	$8,000,000	Stockholders' equity	$8,000,000

In turn, 100 shares of that stock may be sold by an original stockholder (A) to another individual (B) for $92 per share. This is a private transaction; no cash comes to the corporation. Of course, the corporation records the fact that 100 shares originally owned by A are now owned by B, but the corporate financial position is unchanged. Accounting focuses on the business entity; the private dealings of the owners have no direct effect on the financial position of the entity and hence are unrecorded except for detailed records of the owners' identities.

2. Cash receipts and disbursements are not the fundamental basis for the accounting recognition of revenues and expenses. Credit, not cash, lubricates the economy. Therefore, if services or goods have been rendered to a customer, a collectible claim to cash in the form of a receivable is deemed sufficient justification for recognizing revenue; similarly, if services or goods have been used up, an obligation in the form of a payable is justification for recognizing expense.

   This approach to the measurement of net income is known as the accrual basis. Revenue is recognized as it is earned and realized. Expenses or losses are recognized when goods or services are used up in the obtaining of revenue (or when such goods or services cannot justifiably be carried forward as an asset because they have no potential future benefit). The expenses and losses are deducted from the revenue, and the result of this matching process is net income, the net increase in stockholders' equity from the conduct of operations.

3. As the chapter indicated, retained earnings is not cash. It is a stockholders' equity account that represents the accumulated increase in ownership claims because of profitable operations. This claim or interest may be partially liquidated by the payment of cash dividends, but a growing company will reinvest cash in sustaining the added investments in receivables, inventories, plant, equipment, and other assets so necessary for expansion. As a result, the ownership claims reflected by retained earnings may become "permanent" in the sense that, as a practical matter, they will never be liquidated as long as the company remains in business.

   This linking of retained earnings and cash is only one example of erroneous interpretation. As a general rule, there is no direct relationship between the individual items on the two sides of the balance sheet. For example, Walgreens had cash of less than $78 million on the above balance sheet date when its retained earnings were nearly $1.5 billion.

4. Stockholders' equity is a difference, the excess of assets over liabilities. If the assets were carried in the accounting records at their liquidating value today, and the liabilities were carried at the exact amounts needed for their extinguishment, the remark would be true. But such valuations would be coincidental because assets are customarily carried at *historical cost* expressed in an unchanging monetary unit. Intervening changes in markets and general price levels in inflationary times may mean that the assets are woefully understated. Investors may make a critical error if they think that balance sheets indicate current values.

   Furthermore, the "market values" for publicly owned shares are usually determined by daily trading conducted in the financial marketplaces such as the New York Stock Exchange. These values are affected by numerous factors including the *expectations* of (a) price appreciation and (b) cash flows in the form of dividends. The focus is on the future; the present and the past are examined only as clues to what may be forthcoming. Therefore the present stockholders' equity is usually of only incidental concern.

   For example, stockholders' equity for Walgreens was $1,573,640,000 ÷ 123,070,536 shares, or $13 per share, while the company's market price per common share fluctuated between $34 and $43.

Highlights to Remember

An underlying structure of concepts, techniques, and conventions provides a basis for accounting practice. Two basic financial statements, the balance sheet (or statement of financial position) and income statement, are presented in this chapter. Their main elements are assets, liabilities, owners' equity, revenues, and expenses. Income statements and balance sheets are linked because the revenues and expenses appearing on income statements are components of stockholders' equity. Revenues increase stockholders' equity; expenses decrease stockholders' equity.

The accrual basis is the heart of accounting. Under accrual accounting revenues are recognized as earned and expenses as incurred rather than as related cash is received or disbursed. Expense should not be confused with the term *cash disbursement*, and revenue should not be confused with the term *cash receipt*.

The balance sheet equation provides a framework for recording accounting transactions. At the end of each accounting period, adjustments must be made so that financial statements may be presented on a full-fledged accrual basis. The major adjustments are for (1) expiration of unexpired costs, (2) recognition (earning) of unearned revenues, (3) accrual of unrecorded expenses, and (4) accrual of unrecorded revenues. After transactions are recorded and adjustments are made, the data can be compiled into financial statements.

Dividends are not expenses; they are distributions of assets that reduce ownership claims. Similarly, retained income is not cash; it is a claim against total assets.

Entities can be organized as corporations, partnerships, or sole proprietorships. The type of organization does not affect most accounting entries. Only the owners' equity section will differ among organizational types.

Three major conventions that affect accounting are recognition, matching and cost recovery, and stable monetary unit. Recognition affects when revenues will be recorded in the income statement, matching and cost recovery specify when expenses will be recorded, and stable monetary units justify use of a unit of currency (the dollar in the United States) to measure accounting transactions.

Appendix 17A: Additional Accounting Concepts

This appendix describes several concepts that are prominent parts of the body of generally accepted accounting principles: continuity or going concern, objectivity or verifiability, materiality, conservatism, and cost-benefit.

The Continuity or Going Concern Convention

continuity convention (going concern convention)
The assumption that in all ordinary situations an entity persists indefinitely.

The **continuity** or **going concern convention** is the assumption that in all ordinary situations an entity persists indefinitely. This notion implies that existing *resources*, such as plant assets, *will be used* to fulfill the general purposes of a continuing entity *rather than sold* in tomorrow's real estate or equipment markets. It also implies that existing liabilities will be paid at maturity in an orderly manner.

Suppose some old specialized equipment has a depreciated cost (i.e., original cost less accumulated depreciation) of $10,000, a replacement cost of $12,000, and a realizable value of $7,000 on the used-equipment market. The continuity convention is often cited as the justification for adhering to acquisition cost (or acquisition cost less depreciation, $10,000 in this example) as the primary basis for valuing assets such as inventories, land, buildings, and equipment. Some critics of these accounting practices believe that such valuations are not as informative as their replacement cost ($12,000) or their realizable values on sale ($7,000). Defenders of using $10,000 as an appropriate asset valuation argue that a going concern will generally use the asset as originally intended. Therefore the recorded cost (the acquisition cost less depreciation) is the preferable basis for accountability and evaluation of performance. Hence other values are not germane because replacement or disposal will not occur en masse as of the balance sheet date.

The opposite view to this going concern or continuity convention is an immediate-liquidation assumption whereby all items on a balance sheet are valued at the amounts appropriate if the entity's assets were to be sold and its liabilities paid in piecemeal fashion within a few days or months. This liquidation approach to valuation is usually used only when the entity is in severe, near-bankrupt straits.

Objectivity or Verifiability

objectivity (verifiability) Accuracy supported by a high extent of consensus among independent measures of an item.

Users want assurance that the numbers in the financial statements are not fabricated by management or by accountants to mislead or falsify the firm's financial position and performance. Consequently, accountants seek and prize **objectivity** (or **verifiability**) as one of their principal strengths and regard it as an essential characteristic of measurement. A financial statement item is *objective* or *verifiable* if there would be a high extent of consensus among independent measures of the item. For example, the amount paid for assets is usually highly verifiable, but the predicted cost to replace assets often is not.

Many critics of existing accounting practices want to trade objectivity (accuracy) for what they conceive as more relevant or valid information. For example, the accounting literature is peppered with suggestions that accounting should attempt to measure "economic income," even though objectivity may be lessened. This particular suggestion often involves introducing asset valuations at replacement costs when these are higher than historical costs. The accounting profession has generally rejected these suggestions, even when reliable replacement price quotations are available, because no evidence short of a bona fide sale is regarded as sufficient to justify income recognition.

Materiality

materiality The accounting convention that justifies the omission of insignificant information when its omission or misstatement would not mislead a user of the financial statements.

Because accounting is a practical art, the practitioner often tempers accounting reports by applying judgments about **materiality.** A financial statement item is not *material* if it is sufficiently small that its omission or misstatement would not mislead a user of the financial statements. Many outlays that should theoretically be recorded as assets are immediately written off as expenses because of their lack of significance. For example, many corporations have a rule that requires the immediate write-off to expense of all outlays under a specified minimum of, say, $100, regardless of the useful life of the asset acquired.

In such a case, coat hangers may be acquired that may last indefinitely but may never appear in the balance sheet as assets. The resulting $100 understatement of assets and stockholders' equity would be too trivial to worry about.

When is an item material? There will probably never be a universal clear-cut answer. What is trivial to IBM may be material to Joe's Computer Repair Service. A working rule is that an item is material if its proper accounting would probably affect the decision of a knowledgeable user. In sum, although materiality is an important convention, it is difficult to use anything other than prudent judgment to tell whether an item is material.

The Conservatism Convention

conservatism convention

Selecting the method of measurement that yields the gloomiest immediate results.

Conservatism has been a hallmark of accounting. In a technical sense, the **conservatism convention** means selecting the method of measurement that yields the gloomiest immediate results. This attitude is reflected in such working rules as "Anticipate no gains, but provide for all possible losses," and "If in doubt, write it off."

Accountants have traditionally regarded the historical costs of acquiring an asset as the ceiling for its valuation. Assets may be written up only upon an exchange, but they may be written down without an exchange. For example, consider *lower-of-cost-or-market* procedures in which inventories are written down when replacement costs decline, but they are never written up when replacement costs increase.

Conservatism has been criticized as being inherently inconsistent. If replacement market prices are sufficiently objective and verifiable to justify write-downs, why aren't they just as valid for write-ups? Furthermore, the critics maintain, conservatism is not a fundamental concept. Accounting reports should try to present the most accurate picture feasible—neither too high nor too low. Accountants defend their attitude by saying that erring in the direction of conservatism would usually have less severe economic consequences than erring in the direction of overstating assets and net income.

Conservatism that leads to understating net income in one period also creates an overstatement of net income in a future period. For example, if a $100 inventory is written down to $80, net income is reduced by $20 in the period of the write-down but *increased* by $20 in the period the inventory is sold.

Cost-Benefit

cost-benefit criterion

An approach that implicitly underlies the decisions about the design of accounting systems. As a system is changed, its potential benefits should exceed its additional costs.

Accounting systems vary in complexity from the minimum crude records kept to satisfy government authorities to the sophisticated budgeting and feedback schemes that are at the heart of management planning and controlling. As a system is changed, its potential benefits should exceed its additional costs. Often the benefits are difficult to measure but this **cost-benefit criterion** at least implicitly underlies the decisions about the design of accounting systems. Sometimes the reluctance to adopt suggestions for new ways of measuring financial position and performance is because of inertia. More often, it is because the apparent benefits do not exceed the obvious costs of gathering and interpreting the information.

Room for Judgment

Accounting is commonly misunderstood as being a precise discipline that produces exact measurements of a company's financial position and performance. As a result, many individuals regard accountants as little more than mechanical tabulators who grind out financial reports after processing an imposing amount of detail in accordance with stringent predetermined rules. Although accountants take methodical steps with masses of data, their rules of measurement allow much room for judgment. Managers and accountants who exercise this judgment have more influence on financial reporting than is commonly believed. These judgments are guided by the basic concepts, techniques, and conventions called GAAP. Examples of the latter include the basic concepts just discussed. Their meaning will become clearer as these concepts are applied in future chapters.

Appendix 17B: Using Ledger Accounts

Chapter 17 focused on the balance sheet equation, the general framework used by accountants to record economic transactions. This appendix focuses on some of the main techniques that accountants use to record the transactions illustrated in the chapter.

The Account

To begin, consider how the accountant would record the King Hardware Co. transactions that were introduced in the chapter. Exhibit 17-1 (p. 643) showed their effects on the elements of the balance sheet equation:

	A		= L +	SE
	Cash	Inventory	Accounts Payable	Paid-in Capital
1. Initial investment by owners	+100,000		=	+100,000
2. Acquire inventory for cash	− 75,000	+75,000 =		
3. Acquire inventory on credit		+35,000 =	+35,000	

ledger accounts A method of keeping track of how multitudes of transactions affect each particular asset, liability, revenue, and expense.

This balance sheet equation approach emphasizes the concepts, but it can obviously become unwieldy if many transactions occur. You can readily see that changes in the balance sheet equation can occur many times daily. In large businesses, such as in a department store, hundreds or thousands of repetitive transactions occur hourly. In practice, **ledger accounts** must be used to keep track of how these multitudes of transactions affect each particular asset, liability, revenue, expense, and so forth. These accounts used here are simplified versions of those used in practice. These are called T-accounts because they take the form of the capital letter *T*. The preceding transactions would be shown in T-accounts as follows:

Assets			=	Liabilities + Stockholders' Equity		
Cash				**Accounts Payable**		
Increases		Decreases		Decreases	Increases	
(1)	100,000	(2)	75,000		(3)	35,000
Bal.	25,000					
Inventory				**Paid-in Capital**		
Increases		Decreases		Decreases	Increases	
(2)	75,000				(1)	100,000
(3)	35,000					
Bal.	110,000					

double-entry system
A method of record keeping in which at least two accounts are affected by each transaction.

The entries were made in accordance with the rules of a **double-entry system,** whereby each transaction affects at least two accounts. Asset accounts have left-side balances. They are increased by entries on the left side and decreased by entries on the right side.

Liabilities and stockholders' equity accounts have right-side balances. They are increased by entries on the right side and decreased by entries on the left side.

The format of the T-account eliminates the use of negative numbers. Any entry that reduces an account balance is *added* to the side of the account that *decreases* the account balance.

Each T-account summarizes the changes in a particular asset or equity. Each transaction is keyed in some way, such as by the numbering used in this illustration or by date or both. This keying facilitates the rechecking (auditing) process by aiding the tracing of transactions to original sources. A balance of an account is computed by totaling each side of an account and deducting the smaller total amount from the larger. Accounts exist to keep an up-to-date summary of the changes in specific assets and equities.

A balance sheet can be prepared at any time if the accounts are up to date. The necessary information is tabulated in the accounts. For example, the balance sheet after the first three transactions would contain:

Assets		Liabilities and Stockholders' Equity	
Cash	$ 25,000	Liabilities	
Inventory	110,000	Accounts payable	$ 35,000
		Stockholders' equity	
		Paid-in capital	100,000
Total assets	$135,000	Total equities	$135,000

general ledger A collection of the group of accounts that supports the items shown in the major financial statements.

General Ledger

Exhibit 17-7 is the *general ledger* of King Hardware Co. The **general ledger** is defined as a collection of the group of accounts that supports the items shown in

Exhibit 17-7 General Ledger of King Hardware Co.

1. Initial investment
2. Acquire inventory for cash
3. Acquire inventory on credit
4a. Sales on credit
4b. Cost of inventory sold
5. Collect from customers
6. Pay accounts of suppliers
7a. Pay rent in advance
7b. Recognize expiration of rental services

Assets
(Increases on Left, Decreases on Right)

Cash

(1)	100,000	(2)	75,000
(5)	30,000	(6)	10,000
		(7a)	3,000
3/31 Bal.	42,000		

Accounts Receivable

| (4a) | 120,000 | (5) | 30,000 |
| 3/31 Bal. | 90,000 | | |

Inventory

(2)	75,000	(4b)	100,000
(3)	35,000		
3/31 Bal.	10,000		

Prepaid Rent

| (7a) | 3,000 | (7b) | 1,000 |
| 3/31 Bal. | 2,000 | | |

Liabilities and Stockholders' Equity
(Decreases on Left, Increases on Right)

Accounts Payable

| (6) | 10,000 | (3) | 35,000 |
| | | 3/31 Bal. | 25,000 |

Paid-In Capital

| | | (1) | 100,000 |
| | | 3/31 Bal. | 100,000 |

Retained Income

| | | 3/31 Bal. | 19,000* |

Expense and Revenue Accounts

Sales

| | | (4a) | 120,000 |

Cost of Goods Sold

| (4b) | 100,000 | | |

Rent Expense

| (7b) | 1,000 | | |

* The details of the revenue and expense accounts appear in the income statement. Their net effect is then transferred to a single account, Retained Income, in the balance sheet.

the major financial statements.[3] Exhibit 17-7 is merely a recasting of the facts that were analyzed in Exhibit 17-1. Study Exhibit 17-7 by comparing its analysis of each transaction against its corresponding analysis in Exhibit 17-1, page 643.

Debits and Credits

The balance sheet equation has been mentioned often in this chapter. Recall:

$$A = L + \text{owner's equity} \tag{1}$$
$$A = L + \text{paid-in capital} + \text{retained income} \tag{2}$$
$$A = L + \text{paid-in capital} + \text{revenue} - \text{expenses} \tag{3}$$

The accountant often talks about entries in a technical way:

Transposing,

$$A + \text{expenses} = L + \text{paid-in capital} + \text{revenue} \tag{4}$$

Finally,

$$\text{left side } = \text{ right side} \tag{5}$$
$$\text{debit } = \text{ credit}$$

debit An entry on the left side of an account.

credit An entry on the right side of an account.

Debit means one thing and one thing only—"left side of an account" (not "bad," "something coming," etc.). **Credit** means one thing and one thing only—"right side of an account" (not "good," "something owed," etc.). The word *charge* is often used instead of *debit*, but no single word is used as a synonym for *credit*.

For example, if you asked an accountant what entry to make for Transaction 4b, the answer would be: "I would debit (or charge) Cost of Goods Sold for $100,000; and I would credit Inventory for $100,000." Note that the total dollar amounts of the debits (entries on the left side of the account[s] affected) will *always* equal the total dollar amount of credits (entries on the right side of the account[s] affected) because the whole accounting system is based on an equation. The symmetry and power of this analytical debit-credit technique is indeed impressive.

The words *debit* and *credit* have a Latin origin. They were used centuries ago when double-entry bookkeeping was introduced by Pacioli, an Italian monk. Even though *left* and *right* are more descriptive words, *debit* and *credit* are too deeply entrenched to avoid.

Debit and credit are used as verbs, adjectives, or nouns. That is, "debit $1,000 to cash and credit $1,000 to accounts receivable" are examples of uses as verbs, meaning that $1,000 should be placed on the left side of the cash account and on the right side of the accounts receivable account. Similarly, if "a debit is made to cash" or "cash has a debit balance of $12,000," then *debit* is a noun or adjective that describes the status of a particular account.

---

[3] The general ledger is usually supported by various *subsidiary ledgers*, which provide details for accounts in the general ledger. For instance, an accounts receivable subsidiary ledger would contain a separate account for each credit customer. The accounts receivable balance that appears in the Sears balance sheet is in a single account in the Sears general ledger. However, that single balance is buttressed by detailed individual accounts receivable with millions of credit customers. You can readily visualize how some accounts in general ledgers might have subsidiary ledgers supported by sub-subsidiary ledgers, and so on. Thus a subsidiary accounts receivable ledger might be subdivided alphabetically into Customers A–D, E–H, and so forth.

In our everyday conversation we sometimes use the words *debits* and *credits* in a general sense that may completely diverge from their technical accounting uses. For instance, we may give praise by saying "She deserves plenty of credit for her good deed" or "That misplay is a debit on his ledger." When you study accounting, forget these general uses and misuses of the words. Merely think right side or left side.

Assets are traditionally carried as left-side balances. Why do assets and expenses both carry debit balances? They carry left-side balances for different reasons. *Expenses* are temporary stockholders' equity accounts. Decreases in stockholders' equity are entered on the left side of the accounts because they offset the normal (i.e., right-side) stockholders' equity balances. Because expenses decrease stockholders' equity, they are carried as left-side balances.

To recapitulate:

Assets		=	Liabilities		+	Stockholders' Equity	
Increase	Decrease		Decrease	Increase		Decrease	Increase
+	−		−	+		−	+
debit	credit		debit	credit		debit	credit
left	right		left	right		left	right

Because revenues increase stockholders' equity, they are recorded as credits. Because expenses decrease stockholders' equity, they are recorded as debits.

Accounting Vocabulary

More new terms were introduced in this chapter (and its appendices) than in any other, so be sure that you understand the following:

account, *p. 644*
accounts payable, *p. 641*
accounts receivable, *p. 641*
accrual basis, *p. 646*
accrue, *p. 654*
adjustments, *p. 647*
assets, *p. 640*
audit, *p. 660*
balance sheet, *p. 640*
cash basis, *p. 646*
conservatism convention, *p. 667*
continuity convention, *p. 665*
corporation, *p. 641*
cost-benefit criterion, *p. 667*
cost recovery, *p. 662*
credit, *p. 671*
debit, *p. 671*
deferred revenue, *p. 653*
dividends, *p. 657*

double-entry system, *p. 669*
earnings, *p. 645*
equities, *p. 640*
expenses, *p. 645*
Financial Accounting Standards
  Board (FASB), *p. 661*
general ledger, *p. 669*
going concern convention, *p. 665*
income, *p. 645*
income statement, *p. 642*
ledger accounts, *p. 668*
liabilities, *p. 641*
matching, *p. 662*
materiality, *p. 666*
net worth, *p. 660*
objectivity, *p. 666*
owners' equity, *p. 641*
paid-in capital, *p. 641*
partnership, *p. 659*

profits, *p. 645*
residual value, *p. 650*
retained earnings, *p. 641*
retained income, *p. 641*
revenue, *p. 644*
Securities and Exchange
  Commission (SEC), *p. 661*
sole proprietorship, *p. 659*
source documents, *p. 647*
statement of financial condition,
  p. 640
statement of financial position,
  p. 640
stockholders' equity, *p. 641*
transaction, *p. 640*
unearned revenue, *p. 653*
unexpired cost, *p. 648*
verifiability, *p. 666*

Assignment Material

The assignment material for each remaining chapter is divided as follows:

- Fundamental Assignment Material
  General Exercises and Problems
  Understanding Published Financial Reports
- Additional Assignment Material
  Questions
  General Exercises and Problems
  Understanding Published Financial Reports

The "General Exercises and Problems" subgroups focus on concepts and procedures that are applicable to a wide variety of specific settings. Many instructors believe that these "traditional" types of exercises and problems have proved their educational value over many years of use in introductory textbooks.

The "Understanding Published Financial Reports" subgroups focus on real-life situations. They have the same basic aims as the "General Exercises and Problems" subgroups. Indeed, some instructors may confine their assignments to the "Understanding Published Financial Reports" subgroups. The distinctive characteristic of the latter subgroups is the use of actual companies and news events to enhance the student's interest in accounting. Many students and instructors get more satisfaction out of a course that frequently uses actual situations as a means of learning accounting methods and concepts.

Fundamental Assignment Material

General Exercises and Problems

17-A1 Balance Sheet Equation

For each of the following independent cases, compute the amounts (in thousands) for the items indicated by letters, and show your supporting computations:

	Case 1	Case 2	Case 3
Revenues	$140	$ K	$300
Expenses	110	170	270
Dividends declared	–0–	5	Q
Additional investment by stockholders	–0–	30	35
Net income	E	20	P
Retained income			
Beginning of year	40	60	100
End of year	D	J	110
Paid-in capital			
Beginning of year	15	10	N
End of year	C	H	85
Total assets			
Beginning of year	85	F	L
End of year	95	275	M
Total liabilities			
Beginning of year	A	90	105
End of year	B	G	95

17-A2 Analysis of Transactions, Preparation of Statements

The Ekern Company was incorporated on April 1, 19X5. Ekern had ten holders of common stock. Elke Ekern, who was the president and chief executive officer, held 51% of the shares. The company rented space in chain discount stores and specialized in selling ladies' shoes. Ekern's first location was in a store of Nordic Market Centers, Inc.

The following events occurred during April:

1. The company was incorporated. Common stockholders invested $90,000 cash.
2. Purchased merchandise inventory for cash, $35,000.
3. Purchased merchandise inventory on open account, $25,000.
4. Merchandise carried in inventory at a cost of $37,000 was sold for cash for $25,000 and on open account for $65,000, a grand total of $90,000. Ekern (not Nordic) carries and collects these accounts receivable.
5. Collection of the above accounts receivable, $15,000.
6. Payments of accounts payable, $18,000. See transaction 3.
7. Special display equipment and fixtures were acquired on April 1 for $36,000. Their expected useful life was 36 months with no terminal scrap value. Straight-line depreciation was adopted. This equipment was removable. Ekern paid $12,000 as a down payment and signed a promissory note for $24,000.
8. On April 1, Ekern signed a rental agreement with Nordic. The agreement called for a flat $2,000 per month, payable quarterly in advance. Therefore Ekern paid $6,000 cash on April 1.
9. The rental agreement also called for a payment of 10% of all sales. This payment was in addition to the flat $2,000 per month. In this way, Nordic would share in any success of the venture and be compensated for general services such as cleaning and utilities. This payment was to be made in cash on the last day of each month as soon as the sales for the month were tabulated. Therefore Ekern made the payment on April 30.
10. Wages, salaries, and sales commissions were all paid in cash for all earnings by employees. The amount was $38,000.
11. Depreciation expense was recognized. See transaction 7.
12. The expiration of an appropriate amount of prepaid rental services was recognized. See transaction 8.

Required

1. Prepare an analysis of Ekern Company's transactions, employing the equation approach demonstrated in Exhibit 17-1. Two additional columns will be needed: Equipment and Fixtures and Note Payable. Show all amounts in thousands.
2. Prepare a balance sheet as of April 30, 19X5, and an income statement for the month of April. Ignore income taxes.
3. Given these sparse facts, analyze Ekern's performance for April and its financial position as of April 30, 19X5.

17-A3 Cash Basis Versus Accrual Basis

Refer to the preceding problem. If Ekern Company measured income on the cash basis, what revenue would be reported for April? Which basis (accrual or cash) provides a better measure of revenue? Why?

Understanding Published Financial Reports

17-B1 Balance Sheet Equation

Micron Technology is one of the leading producers of semiconductor components. Its net income grew from $7 million in 1985 to more than $1.6 billion in 1994. The company's actual data (in millions of dollars) follow for its fiscal year ended September 1, 1994:

Assets, beginning of period	$ 965.7
Assets, end of period	E
Liabilities, beginning of period	A
Liabilities, end of period	480.4
Paid-in capital, beginning of period	357.0
Paid-in capital, end of period	D
Retained earnings, beginning of period	282.5
Retained earnings, end of period	C
Revenues	1,628.6
Costs and expenses	B
Net income	400.5
Dividends	12.2
Additional investments by stockholders	21.5

Required   Find the unknowns (in millions), showing computations to support your answers.

17-B2 Analysis of Transactions, Preparation of Statements
Hino Motors has maintained its top position in the sales of medium- and heavy-duty diesel trucks in Japan since 1973. The company's actual condensed balance sheet data, March 31, 1994, follows (in billions of Japanese yen):

Assets		Equities	
Cash	¥ 52	Accounts payable	¥ 84
Accounts receivable	64	Other liabilities	86
Inventories	27		
Prepaid expenses and other assets	60	Paid-in capital	44
Property, plant, and equipment	160	Retained earnings	149
Total	¥ 363	Total	¥ 363

The following summarizes some major transactions during April 1994 (in billions of yen):

1. Trucks carried in inventory at a cost of ¥30 were sold for cash of ¥20 and on open account of ¥50, a grand total of ¥70.
2. Acquired inventory on account, ¥50.
3. Collected receivables, ¥30.
4. On April 2, used ¥25 cash to prepay some rent and insurance for 1995.
5. Payments on accounts payable (for inventories), ¥45.
6. Paid selling and administrative expenses in cash, ¥10.
7. A total of ¥9 of prepaid expenses for rent and insurance expired in April 1994.
8. Depreciation expense of ¥18 was recognized for April.

Required
1. Prepare an analysis of the Hino Motors transactions, employing the equation approach demonstrated in Exhibit 17-1, p. 643. Show all amounts in billions of yen. (For simplicity, only a few major transactions are illustrated here.)
2. Prepare a statement of earnings for the month ended April 30, 1994, and a balance sheet as of April 30, 1994. Ignore income taxes.

17-B3 Cash Basis Versus Accrual Basis
Refer to the preceding problem. If Hino Motors measured income on the cash basis, what revenue would be reported for April? Which basis (accrual or cash) provides a better measure of revenue? Why?

Additional Assignment Material

Questions

17-1 What types of questions are answered by the income statement and balance sheet?

17-2 Criticize: "Assets are things of value owned by an organization."

17-3 How are the income statement and balance sheet related?

17-4 Criticize: "Net income is the difference in the ownership capital account balances at two points in time."

17-5 Distinguish between the accrual basis and the cash basis.

17-6 How do adjusting entries differ from routine entries?

17-7 Explain why advertising should be viewed as an asset on acquisition.

17-8 Why is it better to refer to the *costs*, rather than *values*, of assets such as plant or inventories?

17-9 "Depreciation is cost allocation, not valuation." Do you agree? Explain.

17-10 Criticize: "As a stockholder, I have a right to more dividends. You have millions stashed away in retained earnings. It's about time that you let the true owners get their hands on that pot of gold."

17-11 Criticize: "Dividends are distributions of profits."

17-12 Explain the relationship between the FASB and the SEC.

17-13 What is the major criticism of the dollar as the principal accounting measure?

17-14 What does the accountant mean by *going concern*?

17-15 What does the accountant mean by *objectivity*?

17-16 What is the role of cost-benefit (economic feasibility) in the development of accounting principles?

General Exercises and Problems

17-17 True or False
Use *T* or *F* to indicate whether each of the following statements is true or false.

1. Cash should be classified as a stockholders' equity item.
2. Retained earnings should be accounted for as an asset item.
3. Machinery used in the business should be recorded at replacement cost.
4. The cash balance is the best evidence of stockholders' equity.
5. It is not possible to determine changes in the condition of a business from a single balance sheet.
6. From a single balance sheet, you can find stockholders' equity for a period but not for a specific day.

17-18 Nature of Retained Income
This is an exercise on the relationships among assets, liabilities, and ownership equities. The numbers are small, but the underlying concepts are large.

1. Prepare an opening balance sheet of:

Cash	$1,400	Paid-in capital	$1,400

2. Purchase inventory for $600 cash. Prepare a balance sheet. A heading is unnecessary in this and subsequent requirements.
3. Sell the entire inventory for $850 cash. Prepare a balance sheet. Where is the retained income in terms of relationships within the balance sheet? That is, what is the meaning of the retained income? Explain in your own words.
4. Buy inventory for $400 cash and equipment for $750 cash. Prepare a balance sheet. Where is the retained income in terms of relationships within the balance sheet? That is, what is the meaning of the retained income? Explain in your own words.

5. Buy inventory for $450 on open account. Prepare a balance sheet. Where is the retained income and account payable in terms of the relationships within the balance sheet? That is, what is the meaning of the account payable and the retained income? Explain in your own words.

17-19 Income Statement
Here is a proposed income statement of an antiques dealer:

Rhodes Antiques
Statement of Profit
and Loss
December 31, 19X6

Revenues		
Sales	$1,300,000	
Increase in market value of land and building	200,000	$1,500,000
Deduct expenses		
Advertising	$ 100,000	
Sales commissions	60,000	
Utilities	20,000	
Wages	150,000	
Dividends	100,000	
Cost of antiques purchased	800,000	1,230,000
Net profit		$ 270,000

Required   List and describe any shortcomings of this statement.

17-20 Customer and Airline
Suppose Levitz Furniture Company decided to hold a managers' meeting in Hawaii in February. To take advantage of special fares, Levitz purchased airline tickets in advance from American Airlines at a total cost of $90,000. These were acquired on December 1 for cash.

Required   Using the balance sheet equation format, analyze the impact of the December payment and the February travel on the financial position of both Levitz and American.

17-21 Tenant and Landlord
The Handy Hardware Company, a retail hardware store, pays quarterly rent on its store at the beginning of each quarter. The rent per quarter is $9,000. The owner of the building in which the store is located is the Barker Corporation.

Required   Using the balance sheet equation format, analyze the effects of the following on the tenant's and the landlord's financial position:

1. Handy Hardware pays $9,000 rent on July 1.
2. Adjustment for July.
3. Adjustment for August.
4. Adjustment for September.

17-22 Find Unknowns
The following data pertain to Great Barrier Excursions. Total assets at January 1, 19X1, were $100,000; at December 31, 19X1, $120,000. During 19X1, sales were $260,000, cash dividends were $14,000, and operating expenses (exclusive of costs of goods sold) were $50,000. Total liabilities at December 31, 19X1, were $55,000; at January 1, 19X1, $40,000. There was no additional capital paid in during 19X1.

Required   (These need not be computed in any particular order.)
Calculate the following items.

1. Stockholders' equity, for January 1, 19X1
2. Net income for 19X1
3. Cost of goods sold for 19X1

17-23 Balance Sheet Equation; Solving for Unknowns

Compute the unknowns (V, W, X, Y, and Z) in each of the individual cases, Columns 1 through 7.

Given	1	2	3	4	5	6	7
Assets at beginning of period		$9,000				Z	$ 8,200
Assets at end of period		11,000					9,600
Liabilities at beginning of period		6,000				$12,000	4,000
Liabilities at end of period		Y					6,000
Stockholders' equity at beginning of period	$7,000	Z				V	X
Stockholders' equity at end of period	X	5,000				10,000	W
Sales			$15,000		X	14,000	20,000
Inventory at beginning of period			6,000	$ 8,000		Y	
Inventory at end of period			7,000	7,000		7,000	
Purchase of inventory			10,000	12,000		6,000	
Gross profit			Y		3,000	6,000	V
Cost of goods sold*			X	X	4,500	X	Z
Other expenses			4,000			4,000	5,000
Net profit	3,000	X	Z			W	Y
Dividends	2,000	–0–				1,500	400
Additional investments by stockholders						5,000	–0–

* Note that cost of goods sold = beginning inventory + purchases – ending inventory.

17-24 Fundamental Transaction Analysis and Preparation of Statements

Three former college classmates have decided to pool a variety of work experiences by opening a clothing store. The business has been incorporated as The Clothes Hanger. The following transactions occurred during March.

1. On March 1, 19X5, each of the three invested $9,000 in cash in exchange for 1,000 shares of stock each.

2. The corporation quickly acquired $40,000 in inventory, half of which had to be paid for in cash. The other half was acquired on open accounts that were payable after 30 days.

3. A store was rented for $500 monthly. A lease was signed for 1 year on March 1. The first 2 months' rent were paid in advance. Other payments were to be made on the second of each month.

4. Advertising during March was purchased on open account for $3,000 from a news-paper owned by one of the stockholders. Additional advertising services of $6,000 were acquired for cash.

5. Sales were $60,000. Merchandise was sold for twice its purchase cost. Seventy-five percent of the sales were on open account.

6. Wages and salaries incurred in March amounted to $11,000, of which $5,000 was paid.

7. Miscellaneous services paid for in cash were $1,510.

8. On March 1, fixtures and equipment were purchased for $6,000 with a down-payment of $1,000 plus a $5,000 note payable in one year.

9. See transaction 8 and make the March 31 adjustment for interest expense *accrued* at 9.6%. (The interest is not *due* until the note matures.)

10. See transaction 8 and make the March 31 adjustment for depreciation expense on a straight-line basis. The estimated life of the fixtures and equipment is 10 years with no expected terminal scrap value. Straight-line depreciation here would be $6,000 ÷ 10 years = $600 per year, or $50 per month.

11. Cash dividends of $400 were declared and disbursed to stockholders on March 30.

Required

1. Using the accrual basis of accounting, prepare an analysis of transactions, employing the equation approach demonstrated in Exhibit 17-1, page 643. Place your analysis sideways; to save space, use abbreviated headings. Work slowly. Use the following headings: Cash, Accounts Receivable, Inventory, Prepaid Rent, Fixtures and Equipment, Accounts Payable, Notes Payable, Accrued Wages Payable, Accrued Interest Payable, Paid-in Capital, and Retained Income.

2. Prepare a balance sheet and a multiple-step income statement. Also prepare a statement of retained income.

3. What advice would you give the owners based on the information compiled in the financial statements?

17-25 Debits and Credits

Study Appendix 17B. Determine for the following transactions whether the account *named in parentheses* is to be debited or credited.

1. Sold merchandise (Merchandise Inventory), $1,000.

2. Paid Johnson Associates $3,000 owed them (Accounts Payable).

3. Paid dividends (Cash), $500.

4. Bought merchandise on account (Merchandise Inventory), $3,000.

5. Received cash from customers on accounts due (Accounts Receivable), $2,000.

6. Bought merchandise on open account (Accounts Payable), $5,000.

7. Borrowed money from a bank (Notes Payable), $12,000.

17-26 True or False

Study Appendix 17B. Use *T* or *F* to indicate whether each of the following statements is true or false. For each false statement, explain why it is false.

1. Decreases in accounts must be shown on the debit side.

2. Both increases in liabilities and decreases in assets should be entered on the right.

3. Equipment purchases for cash should be debited to Equipment and credited to Cash.

4. Asset credits should be on the right and liability credits on the left.

5. Payments on mortgages should be debited to Cash and credited to Mortgages Payable. Mortgages are long-term debts.

6. Debit entries must always be recorded on the left.

7. Money borrowed from the bank should be credited to Cash and debited to Notes Payable.

8. Purchase of inventory on account should be credited to Inventory and debited to Accounts Payable.

9. Decreases in liability accounts should be recorded on the right.

10. Increases in asset accounts must always be entered on the left.

11. Increases in stockholders' equity always should be entered as credits.

17-27   Use of T-Accounts
Study Appendix 17B. Refer to Problem 17-A2. Make entries for April in T-accounts. Key your entries and check to see that the ending balances agree with the financial statements.

17-28   Use of T-Accounts
Study Appendix 17B. Refer to Problem One of the "Summary Problems for Your Review." The transactions are analyzed in Exhibit 17-2, page 000. Make entries in T-accounts and check to see that the ending balances agree with the financial statements in Exhibits 17-3, 17-4, 17-5 on page 000.

17-29   Use of T-Accounts
Study Appendix 17B. Refer to Problem 17-24. Use T-accounts to present an analysis of March transactions. Key your entries and check to see that the ending balances agree with the financial statements.

17-30   Measurement of Income for Tax and Other Purposes
The following are the summarized transactions of Dr. Sally Schwager, a dentist, for 19X5, her first year in practice.

1. Acquired equipment and furniture for $60,000. Its expected useful life is 5 years. Straight-line depreciation will be used, assuming zero terminal disposal value.

2. Fees collected, $81,000. These fees included $2,000 paid in advance by some patients on December 31, 19X5.

3. Rent is paid at the rate of $500 monthly, payable quarterly on the 25th of March, June, September, and December for the following quarter. Total disbursements during 19X5 for rent were $7,500 including an initial payent on January 1.

4. Fees billed but uncollected, December 31, 19X5, $20,000.

5. Utilities expense paid in cash, $600. Additional utility bills unpaid at December 31, 19X5, $100.

6. Salaries expense of dental assistant and secretary, $16,000 paid in cash. In addition, $1,000 was earned but unpaid on December 31, 19X5.

Dr. Schwager may elect either the cash basis or the accrual basis of measuring income for income tax purposes, provided that she uses it consistently in subsequent years. Under either alternative, the original cost of the equipment and furniture must be written off over its 5-year useful life rather than being regarded as a lump-sum expense in the first year.

Required

1. Prepare income statements on both the cash and accrual bases, using one column for each basis.

2. Which basis do you prefer as a measure of Dr. Schwager's performance? Why? What do you think is the justification for the government's allowing the use of the cash basis for income tax purposes?

Understanding Published Financial Reports

17-31 Balance Sheet Effects
The Wells Fargo Bank showed the following items (among others) on its balance sheet at January 1, 1994:

Cash	$ 2,644,000,000
Total deposits	$41,644,000,000

Required

1. Suppose you made a deposit of $1,000 in the bank. How would each of the bank's assets and equities be affected? How much would each of your personal assets and equities be affected? Be specific.

2. Suppose Wells Fargo makes an $900,000 loan to a local hospital for remodeling. What would be the effect on each of the bank's assets and equities immediately after the loan is made? Be specific.

3. Suppose you borrowed $10,000 from Wells Fargo on a personal loan. How would such a transaction affect each of your personal assets and equities?

17-32 Preparation of Balance Sheet

Georgia-Pacific Corporation is a large producer of timber, wood products, pulp, and paper. Its annual report included the following balance sheet items at December 31 1994 (in millions of dollars):

Various notes payable	$ 915
Cash	(1)
Total stockholders' equity	(2)
Total liabilities	(3)
Long-term debt	4,157
Accounts receivable	377
Common stock	71
Inventories	1,202
Accounts payable	582
Property, plant, and equipment	5,448
Additional stockholders' equity	2,331
Other assets	3,477
Other liabilities	2,489
Total assets	10,545

Required

Prepare a condensed balance sheet including amounts for

1. Cash. What do you think of its relative size?
2. Total stockholders' equity.
3. Total liabilities.

17-33 Net Income and Retained Income

McDonald's Corporation is a well-known fast-foods restaurant company. The following data are from its 1993 annual report (in thousands):

McDonald's
Corporation

Retained earnings,		Dividends paid	$ 197,200
end of year	$7,612,600	General, administrative,	
Revenues	7,408,100	and selling expenses	941,100
Interest and other non-		Retained earnings,	
operating expenses	308,300	beginning of year	6,727,300
Income tax expense	593,200	Other operating expenses	1,456,700
Food and packaging			
expense	1,735,100		
Wages and salaries	1,291,200		

Required

1. Prepare the following for the year:

  a. Income statement. The final three lines of the income statement were labeled as *income before provision for income taxes, provision for income tax expense,* and *net income.*
  b. Statement of retained income.
2. Comment briefly on the relative size of the cash dividend.

17-34 Earnings Statement, Retained Earnings

The Procter & Gamble Company has many well-known products, including Tide, Crest, Jif, and Prell. The following is a reproduction of the terms and amounts in the financial statements contained in a recent annual report regarding the fiscal year ended June 30, 1994 (in millions):

Net sales and other income	$30,544	Retained earnings at	
Cash	2,373	beginning of year	$6,248
Interest expense	482	Cost of products sold	17,355
Income taxes	1,135	Dividends to shareholders	963
Accounts payable—trade	2,604	Marketing, administrative,	
		and other expenses	9,361

Required Choose the relevant data and prepare (1) the income statement for the fiscal year and (2) the statement of retained income for the fiscal year. The final three lines of the income statement were labeled as *earnings before income taxes, income taxes,* and *net earnings.*

18

Understanding Corporate Annual Reports: Basic Financial Statements

An organization's basic financial statements are presented in its annual report. Investors and creditors use annual reports to assess the amounts, timing, and uncertainty of future cash flows. *Courtesy Laima E. Druskis*

Learning Objectives

When you have finished studying this chapter, you should be able to

1 Identify and explain the main types of assets in the balance sheet of a corporation.

2 Identify and explain the main types of liabilities in the balance sheet of a corporation.

3 Identify and explain the main elements of the stockholders' equity section of the balance sheet of a corporation.

4 Identify and explain the principal elements in the income statement of a corporation.

5 Identify and explain the elements in the statement of retained earnings.

6 Identify activities that affect cash, and classify them as operating, investing, or financing activities.

7 Prepare the statement of cash flows using the direct method.

8 Prepare a reconciliation of net income to net cash provided by operations.

9 Explain the role of depreciation in the statement of cash flows.

Investors often use financial statements to assess a company's position and prospects. Consider the financial statements of Microsoft, the world's largest computer software company. The company's income statements show a growth in net income from $279 million in 1990 to $1,146 million in 1994, based on an increase in revenues from $1.2 billion to $4.6 billion. Balance sheets show that total assets grew from $1.1 billion in 1990 to $5.4 billion in 1994, whereas liabilities increased from $.2 billion to $.9 billion. During this 4-year period, optimistic investors bid its price up from under $10 per share to more than $50.

This chapter focuses on what investors and other decision makers can learn from financial statements. It extends the discussion of balance sheets and income statements from the preceding chapter and introduces another major financial statement, the statement of cash flows.

Accounting is commonly misunderstood as being a precise discipline that produces exact measurements of a company's financial position and performance. As a result, many individuals regard accountants as little more than mechanical tabulators who grind out financial reports after processing an imposing amount of detail in accordance with stringent predetermined rules. Although accountants do take methodical steps with masses of data, their rules of measurement allow room for judgment. Managers and accountants who exercise this judgment have more influence on financial reporting than is commonly believed. To understand financial statements fully, you must recognize the judgments that go into their construction.

■ CLASSIFIED BALANCE SHEET

Exhibit 18-1 shows the 1993 and 1994 classified balance sheets for Nike, Inc., maker of athletic footwear. They classify assets and equities into five main sections: current assets, noncurrent assets, current liabilities, noncurrent liabilities, and shareholders' equity. Be sure to locate each of these items in the exhibit when you read the description of the item in the following pages.

Current Assets

current assets Cash and all other assets that are reasonably expected to be converted to cash or sold or consumed during the normal operating cycle.

operating cycle The time span during which cash is spent to acquire goods and services that are used to produce the organization's output, which in turn is sold to customers, who in turn pay for their purchases with cash.

Current assets include cash and all other assets that are reasonably expected to be converted to cash or sold or consumed during the normal operating cycle. An **operating cycle** is the time span during which cash is spent to acquire goods and services that are used to produce the organization's output, which in turn is sold to customers, who in turn pay for their purchases with cash. Consider a retail business. Its operating cycle is illustrated in the following diagram (figures are hypothetical):

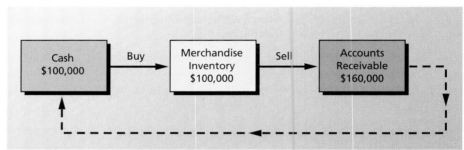

The box for Accounts Receivable (amounts owed to the business by customers) is larger than the other two boxes because the objective of a business is to sell goods at a price higher than acquisition cost. The total amount of profit a firm earns during a particular period depends on how much its selling prices exceed its costs of producing or purchasing the products and additional expenses incurred during the period.

Accountants sometimes assume that an operating cycle is 1 year. But some businesses have several operating cycles during 1 year. Others—such as the distillery, tobacco, and lumber industries—need more than 1 year to complete a single cycle. Inventories in such industries are nevertheless regarded as current assets. Similarly, installment accounts and notes receivable are typically classified as current assets even though they will not be fully collected within 1 year.

cash equivalents
Short-term investments that can easily be converted into cash with little delay.

As Exhibit 18-1 shows, current assets fall into several broad categories, such as cash and cash equivalents, accounts receivable, inventories, prepaid expenses, and other current assets. *Cash* consists of bank deposits in checking accounts plus money on hand. **Cash equivalents** are short-term investments that can easily be converted into cash with little delay.[1] Examples include

---

[1] Short-term investments are frequently called *marketable securities*, but this is a misnomer. Strictly speaking, marketable securities may be held for either a short-term or a long-term purpose. Short-term investments should be distinguished from *long-term investments* in the capital stock or bonds of other companies. The latter are noncurrent assets.

Exhibit 18-1

Nike, Inc.
Balance Sheet

(in thousands)	May 31 1994	May 31 1993
ASSETS		
Current assets		
Cash and equivalents	$ 518,816	$ 291,284
Accounts receivable, less allowance for doubtful accounts of 28,291 and 19,447	703,682	667,547
Inventories	470,023	592,986
Prepaid expenses	40,307	42,452
Other current assets	37,603	23,499
Total current assets	1,770,431	1,617,768
Noncurrent assets		
Property, plant, and equipment		
At cost	639,085	571,032
Less: accumulated depreciation	233,240	193,037
Net property, plant, and equipment	405,845	377,995
Goodwill	157,187	159,579
Other assets	40,352	30,927
Total noncurrent assets	603,384	568,501
Total Assets	$2,373,815	$2,186,269
LIABILITIES AND SHAREHOLDERS' EQUITY		
Current liabilities		
Notes payable	$ 127,378	$ 108,165
Accounts payable	210,576	135,701
Accrued liabilities	181,889	138,563
Income taxes payable	38,287	17,150
Current portion of long-term debt	3,857	52,985
Total current liabilities	561,987	452,564
Noncurrent liabilities		
Long-term debt	12,364	15,033
Deferred income taxes	18,228	31,978
Other non-current liabilities	39,987	43,575
Total noncurrent liabilities	70,579	90,586
Total liabilities	632,566	543,150
Shareholders' equity		
Redeemable preferred stock	300	300
Common stock at stated value	2,863	2,879
Capital in excess of stated value	108,284	108,451
Retained earnings	1,644,925	1,539,279
Foreign currency translation adjustment	(15,123)	(7,790)
Total shareholders' equity	1,741,249	1,643,119
Total liabilities and shareholders' equity	$2,373,815	$2,186,269

money market funds and Treasury bills. They represent an investment of excess cash not needed immediately. These securities are usually shown at cost or market price, whichever is lower. The market price is disclosed parenthetically if it is above cost. In 1994, Nike had $518,816,000 in cash and cash equivalents.

Accounts receivable is the total amount owed to the company by its customers. Because some customers ultimately will not pay their bill, the total is reduced by an allowance or provision for doubtful accounts (i.e., possible "bad debts"). The difference represents the net amount that the company will probably collect. At the end of the 1994 fiscal year[2] Nike had gross accounts receivable of $731,973,000, but after deducting $28,291,000 for doubtful accounts, the company expects to collect $703,682,000 from its accounts receivable.

Inventories consist of merchandise, finished products of manufacturers, goods in the process of being manufactured, and raw materials. Accountants state inventories at their cost or market price (defined as replacement cost), whichever is lower. Cost of manufactured products normally is composed of raw material cost plus the costs of converting it into a finished product (direct labor and manufacturing overhead). Nike's 1994 inventories stood at $470,023,000.

Determining the cost of inventories is not always as easy as it may seem at first glance. When the total cost of goods purchased or produced by a company is measured, how should it be allocated between the goods sold (an expense) and the goods still on hand (an asset)? Allocation is easy if each unit of the product is readily identifiable, like the cars of an automobile dealer or the expensive merchandise of a jewelry store. Advanced data processing systems have made such specific identification possible for more and more organizations. But it is still expensive to have an elaborate identification system for goods that are purchased and sold in vast numbers and variety. Chapter 20 discusses the assumptions that are made to simplify inventory measurement.

Prepaid expenses are advance payments to suppliers. They are usually unimportant in relation to other assets. Examples are prepayment of rent and insurance premiums for coverage over the coming operating cycle. They belong in current assets because, if they were not present, more cash would be needed to conduct current operations. In 1994, Nike shows $40,307,000 of prepaid expenses, which is only 2.3% of total current assets.

Other current assets are miscellaneous current assets that do not fit into the listed categories. They might include *notes receivable* and *short-term investments* that are not cash equivalents. For Nike, such assets amounted to $37,603,000 in 1994.

Property, Plant, and Equipment

fixed assets (tangible assets) Physical items that can be seen and touched, such as property, plant, and equipment.

Property, plant, and *equipment* are sometimes called **fixed assets** or plant assets. Because they are physical items that can be seen and touched, they are also called **tangible assets.** Details about property, plant, and equipment are usually found in a footnote to the financial statements such as the one for Nike shown in Exhibit 18-2. Footnotes are an integral part of financial statements. They contain explanations for the summary figures that appear in the statements.

Land is typically accounted for as a separate item and is carried indefinitely at its original cost.

Buildings and *machinery* and *equipment* are initially recorded at cost: the invoice amount, plus freight and installation, less cash discounts. The major

---

[2] A *fiscal year* is defined as the year established for accounting purposes for the preparation of annual reports. Nike's fiscal year is June 1 through May 31.

difficulties of measurement center on the choice of *depreciation* method (see Chapter 17, page 649)—that is, the allocation of the original cost to the particular periods or products that benefit from the use of the assets. Remember that depreciation only means allocating the original cost of plant and equipment, not valuing them in the ordinary sense of the term. Balance sheets typically do *not* show replacement cost, resale value, or the price changes since acquisition.

Exhibit 18-2

Nike, Inc.
Footnote 5 to the
1994 Financial
Statements

Note 5. Property, Plant, and Equipment (thousands)

	1994	1993
Land	$ 59,761	$ 50,851
Buildings	154,731	152,368
Machinery and equipment	317,782	296,680
Leasehold improvements	54,383	46,611
Construction-in-progress	52,428	24,522
	$639,085	$571,032
Less: accumulated depreciation	233,240	193,037
Net property, plant, and equipment	$405,845	$377,995

The amount of original cost to be allocated over the total useful life of the asset as depreciation is the difference between the total acquisition cost and the estimated *residual value*. The residual value is the amount expected to be received when selling the asset at the end of its economic life. The depreciation allocation to each year may be made on the basis of time or service. The estimate of useful life, which is an important factor in determining the yearly allocation of depreciation, is influenced by estimates of physical wear and tear, technological change, and economic obsolescence. Thus the useful life is usually less than the physical life.

There are three general methods of depreciation: *straight line, accelerated*, and *units of production*. The straight-line method allocates the same cost to each year of an asset's useful life. Accelerated methods allocate more of the cost to the early years and less to the later years.[3] The units-of-production method allocates cost based on the amount of production rather than the passage of time.

Which method is best? It depends on the firm's goal, the asset involved, and the type of financial statement being prepared. The straight-line method is most popular. More than 90% of all firms use it for at least some assets when preparing financial statements for reporting to the public. In contrast, most U.S. firms use accelerated depreciation when preparing financial statements for the IRS.

Suppose a business spends $42,000 to buy equipment with an estimated useful life of 4 years and an estimated residual value of $2,000. Using the straight-line method of depreciation, the annual depreciation expense in each of the 4 years would be:

---

[3] Methods of accelerated depreciation are described in Chapter 12, pages 624-654. Those pages can be studied at this time if desired, but knowledge of accelerated depreciation methods is not necessary for understanding this chapter.

$$\frac{\text{original cost} - \text{estimated residual value}}{\text{years of useful life}}$$

$$= \frac{(\$42,000 - \$2,000)}{4}$$

$$= \$10,000 \text{ per year}$$

Exhibit 18-3 shows how the asset would be displayed in the balance sheet.

		Balances at End of Year		
	1	*2*	*3*	*4*
Plant and equipment (at original acquisition cost)	$42,000	$42,000	$42,000	$42,000
Less: accumulated depreciation (the portion of original cost that has already been charged to operations as expense)	10,000	20,000	30,000	40,000
Net book value (the portion of original cost not yet charged as expense)	$32,000	$22,000	$12,000	$ 2,000

Exhibit 18-3

Straight-line
Depreciation
(figures assumed)

In Exhibits 18-1 and 18-2 the original cost of fixed assets on Nike's 1994 balance sheet is $639,085,000. There is *accumulated depreciation* of $233,240,000, the portion of the original cost of the asset that was previously charged as depreciation expense, so the net property, plant, and equipment at May 31, 1994 is $639,085,000 – $233,240,000 = $405,845,000.

Depreciation is the part of an asset that has been used up. It is gone. It is not a pool of cash set aside to replace the asset. If a company decides to accumulate specific cash to replace assets, such cash should be specifically labeled as a cash *fund* for replacement and expansion. Holiday Inns, Inc., has used such a fund, calling it a *capital construction fund*. Such funds are quite rare because most companies can earn better returns by investing any available cash in ordinary operations rather than in special funds. Typically, companies use or acquire cash for the replacement and expansion of plant assets only as specific needs arise.

Leasehold improvements are investments made by a lessee (tenant) in items such as painting, decorating, fixtures, and air-conditioning equipment that cannot be removed from the premises when a lease expires. The costs of leasehold improvements are written off in the same manner as depreciation, but their periodic write-off is called *amortization*.

Construction in progress is shown separately from other assets because the assets are not yet ready for use. It represents assets that will be part of buildings or machinery and equipment when completed.

Natural resources such as mineral deposits are not illustrated here, but they are typically grouped with plant assets. Their original cost is written off in the form of *depletion* as the resources are used. For example, a coal mine may cost $10 million and originally contain an estimated 5 million tons. The depletion rate would be $2 per ton. If 500,000 tons were mined during the first year, depletion would be $1 million for that year; if 300,000 tons were mined the second year, depletion would be $600,000; and so forth until the entire $10 million has been charged as depletion expense.

Long-term investments are also noncurrent assets. They include long-term holdings of securities of other firms. Accounting for intercorporate investments is discussed in detail in Chapter 19. Nike does not have any long-term investments, unless they are combined with other small, miscellaneous noncurrent assets in the $40,352,000 of *other assets* shown in Exhibit 18-1.

Intangible Assets

intangible assets
Long-lived assets that are not physical in nature. Examples are goodwill, franchises, patents, trademarks, and copyrights.

goodwill The excess of the cost of an acquired company over the sum of the fair market values of its identifiable individual assets less its liabilities.

Tangible assets such as cash or equipment can be physically observed. In contrast, **intangible assets** are a class of *long-lived assets* that are not physical in nature. They are rights to expected future benefits deriving from their acquisition and continued possession. Examples are goodwill, franchises, patents, trademarks, and copyrights. In Exhibit 18-1 goodwill of $157,187,000 at May 31, 1994, is Nike's only intangible asset.

Goodwill, which is discussed in more detail in the next chapter, is the excess of the cost of an acquired company over the sum of the fair market values of its identifiable individual assets less its liabilities. For example, Nike acquired Cole Haan for $95 million. It could assign only $13 million to various identifiable assets such as receivables, plant, and patents less liabilities assumed by Nike; the remainder, $82 million, was recorded as goodwill.

The accounting for goodwill illustrates how an exchange transaction is a basic concept of accounting. After all, many owners could obtain a premium price if they sold their companies. But such goodwill is never recorded. Only the goodwill arising from an *actual acquisition* should be shown as an asset on the purchaser's records.

For shareholder-reporting purposes, goodwill must be amortized (depreciated), generally in a straight-line manner, over the periods benefited. In the United States, the longest allowed amortization period is 40 years; in Japan and France, for example, it is 5 years. Nike is amortizing its $82 million of goodwill from the Cole Haan purchase at the rate of $82,000,000 ÷ 40 = $2,050,000 per year. The shortest amortization period is not specified, but a lump-sum write-off on acquisition is forbidden for U.S. firms.

Many managers and accountants insist that some intangible assets have unlimited lives. Nevertheless, the attitude of the regulatory bodies toward accounting for intangible assets has become increasingly conservative. For example, before 1970, the amortization of goodwill, trademarks, and franchises with indefinite useful lives was not mandatory in the U.S. But in 1970 the regulators ruled that the values of all intangible assets eventually disappear, thus making amortization mandatory.

Companies in many countries regard research and development costs as assets. They assume that research costs are incurred to purchase an asset that would benefit future operations and thus amortize research costs over the years of expected benefit, usually 3 to 6 years. In the U.S., however, the FASB has banned deferral and required write-off of these costs as incurred. The FASB admits that research and development costs may generate many long-term benefits, but the general high degree of uncertainty about the extent and measurement of future benefits has led to conservative accounting in the form of immediate write-off.

Liabilities

Assets are, of course, only part of the picture of any organization's financial health. Its *liabilities*, both current and noncurrent, are equally important.

current liabilities An organization's debts that fall due within the coming year or within the normal operating cycle if longer than a year.

Current liabilities are an organization's debts that fall due within the coming year or within the normal operating cycle if longer than a year. Turn again to Exhibit 18-1 on page 687. *Notes payable* are short-term debt backed by formal promissory notes held by a bank or business creditors. *Accounts payable* are amounts owed to suppliers who extended credit for purchases on open account. *Accrued liabilities* or *accrued expenses payable* are recognized for wages, salaries, interest, and similar items. The accountant recognizes expenses as they occur—regardless of when they are paid for in cash. *Income taxes payable* is a special accrued expense of enough magnitude to warrant a separate classification. The *current portion of long-term debt* shows the payments due within the next year on bonds and other long-term debt.

Some companies also list *unearned revenue*, also called deferred revenue. Such revenue occurs when cash is received before the related goods or services are delivered. For example, *Newsweek* magazine has such an account because it is obligated to send magazines to subscribers with prepaid subscriptions. Nike had no unearned revenue in 1994, but it did have current liabilities totaling $561,987,000.

Objective 2

Identify and explain the main types of liabilities in the balance sheet of a corporation

noncurrent liabilities (long-term liabilities) An organization's debts that fall due beyond one year.

Noncurrent liabilities, also called **long-term liabilities,** are an organization's debts that fall due beyond one year. Exhibit 18-1 shows Nike's noncurrent liabilities for 1994 as $70,579,000, making its total liabilities $632,566,000. Nike has two noncurrent liabilities, long-term debt (which we will discuss in more depth in a moment) and *deferred income taxes*. The latter rather technical and controversial item arises because the financial statements used for reporting to shareholders differ legitimately from those used for reporting to the income tax authorities. Appendix 18 provides more details about deferred taxes.

Exhibit 18-4 is a footnote from the financial statements that further breaks down Nike's long-term debts. Note especially the next to last line in this exhibit, "Less: current maturities." This item refers to payments due in the next year. The $3,857,000 noted on this line is subtracted from long-term debt because it has already been included in current liabilities. The remaining $12,364,000 is shown as "Long-term debt" in Exhibit 18-1.

Exhibit 18-4

Nike, Inc.
Footnote 8 to the
1994 Financial
Statements

Note 8. Long-Term Debt (Thousands)

	May 31	
	1994	*1993*
8.45% unsecured term loan, due July 1993	—	$25,000
7.90% unsecured term loan, due June 1993	—	25,000
9.43% capital warehouse lease, payable in quarterly installments through 2007	$ 9,098	9,628
Other	7,123	8,390
	$16,221	$68,018
Less: Current maturities	3,857	52,985
TOTAL	$12,364	$15,033

Long-term debt may be secured or unsecured. *Secured debt* provides debtholders with first claim on specified assets. Mortgage bonds are an example of secured debt. If the company is unable to meet its regular obligations on the bonds, the specified assets may be sold and the proceeds used to pay off the firm's obligations to its bondholders, in which case secured debt holders have first claim. Nike's obligation for the capital warehouse lease is like a secured debt. If Nike cannot make the installment payments, the warehouse will be returned to the lessor.

debentures Formal certificates of indebtedness that are accompanied by a promise to pay interest at a specified annual rate.

subordinated A creditor claim that is junior to the other creditors in exercising claims against assets.

liquidation Converting assets to cash and using the cash to pay off outside claims.

Unsecured debt consists of **debentures** (e.g., bonds, notes, or loans) which are formal certificates of indebtedness that are accompanied by a promise to pay interest at a specified annual rate. Unsecured debt holders are general creditors who have a general claim against total assets rather than a specific claim against particular assets. Most of Nike's long-term debt is unsecured. Holders of **subordinated** *bonds* or *debentures* are junior to the other creditors in exercising claims against assets.

The following simplified example should clarify these ideas. Suppose a corporation is liquidated. **Liquidation** means converting assets to cash and using the cash to pay off outside claims. The company had a single asset, a building, that was sold for $120,000 cash:

Assets		Liabilities and Stockholders' Equity	
Cash	$120,000	Accounts payable	$ 60,000
		First-mortgage bonds payable	80,000
		Subordinated debentures payable	40,000
		Total liabilities	$180,000
		Stockholders' equity (negative)	(60,000)
Total assets	$120,000	Total liab. and stk. eq.	$120,000

The mortgage (secured) bondholders would be paid in full ($80,000). Trade creditors such as suppliers would be paid the remaining $40,000 for their $60,000 claim ($.67 on the dollar). Other claimants would get nothing. If the debentures were *unsubordinated*, the $40,000 of cash remaining after paying $80,000 to the mortgage holders would be used to settle the $100,000 claims of the unsecured creditors as follows:

To trade creditors	6/10 × $40,000 =	$24,000
To debenture holders	4/10 × $40,000 =	16,000
Total cash distributed		$40,000

To increase the appeal of their bonds, many corporations issue debt that is *convertible* into common stock. Convertibility allows bondholders to participate in a company's success without the risk of holding common stock. Suppose convertible bonds are issued for $1,000 when the stock price is $22, with a provision that each bond can be converted into 40 common shares. If the stock price increases by 50% to $33 a share, the bondholder could exchange the

$1,000 bond for 40 shares worth 40 × $33 = $1,320. If the stock price falls (or does not increase beyond $25 a share), the bondholder can keep the bond and receive $1,000 at maturity.

Stockholders' Equity

The final element of a balance sheet is *stockholders' equity* (also called *share- holders' equity* or *owners' equity* or *capital* or *net worth*), the total residual inter- est in the business. As noted in Chapter 17, it is the excess of total assets over total liabilities. The main elements of stockholders' equity arise from two sources: (1) contributed or paid-in capital, and (2) retained income.

Paid-in capital typically comes from owners who invest in the business in exchange for stock certificates, which are issued as evidence of stockholder rights. Capital stock can be divided into two major classes: *common stock* and *preferred stock*. Some companies have several categories of each, all with a vari- ety of different attributes.

common stock Stock that has no predeter- mined rate of divi- dends and is the last to obtain a share in the assets when the corporation is dis- solved. It usually has voting power in the management of the corporation.

preferred stock Stock that typically has some priority over other shares regarding dividends or the dis- tribution of assets upon liquidation.

par value (legal value, stated value) The value that is printed on the face of the certificate.

limited liability Creditors cannot seek payment from share- holders as individuals if the corporation itself cannot pay its debts.

All corporations have **common stock.** Such stock has no predetermined rate of dividends and is the last to obtain a share in the assets when the corpo- ration is dissolved. Common shares usually have voting power in the manage- ment of the corporation. Common stock is usually the riskiest investment in a corporation, being unattractive in dire times but attractive in prosperous times because, unlike other stocks, there is no limit to the stockholder's potential par- ticipation in earnings.

Exhibit 18-1 shows that Nike has preferred stock, in addition to common stock. About 40% of the major companies in the United States issue **preferred stock.** It typically has some priority over other shares regarding dividends or the distribution of assets on liquidation. For example, Nike pays an annual pre- ferred stock dividend of $.10 per share, or $30,000 in total. These dividends must be paid in full before any dividends are paid to any other classes of stock. Preferred shareholders in Nike, as in most companies with preferred stock, do not have voting privileges regarding the management of the corporation.

Stock frequently has a designated **par** or **legal** or **stated value** that is print- ed on the face of the certificate. For preferred stock (and bonds), par is a basis for designating the amount of dividends or interest. Many preferred stocks have $100 par values. That is, a 9%, $100-par preferred stock would carry a $9 annu- al dividend. Similarly, an 8% *bond* usually means that the investor is entitled to annual interest of $80 because most bonds have par values of $1,000.

In contrast, par value has no practical importance for common stock. Historically, the par amount of common stock was intended only to measure the maximum legal liability of the stockholder in case the corporation could not pay its debts. (Shareholders typically have **limited liability,** which means that creditors cannot seek payment from them as individuals if the corporation itself cannot pay its debts.) Currently, par is set at a nominal amount (e.g., $1) in rela- tion to the market value of the stock on issuance (e.g., $70). It is generally ille- gal for a corporation to sell an original issue of its common stock below par.

Capital in excess of stated value is the excess received over the stated, par, or legal value of the shares issued. Common shares are almost always issued at a price substantially greater than par. Suppose all outstanding common shares of Nike had been issued for cash. The cumulative balance sheet effect at May 31, 1994, would be:

Cash	$111,147,000	Common stock, at stated value	$ 2,863,000
		Capital in excess of stated value	108,284,000
		Total paid-in capital	$111,147,000

Retained earnings, also called *retained income*, is the increase in stockholders' equity caused by profitable operations (see Chapter 17). Retained earnings is the dominant item of stockholders' equity for most companies. For instance, as of May 31, 1994, Nike had common stockholders' equity of $1,741,249,000 of which $1,644,925,000 was retained income.

The final item in Exhibit 18-1, *foreign currency translation adjustment*, exists only for companies with foreign operations. It arises from changes in the exchange rate between the dollar and foreign currencies. Further details are beyond the scope of this book.

treasury stock A corporation's own stock that has been issued and subsequently repurchased by the company and is being held for a specific purpose.

Many companies have **treasury stock,** which is a corporation's own stock that has been issued and subsequently repurchased by the company and is being held for a specific purpose. Such repurchase is a decrease in ownership claims. It should therefore appear on a balance sheet as a deduction from total stockholders' equity. The stock is not retired; it is only held temporarily "in the treasury" to be distributed later, possibly as a part of an employee stock purchase plan or as an executive bonus or for use in acquiring another company. Cash dividends are not paid on shares held in the treasury, but are distributed only to the outstanding shares (those in the hands of stockholders). Treasury stock is usually of minor significance in the financial picture of a corporation. Nike had no treasury stock in 1994.

■ INCOME STATEMENT

Objective 4

Identify and explain the principal elements in the income statement of a corporation

Most investors are vitally concerned about a company's ability to produce long-run earnings and dividends. In this regard, income statements are more important than balance sheets. Revenue is shown first; this represents the total sales value of products delivered and services rendered to customers. Expenses are then listed and deducted.

Use of Subtotals

An income statement can take one of two major forms: single step or multiple step. A single-step statement merely lists all expenses without drawing subtotals, whereas a multiple-step statement contains one or more subtotals. Subtotals highlight significant relationships. As explained in the preceding chapter, sometimes cost of goods sold is deducted from sales to show gross profit or gross margin. The size of the margin above merchandise costs is an important statistic for many managers and analysts.

Exhibit 18-5 illustrates the two most common subtotals: *gross profit* and *income from operations* (also called *operating income*).

Depreciation expense, selling expenses, and administrative expenses are often grouped as "operating expenses" and deducted from the gross profit to obtain operating income, which is also called *operating profit*. (Of course, cost of goods sold is also an operating expense. Why? Because it is also deducted from sales revenue to obtain "operating income.") In 1994, Nike had a gross profit of $1,488,245,000 and operating income of $514,146,000.

		Year Ended May 31	
Exhibit 18-5		*1994*	*1993*
Revenues		$3,789,668	$3,930,984
Cost of sales		2,301,423	2,386,993
Gross profit		$1,488,245	$1,543,991
Selling and administrative expenses		974,099	922,261
Income from operations		$ 514,146	$ 621,730
Other expense (income)			
Interest expense		$ 15,282	$ 25,739
Miscellaneous expense		8,270	1,475
Total other expense		$ 23,552	$ 27,214
Income before provision for income taxes		$ 490,594	$ 594,516
Provision for income taxes		191,800	229,500
Net income		$ 298,794	$ 365,016
Earnings per share*		$ 3.96	$ 4.74

Exhibit 18-5

Nike, Inc.
Statement of Income
(thousands except
per share data)

*Computation of earnings per share:

	1994	1993
Net income	$298,794,000	$365,016,000
Divided by average common shares outstanding	75,456,000	77,063,000
Earnings per share	$ 3.96	$ 4.74

Operating and Financial Management

Operating income is a popular subtotal because of the often made distinction between operating management and financial management. *Operating management* is mainly concerned with the major day-to-day activities that generate sales revenue. In contrast, *financial management* is mainly concerned with where to get cash and how to use cash for the benefit of the organization. That is, financial management attempts to answer such questions as: How much cash should be held in checking accounts? Should we pay a dividend? Should we borrow or issue common stock? The best managers are superb at both operating management and financial management. However, many managers are better operating managers than financial managers, or vice versa.

Because interest income and expense are usually a result of financial rather than operating decisions, they often appear as separate items after operating income. This approach facilitates comparisons of operating income between years and between companies. Some companies make heavy use of debt, which causes high interest expense, whereas other companies incur little debt and interest expense. Other nonoperating items might include gains or losses from foreign exchange transactions or from disposals of fixed assets.

Income, Earnings, and Profits

Although this book tends to use *income* most often, the terms *income*, *earnings*, and *profits* are often used as synonyms. The income statement is also called the *statement of earnings*, the *statement of profit and loss*, and the *P & L statement*. Most companies still use net *income* on their income statements, but the term "earnings" is becoming increasingly popular because it has a preferable image. Nike's 1994 net income was $298,794,000.

net income The popular "bottom line"—the residual after deducting from revenues all expenses, including income taxes.

The term **net income** is the popular "bottom line"—the residual after deducting *all* expenses including income taxes. The term *net* is seldom used for any subtotals that precede the calculation of *net income*. Instead, the subtotals are called *income*. Thus the appropriate term is *operating income* or *income from operations*, not *net operating income*.

Income taxes are often a prominent expense and are not merely listed with operating expenses. Instead, income taxes are usually deducted as a separate item immediately before net income. This expense is often called "provision for income taxes," as in Exhibit 18-5.

earnings per share Net income divided by the average number of common shares outstanding during the year.

Income statements conclude with disclosure of **earnings per share.** Exhibit 18-5 illustrates this as the net income divided by the average number of common shares outstanding during the year. Nike earned $3.96 per share in 1994.

■ STATEMENT OF RETAINED EARNINGS

statement of retained earnings (statement of retained income) A financial statement that analyzes changes in the retained earnings or retained income account for a given period.

Using the net income figure from the income statement enables accountants to analyze the changes in retained earnings. This analysis is frequently placed in a separate statement, the **statement of retained earnings** (also called **statement of retained income**). As Exhibit 18-6 demonstrates, the major reasons for changes in retained earnings are dividends and net income. Note especially that dividends are *not* expenses; they are not deductions in computing net income, as Chapter 17 explained in more detail on page 657. Nike also reduced retained earnings by repurchasing some of its own common stock. The retained earnings associated with the repurchased shares is deducted because those shares are no longer outstanding.

Dividends, you will recall, are distributions of assets to stockholders that reduce retained income.

Objective 5

Identify and explain elements in the statement of retained earnings

Exhibit 18-6

Nike, Inc.
Statement of Retained Earnings for the Year Ended May 31, 1990 (thousands of dollars)

Retained earnings, May 31, 1993	$1,539,279
Net income (Exhibit 18-5)	298,794
Total	1,838,073
Deduct: dividends on common stock	59,485
dividends on preferred stock	30
repurchase of common stock	133,633
Retained earnings, May 31, 1994	$1,644,925

Summary Problems for Your Review

Problem One

"The book value of plant assets is the amount that would be spent today for their replacement." Do you agree? Explain.

Solution to Problem One

Net book value of the plant assets is the result of deducting accumulated depreciation from original cost. This process does not attempt to capture all the technological and economic events that may affect replacement value. Consequently, there is little likelihood that net book value will approximate replacement cost.

Problem Two

On December 31, 19X1, a magazine publishing company receives $150,000 in cash for 3-year subscriptions. This sum is regarded as unearned revenue. Show the balances in that account at December 31, 19X2, 19X3, and 19X4. How much revenue would be earned in each of those 3 years?

Solution to Problem Two

The balance in unearned revenue would decline at the rate of $50,000 yearly; $50,000 would be recognized as earned revenue in each of the 3 years.

	December 31			
	19X1	*19X2*	*19X3*	*19X4*
Unearned revenue	$150,000	$100,000	$50,000	$ 0

■ STATEMENT OF CASH FLOWS

Many decision makers focus primarily on two financial statements, the income statement and the balance sheet. However, another statement, the *statement of cash flows,* is also required as a basic financial statement. The statement has the following purposes:

1. It shows the relationship of net income to changes in cash balances. Cash balances can decline despite positive net income and vice versa.
2. It reports past cash flows as an aid to
   a. Predicting future cash flows
   b. Evaluating management's generation and use of cash
   c. Determining a company's ability to pay interest and dividends, and to pay debts when they are due
3. It reveals commitments to assets that may restrict or expand future courses of action.

Basic Concepts

statement of cash flows A statement that reports the cash receipts and cash payments of an organization during a particular period.

A **statement of cash flows** reports the cash receipts and cash payments of an organization during a particular period. Note that balance sheets show the status of an entity at a day in time. In contrast, statements of cash flows, income statements, and statements of retained income cover periods. They provide the explanations of why the balance sheet items have changed by providing information about operating, investing, and financing activities. This linkage is depicted in the accompanying diagram:

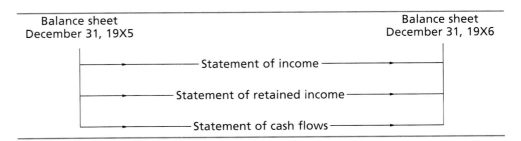

The statement of cash flows explains where cash came from during a period and where it was spent.

One reason for the popularity of cash flow statements is that they show information that readers of financial reports could otherwise obtain only by makeshift analysis and interpretation of published balance sheets and statements of income and retained income.

The statement of cash flows usually explains changes in cash and cash equivalents, both of which can quickly be used to meet obligations. *Cash equivalents*, as noted earlier in this chapter, are highly liquid short-term investments that can easily be converted into cash with little delay. Hereafter, when we refer to cash, we mean both cash and cash equivalents.

Typical Activities Affecting Cash

Objective 6

Identify activities that affect cash, and classify them as operating, investing, or financing activities

The fundamental approach to the statement of cash flows is simple: (1) list the activities that increased cash (i.e., cash inflows) and those that decreased cash (cash outflows), and (2) place each cash inflow and outflow into one of three categories according to the type of activity that caused it: *operating activities*, *investing activities*, and *financing activities*.

The following activities are those found most often in statements of cash flows:

Operating Activities

Cash Inflows	*Cash Outflows*
Collections from customers	Cash payments to suppliers
Interest and dividends collected	Cash payments to employees
Other operating receipts	Interest paid
	Taxes paid
	Other operating cash payments

Investing Activities

Cash Inflows	Cash Outflows
Sale of property, plant, and equipment	Purchase of property, plant, and equipment
Sale of securities that are not cash equivalents	Purchase of securities that are not cash equivalents
Receipt of loan repayments	Making loans

Financing Activities

Cash Inflows	Cash Outflows
Borrowing cash from creditors	Repayment of amounts borrowed
Issuing equity securities	Repurchase of equity shares (including the purchase of treasury stock)
	Payment of dividends

As the lists of activities indicate, cash flows from operating activities are generally the effects of transactions that affect the income statement (e.g., sales and wages). Investing activities include (1) lending and collecting on loans and (2) acquiring and selling long-term assets. Financing activities include obtaining resources from creditors and owners and providing them with returns *of* their investments and owners with returns *on* their investments in the form of cash dividends.

Perhaps the most troublesome classifications are the receipts and payments of interest and the receipts of dividends. After all, these items are associated with investment and financing activities. After much debate, the FASB decided to include these items with cash flows from operating activities. Why? Mainly because they affect the computation of income. In contrast, payments of cash dividends are financing activities because they do not affect income.

Focus of a Statement of Cash Flows

The basic ideas underlying the statement of cash flows are straightforward. Consider the illustration of the hypothetical Balmer Company. Exhibit 18-7 shows the company's condensed balance sheets and income statement. (We will look at the more complex, real statement for Nike at the end of this chapter.)

Because the statement of cash flows explains the *causes* for the change in cash, the first step is to compute the amount of the change (which represents the net *effect*):

Cash, December 31, 19X1	$25,000
Cash, December 31, 19X2	16,000
Net decrease in cash	$ 9,000

Exhibit 18-8 illustrates how this information is often shown at the bottom of a statement of cash flows. The beginning cash balance is added to the net change to compute the ending cash balance. Another common practice is to place the beginning cash balance at the top of the statement and the ending cash balance at the bottom. However, there is no requirement that beginning and ending cash balances be shown explicitly in the statement of cash flows. Showing only the net change is sufficient.

Exhibit 18-7		
Balmer Company Statement of Income for the Year Ended December 31, 19X2 (in thousands)	Sales		$200
	Costs and expenses		
	Cost of goods sold	$100	
	Wages and salaries	36	
	Depreciation	17	
	Interest	4	
	Total costs and expenses		157
	Income before income taxes		43
	Income taxes		20
	Net income		$ 23

Balmer Company
Balance Sheet as of December 31 (in thousands)

Assets				**Liabilities and Stockholders' Equity**			
	19X2	*19X1*	*Increase (Decrease)*		*19X2*	*19X1*	*Increase (Decrease)*
Current assets				Current liabilities			
Cash	$ 16	$ 25	$ (9)	Accounts payable	$ 74	$ 6	$ 68
Accounts receivable	45	25	20	Wages and salaries			
Inventory	100	60	40	payable	25	4	21
Total current assets	161	110	51	Total current liabilities	99	10	89
Fixed assets, gross	581	330	251	Long-term debt	125	5	120
Less accum. depreciation	(101)	(110)	9	Stockholders' equity	417	315	102
Net fixed assets	480	220	260	Total liabilities and			
Total assets	$641	$330	$311	stockholders' equity	$641	$330	$311

When business expansion occurs, as in this case, and where there is a strong cash position at the outset, cash often declines. Why? Because cash is usually needed for investment in various business assets required for expansion, including investment in accounts receivable and inventories.

The statement in Exhibit 18-8 gives a direct picture of where cash came from and where it went. In this instance, the excess of cash outflows over cash inflows reduced cash by $9,000. Without the statement of cash flows, the readers of the annual report would have to conduct their own analyses of the beginning and ending balance sheets, the income statement, and the statement of retained income to get a grasp of the impact of financial management decisions.

Most important, this illustration demonstrates how a firm may simultaneously (1) have a significant amount of net income, as computed by accountants on the accrual basis, and yet (2) have a decline in cash that could become severe. Indeed, many growing businesses are desperate for cash even though reported net income zooms upward.

Exhibit 18-8

Balmer Company
Statement of
Cash Flows
for the Year Ended
December 31, 19X2
(in thousands)

Cash Flows from Operating Activities

Cash collections from customers		$180
Cash payments		
To suppliers	$ 72	
To employees	15	
For interest	4	
For taxes	20	
Total cash payments		(111)
Net cash provided by operating activities		$ 69

Cash Flows from Investing Activities

Purchases of fixed assets	$(287)	
Proceeds from sale of fixed assets	10	
Net cash used in investing activities		(277)

Cash Flows from Financing Activities

Proceeds from issue of long-term debt	$120	
Proceeds from issue of common stock	98	
Dividends paid	(19)	
Net cash provided by financing activities		199
Net decrease in cash		$ (9)
Cash, December 31, 19X1		25
Cash, December 31, 19X2		$ 16

◼ PREPARATION OF A STATEMENT OF CASH FLOWS: THE DIRECT METHOD

Now that you know why statements of cash flow are important, we can consider the preparation of such statements. The first major section in the statement of cash flows in Exhibit 18-8 is **cash flows from operating activities.** The section might also be called *cash flow from operations*, *cash provided by operations*, or, if operating activities decrease cash, *cash used for operations*.

cash flows from operating activities The first major section in the statement of cash flows.

Collections from sales to customers are almost always the major operating activity that increases cash. Correspondingly, disbursements for purchases of goods to be sold and operating expenses are almost always the major operating cash outflows. The excess of collections over disbursements is the net cash provided by operating activities. There are two ways to compute this amount: the *direct method* and the *indirect method*.

Because it is easier to understand, the FASB favors the *direct method*. It is used in Exhibit 18-8: collections minus operating disbursements equals net cash provided by operating activities—$180,000 – $111,000 = $69,000. The *indirect method* is explained later in this chapter.

The second and third major sections of the statement present examples of cash flows from investing activities ($277,000 outflow) and financing activities ($199,000 inflow), respectively.

Working from Income Statement Amounts to Cash Amounts

Objective 7

Prepare the statement of cash flows using the direct method

Many accountants build the statement of cash flows from the *changes* in balance sheet items, a few additional facts, and their familiarity with the typical causes of changes in cash. For instance, for convenience we used $180,000 as the amount of cash collections from Balmer Company customers for 19X2. However, most accounting systems do not provide such a balance. Therefore accountants often compute the collections by beginning with the sales in the income statement (an amount calculated using the accrual basis) and adding (or deducting) the *change* in the accounts receivable balance. A detailed analysis of collections and other operating items follows.

a. Balmer Company recognized $200,000 of revenue in 19X2, but because accounts receivable increased by $20,000, Balmer collected only $180,000 from customers:

Sales	$200,000
+ Beginning accounts receivable	25,000
Potential collections	$225,000
− Ending accounts receivable	45,000
Cash collections from customers	$180,000

Instead of adding the beginning accounts receivable balance and then deducting the ending accounts receivable, we could add the decrease in accounts receivable (or deduct the increase):

Sales	$200,000
Decrease (increase) in accounts receivable	(20,000)
Cash collections from customers	$180,000

b. The difference between the $100,000 cost of goods sold and the $72,000 cash payment to suppliers is accounted for by changes in inventory *and* accounts payable. The $40,000 increase in inventory indicates that purchases exceeded the cost of goods sold by $40,000:

Ending inventory	$100,000
+ Cost of goods sold	100,000
Inventory to account for	$200,000
− Beginning inventory	(60,000)
Purchases of inventory	$140,000

Although purchases were $140,000, payments to suppliers were only $72,000. Why? Because trade accounts payable increased by $68,000, from $6,000 to $74,000:

Beginning trade accounts payable	$ 6,000
+ Purchases	140,000
Total amount to be paid	$146,000
− Ending trade accounts payable	(74,000)
Accounts paid in cash	$ 72,000

The effects of inventory and trade accounts payable can be combined as follows:

Cost of goods sold	$100,000
Increase (decrease) in inventory	40,000
Decrease (increase) in trade accounts payable	(68,000)
Payments to suppliers	$ 72,000

c. Cash payments to employees were only $15,000 because the wages and salaries expense of $36,000 was offset by a $21,000 increase in wages and salaries payable:

Beginning wages and salaries payable	$ 4,000
+ Wages and salaries expense	36,000
Total to be paid	$40,000
− Ending wages and salaries payable	(25,000)
Cash payments to employees	$15,000

or

Wages and salaries expense	$36,000
Decrease (increase) in wages and salaries payable	(21,000)
Cash payments to employees	$15,000

d. Note that both interest payable and income taxes payable were zero at the beginning and at the end of 19X2. Therefore the entire $4,000 interest expense and the $20,000 income tax expense were paid in cash in 19X2.

Exhibit 18-9 summarizes the differences between Balmer Company's net income of $23,000 and net cash provided by operating activities of $69,000 in 19X2. Examine Exhibit 18-8 and confirm that the $69,000 cash inflow from operating activities is shown in the first section of the statement of cash flows.

Investing and Financing Cash Flows

If the necessary information regarding investing and financing cash flows is not directly available, accountants analyze *changes* in all balance sheet items *except* cash. The following rules pertain:

- *Increases in cash (cash inflows)* are from:
  Increases in liabilities or stockholders' equity
  Decreases in noncash assets

Exhibit 18-9

Comparison of Net Income and Net Cash Provided by Operating Activities

	Income Statement	Adjustments	Cash Flows Statement
Sales	$200,000		
Increase in accounts receivable		$ (20,000)	
Cash collections from customers			$180,000
Cost of goods sold	(100,000)		
Increase in inventory		(40,000)	
Increase in accounts payable		68,000	
Cash payments to suppliers			(72,000)
Wages and salaries expense	(36,000)		
Increase in wages and salaries payable		21,000	
Cash paid to employees			(15,000)
Interest: expense equals cash flow	(4,000)		(4,000)
Income taxes: expense equals cash flow	(20,000)		(20,000)
Depreciation: deducted in computing net income but not a cash outflow	(17,000)	17,000	
Net income	$ 23,000		
Total additions (deductions)		$ 46,000	
Net cash provided by operating activities			$ 69,000

- *Decreases in cash (cash outflows)* are from:
  Decreases in liabilities or stockholders' equity
  Increases in noncash assets

Consider Balmer Company's balance sheet (Exhibit 18-7, p. 701). All noncash *current* assets and *current* liabilities of Balmer Company were affected only by operating activities, which we just discussed. Now let's look at three *noncurrent* accounts: fixed assets, long-term debt, and stockholders' equity.

a. Fixed assets increased by $260,000 in 19X2. Three items usually explain changes in net fixed assets: (1) asset acquisitions, (2) asset dispositions, and (3) depreciation expense for the period. Therefore:

   increase in net plant assets = acquisitions – disposals – depreciation expense

   If we had no information about Balmer Company's asset disposals, we could compute the book value of disposals from the above equation and get:

$$\$260,000 = \$287,000 - \text{disposals} - \$17,000$$
$$\text{disposals} = \$287,000 - \$17,000 - \$260,000$$
$$\text{disposals} = \$10,000$$

   Balmer Company received exactly the book value for the assets sold. (We discuss disposals for other than book value later in this chapter.) If we know the amount of disposals, but either acquisitions or depreciation expense were unknown, we could determine the missing item by applying this same equation. Both asset acquisitions and asset disposals are *investing activities* that affect cash.

b. Long-term debt increased by $125,000 – $5,000 = $120,000. Long-term debt was issued, which is a *financing activity* that increased cash.

c. The $102,000 increase in stockholders' equity can be explained by three factors: (1) issuance (or repurchase) of capital stock, (2) net income (or loss), and (3) dividends. Therefore:

increase in stockholders' equity = new issuance + net income – dividends

Suppose data about the issuance of new capital stock has not been provided:

$$\$102{,}000 = \text{new issuance} + \$23{,}000 - \$19{,}000$$
$$\text{new issuance} = \$102{,}000 - \$23{,}000 + \$19{,}000$$
$$\text{new issuance} = \$98{,}000, \text{ an inflow of cash}$$

Both the issuance of new shares and the payment of cash dividends are *financing activities* that affect cash.

Reexamine Exhibit 18-8, page 702. The asset acquisitions and disposals from paragraph **a** are listed with cash flows from investing activities, and the effects of debt and equity issues and dividend payments from paragraphs **b** and **c** are shown with cash flows from financing activities.

Noncash Investing and Financing Activities

Major investment and financing activities that do not affect cash must be reported in a schedule that accompanies the statement of cash flows. For example, consider the acquisition of a $120,000 warehouse in exchange for the issuance of capital stock. The transaction would not be included in the body of the statement of cash flows. Why? Because cash was unaffected. But the transaction is almost identical to one in which capital stock is issued for cash of $120,000, which is immediately used to purchase the warehouse. Therefore such a transaction should be disclosed to readers of a statement of cash flows. Disclosure is made in a schedule that follows directly after the statement. Balmer Company did not have such a transaction in 19X2.

Cash Flow and Earnings

cash flow Usually refers to the net cash flow from operating activities.

A focal point of the statement of cash flows is the net cash flow from operating activities. Frequently, this is called simply **cash flow.** The importance of cash flow has been stressed by Harold Williams, the former chairman of the SEC, quoted in *Forbes*: "If I had to make a forced choice between having earnings information and having cash flow information, today I would take cash flow information." Fortunately, we do not have to make a choice. Cash flow and income both convey useful information about an entity.

Some companies used to stress a cash-flow-per-share figure and provide it in addition to the required earnings-per-share figure. But cash-flow-per-share ignores noncash expenses that are just as important as cash expenses for judging overall company performance. Moreover, a reported cash-flow-per-share says nothing about the cash needed for replacement and expansion of facilities. Thus the entire per-share cash flow from operations may not be available for cash dividends. Because it gives an incomplete picture, a cash-flow-per-share figure can be quite misleading. Accordingly, the FASB has specifically prohibited the reporting of cash-flow-per-share amounts.

Both cash flow and accrual earnings data are useful. As Professor Loyd Heath said, "Asking which one is better, cash flow or earnings, is like asking which shoe is more useful, your right or your left."

■ PREPARATION OF A STATEMENT OF CASH FLOWS: THE INDIRECT METHOD

indirect method In a statement of cash flows, the method that reconciles net income to the net cash provided by operating activites.

Instead of using the direct method of preparing statements of cash flows, accountants often find it convenient to compute cash flows from operating activities by the **indirect method.** The indirect method reconciles net income to the net cash provided by operating activities. It also shows the link between the income statement and the statement of cash flows.

Reconciliation of Net Income to Net Cash Provided by Operations

Objective 8

Prepare a reconciliation of net income to net cash provided by operations

The reconciliation begins with net income. Accountants then make additions or deductions for items that affect net income and net cash flow differently. Using the numbers in our Balmer Company example, Exhibit 18-10 shows the reconciliation. Net cash provided by operating activities exceeds net income by $46,000.

Exhibit 18-10

Supporting Schedule to Statement of Cash Flows Reconciliation of Net Income to Net Cash Provided by Operating Activities (in thousands)

Net income		$23
Adjustments to reconcile net income		
to net cash provided by operating activities		
Depreciation	$17	
Net increase in accounts receivable	(20)	
Net increase in inventory	(40)	
Net increase in accounts payable	68	
Net increase in wages and salaries payable	21	
Total additions and deductions		46
Net cash provided by operating activities		$69

Consider the logic applied in the reconciliation in Exhibit 18-10:

1. Depreciation is added back to net income because it was deducted in the computation of net income. If the purpose is to calculate cash provided by operations, the depreciation of $17,000 should not have been subtracted. Why? Because it was not a cash expense this period. Since it *was* subtracted, it must now be added back to income to get cash from operations. The addback simply cancels the earlier deduction.

2. Increases in noncash current assets such as receivables and inventory result in less cash flow from operations. For instance, suppose the $20,000 increase in receivables resulted from credit sales made near the end of the year. The $20,000 sales figure would be included in the computation of net income, but the $20,000 would not have increased cash flow from operations. Therefore the reconciliation deducts the $20,000 from the net income to help pinpoint the effects on cash.

3. Increases in current liabilities such as accounts payable and wages payable result in more cash flow from operations. For instance, suppose the $21,000 increase in wages payable was attributable to wages earned near the end of the year, but not yet paid in cash. The $21,000 wages expense would be deducted in computing net income, but the $21,000 would not have decreased cash flow from operations. Therefore the reconciliation adds the $21,000 to net income to offset the deduction and thereby shows the effect on cash.

The reconciliation's most common additions or deductions from net income are:

- Add decreases (or deduct increases) in accounts receivable
- Add decreases (or deduct increases) in inventories
- Add increases (or deduct decreases) in accounts payable
- Add increases (or deduct decreases) in wages and salaries payable
- Add increases (or deduct decreases) in unearned revenue

The general rules for reconciling for these items are:

- Deduct increases in noncash current assets
- Add decreases in noncash current assets
- Add increases in current liabilities
- Deduct decreases in current liabilities

A final step is to reconcile for amounts that are included in net income but represent investing or financing activities (in contrast to operating activities). Examples include:

- Add loss (or deduct gain) from sale of fixed assets
- Add loss (or deduct gain) on extinguishment of debt

In our earlier example, Balmer Company had no losses or gains that were a result of investing or financing activities. However, suppose Balmer Company sold another asset for $12,000 cash. The asset had a book value of $8,000, so a gain of $4,000 would be part of pretax income:

Proceeds from sale of fixed asset	$12,000
Book value of asset sold	8,000
Gain on sale of asset	$ 4,000

For simplicity, assume that this sale did not affect income taxes. Therefore Balmer Company's net income would be $23,000 (from Exhibit 18-7, p. 701) *plus* the gain of $4,000, or a total of $27,000.

The sale of the asset is an investing activity, so the entire cash inflow should be listed under investing activities in the statement of cash flows:

Proceeds from sale of fixed asset	$12,000

The section "cash flows from operating activities" should not be affected by this sale. But net income includes the $4,000 gain. In a reconciliation schedule that begins with net income (as in Exhibit 18-10), the gain must be subtracted:

Net income ($23,000 from Exhibit 18-8 plus $4,000 gain)	$27,000
Plus adjustments in Exhibit 18-10	46,000
Less gain on disposal of fixed assets	(4,000)
Net cash provided by operating activities	$69,000

Note that the sale of the asset affected net income because of the gain, but it did not affect net cash provided by operating activities.

Reconciliation Schedule under Direct and Indirect Methods

The FASB requires all preparers of a statement of cash flows to use either the direct or the indirect method. Furthermore, the reconciliation schedule must be included in some fashion under either the direct or the indirect method:

- *Direct Method* (favored by FASB)
    Exhibit 18-8 as the body. Include Exhibit 18-10 as a supporting schedule.
- *Indirect Method* (permitted by FASB)
    Alternative Format 1:
        Exhibit 18-8 as the body. However, replace the first section with a one-line item, net cash provided by operating activities. Include Exhibit 18-10 as a supporting schedule.
    Alternative Format 2:
        Exhibit 18-8, except use Exhibit 18-10 in the body as the first section, cash flows from operating activities. Exhibit 18-11 (p. 710) illustrates this widely used method.

Role of Depreciation

Objective 9

Explain the role of depreciation in the statement of cash flows

The most crucial aspect of a statement of cash flows is how depreciation and other expenses that do not require cash relate to the flow of cash. There is widespread misunderstanding of the role of depreciation in financial reporting, so let us examine this point in detail.

Accountants view depreciation as an allocation of historical cost to expense. Therefore, depreciation expense does not entail a current outflow of cash. Consider again the comparison of Balmer Company's net income and cash flows on page 705. Why is the $17,000 of depreciation added to net income to compute cash flow? Simply to cancel its deduction in calculating net income. Unfortunately, use of the indirect method may at first glance create an erroneous impression that depreciation is added because it, by itself, is a source of cash. If that were really true, a corporation could merely double or triple its bookkeeping entry for depreciation expense when cash was badly needed! What would happen? Income would decline, but cash provided by operations would be unaffected. Suppose depreciation for Balmer Company were doubled:

	With Depreciation of $17,000	With Depreciation of $34,000
Sales	$200,000	$200,000
All expenses except depreciation (including income taxes)*	(160,000)	(160,000)
Depreciation	(17,000)	(34,000)
Net income	$ 23,000	$ 6,000
Nondepreciation adjustments†	29,000	29,000
Add depreciation	17,000	34,000
Net cash provided by operating activities	$ 69,000	$ 69,000

*$100,000 + $36,000 + $4,000 + $20,000 = $160,000
†$(20,000) + $(40,000) + $68,000 + $21,000 = $29,000

The doubling would affect depreciation and net income, but have no direct influence on cash provided by operations, which would still amount to $69,000.

Statement of Cash Flows for Nike, Inc.

Exhibit 18-11 contains the 1994 statement of cash flows for Nike, Inc. Other publicly held corporations may include more details, but the general format of the statement of cash flows is similar to that shown. Note that Nike uses the indirect method in the body of the statement of cash flows to report the cash flows from operating activities. Most companies use this format.

Exhibit 18-11	
Nike, Inc. **Statement of Cash Flows for the Year Ended May 31, 1994** **(thousands)**	

Cash provided (used) by operations	
Net income	$298,794
Income charges (credits) not affecting cash	
Depreciation	64,531
Deferred income taxes	(23,876)
Other, including amortization	4,479
Changes in certain working capital components	
Decrease in inventory	160,823
Decrease in accounts receivable	23,979
Decrease in other current assets	6,888
Increase in accounts payable, accrued liabilities, and income taxes payable	40,845
Cash provided by operations	576,463
Cash provided (used) by investing activities	
Additions to property, plant, and equipment	(95,266)
Disposals of property, plant, and equipment	12,650
Acquisition of subsidiaries	(3,552)
Additions to other assets	(5,450)
Cash used by investing activities	(91,618)
Cash provided (used) by financing activities	
Additions to long-term debt	6,044
Reductions in long-term debt including current portion	(56,986)
Decrease in notes payable	(2,939)
Proceeds from exercise of options	4,288
Repurchase of stock	(140,104)
Dividends—common and preferred	(60,282)
Cash used by financing activities	(249,979)
Effect of exchange rate changes on cash	(7,334)
Net increase in cash and equivalents	227,532
Cash and equivalents, beginning of year	291,284
Cash and equivalents, end of year	$518,816

Most of the items in Exhibit 18-11 have been discussed earlier in the chapter, but three deserve mention here. First, deferred income taxes are added back to net income. These taxes are charged as expense but are not currently payable. Therefore they are a noncash expense, similar to depreciation. Second, proceeds from the exercise of options are *cash received* from issuance of shares to executives as part of a stock option compensation plan. Third, the effect of changes in the exchange rate on cash shows the impact of changes in the relative prices of foreign currencies on multinational operations. It is beyond the scope of this text.

You might also notice that changes in account balances cannot be computed directly from the balance sheets in Exhibit 18-1. This is a result of factors beyond the scope of this text, primarily the incorporation of the accounts of companies acquired by Nike during fiscal 1994.

Highlights to Remember

This chapter explains the meanings of the account titles most often found in the major financial statements. In the balance sheet, assets and liabilities are divided into current and noncurrent items. Stockholders' equity is the residual interest in the business, part arising from paid-in capital and part from retained income. The income statement summarizes performance over a period including operating and financial management.

Statements of cash flows report the cash receipts and cash payments during a period, classified according to the activities that caused the cash flow. Operating activities are the major source of cash inflows for most companies. The largest inflow usually is collections from customers. The largest outflows are generally for purchases of goods to be sold and operating expenses. Investment activities usually create a net cash outflow. These activities include purchases and disposals of land and equipment and long-term investments in other companies. Financing activities are often an important source of cash. Increases in debt and issuance of equity securities for cash provide cash inflows. Retirement of debt or equity and payment of dividends are cash outflows.

The FASB favors use of the direct method for the statement of cash flows, but the indirect method is also acceptable. Whichever form is used, a reconciliation of net income to net cash provided by operations must be included. It is especially important to understand the relationship of depreciation to cash. Depreciation is added back to net income when reconciling net income and net cash provided by operations because depreciation is a noncash expense—*not* because depreciation is a source of cash.

Summary Problem for Your Review

Problems One and Two appeared earlier in the chapter.

Problem Three

The Buretta Company has prepared the data in Exhibit 18-12. In December 19X1, Buretta paid $54 million cash for a new building acquired to accommodate an expansion of operations. This was financed partly by a new issue of long-term debt for $40 million cash. During 19X1 the company also sold fixed assets for $5 million cash which was equal to their book value. All sales and purchases of merchandise were on credit.

Because the net income of $4 million was the highest in the company's history, Mr. Buretta, the chairman of the board, was perplexed by the company's extremely low cash balance.

Required 1. Prepare a statement of cash flows. Ignore income taxes. You may wish to use Exhibit 18-8, page 702, as a guide. Use the direct method for reporting cash flows from operating activities.

2. Prepare a supporting schedule that reconciles net income to net cash provided by operating activities.
3. What is revealed by the statement of cash flows? Does it help you reduce Mr. Buretta's puzzlement? Why?

Exhibit 18-12				
Buretta Co.	Sales			$100
Income Statement	Less cost of goods sold			
and Statement of	Inventory, December 31, 19X0	$ 15		
Retained Earnings	Purchases	104		
for the Year Ended	Cost of goods available for sale	$119		
December 31, 19X1	Inventory, December 31, 19X1	46	73	
(millions)	Gross profit		$ 27	
	Less other expenses			
	General expenses	$ 8		
	Depreciation	8		
	Property taxes	4		
	Interest expense	3	23	
	Net income		$ 4	
	Retained earnings, December 31, 19X0		7	
	Total		$ 11	
	Dividends		1	
	Retained earnings, December 31, 19X1		$ 10	

Balance Sheets as of December 31 (millions)

Assets	19X1	19X0	Increase (Decrease)
Cash	$ 1	$20	$(19)
Accounts receivable	20	5	15
Inventory	46	15	31
Prepaid general expenses	4	2	2
Fixed assets, net	91	50	41
	$162	$92	$ 70

Equities	19X1	19X0	Increase (Decrease)
Accounts payable for merchandise	$ 39	$14	$ 25
Accrued property tax payable	3	1	2
Long-term debt	40	—	40
Capital stock	70	70	—
Retained earnings	10	7	3
	$162	$92	$ 70

Solution to Problem Three

1. See Exhibit 18-13. Cash flows from operating activities were computed as follows (in millions):

Sales	$100
Less increase in accounts receivable	(15)
Cash collections from customers	$ 85
Cost of goods sold	$ 73
Plus increase in inventory	31
Purchases	$104
Less increase in accounts payable	(25)
Cash paid to suppliers	$ 79
General expenses	$ 8
Plus increase in prepaid general expenses	2
Cash payment for general expenses	$ 10
Property taxes	$ 4
Less increase in accrued property tax payable	(2)
Cash paid for property taxes	$ 2
Cash paid for interest	$ 3

Exhibit 18-13

Buretta Company
Statement of
Cash Flows
for the Year Ended
December 31, 19X1
(in millions)

Cash Flows from Operating Activities		
Cash collections from customers		$85
Cash payments		
Cash paid to suppliers	$(79)	
General expenses	(10)	
Interest paid	(3)	
Property taxes	(2)	(94)
Net cash used by operating activities		$ (9)
Cash Flows from Investing Activities		
Purchase of fixed assets (building)	$(54)	
Proceeds from sale of fixed assets	5	
Net cash used by investing activities		(49)
Cash Flows from Financing Activities		
Long-term debt issued	$40	
Dividends paid	(1)	
Net cash provided by financing activities		39
Net decrease in cash		$(19)
Cash balance, December 31, 19X1		20
Cash balance, December 31, 19X2		$ 1

2. Exhibit 18-14 reconciles net income to net cash provided by operating activities.

3. The statement of cash flows shows where cash has come from and where it has gone. Operations used $9 million of cash. Why? Exhibit 18-14 shows that large increases in accounts receivable ($15 million) and inventory ($31 million), plus a $2 million increase in prepaid expenses, used $48 million of cash. In contrast, only $39 million (that is, $4 + $8 + $25 + $2 million) was generated. Exhibit 18-13 explains the $9 million use of cash slightly differently; the $85 million of cash receipts and $94 million in disbursements are shown directly. Investing activities also consumed cash because $54 million was invested in a building, and only $5 million was received

from sales of fixed assets. Financing activities generated $39 million cash, which was $19 million less than the $58 million used by operating and investing activities.

Exhibit 18-14	
Buretta Company Reconciliation of Net Income to Net Cash Provided by Operating Activities for the Year Ended December 31, 19X1 (Millions)	

Supporting Schedule to Statement of Cash Flows	
Net income (from income statement)	$ 4
Adjustments to reconcile net income to net cash provided by operating activities	
Add: depreciation, which was deducted in the computation of net income but does not decrease cash	8
Deduct: increase in accounts receivable	(15)
Deduct: increase in inventory	(31)
Deduct: increase in prepaid general expenses	(2)
Add: increase in accounts payable	25
Add: increase in accrued property tax payable	2
Net cash provided by operating activities	$ (9)

Mr. Buretta should no longer be puzzled. The statement of cash flows shows clearly that cash payments exceeded receipts by $19 million. However, he may still be concerned about the depletion of cash. Either operations must be changed so that they do not require so much cash, or investment must be curtailed, or more long-term debt or ownership equity must be raised. Otherwise Buretta Company will soon run out of cash.

Appendix 18: Shareholder Reporting, Income Tax Reporting, and Deferred Taxes

In the United States, reports to stockholders must abide by "generally accepted accounting principles (GAAP)." In contrast, reports to income tax authorities must abide by the income tax rules and regulations. These rules comply with GAAP in many respects, but they frequently diverge. Therefore there is nothing immoral or unethical about "keeping two sets of records." In fact, it is necessary.

Keep in mind that the income tax laws are patchworks that often are designed to give taxpayers special incentives for making investments. For example, tax authorities in some countries have permitted taxpayers to write off the full cost of new equipment as expense in the year acquired. Although such a total write-off may be permitted for income tax purposes, it is not permitted for shareholder reporting purposes.

Major differences between U.S. GAAP and the U.S. tax laws are found in accounting for amortization and depreciation. For example, consider how the accounting for perpetual franchises, trademarks, and goodwill differs. Their acquisition costs must be amortized for shareholder reporting. However, the IRS will not allow amortization because such assets have indefinite useful lives. Tax reporting and shareholder reporting are *required* to differ.

Depreciation causes the largest differences between tax and shareholder reporting in the United States. Most companies use straight-line depreciation for reporting to shareholders. Why? Managers believe that it best matches expenses with revenues. But companies use accelerated depreciation for tax reporting because it postpones (or defers) tax payments. Congress provided this deferral opportunity to motivate companies to increase their investment.

For reporting to shareholders, accountants must match income tax expense with the revenues and expenses that cause the taxes. When revenues and expenses on the statement to tax authorities differ from the revenues and expenses on the shareholders' report, deferred taxes can arise. Most often deferred taxes arise when tax expenses exceed book expenses. The result is a deferred tax *liability*.

		19X0	19X1	Total
Exhibit 18-15				
Illustration of Deferred Taxes	**Income statement for tax purposes**			
	Revenue	$100,000	$100,000	$200,000
	Expenses, except depreciation	80,000	80,000	160,000
	Depreciation	20,000	0	20,000
	Operating income (or taxable income)	$ 0	$ 20,000	$ 20,000
	Taxes payable @ 40%	0	8,000	8,000
	Net income	$ 0	$ 12,000	$ 12,000
	Income statement for shareholder reporting			
	Revenue	$100,000	$100,000	$200,000
	Expenses, except depreciation	80,000	80,000	160,000
	Depreciation	10,000	10,000	20,000
	Operating income	$ 10,000	$ 10,000	$ 20,000
	Less income taxes			
	Paid or payable almost immediately	0	8,000	8,000
	Deferred	4,000	(4,000)	0
	Net income	$ 6,000	$ 6,000	$ 12,000

	December 31	
	19X0	19X1
Balance sheet effect		
Liability: Deferred income taxes	$4,000	$0

Consider a simple example. The total depreciation on a company's only asset over a 2-year period, 19X0–19X1, was $20,000. Revenue was $100,000 each year, expenses (other than depreciation) were $80,000, and the combined federal and state income tax rate was 40%. For tax purposes, the entire $20,000 of depreciation was charged as an expense in 19X0; for shareholder reporting, $10,000 was charged each year. Such differences in timing of expenses are completely legitimate.

Exhibit 18-15 illustrates tax deferral. Total operating income over the two years was $20,000, and total taxes were $8,000. According to U.S. tax law, all $20,000 of operating income and $8,000 of taxes applied to 19X1. In contrast, for financial reporting, half of the operating income was recognized each year, so half of the taxes should be recognized each year. Although $4,000 of taxes was related to 19X0 revenues and expenses, the *payment* was postponed (*deferred*) to 19X1. A $4,000 *expense* for deferred taxes was included on the 19X0 financial reporting income statement, and the obligation for future payment of the tax became a liability on the balance sheet. In 19X1 $4,000 of tax *expense* was again related to the revenues and expenses of the period. However, the tax *payment* was $8,000. The payment covers the $4,000 expense for 19X1 and pays off the $4,000 of taxes deferred from 19X0.

Accounting Vocabulary

cash equivalents, *p. 686*
cash flow, *p. 706*
cash flows from operating
   activities, *p. 702*
common stock, *p. 694*
current assets, *p. 686*
current liabilities, *p. 692*
debentures, *p. 693*
earnings per share, *p. 697*
fixed assets, *p. 688*
goodwill, *p. 691*

indirect method, *p. 707*
intangible assets, *p. 691*
legal value, *p. 694*
limited liability, *p. 694*
liquidation, *p. 693*
long-term liabilities, *p. 692*
net income, *p. 697*
noncurrent liabilities, *p. 692*
operating cycle, *p. 686*
par value, *p. 694*
preferred stock, *p. 694*

stated value, *p. 694*
statement of cash flows, *p. 699*
statement of retained earnings,
   p. 697
statement of retained income,
   p. 697
subordinated, *p. 693*
tangible assets, *p. 688*
treasury stock, *p. 695*

Fundamental Assignment Material

*General
Exercises
and Problems*

18-A1 Balance Sheet and Income Statement
The Storski Company had the following items on its December 31, 19X0, balance sheet and 19X0 income statement (in dollars except for number of shares outstanding):

Cash and equivalents	$ 39,000
Notes payable	40,000
Revenues	800,000
Long-term debt, excluding current portion	210,000
Accounts receivable, net	63,000
Provision for income taxes	55,000
Other long-term assets	110,000
Interest expense	55,000
Deferred income tax liability	44,000
Retained earnings	202,000
Income taxes payable	37,000
Cost of sales	460,000
Inventories	31,000
Prepaid expenses	15,000
Common stock (50,000 shares outstanding)	25,000
Property, plant, and equipment, at cost	580,000
Accounts payable	49,000
Interest income	20,000
Goodwill, patents, and trademarks	75,000
Current portion of long-term debt	15,000
Less: accumulated depreciation	170,000
Selling and administrative expenses	150,000
Additional paid-in capital	?

Prepare in proper form the December 31, 19X0, balance sheet and the 19X0 income statement for Storski Company. Include the proper amount for *additional paid-in capital*.

18-A2 Prepare a Statement of Cash Flows, Direct Method
The Outdoor Comfort Clothing Stores chain had a cash balance on December 31, 19X5, of $48 thousand. Its net income for 19X6 was $464 thousand. Its 19X6 transactions affecting income or cash were (in thousands):

1. Sales of $1,700, all on credit. Cash collections from customers, $1,450.
2. The cost of items sold, $850. Purchases of inventory totaled $900; inventory and accounts payable were affected accordingly.
3. Cash payments on trade accounts payable, $775.
4. Salaries and wages: accrued, $190; paid in cash, $200.
5. Depreciation, $45.
6. Interest expense, all paid in cash, $11.
7. Other expenses, all paid in cash, $100.
8. Income taxes accrued, $40; income taxes paid in cash, $35.
9. Bought plant and facilities for $435 cash.
10. Issued debt for $120 cash.
11. Paid cash dividends of $39.

Prepare a statement of cash flows using the direct method for reporting cash flows from operating activities. Omit supporting schedules.

18-A3 Reconciliation of Net Income and Net Cash Provided by Operating Activities
Refer to Problem 18-A2. Prepare a supporting schedule that reconciles net income to net cash provided by operating activities.

18-A4 Depreciation and Cash Flows
O'Neill Company had sales of $820,000, all received in cash. Total operating expenses were $620,000. All except depreciation were paid in cash. Depreciation of $90,000 was included in the $620,000 of operating expenses. Ignore income taxes.

1. Compute net income and net cash provided by operating activities.
2. Assume that depreciation is tripled. Compute net income and net cash provided by operating activities.

Understanding Published Financial Reports

18-B1 Balance Sheet Format
Georgia-Pacific Corporation, one of the world's largest forest products companies, lists the following balance sheet items for January 1, 1994 (in millions):

Property, plant, and equipment, at cost	$10,986
Common stock	71
Cash	41
Commercial paper and other short-term notes payable	650
Receivables	377
Prepaid expenses and other current assets	26
Accumulated depreciation	(5,538)
Accounts payable	582
Other long-term liabilities	827
Additional paid-in capital	1,202
Inventories	1,202

Other assets	2,070
Current portion of long-term debt	57
Accrued compensation, interest, and other payables	602
Timber and timberlands, net	1,381
Deferred income tax liability	1,095
Short-term bank loans	173
Long-term debt, excluding current portion	4,157
Retained earnings	?

Required   Prepare a balance sheet in proper form for Georgia-Pacific. Include the proper amount for retained earnings.

18-B2 Preparation of Statement of Cash Flows

Walgreens Co., the largest drugstore chain in the United States, had the following items in its financial statements for the fiscal year ended August 31, 1994 (in thousands):

Net sales	$1,496,721
Net earnings	281,929
Additions to property and equipment	(289,976)
Depreciation and amortization	118,118
Cash dividends paid	(81,226)
Other non-cash expenses	7,880
Increases in inventories	(169,365)
Investment in corporate-owned life insurance	(6,445)
Increases in trade accounts payable	105,631
Increases in other current assets	(3,910)
Payments of long-term obligations	(5,760)
Net proceeds from employee stock plans	948
Increases in accrued expenses and other liabilities	59,507
Net purchases of marketable securities	(815)
Increases in accounts receivable, net	(50,692)
Other investments	444
Retained earnings	1,496,721
Deferred income taxes	5,653
Increases in income taxes payable	693
Proceeds from disposition of property and equipment	13,704
Total assets	2,908,749
Cash and cash equivalents at end of year	77,915
Net decrease in cash and cash equivalents	(13,682)

Required   Select the items from this list that would appear in Walgreens' statement of cash flows and prepare the statement in proper form. Use the indirect method for reporting cash flows from operating activities. (Note: Deferred income taxes is a noncash expense.)

18-B3 Cash Provided by Operations

PepsiCo., Inc., maker of snack foods (for example, Fritos) as well as soft drinks, had net income of $1,784.0 million in 1993. Additional information follows (in millions):

	1993	
Depreciation and amortization	$1,576.5	
Other noncash charges	$ 324.2	
Interest expense	$ 645.0	
Provision for income taxes	$ 880.4	
Changes in noncash working capital accounts		
Accounts and notes receivable	$ 111.8	Increase
Inventories	$ 101.6	Increase
Prepaid expenses	$ 1.2	Decrease
Accounts payable	$ 30.4	Increase
Income taxes payable	$ 54.4	Increase
Other current liabilities	$ 158.7	Increase

Required   Compute the net cash provided by operating activities.

Additional Assignment Material

Questions

18-1. "The operating cycle for a company is one year." Do you agree? Why?

18-2. Why is the term *marketable securities* a misnomer?

18-3. Why should short-term prepaid expenses be classified as current assets?

18-4. Enumerate the items most commonly classified as current assets.

18-5. "Sometimes 100 shares of stock should be classified as current assets and sometimes not." Explain.

18-6. "Accumulated depreciation is the cumulative amount charged as expense." Explain.

18-7. "Accumulated depreciation is a sum of cash being accumulated for the replacement of fixed assets." Do you agree? Explain.

18-8. "Most companies use straight-line depreciation, but they should use accelerated depreciation." Criticize this quote.

18-9. Criticize: "Depreciation is the loss in value of a fixed asset over a given span of time."

18-10. What factors influence the estimate of useful life in depreciation accounting?

18-11. "Accountants sometimes are too concerned with physical objects or contractual rights." Explain.

18-12. "Goodwill may have nothing to do with the personality of the manager or employees." Do you agree? Explain.

18-13. Why are intangible assets and deferred charges usually swiftly amortized?

18-14. What is a subordinated debenture?

18-15. What is the role of the par value of stock or bonds?

18-16. "Common shareholders have limited liability." Explain.

18-17. "Treasury stock is negative stockholders' equity." Do you agree? Explain.

18-18. "The statement of cash flows is an optional statement included by most companies in their annual reports." Do you agree? Explain.

18-19. What are the purposes of a statement of cash flows?

18-20. What three types of activities are summarized in the statement of cash flows?

18-21. Name four major operating activities included in a statement of cash flows.

18-22. Name three major investing activities included in a statement of cash flows.

18-23. Name three major financing activities included in a statement of cash flows.

18-24. Where does interest received or paid appear on the statement of cash flows?

18-25. Why is there usually a difference between the cash collections from customers and sales revenue in a period's financial statements?

18-26. What are the two major ways of computing net cash provided by operating activities?

18-27. The indirect method for reporting cash flows from operating activities can create an erroneous impression about noncash expenses (such as depreciation). What is the impression and why is it erroneous?

18-28. An investor's newsletter had the following item: "The company expects increased cash flow in 1997 because depreciation charges will be substantially greater than they were in 1996." Comment.

18-29. "Net losses mean drains on cash." Do you agree? Explain.

18-30. "Depreciation is an integral part of a statement of cash flows." Do you agree? Explain.

18-31. "Cash flow per share can be downright misleading." Why?

18-32. XYZ Company's only transaction in 19X5 was the sale of a fixed asset for cash of $20,000. The income statement included only "Gain on sale of fixed asset, $4,000." Correct the following statement of cash flows:

Cash flows from operating activities	
Gain on sale of fixed asset	$ 4,000
Cash flows from investing activities	
Proceeds from sale of fixed asset	20,000
Total increase in cash	$24,000

18-33. Why are noncash investing and financing activities listed on a separate schedule accompanying the statement of cash flows?

18-34. The Lawrence Company sold fixed assets with a book value of $5,000 and recorded a $3,000 gain. How should this be reported on a statement of cash flows?

18-35. "The presence of a deferred tax liability on the balance sheet means that cumulative tax payments have exceeded the cumulative tax expense charged on financial reports to shareholders." Do you agree? Explain.

General Exercises and Problems

18-36 Meaning of Book Value

Kuhlman Properties purchased an office building near Frankfurt 20 years ago for 1 million deutsche marks (DM), DM 200,000 of which was attributable to land. The mortgage has been fully paid. The current balance sheet follows:

Cash		DM 400,000	Stockholders'	
Land		200,000	equity	DM 760,000
Building at cost	DM 800,000			
Accumulated depreciation	640,000			
Book value		160,000		
Total assets		DM 760,000		

The company is about to borrow DM 1.8 million on a first mortgage to modernize and expand the building. This amounts to 60% of the combined appraised value of the land and building before the modernization and expansion.

Required   Prepare a balance sheet after the loan is made and the building is expanded and modernized but before any further depreciation is charged. Comment on its significance.

18-37 Balance Sheet and Income Statement

The fiscal year for Arai Company ends on May 31. Results for the year ended May 31, 19X1, included (in millions of Japanese yen except for number of shares outstanding):

Cash and cash equivalents	¥ 29,000
Cost of goods sold	220,000
Inventories	26,000
Other current assets	11,000

Fixed assets, net	217,000
Net sales	440,000
Receivables	22,000
Debentures	77,000
Research and development expenses	42,000
Administrative and general expenses	65,000
Other income (expenses), net	(12,000)
Capital construction fund	28,000
Selling and distribution expenses	41,000
Other current liabilities	9,000
Less: treasury stock	(14,000)
Long-term investments	15,000
Retained income, appropriated for self-insurance	16,000
Accounts payable	19,000
Mortgage bonds	84,000
Deferred income tax liability	12,000
Redeemable preferred stock	15,000
Common stock, at par (50,000 shares outstanding)	5,000
Paid-in capital in excess of par	103,000
Income tax expense	51,000
Accrued expenses payable	16,000
Retained income, unrestricted	27,000
Intangible assets	?

Required Prepare in proper form the balance sheet as of May 31, 19X1, and the income statement for the year ended May 31, 19X1. Include the proper amount for *intangible assets*.

18-38 Cash Received from Customers
Sales for Modern Tiles, Inc., during 19X1 were $572,000, 80% of them on credit and 20% for cash. During the year accounts receivable increased from $66,000 to $72,000, an increase of $6,000. What amount of cash was received from customers during 19X1?

18-39 Cash Paid to Suppliers
Cost of goods sold for Modern Tiles, Inc., during 19X1 was $310,000. Beginning inventory was $105,000 and ending inventory was $120,000. Beginning trade accounts payable were $24,000, and ending trade accounts payable were $47,000. What amount of cash was paid to suppliers?

18-40 Cash Paid to Employees
Modern Tiles, Inc., reported wage and salary expenses of $227,000 on its 19X1 income statement. It reported cash paid to employees of $155,000 on its statement of cash flows. The beginning balance of accrued wages and salaries payable was $20,000. What was the ending balance in accrued wages and salaries payable? Ignore payroll taxes.

18-41 Simple Cash Flows from Operating Activities
Kinserdal and Associates provides consulting services. In 19X0 net income was $200,000 on revenues of $480,000 and expenses of $280,000. The only noncash expense was depreciation of $50,000. The company has no inventory. Accounts receivable increased by $9,000 during 19X0, and accounts payable and salaries payable were unchanged.

Required Prepare a statement of cash flows from operating activities. Use the direct method. Omit supporting schedules.

18-42 Net Income and Cash Flow

Refer to Problem 18-41. Prepare a schedule that reconciles net income to net cash provided by operating activities.

18-43 Net Loss and Cash Flows from Operating Activities

The Lombard Company had a net loss of $40,000 in 19X2. The following information is available:

Depreciation	$23,000
Decrease in accounts receivable	4,000
Increase in inventory	2,000
Increase in accounts payable	17,000
Increase in salaries and wages payable	5,000

Required   Present a schedule that reconciles net income (loss) to net cash provided by operating activities.

18-44 Preparation of a Statement of Cash Flows

Hernandez Auto Parts is a wholesaler of automobile parts. By the end of 19X2 the company's cash balance had dropped to $15 thousand, despite net income of $240 thousand in 19X2. Its transactions affecting income or cash in 19X2 were (in thousands):

1. Sales were $2,503, all on credit. Cash collections from customers were $2,406.
2. The cost of items sold was $1,596.
3. Inventory increased by $56.
4. Cash payments on trade accounts payable were $1,640.
5. Payments to employees were $305; accrued wages payable decreased by $24.
6. Other operating expenses, all paid in cash, were $104.
7. Interest expense, all paid in cash, was $26.
8. Income tax expense was $105; cash payments for income taxes were $108.
9. Depreciation was $151.
10. A warehouse was acquired for $540 cash.
11. Equipment was sold for $37 cash; original cost was $196, accumulated depreciation was $159.
12. Received $28 for issue of common stock.
13. Retired long-term debt for $25 cash.
14. Paid cash dividends of $88.

Required   Prepare a statement of cash flows using the direct method for reporting cash flows from operating activities. Omit supporting schedules.

18-45 Reconciliation of Net Income and Net Cash Provided by Operating Activities

Refer to problem 18-44. Prepare a supporting schedule to the statement of cash flows that reconciles net income to net cash provided by operating activities.

18-46 Depreciation and Cash Flows

The following condensed income statement and reconciliation schedule are from the annual report of Okanagon Company (in millions):

Sales	$180
Expenses	158
Net income	$ 22

Reconciliation Schedule of Net Income to
Net Cash Provided by Operating Activities

Net income	$ 22
Add noncash expenses	
Depreciation	15
Deduct net increase in noncash	
operating working capital	(17)
Net cash provided by operating activities	$ 20

A shareholder has suggested that the company switch from straight-line to accelerated depreciation on its annual report to shareholders. He maintains that this will increase the cash flow provided by operating activities. According to his calculations, using accelerated methods would increase depreciation to $25 million, an increase of $10 million; net cash flow from operating activities would then be $30 million.

Required

1. Suppose Okanagon Company adopts the accelerated depreciation method proposed. Compute net income and net cash flow from operating activities. Ignore income taxes.
2. Use your answer to requirement 1 to prepare a response to the shareholder.

18-47 Cash Flows, Indirect Method

The Pueblo Company has the following balance sheet data (in millions):

	December 31				December 31		
	19X2	*19X1*	*Change*		*19X2*	*19X1*	*Change*
Current assets				Current liabilities			
Cash	$ 13	$ 20	$ (7)	(detailed)	$105	$ 30	$ 75
Receivables, net	66	30	36	Long-term debt	150	—	150
Inventories	100	50	50	Stockholders' equity	224	170	54
Total current assets	$179	$100	$ 79				
Plant assets (net of							
accumulated							
depreciation)	300	100	200				
				Total liabilities and			
Total assets	$479	$200	$279	stockholders' equity	$479	$200	$279

Net income for 19X2 was $60 million. Net cash inflow from operating activities was $69 million. Cash dividends paid were $6 million. Depreciation was $20 million. Fixed assets were purchased for $220 million, $150 million of which was financed via the issuance of long-term debt outright for cash.

Julia Redwing, the president and majority stockholder of Pueblo, was a superb operating executive. She was imaginative and aggressive in marketing and ingenious and creative in production. But she had little patience with financial matters. After examining the most recent balance sheet and income statement, she muttered, "We've enjoyed 10 years of steady growth; 19X2 was our most profitable ever. Despite such profitability, we're in the worst cash position in our history. Just look at those current liabilities in relation to our available cash! This whole picture of the more you make, the poorer you get, just does not make sense. These statements must be cockeyed."

Required

1. Prepare a statement of cash flows using the indirect method. Include a schedule reconciling net income to net cash provided by operating activities in the body of the statement.
2. Using the statement of cash flows and other information, write a short memorandum to Redwing, explaining why there is such a squeeze on cash.

18-48 Preparation of Statement of Cash Flows

The Blue Heron Company has assembled the (a) balance sheet and (b) income statement and statement of retained earnings for 19X1 shown in Exhibit 18-16.

On December 30, 19X1, Blue Heron paid $98 million in cash to acquire a new plant to expand operations. This was partly financed by an issue of long-term debt for $50 million. Plant assets were sold for their book value of $6 million during 19X1. Because net income was $14 million, the highest in the company's history, James Sato, the chief executive officer, was distressed by the company's extremely low cash balance.

Required

1. Prepare a statement of cash flows using the direct method for reporting cash flows from operating activities. You may wish to use Exhibit 18-8, page 702, as a guide.
2. Prepare a schedule that reconciles net income to net cash provided by operating activities.
3. What is revealed by the statement of cash flows? Does it help you reduce Mr. Sato's distress? Why? Briefly explain to Mr. Sato why cash has decreased even though net income was $14 million.

Exhibit 18-16		19X1	19X0	Change
Blue Heron Co.	**Assets**			
Balance Sheet	Cash	$ 10	$ 25	$(15)
December 31, 19X1	Accounts receivable	45	28	17
(in millions)	Inventory	70	50	20
	Prepaid general expenses	4	3	1
	Plant assets, net	202	150	52
		$331	$256	$75
	Liabilities and shareholders' equity			
	Accounts payable for merchandise	$ 74	$ 60	$14
	Accrued tax payable	3	2	1
	Long-term debt	50	—	50
	Capital stock	100	100	—
	Retained earnings	104	94	10
		$331	$256	$75

Blue Heron Co.	Sales		$255
Income Statement	Less cost of goods sold		
and Statement of	Inventory, December 31, 19X0	$ 50	
Retained Earnings	Purchases	160	
for the Year Ended	Cost of goods available for sale	$210	
December 31, 19X1	Inventory, December 31, 19X1	70	140
(in millions)	Gross profit		$115
	Less other expenses		
	General expense	$ 51	
	Depreciation	40	
	Taxes	10	101
	Net income		$ 14
	Dividends		4
	Net income of the period retained		$ 10
	Retained earnings, December 31, 19X0		94
	Retained earnings, December 31, 19X1		$104

18-49 Gain on Disposal of Equipment

Arkansas Life Insurance Company (ALIC) sold a computer. It had purchased the computer four years ago for $660,000, and accumulated depreciation at the time of sale was $490,000.

Required

1. Suppose ALIC received $170,000 cash for the computer. How would the sale be shown on the statement of cash flows?
2. Suppose ALIC received $210,000 for the computer. How would the sale be shown on the statement of cash flows (including the schedule reconciling net income and net cash provided by operating activities)?

Understanding Published Financial Reports

18-50 Various Intangible Assets

Consider the following:

a. (1) Dow Chemical Company's annual report indicated that research and development expenditures were $1,256 million during 1993. How did this amount affect operating income, which was $1,440 million? (2) Suppose the entire $1,256 million arose from outlays for patents acquired from various outside parties on December 30, 1993. What would be the operating income for 1993? (3) How would the Dow balance sheet, December 31, 1993, be affected by (2)?

b. On December 30, 1995, American Telephone & Telegraph Company (AT&T) acquired new patents on some communications equipment for $8 million. Technology changes quickly. The equipment's useful life is expected to be 4 years rather than the 17-year life of the patent. What will be the amortization for 1996?

c. Hilton Hotels has an account classified under assets in its balance sheet called pre-opening costs. A footnote said that these costs "are deferred and charged to income over a three-year period after the opening date." Suppose expenditures for pre-opening costs in 1995 were $2,000,000 and the pre-opening costs account balance on December 31, 1995, was $1,840,000 and on December 31, 1994, it was $2,390,000. What amount was amortized for 1995?

d. Philip Morris purchased Kraft for approximately $13 billion. Of the $13 billion purchase price, only about $2 billion could be assigned to identifiable individual assets. Assume that the acquisition occurred on January 2. What was the total amount of goodwill from the purchase recorded on the Philip Morris balance sheet? What is the minimum amount of amortization of goodwill in the first year? Could the entire amount be written off in the first year? Explain.

18-51 Various Liabilities

For each of the following items, indicate how the financial statements will be affected. Identify the affected accounts specifically.

1. Maytag Corporation sells electric appliances, including automatic washing machines. Experience in recent years has indicated that warranty costs average 3.2% of sales. Sales of washing machines for October were $3 million. Cash disbursements and obligations for warranty service on washing machines during October totaled $82,000.
2. Pepsi-Cola Company of New York gets cash deposits for its returnable bottles. In August it received $100,000 cash and disbursed $91,000 for bottles returned.
3. The Chase Manhattan Bank received a $1,200 savings deposit on April 1. On June 30 it recognized interest thereon at an annual rate of 6%. On July 1 the depositor closed her account with the bank.
4. The Shubert Theater sold for $120,000 cash a "season's series" of tickets in advance of December 31 for four plays, each to be held in successive months beginning in January. (a) What is the effect on the balance sheet, December 31? (b) What is the effect on the balance sheet, January 31?

18-52 Exercises in Assets, Liabilities, and Stockholders' Equity

Apple Computer makes Macintosh, Power Macintosh, and Power-Book computers and Newton MessagePads. The company's 1994 net income was more that $300 million on sales of nearly $10 billion.

Required

1. In 1993 Apple Computer had accounts receivable totaling $1,465,722,000 on its books, and after subtracting estimated uncollectible accounts of $83,776,000 the company reported net accounts receivable of $1,381,946,000 on its balance sheet. In 1994, accounts receivable before subtracting estimated uncollectibles increased by $206,617,000 and estimated uncollectible accounts increased by $7,216,000. What amount was reported for net accounts receivable on Apple's 1994 balance sheet?
2. Apple began the 1994 fiscal year with approximately $7 million in long-term debt. The company repaid $3 million of this debt, and borrowed another $300 million during the year. How much long-term debt was shown on Apple's 1994 balance sheet?
3. Retained earnings at the end of the 1993 fiscal year were shown at $1,842,600,000 on Apple's balance sheet. During 1994 net income was $310,178,000 and dividends amounting to $56,572,000 were paid. What was the balance in retained earnings in Apple's 1994 balance sheet?

18-53 Gain on Airplane Crash

In August 1988 a Delta Airlines 727 crashed in Dallas. The crash resulted in a gain of $.11 per share of Delta. How could this happen? Consider the accounting for airplanes. Airlines insure their craft at market value, $6.5 million for Delta's 727. However, the planes' book values are often much less because of large accumulated depreciation amounts. The book value of Delta's 727 was only $962,000.

Required

1. Suppose Delta received the insurance payment and immediately purchased another 727 for $6.5 million. Compute the effect of the crash on pretax income. Also compute the effect on Delta's total assets.
2. Do you think a casualty should generate a reported gain? Why?

18-54 Identification of Operating, Investing, and Financing Activities

The items listed below were found on the statement of cash flows of the American Telephone and Telegraph Company (AT&T). For each item, indicate which section of the statement should contain the item—the operating, investing, or financing section.

a. Additions to property, plant, and equipment
b. Depreciation
c. Increase in short-term borrowing
d. Redemption of preferred shares
e. Increase in long-term debt
f. Net income
g. Dividends paid
h. Issuance of common shares
i. Retirement of long-term debt

18-55 Interest Expense

In 1993 Alcoa reported interest expense of $87.8 million on its income statement. Suppose that accrued interest, a current liability on the balance sheet, increased from $49.9 million on January 1, 1993, to $57.9 million on December 31, 1993.

Required

1. Describe how the transactions relating to interest would be shown in the body of the statement of cash flows. Assume that Alcoa uses the direct method for reporting cash flows from operating activities.
2. Describe how the transactions relating to interest would be shown on a supplementary schedule that reconciles net income and net cash provided by operating activities.

18-56 Indirect and Direct Cash Flows from Operations

Micron Technology is one of the country's fastest growing makers of semiconductor components. Sales increased from $333 million in 1990 to more then $41.6 billion in 1994. The following items were in the company's statement of cash flows for the fiscal year ending September 1, 1994 (in millions):

Increase in inventories	$ 17.9
Net income	400.5
Depreciation	138.8
Increase in income taxes payable	13.4
Increase in accounts payable	20.5
Amortization	42.4
Increase in receivables	81.0
Increase in accrued operating expenses	11.3

The company's income statement showed (in millions):

Sales	$1,628.6
Cost of goods sold	(789.4)
Other operating expenses	(219.1)
Operating income	620.1
Interest income	5.7
Income before income taxes	625.8
Income tax provision	(225.3)
Net income	$ 400.5

Required

1. Prepare a statement of cash flows from operating activities using the indirect method.
2. Prepare a statement of cash flows from operating activities using the direct method. Assume that all interest income was received in cash and that all depreciation and amortization is included in other operating expenses.

18-57 Statement of Cash Flows, Direct and Indirect Methods

Nordstrom, Inc., the Seattle-based department store, had the following income statement for the year ended January 31, 1994 (in thousands):

Net sales		$3,589,938
Costs and expenses		
Cost of sales	$2,469,304	
Selling, general, and administrative	940,579	
Interest	37,646	
Less: Other income	(88,509)	
Total costs and expenses		3,359,020
Earnings before income taxes		$ 230,918
Income taxes		90,500
Net earnings		$ 140,418

The company's net cash provided by operating activities, prepared using the indirect method, was:

Net earnings	$ 140,418
Adjustments to reconcile net earnings to net cash provided by operating activities	
Depreciation and amortization	103,466
Changes in	
Accounts receivable	16,757
Merchandise inventories	(48,863)
Prepaid expenses	(878)
Accounts payable	43,879
Accrued salaries and wages	(1,081)
Other accrued expenses	4,853
Income taxes payable	3,540
Net cash provided by operating activities	$ 262,091

Required   Prepare a statement showing the net cash provided by operating activities using the direct method. Assume that all "other income" was received in cash and that prepaid expenses, accrued salaries and wages, and other accrued expenses relate to selling, general, and administrative expenses.

18-58 Comprehensive Review: Reconstruct Transactions
Childrobics, Inc. was incorporated in the state of New York on May 7, 1993. The company owns and operates indoor recreation facilities for children and their families in the New York metropolitan area. The company prepared financial statements on February 28, 1994, for the period since incorporation. Slightly revised versions of the company's balance sheet and statement of cash flows follow. Footnotes pointed out that, in exchange for a note payable of $250,000, the creditors supplied $146,000 in cash and $104,000 in property and equipment.

Required   Compute amounts to replace each of the question marks in the Childrobics' balance sheet.

Childrobics, Inc.
Balance Sheet
February 28, 1994

Assets		
Current assets		
Cash		$?
Property and equipment		
At cost	$?	
Accumulated depreciation	?	
Net		?
Other assets		25,300
Total assets		$?
Liabilities and Stockholders' Equity		
Current liabilities		
Accounts payable and accrued expenses	$?	
Deferred revenue	?	
Note payable	?	
Total current liabilities		$?
Stockholders' equity		
Common stock: $.01 par value, 25,000,000 shares authorized, 975,000 shared issued and outstanding	$?	

Additional paid-in capital	?	
Retained Earnings	?	
Total stockholders' equity		?
Total liabilities and stockholders' equity		$?

**Childrobics, Inc.
Statement of
Cash Flows for the
Period Ended
February 28, 1994**

Operating Activities		
Net income	$ 2,516	
Adjustment to reconcile net income to net cash provided by operating activities		
Depreciation	10,947	
Change in assets and liabilities		
Account payable and accrued expenses	59,871	
Deferred revenue—customer deposits	13,450	
Net cash—operating activities		$ 86,784
Investing Activities		
Purchases of property and equipment	$(192,583)	
Expenditures for other assets	(25,300)	
Net cash—investing activities		(217,883)
Financing Activities		
Loans	$146,000	
Common stock	25,000	
Net cash—financing activities		171,000
Net increase in cash		39,901
Cash, beginning of period		0
Cash, end of period		$ 39,901

19 More on Understanding Corporate Annual Reports

Preparing and analyzing financial statements for large corporations with many subsidiaries is a very complex task. Financial accountants use computers to facilitate their work. *Courtesy of Marmon Group, Inc.*

Learning Objectives

When you have finished studying this chapter, you should be able to

1 Contrast accounting for investments using the equity method and the cost method.

2 Explain the basic ideas and methods used to prepare consolidated financial statements.

3 Describe how goodwill arises and how to account for it.

4 Explain and use a variety of popular financial ratios.

5 Identify the major implications that efficient stock markets have for accounting.

This chapter continues the discussion of corporate annual reporting begun in the preceding chapter. Part One covers intercorporate investments, including consolidated statements and goodwill. Part Two covers the analysis of financial statements. *Either part may be studied independently, depending on your specific interest.*

Part One: Intercorporate Investments Including Consolidations

Firms often invest in the equity securities of other companies. The investor may be simply investing excess cash, or it may be seeking some degree of control over the investee. We will consider only investments in the common stock of another company that the investor intends to hold indefinitely—called *held- to- maturity* securities. There are three methods of accounting for such intercorporate investments. We discuss *cost* and *equity* methods in the following section and *consolidation* in the next.

The method of accounting for intercorporate investments depends on the type of relationship between the investor and the investee. An investor that holds less than 20% of another company is assumed to be a passive investor—it cannot significantly influence the decisions of the investee—and it uses the *cost method*. Investors with between 20% and 50% interest use the *equity method*. At such a level of ownership the investor has the ability to exert significant influence on the investee. For example, Ford uses the equity method to account for its 25% interest in Mazda Motor Corporation of Japan. Firms with an interest in excess of 50% must use the consolidation approach.

■ EQUITY AND COST METHODS

cost method The method of accounting for investments whereby the initial investment is recorded at cost and dividends are recognized as income when they are received

The **cost method** records the initial investment at cost and recognizes any dividends as income when they are received. Such investments are often called *marketable securities* in the financial statements.

The **equity method** accounts for the investment at the acquisition cost adjusted for the investor's share of dividends and earnings or losses of the investee after the date of investment. Investors increase the carrying amount of the investment by their share of the investee's earnings and reduce the carrying amount by dividends received from the investee and by their share in the investee's losses.

equity method Accounts for the investment at the acquisition cost adjusted for the investor's share of dividends and earnings or losses of the investee after the date of investment.

Compare the cost and equity methods. Suppose IBM acquires 40% of the voting stock of Start-up Computer Corporation (SCC) for $80 million. In year 1, SCC has a net income of $30 million and pays cash dividends of $10 million. IBM's 40% shares of income and dividends would be $12 million and $4 million, respectively. The balance sheet equation would be affected as follows under each of the methods (in millions):

	Equity Method				Cost Method			
	Assets		=	Equities		Assets	=	Equities
	Cash	Investments		Liab.	Stk. Eq.	Cash	Investments	Liab.	Stk. Eq.
1. Acquisition	−80	+80	=			−80	+80	=	
2. Net income of SCC		+12	=		+12	No entry and no effect			
3. Dividends from SCC	+4	−4	=			+4		=	+4
Effects for year	−76	+88	=		+12	−76	+80	=	+4

The investment account will have a net increase of $8 million for the year. The dividend will increase the cash account by $4 million.	The investment account will be unaffected. The dividend will increase the cash account by $4 million.

Objective 1

Contrast accounting for investments using the equity method and the cost method

Because a 40% ownership share requires use of the equity method, IBM would recognize income as it is earned by SCC rather than when dividends are received. Cash dividends do not affect net income; they increase cash and decrease the investment balance. In a sense, IBM's "claim" on SCC grows by its share of SCC's net income. The dividend is a partial liquidation of IBM's claim. The receipt of a dividend is similar to the collection of an account receivable, from an accounting standpoint. The revenue from a sale of merchandise on account is recognized when the receivable is created, so to include the collection also as revenue would be double-counting. Similarly, it would be double-counting to include the $4 million of dividends as income because the $12 million of income is already recognized as it is earned.

Suppose IBM were allowed to account for this investment using the cost method. The only event subsequent to acquisition that triggers an entry in IBM's accounts is the receipt of dividends from SCC. IBM receives cash and recognizes income at the time of each dividend payment.

The major justification for using the equity method instead of the cost method is that it more appropriately recognizes increases or decreases in the economic resources underlying the investments. Furthermore, the cost method may allow management of the investor company to influence its own reported net income unduly. How? Under the cost method, the reported net income of the investor is directly affected by the dividend policies of the investee, over which the investor might have significant influence. Under the equity method, IBM's reported net income could not be influenced by the manipulation of SCC's dividend policies.

■ CONSOLIDATED FINANCIAL STATEMENTS

When one firm owns more than 50% of the stock in another business, the stockholding firm obviously has a great deal of influence over the other business. The extent of this influence is reflected in the terms used to refer to the two companies. The company owning more than 50% of the other business's stock is called the **parent company.** The company whose stock is owned by the other business is called the **subsidiary.** Although parent and subsidiary companies typically are separate legal entities, in many regards they function as one unit.

parent company A company owning more than 50 percent of another business's stock.

subsidiary A company owned by a parent company that owns more than 50 percent of its stock.

consolidated financial statements Financial statements that combine the financial statements of the parent company with those of various subsidiaries, as if they were a single entity.

Why have subsidiaries? Why not have the corporation take the form of a single legal entity? The reasons include limiting the liabilities in a risky venture, saving income taxes, conforming with government regulations with respect to a part of the business, doing business in a foreign country, and expanding in an orderly way. For example, there are often tax advantages in acquiring the capital stock of a going concern rather than its individual assets.

The parent-subsidiary relationship requires special accounting treatment. Under U.S. regulations, parent companies must issue **consolidated financial statements** that combine the financial statements of the parent company with those of various subsidiaries. That is, the parent and subsidiary companies are accounted for as if they were a single entity. Why? Because consolidated statements give investors a more accurate picture of the whole organization's health.

The Acquisition

Objective 2

Explain the basic ideas and methods used to prepare consolidated finan-cial statements

When consolidating parent and subsidiary financial statements, accountants must avoid double-counting of assets and equities. Suppose Company P (parent) acquired a 100% voting interest in S (subsidiary) for $210 million cash at the beginning of the year.[1] The balance sheet accounts of both companies are analyzed in the next table. (Investment in S appears in the first column because it is a focal point in this chapter, not because it comes first in actual balance sheets.) Figures in this and subsequent tables are in millions of dollars:

---

[1] In this example, the purchase price equals the stockholders' equity of the acquired company. The preparation of consolidated statements in situations in which these two amounts differ is discussed later, in the section "Accounting for Goodwill," pages 741–742.

	Assets			=	Liabilities	+	Stockholders' Equity
	Investment + in S		Cash and Other Assets	=	Accounts Payable, Etc.	+	Stockholders' Equity
P's accounts, January 1							
Before acquisition			650	=	200	+	450
Acquisition of S	+210		−210	=			
S's accounts, January 1			400	=	190	+	210
Intercompany eliminations	−210			=			−210
Consolidated, January 1	0	+	840	=	390	+	450

Note that the $210 million is paid to the *former owners* of S as private investors. The $210 million is *not* an addition to the existing assets and stockholders' equity of S. *That is, the books of S are completely unaffected by P's initial investment and P's subsequent accounting thereof.* S is not dissolved, but it lives on as a separate legal entity. Each legal entity has its individual set of books. The consolidated entity does not keep a separate set of books.

Suppose a consolidated balance sheet were prepared immediately after the acquisition. The consolidated statement would show the details of *all* assets and liabilities of *both* the parent and the subsidiary. The *Investment in S* account on P's books is the evidence of an ownership interest, which is held by P but is really composed of all the assets and liabilities of S. The consolidated statements cannot show both the evidence of interest *plus* the detailed underlying assets and liabilities. To avoid such double-counting, we eliminate the reciprocal evidence of ownership present in two places: (1) the Investment in S on P's books and (2) the Stockholders' Equity on S's books.

In summary, if the $210 million elimination of the reciprocal accounts did not occur, there would be a double-counting in the consolidated statement:

Entity	Types Of Records
P	Parent books
+S	Subsidiary books
= Preliminary consolidated report	No separate books for the consolidated entity, but periodically P and S assets and liabilities are added together via work sheets
−E	"Eliminating entries" to remove double-counting
= Consolidated report to investors	

After Acquisition

Long-term investments in equity securities, such as this investment in S, are carried in the *investor's* balance sheet by the equity method, described earlier in this chapter. Suppose S has a net income of $50 million for the year. If P were reporting alone, it would account for the net income of its subsidiary by increasing its Investment in S account and its Stockholders' Equity account (in the form of Retained Earnings) by 100% of $50 million.

The income statements for the year would be (numbers in millions):

	P	S	Consolidated
Sales	$900	$300	$1,200
Expenses	800	250	1,050
Operating income	$100	$ 50	$ 150
Pro-rata share (100%) of subsidiary net income	50	—	
Net income	$150	$ 50	

P's parent-company-only income statement shows its own sales and expenses plus its pro-rata share of S's net income (as the equity method requires).

Reflect on the changes in P's accounts, S's accounts, and the consolidated accounts (in millions of dollars):

	Assets		=	Liabilities	+	Stockholders' Equity
	Investment + in S	Cash and Other = Assets		Accounts Payable, = Etc.	+	Stockholders' Equity
P's accounts						
Beginning of year	210	+	440 =	200	+	450
Operating income		+100 =				+100*
Share of S income	+50	=				+50*
End of year	260	+	540 =	200	+	600
S's accounts						
Beginning of year		400 =		190	+	210
Net income		+50 =				+50*
End of year		450 =		190	+	260
Intercompany eliminations	−260	=				−260
Consolidated, end of year	0	+	990 =	390	+	600

* Changes in the retained earnings portion of stockholders' equity.

Note that consolidated statements summarize the individual accounts of two or more separate legal entities, eliminating double-counting.[2] The income statement for P shows a $150 million net income; for S, a $50 million net income; for P and S consolidated, a $150 million net income.

---

[2] Another example of double-counting is sales by P to S (or by S to P), which do not exist in this example. A consolidated income statement should not include the sale when P sells the item to S and again when S sells it to an outsider. Suppose P bought an item for $1,000 and sold it to S for $1,200. P recognized revenue of $1,200, cost of goods sold of $1,000, and income of $200. S recorded an inventory item of $1,200. In consolidation, this transaction must be eliminated. After adding together the individual accounts of P and S, you must deduct $1,200 from revenue, $1,000 from cost of goods sold, and $200 from inventory. This eliminates the $200 of income that P recognized and reduces inventory to the original $1,000 that P paid for the item.

Minority Interests

minority interests
An account that
shows the outside
stockholders' interest,
as opposed to the par-
ent's interest, in a sub-
sidiary corporation.

When a parent holds less than 100% of the stock of a subsidiary, a consolidated balance sheet includes an account on the equities side called *Minority Interests in Subsidiaries*, or simply **Minority Interests.** The account shows the outside stockholders' interest, as opposed to the parent's interest, in a subsidiary corporation. It arises because the consolidated balance sheet is a combination of all the assets and liabilities of a subsidiary. Suppose the parent owns 90% of the subsidiary stock, and outsiders to the consolidated group own the other 10%. The Minority Interests account is a measure of the outside stockholders' interest. The diagram that follows shows the area encompassed by the consolidated statements; it includes all the subsidiary assets, item by item. The creation of an account for minority interests, in effect, corrects this overstatement. The remainder after deducting minority interests is P's total ownership interest:

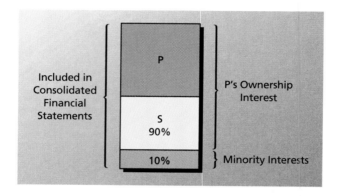

The next table, using the basic figures of the previous example, shows the overall approach to a consolidated balance sheet immediately after the acquisition. Suppose P bought 90% of the stock of S for a cost of 0.90 × $210, or $189 million. The minority interest would be 10%, or $21 million.

	Assets		=	Liabilities	+	Stockholders' Equity		
	Investment + in S	Cash and Other = Assets		Accounts Payable, Etc.	+	Minority + Interest		Stockholders' Equity
P's accounts, January 1								
Before acquisition		650	=	200			+	450
Acquisition of 90% of S	+189	−189	=					
S's accounts, January 1		400	=	190			+	210
Intercompany eliminations	−189		=			+21		−210
Consolidated, January 1	0	+ 861	=	390	+	21	+	450

Again, suppose S has a net income of $50 million for the year. The same basic procedures are followed by P and by S regardless of whether S is 100% owned or 90% owned. However, the presence of a minority interest changes the *consolidated* income statement slightly, as follows:

	P	S	Consolidated
Sales	$900	$300	$1,200
Expenses	800	250	1,050
Operating income	$100	$ 50	$ 150
Pro-rata share (90%) of subsidiary net income	45	—	
Net income	$145	$ 50	
Minority interest (10%) in subsidiaries' net income			5
Net income to consolidated entity			$ 145

Consolidated balance sheets at the end of the year would also be affected, as follows:

	Assets		=	Liabilities	+	Stockholders' Equity	
	Investment + in S	Cash and Other = Assets		Accounts Payable, = Etc.	+	Minority + Interest	Stockholders' Equity
P's accounts							
Beginning of year, before acquisition		650	=	200		+	450
Acquisition	189	−189	=				
Operating income		+100	=				+100
Share of S income	+45		=				+45
End of year	234	+ 561	=	200		+	595
S's accounts							
Beginning of year		400	=	190		+	210
Net income		+50	=				+50
End of year		+ 450	=	190		+	260
Intercompany eliminations	− 234		=			+26*	−260
Consolidated, end of year	0	+ 1,011	=	390	+	26 +	595

* Beginning minority interest plus minority interest in net income: 21 + (0.10 x 50) = 21 + 5 = 26.

As indicated in the table, the entry to consolidate the statements eliminates $260 million of stockholders' equity (on S's books) and $234 million of investment in S (on P's books). The $26 million difference is the minority interest (on consolidated statements). It identifies the interest of those shareholders who own the 10% of the *subsidiary* stockholders' equity that is not eliminated by consolidation.

Perspective on Consolidated Statements

To get a clear idea of the consolidation process and its effect on balance sheets and income statements, consider the following hypothetical relationships that exist for Goliath Corporation, which for more realism could be viewed as a simplified version of General Motors:

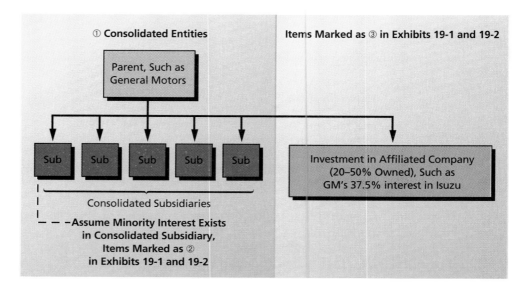

① Consolidated Entities   **Items Marked as ③ in Exhibits 19-1 and 19-2**

Parent, Such as General Motors

Sub   Sub   Sub   Sub   Sub

Consolidated Subsidiaries

– – –Assume Minority Interest Exists
in Consolidated Subsidiary,
Items Marked as ②
in Exhibits 19-1 and 19-2

Investment in Affiliated Company
(20–50% Owned), Such as
GM's 37.5% interest in Isuzu

Exhibits 19-1 and 19-2 provide an overall look at how consolidated balance sheets and income statements for such a company appear in corporate annual reports. The circled items ①, ②, and ③ in the exhibits deserve special mention:

① The headings indicate that these are *consolidated* financial statements.

② On balance sheets, the minority interest typically appears just above the stockholders' equity section, as Exhibit 19-1 shows. On income statements, the minority interest in net income is deducted as if it were an expense of the consolidated entity, as Exhibit 19-2 demonstrates. It generally follows all other expenses. Sometimes you will find minority interest before income taxes and sometimes after. Note that minority interest is a claim of outside stockholders' interest in a *consolidated subsidiary* company. Note also that minority interests arise only in conjunction with *consolidated* financial statements.

③ As described earlier in the chapter, investments in equity securities that represent 20% to 50% ownership are usually accounted for under the equity method. These investments are frequently called **investments in affiliates** or **investments in associates.** General Motors would account for its 37.5% investment in Isuzu in this manner. Exhibit 19-1 shows how the Investment account in the balance sheet has risen by the pro-rata share of the current earnings of affiliates, the $1 million shown in the income statement in Exhibit 19-2.

investments in affiliates (investments in associates) Investments in equity securities that represent 20% to 50% ownership. They are usually accounted for under the equity method.

Some accountants argue against consolidating subsidiaries in businesses totally different from those of the parent. Such 50%- to 100%-owned subsidiaries could be accounted for using the equity method, as if they were affiliated companies. Supporters of this approach maintain that a consolidated statement for such distinctly different businesses would produce a meaningless hodgepodge. For example, they believe that General Motors (GM) should not consolidate the accounts for General Motors Acceptance Corporation (GMAC), a finance company subsidiary, even though GM's interest is 100%.

Exhibit 19-1 Goliath Corporation ① Consolidated Balance Sheets as of December 31 (millions of dollars)

Assets	19X3	19X2
Current assets		
Cash	$ 90	$ 56
Short-term investments in debt securities at cost (which approximates market value)	—	28
Accounts receivable (less allowance for doubtful accounts of $2,000,000 and $2,100,000 at their respective dates)	91	95
Inventories at average cost	120	130
Total current assets	301	309
③ Investments in affiliated companies	10	9
Property, plant, and equipment		
Land at original cost	50	39
Plant and equipment		
	19X3	19X2
Original cost	$255	$190
Accumulated depreciation	126	112
Net plant and equipment	129	78
Total property, plant, and equipment	179	117
Other assets		
Franchises and trademarks	15	16
Deferred charges and prepayments	3	4
Total other assets	18	20
Total assets	$508	$455

Liabilities and Stockholders' Equity	19X3	19X2
Current liabilities		
Accounts payable	$100	$ 84
Notes payable	10	—
Accrued expenses payable	32	22
Accrued income taxes payable	34	38
Total current liabilities	176	144
Long-term liabilities		
First mortgage bonds, 5% interest, due December 31, 19X6	25	25
Subordinated debentures, 6% interest, due December 31, 19X9	30	20
Total long-term liabilities	55	45
Deferred income*	12	9.3
② Minority interest in consolidated subsidiaries	6	5.7
Total liabilities	249	204
Stockholders' equity		
Preferred stock, 100,000 shares, $30 par†	3	3
Common stock, 1,000,000 shares, $1 par	1	1
Paid-in capital in excess of par	55	55
Retained earnings	200	192
Total stockholders' equity	259	251
Total liabilities and stockholders' equity	$508	$455

* Advances from customers on long-term contracts. Other examples are collections for rent and subscriptions, which often are classified as current liabilities.
† Dividend rate is $5 per share; each share is convertible into two shares of common stock. The shares were originally issued for $100. The excess over par is included in "paid-in capital in excess of par." Liquidating value is $100 per share.

739

Nevertheless, the FASB requires all subsidiaries to be consolidated. The major reason for forcing consolidation is to provide a more complete picture of the economic entity. The FASB believes that excluding some subsidiaries from consolidation results in the omission of significant amounts of assets, liabilities, revenues, and expenses from the consolidated statements of many companies.

There are exceptions to the general rule, but they are rare. A subsidiary is not consolidated if control is likely to be temporary or it does not rest with the majority owner. For example, a subsidiary could be in bankruptcy or operating under foreign exchange restrictions or other controls. In these cases, subsidiaries are carried on the cost basis until control by the parent is resumed.

Exhibit 19-2

Goliath Corporation
① Consolidated
Income Statements
for the Years Ended
December 31
(000s Omitted)

	19X3	19X2
Net sales and other operating revenues	$507,000	$609,100
Cost of goods sold and operating expenses, exclusive of depreciation	468,750	554,550
Depreciation	14,000	11,000
Total operating expenses	482,750	565,550
Operating income	24,250	43,550
③ Equity in earnings of affiliates	1,000	900
Total income before interest expense and income taxes	25,250	44,450
Interest expense	2,450	2,450
Income before income taxes	22,800	42,000
Income taxes	12,000	21,900
Income before minority interests	10,800	20,100
② Minority interest in consolidated subsidiaries' net income	300	600
Net consolidated income to Goliath Corporation*	10,500	19,500
Preferred dividends	500	500
Net income to Goliath Corporation common stock	$ 10,000	$ 19,000
Earnings per share of common stock		
On shares outstanding (1,000,000 shares)	$10.00[†]	$19.00
Assuming full dilution, reflecting conversion of all convertible securities (1,200,000 shares)	$8.75[‡]	$16.25

[*] This is the total figure in dollars that the accountant traditionally labels net income. It is reported accordingly in the financial press.
[†] This is the figure most widely quoted by the investment community: $10,000,000 ÷ 1,000,000 = $10.00; $19,000,000 ÷ 1,000,000 = $19.00.
[‡] Computed, respectively: $10,500,000 ÷ 1,200,000 = $8.75; $19,500,000 ÷ 1,200,000 = $16.25.

Exhibit 19-3 summarizes all the relationships depicted in the preceding exhibits. Take a few moments to review Exhibits 19-1 and 19-2 in conjunction with Exhibit 19-3. In particular, note that minority interests arise only in conjunction with *consolidated* subsidiaries. Why? Because consolidated balance sheets and income statements aggregate 100% of the detailed assets, liabilities, sales, and expenses of the subsidiary companies. Thus, if a minority interest were not recognized, the stockholders' equity and net income of the consolidated enterprise would be overstated.

In contrast, minority interests do not arise in connection with the accounting for investments in affiliated companies. Why? Because consolidated statements do not contain detailed assets, liabilities, revenues, and expenses of the affiliated companies. The investor's interests in these companies are recognized on a pro-rata basis only.

Accounting for Goodwill

Objective 3

Describe how goodwill arises and how to account for it

In Chapter 18, we defined goodwill as the excess of cost over fair (market) value of net identifiable assets of businesses acquired. We will now see how goodwill arises when one company purchases another.

Our previous example of Companies P and S assumed that the acquisition cost of S by P was equal to the amount of the stockholders' equity, or the *book value,* of S. However, the total purchase price paid by P often exceeds the book values of the assets acquired. In fact, the purchase price also often exceeds the sum of the fair market values (current values) of the identifiable individual assets less the liabilities. For example, Philip Morris paid $13 billion for Kraft, but assigned only $2 billion to identifiable individual assets. The remainder was assigned to goodwill.

To see the impact of goodwill on the consolidated statements, refer to our initial example on consolidations, where P acquired a 100% interest in S for $210 million. Suppose the price were $40 million higher, or a total of $250 million cash. For simplicity, assume that the fair values of the individual assets of S are equal to their book values. The balance sheets immediately after the acquisition are:

	Assets			= Liabilities +		Stockholders' Equity
	Investment + in S	Goodwill +	Cash and Other = Assets	Accounts Payable, Etc.	+	Stockholders' Equity
P's accounts						
Before acquisition			650 =	200	+	450
Acquisition	+250		−250 =			
S's accounts			400 =	190	+	210
Intercompany eliminations	−250 +	40	=			−210
Consolidated	0 +	40* +	800 =	390	+	450

* The $40 million "goodwill" would appear in the consolidated balance sheet as a separate intangible asset account. It often is shown as the final item in a listing of assets. It is usually amortized in a straight-line manner as an expense in the consolidated income statement over a span of no greater than 40 years.

Exhibit 19-3		Summary of Equity Method and Consolidations		
Item in Exhibits 19-1 and 19-2	**Percentage of Ownership**	**Type of Accounting**	**Balance Sheet Effects**	**Income Statement Effects**
①	100%	Consolidation	Individual assets, individual liabilities added together	Individual revenues, individual expenses added together
②	Greater than 50% and less than 100%	Consolidation	Same as 1, but recognition given to minority interest in liability section	Same as 1, but recognition given to minority interest near bottom of statement when consolidated net income is computed
③	20% to and including 50%	Equity method	Investment carried at cost plus pro-rata share of subsidiary earnings less dividends received	Equity in earnings of *affiliated* or *associated* companies shown on one line as addition to income

What if the book values of the individual assets of S are not equal to their fair values? The usual procedures are:

1. S continues as a going concern and keeps its accounts on the same basis as before.

2. P records its investment at its acquisition cost (the agreed purchase price).

3. For consolidated reporting purposes, the excess of the acquisition cost over the book value of S is identified with the individual assets, item by item. (In effect, they are revalued at the current market prices prevailing when P acquired S.) Any *remaining excess* that cannot be identified is labeled as purchased goodwill.

Suppose the fair value of the assets of S (e.g., machinery and equipment) exceeded their book value by $30 million in our example. The balance sheets immediately after acquisition would be the same as previously, with a single exception. The $40 million goodwill would now be only $10 million. The remaining $30 million would appear in the consolidated balance sheet as an integral part of the individual assets. That is, S's equipment would be shown at $30 million higher in the consolidated balance sheet than the carrying amount on S's books. Similarly, the depreciation expense on the consolidated income statement would be higher. For instance, if the equipment had five years of useful life remaining, the straight-line depreciation would be $30 million ÷ 5 = $6 million higher per year.

As in the preceding tabulation, the $10 million "goodwill" would appear in the consolidated balance sheet as a separate intangible asset account.

Goodwill and Abnormal Earnings

Goodwill is frequently misunderstood. The layperson often thinks of goodwill as being the friendly attitude of the neighborhood store manager. But goodwill can have many aspects. A purchaser may be willing to pay more than the current values of the individual assets received because the acquired company is able to generate abnormally high earnings. The causes of this excess earning power may be traceable to personalities, skills, locations, operating methods, and so forth. For example, a purchaser may be willing to pay extra because excess earnings can be forthcoming from:

1. Saving in time and costs by purchasing a corporation having a share of the market in a type of business or in a geographical area where the acquiring corporation planned expansion
2. Excellent general management skills or a unique product line
3. Potential efficiency by combination, rearrangement, or elimination of duplicate facilities and administration

Of course, "goodwill" is originally generated internally. For example, a happy combination of advertising, research, management talent, and timing may give a particular company a dominant market position for which another company is willing to pay dearly. This ability to command a premium price for the total business creates goodwill. Nevertheless, such goodwill should never be recorded by the selling company. Therefore the *only* goodwill generally recognized as an asset is that identified when one company is purchased by another. The consolidated company must then show the purchased goodwill in its financial statements.

Highlights to Remember: Part One

Nearly all corporate annual reports contain consolidated financial statements, as well as investment accounts of various sorts. Acquiring a fundamental understanding of accounting for intercorporate investments is therefore essential for the intelligent use of financial reports.

To account for ownership interests below 20%, accountants use the cost method. Interests between 20% and 50% generally require use of the equity method, and if ownership interests are above 50%, the statements are consolidated. Under the equity method and under consolidation, the investor's net income includes its proportionate share of the investee's net income. In contrast, income under the cost method includes only the dividends received from investees.

Consolidated statements combine the statements of a parent company with those of subsidiaries, and double-counting must be eliminated. If ownership is less than 100%, a minority interest is recognized. If the purchase price exceeds the fair market value of net assets acquired, the difference is recorded as an asset called goodwill.

Summary Problem for Your Review

Problem One

1. Review the section on minority interests, pages 736–737. Suppose P purchases 60% of the stock of S for a cost of .60 × $210, or $126 million. The total assets of P consist of this $126 million plus $524 million of other assets, a total of $650 million. The assets, liabilities, and shareholders' equity of S are unchanged from the amounts

given in the example on page 736. Prepare an analysis showing what amounts would appear in a consolidated balance sheet immediately after the acquisition.

2. Suppose S has a net income of $50 million for the year, and P has an operating income of $100 million. Other details are described in the example on page 735. Prepare an analysis showing what amounts would appear in a consolidated income statement and year-end balance sheet.

Solution to Problem One

1.

	Assets		=	Liabilities	+	Stockholders' Equity		
	Investment + *in S*	*Cash and Other Assets*	=	*Accounts Payable, Etc.*	+	*Minority Interest*	+	*Stockholders' Equity*
P's accounts, January 1:								
before acquisition		650	=	200			+	450
Acquisition of 60% of S	+126	−126	=					
S's accounts, January 1		400	=	190			+	210
Intercompany eliminations	−126		=			+84		−210
Consolidated, January 1	0	+ 924	=	390	+	84	+	450

2.

	P	S	Consolidated
Sales	$900	$300	$1,200
Expenses	800	250	1,050
Operating income	$100	$ 50	$ 150
Pro-rata share (60%) of unconsolidated subsidiary net income	30	—	
Net income	$130	$ 50	
Minority interest (40%) in consolidated subsidiary net income			20
Net income to consolidated entity			$ 130

	Assets		=	Liabilities	+	Stockholders' Equity		
	Investment + *in S*	*Cash and Other Assets*	=	*Accounts Payable, Etc.*	+	*Minority Interest*	+	*Stockholders' Equity*
P's accounts								
Beginning of year, before acquisition		650	=	200			+	450
Acquisition	126	−126	=					
Operating income		+100	=					+100
Share of S income	+30		=					+ 30
End of year	156	+ 624	=	200			+	580

(Continued)

S's accounts								
Beginning of year			400	=	190		+	210
Net income			+ 50	=				+ 50
End of year			450	=	190		+	260
Intercompany eliminations	−156			=		+104*		−260
Consolidated, end of year	0	+	1,074	=	390	+	104	+	580

* 84 beginning of year + (0.40 x 50) = 84 + 20 = 104.

Accounting Vocabulary: Part One

consolidated financial statements
  p. 733
cost method *p. 732*

equity method *pp. 732*
investments in affiliates *p. 738*
investments in associates *p. 738*

minority interests *p. 736*
parent company *p. 733*
subsidiary *p. 733*

Part Two: Analysis of Financial Statements

As you have seen, constructing financial statements is no easy task. Analyzing and interpreting such statements can also be difficult. But managers, investors, and other users of financial statements find the effort worthwhile. Why? Because careful analysis of financial statements can help decision makers evaluate an organization's past performance and predict its future performance. Such evaluations help managers, investors, and others make intelligent, informed financial decisions. We use the 1993 and 1994 financial statements of Microsoft Corporation in Exhibits 19-4 and 19-5 to focus on financial statement analysis.

Decisions based on comparisons of financial statements span a wide range. For example, investors use them to decide whether to buy, sell, or hold common stock. Managers and the financial community (such as bank officers and stockholders) use them as clues to help evaluate the operating and financial outlook for an organization. Budgets or pro forma statements—carefully formulated expressions of predicted results including a schedule of the amounts and timing of cash repayments—are helpful to extenders of credit, who want assurance of being paid in full and on time. For example, a set of budgeted financial statements is one of the first things a banker will request from an entrepreneur proposing a new business. Even well established companies usually need to provide pro forma statements to assure creditors that the company will pay back the amounts borrowed.

component percentages Analysis and presentation of financial statements in percentage form to aid comparability, frequently used when companies differ in size.

common-size statements Financial statements expressed in component percentages.

■ COMPONENT PERCENTAGES

When comparing companies that differ in size, analysts often apply percentage relationships, called **component percentages,** to income statements and balance sheets (see Exhibit 19-6). The resulting statements are called **common-size statements.** For example, it is difficult to compare Microsoft's 1994 $4.312 billion of current assets with the $17.9 million of Interlinq, a smaller software company. It's much easier to compare Microsoft's 1994 81% current asset *percentage* (shown in Exhibit 19-6) with Interlinq's $17.9 million ÷ $23.8 million = 75%.

Income statement percentages are usually based on sales = 100%. Microsoft seems reasonably profitable, but such percentages would have more meaning when compared with the *budgeted* performance for the current year (not shown here). Both the gross margin rate and net income percentage seem satisfactory. However, averages for these items vary greatly by industry. Comparison with other similar firms or industry averages is necessary to interpret the rates fully. Changes between one year and the next can also reveal important information. Microsoft's net income remained at 25% of sales, despite a small increase in gross margin. The main reason income did not increase was a decrease in other income (from 2% to 0% of sales).

Balance sheet percentages are usually based on total assets = 100%. Note in Exhibit 19-6 that Microsoft's current assets and current liabilities increased while the plant, property, and equipment, and stockholders' equity decreased.

Corporate annual reports to the public must contain a section that is usually labeled *management's discussion and analysis*. This section concentrates on explaining the major changes in the income statement, changes in liquidity and capital resources, and the impact of inflation. The focus is on a comparison of one year with the next. For example, Microsoft's annual report had seven pages of detailed discussions, including:

> "Net revenues [increased] 24% [in 1994].... Cost of revenues as a percentage of net revenues was 16.4% in 1994, down from 16.9% in 1992 and 1993. The percentage decreased due to lower disk prices from vendors and a greater percentage of sales of licenses to OEMs and corporations, offset by increased sales of lower-margin Microsoft Office and upgrade products.... Net income as a percentage of net revenues decreased [from 25.4% to 24.7%] in 1994, primarily due to the Stac Electronics patent litigation charge and increased research and development expenses, offset by the lower relative level of sales and marketing expenses.... The company's cash and short-term investments totaled $3,614 million at June 30, 1994 and represented 67% of total assets.... Cash generated from operations has been sufficient to fund the company's investment in research and development activities and facilities expansion."

Exhibit 19-4

Microsoft
Corporation
Balance Sheet
(millions)

	June 30			
	1994		1993	
Assets				
Current assets				
Cash and short-term investments	$3,614		$2,290	
Accounts receivable	475		338	
Inventories	102		127	
Other	121		95	
Total current assets		$ 4,312		$ 2,850
Long-term assets*				
Plant, property, and equipment, net		930		867
Other assets		121		88
Total assets		$ 5,363		$ 3,805
Liabilities and Stockholders' Equity				
Current liabilities				
Accounts payable	$ 324		$ 239	
Income taxes payable	305		127	
Accrued compensation	96		86	
Other	188		111	
Total current liabilities		$ 913		$ 563
Long-term debt		0		0
Total liabilities		$ 913		$ 563
Stockholders' equity				
Paid-in capital	$1,500		$1,086	
Retained earnings	2,950		2,156	
Total shareholders' equity		4,450		3,242
Total liabilities and shareholders' equity		$5,363		$3,805

* This caption is frequently omitted. Instead, the long-term assets are merely listed as separate items following the current assets.

Exhibit 19-5

Microsoft
Corporation
Statement of Income
(millions except
earnings per share)

		For the Year Ended June 30			
		1994		**1993**	
Net Revenues			$4,649		$3,753
Cost of revenues*			763		633
Gross profit			$3,886		$3,120
Operating expenses:					
General and administrative	166			119	
Research and development	610			470	
Sales and marketing	1,384	2,160		1,205	1,794
Operating income			1,726		1,326
Other income (expense)†			(4)		75
Income before income taxes			1,722		1,401
Provision for income taxes			576		448
Net income			$1,146		$ 953
Earnings per share‡			$ 1.88		$ 1.57

* Also called cost of goods sold.
† Primarily interest revenue and litigation charges.
‡ Microsoft pays no dividends. Publicly held companies must show earnings per share on the face of the income statement, but it is not necessary to show dividends per share. Average shares outstanding are approximately 610 million in 1994 and 606 million in 1993.

Exhibit 19-6

Microsoft
Corporation
Common-Size
Statements (millions
except percentages)

	For the Year Ended June 30			
Statement of Income	**1994**		**1993**	
Net revenues	$4,649	100%	$3,753	100%
Cost of revenues	763	16	633	17
Gross profit (or gross margin)	$3,886	84%	$3,120	83%
General and administrative	$ 166	4%	$ 119	3%
Research and development	610	13	470	13
Sales and marketing	1,384	30	1,205	32
Operating expenses	$2,160	47%	$1,794	48%
Operating income	$1,726	37%	$1,326	35%
Other income (expense)	(4)	0	75	2
Income before income taxes	$1,722	37%	$1,401	37%
Provision for income taxes	576	12	448	12
Net income	$1,146	25%	$ 953	25%
Balance Sheet				
Current assets	$4,312	81%	$2,850	75%
Plant, property, and equipment, net	930	17	867	23
Other assets	121	2	88	2
Total assets	$5,363	100%	$3,805	100%
Current liabilities	$ 913	17%	$ 563	15%
Long-term liabilities	0	0	0	0
Total liabilities	$ 913	17%	$ 563	15%
Stockholders' equity	4,450	83	3,242	85
Total equities	$5,363	100%	$3,805	100%

*Note the use of dollar signs in columns of numbers. Frequently, they are used at the top and bottom only and not for every subtotal. Their use by companies depends on the preference of management.

■ USES OF RATIOS

Objective 4

Explain and use a variety of popular financial ratios

In addition to or instead of budgets and common-size statements, investors and creditors often use ratios computed from published financial statements. Exhibit 19-7 on page 750 shows how some typical ratios are computed. Many more ratios could be computed. For example, Standard & Poor's Corporation sells a COMPUSTAT service which, via computer, can provide financial and statistical information for thousands of companies. The information includes 175 financial statement items on an annual basis and 100 items on a quarterly basis, plus limited footnote information. Exhibit 19-7 contains only the most popular ratios.[3]

Comparisons

Evaluation of a financial ratio requires a comparison. There are three main types of comparisons: (1) with a company's own historical ratios (called **time-series comparisons**), (2) with general rules of thumb or **bench marks,** and (3) with ratios of other companies or with industry averages for the same period (called **cross-sectional comparisons**).

time-series comparisons
Comparison of a company's financial ratios with its own historical ratios.

bench marks
General rules of thumb specifying appropriate levels for financial ratios.

cross-sectional comparisons
Comparisons of a company's financial ratios with ratios of other companies or with industry averages for the same period.

Consider first *time-series comparisons*. Much can be learned by examining the trend of a company's ratios. This is why annual reports typically contain a table of comparative statistics for 5 or 10 years. For example, consider the trends in three of Microsoft's profitability ratios:

	1990	1991	1992	1993	1994
Return on sales	23.6%	25.1%	25.7%	25.4%	24.7%
Return on stockholders' equity	37.7%	40.8%	40.0%	35.1%	29.8%
Earnings per share	$0.52	$0.82	$1.20	$1.57	$1.88

Note that return on sales peaked in 1992 and return on stockholders' equity peaked in 1991; both have fallen since. Earnings per share has increased substantially each year.

The second type of comparison uses broad rules of thumb as *bench marks*. For instance, the most quoted bench mark is a current ratio of 2 to 1. Others are described in *Key Business Ratios* by Dun & Bradstreet, a financial services firm. For example:

- *Fixed assets to tangible net worth*. Ordinarily this relationship should not exceed 100% for a manufacturer and 75% for a wholesaler or retailer.
- *Current debt to tangible net worth*. Ordinarily a business begins to pile up trouble when this relationship exceeds 80%.

---

[3] For more details, see George Foster, *Financial Statement Analysis*, 2d ed. (Upper Saddle River, NJ: Prentice Hall, 1986).

Exhibit 19-7 Some Typical Financial Ratios

Typical Name of Ratio	Numerator	Denominator	Appropriate Microsoft Numbers Applied to June 30 of Year	
			1994	1993
Short-term ratios				
Current ratio	Current assets	Current liabilities	4,312 ÷ 913 = 4.7	2,850 ÷ 563 = 5.1
Inventory turnover	Cost of goods sold	Average inventory at cost[†]	763 ÷ ½ (102 + 127) = 6.7 times	633 ÷ ½ (127 + 86) = 5.9 times
Average collection period in days	Average accounts receivable[†] × 365	Sales on account	[½(475 + 338) × 365] ÷ 4,649 = 32 days*	[½(338 + 270) × 365] ÷ 3,753 = 30 days
Debt-to-equity ratios				
Current debt to equity	Current liabilities	Stockholders' equity	913 ÷ 4,450 = 20.5%	563 ÷ 3,242 = 17.4%
Total debt to equity	Total liabilities	Stockholders' equity	913 ÷ 4,450 = 20.5%	563 ÷ 3,242 = 17.4%
Profitability ratios				
Gross profit rate or percentage	Gross profit or gross margin	Sales	3,886 ÷ 4,649 = 83.6%	3,120 ÷ 3,753 = 83.1%
Return on sales	Net income	Sales	1,146 ÷ 4,649 = 24.7%	953 ÷ 3,753 = 25.4%
Return on stockholders' equity	Net income	Average stockholders' equity[†]	1,146 ÷ ½(4,450 + 3,242) = 29.8%	953 ÷ ½(3,242 + 2,193) = 35.1%
Earnings per share	Net income less dividends on preferred stock, if any	Average common shares outstanding	1,146 ÷ 610 = $1.88	953 ÷ 606 = $1.57
Price earnings	Market price per share of common stock[‡]	Earnings per share	51 ÷ 1.88 = 27.1	44 ÷ 1.57 = 28.0
Dividend ratios				
Dividend yield	Dividends per common share	Market price per common share[‡]	0 ÷ 51 = 0.0%	0 ÷ 44 = 0.0%
Dividend payout	Dividends per common share	Earnings per share	0 ÷ 1.88 = 0.0%	0 ÷ 1.57 = 0.0%

* This may be easier to see as follows:
Average receivables = ½ (475 + 338) = 406.5
Average receivables as a percentage of annual sales = 406.5 ÷ 4,649 = 8.7%
Average collection period = 8.7% x 365 days = 32 days
[†] Relevant 1992 amounts: accounts receivable, $270 million; inventory, $86 million; and stockholders' equity, $2,193 million.
[‡] Market price: June 30, 1994, $51; June 30, 1993, $44.

Obviously, such bench marks are only general guides. More specific analyses come from the third type of comparisons, *examining ratios of similar companies or industry averages*. Dun & Bradstreet informs its subscribers of the credit-worthiness of thousands of individual companies. In addition, the firm regularly compiles many ratios of the companies it monitors. Each ratio in Exhibit 19-7 can be compared with industry statistics. For example, some of the Dun & Bradstreet ratios for 419 prepackaged software companies showed:

	Current Ratio	Collection Period	Current Debt to Equity	Total Debt to Equity	Return on Sales	Return on Stockholders' Equity
	(Times)	*(Days)*	*(Percent)*	*(Percent)*	*(Percent)*	*(Percent)*
419 companies						
Upper quartile*	3.0	39	23.0	37.3	11.5	58.2
Median	2.2	52	47.2	64.0	6.0	26.4
Lower quartile	1.4	83	120.0	170.0	2.6	5.4
Microsoft†	4.7	32	20.5	20.5	24.7	29.8

* The individual ratios are ranked from best to worst. The middle figure is the median. The figure ranked halfway between the median and the best is the upper quartile. Similarly, the figure ranked halfway between the median and the worst is the lower quartile.

† Ratios are from Exhibit 19-7. Please consult that exhibit for an explanation of the components of each ratio.

Our illustrative analysis focuses on one company, and 1 or 2 years. This is sufficient as a start, but analysts also examine other firms in the industry, industry averages, and a series of years to get a better perspective. Above all, recognize that a ratio by itself is of limited use. There must be a standard for comparison—a history, a similar entity, an industry average, a bench mark, or a budget.

Discussion of Specific Ratios

Consider again the ratios in Exhibit 19-7. Shown first is the current ratio, a widely used statistic. Other things being equal, the higher the current ratio, the more assurance the creditor has about being paid in full and on time. Microsoft's current ratio of 4.7 has declined from 5.1 but is still well above the industry median of 2.2.

The inventory turnover rate is not available from Dun & Bradstreet on an industry-comparable basis. However, it can be an important signal. For example, a decrease in inventory turnover may suggest slower-moving (or even unsalable) merchandise or a worsening coordination of the buying and selling functions. Many companies have improved their inventory turnover by installing just-in-time inventory systems. Microsoft's inventory turnover increased from 5.9 to 6.7 in 1994. Whether that rate is "fast" or "slow" depends on past performance and the performance of similar companies. For comparison, Lotus has an inventory turnover of 9.0.

Microsoft's average collection period of 32 days is less favorable than the 30 days in 1993, but it places Microsoft well into the upper quartile of prepackaged software firms according to Dun & Bradstreet's industry data. A lengthening collection period might indicate increasing acceptance of poor credit risks or less energetic collection efforts.

Note how the average collection period depends on sales *on account*. The computation in Exhibit 19-7 assumes that all sales are credit sales. However, if we relax our assumption, the 32-day period would rise markedly. For example, if half the sales were for cash, the average collection period for accounts receivable would change from 32 to 64 days:

$$\frac{\frac{1}{2}\,(475\ +\ 338)\ \times\ 365}{\frac{1}{2}\,(4{,}649)} = 64\ \text{days}$$

The third and fourth columns of the Dun & Bradstreet tabulation show debt-to-equity ratios. Both creditors and shareholders watch these ratios to judge the degree of risk of insolvency and stability of profits. Typically, companies with heavy debt in relation to ownership capital are in greater danger of suffering net losses or even bankruptcy when business conditions sour. Why? Because revenues and many expenses decline, but interest expenses and maturity dates do not change. Microsoft's ratios of 20.5% for both ratios are well below the medians for the industry; they reflect low levels of risk or uncertainty concerning the company's ability to pay its debts on time.

Investors find profitability ratios especially helpful. Examine the gross profit rate and the return on sales. Microsoft's gross profit rate increased from 83.1% in 1993 to 83.6% in 1994, but its return on sales declined from 25.4% to 24.7%. These are both measures of *operating success*. Dun & Bradstreet does not report gross profit rates, but Microsoft's return on sales is high enough to rank high in the top quartile of prepackaged software companies.

More important to shareholders is the rate of return on their invested capital, a measure of *overall accomplishment*. Microsoft's 1994 rate of 29.8% is down from the 35.1% of 1993, and it is barely above the industry median of 26.4%.

The final four ratios in Exhibit 19-7 are based on earnings and dividends. The first, earnings per share of common stock (EPS), is the most popular of all ratios. This is the only ratio that is required as part of the body of financial statements of publicly held companies in the United States. The EPS must be presented on the face of the income statement. For most companies it is calculated as in Exhibit 19-7: net income less dividends on preferred stock divided by average common shares outstanding. For companies holding securities that can be exchanged for or converted to common shares, EPS calculations are more complex. Such computations are beyond the scope of this discussion.

The computation of three other ratios is shown in Exhibit 19-7: price earnings, dividend yield, and dividend payout. These ratios are especially useful to investors in the common stock of the company. Because Microsoft pays no dividends, the last two ratios are both zero.

Operating Performance Ratios

In addition to the more focused ratios just cited, businesspeople often look at the rate of return on invested capital as an important measure of overall accomplishment:

$$\text{rate of return on investment} = \frac{\text{income}}{\text{invested capital}} \tag{1}$$

On the surface, this measure is straightforward, but its ingredients may differ according to the purpose it is to serve. What is invested capital, the denominator of the ratio? What income figure is appropriate?

The measurement of *operating* performance (how profitably assets are employed) should not be influenced by the management's *financial* decisions (i.e., how assets are obtained). Operating performance is best measured by pretax operating rate of return on average total assets:

$$\frac{\text{pretax operating rate}}{\text{of return on average total assets}} = \frac{\text{operating income}}{\text{average total assets}} \qquad (2)$$

For Microsoft, this ratio is $1,726 \div \$4,584 = 37.7\%$.

The right-hand side of equation 2 consists, in turn, of two important ratios:

$$\frac{\text{operating income}}{\text{average total assets}} = \frac{\text{operating income}}{\text{sales}} \times \frac{\text{sales}}{\text{average total assets}} \qquad (3)$$

The right-hand terms in equation 3 are often called the *operating income percentage on sales* and *total asset turnover*, respectively. Therefore, Microsoft's operating performance can be expressed as:

$$\frac{\text{pretax operating rate}}{\text{of return on average total assets}} = \frac{\text{operating income}}{\text{percentage on sales}} \times \frac{\text{total asset}}{\text{turnover}} \qquad (4)$$

$$= \frac{\$1,726}{\$4,649} \times \frac{\$4,649}{\frac{1}{2}(\$5,363 + \$3,805)}$$

$$= 37.13\% \times 1.0142 = 37.7\%$$

If ratios are used to evaluate operating performance, they should exclude extraordinary items. Such items are not expected to recur, and therefore they should not be included in measures of normal performance.

A scrutiny of equation 4 shows that there are two basic factors in profit making: operating margin percentages and turnover. An improvement in either will, by itself, increase the rate of return on total assets.

The ratios used can also be computed on the basis of figures after taxes. However, the peculiarities of the income tax laws may sometimes distort results—for example, the tax rate may change, or losses carried back or forward might eliminate the tax in certain years.

■ EFFICIENT MARKETS AND INVESTOR DECISIONS

Much recent research in accounting and finance has concentrated on whether the stock markets are "efficient." An **efficient capital market** is one in which market prices "fully reflect" all information available to the public. Therefore searching for "underpriced" securities in such a market would be fruitless unless an investor has information that is not generally available. If the real-world markets are indeed efficient, a relatively inactive portfolio approach would be an appropriate investment strategy for most investors. The hallmarks of the approach are risk control, high diversification, and low turnover of securities. The role of accounting information would mainly be in identifying the different degrees of risk among various stocks so that investors can maintain desired levels of risk and diversification.

Research in finance and accounting during the past 30 years has reinforced the idea that financial ratios and other data such as reported earnings provide inputs to predictions of such economic phenomena as financial failure or earnings growth. Furthermore, many ratios are used simultaneously rather than one at a time for such predictions. Above all, the research shows that accounting reports are only one source of information and that in the aggregate the market is not fooled by companies that choose the least-conservative accounting policies. In sum, the market as a whole generally sees through any attempts by companies to gain favor through the choice of accounting policies that tend to boost immediate income. Thus there is evidence that the stock markets may indeed be "efficient," at least in their reflection of most accounting data.[4]

Suppose you are the chief executive officer of a company with reported earnings of $4 per share and a stock price of $40. You are contemplating changing your method of depreciation for investor-reporting purposes from accelerated to straight-line. Your competitors use straight-line. You think your company's stock price unjustifiably suffers in comparison with other companies in the same industry.

If straight-line depreciation is adopted, your company's reported earnings will be $5 instead of $4 per share. Would the stock price rise accordingly from $40 to $50? No, the empirical research on these issues indicates that the stock price would remain at $40 (all other things equal).

The chief executive's beliefs as shown in the preceding example are shared by many managers, who essentially adhere to an extremely narrow view of the role of an income statement. Such a "bottom-line" mentality is slowly, surely, and sensibly falling into disrepute. At the risk of unfair exaggeration, the view is summarized as:

1. The income statement is the sole (or at least the primary) source of information about a company.
2. Lenders and shareholders invest in a company because of its reported earnings. For instance, the higher the reported earnings per share, the higher the stock price, and the easier it is to raise capital.

Basically, these arguments assume that investors can be misled by how reported earnings are measured. But there is considerable evidence that securities markets are not fooled with respect to accounting changes that are devoid of economic substance (i.e., have no effect on cash flows). Why? Because the change generally reveals no new information, so no significant change in stock price is likely.

Remember that the market is efficient only with respect to *publicly available* information. Therefore significant accounting issues deal primarily with the disclosure of new information, not the format for reporting already available data.

Be aware also that accounting statements are not the only source of financial information about companies. Some alternative sources are the following: company press releases (e.g., capital expenditure announcements); trade association publications (e.g., reports with industry statistics); brokerage house analyses (e.g., company or industry studies); and government economic reports (e.g., gross national product and unemployment figures). If accounting reports are to be useful, they must have some advantage over alternative sources in disclosing new information. Financial statement information may be more directly related to the item of interest, and it may be more reliable, less costly, or more timely than information from alternative sources.

---

[4] Several "anomalies" prevent unqualified endorsement of stock market efficiency. Recent research shows that accounting data may be combined to yield information that is not reflected in stock prices. Nevertheless, the evidence that stock prices efficiently reflect basic *accounting data* is quite strong.

The research described previously concentrates on the effects of accounting on investors in the aggregate. Individual investors vary in how they analyze financial statements. One by one, individual users must either incur the costs of conducting careful analyses or delegate that chore to professional analysts. In any event, intelligent analysis cannot be accomplished without an understanding of the assumptions and limitations of financial statements including the presence of various alternative accounting methods.

Highlights to Remember: Part Two

Financial ratios aid the intelligent analysis of financial statements. To compare companies that differ in size, analysts use component percentages. They also prepare a variety of ratios and compare them with the company's own historical ratios, with general bench marks, and with ratios of other companies or industry averages. They use short-term ratios, debt-to-equity ratios, profitability ratios, and dividend ratios. An especially important ratio for assessing operating performance is the rate of return on invested capital.

Annual reports and the financial statements contained therein are only one source of information used by investors. Evidence indicates that stock prices fully reflect most publicly available information, including accounting numbers. Investors apparently are not fooled by the format of the information. Therefore, accounting regulators should focus on disclosure issues, not format.

Summary Problem for Your Review

Problem One appeared earlier in the chapter.

Problem Two

Examine Exhibits 19-4 and 19-5, pages 747–48. Assume some new data in place of certain old data for the June 30, 1994, balance sheet (in millions):

	Old Data	New Data
Accounts receivable	$ 475	$ 525
Inventories	102	121
Total current assets	4,312	4,600
Paid-in capital	1,500	1,700
Total stockholders' equity	4,450	4,900

Required   Compute the following ratios applicable to June 30, 1994, or to the fiscal year 1994, as appropriate: current ratio, inventory turnover, average collection period, and return on stockholders' equity. Compare this new set of ratios with the old set of ratios. Are the new ratios more desirable? Explain.

Solution to Problem Two

All the ratios would be affected.

$$\text{current ratio} = \frac{\text{current assets}}{\text{current liabilities}}$$

$$= \frac{\$4,600}{\$913} = 5.0 \text{ instead of } 4.7$$

$$\text{inventory turnover} = \frac{\text{cost of goods sold}}{\text{average inventory}}$$

$$= \frac{\$763}{\frac{1}{2}(\$121 + \$127)}$$

$$= \frac{\$763}{\$124} = 6.2 \text{ times instead of } 6.7 \text{ times}$$

$$\frac{\text{average collection}}{\text{period}} = \frac{\text{average accounts receivable}}{\text{sales on account}} \times 365$$

$$= \frac{\frac{1}{2}(\$525 + \$338)}{\$4,649} \times 365$$

$$= \frac{431.5 \times 365}{\$4,649} = 34 \text{ days instead of } 32 \text{ days}$$

$$\frac{\text{return on}}{\text{stockholders' equity}} = \frac{\text{net income}}{\text{average stockholders' equity}}$$

$$= \frac{\$1,146}{\frac{1}{2}(\$4,900 + \$3,242)}$$

$$= 28.2\% \text{ instead of } 29.8\%$$

The new set of ratios has good news and bad news. The good news is that the company would appear to be slightly more liquid (a current ratio of 5.0 instead of 4.7). The bad news is that the inventory turnover, the average collection period, and the rate of return on stockholders' equity are less attractive.

Accounting Vocabulary: Part Two

For various financial ratios, see Exhibit 19-7, page 750. Also become familiar with:

bench marks, *p. 749*
common-size statements, *p. 745*

component percentages, *p. 745*
cross-sectional comparisons, *p. 749*

efficient capital market, *p. 753*
time-series comparisons, *p. 749*

Fundamental Assignment Material

Special Note: Problems relating to Part One of the chapter are presented first in each subgrouping of the assignment material.

General Exercises and Problems

Required

19-A1 **Cost or Equity Method**

Suppose General Motors acquired 25% of the voting stock of Dearborn Tire Co. for $60 million cash. In year 1, Dearborn Tire had a net income of $48 million and paid a cash dividend of $32 million.

Using the equity and the cost methods, show the effects of the three transactions on the accounts of General Motors. Use the balance sheet equation format.

19-A2   Consolidated Financial Statements

Suppose Brentwood Publishing Company acquired a 100% voting interest in Mendoza Book Company for $50 million cash at the start of the year. Immediately before the business combination, each company had the following condensed balance sheet accounts (in millions):

	Brentwood	Mendoza
Cash and other assets	$250	$70
Accounts payable, etc.	$100	$20
Stockholders' equity	150	50
Total equities	$250	$70

1. Prepare a tabulation of the consolidated balance sheet accounts immediately after the acquisition. Use the balance sheet equation format.
2. Suppose Brentwood and Mendoza have the following results for the year:

	Brentwood	Mendoza
Sales	$310	$100
Expenses	225	90

Prepare income statements for the year for Brentwood, Mendoza, and the consolidated entity. Assume that neither Brentwood nor Mendoza sells items to the other.

3. Present the effects of the operations for the year on Brentwood's accounts and on Mendoza's accounts, using the balance sheet equation. Also tabulate the consolidated balance sheet accounts at the end of the year. Assume that liabilities are unchanged.
4. Suppose Mendoza paid a cash dividend of $8 million. What accounts in requirement 3 would be affected and by how much?

19-A3   Minority Interests

This extends the preceding problem. However, this problem is self-contained because all the facts are reproduced below. Brentwood Publishing Company acquired an 80% voting interest in Mendoza Book Company for $40 million cash at the start of the year. Immediately before the business combination, each company had the following condensed balance sheet accounts (in millions):

	Brentwood	Mendoza
Cash and other assets	$250	$70
Accounts payable, etc.	$100	$20
Stockholders' equity	150	50
Total equities	$250	$70

1. Prepare a tabulation of the consolidated balance sheet accounts immediately after the acquisition. Use the balance sheet equation format.
2. Suppose Brentwood and Mendoza have the following results for the year:

	Brentwood	Mendoza
Sales	$310	$100
Expenses	225	90

Prepare income statements for the year for Brentwood, Mendoza, and the consolidated entity.

3. Using the balance sheet equation format, present the effects of the operations for the year on Brentwood's accounts and Mendoza's accounts. Also tabulate consolidated balance sheet accounts at the end of the year. Assume that liabilities are unchanged.
4. Suppose Mendoza paid a cash dividend of $8 million. What accounts in requirement 3 would be affected and by how much?

19-A4   Goodwill and Consolidation

 This extends Problem 19-A2. However, this problem is self-contained because all the facts are reproduced below. Brentwood Publishing Company acquired a 100% voting interest in Mendoza Book Company for $80 million cash at the start of the year. Immediately before the business combination, each company had the following condensed balance sheet accounts (in millions):

	Brentwood	Mendoza
Cash and other assets	$250	$70
Accounts payable, etc.	$100	$20
Stockholders' equity	150	50
Total equities	$250	$70

Assume that the fair values of Mendoza's individual assets were equal to their book values.

Required

1. Prepare a tabulation of the consolidated balance sheet accounts immediately after the acquisition. Use the balance sheet equation format.
2. If goodwill is going to be amortized over 40 years, how much was amortized for the first year? If over 5 years, how much was amortized for the first year?
3. Suppose the book values of Mendoza's individual assets are equal to their fair market values except for equipment. The net book value of equipment is $15 million and its fair market value is $25 million. The equipment has a remaining useful life of 4 years. Straight-line depreciation is used.

   a. Describe how the consolidated balance sheet accounts immediately after the acquisition would differ from those in requirement 1. Be specific as to accounts and amounts.

   b. By how much will consolidated income differ in comparison with the consolidated income that would be reported in requirement 2? Assume amortization of goodwill over a 40-year period.

19-A5   Rate-of-Return Computations

1. Baiol Chemical Company reported a 5% operating margin on sales, a 10% pretax operating return on total assets, and $600 million of total assets. Compute the (a) operating income, (b) total sales, and (c) total asset turnover.
2. Ito Electronics Corporation reported ¥600 million of sales, ¥18 million of operating income, and a total asset turnover of 5 times. (¥ is Japanese yen.) Compute the (a) total assets, (b) operating margin percentage on sales, and (c) pretax operating return on total assets.

Understanding Published Financial Reports

19-B1 Equity Method

Suppose Sears acquired one-third of the voting stock of Maytag Corporation for $50 million cash. In year 1, Maytag had a net income of $45 million and paid cash dividends of $24 million.

Required

Prepare a tabulation that compares the equity method and the cost method of accounting for Sears's investment in Maytag. Show the effects on the balance sheet equation under each method. What is the year-end balance in the Investment in Maytag account under the equity method? Under the cost method? Which method should Sears use for reporting its investment in Maytag?

19-B2 Consolidated Financial Statements

Consider the actual purchase of boat maker Bayliner, Inc., by Brunswick Corporation. The purchase price was $400 million for a 100% interest.

Assume that the book value and the fair market value of Bayliner's net assets was $400 million. The balance sheet accounts immediately after the transaction were approximately (in millions):

	Brunswick	Bayliner
Investment in Bayliner	$ 400	—
Cash and other assets	1,000	$600
Total assets	$1,400	$600
Liabilities	$ 800	$ 200
Stockholders' equity	600	400
Total equities	$1,400	$600

Required

1. Using the balance sheet equation format, prepare a tabulation of the consolidated balance sheet accounts immediately after the acquisition.
2. Suppose Bayliner had sales of $600 million and expenses of $500 million for the year, and Brunswick had sales of $1,800 million and expenses of $1,300 million. Prepare income statements for Brunswick, for Bayliner, and for the consolidated company. Assume that neither Brunswick nor Bayliner sold items to the other.
3. Using the balance sheet equation, present the effects of the operations for the year on the accounts of Bayliner and Brunswick. Also tabulate the consolidated balance sheet accounts at the end of the year. Assume that liabilities are unchanged.
4. Suppose Bayliner paid a cash dividend of $12 million. What accounts in requirement 3 would be affected and by how much?

19-B3 Investment in Equity Securities

Ford owns 25% of the stock of Mazda Motor Corp. In 1993 Mazda reported net income of $12 million and declared cash dividends of $64 million. Ford accounted for its investment in Mazda by the equity method.

Required

1. Compute the amount of income recognized by Ford in 1993 from its investment in Mazda.
2. Assume that Ford had a balance of $900 million in its "Investment in Mazda" account at the beginning of 1993. Compute the balance in the account at the end of 1993.

3. Suppose Ford had used the cost method to account for its investment in Mazda:

    a. Compute the amount of income recognized by Ford in 1993 from its investment in Mazda.

    b. Assume that Ford had a balance of $800 million in its "Investment in Mazda" account at the beginning of 1993. Compute the balance in the account at the end of 1993.

4. Indicate briefly how the following three classes of investments should be accounted for: (a) greater than 50% interest, (b) 20% through 50% interest, and (c) less than 20% interest.

19-B4 Income Ratios and Asset Turnover

A semiannual report to the stockholders of Texaco included the following comments on earnings:

> On an annualized basis, net income represented an 8.9% return on average total assets of approximately $27.3 billion and an 18.9% return on average stockholders' equity.... Net income per gallon on all petroleum products sold worldwide averaged 3.6 cents. Net income was 4 cents on each dollar of revenue.

Required Using only this information, compute the (1) total asset turnover, (2) net income, (3) total revenues, (4) average stockholders' equity, and (5) gallons of petroleum products sold.

19-B5 Financial Ratios

Albertson's has 676 stores and is the fourth largest retail food and drug chain in the United States. Excerpts from the company's 1994 annual report are in Exhibit 19-8. Albertson's paid cash dividends of $.44 per common share in fiscal 1994, and an average of 254,227,000 shares were outstanding during the year. Assume that Albertson's has no stock options or convertible securities. The company's current market price is $30 per share.

Required Compute the following financial ratios for fiscal 1994:

1. Current ratio
2. Inventory turnover
3. Current debt to equity
4. Total debt to equity
5. Gross profit rate
6. Return on sales
7. Return on stockholders' equity
8. Earnings per share
9. Price earnings
10. Dividend yield
11. Dividend payout

Additional Assignment Material

Questions

19-1. What is the equity method?

19-2. Contrast the cost method and the equity method.

19-3. "The equity method is usually used for long-term investments." Do you think this is appropriate? Explain.

19-4. Distinguish between control of a company and a significant influence over a company.

19-5. What criterion is used to determine whether a parent-subsidiary relationship exists?

19-6. Why have subsidiaries? Why not have the corporation take the form of a single legal entity?

19-7. "A consolidated financial statement simply adds together the separate accounts of a parent company and its subsidiaries." Do you agree? Explain.

19-8. What is a minority interest?

19-9. "The lower-of-cost-or-market rule is applied to short-term investments in marketable equity securities." Do you agree? Explain.

19-10. "Goodwill is the excess of purchase price over the book values of the individual assets acquired." Do you agree? Explain.

19-11. "It is better to write off goodwill immediately, even though it can be amortized over 40 years." Do you agree? Why?

19-12. "Pro forma statements are the formal financial statements that companies file with the Securities and Exchange Commission." Do you agree? Explain.

Exhibit 19-8	
Albertson's, Inc. Income Statement and Balance Sheet (in millions)	

Income Statement for the Year Ended February 3, 1994

Sales	$11,284
Cost of sales	8,493
Gross profit	$ 2,791
Other expenses (summarized)	2,239
Earnings before income taxes	$ 552
Income taxes	212
Net earnings	$ 340

	February 3, 1994	January 28, 1993
Balance Sheet		
Assets		
Inventories	$ 872	$ 830
Other current assets (summarized)	250	183
Total current assets	$ 1,122	$1,013
Land, buildings, and equipment (net)	2,082	1,845
Other assets	91	88
Total assets	$ 3,295	$2,946
Liabilities and stockholders' equity		
Current liabilities (summarized)	$ 990	$ 813
Long-term liabilities (summarized)	916	744
Total liabilities	$ 1,906	$1,557
Stockholders' equity (summarized)	1,389	1,389
Total liabilities and stockholders' equity	$ 3,295	$2,946

19-13. Name the three types of comparisons made with ratios.

19-14. Why is it useful to analyze income statements and balance sheets by component percentages?

19-15. What two ratios are multiplied together to give the pretax operating rate of return on average total assets?

19-16. "Ratios are mechanical and incomplete." Explain.

19-17. "An efficient capital market is one where securities are traded through stockbrokers." Do you agree? Explain?

19-18. Give three sources of information for investors besides accounting information.

19-19. Evaluate the following quotation from *Forbes*: "If IBM had been forced to expense [the software development cost of] $785 million, its earnings would have been cut by 72 cents a share. With IBM selling at 14 times earnings, expensing the costs might have knocked over $10 off IBM's share price."

19-20. Is return on sales a good measure of a company's performance?

19-21. Suppose the president of your company wanted to switch depreciation methods to increase reported net income: "Our stock price is 10% below what I think it should be; changing depreciation method will increase income by 10%, thus getting our share price up to its proper level." How would you respond?

**General
Exercises and
Problems**

Required

19-22   Equity Method

Company X acquired 25% of the voting stock of Company Y for $90 million cash. In year 1, Y had a net income of $40 million and paid cash dividends of $24 million.

Prepare a tabulation that compares the equity method and the cost method of accounting for X's investment in Y. Show the effects on the balance sheet equation under each method. What is the year-end balance in the investment in Y account under the equity method? Under the cost method?

19-23   Consolidated Financial Statements

Sacramento Company (the parent) owns 100% of the common stock of Valley Apricot Company (the subsidiary), which was acquired at the start of 19X0. Their financial statements follow:

	Sacramento (Parent)	Valley Apricot (Subsidiary)
Income Statement for 19X0		
Revenue and "other income"	$4,100,000	$1,000,000
Expenses	3,800,000	900,000
Net income	$ 300,000	$ 100,000
Balance Sheets, December 31, 19X0		
Assets	$1,000,000	$ 400,000
Liabilities to creditors	$ 450,000	$ 100,000
Stockholders' equity	550,000	300,000
Total liabilities and stockholders' equity	$1,000,000	$ 400,000

Required

1. Valley Apricot had enjoyed a fantastically profitable year in 19X0. Sacramento's income statement had been prepared by showing its claim to Valley Apricot's income as part of "other income." On the other hand, Sacramento's balance sheet is really not completed. The $1 million of assets of Sacramento includes a $200,000 investment in Valley Apricot and does not include Sacramento's claim to Valley Apricot's 19X0 net income.

   Prepare a consolidated income statement and a consolidated balance sheet. Use the balance sheet equation format for the latter.

2. Suppose Sacramento Company owned 60% of Valley Apricot Company. Liabilities to creditors are unchanged. The assets of Sacramento include a $120,000 investment in Valley Apricot instead of $200,000. However, assume the total assets are $1 million. The balance sheet is really not completed because the investment account does not reflect the claim to Valley Apricot's 19X0 net income. Similarly, Sacramento's revenue and other income is $4.06 million, not $4.1 million, but expenses remain at $3.8 million as in requirement 1.

   Prepare a consolidated income statement and a consolidated balance sheet. Use the balance sheet equation format for the latter.

19-24   Determination of Goodwill

Refer to the preceding problem, requirement 1. Suppose the investment in Valley Apricot in requirement 1 was $280,000 instead of the $200,000 as stated. This would mean that the "other assets" would be $720,000 instead of $800,000. Would the consolidated income differ? How? Be as specific as possible. Would the consolidated balance sheet differ? How? Be as specific as possible.

19-25 Purchased Goodwill

Consider the following balance sheets (in millions):

	Quinn Chemical Company	Anderson Drug Company
Cash	$ 720	$ 80
Inventories	360	70
Plant assets, net	360	60
Total assets	$1,440	$210
Common stock and paid-in capital	$ 470	$120
Retained income	970	90
Total liabilities and stockholders' equity	$1,440	$210

Quinn paid $290 million to Anderson stockholders for all their stock. The "fair value" of the plant assets of Anderson is $140 million. The fair value of cash and inventories is equal to their carrying amounts. Quinn and Anderson continued to keep separate books.

Required

1. Prepare a tabulation showing the balance sheets of Quinn, of Anderson, Intercompany Eliminations, and Consolidated immediately after the acquisition.
2. Suppose only $100 million rather than $140 million of the total purchase price of $290 million could be logically assigned to the plant assets. How would the consolidated accounts be affected?
3. Refer to the facts in requirement 1. Suppose Quinn had paid $330 million rather than $290 million. State how your tabulation in requirement 1 would change.

19-26 Amortization and Depreciation

Refer to the preceding problem, requirement 3. Suppose a year passes, and Quinn and Anderson generate individual net incomes of $90 million and $45 million, respectively. The latter is after a deduction by Anderson of $12 million of straight-line depreciation. Compute the consolidated net income if goodwill is amortized (1) over 40 years and (2) over 10 years. Ignore income taxes.

19-27 Allocation of Total Purchase Price to Assets

Western Electronics and Paramount Cinema had the following balance sheet accounts as of December 31, 19X3 (in millions):

	Western Electronics	Paramount Cinema		Western Electronics	Paramount Cinema
Cash and receivables	$ 30	$ 22	Current liabilities	$ 50	$ 20
Inventories	120	3	Common stock	100	10
Plant assets, net	150	95	Retained income	150	90
Total assets	$300	$120	Total liabilities and stockholders' equity	$300	$120
Net income for 19X3	$ 19	$ 4			

On January 4, 19X4, these firms merged. Western issued $160 million of its shares (at market value) in exchange for all the shares of Paramount, a motion picture division of a large company. The inventory of films acquired through the combination had been fully amortized on Paramount's books.

During 19X4, Paramount received revenue of $22 million from the rental of films from its inventory.

Western earned $25 million on its other operations (i.e., excluding Paramount) during 19X4. Paramount broke even on its other operations (i.e., excluding the film rental contracts) during 19X4.

1. Prepare a consolidated balance sheet for the combined company immediately after the combination on a purchase basis. Assume that $60 million of the purchase price was assigned to the inventory of films.
2. Prepare a comparison of Western's net income between 19X3 and 19X4 where 25% of the cost of the film inventories would be properly matched against the revenue from the film rentals. What would be the net income for 19X4 if the $60 million were assigned to goodwill rather than to the library of films, and goodwill were amortized over 40 years?

19-28   Preparation of Consolidated Financial Statements

The Purdy Medical Instruments Company's fiscal year ends on December 31. The company had the following items on its 19X3 income statement and balance sheet (in millions):

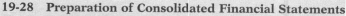

Net sales and other operating revenue	$890
Investments in affiliated companies	100
Common stock, 10,000,000, $1 par	10
Depreciation and amortization	20
Accounts payable	210
Cash	25
Paid-in capital in excess of par	102
Interest expense	25
Retained income	198
Accrued income taxes payable	20
Cost of goods sold and operating expenses, exclusive of depreciation and amortization	640
Subordinated debentures, 11% interest, due December 31, 19X9	100
Minority interest in consolidated subsidiaries' net income	20
Goodwill	100
First-mortgage bonds, 10% interest, due December 31, 19Y3	80
Property, plant, and equipment, net	120
Preferred stock, 2,000,000 shares, $50 par, dividend rate is $5 per share, each share is convertible into one share of common stock	100
Short-term investments at cost, which approximates current market	45
Income tax expense	90
Accounts receivable, net	180
Minority interest in subsidiaries	90
Inventories at average cost	340
Dividends declared and paid on preferred stock	10
Equity in earnings of affiliated companies	20

Required Prepare Purdy's consolidated 19X3 income statement and its consolidated balance sheet for December 31, 19X3.

19-29 Financial Ratios

The annual reports of Trondheim Fiske, a Norwegian fishing supply company, included the following selected data (in millions):

	19X3	19X2	19X1
Annual amounts:			
Net income	Nkr 95*	Nkr 60	Nkr 25
Gross margin on sales	520	380	200
Cost of goods sold	980	620	300
Operating expenses	380	295	165
Income tax expense	45	25	10
Dividends declared	30	15	5
End-of-year amounts:			
Long-term assets	Nkr 250	Nkr 220	Nkr 180
Long-term debt	80	65	40
Current liabilities	70	55	35
Cash	10	5	10
Accounts receivable	95	70	40
Merchandise inventory	120	85	60
Paid-in capital	205	205	205
Retained income	120	55	10

* Nkr is Norwegian kroner. In recent years the exchange rate has varied between five and seven Nkr per dollar.

During each of the 3 years, there were outstanding 10 million shares of capital stock, all common. Assume that all sales were on account and that the applicable market prices per share of stock were Nkr30 for 19X2 and Nkr40 for 19X3.

Required
1. Compute each of the following for each of the last 2 years, 19X2 and 19X3:

    a. Rate of return on sales
    b. Rate of return on stockholders' equity
    c. Inventory turnover
    d. Current ratio
    e. Ratio of total debt to stockholders' equity
    f. Ratio of current debt to stockholders' equity
    g. Gross profit rate
    h. Average collection period for accounts receivable
    i. Price-earnings ratio
    j. Dividend-payout percentage
    k. Dividend yield

2. Answer yes or no to each of these questions and indicate which of the computations in requirement 1 support your answer:

    a. Has the merchandise become more salable?
    b. Is there a decrease in the effectiveness of collection efforts?
    c. Has gross profit rate improved?

   d. Has the rate of return on sales deteriorated?

   e. Has the rate of return on owners' investment increased?

   f. Are dividends relatively more generous?

   g. Have the risks of insolvency changed significantly?

   h. Has the market price of the stock become cheaper relative to earnings?

   i. Have business operations improved?

   j. Has there been a worsening of the company's ability to pay current debts on time?

   k. Has there been a decline in the cash return on the market value of the capital stock?

   l. Did the collectibility of the receivables improve?

3. Basing your observations on only the available data and the ratios you computed, prepare some brief comments on the company's operations and financial changes during the 3 years.

Understanding Published Financial Reports

19-30   Classification on Balance Sheet

The following accounts appeared in the annual report of the Mitsubishi Kasei Corporation, Japan's premier integrated chemical company:

1. Minority interests in consolidated subsidiaries

2. Current maturities of long-term debt

3. Investments in and advances to nonconsolidated subsidiaries and affiliates

4. Prepaid expenses

5. Accrued income taxes

6. Treasury stock at cost

Required   Indicate in detail in which section of the balance sheet each account should appear.

19-31   Meaning of Account Descriptions

The following account descriptions were found in an annual report of E. I. duPont de Nemours Company:

- Minority interests in earnings of consolidated subsidiaries
- Minority interest in consolidated subsidiaries
- Investments in affiliates
- Equity in earnings of affiliates

In your own words, explain what each type of account represents. Indicate whether the item appears on the balance sheet or the income statement.

19-32   Affiliated Companies

Seagram Company Ltd. owns 24.5% of E. I. duPont de Nemours (usually called simply Du Pont). Seagram's fiscal 1994 income statement included the following two items:

- Dividend income from E.I. duPont de Nemours & Co. $ 295,000,000
- Equity in unremitted Du Pont earnings   160,000,000

The balance sheet included the following:

- Common stock of E. I. duPont de Nemours $3,154,000,000

Required

1. Compute Du Pont's net earnings and total cash dividends declared.

2. Assume that Seagram neither purchased nor sold common stock in Du Pont during fiscal 1994. Compute the balance in the "Common stock of E. I. duPont de Nemours" at the beginning of fiscal 1994.

3. Suppose Seagram purchased its Du Pont stock on the first day of fiscal 1994 for the amount computed in requirement 2 and accounted for Du Pont using the cost method instead of the equity method. What amounts would be shown in Seagram's financial statements for the following: (a) total income from E.I. duPont de Nemours in fiscal 1994, and (b) investment in common stock of E. I. duPont de Nemours at the end of fiscal 1994.

19-33   Consolidations in Japan

A few years ago Japan's finance ministry issued a directive requiring the 600 largest Japanese companies to produce consolidated financial statements. The previous practice had been to use parent-company-only statements. A story in *Business Week* said: "Financial observers hope that the move will help end the tradition-honored Japanese practice of 'window dressing' the parent company financial results by shoving losses onto hapless subsidiaries, whose red ink was seldom revealed.... When companies needed to show a bigger profit, they would sell their product to subsidiaries at an inflated price.... Or the parent company charged a higher rent to a subsidiary company using its building."

Required   Could a parent company follow the quoted practices and achieve window dressing in its parent-only financial statements if it used the equity method of accounting for its intercorporate investments? The cost method? Explain.

19-34   Minority Interests

Dow Chemical Company owns 72% of Marion Merrell Dow, a consolidated subsidiary. In 1993 Marion Merrell Dow had net income of $362 million and paid dividends of $274 million. Dow Chemical had net income of $644 million. Assume that Marion Merrell Dow was the only consolidated subsidiary of Dow Chemical that was not 100% owned.

Required   1. Dow Chemical's income statement included an amount labeled "Minority interests' share in income." Compute its amount.
2. Compute Dow Chemical's "Income before minority interests." Explain your computation.
3. Does Dow Chemical's consolidated balance sheet contain an asset such as "Investment in Marion Merrell Dow"? Explain.
4. Dow Chemical's balance sheet includes the following:
   * Minority interest in subsidiary companies $2,439,000,000

Where on the balance sheet do you expect to find this item? Explain.

19-35   Minority Interest

The consolidated financial statements of Caesars World, Inc., the casino company, included the accounts of Caesars New Jersey, Inc., an 86.6%-owned subsidiary. Assume that Caesars New Jersey was Caesars World's only consolidated subsidiary. Caesars World's income statement contained the following (in thousands):

Income before minority interest	$40,793
Minority interest in earnings of consolidated subsidiary	3,990
Net income	$36,803

Caesars World's account "Minority interest in consolidated subsidiary" listed $25,112,000 at the beginning of the year. Caesars New Jersey paid no dividends. Assume that Caesars World did not buy or sell any of its interest in Caesars New Jersey during the year.

Required   1. Compute the net income of Caesars New Jersey.
2. What proportion of Caesars World's $36,803,000 net income was contributed by Caesars New Jersey?

3. Compute Caesars World's balance in "Minority interest in consolidated subsidiary" at the end of the year.
4. Comment on the reason for including a line for minority interest in the income statement and balance sheet of Caesars World.

19-36 Income Ratios and Asset Turnover

Briggs & Stratton is the world's largest producer of air-cooled gasoline engines for outdoor power equipment. Its 1994 annual report to stockholders included the following data:

Net income	$ 69,923,000
Total assets	
Beginning of year	777,355,000
End of year	656,107,000
Net income as a percent of	
Total revenue	5.44%
Average stockholders' equity	18.31%

Required

Using only the data given, compute the (1) net income percent of average assets, (2) total revenues, (3) average stockholders' equity, and (4) asset turnover (using two different approaches).

19-37 Financial Ratios

Kobe Steel, Ltd., a diversified Japanese company, is one of the world's top 20 producers of iron and steel. The company's income statement and balance sheet for the year ended March 31, 1993, are shown in Exhibits 19-9 and 19-10. Monetary amounts are in Japanese yen (¥).

Required

1. Prepare a common-size income statement, that is, one showing component percentages.
2. Compute the following ratios:

    a. Current ratio
    b. Inventory turnover (1992 inventory was ¥227,681,000,000)
    c. Total debt to equity
    d. Gross profit rate
    e. Return on stockholders' equity (1992 stockholders' equity was ¥428,735,000,000)
    f. Price-earnings ratio (the market price was ¥300 per share)
    g. Dividend-payout ratio
3. What additional information would help you interpret the percentages and ratios you calculated?

Exhibit 19-9

Kobe Steel, Ltd.
Income Statement
for the Year Ended
March 31, 1993
(millions)

Net sales	¥1,177,290
Cost of sales	977,183
Gross profit	¥ 200,107
Selling and administrative expenses	127,305
Operating income	¥ 72,802
Other income (expenses)	
Interest and dividend income	¥ 12,176
Interest expense	(61,896)
Other	16,483
Total	(33,237)
Income before income taxes	¥ 39,565
Income taxes	27,800
Net income	¥ 11,765
Amounts per share	
Net income	¥ 4.149
Cash dividends	¥ 6.000

Exhibit 19-10

Kobe Steel, Ltd.
Balance Sheet
March 31, 1993
(millions)

Assets

Current assets	
Cash and marketable securities	¥ 314,723
Receivables	279,119
Inventories	239,853
Other	29,531
Total current assets	¥ 863,226
Property, plant, and equipment, net	940,934
Investments	207,517
Other assets	74,943
Total assets	¥2,086,620

Liabilities and Stockholders' Equity

Current liabilities	
Bank loans	¥ 182,124
Payables	345,942
Advances and deposits from customers	70,750
Long-term debt due within 1 year	109,560
Other	90,889
Total current liabilities	¥ 799,265
Long-term liabilities	
Long-term debt due after 1 year	¥ 717,809
Employees' retirement benefits	73,375
Other	72,742
Total long-term liabilities	¥ 863,926
Stockholders' equity	
Common stock (2,835,436,826 shares outstanding)	¥ 213,640
Additional paid-in capital	132,283
Retained earnings	77,506
Total stockholders' equity	¥ 423,429
Total liabilities and stockholders' equity	¥2,086,620

20 Difficulties in Measuring Net Income

The inventory of this appliance store represents a large investment. The choice among inventory valuation methods has a significant effect on both the store's balance sheet and income statement.
Courtesy Marmon Group, Inc.

Learning Objectives

When you have finished studying this chapter, you should be able to

1 Describe the four major methods of accounting for inventories.

2 Compare FIFO and LIFO, and explain why most U.S. firms use LIFO.

3 Explain the lower-of-cost-or-market method.

4 Distinguish between financial capital maintenance and physical capital maintenance.

5 Explain and illustrate four methods of measuring income: historical cost/nominal dollars, current cost/nominal dollars, historical cost/constant dollars, and current cost/constant dollars.

The income statement summarizes the performance of an organization over a specified period. This chapter focuses on how choices among alternative accounting methods affect the measurement of income. The focus is on the assumptions and limitations of generally accepted accounting methods.

The two major parts of this chapter examine the controversial effects on income of (1) the principal inventory methods and (2) various measurements of changes in price levels. Each major part may be studied independently.

Part One: Principal Inventory Methods

Each period, accountants must divide the costs of merchandise acquired between cost of goods sold and cost of items remaining in ending inventory. Various inventory methods accomplish this division. If unit prices and costs did not fluctuate, all inventory methods would show identical results. But prices change, and these changes raise central issues regarding cost of goods sold (income measurement) and inventories (asset measurement).

To explore inventory accounting, consider a new vendor of a cola drink at the fairgrounds. He began the week with no inventory. He bought one can of cola on Monday for 30 cents; a second can on Tuesday for 40 cents; and a third can on Wednesday for 56 cents. He then sold one can on Thursday for 90 cents. What is his gross profit? What is his ending inventory?

Before reading through this chapter, consider how you would answer these questions. Then ask a classmate or two how they would respond. Chances are your answers will differ from those of your colleagues. Who is right and who is wrong? It is not easy to say. In fact, accountants would not all agree on the appropriate answers.

■ FOUR MAJOR INVENTORY METHODS

Objective 1

Describe the four
major methods of
accounting for
inventories

Four principal inventory methods are generally accepted in the United States:
specific identification, weighted average, FIFO, and LIFO. Panel I of Exhibit 20-
1 provides a quick glimpse of the nature of these generally accepted methods
and applies them to our opening example of the cola vendor. (Panel II of
Exhibit 20-1 is described on page 775.) As you can readily see, the choice of an
inventory method often can significantly affect gross profit and hence net
income (and also ending inventory valuation for balance sheet purposes).

Exhibit 20-1   Comparison of Inventory Methods for Cola Vendor (all monetary amounts are in cents)

	(1) Specific Identification			(2) FIFO	(3) LIFO	(4) Weighted Average
	(1A)	(1B)	(1C)			
Panel I						
Income Statement for the Period Monday Through Thursday						
Sales	90	90	90	90	90	90
Deduct cost of goods sold:*						
1 30-cent (Monday) unit	30			30		
1 40-cent (Tuesday) unit		40				
1 56-cent (Wednesday) unit			56		56	
1 weighted-average unit [(30 + 40 + 56) ÷ 3 = 42]						42
Gross profit for Monday through Thursday	60	50	34	60	34	48
Ending Inventory, Thursday, 2 units/ [(30 + 40 + 56) – cost of goods sold]	96	86	70	96	70	84
Panel II						
Income Statements for Friday Only and for Monday Through Friday						
Sales, 2 units @ 90 on Friday	180	180	180	180	180	180
Cost of goods sold (Thursday ending inventory from above)	96	86	70	96	70	84
Gross profit, Friday only	84	94	110	84	110	96
Gross profit, Monday through Thursday (from above)	60	50	34	60	34	48
Gross profit, Monday through Friday (3 cans sold)	144	144	144	144	144	144

* The cost of goods sold can also be computed as follows, using FIFO cost of goods sold as an example:

Beginning inventory	0
+ Purchases	126
= Cost of goods available for sale	126
– Ending inventory	96
= Cost of goods sold	30

Specific Identification

specific identification An inventory method that recognizes the actual cost paid for the specific item sold.

The **specific identification** method (column 1) recognizes the actual cost paid for the specific physical item sold. Gross profit depends on which can the vendor sells. As Panel I of Exhibit 20-1 shows, gross profit for operations of Monday through Thursday could be 60 cents, 50 cents, or 34 cents, depending on the particular can handed to the customer. By reaching for the "Monday" can instead of the "Wednesday" can, the vendor makes a gross profit of 60 cents instead of 34 cents.

Specific identification, which uses physical observation or the labeling of items in stock with individual numbers or codes, is easy and economically justifiable for relatively expensive merchandise such as custom artwork, diamond jewelry, and automobiles. However, most organizations have vast segments of inventories that are too numerous and insufficiently valuable per unit to warrant such individualized attention. In addition, because the cost of goods sold is determined by the specific item handed to the customer, this method permits managers to manipulate income and inventory values by filling a sales order from several physically equivalent items with different historical costs.

First-in, First-out (FIFO) Method

first-in, first-out (FIFO) An inventory method that assumes that the stock acquired earliest is sold (used up) first.

The **first-in, first-out (FIFO)** method (column 2) assumes that the stock acquired earliest is sold (used up) first. Thus the "Monday" can is deemed to have been sold before the "Tuesday" can regardless of the actual can the vendor delivers to the customer. In times of rising prices, FIFO usually shows the largest gross profit (60 cents in Panel I of Exhibit 20-1).

By using the latest costs to measure the ending inventory, FIFO tends to provide inventory valuations that closely approximate the actual market value of the inventory at the balance sheet date. In addition, in periods of rising prices, FIFO leads to higher net income. Why? Because older, lower costs are charged as cost of goods sold.

Higher reported incomes may favorably affect investor attitudes toward the company. Similarly, higher reported incomes may lead to higher salaries, higher bonuses, or higher status for the management of the company. Unlike specific identification, FIFO specifies the order in which acquisition costs will become cost of goods sold. Thus managers cannot affect income by choosing to sell one item rather than another identical one.

Last-in, First-out (LIFO) Method

last-in, first-out (LIFO) An inventory method that assumes that the stock acquired most recently is sold (used up) first.

Objective 2

Compare FIFO and LIFO, and explain why most U.S. firms use LIFO

The **last-in, first-out (LIFO)** method (column 3) assumes that the stock acquired most recently is sold (used up) first. That is, FIFO associates the most recent costs with inventories, whereas LIFO treats the most recent costs as cost of goods sold. Thus the "Wednesday" can is deemed to have been sold regardless of the actual can delivered. Many accountants believe that LIFO provides a more realistic income number because net income measured using LIFO combines current sales prices and current acquisition costs.

In contrast, LIFO inventory values on the balance sheet are less realistic because they are older costs. In a period of rising prices and constant or growing inventories, LIFO yields lower net income than the other inventory methods (34 cents in Panel I of Exhibit 20-1) because recent higher costs are charged as cost of goods sold. Why is lower net income such an important feature of LIFO? Because LIFO is an acceptable inventory accounting method for U.S. income tax purposes, and when lower income is reported to the tax authorities, lower taxes are paid. Because the Internal Revenue Code requires that LIFO be used for financial reporting purposes if it is used for tax purposes, it is not surprising that almost two-thirds of U.S. corporations use LIFO for at least some of their inventories.

Inflationary periods often cause firms to change from FIFO to LIFO. For example, the *Wall Street Journal* reported that Chicago Heights Steel Co. "boosted cash by 5% to 10% by lowering income taxes when it switched to LIFO." When Becton, Dickinson and Company changed to LIFO, its annual report stated that its "change to the LIFO method . . . for both financial reporting and income tax purposes resulted in improved cash flow due to lower income taxes paid." Indeed, some observers maintain that executives are guilty of mismanagement if they do not adopt LIFO when FIFO produces significantly higher taxable income.

A disadvantage of LIFO is that it permits management to influence income by the timing of purchases of inventory items. Consider our cola vendor. Suppose acquisition prices increase from 56 cents on Wednesday to 68 cents on Thursday, the day of the sale of the one unit. How is net income affected if one more unit is acquired on Thursday? Under LIFO, cost of goods sold would change from 56 cents to 68 cents (the cost of the last unit purchased, the one bought on Thursday), and profit would fall by 12 cents. In contrast, a FIFO valuation of the cost of goods sold and gross profit would be unchanged:

	LIFO		FIFO	
	Without Thursday Purchase (cents)	With Thursday Purchase (cents)	Without Thursday Purchase (cents)	With Thursday Purchase (cents)
Sales	90	90	90	90
Cost of goods sold	56	68	30	30
Gross profit	34	22	60	60
Ending inventory (cents)				
(30 + 40)	70			
(30 + 40 + 56)		126		
(40 + 56)			96	
(40 + 56 + 68)				164

LIFO layers (LIFO increments)
Separately identifiable additional layers of LIFO inventory.

Another disadvantage of LIFO is that income can soar when inventories are depleted. Under LIFO, inventory consists of **LIFO layers** (or **LIFO increments**), which are identifiable additions to inventory. For example, on Wednesday our cola vendor had three LIFO layers:

- Layer 1: 30-cent unit purchased on Monday
- Layer 2: 40-cent unit purchased on Tuesday
- Layer 3: 56-cent unit purchased on Wednesday

As a company grows, the LIFO layers tend to pile on one another as the years go by. Thus many LIFO companies will show inventories that may have ancient layers (going back to 1940 in some instances). The reported LIFO value may therefore be far below what FIFO values might otherwise show.

When inventory is reduced, old LIFO layers become the cost of goods sold. These old values may be much below current replacement values, leading to *overstatement* of income. In other words, the LIFO method usually gives lower net income because most recent values are used for the cost of goods sold. But *when inventories are reduced*, LIFO can lead to just the *opposite* effect. Old values are used for cost of goods sold and net income is higher under LIFO than under other methods.

For example, suppose a new company bought 100 units of inventory in 1960 for $10 per unit. Each year since, the company purchased and sold exactly 200 units. In 1995 the purchase price was $40 per unit. In early 1996 a new inventory system was installed, reducing the needed level of inventory to 50 units. Therefore, in 1996 the company purchased only 150 units at $40 per unit, even though sales remained at 200 units. The 1996 sales price is $50 per unit. Gross profit for 1996 under FIFO and LIFO would be:

	FIFO	LIFO
Sales	$10,000	$10,000
Deduct cost of goods sold		
100 1995 units	(4,000)	
100 1996 units	(4,000)	
150 1996 units		(6,000)
50 1960 units		(500)
Gross profit	$ 2,000	$ 3,500

This disadvantage of LIFO is especially relevant in today's environment because many companies are increasingly concerned with reducing inventory levels.

Weighted-Average Cost

weighted-average cost The inventory method that assigns the same unit cost to each unit available for sale. The unit cost is computed by dividing the cost of all units available for sale by the number of units available.

The **weighted-average cost** method assigns the same unit cost to each unit available for sale. The unit cost is computed by dividing the cost of all units available for sale by the number of units available as shown in Exhibit 20-1. The weighted-average method usually produces a gross profit somewhere between that obtained under FIFO and LIFO (48 cents as compared with 60 cents and 34 cents in Panel I of Exhibit 20-1).

To understand better the term *weighted average*, assume that our cola vendor bought two cans rather than one on Monday at 30 cents each. To get the weighted average, we must consider not only the price paid, but also the number of units purchased:

weighted average = cost of goods available for sale ÷ units available for sale

weighted average = [(2 × 30 cents) + (1 × 40 cents) + (1 × 56 cents)] ÷ 4

= 156 cents ÷ 4 = 39 cents

The weighted-average method produces less extreme results than either LIFO or FIFO on both the income statement and the balance sheet, as the comparisons in Exhibit 20-1 show. Also, the weighted average is subject to minimal manipulation by managers.

Choice and Use of Inventory Methods

Each of the four inventory methods has different strengths and weaknesses. Among the issues facing management when choosing a method are such questions as: Which method provides the highest reported net income? Which method provides management the most flexibility to affect reported earnings? How do the methods affect income tax obligations? Which method produces an inventory valuation that approximates the actual value of the inventory?

In choosing an inventory method, it is important to recognize the link between the cost of goods sold and the valuation of ending inventory. The cola vendor began his business, acquired three cans of cola during the week, and had a total cost of goods available for sale of $1.26. At the end of the period, this $1.26 must be allocated either to cans sold or to cans in ending inventory. The higher the cost of goods sold, the lower the ending inventory. Exhibit 20-2 illustrates this interdependence. At one extreme, FIFO treats the 30-cent cost of the first can acquired as the cost of goods sold and 96 cents as ending inventory. At the other extreme, LIFO treats the 56-cent cost of the last can acquired as the cost of goods sold and the 70 cents as ending inventory.

Exhibit 20-2				
Diagram of Inventory Methods (data are from Exhibit 20-1; monetary amounts are in cents)	Beginning inventory	+ Merchandise purchases	=	Cost of goods available for sale
	0	+ 126	=	126
	Cost of goods available for sale	− Cost of goods sold	=	Ending inventory

1 @ 30	$\begin{bmatrix} 30 \\ \text{or} \end{bmatrix}$		$\begin{bmatrix} 96 \\ \text{or} \end{bmatrix}$
1 @ 40	− 40	=	86	Specific identification
1 @ 56	$\begin{bmatrix} \text{or} \\ 56 \end{bmatrix}$		$\begin{bmatrix} \text{or} \\ 70 \end{bmatrix}$
126	− 30	=	96	FIFO
	− 56	=	70	LIFO
	− 42	=	84	Weighted average

One thing to consider in choosing among inventory methods is how physical units flow. Consider four different ways that our cola vendor might physically store and sell his cola. One way—specific identification—would be to mark each can with its cost, and record that cost as a cost of goods sold when the can is handed to a customer. This method can be used only when the physical procedure allows the seller to track each item of inventory. Another way— LIFO—would be to put each new can acquired into the top of a cooler. As each customer arrives, the top can is the one sold. In contrast, if each new can is placed at the back of the cooler to chill, and the oldest, coldest can is sold first, FIFO captures the physical flow. Finally, if the cans are just mixed together, the weighted-average method is a rough approximation of what is known about the cost of the can sold.

Although we can relate the four methods to the physical flow of the cola cans, the accounting profession has concluded that this is not important to the choice of the inventory accounting method. Why? Many vendors have substantial choice over the physical flow of their products, but that choice often has little importance to the financial success of the business. Therefore companies may choose any of the four methods to record the cost of goods sold, but the method must be applied *consistently*. That is, the choice of method cannot be changed from period to period. Because the method is not linked to the physical flow of the merchandise, inventory methods are often referred to as *cost flow assumptions*. For example, when we decide that the cost of the first inventory item purchased will be matched with the sales revenue from the first item sold to calculate the gross profit from the sale, we are adopting the FIFO cost flow assumption.

Panel II of Exhibit 20-1 shows the results of selling the remaining two cans of inventory on Friday. Note that cumulative gross profit over the life of the vendor's business would be the same $1.44 under any of the inventory methods. These methods are important because we must match particular costs to particular periods during the life of the business to prepare financial statements and evaluate performance. We must understand how the inventory cost flow assumption affects a company's financial statements before we can use the statements to evaluate performance.

As mentioned earlier, taxes have a major influence on the choice of inventory methods. LIFO is the most popular inventory method for large U.S. companies, but it is seldom used in countries where it is not allowed for tax purposes. About two-thirds of large U.S. companies use LIFO for at least some of their inventories. More than 60% use FIFO, and 40% use weighted average for part of their inventories. Less than 10% use any other method including specific identification. More than half the companies use more than one inventory method.

A recent study showed that fewer than 25% of the responding companies in the U.S. electronics, business equipment, ship building, and railway equipment industries use LIFO. If tax benefits are so important, why doesn't everyone use LIFO? Recall that LIFO yields lower net income and lower taxes *in a period of rising prices and constant or growing inventories*. One answer is that some industries do not face rising prices. For such industries, FIFO yields lower net income and lower taxes. In electronics, for example, technology has been a consistent force driving prices down. Think back to 10 years of constant reductions in prices for radios, stereo systems, clocks, and watches. The situation is similar for business equipment such as word processors and computers. Ship building and railway equipment companies use specific identification instead of LIFO because each unit is large and expensive.

Objective 3

Explain the lower-of-cost-or-market method

■ LOWER OF COST OR MARKET

Regardless of the inventory method used, accountants must decrease the inventory value if the inventory's market price drops below its acquisition cost. Therefore, the acquisition cost provides a ceiling for the valuation of assets;

their balance sheet values can be increased only upon an exchange. However, asset values can be decreased without an exchange.

Inventory accounting uses the **lower-of-cost-or-market (LCM)** method, whereby the current market price of inventory is compared with its cost (derived by specific identification, FIFO, LIFO, or weighted average), and the lower of the two is selected as the basis for the valuation of goods at a specific inventory date.

Market generally means the *current replacement cost* or its equivalent. It ordinarily does *not* mean the ultimate selling price to customers. Consider the following facts. A company has 100 units in its ending FIFO inventory on December 31, 19X3. Its gross profit for 19X3 has been tentatively computed as follows:

lower-of-cost-or-market (LCM) An inventory method in which the current market price of inventory is compared with its cost (derived by specific identification, FIFO, LIFO, or weighted average) and the lower of the two is selected as the basis for the valuation of goods at a specific inventory date.

Sales	$2,180
Cost of goods available for sale	$1,980
Ending inventory, at cost of 100 units	790
Cost of goods sold	$1,190
Gross profit	$ 990

However, market prices during the final week of December suddenly declined to $4 per unit. If the lower market price is indicative of lower ultimate sales prices, an inventory write-down of $790 – (100 × $4), or $390, is in order. Therefore reported income for 19X3 would be lowered by $390:

	Before $390 Write-Down	After $390 Write-Down	Difference
Sales	$2,180	$2,180	
Cost of goods available	$1,980	$1,980	
Ending inventory	790	400	– $390
Cost of goods sold	$1,190	$1,580	+ $390
Gross profit	$ 990	$ 600	– $390

The theory states that of the $790 cost, $390 is considered to have expired during 19X3 because the cost cannot be justifiably carried forward to the future as an asset.

Now suppose the replacement prices rise to $8 per unit in January 19X4. No restoration of the December write-down will be permitted. In short, the lower-of-cost-or-market method would regard the $4 cost as of December 31 as the "new cost" of the inventory. Original acquisition cost is the ceiling for valuation under generally accepted accounting principles.

Highlights to Remember: Part One

Four principal inventory methods are used in the United States: specific identification, weighted average, FIFO, and LIFO. These methods measure the cost of goods sold that is recognized when an item is delivered to a customer. Each of the methods represents a specific physical flow of inventory, but a method can be used even if it doesn't match the actual physical flow.

LIFO is the most popular inventory method in the United States because it offers income tax advantages that become most pronounced during times of steady or rising inventories combined with rising prices. Unfortunately, LIFO also allows management to influence income by the timing of purchases of inventory items, and income can soar if old, low-cost LIFO layers are penetrated.

Accountants apply the lower-of-cost-or-market method to inventories. Inventories are not written up above cost, but they are written down if replacement costs fall below acquisition costs.

Summary Problem for Your Review

Problem One

Refer to Exhibit 20-1, page 772. Suppose the vendor sold two cans on Thursday for 90 cents each. All other data are unchanged.

1. Compute (a) the gross profit for Monday through Wednesday, (b) the gross profit for Thursday, and (c) the ending inventory on Thursday, under FIFO and under LIFO.
2. Assume the same facts as in requirement 1 except that the vendor purchased one additional can of cola on Thursday for 65 cents. Compute Thursday's gross profit under FIFO and under LIFO.

Solution to Problem One

All amounts are in cents.

1. **a.** No gross profit would be recognized on Monday through Wednesday because there were no sales.

	FIFO		LIFO	
b. Sales		180		180
Cost of goods sold				
Beginning inventory (from Exhibit 20-1)	126		126	
Purchases	0		0	
Cost of goods available for sale	126		126	
Ending inventory	56		30	
Cost of goods sold		70		96
Gross profit, Thursday		110		84

   c. The ending inventory on Thursday was one Wednesday unit @ 56 cents under FIFO and one Monday unit @ 30 cents under LIFO.

2. Note how the late purchase affects LIFO gross profit but not FIFO gross profit:

	FIFO		LIFO	
Sales		180		180
Cost of goods sold				
Beginning inventory (from Exhibit 20-1)	126		126	
Purchases	65		65	
Cost of goods available for sale	191		191	
Ending inventory*	121		70	
Cost of goods sold		70		121
Gross profit, Thursday		110		59

* Wednesday and Thursday units for FIFO (56 cents + 65 cents) and Monday and Tuesday units for LIFO (30 cents + 40 cents).

Accounting Vocabulary: Part One

first-in, first-out (FIFO), *p. 773*
last-in, first-out (LIFO), *p. 773*
LIFO increments, *p. 774*

LIFO layers, *p. 774*
lower-of-cost-or-market (LCM),
  p. 778

specific identification, *p. 773*
weighted-average cost, *p. 775*

Part Two: Changing Prices And Income Measurement

The use of historical cost in measuring income is one of the most controversial subjects in accounting. The remainder of this chapter focuses on how inflation affects the income statement.

■ COMPLAINTS ABOUT HISTORICAL COST

Accountants have traditionally maintained that net income is a return on the capital invested by shareholders. Suppose an amount equal to the net income of a period is returned to the shareholders as dividends. In the absence of inflation, such a payment leaves the shareholders' invested capital at the end of the period equal to the beginning capital. However, when prices change, this relationship between income and capital is altered. In times of generally rising prices, paying dividends equal to net income, as conventionally measured, usually amounts to paying out some capital itself as well as the return on capital.

In particular, industries with huge investments in plant and equipment claim that their profits in times of inflation are badly misstated by generally accepted accounting principles. For instance, consider NYNEX, a company that emerged from the breakup of the Bell System. NYNEX recently reported net income of $1,095 million, which would have been a net loss of $82 million if depreciation had been adjusted for inflation.

Because of the soaring inflation of the late 1970s in the United States, the FASB issued *Statement No. 33*, "Financial Reporting and Changing Prices." The statement required no changes in the primary financial statements. However, it required large companies to include supplementary inflation-adjusted schedules in their annual reports.

Statement No. 33 was experimental, and its requirements were in place for 8 years. By then inflation had subsided, and the FASB decided that inflation-adjusted disclosures would no longer be required. Although U.S. companies do not need to report inflation-adjusted numbers, a basic knowledge about reporting the effects of changing prices is useful for at least three reasons: (1) High inflation is still present in many countries, and accounting reports in those countries must cope with the effects of inflation; (2) if history is any indication, higher inflation rates will return to the United States sooner or later, and when they do, users of financial statements will again become concerned with inflation-adjusted statements; and (3) understanding the limitations of traditional financial statements is enhanced by knowing how inflation affects (or does not affect) such financial statements.

■ INCOME OR CAPITAL

Objective 4

Distinguish between financial capital maintenance and physical capital maintenance

Before exploring alternatives to historical-cost accounting, consider the concepts of income and capital. Financial resources (capital) are invested with the expectation of an eventual return *of* that capital together with additional amounts representing the return *on* that capital (income). Controversies have arisen regarding whether the financial resources generated by the invested capital qualify as returns *of* or *on* capital.

Consider an example where a company begins with owners' investment (capital) of $1,000, which is used immediately to purchase inventory. The inventory is sold a year later for $1,500. Meanwhile, the cost of replacing the inventory has risen to $1,200.

financial capital maintenance The concept that income emerges after financial resources are recovered.

	Financial Capital Maintenance	Physical Capital Maintenance
Sales	$1,500	$1,500
Cost of goods sold	1,000	1,200
Income	$ 500	$ 300

Most accountants and managers believe that income emerges after financial resources are recovered, a concept called **financial capital maintenance.** Because the $1,000 capital has been recovered, $500 is the measure of income. This is the concept underlying traditional historical-cost accounting.

physical capital maintenance The concept that income emerges only after recovering an amount that allows physical operating capability to be maintained.

On the other hand, some accountants believe that income emerges only after recovering an amount that allows physical operating capability to be maintained, called **physical capital maintenance.** Because $1,200 is the current cost of inventory (cost of maintaining physical capability) at the date of sale, $300 is the measure of income.

■ MEASUREMENT ALTERNATIVES UNDER CHANGING PRICES

nominal dollars
Dollar measurements that are not restated for fluctuations in the general purchasing power of the monetary unit.

constant dollars
Nominal dollars that are restated in terms of current purchasing power.

historical cost The amount originally paid to acquire an asset.

current cost The cost to replace an asset, as opposed to its historical cost.

Changing prices, and in particular *inflation,* which is a general decline in the purchasing power of the monetary unit, have caused accountants to consider two types of changes in financial reporting:

1. Switch from measuring transactions in **nominal dollars,** which are dollar measurements that are not restated for fluctuations in the general purchasing power of the monetary unit, to **constant dollars,** which are nominal dollars that are restated in terms of current purchasing power.

2. Instead of reporting the **historical cost** of an asset, which is the amount originally paid to acquire it, use the **current cost,** which is generally the cost to replace it.

Traditional accounting uses *nominal* (rather than constant) dollars and *historical* (rather than current) costs. Using historical costs implies maintenance of *financial* capital; current costs imply *physical* capital maintenance. Historical cost/nominal dollar accounting has almost exclusively dominated financial reporting throughout this century. Yet, as noted earlier, criticism of this type of accounting abounds when inflation is present.

The two nontraditional alternatives, which can be applied separately or in combination, address separate but related problems caused by inflation: (1) constant-dollar disclosures account for *general* changes in the purchasing power of the dollar, and (2) current-cost disclosures account for changes in *specific* prices. The two approaches create the following four alternatives for measuring income:

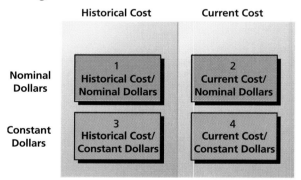

In the following discussion of these approaches, we will consider the situation of the Marsalis Company to compare various concepts of income and capital. Marsalis has the following comparative balance sheets at December 31 (based on historical costs in nominal dollars):

	19X1	19X2
Cash	$ 0	$10,500
Inventory, 400 and 100 units, respectively	8,000	2,000
Total assets	$8,000	$12,500
Original paid-in capital	$8,000	$ 8,000
Retained income	—	4,500
Stockholders' equity	$8,000	$12,500

The company had acquired all 400 units of inventory at $20 per unit (total of $8,000) on December 31, 19X1, and had held the units until December 31, 19X2. Three hundred units were *sold* for $35 per unit (total of $10,500 cash) on December 31, 19X2. The replacement cost of the inventory at that date was $30 per unit. The general-price-level index was 100 on December 31, 19X1, and 110 on December 31, 19X2. Assume that these are the only transactions. Ignore income taxes.

EXHIBIT 20-3	Four Major Methods to Measure Income and Capital (dollars)

	Nominal Dollars*				Constant Dollars*			
	(Method 1)		(Method 2)		(Method 3)		(Method 4)	
	Historical Cost		Current Cost		Historical Cost		Current Cost	
Balance Sheets as of								
December 31	19X1	19X2	19X1	19X2	19X1	19X2	19X1	19X2
Cash	—	10,500	—	10,500	—	10,500	—	10,500
Inventory, 400 and 100 units, respectively	8,000	2,000[b]	8,000	3,000[c]	8,800[e]	2,200[e]	8,800[e]	3,000[c]
Total assets	8,000	12,500	8,000	13,500	8,800	12,700	8,800	13,500
Original paid-in capital	8,000	8,000	8,000	8,000	8,800[f]	8,800[f]	8,800[f]	8,800[f]
Retained income (confined to income from continuing operations)		4,500		1,500		3,900		1,500
Revaluation equity (accumulated holding gains)				4,000				3,200
Total liabilities and shareholders' equity	8,000	12,500	8,000	13,500	8,800	12,700	8,800	13,500
Income Statements for 19X2								
Sales, 300 units @ $35		10,500		10,500		10,500		10,500
Cost of goods sold, 300 units		6,000[b]		9,000[c]		6,600[e]		9,000[c]
Income from continuing operations (to retained income)		4,500		1,500		3,900		1,500
Holding gains[a]								
On 300 units sold				3,000[d]				2,400[g]
On 100 units unsold				1,000[d]				800[g]
Total holding gains[a] (to revaluation equity)				4,000				3,200

* Nominal dollars are not restated for a general price index, whereas constant dollars are restated.
[a] Many advocates of this current-cost method favor showing these gains in a completely separate statement of holding gains rather than as a part of the income statement. Others favor including some or all of these gains as a part of income for the year.

[b] 100 × $20,   [c] 100 × $30,   [d] 300 × ($30 − $20),   [e] 110/100 × $8,000,   [f] 110/100 × $8,000.
   300 × $20,   300 × $30,   100 × ($30 − $20).   110/100 × $2,000,
                                                                 110/100 × $6,000.

[g] $9,000 − [(110/100) × $6,000] = $2,400 $3,000 − [(110/100) × $2,000] = $800
or   or
300 × [$30 − (110/100) × $20] = $2,400.   100 × [$30 − (110/100) × $20] = $800.

Objective 5

Explain and illustrate four methods of measuring income: historical cost/nominal dollars, current cost/nominal dollars, historical cost/constant dollars, and current cost/constant dollars

Historical Cost/Nominal Dollars

Exhibit 20-3 is the basis for the explanations that follow in the next several pages. The first two columns of Exhibit 20-3 show financial statements prepared using the time-honored historical cost/nominal dollars approach (method 1). This method measures invested capital in nominal dollars. It is the most popular approach to income measurement and is commonly called the historical-cost method. Operating income (equal to net income in this case) is the excess of revenue ($10,500 in 19X2) over the "not restated" historical costs of assets used in obtaining that revenue. As we have already seen, when the conventional accrual basis of accounting is used, an exchange transaction is ordinarily necessary before revenues (and resulting incomes) are recorded. Thus no income generally appears until the asset is sold. Intervening price fluctuations are ignored.

Current Cost/Nominal Dollars

current-cost method
The measurement method that uses current costs and nominal dollars.

The second set of financial statements in Exhibit 20-3 illustrates a **current-cost method** that has especially strong advocates in the United Kingdom and Australia (method 2). This method uses current cost/nominal dollars. The focus is on income from continuing operations. This model emphasizes that operating income should be "distributable" income. That is, Marsalis Company could pay dividends in an amount of only $1,500, leaving enough assets to allow for replacement of the inventory that has just been sold.

Critics of traditional accounting claim that the $4,500 historical-cost measure of income from continuing operations is misleading because it overstates the net increment in distributable assets. If a $4,500 dividend were paid, the company would not be able to continue operations at the same level as before. The $3,000 difference between the two operating incomes ($4,500 − $1,500 = $3,000) is frequently referred to as an "inventory profit" or an "inflated profit." Why? Because $9,000 instead of $6,000 is now necessary to replace the 300 units sold (300 × the increase in price from $20 to $30 equals the $3,000 difference).

holding gains (or losses) Increases (or decreases) in the replacement costs of the assets held during the current period.

The current-cost method stresses a separation between *income from continuing operations*, which is defined as the excess of revenue over the current costs of the assets consumed in obtaining that revenue, and **holding gains** (or **losses**), which are increases (or decreases) in the replacement costs of the assets held during the current period. Accountants differ sharply on how to account for holding gains or losses. The "correct" accounting depends on distinctions between capital and income. That is, income cannot occur until invested capital is "recovered" or "maintained." The issue of capital versus income is concretely illustrated in Exhibit 20-3. Advocates of a physical concept of capital maintenance claim that *all* holding gains (both those gains related to the units sold and the gains related to the units unsold) should be excluded from income and become a part of stockholders' equity called **revaluation equity.** Why? Because holding gains represent the amount that must be reinvested to maintain physical capital at its beginning-of-the-year level. Holding gains become part *of* capital, not a return *on* capital.

revaluation equity A portion of stockholders' equity that shows all accumulated holding gains.

Historical Cost/Constant Dollars

Method 3 of Exhibit 20-3 shows the results of applying a *general price index* adjustment to historical costs. Essentially, the income measurements in each year are restated in terms of *constant dollars* (possessing the same general purchasing power of the current year) instead of *nominal dollars* (possessing different general purchasing power of various years). Because of inflation, dollars spent or received in 19X2 have a different value than dollars spent or received in 19X1. Adding 19X1 dollars to 19X2 dollars is like adding apples and oranges. Constant-dollar accounting measures all items on the 19X2 financial statements in 19X2 dollars.

Consider the objections to method 1. Deducting 6,000 19X1 dollars from 10,500 19X2 dollars to obtain $4,500 is akin to deducting 60 *centimeters* from 105 *meters* and calling the result 45. In either case, the result is nonsense.

Method 3, historical cost/constant dollars, shows how to remedy the foregoing objections. *General price indexes* may be used to restate the amounts of the historical cost/nominal dollar method. Examples of such indexes are the Gross National Product Implicit Price Deflator and the Consumer Price Index for All Urban Consumers (CPI). Anyone who has lived long enough to be able to read this book is aware that the purchasing power of the dollar is unstable. Index numbers are used to gauge the relationship between current conditions and some norm or baseline condition (which is assigned the index number of 100). For our purpose, a **general price index** compares the average price of a group of goods and services at one date with the average price of a similar group at another date.

A price index is an average. It does not measure the behavior of the individual component prices. Some individual prices may move in one direction and some in another. The general consumer price level may soar while the prices of eggs and chickens decline.

Do not confuse *general* indexes, which are used in constant-dollar accounting, with *specific* indexes. The two have entirely different purposes. Sometimes **specific price indexes** are used to approximate the *current costs* of particular assets or types of assets. That is, companies use specialized indexes to get low cost approximations of current costs without professional appraisers. For example, Inland Steel used the *Engineering News Record* Construction Cost Index to value most of its property, plant, and equipment for purposes of using the current-cost method.

Note that the historical-cost/constant-dollar approach (method 3) is *not* a fundamental departure from historical costs. Instead, it maintains that all historical costs to be matched against revenue should be restated on some constant-dollar basis so that all revenues and all expenses can be expressed in dollars of the same (usually current) purchasing power. The restated figures *are historical costs* expressed in constant dollars via the use of a general price index.

The *most recent* dollar is typically employed because users of financial statements tend to think in such terms instead of in terms of old dollars with significantly different purchasing power. The original units in inventory would be updated on each year's balance sheet along with their effect on stockholders' equity. For example, the December 31, 19X1, balance sheet would be stated for comparative purposes on December 31, 19X2:

general price index
A comparison of the average price of a group of goods and services at one date with the average price of a similar group at another date.

specific price index
An index used to approximate the current costs of particular assets or types of assets.

	Unrestated Cost	Multiplier	Restated Cost
Inventory	$8,000	110/100	$8,800
Original paid-in capital	8,000	110/100	8,800

To extend the illustration, suppose all the inventory was held for 2 full years and that the general price index rose from 110 to 132 during 19X3. The December 31, 19X2, balance sheet items would be restated for comparative purposes on December 31, 19X3, using 19X3 dollars:

	Restated Cost 12/31/X2	Multiplier	Restated Cost 12/31/X3
Inventory	$8,800	132/110	$10,560*
Original paid-in capital	8,800	132/110	10,560*

* The same result could be tied to the year of acquisition:
Inventory $8,000 × 132/100 = $10,560
Original paid-in capital $8,000 × 132/100 = $10,560

The restated amount is just that—a restatement of original *cost* in terms of current (19X3) dollars. It is not a gain in any sense. Therefore this approach should *not* be labeled as an adoption of "current-cost" accounting. Using this approach, if the specific current cost of the inventory goes up or down, the restated cost is unaffected.

The restated historical-cost approach harmonizes with the concept of *maintaining the general purchasing power* of the invested capital (a *financial* concept of capital maintenance) in total rather than maintaining "specific invested capital," item by item.

Current Cost/Constant Dollars

Method 4 of Exhibit 20-3 shows the results of applying general index numbers to current costs. As the footnotes of the exhibit explain in more detail, the nominal gains reported under method 2 are adjusted so that only gains in constant dollars are reported. For example, suppose you buy 100 units on December 31, 19X1, for $2,000 cash. If the current replacement cost of your inventory at December 31, 19X2, is $3,000 but the general price index has risen from 100 to 110, your nominal gain is $1,000, but your "real" gain in constant dollars in 19X2 is only $800: the $3,000 current cost minus the restated historical cost of $2,000 × 1.10 = $2,200.

Suppose the 100 units are held throughout 19X3. The general price index rises from 110 to 132. The replacement cost rises from $30 to $34, a nominal holding gain for 19X3 of $4 × 100 = $400. However, because the original cost adjusted for price increases is $2,200 × (132 ÷ 110) = $2,640 at the end of 19X2, an increase of $440 over the 19X1 amount, the current-cost/constant-dollar approach (method 4) would report a real holding loss:

	12/31/X0	12/31/X1	12/31/X2
Original cost restated for changes in the price level	$2,000	$2,200	$2,640
Current cost	2,000	3,000	3,400
Increase in current cost		1,000*	400*
Increase due to price level		200**	440**
Holding gain (loss)		$ 800	$ (40)

* 3,000 − 2,000 = 1,000, and 3,400 − 3,000 = 400
** 2,200 − 2,000 = 200, and 2,640 − 2,200 = 440

Many theorists disagree on the relative merits of historical-cost approaches versus miscellaneous versions of current-cost approaches to income measurement. But there is general agreement among the theorists that restatements in constant dollars would be an improvement regardless of whether historical or current costs are used (ignoring practical barriers), because otherwise income includes illusory gains caused by using an unstable measuring unit.

Highlights to Remember: Part Two

The matching of historical costs with revenue is the generally accepted means of measuring net income. Such net income assumes a goal of financial capital maintenance. However, this method is often criticized in times of high inflation. Some critics suggest using a concept of physical capital maintenance instead of financial capital maintenance. Others simply want to use a common unit of measure. These alternatives can be summarized as follows:

	Financial Capital Maintenance	Physical Capital Maintenance
Mixed measuring unit	Historical cost/nominal dollars	Current cost/nominal dollars
Common measuring unit	Historical cost/constant dollars	Current cost/constant dollars

Historical cost/nominal dollars is the traditional method of measuring income. Historical cost/constant dollars uses a general price index to create a common measuring unit, dollars of the same purchasing power, but it is not a departure from historical cost. A more fundamental change is to use current costs instead of historical costs. Proponents claim that such a measure, based on physical capital maintenance, is a better gauge of the distinction between income (the return *on* capital) and capital maintenance (the return *of* capital).

Summary Problem for Your Review

Problem One appeared earlier in the chapter.

Problem Two

In 1975 a parcel of land, call it parcel 1, was purchased for $1,200. An identical parcel, 2, was purchased today for $3,600. The general-price-level index has risen from 100 in

1975 to 300 now. Fill in the blanks in the following table.

Parcel	(1) Historical Cost Measured in 1975 Purchasing Power	(2) Historical Cost Measured in Current Purchasing Power	(3) Historical Cost as Originally Measured
1			
2			
Total	_____	_____	_____

1. Compare the figures in the three columns. Which total presents a nonsense result? Why?
2. Does the write-up of parcel 1 in column 2 result in a gain? Why?
3. Assume that these parcels are the only assets of the business. There are no liabilities. Prepare a balance sheet for each of the three columns.

Solution to Problem Two

Parcel	(1) Historical Cost Measured in 1975 Purchasing Power	(2) Historical Cost Measured in Current Purchasing Power	(3) Historical Cost as Originally Measured
1	$1,200	$3,600	$1,200
2	1,200	3,600	3,600
Total	$2,400	$7,200	$4,800

1. The addition in column 3 produces a nonsense result. In contrast, the other sums are the results of applying a standard unit of measure. The computations in columns 1 and 2 are illustrations of a restatement of historical cost in terms of a common dollar, a standard unit of measure. Such computations have been frequently called adjustments for changes in the general price level. Whether the restatement is made using the 1975 dollar or the current dollar is a matter of personal preference; columns 1 and 2 yield equivalent results. Restatement in terms of the current dollar (column 2) is most popular because the current dollar has more meaning than the old dollar to the reader of the financial statements.

2. The mere restatement of identical assets in terms of different but equivalent measuring units cannot be regarded as a gain. Expressing parcel 1 as $1,200 in column 1 and $3,600 in column 2 is like expressing parcel 1 in terms of, say, either 1,200 square yards or 9 × 1,200 = 10,800 square feet. Surely, the "write-up" from 1,200 square yards to 10,800 square feet is not a gain; it is merely another way of measuring the same asset. The 1,200 square yards and the 10,800 square feet are equivalent; they are different ways of describing the same asset. That is basically what general-price-level accounting is all about. It says you cannot measure one plot of land in square yards and another in square feet and add them together before converting to some common measure. Unfortunately, column 3 fails to perform such a conversion before adding the two parcels together; hence the total is internally inconsistent.

3. The balance sheets would be:

	(1)	(2)	(3)
Land	$2,400	$7,200	$4,800
Paid-in capital	$2,400	$7,200	$4,800

Note that (1) is expressed in 1975 dollars, (2) is in current dollars, and (3) is a mixture of 1975 and current dollars.

Accounting Vocabulary: Part Two

constant dollars, *p. 782*	general price index, *p. 785*	physical capital maintenance,
current cost *p. 782*	historical cost, *p. 782*	*p. 781*
current-cost method, *p. 784*	holding gains (or losses), *p. 784*	revaluation equity, *p. 784*
financial capital maintenance,	inflation, *p. 782*	specific price index, *p. 785*
p. 781	nominal dollars, *p. 782*	

Fundamental Assignment Material

Special Note: Problems relating to Part One of the chapter are presented first in each subgrouping of the assignment material. For coverage of the basic ideas of inflation accounting, Problem 20-A2 is especially recommended; for a closer but still fundamental look, Problem 20-33 is especially recommended.

General Exercises and Problems

20-A1   LIFO, FIFO, Cash Effects

Aesop Company had sales revenue of $390,000 in 19X5 for a line of hardware supplies. Pertinent data for 19X5 included:

Inventory, December 31, 19X4	14,000 units @ $6	$ 84,000
January purchases	20,000 units @ $7	140,000
July purchases	32,000 units @ $8	256,000
Sales for the year	30,000 units	

Required

1. Prepare a statement of gross margin for 19X5. Use two columns, one assuming LIFO and one assuming FIFO.
2. Assume a 40% income tax rate. Suppose all transactions are for cash. Which inventory method results in more cash for Aesop Company? By how much?

20-A2   Four Versions of Income and Capital

Matsunaga Company has the following comparative balance sheets as of December 31 (based on historical costs in nominal dollars):

	19X0	19X1
Cash	$ —	$4,200
Inventory, 100 and 40 units, respectively	5,000	2,000
Total assets	$5,000	$6,200
Paid-in capital	$5,000	$5,000
Retained income	—	1,200
Stockholders' equity	$5,000	$6,200

The general-price-level index was 140 on December 31, 19X0, and 161 on December 31,

19X1. The company had acquired 100 units of inventory on December 31, 19X0, for $50 each and had held them throughout 19X1. Sixty units were sold on December 31, 19X1, for $70 cash each. The replacement cost of the inventory at that date was $60 per unit. Assume that these are the only transactions. Ignore income taxes.

Required

Use four columns to prepare comparative balance sheets as of December 31, 19X0 and 19X1, and income statements for 19X1 under (1) historical cost/nominal dollars, (2) current cost/nominal dollars, (3) historical cost/constant dollars, and (4) current cost/constant dollars.

Understanding Published Financial Reports

20-B1   Comparison of Inventory Methods

Unisys Corporation is a producer of computer-based information systems. The following actual data and descriptions are from the company's fiscal 1993 annual report (in millions):

	December 31	
	1993	**1992**
Inventories	$753.9	$873.8

A footnote states: "Inventories are valued at the lower of cost or market. Cost is determined principally on the first-in, first-out method."

The income statement for the fiscal year ended December 31, 1993, included (in millions):

Total revenues	$7,742.5
Cost of sales and services	4,844.3

Suppose a division of Unisys had the accompanying data regarding computer parts that it acquires and resells to customers for maintaining equipment (dollars are *not* in millions):

	Units	Total
Inventory (December 31, 1992)	100	$ 400
Purchase (February 20, 1993)	200	1,000
Sales, March 17 (at $8 per unit)	150	
Purchase (June 25, 1993)	140	840
Sales, December 7, 1993 (at $9 per unit)	160	

Required

1. For these computer parts only, prepare a tabulation of the cost-of-goods-sold section of the income statement for the year ended December 31, 1993. Support your computations. Round totals to the nearest dollar. Show your tabulation for four different inventory methods: (a) FIFO, (b) LIFO, (c) weighted-average, and (d) specific identification.

   For requirement *d*, assume that the purchase of February 20 was identified with the sale of March 17. Also assume that the purchase of June 25 was identified with the sale of December 7; the additional units sold were identified with the beginning inventory.

2. By how much would income taxes differ if Unisys used (a) LIFO instead of FIFO for this inventory item? (b) LIFO instead of weighted average? Assume a 40% tax rate.

20-B2   Effects of Late Purchases

Refer to the preceding problem. Suppose Unisys acquired 60 extra units at $7 each on December 29, 1993, a total of $420. How would gross margin and income taxes be affected under FIFO? That is, compare FIFO results before and after the purchase of 60 extra units. Under LIFO? That is, compare LIFO results before and after the purchase of 60 extra units. Show computations and explain.

20-B3   Accounting for Changing Prices

H.J. Heinz, the food products company, had historical cost inventory on April 27, 1994, of $1,150 million and on April 28, 1993, of $1,190 million. Suppose the entire 1993 inventory was purchased on April 28 when the price index was 100. Half the inventory was sold for $750 million on April 27, 1994, when the price index was 110; the other half remained in inventory. An amount of inventory identical to the amount sold was immediately purchased for $700 million.

Required

1. Compute the amount Heinz would show in its 1994 annual report for (a) inventory, April 28, 1993; (b) inventory, April 27, 1994; (c) cost of goods sold for the year ended April 27, 1994; and (d) holding gains (losses) for the year ended April 27, 1994, under each of the following four measurement methods: historical cost/nominal dollars, current cost/nominal dollars, historical cost/constant dollars, and current cost/constant dollars.
2. Suppose the sale and purchase of this inventory was Heinz's only activity in fiscal 1994. Compute income from continuing operations under historical cost/nominal dollars, current cost/nominal dollars, historical cost/constant dollars, and current cost/constant dollars.

Additional Assignment Material

Questions

20-1. Name and briefly describe each of the four inventory methods that are generally accepted in the United States.

20-2. Suppose prices are rising and inventories are increasing. Which of the four generally accepted inventory methods will usually result in the highest net income? Explain.

20-3. Which inventory method, FIFO or LIFO, comes closer to describing what operating managers actually do? Explain.

20-4. "FIFO produces more net income than LIFO over the life of the business." Do you agree? Explain.

20-5. LIFO sometimes produces absurd inventory valuations. Why?

20-6. "Purchases of inventory at the end of a fiscal period can have a direct effect on income under LIFO." Do you agree? Explain.

20-7. "There is a single dominant reason why more and more U.S. companies have adopted LIFO." What is the reason?

20-8. "Switching from FIFO to LIFO will lower our profits. Therefore the stockholders would be hurt by such a switch." Do you agree? Explain.

20-9. "LIFO is desirable only as long as inventories continue to increase." Explain.

20-10. "In applying the lower-of-cost-or-market method to inventories, inventory values are written down when replacement cost falls. If the replacement cost then increases, inventory values are written up, but not to an amount greater than the original cost." Do you agree? Explain.

20-11. Explain the difference between return *on* capital and return *of* capital.

20-12. "Because of pressure from the SEC, the FASB issued a revolutionary statement in 1979 abandoning the historical-cost method of income measurement and replacing it with a current-cost method." Do you agree? Explain.

20-13. Distinguish between the physical and the financial concepts of maintenance of invested capital.

20-14. What are the two major approaches to recognizing changing prices in measuring income?

20-15. "The choice among accounting measures of income is often expressed as either historical-cost accounting or general-price-level accounting or current-cost accounting." Do you agree? Explain.

20-16. "General-price-level accounting is a loose way of achieving replacement-cost accounting." Do you agree? Explain.

20-17. Explain what a general price index represents.

20-18. Explain how net income is measured under the current-cost approach.

20-19. What is the common meaning of *current* cost?

20-20. "All holding gains should be excluded from income." What is the major logic behind this statement?

20-21. "A holding gain can be recognized but unrealized." Do you agree? Explain.

20-22. Why do managers in heavy industries such as steel favor the current-cost concept for income tax purposes?

General Exercises and Problems

20-23 LIFO and FIFO

The inventory of the Puckett Gravel Company on June 30 shows 500 tons at $7 per ton. A physical inventory on July 31 shows a total of 600 tons on hand. Revenue from sales of gravel for July totals $17,500. The following purchases were made during July:

July 5	1,000 tons @ $8 per ton
July 15	250 tons @ $9 per ton
July 25	300 tons @ $10 per ton

Required

1. Compute the inventory value as of July 31, using (a) FIFO and (b) LIFO.
2. Compute the gross profit using each method.

20-24 Comparison of Inventory Methods

The Hrbeck Co. is a wholesaler of farm implements. The company uses a periodic inventory system. The data concerning Silverton Sprayer model Z66 for the year 19X2 follow:

	Purchases	Sold*	Balance
December 31, 19X1			150 @ $40 = $6,000
January 20, 19X2	90 @ $50 = $ 4,500		
February 5		80	
May 20	100 @ $60 = $ 6,000		
June 17		110	
October 24	80 @ $70 = $ 5,600		
November 29		60	
Total	270	$16,100	250
December 31, 19X2			170 @ ?

* The sales during 19X2 were made at the following selling prices:

80 @ 70	=	$ 5,600
110 @ 80	=	$ 8,800
60 @ 100	=	$ 6,000
250		$20,400

Required

1. Prepare a comparative statement of gross profit for the year ended December 31, 19X2, using FIFO, LIFO, and weighted-average inventory methods.
2. By how much would income taxes differ if Hrbeck used LIFO instead of FIFO for Silverton Sprayer model Z66? Assume a 40% income tax rate.

20-25 Effects of Late Purchases
Refer to the preceding problem. Suppose 100 extra units were acquired on December 30 for $70 each, a total of $7,000. How would net income and income taxes be affected under FIFO? Under LIFO? Show a tabulated comparison.

20-26 LIFO, FIFO, Purchase Decisions, and Earnings per Share
Suppose the Visser company has 1 million shares of common stock outstanding and has had the following transactions during 19X1, its first year in business:

Sales:	1,000,000 units @ $7
Purchases:	800,000 units @ $3
	300,000 units @ $4

The current income tax rate is a flat 50%; the rate next year is expected to be 40%. Prices on inventory increased from $3 to $4 during the year and are not expected to decline next year.

It is December 20, and, as the president, you are trying to decide whether you should buy the 600,000 units you need for inventory now or early next year. The current price is $5 per unit. Prices on inventory are expected to remain stable; in any event, no decline in prices is anticipated.

You have not chosen an inventory method as yet, but you will pick either LIFO or FIFO.

Other expenses for the year will be $2.4 million.

Required

1. Using LIFO, prepare a comparative income statement assuming the 600,000 units (a) are not purchased, (b) are purchased. The statement should end with reported earnings per share.
2. Repeat requirement 1, using FIFO.
3. Comment on the results obtained. What method would you choose? Why? Be specific.
4. Suppose that in year 2 the tax rate drops to 40%, prices remain stable, 1 million units are sold at $7, enough units are purchased at $5 so that the ending inventory will be 700,000 units, and other expenses are reduced to $1,800,000.
   a. Prepare a comparative income statement for the second year showing the impact of each of the four alternatives in requirements 1 and 2 on net income and earnings per share for the second year.
   b. Explain any difference in net income that you encounter among the four alternatives.
   c. Why is there a difference in ending inventory values under LIFO even though the same amount of physical inventory is in stock?
   d. What is the total cash outflow for income taxes for the two years together under the four alternatives?
   e. Would you change your answer in requirement 3 now that you have completed requirement 4? Why?

20-27 LIFO, FIFO, Prices Rising and Falling
The Gahagan Fertilizer Company has a periodic inventory system. Inventory on December 31, 19X4, consisted of 10,000 bags at $10 = $100,000. Purchases during 19X5 were 15,000 bags. Sales were 14,000 bags for sales revenue of $18 per bag.

Prepare a four-column comparative statement of gross margin for 19X5:

1. Assume that purchases were at $12 per unit. Assume FIFO and then LIFO (columns 1 and 2).
2. Assume that purchases were at $8 per unit. Assume FIFO and LIFO (columns 3 and 4).
3. Assume an income tax rate of 40%. Suppose all transactions are for cash.
   a. Which inventory method in requirement 1 results in more cash for Gahagan Company? By how much?
   b. Which inventory method in requirement 2 results in more cash for Gahagan Company? By how much?

20-28   FIFO and LIFO

Two divisions of Diversified Metals, Inc., are in the scrap metal warehousing business, the Trenton Division on the East Coast and the Long Beach Division in the West. The manager of each division receives a bonus based on the division's pretax income. The divisions are about the same size and in 19X4 coincidentally encountered seemingly identical operating situations. However, their accounting systems differ; Trenton uses FIFO and Long Beach uses LIFO.

Both divisions reported the following data for 19X4:

Beginning inventory, 10,000 tons @ $50 per ton	$ 500,000
Purchase, February 15, 19X4, 20,000 tons @ $70 per ton	1,400,000
Purchase, October 6, 19X4, 30,000 tons @ $90 per ton	2,700,000
Sales, 45,000 tons @ $100 per ton	4,500,000
Other expenses (in addition to cost of goods sold but excluding income taxes)	690,000

The income tax rate is 35%.

1. Compute net income for the year for each division. Show your calculations.
2. Which division had the better performance for the year? Which accounting system would you prefer if you were manager of one of the divisions? Why? Explain fully. Include your estimate of the overall effect of these events on the cash balance of each division, assuming that all transactions during 19X4 were direct receipts or disbursements of cash.

20-29   Effects of LIFO and FIFO

(Adapted from a problem originated by George H. Sorter.) The New Delhi Trading Company is starting in business on December 31, 19X0. In each *half year*, from 19X1 through 19X4, it expects to purchase 1,000 units and sell 500 units for the amounts listed below. In 19X5, it expects to purchase no units and sell 4,000 units for the amount indicated below. Monetary amounts are in thousands of rupees (R).

	19X1	19X2	19X3	19X4	19X5
Purchases					
First 6 months	R 2,000	R 4,000	R 6,000	R 6,000	R 0
Second 6 months	4,000	9,000	6,000	8,000	0
Total	R 6,000	R13,000	R12,000	R14,000	R 0
Sales (at selling price)	R10,000	R10,000	R10,000	R10,000	R40,000

Assume that there are no costs or expenses other than those shown. The income tax rate is 55%, and taxes for each year are payable on December 31 of that year. New Delhi Trading Company is trying to decide whether to use FIFO or LIFO throughout the 5-year period.

Required

1. What was net income under FIFO for each of the 5 years? Under LIFO? Show calculations.
2. Explain briefly which method, LIFO or FIFO, seems more advantageous, and why.

20-30 Effects of LIFO on Purchase Decisions

The Obel Corporation is nearing the end of its first year in business. The following purchases of its single product have been made:

	Units	Unit Price	Total Cost
January	400	$20	$ 8,000
March	400	20	8,000
May	400	22	8,800
July	400	26	10,400
September	400	28	11,200
November	400	30	12,000
	2,400		$58,400

Sales for the year will be 2,000 units for $96,000. Expenses other than cost of goods sold will be $16,000.

The president is undecided about whether to adopt FIFO or LIFO for income tax purposes. The company has ample storage space for up to 3,000 units of inventory. Inventory prices are expected to stay at $30 per unit for the next few months.

Required

1. If the president decided to purchase 1,600 units @ $30 in December, what would be the net income before taxes, the income taxes, and the net income after taxes for the year under (a) FIFO and (b) LIFO? Assume that income tax rates are 30% on the first $25,000 of net taxable income and 40% on the excess.
2. If the company sells its year-end inventory in year 2 @ $48 per unit and goes out of business, what would be the net income before taxes, the income taxes, and the net income after taxes under (a) FIFO and (b) LIFO? Assume that other expenses in year 2 are $16,000.
3. Repeat requirements 1 and 2, assuming that 1,600 units, @ $30, were not purchased until January of the second year. Generalize on the effect on net income of the timing of purchases under FIFO and LIFO.

20-31 Lower of Cost or Market

Penn Wood Products Company uses cost or market, whichever is lower, for its inventories. There were no sales or purchases during the periods indicated, although selling prices generally fluctuated in the same directions as replacement costs. At what amount would you value merchandise on the dates listed below?

	Invoice Cost	Replacement Cost
December 31, 19X0	$100,000	$ 75,000
April 30, 19X1	100,000	90,000
August 31, 19X1	100,000	110,000
December 31, 19X1	100,000	65,000

20-32   Meaning of General Price Index Applications and Choice of Base Year
Kemper Real Estate Company acquired land in mid-1976 for $3 million. In mid-1996 it acquired a substantially identical parcel of land for $8 million. Suppose the general price index annual averages were:

1996–350.0	1986–175.0	1976–105.0

Required

1. In four columns, show the computations of the total cost of the two parcels of land expressed in (a) costs as traditionally recorded, (b) dollars of 1996 purchasing power, (c) 1986 purchasing power, and (d) 1976 purchasing power.
2. Explain the meaning of the figures that you computed in requirement 1.

20-33   Concepts of Income
Suppose you are in the business of investing in land and holding it for resale. On December 31, 19X0, a parcel of land has a historical cost of $100,000 and a current value of $400,000; the general price index had tripled since the land was acquired. Suppose also that the land is sold on December 31, 19X1, for $460,000. The general price level rose by 5% during 19X1.

Required

1. Prepare a tabulation of income from continuing operations and holding gains for 19X1, using the four methods illustrated in Exhibit 20-3, page 783.
2. In your own words, explain the meaning of the results, giving special attention to what income represents.

20-34   Four Versions of Income and Capital
Reexamine Exhibit 20-3, page 783. Suppose the replacement cost at December 31, 19X2, had been $25 instead of $30. Suppose also that the general price index had been 120 instead of 110. All other facts are unchanged. Use four columns to prepare balance sheets as of December 31, 19X2 (only), and income statements for 19X2 under the four concepts shown in Exhibit 20-3. Explain the differences between your solution and the results shown in Exhibit 20-3.

Understanding
Published
Financial Reports

20-35   Switch from LIFO to FIFO
This is a classic problem. Effective January 1, 1970, Chrysler Corporation adopted the FIFO method for inventories previously valued by the LIFO method. The 1970 annual report stated: "This . . . makes the financial statements with respect to inventory valuation comparable with those of the other United States automobile manufacturers."

The *Wall Street Journal* reported:

The change improved Chrysler's 1970 financial results several ways. Besides narrowing the 1970 loss by $20 million it improved Chrysler's working capital.

The change helped Chrysler's balance sheet by boosting inventories, and thus current assets, by $150 million at the end of 1970 over what they would have been under LIFO. As Chrysler's profit has collapsed over the last two years and its financial position tightened, auto analysts have eyed warily Chrysler's shrinking ratio of current assets to current liabilities.

Chrysler's short-term debt stood at $374 million at year-end, down from $477 million a year earlier but up slightly from $370 million on September 30. Chrysler's cash and marketable securities shrank during the year to $156.4 million at year-end, down from $309.3 million a year earlier and $220 million on Sept. 30.

To get the improvements in its balance sheet and results, however, Chrysler paid a price. Roger Helder, vice president and comptroller, said Chrysler owed the government $53 million in tax savings it accumulated by using the LIFO method since it switched from FIFO in 1957. The major advantage of LIFO is that it holds down profit and thus tax liabilities. The other three major auto makers stayed on the FIFO method. Mr. Helder said Chrysler now has to pay back that $53 million to the government over 20 years, which will boost Chrysler's tax bills about $3 million a year.

Required   Given the content of this text chapter, do you think the Chrysler decision to switch from LIFO to FIFO was beneficial to its stockholders? Explain, being as specific and using as many data as you can.

20-36   Effect of LIFO

General Mills, producer of Wheaties, Cheerios, Gold Medal Flour, and many other food products, reported 1994 operating income of $753 million. Part of footnote 1 to the financial statements stated:

> Certain domestic inventories are valued using the LIFO method, while other inventories are generally valued using the FIFO method.

> Inventories are valued at the lower of cost or market as follows:

	May 29, 1994	May 30, 1993
Inventories	$488,000,000	$439,000,000

If LIFO inventories were valued at the lower of FIFO cost or market, the inventories would have been $53 million and $60 million higher than those reported for fiscal 1994 and 1993, respectively.

Required   Suppose the FIFO method had always been used for all inventories. Calculate General Mills's operating income for fiscal 1994. By how much would the cumulative operating income for all years through 1994 differ from that reported? Would it be more or less than that reported?

20-37   LIFO Liquidation

E.I. duPont de Numours Co., reported 1993 net income of $555 million and included the following footnote in its 1993 annual report:

> Liquidation of LIFO inventory quantities... increased 1993 net income by about $50 million.

Required
1. Compute the percentage increase in net income caused by the LIFO liquidation.
2. Suppose the income tax rate was 40%. What was the effect of the LIFO liquidations on the (before tax) operating income? What was the effect on taxes?
3. How could duPont have avoided the extra taxes?

20-38   Lower of Cost or Market

Polaroid Corporation's annual report stated: "Inventories are valued on a first-in, first-out basis at the lower of cost or market value. Market value is determined by replacement cost or net realizable value." Assume that severe price competition in 1995 necessitated a write-down on December 31 for a class of camera inventories bearing a standard cost of $10 million. The appropriate valuation at market was deemed to be $8 million.

Suppose the product line had been terminated in early 1996 and the remaining inventory had been sold for $8 million.

Required

1. Assume that sales of this line of camera for 1995 were $21 million and cost of goods sold was $16 million. Prepare a statement of gross margin for 1995 and 1996. Show the results under a strict FIFO cost method in the first two columns and under a lower-of-FIFO-cost-or-market method in the next two columns.
2. Assume that Polaroid did not discontinue the product line. Instead a new marketing campaign spurred market demand. Replacement cost of the cameras in the December 31 inventory was $9 million on January 31, 1996. What inventory valuation would be appropriate if the inventory of December 31, 1995, was still held on January 31, 1996?

20-39   Effects of General Versus Specific Price Changes
The following data are from the annual reports of Gannett Co. (owner of 125 newspapers), Zayre Corp. (operator of over 360 discount stores and over 700 specialty stores), and Goodyear Tire and Rubber Company, respectively (in millions):

	Gannett	Zayre	Goodyear
Increase in specific prices of assets held during the year	$45.8	$24.9	$ (4.7)
Less: effect of increase in general price level	37.5	55.5	252.0
Excess of increase in specific prices over increase in the general price level	$ 8.3	$(30.6)	$(256.7)

Required

Compare and contrast the relationship between changes in the general price level and changes in the price of specific assets of each of the three companies.

Recommended Readings

The following readings will aid readers who want to pursue some topics in more depth than is possible in this book. There is a hazard in compiling a group of recommended readings. Inevitably, some worthwhile books or periodicals are omitted. Moreover, such a list cannot include books published subsequent to the compilation date. The list is not comprehensive, but it suggests many excellent readings.

PERIODICALS

Professional Journals

The following professional journals are typically available in university libraries and include articles on the application of management accounting:

- *Accounting Horizons.* Published by the American Accounting Association; stresses current practice-oriented articles in all areas of accounting.
- *CMA: The Management Accounting Magazine.* Published by The Society of Management Accountants of Canada; includes much practice-oriented research in management accounting.
- *Financial Executive.* Published by the Financial Executives Institute; emphasizes general policy issues for accounting and finance executives.
- *GAO Journal.* Covers managerial accounting issues of interest to the General Accounting Office of the U.S. government.
- *Harvard Business Review.* Published by Harvard Business School; directed to general managers, but contains excellent articles on applications of management accounting.
- *Journal of Accountancy.* Published by the American Institute of CPAs; emphasizes financial accounting and is directed at the practicing CPA.
- *Journal of Cost Management.* Published by CAM-I; covers new developments in cost management practice and theory.
- *Management Accounting.* Published by the Institute of Management Accountants; many articles on actual applications by individual organizations.
- *Planning Review.* Published by the Planning Executives Institute; a journal designed for business planners.
- *Business Week, Forbes, Fortune, The Economist, The Wall Street Journal.* Popular publications that cover a variety of business and economics topics; often their articles relate to management accounting.

Academic Journals

The academic journal that focuses most directly on current management and cost accounting research is the *Journal of Management Accounting Research*, published by the Management Accounting section of the American Accounting Association. *The Accounting Review*, the general research publication of the American Accounting Association, and *Journal of Accounting Research*, published at the University of Chicago, and *Contemporary Accounting Research*, published by the Canadian Academic Association, cover all accounting topics at a more theoretical level. *Accounting, Organizations and Society*, a British journal, publishes much research on behavioral aspects of management accounting. The *Journal of Accounting and Economics* covers economics-based accounting research. The *Journal of Accounting Literature* presents reviews of accounting research.

BOOKS IN MANAGEMENT ACCOUNTING

Most of the topics in this text are covered in more detail in the many books entitled *Cost Accounting* including *Cost Accounting: A Managerial Emphasis* by C. T. Horngren, G. Foster, and Srikant Datar (Prentice Hall, 1990). You can find more advanced coverage in *Advanced Managerial Accounting*, 2nd ed. by R. S. Kaplan and Anthony A. Atkinson (Prentice Hall, 1989) and R. Magee, *Advanced Cost Accounting* (Harper and Row, 1986).

The Financial Executives Institute, 10 Madison Avenue, P.O. Box 1938, Morristown, NJ 07960, and the Institute of Management Accounting, 10 Paragon Drive, P.O. Box 433, Montvale, NJ 07645-0433, have long lists of accounting research publications.

Handbooks and General Texts, Readings, and Case Books

The books in this list have wide application to management accounting issues. The handbooks are basic references. The textbooks are designed for classroom use but may be useful for self-study. Readings books are collections of some of the better periodical articles. The case books present applications from real companies.

- BARRETT, M., AND W. BRUNS, JR., *Case Problems in Management Accounting*. Homewood, IL: Irwin, 1984.
- BIERMAN, H., JR., C. BONINI, AND W. HASEMAN, *Quantitative Analysis for Business Decisions*, 8th ed. Homewood, IL: Richard D. Irwin, 1991.
- BIERMAN, H., JR., AND S. SMIDT, *The Capital Budgeting Decision*, 8th ed. New York: Macmillan, 1993. Expands the capital budgeting discussion in Chapters 11-12.
- CAPLAN, E., AND J. CHAMPOUX, *Cases in Management Accounting: Context and Behavior*. New York: National Association of Accountants, 1983.
- COOPER, D., R. SCAPENS, AND J. ARNOLD, eds., *Management Accounting Research and Practice*. London: Institute of Cost and Management Accountants, 1983.
- COOPER, R., *The Design of Cost Management Systems: Text, Cases and Readings*. Upper Saddle River, NJ: Prentice Hall, 1991.
- DAVIDSON, S., AND R. WEIL, eds., *Handbook of Modern Accounting*. New York: McGraw-Hill, 1983.

- Demski, J. S., *Information Analysis*, 2nd ed. Reading, MA: Addison-Wesley, 1980. A rigorous theoretical discussion of the value of information.
- Fremgen, J. M., and S. S. Liao, *The Allocation of Corporate Indirect Costs*. New York: National Association of Accountants, 1981.
- Brinker, B. ed. *Handbook of Cost Management*. New York: Warren, Gorham and Lamont, 1993.
- Holmes, J. R., G. H. Lander, M. A. Tipgos, and M. G. Wallace, Jr., *Profile of the Management Accountant*. New York: National Association of Accountants, 1982.
- Kaplan, R., and W. Bruns, eds., *Accounting and Management: Field Study Perspectives*. Boston, MA: Harvard Business School Press, 1988.
- Rotch, W., B. Allen, and C. Smith *Cases in Management Accounting and Control Systems* 3rd ed., Upper Saddle River, NJ: Prentice Hall, 1994.
- Seed, A. H., III, *The Impact of Inflation on Internal Planning and Control*. New York: National Association of Accountants, 1981.
- Shank, J., *Contemporary Managerial Accounting: A Casebook*. Upper Saddle River, NJ: Prentice Hall, 1981.
- Thomas, W., ed., *Readings in Cost Accounting, Budgeting and Control*. Cincinnati, OH: South-Western Publishing, 1988.

Strategic Nature of Management Accounting

Management accountants realize that cost and performance information is most useful to organizations when it helps define strategic alternatives and helps in the management of resources to achieve strategic objectives. The books in this list, though not necessarily accounting books, provide valuable foundation to the interaction of strategy and accounting information.

- Kaplan, R., and H. T. Johnson, *Relevance Lost: The Rise and Fall of Management Accounting*. Boston, MA: Harvard Business School Press, 1987.
- Porter, M., *Competitive Strategy*. New York: Free Press, 1980.
- Porter, M., *Competitive Advantage*. New York: Free Press, 1985.
- Rappaport, A., *Creating Shareholder Value: The New Standard for Business Performance*. New York: Free Press, 1986.
- Shank, J., and V. Govidarajan, *Strategic Cost Analysis: The Evolution from Managerial to Strategic Accounting*, Homewood, IL: Irwin, 1989.

Modern Manufacturing

The following books provide background on the nature of modern manufacturing.

- Chase, R., and N. Aquilano, *Production and Operation Management*. Homewood, IL: Irwin, 1989.
- Hayes, R., S. Wheelright, and K. Clark, *Dynamic Manufacturing*. New York, Free Press, 1988.
- Schonberger, R., *World Class Manufacturing*. New York, Free Press, 1986.
- Skinner, W., *Manufacturing: The Formidable Competitive Weapon*. New York: Wiley, 1985.
- Teece, P., *The Competitive Challenge: Strategies for Industrial Innovation and Renewal*. Cambridge, MA: Ballinger, 1987.
- Zuboff, S., *In the Age of the Smart Machine*. New York: Basic Books, 1984.

Management Accounting in Modern Manufacturing Settings

These books present relatively recent responses of management accountants to changes in manufacturing methods and practices.

- ATKINSON, A., R. BANKER, R. KAPLAN, AND S. YOUNG, *Management Accounting*, Upper Saddle River, NJ: Prentice Hall, 1995
- BENNETT, E., B. FOSSUM, R. HARRIS, D. ROBERTSON, AND F. SKIPPER, *Financial Practices in a Computer Integrated System (CIS) Environment*. Morristown, NJ: Financial Executives Research Foundation, 1987.
- BENNETT, R., J. HENDRICKS, D. KEYS, AND E. RUDNICKI, *Cost Accounting for Factory Automation*. Montvale, NJ: National Association of Accountants, 1987.
- BERLINER, C., AND J. BRIMSON, eds., *Cost Accounting for Today's Advanced Manufacturing: The CAM-I Conceptual Design*. Boston, MA: Harvard Business School Press, 1988.
- CAPETTINI, R., AND D. CLANCY, eds., *Cost Accounting, Robotics, and the New Manufacturing Environment*. Sarasota, FL: American Accounting Association, 1987.
- GOLDRATT, E., AND J. COX, *The Goal. Croton-On-Hudson*, NY: North River Press, Inc., 1984. A novel illustrating the new manufacturing environment.
- HOWELL, R., J. BROWN, S. SOUCY, AND A. SEED, *Management Accounting in the New Manufacturing Environment*. Montvale, NJ: National Association of Accountants, 1987.
- HOWELL, R., AND S. SOUCY, *Factory 2000 +* . Montvale, NJ: National Association of Accountants, 1988. A collection of five articles by the authors originally published in *Management Accounting*.
- KAPLAN, R., ed., *Measuring Manufacturing Performance*, Boston, MA: Harvard University Press, 1990.
- LEE, J., *Managerial Accounting Changes for the 1990s*. Artesia, CA: McKay Business Systems, 1987.
- MCNAIR, C., W. MOSCONI, AND T. NORRIS, *Meeting the Technology Challenge: Cost Accounting in a JIT Environment*. Montvale, NJ: National Association of Accountants, 1987.
- NATIONAL ASSOCIATION OF ACCOUNTANTS, *Cost Accounting for the 90s: Responding to Technological Change*. Montvale, NJ, 1988.
- TURNEY, P., *Performance Excellence in Manufacturing and Service Organizations*. Sarasota, FL: American Accounting Association, 1990.

Management Control Systems

The topics of Chapters 7 to 10 can be explored further in several books, including:

- ANTHONY, R. N., J. DEARDEN, AND V. GOVINDARAJAN, *Management Control Systems*. Homewood, IL: Irwin, 1992. A popular textbook that includes many cases.
- ARROW, K. J., *The Limits of Organization*. New York: Norton, 1974. A readable classic by the Nobel laureate.
- BENKE, R., AND J. D. EDWARDS, *Transfer Pricing: Techniques and Uses*. New York: National Association of Accountants, 1980.
- ECCLES, ROBERT G., *The Transfer Pricing Problem: A Theory for Practice*. Lexington, MA: Lexington Books, 1985.
- EMMANUEL, C., K. MERCHANT, AND D. OTLEY, *Accounting for Management Control*. Chapman & Hall, 1990.

- EUSKE, K., *Management Control: Planning, Control, Measurement, and Evaluation*. Reading, MA: Addison-Wesley, 1984.
- MACIARIELLO, J. A. AND C. KIRBY, *Management Control Systems: Using Adaptive Systems to Attain Control*, Upper Saddle River, NJ: Prentice Hall, 1984.
- MAUTZ, R. K., AND J. WINJUM, *Criteria for Management Control Systems*. New York: Financial Executives Institute, 1981. Focus on internal control.
- SOLOMONS, D., *Divisional Performance: Measurement and Control*. New York: Markus Wiener, 1983. A reprint of a 1965 classic that is still relevant.

Management Accounting in Nonprofit Organizations

Many books discuss management accounting in nonprofit organizations, especially in health care. Four examples are

- ANTHONY, R. N., AND D. W. YOUNG, *Management Control in Nonprofit Organizations*, 5th ed. Homewood, IL: Irwin, 1994.
- HERZLINGER, R. AND D. NITTERHOUSE, *Financial Accounting and Managerial Control for Nonprofit Organizations*. Cincinnati, OH: Southwestern Publishing Co., 1994.
- RAMANATHAN, K. V., *Management Control in Nonprofit Organizations*. New York: Wiley, 1982.
- SCHAFER, E. L., AND M. E. GOCKE, *Management Accounting for Health Maintenance Organizations*. Denver: Center for Research in Ambulatory Health Care Administration, 1984.
- SUVER, J. D., AND B. R. NEUMANN, *Management Accounting for Healthcare Organizations*. Chicago, IL: Precept Press, 1992.

BOOKS IN FINANCIAL ACCOUNTING

This book's companion volume, *Introduction to Financial Accounting*, provides an expansion of the financial accounting material (Chapters 17-20). A more detailed coverage of the topics can be found in books entitled *Intermediate Accounting* including that by T.R. DYCKMAN, R.E. DUKES, and C.J. DAVIS (Irwin, 1995).

Opinions of the Accounting Principles Board are available from the American Institute of CPAs, 1211 Avenue of the Americas, New York, NY 10036-8775. The institute also has a series of research studies on a variety of topics. The pronouncements of the Financial Accounting Standards Board are available from the board's offices, 401 Merritt 7, P.O. Box 5116, Norwalk, CT 06856-5116.

Financial accounting has such an extensive literature that it is impossible to provide a short list of books that adequately covers the field. However, we will mention four books that cover a wide range of issues. For a perspective on the large firms practicing accounting, see two books by M. STEVENS, *The Accounting Wars* (Macmillan, 1985) and *The Big Six* (Touchstone Books, 1992).

Research relating financial reporting to the capital markets is summarized in T. R. DYCKMAN and D. MORSE, *Efficient Capital Markets and Accounting: A Critical Analysis* (Prentice Hall, 1986). The interaction of financial reporting and management's economic incentives is covered in text and readings in R. BALL and C. SMITH, *The Economics of Accounting Policy Choice*, New York: McGraw-Hill, 1992. Application of this research to financial statement analysis is provided in C. STICKNEY, *Financial Statement Analysis* (Dryden Press, 1990).

Fundamentals of Compound Interest and the Use of Present-Value Tables

NATURE OF INTEREST

Interest is the cost of using money. It is the rental charge for cash, just as rental charges are often made for the use of automobiles or boats.

Interest does not always entail an outlay of cash. The concept of interest applies to ownership funds as well as to borrowed funds. The reason why interest must be considered on *all* funds in use, regardless of their source, is that the selection of one alternative necessarily commits funds that could otherwise be invested in some other opportunity. The measure of the interest in such cases is the return foregone by rejecting the alternative use. For instance, a wholly owned home or business asset is not cost free. The funds so invested could alternatively be invested in government bonds or in some other venture. The measure of this opportunity cost depends on what alternative incomes are available.

Newspapers often contain advertisements of financial institutions citing interest rates that are "compounded." This appendix explains compound interest, including the use of present-value tables.

Simple interest is calculated by multiplying an interest rate by an unchanging principal amount. In contrast, *compound interest* is calculated by multiplying an interest rate by a principal amount that is increased each interest period by the previously accumulated (unpaid) interest. The accumulated interest is added to the principal to become the principal for the new period. For example, suppose you deposited $10,000 in a financial institution that promised to pay 10% interest per annum. You then let the amount accumulate for three years before withdrawing the full balance of the deposit. The *simple-interest* deposit would accumulate to $13,000 at the end of three years:

	PRINCIPAL	SIMPLE INTEREST	BALANCE, END OF YEAR
Year 1	$10,000	$10,000 × 0.10 = $1,000	$11,000
Year 2	10,000	10,000 × 0.10 = 1,000	12,000
Year 3	10,000	10,000 × 0.10 = 1,000	13,000

Compound interest provides interest on interest. That is, the principal changes from period to period. The deposit would accumulate to $10,000 × $(1.10)^3 = \$10,000 \times 1.331 = \$13,310$:

	PRINCIPAL	COMPOUND INTEREST	BALANCE, END OF YEAR
Year 1	$10,000	$10,000 × 0.10 = $1,000	$11,000
Year 2	11,000	11,000 × 0.10 = 1,100	12,100
Year 3	12,100	12,100 × 0.10 = 1,210	13,310

The "force" of compound interest can be staggering. For example, the same deposit would accumulate as follows:

	AT END OF		
	10 Years	20 Years	40 Years
Simple interest			
$10,000 + 10 ($1,000) =	$20,000		
10,000 + 20 ($1,000) =		$30,000	
10,000 + 40 ($1,000) =			$ 50,000
Compound interest			
$10,000 × $(1.10)^{10}$ = $10,000 × 2.5937 =	$25,937		
$10,000 × $(1.10)^{20}$ = $10,000 × 6.7275 =		$67,275	
$10,000 × $(1.10)^{40}$ = $10,000 × 45.2593 =			$452,593

Hand calculations of compound interest quickly become burdensome. Therefore compound interest tables have been constructed to ease computations. (Indeed, many hand-held calculators contain programs that provide speedy answers.) Hundreds of tables are available, but we will use only the two most useful for capital budgeting.[1]

TABLE 1: PRESENT VALUE OF $1

How shall we express a future cash inflow or outflow in terms of its equivalent today (at time zero)? Table 1 provides factors that give the present value of a single, lump-sum cash flow to be received or paid at the end of a future period.[2]

Suppose you invest $1.00 today. It will grow to $1.06 in one year at six percent interest; that is, $1 × 1.06 = $1.06. At the end of the second year its value is ($1 × 1.06) × 1.06 = $1 × $(1.06)^2$ = $1.124, and at the end of the third year it is $1 × $(1.06)^3$ = 1.191. In general, $1.00 grows to $(1 + i)^n$ in n years at i percent interest.

---

[1] For additional tables, see R. Vichas, *Handbook of Financial Mathematics, Formulas and Tables* (Upper Saddle River, NJ: Prentice Hall, 1979).

[2] The factors are rounded to four decimal places. The examples in this text use these rounded factors. If you use tables with different rounding, or if you use a calculator or personal computer, your answers may differ from those given because of a small rounding error.

To determine *the present value*, you reverse this accumulation process. If $1.00 is to be received in one year, it is worth $1 ÷ 1.06 = $0.9434 today at an interest rate of 6%. Suppose you invest $0.9434 today. In one year you will have $0.9434 × 1.06 = $1.00. Thus $0.9434 is the *present value* of $1.00 a year hence at 6%. If the dollar will be received in two years, its present value is $1.00 ÷ (1.06)² = $0.8900. The general formula for the present value *(PV)* of an amount S to be received or paid in n periods at an interest rate of i% per period is

$$PV = \frac{S}{(1+i)^n}$$

Table 1 gives factors for the present value of $1.00 at various interest rates over several different periods. Present values are also called *discounted* values, and the process of finding the present value is *discounting*. You can think of this as discounting (decreasing) the value of a future cash inflow or outflow. Why is the value discounted? Because the cash is to be received or paid in the future, not today.

Assume that a prominent city is issuing a 3-year non-interest-bearing note payable that promises to pay a lump sum of $1,000 exactly three years from now. You desire a rate of return of exactly 6%, compounded annually. How much would you be willing to pay now for the 3-year note? The situation is sketched as follows:

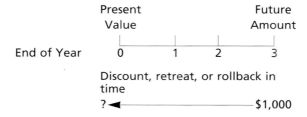

The factor in the period 3 row and 6% column of Table 1 is 0.8396. The present value of the $1,000 payment is $1,000 × 0.8396 = $839.60. You would be willing to pay $839.60 for the $1,000 to be received in three years.

Suppose interest is compounded semiannually rather than annually. How much would you be willing to pay? The three years become six interest payment periods. The rate per period is half the annual rate, or 6% ÷ 2 = 3%. The factor in the period 6 row and 3% column of Table 1 is 0.8375. You would be willing to pay $1,000 × 0.8375 or only $837.50 rather than $839.60.

As a further check on your understanding, review the earlier example of compound interest. Suppose the financial institution promised to pay $13,310 at the end of three years. How much would you be willing to deposit at time zero if you desired a 10% rate of return compounded annually? Using Table 1, the period 3 row and the 10% column show a factor of 0.7513. Multiply this factor by the future amount:

$$PV = 0.7513 \times \$13,310 = \$10,000$$

A diagram of this computation follows:

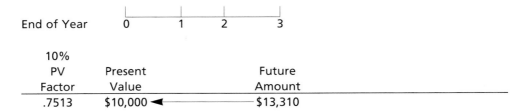

End of Year	0	1	2	3

10% PV Factor	Present Value			Future Amount
.7513	$10,000 ◄			$13,310

Pause for a moment. Use Table 1 to obtain the present values of

1. $1,700, at 20%, at the end of 20 years
2. $8,300, at 10%, at the end of 12 years
3. $8,000, at 4%, at the end of 4 years

Answers:

1. $1,700 (0.0261) = $44.37
2. $8,300 (0.3186) = $2,644.38
3. $8,000 (0.8548) = $6,838.40

TABLE 2: PRESENT VALUE OF AN ORDINARY ANNUITY OF $1

An ordinary annuity is a series of equal cash flows to take place at the end of successive periods of equal length. Its present value is denoted PV_A. Assume that you buy a note from a municipality that promises to pay $1,000 at the end of *each* of three years. How much should you be willing to pay if you desire a rate of return of 6%, compounded annually?

You could solve this problem using Table 1. First, find the present value of each payment, and then add the present values as in Exhibit B-1. You would be willing to pay $943.40 for the first payment, $890.00 for the second, and $839.60 for the third, a total of $2,673.00.

Since each cash payment is $1,000 with equal 1-year periods between them, the note is an ordinary annuity. Table 2 provides a shortcut method. The present value in Exhibit B-1 can be expressed as

$$PV_A = \$1,000 \times \frac{1}{1.06} + \$1,000 \times \frac{1}{(1.06)^2} + \$1,000 \times \frac{1}{(1.06)^3}$$

$$= \$1,000 \left[\frac{1}{1.06} + \frac{1}{(1.06)^2} + \frac{1}{(1.06)^3} \right]$$

The three terms in brackets are the first three numbers from the 6% column of Table 1, and their sum is in the third row of the 6% column of Table 2: .9434 + .8900 + .8396 = 2.6730. Instead of calculating three present values and adding them, you can simply multiply the PV factor from Table 2 by the cash payment: 2.6730 × $1,000 = $2,673.

Payment	End of Year Table One Factor	0 Present Value	1	2	3
1	$\frac{1}{1.06} = .9434$	$ 943.40	$1,000		
2	$\frac{1}{(1.06)^2} = .8900$	890.00		$1,000	
3	$\frac{1}{(1.06)^3} = .8396$	839.60			$1,000
Total		$2,673.00			

This shortcut is especially valuable if the cash payments or receipts extend over many periods. Consider an annual cash payment of $1,000 for 20 years at 6%. The present value, calculated from Table 2, is $1,000 × 11.4699 = $11,469.90. To use Table 1 for this calculation, you would perform 20 multiplications and then add the twenty products.

The factors in Table 2 can be calculated using the following general formula:

$$PV_A = \frac{1}{i}\left[1 - \frac{1}{(1+i)^n}\right]$$

Applied to our illustration:

$$PV_A = \frac{1}{.06}\left[1 - \frac{1}{(1.06)^3}\right] = \frac{1}{.06}(1 - .8396) = \frac{.1604}{.06} = 2.6730$$

Use Table 2 to obtain the present values of the following ordinary annuities:

1. $1,600 at 20% for 20 years
2. $8,300 at 10% for 12 years
3. $8,000 at 4% for 4 years

Answers:

1. $1,600 (4.8696) = $7,791.36
2. $8,300 (6.8137) = $56,553.71
3. $8,000 (3.6299) = $29,039.20

In particular, note that the higher interest rate, the lower the present value.

Table 1 — Present Value of $1

$$PV = \frac{1}{(1+i)^n}$$

PERIODS	3%	4%	5%	6%	7%	8%	10%	12%	14%	16%	18%	20%	22%	24%	25%	26%	28%	30%	40%
1	.9709	.9615	.9524	.9434	.9346	.9259	.9091	.8929	.8772	.8621	.8475	.8333	.8197	.8065	.8000	.7937	.7813	.7692	.7143
2	.9426	.9246	.9070	.8900	.8734	.8573	.8264	.7972	.7695	.7432	.7182	.6944	.6719	.6504	.6400	.6299	.6104	.5917	.5102
3	.9151	.8890	.8638	.8396	.8163	.7938	.7513	.7118	.6750	.6407	.6086	.5787	.5507	.5245	.5120	.4999	.4768	.4552	.3644
4	.8885	.8548	.8227	.7921	.7629	.7350	.6830	.6355	.5921	.5523	.5158	.4823	.4514	.4230	.4096	.3968	.3725	.3501	.2603
5	.8626	.8219	.7835	.7473	.7130	.6806	.6209	.5674	.5194	.4761	.4371	.4019	.3700	.3411	.3277	.3149	.2910	.2693	.1859
6	.8375	.7903	.7462	.7050	.6663	.6302	.5645	.5066	.4556	.4104	.3704	.3349	.3033	.2751	.2621	.2499	.2274	.2072	.1328
7	.8131	.7599	.7107	.6651	.6227	.5835	.5132	.4523	.3996	.3538	.3139	.2791	.2486	.2218	.2097	.1983	.1776	.1594	.0949
8	.7894	.7307	.6768	.6274	.5820	.5403	.4665	.4039	.3506	.3050	.2660	.2326	.2038	.1789	.1678	.1574	.1388	.1226	.0678
9	.7664	.7026	.6446	.5919	.5439	.5002	.4241	.3606	.3075	.2630	.2255	.1938	.1670	.1443	.1342	.1249	.1084	.0943	.0484
10	.7441	.6756	.6139	.5584	.5083	.4632	.3855	.3220	.2697	.2267	.1911	.1615	.1369	.1164	.1074	.0992	.0847	.0725	.0346
11	.7224	.6496	.5847	.5268	.4751	.4289	.3505	.2875	.2366	.1954	.1619	.1346	.1122	.0938	.0859	.0787	.0662	.0558	.0247
12	.7014	.6246	.5568	.4970	.4440	.3971	.3186	.2567	.2076	.1685	.1372	.1122	.0920	.0757	.0687	.0625	.0517	.0429	.0176
13	.6810	.6006	.5303	.4688	.4150	.3677	.2897	.2292	.1821	.1452	.1163	.0935	.0754	.0610	.0550	.0496	.0404	.0330	.0126
14	.6611	.5775	.5051	.4423	.3878	.3405	.2633	.2046	.1597	.1252	.0985	.0779	.0618	.0492	.0440	.0393	.0316	.0254	.0090
15	.6419	.5553	.4810	.4173	.3624	.3152	.2394	.1827	.1401	.1079	.0835	.0649	.0507	.0397	.0352	.0312	.0247	.0195	.0064
16	.6232	.5339	.4581	.3936	.3387	.2919	.2176	.1631	.1229	.0930	.0708	.0541	.0415	.0320	.0281	.0248	.0193	.0150	.0046
17	.6050	.5134	.4363	.3714	.3166	.2703	.1978	.1456	.1078	.0802	.0600	.0451	.0340	.0258	.0225	.0197	.0150	.0116	.0033
18	.5874	.4936	.4155	.3503	.2959	.2502	.1799	.1300	.0946	.0691	.0508	.0376	.0279	.0208	.0180	.0156	.0118	.0089	.0023
19	.5703	.4746	.3957	.3305	.2765	.2317	.1635	.1161	.0829	.0596	.0431	.0313	.0229	.0168	.0144	.0124	.0092	.0068	.0017
20	.5537	.4564	.3769	.3118	.2584	.2145	.1486	.1037	.0728	.0514	.0365	.0261	.0187	.0135	.0115	.0098	.0072	.0053	.0012
21	.5375	.4388	.3589	.2942	.2415	.1987	.1351	.0926	.0638	.0443	.0309	.0217	.0154	.0109	.0092	.0078	.0056	.0040	.0009
22	.5219	.4220	.3418	.2775	.2257	.1839	.1228	.0826	.0560	.0382	.0262	.0181	.0126	.0088	.0074	.0062	.0044	.0031	.0006
23	.5067	.4057	.3256	.2618	.2109	.1703	.1117	.0738	.0491	.0329	.0222	.0151	.0103	.0071	.0059	.0049	.0034	.0024	.0004
24	.4919	.3901	.3101	.2470	.1971	.1577	.1015	.0659	.0431	.0284	.0188	.0126	.0085	.0057	.0047	.0039	.0027	.0018	.0003
25	.4776	.3751	.2953	.2330	.1842	.1460	.0923	.0588	.0378	.0245	.0160	.0105	.0069	.0046	.0038	.0031	.0021	.0014	.0002
26	.4637	.3607	.2812	.2198	.1722	.1352	.0839	.0525	.0331	.0211	.0135	.0087	.0057	.0037	.0030	.0025	.0016	.0011	.0002
27	.4502	.3468	.2678	.2074	.1609	.1252	.0763	.0469	.0291	.0182	.0115	.0073	.0047	.0030	.0024	.0019	.0013	.0008	.0001
28	.4371	.3335	.2551	.1956	.1504	.1159	.0693	.0419	.0255	.0157	.0097	.0061	.0038	.0024	.0019	.0015	.0010	.0006	.0001
29	.4243	.3207	.2429	.1846	.1406	.1073	.0630	.0374	.0224	.0135	.0082	.0051	.0031	.0020	.0015	.0012	.0008	.0005	.0001
30	.4120	.3083	.2314	.1741	.1314	.0994	.0573	.0334	.0196	.0116	.0070	.0042	.0026	.0016	.0012	.0010	.0006	.0004	.0000
40	.3066	.2083	.1420	.0972	.0668	.0460	.0221	.0107	.0053	.0026	.0013	.0007	.0004	.0002	.0001	.0001	.0001	.0000	.0000

Table 2 Present Value of Ordinary Annuity of $1

$$PV_A = \frac{1}{i}\left[1 - \frac{1}{(1+i)^n}\right]$$

Periods	3%	4%	5%	6%	7%	8%	10%	12%	14%	16%	18%	20%	22%	24%	25%	26%	28%	30%	40%
1	.9709	.9615	.9524	.9434	.9346	.9259	.9091	.8929	.8772	.8621	.8475	.8333	.8197	.8065	.8000	.7937	.7813	.7692	.7143
2	1.9135	1.8861	1.8594	1.8334	1.8080	1.7833	1.7355	1.6901	1.6467	1.6052	1.5656	1.5278	1.4915	1.4568	1.4400	1.4235	1.3916	1.3609	1.2245
3	2.8286	2.7751	2.7232	2.6730	2.6243	2.5771	2.4869	2.4018	2.3216	2.2459	2.1743	2.1065	2.0422	1.9813	1.9520	1.9234	1.8684	1.8161	1.5889
4	3.7171	3.6299	3.5460	3.4651	3.3872	3.3121	3.1699	3.0373	2.9137	2.7982	2.6901	2.5887	2.4936	2.4043	2.3616	2.3202	2.2410	2.1662	1.8492
5	4.5797	4.4518	4.3295	4.2124	4.1002	3.9927	3.7908	3.6048	3.4331	3.2743	3.1272	2.9906	2.8636	2.7454	2.6893	2.6351	2.5320	2.4356	2.0352
6	5.4172	5.2421	5.0757	4.9173	4.7665	4.6229	4.3553	4.1114	3.8887	3.6847	3.4976	3.3255	3.1669	3.0205	2.9514	2.8850	2.7594	2.6427	2.1680
7	6.2303	6.0021	5.7864	5.5824	5.3893	5.2064	4.8684	4.5638	4.2883	4.0386	3.8115	3.6046	3.4155	3.2423	3.1611	3.0833	2.9370	2.8021	2.2628
8	7.0197	6.7327	6.4632	6.2098	5.9713	5.7466	5.3349	4.9676	4.6389	4.3436	4.0776	3.8372	3.6193	3.4212	3.3289	3.2407	3.0758	2.9247	2.3306
9	7.7861	7.4353	7.1078	6.8017	6.5152	6.2469	5.7590	5.3282	4.9464	4.6065	4.3030	4.0310	3.7863	3.5655	3.4631	3.3657	3.1842	3.0190	2.3790
10	8.5302	8.1109	7.7217	7.3601	7.0236	6.7101	6.1446	5.6502	5.2161	4.8332	4.4941	4.1925	3.9232	3.6819	3.5705	3.4648	3.2689	3.0915	2.4136
11	9.2526	8.7605	8.3064	7.8869	7.4987	7.1390	6.4951	5.9377	5.4527	5.0286	4.6560	4.3271	4.0354	3.7757	3.6564	3.5435	3.3351	3.1473	2.4383
12	9.9540	9.3851	8.8633	8.3838	7.9427	7.5361	6.8137	6.1944	5.6603	5.1971	4.7932	4.4392	4.1274	3.8514	3.7251	3.6059	3.3868	3.1903	2.4559
13	10.6350	9.9856	9.3936	8.8527	8.3577	7.9038	7.1034	6.4235	5.8424	5.3423	4.9095	4.5327	4.2028	3.9124	3.7801	3.6555	3.4272	3.2233	2.4685
14	11.2961	10.5631	9.8986	9.2950	8.7455	8.2442	7.3667	6.6282	6.0021	5.4675	5.0081	4.6106	4.2646	3.9616	3.8241	3.6949	3.4587	3.2487	2.4775
15	11.9379	11.1184	10.3797	9.7122	9.1079	8.5595	7.6061	6.8109	6.1422	5.5755	5.0916	4.6755	4.3152	4.0013	3.8593	3.7261	3.4834	3.2682	2.4839
16	12.5611	11.6523	10.8378	10.1059	9.4466	8.8514	7.8237	6.9740	6.2651	5.6685	5.1624	4.7296	4.3567	4.0333	3.8874	3.7509	3.5026	3.2832	2.4885
17	13.1661	12.1657	11.2741	10.4773	9.7632	9.1216	8.0216	7.1196	6.3729	5.7487	5.2223	4.7746	4.3908	4.0591	3.9099	3.7705	3.5177	3.2948	2.4918
18	13.7535	12.6593	11.6896	10.8276	10.0591	9.3719	8.2014	7.2497	6.4674	5.8178	5.2732	4.8122	4.4187	4.0799	3.9279	3.7861	3.5294	3.3037	2.4941
19	14.3238	13.1339	12.0853	11.1581	10.3356	9.6036	8.3649	7.3658	6.5504	5.8775	5.3162	4.8435	4.4415	4.0967	3.9424	3.7985	3.5386	3.3105	2.4958
20	14.8775	13.5903	12.4622	11.4699	10.5940	9.8181	8.5136	7.4694	6.6231	5.9288	5.3527	4.8696	4.4603	4.1103	3.9539	3.8083	3.5458	3.3158	2.4970
21	15.4150	14.0292	12.8212	11.7641	10.8355	10.0168	8.6487	7.5620	6.6870	5.9731	5.3837	4.8913	4.4756	4.1212	3.9631	3.8161	3.5514	3.3198	2.4979
22	15.9369	14.4511	13.1630	12.0416	11.0612	10.2007	8.7715	7.6446	6.7429	6.0113	5.4099	4.9094	4.4882	4.1300	3.9705	3.8223	3.5558	3.3230	2.4985
23	16.4436	14.8568	13.4886	12.3034	11.2722	10.3711	8.8832	7.7184	6.7921	6.0442	5.4321	4.9245	4.4985	4.1371	3.9764	3.8273	3.5592	3.3254	2.4989
24	16.9355	15.2470	13.7986	12.5504	11.4693	10.5288	8.9847	7.7843	6.8351	6.0726	5.4509	4.9371	4.5070	4.1428	3.9811	3.8312	3.5619	3.3272	2.4992
25	17.4131	15.6221	14.0939	12.7834	11.6536	10.6748	9.0770	7.8431	6.8729	6.0971	5.4669	4.9476	4.5139	4.1474	3.9849	3.8342	3.5640	3.3286	2.4994
26	17.8768	15.9828	14.3752	13.0032	11.8258	10.8100	9.1609	7.8957	6.9061	6.1182	5.4804	4.9563	4.5196	4.1511	3.9879	3.8367	3.5656	3.3297	2.4996
27	18.3270	16.3296	14.6430	13.2105	11.9867	10.9352	9.2372	7.9426	6.9352	6.1364	5.4919	4.9636	4.5243	4.1542	3.9903	3.8387	3.5669	3.3305	2.4997
28	18.7641	16.6631	14.8981	13.4062	12.1371	11.0511	9.3066	7.9844	6.9607	6.1520	5.5016	4.9697	4.5281	4.1566	3.9923	3.8402	3.5679	3.3312	2.4998
29	19.1885	16.9837	15.1411	13.5907	12.2777	11.1584	9.3696	8.0218	6.9830	6.1656	5.5098	4.9747	4.5312	4.1585	3.9938	3.8414	3.5687	3.3317	2.4999
30	19.6004	17.2920	15.3725	13.7648	12.4090	11.2578	9.4269	8.0552	7.0027	6.1772	5.5168	4.9789	4.5338	4.1601	3.9950	3.8424	3.5693	3.3321	2.4999
40	23.1148	19.7928	17.1591	15.0463	13.3317	11.9246	9.7791	8.2438	7.1050	6.2335	5.5482	4.9966	4.5439	4.1659	3.9995	3.8458	3.5712	3.3332	2.5000

Glossary

absorption approach (p. 133) A costing approach that considers all factory overhead (both variable and fixed) to be product (inventoriable) costs that become an expense in the form of manufacturing cost of goods sold only as sales occur.

accelerated depreciation (p. 462) Any pattern of depreciation that writes off depreciable assets more quickly than does ordinary straight-line depreciation.

account (p. 644) Each item in a financial statement.

account analysis (p. 91) Selecting a volume-related cost driver and classifying each account as a variable cost or as a fixed cost.

accounting rate-of-return (ARR) model (p. 432) A non–DCF capital-budgeting model expressed as the increase in expected average annual operating income divided by the initial increase in required investment.

accounting system (p. 5) A formal mechanism for gathering, organizing, and communicating information about an organization's activities.

accounts payable (p. 641) Amounts owed on open accounts whereby the buyer pays cash some time after the date of sale.

accounts receivable (p. 641) Amounts owed to a company by customers who buy on open account.

accrual basis (p. 646) A process of accounting that recognizes the impact of transactions on the financial statements in the time periods when revenues and expenses occur instead of when cash is received or disbursed.

accrue (p. 654) To accumulate a receivable or payable during a given period even though no explicit transaction occurs.

activity analysis (p. 88) The process of indentifying appropriate cost drivers and their effects on the costs of making a product or providing a service.

activity-based accounting (ABA) (p. 135) A system that first accumulates overhead costs for each of the activities of an organization, and then assigns the costs of activities to the products, services, or other cost objects that caused that activity.

activity-based costing (ABC) *See* activity-based accounting.

activity-level variances (p. 298) The differences between the master budget amounts and the amounts in the flexible budget.

adjustments (p. 647) Recording of implicit transactions, in contrast to the explicit transactions that trigger nearly all day-to-day routine entries.

agency theory (p. 385) A theory used to describe the formal choices of performance measures and rewards.

assets (p. 640) Economic resources that are expected to benefit future activities.

attention directing (p. 6) Reporting and interpreting information that helps managers to focus on operating problems, imperfections, inefficiencies, and opportunities.

audit (p. 660) An examination or in-depth inspection that is made in accordance with generally accepted auditing standards. It culminates with the accountant's testimony that management's financial statements are in conformity with generally accepted accounting principles.

avoidable costs (p. 178) Costs that will not continue if an ongoing operation is changed or deleted.

backflush costing (p. 584) An accounting system that applies costs to products only when the production is complete.

balance sheet (p. 640) A snapshot of financial status at an instant of time.

balanced scorecard (p. 355) A performance measurement system that strikes a balance between financial and operating measures, links performance to rewards, and gives explicit recognition to the diversity of stakeholder interests.

behavioral implications (p. 10) The accounting system's effect on the behavior (decisions) of managers.

bench marks (p. 749) General rules of thumb specifying appropriate levels for financial ratios.

book value (p. 226) The original cost of equipment less accumulated depreciation, which is the summation of depreciation charged to past periods.

break-even point (p. 42) The level of sales at which revenue equals expenses and net income is zero.

budget (p. 11) A quantitative expression of a plan of action, and an aid to coordinating and implementing the plan.

budgeted factory-overhead rate (p. 538) The budgeted total overhead divided by the budgeted cost driver activity.

by-product (p. 510) A product that, like a joint product, is not individually identifiable until manufacturing reaches a split-off point, but has relatively insignificant total sales value.

capacity costs (p. 83) The fixed costs of being able to achieve a desired level of production or to provide a desired level of service while maintaining product or service attributes, such as quality.

capital budget (p. 255) A budget that details the planned expenditures for facilities, equipment, new products, and other long-term investments.

capital turnover (p. 387) Revenue divided by invested capital.

capital-budgeting decisions (p. 413) Decisions that have significant financial effects beyond the current year.

cash basis (p. 646) A process of accounting where revenue and expense recognition would occur when cash is received and disbursed.

cash budget (p. 265) A statement of planned cash receipts and disbursements.

cash equivalents (p. 686) Short-term investments that can easily be converted into cash with little delay.

cash flow (p. 706) Usually refers to the net cash flow from operating activities.

cash flows from operating activities (p. 702) The first major section in the statement of cash flows.

cellular manufacturing (p. 145) A production system where machines are organized in cells according to the specific requirements of a product family.

Certified Management Accountant (CMA) (p. 18) The management accountant's counterpart to the CPA.

Certified Public Accountant (CPA) (p. 18) In the United States, an accountant earns this designation by a combination of education, qualifying experience, and the passing of a two-day written national examination.

coefficient of determination (R^2) (p. 96) A measurement of how much of the fluctuation of a cost is explained by changes in the cost driver.

committed fixed costs (p. 84) Costs arising from the possession of facilities, equipment, and a basic organization: large, indivisible chunks of cost that the organization is obligated to incur or usually would not consider avoiding.

common costs (p. 178) Those costs of facilities and services that are shared by users.

common stock (p. 694) Stock that has no predetermined rate of dividends and is the last to obtain a share in the assets when the corporation is dissolved. It usually has voting power in the management of the corporation.

common-size statements (p. 745) Financial statements expressed in component percentages.

component percentages (p. 745) Analysis and presentation of financial statements in percentage form to aid comparability, frequently used when companies differ in size.

computer-integrated manufacturing (CIM) systems (p. 21) Systems that use computer-aided design and computer-aided manufacturing, together with robots and computer-controlled machines.

conservatism convention (p. 667) Selecting the method of measurement that yields the gloomiest immediate results.

consolidated financial statements (p. 733) Financial statements that combine the financial statements of the parent company with those of various subsidiaries, as if they were a single entity.

constant dollars (p. 782) Nominal dollars that are restated in terms of current purchasing power.

continuity convention (p. 665) The assumption that in all ordinary situations an entity persists indefinitely.

continuous budget (p. 255) A common form of master budget that adds a month in the future as the month just ended is dropped.

contribution approach (p. 133) A method of internal (management accounting) reporting that emphasizes the distinction between variable and fixed costs for the purpose of better decision making.

contribution margin (p. 44) The sales price minus the variable cost per unit.

controllable cost (p. 342) Any cost that is influenced by a manager's decisions and actions.

controller/comptroller (p. 14) The top accounting officer of an organization. The term comptroller is used primarily in government organizations.

conversion costs (p. 125) Direct labor costs plus factory overhead costs.

corporation (p. 641) A business organized as a separate legal entity and owned by its stockholders.

cost (p. 122) A sacrifice or giving up of resources for a particular purpose, frequently measured by the monetary units that must be paid for goods and services.

cost accounting (p. 122) That part of the accounting system that measures costs for the purposes of management decision making and financial reporting.

cost accounting systems (p. 489) The techniques used to determine the cost of a product, service, or other cost objective by collecting and classifying costs and assigning them to cost objects.

cost accumulation (p. 123) Collecting costs by some natural classification such as materials or labor.

cost allocation (p. 123) Tracing and reassigning costs to one or more cost objectives such as departments, customers, or products.

cost allocation base (p. 490) A cost driver when it is used for allocating costs.

cost application (p. 501) The allocation of total departmental costs to the revenue-producing products or services.

cost behavior (p. 37) How the activities of an organization affect its costs.

cost center (p. 338) A responsibility center for which costs are accumulated.

cost drivers (p. 38) Activities that affect costs.

cost function (p. 86) An algebraic equation used by managers to describe the relationship between a cost and its cost driver(s).

cost measurement (p. 86) The first step in estimating or predicting costs as a function of appropriate cost drivers.

cost method (p. 732) The method of accounting for investments whereby the initial investment is recorded at cost and dividends are recognized as income when they are received

cost object *See* cost objective.

cost objective (p. 122) Any activity or resource for which a separate measurement of costs is desired. Examples include departments, products, and territories.

cost of capital (p. 388) What a firm must pay to acquire more capital, whether or not it actually has to acquire more capital to take on a project.

cost of goods sold (p. 54) The cost of the merchandise that is acquired or manufactured and resold.

cost of quality report (p. 347) A report that displays the financial impact of quality.

cost pool (p. 490) A group of individual costs that is allocated to cost objectives using a single cost driver.

cost prediction (p. 88) The application of cost measures to expected future activity levels to forecast future costs.

cost recovery (p. 662) A concept in which assets such as inventories, prepayments, and equipment are carried forward as assets because their costs are expected to be recovered in the form of cash inflows (or reduced cash outflows) in future periods.

cost-allocation base (p. 490) A cost driver when it is used for allocating costs.

cost-benefit balance (p. 9) Weighing estimated costs against probable benefits, the primary consideration in choosing among accounting systems and methods.

cost-benefit criterion (p. 667) An approach that implicitly underlies the decisions about the design of accounting systems. As a system is changed, its potential benefits should exceed its additional costs.

cost-management system (p. 143) Identifies how management's decisions affect costs, by first measuring the resources used in performing the organization's activities and then assessing the effects on costs of changes in those activities.

cost-volume-profit (CVP) analysis (p. 42) The study of the effects of output volume on revenue (sales), expenses (costs), and net income (net profit).

credit (p. 671) An entry on the right side of an account.

cross-sectional comparisons (p. 749) Comparisons of a company's financial ratios with ratios of other companies or with industry averages for the same period.

current assets (p. 686) Cash and all other assets that are reasonably expected to be converted to cash or sold or consumed during the normal operating cycle.

current cost (p. 782) The cost to replace an asset, as opposed to its historical cost.

current liabilities (p. 692) An organization's debts that fall due within the coming year or within the normal operating cycle if longer than a year.

current-cost method (p. 784) The measurement method that uses current costs and nominal dollars.

currently attainable standards (p. 303) Levels of performance that can be achieved by realistic levels of effort.

cycle time (p. 350) The time taken to complete a product or service, or any of the components of a product or service.

debentures (p. 693) Formal certificates of indebtedness that are accompanied by a promise to pay interest at a specified annual rate.

debit (p. 671) An entry on the left side of an account.

decentralization (p. 373) The delegation of freedom to make decisions. The lower in the organization that this freedom exists, the greater the decentralization.

decision making (p. 10) The purposeful choice from among a set of alternative courses of action designed to achieve some objective.

decision model (p. 170) Any method for making a choice, sometimes requiring elaborate quantitative procedures.

deferred revenue *See* unearned revenue.

depreciation (p. 226) The periodic cost of equipment which is spread over (or charged to) the future periods in which the equipment is expected to be used.

differential approach (p. 426) An approach that compares two alternatives by computing the differences in cash flows between alternatives and then converting these differences in cash flows to their present values.

differential cost (p. 218) The difference in total cost between two alternatives.

direct costs (p. 124) Costs that can be identified specifically and exclusively with a given cost objective in an economically feasible way.

direct method (p. 498) A method for allocating service department costs that ignores other service departments when any given service department's costs are allocated to the revenue-producing (operating) departments.

direct-labor costs (p. 125) The wages of all labor that can be traced specifically and exclusively to the manufactured goods in an economically feasible way.

direct-material costs (p. 125) The acquisition costs of all materials that are physically identified as a part of the manufactured goods and that may be traced to the manufactured goods in an economically feasible way.

discount rate *See* required rate of return.

discounted-cash-flow (DCF) models (p. 414) A type of capital-budgeting model that focuses on cash inflows and outflows and explicitly and systematically incorporates the time value of money.

discretionary fixed costs (p. 84) Costs determined by management as part of the periodic planning process in order to meet the organization's goals.

discriminatory pricing (p. 186) Charging different prices to different customers for the same product or service.

dividends (p. 657) Distributions of assets to stockholders that reduce retained income.

double-entry system (p. 669) A method of record keeping in which at least two accounts are affected by each transaction.

dysfunctional behavior (p. 380) Any action taken in conflict with organizational goals.

earnings *See* profits.

earnings per share (p. 697) Net income divided by the average number of common shares outstanding during the year.

effectiveness (p. 298) The degree to which a goal, objective, or target is met.

efficiency (p. 298) The degree to which inputs are used in relation to a given level of outputs.

efficiency variance *See* usage variance.

efficient capital market (p. 753) A market in which market prices fully reflect all information available to the public.

engineering analysis (p. 90) The systematic review of materials, supplies, labor, support services, and facilities needed for products and services: measuring cost behavior according to what costs should be, not by what costs have been.

equities (p. 640) The claims against, or interests in, an organization's assets.

equity method (p. 732) Accounts for the investment at the acquisition cost adjusted for the investor's share of dividends and earnings or losses of the investee after the date of investment.

equivalent units (p. 573) The number of completed units that could have been produced from the inputs applied.

expected cost (p. 301) The cost most likely to be attained.

expenses (p. 645) Gross decreases in assets from delivering goods or services.

factory burden *See* factory-overhead costs.

factory-overhead costs (p. 125) All costs other than direct material or direct labor that are associated with the manufacturing process.

favorable expense variable (p. 294) A variance that occurs when actual expenses are less than budgeted expenses.

Financial Accounting Standards Board (FASB) (p. 661) The primary regulatory body over accounting principles and practices. Consisting of seven full-time members, it is an independent creation of the private sector.

financial accounting (p. 5) The field of accounting that develops information for external decision makers such as stockholders, suppliers, banks, and government regulatory agencies.

financial budget (p. 256) The part of a master budget that focuses on the effects that the operating budget and other plans (such as capital budgets and repayments of debt) will have on cash.

financial capital maintenance (p. 781) The concept that income emerges after financial resources are recovered.

financial planning models (p. 270) Mathematical models of the master budget that can react to any set of assumptions about sales, costs, or product mix.

first-in, first-out (FIFO) (p. 773) An inventory method that assumes that the stock acquired earliest is sold (used up) first.

first-in, first-out (FIFO) process-costing method (p. 578) A process-costing method that sharply distinguishes the current work done from the previous work done on the beginning inventory of work in process.

fixed assets (p. 688) Physical items that can be seen and touched, such as property, plant, and equipment.

fixed cost (p. 38) A cost that is not immediately affected by changes in the cost driver.

fixed overhead rate (p. 605) The amount of fixed manufacturing overhead applied to each unit of production. It is determined by dividing the budgeted fixed overhead by the expected volume of production for the budget period.

flexible budget (p. 295) A budget that adjusts for changes in sales volume and other cost-driver activities.

flexible-budget variances (p. 298) The variances between the flexible budget and the actual results.

Foreign Corrupt Practices Act (p. 8) U.S. law forbidding bribery and other corrupt practices, and requiring that accounting records be maintained in reasonable detail and accuracy, and that an appropriate system of internal accounting controls be maintained.

full cost (p. 188) The total of all manufacturing costs plus the total of all selling and administrative costs.

fully allocated cost *See* full cost.

general ledger (p. 669) A collection of the group of accounts that supports the items shown in the major financial statements.

general price index (p. 785) A comparison of the average price of a group of goods and services at one date with the average price of a similar group at another date.

generally accepted accounting principles (GAAP) (p. 6) Broad concepts or guidelines and detailed practices, including all conventions, rules, and procedures that together make up accepted accounting practice at a given time.

goal congruence (p. 339) A condition where employees, working in their own personal interests make decisions that help meet the overall goals of the organization.

going concern convention *See* continuity convention.

goodwill (p. 691) The excess of the cost of an acquired company over the sum of the fair market values of its identifiable individual assets less its liabilities.

gross book value (p. 393) The original cost of an asset before deducting accumulated depreciation.

gross margin (p. 54) The excess of sales over the total cost of goods sold.

gross profit *See* gross margin.

half-year convention (p. 473) A requirement of the modified accelerated cost recovery system that treats all assets as if they were placed in service at the midpoint of the tax year.

high-low method (p. 93) A simple method for measuring a linear cost function from past cost data, focusing on the highest-activity and lowest-activity points and fitting a line through these two points.

historical cost (p. 782) The amount originally paid to acquire an asset.

holding gains (or losses) (p. 784) Increases (or decreases) in the replacement costs of the assets held during the current period.

hurdle rate *See* required rate of return.

hybrid-costing system (p. 586) An accounting system that is a blend of ideas from both job costing and process costing.

ideal standards *See* perfection standards.

idle time (p. 148) An indirect labor cost consisting of wages paid for unproductive time caused by machine breakdowns, material shortages, and sloppy scheduling.

imperfect competition (p. 183) A market in which a firm's price will influence the quantity it sells.

incentives (p. 384) Those formal and informal performance-based rewards that enhance managerial effort toward organizational goals.

income *See* profits.

income percentage of revenue (p. 387) Income divided by revenue.

income statement (p. 642) A statement that measures the performance of an organization by matching its accomplishments (revenue from customers, which is usually called sales) and its efforts (cost of goods sold and other expenses).

incremental cost *See* differential cost.

incremental effect (p. 49) The change in total results (such as revenue, expenses, or income) under a new condition in comparison with some given or known condition.

indirect costs (p. 124) Costs that cannot be identified specifically and exclusively with a given cost objective in an economically feasible way.

indirect labor (p. 148) All factory labor wages, other than those for direct labor and manager salaries.

indirect method (p. 707) In a statement of cash flows, the method that reconciles net income to the net cash provided by operating activites.

inflation (p. 457, 782) A general decline in the purchasing power of the monetary unit.

Institute of Management Accountants (IMA) (p. 18) The largest U.S. professional organization of accountants whose major interest is management accounting.

intangible assets (p. 691) Long-lived assets that are not physical in nature. Examples are goodwill, franchises, patents, trademarks, and copyrights.

internal control system (p. 340) Methods and procedures to prevent errors and irregularities, detect errors and irregularities, and promote operating efficiency.

internal rate of return (IRR) (p. 418) The discount rate that makes the net present value of the project equal to zero.

inventory turnover (p. 181) The number of times the average inventory is sold per year.

investment center (p. 339) A responsibility center whose success is measured not only by its income but also by relating that income to its invested capital, as in a ratio of income to the value of the capital employed.

investments in affiliates (p. 738) Investments in equity securities that represent 20% to 50% ownership. They are usually accounted for under the equity method.

investments in associates *See* investments in affiliates.

job costing *See* job-order costing.

job order *See* job-cost record.

job-cost record (p. 532) A document that shows all costs for a particular product, service, or batch of products.

job-cost sheet *See* job-cost record.

job-order costing (p. 532) The method of allocating costs to products that are readily identified by individual units or batches, each of which requires varying degrees of attention and skill.

joint costs (p. 222) The costs of manufacturing joint products prior to the split-off point.

joint products (p. 222) Two or more manufactured products that (1) have relatively significant sales values and (2) are not separately identifiable as individual products until their split-off point.

just-in-time (JIT) philosophy (p. 20) A philosophy to eliminate waste by reducing the time products spend in the production process and eliminating the time products spend on activities that do not add value.

just-in-time (JIT) production system (p. 144) A system in which an organization purchases materials and parts and produces components just when they are needed in the production process, the goal being to have zero inventory, because holding inventory is a non-value-added activity.

labor time tickets (p. 533) The record of the time a particular direct laborer spends on each job.

last-in, first-out (LIFO) (p. 773) An inventory method that assumes that the stock acquired most recently is sold (used up) first.

least-squares regression (p. 96) Measuring a cost function objectively by using statistics to fit a cost function to all the data.

ledger accounts (p. 668) A method of keeping track of how multitudes of transactions affect each particular asset, liability, revenue, and expense.

legal value *See* par value.

liabilities (p. 641) The entity's economic obligations to nonowners.

LIFO layers (p. 774) Separately identifiable additional layers of LIFO inventory.

LIFO increments *See* LIFO layers.

limited liability (p. 694) Creditors cannot seek payment from shareholders as individuals if the corporation itself cannot pay its debts.

limiting factor (p. 180) The item that restricts or constrains the production or sale of a product or service.

line authority (p. 14) Authority exerted downward over subordinates.

linear-cost behavior (p. 80) Activity that can be graphed with a straight line when a cost changes proportionately with changes in a cost driver.

liquidation (p. 693) Converting assets to cash and using the cash to pay off outside claims.

long-range planning (p. 255) Producing forecasted financial statements for five- or ten-year periods.

long term liabilities *See* noncurrent liabilities.

lower-of-cost-or-market (LCM) (p. 778) An inventory method in which the current market price of inventory is compared with its cost (derived by specific identification, FIFO, LIFO, or weighted average) and the lower of the two is selected as the basis for the valuation of goods at a specific inventory date.

management accounting (p. 4) The process of identifying, measuring, accumulating, analyzing, preparing, interpreting, and communicating information that helps managers fulfill organizational objectives.

management audit (p. 8) A review to determine whether the policies and procedures specified by top management have been implemented.

management by exception (p. 11) Concentrating on areas that deviate from the plan and ignoring areas that are presumed to be running smoothly.

management by objectives (MBO) (p. 394) The joint formulation by a manager and his or her superior of a set of goals and plans for achieving the goals for a forthcoming period.

management control system (p. 334) A logical integration of management accounting tools to gather and report data and to evaluate performance.

managerial effort (p. 339) Exertion toward a goal or objective including all conscious actions (such as supervising, planning, and thinking) that result in more efficiency and effectiveness.

manufacturing overhead *See* factory overhead costs.

margin of safety (p. 44) Equal to the planned unit sales less the break-even unit sales; it shows how far sales can fall below the planned level before losses occur.

marginal cost (p. 182) The additional cost resulting from producing and selling one additional unit.

marginal income *See* contribution margin.

marginal income tax rate (p. 458) The tax rate paid on additional amounts of pretax income.

marginal revenue (p. 183) The additional revenue resulting from the sale of an additional unit.

markup (p. 186) The amount by which price exceeds cost.

master budget (p. 255) A budget that summarizes the planned activities of all subunits of an organization.

master budget variance (p. 294) The variance of actual results from the master budget.

matching (p. 662) The relating of accomplishments or revenues (as measured by the selling prices of goods and services delivered) and efforts or expenses (as measured by the cost of goods and services used) to a particular period for which a measurement of income is desired.

materiality (p. 666) The accounting convention that justifies the omission of insignificant information when its omission or misstatement would not mislead a user of the financial statements.

materials requisitions (p. 533) Records of materials issued to particular jobs.

measurement of cost behavior (p. 79) Understanding and quantifying how activities of an organization affect levels of costs.

minority interests (p. 736) An account that shows the outside stockholders' interest, as opposed to the parent's interest, in a subsidiary corporation.

mixed costs (p. 82) Costs that contain elements of both fixed and variable-cost behavior.

motivation (p. 340) The drive for some selected goal that creates effort and action toward that goal.

net book value (p. 393) The original cost of an asset less any accumulated depreciation. *See* book value.

net income (p. 697) The popular "bottom line"—the residual after deducting from revenues all expenses, including income taxes.

net worth (p. 660) A synonym for owner's equity.

net-present-value (NPV) method (p. 415) A discounted-cash-flow approach to capital budgeting that discounts all expected future cash flows to the present using a minimum desired rate of return.

nominal dollars (p. 782) Dollar measurements that are not restated for fluctuations in the general purchasing power of the monetary unit.

nominal rate (p. 468) Quoted market interest rate that includes an inflation element.

non-value-added costs (p. 143) Costs that can be eliminated without affecting a product's value to the customer.

noncurrent liabilities (p. 692) An organization's debts that fall due beyond one year.

normal costing (p. 611) A cost system that applies actual direct materials and actual direct-labor costs to products or services but uses standards for applying overhead.

normal costing system (p. 545) The cost system in which overhead is applied on an average or normalized basis, in order to get representative or normal inventory valuations.

objectivity (p. 666) Accuracy supported by a high extent of consensus among independent measures of an item.

operating budget (p. 256) A major part of a master budget that focuses on the income statement and its supporting schedules.

operating cycle (p. 686) The time span during which cash is spent to acquire goods and services that are used to produce the organization's output, which in turn is sold to customers, who in turn pay for their purchases with cash.

operating leverage (p. 53) A firm's ratio of fixed to variable costs.

operation costing (p. 586) A hybrid-costing system often used in the batch or group manufacturing of goods that have some common characteristics plus some individual characteristics.

opportunity cost (p. 218) The maximum available contribution to profit forgone (or passed up) by using limited resources for a particular purpose.

outlay cost (p. 218) A cost that requires a cash disbursement.

overapplied overhead (p. 542) The excess of overhead applied to products over actual overhead incurred.

overtime premium (p. 148) An indirect labor cost, consisting of wages paid to all factory workers in excess of their straight-time wage rates.

owners' equity (p. 641) The excess of the assets over the liabilities.

paid-in capital (p. 641) The ownership claim against, or interest in, the total assets arising from any paid-in investment.

par value (p. 694) The value that is printed on the face of the certificate.

parent company (p. 733) A company owning more than 50 percent of another business's stock.

participative budgeting (p. 269) Budgets formulated with the active participation of all affected employees.

partnership (p. 659) An organization that joins two or more individuals together as co-owners.

payback period *See* payback time.

payback time (p. 431) The measure of the time it will take to recoup, in the form of cash inflows from operations, the initial dollars of outlay.

payroll fringe costs (p. 149) Employer contributions to employee benefits such as social security, life insurance, health insurance, and pensions.

perfect competition (p. 182) A market in which a firm can sell as much of a product as it can produce, all at a single market price.

perfection standards (p. 302) Expressions of the most efficient performance possible under the best conceivable conditions, using existing specifications and equipment.

performance reports (p. 11) Feedback provided by comparing results with plans and by highlighting variances.

period costs (p. 127) Costs that are deducted as expenses during the current period without going through an inventory stage.

physical capital maintenance (p. 781) The concept that income emerges only after recovering an amount that allows physical operating capability to be maintained.

postaudit (p. 435) A follow-up evaluation of capital-budgeting decisions.

practical capacity (p. 610) Maximum or full capacity.

predatory pricing (p. 185) Establishing prices so low that competitors are driven out of the market so that the predatory pricer then has no significant competition and can raise prices dramatically.

preferred stock (p. 694) Stock that typically has some priority over other shares regarding dividends or the distribution of assets upon liquidation.

price elasticity (p. 183) The effect of price changes on sales volumes.

price variance (p. 307) The difference between actual input prices and expected input prices multiplied by the actual quantity of inputs used.

prime costs (p. 125) Direct labor costs plus direct materials costs.

pro forma statement *See* master budget.

problem solving (p. 6) Aspect of accounting that quantifies the likely results of possible courses of action and often recommends the best course of action to follow.

process costing (p. 532) The method of allocating costs to products by averaging costs over large numbers of nearly identical products.

product costs (p. 127) Costs identified with goods produced or purchased for resale.

product life cycle (p. 13) The various stages through which a product passes, from conception and development through introduction into the market through maturation and, finally, withdrawal from the market.

production cycle time (p. 145) The time from initiating production to delivering the goods to the customer.

production-volume variance (p. 605) A variance that appears whenever actual production deviates from the expected volume of production used in computing the fixed overhead rate. It is calculated as (actual volume − expected volume) × fixed-overhead rate.

productivity (p. 353) A measure of outputs divided by inputs.

profit centers (p. 338) A responsibility center for controlling revenues as well as costs (or expenses)—that is, profitability.

profit plan *See* operating budget.

profits (p. 645) The excess of revenues over expenses.

prorate (p. 543) To assign underapplied overhead or overapplied overhead in proportion to the sizes of the ending account balances.

prorating the variance (p. 617) Assigning the variances to the inventories and cost of goods sold related to the production during the period the variances arose.

quality control (p. 346) The effort to ensure that products and services perform to customer requirements.

quality-control chart (p. 350) The statistical plot of measures of various product dimensions or attributes.

quantity variance *See* usage variance.

recovery period (p. 459) The number of years over which an asset is depreciated for tax purposes.

regression analysis *See* least-squares regression.

relevant information (p. 168) The predicted future costs and revenues that will differ among alternative courses of action.

relevant range (p. 40) The limit of cost-driver activity within which a specific relationship between costs and the cost driver is valid.

required rate of return (p. 415) The minimum desired rate of return, based on the firm's cost of capital.

residual income (p. 388) Net income less "imputed" interest.

residual value (p. 650) The predicted sales value of a long-lived asset at the end of its useful life.

responsibility accounting (p. 338) Identifying what parts of the organization have primary responsibility for each objective, developing measures of achievement of objectives, and creating reports of these measures by organization subunit or responsibility center.

responsibility center (p. 338) A set of activities assigned to a manager, a group of managers, or other employees.

retained earnings *See* retained income.

retained income (p. 641) The ownership claim arising as a result of profitable operations.

return on investment (ROI) (p. 387) A measure of income or profit divided by the investment required to obtain that income or profit.

return on sales *See* income percentage of revenue.

revaluation equity (p. 784) A portion of stockholders' equity that shows all accumulated holding gains.

revenue (p. 644) A gross increase in assets from delivering goods or services.

rolling budget *See* continuous budget.

sales budget (p. 268) The result of decisions to create conditions that will generate a desired level of sales.

sales forecast (p. 268) A prediction of sales under a given set of conditions.

sales mix (p. 48) The relative proportions or combinations of quantities of products that constitute total sales.

sales-activity variances (p. 301) Variances that measure how effective managers have been in meeting the planned sales objective, calculated as actual unit sales less master budget unit sales times the budgeted unit contribution margin.

scarce resource *See* limiting factor.

scorekeeping (p. 6) The accumulation and classification of data.

Securities and Exchange Commission (SEC) (p. 661) By federal law, the agency with the ultimate responsibility for specifying the generally accepted accounting principles for U.S. companies whose stock is held by the general investing public.

segment autonomy (p. 376) The delegation of decision-making power to managers of segments of an organization.

segments (p. 343) Responsibility centers for which a separate measure of revenues and costs is obtained.

sensitivity analysis (p. 277) The systematic varying of budget data input to determine the effects of each change on the budget.

separable costs (p. 222) Any cost beyond the split-off point.

service departments (p. 491) Units that exist only to support other departments.

sole proprietorship (p. 659) A business entity with a single owner.

source documents (p. 647) Explicit evidence of any transactions that occur in the entity's operation, for example, sales slips and purchase invoices.

specific identification (p. 773) An inventory method that recognizes the actual cost paid for the specific item sold.

specific price index (p. 785) An index used to approximate the current costs of particular assets or types of assets.

split-off point (p. 222) The juncture of manufacturing where the joint products become individually identifiable.

staff authority (p. 14) Authority to advise but not command. It may be exerted downward, laterally, or upward.

standard cost (p. 301) A carefully determined cost per unit that should be attained.

standard cost systems (p. 301) Accounting systems that value products according to standard costs only.

Standards of Ethical Conduct for Management Accountants (p. 22) Codes of conduct developed by the Institute of Management Accountants, which include competence, confidentiality, integrity, and objectivity.

stated value *See* par value.

statement of cash flows (p. 699) A statement that reports the cash receipts and cash payments of an organization during a particular period.

statement of financial condition *See* balance sheet.

statement of financial position *See* balance sheet.

statement of retained earnings (p. 697) A financial statement that analyzes changes in the retained earnings or retained income account for a given period.

statement of retained income *See* statement of retained earnings.

static budget variance *See* master budget variance.

step costs (p. 81) Costs that change abruptly at intervals of activity because the resources and their costs come in indivisible chunks.

step-down method (p. 498) A method for allocating service department costs that recognizes that some service departments support the activities in other service departments as well as those in production departments.

stockholders' equity (p. 641) The excess of assets over liabilities of a corporation.

strategic plan (p. 254) A plan that sets the overall goals and objectives of the organization.

subordinated (p. 693) A creditor claim that is junior to the other creditors in exercising claims against assets.

subsidiary (p. 733) A company owned by a parent company that owns more than 50 percent of its stock.

sunk cost (p. 226) A cost that has already been incurred and, therefore, is irrelevant to the decision making process. Synonyms are historical cost or past cost.

tangible assets *See* fixed assets.

target costing (p. 187) A strategy in which companies first determine the price at which they can sell a new product or service and then design a product or service that can be produced at a low enough cost to provide an adequate profit margin.

tax shields (p. 459) Depreciation deductions and similar deductions that protect that amount of income from taxation. All allowable expenses, both cash and noncash items, could be called tax shields because they reduce income and thereby reduce income taxes.

time cards *See* labor time tickets.

time-series comparisons (p. 749) Comparison of a company's financial ratios with its own historical ratios.

total project approach (p. 426) An approach that compares two or more alternatives by computing the total impact on cash flows for each alternative and then converting these total cash flows to their present values.

total quality management (TQM) (p. 350) The application of quality principles to all of the organization's endeavors to satisfy customers.

transaction (p. 640) Any event that affects the financial position of an organization and requires recording.

transaction-based costing (p. 503) Activity-based costing.

transfer price (p. 377) The amount charged by one segment of an organization for a product or service that it supplies to another segment of the same organization.

transferred-in costs (p. 581) In process costing, costs incurred in a previous department for items that have been received by a subsequent department.

treasury stock (p. 695) A corporation's own stock that has been issued and subsequently repurchased by the company and is being held for a specific purpose.

unavoidable costs (p. 178) Costs that continue even if an operation is halted.

uncontrollable cost (p. 342) Any cost that cannot be affected by the management of a responsibility center within a given time span.

underapplied overhead (p. 542) The excess of actual overhead over the overhead applied to products.

unearned revenue (p. 653) Collections from customers received and recorded before they are earned.

unexpired cost (p. 648) Any asset that ordinarily becomes an expense in future periods, for example, inventory and prepaid rent.

unfavorable expense variance (p. 294) A variance that occurs when actual expenses are more than budgeted expenses.

usage variance (p. 307) The difference between the quantity of inputs actually used and the quantity of inputs that should have been used to achieve the actual quantity of output multiplied by the expected price of input.

value chain (p. 357) The sequence of functions that adds value to the company's products or services.

value-added cost (p. 143) The necessary cost of an activity that cannot be eliminated without affecting a product's value to the customer.

variable budget *See* flexible budget.

variable cost (p. 38) A cost that changes in direct proportion to changes in the cost driver.

variable-cost percentage *See* variable-cost ratio.

variable-cost ratio (p. 54) All variable costs divided by sales.

variable-overhead efficiency variance (p. 310) When actual cost-driver activity differs from the standard amount allowed for the actual output achieved.

variable-overhead spending variance (p. 310) The difference between the actual variable overhead and the amount of variable overhead budgeted for the actual level of cost-driver activity.

variances (p. 11) Deviations from plans.

verfiability *See* objectivity.

visual-fit method (p. 95) A method in which the cost analyst visually fits a straight line through a plot of all the available data, not just between the high point and the low point, making it more reliable than the high-low method.

Index

INDEX OF COMPANIES